SEVENTH EDITION

7

The Informed Argument

ROBERT K. MILLER

University of St. Thomas

HEINLE
CENGAGE Learning

Australia • Brazil • Japan • Korea • Mexico • Singapore • Spain • United Kingdom • United States

The Informed Argument, Seventh Edition
Robert K. Miller

Publisher: Michael Rosenberg

Acquisitions Editor: Aron Keesbury

Development Editor: Maggie Barbieri

Managing Marketing Manager: Mandee Eckersley

Assoc. Marketing Communications Manager:
  Patrick Rooney

Assoc. Content Project Manager: Sarah Sherman

Manufacturing Manager: Marcia Locke

Permissions Editor: Ron Montgomery

Permissions Researcher: Karyn Morrison

Production Service/Compositor:
  Graphic World Inc.

Text Designer: Linda Beaupre

Photo Manager: Sheri Blaney

Photo Researcher: Sharon Donahue

Cover Designer: Ox and Company

Cover Printer: Phoenix Color

Printer: Quebecor World

Cover Art: © Wally McNamee/CORBIS

For product information and technology assistance, contact us at
Cengage Learning Customer & Sales Support, 1-800-354-9706
For permission to use material from this text or product,
submit all requests online at **cengage.com/permissions**
Further permissions questions can be emailed to
permissionrequest@cengage.com

Library of Congress Control Number: 2006923441
ISBN-13: 978-1-4130-1611-6
ISBN-10: 1-4130-1611-1

Heinle
25 Thomson Place
Boston, MA 02210-1202
USA

Credits appear on pages 723–730, which constitute a continuation of the copyright page.

Printed in the United States of America
3 4 5 6 7 09 08

Contents

Preface   ix

Part I: *Understanding Arguments*   1
Chapter 1:   **The Purposes of Argument**   2
Chapter 2:   **The Contexts of Argument**   16
Chapter 3:   **The Media for Argument**   34
Chapter 4:   **The Strategies for Argument**   70

Part II: *Composing Arguments*   109
Chapter 5:   **Constructing Arguments**   110
Chapter 6:   **Doing Research**   152
Chapter 7:   **Documenting Your Sources**   180

Part III: *Negotiating Differences*   207
Chapter 8:   Ownership   208
             Cluster 1. Who Owns Words and Ideas?   210
             1. Jay Mathews, "Standing Up for the Power of Learning"   212
             2. Ralph Caplan, "What's Yours?
                (Ownership of Intellectual Property)"   217
             3. David Gibson, "Copyright Crusaders"   222
             4. Abigail Lipson and Sheila M. Reindl,
                "The Responsible Plagiarist"   226
             Cluster 2. Who Owns Music?   236
             1. Janis Ian, "Free Downloads Play Sweet Music"   239
             2. Tom Lowry, "Ringtones: Music to Moguls' Ears"   244

3. James Surowiecki, "Hello, Cleveland" 247
4. Tom McCourt, "Collecting Music in the Digital Realm" 250
Cluster 3. Who Owns the Media? 256
1. Jenny Toomey, "Empire of the Air" 257
2. Gal Beckerman, "Tripping Up Big Media" 263
3. Laura Peterson, "The Moguls Are the Medium" 272
4. Tom Lowry and Ron Grover, "Breaking Up Is Easy to Do" 275

Chapter 9: **Body Image** **280**
Cluster 1. How Do the Media Influence Body Image? 282
1. Sascha de Gersdorff, "Fresh Faces" 283
2. Graham Lawton, "Extreme Surgery" 287
3. Joyce McMillan, "The Brutality of Celebrity Culture" 291
4. Marika Tiggemann, "Media Influences on Body
   Image Development" 294
Cluster 2. Why Are So Many Americans Overweight? 302
1. Susan Brink and Elizabeth Querna, "Eat This Now!" 303
2. Barbara Wickens, "How Your Brain Makes You Fat" 307
3. W. Wayt Gibbs, "Obesity: An Overblown Epidemic?" 311
4. Jeffrey P. Koplan, Catharyn T. Liverman, and
   Vivica I. Kraak, "Preventing Childhood Obesity" 318
Cluster 3. When Does Being "Fit" Become "Unfit"? 330
1. Heather Beresford, "I Was an Idiot to Take It So Far" 331
2. Christopher McDougall and Lou Schuler, "Buyin' Bulk" 334
3. Harrison G. Pope, Jr., Katherine A. Phillips,
   and Roberto Olivardia, "The Adonis Complex" 342
4. Sarah Grogan, Ruth Evans, Sam Wright,
   and Geoff Hunter, "Femininity and Muscularity:
   Accounts of Seven Women Body Builders" 353

Chapter 10: **Relationships** **366**
Cluster 1. Is Anyone Really 'Dating' Anymore? 368
1. Beth Bailey, "From Front Porch to Back Seat:
   A History of the Date" 369
2. Darryl James, "Get Your Hand Out of My Pocket" 377
3. Vigen Guroian, "Dorm Brothel" 380
4. Phillip Vannini, "Will You Marry Me? Spectacle and
   Consumption in the Ritual of Marriage Proposals" 389
Cluster 2. What Does Marriage Require? 402
1. Stephanie Coontz, "Great Expectations" 403
2. Christina Nehring, "Fidelity with a Wandering Eye" 406
3. Jonathan Rauch, "A More Perfect Union" 411
4. Phillip Hodson, "Baby, This Is For Ever" 419

Cluster 3. What Does It Mean to Be a Good Parent? 424
1. Maureen Freely, "Designer Babies
and Other Fairy Tales" 425
2. Wendy McElroy, "Victims from Birth" 429
3. Anna Quindlen, "The Good Enough Mother" 432
4. Steven E. Rhoads, "What Fathers Do Best" 435

Chapter 11: **Education** 440
Cluster 1. What Should Students Be Taught? 442
1. Rick Livingston, "The Humanities for Cocktail Parties
and Beyond" 444
2. Stanley N. Katz, "Liberal Education on the Ropes" 448
3. Ronald Takaki, "An Educated and Culturally Literate
Person Must Study America's Multicultural Reality" 458
4. Stephen L. Trainor, "Designing a Signature General
Education Program" 463
Cluster 2. How Should Students Be Taught? 470
1. Bill Coplin, "Lost in the Life of the Mind" 471
2. Mano Singham, "Moving Away from the Authoritarian
Classroom" 475
3. bell hooks, "Toward a Radical Feminist Pedagogy" 484
4. Lewis Thomas, "The Art of Teaching Science" 490
Cluster 3. How Should Learning Be Measured? 498
1. Patricia Williams, "Tests, Tracking, and Derailment" 499
2. Gregory Cizek, "Unintended Consequences
of High-Stakes Testing" 503
3. Bertell Ollman, "Why So Many Exams?
A Marxist Response" 514
4. Peter Elbow, "Getting Along without Grades—
and Getting Along with Them, Too" 521

Chapter 12: **American National Identity** 540
Cluster 1. Who Gets to Be an American? 542
1. Celia C. Perez-Zeeb, "By the Time I Get to Cucaracha" 544
2. Peter Brimelow, "A Nation of Immigrants" 549
3. Jacob G. Hornberger, "Keep the Borders Open" 555
4. Steven Camarota, "Too Many: Looking Today's
Immigration in the Face" 560
Cluster 2. What Does It Mean to Be a Good
American Citizen? 568
1. John Balzar, "Needed: Informed Voters" 570
2. Wilfred M. McClay, "America: Idea or Nation?" 573
3. Michael Kazin, "A Patriotic Left" 582
4. Josiah Bunting, III, "Class Warfare" 589

Cluster 3. What Kind of Power Should We Give
        Our Government?   598
  1. Martin Luther King, Jr., "Letter from a Birmingham Jail"   600
  2. Heather Green, "Databases and Security vs. Privacy"   612
  3. Alan M. Dershowitz, "Why Fear National ID Cards?"   616
  4. David J. Barron, "Reclaiming Federalism"   619

Chapter 13: **Environment**   **630**
Cluster 1. How Can We Improve the Cyber Environment?   632
  1. Cass Sunstein, "The Daily We: Is the Internet
     Really a Blessing for Democracy?"   633
  2. Danny O'Brien, "How to Mend a Broken Internet"   646
  3. Andrew K. Pace, "Surviving Chronic E-Mail Fatigue"   651
  4. John Tierney, "Making Them Squirm"   655
Cluster 2. How Do We Design Communities?   660
  1. Stuart Meck, "Getting on the Case"   662
  2. Jane Holtz Kay, "The Lived-In City: A Place in Time"   668
  3. Donella Meadows, "So What Can We Do—Really Do—
     about Sprawl?"   676
  4. Robert Wilson, "Enough Snickering. Suburbia Is More
     Complicated and Varied Than We Think"   682
Cluster 3. What is Our Relationship to Nature?   688
  1. Rachel Carson, "The Obligation to Endure"   690
  2. Ronald Bailey, "Silent Spring at 40"   697
  3. Jack Turner, "In Wildness Is the Preservation
     of the World"   702
  4. Charles Petit, "Hazy Days in Our Parks"   712

Credits   **723**

Photo Credits   **729**

Index   **731**

Preface

Like the previous editions, *The Informed Argument*, Seventh Edition, grows out of the belief that argumentation can be a powerful vehicle for individual learning and for social transformation. The book is designed to help students see that arguments involve much more than trying to win a debate. They can be a way to discover truth and to solve problems. The opening chapter makes this clear by discussing not only arguments designed to assert a claim or to advance a proposition but also arguments that operate as means of inquiry and vehicles for reconciling differences.

This book encourages students to read, to analyze, to reflect, and to write by drawing upon the strategies and conventions of effective argumentation in different media—media ranging from advertisements and web pages to editorials and scholarly articles. The ultimate goal of this effort is to help students become literate and responsible citizens in a complex and changing society, a society in which arguments of one kind or another abound and in which increasing discord threatens the common good. Accordingly, this edition emphasizes that argumentation should be a means of negotiating differences to address the problems we face as consumers, citizens, and members of various communities.

The book is organized so that students can begin by addressing issues in popular culture and gradually move toward those that are more central to public policy, such as who gets to immigrate to the United States and how cities should be planned. In other words, the sequence of chapters is designed to engage students by focusing initially on concerns that they are likely to have at the beginning of a college course and then showing how the ethical, economic, and social implications of these concerns link to those of the larger world to which both students and teachers belong.

This edition of *The Informed Argument* incorporates recent scholarly thinking about the nature of argument—including significant attention to the importance of visual rhetoric—into a framework based on such principles of classical rhetoric as ethos, logos, and pathos and the importance of arrangement or organization. By bringing a contemporary understanding of the way cultural context shapes arguments to the application of classical rhetoric, the book provides students with a sophisticated but, nevertheless, accessible perspective through which to view the arguments they see, read, and write.

A Contemporary Perspective on Traditional Argumentation

Throughout the book, argument is presented as an activity that occurs within specific contexts and is intended to serve a wide range of special and political purposes. The first four chapters, located within "Part 1: Understanding Arguments," introduce students to concepts that can help them to evaluate arguments composed by others and to compose arguments of their own. Chapter 1, "The Purposes of Argument," will help students appreciate how argumentation occurs for a variety of ends and how purpose shapes many of the rhetorical choices writers need to make. Chapter 2, "The Contexts of Argument," explores how the different aspects of context, including cultural diversity, influence argumentation. Chapter 3, "The Media for Argument," examines how various media shape argumentation and can be powerful tools for argument in their own right. This chapter has been expanded to include additional attention to visual rhetoric, an area of increasing interest to scholars and one that appeals to students because they recognize how images confront them almost everywhere they turn. Chapter 4, "The Strategies for Argument," introduces students to logic and logical fallacies—areas that can too easily inhibit interest in argumentation if emphasized at the beginning of a course, giving students the impression that arguments are either correct or incorrect because of fixed laws. This chapter (which was Chapter 2 in the sixth edition) is now positioned so that it is closer to those that focus on composing written arguments because logic can help students decide how to organize an argument. Part 1 is followed by three chapters grouped together as "Part 2: Composing Arguments." Chapter 5, "Constructing Arguments," discusses how the process of writing is an integral part of inquiry and of successfully communicating the results of that inquiry. As in previous editions, student essays illustrate the importance of revision and organization. Two versions of a student argument on class attendance policies illustrate what can be accomplished through revision. And four works by other students demonstrate how to organize arguments according to widely recognized plans.

Research as an Integral Part of Argument

Like all previous editions, the seventh edition includes substantial treatment of research—from exploring a topic to finding and documenting sources. Because effective argumentation is informed argumentation, research is an integral part of the process of writing a good argument. In Chapter 6, "Doing Research," and Chapter 7, "Documenting Your Sources," students will find useful advice for discovering relevant sources, incorporating material from these sources into works that are clearly their own, and honoring academic conventions for documentation. Both MLA and APA style documentation are discussed in detail within Chapter 7, and arguments that model documented research can be found throughout the book.

Diverse Readings

The readings are organized around six main themes, each of which is further divided into three sub-themes, or "clusters," that respond to questions that cannot be answered simply. For example, the book includes clusters in response to questions such as "Who owns words and ideas?" and "What kind of power should we give our government?" but not questions like "Are you for or against the death penalty?" This organizing scheme grows out of my view that anthologies that pair for-and-against arguments tend to oversimplify important issues, deepen divisions, and thus work against problem solving. Accordingly, while the readings represent diverse points of view, they cannot be easily classified as pro or con advocacy. Moreover, while most of the readings are arguments, some are reports that provide students with backgrounds upon which they can draw when composing arguments of their own. Although each cluster of readings can stand on its own, the three clusters in each chapter are closely related. This pattern of organization allows students to reflect upon a range of different issues while nevertheless seeing how many of these issues intersect. Moreover, the number of readings included provide instructors with options for selecting the pieces that are best suited for their own courses.

The themes of these six chapters are also diverse. In response to both reviewers and students, this edition gives more attention to issues from popular culture—such as the cultural and psychological impact of obsession with body image and the ethical and social consequences of trying to create relationships through dating, marriage, and parenting. Other chapters focus on issues more frequently addressed in textbooks on argumentation, issues such as educational reform and environmental regulation. But even these more traditional chapters offer fresh perspectives. For example, the chapter on the environment now includes a new cluster focusing on the nature of the cyber environment, an environment in which increasing numbers of people now dwell for large parts of their day. And the chapter on education, which previously addressed both secondary and higher education, is now focused exclusively on higher education, with readings arranged in response to three closely related questions: What should students be taught? How should students be taught? And, how should learning be measured?

The writers included in the book represent a range of interests, professions, perspectives, and cultural backgrounds. They also differ in the proficiency with which they present their ideas. A collection of equally compelling arguments would not prepare students to evaluate the diverse arguments they encounter in life. Students using this edition should come to see that some arguments are more persuasive than others—a useful development in critical thinking—but all of the readings are treated respectfully in the apparatus. Most of the readings are recent, reflecting contemporary points of view. They also reflect a diversity of media: There are selections from traditional print publications such as the *New York Times,* newer publications such as *Z Magazine,* and online journals. Some classic arguments, such as Martin Luther King, Jr.'s "Letter from a Birmingham Jail" and an excerpt from Rachel Carson's *Silent Spring* have been retained from previous editions because they have proven records of teaching well and remind students that arguments occur in a historical context. In most clusters, the selections by these writers have been arranged so that short and accessible readings lead to longer and more challenging pieces.

Innovative Pedagogical Features

- Historically significant excerpts that help establish how the readings in each chapter are part of an ongoing discussion.
- Accessible introductions to each cluster of readings that orient students to what they are about to read.
- Four kinds of supplementary boxes for each reading selection to help students better understand each piece:
    - *Gloss:* Information on specific people, events, or concepts in the reading. Glosses are linked to the text with reference marks (e.g., asterisk and dagger symbols).
    - *Context:* Background on issues, ideas, events, or persons in the reading.
    - *Sidebar:* Excerpts from texts referred to in the reading.
    - *Complication:* Information that complicates the argument made in the reading.
- Context, Sidebar, and Complication boxes are color keyed to the text.
- Questions for Discussion for each reading that include three main kinds of questions:
    - Questions to help students understand the selection.
    - Questions that focus attention on argumentative strategies and context.
    - Questions that encourage students to be self-reflective about their views.
- Negotiating Differences assignments at the end of each cluster that engage students in argumentation as a way to solve a problem related to the cluster topic.

New to This Edition

- Changes in organization that make the principles of argument easier to grasp
- Two new chapters: "Body Image" and "Relationships"
- Forty new reading selections
- Forty-four new images
- Expanded discussion of visual rhetoric, including advertisements, cartoons, graphs, icons, paintings, photographs, posters, and websites
- Expanded discussion of the uses of evidence in argumentation
- New student essays that provide models of different approaches to argument
- A refined design, including a new second color, to make the text easier to read and to annotate

Acknowledgments

When preparing this edition, I had the counsel of two good friends: Erika Scheurer and Mary Rose O'Reilley. Few weeks pass when I do not benefit from their advice and support, but I especially want to thank Erika for lending me reading material and for introducing me to Peter Elbow—who, in turn, offered thoughtful suggestions when I was working on the chapter focused on education. And I want to thank Mary Rose for contributing the discussion of portfolios that is inserted within Peter's argument in Chapter 11 and also for the dedication she composed for *The Garden at Night*, her most recent book on teaching English and a gift beyond measure.

Robert P. Yagelski of the State University of New York at Albany deserves acknowledgment for the extensive and labor-intensive work he did when we collaborated on the sixth edition of this book. Although Bob did not work on the seventh edition, much of the material that he introduced into the book remains in it, and I am grateful for this legacy.

I also want to acknowledge another kind of legacy: the insight I have gained from teaching argument for many years. Much of my work on this edition has been guided by classroom experience, and I wish to thank the many students who have helped me see what to retain and what to revise. Those students who contributed arguments to the book deserve special recognition, for they know that preparing a paper for publication takes considerable effort: Kristen Brubaker, James Fowler, Rachel Guetter, Karen Rivedal, and Tyler Sunderman.

I also benefited from the assistance of a former student: David Doody, who, as my efficient and good-natured research assistant, located several of the new selections and provided me with information upon which I drew when writing head notes and other parts of the apparatus. In addition, David skillfully composed marginalia to accompany many of the new readings.

At Wadsworth, both Karen Judd, Managing Development Editor, and Isabel Alves, Senior Permissions Editor, provided much appreciated assistance on many occasions. Isabel worked with Karyn Morrison on securing the many permissions agreements necessary for bringing this edition into print. I also want to thank Sarah Sherman, Associate Content Project Manager, and Bruce Bond, Senior Art Director, for overseeing the production and design process. Dickson Musslewhite, my acquisitions editor at Wadsworth, has been a strong advocate for this book, and I wish to thank him in particular for bringing me together with Maggie Barbieri—who served as my development editor. During every stage of this edition's development and production, Maggie provided attention, guidance, insight, and unfailing commitment to completing this project—doing so with professionalism infused with humor and grace even when she had other pressing concerns to address.

When the book went into production, the able assistance of Lisa Royse and Anne Williams of Graphic World Publishing Services ensured that the various components of the book got where they needed to be when they needed to be there during the long process of bringing manuscript and images into print. I also want to acknowledge the copyedit done by Julie Laing.

In addition, I am grateful to the following reviewers who offered useful suggestions as I undertook this edition:

Carolyn A. Embree, *University of Akron*
Rita Hendin, *Arizona State University*
Katherine M. Kapitan, *Buena Vista University*
Mary Kilgallen, *Ferris State University*
Mary R. Lamb, *Georgia State University*

Dr. Martha Macdonald, *York Technical College*
Elizabeth Mandrell, *Morehead State University*
David Silverstein, *The Pennsylvania State University*
Joanna Wolfe, *University of Louisville*
Their thoughtful comments guided me as I worked and affirmed the importance of this endeavor.

The Informed Argument

Understanding Arguments

1 ■ The Purposes of Argument

2 ■ The Contexts of Argument

3 ■ The Media for Argument

4 ■ The Strategies for Argument

1

The Purposes of Argument

Almost anything can be argued, but not everything *should* be argued. The decision about what to argue and how to make an argument not only is a practical one (What topic can I do justice to in the week I have for an argument assigned in my writing class? Will I be able to find the resources to complete this assignment?) but also can be an ethical one (What position should I take on stem-cell research? What are the potential consequences of opposing an increase in tuition at my school?). To make an argument is to engage in a social activity that can have consequences for you and others, and it's part of your responsibility as a writer to consider those consequences as you decide what to argue and how to do so. To make such a decision, it is helpful to consider why people engage in argument.

People engage in argumentation in diverse circumstances and to achieve different goals. Consider the following situations:

Example 1. A controversial radio personality recently spoke on campus at the invitation of a student group affiliated with one of the national political parties. The event was not sponsored by the university, but university facilities were used. Moreover, the student group that extended the invitation used university resources (such as a systemwide message delivered by e-mail) to publicize the event. The university, however, did not contribute any money for this event, nor did any academic department. The student group raised the money to fund part of the speaker's fee; the balance was contributed by private donors who chose to be anonymous. The event drew a large crowd. Many students present were shocked by views that seemed extreme to them and by crude language used to describe members of the government known for taking positions different from those of the speaker. Students were especially upset because they felt that the speaker twisted and ridiculed questions during the question-and-answer period that followed the speech, and you were one of the students who felt mocked. During the next several days, there was much discussion of the event, and a news report of the controversy it prompted appeared in a local newspaper. At this point, the university's president, who had not been present at the event, sent a message to all students, faculty, and staff. He said he "deeply regretted" the controversy and emphasized that the event had not been sponsored by the university. Unsatisfied by this official response, you decide to write a letter to the school newspaper. You assert that you are not paying tuition so that you can be insulted when you ask a reasonable question and that the university should not have allowed its facilities to be used for a speaker who has a history of being controversial.

Example 2. You have been working full time for the same company for more than three years, doing well at your job but feeling that it's not the kind of work you envisioned when you chose to major in marketing. During your years at the company you have received several raises, but you are still doing essentially the same kind of work and you have no reason to expect a promotion within the next year. When a friend at another company tells you about a position opening up at her firm, you are intrigued and ask whether she can provide additional information. She responds the next day by e-mail, attaching a link that provides the job description and the qualifications expected for candidates. The job sounds ideal for you, and the description leads you to think that it would offer opportunities for further growth. You update your resume and carefully write a letter of application. In preparation for writing your letter, you visit the company's home page and research the World Wide Web for information about how the company is doing. You then make several drafts of your letter, consulting with friends in the workplace who write well. You focus on your experience and abilities but also draw upon what you have learned about the position and the company so that your audience can see that you are a good fit.

NATURE OF ARGUMENT

Your letter would be an **argument to assert,** which means to make a claim or to state an opinion. Asserting your opinion in this case cannot undo what has already happened. You are simply explaining the nature of your concerns so that they can be understood by others. It is possible, however, that your assertion will influence the selection of future speakers or the guidelines made available to them when an invitation to speak is extended.

NATURE OF ARGUMENT

Your letter would be an **argument to prevail,** which means to achieve a specific goal based upon an assertion, a goal that once achieved is a victory of some kind. Eventually, the job in question will be given to only one person, no matter how many people apply for it. To obtain that job, you will need to prevail over other candidates. Although securing the job you want will require several arguments—such as those that you might need to make during the interview—you do not need to make them all at once. The first step is to write well enough to obtain an interview. Some applicants will be interviewed; others will not. You are determined to be among those selected.

Example 3. You and your partner have been together for five years, and you are still living in the apartment you rented when you graduated from the college where you met. You have happy memories of your years in this apartment and continue to enjoy the neighborhood. Located midway between campus (where you still attend occasional events) and downtown (where you both work), it is within walking distance of several shops, coffeehouses, and small restaurants. Unfortunately, your rent has increased substantially and you both feel the need for more space. Moreover, you realize that home ownership would provide tax advantages and help you build equity. It might also prove to be a good investment if the property you buy increases in value. Raising the down payment will be a challenge, and you may have to leave the neighborhood where you are living because it has become more popular (and thus more expensive) since you moved there. You want to explore the possibility of home ownership but feel that it is premature to call a real estate agent until you have a clearer sense of what you want and where you want it. What would be best for you: a duplex, a single-family house, a townhouse, or a condo? Then there is the issue of location: Do you want to remain in the city, finding housing in your current neighborhood or in a redeveloping neighborhood where property might still be undervalued? Or should you move to one of the city's many suburbs, each of which has a different profile? You and your partner discuss these questions daily and talk with friends who live in different parts of the metropolitan area. You both follow online listings posted by real estate agents and visit several properties around town when real estate agents host open houses. As your search continues, you come to agree that location is more important to you than the nature of the housing, and you have clarified your criteria—identifying three attractive locations where crime is low, public services are good, property values are increasing, and property sells quickly once listed. (This last factor matters to you because you both recognize that the job market may require you to relocate within the next five to ten years.) At this point, you contact one of the real estate agents you met at an open house—someone who impressed you as well informed and reliable. Working with this real estate agent over the next two months, you view several properties that come close to meeting your needs, and you benefit from ongoing dialogue with the real estate agent, noting that she has been paying close attention to your responses. Eventually you find a property that you love and can afford. The real estate agent confirms that the property is a good value and offers to help you arrange the financing. You make a small payment to hold the property until you can arrange for a building inspector to evaluate it. You also arrange a time when you can revisit the property with a few close friends and family members so that they feel part of the process and you can learn whether they see any problems you may have overlooked. All goes well, and you purchase the property in question.

Example 4. You are a member of the school board that makes decisions for a large district. Both of your children are attending public schools in this district, which has the reputation of being one of the best in the state. During this school year, the board must approve the use of a new textbook for American history for

NATURE OF ARGUMENT

The process you have just completed provides an example of an **argument to inquire,** which means that you use research and dialogue to discover the best of many possible answers. Other people may reach a conclusion that is different from your own, and you see no reason to prevail over them, insisting that the location and housing you chose would be ideal for anyone. But by debating questions such as "Do we want housing that is in move-in condition, or would it make more sense to buy something that needs renovation that we could undertake in stages?" you are able to discover what works best for you. A written transcript of all your conversations—or even a hard copy of the e-mail on your search—would show others how inquiry leads to discovery. You might even create a website with links that would help others successfully navigate the process you have just completed. If you urged others to make the same choice you did, you would be writing to prevail. But if you help them make the choice that works best for them, you are arguing to inquire.

high school seniors. Administrative policy calls for reconsideration of authorized textbooks every five years. The current textbook has been used for more than four years, and the selection of a new text will be difficult. Many parents have formed a group called Citizens for American Education and have launched a campaign against the current text, a new edition of which will be out within a year. They complain that this text is "un-American" because it gives extensive coverage to issues such as slavery, the treatment of Native Americans, and the imprisonment of Japanese Americans during the Second World War. Arguing that emphasis on issues such as these demoralizes students and turns them against their own country, this group of parents has endorsed an alternative textbook—one that emphasizes the nation's positive achievements. This textbook has received poor reviews from historians, but it is visually attractive because it has a good design and includes many illustrations in color. Teachers, however, argue that the adoption of this proposed text would contribute to "dumbing down" of the curriculum and would leave students with a distorted vision of the past. Moreover, some members of the community (including teachers and parents) are concerned about the rising price of textbooks, noting that the use of color and art contributes to making a text more expensive than a text without colorful illustrations. Some educators insist that color and art are essential for holding students' attention; others argue that attention can be gained in other ways. You note that at least two separate issues need to be resolved. You must be able to negotiate with parents and teachers who have ideological differences about what is most significant about the past. This will be a challenge, because the extent to which the new text is "political" (and what kind of political) could deepen and harden mistrust that already exists within the district. By comparison, it seems that it should be easier to negotiate the issue of what a text costs and how the material is presented visually. With these concerns in mind, you convince the school board to convene a special meeting at which concerned teachers, parents, and students can express their views to the board—with the assurance that they will be given a fair hearing but will be expected to listen to others and to avoid attacking people with whom they disagree. Subsequent to this meeting, and working closely with your fellow board members, you arrange for publishers to provide sample copies of all current and forthcoming texts for American history for the twelfth grade. You invite volunteers to join two committees. One of these will assess the clarity, accuracy, and balance of the books available; the other will research and report upon the relationship between visual presentation and learning. To make sure that these committees are balanced and representative, you recruit additional members when necessary and arrange for consultations with history and education professors at a college widely respected in the community. By sharing power and listening to diverse voices, you eventually help the board make a decision that pleases people who thought they had irreconcilable differences: The board authorizes the use of an ideologically balanced and clearly written text that is less expensive than many of the texts with which it is competing for market share. Recognizing that this text, like any text, cannot fully address all parts of American history, you help set up a website that parents,

NATURE OF ARGUMENT

The role that you have fulfilled provides an example of an **argument to negotiate differences,** which means reconciling people engaged in some kind of conflict. You did not begin with a fixed position (as in arguing to assert or to prevail). Instead, you listened carefully to what others had to say and created forums in which a productive exchange of views could be continued. You and your colleagues then worked with what was generated through discussion and research to reconcile differences with a multilayered solution. Had you simply "compromised" by pushing for a middle-of-the-road text that split the difference between those who wanted a more conservative text and those who wanted a more progressive one, you might have achieved a short-term solution. The problem with compromise, however, is that no one really gets what he or she wants. By launching an educational website and a new program for parents, you provided conflicting parties with the sense that they are part of the solution.

teachers, and students can access and on which they can post links to additional documents, images, and articles. You also launch a program in which concerned parents are invited to visit classes and speak about what they liked and disliked about the way they learned history—thus including diverse voices but fostering discussion of learning rather than political or religious ideology.

As these four examples show, people engage in argument for many reasons:

- To assert
- To prevail
- To inquire
- To negotiate differences

These purposes may overlap. It is necessary, for example, to assert when arguing to prevail, and it is often necessary to inquire before you can negotiate differences. You will examine arguments that illustrate these points later in this book. You will also consider other issues, such as how to organize and to support an argument. But before you do so, some additional consideration of purpose will help you analyze arguments written by others and compose arguments of your own.

The preceding examples are arranged in a sequence that seems to move from the simplest to the most complex—and this sequence reflects a rhetorical principle that is true to an extent. It is often easier to make an assertion than to reconcile differences. The extent to which any argument is challenging, however, depends upon your rhetorical situation as a whole: your audience, your topic, and the context in which you are composing. (For a discussion of the rhetorical situation, see Chapter 2.) So, difficulty cannot be accessed by purpose alone. The examples have also been arranged in a sequence that suggests that the older you become, the more complicated the purpose you can undertake. Again, there is a social reality behind this sequence. One of the first words learned by young children is "no"—and that is a kind of assertion. But parents also have to assert themselves, and arguments to fulfill any of the purposes listed previously can be necessary at almost any stage in life. For example, if you are living in a dorm or apartment with students who have conflicting values or habits, there may be an occasion in which you argue to negotiate differences before you stop speaking to each other.

Arguments To Assert

In the first example, when you complained about the behavior of an on-campus speaker, you saw the need to publicize your view. You wished to assert your position so that others would understand how you felt, and you saw this as part of a wider discussion at your school. Your letter may influence others and have unexpected consequences in the future if it made a memorable impression, but your primary purpose was simply to assert—not to argue for a specific reform and provide evidence that such a reform would be helpful. Nor were you trying (at this point, at least) to use argument to inquire as a way to work out a better policy for governing campus life. You were upset, you had reason to be upset, and you wanted others to know it. Fair enough. That's much better than bottling up feelings or being afraid to express an opinion.

You can probably imagine many situations in which your primary goal is to assert a position on which there may be disagreement or controversy:

- In a class discussion about gay marriage
- In a meeting of a student organization that is considering whether to call for a boycott of local stores that sell goods produced in sweatshops
- In your place of employment as your coworkers decide how to respond to a new overtime policy
- In a relationship in which you have been asked what you think would be necessary to improve it

FIGURE 1-1

Advertising as Arguing to Assert

This advertisement for a climbing rope manufacturer might be seen as an argument to assert a particular point of view about women. It plays off cultural stereotypes about women as passive and presents a different view of women as aggressive and athletic.

In such situations, more than one assertion is likely to arise, because more than one person is involved in each of these discussions and one assertion can easily trigger another. To assert what you think and believe can help you gain credibility as a thoughtful participant in discussion and contribute toward arguing to inquire. In short, honest assertions can be useful to offer and helpful to learn. Almost any assertion can lead to a prolonged discussion or a well-developed piece of writing. But arguments to assert usually begin with an assertion instead of being composed to arrive at one.

In some ways, all arguments are arguments to assert. Even advertisements whose primary purpose is to persuade people to purchase a product, often assert a position or perspective (see Figure 1-1).

Arguments to Prevail

When most people think of formal arguments, they think of arguments whose primary purpose is to prevail. The most common example is an argument made in a legal case. A lawyer might be arguing before a judge to grant bail to her client—say, a young man accused of rape—so that the client will not have to remain in jail while waiting for the trial to begin. In such a case, the lawyer has one main goal: to win. She wishes only to convince the judge that the client should be free on bail. Her opponent, the prosecutor, will try to counter the defense lawyer's argument so that the young man remains imprisoned. When this case goes to trial, arguments designed to prevail will continue to be made. The defense attorney will try to win an acquittal, and the prosecutor will try to win a conviction. In most such cases, the arguments tend to be adversarial and the opponents easily identified.

But legal cases are not always so clear-cut. Consider a different example of a young man pulled over for drunk driving:

> A man in his twenties with no criminal record and a clean driving record is driving home late at night from a party celebrating his company's recent increase in sales. On the way home he realizes that he has had too much to drink and that it is dangerous for him to be driving. So he pulls onto the shoulder of the road, puts the car in park, and then falls asleep with the car still idling. Later, a police officer stops to investigate and, realizing that the young man has been drinking, arrests him for drunk driving.

According to the laws in that state, the young man is guilty of driving while intoxicated, because he was seated behind the wheel of the car while the car was still running. In the eyes of the law, it doesn't matter that the car was parked and not moving at the time the officer found the man. In his summary argument to the jury,

FIGURE 1-2

A Poster Opposing Drunk Driving

Drawing upon the simplicity of a road sign, the designer of this poster makes an argument to prevail: Driving after drinking alcohol should be stopped. MADD stands for "Mothers Against Drunk Driving," and the initials contribute to this argument by indicating that drunk driving is "mad" (or insane) as well as indicating that mothers and those who sympathize with them are "mad" (or angry) about the consequences of drunk driving.

the defense lawyer pointed out that his client is indeed technically guilty but that convicting him would amount to penalizing him for realizing that he shouldn't have been driving; a conviction would punish him for making the safe and responsible decision to stop his car and wait until he sobered up before continuing to drive home. In other words, the lawyer argued that his client did the right thing, even though he was legally guilty of driving while intoxicated. Why, he asked, should this young man, with no prior offenses, be punished for making the right decision?

In this case, the lawyer's purpose was to win—to prevail over his opponent, the prosecutor—by convincing the jury that they should find the defendant not guilty. And his argument that his client did the "right" thing—if not the legal thing—can be seen as a strategy to win the jury's sympathy and appeal to their sense of justice. But if you consider the argument in the larger context of the state's efforts to impose laws that will reduce drunk driving accidents, then the lawyer argued in a way that contributes to that larger purpose. He tried to persuade the jury that what his client did—pulling over his car so that he would avoid an accident—was really what the drunk driving laws are all about. Punishing the young man for his decision therefore would make no sense. In short, the social and ethical considerations of the case go beyond the immediate goal of winning the argument and the case.

As the example of the job applicant (on page 4) suggests, you can make an argument to prevail for personal and professional reasons. Moreover, arguing to prevail does not necessarily mean putting yourself in an adversarial position. Someone who comes on too strong when applying for a job is unlikely to get it—unless the position is for a bouncer at a bar. If you were to claim that you alone were capable of filling the position and were to ignore what could be seen as problems in your background, you probably would not be taken seriously. Instead, by demonstrating good credibility (what is called *ethos* in classical rhetoric), you would claim no more than you can support, present yourself as respectful and professional, and frankly acknowledge areas in which you need to gain more experience. Recognizing a potential weakness can be taken as a sign of strength—especially if you can explain why those areas should not pose concern—a strategy known as anticipating and responding to opposition (which will be described in Chapters 2 and 5). Even if you lose the immediate argument—by failing to get the job you are seeking—you can achieve a larger purpose: understanding what kind of rhetoric works in the job market so that you approach your next application with more experience and, in time, expertly assess the people you interview when you are in a position of authority.

You can probably think of many occasions during which you might need to use argument to prevail. For example:

- Getting admitted to a school to which you want to transfer
- Winning a required debate in a course in political science or communications
- Retaining your ability to drive after having been ticketed for speeding
- Convincing someone you love to accept a marriage proposal

At some point you will likely find yourself in a situation in which winning an argument is extremely important to you. Understanding arguments to prevail can help you construct an effective argument in that situation.

Arguments To Inquire

In the third example provided earlier, the search undertaken by a couple looking for new housing does not argue on behalf of a specific position that others should accept (as in arguing to prevail). Its primary purpose is to explore the complexities of their needs and the variety of options available to them. This exploration—which involves both research and give and take in discussion (or what is called *dialectic* in classical rhetoric)—helps the couple make a good decision. In other words, instead of emphasizing an assertion as the foundation for their process (as in arguing to assert or to prevail), they have reached an assertion as a result of their efforts—an assertion informed by a series of other assertions that emerged through dialogue.

You probably engage in similar kinds of arguments. Perhaps the best example is class discussion. In a sociology course, for instance, you might discuss foster care. As a student in the class, you are not considered an expert on foster care, nor do your arguments or your classmates' arguments have consequences outside your class (unlike, say, a social worker's arguments to a family court judge about a specific case). Most important, your arguments in this situation are not necessarily intended to convince your classmates to support or oppose a particular position about when it is appropriate to remove children from their families of origin; rather, in making arguments and listening to those of your classmates, you are engaged in a collective inquiry into the sociological issues surrounding child care. You are arguing to learn and understand.

As a college student, you will probably find that much academic writing can be characterized as arguments to inquire. Arguments in the natural and social sciences, for example, often cite previous studies and reach tentative conclusions that recognize the need for additional research. Such arguments are exploratory and informative, implicitly inviting readers to join the inquiry at hand. With this in mind, consider the following excerpt from the opening chapter of *Writing Space,* a book by Jay David Bolter about how new computer technologies are changing the nature of writing. As this excerpt suggests, Bolter believes that computers are fostering dramatic changes in how and what people write. His position is not universally shared, however. Bolter knows this. He isn't concerned about convincing other scholars that he's right and they're wrong; rather, he wishes to examine a complex issue that other scholars want to understand better.

In Victor Hugo's novel *Notre-Dame de Paris, 1482,* the priest remarked "Ceci tuera cela": this book will destroy that building. He meant not only that printing and literacy would undermine the authority of the church but also that "human thought . . . would change its mode of expression, that the principal idea of each generation would no longer write itself with the same material and in the same way, that the book of stone, so solid and durable, would give place to the book made of paper, yet more solid and durable" (p. 199). The medieval cathedral crowded with statues and stained glass was both a symbol of Christian authority and a repository of medieval knowledge (moral knowledge about the world and the human condition). The cathedral was a library to be read by the religious, who walked through its aisles looking up at the scenes of the Bible, the images of saints, allegorical figures of virtue and vice, visions of heaven and hell. . . . Of course, the printed book did not eradicate the encyclopedia in stone; it did not even eradicate the medieval art of writing by hand. People continued to contemplate their religious tradition in cathedrals, and they continued to communicate with pen and paper for many purposes. But printing did displace handwriting: the printed book became the most valued form of handwriting. And printing certainly helped to displace the medieval organization and expression of knowledge. As Elizabeth Eisenstein has shown, the modern printing press has been perhaps the most important tool of the modern scientist. (See *The Printing Press as an Agent of Change* by Elizabeth Eisenstein, 1979, especially vol. 2, pp. 520ff.)

Hugo himself lived in the heyday of printing, when the technology had just developed to allow mass publication of novels, newspapers, and journals. Hugo's own popularity in France (like Dickens' in England) was evidence that printed books were reaching and defining a new mass audience. Today we are living in the late age of print. The evidence of senescence, if not senility, is all around us. And as we look up from our computer keyboards to the books on our shelves, we must ask ourselves whether "this will destroy that." Computer technology (in the form of word processing, databases, electronic bulletin boards and mail) is beginning to displace the printed book. . . .

The printed book, therefore, seems destined to move to the margin of our literate culture. . . . The shift to the computer will make writing more flexible, but it will also threaten the definitions of good writing and careful reading that have been fostered by the technique of printing. The printing press encouraged us to think of a written text as an unchanging artifact, a monument to its author and its age. . . . Electronic writing emphasizes the impermanence and changeability of text, and it tends to reduce the distance between author and reader by turning the reader into an author. It is changing the cultural status of writing as well as the method of producing books. It is changing the relationship of the author to the text and of both the author and text to the reader.

To write an effective argument of inquiry requires researching the topic and examining the issues surrounding it. It might require using evidence, but the evidence might be used to *illustrate* a point rather than to support it. For example, in the preceding excerpt, Bolter refers to historian Elizabeth Eisenstein to help him develop his point about the important effect of the printing press. He does this not as a way to say, "I'm right," but as a way to lend credibility to his main point about writing and technology.

What is especially noteworthy about an argument to inquire is that your own position might change or evolve as you examine the topic and go through the process of planning, writing, and revising your argument. In fact, you might begin the process of writing this kind of argument without a clear position on the topic. Your position will emerge through the process of writing. These arguments, then, are exploratory in two ways: (1) They encourage the writer to explore a topic in order to arrive at a reasonable position, and (2) they invite other writers to engage in exploring that topic.

As noted earlier, arguing to inquire is common in academic writing. Other situations in which you might find it useful include the following:

- Discovering the right major for you
- Deciding what kind of car to buy
- Focusing on what you can contribute to a relationship
- Figuring out how to raise children

Arguments To Negotiate and Reconcile

Glance through your morning newspaper, and you will quickly find examples of situations in which people have seemingly irreconcilable or even intractable differences about an issue or occupy such divergent perspectives that no option seems to exist except for one side defeating or silencing the other. At the same time, communications technologies have brought people into more frequent contact with one another, so we now routinely confront all kinds of differences—social, cultural, religious, political, ethnic, regional, and so on. Such diversity enriches our lives, but it also challenges us to learn how to live together peacefully. In this sense, one of the main purposes of argument is to confront the complexity that arises from diversity in order to negotiate and, ideally, to reconcile differences. This might be the most difficult kind of argument.

The school board example on pages 5–7 shows how the need to negotiate and reconcile is especially important in situations involving multiple parties with multiple points of view—all of which need to be respected. The solution in this case required a lengthy process, and the process of negotiating differences is likely to become more complex and lengthy as the number of people involved increases or the differences of opinions deepen. Although the solution achieved in the example may need to be renegotiated (such as the next time the board must choose an American history textbook for high school seniors), sustained effort reduced conflict and led to widely accepted decisions.

Such an outcome might sound idealistic, but many situations are argued in this way. For example, lawyers representing different sides in a legal case do not always argue to prevail. It is quite common for defense lawyers and prosecutors to negotiate a plea bargain, which amounts to a compromise in which each side gains something and neither side loses everything. In such a situation, both sides would argue in front of a judge in a way intended to work out an agreement that is fair and appropriate. That agreement usually involves the defendant pleading guilty to a lesser charge, and it would appeal to prosecutors who are uncertain about prevailing in court when arguing for a more serious charge. It would also appeal to prosecutors who believe they can resolve other cases through information provided by the defendant as part of the plea bargain—thus advancing the common good, even if a specific individual may be getting off lightly.

Arguing to negotiate differences is sometimes called *Rogerian argument,* after the influential psychotherapist Carl Rogers, who emphasized the importance of communication to resolve conflicts. Rogers believed that most people are so ready "to judge, to evaluate, to approve or disapprove" that they fail to understand what others think. He urged people to "listen with understanding" and recommended a model for communication in which listeners are required to restate what others have said before offering their own views. This restatement should be done fairly and accurately, without either praise or blame, so that the original speaker is able to confirm, "Yes, that is what I said."

Although this model might seem simple, Rogers cautioned that it takes courage to listen carefully to views that are contrary to one's own, especially in volatile situations or on charged and difficult issues (such as abortion or capital punishment). It is extremely hard to listen when feelings are strong. The greater the conflict, the greater the chance of misinterpreting what others have said. Moreover, it's easy to think of situations in which any kind of listening seems impossible because the people involved are engaged in such deep conflict. Rogers envisioned situations in which individuals are engaged in dialogue, and his commitment to the importance of restating others' ideas (without evaluating them) rests on the assumption that language can be neutral—an idea that has been seriously questioned by modern linguists and philosophers. And Rogers's emphasis on the importance of listening may be more helpful to people who are used to speaking than to those who have been silenced. Feminists, for instance, have argued that because public discourse has long been dominated by men, women need to learn how to assert themselves and men need help in learning to listen. For these reasons, many scholars questioned the extent to which Rogers's ideas can be applied to written arguments.

Nevertheless, if you think carefully about the role of argument in resolving conflict and achieving social cooperation, Rogers's perspective on communication can be useful in helping you formulate effective arguments. And the examples cited here underscore the advantages of approaching argument in this way when a situation is characterized by a difficult conflict. Indeed, given the scale of the conflicts we face today within our communities, in our cultures, and in the world, a Rogerian perspective might be the most ethical way to approach an argument and might offer the only viable alternative available in certain situations. Think, for example, of the situation faced by Nelson Mandela as the new president of South Africa after the previous apartheid government was dismantled (see Figure 1-3). The long history of oppression and conflict that characterized South Africa and the terrible struggle that Mandela and his supporters endured to defeat apartheid and achieve equality would have made it easy for Mandela to argue for his new government's policies with only the goal of domination and victory in mind. Instead, Mandela recog-

FIGURE 1-3

Nelson Mandela

In helping reconstruct his country after apartheid was dismantled in 1991, former president of South Africa Nelson Mandela made many speeches that can be considered Rogerian argument.

nized that even supporters of the defeated apartheid government were citizens of his country and that it was in everyone's interest to confront and negotiate their differences. As a result, he often argued with the goal of resolution in mind.

The usefulness of an approach to argument that emphasizes negotiating differences extends to more common situations. For example, neighbors in conflict over a drainage problem on the boundary between their properties might be better served by arguing to their town supervisor for a resolution that fairly addresses the problem on both sides of the boundary rather than by one neighbor trying to force the other to fix the problem by winning the case in court. Or you might find yourself working with classmates as part of a group project for one of your college courses; if a conflict arises between group members, it's possible that a "victory" by one group member over another could result in a project that is less effective and therefore earns a lower grade for all group members. In short, arguing to negotiate differences rather than to defeat an opponent might best serve your interests and those of the other people involved, and it may be the best way to avoid further conflict.

There is no question that some differences may be irreconcilable. The news headlines about bombings in the Middle East or religious conflict in Europe remind us that no matter how genuinely we engage with one another in arguments, negotiation and resolution might not always be possible. And there are times when winning an argument, rather than negotiating differences, may be ethical. Still, in all but the most extreme situations, genuine engagement in argument as a way to solve a problem, negotiate serious differences, and work toward resolution can offer the best alternative for all concerned. As a writer, you also benefit from writing arguments in this way, in the sense that your engagement in such argumentation may lead to a greater understanding of the situation, which can enrich your perspective on conflict and enhance your ability to engage in future arguments.

Although arguing to negotiate differences is especially useful in public affairs, such as the school board example (on pages 5–7) and the way Nelson Mandela guided his country in the years immediately after the formal end of apartheid, it can also be useful when resolving differences that may arise in your daily life. Examples include the following:

- Establishing helpful rules that can keep roommates living together peacefully
- Distributing responsibilities fairly among coworkers to improve morale
- Convincing your family to stop fighting with one another to develop a better relationship

Again, understanding the purposes of argument introduced in this chapter is likely to help you compose arguments that are useful not only in your personal and professional lives but also in discussion of important social issues. You may emphasize one purpose on one occasion and another purpose at another time. You may also combine these purposes in different ways depending on the context of your argument (see Chapter 2), the media of your argument (see Chapter 3), and the strategies you choose to employ (see Chapter 4). But whatever you decide, remember that arguing is not the same as quarreling—it is a means for conveying what you believe, achieving specific goals, clarifying what you think, and solving problems in a troubled world.

2

The Contexts of Argument

W henever we engage in argumentation, we must do more than examine the topic carefully and construct a sound argument in support of our position. We must also take into account our audience, the specific situation we and they are in, the cultural factors that might affect how an audience responds to a particular argument, even the historical moment we are in as we argue. In short, we always argue within a context—actually, within several contexts simultaneously—and we must consider context if we expect to argue effectively.

Imagine that you have been given an assignment to assert a position on the federal government's ability to access personal e-mail for reasons of national security and to write an argument justifying your position. Assume further that your essay will be read to your class, which includes students who differ in terms of gender, religion, and political principles. The electronic surveillance of personal mail is a controversial topic for at least two reasons: it concerns "national security," which is important but could be challenged by students who question the integrity of law enforcement officials, and people vary in terms of how strongly they feel about the right to privacy. After reading a number of articles and essays, you decide that despite some problems with electronic surveillance, you believe that it can be an important tool for fighting terrorism. You write an argument in which you acknowledge the serious problems that can occur as a result of electronic surveillance by law enforcement agencies, but you justify its use on the grounds of security and public safety. In your argument you try to address your teacher and your classmates, some of whom have voiced strenuous opposition to electronic surveillance. You wish to make an effective argument that your classmates, even those opposed to electronic surveillance, will take seriously, though you are mindful that some of them might reject what you have to say because of their own passionate engagement with the issue. You also know that your teacher will be assessing your argument and that your classmates' reactions might influence her assessment. So you gather some evidence that surveillance has prevented violence, and you identify what you consider to be good arguments in support of policies that can protect citizens' privacy and civil rights. But you also know that the charged nature of the topic will make some of these arguments seem less than convincing to some of your classmates. What will you write?

As a writer you might not have faced a situation quite as challenging as the one described here, but if you have engaged in argument, you have had to think about some of the same problems you would encounter in this situation. The answer to the question "What will you write?" in a given situation requires that you consider the context of your argument. No matter what kind of argument you wish to make, no matter what your purpose, there are at least three main contexts you should consider as you construct an argument:

- The rhetorical situation
- The cultural context
- The moment in which you are arguing, which we can call the *historical context*

The Rhetorical Situation

Rhetoricians have long used the metaphor of a triangle to help define the rhetorical situation (see Figure 2-1). The classical rhetorical triangle reminds us that when we write an argument, we are engaged in an interaction with a particular audience about a particular subject. Both audience and writer have a connection to the subject matter in the form of knowledge about the subject, opinions about it, experience with it, and so on. But the writer and the audience will never have identical connections to that subject. A big part of the challenge, then, is to try to understand your audience and its connection to your subject so that you can address your audience effectively as you construct your argument.

Analyzing Your Audience

The audience for an argument can vary dramatically from one situation to another, and as will be explained in more detail later in this chapter, the specific characteristics of the rhetorical situation (when and where someone is making an argument, for example) can profoundly affect how a writer addresses an audience and how an audience might respond to an argument. But because an argument is often an attempt to communicate with an audience about a conflict or a problem, and because ideally an argument will effectively address that conflict or resolve the problem, it is essential for writers to try to understand their audience to the extent that they can. There are some general guidelines for doing so.

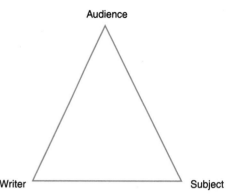

FIGURE 2-1
The Rhetorical Situation

First, try to determine what you already know about your intended audience. In some cases, the audience for an argument will be specific. In the hypothetical example on page 18, you would be familiar with your audience (your teacher and your classmates), and you would have some sense of their knowledge and opinions about your subject (electronic surveillance). Moreover, because you would have engaged in class discussion about this topic, you might even know how some of your classmates (and perhaps your teacher) might react to specific arguments in favor of or against electronic surveillance. You can imagine other situations in which you might know your audience well. For instance, if you were writing a letter to your school newspaper in support of a proposal for a new swimming pool, you would know something about the people who might read your letter. You might even know them personally. You would have a good sense of who the readers would be because you see and hear them whenever you are on campus. A writer can draw on such knowledge to identify effective arguments. In some ways this is almost an ideal situation for a writer, because there would be little of the uncertainty about the audience that writers usually face in writing an argument. If the goal is to try to solve a problem, then knowing the audience can lead to a better understanding of their positions and a more genuine engagement with them about the issue.

It is important to remember, however, that there is much that you may not know about an audience with which you are familiar. Differences or similarities in gender and race may be relatively easy to determine. But the nature of someone's spiritual life or sexual orientation depends in good measure on how much information others choose to disclose to you. Even a close friend may choose not to disclose something that is troubling him. So when addressing a familiar audience, draw upon what you know but do not make assumptions about what you do not know for certain.

In many cases, however, writers are likely to have only limited knowledge about their audience. Imagine the difference between writing a letter to the editor of a newspaper, which is read by a few hundred people who live in the same town, and writing a letter to the editor of a national publication such as *USA Today*, which is read by millions of people from all over the country. The assumptions that you can reasonably make about these audiences can differ dramatically. But it is not feasible to analyze a general audience, such as the readership of *USA Today*, in depth because that audience is far too diverse for you to know anything about it in detail. Nevertheless, you can approach such an audience in a way that is likely to engage a majority of readers and address them effectively. In other words, even though there is a limit to what you can know about an audience (after all, even a close friend can surprise you), you can make some general assumptions about your audience that will help you argue effectively.

You can begin by assuming an intelligent and fair-minded audience. Assume as well that intelligent and fair-minded people tend to be skeptical about sweeping generalizations and unsupported claims. In some cases you might be able to expect your audience to agree with you. For example, if you are the keynote speaker at a political convention, chances are that most people in the audience will share your viewpoint. But if you are attempting to reconcile differences or solve a conflict through argument, you should probably assume that your audience will disagree with you. Some members of your audience might be neutral about the issue you're addressing. But imagining a skeptical audience will enable you to anticipate and respond to opposing views or objections to your position, thus building a stronger case.

Imagining Your Audience

In some ways, imagining an audience is a creative act. The twentieth-century scholar Walter Ong wrote a famous article called "The Writer's Audience Is Always a Fiction," in which he argued that when writers write, they must always create a sense of an audience that doesn't necessarily correspond directly to a "real" audience. This act of "fiction," Ong maintained, is necessary because rarely do writers know in detail just whom they are writing to or for. But this imagined audience is always based on a general sense of who might read what you are writing, your experiences with people in general, your experiences as readers of other people's writing, and your knowledge of the conventions of writing. All these figure into the imagined audience. In other words, the imagined audience is based on real experiences with writing and with other people. When it comes to argument, this act of imagining an audience influences the specific arguments you will make in support of your position on an issue. It can also inform you about how readers respond to your argument. Just as you may be creating a sense of audience, your real audience may (or may not) choose to participate in the fiction you create. For example, if you convey the sense that you are addressing a thoughtful and fair-minded audience, readers who sometimes fail to demonstrate these qualities may rise to the standard you have set for them.

Even when imagining a general audience, writers often make specific assumptions about their readers, beyond assuming that they are intelligent but skeptical. Consider, for example, the following letter, which was written to the editors of *Newsweek* in response to an essay by columnist Allan Sloan criticizing greed and unethical behavior by large corporations:

> Right on, Allan Sloan! I have long thought that no economic system, certainly not capitalism, can function successfully without the moderating effects of virtuous, ethical behavior on the part of the key players. That said, I'm afraid that we have yet to widely acknowledge that such behavior can never be reliably coerced by endless rounds of civil regulation. In a free society there will always be loopholes to be identified and exploited by those with selfish, greedy attitudes.

Notice that this writer implicitly assumes that his readers are not necessarily those with "selfish, greedy attitudes"; nor are they likely to be the "key players" in the capitalist system. In other words, he assumes that his readers are "average" people who share his basic values regarding ethical behavior. He can further assume that his readers have read Allan Sloan's essay and that they probably have a basic understanding of the principles of capitalism that Sloan discussed. Even a "general" audience can be specific in certain respects. Narrowing an audience in this way can help a writer determine how to cast an argument so that it effectively addresses that general audience.

Sometimes, a writer can define a general audience more directly by explicitly excluding specific kinds of readers. In the following letter, which was also written to the editors of *Newsweek,* the writer is responding to an article about electroshock therapy:

> I was surprised to find no mention of neurofeedback in your article "Healthy Shocks to the Head." Noninvasive, relatively inexpensive and proving to be effective with a long list of central nervous-system disorders, this procedure should be given an opportunity to demonstrate its effectiveness before more invasive procedures are tried. It's too bad the medical community is so enamored with drugs and surgery.

Notice that this writer refers to "the medical community" in a way that excludes members of that community from his audience. In effect, he is addressing everyone outside the medical community. This writer probably knows that members of that community are likely to read his letter, too, so indirectly he is addressing them—as well as criticizing them—and perhaps inspiring an Ong-like fiction: "You're a *good* doctor or nurse, not one of those types I am referring to here." But by referring to them as he does, he defines his intended audience as those readers who are not members of that community, thus narrowing his "general" audience and assuming that they might share his concerns.

It is worth noting that if the writer in the preceding example hoped to try to negotiate the apparent conflict that exists between those who advocate noninvasive techniques for treating disorders of the central nervous system, as he does, and those in the medical community who might have a different view, then he would need to address the medical community directly. In other words, a sense of purpose for an argument will shape the writer's sense of audience.

The audience for an argument is also influenced by the specific circumstances in which the argument is being made. In the previous example, the writer is addressing a general audience made up of readers of *Newsweek,* and he is doing so in response to a specific article that appeared in that magazine. Imagine if he were making the same argument—in favor of noninvasive techniques for treating disorders of the central nervous system—in a letter written to the *Journal of Mental Health.* In that case the audience would likely include some of the same readers of *Newsweek,* but it would now be composed primarily of mental health professionals who read that journal—that is, members of the medical community that he criticized in his original letter. Although his argument might not change, this writer would now be able to use more technical language and would likely have to address his readers differently if he wished them to take him seriously. Imagine further that he is not responding to an article in *Newsweek* but is writing about the issue of electroshock therapy in general. In this case he must introduce his topic differently, because he would not be able to refer to a specific article that he could assume his readers had read. But he *could* assume that his audience knew more about these treatments than the readers of *Newsweek* are likely to know, which would affect what information he might include in his argument and how he might present it. The circumstances for his argument would therefore affect several important aspects of his argument even if his basic position is the same.

As these examples suggest, the circumstances within which an audience is being addressed can have a big effect on how that audience will respond to a specific argument. It is impossible for a writer to know about everything that is part of a rhetorical situation, just as it is impossible for a writer to be able to anticipate how every member of the audience will react to a specific word, phrase, tone, fact, or line of argumentation. Human beings are simply too complex. But effective arguments are usually effective only within a specific rhetorical situation. What works in one situation might not work in another. So it is crucial for writers of arguments to examine the rhetorical situation they are in and make their best judgments about how to address their audience in that situation. Although trying to understand an audience takes time and effort, it offers a great reward: knowledge about human nature that can make it easier to live and work with others.

Cultural Context

When writers engage a particular audience in argumentation, they never address generic readers, even when they are addressing the kind of general audience described in the previous section. Instead, they address individuals, each of whom brings a different set of experiences, knowledge, beliefs, and background to the interaction. In other words, who we are as individuals shapes how we will react to an argument. And who we are is a complex matter that encompasses race, gender, and other aspects of cultural identity. In this regard, culture will always be part of any rhetorical situation and thus shape any argument.

Understanding Culture

Culture can be understood in several ways when it comes to argumentation. As suggested in the preceding paragraph, culture is your sense of identity as it relates to your racial and ethnic backgrounds, your religious upbringing (if any), your membership in a particular social class (working class, for example), and the region where you live (for example, rural West Virginia versus urban Los Angeles). These aspects of our identity affect how individuals understand themselves in relation to others and as members of various communities. Culture in this sense will shape how you view the world, what you believe and value, and how you experience various aspects of life. Culture can also be envisioned as the nation in which you live and interact with others, as in the culture of the United States or the culture of Japan. These ways of understanding culture overlap, but they provide a sense of the powerful influence that culture will have on individual writers and readers as they engage in argumentation.

Consider how classmates with different cultural backgrounds might react to an argument in favor of racial profiling (or the police practice of stopping and searching people because of their race or ethnicity rather than because of evidence of criminal behavior). An African American student might be highly sensitive to the subject—and perhaps passionate about it—because the controversy about the subject has directly involved people with an appearance similar to his or her own. In addition, if that student grew up in an urban neighborhood where relations between residents and police are strained, geography is also likely to shape his or her views. Compare that student to, say, an exchange student from Japan, where racial issues have a different history. A Japanese student might also have a different sense of authority and of the relationship between individuals and the government than Americans students have. To invoke a somewhat different example, what if one of your white classmates was raised in a Quaker household that emphasized a lifestyle based on nonviolence? How might that person react to an argument in favor of racial profiling? All of these hypothetical examples indicate the various ways in which culture can influence both the writing and the reading of an argument.

These examples tell us something else: that culture is complex. The student who was raised as a Quaker, for example, is white but can legitimately claim a different cultural identity from other white students in your class, even though all of them can claim to be part of American culture. The same can be said of two different black students: one who might have grown up in a middle-class suburb and another whose parents might be working-class immigrants from the Caribbean. In other words, even if two people have similar cultural backgrounds, they will not have *identical* cultural backgrounds and will not have identical experiences as members of that culture. As a writer of arguments you can't be expected to sort out all of these subtle complexities, but you should always be sensitive to culture and assume that culture will play an important role in argumentation. Brian Fay, a philosopher of social science, describes the influence of culture in this way:

> My experience has been deeply shaped by the fact that I am male, a (former) Catholic, American, and middle class. Because of these characteristics I look at the world in a certain way, and people treat me in a particular manner. My Catholic upbringing, for example, gave me a view of myself as fallen and as needing to be redeemed by something other than myself or the natural world; it made me think that certain desires and behaviors are bad, and led me to (try to) repress them; even my body was shaped by certain typical Catholic disciplines (kneeling, for instance). Even when in later life I reacted against this upbringing, I was still reacting against my particular Catholic heritage, and in this way this heritage continues to shape me; it will do so until I die.
>
> It seems obviously true that I am in part who and what I am in strong measure because of the groups to which I belong (to which in many cases I had no choice but to belong). If I had been born and raised in New Guinea then I would be quite other than what I am: I would not only describe the world differently, I would experience it differently.

Fay does not use the term *culture* in this passage, but he is referring to aspects of one's background—such as religious upbringing, social class, gender, and national origin—usually associated with culture and considered part of one's cultural identity. Think of how these aspects of Fay's cultural identity might affect his reaction to an argument about racial profiling.

Considering Culture in Argument

The role of culture in argument is clearly illustrated in the following editorial by sports columnist Harvey Araton about how two tennis players—one an Israeli and the other a Pakistani—played together successfully at Wimbledon in 2002 at a time when the conflict in the Middle East between Arabs and Jews was becoming especially bloody. (See Figure 2-2.)

They played together, then sat together, Pakistani and Israeli, Muslim and Jew, and wanted everyone to know it was no big deal. There was no statement made, no cause advanced, other than the bid to go as far as they could in the Wimbledon draw. Pragmatism, not peace-making, made doubles partners of Aisam ul-Haq Qureshi and Amir Hadad.

"We are not here to change anything," said Qureshi, 22, of Lahore, Pakistan. "I don't like to interfere religion or politics into sport."

Hadad, 24, of Ramala, Israel, near Tel Aviv, said: "I know Aisam is very good on grass, one serve, good volley, and also I like him as a person. When he asked me to play, we didn't even think it's going to get so big."

Then they survived the qualifying tournament and won two rounds in the main draw last week. No Pakistani had lasted past this round at Wimbledon, or in any Grand Slam event. What would have been a feel-good story in Pakistan became an inflamed issue when Qureshi, the country's No. 1 player, from a family with a rich tennis history, made a bit of his own history with Hadad—until they were dispatched by the Czechs Martin Damm and Cyril Suk yesterday, 6-1, 7-6 (5), 6-4.

It was, for them, a productive pairing, one they said they might reprise at the United States Open next month, no matter the ominous reports from Pakistan that Qureshi has read on the Internet.

His family, stationed by Court 5 yesterday in the shadow of Center Court, was only inter-ested in what was happening here, saying they had received support from Pakistanis all over London. His mother, Nosheen, formerly No. 1 in Pakistan and still an active player at 41, kissed the Israeli, Hadad, on the cheek and called him a good boy. The father, Ihtsham, a 50-year-old businessman, videotaped the thirdround match, right down to the volley his son mis-played on match point. An uncle, Khalid Rashid, dismissed the protests, calling them the work of "Al Qaeda and extremists in the north."

The reports, without subtlety, said otherwise. A former Pakistani champion, Saeed Haid, was quoted in *The Times* of London saying, "The bloodshed in the Middle East means his pairing with an Israeli is wrong." A director of the country's official Sports Board, Brig. Saulat Abbas, told Agence France-Presse: "Although he is playing in his private capacity, we officially condemn his playing with an Israeli player and an explanation has been sought from him. Since we have no links with Israel, Qureshi may face a ban."

In the heart of aristocratic-mandated civility, the lawns neatly manicured and the sports-wear lily white, this sounded like hardened geopolitical zealotry bordering on lunacy. A cau-tious Ihtsham Qureshi said it was his understanding that the Pakistani news media were supporting his son, and many positive e-mail messages had been received. His wife, whose father was the best player in India before partition in 1947, said "People with the right per-spective don't think like that."

Within this insular sport, which rears wandering citizens of the world, the players sounded mature and wise as they spoke of a friendship formed along the endless road of small-time events for those on the far periphery of fame. They joked about how their greatest faith must be in their ability to stay fit and focused in the pursuit of almighty computer points.

"I don't pray at all, but I practice a lot," Hadad said.

Araton's essay was published in the *New York Times,* whose readership includes Arabs and Jews, both in the United States and abroad. But that readership is composed primarily of people living in the United States, most of whom are American citizens. Those in that audience who are neither Jewish nor Muslim are likely to react differently to Araton's argument than Jews or Muslims will. Araton quotes former Pakistani tennis champion Saeed Haid as criticizing Aisam ul-Haq Qureshi, the current Pakistani tennis player, for playing with a Jewish partner in view of the bloodshed between Arabs and Jews; Araton quotes the Pakistani sports director as condemning Qureshi. Araton suggests that these criticisms amount to zealotry and lunacy, but his argument grows out of a cultural context (that of the United States) in which pluralism and religious diversity are deeply held values. The former Pakistani tennis champion and sports director are arguing out of a different cultural context (that is, an Arab and Muslim nation) that does not necessarily share those values. In such a context, the criticisms of Qureshi would not sound like zealotry. As is often the case in situations in which different cultures come into conflict, this situation is not simply a matter of differing opinions or a disagreement about whether Qureshi was right to take Amir Hadad as his doubles partner; rather, the different cultural contexts complicate the matter. Araton brings to his argument a different worldview, which grows out of his cultural identity, from that of the Pakistani tennis champion or the sports director. These cultural differences profoundly shape not only how these individuals view the situation with Qureshi and Hadad but also what kinds of claims or assertions are likely to be persuasive to each. (See Figure 2-2.)

FIGURE 2-2

Aisam ul-Haq Qureshi (left) and Amir Hadad

SOURCE: AP, July 4, 2002.

Culture not only influences how individual readers or writers might react to an argument but also can affect how people engage in argumentation. Different cultures might have different values, as you saw in the example of the Pakistani tennis player Qureshi, and they might have different ways of engaging in argument. For example, in some cultures it is considered impolite or even disrespectful to question another's statements, claims, or credibility. In such cultures, people follow certain implicit protocols that govern what they can say to each other. In Japan, for example, if it is raining and you are without an umbrella, it would be impolite to directly ask a person who has an umbrella if you may borrow it. Instead, you would be expected to make a statement such as "It's raining very hard" or "We are likely to get wet," which the other person would know to interpret as a request to borrow the umbrella. Such cultural protocols govern how a writer might structure an argument and support a position on an issue. A Japanese writer arguing in favor of, say, having American troops leave Okinawa, which is a Japanese-controlled island, might focus his argument on the capabilities of the Japanese security forces to protect Okinawa rather than asserting that Americans have no business occupying that island.

Considering Gender

We can also think of culture as encompassing important aspects of our identity such as gender, sexual orientation, and age. It is risky to generalize about such things, and many arguments are directed toward audiences without regard to such factors. But it is important to be sensitive to how these factors can influence the way an audience might react to an argument. Moreover, there are times when it is appropriate to take these factors into account in making an argument. Sometimes an argument is intended specifically for an audience of, say, young women or retired men. Sometimes the topic might be one that has different implications for different audiences. An argument in favor of a woman's right to choose an abortion will mean something different to women than it will to men, and it will mean something different to young women than it will to older women—no matter whether men and women of any age agree with the argument. In such cases, writers will make certain assumptions based on these important aspects of their readers' identities and will adjust their claims and appeals accordingly.

Consider the following two examples, both of which are arguments about differences in how men and women are treated. The first is a letter written to the editor of *Health* magazine, which is devoted to health-related and lifestyle issues for women. The writer was responding to an article about changing ideas of beauty:

Dorothy Foltz-Gray's article "The Changing Face of Beauty" [July/August] is a stunning example of a woman co-opted by our patriarchal society's focus on skin-deep appearance.

She writes that the power of beauty gets you "more than just admiration." And that "it was exhilarating to think I had a little of that power, too."

After 15 years in the corporate world, I have had my fill of women getting ahead because of their looks. Foltz-Gray was careful to assert that she got the "homely" woman's job based upon her own merits, even though she does acknowledge that her looks played a part. She did "feel uncomfortable" with that but accepted the job.

I would have liked to see the article point the finger at the real culprit (men in power) and advocate for change, rather than continuing to accept the status quo. I believe that the media has an obligation to expose abuses of power, especially a magazine devoted to women's total wellness.

This writer is addressing the magazine's editors directly, but she makes it clear that she assumes *Health* to be a magazine for and about women. She also makes an assertion that might be acceptable to most readers of this magazine (most of whom are women) but would be controversial for other audiences: that "men in power" are the reason for women's struggles to advance in the workplace. Given the audience for *Health,* she perhaps doesn't need to worry about alienating male readers. She seems to be saying to her female readers, "C'mon, let's call this problem what it is!" If she were writing for a different audience—say, a more general audience that would include as many men as women or readers of a business-oriented publication such as the *Wall Street Journal*—she would have to assume that her assertion would not be accepted by many in her audience, and she would probably have to defend it.

The second example also addresses the issue of differences in how men and women are treated, but it does so in a less strident way and for a less specific audience. Nevertheless, although the writer, Susan Brownmiller, is addressing a broader audience than the readers of *Health* magazine, she seems to address male and female readers differently. This excerpt is taken from her book *Femininity*:

We are talking, admittedly, about an exquisite esthetic. Enormous pleasure can be extracted from feminine pursuits as a creative outlet or purely as relaxation; indeed, indulgence for the sake of fun, or art, or attention, is among femininity's great joys. But the chief attraction (and the central paradox, as well) is the competitive edge that femininity seems to promise in the unending struggle to survive, and perhaps to triumph. The world smiles favorably on the feminine woman: it extends little courtesies and minor privilege. Yet the nature of this competitive edge is ironic, at best, for one works at femininity by accepting restrictions, by limiting one's sights, by choosing an indirect route, by scattering concentration and not giving one's all as a man would to his own, certifiably masculine, interests. It does not require a great leap of imagination for a woman to understand the feminine principle as a grand collection of compromises, large and small, that she simply must make in order to render herself a successful woman. If she has difficulty in satisfying femininity's demands, if its illusions go against her grain, or if she is criticized for her shortcomings and imperfections, the more she will see femininity as a desperate strategy of appeasement, a strategy she may not have the wish or the courage to abandon, for failure looms in either direction.

Brownmiller is addressing the same basic issue as the previous writer: the potential effect of being a woman on success in life. Brownmiller knows that her readers will be both men and women. Yet there seems to be a subtle difference in the way she addresses readers who are men compared with readers who are women. For one thing, she is writing as a woman, and in doing so, she refers to experiences that only women readers will be able to relate to. For example, she describes the "enormous pleasure" of "feminine pursuits." Although she always uses the third person and never speaks of women as "we," these references to the female experience seem to create a bond between her and women readers that cannot exist with male readers because women readers will be able to share these experiences with her. But she makes these references without referring to men in a way that might alienate them (as the previous writer seems to do). No doubt Brownmiller understands that men and women might react differently to her argument, but she takes advantage of those different reactions in presenting her argument—assuming, it seems, that women will know what she is talking about and perhaps inviting men to try to understand the experience of femininity that she is describing.

Considering Age

Look again at the passage written by Susan Brownmiller and imagine that she is writing for an audience composed mostly of older readers—for example, the readers of *AARP The Magazine,* published by the American Association of Retired Persons. She might wish to handle the issue of femininity somewhat differently, because many of those readers would probably experience gender in different ways than younger readers would. (See Figure 2-3.) In this sense the age of an intended audience can influence how a writer makes an argument. In some cases an argument is intended for readers of a specific age, and the writer's language, strategies, and even topics will be shaped accordingly. An argument in favor of a particular kind of retirement fund might play well with readers of *AARP The Magazine,* but it wouldn't appear in *Seventeen* magazine or in a flyer from a college career development service. Sometimes, the effect of the age of intended readers is more subtle. Consider what assumptions journalist Camille Sweeney makes about the age of her readers in the following passage, taken from the beginning of an article in which Sweeney argues that the appeal of Internet chat rooms for teens has to do with the age-old adolescent struggle to establish an identity:

☐ wrinkled?
☐ wonderful?

Will society ever accept
old can be beautiful?

FIGURE 2-3

This image originally appeared as part of an advertising campaign by Dove that was designed to challenge conventional representations of how women appear in advertisements for products such as shampoo. Note how this woman does not regret being "old" and is beautiful in her own way.

"Yo yo yo, what's up what's up?" The lines scroll up my screen. Different fonts, different colors, the words whiz by, everyone's screen name sounding vaguely pornographic. I'm on America Online, in a chat room for young adults. There are hundreds of such chat rooms on AOL, and it has taken a lot of Net navigating simply to find one that has room enough to let me in.

For all the crowds and clamoring, there's not much being said in this chat room, or rather, not much that's being paid attention to. A 16-year-old girl is talking about her baby due in two months. A grumpy 15-year-old guy reluctantly wishes her well. Another girl, 17, asks, "Are your parents cool with it?" The lines continue to scroll, a word here, a phrase there, live text that reads much like a flow of conversation you might overhear in a crowded high-school hallway or parking lot between classes in old-fashioned meat space (that is, anyplace not in the cyberworld).

Sweeney goes on to tell readers that she spent several months visiting chat rooms in an effort to "determine if there is such a thing as a cyberself," and she ultimately takes the position that what goes on in cyberspace with teens isn't new: Teens are just trying to discover who they are. Sweeney isn't addressing her essay to teens themselves; she knows that teenagers will make up only a small number of her readers. But older readers might be less familiar with the cyberworld Sweeney is describing. As a result, she not only must try to give her readers a sense of what happens in chat rooms but also must explain some terms (such as *meat space*). Perhaps more important, Sweeney refers to teens as "other"—that is, she discusses teens as if they are different from her readers. In this way, she tries to connect with her readers on the basis of age. And that sense of connection—of older readers observing unfamiliar teen social behavior—runs throughout her essay and gives it some of its persuasive impact. To appreciate that impact, imagine how different her opening paragraphs might be if they had been written for readers of *Teen* magazine.

Considering Sexual Orientation

To turn to another kind of cultural context, consider the implications of the simple question "Do you have a family?" When one adult asks it of another in the United States, the question usually means "Are you married with children?" So how is a single gay man to respond? He might cut the conversation short by interpreting it to be a query about marriage and children and simply respond, "No." Or he might take the question literally (or subversively) by saying, "Yes, I have two brothers and several nieces," although this response could trigger annoyance, confusion, or a more direct question about his household.

What might happen, then, if you use an expression such as "family values" or "our children" in an argument? Strictly speaking, no one is excluded from these words on the basis of sexual orientation. Anyone can create a family, and increasing numbers of same-gender couples are adopting children. Nevertheless, someone who is gay, lesbian, bisexual, or transgendered might associate expressions such as "family values" and "our children" with a heterosexual majority to which they do not belong. The phrase "family values" is especially problematic because it has often been used in rhetoric designed to limit the rights of minorities—as in the campaign that led to the Defense of Marriage Act, a 1996 federal law that excludes same-gender couples from the right to have a civil marriage.

If it can be problematic for writers to assume that all members of their audience are heterosexual, it can be challenging to write about sexual orientation. Words such as *gay* and *queer* are emotionally charged, and occasions for stereotyping abound. For example, a reference to the "gay community" implies that all gay individuals (regardless of religion, race, or social class) socialize together. It might not be clear whether the "gay community" includes women, because there are women who describe themselves as gay and others who insist on the use of *lesbian* on the grounds that *gay* was taken over by men. Unless we assume that it is reasonable to write about the "heterosexual community," which would be a big community indeed, it is better to write about "gay and lesbian communities" instead of lumping diverse people into a single group about which a generalization is going to be made.

In the introduction to *A Queer Geography*, Frank Browning writes,

As an American, as a white man, as a creature of the late twentieth century, as a male who grew up when the *New York Times, Time, Life, Newsweek,* and all of television and radio regarded homosexuality as either criminal or diseased, I am incapable of experiencing my desires as either a young Neapolitan in Italy or a Sambia tribesman in New Guinea—two places where homosexuality has a rich and ancient history and few make much effort to disguise. The strategies of social and psychological survival I have employed set me apart radically from middle-class Brazilians or Filipinos and even from most of the young men I write about in this book.

In other words, Browning sees his cultural context as being defined by nationality (American), race (white), gender (male), and age (being no longer young in the late twentieth century) in addition to sexual orientation (homosexual). As you read and write arguments, recognize that sexual orientation is an element of culture but cannot exist separately from other aspects of cultural context. It would be risky to assume that anyone could be either completely defined by sexual orientation or completely understood without some consideration of it.

Historical Context

The earlier example of Harvey Araton's essay about Qureshi, the Pakistani tennis player (see pages 23–25), points to another crucial kind of context for argumentation: the moment at which an argument is being made. Araton's essay might have had a certain effect because it was published in the midst of intense, terrible fighting between Israelis and Palestinians in the Middle East in 2002. It was also published during the Wimbledon tennis championship, the world's most prestigious tennis tournament. If Araton had written his essay a year earlier (assuming that Qureshi and Hadad were playing as doubles partners at that time), when the conflict in the Middle East was not as intense and when international attention was not focused on that part of the world, his argument might have been less provocative or persuasive for many readers. It might even have had an entirely different significance. Araton's main argument, which focused on achieving a peaceful solution to a long-standing and bloody conflict, was really not about tennis, but he used the decision by Qureshi and his tennis partner Hadad—and the controversy surrounding their decision—to give his argument a timeliness and force it might not otherwise have had. In other words, *when* an argument is made can be as important as *how* it is made.

The ancient Greek rhetoricians used the term *kairos* to describe an opportune moment for making a specific argument or trying to persuade an audience to act in a specific situation. We might think of *kairos* as making the right argument at the right time. Araton's essay is a good example of an author taking advantage of a particular moment to make an argument. Historical context, then, can refer to understanding when to make a particular argument. A particular appeal might be persuasive at one time but not at another. Circumstances change, and that change can affect what a writer chooses to write in an argument, as well as how readers respond to that argument. After the horrible events of September 11, 2001, for example, many people thought that certain kinds of statements and criticisms were inappropriate. Comedians refrained from skewering politicians, especially President George W. Bush; editorialists and political commentators did likewise. In such a climate, arguments that relied on criticisms of the President would widely be considered not only ineffective but also inappropriate and even disrespectful. Indeed, filmmaker and political essayist Michael Moore found himself in this situation when his publisher hesitated to release Moore's book *Stupid White Men* after the events of September 11. Given the sudden change in the American political climate as a result of September 11, the publisher asked Moore to rewrite the book, which was a humorous but irreverent attack on the Bush presidency. In effect, Moore was asked to change his argument about the Bush administration because the times had changed. Although Moore refused to do so, it took many months before his book was made available for sale to the public. Three years later, however, Moore was able to release *Fahrenheit 9/11,* a widely distributed film highly critical of President Bush and the policies that led to the invasion of Iraq. The context had changed. The sense of national unity felt immediately after the terrorist attacks of September 11 had given way to increasing controversy as a presidential election approached. Moore's experience is a dramatic but revealing example of how events can profoundly affect what audiences will accept as appropriate in argumentation.

Historical context encompasses more than just making the right argument at the right time. The time in which an argument is made can profoundly affect not only how an audience reacts to it but also its meaning and import. Consider the opening paragraph of the Declaration of Independence, one of the most famous arguments ever written:

> When in the Course of human events, it becomes necessary for one people to dissolve the political bands which have connected them with another, and to assume among the powers of the earth, the separate and equal station to which the Laws of Nature and Nature's God entitle them, a decent respect to the opinions of mankind requires that they should declare the causes which impel them to the separation.

Thomas Jefferson's well-known words are general, even abstract, but we know that they refer to a specific situation and to specific events that occurred in 1776 and before. But some of the abstract ideas in this passage carried different meanings in 1776 than they do today. For example, the idea of a colony or state separating from a monarchy such as ruled Great Britain at that time was radical and even unthinkable to many people. Today, such a notion does not seem so radical. Similarly, what Jefferson meant by "Nature" and "Nature's God" is not necessarily what we might mean if we used those terms today. Indeed, "Nature's God" may be problematic for conservatives who insist that the Founding Fathers intended the United States to be a Christian country. The most famous lines from the Declaration of Independence make an argument that most Americans probably accept as universal but which Jefferson knew to be extremely radical in his day:

> We hold these truths to be self-evident, that all men are created equal, that they are endowed by their Creator with certain unalienable Rights, that among these are Life, Liberty and the pursuit of Happiness.

Such "truths" were not widely considered "self-evident," as Jefferson surely knew, which gave his argument a kind of shock value it would not have today. Perhaps an even more revealing illustration of how the historical context can affect the meaning of an assertion is contained in the famous statement that "all men are created equal." Today such a statement might carry a sexist message that it would not have had for readers in 1776. Indeed, today this statement might be interpreted as a negative one because of what we now consider to be sexist language.

We need not look back 200 years for examples of how historical context can alter meanings in this way. Think of the connotations of the phrase "support our troops." In times of peace, these words may enjoy wide appeal. In time of war, however, these same words can inspire significantly different responses. Even if there is general agreement that troops in the field should be well equipped and receive reassuring messages from home, critics of a war may wonder if "support our troops" is code for "support the political decisions that sent the troops into battle." Accordingly, phrases such as "God support *our* troops," and "support our troops—bring them home" appeared on bumper stickers during the second war against Iraq. The former implies that God should abandon the people against whom "our troops" are fighting; the latter calls for an end to war. Even in cases that are not quite as dramatic as these, historical context is part of any argument and affects how that argument works and what it means. Good writers attend to historical context, and careful readers are attuned to it.

In composing an argument, you can never address every possible contextual factor. But you will always be making your argument about a specific issue at a specific moment in a specific rhetorical situation. The more carefully you consider those factors, the more effective your argument is likely to be.

3

The Media for Argument

D avid Brooks is a well-known conservative commentator who appears regularly on television shows devoted to political affairs. Brooks also writes a syndicated column for newspapers. His arguments about political and social issues are conservative; his basic message regarding the limits of government in American social and economic life is constant. But do his arguments change in any way when he is making them on a political affairs television show as compared with his columns or essays? Here is a paragraph from a column Brooks wrote in 2006.

> Plato famously divided the soul into three parts: reason, eros (desire), and thymos (the hunger for recognition). Thymos is what motivates the best and worst things men do. It drives them to seek glory and assert themselves aggressively for noble causes. It drives them to rage if others don't recognize their worth. Sometimes it even causes them to kill over a trifle if they feel disrespected.

In the argument that follows, Brooks defines politics as "a competition for recognition," notes that thymos is not limited to men, and claims that understanding the "the thymotic urge" can lead to understanding many contemporary conflicts. It is unlikely, however, that he would have used a term such as *thymos* when speaking spontaneously during a televised discussion of current events. He is able to do so in print, however, because punctuation—one of the conventions of print—helps him to define his terms. Note how he uses a colon and parentheses to make a complex point efficiently. Note also the length of his paragraph. When writing a newspaper column, Brooks knows that readers will expect frequent paragraph breaks because short paragraphs are usually easier to read than long paragraphs—and many people read the newspaper quickly. So this example leads to the question, which is the focus for this chapter: What role does the medium play in argument?

As you will see, many elements of argumentation, such as addressing an audience appropriately and using evidence effectively, apply to all media. So some of what I describe in relation to print will be important for arguments in any medium. But although print remains an important medium for making arguments, other media, including television, radio, and newer online media such as Internet discussion groups and the World Wide Web, have become increasingly significant as forums for public discourse. To argue effectively in these media, you need an understanding of how media might influence or change the way you construct and present an argument.

Analyzing Arguments in Print

We live in a world in which there is so much material available in print that we tend to see print as a natural medium for communication. But print isn't natural. It is technological—or rather, a set of technologies that have evolved from the invention of the printing press in the fifteenth century, to the typewriter in the nineteenth, to the word-processing programs with adjustable fonts and margins in the twentieth. The technology has changed, but certain concerns—such as what font to use and how many columns to set per page—have remained essentially the same. You probably engage in written argumentation without pausing to think about how the conventions of print shape the arguments you write and how the volume of material in print influences the cultures through which you try to make yourself heard. Pausing for such thought would be useful.

The extent to which material is available in print is never discernable to the human eye. The best bookstore in town carries only a small fraction of titles in print, and most library collections are highly selective. Chapter 6 will address how you can efficiently locate print sources when conducting research. For the moment, consider these two truths: printed text continues to be a major medium for communication, and the extent to which such material is available can be seen as both a blessing and a curse.

Print can influence arguments in other media. For example, arguments delivered as speeches are usually written out first; similarly, a radio or television report is often crafted in written form before it is broadcast. But print is not a monolithic medium for arguments. There are countless varieties of print forums within which people can argue:

- Magazines and newspapers of all kinds
- Flyers and circulars

- Memos, letters, and pamphlets
- Financial reports
- Essays written for college classes
- Books

Accordingly, you cannot expect to read everything available in print; nor can what you choose be read with equal degrees of attention. An unsolicited catalog that shows up in your mailbox can be skimmed quickly and tossed away. But sources relevant to written argumentation must be read with care.

Reading Arguments Critically

Reading is not a passive activity. When you read a newspaper editorial, for example, you are not simply trying to understand the writer's point. You are also engaged in a sophisticated intellectual and social activity in which you try to analyze, evaluate, and react to the argument. The more carefully you do so, the more substantive will be your engagement with the argument and the better will be your understanding of the issue under discussion. Ideally, reading an argument should be as careful and sophisticated an act as writing an argument.

The more you know about the strategies writers use in constructing their arguments, the better able you will be to analyze and evaluate those arguments (see Chapter 4). In addition, the more you know about yourself as a reader, the easier it will be for you to identify appeals or lines of reasoning that might be questionable or flawed.

In reading an argument critically, you should try to account for these strategies and be aware of how an argument can be shaped by the specific print publication for which it is written. Some teachers might advise you always to read skeptically, and that can be good advice because it can help you guard against subtle but powerful appeals that can shape your reaction to an argument. Reading critically means looking carefully at the way a writer tries to address a specific audience for a specific publication; it means being aware of how your perspective, beliefs, and values might influence your reaction to particular arguments.

Reading an argument carefully requires you to take into account the specific print forum in which that argument appears, because different forums lend themselves to different kinds of arguments. For example, an editorial in the conservative business newspaper the *Wall Street Journal* will usually differ in tone, style, and content from an essay in the left-leaning magazine *Mother Jones*. Each of these publications has a different purpose and addresses a somewhat different audience. To understand an argument published in each of these print forums you must have some sense of those differences.

Let's turn to a specific example: the full text of an argument published in the *New York Times Magazine* on July 10, 2005. It is by Randy Cohen, who contributes a weekly column on ethics. The argument that follows consists of only seven paragraphs, yet within this small amount of space, Cohen establishes the historical context of a passage that has drawn his attention and shows how it was designed for a specific audience (see Chapter 2). He also establishes why the passage in question is still worthy of careful consideration, even though he raises and addresses several concerns about it.

A Founder's Advice

Never suffer a thought to be harbored in your mind which you would not avow openly. When tempted to do anything in secret, ask yourself if you would do it in public. If you would not, be sure it is wrong. LETTER FROM THOMAS JEFFERSON TO HIS GRANDSON FRANCIS EPPES, AGE **14**, MONTICELLO, MAY **21, 1816**

Jefferson's 19th-century advice would undoubtedly forestall much contemporary misconduct. It would also eliminate most showers—that's one limitation of an ethics of transparency: the desire for privacy need not be an acknowledgment of wrongdoing. Many benign activities are quite sensibly conducted out of public view—for example, bathing, the pursuit of sexual happiness or the design of the next iMac—and our language reflects this. To act in secret (Jefferson's word) can connote the illicit, suggesting shame, furtiveness and criminality (although not for the iMac designer); to act in private implies modesty, dignity and self-reliance. Unfortunately, Jefferson didn't give young Francis a way to distinguish between the two.

Jefferson's advice has a more serious shortcoming: it demands only that we conform to local custom. Jefferson lived in a slave-owning society, and he owned slaves—openly, in public. He did so with some remorse, perhaps, but without sufficient moral urgency to free them (excepting a few), something his contemporary, George Washington, was able to do, if only upon his death. Jefferson's system of moral thought did not equip him to transcend the behavior of his neighbors, in this regard at least.

It is noteworthy that Jefferson would regulate not only deeds but also thoughts, even though there are honest thoughts that we wisely decline to avow openly. (Why, yes, that does make you look fat.) Civility relies on restraint, on not voicing every passing idea, not because it is false but because its utterance may be hurtful.

But Jefferson was not instructing Eppes in social niceties; neither was he denying him the privacy of his own mind nor cautioning him against hypocrisy. Jefferson was suggesting that by nurturing unexpressed ideas, each of us risks becoming a cult of one, our beliefs untested and unsupported. It is by airing our thoughts that we can discover their flaws and our fatuities. In this we can see Jefferson as an enlightenment figure, applying something like the scientific method to his own mind.

Jefferson's enthusiasm for discourse and debate had its limits, notes Herbert Sloan of the Barnard College history department: "Jefferson deplored the way antiadministration newspapers were corrupting the public mind and urged the governor of Pennsylvania to undertake prosecutions for seditious libel." But Jefferson's inability always to heed his own advice makes him not hypocritical but human, and it does not gainsay the wisdom of that advice.

An ethics based on imagined public scrutiny is not infallible, but it is a fine guide for a young man starting out in life. Jefferson sent his grandson this counsel along with a volume of Greek grammar ("You might, while at home, amuse yourself with learning the letters and spelling"), believing that both would be useful as he undertook his studies at the New London Academy. True education, Jefferson wrote in the same letter, means "uniting merit with your learning."

Apparently Jefferson and the masters at New London provided Eppes a reasonable amount of both. After completing his education, he eventually moved to Florida, where he was elected mayor of Tallahassee and helped found what would become Florida State University; establishing universities seems to have run in the family. If his accomplishments were less than his grandfather's, well, whose aren't?

If you reread this argument, you will find that Cohen emphasizes the shortcomings of a position to which he has given careful consideration, but he does so respectfully without making Jefferson seem foolish. For example, he describes Jefferson as "human" rather than "hypocritical." He also indicates that the idea in question is still relevant by placing "showers" and "iMac" in the opening paragraph. But relevance was also established by the historical context in which this piece was first published. Americans reading it during the summer of 2005 would have been mindful of ongoing debates about the right to privacy and the extent to which both business and government should publicly disclose information for which there may be a reason to keep secret. In this context, the title "A Founder's Advice" has more than one meaning. The title signals that the argument will concern advice from one of the men traditionally called the Founding Fathers of the United States, but the argument as a whole suggests that the Founding Fathers may not always be the best source for determining how Americans should govern themselves in the future. As Cohen points out, both Jefferson and Washington owned slaves. Advice given to a specific audience in a specific context (a grandson going off to school in the eighteenth century) may not be appropriate for another audience in another context (American citizens in the twenty-first century).

Cohen's argument has been reprinted here in two parallel columns, as it was when first published, and with the philosopher-like icon that appears at the opening of his contributions to the *Times* (which run under the title "The Ethicist"). Whether or not you agree with the assertion Cohen has made and supported in this argument, you should recognize that this argument is shaped by the conventions of print—not only in its visual appearance but also in its clarity and succinctness. It is highly unlikely that Cohen could speak these words spontaneously. They are almost certainly the product not only of learning and reflection but also of print-related benefits, such as the ability to revise prose and have it reviewed by an editor.

The reading selections provided in Chapters 8–13 come from many kinds of publications—ranging from popular magazines to academic journals. When you read them, consider how the nature of different print forums influences the nature of the argument.

Analyzing Arguments in Visual Media

Although images have always had power, they have become increasingly powerful as more people are exposed to them on a regular basis. That exposure now comes in many forms—among them: photographs, advertisements, icons, and art.

Photographs as Argument

To appreciate the power of images to convey ideas, look at the photograph of President George W. Bush in Figure 3-1, which appeared in August 2002 when the President was trying to generate support for his proposed new Department of Homeland Security. This photo was taken by an Associated Press photographer, but it was certainly set up by the

FIGURE 3-1

President George W. Bush at a News Conference at Mount Rushmore

What does this photograph communicate about President Bush? What argument does it seem to make?

President's staff. For example, the staff would have determined where photographers could stand during the news conference; in that way, they set the angle from which photographs of the President could be taken. Those photographs would thus produce the desired effect: to show the President alongside with the famous faces of past American presidents carved into Mount Rushmore.

What does such a photograph communicate about President Bush? How might it have influenced readers' opinions about him and about his proposal for a Department of Homeland Security? Consider the cultural significance of the Mount Rushmore national monument and what it means to Americans. It not only invokes the idea of patriotism for many Americans but also suggests greatness with its gigantic figures of four revered American presidents. The photograph associates President Bush—and, by extension, his proposal—with those ideas of patriotism and greatness. Now consider how different the impact of a photograph of the President might be if the background at his press conference had been a wall at an airport or a dark blue curtain in a hotel conference room rather than the striking and deeply symbolic stone visages of Mount Rushmore.

Although President Bush is prominent and easily recognizable in this photograph, the setting is clearly important as well. In Figure 3-2, however, the photographer has provided almost no setting, choosing instead to provide a close-up of a mother and children. It is a famous photograph, taken in 1936 by Dorothea Lange—a photographer commissioned by the federal government to document the effects of the Great Depression on the rural poor. Scholars are familiar with the historical context of this image and with the setting: a camp in

FIGURE 3-3
"Migrant Mother" Postage Stamp

FIGURE 3-2
"Migrant Mother"

By Dorothea Lange.

California for migrant farm workers. If read as an argument to assert (see pages 7–9), the image can be seen as asserting that the American economy was having a devastating affect on the family and that the mother remained central to holding the family together. If read as an argument to negotiate differences (see pages 13–15), the image could be seen as a case for providing government relief. In either case, the photograph is designed to evoke compassion, so *pathos* plays an important role in this image (see pages 103–108).

But what happens when the presentation and context of an image changes? In 1998, Lange's photograph was used on a U.S. postage stamp (see Figure 3-3). Because you can visualize the size of a postage stamp, ask yourself what happens when the photograph is reduced in scale, has letters and numbers imposed upon it, and becomes an object designed to be licked and postmarked. Does this presentation honor the photograph or degrade it? How does your response to both the photograph and the stamp change with additional context: testimony in 1998 from Katherine McIntosh, the woman who was once the girl hiding behind the mother's right shoulder?

CONTEXT

I was about five years old when the photograph was taken. We were on the way to a camp at Nipoma to work picking peas, but the peas had frozen over. We camped under a kind of lean-to we carried in the car. I remember a lady came and took photographs. My mother was about 34 at the time.

She had earlier lost two children, a little girl aged six and a boy who was stillborn. She had five children by my father, Leo Owens, who died before I was born, and three more by Jim Hill, my step-dad.

Ma is exactly as the picture showed, except that she had a great sense of humour, which doesn't show. She was beautiful. She had long hair and I can remember when I was in high school, aged about 12, I had to get up at 4 a.m. and fix her hair in rollers.

The stoic image of my mother is true to her. When she was pregnant, she would continue working in the fields until she started labour. Then she'd go home and have a baby and in no time—a week or 10 days later—she would be back out there, working. If there was something wrong with you in those days, you didn't survive. She finally quit work in her seventies. My mother died of cancer, aged 80.

Last September the U.S. Post Office issued a stamp with the picture on it. But they did not even invite us to the launching. In October a copy of the picture with Lange's writing on it was sold at Sotheby's in New York for $244,500. What upsets us is that people are making money out of our mother's pain. But we are proud that she has become a part of history.

From an interview of Katherine McIntosh by Peter Lennon published in *The Guardian,* a well-respected British newspaper.

PHOTOGRAPHY AS ARGUMENT

This photograph was taken several months after U.S. armed forces defeated the Taliban, a group that had previously imposed a strict Islamic government on Afghanistan. What argument does this photograph make? In answering that question, consider the contrast between the traditional dress of the girls in the photograph, which is intended to hide a woman's physical appearance, and the Western beauty items on the shelf, which are intended to enhance physical beauty. Consider, too, the uncovered face of the girl, placed at the center of the photo, just in front of her companion, whose face remains obscured by the traditional dress. How do these elements help make a statement?

Kabul, Afghanistan. September 13, 2002. Manizha, 13 (center), and Mina, 16, in front of an array of beauty products that were not openly available under Taliban rule.

Advertisements as Argument

Images also play an important role in another form of persuasion: advertisements designed to promote a product or to influence behavior. Flip through the pages of popular magazines, and you are likely to find many ads that feature young and attractive models to draw people's attention to a diverse range of products. Repeated exposure to unusually fit or thin models can damage self-esteem when people compare their own bodies to those that are being used to sell things. (See pages 294–300 and 342–351.) So let's consider two advertisements that do not make direct use of the human body.

Figures 3-4 and 3-5 illustrate the importance of color and design in advertisement. Both use red, white, and blue, although Figure 3-4 is primarily blue and white (with a little red, silver, and gold shown in the container of cream cheese). Figure 3-5 uses red more prominently, and in this case, the colors are clearly those of the American flag (in addition to being the colors of the Tommy Hilfiger logo). If you look closely at Figure 3-4, you will see that the container of cream cheese appears slightly above the exact center of the advertisement and that it is being lifted up (or supported) by a feather (which makes it very light, indeed). This design gives prominence to the product, almost as if it has been located on a pedestal. Design also gives prominence to the bottle of "tommy girl" cologne.

FIGURE 3-4

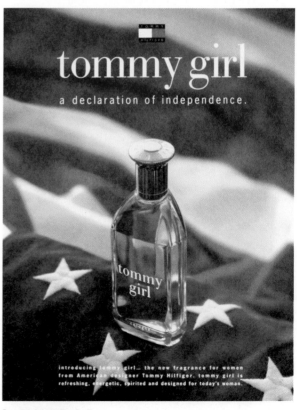

FIGURE 3-5

Although the bottle is placed toward the bottom of the advertisement, it is tall enough to rise above the center. Moreover, the stripes and folds in the American flag are angled so that those on the left side point toward the product. In both cases, color and design are sufficiently strong to command at least brief attention.

When seen as arguments, what kind of claims do these ads make? Figure 3-4 claims that Philadelphia Extra Light cream cheese is "so light" that is unlikely to weigh someone down. Implicit in this claim is another: "If you are worried about your weight, this is a good product to buy." Of course, the product would have to be lighter than it actually is for it to be able to ascend into heaven on its own accord. The design conveys the impression that the product is making good progress on its upward flight because the container of cream cheese is already above the clouds. The feather reinforces the claim about lightness, as in the cliché about something being "light as a feather." And it's possible that the feather, when linked to a word like "heavenly," belonged to an angel (who is perhaps shedding feathers while shedding pounds). The final line of text returns to the concept of the "heavenly" by claiming that the cream cheese in question provides "a little taste of heaven." Taken literally, a claim like this makes no sense. No one who takes religion seriously—whatever their faith tradition may be—is likely to believe that tasting cream cheese is like being in heaven. But in American English, words like "heavenly," "divine," and "adore" have come to be used so casually that their spiritual significance is often overlooked. So the copywriter for this advertisement probably assumed that "heavenly" would be taken as a synonym for "delicious," whereas the design of the ad as a whole suggests that paradise is a light-filled place above the earth that consumers can reach by virtuously eating the right foods.

The text at the bottom of Figure 3-5 reads, "introducing tommy girl—the new fragrance for women from the American designer Tommy Hilfiger. tommy girl is refreshing, energetic, spirited, and designed for today's woman." These adjectives—which differ from words like *romantic, sensual,* or *sexy* that often appear in perfume ads—support the claim that women purchasing this product are making "a declaration of independence." And it is the evocation of the Declaration of Independence that provides the tenuous justification for using the American flag (which is flown on Independence Day, or the 4th *of July* as many people now call it) to support this product. Advertisements often make patriotic appeals—appeals that suggest buying a product (or supporting a political policy) is good for our country. It is difficult to imagine, however, how wearing a particular cologne (or any cologne at all) contributes to our nation's well-being, so the implicit claim in this advertisement does not hold up under analysis.

Relying heavily on color and design, both Figure 3-4 and Figure 3-5 use very little text, and thus make a similar assump-

TWISTING AN IMAGE TO MAKE A POINT

This ad by a group called Adbusters (http://adbusters. org) makes a statement by altering an image from an advertisement for a popular vodka. The ad uses the same layout and color scheme as the original ad, the same image of the vodka bottle, and even the name of the vodka itself. But here the image of a sagging bottle and the advertising tag line ("Absolut impotence"), which parodies the original tag line, create an association between vodka and sexual dysfunction. Consider how effectively this ad employs visual elements to make its argument. Would a print advertisement explaining the connection between alcohol and impotence work in the same way?

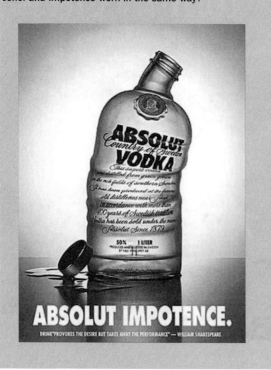

tion about their audience: someone glancing through a magazine is more likely to be interested by strong color and effective design than by a word-heavy text. Those words that have been used make another assumption about audience: language can be used playfully because few people expect an advertisement to be entirely truthful. Cream cheese is unlikely to taste like heaven, and wearing a widely marketed cologne from a major manufacturer is unlikely to make anyone truly independent. Common sense tells us this. But an effective advertisement can prompt people to make decisions that have little to do with common sense.

Icons as Argument

The icons created by corporations can also make implied arguments, arguments that can be deciphered by people who are attentive to visual rhetoric. Consider, for example, what is implied by associating a computer with an apple or a television network with an eye.

If you examine the packaging of name-brand products the next time you are in a grocery story, you will see icons that have become so familiar that they rarely get a second glance. A brand of tuna fish features a mermaid, a brand of salt shows a girl beneath an umbrella, and a variety of vegetables are presented with the image of an unusually tall man with a green complexion. When these icons change, the changes reflect a change in argument.

Closely related to advertisements, icons can also be used subversively. Consider Figure 3-6, in which Iraq is presented as iRaq, mimicking the look and cadence of iPod. The apple icon associated with iPod has become a bomb in this case, creating a line that could be read as "Bomb Iraq" or "Iraq has turned into a bomb." The latter reading is more likely given the message that appears at the bottom of the poster. The bright pink background suggests pop art, as well as a world in which some people are more concerned about finding the right shade of lip gloss than fighting for human rights. And central to the poster is an image that began as a photograph but became an icon for reasons explained by Sarah Boxer. Different forms of visual rhetoric have come together to make a powerful statement.

Art as Argument

You might not associate art with argument, but the design principles discussed in the previous sections apply to paintings and other kinds of art. You can think of any painting as an argument for the artist's vision. The painting shown in Figure 3-7 was completed in 1816, eight years after Spanish troops had suppressed a revolt in Mexico, which was still part of the Spanish Empire at the time. It is the work of Francisco José de Goya,

FIGURE 3-6
Antiwar Poster

By Cooper Greene.

iRaq

10,000 volts in your pocket, guilty or innocent.

Torture Incarnate and Propped on a Pedestal

Icons live their own lives. Of all the photographs of American soldiers tormenting Iraqi prisoners in the Abu Ghraib prison, one alone has become the icon of the abuse.

The image appears in mock advertisements in New York, in paintings in San Francisco, on murals in Tehran and on mannequins in Baghdad. It shows no dogs, no dead, no leash, no face, no nakedness, no pileup, no thumbs-up. It is the picture of a hooded prisoner standing on a box, electrodes attached to his outstretched arms.

Why this image above all the rest? It is far from the most violent, but easily the most graphic. You need less than a second's glance to know exactly what it is. The triangle of the hood silhouettes sharply against the hot pink or chartreuse background of a fake iPod ad. Andy Warhol himself could not have done better. It holds its own on murals meant to be read from far away. It plays well against the Statue of Liberty. It suggests Christ on the cross. And, best yet, the hooded figure in the photograph is on a pedestal. It is already an icon.

As a symbolic shape, the hood is almost as strong as a cross. The difference is that the hood has generally been the sign of the persecutor, not of the victim. It is the uniform of the executioner, the sheet of the Klansman, the mask of Death. Until now. In these images, you can see the hood's meaning begin to change and take root.

Sarah Boxer

FIGURE 3-7

Painting a Subversive Argument

Francisco José de Goya's famous 1816 painting of an execution in Mexico might be seen as an argument against government oppression.

one of the great European painters of the nineteenth century. Because he was such a good painter, Goya was frequently commissioned to paint portraits of Spanish royalty and aristocrats, but his sympathies were with people who struggled for freedom. This sympathy is evident in his painting of an execution in Mexico. Most of the painting is dark, symbolizing the darkness of the event. Bright color is reserved for the man who is about to be shot. He is wearing a white shirt, which implies purity, and gold trousers, a warm color that contributes to the sense that he is someone worthy of sympathy. The coloring of the lantern illuminating the execution echoes the color of his clothing. Light has positive connotations, especially when surrounded by darkness. So the man in white and gold is in the light created by the white and yellow lantern.

Other aspects of the design direct attention to this man, whose complexion suggests that he is a person of color. His arms are raised in what could be seen as either a gesture of surrender or an embrace that encompasses the soldiers and anyone viewing the picture. The guns are not only aimed at him; they also visually direct the viewers' eyes to him. Furthermore, the man in the white shirt is one of the few figures with eyes the viewers can see. (The other two are also victims.) The expression in his eyes seems tender rather than fierce, contributing to the sympathy Goya creates for him. Significantly, you cannot see the eyes of any of the soldiers; they are presented as part of a faceless mass.

What claim does this painting make? Interpretations vary. But the painting clearly conveys sympathy for the victim. It is arguing that the repression of the revolt was brutal, that governments do wicked things under the cover of night, or that the repression of native

PAINTING AS ARGUMENT

The landscape paintings of the famous Hudson Valley School in the nineteenth century are sometimes described as making a case for environmental conservation. They presented an idealized version of nature as beautiful and sublime, worthy of admiration and protection, when many people were concerned about the destructive effects of industrialization. Consider what claim Thomas Cole might be making in this painting of a well-known mountain along the Hudson River. How does his depiction of Storm King Mountain make a case for a particular view of nature?

people cannot last forever. It is worth noting, in this respect, that although the soldiers have all the guns, there are more victims than soldiers—a fact that suggests that the imperial authority is outnumbered. (The drama of this painting is reinforced by its size, approximately six feet by eight feet. If you ever have the chance to view the original in Madrid, you will feel as if you are witnessing a life-size event.)

Sometimes art is enlisted directly in an effort to persuade or to put forth a particular position on an issue or situation. A poster designed to advertise the French State Railways (Figure 3-8) makes more than one visually compelling argument. Train service is associated with *exactitude*, which is French for "getting things exactly right" or, more precisely, *precision*. The streamlined appearance of the train and the uncluttered look of the platform convey the sense that the technology in question is efficient and reliable. The clock positioned above the engineer's head suggests that this train will leave the station at exactly the right time. Addressed to travelers, the poster makes the claim: "You can count on us."

Another argument conveyed by the poster's design emerges when you consider its historical context. The poster was published in 1932, when the economies of Western nations were in deep depression and democratic governments were at risk. In Italy, one of France's neighbors, Benito Mussolini had won respect for his fascist government by fulfilling his promise "to make the trains run on time." One year after this poster appeared, Hitler would seize power in Germany, bringing fascism to another of France's neighbors. The fascists came to power in part because they offered a message that appealed to people during troubled times. The heart of that message was that strong government, represented by a strong leader, could preserve both capitalism and nationalism by repressing communists and any social group considered a threat to economic growth. It would do so through the imposition of a new order suitable for a new age. In the early 1930s fascism, like the train, could claim to be modern and efficient.

With this in mind, take another look at the poster. Most of the colors are muted; the boldest

FIGURE 3-8

Poster as Argument

This poster for the French State Railways in the 1930s may be making several arguments. What are they?

PIERRE-FÉLIX FIX-MASSEAU (1905–1994) French
Exactitude, 1932. Poster / color lithograph. Printer: Edita, Paris. Designed as an advertisement for the French State (État) Railways. H: 39^1/$_4$ in (99.7 cm) × W: 24^1/$_4$ in (61.6 cm) // 44 in (111.8 cm) × 29^1/$_2$ in (74.9 cm)

color, red, highlights the word *etat,* which means "state." The train becomes a metaphor for the power of the state. It is long, massive, and potentially dangerous. As the viewer, you see the train from a position on the platform that is precariously close to the edge. One false step, and you might fall beneath the power of the state. You are, moreover, alone on the platform. Everyone else seems to have already boarded the train. Do you want to be left behind? Do you want to get hurt? So in addition to urging people to travel by train, which continues to be a widely used means of transportation in Europe, this poster argues, "Get on board for the future, or get out of my way. The government is powerful; you are not. It will be dangerous for you to resist." The future is either the technology or the power of a strong central government—or both, as is the case when a central government uses technology to increase its power.

The U.S. government also used paintings and sketches during World War II to encourage enlistment in the armed forces, sell war bonds, publicize efforts to conserve items such as gasoline and butter, and generally exhort citizens to support the war effort. You might think of these images in the same way that you think of contemporary print or television advertisements: as propaganda whose purpose was to persuade rather than to engage viewers in serious argumentation. However, if you understand World War II as a moral endeavor to combat the evils of totalitarianism and ethnic extermination, then you might view these posters as part of a larger attempt to engage U.S. citizens in a collective effort to oppose evil. From such a perspective, individual posters can be seen as making an argument for a particular kind of activity associated with the war effort. Each poster might be posing a version of the question "Won't this particular activity help in the war effort?"

For example, the message in the poster in Figure 3-9 seems clear: Buy war bonds to help the U.S. airmen. In a sense the claim made in this poster is that war bonds will help the war effort by keeping U.S. airmen flying; the warrant, or fundamental assumption on which a statement of belief can be made, is that sustaining the war effort is desirable. The image of the airman in the poster, with his eyes looking skyward, his hands holding his combat equipment, a determined expression on his face, is noble and inspiring. The phrase at the top of the poster seems to be a statement this airman would make, and the large, bright words at the bottom of the poster drive the argument home. But notice that this airman is African American. At a point in history (the 1940s) before the civil rights movement and before the landmark U.S. Supreme Court rulings that helped guarantee rights to African Americans, this image would have struck many citizens as unusual and even disturbing, because this airman was fighting for a country that did not extend full rights to people of his racial background. Indeed, at that time the U.S. armed forces were still segregated. Yet the poster seems to suggest that *all* Americans are part of the war effort. And it might have spoken especially powerfully to Black Americans, whose experience of racism might have made them hesitant to support the U.S. government's efforts. The airman in this poster might suggest to those citizens that their support is needed and appropriate.

The poster in Figure 3-10 can also be seen as presenting an argument rather than simply trying to persuade. This poster was used in General Motors automobile factories in 1942, when that company was producing vehicles for the war effort. However, even during the war, companies and workers faced many of the same challenges that they face in peacetime, and labor relations were always a potentially difficult matter. Strikes by auto workers in the 1930s had a serious economic and social effect on the country. But a labor conflict—especially a strike—during war time could have been disastrous. In such a context you might see this poster as making an argument about the need for good relations

Art in Support of a War Effort

These posters were distributed by the U.S. government during World War II. Their message of support for the U.S. war effort is obvious, but what specific arguments do these posters make?

I FIGURE 3-9

I FIGURE 3-10

between workers and their employers. The claim might be stated as follows: Avoiding labor conflict will aid the U.S. war effort because it will enable the company to continue production of military vehicles. Again, the warrant is that aiding the war effort is desirable for all Americans. The design of the poster is intended to present that claim effectively. The most noticeable item is the word *together,* which appears in large red letters at the top of the page. The images of the two fists—both clenched, both exuding strength, both exposed by rolled-up sleeves as if to suggest getting down to work—reinforce the idea of working together. Both are identical in every respect except for the color of their shirt sleeves, which are used to reinforce their respective positions: blue for the blue-collar workers, white for management. The light yellow background not only highlights the arms by bringing them into relief but also conveys a sense of possibility: yellow is associated with the sun, with the idea of a new day. Notice, too, that aside from that background color and the green tank and fighter aircraft, everything else on the poster is red, white, or blue, colors associated with patriotism. Every element of the design thus supports the poster's claim.

Integrating Visual Elements and Text

The examples included so far in this chapter reveal that combining text and visual elements can be an extremely effective technique for argumentation. You probably have noticed a trend in television advertising in recent years toward structuring commercials around text. One widely broadcast ad for Nike shoes, for example, included a series of images of world-class athletes in many different sports preparing for their respective events: a sprinter getting ready at the starting blocks, a swimmer stretching at the edge of the pool before the start of the race, an archer drawing her bow. As these images appear in quick succession on the screen, the sound of an orchestra warming up grows louder. As the sound reaches a crescendo and then suddenly stops, the images also disappear, leaving a black screen on which only the words "Just do it," the famous Nike slogan, appear, with the equally famous Nike swoosh logo above them. The words on the screen seem to have greater impact without sound and color.

When you encounter textual arguments that incorporate visual elements, it is important to be aware of the effect that the combination of text and image can have on you as a reader or viewer. Engaging these arguments critically includes assessing visual elements and what they might contribute to the author's claims. Consider, for example, the open letter in Figure 3-11, which was distributed as a newspaper advertisement by St. Lawrence Cement, a company that found itself in an environmental controversy in 2002 when it sought to build a cement plant in upstate New York. The letter includes an extended written argument in which the company presents its claim that its proposed plant will not harm the environment. You might see this argument as an example of an argument to negotiate differences (see pages 13–15): it addresses its audience in a way that is respectful and direct, acknowledging the validity of its opponents' concerns; it presents evidence that supports its central claim that its plant will not cause environmental damage; and it rests this claim on a warrant that seems acceptable to its intended audience (that all residents want and will benefit from a healthy environment).

But the text of the letter in this advertisement is only part of the argument. The ad also includes a photograph, along with several graphs that reinforce the claim. Those graphs ostensibly present factual evidence that the company's new plan will significantly reduce its effect on the environment. Note that the visual form of the graphs highlights facts that might otherwise be harder for readers to pick out of the lengthy text. The photograph doesn't present evidence in the way the graphs do, but it reinforces the company's message that it is staffed by concerned and competent professionals. Notice that the four people in the photograph represent racial and gender diversity as well, sending a further positive message about the company to readers. The layout of the ad also contributes to the argument. Because the photo is placed before the first paragraph, readers are likely to view it before reading the text. If they have a positive reaction to that image, they might be agreeable to the company's argument. In addition, the letter discusses environmental issues before economic ones, which seems to reinforce the company's claim that it is concerned about the environment. The subheadings ("Environmental Benefits," "Economic Benefits") highlight these concerns and make them easier for readers to access. In short,

FIGURE 3-11

Enhancing an Argument with Graphic Elements

In this "open letter to the community," the St. Lawrence Cement company uses graphs and a photograph to help make its argument in favor of a new plant.

An Open Letter to the Community:

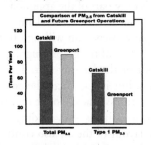

The community plays an important role in shaping the quality of life for the individuals and families who live there. Communities, and all the people who make them up, are concerned with whether a new facility, such as the St. Lawrence Cement Greenport replacement plant, will be good for the environment. They want to know if the project will stimulate the local economy and create new jobs, and whether the company will operate as a responsible community member. Overall, the community wants to be assured that any proposed facility is safe and that it upholds the high environmental standards that many have worked hard to establish.

At St. Lawrence Cement, we believe that this is all as it should be. We regard ourselves as part of this community, both Hudson and Greenport locally as well as New York State. We believe that we should be open with the community and share our plans for the new Greenport facility and its benefits. We also feel compelled to correct misinformation, misleading statements and untruths about the plant. This is especially important when issues begin to drive a wedge between community members. Finally, we are convinced that our proposed project to replace the existing Catskill plant with the new Greenport facility will provide an overall net benefit to the communities and regions in which we operate.

St. Lawrence Cement has been a community member for nearly two decades, operating a cement facility at Catskill since 1984. We are proud of our track record in Catskill, and we hold it up to the community as an indicator of the commitment we have to meet and exceed the most rigorous environmental standards in the country.

Environmental Benefits

While the current Catskill plant is safe and emissions are well under the allowable standards, the Catskill plant is also older and unable to accommodate new environmental control technologies that are now available. Economically, it is not feasible to try to retro-fit the existing plant. This is why St. Lawrence Cement has proposed to build a replacement facility at Greenport—a new plant for a new age.

Our proposed Greenport replacement facility will incorporate a unique combination of environmental control technologies, making it one of the most environmentally friendly cement plants in the world. The replacement of Catskill with the new state-of-the-art Greenport plant will allow us to substantially lower those emissions that the public tends to be most concerned about.

Emissions of fine particulates (most commonly referred to as PM 2.5) will be cut by 14%, with the most troublesome combustion-related particulate matter dropping by 40%. Emissions of mercury will be reduced by 95% and lead emissions by 94%. Similarly, the emissions that cause acid rain—

sulfur dioxide and nitrogen oxides emissions—will be reduced by 45%. Studies by the EPA and NYSDEC corroborate these figures, providing credible and expert third-party validation that the environmental benefits we promise are real.

St. Lawrence also recognizes the community's concerns about the impact of plant emissions on historic structures and facades. Emissions from our Catskill plant are already well below allowable limits, and do not accelerate the deterioration of historic buildings and facades. The even lower emissions at Greenport should re-assure the community that St. Lawrence Cement is committed to the community and the preservation of our historic buildings—valuable community assets that enrich our area and attract tourists.

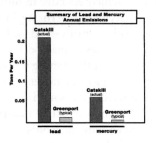

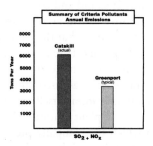

Economic Benefits

The history of this region is grounded in the cement industry. The community recognizes the importance of industry to create a diverse economy, one that takes advantage of tourism while also providing meaningful jobs for the families who live here. The Greenport replacement plant respects this need for balance, and promises to bring economic improvements to the area while preserving and enhancing the community's overall appeal.

The replacement plant, for example, will use a different process for cement production than the Catskill facility. Instead of the current 'wet' process utilized at Catskill, the Greenport plant will employ a dry process. The net benefit here is that the replacement facility will use 99% less Hudson River water and discharge absolutely nothing back into the River. Add to this St. Lawrence's restoration of 3.0 acres of former inter-tidal wetland in South Bay, an area filled over a half-century ago (long before St. Lawrence bought the property) that has been deemed extremely well-suited, if restored, for fish and wildlife habitation.

Of course, the Greenport replacement plant also holds enormous economic promise for the community, Columbia County and upstate New York. In addition to the costs of constructing the new facility (much of which will be spent right here in Greenport), jobs will be both preserved and created, a host of products and services will be required, and local, county and state taxes will be paid. St. Lawrence Cement is committed to the local community, its economy and its future, and we've proposed a project that promises multiple benefits for all of us.

St. Lawrence Cement welcomes this opportunity to provide our community with important facts and information that will help the community better understand the environmental and economic impact of our proposed replacement plant in Greenport. For certain, we want to see a successful conclusion to the process, but we also want our fellow members of the local and regional community to know the facts, recognize the benefits and support the plant.

the combination of these visual elements with the text of the letter contributes subtly to the effectiveness of this argument.

This example illustrates both the importance and the potential risks of using visual elements in genuine argumentation about controversial issues. If you engage in argument with an honest intent to address difficult problems, then it makes sense to employ whatever strategies and resources are available, including visual elements, to make the argument as effectively as possible. In the case of the St. Lawrence Cement company, it is easy to suspect the company's motives and accuse it of trying to manipulate public opinion. (Of course, the same can be true of the company's opponents.) From such a perspective, you might see the use of visual elements as part of an effort to win at any cost, and you might be right. One element in analyzing the argument in a case like this is the company's track record in such disputes. Has the company been unforthcoming about the environmental effect of its plants in the past? Has it engaged in underhanded tactics to manipulate public opinion? If so, you would have reason to be skeptical of the company's motives and you should assess its argument accordingly. You might, for example, view the photograph negatively because you may suspect that the company is trying to soften its image and divert attention from its environmental record.

But it might also be true that many long-time residents of the town work for the company and therefore have a sincere interest in ensuring that the new plant will not harm the local environment. Because those workers live in the community where the plant will be built, their interests will be similar to those of opponents of the plant who hope to preserve the health of the local environment. From this perspective, the argument made by the company—and arguments made by other parties in the conflict—can be seen as negotiating differences among the participants. Visual elements become tools that all participants employ as they seek to resolve the problems created by the company's plans to build the new plant. If it turned out that the company or other parties in the controversy did not have honorable motives, you could still engage their arguments thoughtfully and decide on their merits accordingly. Your attention to the visual elements is an important part of the process by which you make that decision.

Analyzing Arguments in Electronic Media

Because they offer capabilities that are not available in print forms, electronic media provide a rich context for argumentation that can differ significantly from print media. For example, radio allows speech, music, and other sound effects to be used in arguments in ways that cannot be reproduced in print. Television enables the use of sound in addition to moving images and text. And the computer-based media on the Internet and World Wide Web offer previously unseen configurations of text, image, and sound that can be more interactive than other media. Moreover, the specific characteristics of communication in these new electronic media, especially their speed and availability, might be changing the nature of communication itself.

Because of the rapid development of new technologies (such as multimedia online capabilities, digital video and audio technologies, and high-definition TV), the characteristics of electronic media are changing constantly. No one can anticipate how these media will influence the ways you engage in argumentation about important issues. (Who could have predicted twenty years ago that e-mail and cell phones would become as commonplace as the traditional telephone?) But what you can do is examine some of the important features of these media and begin to explore how they can be used to make effective arguments.

The Internet

Because the Internet has become so important in how people interact and communicate with each other, it is inevitably influencing how arguments are made.

You can use the Internet to discover images that will help you when you are arguing to inquire (see pages 11–12) or writing an argument to fulfill any of the purposes described in Chapter 1—images that can be downloaded and analyzed at your convenience. But the technologies that contribute to the Internet also lead to the presentation of images in ways that must be experienced online rather than in print. Consider, in this respect, Figure 3-12: the home page for the U.S. Army website. Like Figures 3-9 and 3-10, this site is designed to encourage support for the military. If you examine it, you will see lots of links that would call up different screens, each of which have additional images. Caught and frozen in print, as it is here, and considered only as a piece of graphic design, Figure 3-12 seems more cluttered than the posters you have already seen. But it was not designed to appear as it is here. When called up though the Internet, it was accompanied by military

FIGURE 3-12
U.S. Army Home Page

music and moving pictures—features that invite additional attention, whether it take the form of quickly clicking on various links or carefully examining information about issues such as benefits. In other words, images on the Internet, like images on television and in the movies, are dynamic rather than static. You can analyze any single image or screen, but you can also analyze the larger work of which these components are a part.

The emergence of the Internet and the World Wide Web as a means of communication and as a forum for public discussion has been touted by some observers as a watershed development for democratic societies, which—in theory, at least—are built around the idea that citizens make collective decisions about how they should be governed. Some believe that Internet technologies like e-mail and the multimedia capabilities for transmitting ideas and information on the World Wide Web will eventually enable many more people to participate directly in the political process than they could have without these technologies. Today, newsgroups, e-mail discussion lists (such as listserv), web-based bulletin boards, and online chat rooms enable millions of people to join in discussions about current issues that affect their lives. With access to these online forums, you can debate a recent congressional decision or political election with someone from across the country almost as easily as—indeed, perhaps *more* easily than—you can debate your neighbors or roommate. Moreover, the Internet and World Wide Web enable people with similar interests or concerns to form "virtual communities," in which they can share ideas quickly and easily without having to be in the same place at the same time. Online forums now exist for every imaginable kind of group, from anthropologists to zoologists, from sales to sailing. These forums allow participants to engage in conversations about issues important to them, and many professional organizations use online forums for conducting meetings, circulating petitions, voting, and similar activities. In these ways, Internet technologies help people form and maintain communities by providing a ready medium for communication, discussion, and debate.

Chances are that you have participated in one or more of the online forums now available on the Internet or World Wide Web. If so, you might share the enthusiasm expressed by many commentators for these technologies. You might also have experienced the "flame wars" that frequently occur in newsgroups, mailing lists, and chat rooms. Visit a chat room or skim the messages posted to a mailing list or newsgroup, and you quickly see that much of the discussion that occurs in some of these forums is not argumentation but more like the quarreling you see on television talk shows. This is true even in online forums devoted to serious issues and maintained by professionals such as lawyers or academics. Many critics have expressed skepticism about the possibilities of these forums to enhance public debate about serious issues. They worry about the overwhelming volume of online discussion and of information on the Internet and World Wide Web, and they raise questions about the usefulness of online discussion. Here, for example, is Mark Slouka, a well-known writer specializing in issues related to these new technologies:

> Will virtual communities help us "reclaim democracy, vent our opinions about the OJ trial, and circumvent Op-Ed newspaper editors," etc.? Clearly, there's something very powerful (and potentially very positive) about a technology that allows millions of people to share ideas and allows them to side-step the occasionally ignorant or biased "filters" like magazine Op-Ed editors. My concern (a viable one, to judge from the mass of stuff online) is that the Net will privilege "venting" over debate and knee jerk speed over reflection. There's a very real chance that what the Net will produce is not "tons of useful information," but virtual

mountains of babble among which the occasionally useful tidbit of information (the kind not available in the local library) will be as easy to find as a nickel in a landfill.

Slouka expresses two of the main concerns skeptics often cite in their criticism of online forums for public discourse: the questionable nature of much of the discussion that occurs online and the sheer volume of online discussions. A single newsgroup or mailing list can generate hundreds of messages in one day, far too many for any person to sort through carefully. In addition, as Slouka notes, many online discussions are characterized by superficial exchanges of opinions instead of careful, considered debate. Genuine argumentation is often as hard to find online as it is on popular talk radio.

What does all this mean for those who are interested in argument? No one can be sure, despite the enormous amount of discussion among scholars, critics, and policymakers about the role of electronic technologies in public discourse. But the Internet and World Wide Web are not likely to disappear. They will continue to evolve, and they will very likely become more important for communication and argumentation in our society. The capabilities of these technologies seem to promise new ways of engaging in argument for the purpose of solving problems and negotiating differences. But it is also true that these technologies will complicate argumentation in ways that we cannot anticipate. In the meantime you will almost certainly encounter arguments in online forums, and you might present your own arguments in such forums. In many respects, engaging in genuine argumentation online is similar to engaging in argumentation in other forums, and the advice offered in this chapter and elsewhere in this book will generally apply to online forums as well. But there are some characteristics of online technologies that can shape argumentation, and you should be aware of how these characteristics might affect arguments online.

Not all online forums are alike, and online forums used primarily for discussion—including e-mail mailing lists, newsgroups or web-based bulletin boards, and chat rooms—must be distinguished from websites, which can advance arguments but do not necessarily involve discussion and which have multimedia capabilities that most discussion forums lack.

Websites

The World Wide Web represents a potentially unprecedented medium for argument. Because of the Web's complexity and because of the rapid pace at which Web technologies are evolving, no one can predict how its role as a medium for argument might grow or change. But it is clear that the Web offers intriguing possibilities for structuring and presenting arguments. This section reviews some of the characteristics of the Web and their implications for argument.

Online Versions of Print Arguments   To begin, it is important to point out that there are different kinds of websites. Some websites essentially offer online versions of print documents. For example, many newspapers and magazines are available on the Web in more or less the same format as their print versions. If you visit a site such as the *Los Angeles Times* online, you will find the same articles that appear in the printed newspaper. Although the online versions of these articles might have links to other websites and might include graphics that do not appear in the print versions, their content and format are essentially the same as the printed versions. In terms of structure, content, and related matters, therefore, arguments on such websites are not very different from arguments in a print medium. An editorial essay in the *Los Angeles Times* is the same essay online and in print. Currently, most arguments on the Web are of this kind (Figure 3-13).

Hypertextual Websites   True hypertext is another matter. **Hypertext** refers to the capacity to link documents through **hyperlinks** that a user clicks to move from one document to another. Websites that are truly hypertextual can differ dramatically from a print document (or an online version of a print document) in the way they are structured. Hypertextual documents need not be organized in a linear fashion, as most print essays are; rather, links can be embedded on web pages so that users can move from one page to another in the website in a variety of ways: hierarchically, in a radial fashion, or randomly. The possibilities for arranging textual and graphical information in a hypertext are endless. Moreover, hypertexts can be more interactive than print text in the sense that readers select which links they will follow as they move through a document. In a print essay, readers generally move from the opening paragraph to the final paragraph. By contrast, true hypertexts offer countless ways for readers to move through them, so it is possible that no two readers will read a hypertext in exactly the same way.

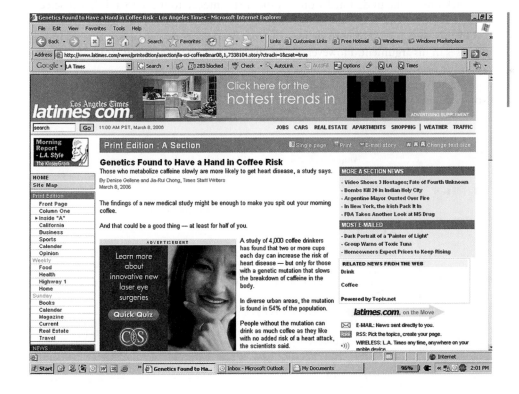

FIGURE 3-13

Print Publications on the Web

This screenshot shows part of an article from the *Los Angeles Times* website.

These features of hypertext offer new possibilities for authors to present their arguments. In addition to enabling authors to incorporate graphics and sound easily into an argument, hypertext allows authors to structure an argument in a variety of ways that affect the impact of the argument. Keeping in mind that arguments in print form tend to be organized in a linear fashion, consider the following example of a hypertextual website titled "Argumentation on the World Wide Web," by Tom Formaro. In this hypertext, Formaro examines the implications of using hypertext for argumentation, actually demonstrating his argument by presenting it in hypertext. Formaro might have made the same argument in a conventional print format. But hypertext offers options for presenting his argument that would not be possible in print.

Figure 3-14 shows the first screen of his hypertext. Notice that this web page doesn't really introduce Formaro's topic; rather, it gives you advice on how to move through, or navigate, his hypertext. Notice, too, the links on the left side of the screen. As you'll see, those links will remain visible no matter which web page you visit in this hypertext; they help you find your way to specific pages in the document. However, Formaro has also embedded links within each page. Those links function differently within his argument than the links on the left side of the screen. For example, a few links from this first screen will bring you to the screen in Figure 3-15. Here, Formaro raises questions that are central to his main argument—questions about the meaning of a "beginning" in a text and how the idea of a beginning or introduction can be complicated by hypertext. You can read this paragraph and then click one of the links at the bottom of the screen, which will take you to another screen related to this one—almost like turning a page in a book. But you can also click one of the underlined words in the first sentence to move to a different screen. If you click the word *postmodern,* for instance, you'll see the screen in Figure 3-16.

On this web page, Formaro defines the term *postmodernism* in a way that serves his purposes in his argument. However, if you clicked the word *hypertext* instead of *postmodern* in the previous screen, you would see the screen in Figure 3-17.

Here Formaro discusses what he sees as the key feature of hypertext for argumentation. Notice the many underlined words on this screen. Each of them is a link that leads to a

FIGURE 3-14

Opening Screen of "Argumentation on the World Wide Web"

ARGUMENTATION ON THE World Wide Web

Links

Sections

General Index

Authors Index

Topics Index

Bibliography

Navigation Tips

How to Use This Hypertext

A Caveat

I've chosen to use frames because of the effect frames have on the boundaries of a work. What you'll notice throughout this piece is that when you jump to other sites from links I've provided, you haven't really left this work at all. The Links sidebar and the title remain visible. The boundary between my work and the work of others becomes difficult to discern.

Blurring the boundaries between works is the reason for the frames and illustrates an important point about hypertext on the World Wide Web. I'll discuss this idea formally throughout the work, especially when considering the World Wide Web and texts. If you are not using a frames compatible browser, you will still be able to view the work, but the boundary between this piece and others to which it is linked will be more distinct.

Navigation Tips

Receiving image (0 bytes of 821 bytes, 0 bytes/sec): button.home.gif

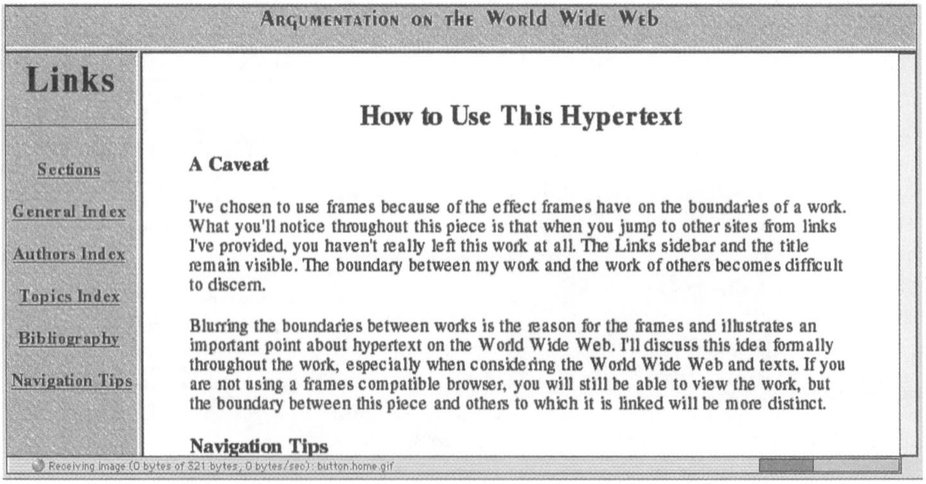

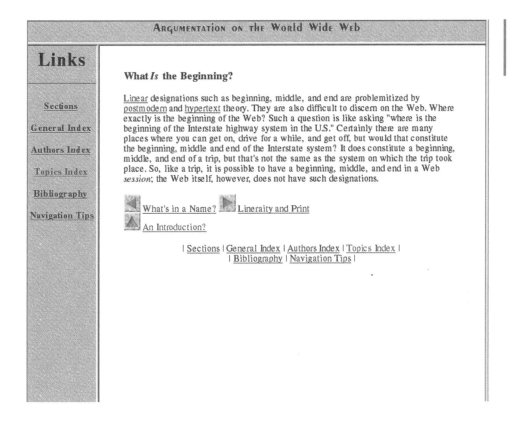

FIGURE 3-15

A "Beginning" Web Page
in "Argumentation on the
World Wide Web"

different screen. As a reader you make choices about which links to follow, and these choices affect how you engage Formaro's argument. Different readers will follow different links, thus reading Formaro's text in different ways, in effect deciding how to organize Formaro's argument. As a writer, Formaro creates these links as transitions to various parts of his argument. In this sense, his links are not only a means of moving through his document but also a way to connect ideas. He can thus use them to help make his claims or provide evidence.

Because we are so used to the conventions of print and its usual linear structure, reading through a complicated argument in a hypertext such as Formaro's can be disconcerting. Hypertext forces us to read differently. It also forces the writer to think differently about how to present an argument. Because the author does not determine the precise order in which each reader will read the various pages in a hypertext, the author cannot think of his or her argument in a linear way, in which every reader moves from point to point in the same way. Instead, the author may think of an argument as a collection of large pieces, each representing a distinct topic, point, or claim. The author must then decide how those pieces relate to each other so that the overall argument makes sense to readers, each of whom might experience the argument differently. Should a particular claim or bit of evidence appear on a main page or on a page linked to that main page? Why? What pieces of an argument should *every* reader see? Which pieces can be skipped without weakening the argument? Such questions can encourage a writer—and readers—

ARGUMENTATION ON THE WORLD WIDE WEB

Links

Sections

General Index

Authors Index

Topics Index

Bibliography

Navigation Tips

Defining Postmodernism

A definition of postmodernism I find useful comes from Jean-Francoise Lyotard: "I define *postmodernism* as incredulity toward metanarratives" (*The Postmodern Condition* xxiv). Lyotard argues that no one set of rules, no one story, no one condition accurately explains knowledge and communication. "Universal and eternal truths," as David Harvey notes, "if they exist at all, cannot be specified. Condemning meta-narratives . . . as 'totalizing,' [postmodernists] insist upon the plurality of 'power-discourse' formations (Foucault), or of 'language games' (Lyotard)" ("Postmodernism" 45). Essentially, these theorists point to the fact that we should be aware of instances of privileging one set of ideas over another.

Lyotard also suggests postmodernism is continually redefined: "The emphasis can be placed on the powerlessness of the faculty of presentation, on the nostalgia for presence felt by the human subject, on the obscure and futile will which inhabits him in spite of everything." What at one moment challenges our ideas, our sense of how things are, becomes, at the next moment, that which we seek to challenge. (*The Postmodern Condition* 79).

Postmodern and Web Theory The Implications of Postmodernism

An Introduction?

| Sections | General Index | Authors Index | Topics Index |
| Bibliography | Navigation Tips |

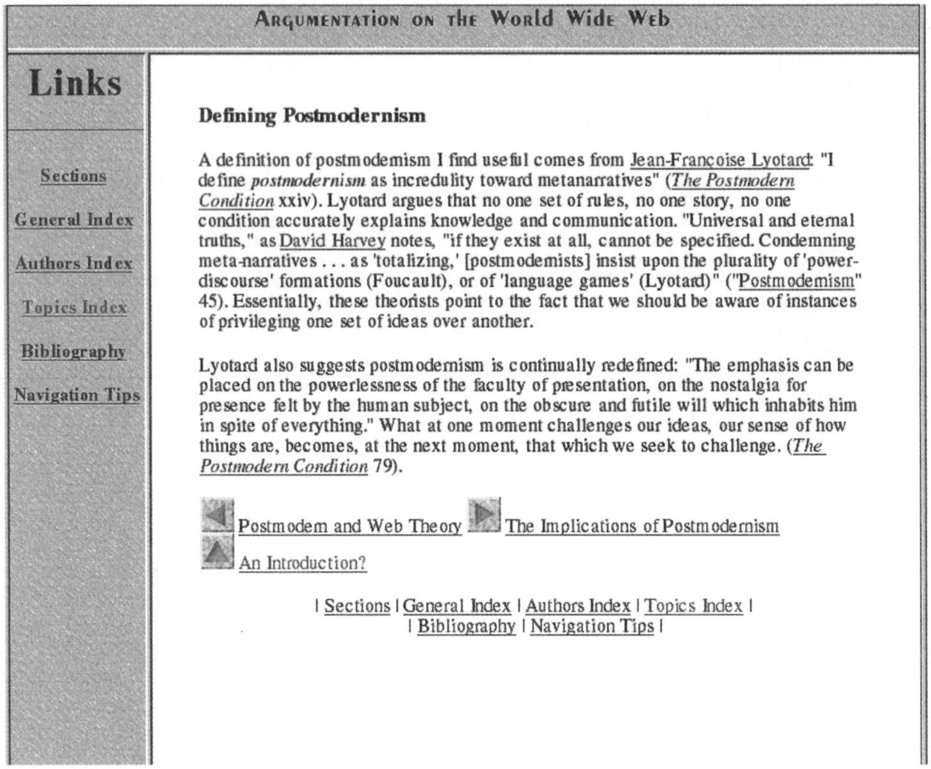

FIGURE 3-16

One Link from the "Beginning"

ARGUMENTATION ON THE WORLD WIDE WEB

Links

Sections

General Index

Authors Index

Topics Index

Bibliography

Navigation Tips

Hypertext Theory

The core of hypertext and the Web can be summed up in one word: freedom. Freedom for authors, for readers, for texts, freedom for the argument, and even freedom for the technology (the relationship among each of these elements relates to Burke's concept of container and the thing contained). There are some exceptions to the freedom of hypertext on the World Wide Web. However, together with my conception of privileging as the core of postmodern theory, freedom in hypertext--and particularly on the Web--are the theoretical legs on which my discussion stands.

Freedom and the Author

An Introduction?

| Sections | General Index | Authors Index | Topics Index |
| Bibliography | Navigation Tips |

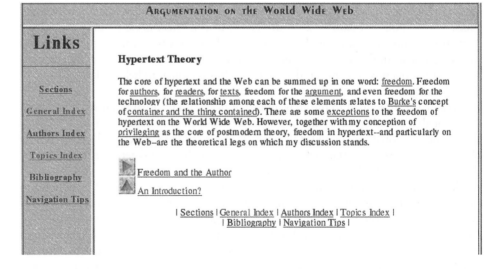

FIGURE 3-17

A Different Link from the "Beginning"

to reexamine how an argument fits together. And the links themselves represent transitions that can support or enhance an argument. For example, an author can make a claim based on an implied warrant then create a link to a page that defends that warrant. In a print article, such a defense would have to be incorporated into the text (or perhaps included in a footnote or sidebar), which perhaps would interrupt the flow of the author's argument. Hypertext enables authors to decide on alternative ways of presenting claims, evidence, and warrants.

Notice, too, that hypertext enables an author to embed multimedia in a website to help support an argument. The Web enables Formaro to use color and design easily to present and enhance his argument in ways described earlier in this chapter. If he desired, he could also link video or audio clips to specific points in his argument. These features can become powerful tools in an author's efforts to present his or her argument.

It remains to be seen whether the potential of hypertext to enhance arguments will be realized in a widespread way in the years ahead. Formaro's website represents a use of hypertext for argumentation that is still quite rare, despite the rapid growth of the Web. But as his hypertext suggests, the Web offers intriguing new possibilities for people to address complex issues and try to solve problems through argumentation.

Websites as Arguments   We have been discussing websites in which authors make arguments in hypertextual form. But websites themselves can also be seen as making arguments in the way that a brochure or a flyer does. Today, advocacy groups, political organizations, government and nongovernmental agencies, institutions, and community groups of all kinds maintain websites on which they present themselves to the public. But individuals or groups can take advantage of the Web's capabilities to make implicit arguments. Consider the home page of the website for the University of St. Thomas (Figure 3-18), the largest private university in Minnesota. The school's colors are purple and gray; purple was chosen as the principal color for the home page because it is more assertive than gray. The text at the center of the principal box provides a summary of the school's mission and location, and it establishes the size of enrollment and that the university serves both undergraduate and graduate students. Running horizontally along the top of the site, links provide access to information such as maps and directories. Additional links are listed in a column immediately below the first bar, and two images appear to the right of this column: a picture of arches and a picture of an academic building with office towers in the background. Users familiar with St. Thomas would recognize the arches as the principal entrance to the school's main campus near the Mississippi River in St. Paul, Minnesota, and the urban view to be part of the school's campus in downtown Minneapolis. (Minneapolis and St. Paul are called the Twin Cities because one begins where the other ends, and they share a number of services, such as an international airport.) Visitors to this site who are only beginning to learn about St. Thomas would not be able to place these images precisely, but they could grasp what is conveyed by them. The arches suggest a welcoming entrance to an academic environment; the downtown view supports the text about how the Twin Cities provide "employment opportunities" and "cultural events." Part of the school's motto appears to the right of the architectural images, and different fonts are used to suggest that it is important to challenge yourself but even more important to change the world.

I FIGURE 3-18

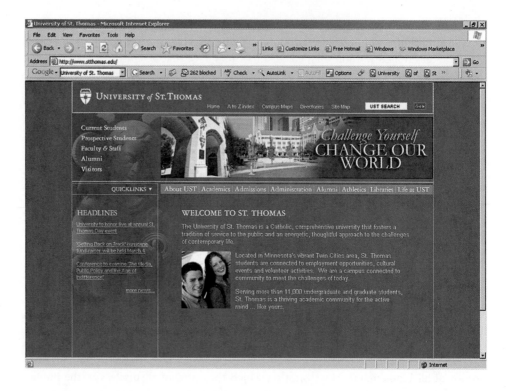

An additional horizontal line of links appears immediately below the architectural images, and each of these leads to a variety of other links. Daily news stories can be easily accessed by clicking on one of the story lines in a box on the left side of the page. And two other images contribute to the school's presentation of itself: a photograph of a young man and woman suggests that students are happy at St. Thomas and that the student body is equally composed of men and women. It also suggests that the majority of students at St. Thomas are of European descent, even though the school does not discriminate on the basis of race, color, or national origin as noted at the bottom of the page.

Finally, a sculptured representation of St. Thomas Aquinas, after whom the school is named, appears in soft gray as part of the background for the left size of the page. This image is a close-up of the sculpture that can be seen in the image of the arches. Widely respected as one of the great philosophers of the Middle Ages, and a saint in Catholic teaching, Aquinas quietly asserts the school's Catholic identity—which is otherwise established only by a single reference to "Catholic" in the principal text. The home page thus establishes that St. Thomas is a Catholic university, but it is also a university that does not discriminate on the basis of religion (as noted at the bottom of the page).

Online Discussion Forums

Online discussion forums have proliferated dramatically in the past few years. Today you can find a newsgroup, mailing list, or web board on any imaginable topic. In addition, college instructors now commonly set up online forums as a component of their courses. (In courses offered exclusively online, online forums often replace traditional face-to-face classroom discussion.) A common use of such forums is to foster discussion among students about important course topics. In effect, students often go online to engage in argumentation about course-related issues.

One obvious advantage that an online forum has over a more traditional print medium (such as a newspaper editorial page) is that it is more immediate and opens the possibility for more voices to enter the conversation. You can post a message to a newsgroup in which you defend a position on an issue, and within a few hours or even minutes several people might have responded to your post. Many more people can join in the conversation in this way than could possibly do so on a newspaper editorial page or in the letters-to-the-editor section of a magazine. In **asynchronous** forums such as mailing lists, newsgroups (in which messages remain available to participants anytime they log on—the electronic equivalent of a bulletin board containing many messages pinned to it), or web boards, readers can sort through messages and analyze them before posting a response. In this respect, asynchronous forums have an advantage over face-to-face discussion (such as in a classroom or at a public meeting) in that they allow participants time to consider their responses before posting them. Usually, in a face-to-face discussion a response must be made soon after someone has spoken, providing little time for discussants to formulate their responses carefully. If the conversation moves quickly, you might not even get the chance to make your comment before the conversation moves to another point. On a mailing list, newsgroup, or web board, by contrast, you can write and even revise your response offline before posting it. Of course, it's possible to respond prematurely in an asynchronous forum, just as it is possible to respond rashly in a face-to-face discussion or to damage a relationship by responding to an e-mail in anger.

Here's part of a discussion about plagiarism that occurred on the Usenet newsgroup **soc.college.admissions**. The discussion began when one participant posted part of a news report about plagiarism in American colleges and universities. Several other people joined in. (The lines preceded by >'s are quoted passages from previous messages.)

> Plagiarism is running rampant on American college campuses, and everyone
> knows that technology is partly to blame. After all, any student with a few
> dollars can go to one of the many Web sites that sell research papers and
> buy the perfect paper for the assignment.

I fail to understand why plagiarism is so hard to define and understand. If every teacher in every class started out on the first day of class to define plagiarism as:
1. submitting ideas or words that are not one's own without properly and accurately attributing them to their true author
2. papers that are copies of papers someone else wrote or which have been previously submitted to another class
3. whatever else the teacher does not want in original works (specifically "cut and paste" items from the Internet)
along with examples of what is permitted and what is not permitted, the students would know upfront specifically what is allowed and not allowed.

Each student should then be required to write a brief summary of the rules in his/her own handwriting, sign it and turn it into the teacher. This can be done even by very young children. Nothing affects understanding so much as having to put it in one's own words (how ironic for a definition of plagiarism). Then if someone is found to have violated the rules, he or she fails the class. And schools must back up the teachers, not be weakened by litigious parents.

Kate

_____

"Kate" wrote in #1

> I fail to understand why plagiarism is so hard to define and understand.
> If every teacher in every class started out on the first day of class to
> define plagiarism as:
> 1. submitting ideas or words that are not one's own without properly and
> accurately attributing them to their true author

This is precisely why it's so hard to define. Most students (or people for that matter) go through entire days without thinking a single original thought. How is a student expected to write an entire paper of almost entirely unoriginal ideas and credit every single 'true author'? I obviously know what your point is, I'm just saying the line isn't that clear. I know that one of the greatest feelings for a teacher is discovering new ideas coming from his students, but can you really expect this from everyone (the C student as well as the B and A students)?

How strict would you propose enforcing your Rule No. 1? Would you like to end up with papers with citations noted after every single sentence? I think plagiarism is awful, I just think its not as clear-cut as you say.

matt

_____

> I think plagiarism is awful, I just think its not as clear-cut as you say.

Hmmm. I find that I agree with a lot of this. How about: 1) I read Joe Expert's book and he lays out a few facts. I think to myself, "(Insert some conclusion from those facts here)." Then, I turn the page and Joe Expert reaches the same conclusion. Do I need to cite that? (I would, to be on the safe side, but I'm not sure I should have to.)

Also, how about the line between "common knowledge" and what needs to be cited? Interestingly, Vanderbilt University defines this specifically in their honor code documentation: common knowledge is an idea that appears in 3 or more distinct sources. This is the first time in my life I have seen such a clear cut definition.

Joe

_____

"Joe" wrote in message #3

> How about: 1) I read Joe Expert's book and he lays out a few facts. I think
> to myself, "(Insert some conclusion from those facts here)." Then, I turn
> the page and Joe Expert reaches the same conclusion. Do I need to cite
> that? (I would, to be on the safe side, but I'm not sure I should have to).

It's not plagiarism to use the same idea another person had if you put it into your own words and ex-pand upon it or criticize it positively or negatively. Such as: "Joe Expert says George Bush is the Anti-Christ [cite]. Many people may believe this to be true but I disagree for several reasons." . . .

The problem with plagiarism today is that it is far easier to heist information from the Internet in one's bedroom than it is to crawl through dusty library stacks before computers were everywhere. Perhaps, teachers can require that a certain percentage of citations in a paper must be from real books—which requires real page numbers; maybe require a few xeroxed book pages in support. Maybe that's all too much.

Kate

———————————-

"Kate" wrote:

> The problem with plagiarism today is that it is far easier to heist
> information from the Internet in one's bedroom than it is to crawl through
> dusty library stacks before computers were everywhere.

Wait, is this a bad thing . . . ?

> Perhaps, teachers
> can require that a certain percentage of citations in a paper must be from
> real books—which requires real page numbers; maybe require a few xeroxed
> book pages in support. Maybe that's all too much.

If the information is appropriate for the paper, accurate, and from a credible source, does it matter where it came from? I think it would be unhealthy to search for reasons to cling to real books (espe-cially when the whole world is opting for change.) After all, 'real' (or perhaps not so real) books are now being published over the Net.

This excerpt is a good example of the way argumentation can occur in asynchronous online forums. The participants seem genuinely concerned about plagiarism, and the dis-cussion seems to move toward a loose consensus about how schools might solve the prob-lem. Notice that the participants follow some of the conventions of traditional argument. For example, they present claims (for example, plagiarism is hard to define), support their claims (for example, students do not generally work with original ideas, so identifying what is original and what is not can become a problem), and imply warrants (for exam-ple, plagiarism is bad). In addition, participants address their audience—indeed, they do so directly by responding to points made by other participants. And they seem to make certain assumptions about that audience and about the larger context of the discussion. For example, the participants all seem familiar with American higher education, and they are responding to recent events involving plagiarism at American universities. In these ways, this newsgroup discussion resembles traditional argumentation.

It is easy to see some of the advantages of arguing in such a forum. The medium al-lows for a great deal of back-and-forth discussion in a way that simply is not possible in traditional print forums. And many people can participate without the discussion becoming overwhelming. The immediacy of the forum allows participants to focus nar-rowly on specific claims or evidence, as you might in a face-to-face debate but without the pressure of having to respond immediately to someone else's challenge or rebuttal.

But notice that argument in this forum tends to be more informal and less rigorous than it can be in print media. Because messages tend to be relatively short, and because active discussions can generate many messages quickly, claims and evidence need to be presented concisely, without the lengthy explanations and extensive support that might be expected in the formal essays you write for your college courses. For the most part participants understand and accept this fact. But if you engage in discussions in online forums, it is worth remembering that the principles of genuine argumentation don't always apply.

The matter of credibility can also be complicated in online forums. Generally, there is no way of knowing who participants really are, whether they have any legitimate knowledge or experience related to the topic at hand, and whether they are being honest about what they say. Determining the credibility of the author of an argument is an important part of analyzing that argument, and you will find advice in Chapter 4 for how to do so. Participants in online forums can establish their own credibility over time through the messages they post, but you usually have no way to verify what others say in their messages. To an extent, one's credibility is always constructed, even in a respected print medium. But writers whose essays appear in a magazine such as the *Atlantic Monthly* or a newspaper such as the *Wall Street Journal* must work with editors and generally have well-established credentials. Just being published in a respected magazine gives them a measure of credibility. By contrast, anyone can log into a newsgroup such as **soc.college.admissions** and post a message. And a participant can claim to be a college instructor or an admissions officer without having to provide proof. If you know that people are who they claim to be, you are more likely to take those people's arguments seriously. But without a way to verify their claims, you should always view their messages with at least a small measure of skepticism.

It goes without saying that your own credibility can be questioned, too. As a participant in an online discussion, you are likely to be more effective in making your arguments if you can establish credibility, just as you would in a print medium. Keep in mind that other participants might take your claims about who you are with a grain of salt. Keep in mind, too, that following the protocols of arguing in online forums is one of the best ways to establish your credibility in such a forum. Posting relatively brief messages that respond to previous messages, keeping your responses to the point, and avoiding criticism or ridicule of other participants (that is, avoiding flame wars) will likely encourage others to take your arguments more seriously.

Synchronous forums, such as chat rooms, instant messaging, or multiuser domains (MUDs), differ from asynchronous forums in that participants post and read messages in "real time." In other words, when you are logged onto a chat room or other kind of synchronous forum, your message appears on the screens of all other logged-on participants as soon as you write it on your computer; any messages posted by other participants appear on your screen immediately as well. And those messages do not remain available once the conversation has ended; that is, you cannot always retrieve them later, as you can on a newsgroup or mailing list.

The experience of engaging in a synchronous discussion is much like having a face-to-face conversation, except that you are reading and writing comments rather than speaking or hearing them. As a result, discussions in synchronous forums tend to be somewhat slower than face-to-face discussions. And usually several different topics—or "threads"—occur simultaneously. These characteristics of synchronous forums result in messages that tend to be short and, ideally, concise. Longer messages, even messages of a few sentences, can slow the discussion and make it harder for participants to keep up with the conversation. Consequently, synchronous forums do not lend themselves to considered debate about complex issues that require participants to present lengthy arguments or cite extensive evidence to support their arguments. If you engage in synchronous discussions, you will be most effective if you can keep your statements short but clear and if you can focus on one claim at a time. Similarly, offer clearly identifiable support for a claim that can be easily digested by other participants.

Although the advice offered here applies generally to any kind of online discussion forum, all online forums are not the same. Public newsgroups such as **soc.college. admissions** tend to be much more freewheeling and informal than specialized newsgroups for professionals, which are often moderated (that is, a moderator reviews messages and decides whether they are appropriate for the forum; the moderator is the equivalent of a newspaper or magazine editor). The protocols governing online behavior can vary widely from one forum to another. Sarcasm and ad hominem attacks that are common on many public newsgroups might result in your removal from a moderated academic mailing list. The audiences for online forums can differ dramatically as well. Participants in a newsgroup such as **soc.law** may include lawyers and other legal professionals, but participants are just as likely to be people with little or no knowledge of the law. By contrast, a mailing list maintained by the American Bar Association will probably be made up mostly of lawyers. The nature of the audience will affect the kinds of topics discussed in a forum and the ways in which participants engage with each other. Flame wars, for example, are much less common in specialized professional forums than in public newsgroups and chat rooms. The expectations for claims and evidence are likely to be more rigorous in a professional forum as well. Even the length of messages and the conventions for how people identify themselves can be different in these different forums. Because of these differences, to engage effectively in argumentation in any online forum, you need to become familiar with the forum and its protocols. It makes sense to read a newsgroup or mailing list for several days or even weeks before jumping into the discussion. If you do so, you will probably find that online discussions can be fruitful and interesting and can be part of your effort to solve problems and negotiate difference through argument.

Radio and Television

The differences between these two media are obvious; most important, radio is not a visual medium. When television began to come into widespread use in the 1950s, many critics feared that it would mean the end of radio. However, radio has thrived since that time, suggesting that it has characteristics as a medium for communication that television lacks. At the same, time radio and television share many characteristics that can escape our notice.

Perhaps the most important feature of radio and television is their reach: they are available to hundreds of millions of people worldwide—many more people than currently have access to the Internet. This reach gives them enormous power for making an argument available to a large audience. Moreover, radio and television are local, national, and international at the same time. Your local talk-radio station might have a host who addresses issues of importance to residents of your region. At the same time, the station might be part of a national network, enabling it to broadcast national (and possibly international) shows. So someone can direct an argument to a specific audience or to a much wider national audience on the same station. The same can be said of most television stations. Although it is true that local newspapers and other print forums also print local, national, and international news, more people listen to radio shows and watch television news programs than read newspapers and newsmagazines. The easy availability of radio and TV seems to matter. And that ease becomes a factor in making an argument in these media.

The immediacy of radio and television is also important. If you are listening to an editorial on radio or on a television news program, you are hearing an electronic version of a speech. In most cases, you will not have access to a printed version of the editorial, so you will not be able to rehear it or reread sections of it (unless you record it). This characteristic of radio or television arguments requires the speaker to adjust diction, style, and arrangement so that listeners can follow the argument easily. Long, complex sentences can be difficult for an audience to follow in oral arguments, and complicated reasoning or detailed evidence can be lost on listeners. For these reasons constructing an argument in these media usually means choosing accessible words, crafting relatively simple sentences, perhaps repeating key phrases, and generally being more succinct than you might be in, say, a research paper for a college course or a newspaper editorial.

Sound is a powerful tool in both television and radio. Listen to any commercial, an announcement for an upcoming program, or a political advertisement, and you will almost certainly hear music or some other sound effect that was specifically chosen for that spot. Political advertisements, for example, are often accompanied by patriotic music or other kinds of music intended to influence listeners positively. Television commercials for sporty cars use contemporary rock music that appeals to younger people who are likely to buy such cars. Similarly, ads for many products now include popular songs from the 1970s that would have positive connotations for viewers who grew up during that decade. As a listener or viewer you might find yourself reacting to such sound effects in ways that might influence how you think about the claim being made on behalf of a political candidate or for a particular car. Would you react to the pitch in the same way if it did not incorporate that favorite song of yours? Would your feelings about the political candidate be different if no music were played during the radio ad? Being aware of the effect of such uses of sound is part of being able to engage public arguments critically.

The video and sound capabilities of television make it an enormously powerful medium, and it is important to keep in mind that much of what appears on television should be the subject of careful analysis when it is a source for information. Aside from editorials on news programs, discussions on some public affairs programs (such as *Face the Nation*), and some special documentary programs, little of what appears on television can be described as genuine argumentation of the kind explored in this book. At the same time the power of this medium, its ubiquitous nature, and even its seductiveness are compelling reasons for you to be aware of its persuasive qualities and to be able to distinguish between the many kinds of persuasion on television and the few genuine arguments appearing in that medium.

Perhaps the most obvious instance of argumentation on television occurs during political conventions, especially during presidential elections. When the major political parties convene, they take great pains to present themselves in a certain light on the extensive television coverage of those events. The stage and backdrop for speeches, the music, the colors of banners and signs, and the camera angles are all carefully arranged to communicate certain messages to voters. When a candidate addresses the convention, his or her appearance on the television screen is as important as the speech. Think of your reaction to a televised political speech. How much was it influenced by your feelings about the appearance of the candidate? By his or her delivery? How much attention did you pay to the words themselves? How closely did you follow the argument, identifying and evaluating claims and evidence? Chances are that for many viewers the messages communicated by the candidate's appearance and presentation overshadow the specific claims made in the speech. A candidate's confident and trustworthy appearance might impress the viewer more than his or her specific arguments about, say, tax reform. The power and subtlety of visual messages thus present a challenge to those who wish to engage in genuine argumentation in this important medium.

You might never have an opportunity to make an argument on radio or television, but you will certainly encounter arguments in those media. And many of those arguments will be about important matters in your life, including political elections. Being aware of the way these media are used to communicate and persuade—as well as to argue—will make you a more savvy citizen.

The well-known critic Marshall McLuhan once famously asserted that the medium *is* the message. This chapter has examined some ways in which McLuhan may have been right.

We live in an age of multimedia communications, and we are surrounded by images on television, in print, and on the World Wide Web; on signs and billboards; on flyers and pamphlets; and from the logos on race cars to the Nike swoosh on golfer Tiger Woods's ever-present baseball cap. Not only advertisers but also politicians, advocates for all kinds of causes, institutions like schools and hospitals, and even individuals use and manipulate visual elements to communicate an idea or position and to influence a particular audience. They all use visual rhetoric to make an argument.

4

The Strategies for Argument

W hen you write an argument, you might feel confident about what you want to say or about the position you wish to take on an issue. In such a case your primary challenge is to examine the issue carefully so that you can develop the most effective argument. In other situations you might be faced with the prospect of arguing about an issue about which you are unsure or have mixed emotions. In that case writing your argument will involve exploring the issue more fully and perhaps even discovering your position as you write. In both cases, however, you are engaged in what classical rhetoricians termed **invention,** that is, exploring and developing ideas about a specific topic to make an effective argument about it. Aristotle, whose treatise on rhetoric is still an important work for rhetoricians today, defined **rhetoric** as "the faculty of observing in any given case the available means of persuasion." In other words, rhetoric is finding an effective way to persuade other people to believe or do something. You can usefully think of argumentation in similar terms.

In his *Rhetoric,* Aristotle identified three primary modes of persuasion:

- Ethical, or arguments based on the speaker's character
- Logical, or arguments based on reason and evidence
- Emotional, or arguments that appeal to the emotions

Scholars continue to refer to these modes by their names in Greek: *ethos* (from which *ethical* derives), *logos* (from which *logic* derives) and *pathos* (from which *pathetic* derives). Effective arguments usually include all of these modes. Logic alone works as a kind of mathematical proof, and an illogical argument is unlikely to be convincing. But because humans have values and feelings, an argument that appeals to the mind alone may not be as successful as an argument that speaks to the heart and soul as well. Moreover, no matter how clever an argument may be, it is unlikely to endure if it is unethical. Misrepresentation and manipulation can sometimes secure a short-term victory, but truth ultimately prevails.

Accordingly, this book takes the position that the ethical dimension of an argument is of primary importance. But an ethically based argument implies that claims can be supported by evidence and clear thinking has led to reasonable conclusions. *Ethos* and *logos* are thus closely related. This chapter will describe the principles of logical reasoning (as well as the use of emotional appeals) after beginning with an explanation of how writers convey ethos to readers.

Understanding Ethos

"You can count on her."

"I wouldn't trust a word he says."

How many times have you heard—or spoken—some version of those two statements? Very likely, you have done so often, perhaps without realizing that you were engaging in one of the most basic and long-standing strategies for argument: invoking character. Aristotle identified character, or ethos, as one of the most powerful components of persuasion available to a speaker: "We believe good men [and women] more fully and more readily than others," he wrote, adding that a speaker's character "may almost be called the most effective means of persuasion he [or she] possesses" (*Rhetoric*). But character is not just a strategy; it is also a quality. Like Aristotle, the famous Roman rhetorician Quintillian believed that the most effective orator is a "good" person. Above all, Quintillian wrote, the effective orator "must possess the quality which . . . is in the very nature of things the greatest and most important, that is, he [or she] must be a good man [or woman]" (*Institutio Oratoria,* Book XII). In short, the best way to sound or appear ethical in an argument is to *be* ethical.

We often rely on our sense of someone's character when making decisions in our daily lives. For example, you might seek advice about attending graduate school from a relative or a teacher you trust and whom you know to be careful with advice about such matters. In some cases character might grow out of authority and expertise: Your professor's knowledge of universities and education can lead to useful advice about graduate school. You wouldn't necessarily have the same confidence about such advice from, say, a friend who is a chef. From her you might seek suggestions for a good restaurant or recipe. Authority or expertise is not the same thing as character (a professor can be unethical and untrust-worthy, for instance), but it is usually part of character and can be a powerful source of appeals in argument.

This kind of appeal is common in advertising. Corporations select celebrities to represent them or their products—for example, basketball star Michael Jordan for Nike shoes. The implicit argument is that if someone like Jordan endorses this product, it must be good. An advertising campaign for the soft drink Sprite even parodied this strategy. In several television ads, professional basketball players, such as Grant Hill, were shown drinking Sprite. The ads seemed to suggest that drinking Sprite would enable anyone to perform the athletic feats of a player like Hill. But at the end of the ad, a person fails to perform such a feat after drinking Sprite. The ads end with the line "Obey your thirst." The suggestion was that you shouldn't trust a celebrity for advice about how to quench your thirst. These ads presented a twist on the common approach to using celebrities to sell products, suggesting how routine that approach has become in American culture.

Character is especially important in the arenas of law and politics. In court, for instance, lawyers will try to establish or undermine the credibility of witnesses as they try to convince a judge or jury about a person's guilt or innocence. Defense lawyers sometimes call "character witnesses" to establish that the defendant was a particular kind of person (usually a good person). Similarly, when it comes to politics, character often looms large. Consider how often candidates for elected office try to establish their credibility as trustworthy and dependable. Advertisements showing a candidate's family, for example, are standard fare in U.S. elections. Such advertisements intend to convey that politicians who are married and have children are more reputable than candidates who are single—an old-fashioned idea that has been strangely enduring even though most people these days recognize that there's nothing necessarily odd about being single and that families who smile together are not necessarily happy. Just as common are advertisements attacking an opponent's credibility. Often such "attack ads" will suggest that a candidate is not concerned with issues affecting voters and therefore isn't to be trusted.

A writer can raise questions about someone's credibility to support a particular point or position on an issue. Consider, for instance, the following excerpt from an editorial by *Chicago Tribune* columnist Clarence Page. Page is arguing in favor of a controversial policy at the University of North Carolina requiring all incoming first-year students in 2002 to read a book about the Koran. The purpose was to encourage students to learn and think carefully about an important book that they might not be familiar with. Page is reacting specifically to an appearance by a University of North Carolina professor on *The O'Reilly Factor,* a popular television news talk show hosted by journalist Bill O'Reilly:

The important thing, as Robert Kirkpatrick, the professor who chose the book, explained on "The O'Reilly Factor" TV show is this: First-year students need to know that "as a member of an academic community they have to learn to think and to read and to write and to defend their opinions."

That's right. Start pushing a book on college freshmen and, who knows? They might try reading another one.

That's what college is supposed to be about. It is not just a time for learning but a time to arouse curiosity in preparation for a lifetime of learning.

That process begins when you learn not only to have opinions but also how to express and defend them.

"And defending the right not to read the book is something that will be very interesting to read," the professor said.

Indeed, it should be at least as interesting as listening to showman-journalist O'Reilly explain why he will not read the book. According to a Fox transcript, he called UNC's assignment "unbelievable," compared it to assigning "Mein Kampf" during World War II and asked why should freshmen be required to study "our enemy's religion."

Yes, there is a lot more to Islam than Osama bin Laden and his violent brethren, but apparently not in O'Reilly's mind.

"I mean, I wouldn't give people a book during World War II on [how] the emperor is God in Japan. Would you?"

"Sure," Kirkpatrick said. "Why not? Wouldn't that have explained kamikaze pilots?"

That's a sensible answer, not that sensibleness gets you anywhere on high-energy cable TV news-talk shows these days or, for that matter, in politics—especially religious politics.

Here, Page supports his own position in favor of the reading requirement by questioning O'Reilly's credibility (and even his common sense) on the issue. He suggests that O'Reilly's interest as a TV talk-show host is not in arriving at a "sensible" answer to the question raised by the University of North Carolina requirement but rather in being a "showman." Such a strategy can be effective when a person advocating a certain position is well-known and likely to be considered credible by many people. Because of his television show, O'Reilly was widely known in the United States in 2002, and it is likely that many of his viewers saw him as an important voice on issues such as public education. By calling O'Reilly's credibility on the issue into question, Page could weaken O'Reilly's position and strengthen his own argument that the reading requirement is justified and sound.

Let us now turn to a longer and more subtle example, an argument that does not raise the question of *ethos* by directly praising anyone or questioning anyone's credibility. James Surowiecki published "A Farewell to Alms?" in the *New Yorker* in July 2005, a few weeks after a giant rock festival had focused international attention on poverty in Africa. This event provided the occasion for Surowiecki to assert and support a position about foreign aid to developing countries. Much could be said about how carefully he put his argument together—beginning with how the title alludes to *A Farewell to Arms*, a novel by Ernest Hemingway about a young man who becomes disenchanted with war after serving in the military. But as you read it now, be alert for how Surowiecki establishes his own credibility in this piece without announcing, "I am a credible person with excellent *ethos*." Note how he recognizes that foreign aid can be abused and offers specific examples of such abuse but also points to cases where foreign aid has helped lift countries out of poverty.

A Farewell to Alms?

In 1985, when Bob Geldof organized the rock spectacular Live Aid to fight poverty in Africa, he kept things simple. "Give us your fucking money" was his famous (if apocryphal) command to an affluent Western audience—words that embodied Geldof's conviction that charity alone could save Africa. He had no patience for complexity: we were rich, they were poor, let's fix it. As he once said to a luckless official in the Sudan, after seeing a starving person, "I'm not interested in the bloody system! Why has he no food?"

Whatever Live Aid accomplished, it did not save Africa. Twenty years later, most of the continent is still mired in poverty. So when, earlier this month, Geldof put together Live 8, another rock
spectacular, the utopian rhetoric was ditched. In its place was talk about the sort of stuff that
Geldof once despised—debt-cancellation schemes and the need for "accountability and transparency" on the part of African governments—and, instead of fund-raising, a call for the leaders
of the G-8 economies to step up their commitment to Africa. (In other words, don't give us your
fucking money; get interested in the bloody system.) Even after the G-8 leaders agreed to double aid to Africa, the prevailing mood was one of cautious optimism rather than euphoria.

That did not matter to the many critics of foreign aid, who mounted a lively backlash
against both Live 8 and the G-8 summit. For them, continuing to give money to Africa is simply "pouring billions more down the same old ratholes," as the columnist Max Boot put it. At
best, these critics say, it's money wasted; at worst, it turns countries into aid junkies, cling-
ing to the World Bank for their next fix. Instead of looking for help, African countries need to
follow the so-called Asian Tigers (countries like South Korea and Taiwan), which overcame
poverty by pursuing what Boot called "superior economic policies."

Skepticism about the usefulness of alms to the Third World is certainly in order. Billions
of dollars have ended up in the pockets of kleptocratic rulers—in Zaire alone, Mobutu Sese
Soko stole at least four billion—and still more has been misspent on massive boondoggles
like the twelve-billion-dollar Yacreata dam between Argentina and Paraguay, which Argentina's
former President called "a monument to corruption." And historically there has been little correlation between aid and economic growth.

This checkered record notwithstanding, it's a myth that aid is doomed to failure. Foreign
aid funded the campaign to eradicate smallpox, and in the sixties it brought the Green
Revolution in agriculture to countries like India and Pakistan, lifting living standards and life
expectancies for hundreds of millions of people. As for the Asian nations that Africa is being
told to emulate, they may have pulled themselves up by their bootstraps, but at least they
were provided with boots. In the postwar years, South Korea and Taiwan had the good fortune to become, effectively, client states of the U.S. South Korea received huge infusions of
aid, with which it rebuilt its economy after the Korean War. Between 1946 and 1978, in fact,
South Korea received nearly as much U.S. aid as the whole of Africa. Meanwhile, the billions
that Taiwan got allowed it to fund a vast land-reform program and to eradicate malaria. And
the U.S. gave the Asian Tigers more than money; it provided technical assistance and some
military defense, and it offered preferential access to American markets.

Coincidence? Perhaps. But the two Middle Eastern countries that have shown relatively
steady and substantial economic growth—Israel and Turkey—have also received tens of billions in U.S. aid. The few sub-Saharan African countries that have enjoyed any economic success at all of late—including Botswana, Mozambique, and Uganda—have been major aid
recipients, as has Costa Rica, which has the best economy in Central America. Ireland (which
is often called the Celtic Tiger), has enjoyed sizable subsidies from the European Union.
China was the World Bank's largest borrower for much of the past decade.

Nobody doubts that vast amounts of aid have been squandered, but there are reasons to think that we can improve on that record. In the first place, during the Cold War aid was more often a geopolitical tool than a well-considered economic strategy, so it's not surprising that much of the money was wasted. And we now understand that the kind of aid you give, and the policies of the countries you give it to, make a real difference. A recent study by three scholars at the Center for Global Development found that, on average, foreign aid that was targeted at stimulating immediate economic growth (as opposed to, say, dealing with imminent crises) has had a significantly beneficial effect, even in Africa.

There's still a lot wrong with the way that foreign aid is administered. Too little attention is paid to figuring out which programs work and which don't, and aid still takes too little advantage of market mechanisms, which are essential to making improvements last. There's plenty we don't know about what makes one country succeed and another fail, and, as the former World Bank economist William Easterly points out, the foreign-aid establishment has often promised in the past that things would be different. So we should approach the problem of aid with humility. Yet humility is no excuse for paralysis. In 2002, President Bush created the Millennium Challenge Account, which is designed to target assistance to countries that adopt smart policies, and said that the U.S. would give five billion dollars in aid by 2006. Three years later, a grand total of $117,500 has been handed out. By all means, let's be tough-minded about aid. But let's not be hardheaded about it.

—*James Surowiecki*

Early in his argument, Surowiecki emphasizes that billions of dollars of foreign aid have been stolen. He later returns to this problem. His last two paragraphs begin with lines that link back to the waste he recognizes: "Nobody doubts that vast amounts of aid have been squandered. . . ." and "There's still a lot wrong with the way that aid is administered." Nevertheless, the success stories that he mentions show that foreign aid can be effective. This balanced approach suggests that Surowiecki is credible because he is a fair-minded person who can look at a problem from more than one side and then reach a reasonable conclusion: "By all means, let's be tough-minded about aid. But let's not be hardheaded about it." Moreover, the topic itself helps establish Surowiecki's *ethos*. Arguing to reduce poverty in Africa is nobler than arguing how to get a tax break.

As the previous example shows, readers who don't know anything about James Surowiecki can find his argument convincing because of the way he presents himself, in addition to the way he presents information. Many arguments have force because of the authority or character of the writer. Consider the following letter to the editor of the *Cleveland Plain Dealer*, written in response to an editorial about the promise of medical technology:

The *Plain Dealer's* Aug. 13 editorial "Miracles on demand" was right that emerging medical breakthroughs hold incredible promise in overcoming serious diseases like cancer and heart failure. And it was right that, in our imperfect world, it is impossible to provide an absolute guarantee of the safety of medical technology. But it missed the fact that manufacturers and the Food and Drug Administration are doing an excellent job making sure new tests and treatments are as safe as possible. . . .

FDA data on product recalls show that the agency's system of pre-market and post-market regulations is working well. Even as the number and complexity of medical technologies has increased, the total number of recalls has remained steady over the last 10 years. The vast majority of recalls are not considered a serious public-health issue and are due to issues like labeling errors that can be easily corrected. Are medical technologies always perfect? Unfortunately, no. But manufacturers and the FDA have maintained an impressive safety record as a result of their mutual commitment to the safest possible products.

The agency itself concludes: "The public's confidence in FDA is well justified." After examining the facts, we wholeheartedly agree.

The letter was signed as follows:

Pamela G. Bailey.

Bailey is president of the Advanced Medical Technology Association, which represents more than 1,100 innovators and manufacturers of medical devices, diagnostic products and medical information systems.

Bailey is making a logical argument about the safety of medical technologies. But her argument might have greater impact on readers who notice that she is president of an organization of medical technology professionals. You might consider whether you assign greater credibility to this argument on the basis of your knowledge of Bailey's position. (Your reaction would depend in part on your opinion of large companies that manufacture medical technologies. For some readers, knowing who Bailey is will undermine her argument.)

The public prominence of a person can work in much the same way in an argument. In the summer of 2002, the *New York Times* published an essay in favor of school vouchers by the famed economist Milton Friedman. After the Supreme Court decision in June 2002 upholding the voucher program in Cleveland, Ohio, city schools, many editorialists wrote arguments supporting or opposing the court's ruling. Many of those writers had no authority as either legal experts or educators. In that regard, their character probably did not figure prominently into their arguments—or in readers' reactions to their arguments. Friedman, by contrast, is an internationally known figure who is one of the most influential economists of the twentieth century. Consider how this blurb, which was included at the end of his essay, might influence your reaction to his argument:

Milton Friedman, the 1976 recipient of the Nobel Prize in economics, is a senior research fellow at the Hoover Institution.

Writers of arguments need not have such impressive reputations as Friedman's to employ character effectively. Establishing credibility is an important strategy in argumentation that all writers can use. When you refer to your experiences, for example, as a way to indicate to your readers that you know something about a situation or an issue, you are establishing credibility that can give your argument greater weight. Here is writer Joshua Wolf Shenk, addressing the issue of legalizing drugs:

There's no breeze, only bare, stifling heat, but Kevin can scarcely support his wispy frame. He bobs forward, his eyes slowly closing until he drifts asleep, in a 45-degree hunch. "Kevin?" I say softly. He jerks awake and slowly rubs a hand over his spindly chest. "It's so hot in here I can hardly think," he says. . . .

This July I spent a long, hot day talking to junkies in New York City, in a run-down hotel near Columbia University. Some, like Kevin, were reticent. Others spoke freely about their lives and addictions. I sat with Melissa for 20 minutes as she patiently hunted her needle-scarred legs for a vein to take a spike. She had just fixed after a long dry spell. "I was sick," she told me. "I could hardly move. And Pap"—she gestures toward a friend sitting across from her—"he helped me out. He gave me something to make me better. . . ."

Making drugs legally available, with tight regulatory controls, would end the black market, and with it much of the violence, crime, and social pathology we have come to understand as "drug-related." And yet, history shows clearly that lifting prohibition would allow for more drug use, and more abuse and addiction.

I spent that day in New York to face this excruciating dilemma. It's easy to call for an end to prohibition from an office in Washington, D.C. What about when looking into Kevin's dim eyes, or confronting the images of crack babies, shriveled and wincing?

Shenk uses his own experience not only to make his point about the horrors of drug addiction but also to establish himself as someone who knows about this problem from direct experience. Notice, too, that Shenk's gentle, sympathetic descriptions of the addicts he met help convey a sense of him as caring and deeply concerned, which might add to his credibility for many readers. (There is an emotional appeal here, too.)

If writers of arguments try to connect with readers by establishing credibility, readers have the option of resisting that connection. In other words, they might not identify with the writer—or with the audience he or she directly addresses—or they might not *wish* to identify with the writer. There can be many reasons to resist such a connection, but one important reason has to do with how readers perceive the writer's credibility. As a reader, you are not likely to be persuaded by a writer whose credibility you question, no matter how inclined you might be to agree with his or her argument. But as a writer, you cannot automatically assume that readers will find you credible just because you believe in yourself and know that you are telling the truth.

Writers can establish their ethos in a variety of ways. For example, the following excerpt is the opening paragraph of an essay titled "The Laments of Commuting" by Daisy Hernandez, which was published in the *New York Times:*

> It's hard to make commuters happy. So much is working against us. Virtually no subway platforms have air conditioning. Express lines suddenly go local. And it's a long-distance hike through the underground pedestrian connection between ACE and the NRQWS1237 trains.

Notice that Hernandez immediately identifies herself as a commuter in her essay. Readers will be more likely to consider her credible because of her knowledge and her experience as a commuter. In addition, her conversational tone suggests that she is reasonable and personable—someone you might find yourself sitting next to on the train as you commute to work. Even though commuting is a serious matter for millions of people, Hernandez adopts a tone that isn't overly serious, and her lighter tone might invite readers—especially those who do not commute—to engage her argument. Hernandez's experience as a commuter and her tone may help establish her credibility with readers. As a reader, you will want to take note of your reaction to Hernandez's experience and tone and decide whether they make her a more credible writer in this instance.

Compare Hernandez's approach with that of the following writer, whose letter to the editor of *USA Today* was written in response to an article about actor Mike Myers:

> The sheer stupidity of what many Americans find entertaining never ceases to amaze me. Another tired, hackneyed sequel to the foolish *Austin Powers* series is dragged out for the

people who wouldn't get a joke if it didn't include obvious "you're-supposed-to-laugh-now" cuts.

The debate still rages as to who is less funny: Jim Carrey or *Austin Powers'* Mike Myers. Both couldn't act their way out of a wet paper bag, so instead they pump out inane movies with a grade-school humor level. It's as if IQ is unwelcome in movie production these days.

Honestly, who couldn't star in *Austin Powers?* The only difference between Myers' embarrassing himself and any number of fools we've all had to tolerate is that Myers has cultivated an entire career by being gratingly unfunny.

I gave in this past weekend and managed to suffer through about 15 minutes of *The Spy Who Shagged Me,* playing on cable. I want my 15 minutes back, Mr. Myers.

This writer's opening sentence immediately creates a distinction between him and the "many Americans" who find Myers' movies entertaining. That distinction might serve the writer's purpose, because he obviously excludes himself from that category of readers. So he might not be concerned if such readers dismiss his argument. However, consider how the writer's tone might affect his ethos among other readers, who might even agree with his assessment of Myers. This writer criticizes Myers's comedy, but he offers no evidence to support his main contention that Myers's acting ability is poor; instead, he offers simple assertions to that effect. Although readers who share the writer's opinion might nod in agreement, it is worth considering how other readers, who might have no strong opinion about Myers, might react to this argument. For such readers this writer might sound arrogant or unreasonable, and his credibility therefore suffers. In this case, then, the writer's ethos might undermine his argument for some readers but enhance it for others.

Establishing an honest, straightforward voice as a writer can help convince readers that you are credible and believable and that they can take you seriously. Indeed, the quality of your writing can help establish your credibility by demonstrating your competence to readers. Acknowledging your own limitations can be an effective strategy for establishing credibility, too. For example, imagine that you wish to contribute to a discussion of standardized testing in your community, an important educational issue that affects all students (including you). In writing a letter to your local school board, for instance, you might concede at the outset that you are not an expert in educational testing but that your experiences as a student give you insight into the problems associated with testing. Such a statement can gain you credibility by showing that you are not trying to claim expertise that you don't have yet you are genuinely concerned about the issue at hand. In this sense you are being honest with your readers and thereby communicating to them that they can trust you. You are, in other words, establishing your character as the writer of an argument.

Sometimes, claiming authority as the writer of an argument can backfire. You have no doubt heard or read statements by someone engaged in argument who claims to know more than someone else about the issue being discussed. For instance, return to the example in the previous paragraph. Imagine that your letter to the school board has provoked a response from a school board member who is an expert in educational testing. Imagine further that he explicitly refers to that expertise in his attempt to call your position into question. In effect, he says, "I know what I'm talking about, because I'm an expert in this area. This other person, on the other hand, doesn't know what he or she is talking about." Even if the board member's purpose is to prevail, such an approach can undermine his credibility, because readers could find him arrogant. The school board member in this example might have expertise in testing, but residents of the school district might reject his position if they believe that his arrogance gets in the way of the best interests of the students. If his purpose in this argument, by contrast, is to address a problem involving the testing of students in his school district, then perhaps the strategy is inappropriate. Like all appeals, the appeal to character can be complicated and should always be assessed in terms of the specific situation at hand.

Understanding Logos

Because *logos* sounds so much like logic, it is easy to assume that the two are synonymous. They are certainly similar. Classical rhetoricians such as Aristotle devoted much attention to how to reason logically and how to use logic to persuade an audience. But in addition to logic, *logos* involves having good command of information and language. It is impossible to argue logically, after all, if you use words imprecisely or cannot support your claims with evidence.

Logic is often associated with objectivity, and logical arguments are traditionally considered those based on facts and reason rather than emotion. Of course, the very idea of objectivity can be (and has been) questioned, and because we often engage in arguments over complex and important issues that matter deeply to us, avoiding emotion is rarely possible and not necessarily even desirable. Nevertheless, logic can be a powerful component in a writer's effort to engage in argumentation, and even when you make arguments that appeal to ethics and emotions, you will usually need to incorporate some elements of logic. The most important of these is evidence that supports whatever you claim. That evidence can take different forms and then be arranged in different patterns. These patterns, in turn, can help you discover where you may need additional evidence and where you may need to modify what you claim.

Appraising Evidence

One of the most important—and difficult—aspects of making effective arguments is identifying and using appropriate evidence. Being able to appraise evidence is a crucial part of evaluating arguments, but appraising evidence can be challenging. Consider the following examples. The first is a letter to the editors of *Consumer Reports* magazine; in this letter the writer challenges a recommendation the magazine made in a report on how to save money:

> I disagree with your money-saving recommendation to stick with regular gasoline. I own a 2001 Chrysler Sebring and a 1996 Ford Taurus GL, both of which are supposed to use regular. But I've found that using midgrade 89-octane fuel increases highway mileage by 2 to 5 mpg.

Here's the editors' response:

> It's good to hear that something yields better fuel economy, but we wouldn't credit the fuel. We have found that temperature and climate conditions affect mileage more than octane.

Who is right? Or, to rephrase the question, whose evidence is more convincing? The writer of the letter provides evidence of good fuel economy using a higher-octane fuel; the magazine editors refer to their own tests as evidence suggesting otherwise. How do you judge the evidence in such a case?

As these examples suggest, almost anything can be used as evidence: statistics, opinions, observations, theories, anecdotes. It is not always easy to decide whether a particular kind of evidence might be appropriate for a specific claim. Moreover, what counts as appropriate and persuasive evidence always depends upon context. Personal experience might be acceptable to readers of a popular consumer magazine but not necessarily for a technical report on fuel economy for a government agency. The rhetorical situation in which an argument is made will help determine not only what kinds of evidence are most appropriate for that argument but also whether that evidence is likely to be persuasive.

With that in mind, look at four commonly used kinds of evidence:

- Facts or statistics
- Personal experience
- Authority
- Values

Facts as Evidence　　In the following excerpt from an essay published in the online public interest journal *TomPaine.com,* writer Joan Wile argues against a tax refund that President George W. Bush sponsored in 2001. Wile contends that opposition to the Bush tax policies is important, even a year after the policy was adopted. Writing in 2002, she asserts,

> However, the tax abatement issue is still, if not more, critical today than a year ago. Our needs are even greater but with less revenue to address them—our receding economy; our health care crisis; our worsening environment; our failing education system; the reestablished deficit; our increasing numbers of poor with the concomitant smaller numbers of rich controlling greater amounts of wealth, as well as the necessity for greater defense (but sane and non-threatening to our civil liberties) measures against terrorism.

Wile tries to establish the importance of the tax abatement issue by presenting evidence that the nation's ongoing "needs" continue to be great. Her evidence consists of references to the problems facing the United States: "our receding economy; our health care crisis; our worsening environment; our failing education system; the reestablished deficit; our increasing numbers of poor." Notice that Wile refers to these problems as facts without necessarily establishing them as such. For example, she refers to the "receding economy" without providing, say, statistics on economic activity or stock market performance to demonstrate that the economy is indeed in recession. She can do so because in September 2002, when her essay was published, the U.S. economy was in recession. So simply referring to the economic situation suffices as evidence in this instance. Similarly, she cites "our worsening environment" and "failing education system" without specific information about them. Given the audience for *TomPaine.com,* Wile can assume that most of her readers will accept these references as adequate evidence, because she knows that those readers are likely to view both the environment and the education system as being in crisis; they will not demand further information to support her assertions. But what if she were writing for a politically conservative journal? In that case she would most likely have to supply additional evidence—perhaps in the form of figures indicating increased air and water pollution or declining scores on standardized educational tests—to persuade readers that such crises do exist. In short, what counts as a fact and what is considered ample evidence depend on context and audience.

Whatever the writer's intended audience, a reader must decide whether the evidence presented in support of a claim is adequate. In this example, Wile's argument that the tax refund was a bad idea rests on her claim that the nation has pressing problems that require tax dollars. She supports that claim by listing those problems. If you agree that the problems she lists are real and pressing, then you will likely accept her claim and find her argument persuasive. If you don't agree that such problems exist, her evidence will not be adequate to persuade you that the tax refund should be opposed. Sometimes, simply referring to something won't suffice. More specific evidence is required. Here is part of an essay by a college president who believes that the problems in U.S. schools will not be solved unless teachers are adequately supported in their work:

> We often marginalize our teachers rather than celebrate and reward their contributions. Recent national data reveal that the average annual earnings of young teachers between the ages of 22 and 28 was 30 percent less than similarly aged professionals in other fields. By the time these teachers reach 50, the salary gap almost doubles—a little more than $45,000 for veteran teachers versus almost $80,000 for non-teachers. Of course, many of these new teachers don't stay in the profession to age 50. We lose 30 percent of our new teachers in their first five years of teaching and more than 40 percent in large metropolitan areas like New York City.

This writer, R. Mark Sullivan, provides statistical data to support his claim that teachers are not celebrated and rewarded for their contributions. His audience is a general one: the readers of a regional newspaper. He can assume that they will be familiar with some of the problems facing schools, but he probably cannot assume that all his readers will accept his claim that teachers are not supported adequately. To establish that point, he cites evidence showing income disparities between teachers and other professionals. For many readers such figures can be compelling, because income is such an important factor in most people's lives. As a result, many readers will likely see figures demonstrating lower incomes for teachers as good evidence that teachers are not well supported.

But look carefully at the second set of statistics Sullivan offers: the percentage of new teachers who quit teaching within five years. Does this evidence really support his claim that teachers are not well supported? On the surface it might seem so. One explanation for the seemingly high number of teachers leaving the profession might be their low salaries (which is what Sullivan suggests). Another explanation (which Sullivan does not suggest) might be that teachers' working conditions are difficult. These figures might also suggest that not everyone can be a good teacher, and you might believe that those who quit shouldn't be teaching anyway. If it is true that these young teachers quit because they simply have not been effective teachers, then the figures Sullivan cites might work against his claim: They could suggest that the best teachers remain in the classroom and the ineffective ones leave. Moreover, Sullivan never gives the attrition rates for other professions. How many accountants or engineers quit their jobs within five years, for example? That information could change the significance of the figures that Sullivan cites. If 25 percent of accountants or engineers quit in their first five years, then 30 percent of teachers might not seem so high a number—in which case it would not be persuasive evidence for Sullivan's claim.

This example suggests the importance of examining evidence carefully to determine whether it supports a claim. As a reader, you should pay close attention to *how* a writer is using evidence, as well as to *what* evidence is presented. In this example Sullivan uses statistical evidence, which is usually considered valid and can be persuasive for many audiences. But as noted, it is important to examine just what the statistics might indicate. Even if statistical evidence is accepted as true, it may be open to interpretation. Think about the ongoing debates about global warming. In these debates participants often point to statistics showing the rising average temperature of the earth. Most scientists seem to agree that the average global temperature has increased in the past century, but they do not agree about what that means. Do rising global temperatures *prove* that humans have caused global warming? Or do they reflect natural cycles of warming and cooling? A statistical fact by itself has no inherent significance. How it is used and in what context it is used make all the difference.

Personal Experience as Evidence   In the previous example, writer R. Mark Sullivan's use of statistics can be seen as a savvy strategy because many readers are likely to accept statistical evidence as valid. But Sullivan might have used other kinds of evidence to support his claim that teachers are not adequately rewarded for their work. For example, he might have included statements from people who have left teaching because they didn't feel supported. Or he might have referred to his own experience as a teacher (assuming that he had such experience) or perhaps to the experience of someone he knows well—say, a brother or neighbor—who left teaching for that reason. The readers of a regional newspaper might find that kind of evidence as compelling as statistical evidence. Consider how the writer of the following passage uses his own experience as evidence; the passage is taken from an essay that argues against the designation of New York's Adirondack Mountains as "wilderness":

> The irony is that one actually has a truer "wilderness experience" in Adirondack lands designated "wild forest" than in those designated "wilderness." How can this be? The answer is in the numbers—of people, that is. Without the "status" of wilderness, the lowly wild forest just grows on, with little to no human molestation. While there may be a road or two, it is the road less traveled. There may not be a High Peak to bag, but chances are you'll see real wildlife . . . and some lower elevation vistas that fewer eyes have seen. And amazingly enough, you will probably not see another human. I can say this because I have experienced it.

This writer supports his claim about the wilderness experience in "wild forest" areas by stating that he has had that experience. It can be hard to deny the validity of such experience. Think of the weight often given to eyewitness testimony in legal cases: if a person saw something, it must be true. But the extent to which readers will find such firsthand evidence compelling will vary. And readers can question this kind of evidence, just as they can question statistical data. For one thing, where exactly did this writer go in the Adirondacks? It's possible that he visited a few unusual locations that are not representative of most "wild forest" areas. Also, when did he go? He would almost certainly encounter fewer (or no) other hikers in February than he would in July. And how often did he visit these places? If he visited them only once or twice, then his experience might not be typical for those areas. If so, that experience becomes much less forceful as evidence for his claim than it would be if he regularly visited these areas throughout the year. As a reader, raising questions like these will help you evaluate personal experience used as evidence. It can also keep you alert to questionable evidence and help you spot evidence that simply does not support the claim being made.

Authority as Evidence   Citing experts or authorities as evidence is common in all kinds of arguments, but it is especially important in many academic disciplines. Here is an excerpt from *Ecological Literacy,* in which environmental studies scholar David Orr argues that perpetual economic growth cannot be sustained without irreparable damage to the earth's ecosystems:

> In a notable book in 1977, economist Fred Hirsch described other limits to growth that were inherently social. As the economy grows, the goods and services available to everyone theoretically increase. . . . After basic biological and physical needs are met, an increasing portion of consumption is valued because it raises one's status in society. But, "If everyone in a crowd stands on tiptoe," as Hirsch puts it, "no one sees better." Rising levels of consumption do not necessarily increase one's status.

In this passage, Orr draws on the work of a respected economist to support his claim about the dangers of constant economic growth. Notice that Orr underscores the authority of Hirsch's work by describing his book as "notable." Then he presents Hirsch's views about economic growth. Following this passage, Orr summarizes what Hirsch describes as the effects of the desire for more consumption, including such unhappy consequences as "a decline in friendliness, the loss of altruism and mutual obligation, increased time pressures," and so on. Then Orr concludes, "In short, after basic biological needs are met, further growth both 'fails to deliver its full promise' and 'undermines its social foundations.'"

In this case Orr does not offer factual evidence; rather, he cites Hirsch's theories to make the claim that unchecked economic growth is undesirable. In effect, Orr is deferring to Hirsch's expertise as an economist to support this claim. Although what Hirsch offers is essentially an interpretation of economic data and social and economic developments, rather than the data themselves, his status as an expert gives his interpretation weight. Orr relies on that status in using Hirsch's ideas as evidence.

In evaluating an argument like Orr's, you must decide how credible the authority or expert really is. If you know nothing about the work of Hirsch, you have to take Orr's word for it or find Hirsch's book and examine it for yourself. Notice that Orr summarizes Hirsch's key ideas in this passage. He probably assumed that many of his readers would not be familiar with Hirsch's theories. So telling us that Hirsch is an economist who authored a "notable" book helps establish Hirsch's authority on the subject. Orr's claim depends largely on whether his readers accept that authority as credible.

In many cases, writers cite a well-known authority or expert in supporting a claim. Using such an authority to support a claim has obvious advantages. Not only will readers be familiar with the authority, but a widely accepted authority can have an established credibility that a writer can rely on. Consider how Martin Luther King, Jr., in this passage from his famous "Letter From a Birmingham Jail," draws on biblical and historical figures to support his claim that being an extremist for freedom is just and right:

> But though I was initially disappointed at being categorized as an extremist, as I continued to think about the matter I gradually gained a measure of satisfaction from the label. Was

not Jesus an extremist for love: "Love your enemies, bless them that curse you, do good to them that hate you, and pray for them which despitefully use you, and persecute you." Was not Amos an extremist for justice: "Let justice roll down like waters and righteousness like an overflowing stream." Was not Paul an extremist for the Christian gospel: "I bear in my body the marks of the Lord Jesus." Was not Martin Luther an extremist: "Here I stand; I cannot do otherwise, so help me God." And John Bunyan: "I will stay in jail to the end of my days before I make a butchery of my conscience." And Abraham Lincoln: "This nation cannot survive half slave and half free." And Thomas Jefferson: "We hold these truths to be self-evident, that all men are created equal."

Clearly, King expects these names to have credibility with his readers. The moral weight of the names he cites will give force to the quotations he uses as evidence in this passage.

Values as Evidence   The passage from King's "Letter From a Birmingham Jail" points to a final kind of evidence: values or beliefs. (You can read King's "Letter From a Birmingham Jail" on pages 600–610.) Although King uses the authority of the names he cites in this passage, he is also invoking deeply held moral values. Elsewhere in his "Letter" he uses these values directly as evidence to support specific claims. For example, in arguing that he and his followers were justified in breaking laws prohibiting Blacks from visiting public places, King cites a moral principle:

> One has not only a legal but a moral responsibility to obey just laws. Conversely, one has a moral responsibility to disobey unjust laws. I would agree with St. Augustine that "an unjust law is no law at all."

In effect, King uses the value of justice as evidence that his disobedience was justified and even necessary. Using values or beliefs as evidence can be tricky. If you invoke a principle or value that your readers do not share, your evidence will not be persuasive to them and your argument may be weakened. In addition, values and beliefs can be open to interpretation, just like factual evidence or personal experience. Consider, for example, the ongoing controversies about capital punishment. Both opponents and supporters of capital punishment cite moral values to support their arguments—sometimes, the same value or principle (for example, "Thou shalt not kill"). In assessing such evidence, be aware of how it might be received by readers.

Presenting Evidence in Visual Form   Evidence, especially factual or statistical evidence, is sometimes presented in visual formats within a written argument. In some cases presenting evidence graphically can be more effective than simply incorporating it into the text.

Word processing and desktop publishing computer software, along with the rise of the World Wide Web as a medium with multimedia capabilities, make it easy for writers to incorporate visual elements into their arguments. At the same time, these technologies make it even more important for readers to develop the ability to evaluate evidence carefully. Evidence presented visually, as in Figure 4-1, can be appealing and persuasive, but it should be subjected to the same careful scrutiny that you would use to assess any evidence.

FIGURE 4-1

Presenting Information Visually

Charts such as this, which shows the significant increase in gasoline prices that occurred in the United States between 2004 and 2006, present information efficiently and effectively.

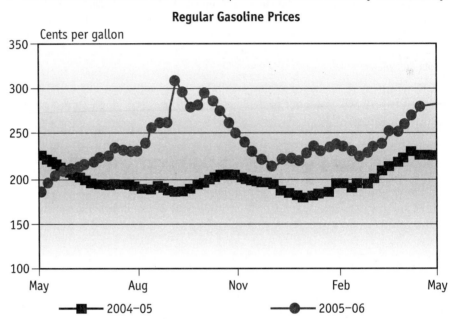

SOURCE: U.S. Department of Energy

Patterns of Logic

Logical arguments can take several forms. The most common are those derived from classical rhetoric: inductive and deductive reasoning. In the late-twentieth century, however, communication specialists became interested in a pattern of reasoning called the Toulmin method. This chapter introduces all three of these approaches.

Reasoning Inductively

When you use induction, you are drawing a conclusion based on specific evidence. Your argument rests on a foundation of details accumulated for its support. This is the type of reasoning used most frequently in daily life. In the morning you look at the sky outside the window, check the outdoor temperature, and perhaps listen to a weather forecast before dressing for the day. If the sun is shining, the temperature is high, and the forecast is favorable, you are drawing a reasonable conclusion if you decide to dress lightly and leave the umbrella at home. You haven't *proved* that the day will be warm and pleasant; you have only *concluded* that it will be. This is all you can usually do in an inductive argument: arrive at a conclusion that seems likely to be true on the basis of available evidence. Ultimate and positive proof is usually beyond reach. In this sense, induction can be seen as a way for a writer of an argument to deal with probability.

Listen, for example, to literary critic Sven Birkerts as he considers the technological changes he saw around him in the 1990s. Birkerts is concerned that new electronic media, especially those driven by computers, are adversely affecting our lives, in particular how we read and write, without our being aware of it. "A change is upon us," he asserts, "away from the patterns and habits of the printed page and toward a new world distinguished by its reliance on electronic communication":

> The evidence of the change is all around us, though possibly in the manner of the forest that we cannot see for the trees. The electronic media, while conspicuous in gadgetry, are very nearly invisible in their functioning. They have slipped deeply and irrevocably into our midst, creating sluices and circulating through them. I'm not referring to any one product or function in isolation, such as television or fax machines or the networks that make them possible. I mean the interdependent totality that has arisen from the conjoining of parts—the disk drives hooked to modems, transmissions linked to technologies of reception, duplication, and storage. Numbers and codes and frequencies. Buttons and signals. And this is no longer "the future," except for the poor or the self-consciously atavistic—it is now. Next to the new technologies, the scheme of things represented by print and the snailpaced linearity of the reading act looks stodgy and dull. Many educators say that our students are less and less able to read, or analyze, or write with clarity and purpose. Who can blame the students? Everything they meet with in the world around them gives them the signal: That was then, and electronic communications are now.

Notice that Birkerts offers a series of observations about the effect of the technological changes he sees in our lives. He cites examples to illustrate the effects that these changes seem to be having on how we communicate. He then concludes that students no longer learn to read and write as they did before the advent of these new technologies. He cannot be certain of this result; no one can. But the evidence around him suggests that such a result is not only possible but perhaps even likely.

This kind of reasoning is common in scientific research. Scientists may have a theory that explains some phenomenon, but they must carry out many experiments to prove the theory is valid. These experiments will enable the scientists to eliminate certain variables and gather enough data to justify a generally applicable conclusion. Ideally, a well-researched scientific conclusion will reach a point at which it seems uncontestable. One such example is the warning on cigarette packages. Over the years so much evidence has accumulated to link cigarette smoking to cancer that the warning has evolved from a probability to a veritable certainty. Most writers of arguments cannot hope to reach such certain conclusions through induction. Instead, like Birkerts, they try to draw reasonable conclusions based on their observations and the evidence they present. If writers are careful and thorough and have gathered sufficient evidence, their conclusions will usually seem valid to readers.

But beliefs established over many generations can be overturned by a new discovery. Within a few years that "new discovery" can also come under challenge. So serious researchers go back to the lab and keep working—ever mindful that the unknown is almost always greater than the known. Lewis Thomas discusses this aspect of science in an essay included in Chapter 11 (see pages 490–495) and sees it as a source for wonder rather than worry, arguing that science is most exciting when focused on what is not yet understood.

Induction is also essential in law enforcement. Police officers are supposed to have evidence against someone before making an arrest. Consider, for example, the way a detective works. A good detective does not arrive at the scene of a crime already certain about what happened. If the crime seems to be part of a pattern, the detective may already have a suspicion about who is responsible. But an expert investigator will want to make a careful study of every piece of evidence that can be gathered. A room may be dusted for fingerprints, a murder victim photographed as found, and every item in the vicinity examined for clues. Neighbors, relatives, friends, and colleagues will be questioned. The best detective is usually the one with the best eye for detail and the greatest determination to keep searching for the clues that will lead to an accurate and successful prosecution. Similarly, a first-rate detective will be honest enough never to overlook a fact that does not fit with the rest of the evidence. The significance of every loose end must be examined to avoid the possibility of an unfair arrest and unjust verdict.

In making an inductive argument, you will reach a point at which you will decide that you have offered enough evidence to support your conclusion. When you are writing a college paper, you will probably decide that you have reached this point sooner than a scientist or detective might. But whether you are writing a short argument or conducting a major investigation, the reasoning process is essentially the same. When you stop citing evidence and move on to your conclusion, you have made what is known as an *inductive leap.* In an inductive argument, you must always offer interpretation or analysis of the evidence you have introduced; there will always be a slight gap between your evidence and your conclusion. It is over this gap that you must leap; the challenge is to do it agilely. Good writers know that their evidence must be in proportion to their conclusion: The bolder the conclusion, the more evidence is needed to back it up. Remember the old adage about "jumping to conclusions," and realize that you'll need the momentum of a running start to make more than a moderate leap at any one time.

If you listen closely to the conversations of people around you, chances are good that you'll hear examples of inductive reasoning that lack adequate support. When someone says, "I don't like Mexican food," and reveals under questioning that his only experience with Mexican food has been eating a taco from a fast-food chain, you cannot take this judgment seriously. A sweeping conclusion has been drawn from flimsy evidence. People who claim to know "all about" complex subjects often reveal that they know little. Good writers are careful not to overgeneralize.

When you use inductive reasoning to compose an argument, you might cite a particular observation that strikes you as especially important. You might even begin with a short anecdote. An inductive argument would then expand as the evidence accumulates so that the conclusion is well supported.

Reasoning Deductively

When an argument rests on a fundamental truth, right, or value, rather than on available evidence, it employs deductive reasoning. Whereas in inductive reasoning a writer begins with observations or evidence and draws conclusions from those, in deductive reasoning the writer begins with a basic truth or belief and proceeds from there. Evidence is still cited in support of the argument, but evidence is of secondary importance. The writer's first concern is to define a commonly accepted value or belief that will prepare the way for the argument she or he wants to make.

One of the most famous examples of an argument based on deductive reasoning is the Declaration of Independence, written by Thomas Jefferson. (To read the Declaration of Independence, go to page 599.) Although Jefferson cited numerous grievances against England, he rested his argument on the belief that "all men are created equal" and that they have "certain unalienable Rights," which King George III had violated. This was a revolutionary idea in the eighteenth century, and even today there are people who question it. But if you accept the idea that all people are created equal and have an inherent right to "Life, Liberty, and the pursuit of Happiness," as Jefferson asserted, then certain conclusions follow. The writer's task is to work logically toward those conclusions. Accordingly, Jefferson argued for a specific action—the separation of the colonies from England—based on the basic idea of equality. In other words, having established the fundamental truth of the equality of all people, he reasoned that the king's actions were unacceptable and concluded that the colonies must become independent.

The truth, right, or belief from which a writer deduces an argument is called the **premise.** Often, the main premise of a deductive argument is not immediately obvious, but even when you don't recognize it, it is the crucial element holding together the argument. Look at a more current example of an argument based on deductive reasoning, a *New York Times* editorial written in 2002 in response to a controversial court ruling that declared the Pledge of Allegiance unconstitutional:

Half a century ago, at the height of anti-Communist fervor, Congress added the words "under God" to the Pledge of Allegiance. It was a petty attempt to link patriotism with religious piety, to distinguish us from the godless Soviets. But after millions of repetitions over the years, the phrase has become part of the backdrop of American life, just like the words "In God We Trust" on our coins and "God bless America" uttered by presidents at the end of important speeches.

Yesterday, the United States Court of Appeals for the Ninth Circuit in California ruled 2 to 1 that those words in the pledge violate the First Amendment, which says that "Congress shall make no law respecting an establishment of religion." The majority sided with Michael Newdow, who had complained that his daughter is injured when forced to listen to public school teachers lead students daily in a pledge that includes the assertion that there is a God.

This is a well-meaning ruling, but it lacks common sense. A generic two-word reference to God tucked inside a rote civic exercise is not a prayer. Mr. Newdow's daughter is not required to say either the words "under God" or even the pledge itself, as the Supreme Court made clear in a 1943 case involving Jehovah's Witnesses. In the pantheon of real First Amendment concerns, this one is off the radar screen.

The practical impact of the ruling is inviting a political backlash for a matter that does not rise to a constitutional violation. We wish the words had not been added back in 1954. But just the way removing a well-lodged foreign body from an organism may sometimes be more damaging than letting it stay put, removing those words would cause more harm than leaving them in. By late afternoon yesterday, virtually every politician in Washington was rallying loudly behind the pledge in its current form.

Most important, the ruling trivializes the critical constitutional issue of separation of church and state. There are important battles to be fought virtually every year over issues of prayer in school and use of government funds to support religious activities. Yesterday's decision is almost certain to be overturned on appeal. But the sort of rigid overreaction that characterized it will not make genuine defense of the First Amendment any easier.

Obviously, the editors of the *New York Times* disagree with the court's ruling. They support the idea of the separation of church and state, which is a fundamental principle contained in the U.S. Constitution. Notice that they are not arguing for or against this principle; they accept it as true and good. Their argument proceeds from that principle. They criticize the ruling not because it violates this principle but because they see no genuine threat to this principle that would justify the court's decision. According to the editors, the ruling is intended to help maintain the constitutional separation of church and state, which they believe is admirable. But in their view, common sense indicates that the words "under God" in the Pledge of Allegiance do not represent a significant threat to that constitutional principle. So you might articulate the editors' main premise as follows:

> Premise: Serious threats to the constitutional separation of church and state should be opposed.

In this instance no serious threat exists in the editors' view; therefore, the ruling makes no sense. They develop their argument by examining what they consider to be some of the negative consequences of the ruling.

This kind of argumentation is quite common. Glance at an editorial page of any newspaper, and you're likely to see one or more examples of an argument based on deductive reasoning. But as the preceding example shows, formulating—or identifying—a good premise can be a challenge. A good premise should satisfy at least two basic requirements:

- It should be general enough that an audience is likely to accept it, thus establishing a common ground between writer and audience.
- It should be specific enough to prepare the way for the argument that will follow.

In this example, the editors can be confident that most of their readers will understand the idea of the separation of church and state. Certainly, not all of their readers will agree that this principle is a good one that should be maintained, but most readers very likely will agree. So the editors' task is to build an argument that might convince those readers that no threat to that principle exists in this case.

What makes formulating a good premise difficult is that a premise usually refers to or invokes fundamental values or beliefs that we don't often examine consciously. In the case of the Declaration of Independence, Jefferson clearly articulated a fundamental belief in equality, which most of us today understand and accept. The *New York Times* editors invoke a constitutional principle that, while controversial, is nevertheless well-known and easily identified. In some cases the premise will be harder to identify. But being able to identify the basic premise of an argument is an important skill that will help you more effectively evaluate arguments you encounter; it will also help you write effective arguments.

The Syllogism   If you look closely at the examples in this section, you'll notice that having a main premise is only part of the writer's task. Deductive reasoning often follows a pattern of what is called a **syllogism,** a three-part argument in which the conclusion rests on two premises, the first of which is the **major premise,** because it is the main assumption on which the argument rests. Here's a simple example of a syllogism:

Major Premise:	All people have hearts.
Minor Premise:	John is a person.
Conclusion:	Therefore, John has a heart.

If both premises are true—as they are in this case—then the conclusion should also be true. Note that the major and minor premises have a term in common (in this example, *people* or *person*). In a written argument the minor premise usually involves a specific case that relates to the more general statement with which the essay began. For instance, you might set up a syllogism based on the *New York Times* editorial on pages 89–90 like this:

Major Premise:	Serious threats to the constitutional separation of church and state should be opposed.
Minor Premise:	The phrase "under God" in the Pledge of Allegiance does not constitute a serious threat to the constitutional separation of church and state.
Conclusion:	Therefore, the Pledge of Allegiance should not be opposed. (That is, the appeals court ruling that the Pledge is unconstitutional is incorrect.)

Notice that the minor premise cites a specific threat, whereas the major premise refers to a more general principle or belief. You can see from this example, however, how quickly syllogistic reasoning can become complicated. You can also see that the major and minor premises are not universally held to be true or valid; many people may disagree with either or both of them. The writers of this editorial surely knew that, and they probably calculated that most of their readers would accept their major premise as true.

The Enthymeme   Because it can be difficult to follow the rules of logic, faulty reasoning is common. Consider another simple example:

Major Premise:	All women like to cook.
Minor Premise:	Elizabeth is a woman.
Conclusion:	Therefore, Elizabeth likes to cook.

Technically, the form here is correct. The two premises have a term in common, and if you accept both premises as true, then you also have to accept the conclusion. But the major premise is faulty. Elizabeth, like many women (and men) might hate to cook, preferring to go out bowling at night or to read the latest issue of the *Journal of Organic Chemistry*. A syllogism may be valid in terms of its organization, but it can be untrue if it rests on a major premise that can easily be disputed. Usually, the major premise is a generalization, as in this example, but some generalizations make sense and will be widely accepted and others will not. And it is easy to confuse generally accepted truths with privately held beliefs. In this case some people might believe that all women like to cook, but many will not hold that belief. You can argue in favor of a private belief, but you cannot expect an audience to accept an easily debatable opinion as the foundation for an argument on behalf of yet another opinion.

It is also important to realize that in many arguments a premise might be implied but not stated. You might overhear a conversation like this one:

"I hear you and Elizabeth are getting married."

"Yes, that's true."

"Well, now that you've got a woman to cook for you, maybe you could invite me over for dinner sometime."

"Why do you think that Elizabeth will be doing the cooking?"

"Because she's a woman."

The first speaker has made a number of possible assumptions. He or she might believe that all women like to cook or perhaps that all women are required to cook whether they like it or not. But these assumptions were not stated. If they were, it would be easy for the other speaker to point out the flaw in the first speaker's reasoning.

This example suggests why many people see formal logic as too rigid for everyday arguments. Although formal logic can help us understand arguments and identify the assumptions used in argument, rarely do writers of arguments consciously try to follow its rules. However, we routinely use logic in our day-to-day discussions and arguments, though more informally. We regularly make and support claims, make and evaluate assumptions, and draw or oppose conclusions, and are doing so according to the rules of formal logic would be cumbersome and perhaps even silly. Consider the following statement:

"I'd better close the windows, because the sky is getting darker."

If you examined this statement carefully, you could devise a syllogism to reveal the logic inherent in the statement:

Major Premise:	A dark sky indicates rain.
Minor Premise:	The sky is getting darker.
Conclusion:	Therefore, it will probably rain (and I should close the windows).

You'll notice that in the original statement the major premise is implicit. Yet the statement is a form of logic nonetheless. Indeed, it would sound silly if we spoke in formal syllogisms in such situations. The point is that we need to make claims and provide reasons as we conduct our day-to-day affairs, but we need to do so efficiently. And we can usually assume certain beliefs or knowledge on the part of our listeners without having to state them explicitly.

For centuries theorists have been exploring the uses of such informal logic in arguments. Aristotle called this kind of informal logic a rhetorical syllogism, or an **enthymeme.** You might think of an enthymeme as a syllogism that consists of only two parts. In the preceding example, the major premise is missing. But it might be more helpful to think in terms of practical logic. In other words, rather than trying to follow the rigid rules of formal logic when making an argument, you are applying logic where it is most useful to you. Aristotle understood that in most situations such informal uses of logic are not only efficient and practical but effective as well.

There are two important ways in which understanding logic and employing informal logic, such as enthymemes, can be helpful to you: (1) as a reader (or listener) who is trying to make sense of and evaluate an argument and (2) as a writer who is trying to construct an effective argument. As a reader, you are often confronted with arguments—on a newspaper editorial page, in a reading assignment for a college course, in a political flyer you received in the mail. Being able to identify the premises on which an argument is based, especially when they are implicit, enables you to evaluate the argument and perhaps to uncover problems or flaws in the argument. For writers, logic can be a powerful way not only to make a persuasive case for a position but also to organize an argument. (See pages 123–146 for a discussion of organizing an argument.)

Cultural Differences in Logical Arguments   It is also important to keep in mind that people from different cultural backgrounds might make different assumptions that they take for granted their audience shares. For example, in making an argument against sweatshops in which U.S. corporations employ young workers in Asian countries, an American writer might assume that his or her readers share his or her belief that child labor is a bad thing. Indeed, that would be a safe assumption with an American audience; child labor has long been illegal in the United States (except under certain circumstances), and Americans generally seem to agree that it should be illegal. However, a reader from a rural community in Bangladesh, for instance, where children routinely work on local farms, might not share that assumption. In such a case the writer's argument would likely have different effects on these different readers. You can easily think of more dramatic examples of such cultural differences and how they might affect logical argument. The suicide bombings taking place in the struggle between Israelis and Palestinians in the Middle East have been the subject of intense debate, which has revealed deep differences in how the participants view violence, suicide, national identity, and religious belief. In such a charged and difficult context a writer cannot safely assume, for instance, that his or her readers will accept the view that suicide is inherently wrong. You might not often engage in argumentation about such difficult issues, but you will almost certainly encounter the need to understand how cultural difference might influence the way readers will react to your assumptions.

The Toulmin Model of Argumentation

Formal logic, although it is a powerful framework for argumentation, has its limitations. Most people prefer not to be bound by a predetermined method of structuring an argument and regard the syllogism, in particular, as unnecessarily rigid. Many writers therefore combine inductive and deductive reasoning in making an argument and often make arguments without the use of formal logic. Partly for these reasons scholars have long explored alternative ways of employing logic so that it becomes more practical and effective in arguments. One of the best-known systems for doing so was developed by a British philosopher named Stephen Toulmin in the 1950s. Emphasizing that logic is concerned with probability more often than with certainty, Toulmin provided a new way of analyzing arguments that focused on the nature of claims.

Toulmin's model includes three main components: the claim, the data or reasons, and the warrant. According to Toulmin, the basis of all arguments is the **claim,** which is the writer's (or speaker's) statement of belief—the conclusion or point he or she wishes to prove. The **data** or reasons are the evidence or information a writer or speaker offers to support the claim. The **warrant** is a general

ELEMENTS OF THE TOULMIN SYSTEM OF ARGUMENT	
Claim:	The conclusion or the main point being argued.
Data:	The evidence supporting the claim. Also called the *reasons*.
Warrant:	Basic principle or assumption that connects the data and the claim.

statement that establishes a trustworthy relationship between the data and the claim; it is a fundamental assumption (similar to the major premise in formal logic) on which a claim can be made and supported. In an argument the claim and data will be explicit, but the warrant is often implied, especially if the person making the argument assumes that the audience accepts the warrant. In that case the task is simply to present sufficient evidence to support the claim. However, if the audience disagrees with the warrant or finds it unacceptable, then the writer must defend it to make the claim.

To better understand these terms, consider an example adapted from one of Toulmin's examples:

Claim: Raymond is an American citizen.

Data: Raymond was born in Puerto Rico.

Warrant: Anyone born in Puerto Rico is an American citizen.

These three statements might remind you of the three elements in a deductive argument. If arranged as a syllogism, they might look like this:

Major Premise: Anyone born in Puerto Rico is an American citizen.

Minor Premise: Raymond was born in Puerto Rico.

Conclusion: Raymond is an American citizen.

The advantage of Toulmin's model becomes apparent when you realize that the major premise here might not be true. For example, Raymond might have been born to French parents who were vacationing in Puerto Rico, or perhaps he was an American citizen but became a naturalized citizen of another country. Because the rigid logic of the syllogism is designed to lead to a conclusion that is *necessarily* true, Toulmin argued that it is ill suited for working toward a conclusion that is *probably* true. Believing that the syllogism was overemphasized in the study of logic, Toulmin saw a need for a "working logic" that would be easier to apply in the rhetorical situations in which most people find themselves—a kind of logic that would function in the kinds of arguments that people engage in every day. His model therefore easily incorporates **qualifiers** such as "probably," "presumably," and "generally." Here is a revision of the first example, employing Toulmin's model:

Claim: Raymond is probably an American citizen.

Data: Raymond was born in Puerto Rico.

Warrant: Anyone born in Puerto Rico is entitled to American citizenship.

Both the claim and the warrant have been modified. Toulmin's model does not dictate any specific pattern in which these elements must be arranged, which is a great advantage for writers. The claim can be made at the beginning of an argument, or it can just as easily be placed after a discussion of the data and the warrant. Similarly, the warrant may precede the data, it may follow it, or it may be implied, as we already noted.

It is easy to see that claims and warrants can be extremely complicated and controversial, and one advantage of Toulmin's system is that it not only offers writers great flexibility in constructing effective arguments but also provides readers with a way to evaluate arguments carefully. Chapter 5 discusses how Toulmin's model can help you structure your own arguments. For now it's important to examine some of the complexities of claims and warrants.

Understanding Claims and Warrants   There are different kinds of claims: claims supported by facts, claims supported by expert opinion, claims supported by values. For example, if you wanted to argue that the stock market should be subject to greater regulation, you could base your claim primarily on facts: You could define current regulations, report on laws governing markets, cite specific abuses and scandals involving insider trading, and include figures for the money lost to investors as a result of unethical trading practices. You would present these various facts to support your claim that greater regulation is needed. By contrast, another writer might argue in favor of regulating the stock market on the basis of the values of honesty and fair play. Of course, when we argue, we often use several different kinds of claims. For example, if you wanted to argue against capital punishment, your data might consist of facts (such as the numbers of executions performed annually, differences in these figures by state or by race, and the number of death row inmates), the views of criminologists or legal experts regarding the death penalty, and an appeal to a moral value (such as the sanctity of human life) that you believe your audience might share. In short, you would present different types of data depending on the nature of the claim you are making.

Warrants are also complex, and the nature of a warrant will differ from one argument to another. Some warrants may be relatively straightforward. For example, law often constitutes a warrant. A lawyer arguing on behalf of someone claiming American citizenship might invoke the Jones Act of 1917, which guarantees U.S. citizenship to citizens of Puerto Rico. That law would become the lawyer's warrant for the claim that a person born in Puerto Rico should be considered a U.S. citizen. But because warrants sometimes reflect assumptions or beliefs, they can be disputable and controversial. If you base a claim that capital punishment should be banned in the United States on a belief that taking any human life is wrong, you should be prepared to defend that warrant, because many people would not accept it. In such a case you would strengthen your argument against capital punishment if you explained and defended your view about the wrongness of taking human life. Simply stating or implying such a controversial warrant would likely result in some readers dismissing your argument altogether.

These examples reflect the challenges that writers—and readers—can often face when they engage in argumentation about difficult or charged issues, and they are reminders that no model, including Toulmin's, will always lead to effective arguments. But if the goal is to understand the issues adequately in order to address a problem or negotiate differences that create conflict or discord, then Toulmin's model can be a useful framework for both writers and readers.

Evaluating Claims and Warrants   Being able to make strong claims and support them adequately is a crucial part of what makes an argument effective. It is also a challenge, largely because most claims deal with probability rather than certainty. If you engage in serious argumentation out of a desire to address an important issue or solve a problem, you need to understand how claims function and how to evaluate claims effectively. Toulmin's ideas about claims, data, and warrants can be useful tools in helping you make and evaluate claims.

Look at an example of an argument about an issue that became deeply important to Americans after the terrorist attacks on the United States on September 11, 2001: national security. In response to those attacks, the U.S. government began removing information that had previously been available on many of its websites. Among the kinds of information removed were environmental statistics, emergency plans, and data on health and safety risks to Americans. A year after the attacks and several months after the government began censoring its websites, writer Mary Graham argued in the *Atlantic Monthly* that keeping such information secret in the interest of national security is not only wrong but also dangerous. She asserted that "the wholesale censorship of information on Web sites carries insidious costs." To support this central claim, Graham describes how this censorship policy can undermine, rather than increase, national security. She also asserts that this kind of censorship is unfair, and she questions whether secrecy will actually accomplish the goal of enhancing security: "National security is everyone's concern, and the idea that openness can be more effective than secrecy in reducing risks has received too little attention."

Evaluating Graham's argument requires us to examine how these assertions relate to her central claim. You might restate her claim as follows:

Claim: The censorship of information on U.S. government websites should end because it is unfair to Americans and does not necessarily increase Americans' security.

Graham offers two main reasons for her claim: (1) Censorship is unfair, and (2) secrecy might not enhance security. So far so good. But this claim rests on a basic assumption— her warrant—that isn't as obvious. You might state her warrant as follows:

Warrant: Americans have a right to information related to their security.

Notice that this warrant invokes a legal principle (a specific legal right that Americans have to information); it also invokes more general ethical values (openness and fairness). Because such a warrant is likely to be acceptable to most readers of the *Atlantic Monthly,* Graham need not defend it and can therefore concentrate on supporting her claim by offering reasons the government's censorship policy won't achieve its goal of enhancing security. In short, her claim is clear, supported with various reasons, and strengthened by a warrant that is generally acceptable to her intended audience. As a reader, you can disagree with her claim, and no doubt some readers will also disagree with her warrant (believing, for example, that only government officials should have access to the kinds of information that has been censored from government websites). But if you accept her warrant, you can evaluate her argument against censorship on the basis of the evidence she presents.

If a claim is based on a warrant that isn't necessarily acceptable to an audience, the writer might have to defend that warrant. Otherwise, the argument for the claim might be less persuasive to the audience. Sometimes, it is the warrant and not the claim that is problematic for an audience. Examine an example in which the writer might have misjudged his audience and relied on a warrant that might be questionable for that audience. The following passage was taken from an essay arguing against a national boycott of gasoline— called a "gas out"—that some consumer advocates and environmental groups proposed in 2000, when gas prices were rising quickly in the United States. The writer, Gary Foreman, disagreed with this proposal. Because gas prices have climbed even higher since then, his argument is still relevant. He made this claim against the boycott:

I can pretty much tell you that "Gas Out 2000" won't work. It might draw some media attention. But it won't change the price you pay at the pump by one penny. And if you'll consider the facts you'll understand why.

Restate Foreman's claim:

Claim: It's useless to participate in "Gas Outs," because they won't reduce the price of gas.

If you restate his claim in this way, his main reason supporting his claim also becomes clear: The boycott won't reduce gas prices. Most of Foreman's essay is devoted to an explanation of the economics of gasoline production and distribution, which he uses to support his claim. In other words, he relies on facts about the economics of the gasoline market to demonstrate why a boycott cannot reduce prices. But what is his warrant? Later in his essay he writes,

> So if a "Gas Out" won't help, what can you do? One very practical thing. Use less gas. Carpool, take public transportation, combine trips or get your car tuned up. Anything you can do to save gas will put more money in your pocket. And that's the one "statement" that oil producers will notice. More importantly, you'll notice it in your wallet, too.

Here he implicitly conveys his warrant, which you can restate as follows:

Warrant: Paying less money for gas is desirable.

Notice that this warrant is likely to be acceptable to many people. But this essay was published in a newsletter called *Simple Living*, which promotes an environmentally sound lifestyle. The readers of that newsletter are likely to be as concerned about the environmental effects of gasoline combustion as they are about gasoline prices. In other words, for such an audience, Foreman could safely use a more environmentally conscious warrant; he could have made an argument that focused on environmental impact, as well as price. Such an argument would likely have resonated with the readers of *Simple Living*. In fact, it is likely that many of those readers would find Foreman's argument *less* persuasive precisely because he focuses on reducing gas prices and ignores the ethical and environmental concerns that those readers probably share. In this case, readers of *Simple Living* might accept Foreman's claim that a boycott may not be a good idea but resist his warrant.

This last example highlights that claims and warrants, like other aspects of argument such as style or tone, must be understood in rhetorical context. No claim is universally valid; no warrant is universally acceptable. The audience, the cultural context, and the rhetorical situation all influence the effect of an argument. It's worth noting here, too, that because this newsletter was published on the World Wide Web, the writer might have assumed his audience to be much larger than just the subscribers to the newsletter. If so, you can see how the medium can influence an argument's warrant. (See Chapter 3 for a discussion of how media can affect argument.)

Recognizing Logical Fallacies

If you look closely at some of the examples in this chapter, you can find problems with the arguments. Any apparently logical argument can reveal serious flaws if you take the trouble to examine it carefully. Here is an excerpt from a letter written by a person opposed to a federal appeals court decision in 2002 ruling that the phrase "under God" in the Pledge of Allegiance is unconstitutional:

> In light of the events of this past September (9/11/01), I think it would be hypocrisy to omit an acknowledgement of a divine being under which the ideals and beliefs of this nation were created. And if you don't think so, ask everyone how many of them prayed to God that day.

This writer suggests that a large number of people praying is evidence of the existence of God. Whether or not you agree with him that there is a God, you can easily see that the number of people who pray does not necessarily prove God's existence. This flaw in the writer's reasoning is called a **logical fallacy** (specifically **attributing false causes,** which is discussed on pages 100–101). Fallacies are often unintentional. You might think that you are making a strong argument but have actually engaged in flawed reasoning without realizing it, as is likely to have been the case with the writer in this example. Sometimes, however, writers know that their reasoning may be suspect but deliberately use it to win an argument. Some fallacies can be powerful strategies for writers of arguments. But if you are concerned about truth—about addressing a problem or negotiating a conflict—then it makes sense to guard against fallacies so that you do not undermine your efforts to come to a reasonable resolution. And it is important to be able to identify fallacies in the arguments of others. This section discusses some common fallacies.

Appealing to Pity

Writers are often justified in appealing to the pity of their readers when the need to inspire this emotion is closely related to whatever they are arguing for and when the entire argument does not rest on this appeal alone. For example, someone who is attempting to convince you to donate one of your kidneys for a medical transplant would probably assure you that you could live with only one kidney and that there is a serious need for the kidney you are being asked to donate. In addition to making these crucial points, the arguer might move you to pity by describing what will otherwise happen to the person who needs the transplant.

When the appeal to pity stands alone, even in charitable appeals in which its use is fundamental, the result is often questionable. Imagine a large billboard advertisement for the American Red Cross. It features a close-up photograph of a distraught (but nevertheless good-looking) man, beneath which, in large letters, runs this caption: PLEASE, MY LITTLE GIRL NEEDS BLOOD. Although we might already believe in the importance of donating blood, we should question the implications of this ad. Can we donate blood and ask that it be reserved for the exclusive use of children? Are the lives of children more valuable than the lives of adults? Few people would donate blood unless they sympathized with those who need transfusions, and it might be unrealistic to expect logic in advertising. But consider how weak an argument becomes when the appeal to pity has little to do with the issue in question. Someone who has seldom attended class and has failed all his examinations but then tries to argue, "I deserve to pass this course because I've had a lot of problems at home," is making a fallacious appeal to pity. The "argument" asks the instructor to overlook relevant evidence and make a decision favorable to the arguer because the instructor has been moved to feel sorry for him. You should be skeptical of any appeal to pity that is irrelevant to the conclusion or that seems designed to distract attention from the other factors you should be considering.

Appealing to Prejudice

Writers of argument benefit from appealing to their readers' values. Such appeals become fallacious, however, when couched in inflammatory language or when offered as a crowd-pleasing device to distract attention from whether the case at hand is reasonable and well informed. A newspaper that creates a patriotic frenzy through exaggerated reports of enemy "atrocities" is appealing to the prejudices of its readers and is making chances for reasonable discussion less likely. Racist, sexist, classist, and homophobic language can also be used to incite a crowd—something responsible writers should take pains to avoid doing. Appeals to prejudice can also take more subtle forms. Politicians might remind you that they were born and raised in "this great state" and that they love their children and admire their spouses—all of which are factors believed to appeal to the average voter but nevertheless are unlikely to affect performance in office. When candidates linger on what wonderful family life they enjoy, it might be time to ask a question about the economy.

Appealing to Tradition

Although you can learn from the past and often benefit from honoring tradition, you can seldom make decisions based on tradition alone. Appealing to tradition is fallacious when tradition becomes the only reason for justifying a position. "We cannot let women join our club because we've never let women join in the past" is no less problematic than arguing, "We shouldn't buy computers for our schools because we didn't have computers in the past." The world changes, and new opportunities emerge. What people have done in the past is not necessarily appropriate for the future. If you believe that a traditional practice can guide people in the future, you need to show why this is the case. Do not settle for claiming, "This is the way it always has been, so this is the way it always has to be."

Arguing by Analogy

An analogy is a comparison that works on more than one level, and it is possible to use analogy effectively when reasoning inductively. You must first be sure that the things you are comparing have several characteristics in common and that these similarities are relevant to the conclusion you intend to draw. For example, you might argue that competition is good for schools, because it is considered to be good for businesses. But the strength of this argument would depend on the degree to which schools are analogous to businesses, so you would need to proceed with care and demonstrate that there are important similarities between the two. When arguing from analogy, it is important to remember that you are speculating. As is the case with any type of inductive reasoning, you can reach a conclusion that is likely to be true but is not guaranteed to be true. It is always possible that you have overlooked a significant factor that will cause the analogy to break down.

Unfortunately, analogies are often misused. An argument from analogy that reaches a firm conclusion is likely to be fallacious, and it is certain to be fallacious if the analogy itself is inappropriate. If a congressional candidate asks people to vote for him because of his outstanding record as a football player, he might be able to claim that politics, like football, involves teamwork. But because a successful politician needs many skills and will probably never need to run across a field or knock someone down, it would be foolish to vote on the basis of this questionable analogy. The differences between football and politics outweigh the similarities, and it would be fallacious to pretend otherwise.

Attacking the Character of Opponents

If you make personal attacks on opponents but ignore what they have to say or distract attention from it, you are using what is often called an *ad hominem* argument (Latin for "to the man"). Although an audience often considers the character of a writer or speaker in deciding whether to trust what he or she has to say, most of us realize that good people can make bad arguments and even a crook can sometimes tell the truth. It is always better to give a thoughtful response to an opponent's arguments than to ignore those arguments and indulge in personal attacks.

Attributing False Causes

If you assume that an event is the result of something that merely occurred before it, you have committed the fallacy of false causation. Assumptions of this sort are sometimes called *post hoc* reasoning, from the Latin phrase *post hoc, ergo propter hoc,* which means "after this, therefore because of this." Superstitious people offer many examples of this type of fallacious thinking. They might tell you, "Everything was going fine until the lunar eclipse last month; *that's* why the economy is in trouble." Or personal misfortune might be traced back to spilling salt, stepping on a sidewalk crack, or walking under a ladder.

Such fallacy is often found in the arguments of writers determined to prove the existence of various conspiracies. They often seem to amass an impressive amount of "evidence," but their evidence is frequently questionable. Or, to take a comparatively simple example, someone might be suspected of murder simply because he or she was seen near the victim's house a day or two before the crime occurred. This suspicion might lead to the discovery of evidence, but it could just as easily lead to the false arrest of the meter reader from the electric company. Being observed near the scene of a crime proves nothing by itself. A prosecuting attorney who would be foolish enough to base a case on such a flimsy piece of evidence would be guilty of post hoc reasoning. Logic should always recognize the distinction between *causes* and what might simply be *coincidences*. Sequence is not a cause because every event is preceded by an infinite number of other events, not all of which can be held responsible for whatever happens today.

This fallacy can be found in more subtle forms in essays on abstract social problems. Writers who blame contemporary problems on such instant explanations as "the rise of violence on television" or "the popularity of computers" are no more convincing than the parent who argues that all difficulties of family life can be traced to the rise of rock and roll. It is impossible to understand the present without understanding the past, but don't isolate at random any one event in the past and then try to argue that it explains everything. And be careful not to accidentally imply a cause-and-effect relationship where you did not intend to do so.

Attributing Guilt by Association

This fallacy is frequently apparent in politics, especially toward the end of a close campaign. A candidate who happens to be religious, for example, might be maneuvered by opponents into the false position of being held accountable for the actions of all men and women who hold to that particular faith. Nothing specific has been argued, but a negative association has been either created or suggested through hints and innuendo.

Begging the Question

In the fallacy known as begging the question, a writer begins with a premise that is acceptable only to anyone who will agree with the conclusion subsequently reached—a conclusion often similar to the premise. Thus, the argument goes around in a circle (and is sometimes referred to as **circular reasoning**). For instance, someone might begin an essay by claiming, "Required courses like first-year composition are a waste of time" and end with the conclusion that "first-year composition should not be a required course." It might indeed be arguable that first-year composition should not be required, but the author who begins with the premise that first-year composition is a waste of time has assumed what the argument should be devoted to proving. Because it is much easier to *claim* something is true than to *prove* it is true, you may be tempted to beg the question you set out to answer. This temptation should always be avoided.

Equivocating

Someone who equivocates uses vague or ambiguous language to mislead an audience. In argumentation, equivocation often takes the form of using one word in several senses without acknowledging the change in meaning. It is especially easy to equivocate when using abstract language. Watch out in particular for the abuse of such terms as *right, society, freedom, law, justice,* and *real.* When you use words like these, make sure your meaning is clear. And make doubly sure your meaning doesn't shift when you use the term again.

Ignoring the Question

When someone says, "I'm glad you asked that question!" and then promptly begins to talk about something else, that person is guilty of ignoring the question. Politicians are famous for exploiting this technique when they don't want to be pinned down on a subject. Students (and teachers) sometimes use it when asked a question that they want to avoid. Ignoring the question is also likely to occur when friends or partners have a fight. In the midst of a quarrel, you might hear remarks like "What about you?" or "Never mind the budget! I'm sick of worrying about money! We need to talk about what's happening to our relationship!"

Jumping to Conclusions

This fallacy is so common that it has become a cliché. It means that the conclusion in question has not been supported by an adequate amount of evidence. Because one green apple is sour, it does not follow that all green apples are sour. Failing one test does not mean that you will necessarily fail the next. An instructor who seems disorganized on the first day of class might eventually prove to be the best teacher you ever had. You should always try to have more than one example to support an argument. Be skeptical of arguments that seem heavy on opinion but weak on evidence.

Opposing a Straw Man

Because it is easier to demolish a man of straw than to address a live opponent fairly, arguers are sometimes tempted to pretend that they are responding to the views of their opponents when they are only setting up a type of artificial opposition that they can easily refute. The most common form of this fallacy is to exaggerate the views of others or to respond only to an extreme view that does not adequately represent the arguments of opponents. If you argue against abolishing Social Security, you should not think that you have effectively defended that program from all criticisms of it. By responding only to an extreme position, you are doing nothing to resolve specific concerns about how Social Security is financed and administered.

Presenting a False Dilemma

A false dilemma is a fallacy in which a speaker or writer poses a choice between two alternatives but overlooks other possibilities and implies that no other possibilities exist. A college freshman who receives low grades at the end of the first semester and then claims, "What's wrong with low grades? Is cheating any better?" is pretending that there is no possibility other than cheating or earning a low grade—such as that of earning higher grades by studying harder, a possibility recognized by most students and teachers.

Reasoning That Does Not Follow

Although almost any faulty argument is likely to have gaps in reasoning, this fallacy, sometimes called the *non sequitur* (Latin for "it does not follow"), describes a conclusion that does not follow logically from the explanation given for it.

Gaps of this sort can often be found within specific sentences. The most common type of non sequitur is a complex sentence in which the subordinate clause does not clearly relate to the main clause, especially where causation is involved. An example of this type of non sequitur would be "Because the teacher likes Joe, Joe passed the quiz in calculus."

Here a cause-and-effect relationship has been claimed but not explained. It might be that Joe studied harder for his quiz because he believes that his teacher likes him, and that in turn resulted in Joe passing the quiz. But someone reading the sentence as written could not be expected to know this. A non sequitur can also take the form of a compound sentence: "Mr. Blandshaw is young, so he should be a good teacher." Mr. Blandshaw might indeed be a good teacher but not just because he is young. On the contrary, young Mr. Blandshaw might be inexperienced, anxious, and humorless. He might also give unrealistically large assignments because he lacks a clear sense of how much work most students can handle.

Non sequiturs sometimes form the basis for an entire argument: "William Henderson will make a good governor because he is a friend of working people. He is a friend of working people because he has created hundreds of jobs through his contracting business." Before allowing this argument to go any further, you should realize that you've been asked to swallow two non sequiturs. Being a good governor involves more than being "a friend of working people." Furthermore, there is no reason to assume that Henderson is "a friend of working people" just because he is an employer. He might have acquired his wealth by taking advantage of the men and women who work for him.

Sliding Down a Slippery Slope

According to this fallacy, one step will inevitably lead to an undesirable end. An example would be claiming that legalized abortion will lead to euthanasia or that censoring pornography will lead to the end of freedom of the press. Although it is important to consider the probable effects of any step that is being debated, it is fallacious to claim that people will necessarily tumble downhill as the result of any one step. There is always the possibility that we'll be able to keep our feet firmly on the ground even though we've moved them from where they used to be.

Understanding Pathos

There is perhaps no more powerful way to construct an argument than to appeal to readers' emotions. No argument is devoid of emotional appeal. But some arguments rely on emotions more than others do. And because emotional appeals can be so powerful, they carry risk for both writer and reader.

One reason that emotional arguments don't work in all circumstances is that emotion is so complex and often poorly understood. Think for a moment about the range of emotions that might figure into an argument about, say, capital punishment: anger, pity, worry, fear, sadness, relief. Trying to anticipate how readers might react emotionally to a specific point about such charged issues can be daunting. You might try to inspire sympathy among your readers by, for instance, invoking a call to patriotism in an argument about measures to be taken against terrorism but find that your argument sparked anger among some readers instead. It is impossible to know with certainty what emotional responses you might elicit with a particular line of argument; you can only try to anticipate responses on the basis of your experience, your knowledge of your readers, and your understanding of the rhetorical context.

Because of this uncertainty and because emotions will very likely be involved in any argument, it is a good idea to think of the use of emotion in argument as an ethical matter. You might suspect that a line of argument may evoke strong emotions in some readers and, as a result, make those readers more susceptible to that line of argument. In other words, you might be able to "push the buttons" of your readers intentionally to elicit strong emotions. Doing so might enable you to win the argument, but will it truly solve the problem about which you are arguing? Is it the right way to address the issue at hand?

Used carefully and ethically, emotional appeals can be effective. Consider how one writer employs emotion in an argument about the ongoing controversy over gun control. In this case the writer, Jeanne Shields, argues in favor of restricting the sale and ownership of handguns. But she writes from an especially wrenching position: Her own son was murdered by someone using a handgun. Here is her argument, first published in 1978 when many Americans were concerned about a high rate of violent crime.

Why Nick?

If the telephone rings late at night, I always mentally check off where each child is, and at the same time get an awful sinking feeling in the pit of my stomach.

Four years ago, April 16, we had a telephone call very late. As my husband answered, I checked off Pam in Long Beach (California), Nick in San Francisco, David in New Brunswick (New Jersey) and Leslie outside Boston. The less my husband spoke, the tighter the knot got in my stomach. Instinctively, I knew it was bad news, but I wasn't prepared for what he had to tell me. Our eldest son, Nick, 23, had been shot dead on a street in San Francisco.

Nick was murdered at about 9:30 p.m. He and a friend, Jon, had come from lacrosse practice and were on their way home. They stopped to pick up a rug at the home of a friend. While Jon went in to get the rug, Nick rearranged the lacrosse gear in the back of their borrowed Vega. He was shot three times in the back of the head and died instantly, holding a lacrosse stick.

Nick was the fourteenth victim of what came to be called the "Zebra killers." Between the fall of 1973 and April 16, 1974, they had randomly killed fourteen people and wounded seven others—crippling one for life. Four men were subsequently convicted of murder in a trial that lasted thirteen months.

My son was tall, dark and handsome, and a good athlete. He was particularly good at lacrosse and an expert skier. Nick was an ardent photographer and wrote some lovely poetry. He was a gentle and sensitive man with an infectious grin and the capacity to make friends easily. It was hard for me to believe he was gone.

The generous support and love of our friends gave us the strength to go on during those days. The calls and letters that poured in from those who knew Nick were overwhelming. In his short life, Nick had touched so many people in so many ways. It was both heartwarming and very humbling.

But always, running through those blurred days was the question. Why? Why Nick? My deep faith in God was really put to the test. Yet, nothing that I could do or think of, or pray for, was ever going to bring Nick back.

Because Nick was shot two days after Easter, the funeral service was filled with Easter prayers and hymns. Spring flowers came from the gardens of friends. The day was mild, clear and beautiful, and a kind of peace and understanding seeped into my aching heart.

No matter how many children you have, the death of one leaves a void that cannot be filled. Life seems to include a new awareness, and one's philosophy and values come under sharper scrutiny. Were we just to pick up the pieces and continue as before? That choice became impossible, because a meaning had to be given to this vicious, senseless death.

That summer of 1974, the newspapers, magazines and television were full of Watergate. But I couldn't concentrate on it or anything else. Instead I dug hard in the garden for short periods of time, or smashed at tennis balls.

On the other hand, my husband, Pete, immersed himself in a study of the gun-control issue. Very near to where Nick had died, in a vacant lot, two small children found a gun—*the* gun. It was a .32-caliber Beretta. Police, in tracing it, found that initially it had been bought legally, but then went through the hands of seven different owners—most of whom had police records. Its final bullets, fired at close range, had killed my son—and then it was thrown carelessly away.

Pete's readings of Presidential commission recommendations, FBI crime statistics and books on the handgun issue showed him that our Federal laws were indeed weak and ineffective. He went to Washington to talk to politicians and to see what, if anything, was being done about it. I watched him wrestle with his thoughts and spend long hours writing them down on paper—the pros and cons of handgun control and what could logically be done about the proliferation of handguns in this nation.

Through friends, Pete had been introduced in Washington to the National Council to Control Handguns, a citizens' lobby seeking stricter Federal controls over handguns. As Pete became more closely associated with the NCCH as a volunteer, it became increasingly obvious that he was leaning toward a greater involvement.

Consequently, with strong encouragement from me and the children, Pete took a year's leave of absence from his job as a marketing executive so that he could join NCCH full time. A full year and a half later, he finally resigned and became the NCCH chairman.

The main adversaries of handgun control are members of the powerful and financially entrenched National Rifle Association, macho men who don't understand the definition of a civilized society. They are aided by an apathetic government which in reality is us, because we citizens don't make ourselves heard loud and clear enough. How many people are in the silent majority, who want to see something done about unregulated sale and possession of handguns? Why do we register cars and license drivers, and not do the same for handguns? Why are the production and sale of firecrackers severely restricted—and not handguns?

I now work in the NCCH office as a volunteer. One of my jobs is to read and make appropriate card files each day from a flood of clippings describing handgun incidents. The daily newspapers across the country recount the grim litany of shootings, killings, rapes, and robberies at gun point. Some of it's tough going, because I am poignantly aware of what a family is going through. Some of it's so appalling it makes me literally sick.

Some people can no longer absorb this kind of news. They have almost become immune to it, because there is so much violence. To others, it is too impersonal; it's always something that happens to somebody else—not to you.

But anybody can be shot. We are all in a lottery, where the likelihood of your facing handgun violence grows every day. Today there are 50 million handguns in civilian hands. By the year 2000, there will be more than 100 million.

So many families have given up so much to the deadly handgun. It will take the women of this country—the mothers, wives, sisters and daughters—to do something about it. But when will they stand up to be counted and to be heard? Or will they wait only to hear the telephone ringing late at night?

—Jeanne Shields

In setting up her argument, Shields describes a situation that she knows is likely to evoke strong emotions among her readers. Readers who are parents themselves will surely identify with Shields and her husband, and other readers are likely to feel empathy for them. Those feelings can make readers more likely to be open to Shields's support for tougher gun laws, even if those readers are not in favor of gun control in principle. Notice how the opening paragraphs of her essay describe two vivid scenes: two parents receiving a dreaded late-night phone call and an innocent young man shot in cold blood while doing an everyday task. Such a strategy is likely to give many readers pause, because the emotions surrounding these scenes can be deep and powerful.

In short, her emotional appeal becomes an integral part of the argument she makes regarding gun control.

Shields also evokes feeling through her reference to Easter and spring flowers—as well as through her references to the "generous support and love of our friends" and the "heartwarming" calls and letters she received.

Unfortunately, Shields was so close to the loss that prompted her argument that her emotions interfered with her ability to reason logically. After recognizing that the gun used to kill her son had been initially purchased legally, she does not explain how gun control would prevent a legally purchased weapon from falling into the hands of criminals. More disturbingly, she makes the unsupported claim that it will take the "women of this country" to control handguns immediately after emphasizing that her husband had resigned from a well-paying job to lobby for stricter gun laws (while she gardened and played tennis). And in describing the members of the National Rifle Association as "macho men who don't understand the definition of a civilized society" she makes a sexist claim (because women also belong to the NRA) that is an *ad hominem* argument (see page 100) directed against the very people she most needs to persuade.

It is also worth noting what Shields does *not* report. There were seventy-one "Zebra killings," and these killings were racially motivated. The killers were black, and the victims were white. So there is an unspoken argument here about race and social class, because the killers were members of an extremist group enraged by the unequal distribution of power in the United States. Shields recognizes that her son was the fourteenth victim of this killing spree, but she does not establish how many killings occurred as a whole—perhaps because the total number could lead some readers to focus on the entire situation rather than the death of an individual. But by choosing to say nothing about race, she ignores the social complexity of the killings. The individual victims were chosen at random, but those random killings were the result of a specific ideology. The 1970s may seem like a long time ago. But ask yourself how effective the war on terror being fought today would be if it focused only on the weapons used by terrorists and ignored the beliefs that have motivated people to turn themselves into suicide bombers.

This example illustrates that emotional appeals must be used judiciously and ethically. It is easy to imagine some readers rejecting Shields's argument in favor of gun control and turning her appeal to the opposite position. The same emotions she invokes in favor of gun control can be used in an argument opposing it. For example, a parent whose child was murdered might take the position that arming oneself with a handgun can help prevent violent crime and might have saved his or her child. In evaluating positions like these, it is important to sort out the emotional appeals, as well as the specific logical arguments, each person is making.

Arguments about controversial issues such as gun control are fertile ground for emotional appeals, but emotion can be used in any argument. Here's an excerpt from an essay by Filip Bondy published the day after Brazil's soccer team won the 2002 World Cup:

> He cried, he laughed, he scored. Ronaldo put his mark on this special World Cup Sunday with a redemptive samba—two second-half goals in the 2-0 championship victory by Brazil over Germany, and eight goals in seven matches.
>
> Ronaldo's tale is now one for the ages, from the streets of Rio to the Yokohama stadium where he trotted about the field in triumph, hugging everyone, with a Brazil flag draped from his broad shoulders.
>
> The son of a drug-addicted father and a rock-steady mother, Ronaldo had blown off school as a youngster to play street soccer, to become that odd athletic combination of bull and gazelle that made him such a unique talent.
>
> He wouldn't listen to his mother, who wanted him to study hard and to become a doctor. Instead, he aimed for something even more impossible—a career in soccer—and somehow succeeded. The trail, however, was not always as direct as his style.

In this argument celebrating Ronaldo, Bondy appeals not only to his readers' admiration for Ronaldo's achievement but also to the joy that sports fans so often feel when they witness a victory by a great champion. In addition, in referring to the story of Ronaldo's difficult childhood, Bondy is also likely to stir up positive feelings about family, hard work, and the pursuit of individual dreams. Although he is not writing about something as complex and controversial as gun control, Bondy's appeal to these emotions may help make his argument about Ronaldo's achievement more convincing to his readers, whether they are fans of Brazil's soccer team or not.

This example illustrates that emotional appeals can work on several levels. Notice, for example, that the idea of a world championship in sports can be used to evoke pride or admiration in readers. A writer like Bondy can try to employ that emotion throughout argument. In other words, the very idea of a championship elicits certain emotions that become integral to the entire argument. By contrast, the brief descriptions in Bondy's essay of Ronaldo's childhood can elicit different emotions, which the writer uses for different purposes—in this case, to help support his point that Ronaldo's achievement is a special one and perhaps to create additional admiration for Ronaldo as an individual. Visual details and individual words or phrases can have the same effect. For example, think about your own reaction to the description of Ronaldo "hugging everyone, with a Brazil flag draped from his broad shoulders" or of Ronaldo's father as "drug-addicted." Certain words have powerful associations; in this case "drug-addicted" might create greater sympathy for Ronaldo. Terms such as *family values, environmentally friendly, freedom of choice,* and *American* are often used precisely because of the emotions they evoke. As a writer, you can employ such carefully chosen words as you build your argument. But be mindful of the potential pitfalls of doing so. A single word, such as *drugs,* can elicit different responses in different readers, and it is important to try to understand the associations that a particular word or phrase might carry for readers. It is equally important to recognize how such words might influence you when you encounter them in someone else's argument.

How you use the power of emotion in an argument depends not only on your ability to assess the impact of a line of reasoning or an emotional appeal on your audience but also on what you hope to accomplish with an argument. If your purpose is to address a problem or to negotiate differences regarding a difficult or complex issue, then you must take care to employ emotional appeals appropriately and ethically.

Earlier in this chapter, the close connection between *ethos* and *logos* was noted: a writer is not likely to be credible if he or she is unable to support claims with evidence or to reason logically. But there is also a close connection between *ethos* and *pathos.* Although a credible writer comes across as fair-minded, being fair-minded does not require a hard heart. Indeed, a writer who seems capable of empathy is more likely to be convincing than one who seems cold-blooded. The challenge, when drawing upon *pathos,* is to make sure that the feelings being expressed or evoked contribute to the argument rather than distract from it. Moreover, *pathos* should be used in moderation: appeal to the feelings of your audience when you can do so effectively, but do not lose sight of your responsibility to communicate accurate and relevant information in a pattern that readers can follow.

Finally, reflect upon the distinction between a strategy and a strength. When composing an argument, you can employ *ethos, logos,* and *pathos* as strategies to achieve your purpose—whether it is to assert, prevail, inquire, or reconcile. Ideally, however, you should be able to employ these strategies because they spring naturally from the person you have become. If you are ethical, logical, and compassionate, you will be more convincing that someone who lacks these strengths and strategically plans to simulate them as part of a game in which winning a victory matters more than furthering the understanding of truth or reconciling differences.

Composing Arguments

5 ■ Constructing Arguments

6 ■ Doing Research

7 ■ Documenting Your Sources

5

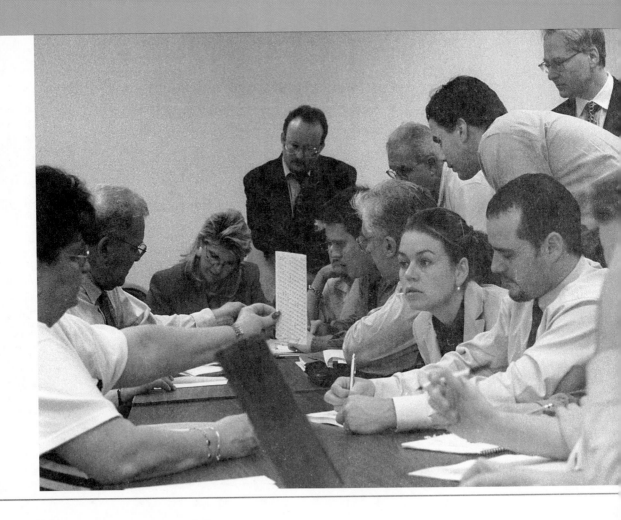

Constructing Arguments

A n assignment for your cultural anthropology course requires you to write an essay examining the ethical issues faced by Western anthropologists who study nonindustrialized societies in places such as the Amazon basin. In your essay you are to take a position on the ethical guidelines for such research that have been proposed by a professional organization for anthropologists.

- You have been asked by other residents of your college dormitory to write a letter to the campus director of residential life to urge him not to implement new security measures that the college is considering. These measures include a new policy that would prohibit students from having visitors in their dorms except during specified hours in the early evening. You and your dormmates oppose these measures. Your letter to the director of residential life will try to convince him that the proposed measures would significantly restrict students' social activities without enhancing campus security.
- A local organization that you belong to advocates sustainable community development. A national retail business has requested a permit to build a large store on farmland near a residential neighborhood in your community.

Many residents are pleased because they believe that the new store will improve the community's economic status. Others worry about the effect of the new store on surrounding land, especially regarding water runoff into a nearby marsh that is part of a community park and natural area. Your organization has decided to oppose the building of the new store on the proposed site unless certain measures to protect the marsh are required. You are part of a team that will create a new website devoted to presenting your organization's perspective on the new store.

How do you proceed?

The answer to that question is the same for each of these situations. It is also different for each of them.

In each of these cases you would try to present and support your claims to your intended audience in a way that is persuasive. To make an effective argument, you must examine the issue carefully so that you understand it well, which might require some research. You must also gather and present evidence to support the claims you will make in your argument. You will want to consider how your intended audience is likely to respond to your claims and warrants in each case. And you must adopt a style—and, in the case of the website, a design—that most effectively presents your case.

But each of these situations is different, and arguing effectively means understanding the specific factors involved in each case.

1. *The rhetorical situation.* The audience and circumstances for each of these writing tasks are different. Your anthropology teacher, for instance, will have different expectations for your paper than the director of residential life will have for your letter. And the audience for the website would be an entire community, with complex and perhaps divergent expectations for a persuasive argument.

2. *The goals for argument.* Although you can see each of these arguments as part of an effort to solve a problem, the problems in each instance represent different challenges to you as writer. In your anthropology course you hope to understand the ethical issues of anthropology research sufficiently to make an effective argument to earn you a good grade. Your letter to the residential life director is intended to convince him not to implement new security rules that would have a direct impact on your living situation. And your organization hopes that its website will generate support among community residents for environmental restrictions on a large construction project.

3. *The medium.* The anthropology paper will have to adhere to the conventions of academic writing in the field of anthropology. The letter to the residential life director is also a print document, but one that follows different conventions for writing. And the website is an entirely different medium that requires you to consider such matters as layout, color, and hyperlinks.

Adapting to different situations like these is part of making effective arguments. Everything included in the first four chapters of this book is intended to help you understand argumentation in order to construct effective arguments in any situation. The principles examined apply to all kinds of arguments. But this chapter offers a more focused discussion of how to construct arguments, whatever the situation.

Managing the Composing Process

Understanding the Relationship between Writing and Thinking

In some ways composing an argument, whatever the medium, is like any other kind of writing: You must define your topic, develop your ideas, gather sufficient information, organize your material, revise accordingly, and edit so that your writing is accurate and effective. In other words, you must move through the composing process. Composing arguments can make that process both easier and harder. It can make the process easier in the sense that some of the conventions of argumentation will help you determine what you will say and how you will say it. For example, in an argument you will generally be expected to make your claims clearly and support them with adequate evidence. Knowing that can help you generate ideas and organize the information more easily. But argumentation involves confronting the complexities of human beliefs and opinions. Part of your challenge in composing your argument is managing that complexity and showing that you are knowledgeable and fair-minded. For example, the essay for your anthropology course will probably address issues of racial diversity, and you will have to consider how the controversial nature of race relations might figure into your argument. In addition, if your goal is to address a serious issue and try to solve a problem through argumentation, you will always be concerned about arguing ethically and honestly. In other words, your goal is to engage with others in order to work through a difficult problem. That goal requires you to consider the implications of your argument and the potential effects of your claims on your audience.

Of course, you can't hope to do everything at once. Think of the process of composing an argument as an ongoing process of inquiry. By composing an argument, you are carefully exploring an issue, learning about that issue and about yourself and others. That learning might require you to rethink your claims or your position on the issue at hand. For instance, you might begin your essay for your anthropology course believing that strict ethical guidelines for anthropology research are not necessary, but you might find as you compose your essay that the issue is more complicated than you initially thought. That process of inquiry might therefore lead you to revise your original position.

If you approach the writing of an argument in this way, you are more likely to construct effective arguments. Moreover, you might gain a deeper understanding of the issue at hand and perhaps address the problem more effectively.

Defining Your Topic

In the scenarios at the beginning of this chapter, the topic for argument in each case may seem clear. But it is important to distinguish between a *subject* and a *topic*. That distinction is even more important if you are faced with a situation in which you are asked to write an argument about anything you want (which is not uncommon in a college writing class). In the case of the anthropology essay, for example, the subject is anthropology, or more specifically, anthropology research; you might define the topic as the ethical problems facing anthropologists who study other cultures. You can narrow that topic even further: the specific ethical problem of the relationship between the anthropologist and the people he or she is studying. Because issues like this are so complex, narrowing the topic will enable you to address it adequately in your essay. It would be impossible to write anything but a superficial five-page essay about an issue as big as the ethics of anthropological research. Entire books have been written about that issue. But you can feasibly write a five-page essay arguing for specific ethical guidelines relating to the personal relationship between an anthropologist and the people being studied in a specific situation.

If you are given the flexibility to write an argument on any topic, part of your challenge is to select a suitable topic worth arguing about. The best topics are complex: they are about issues that matter to people; they generate controversy; and usually there is a variety of views about them. The topics in the scenarios at the beginning of this chapter are good topics for those reasons. But it is important that the topic you choose matters to *you*. Composing an effective argument is an intellectually rigorous process. There is no point in carefully examining an issue that you're not interested in or concerned about.

Almost all intelligent arguments involve *opinions,* but not all opinions lead to good arguments. Simply having an opinion about something is not the same thing as being able to make a considered argument about it. And some opinions are just not worth arguing. What would be the point of making an argument that golden retrievers are more handsome dogs than poodles? You might love golden retrievers, but will such a topic generate much interest among your classmates? Probably not. It would be better to choose a topic that will matter to others.

Be careful to distinguish between opinions that are a matter of taste and those that are a question of judgment. Some things—whether broccoli tastes good, for example—are a matter of personal preference. You might be able to write an amusing essay about broccoli, but no matter how hard you try, you will not convince someone who hates green vegetables to rush to the produce department of the nearest supermarket. And why would you want to? Questions of judgment, on the other hand, are more substantial. Judgments are determined by beliefs, which in turn grow out of basic principles to which people try to remain consistent. These principles lead people to decide that some judgments are correct and others are not. Should a university require first-year students to live in dormitories? Should it restrict their social activities? Does the state have a right to execute criminals? Should couples live together before getting married? All of these are to a great extent questions of judgment.

Questions like these provide rich topics for argumentation because they are complex and offer many avenues to explore. But the richness of these topics can be challenging when you are composing an argument. Arguments written about these topics can take many directions. Trying to explore too many directions at once can lead to confusing and ineffective arguments. For this reason defining your topic is only one step in the process of composing an argument. As noted earlier, composing an argument includes exploring your topic fully and perhaps changing it along the way. In some cases you might have a clearly defined topic even before you begin to write. The letter to the director of residential life in the example at the beginning of this chapter is one such instance. But often you will find that your specific topic will change as you explore the issue you are writing about.

Whatever your topic, the following questions can help you define it carefully and begin to explore it:

- Do I know what my specific topic is?
- Is the topic suitable for the assignment or situation for which I am writing?
- Do I have an opinion about this topic? What is that opinion based on?
- On what grounds might anyone disagree with my opinion?
- Can I hope to persuade others to agree with my opinion?
- Can I support my opinion with evidence?

Considering Audience

The questions in the previous section are reminders that an argument is always made with an audience in mind. That audience will shape an argument from the beginning of the composing process. So, carefully considering your audience is an important part of the process of exploring your topic and developing your argument. Chapter 2 examined the rhetorical context of argument and discussed the role of audience in argumentation. As you prepare to compose an argument of your own, you might find it useful to review that chapter. This chapter will focus on how audience considerations will affect how you compose your argument.

Identifying Your Audience   In some situations your audience is already well defined. That letter in which you argue against new dormitory restrictions has a specific audience: the director of residential life. Your essay about the ethical problems facing anthropologists also has a specific audience: your teacher, though your teacher will probably expect you to assume a larger audience (for example, people interested in anthropology). The website about the new store proposed for your town has a more general audience, though even this audience is relatively specific (residents of your community). As you work through the process of composing your argument, try to identify what you know about your audience's interests, views, and knowledge of the topic you are addressing. Your sense of what your audience knows or believes can help you define your topic in a way that will connect with that audience; it can also help you explore your topic so that you can develop ideas for making your argument. For example, in writing the letter to the director of residential life at your college, you can assume that your audience (the director) has detailed knowledge of the problems associated with security in campus housing. He most likely feels a great sense of responsibility for the security of students living on campus. And he probably wants students not only to feel secure on campus but to enjoy their living arrangements as well. As you develop your argument against new restrictions on dormitory visitors, you can use these assumptions to identify claims and warrants likely to be acceptable to the director, and you can more easily identify common ground. For example, you might point out that you and the other students in your dorm share his concerns about safety in the dorms. You can research problems with security on your campus and use that information to support your contention that the new visitor restrictions will not likely enhance security. In short, your understanding of your audience can help you generate specific ideas for your argument and formulate those ideas in ways that might resonate with that audience. Moreover, if you approach argumentation as problem solving, you will tend to see your audience not as an opponent but as a partner in your effort to address the issue at hand. You and your dormmates might have different priorities than the residential life director, and your responsibilities are different. But all of you care about safety, and all of you hope for a pleasant and enjoyable campus lifestyle. Understanding that shared ground can lead you to formulate an argument that works toward a solution rather than a victory. The same can be true even when your audience is more general.

At times, you and your audience might hold different views on an issue, and your respective positions can seem irreconcilable. Because arguments are so often made about controversial matters, it is quite likely that you will find yourself constructing an argument for an audience that might be passionately opposed to your point of view. Just skim the newspaper on any morning, and you'll quickly find such issues: abortion, capital punishment, tax increases, religious freedom, stem-cell research. Because such issues are so important to people, they can make the process of considering your audience more complicated, and they require that you take greater care in understanding your audience.

Imagine, for instance, that you are making an argument to a general audience—say, in an article for your local newspaper—about an issue as emotional and complicated as capital punishment. You can be certain that some members of that audience will hold views opposed to your own. As you develop your argument, assume that such readers will be skeptical. But don't dismiss their views; rather, consider their reasons for opposing your viewpoint, and try to address their concerns as you build your case. Doing so not only will help you make a more convincing argument but also might enable you to find common ground with those readers.

A METHOD FOR EXPLORING YOUR IDEAS AND YOUR AUDIENCE IN ARGUMENT

Whenever you are making any argument, it can be useful to make a list of the reasons you believe as you do about the issue. You will probably not be able to discuss, in a short essay, all points you have listed about the issue, and it is likely that as you compose and revise your argument, you will generate even more ideas—ideas that might prove to be even more important than those on your list. But you can benefit from identifying the reasons for your position, ranking them in order of their importance, and considering the impact they might have on your intended audience. In the case of an essay opposing capital punishment, you might list as one of your reasons "Killing is always morally wrong." If you think about how readers who support the death penalty might react to such a statement, you can begin to anticipate their objections (for example, that killing can be justified in certain cases) or even discover common ground (the idea that human life is sacred).

You can also benefit from making another list: reasons why people might disagree with your position. Then, having explored opposing points of view, you can ask yourself why you have not been persuaded by those reasons. Are there flaws in those reasons? Do you hold beliefs that make it impossible for you to accept those reasons? Adding a brief response to each of these reasons can help you anticipate objections to your position and generate ideas for presenting and supporting your claims. And you are likely to discover that those who hold views opposed to yours have at least one good argument that you cannot answer.

Making Concessions   Often, especially when addressing complex and controversial issues such as capital punishment, you can find yourself believing that your position is right and those who believe otherwise are simply ignorant or harbor dubious motives. But serious controversies almost always continue because each side of the issue has valid concerns that cannot be dismissed. Identifying these concerns enables you to understand the issue better and to construct an argument that might be not only more convincing but also more useful. This might mean conceding a point or two to those who oppose your position. If you have no rebuttal to a particular point and recognize that your opponents' case has some merit, be honest and generous enough to say so. Making such a concession should not be considered simply a strategic move on your part. It also signals your willingness to take the members of your audience seriously, even when they disagree with you, and it reflects your genuine interest in addressing the problem at hand effectively and ethically. In this way you might bridge the gap between you and members of your audience who oppose your position, making it easier to reach a more substantial agreement.

Insisting in a belligerent way that your opponents are completely wrong will hardly convince them to take you seriously. Life is seldom so simple that one side is unequivocally right and the other wrong.

Having a good sense of your audience will help you decide what concessions to make. Different audiences will have different expectations. Some might want to hear concessions before listening to opposing views. Some might expect lengthy discussions of conceded points; others might not. When making concessions, address what you think are your audience's most pressing concerns. Doing so can help you develop important points in your argument and organize them more effectively.

Understanding Audience Expectations   Having a good sense of audience can also help you decide on the examples and evidence that will best illustrate and support your claims. You will want to use examples that your audience will understand, and you will want evidence that will be convincing to them. Examples of actual cases in an argument opposing capital punishment can be persuasive for a general audience, such as readers of your local newspaper. For a college course in legal theory, however, you will probably need to use a court's formal opinion or statistical data if you wish to be persuasive.

There is a great difference, however, between responding to the interests of your audience by discussing what it wants to know and twisting what you say to please an audience with what it wants to hear. A writer should try to tell the truth as he or she sees it. "Truth" can have many dimensions. When limited space forces you to be selective, it is wise to focus on the facets of a topic that will be most effective with the audience you are hoping to convince. But it is one thing to focus and another to mislead. Never present anything to one audience that you would be compelled to deny to another. Doing so not only damages your credibility but also undermines any legitimate effort to solve problems through argumentation.

You should bear in mind, too, that advice about considering audience can be profoundly influenced by culture. The idea of truth, for example, can vary from one culture to another or between two people who follow different religious practices. Even the idea of "factual evidence" can be shaped by cultural background. Western societies such as the United States place a high value on scientific evidence, but some cultures do not share that faith in science. Indeed, even in the United States there are communities that, because of religious beliefs or ideological leanings, harbor a deep mistrust of science. You might never have to address such audiences in an argument, but it is always important to remember that whenever you make an argument to an audience, you do so in a cultural context.

How One Student Addresses Her Audience   The following essay, which was originally published as an editorial in a college newspaper, illustrates the importance of taking audience into account in argumentation.

In this essay Karen chose a topic that would certainly interest many college students, the audience for whom she saw herself writing. Her thesis is clear: Class attendance should not be required of college students. And her writing is lively enough to hold the attention of many readers. All this is good.

But Karen's argument also has some weaknesses. In her sixth paragraph she offers what logicians call a *false dilemma:* offering a choice between only two alternatives when others exist (see page 102). By asking, "So who's the better student—the one who makes

To Skip or Not to Skip: A Student Dilemma

This is college, right? The four-year deal offering growth, maturity, experience, and knowledge? A place to be truly independent?

Because sometimes I can't tell. Sometimes this place downright reeks of paternal instincts. Just ask the freshmen and sophomores, who are by class rank alone guaranteed two full years of twenty-four-hour supervision, orchestrated activities, and group showers.

But the forced dorm migration of underclassmen has been bitched about before, to no avail. University policy is, it seems, set in stone. It ranks right up there with ingrown toe nails for sheer evasion and longevity.

But there's another university policy that has no merit as a policy and no place in a university. Mandatory Attendance Policy: wherein faculty members attempt the high school hall monitor–college instructor maneuver. It's a difficult trick to justify as professors place the attendance percentage of their choice above a student's proven abilities on graded material.

Profs rationalize out a lot of arguments to support the policy. Participation is a popular one. I had a professor whose methods for lowering grades so irritated me I used to skip on purpose. He said, "Classroom participation is a very important part of this introductory course. Obviously, if you are not present, you cannot be participating."

Equally obvious, though not stated by the prof, is the fact that one can be perpetually present but participate as little as one who is absent. So who's the better student—the one who makes a meaningless appearance or the one who is busy with something else? And who gets the points docked?

The rest of his policy was characteristically vague, mentioning that absences "could" result in a lower grade. Constant ambiguity is the second big problem with formal policies. It's tough for teachers to figure out just how much to let attendance affect grade point. So they doubletalk.

According to the UWSP catalog, faculty are to provide "clear explanation" of attendance policy. Right. Based on the language actually used, ninety-five percent of UWSP faculty are functionally incapable of uttering a single binding statement. In an effort to offend no one while retaining all power of action, profs write things like (these are actual policies): "I trust students to make their own judgments and choices about coming, or not coming, to class." But then continues: "Habitual and excessive absence is grounds for failure." What happened to trust? What good are the choices?

Or this: "More than three absences may negatively affect your grade." Then again, they may not. Who knows? And this one: "I consider every one of you in here to be mature adults. However, I reserve the right to alter grades based on attendance."

You reserve the right? By virtue of your saying so? Is that like calling the front seat? Another argument that profs cling to goes something like, "Future employers, by God, aren't going to put up with absenteeism." Well, let's take a reality pill. I think most students can grasp the difference between cutting an occasional class, which they paid for, and cutting at work, when they're the ones on salary. See, college students are capable of bi-level thought control, nowadays. (It's all those computers.)

In summary, mandatory attendance should be abolished because:

1. It is irrelevant. Roughly the same number of students will either skip or attend, regardless of what a piece of paper says. If the course is worth anything.

2. It is ineffective. It automatically measures neither participation, ability, or gained knowledge. That's what tests are for. Grades are what you end up knowing, not how many times you sat there to figure it out.

3. It is insulting. A college student is capable of determining a personal schedule, one that may or may not always meet with faculty wishes. An institution committed to the fostering of personal growth cannot operate under rules that patronize or minimize the role an adult should claim for himself.

4. It is arbitrary. A prof has no right and no ability to factor in an unrealistic measure of performance. A student should be penalized no more than what the natural consequence of an absence is—the missing of one day's direct delivery of material.

5. It abolishes free choice. By the addition of a factor that cannot be fought. We are not at a university to learn conformity. As adults, we reserve the right to choose as we see fit, even if we choose badly.

Finally, I would ask the faculty to consider this: We have for some time upheld in this nation the sacred principle of separation of church and state; i.e., You are not God.

Karen Rivedal

Editor

a meaningless appearance or the one who is busy with something else?," she has ignored at least two other possibilities. Appearance in class is likely to be meaningful to at least some students, and cutting class may be meaningless if the "something else" occupying a student's attention is a waste of time. The comparison in the tenth paragraph between reserving the right to lower grades because of poor attendance and "calling the front seat" is confusing. In point 1 of her summary, Karen claims, "Roughly the same number of students will either skip or attend, regardless of what a piece of paper says," but she offers no evidence to support this claim, which is really no more than guesswork. And because Karen admits that many students skip class despite mandatory attendance policies, her claim in point 5 that required attendance "abolishes free choice" does not hold up.

These lapses in logic aside, the major problem with Karen's argument is that she misjudged her audience. She forgot that professors, as well as students, read the school newspaper. Students cannot change the policies of their professors, but the professors themselves usually can, so she has overlooked the very audience that she most needs to reach. Moreover, not only has she failed to include professors within her audience, but she has actually insulted them. Although her criticisms of professors will strike some students as funny, a professor who is told that she or he is "functionally incapable of uttering a single binding statement" (paragraph 8) is unlikely to feel motivated to change. Only in the last paragraph does Karen specifically address the faculty, and this proves to be simply the occasion for a final insult. There may be professors who take themselves too seriously, but are there really that many who believe that they are divine?

Although it might be easy to poke holes in this argument, Karen deserves credit for boldly calling attention to policies that might indeed be wrong. Recognizing that her original argument could be stronger but still firmly believing that mandatory class attendance is inappropriate for college students, Karen decided to rewrite her editorial as an essay. Here is her revision.

Absent at What Price?

by Karen Rivedal

This is college, right? A place to break old ties, solve problems, and make decisions? Higher education is, I always thought, the pursuit of knowledge in a way that's a step beyond the paternal hand-holding of high school. It's the act of learning performed in a more dynamic atmosphere, rich with individual freedom, discourse, and debate.

But sometimes I can't tell. Some university traditions cloud the full intent of higher education. Take mandatory attendance policies, wherein faculty members attempt the high school hall monitor–college instructor maneuver. It's a difficult trick to justify as professors place the attendance percentage of their choice above a student's proven abilities on graded material.

This isn't to say that the idea of attendance itself is unsound. Clearly, personal interaction between teacher and students is preferable to textbook teaching alone. It's the *mandatory* attendance policy, within an academic community committed to the higher education of adults, that worries me.

Professors offer several arguments to support the practice. Participation is a popular one. I had a professor whose methods for lowering grades so irritated me that I used to skip class out of spite. He said, "Classroom participation is a very important part of this introductory course. Obviously, if you are not present, you cannot be participating."

Equally obvious, though, is the fact that one can be perpetually present, but participate as little as one who is absent. Participation lacks an adequate definition. There's no way of knowing, on the face of it, if a silent student is necessarily a learning student. Similarly, an instructor has no way of knowing for what purpose or advantage a student may miss a class and therefore no ability to determine its relative validity.

As a learning indicator, then, the mandatory attendance policy is flawed. It automatically measures neither participation nor ability. That's what tests are for. A final grade should reflect what a student ends up knowing rather than the artificial consequences of demerit points.

Some faculty recognize the shortcomings of a no-exceptions mandatory attendance policy and respond with partial policies. Constant ambiguity is characteristic of this approach and troublesome for the student who wants to know just where he or she stands. It's tough for teachers to figure out just how much to let attendance affect grade point. So they double-talk.

This, for example, is taken from an actual policy: "I trust students to make their own judgments and choices about coming, or not coming, to class." It then continues: "Habitual and excessive absence is grounds for failure." What happened to trust? What good are the choices?

Or this: "More than three absences may negatively affect your grade." Then again, they may not. Who knows? And this one: "I consider every one of you in here to be mature adults. However, I reserve the right to alter grades based on attendance."

This seems to say, what you can prove you have learned from this class takes a back seat to how much I think you should know based on your attendance. What the teacher says goes—just like in high school.

Professors who set up attendance policies like these believe, with good reason, that they are helping students to learn by ensuring their attendance. But the securing of this end by requirement eliminates an important element of learning. Removing the freedom to make the decision is removing the need to think. An institution committed to fostering personal growth cannot operate under rules that patronize or minimize the role an adult should claim for himself or herself.

A grading policy that relies on the student's proven abilities certainly takes the guess work out of grade assigning for teachers. This take-no-prisoners method, however, also demands a high, some say unfairly high, level of personal student maturity. Younger students especially may need, they say, the extra structuring that a policy provides.

But forfeiting an attendance policy doesn't mean that a teacher has to resign his humanity, too. Teachers who care to can still take five minutes to warn an often-absent student about the possible consequences, or let the first test score tell the story. As much as dedicated teachers want students to learn, learning is still a personal choice. Students must want to.

A "real-world" argument that professors often use goes something like "Future employers aren't going to put up with absenteeism, so get used to it now." Well, let's take a reality pill. I think most students can differentiate between cutting an occasional class, which they paid for, and missing work, when they're the ones on salary.

Students who intelligently protest an institution's policies, such as mandatory attendance requirements, are proof-in-action that college is working. These students are thinking; and learning to think and question is the underlying goal of all education. College is more than its rules, more than memorized facts. Rightly, college is knowledge, the testing of limits. To be valid, learning must include choice and the freedom to make mistakes. To rely on mandatory attendance for learning is to subvert the fullest aims of that education.

In revising her essay, Karen has retained both her thesis and her own distinctive voice. Such phrases as "the high school hall monitor–college instructor maneuver," the "take-no-prisoners method," and "let's take a reality pill" are still recognizably her own. But her argument is now more compelling. In addition to eliminating the fallacies that marred her original version, Karen included new material that strengthens her case. The third paragraph offers a much needed clarification, reassuring readers that an argument against a mandatory attendance policy is not the same as an argument against attending class. The seventh paragraph begins with a fairly sympathetic reference to professors, and the eleventh paragraph opens with a clear attempt to anticipate opposition. The twelfth paragraph includes another attempt to anticipate opposition, and the thirteenth paragraph, with its reference to "dedicated teachers," is much more likely to appeal to the professors in Karen's audience than any statements in the original version did. She still makes a forceful argument, but she doesn't lapse into insults. Finally, the conclusion of this essay is much improved. It successfully links the question of mandatory attendance policies with the purpose of higher education as defined in the opening paragraph.

You might think that Karen's revision has suppressed the strong, critical voice of her original version. As a result, you might feel that her revised essay will not resonate as well with students. However, ask yourself this: If Karen's essay is an effort to address a legitimate concern for both students *and* faculty, is her revised version a more effective attempt to solve the problem of cutting classes?

Defining Your Terms

To make sure that your ideas are understandable in an argument, it is important to clarify any terms essential to your argument. Unfortunately, many writers of argument fail to define the words they use. It is not unusual, for example, to find writers advocating (or opposing) gun control without defining exactly what they mean by *gun control*. Many arguments use words such as *censorship, society, legitimate,* and *moral* so loosely that it is impossible to decide exactly what the writer means. When this happens, the entire argument can break down.

Don't feel that you need to define every word you use, but you should define any important term that your audience might misunderstand. Avoid defining a word by using the same term or another term that is equally complex. For example, if you are opposed to the sale of pornography, you should be prepared to define what you mean by *pornography*. It would not be helpful to tell your audience that pornography is "printed or visual material that is obscene" because this

USING A DICTIONARY

If you consult a dictionary to help you define a term, remember that dictionaries are not all the same. For daily use, most writers usually refer to a good desk dictionary such as *The American Heritage Dictionary, The Random House Dictionary,* or *Merriam Webster's Collegiate Dictionary*. A good general dictionary of this sort will usually provide you with an adequate working definition. You might also want to consider consulting the multivolume *Oxford English Dictionary,* which is available in most college libraries and is especially useful in showing how the usage of a word has changed over the years. Your audience might also appreciate the detailed information that specialized dictionaries in various subject areas can provide. Many such dictionaries are likely to be available in your college library. For example, if you are working on an English literature paper, you might consult *A Concise Dictionary of Literary Terms* or *The Princeton Handbook of Poetic Terms*. For a paper in psychology, you might turn to *The Encyclopedic Dictionary of Psychology,* or for a paper on a musical topic, you could consult *The New Grove's Dictionary of Music and Musicians*. There are also dictionaries for medical, legal, philosophical, and theoretical terms as well as for each of the natural sciences. When using specialized dictionaries, you will often find valuable information, but remember that the definition that appears in your paper should not be more difficult than the word or phrase you originally set out to define.

only raises the question: What is obscene? In an important ruling, the U.S. Supreme Court defined *obscene* as material that "the average person, applying community standards, would find . . . as a whole, appeals to the prurient interest," but even if you happened to have this definition at hand, you should ask yourself whether "the average person" understands what *prurient* means—not to mention what the court might have meant by *community standards.* Unless you define your terms carefully, avoiding unnecessarily abstract language, you can end up writing an endless chain of definitions that require further explanation.

Dictionaries can be helpful when you're defining your terms. But often the important terms in an argument cannot be satisfactorily defined with a dictionary. Consider the term *sustainability,* which is sometimes used in arguments about environmental issues. Such a term has specific and specialized meanings in environmental debates, and it would not suffice to supply only a dictionary definition. So instead of relying exclusively on dictionaries, try to define such key terms in your own words. You can choose from among several strategies:

- Give synonyms.
- Compare the term with other words with which it is likely to be confused, and show how your term differs.
- Define a word by showing what it is *not.*
- Provide examples.

Writers frequently use several of these strategies to create a single definition. Sometimes an entire essay is devoted to defining one term; in doing so, the writer makes an argument in which that term is central. For example, a writer can focus an essay on defining *free speech,* in the process making an argument for a particular conception of that term.

When writing an argument, you will usually need to define your terms within a paragraph or two. In addition to achieving clarity, definition helps control an argument by eliminating misunderstandings that can cause an audience to be inappropriately hostile or to jump to a conclusion different from your own. By carefully defining your terms, you limit a discussion to what you want to discuss. This increases the likelihood that you will gain a fair hearing for your views.

Structuring an Argument

One of the biggest challenges in composing an argument is structuring it. Once you have explored your topic and developed your ideas, you will need to consider the following questions:

- How should I begin my argument?
- In what order should I arrange the points I want to make?
- How can I most efficiently respond to opposing arguments?
- How should I conclude?

The answers to these questions will vary from one essay to another and from one kind of argument (such as a newspaper editorial) to another (a web page). Even if no single plan will work for all arguments, you can benefit from being familiar with some basic principles of argumentation that may help you organize your argument effectively. This chapter explains three traditional ways of structuring an argument:

- Classical arrangement
- Rogerian argument
- Logical arrangements

Making an Outline

Many students think of outlines as extra work. But using an outline can save you time and help you write a more effective argument. It can help you keep track of your main ideas and make sure that the important parts of your argument fit together effectively. It can also help you identify areas in which you may need to do more research.

Depending on your writing process, you can outline before attempting to write or after you have completed a first draft. If you create an outline before you begin writing, the patterns for classical arrangement and Rogerian argument (pages 126–131 and 131–137), which can be adopted for papers of almost any length, may be useful to you. You can also use a standard formal outline:

I. Major idea

   A. Supporting idea

      1. Minor idea

         a. Supporting detail

         b. Supporting detail

      2. Minor idea

         a. Supporting detail

         b. Supporting detail

   B. Supporting idea

II. Major idea

PLANNING AHEAD

When planning a paper, allow ample time for drafting and revising. Ideas often evolve during the writing process. Even if you have extensive notes, you might discover that you lack information to support a claim that occurred to you when you sat down to write. You would then need to do research or modify your claim. The first draft might also include material that, on rereading, you decide does not relate to the focus of your paper and should therefore be removed. Cutting and adding are normal parts of the writing process, so expect to make changes.

And so forth. Subdivisions make sense only when there are at least two categories; otherwise, there would be no need to subdivide. Roman numeral I usually implies the existence of Roman numeral II, and supporting idea A implies the existence of supporting idea B. Formal outlines are usually parallel, each part being in balance with the others.

Many writers prefer to work with less formal outlines. Two widely used alternatives to a formal outline are listing and mapping. When organizing a paper by **listing,** writers simply create a list of the various points they want to make without worrying about Roman numerals or indentation. They then number the points on the list in the order in which they plan to discuss them. When **mapping,** you can create circles or blocks on a page, starting with a main idea. Each different idea is noted in a separate circle or block, and then lines are drawn to connect related ideas.

There is no single method that works equally well for all writers. Unless you are specifically instructed to complete a certain type of outline, practice whatever kind of outlining works best for you. And keep in mind that an outline is not an end in itself; it is only a tool to help you write a good paper. You can rewrite an outline more easily than you can rewrite a paper, so be prepared to rework any outline that does not help you write better.

Integrating Source Material into Your Paper

One of the challenges of writing an argument involving research is integrating source material effectively into a work that remains distinctively your own. The most effective source-based arguments include source material woven smoothly into the paper with well-chosen quotations that are clearly introduced and properly documented. Papers with too many long quotations or quotations that seem arbitrarily placed are weaker; they lack the student's voice and might lead an instructor to be suspicious about how much of the paper is the student's own. You can avoid such problems if you work with your source material to support your own position in an argument and if you follow some basic advice for quoting and citing source material.

First, make sure that any quotations you use fit smoothly into your essay as a whole. Provide transitions that link quotations to whatever has come before them. As a general rule, anything worth quoting at length requires some discussion. After you have quoted someone, you should usually include some analysis or commentary that will make the significance of the quotation clear. Notice how Rachel Guetter, whose essay appears on pages 133–136, follows this advice to weave a quote from one of her sources effectively into her discussion of problems facing gay parents:

> Often, one person in a same-sex relationship is the biological parent and the other will help raise the child as his or her own. According to the American Academy of Pediatrics (AAP), children in this situation lose "survivor benefits if a parent dies and legal rights if the parents break up" (Berman 1). Both situations leave a dramatic impact on the child, who then is caught in the middle of legal battles.

To help keep your paper your own, try to avoid using long quotations. Quote only what you need most, and edit long quotations whenever possible. Use the ellipsis (. . .) to indicate that you have omitted a word or phrase within a sentence, leaving a space before and after each period. (When the ellipsis follows a completed sentence, include the sentence's period before the ellipsis.) When editing quotations in this way, make sure that they remain clear and grammatically correct. If the addition of an extra word or two would help make the quotation more easily understandable, you should enclose the inserted material within square brackets [ ] to let your readers know what had been added to the quotation. Here is another passage from Rachel Guetter's essay illustrating these points:

> Until homosexuality is more widely received, children with gay and lesbian parents will have to deal with the fact that their family is viewed as pejoratively different. Glenn Stanton, se-

nior research analyst for Focus on the Family, says, "While there may be very nice people who are raising kids in homosexual situations, the best model for kids is to grow up with mom and dad" (Stanton). It seems reasonable to believe that having both a mother and father benefits children. Women and men have different parenting traits that give a strong balance for the development of a child. Stanton also states, "Fathers encourage children to take chances . . . mothers protect and are more cautious." There exist in parents different disciplining, communication, and playing styles that can be advantages in raising a child.

Paraphrasing and summarizing are important writing skills. They can help you avoid writing a paper that sounds like nothing more than one quotation after another or using quotations that are so heavily edited that readers start wondering about what you have cut out. When you put another writer's ideas into your own words (being careful, of course, to provide proper documentation), you are demonstrating that you have control over your material, and by doing so, you can often make your paper more readable.

Above all, remember that you are the writer of your argument. You are using the sources you have found to support your position or to enhance your own ideas.

Classical Arrangement

Because classical theories of rhetoric developed when most arguments were oral, the great works of classical rhetoric recommended strategies that could be easily understood by listeners. If speakers adhered to essentially the same plan, listeners were able to follow long, complex arguments because the main components were easily recognizable and the order in which they appeared signaled what was likely to follow.

The common plan for organizing an argument along classical lines included six main components: introduction, statement of background, proposition, proof, refutation, and conclusion, as follows:

Introduction (*Exordium*) In the introduction you urge your audience to consider the case that you are about to present. This is the time to capture your readers' attention and introduce your issue.

Statement of Background (*Narratio*) In the statement of background you narrate, or tell, the key events in the story behind your case. This is the time to provide information so that your audience will understand the nature of the facts in the case.

Proposition (*Partitio*) This component divides (or partitions) the part of the argument focused on information from the part focused on reasoning, and it outlines the major points that will follow. You must state the position you are taking, based on the information you have presented, and then indicate the lines the rest of your argument will follow.

Proof (*Confirmatio*) Adhering carefully to your outline, you now present the heart of your argument: you make (or confirm) your case. You must discuss the reasons you have taken your position and cite evidence to support each of those reasons.

Refutation
(Refutatio)

In this key section you anticipate and refute opposing views. By showing what is wrong with the reasoning of your opponents, you demonstrate that you have studied the issue thoroughly and have reached the only acceptable conclusion in this case.

Conclusion
(Peroratio)

The concluding paragraph(s) should summarize your most important points. In addition, you can make a final appeal to values and feelings that are likely to leave your audience favorably disposed toward your case.

Classical rhetoricians allowed variations on this plan, depending on, as the great Roman orator and scholar Cicero wrote, "the weight of the matter and the judgment of the speaker." For example, a speaker was encouraged to begin with refutation when an audience was already strongly committed to an opposing point of view. But because this basic plan remains strong and clear, it can still help writers organize their thoughts.

One advantage of this method of arrangement is that it helps writers generate ideas for their arguments. If you follow the common classical plan for organizing your argument, you will have to generate ideas for each of the main parts. For example, you will have to provide background information about the issue at hand and include arguments to refute opposing points. As a result, your argument will tend to be thorough.

Much of classical rhetoric focused on political discourse, in which speakers publicly debated issues that required action by elected officials or legislatures. Because of this, classical arrangement can be especially useful when you feel strongly about an issue and you are trying to convince an audience to undertake a proposed course of action. Because classical rhetoric tends to assume that an audience can be persuaded when it is presented with solid evidence and a clear explanation of the flaws in opponents' reasoning, this plan for arranging an argument might be most effective when you are writing for people who share your basic values.

The following essay by Tyler Sunderman provides an example of an argument constructed according to classical arrangement. It advocates snowmobiling in Yellowstone National Park and was composed for an audience that included people who care about enjoying the outdoors and protecting the environment. As you read this argument, be alert for where Tyler moves from providing background to introducing his proposition and how he responds to views other than his own—advancing a clear proposition yet conveying respect for both the environment and the people who have opposed the stand he is taking.

Snowmobiles in Yellowstone: The Case for Fair Access

by Tyler Sunderman

In 1872, Congress set aside the Northwestern corner of the Wyoming Territory as our first National Park. Yellowstone was to be administered by the Department of the Interior for the purpose of being "a public park or pleasuring-ground for the benefit and enjoyment of the people" (Our Mission). With the designation of these 2.2 million acres, Congress created a vast public property that has become part of the culture of our nation (History Page).

Comprised of geysers, old-growth forests, rivers and gorges, Yellowstone has become the destination of generations of American travelers. Setting out in wagons, then automobiles, and then mini-vans and motor homes, Americans have taken to the road to experience the ruggedness of the American West in Yellowstone National Park.

Many Americans, when thinking about Yellowstone remember the family road trips of their childhood, singing the "Fifty, Nifty, United States," and waiting for the next Wall Drug sign as they headed toward the land of Old Faithful and the bubbling mud pots. For the inn keepers and restauranteurs of West Yellowstone, Montana, this is only a part of the tourist season. As the vanloads of families from all corners of America begin to wane in the fall of each year, the locals prepare for the arrival of the snowmobilers.

Since 1968, when the snowmobile was in its infancy, enthusiasts have been permitted to ride on the snow atop the blacktop roads that traverse the park, allowing many Americans to experience the wildlife and scenery of Yellowstone in the winter (Yellowstone Snowmobile). For many years, the economy in the gateway community of West Yellowstone survived by the steady flow of year round tourists, who allowed the local motels and restaurants and filling stations to remain open throughout the year. Generations of Americans have traveled to Yellowstone to see the steam rising from the geysers, the Bison plowing through the snow, and the moose wading in the steaming geyser-fed rivers.

Today, this tradition is under attack. Seven years ago, the Fund for Animals filed suit against the National Park Service, seeking to stop all motorized winter recreation in Yellowstone National Park. The group claimed that the snowmobiles, even though only allowed on the roadways, were harmful to the environment and the wildlife that inhabit the park. In the aftermath of the lawsuit, the National Park Service (NPS) announced in 2000 that it would begin the process of eliminating snowmobile travel within the park. Under this plan, there was to be no further winter travel in Yellowstone by the winter of 2003–2004. The snowmobile industry took action in response, however, and the U.S. District Court for Wyoming found that the NPS had not properly conducted its environmental impact studies. After further examination, the court found limited winter travel to be acceptable, creating provisions to make sure that snowmobiles were operating in the most environmentally friendly way (Yellowstone Snowmobile). Despite the declaration by the NPS in November of 2003 that snowmobiling was to be allowed in the park, litigation has continued, and the future of motorized winter recreation in Yellowstone National Park is still in doubt.

On one side of the argument are environmental advocacy groups that have been attempting to stop motorized travel in Yellowstone in the winter, allowing only snowshoes and cross-country skiing. In direct opposition are the snowmobilers and local businesses, who are trying to keep the park open to motorized recreation. The NPS has attempted to forge a compromise that allows motorized winter recreation, while protecting the environment from as much disruption as possible. Under the most recent proposal, the NPS plans to allow up to 720 snowmobiles into the park each day, led by professional guides who will assure that all park policies are followed. In addition, the NPS will only allow snowmobiles that employ state-of-the-art emissions control technology (Bohrer).

Despite the fact that environmental groups such as the Sierra Club have continued to protest the presence of snowmobiles, I believe that we must continue to allow snowmobiles in Yellowstone National Park. The proposal that has been put forward by the NPS has taken significant steps to meet the needs of both the environment and the local businesses that rely on the park for their livelihood. To lose the right to visit the park on snowmobiles would be to deny the purposes for which Yellowstone was established. The national park system was created for the recreation and enjoyment of the American people. We must work to find ways to co-exist with nature, not to seal ourselves away from it. With modern technological advances, it is possible to limit our impact on the environment, while retaining our rights as citizens to have access to our national treasures.

When Yellowstone National Park was first created, the horse was the primary mode of transportation, and it is unlikely that any member of Congress who voted to establish Yellowstone could have foreseen such an invention as the snowmobile. However, the presence of the snowmobile is in keeping with the original intentions of the park's creation. Yellowstone National Park was created for the purpose of recreation. It was created as a place where nature could be preserved, and the American people would be able to experience it first hand. This experience has always taken on many different forms, from hiking, to boat tours, camping, and yes, even snowmobiles.

Under the policies that have been in place since snowmobiles entered the park in 1968, snowmobiles have been restricted to the paved road surfaces. The NPS does not plow the roads in the winter, allowing snow to accumulate, providing an excellent place for snowmobiles to ride. The 185 miles of roads within the park provide an excellent way for snowmobilers to experience the park. This is not altogether different from the experiences of motorists in the summer months, who are restricted to paved road surfaces. The snowmobile essentially provides an opportunity for visitors to experience the park with personal freedom and ease.

Snowmobiling tourists are key to the survival of the local economy. The money that is spent on motel rooms, fuel, and food helps to ensure the survival of many small businesses in the city of West Yellowstone. The effect that a park closure would have on the local economy would be significant. Many of the snowmobilers that enter the park are new to the sport, and it is necessary for them to rent the necessary equipment for the trip, which generates a great deal of local business. The closing of the park to snowmobiles would remove one of the largest tourist attractions from the community and leave it reeling. In addition, the states of Wyoming and Idaho generate a great deal of their state revenue from the sales taxes collected in the region. As states that rely on tourism for their economic wellbeing, the restriction of motorized recreation would have a negative impact on the states' economic wellbeing.

The environmental groups that oppose motorized winter recreation in Yellowstone have several primary justifications. The number one issue cited by the Sierra Club is the issue of air pollution as a result of snowmobiles in Yellowstone. They point out the fact that snowmobiles emit 68% of all carbon monoxide emissions within the park (Libkind). Furthermore, they claim that snowmobiles account for an even larger share of the hydrocarbon emissions. This data, however, is based on old technology in the snowmobile industry.

For years, snowmobiles employed two cycle engines that are less fuel efficient and more polluting. In recent years, there have been giant leaps in emissions control technology and the development of four cycle engines that will minimize the amount of air pollution, while maximizing fuel efficiency. For example, the manufacturer Arctic Cat recently announced that three of its models have been approved for use in National Parks by the U.S. Department of the Interior. The Arctic Cat T660 model, which is equipped with a four cycle engine, reduces carbon monoxide emissions by over

70%, and hydrocarbons by a factor of 90% (Arctic Cat). These new stringent requirements are assuring that the environmental impact of snowmobiles is minimal. Though older models were responsible for significant emissions, the problem has been mitigated by technological advancement.

When speaking about the Yellowstone snowmobiling issue, Marcus Libkind, President of the Snowlands Network, claimed that snowmobiles "harm soils, vegetation, and wildlife. Their use with insufficient snow-cover leads to compaction of the soil, damage to vegetation, and stresses on sub-nivean animals" (Libkind). While this may be the case, it is not an applicable argument in Yellowstone, where snowmobiles ride atop hard packed snow covering the paved road that cars use in the summer months. The damage that is posed to soil and vegetation is negligible given the fact that snowmobiles are not allowed to ride in meadows or wooded areas where such habitats exist. This is enforced by constant patrols by park rangers. Furthermore, under new National Park Service guidelines, all snowmobilers allowed in Yellowstone are under the supervision of professional guides. This will assure that all policies are followed.

Yellowstone is the home to many animal species, which range from moose and bison, to the newly re-introduced wolves. Many groups have claimed that snowmobiles disrupt and harass wildlife within the park. From my own personal experience as a wintertime visitor to the park, I have seen that this is not the case. While traveling through Yellowstone several years ago on my snowmobile, my uncle and I came along a herd of bison that were walking slowly down the road. Along the side of the trail, all of the snowmobilers shut off their machines and waited, allowing the herd to pass. When we entered the park, we were told that if we encountered a herd of wildlife, we should be respectful of their space, and allow them to pass. This was the case with the approximately 50 snowmobiles stopped on the side of the trail. Though it would be ridiculous to argue that wildlife is never bothered by snowmobilers, it should be noted that there are many instances each year when wildlife is antagonized by summer visitors. It is therefore unfair to blame snowmobiles en-masse for the disruption of the park's wildlife.

As the debate continues over whether the National Park Service should allow snowmobiles in Yellowstone National Park, it is important to be informed about the ways in which the environment is impacted. Though older snowmobiles have caused pollution, new technology has emerged that makes snowmobiles much more environmentally friendly. Therefore, it would make no sense to ban motorized winter recreation based on outdated information. Claims that have been made with regard to the effect that snowmobiles have on native flora and fauna are based on a misunderstanding of the actual rules in the park. All motorized travel is restricted to the paved roadways, thus avoiding increased erosion and damage to native species. In addition, only 720 snowmobiles are to be allowed within the park each day, which is infinitesimal compared with the invasion of cars, motor homes and SUVs in the summer months.

The National Park System was created for the use of the American people. It was created as a place where the citizens of our country could experience a piece of wild America. The ability of snowmobilers to traverse the roads of the park is crucial to keeping with this tradition. Modern technological advances are allowing cleaner, more fuel efficient snowmobiles to be produced. The National Park Service has worked to develop a proposal that limits the number of snowmobiles and mandates emissions control technology, while requiring guided tours of the park. This proposal should be reasonable for all parties, because it retains the rights of the snowmobilers to access the park, while addressing the concerns of environmental groups. This is the best option for Yellowstone and its local economy, and the best option for America.

WORKS CITED

"Arctic Cat 4-Stroke Snowmobiles Certified by U.S. Department of the Interior." Press Release. Arctic Cat Inc. 5 September 2003 <http://www.indianasnowmobilers.com/arcticcatcertified.htm>.

Bohrer, Becky. "Park Service Proposes Allowing Snowmobiles in Yellowstone." *Billings Gazette and Associated Press* 9 August 2004.

Libkind, Marcus. "Defending Winter from the Roar and Stench of Snowmobiles." *San Francisco Sierra Club Yodeler* November 2003.

"The National Park Service—Our Mission." 10 November 2004 <http://www.nps.gov/legacy/mission.html.>

"Yellowstone National Park History." 10 November 2004 <http://www.yellowstone.net/history.htm#1872.>

"Yellowstone Snowmobile History." *Yellowstone Park Winter Guide* 10 November 2004 <http://www.yellowstonewinterguide.com/snowmobiling/snowmobiling_history.php.>

The background that Tyler provides for his argument consists of information unlikely to alienate the readers he needs to persuade, but it is nevertheless useful for the case he is about to make. For example, the first quotation in the paper establishes that Yellowstone was intended to give people pleasure when they visit the park—that's a different mission from what would inspire the creation of a wildlife sanctuary. And by establishing early on that snowmobiling has been practiced in Yellowstone since 1968, Tyler shows that he is arguing to preserve a tradition rather than to violate one. But as he develops his argument, he does not confine himself to arguing that snowmobiling should be allowed in Yellowstone because it is fun. He emphasizes that snowmobilers generate winter revenue for the owners of small businesses near the park and that snowmobiles now benefit from improved technology, so they produce less pollution than they once did. He also draws upon relevant personal experience to show how snowmobilers can treat wildlife with respect. Personal experience alone would not be sufficient to make a convincing case about the use of land owned by the federal government, but this experience contributes to the author's credibility—credibility also established by drawing upon relevant sources and treating opposition arguments with respect.

Rogerian Argument

Chapter 1 introduced how the ideas of psychotherapist Carl Rogers have influenced scholars interested in argumentation. Rogers focused on listening with understanding to avoid miscommunication that can too often accompany serious conflicts. For Rogers the key to resolving conflict is to try honestly to understand what others mean.

Despite questions raised by some scholars about the extent to which Rogers's ideas can be applied to written arguments, you can benefit from viewing persuasion as a means to resolve conflict and achieve social cooperation instead of thinking that the point of an argument is to defeat your opponents. Accordingly, planning a Rogerian argument means emphasizing concessions rather than refutations and placing concessions early in your essay. Like classically arranged arguments, Rogerian arguments have six identifiable parts, as follows:

Introduction	State the problem that you hope to resolve. By presenting your issue as a problem in need of a solution, you raise the possibility of positive change. This strategy can interest readers who would not be drawn to an argument that seems devoted to tearing something down.
Summary of Opposing Views	As accurately and neutrally as possible, state the views of people with whom you disagree. By doing so, you show that you are capable of listening without judging and that you have given a fair hearing to people who think differently from you—the people you most need to reach.
Statement of Understanding	Having summarized views different from your own, you now show that you understand that there are situations in which these views are valid. In other words, you are offering a kind of concession. You are not conceding that these views are always right, but you are recognizing that there are conditions under which you would share the views of your opponents.
Statement of Your Position	Having won the attention of both your opponents and those readers who do not have a position on your issue, you have secured a hearing from an audience that is in need of or is open to persuasion. Now that these readers know that you've given fair consideration to views other than your own, they should be prepared to listen fairly to your views.
Statement of Contexts	Similar to the statement of understanding, in which you have described situations where you would be inclined to share the views of your opponents, the statement of contexts describes situations in which you hope your views would be honored. By showing that your position has merit in a specific context or contexts, you establish that you don't expect everyone to agree with you all the time. The limitations you recognize increase the likelihood that your opponents will agree with you at least in part.
Statement of Benefits	You conclude your argument by appealing to the self-interest of people who do not already share your views but are beginning to respect them because of your presentation. When you conclude by showing how such readers would benefit from

accepting your position, your essay's ending is positive and hopeful.

(Adapted from Richard Coe, *Form and Substance.* New York: Wiley, 1981.)

Depending on the complexity of the issue, the extent to which people are divided about it, and the points you want to argue, any part of a Rogerian argument can be expanded. It is not necessary to devote precisely the same amount of space to each part. You should try to make your case as balanced as possible, however. If you seem to give only superficial consideration to the views of others and then linger at length on your own, you are defeating the purpose of a Rogerian argument.

This book advocates an approach to argumentation that draws on some of the principles of Rogerian argument, especially the importance of working toward solutions to conflicts. Any style of arrangement—classical, Rogerian, or otherwise—can strive toward the goal of solving problems through argumentation. But a Rogerian argument might be most effective in situations in which people are deeply divided as a result of different values or perceptions. It is especially useful when you are trying to reconcile conflicting parties and achieve a compromise. However, there will be situations in which such an approach might not be the most effective one. If you hold strong views about a particular issue, for instance, you might find that it is better to consider other ways of organizing your argument. In some situations presenting a strong argument for a specific course of action or viewpoint might be the most ethical way to proceed, even if the goal is to resolve a conflict. The point is that planning and organizing your argument should be thought of in the larger context of your purposes for engaging in argument.

Here is a student essay about a complicated and controversial issue: gay adoption. As you'll see, Rachel uses the principles of Rogerian argument to make her case in favor of a national policy for adoption by same-sex couples.

A Reasonable Approach to Gay Adoption

by Rachel Guetter

Adoption by gay parents recently became an open topic with the help of talk show host Rosie O'Donnell. O'Donnell, who went public with her sexuality in 2001, has adopted several children and is a foster mother (Huff and Gest 2). She is currently taking on a Florida law that bans homosexuals from adopting. In doing so, she is prompting everyone to address a situation that is likely to become more common: gay couples seeking to adopt children.

Currently, there is no national policy regarding gay adoptions, and state laws offer a mixed bag of approaches and restriction. For example, Florida is the only state that has enacted a law explicitly banning gay adoptions. In the states that do not have prohibitory laws, gays and lesbians can file for adoption in court (Maxwell, et al.). It is then up to each court to decide whether a petition for adoption meets the state's adoption policies. Many homosexuals have children from previous marriages, or they become parents by donating their own sperm or egg. Only California, Connecticut, and Vermont have legislation that would allow gays and lesbians to adopt their partner's child (Berman). The forty-six other states must rely on their individual judges to consider the petition. One would hope that a judge would not let personal preference get in the way of a fair ruling, but unfortunately this does not always happen.

The many different state laws may reflect the resistance of many Americans to the idea of gay adoption. Those who feel that children should not be brought up in homosexual households state that their concerns are not the product of homophobia, but are the product of what they find to be in the best interest of the children. These people believe that the best way for a child to be raised is in a family with married mother and father. Also, some opponents of gay adoption argue that children who grow up with same-sex parents are not provided with the same legal benefits and securities as those who are raised in heterosexual, married households.

One reason for this resistance is that America is still dealing with the lack of acceptance for and recognition of homosexuals. Until homosexuality is more widely received, children with gay and lesbian parents will have to deal with the fact that their family is viewed as pejoratively different. Glenn Stanton, senior research analyst for Focus on the Family, says, "While there may be very nice people who are raising kids in homosexual situations, the best model for kids is to grow up with mom and dad" (Stanton). It seems reasonable to believe that having both a mother and father benefits children. Women and men have different parenting traits that give a strong balance for the development of a child. Stanton also states, "Fathers encourage children to take chances . . . mothers protect and are more cautious." There exist in parents different disciplining, communication, and playing styles that can be advantages in raising a child. Sandy Rios, president of Concerned Women for America, agrees, "As the single mother of a son, I can see quite clearly that having a mother and father together would be far better for my son" ("Pediatrics").

Another problem is that children who have gay and lesbian parents are not necessarily given the same benefits as children from two-parent, heterosexual families. Often, one person in a same-sex relationship is the biological parent and the other will help raise the child as his or her own. According to the American Academy of Pediatrics (AAP), children in this situation lose "survivor benefits if a parent dies and legal rights if the parents break up" (Berman 1). Both situations leave a dramatic impact on the child, who then is caught in the middle of legal battles. Another benefit that the child would not be given is health insurance from both parents. In all of these cases, the child is not given the same economic stability as one who has a married mother and father.

Many gays and lesbians are like any other people who dream of one day having a family. But they face great obstacles. Often, one parent in a same-sex family is not given the same rights as the other when one partner has a biological child. Sometimes neither partner in a same-sex family is able to obtain a child through adoption. Despite such obstacles, it cannot be denied that homosexual families exist. Depending on which study you consult, there are anywhere from 1.5 to 5 million children being raised in gay and lesbian families (Maxwell, et al.). The children, however, are the ones who are being hurt by the lack of legality of the situation that they are in. We owe it to these children—and to the same-sex couples who are committed to raising them—to address this problem in a way that is satisfactory for all concerned.

This issue needs to be examined from a national point of view for two reasons. First of all, people who wish to adopt a child are not restricted to adopting within their own states. Often, the demand for certain children requires couples to look in another state. Secondly, people tend to move from state to state. A couple may adopt a child in one state and later decide to move to another with different laws governing parenthood. The adoption needs to be legally recognized in all states, so if a couple adopts in one state, they can move to another and still be protected by law as legal parents. Instead of allowing each state to make its own decision concerning this matter, federal legislation needs to be enacted that would not only permit homosexuals to adopt their partner's child, but also allow gay couples to adopt children together. Obviously, such legislation would make it easier for same-sex families to raise their children in safe and happy homes. But it might also address the problem of children who need to be adopted. If homosexuals are legally permitted to adopt, more children waiting to be adopted can be given homes and the homosexual families that currently exist will become legally recognized.

There are children who are constantly being shifted from one foster home to another and deservingly need to be placed in a permanent and stable environment. There are currently not enough homes that children can be adopted into. In 1999, about 581,000 children were a part of the U.S. foster care system. Of those, 22 percent were available for adoption ("Foster Care Facts"). A report by the Vera Institute of Justice states that children raised without a permanent home are more likely to exhibit emotional and behavioral problems and be involved with the juvenile justice system ("Safe and Smart"). This is not to say that the foster care system is bad, but it suggests how important a permanent home and family are for children. Same-sex couples could provide such a home for many of these children.

Florida, the state that bans homosexuals from adopting, nevertheless allows homosexuals to become foster parents (Pertman). It is interesting to think that someone could be allowed to clothe, feed, discipline, and love a child yet not be allowed to call that child their own. By allowing a couple to be foster parents, the state has made a statement about what kind of people those foster parents are: responsible and caring and able to provide a good home and family environment. Why should they not be allowed to become legal parents of their own adopted children?

Both sides agree that children need to be raised in loving and caring families. It is wrong to think that a gay couple cannot provide that. A study in Minnesota shows that "in general, gay/lesbian families tended to score the most consistently as the healthiest and strongest of the family structures" (Maxwell, et al.). Married couples placed a strong second, and unmarried heterosexual couples were found to be the least healthy and least strong, especially when children were a part of the family (Maxwell, et al.). The study done by the courts discloses that homosexual couples deliberately plan to have children and arrange their lives so that both parents are significantly involved with raising the child (Maxwell, et al.). Opponents say that it takes more than just a loving environment; it takes both a mom and dad. As the Minnesota study proved, though, perhaps mother–father households are not as stable as once thought. Gays and lesbians have to make extensive plans in order to obtain or even conceive a child, so the likelihood that a child was an "accident" or unwanted is rare.

In February 2002, AAP issued a new statement titled, "Coparent or Second-Parent Adoption by Same-Sex Parents." It explains the AAP's stance on what is in the best interest of children being raised in same-sex families. Dr. Steven Berman offers a summary: "The AAP concluded that legalizing second-parent adoptions is in the best interest of the children" (Berman). Also in this statement is the reassurance that children are not more inclined to become homosexual or to possess homosexual tendencies from being raised by homosexual parents. Although the AAP does not endorse or condemn homosexuality, they, like the rest of the U.S., cannot ignore the growing number of same-sex families and must deal with what truly would be in the best interest of the children who are caught in the middle.

Whether the stance is for or against gay and lesbian adoption, both sides base their reasoning on what is in the best interest for the children. It would be safe to say that most would agree that having a child brought up in a loving, same-sex family is better than having a child moved from foster home to foster home or raised in an abusive home. Being homosexual does not mean that one loses the right to raise a child. Being an unwanted child does not mean that one loses the right to find a loving home, whether that home is single parent, married, heterosexual or even homosexual.

WORKS CITED

Berman, Steven. "Homosexuals and Adoption." *Rocky Mountain News* 23 Feb. 2002:1, final ed.: 1W.

"Foster Care Facts." The Evan B. Donaldson Adoption Institute. 10 Apr. 2002 <http://www.adoptioninstitute.org/FactOverview/foster.html.>

Huff, Richard, and Emily Gest. "Rosie Takes on Prez About Gay Adoption." *New York Daily News* 14 Mar. 2002, final ed.: 2.

Maxwell, Nancy G., Astrid A.M. Mattijssen, and Charlene Smith. "Legal Protection for All the Children: Dutch-American Comparison of Lesbian and Gay Parent Adoptions." *Electronic Journal of Comparative Law* 3.1 (August 1999) 20 Sept. 2002 <http://www.ejcl.org/ ejcl/31/art31-2.html.>

"Pediatrics Academy's Endorsement of Homosexual Adoption." *US Newswire* 04 Feb. 2002.

Pertman, Adam. "Break Down Barriers to Homosexual Adoption." *The Baltimore Sun* 20 Mar. 2002, final ed.: A23.

"Safe and Smart." Vera Institute of Justice. 10 Apr. 2002 <http://www.vera.org/project/project1_1.asp?section_id=6&project_id=5.>

Stanton, Glenn T. "Why Children Need a Male and Female Parent." Focus on the Family. 13 May 2002 <http://www.family.org/cforum/tempforum/A0020006.html.>

Notice that Rachel follows the Rogerian structure described on pages 131–133. After her introduction she presents the views of those who oppose gay adoptions, and she does so without criticism. She offers a statement of understanding, conceding that the concerns of opponents are valid. But she also offers her own concerns, which are based on the same basic goal of protecting children that opponents of gay adoptions hold. This is the common ground that enables her to present her proposal for national legislation regarding gay adoptions—legislation that she believes will protect children in such situation, as well as foster children waiting to be adopted. She clearly lays out the benefits of such legislation.

Although you do not need to follow the Rogerian structure, you can see that it might help you organize your argument in a way that is likely to connect with your opponents—which is one of the goals of Rogerian argument. As in the case of Rachel's essay, an argument structured according to a Rogerian approach places your opponents' concerns first. Notice, too, that Rachel's tone is measured, respectful, and concerned throughout her essay, another indication of her desire to seek common ground and find a solution to the problem she is writing about.

Logical Arrangements

Arguments can also be shaped by the kind of reasoning a writer employs. Chapter 4 discussed the two basic kinds of logic: **inductive reasoning** and **deductive reasoning.** It also discussed informal logic, in particular the Toulmin model. These kinds of logic represent strategies that you can use to make your arguments, and like the classical and Rogerian approaches, they can be helpful in deciding how to structure an argument.

Inductive Reasoning   When you base an argument on inductive reasoning, you are drawing a conclusion based on evidence that you present. Say you are making an argument for more stringent enforcement of driving laws in your state. In doing so, you might present a variety of relevant information:

- Experiences you've had with speeding drivers
- Anecdotes about friends or family members who have been in accidents that resulted from reckless driving
- Statistics from the U.S. Department of Transportation about automobile accidents and their relationship to speed limits
- Quotations from law enforcement officials or experts who advocate lower speed limits but admit that posted speed limits are often not vigorously enforced

From all this evidence you draw the conclusion that higher speed limits are dangerous and that drivers would be safer if laws were enforced more rigorously. Such an argument would be based on inductive reasoning.

In making an argument based on inductive reasoning, keep the following considerations in mind:

- *Try to arrange your evidence so that it leads your readers to the same conclusion you have reached.* You need to introduce the issue and demonstrate to your readers that it is a problem worthy of attention. But the primary challenge will be to decide which evidence to present first and in what order the remaining evidence will be presented. Consider, too, how best to begin. You might, for example, cite a particular observation that strikes you as especially important. Or you might begin with an anecdote. Whatever approach you use, your introduction should address the members of your particular audience so that they will want to continue reading. A well-structured inductive essay would then gradually expand as the evidence accumulates so that the conclusion is supported by numerous details.
- *Consider how specific kinds of evidence you have gathered will affect your readers.* Will some kinds of evidence likely be more compelling to them than others? If so, will it be more effective to present such evidence earlier or later in the argument? Answering those questions not only can help you decide how best to organize your essay but also can generate additional ideas for evidence that will make your conclusion as persuasive to your audience as possible.

- *Decide how much evidence is enough.* Eventually, you will reach a point at which you decide that you have offered enough evidence to support your thesis. You might reach this point sooner in some contexts than others. For example, in an essay for your college writing class, you are not likely to cite as much evidence as you might be expected to include in a research report for a course in freshwater ecology; an essay in a respected political journal such as *Foreign Affairs* will include more extensive evidence than an editorial in your local newspaper. But whatever the context, the process is essentially the same.

- *Interpret and analyze your evidence for your audience.* It is your responsibility not only to provide evidence that supports the claims you make but also to explain why the evidence is significant. According to an old cliché, "the facts speak for themselves." In practice, however, this is rarely true. If it were true, there would be no need for attorneys, judges, juries, or scholars—and lists could be substituted for carefully written arguments. Facts, quotations, and other pieces of evidence can be presented and interpreted in different ways depending upon how a writer or speaker uses them and how well prepared an audience is to understand them. Although you should not feel compelled to explain the significance of every piece of data you cite, you should make an effort to explain any piece of evidence that is especially important or that your audience may not fully understand.

The advice offered here suggests that organizing an argument inductively gives you a great deal of flexibility. As always, the decisions you make will reflect your purpose and your sense of how best to address your audience.

Deductive Reasoning   Deductive reasoning begins with a generalization and works to a conclusion that follows from that generalization. In that respect it can be thought of as the opposite of inductive reasoning, which begins with specific observations and ends with a conclusion that goes beyond those observations. The generalization you start with in a deductively arranged argument is called a **premise** and is the foundation for your argument. As you saw in Chapter 4, it takes much careful thought to formulate a good premise. Nevertheless, because so many arguments employ this kind of logic, deductive reasoning can be a powerful way to construct an effective argument.

The process of reasoning deductively might be difficult to grasp in the abstract, but you can follow some general steps that will help you explore your topic and generate an outline for your argument. In effect, you work backward from the conclusion you wish to reach:

1. *Identify your conclusion.* Suppose that you have become concerned about the consequences of eating meat. Because of worries about your own health, you have reconsidered eating meat, and you have begun to adopt a plant-based, or vegetarian, diet. But in exploring a vegetarian diet, you have also learned that meat production has potentially harmful environmental consequences. In particular, you are concerned about the destruction of forests cut down to allow cattle to graze. You believe that if eating meat leads to such environmental damage, it should be stopped.

   Given how prevalent meat consumption is and its prominent place in the American diet, you can't reasonably argue for eating meat to be made illegal or restricted by law in some way. But you can argue that it should be discouraged—

perhaps in the same way that smoking is discouraged. Most important, you believe that people should at least eat much less meat than they currently do.

So your conclusion is clear: People should eat less meat. Now you begin to write down your outline in reverse:

3. Americans should not consume so much meat.

2. Consuming meat can be unhealthy, and meat production damages the environment.

2. *Examine your reasons carefully.* Before going any further, you realize that not all of your reasons for opposing meat consumption can be taken with equal degrees of seriousness. For one thing, diet can be a personal choice, and your concerns about your own health are not sufficient grounds to argue against other people eating meat. So you need to make sure that your point about the health risks of eating meat does not sound self-serving but has validity for others. Your own research has shown that eating meat involves a number of health risks. You also know that a vegetarian diet has health benefits. You will want to discuss these risks and benefits in a way that makes them relevant to people in general so that you are not simply discussing your own health choices.

Your greater concern is the possible environmental damage associated with meat production. Here, too, it might be difficult to convince people who enjoy eating meat that the loss of forests thousands of miles away from their backyard grill should concern them. So it will be important for you to establish not just that meat production leads to the loss of forest but also that there might also be other environmental consequences closer to home. For example, most livestock in the United States is fed grain, and the production of feed grain not only uses up vast amounts of farmland but also contributes to pollution through agricultural runoff. Furthermore, the raising of livestock generates pollution in the form of animal waste. There is, as well, the problem of the chemicals and drugs that are used on livestock, which you have heard can be risky for humans who eat meat. All of these reasons can be compelling to others who might enjoy eating meat but might be unaware of the problems that can be caused by meat production.

3. *Formulate your premise.* You should now be ready to formulate your premise. Your conclusion is that eating meat should be curtailed, and you will urge others to stop or reduce their meat consumption and adopt an alternative diet. Near the beginning of your argument, you need to establish the principle that supports this conclusion. In this case you believe that it is wrong for people to engage in a practice that is destructive of the environment, especially when there is an alternative to that practice. In effect, you are suggesting that if what we do has damaging consequences (in this case eating meat has negative consequences for the environment and our health), then it is unethical to continue doing it when we have other options. This is your main premise.

A METHOD FOR REASONING DEDUCTIVELY

Because it can be difficult to formulate a good premise, it is often useful to work backward when you are planning a deductive argument. If you know the conclusion you want to reach, write it down, and number it as statement 3. Now ask yourself why you believe statement 3. That question should prompt a number of reasons; group them together as statement 2. Now that you can see your conclusion, as well as some reasons that seem to justify it, ask yourself whether you've left anything out—something basic that you skipped over, assuming that everyone would already agree with it. When you can think back successfully to what this assumption is, knowing that it will vary from argument to argument, you have your premise, at least in rough form.

A premise can be a single sentence, a full paragraph, or more, depending on the length and complexity of the argument. The function of a premise is to establish a widely accepted value that even your opponents should be able to share. You would probably be wise, therefore, to make a fairly general statement early in your argument—something like this:

It is unethical to continue engaging in an activity that is harmful and environmentally destructive.

Such a statement needs to be developed, and you will do so not only by showing how destructive meat production and consumption can be but also by offering alternatives to eating meat. You will want to suggest that individual choices about things like diet can affect others. That makes those choices ethical ones. Now you have the foundation for a logical argument:

If engaging in a practice or activity is harmful to people and their environment, then it should be stopped. Eating meat is such an activity; therefore, we should avoid eating meat and instead adopt an alternative diet.

This example can help you see the utility of structuring an argument deductively. You can see, too, that generating an argument in this way can deepen your engagement with your topic and eventually lead to a more substantive and persuasive essay.

Using the Toulmin Model   Even when you are using a logical arrangement to organize your argument, you will rarely follow the rules of logic rigidly. Because most people use logic informally in arguments, the Toulmin model (see pages 93–97) can be extremely useful in helping you construct your argument. The Toulmin model focuses on the claim you want to make—that is, the conclusion you are trying to reach or the assertion you hope to prove. Your task, simply put, is to state your claim clearly and offer persuasive reasons (what Toulmin calls *data*) for that claim. The third element in the Toulmin system is the warrant, which is the assumption that connects the claim and the data. As noted in Chapter 4, the warrant is usually a fundamental value or belief that, ideally, is shared by writer and audience (like the premise in the preceding section on deductive reasoning).

This model dictates no specified pattern for organizing an argument, so the challenge is to determine how best to present your claim to your intended audience and then to offer adequate reasons for your claim. But the value of this model for constructing an argument lies in the way it requires you to articulate your claim precisely and to pay close attention to the adequacy of your reasons and your evidence, without having to follow the rigid rules of formal logic. In this way the Toulmin model can help you refine your claim and develop convincing support for it. This model also encourages you to think through the often unstated assumptions that lie behind your claim: the warrants. Identifying your warrant can lead to a more effective argument because it can help you see points of possible contention between you and your audience.

Imagine that you live in a small town where a businessperson wishes to build a large meat-processing facility. This person has recently applied to the town board for a permit to begin construction of the plant. As a resident who values the quiet lifestyle of your town, as well as its clean and safe environment, you worry about the social and environmental damage the plant might cause. So you decide to write to the town supervisor to express your concerns and urge him to reject the permit for the plant.

Using the Toulmin model for your letter, your first step would be to try to articulate your central claim clearly. You might state your claim as follows:

Claim: We should not allow a meat-processing facility to be built in our town.

Before moving to your reasons for your claim, you should consider carefully whether that statement accurately represents the position you want to take. Can you be more specific? Can you focus the claim even more narrowly? In thinking about these questions, you might amend your claim as follows:

Claim: Building a meat-packing facility would damage the quality of life and the environment of our town.

Notice that although this version of your claim is related to the first version, it is a bit narrower and more precise. It also points directly to the kinds of data or the reasons you can offer to support the claim. Being clear about your claim is crucial because your reasons must fit that claim closely to be persuasive. Now you can begin exploring your reasons.

At this point it is a good idea to brainstorm, listing the main reasons for your belief that the plant should not be built in your town. You have many reasons: the possible damage to local streams from the waste and runoff from the plant, the increased traffic to and from the plant, the odor, the negative impact of a large plant on the quality of life in a small town. You should examine these reasons and try to identify those that are most compelling. Now you have your claim and main reasons for it:

Claim: Building a meat-packing facility would damage the quality of life and the environment of our town.

Reasons: Meat-packing facilities can cause pollution, endanger the health of local residents, and increase truck traffic on local roads.

Before you begin to develop evidence to support these reasons for your claim, you should think about your warrant—the assumptions that lie behind the claim and connect your reason and claim. This is a crucial step in using the Toulmin model because it helps you identify the assumptions behind your claim or the principles on which you base your claim. In Toulmin's model, the warrant is what provides the basis for a claim. Without an acceptable warrant, the claim becomes weak or even invalid. In this case you might state your warrant as follows:

Claim: Warrant: We all have a right to live in clean, safe environments.

You can probably be confident that your audience—the town supervisor—would accept this warrant, so you probably don't need to defend it. However, you might decide to state it in your letter, and you might even defend it to drive it home. The point is that you have identified a basic value or belief that you assume others share and without which your claim has no foundation.

Now you can begin developing specific evidence to support your claim and your reasons. The preceding reasons suggest the kinds of evidence you might gather. For example, to support the assertion that meat-processing facilities damage the environment, you might find reports of increased pollution in streams near existing meat-packing plants. You can perhaps find similar reports about the effect of truck traffic around such plants.

Evidence to support the assertion that your town's lifestyle would be adversely affected might be trickier. First, you will want to establish the character of the town as it is. That might mean providing facts about the number of residences compared with businesses, the size and use of roads, and so on. The point is to identify specific and persuasive evidence that fits your reasons for your claim—and to gather evidence that will be acceptable and convincing to your audience.

Here's a letter by a student that takes up this issue. In this letter Kristen Brubaker is writing to the supervisor of her small town in rural Pennsylvania. She expresses concern about a resident's request to build a factory hog farm in the town.

Dear Mr. Smithson:

As township supervisor of Wayne Township, you have had a great impact on our community for the past several years. In the coming months, your service will be needed more than ever. Jack Connolly, a resident of our township, has put forth a plan to build a factory hog farm, called a CAFO. His proposed facility will house 5,600 breeding sows, 100,000 piglets, and will cover nearly five acres of buildings (Weist). I am aware that you support this project, but I think there are some points you may be overlooking. We need to work together to ensure that our basic rights as property owners and citizens are not infringed upon and to protect the quality of life in our community.

I know we share similar values when it comes to the protection of our environment. In fact, you are one of the people who helped to shape my view of the environment. When I was younger, I attended the Dauphin County Conservation Camp that you helped to sponsor. I remember several of our activities, including the stream improvement project we completed and the stocking of trout in Powells Creek. Because of these experiences, I was surprised to find out you did not strongly oppose this project. Were you aware that CAFOs have caused extensive damage to trout streams in many states? I hope we don't have to face the destruction of our creek and surrounding valley before we realize that we made a mistake.

Although the risks to our environment are numerous, the first problem most people associate with CAFOs is the smell. In Powells Valley, we have traditionally been an agricultural community, so we're not afraid of the natural, inevitable odor of farms. Although factory farmers argue that the odor of animal waste is simply part of living in a rural, agricultural area, the air pollution caused by CAFOs is often more than a minor inconvenience. Imagine being unable to hang your clothes out to dry because of a thick, permeating smell that saturates everything it touches. The smell is not harmless either. CAFOs produce dangerous levels of ammonia and methane, gases suspected of causing nausea, flu-like symptoms, and respiratory illness, especially in children or the elderly. These chemicals also return to the ground as rain, polluting our water (Satchell). Another potentially harmful gas produced is hydrogen sulfide. In as small a concentration as 10 parts per million, it causes eye irritation. At 50 parts per million, it causes vomiting, nausea, and diarrhea. At 500 parts per million, hydrogen sulfide causes rapid death (Weist).

Another problem with the proposed location of this facility is its close proximity to houses and the small size of the valley. More than 35 houses are located within a half-mile radius of the proposed operation. Our valley is only a mile wide, so there will be nowhere for the odor to go. It will sit in our valley on hot summer days, saturating the air and everything in it. If this facility must be built, why can't it go somewhere less densely populated or somewhere that would handle odors more effectively?

But the most frightening aspect of having a CAFO in our valley is the strong possibility that we would face severe water pollution. Because of the immense scale of CAFOs, they often produce much more manure than the surrounding land can handle effectively. In cases where overspreading occurs, excess nutrients can run into the streams, disrupting the ecological balance and killing fish. Powells Creek, like most small creeks, sits in a very delicate balance and a small increase of nutrients can seriously alter the habitat of the stream. Nutrients contribute to increased plant and algae life, which can clog waterways and rob them of oxygen. Excess nutrients can also seep into the ground water, creating a problem with illness-causing pathogens such as salmonella (Satchell).

Another cause of water pollution among CAFOs is the waste lagoons used to store manure. Because fields may be spread only certain times of the year, there is a need for immense storage facilities. Most farms use lagoons that can be several acres long, sometimes holding up to 25 million gallons of waste. In North Carolina, waste lagoons are being blamed for the catastrophic fish kills and pollution of the coastal waters that took place in 1996 (Satchell). In the recent flooding in North Carolina due to Hurricane Floyd, over 50 lagoons overflowed, and one burst. Although it is not yet known how these recent spills will affect the environment, more fish kills and contaminated drinking water supplies are virtually guaranteed (Wright).

There are many other problems Powells Valley could face as a result of this facility. The operation that Mr. Connolly is proposing would produce 12 million gallons of waste per year. This waste is going to be spread throughout three townships in our valley. This is a lot of waste for one small stream, yet this is the best-case scenario. Can you imagine what would happen in the case of a leak or spill? Powells Creek is located about 350 feet downhill from these proposed facilities. In the case of an overflow, flood, or leak, the waste would go directly into the creek. To make matters worse, this operation is going to be located in an area that has frequent problems with flooding. In 1996, a small flood destroyed the bridge that crosses Powells Creek just below the proposed operation. If a spill or leak were to occur, the creek's aquatic life would be destroyed. If this facility is approved, we may not have to worry about stocking Powells Creek anymore.

The local increase in traffic is another issue that must be addressed. If this facility goes into operation, there would be approximately 1,750 truck trips per year delivering feed and supplies and transporting the 100,000 piglets to finishing operations. In addition to this, there will be an estimated 3,500 trailer truck trips needed to transport the 12 million gallons of waste (Weist). The roads in our area are not equipped for this kind of traffic. It would put a much greater burden on Wayne Township for the upkeep of its roads. The Carsonville Fire Company, which would be charged with the responsibility of handling any accidents, is dangerously underequipped to handle a large spill. Additionally, the roads entering the area of the proposed operation are small, curvy, and unsafe for large trucks. There are school busses from two school districts traveling these roads. The risk of having a serious accident is simply too high to justify this operation.

One of the key factors that allows these problems to exist largely unchallenged is the lack of regulation for these factory farms. If someone were to build a factory producing the same amount of contaminating waste, they would face numerous regulations. Human waste treatment plants also follow strict environmental controls that ensure that they do not pollute. Because CAFOs are technically agriculture, and not industry, they face virtually no regulations. They are also protected by the "Right to Farm Act," which was originally passed to protect family farms from harassment and lawsuits by developers. This law is making us defenseless because it will back any lawsuit we could make against the owner of the CAFO. Although nutrient management plans are required for a large operation, such a requirement is not enough protection.

As expected, Jack Connolly's plans have not been stifled by the protests of over 100 citizens. His nutrient management plan was recently rejected by the Dauphin County Conservation District, but he continues to build. He realizes that although many people in the community are afraid of his plans, just as many are unwilling to interfere with his right to do what he wants with his property. We don't like being told what we can and cannot do with our land, and when we give up those rights, we feel it starts a dangerous trend. At the same time, we must think of the property rights of those who have inhabited this valley their whole lives. Operations like this can seriously lower property values. People who can't stand the smell would have two choices. They could sell their homes, their sole investments, for a fraction of their worth or live with the smell.

There are some possible benefits to having this operation in our valley. For one, the factory is expected to create between 20 and 30 local jobs. We don't have a problem with unemployment in our valley, though, so it's likely that these jobs will be filled with outsiders. Also, they aren't going to be the high-quality jobs that most of us would want. Another possible benefit, one I'm sure you're aware of, is the possibility of cheap fertilizer. I noticed on the nutrient plan that you were listed among the recipients. Are you aware that if there is an accident with the waste on your land, you are responsible, not Mr. Connolly? If you still decide that this plan is in the best interests of everyone it will affect, do some research of your own to ensure you're not part of the problem by accepting more manure than your land can safely handle. Also, make sure Mr. Connolly hasn't increased your projected amount without your knowledge in order to satisfy his nutrient management plan.

If you agree that his CAFO is not good for our community, there are steps you should take to postpone, or even reject, this proposal. First, you, as township supervisor, can reject his building permits until he gets the necessary approval from the county and state. These agencies will be more likely to approve his plan if he already has a multi-million dollar complex built to house it. You could also pass ordinances to prevent the growth of this "farm." A common scenario is that after the nearby property values are sufficiently lowered due to the offensive smell, a factory farm owner will buy the surrounding land and build more operations. It only makes sense when you consider that the operation Mr. Connolly has proposed is a breeding facility. This means that the piglets will need to be transported to a finishing facility. Wouldn't it be cheaper and more cost effective to build a near-by facility that could house the hogs as they were prepared for slaughter? After that, why not just build a slaughtering facility as well? It's happened before, and it could happen in our valley. Although people tend to be against zoning in rural communities such as ours, sometimes it is imperative to prevent negative changes.

Please think about the possible effects this will have on our valley. As a life-long resident, you must value its beauty. I also assume that you value the right of every person in this community to live in a safe and clean environment.

Imagine a day when you couldn't sit on your porch to eat breakfast because of the overwhelming odor that permeates everything it touches. Imagine your grandchildren getting ill because of water-borne bacteria caused by this CAFO. Imagine the day when you can no longer fish in the creek you helped improve. This day could be upon us if we don't take action now. You're a vital part of this equation, and I trust that we can count on you to help us maintain the land that raised us.

Sincerely,

Kristen Brubaker

REFERENCES

Cauchon, Dennis. "N.C. Farmers, Scientists Begin Taking The Toll." *USA Today* 27 Sept. 1999: 6A.

"Hog Factories vs. Family Farms and Rural Communities." Powells Valley Conservation Association. 8 Oct. 1999. Pennsylvania Department of Environmental Protection. 15 Oct. 1999 <http://www.dep.state.pa.us.>

Satchell, Michael. "Hog Heaven—and Hell." *U. S. News and World Report* 22 Jan. 1996: 57.

Weist, Kurt. "Petition to Intervene of the Powells Valley Conservation Association, Inc." Powells Valley Conservation Association, Inc. 1999.

Wright, Andrew G. "A Foul Mess." *Engineering News Record* 4 Oct. 1999: 26.

Notice that Kristen's claim is implicit in her first paragraph, in which she indicates concern about the hog farm, but she doesn't explicitly state that the permit should be denied until the second-to-last paragraph. Notice, too, that she states her warrant in her second paragraph and then reinforces it in her final paragraph. The Toulmin model does not require that the essay be structured in this way. Kristen might just as easily have begun by stating her claim explicitly and proceeded from there; similarly, she might have left her warrant unstated or waited until the final paragraph to state it. Those choices are up to the writer. But using the Toulmin model can help identify these elements so that you can work with them in constructing an argument.

Also note that Kristen has chosen to document her evidence with a list of references, an unusual step in a letter. However, that decision can make her letter more persuasive, because it indicates to the town supervisor not only that Kristen has taken the time to research this issue thoroughly but also that her facts and figures have been taken from reputable sources.

In considering these different models for arranging an argument, you should understand that they are not mutually exclusive. In a classically arranged argument, for example, the statement of background can be done in the kind of nonjudgmental language emphasized in Rogerian argument. Similarly, the summary of opposing views in a

Rogerian argument requires the kind of understanding that a writer following a classical arrangement would need to have before engaging in refutation. In both cases, the writers need to be well informed and fair-minded. And both classical arrangement and Rogerian argument encourage the use of concessions. The difference between the two is best understood in terms of purpose. Although any argument is designed to be persuasive, the purpose of that persuasion varies from one situation to another (see Chapter 1). You might be writing to assert a position or to inquire into a complex issue. Your plan should fit your purpose.

It is also worth remembering that contemporary arguments rarely follow rigid guidelines, except in certain academic courses or in specialized documents, such as legal briefs, or situations like formal debates. For that reason many teachers today advocate the Toulmin model, emphasizing its flexibility in adapting an argument to a specific situation. Moreover, different media represent different opportunities and challenges for how to present an argument (see Chapter 3). All of this means that you have many options for structuring your argument. The more familiar you are with the principles of organization in argumentation, the more likely it is that you will be able to structure your argument effectively.

Supporting Claims and Presenting Evidence

The arguments by Tyler Sunderman, Rachel Guetter, and Kristen Brubaker highlight the importance of presenting good evidence to support your argument. Without compelling evidence even the most carefully articulated claim won't be persuasive. But as noted in Chapter 4 (pages 70–108), what counts as good evidence will vary from one context to another. An important part of generating evidence for your argument is considering your audience and its expectations for evidence, as well as the rhetorical situation in which you are making your argument.

In Kristen Brubaker's case the audience is specific: her town supervisor. And she offers evidence that directly addresses a number of issues regarding quality of life that would concern a person in his position. Indeed, one of the strengths of Kristen's argument is that her evidence fits her audience. Another strength is the amount of evidence she provides. She includes statistics and other facts to support her assertions about pollution, road use, odor, and health problems. She also uses values as evidence, appealing to the supervisor's sense of the importance of private property and community well-being (see pages 142–145). Moreover, the amount of evidence suggests that Kristen has done her homework. By presenting so much appropriate evidence so carefully, she helps establish her credibility. And although she is writing specifically to one person, Kristen's evidence would probably resonate with a broader audience—say, readers of the local newspaper—if Kristen were addressing such an audience. Implicitly addressing a broader audience might strengthen her argument as well, because the supervisor will probably be sensitive to the views of other people in the community.

Your audience can affect not just the kind of evidence you use but also whether you need evidence for a particular point. For example, if you are confident that your readers will accept your warrant, then you might decide that you don't need to support it. If it is likely that your audience will disagree with your warrant, then you will need evidence to back it up. Imagine, for instance, if Kristen were writing for a much broader audience—say she was making an argument against CAFOs for a newspaper like *USA Today.* Some of her readers might be willing to give up some of the characteristics of a small town for greater economic development. For such readers Kristen might want to defend her warrant about a clean environment, perhaps showing that economic development doesn't have to mean damaging the environment. The point is that your sense of audience and its expectations will affect what you decide to present as evidence and even *whether* some kinds of evidence should be included in your essay.

As you construct your argument and develop your supporting evidence, consider the following questions:

- What specific claims and/or warrants am I making that will need supporting evidence?
- What kinds of evidence are available for those claims or warrants?
- Where can I find such evidence?
- What expectations will my audience have for the evidence I present?
- Have I included sufficient evidence for my audience?
- Does the kind of evidence I have included (factual, firsthand experience, philosophical reasoning, expert testimony) make sense for the claims I am making?

Using Language Effectively

In his famous *Rhetoric,* Aristotle wrote that "the way in which a thing is said affects its intelligibility." The way in which something is stated also affects its impact and, potentially, its persuasive force. Style matters. It matters because it is sometimes a reflection of the fact that you have followed the appropriate conventions for a particular argument—for example, you have used the right legal terminology in a letter to your insurance company about a pending lawsuit. And it matters because the way an idea or opinion is presented can profoundly affect how an audience reacts to it. In constructing an effective argument, you should attend to how you employ the power of language—how you use diction, sentence structure, tone, rhythm, and figures of speech. Usually, these are matters you can focus on once you have defined your topic, developed your claims and supporting evidence, and arranged your argument appropriately. But how you use language can be an important consideration in constructing an argument, even from the beginning.

As always, audience is a primary consideration as you decide upon an appropriate style for your argument. Different audiences will have different expectations for what is acceptable—and persuasive—when it comes to your use of language in an argument. You will want to use more formal language in a cover letter to a potential employer (which is a common kind of argument) than you might in a letter to the editor of your school's newspaper. Similarly, an essay advocating a specific research method in a biology class will require a different kind of language than an argument in favor of decriminalizing marijuana laws for the campus newsletter of a student advocacy organization. The specific medium in which you are presenting your argument will also influence your decisions about language. *Wired* magazine publishes writing that is noticeably different in style and tone from those of the essays that appear in public affairs magazines such as *Commentary.*

The audiences for each magazine are different, but so is each magazine's sense of purpose. *Wired* sees itself as techy, edgy, and hip, and the language its writers use reflects that sense of itself. By contrast, *Commentary* is a more erudite, staid publication, and the writing style reflects its seriousness. As you work through your argument, think carefully about what kind of language will be most effective for the specific audience, rhetorical situation, and medium you are encountering.

Even within a specific rhetorical situation you have a great deal of latitude in deciding on the style and tone you will adopt for your argument. Consider the following excerpts from an essay that appeared on *Commondreams.org,* a website that publishes essays and news with alternative views about important social and political issues. In the essay from which the following excerpts were taken, the writer, John Borowski, a science teacher from Oregon, harshly criticizes efforts by interest groups to ban school science books that present an environmentalist perspective, and he argues for parents and others to oppose such efforts:

> Remember this phrase: "Texas is clearly one of the most dominant states in setting textbook adoption standards," according to Stephen Driesler, executive director of the American Association of Publisher's school division. And this November the Texas school board inflamed by the anti-environmental science rhetoric by the likes of Texas Citizens for a Sound Economy and Texas Public Policy Foundation (TPPF) may bring Ray Bradbury's "Fahrenheit 451" to life. Recall that "Fahrenheit 451" (the temperature at which paper bursts into flames) depicts a society where independent thought is discouraged, wall-to-wall television and drugs sedate a numb population and "firemen" burn books.
>
> This past fall "book nazis" at the TPPF, led by Republican Senator Phil Gramm's wife (Wendy) and Peggy Venable, director of the 48,000 member Texas Citizens for a Sound Economy, put several environmental textbooks in their "crosshairs." *Environmental Science: Toward a Sustainable Future* published by Massachusetts-based publisher Jones and Bartlett was canned due to political "incorrectness."
>
> We as parents, defenders of the constitution and the vigilant flame-keepers of the light of democracy must rise to meet the challenge.

There is no doubt about how Borowski feels about groups like TPPF. Nor is there any doubt about his goal: to exhort people who share his concerns to action against such efforts to ban books from schools. You might find Borowski's language inflammatory. There is a good chance that he intended it to be so. He certainly knew that the audience for *Commondreams.org* would not likely include many people from organizations such as TPPF. Rather, it would be composed mostly of people who share his political perspective and are likely to be as appalled as he is about these efforts to ban textbooks. Nevertheless, you can ask how those sympathetic readers might react to the strong and critical language Borowski employs. Will such language be more likely to convince those readers that Borowski is right than a more measured style and a less derogatory tone might be? How does it affect his credibility with his readers? Sometimes, provocative language may be warranted. Is this one of those times?

Posing such questions about your own use of language in constructing your argument can lead to a more effective argument. The rhetorical situation and the issue being addressed will help determine your approach to using language from the outset. In this case Borowski might have been angry and concerned enough to have decided, even before he began writing his essay, to adopt a harsh and sarcastic tone. Sometimes, however, you might not have a clear sense of the most appropriate tone or style until after you have completed a draft. And often you will have much less flexibility in adopting a tone or style. (A science report or legal brief, for example, has strict conventions for such matters.) And bear in mind that at times the choice of a single word can make a great difference in the effect a statement will have on an audience. For example, consider how different this sentence of Borowski's might be if the verb *canned* were replaced by *removed:*

> *Environmental Science: Toward a Sustainable Future* published by Massachusetts-based publisher Jones and Bartlett was canned due to political "incorrectness."

The passage from Borowski's essay illustrates another set of concerns about language in argument: the use of figurative language. At one point Borowski writes that "the vigilant flame-keepers of the light of democracy must rise to meet the challenge." Here he invokes the common metaphors of light and dark to suggest good opposed to evil, right against wrong. Those who share his concerns are "flame-keepers of the light of democracy," a figurative phrase clearly intended not only to address his audience in a positive way but also to stir them to action. Borowski's essay is a rather extreme example of the use of figurative language, and it suggests the power such uses of language can have in efforts to move an audience. But figurative language can also have a more subtle but no less important impact in helping to clarify an important point or emphasizing an idea. Here, for example, is *USA Today* sports columnist Mike Lopresti in an essay about the significance of a loss by an American basketball team to Yugoslavia in the 2002 World Championships:

> But the big issue is the big picture. The years, the Olympiads, and the World Championships ahead. Because American basketball is like an empty soda cup on the field house floor.

Lopresti's use of a simile—in which he compares the international status of American basketball to an empty soda cup—vividly drives home his point with an appropriate image that readers who follow sports will quickly recognize. (Notice, too, the informal style of his writing, which is typical of many sports columnists.)

When deciding how to use language effectively, writers may also draw upon the conventions of argument and use them dramatically. Consider the following excerpt from a review of *The Truth about Hillary: What She Knew, When She Knew It, and How Far She'll Go to Become President,* a book by Edward Klein published in 2005. As you read, note how the first four sentences each begin with "Granted"—an expression that writers frequently use when conceding a point and an illustration, in this case, of anaphora (which means using the same word or phrase at the beginning of a series of sentences or clauses to achieve emphasis):

FIGURATIVE LANGUAGE

For an example of the use of metaphor in an argument, see Gregory Cizek's essay, "Unintended Consequences of High Stakes Testing," on pages 503–512. Cizek uses religion as a metaphor for the debates about standardized tests.

> Granted, it is a very bad book. Granted, it is a lazy, cut-and-paste recycling of other people's work. Granted, it relies too much on nasty personal comments about Senator Clinton provided by anonymous sources. Granted, it sleazily intimates that Hillary Clinton is a lying, scheming, smelly, left-leaning lesbian and a non-maternal parent who consorts with lawyers who defend mobbed-up unions and bears a striking character resemblance to both Richard Nixon and Madonna, and who tacitly approved of her husband's rape of a young woman at a time when Mrs. Clinton may or may not have been bathing, washing her hair or shaving her underarms, while hanging out with short-haired women from the sapphic charnel house

Wellesley College. But to suggest, as the talented John Podhoretz did in The New York Post, that this is "one of the most sordid volumes I have ever waded through" is to raise serious questions about Podhoretz's sordid wading experiences.

As an expert on sordid non-fiction, I would not put "The Truth About Hillary" anywhere near the top of my list; it pales by comparison with Geraldo Rivera's sublimely vile autobiography, "Exposing Myself," and seems demure, nuanced and levelheaded by comparison with masterpieces of partisan venom like the 60's cold-war classic "None Dare Call It Treason."

No, I am not suggesting that Edward Klein is a fair, balanced, persuasive, scrupulously honest reporter or a gifted writer. Resorting to chilling Rip Van Winklisms like "Bill and Hillary often grooved the night away at Cozy Beach, spinning the latest Jefferson Airplane platters," Klein sometimes sounds like a cryogenically preserved Maynard G. Krebs. Like, dig: the cat is far out.

What I am saying is that if Klein purposely set out to write the sleaziest, most derivative, most despicable political biography ever, he has failed both himself and his readers miserably. "The Truth About Hillary" is only about the 16th sleaziest book I have ever read. Though, in fairness to the author, reading creepy, cut-and-paste books is my hobby.

In an argument of your own, you are unlikely to be able to present yourself as "an expert in sordid nonfiction"—something this reviewer—Joe Queenan, does in the *New York Times Book Review* to establish just how bad he thinks Klein's book is. Queenan is establishing ethos (see pages 72–80) by saying, in effect, "I have the credentials to say this is a sordid book because I have read lots of such books." Queenan is clearly having fun with language, coining such phrases as "Rip Van Winklisms" (an allusion to a character in a nineteenth-century story who falls asleep for twenty years and cannot adjust to the change that he sees when he wakes up) and "a cryogenically preserved Maynard G. Krebs" (an allusion to a television character on a 1960s situation comedy who was the cool, hippy-like buddy of a super-straight guy named Dobbie Gillis). The extent to which you can experiment with language will depend on your rhetorical situation (see pages 18–22). But even if you need to sound "nuanced and levelheaded," you can benefit from the strategy Queenan uses in the last two paragraphs reprinted here: clarifying your argument by contrasting what you are saying with what you are not saying. When you write something like "I am not saying *x*; I am saying *y*," you are not only clarifying your position. You are also defining the boundaries that frame your argument. Establishing these boundaries can be especially useful when you expect others to respond to what you have composed, because you are avoiding the potential for unnecessary conflict.

Writers can also make references to myths, literature, or legends that will have significance for readers. Henry David Thoreau, for example, in criticizing what he believed was the wasteful and wasting lifestyle of his fellow citizens, wrote,

> The twelve labors of Hercules were trifling in comparison to those which my neighbors have undertaken.

The reference to the well-known Greek myth would have driven home his point to his readers. And his use of farm labor as metaphor for life in the following sentence not only emphasized his primary claim but did so elegantly:

> The better part of the man is soon ploughed into soil for compost.

As these examples show, a few carefully chosen words can do a great deal of work as you build your argument.

When you are constructing your own argument, pay close to attention to your tone and style. Asking yourself the following questions can help you determine whether your style and tone are appropriate for your purpose, your audience, and the situation about which you are arguing:

- Is my overall tone likely to offend my intended audience? If so, what specifically about my tone might be offensive to my audience? How can I revise to avoid that problem?
- Have I used appropriate words and phrases? Will my audience understand the key terms I have used? Will my audience expect me to use any special language that I have not used?
- Can I use figurative language to enhance my argument? In what way can I do so?

6

Doing Research

W riting effective arguments requires being able to locate and draw on information that will help you develop and support your ideas. Often, you will discover that you must look beyond yourself to gather the necessary information—you must engage in research.

You might think of research as what you do when you are assigned long papers due at the end of a semester, but there are many other occasions when you engage in research. Any time you look for information before making a decision, you are doing research. If you are trying to decide whether to buy a particular car, for example, you might talk to people who already own the same model, read magazine articles about the car, search the Internet for other drivers' opinions about the car, and take a dealer's vehicle for a test drive. In other words, you interview people with expertise on your topic, you conduct a periodical search, you search electronic resources, and you undertake trial testing. Academic research requires all of these activities and more, although the degree to which you need to pursue a specific research activity is likely to vary as you move from one project to another. Academic research also requires that you follow specific conventions by using sources responsibly and documenting where your information comes from. But the prospect of doing research shouldn't be intimidating. The key to successful research is simple: Be curious enough about your topic to look in different places until you find what you need.

Traditionally, academic researchers distinguish between primary and secondary research:

1. **Primary research** requires firsthand experimentation or analysis. This is the sort of research that is done in laboratories, in field locations, or in libraries or archives that house original manuscripts. If you interview someone, design and distribute a survey, conduct an experiment, or analyze data that have not been previously published, you are conducting primary research.

2. **Secondary research** involves investigating what other people have already published on a given subject—in other words, finding information about your topic in books, magazine or journal articles, websites, and similar sources. College students are usually expected to be proficient at secondary research.

Writing arguments often requires secondary research, and to do such research efficiently, you must know how to develop a search strategy. Different projects will require different strategies. The strategy outlined in this part of the book assumes that you will be writing arguments using material from Part III of *The Informed Argument* and that you will supplement this material with additional information you find elsewhere. As your research needs change from one assignment to another, you will probably use different sources. But the illustrations in this chapter will provide you with sufficient information to help you proceed efficiently when you decide to move beyond the articles gathered in Part III of this book.

Reading Critically

Secondary research involves reading, but it requires a kind of reading that might differ from the way you read the morning paper or an article about your favorite musician on a website. The kind of critical reading required for good research is active and engaged; it involves careful thinking about what you are reading. Critical reading begins with understanding the key points of a text and determining whether there are any points that you do not understand. If there are such points do you not understand them because the material is complex or because the author has failed to communicate effectively? Critical reading thus involves evaluating what you read. This means not only being able to determine quality in terms of ethos and logos (see pages 72–86) and style (see pages 126–146) but also considering whether a source raises any unanswered questions. As a student, you will sometimes be confronted with more information than you can digest with ease. You will also find that different writers might make contradictory statements. Being able to recognize what material deserves the closest reading and what sources are the most reliable is essential to coping successfully with the many academic demands made on your time. By learning to read critically, you will acquire a skill that will help you in any college course. And you will be developing an ability that will enable you to write more effective arguments.

You can learn to read critically by engaging in four related activities:

- Previewing
- Annotating
- Summarizing
- Synthesizing

Previewing

Even before you begin to read, you can take steps to help you better understand the reading you are about to undertake and to place it in rhetorical context (see pages 16–31). A quick preview or survey of a written text should give you an idea of how long it will take to read, what the reading will probably reveal, and how useful the reading is likely to be. When you glance through a newspaper to identify which stories you want to read and which you want to skip, you are practicing a simple type of preview, one often guided primarily by your level of interest in various issues. But when previewing reading material in college, it is usually wise to ask yourself some questions that go beyond whether you happen to find a topic appealing:

- *How long is this work?* By checking the length of a work before you begin to read, you can estimate how much reading time the material will demand, based on the speed and ease with which you normally read. The length might also be a clue in determining how useful a text may be. Although quantity is no sure guide to quality, a long work might contain more information that is useful for your topic than a short work. And when doing research, you can usually learn the length of a work before you even hold it in your hand. This information is included in periodical indexes, book catalogs, and many websites.
- *What can I learn from the title?* Although some titles are too general to convey adequately the content of an article or book, a title often reveals an author's focus. An article called "Drugs and the Modern Athlete" will differ in focus from one called "Drug Testing and Corporate Responsibility." Moreover, a title can often indicate the author's point of view. For example, an essay titled "Keep the Borders Open" tells you quite clearly what the author's position on immigration will be. Be aware, however, that titles can sometimes be misleading.
- *Do I know anything about the author?* Recognizing the names of established authorities in a field becomes easier as you do more reading, but many written sources offer information that can help you estimate an author's credibility even when that author is unfamiliar to you. A journal article might identify the author at the beginning or the end of the piece or on a separate page (often called "Notes on Contributors" and listed in the table of contents). A biographical sketch of the author can usually be found on a book jacket, and a list of his or her other published works sometimes appears at the front or the back of the book. Anthologies often include introductory headnotes describing the various writers whose work has been selected. You can also learn more about an author's credibility by using a search engine such as Google to retrieve information from the World Wide Web.

■ *What do I know about the publisher?* An important work can be published by an obscure publisher, and a small magazine might be the first to publish an author who is destined to win a Pulitzer Prize. The publisher's reputation is not an automatic guide to the reliability of a source, but there are a few factors that can help you determine whether a source is likely to be worthwhile. University presses tend to expect a high degree of scholarship, and academic journals usually publish articles only after they have been examined by two or three other experts in that field. If you read widely in periodicals, you will eventually find that some magazines and newspapers consistently reflect political positions that might be characterized as either liberal or conservative. Once you get a sense of the general orientation of such publications, you can usually anticipate what kind of stand will be taken by authors whose articles appear in one of these periodicals. This will help you be sensitive to any bias that the author might hold on the topic at hand. Again, remember that you are only making a preliminary estimate when previewing. The best way to judge a work is to read it carefully.

■ *Is there anything else I can discover by skimming through the material?* A quick examination of the text can identify a number of other features that can help you orient yourself to what you are about to read:

- *Average paragraph length.* Long paragraphs might indicate a densely written text that you will need to read slowly.

- *Special features.* Tables, figures, or illustrations can provide visual aids for the content.

- *Subtitles.* Subtitles can provide you with a rough outline of the work and the main topics it addresses.

- *Abstracts.* In some cases, a writer will provide you with a summary. Articles from scholarly journals are often preceded by an **abstract** (or summary) that can help you understand the article and determine whether it will be useful to you. Many magazines include brief summaries with each article, usually at the beginning of the text. Often, checking the first few and last few paragraphs can give you a good sense of what the article is about and the stance the writer has taken on the topic.

- *Bibliography.* Check to see whether the work includes a reference list. Scanning a bibliography, noting both how current the research seems and how extensive it is, can help you appraise a writer's scholarship and alert you to other sources that you may want to read on your own.

Annotating

Marking a text with notes, or **annotating** it, can be a great help when you are trying to understand your reading. Annotation can also help you discover points that you might want to question when you evaluate this work. One of the advantages of owning a book or having your own photocopy of an excerpt from a book or magazine is that you can mark it as much as you wish. When you are annotating a text that is important to you,

you will usually benefit from reading that text more than once and adding new annotations with each reading.

When you are able to spend more time with a text and want to be sure that you understand not only its content but also its strengths and weaknesses, then additional annotations are in order:

- Use the margins to define new words and identify unfamiliar allusions.
- Write comments that will remind you of what is discussed in various paragraphs.
- Jot down questions that you might subsequently raise in class or explore in a paper.
- Make cross-references to remind yourself of how various components of the work fit together and identify apparent contradictions within the work.
- Write your own response to an important point in the text before you lose the thought. An annotation of this sort can be useful when you are reviewing material before an exam, and it might be the seed from which a paper will later grow.

HIGHLIGHTING VERSUS SIMPLE ANNOTATING

Many students use colored highlighter pens to mark passages that seem important to their research. Highlighting makes these passages easy to find if you need to return to them for specific information or quotations. But highlighters can be hard to write with. So consider reading with a pen or pencil, too. As you read, you can make notes or marks in the margins:

- A check when a line seems important
- An exclamation point when you find surprising information or an unusually bold claim
- A question mark when you have trouble understanding a particular passage or find yourself disagreeing with what it says

This simple form of annotation can be done easily, and if you use a pencil, you will be able to erase any marks that you later find distracting.

Figure 6-1 shows an annotated excerpt from the Declaration of Independence. As you examine it, remember that different readers annotate a text in different ways. Some annotations are more thorough and reflective than others, but there are no "correct" responses against which your own annotations must be measured. You might notice different aspects of a text each time you reread it, so your annotations are likely to accumulate in layers.

Summarizing

On many occasions, you will be required to summarize what others have said or written— or even what you have said or written. This skill is especially important in argumentation. You will have to be able to summarize the main arguments of your opponents if you want to write a convincing argument of your own. And researched papers will become long, obscure, and unwieldy if you lack the ability to summarize your reading.

There is no clear rule to determine which passages are more significant than others. The first sentence of a paragraph might be important if it introduces a new idea, but sometimes it is simply a transitional sentence, linking the new paragraph with whatever has preceded it. Often, a paragraph will have a **topic sentence,** which may appear anywhere in the paragraph, that states the key idea or point of the paragraph.

When writing a summary, be prepared to **paraphrase**—to restate in your own words something you've read or heard. There are many reasons for paraphrasing, and you've probably been practicing this skill for a long time—for example, paraphrasing the words of others to soften an unpleasant fact. But in writing a summary, you should usually paraphrase

FIGURE 6-1

An Annotated Text

1776 | When in the Course of human events, it becomes nec- *such as*
essary for one people to dissolve the political bands *Americans*
Why should which have connected them with another, and to as- *such as*
nations have sume among the powers of the earth, the separate and *English*
"equal equal station to which the Laws of Nature and of Na- *As "Nature's*
Station" ture's God entitle them, a decent respect to the opin- *God" different*
when some ions of mankind requires that they should declare the *from*
are more causes which impel them to the separation. *"God"?*
powerful
than others?
                  We hold these truths to be self-evident, that all *Why "self-*
Does this men are created equal, that they are endowed by their *evident"?*
include Creator with certain unalienable Rights, that among *Couldn't he*
women ??? these are Life, Liberty and the pursuit of Happiness. *prove them?*
                  That to secure these rights, Governments are insti- *Permanent,*
If the tuted among Men, deriving their just powers from the *"not to be*
rights to consent of the governed. That whenever any Form of *separated"*
life & Government becomes destructive of these ends it is
liberty are the Right of the People to alter or to abolish it, and to *So the*
"unalienable" institute new Government, laying its foundation on *Civil War*
how come such principles and organizing its powers in such *was ok?*
we have form, as to them shall seem most likely to effect their
capital Safety and Happiness. Prudence, indeed, will dictate
punishment that Governments long established should not be
and prisons? changed for light and transient causes; and accordingly
                  all experience has shewn, that mankind are more dis-
                  posed to suffer, while evils are sufferable, than to right
                  themselves by abolishing the forms to which they are
                  accustomed. But when a long train of abuses and
wrongful usurpations, pursuing invariably the same Object
seizure evinces a design to reduce them under absolute *What's the*
                  Despotism, it is their right, it is their duty, to throw *difference*
                  off such Government, and to provide new Guards for *between a*
                  their future security. Such has been the patient suffer- *"right" and*
                  ance of these Colonies; and such is now the necessity *a "duty"?*
                  which constrains them to alter their former Systems of
                  Government. The history of the present King of Great *George III*
                  Britain is a history of repeated injuries and usurpa- *(ruled from*
                  tions, all having in direct object the establishment of *1760 to 1820)*
                  an absolute Tyranny over these States. To prove this,
impartial let Facts be submitted to a candid world.

                  Why is the capitalization so weird?

to make complex ideas more easily understandable. In addition, you may also find occasions when paraphrasing can help you to avoid making what your audience could consider a sudden shift in tone.

Summarizing requires good editorial judgment. A writer has to be able to distinguish what is essential from what is not. If the material being summarized has a particular bias, a good summary should indicate that the bias is part of the work in question. *But writers should not interject their own opinions into a summary of someone else's work.* The tone of a summary should be neutral. You might choose to summarize someone's work so that you can criticize it later, but do not confuse summary with criticism. When summarizing, you are taking the role of helping other writers speak for themselves. Don't let your own ideas get in the way.

Summaries vary in length, depending on the length and complexity of the original material and on how much time or space is available for summarizing it. When summary is being used as a preliminary to some other type of work, such as argument or analysis, it is especially important to be concise. For example, if you are summarizing an argument before offering a counterargument of your own, you may be limited to a single paragraph. The general rule to follow is this: Try to do justice to whatever you are summarizing in as few words as possible, and make sure that you have a legitimate reason for writing any summary that goes on for more than a page or two.

Experienced writers know that summary is a skill worth practicing. If you find summary difficult, try the method described in the sidebar on page 160.

SUMMARY VERSUS PARAPHRASE

The distinction between summary and paraphrase can be subtle and sometimes confusing, but it is important to understand. A summary is a brief statement, usually no more than a paragraph or two, summing up the main points or ideas of a text. A summary may include direct quotations from the original text, and it will often include paraphrase.

A paraphrase, by contrast, is a restatement—a rephrasing—in your own words of something you've read. A paraphrase can be as long as the original material; under some circumstances it can even be longer.

A paraphrase of a text is not a summary of it. In a paraphrase you restate a specific quotation or passage from a book or article in your own words; you don't necessarily sum up the entire book or article, as you would in a summary.

Summary is important in research in part because it enables you to make the ideas in a long work manageable and accessible in your own essay. Paraphrase is important because it helps you understand what you have read and avoid plagiarizing (see pages 163–165).

Synthesizing

Synthesizing ideas from two or more sources is an essential skill in constructing effective arguments. Synthesis requires identifying related material in two or more works and tying them together smoothly. Synthesis is often an extension of summary because writers may need to summarize various sources before they can relate these sources to one another. However, synthesis does not necessarily require you to cover *all* the major points of the individual sources. You might go through an entire article or book and identify only one point that relates to another work you have read. And the relationships involved in your synthesis may be of various kinds. For example, two authors might have made the same claim, or one might provide specific information that supports a generalization made by the other. On the other hand, one author might provide information that makes another author's generalization seem inadequate or even wrong.

When reading material that you need to synthesize, ask yourself, "How does this material relate to whatever else I have already read on this topic?" If you are unable to answer this question, consider a few more specific questions:

For a good example of how summary can be used effectively in an argument, see "America: Idea or Nation?" by Wilfred M. McClay (pages 573–581). McClay's summary of *Making Patriots*, by Walter Berns, is a key component of his argument.

- Does the second of two works offer support for the first, or does it reflect an entirely different thesis?
- If the two sources share a similar position, do they arrive at a similar conclusion by different means or do they overlap at any points?
- Would it be easier to compare the two works or to contrast them?

This process of identifying similarities and differences is essentially what synthesis is all about.

When you have determined the points that link your various sources to one another, you are ready to write a synthesis. One challenge in writing a synthesis is organizing it. For example, suppose you have read four articles on the subject of AIDS written, respectively, by a scientist, a clergyman, a gay activist, and a government official. You were struck by how differently these four writers responded to the AIDS epidemic. Although they all agreed that AIDS is a serious problem, each writer advanced a different proposal for fighting the disease. Your synthesis might begin with an introductory paragraph that includes a thesis statement such as "Although there is widespread agreement that AIDS is a serious problem, there is no consensus about how this problem can be solved." Each of the next four paragraphs could then be devoted to a brief summary of one of the different points of view. A final paragraph might emphasize the relationship that exists among the several sources, either by reviewing the major points of disagreement among them or by empha-

A METHOD FOR SUMMARIZING

A summary should be clear, concise, and easy to read. There is no right way to summarize a text, but here is a general method for summarizing that is straightforward and useful:

1. Identify the topic sentences of the paragraphs you are summarizing, and mark any important supporting details. Limit yourself to marking no more than one or two sentences per paragraph.
2. Copy the material you have noted onto a separate sheet of paper. What you now have are the notes for a summary: a collection of short quotations that are unlikely to flow smoothly together.
3. Read over the quotations you have compiled, and look for lines that seem too long and ideas that seem unnecessarily complicated. Paraphrase these lines. As you do, you might also be able to include important details that appeared elsewhere in the paragraph. Keep in mind that you should not have to restate everything that someone else has written. A summary can include direct quotations, as long as the quotations are relatively short and have a clarity that you cannot surpass.
4. Reread your paraphrasing and any quotations that you have included. Look for gaps between sentences, where the writing seems awkward or choppy. Eliminate all repetition, and subordinate any ideas that do not need to stand alone as separate sentences.
5. Check to be sure that any direct quotations are placed within quotation marks.
6. Rearrange any sentences that would flow better in a different sequence, and add transitional phrases wherever they can help smooth the way from one idea to the next.
7. Make sure that your sentences follow in a clear and readable sequence, and correct any errors in grammar, spelling, or syntax.
8. Read over your summary one more time, making sure that the content accurately reflects the nature of the text you are summarizing.

sizing one or two points about which everyone agreed. Your outline for this type of synthesis would be as follows:

Paragraph 1: Introduction
Paragraph 2: Summary of first writer (scientist)
Paragraph 3: Summary of second writer (clergyman)
Paragraph 4: Summary of third writer (gay activist)
Paragraph 5: Summary of fourth writer (government official)
Paragraph 6: Conclusion

Any good outline allows for some flexibility. Depending on the material and what you want to say, your synthesis might have fewer than or more than six paragraphs. For example, if two of your sources were especially long and complex, there is no reason you couldn't devote two paragraphs to each of them, even though you were able to summarize your other two sources within single paragraphs.

An alternative method for organizing a synthesis involves linking two or more writers within paragraphs that focus on specific issues or points. This type of organization is especially useful when you have detected a number of similarities that you want to emphasize. Suppose that you have read six essays about increasing the minimum age for obtaining a driver's license. Three writers favored increasing the minimum age, at least to 18, for much the same reasons; three writers opposing such an increase offered arguments that they shared in common. Your assignment is to identify the arguments most used by people who favor increasing the minimum driving age and those most used by people who oppose it. Your outline for synthesizing this material might be organized like this:

Paragraph 1: Introduction
Paragraph 2: One argument in favor of increasing the minimum driving age that was made by different writers
Paragraph 3: A second argument in favor of increasing the minimum driving age that was made by different writers
Paragraph 4: One argument against increasing the minimum driving age that was made by different writers
Paragraph 5: A second argument against increasing the minimum driving age that was made by different writers
Paragraph 6: Conclusion

There are other ways of organizing a passage of synthesis in your argument, but however you do so, the key is to present the ideas of the other writers clearly and draw connections among them in a way that will support your argument.

The ability to synthesize arguments is especially useful when writing to reconcile differences (see pages 13–15) or constructing a Rogerian argument (see pages 131–137). And because classical arrangement (see pages 126–131) emphasizes the importance of refutation, the ability to synthesize diverse arguments can be useful when using that writing plan.

Taking Notes

Note taking is essential to research. Unfortunately, few researchers can tell in advance exactly what material they will want to include in their final paper. Especially during the early stages of your research, you might record information that will seem unnecessary when you have become more expert on your topic and have a clear thesis. So you will probably have to discard some of your notes when you are ready to write your paper.

It is important to distinguish between note taking and annotating, described on pages 156–157. **Annotating** involves making notes in the margins of a specific text; **note taking** involves keeping notes about all your sources, ideas, and information for a single essay or project.

Some writers simply make notes in notebooks, on loose-leaf paper, or on legal pads. Many writers now make their notes using a word processing program such as Microsoft Word. Such programs make it easy to keep separate files for different kinds of notes. (There are also specialized computer programs designed to help researchers organize their notes.) Unless you have a laptop computer, however, using a word processing program might not be practical if you must take notes in a library or somewhere else outside your home. Newer technologies called **personal digital assistants** are small but powerful alternatives to computers; many of them allow users to make notes.

A more traditional note card system can also be an effective means of taking notes. Such a system allows flexibility when you are ready to move from research to composition. By spreading out your note cards on a desk or table, you can study how they best fit together. You can arrange and rearrange the cards until you have them in a meaningful sequence. This system works, however, only when you have the self-restraint to limit yourself to recording one fact, one idea, or one quotation on each card, as shown in Figure 6-2. Whether you use a note card system, a word processing program, or some other system of note taking, sorting your notes is one of the easiest ways to determine whether you have enough material to write a good paper.

FIGURE 6-2

A Sample Note Card

This note card includes a quotation from the writer's source. Notice that the topic and source information are included at the top of the card.

Prison as Deterrent (Currie 161)

"But prison may not only fail to deter; it may make matters worse. The overuse of incarceration may strengthen the links between street and prison and help to cement users' and dealer's identity as members of an oppositional drug culture, while simultaneously shutting them off from the prospect of successfully participating in the economy outside the prison."

Avoiding Plagiarism

Plagiarism is a legitimate concern for anyone engaged in research. To plagiarize (from *plagiarius,* the Latin word for *kidnapper*) is to steal—to be guilty of what the Modern Language Association calls "intellectual theft." Plagiarism is also a form of cheating; someone who plagiarizes a paper is losing an opportunity for learning in addition to running a serious risk. In the workplace, intellectual theft (of an essay, a song, or a proposal) can lead to lawsuits and heavy financial penalties. In a college or university, students who commit intellectual theft face penalties ranging from a failing grade on a paper to expulsion from the school. They are not the only ones who are hurt, however. In addition to hurting themselves, plagiarists injure the people they steal from; the professors who take the time to read and respond to the work of writers who are not their own students;

Consequences of Plagiarism

AN EXCERPT FROM THE STATEMENT ON PLAGIARISM PUBLISHED BY THE MODERN LANGUAGE ASSOCIATION (MLA):

Plagiarism is almost always seen as a shameful act, and plagiarists are usually regarded with pity and scorn. They are pitied because they have demonstrated their inability to develop and express their own thoughts. They are scorned because of their dishonesty and their willingness to deceive others for personal gain. . . .

The charge of plagiarism is a serious one for all writers. Students exposed as plagiarists suffer severe penalities, ranging from failure in the assignment or in the course to expulsion from school. They must also live with the distrust that follows an attempt to deceive others for personal gain. When professional writers, like journalists, are exposed as plagiarists, they are likely to lose their jobs, and they are certain to suffer public embarrassment and loss of prestige. For example, a well-known historian charged with plagiarism was asked to resign from prominent public positions even though she admitted responsibility for the theft, compensated the author whose work she took, and announced her intention to issue a corrected edition of her book. Almost always, the course of a professional writer's career is permanently affected by a single act of plagiarism.

The serious consequences of plagiarism reflect the value the public places on trustworthy information. A complex society that depends on well-informed citizens maintains high standards of quality and reliability for documents that are publicly circulated and used in government, business, industry, the professions, higher education, and the media. Because research has the power to affect opinions and actions, responsible writers compose their work with great care. They specify when they refer to another author's ideas, facts, and words, whether they want to agree with, object to, or analyze the source. This kind of documentation not only recognizes the work writers do; it also tends to discourage the circulation of error, by inviting readers to determine for themselves whether a reference to another text presents a reasonable account of what that text says. Plagiarists undermine these important public values.

classmates, whose grades might suffer from comparison if a clever plagiarism goes unde-tected; and the social fabric of the academic community, which becomes torn when val-ues such as honesty and mutual respect are no longer cherished.

The grossest form of plagiarism involves submitting someone else's paper as your own. Services that sell papers advertise on many college campuses, and obliging friends or roommates can sometimes be persuaded to hand over one of their own papers for resub-mission. In cyberspace, the World Wide Web provides ample opportunities for down-loading a paper written by someone else. Those who are electronically sophisticated can also piece a paper together by lifting paragraphs from a number of sources on the Internet. No one engages in such overt plagiarism accidentally.

On the other hand, it is also possible to plagiarize without meaning to do so. Students sometimes plagiarize by drawing too heavily on their sources. They might forget to put quotation marks around lines that they have taken word for word from another source, or they might think they don't need to quote if they have changed a few words. The im-portant point to keep in mind is that you must give credit for the *ideas* of others, as well as for their *words,* when you are using sources in your writing. If you take most of the in-formation another writer has provided and repeat it in essentially the same pattern, you are only a half-step away from copying the material, even if you have changed the exact wording.

Here is an example.

Original Source

Hawthorne's political ordeal, the death of his mother—and whatever guilt he may have harbored on either score—afforded him an understanding of the secret psychological springs of guilt. *The Scarlet Letter* is the book of a changed man. Its deeper insights have nothing to do with orthodox morality or religion—or the universal or allegorical applica-tions of a moral. The greatness of the book is related to its sometimes fitful characterizations of human nature and the author's almost uncanny intuitions: his realization of the bond between psychological malaise and physical illness, the nearly perfect, if sinister, outlining of the psychological techniques Chillingworth deployed against his victim.

Plagiarism

Nathaniel Hawthorne understood the psychological sources of guilt. His experience in politics and the death of his mother brought him deep insights that don't have anything to do with formal religion or morality. The greatness of *The Scarlet Letter* comes from its characters and the author's brilliant intuitions: Hawthorne's perception of the link between psycho-logical and physical illness and his almost perfect description of the way Roger Chillingworth persecuted his victim.

This student has simplified the original material, changing some of its wording. But he is still guilty of plagiarism. Pretending to offer his own analysis of *The Scarlet Letter,* he in fact owes all of his ideas to another writer, who is unacknowledged. Even the organization of the passage has been followed. This "paraphrase" would still be considered plagiarism even if it ended with a reference to the original source (page 307 of *Nathaniel Hawthorne in His Times,* by James R. Mellow). A reference or footnote would not reveal the full extent to which this student is indebted to his source.

Here is an acceptable version:

Paraphrase

As James R. Mellow has argued, *The Scarlet Letter* reveals a profound understanding of guilt. It is a great novel because of its insight into human nature—not because of some moral about adultery. The most interesting character is probably Roger Chillingworth because of the way he was able to make Rev. Dimmesdale suffer (307).

This student has not only made a better effort to paraphrase the original material but also introduced it with a reference to the original writer. The introductory reference to Mellow, coupled with the subsequent page reference, clearly shows us that Mellow deserves the credit for the ideas in this passage. Additional bibliographical information about this source is provided by the list of works cited at the end of the paper:

Mellow, James. *Nathaniel Hawthorne in His Times.* Boston: Houghton, 1980.

One final caution: It is possible to subconsciously remember a piece of someone else's phrasing and inadvertently repeat it. You would be guilty of plagiarism if the words in question embodied a critically important idea or reflect a distinctive style or turn of phrase. When you revise your draft, look for such unintended quotations. If you use them, show who deserves the credit for them, and *remember to put quoted material within quotation marks.*

Finding Relevant Material

Up to this point the chapter has focused on how to read and use sources. But you must have relevant sources before you can read them critically and use them effectively. Finding those relevant sources encompasses an important set of research skills.

Getting Started

One of the first goals of any researcher is to decide where to begin. The more specific your search, the greater your chance for efficiently locating the material you need and then writing a well-supported paper. When you know what you are looking for, you can gauge what you should read and what you can probably afford to pass over—a great advantage when you are confronted by the staggering amount of information that a good college library, or the Internet, makes available.

In many cases you will begin your research with your topic already identified. For instance, you might be assigned to write about a specific issue. Or your class might have discussed an issue that interests you enough to want to write an argument about it. Or you might be addressing a problem for which you are seeking a solution, such as a controversy on campus involving a dorm policy or an inflammatory editorial in the student newspaper. In such cases you have a good starting point for your research.

But sometimes you might find yourself in a situation in which you have no clear topic. In such a situation you can take steps to identify a workable topic for your argument. Sometimes, for example, a specific topic will emerge as you scan information on your subject area by using periodical indexes, online databases, and search engines for navigating the Internet. By beginning with a general idea of what you plan to write about and then using key words to check different sources, you can refine your topic or even discover topics that have generated recent interest—topics that will interest you as well. You can judge, at this point, which topics would be the most manageable ones to research. As you proceed, keep two general rules in mind:

- If you are overwhelmed by the number of citations you find in your research area, you probably need to *narrow your topic*.
- If you have difficulty finding material, you might need to *broaden your search*.

If you're unsure about your topic, consider discussing it with other people—in particular, your instructor. (For additional information on choosing a topic, see pages 113–115.)

Avoiding Selective Research

Although you might have a tentative thesis in mind when you begin your search, it's often a good idea to delay formulating your final thesis until your research is complete. Think of your search strategy as an attempt to answer a question. For instance, suppose you are writing an argument about drug-related crime. You can proceed as if you are addressing the following question: "What can be done to reduce drug-related crime?" This is different from starting your research with your thesis predetermined. If you begin already convinced that the way to reduce drug-related crime is to legalize drugs, you might be tempted to take notes only from sources that advocate this position, rejecting as irrelevant any source that discusses problems with this approach. In this case, research is not leading to greater knowledge or understanding. On the contrary, it is being used to reinforce personal beliefs that might border on prejudice. Even if you feel strongly about the issue at hand, keeping an open mind during your research can often lead to a better understanding of that issue—and a more effective argument.

You have seen that anticipating the opposition (see sidebar on page 116) is important even in short arguments. It is no less important in a researched paper. Almost any topic worth investigating will yield facts and ideas that could support different conclusions. It is possible to take significantly different positions on issues such as immigration law, environmental protection, and higher education. These are extremely complex issues, and it is important to remember that fact as you conduct your research. Your own research might ultimately support a belief that you already hold, but if you proceed as if you are genuinely trying to solve a problem or answer a question, your research might deepen your understanding of the issue and lead you to realize that you were previously misinformed. For this reason, try not to overlook relevant material just because you don't agree with it. Your argument will be stronger if you recognize that disagreement about your topic exists and then demonstrate why you favor one position over another or show how different positions can be reconciled.

This effort, essential to learning, is more important than ever because of changes in technology and the distribution of information. Large corporations have come to control what used to be independent publishers and radio stations (see pages 67–69), and the Internet provides numerous ways for customizing the news sent to an individual (see pages 54–67). These business and technological changes can do cultural damage when citizens learn only what confirms their existing beliefs without ever challenging them with information that would expand or reconfigure the box in which they dwell.

With this advice in mind you can more effectively use the many resources now available as you research your topic. In addition to more traditional sources such as books and articles in magazines, journals, and newspapers, you have access to an astonishing amount of information on the Internet. In the remainder of this chapter, we will discuss how best to use these resources.

Using the Internet

The kind of information that can be found on the Internet is incredibly diverse; it includes library catalogs, government documents and data, newspaper and magazine articles, excerpts from books and even entire books, and all kinds of information and material published by commercial organizations, special interest groups, and even individuals who wish to make contact with others who share their concerns.

Today, most of us access all this information through the World Wide Web, which is a graphical interface for navigating the Internet. Current software, such as Internet Explorer or Netscape Navigator, makes it easy to browse the Web. But the enormous scale of the Web can also make it difficult to find relevant information easily. The very richness of the Web can be its drawback, and searching for the right information can be time-consuming and sometimes frustrating. You might find yourself scrolling through an

LEARNING TO SEARCH THE WEB

To learn more about efficiently searching the World Wide Web, check to see whether your library or academic computing office provides workshops or similar services. These workshops can help you learn about various search engines available on the Web and sophisticated strategies for searching the Web.

endless series of documents and losing sight of your main objective while pursuing an elusive loose end. For this reason it's important to understand some basic principles for searching the Web.

You should also be aware of a key difference between much of the material published on the Internet and material published in print. Writers who publish in print receive professional editorial support. Editors decide what material is worth printing and then assist writers in preparing work for publication. Most of the Internet operates without editors, however. Anyone with a little knowledge of computers can publish whatever comes to mind. In a sense the Internet is wonderfully democratic, and many people have enjoyed activities such as creating a website for their cat and connecting with other cat fanciers. On the other hand, the Internet also carries a great deal of misinformation, hate speech, and crank editorials. When searching the Internet, you must carefully evaluate the material you locate and recognize that this material can range from first-rate scholarship to utter trash.

Despite these potential problems, the Internet is an increasingly important resource for research. The challenge is finding your way through the huge amount of material floating around in cyberspace. Computer experts have developed systems called **search engines** that work as indexing services for the World Wide Web. The most commonly used today is Google. Others include Yahoo!, AltaVista, and Lycos. Once you learn how to use one of these systems, you can easily learn how to adapt to the others. No search engine provides a complete, error-free index to electronic documents, so you might have to use more than one system, just as you would use more than one periodical index when looking for information in your library.

EVALUATING INTERNET RESOURCES

The advice provided earlier about reading critically (see pages 154–161) applies to Internet resources as well. But because of the dizzying variety of material on the Internet and because anyone can publish anything on a website, you might have to take special care in evaluating the reliability of information you find on the Web. Most libraries have information on their own websites about evaluating Internet resources. Here are a few good ones:

- *Evaluating Information Found on the Internet,* Sheridan Libraries, Johns Hopkins University: <http://www.library.jhu.edu/researchhelp/general/evaluating>
- *Evaluating Web Resources,* Wolfgram Memorial Library, Widener University: <http://www.widener.edu/659>
- *Thinking Critically About World Wide Web Resources,* UCLA College Library: <http://www.library.ucla.edu/libraries/college/help/critical/index.htm>

Search engines require you to identify your research topic by typing key words or phrases into an entry box. After you have entered your search terms, you will be given a list of websites that match your request. Each of these sites can, in turn, lead you to others. Many search engines also enable you to refine your search by entering more specific information, such as dates or kinds of publications. And Internet directories allow you to browse through broad subject categories to find subtopics that you might be looking for. Like other electronic resources, search engines provide help screens with instructions on the best ways to search. These instructions change as the technology changes, and it is wise to review them whenever you are in doubt about how to proceed.

Remember that the Internet is constantly changing. New sites are launched on the Web constantly—literally every minute. And new search systems are always being developed; hundreds now exist. Because the Internet contains so much information, some researchers make the mistake of thinking that anything they need to find must be available electronically. Not every scholar chooses to make completed work available electronically, so you can miss important material if you try to do all your research on the Internet.

At the same time, many resources that have traditionally been available only in print form are becoming available on the Internet. Many journals, newspapers, and magazines now offer full-text articles online, which means that you don't always have to go to your library to get a copy of an article you might need for your research. In addition, some publications appear only online. For example, *Slate* magazine and *Salon.com* are two respected publications that do not appear in print form; you can access their articles only through the Internet. And organizations of all types sponsor online archives and other sources related to their areas of interest. For example, you can visit the website of the U.S. Department of Health and Human Services to find a great deal of information on a range of topics related to health issues. Thousands of such sites exist on the Web. Once you learn to navigate the Web efficiently and to evaluate Internet sources carefully, the wealth of information available online can enrich your research.

TIPS FOR EFFICIENT WEB SEARCHING

Doing research on the Web is more than visiting a popular search engine such as Google and typing in your topic. Here are a few suggestions for making your Web searching more efficient and successful:

- Visit your library's website to see whether it has information about searching the Web. Many libraries offer excellent advice for using the Web effectively.
- Read the search tips that are usually available on the websites of search engines. These tips can help you learn to use specific search engines more efficiently.
- Learn how to use **Boolean operators** in your searches. Most search tools support Boolean, or logical, operators, such as AND, OR, and NOT. These terms help you narrow your search so that the search tools will return the most relevant documents. Most search engines include basic instructions for using Boolean terms.
- Learn to recognize Internet *domains* in Web addresses, such as .com, .edu., .gov, and .org. Understanding what these domains mean can help you decide whether to visit specific websites that you find with a search engine.

Searching for Magazine and Journal Articles

Magazines, bulletins, and scholarly journals are all called **periodicals** because they are published on a regular schedule—once a week, once a month, and so on. Although researchers can seldom afford to rely exclusively on periodicals for information, the indexes and abstracting services that enable them to locate relevant periodical articles are essential in most searches. Periodicals often include the most current information about a research area, and they can alert you to other important sources through book reviews and through the citations that support individual articles. In addition, as noted in the previous section, many periodicals are now available on the Internet, which makes them easily accessible to researchers.

A good place to start when searching for periodical literature is Expanded Academic ASAP, a version of InfoTrac designed for college-level research. Figure 6-3 shows the opening page for this system. In this case, a researcher began to search for information on childhood obesity, one of the subjects in Chapter 9. For this preliminary search, the individual in question has decided to access only sources from two years and to examine only those sources for which full text is available online. Since this database was offering almost 17 million articles on the day this search was conducted, putting some limits on the search was sensible. The search could have been further controlled by checking "peer-reviewed publications"—a choice that would lead to scholarly sources while eliminating those from general-circulation magazines.

FIGURE 6-3

Opening Screen for
Expanded Academic ASAP

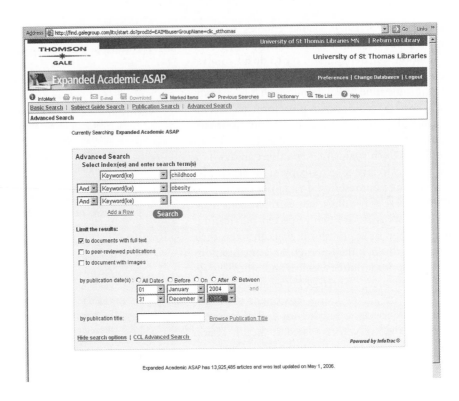

Expanded Academic ASAP has 13,925,485 articles and was last updated on May 1, 2006.

Academic Search Premier is a widely used alternative to Expanded Academic ASAP. Figure 6-4 shows the beginning of a search for information on childhood obesity. In this case, the researcher checked both "full text" and "Scholarly (Peer-Reviewed) Journals." "Default Fields" would generate a list of sources in which the terms *childhood* and *obesity* appeared anywhere in a document. To obtain the most relevant sources, this researcher had directed the system to look for sources in which "childhood" is sufficiently important to appear in the abstract or summary of a source and "obesity" appears in the title. As with any other search, this search could be either expanded or further limited depending upon the number and quality of the sources located.

If your college library does not provide access to either of these databases, it might well provide access to OLLC FirstSearch, which operates according to a similar procedure.

Many colleges and universities allow students and faculty to access databases from personal computers (in addition to the computers provided in the library for searching at the site). To see an example of how this can be done, turn back to page 62 and note how the home page for the University of St. Thomas provides a link to "Libraries." Using this link provided access to both Expanded Academic ASAP and Academic Premier Search; but also to the list featured in Figure 6-5. Clicking on "Psychology & Counseling" led to the choices in Figure 6-6. PsycINFO would lead to sources on a topic like "childhood obesity" written by psychologists; three additional databases would lead to sources discussing how sociologists and social workers view this topic.

Returning to the list featured in Figure 6-5 and clicking "Newspapers/Current Events" led to fourteen choices, the first five of which appear in Figure 6-7. Proquest is highly useful because it searches for information in major newspapers around the

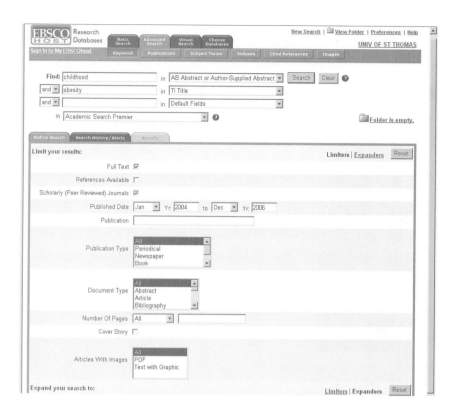

FIGURE 6-4

Opening Screen for Academic Search Premier

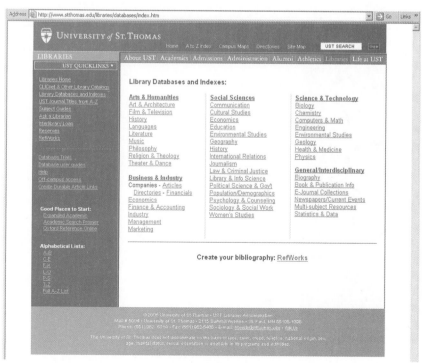

FIGURE 6-5

Areas in which Databases Are Available

FIGURE 6-6

The "Psychology & Counseling" Database

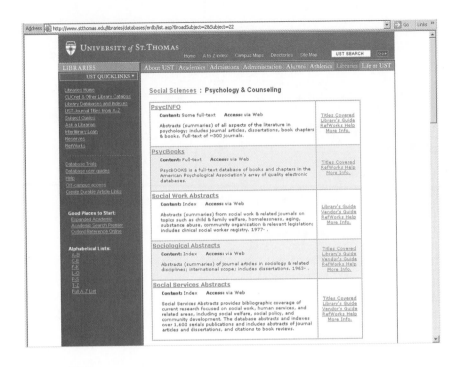

FIGURE 6-7

The "Newspapers/ Current Events" Database

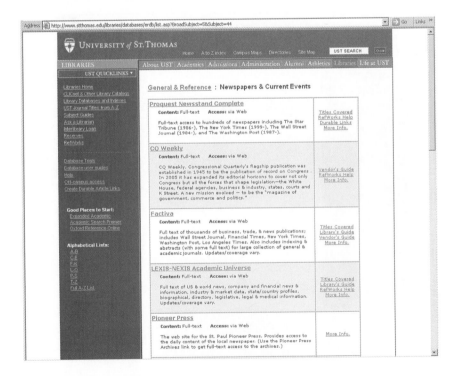

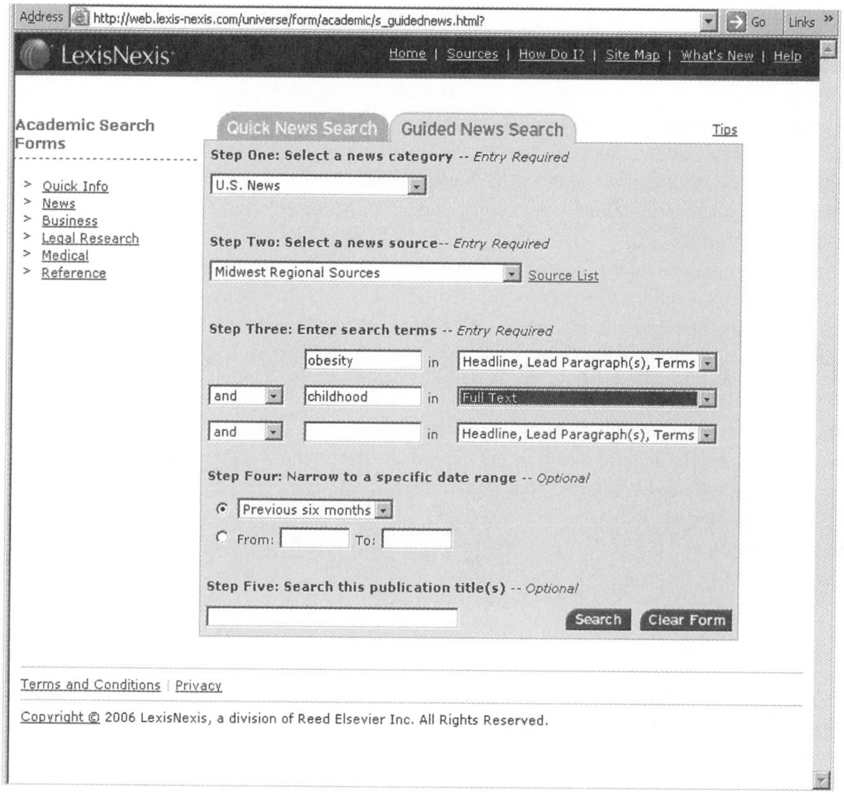

FIGURE 6-8

Opening Screen for
LexisNexis

country. LexisNexis, however, is potentially more useful because it provides access to a larger number of papers and even includes news releases for stories that have not yet made their way into print. Access is also provided to the *Pioneer Press,* the daily newspaper of the city in which this library is located. Searching the city's paper would be useful for students constructing an argument about a local topic.

Figure 6-8 shows how a researcher was beginning to access information through Lexis-Nexis. Because this database provides entry into so many sources around the world, the researcher has chosen to limit the initial search to "U.S. News" and to further limit it by requesting sources only from the Midwest, the part of the country where the researcher lived and wanted to use when focusing an argument. To make sure that only relevant sources were called up, the researcher has specified that "obesity" must appear in either the headline or the lead paragraph and "childhood" must appear within the text.

Although there is some overlapping from one index to another, each index covers different periodicals. The records that you find in one will usually vary from the records that you find in another. This is worth remembering, for two reasons:

1. If you cannot locate any material in the past few years of one index, you can try another index that seems as if it might include records on your subject.

2. Many subjects of general interest will be found in more than one index. If you consult more than one index, you are increasing the likelihood of being exposed to different points of view.

USING BOOLEAN OPERATORS

Boolean, or logical, operators are words that command a search engine to define a search in a specific way. The most common Boolean operators are *AND, OR,* and *NOT.* Understanding how they work can help you search the Internet and databases more efficiently:

- *AND* tells the search engine to find only sources that contain both words in your search. For example, if you entered *sports AND steroids,* your search would yield sources that deal with steroids in sports and would not necessarily return sources that deal with steroids or sports in general.
- *OR* broadens a search by telling the search engine to return sources for either term in your search. Entering *sports OR steroids,* for instance, would yield sources on either of those topics.
- *NOT* can narrow a search by telling the search engine to exclude sources containing a specific keyword. For example, entering *steroids NOT sports* would yield sources on steroids but not sources that deal with steroids in sports.

In addition, keep these tips in mind:

- You can use parentheses for complex searches: *(sports AND steroids) NOT (medicine OR law);* this entry would narrow the search to specific kinds of sources about sports and steroids that did not include medical or legal matters.
- With most search engines you can use quotation marks to find a specific phrase. For example, "steroid use in sports" would return sources that included that exact phrase.
- Generally, you should capitalize Boolean operators.

Using Abstracting Services

Although many electronic indexing services such as *Social Science Abstracts* are now offering summaries of current articles with the citations a search identifies, they do not consistently provide abstracts for all material they index. There are other services that specialize in abstracts. Important abstracting services in printed volumes include the following:

Abstracts in Anthropology	*Biological Abstracts*
Historical Abstracts	*Psychological Abstracts*
Academic Abstracts	*Chemical Abstracts*
Physics Abstracts	*Sociological Abstracts*

These abstracts are organized in different ways, and you might need to consult one volume for the index and another volume for the matching abstracts. When using bound volumes, consult the instructions that can be found within them. However, there is no reason to consult printed volumes of abstracts unless you do not have access to electronic databases. Almost all college libraries provide access to at least a few electronic databases. Ask your reference librarian whether there are electronic resources in your library appropriate to your research.

Because it can be hard to tell from a title whether an article will be useful, abstracts offer an advantage over simple bibliographical citations. The summary provided by an abstracting service can help you decide whether you want to read the entire article. Keep in mind that an abstract written in English does not mean that the article is also in English; be alert for notations such as *(Chin), (Germ),* or *(Span),* which indicate when an article is published in another language. Also, remember that good researchers never pretend to have read an entire article when they have read only an abstract of it. Use abstracts as a tool for locating material to read, not as a substitute for a full-length reading.

Looking for Books

The convenience of the Internet and online databases can tempt you to avoid looking for books on a subject. Yet books remain essential to research. Although the books you locate in your library might vary in quality, they often represent the final and most prestigious result of someone else's research. It is common, for example, for a scholar to publish several journal articles in the process of writing a book. Much of the best information you can find appears somewhere in a book, and you should not assume that your research subject is so new or so specialized that your library will not have books on it. A topic that seems new to you is not necessarily new to others.

Because books take time to read, some researchers look for books at the beginning of their search. Others turn to books after they have investigated the periodical literature to focus their interests and identify the most influential works in their field. Whenever you choose to look for books on your topic, be sure that you do so well before your paper is due. A book full of important information will be of little help if you haven't left yourself time to read it.

Most college libraries have electronic catalogs, which are usually accessible both within the library and through the Internet. This accessibility makes it convenient to search the library catalog without having to go to the library itself. Computerized catalogs enable users to search for books by author, title, or subject. Most of these catalogs also permit a search for material using a call number or a **key word**—a word that is likely to appear somewhere in the title or description. In addition to providing all of the information about a book that could be obtained from a card catalog, computerized catalogs are usually designed to report whether the book is currently available.

Figure 6-9 shows the catalog entry for a book titled *Urban Sprawl.* It contains information about the author, when and where the book was published, and whether it is available in the library. Every library has its own system for displaying information about the books it holds. As you do research, you should expect to find variations on this example. The precise format of a computerized entry depends on the program employed by the library you are using. (If your library still uses index cards in a card catalog, you will find the same basic information displayed on those cards.)

There is no foolproof method for determining the quality or usefulness of a book from a catalog entry. The best way to judge a book's usefulness is to read it. But a catalog listing can reveal some useful clues if you know how to find them:

USING OTHER LIBRARY RESOURCES

Because of the great amount of material being published, libraries save space in several ways, most commonly by using microform, digital technology, and interlibrary loan. In doing research, you might need to use one or more of these resources.

Microform is printed material that has been reduced in size through microphotography. Libraries that use microform provide users with special devices to read the material, whether it is available on microfilm or microfiche (which is a flat sheet of microfilm).

Digital technology, in the form of CD-ROMs or online media, makes articles and other resources available to users electronically rather than in print form. Sometimes, you must read these resources at a computer terminal.

Interlibrary loan enables libraries to give their users access to books held at other libraries. You can usually request articles and books through this service, and today many libraries enable you to make your requests online. Keep in mind, however, that it can take several days or weeks for requested materials to arrive.

FIGURE 6-9

Catalog Entry

This screen shows an entry for a book found by searching this library's online catalog.

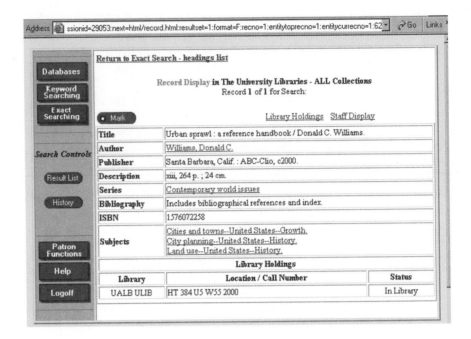

- *The date of publication.* There is no reason to assume that new books are always better than old books, but unless you are researching a historical or literary topic, you should be careful not to rely heavily on material that may be out of date.
- *The length of the book.* A book with 300 pages is likely to provide more information than a book half that size. A book with a bibliography might help you find more material.
- *The reputation of the publisher.* Academic publishers generally publish books that have gone through rigorous review, which is not always the case with some commercial publishers.

Conducting Interviews and Surveys

In some cases, you might want to conduct original research on your topic. For example, if you are writing an argument about a campus controversy over new parking fees, you can gather useful information by talking to people on campus (such as the person in charge of parking) or soliciting opinions by those affected by the new fees. There are many kinds of original research, but two of the most common are interviews and surveys.

Interviews might be inappropriate for some kinds of papers (for example, science reports), but they can often be useful sources of information. If you are writing a paper on identity theft, for example, you might interview someone working in law enforcement, such as a police officer or a public defender. You might also interview professionals at a bank or credit card company who deal with identity theft. Whom you interview will depend largely on your topic, but you should always evaluate the credibility of anyone you interview. Here are some other tips for interviewing:

- *Plan ahead for your interviews.* It's a good idea to prepare a list of questions before you go. It also helps to learn something about the person or people you will interview so that you can ask appropriate questions and avoid inappropriate ones.
- *Ask good questions.* Try to compose questions that will take several sentences to answer rather than questions that might be answered with a single word. Good questions usually elicit more useful responses for your research.
- *Be flexible.* Don't necessarily adhere rigidly to the questions you prepare in advance. A good interviewer knows how to ask a follow-up question inspired by a provocative response to an earlier question. However, try not to become so caught up in the interview that you forget to take careful notes.
- *Consider using a tape recorder.* A tape recorder will usually preserve more of the interview than you can preserve in your notes, and it will enable you to take notes on important points without having to write everything down. If you want to use a tape recorder, ask permission to do so when you arrange for the interview. Also, make sure that the recorder is working properly before you begin the interview, and check your batteries.
- *Record the date of the interview and the full name and credentials or position of the person you interviewed.* You will need to include this information in your bibliography.

When you ask the same questions of several different people, you are conducting a **survey.** When a survey is long, complex, and administered to a large sample group, researchers seeking to analyze the data they have gathered will benefit from having a working knowledge of statistics. But for many undergraduate research projects, a relatively simple survey can produce interesting and useful data. The earlier hypothetical example of a campus controversy about new parking fees illustrates the usefulness of a survey. If you were writing an argument about that controversy, you could gather information about students' attitudes toward the new fees. Such information can be important and potentially persuasive support for your position on the controversy.

Here are some things to consider if you want to use a survey:

- *Carefully compose a list of relevant questions.* Each question should be designed to elicit a clear answer directly related to the purpose of the survey. This is more complicated than it might seem, because the kind of questions you ask will determine what results you get. For example, if you ask students whether they agree with the parking fees, you will get a basic yes-or-no response. However, if you ask students whether they would pay higher fees if they were guaranteed a parking space, you might get different results.
- *Decide whether you want to administer the survey orally or distribute it in a written form.* One advantage of an oral survey is that you get your results immediately; with a written survey, weeks can pass before you discover how many people responded to your request for information. On the other hand, written surveys give you clear records to work from. A good rule to follow when conducting a written survey is to distribute at least twice as many copies as you need to have returned to you.

- *Decide how many people you will need to survey to have a credible sample of the population that concerns you.* For example, in the case of the campus parking fees, say there are 4,000 students at your school but only 1,000 drive to campus. You might want to survey both drivers and nondrivers to see whether you get different results. In that case, if you surveyed 100 students, you might want to make sure that 25 of them are drivers (which would match the 25 percent of student drivers on your campus).
- *Consider whether it would be useful to analyze your results in terms of such differences as gender, race, age, income, or religion.* If so, you must design a questionnaire that will provide this information. In the campus parking controversy it might be that older students are most affected, so you would want to account for the age of your respondents.
- *Take steps to protect the privacy of your respondents.* Ask for no more information than you need, and ask respectfully for that information. Give respondents the option of refusing to answer any question that makes them uncomfortable, and honor any promises you make about how you will use the data you gather.

As this chapter reveals, there are many aspects to doing research and many kinds of resources for the information you need. Which resources you consult and how you search for them will depend on your topic and the specifics of your assignment, such as your deadline and the length of the argument you are writing. But whether you will engage in extensive research or simply look for a few articles about your topic, the general principles guiding research are the same. And the more effective you are as a researcher, the more likely you will be to find the information you need to write an effective argument.

7

Documenting Your Sources

C hapter 6 surveyed many of the strategies that you can use to conduct research for an argument. Doing such research is part of the process of inquiry that you engage in when you make an argument. By researching an issue or controversy carefully, you can gain a better understanding of that issue or controversy and construct a more effective argument that may lead to a satisfactory resolution. That's the goal. But when you draw upon sources for an argument you are composing, you must document those sources properly. In most cases, that means providing both the bibliography that contains all the works you used and the citations within your argument that establish what part of each source is being drawn upon in any particular instance.

Compiling a Preliminary Bibliography

As you use the strategies described in Chapter 6 to begin locating sources of possible value for your paper, it is important to record certain essential information about the books and articles you have discovered. You will need this information to compile a preliminary bibliography. Here are some things to keep in mind as you work with your sources:

- For books, record the full title, the full name of the author or authors, the city of publication, the publisher, and the date of publication.
- If you are using a particular part of a book, be sure to record the pages in question.
- When you have located articles in periodicals, record the author(s) of the article, the title of the article, the title of the journal in which it was published, the volume number, the issue number (if there is one), the date of the issue, and the pages between which the article can be found.
- If you are using an article or a story from an anthology edited by someone other than the author of the material you are using, make the distinction between the author and title of the selection and the editor and title of the volume.
- For electronic resources, such as websites, be sure to record the Internet address, or URL, accurately and make a note of the date you accessed the site. Note also when the site was posted or last updated.

Today, researchers often use a computer program to keep track of sources. You can easily use certain features of a word processing program such as Microsoft Word to maintain your preliminary bibliography, or you can use specialized software such as EndNote that is designed specifically for constructing bibliographies. Whatever method you use, be sure to keep accurate records. It can be frustrating to discover that you neglected to record an important reference, especially if this discovery comes after the paper is written and shortly before it is handed in.

Citing Sources

Anytime you use material from another source, you must cite it properly. Citing your sources simply means revealing the source of any information you report. When you cite your sources, you are providing your readers with information to help them evaluate the credibility of your sources, crediting the authors whose work you are citing, and making it possible for readers to find your sources themselves. In general, you must provide documentation for the following:

- Any direct quotation
- Any idea that has come from someone else's work
- Any fact or statistic that is not widely known

There are several styles for documenting your sources; these styles are usually associated with different disciplines or professions. Writers in the humanities usually follow the form of the Modern Language Association (MLA). In the social sciences writers are often expected to follow the format of the American Psychological Association (APA). MLA and APA are the two most widely used systems for documenting sources, and chances are that you will be asked to use one of them for papers you write for your college courses. *The Chicago Manual of Style* (CMS) is another widely used system, though college instructors are less likely to use that system than MLA or APA. When you are writing a source-based paper, check with your instructor to see which system you should use. (If you are writing a source-based argument for publication, check with the editor about that publication's preferred system for documenting sources.)

Whichever system you use to document your sources, remember that the purpose of all these systems is the same: to provide appropriate information about your sources. And be sure to understand the relationship between the parenthetical, or in-text, citations and the Bibliography, Works Cited, or References page of your essay. When you cite a source in the body of your essay, you are telling your readers where you obtained the quotation or information you are using; your readers can then go to your bibliography for more information about that source.

The remainder of this chapter explains the basic features of the MLA and APA systems of documentation and provides model entries for the most frequently used sources. However, a detailed discussion of these systems is beyond the range of this chapter. If you need more information about either MLA or APA format, consult the official sources for each (see sidebar on this page).

For examples of how MLA-style documentation is used in written argument, see pages 185–195. For an example of an APA-style paper, see pages 196–204.

Using Footnotes and Content Notes

Traditionally, footnotes were used to document sources. Strictly speaking, a **footnote** appears at the foot of the page, and an **endnote** appears at the end of the paper. However, both MLA and APA now recommend that writers use parenthetical, or in-text, citations of the kind described here; traditional footnotes are not used for documenting sources. Instead, numbered notes are reserved for additional explanation or discussion that is important but cannot be included within the actual text without a loss of focus. Such notes are called **content notes.** APA discourages the use of such notes unless they are essential to the discussion. If you do use content notes, APA format requires

---

MLA AND APA SOURCES

You can find more extensive information about the MLA and APA documentation systems by consulting the official publications for each system. Notice that the following citations are the appropriate format for each system:

Gibaldi, Joseph. <u>MLA Style Manual and Guide to Scholarly Publishing.</u> 2nd ed. New York: MLA, 1998.

Gibaldi, Joseph. <u>MLA Handbook for Writers of Research Papers.</u> 6th ed. New York: MLA, 2003.

American Psychological Association. (2001). *Publication manual of the American Psychological Association* (5th ed.). Washington, DC: Author.

You can also visit their websites: <<u>http://mla.org</u>> or <<u>http://ww.apastyle.org</u>>

COMMONLY USED STYLE MANUALS

MLA and APA are the two most popular style guides, but there are other manuals that you may need to consult. Here is a list of other commonly used manuals:

The Chicago Manual of Style, 14th ed. (Chicago: University of Chicago Press, 1993).

Huth, Edward J. *Scientific Style and Format: The CBE Manual for Authors, Editors, and Publishers.* 6th ed. New York: Cambridge University Press, 1994.

Dodd, Janet S., ed. *The ACS Style Guide: A Manual for Authors and Editors,* 2nd edition. New York: Oxford UP, 1997.

American Institute of Physics. *AIP Style Manual.* 4th ed. New York: Amer. Inst. of Physics, 1990.

Iverson, Cheryl, ed. *American Medical Association Manual of Style: A Guide for Authors and Editors.* 9th ed. Baltimore: Williams & Wilkins, 1998.

Harvard Law Review Association. *The Bluebook: A Uniform System of Citation.* 17th ed. Cambridge: Harvard Law Review Assn., 2000.

them to be placed on a separate page at the end of the essay (rather than at the bottom of the page as footnotes).

If you are using MLA style, use footnotes or endnotes to provide additional information about sources or topics discussed in your essay.

Using Parenthetical (In-Text) Documentation

As noted earlier in this chapter, the two most common systems for documenting sources, MLA and APA, both recommend the use of parenthetical, or in-text, citations to cite sources. The basic principle for using these parenthetical citations is the same for both MLA and APA styles: you are providing readers with information about a source included in your bibliography. However, there are differences between the two systems. These differences reflect conventions within academic fields regarding which information about a source is most important:

- **MLA style,** which tends to reflect the conventions of the humanities (including the arts, literature, history, and philosophy), emphasizes the author and the author's work and places less emphasis on the date of publication.
- **APA style** emphasizes the author and the date of publication, which are more important in the social science disciplines (for example, psychology, sociology, education, and anthropology).

If you understand these basic differences, you might find it easier to become familiar with the specific differences in the formats used by each documentation system.

Organizing a Bibliography

A bibliography is an essential component of any essay or report that includes references to sources. The bibliography, also called a Works Cited or References page, lists all sources that you have cited in your essay or report. The purpose of a bibliography is to provide information about your sources for your readers.

MLA and APA styles for formatting the entries in your bibliography are described in this chapter. As you'll see, there are some differences between MLA and APA styles. No matter which style you use, your bibliography provides the same basic information about your sources:

- The author's name
- The title of the work
- The date of publication

In addition, entries in your bibliography will provide the name of the magazine, newspaper, or journal for any articles you cite, as well as page numbers (unless you are citing an electronic source without page numbers, such as a web page).

ITALICS OR UNDERLINES

Traditionally, both APA and MLA recommended underlining titles of books, journals, magazines, and newspapers. However, with the widespread use of word processing, it is now as easy to use italics as it is to underline, and either is generally acceptable. Nevertheless, MLA still recommends the use of underlining to avoid ambiguity; it suggests that students who wish to use italics check with their instructors first.

MLA-Style Documentation

Now that you have been introduced to the basic principles of documentation, you will probably find it useful to have examples of how various sources look when cited. This section begins with a discussion of the MLA author/work style used for citations within the text of an argument and then turns to how citations should appear in an MLA-style bibliography.

The MLA Author/Work Style   In a parenthetical (or in-text) citation in MLA form, the author's last name is followed by a page reference; in some cases a brief title should be included after the author's name. It is not necessary to repeat within the parentheses information already provided in the text.

A. WORK BY ONE AUTHOR

If you were citing page 133 of a book called *Ecological Literacy* by David W. Orr, the parenthetical citation would look like this:

> The idea of environmental sustainability can become the centerpiece of a college curriculum (Orr 133).

Alternatively, you could use Orr's name in your sentence, in which case the citation would include only the page reference:

> David Orr has argued persuasively that that the idea of environmental sustainability should be the centerpiece of a college curriculum (133).

There is no punctuation between the author's name and the page reference when both are cited parenthetically. Note also that the abbreviation *p.* or *pp.* is not used before the page reference.

B. WORK WITH MORE THAN ONE AUTHOR

If the work you are citing has two or three authors, use the complete names of all of them in your sentence or include their last names in the parentheses:

> Cleanth Brooks and Robert Penn Warren have argued that "indirection is an essential part of the method of poetry" (573).

or

> Although this sonnet may seem obscure, its meaning becomes clearer when we realize "indirection is an essential part of the method of poetry" (Brooks and Warren 573).

Note that when a sentence ends with a quotation, the parenthetical reference comes before the final punctuation mark. Note also that the ampersand (&) is not used in MLA style.

If you are referring to a work by more than three authors, you can list only the first author's name followed by *et al.* (Latin for "and others"):

> These works "derive from a profound disillusionment with modern life" (Baym et al. 910).

C. WORK WITH A CORPORATE AUTHOR

When a corporate author has a long name, you should include it within the text rather than within parentheses. For example, if you were citing a study by the Council on

Environmental Quality called "Ground Water Contamination in the United States," you would do so as follows:

> The Council on Environmental Quality has reported that there is growing evidence of ground water contamination throughout the United States (81).

You could also include the corporate author in the parentheses; omit any initial article:

> There is growing evidence of ground water contamination throughout the United States (Council on Environmental Quality 81).

Although both of these forms are technically correct, the first is preferred because it is easier to read.

D. WORK WITH MORE THAN ONE VOLUME

When you wish to cite a specific part of a multivolume work, include the volume number between the author and the page reference. This example quotes a passage from the second volume of a two-volume book by Jacques Barzun:

> As Jacques Barzun has argued, "The only hope of true culture is to make classifications broad and criticism particular" (2: 340).

Note that the volume number is given an arabic numeral and a space separates the colon and the page reference. The abbreviation *vol.* is not used unless you wish to cite the entire volume: (Barzun, vol. 2).

E. MORE THAN ONE WORK BY THE SAME AUTHOR

If you cite more than one work by the same author, you need to make your references distinct so that readers will know exactly which work you are citing. You can do so by putting a comma after the author's name and then adding a shortened form of the title. For example, if you are discussing two novels by Toni Morrison, *Song of Solomon* and *The Bluest Eye,* your citations might look like this:

> Toni Morrison's work is always concerned with the complexities of racial identity. This theme is perhaps explored most painfully in the character of Pecola Breedlove (Morrison, <u>Bluest</u>). But even a crowd of unnamed characters gathered near a hospital, listening to a woman break spontaneously into song and wondering "if one of those things that racial-uplift groups were always organizing was taking place," can become a reminder that race is always part of the picture (Morrison, <u>Song</u> 6).

If it is clear from the context that the quotation is from a work by Morrison, there is no need to include her name in the parentheses. If you're not sure, however, include it. This example could have left Morrison's name out of the parentheses because it is clear that it is citing her works.

F. QUOTATION WITHIN A CITED WORK

If you want to use a quotation that you have discovered in another book, your reference must show that you acquired this material secondhand and that you have not consulted the original source. Use the abbreviation *qtd. in* (for "quoted in") to make the distinction between the author of the passage being quoted and the author of the work in which you found this passage.

For example, say you were reading a book called *The Abstract Wild* by Jack Turner and you came across a quotation by the naturalist William Kittredge that you wanted to use in your argument. You would cite the Kittredge quotation as follows:

> Many people misquote Henry David Thoreau's famous line about wildness and the preservation of the world. William Kittredge has admitted to making this very mistake: "For years I misread Thoreau. I assumed he was saying wilderness. . . . Maybe I didn't want Thoreau to have said wildness, I couldn't figure out what he meant" (qtd. in Turner 81).

G. WORK WITHOUT AN AUTHOR LISTED

Sometimes a newspaper or magazine article does not include the name of an author. In such a case, include a brief version of the title in parentheses. For example, say you wanted to cite an article from *Consumer Reports* titled "Dry-Cleaning Alternatives" that listed no author:

> Conventional dry-cleaning, which requires the use of dangerous solvents, can result in both air and water pollution. However, if you are concerned about potential environmental damage caused by dry-cleaning your garments, you have several environmentally friendly options, including methods using carbon dioxide and silicone-based methods ("Dry-Cleaning" 10).

H. ELECTRONIC SOURCES

When citing electronic sources, you should follow the same principles you would use when citing other sources. If you are citing an article from an online journal or newspaper, cite it as you would any print article, using the author's last name or, if you don't know the author, a brief version of the title of the article. However, there are many different kinds of electronic sources, and you might not have access to the same kinds of information that are available for a published book or journal article. For example, websites don't usually have page numbers, and you might not be able to determine the author of an online source. In such cases incorporate sufficient information about the source into your sentence so that readers can easily find the citation in your bibliography:

> On its website, the Sustainability Institute maintains information about global climate change ("Research").

In this case the author of the web page being cited is unknown, so a brief version of the title of the web page, "Research at the Sustainability Institute," is included in parentheses. Notice that the title of a website is enclosed in quotation marks, just like the titles of articles in periodicals.

In most cases, a citation of an electronic source appears without a page reference because such sources are rarely numbered. You cannot add a page number based on a printout because readers accessing the same source from a different system may find a different page configuration. But if a page number is included in the source (as in the case of an electronic book) or if paragraphs are numbered, you should provide that information:

(Dickens 134)
(Martinez par. 8)

When online sources have page numbers, the parenthetical citation follows the same conventions as those for print sources. If paragraphs are numbered, it is necessary to add the abbreviation *par.* (or *pars.*) so that readers can see that you are not citing page numbers.

Works Cited in MLA Style   In an MLA-style bibliography, the works cited are arranged in alphabetical order by the author's last name. Here are the main things to remember when you are creating a bibliography in MLA style:

■ Provide the author's first and last name for each entry.
■ Capitalize every important word in the titles of books, articles, and journals.
■ Underline (or italicize) the titles of books, journals, and newspapers.
■ Place the titles of articles, stories, and poems in quotation marks.
■ Indent the second and any subsequent lines one-half inch (or five spaces).

Here's how a typical entry for a single-authored book appears in an MLA-style bibliography:

Abram, David. <u>The Spell of the Sensuous</u>. New York: Random, 1996.

Here are the important parts of the entry:

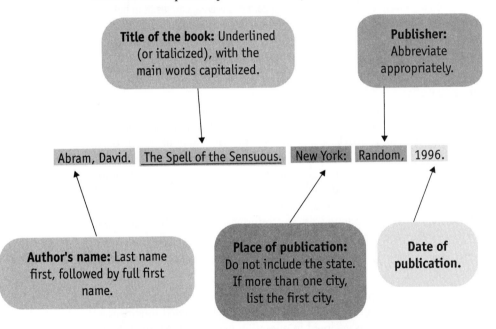

Notice that there are no page numbers for this entry.

If the work you are citing is a journal article, the entry would look like this:

George, Diana. "From Analysis to Design: Visual Communication in the Teaching of Writing." <u>College Composition and Communication</u> 54.1 (2002): 11–39.

Here are the parts of this entry:

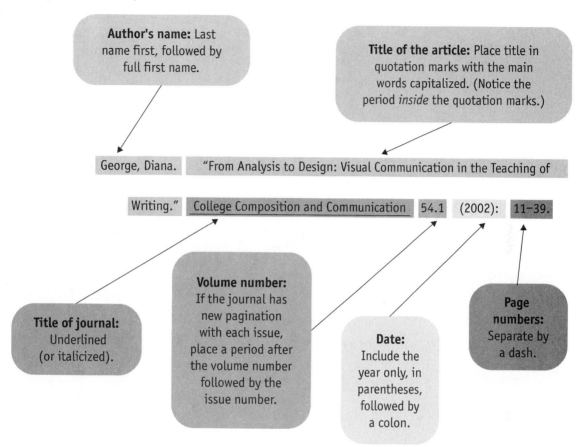

Author's name: Last name first, followed by full first name.

Title of the article: Place title in quotation marks with the main words capitalized. (Notice the period *inside* the quotation marks.)

George, Diana. "From Analysis to Design: Visual Communication in the Teaching of Writing." College Composition and Communication 54.1 (2002): 11–39.

Title of journal: Underlined (or italicized).

Volume number: If the journal has new pagination with each issue, place a period after the volume number followed by the issue number.

Date: Include the year only, in parentheses, followed by a colon.

Page numbers: Separate by a dash.

For online sources, you must include the Internet address, or URL, and two dates: the publication date (if available) and the date you accessed the site. Here's an entry for an online journal article:

Luebke, Steven R. "Using Linked Courses in the General Education Curriculum." Academic Writing 3 (2002). 16 Dec. 2002, <http://aw.colostate.edu/articles/luebke_2002.htm.>

Notice where the dates and URL are placed in this entry:

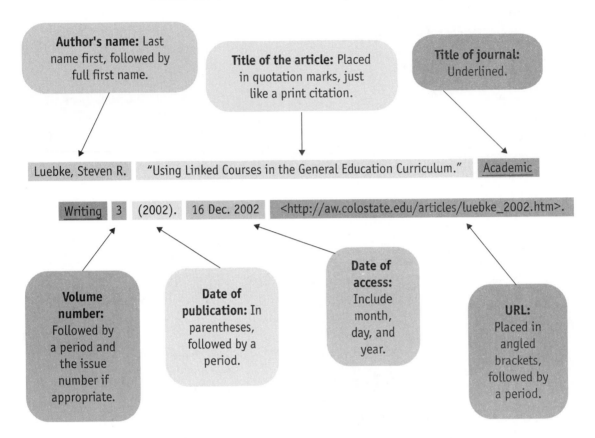

Author's name: Last name first, followed by full first name.

Title of the article: Placed in quotation marks, just like a print citation.

Title of journal: Underlined.

Luebke, Steven R.   "Using Linked Courses in the General Education Curriculum."   Academic

Writing 3 (2002). 16 Dec. 2002 <http://aw.colostate.edu/articles/luebke_2002.htm>.

Volume number: Followed by a period and the issue number if appropriate.

Date of publication: In parentheses, followed by a period.

Date of access: Include month, day, and year.

URL: Placed in angled brackets, followed by a period.

All entries in MLA format follow these basic principles, but each entry will contain slightly different information, depending on the kind of source cited. Keep that in mind as you look for the correct format for the sources you are citing in your bibliography.

A. BOOK WITH ONE AUTHOR

Harrison, Kathryn. <u>Envy</u>. New York: Random, 2005.

B. BOOK WITH TWO OR THREE AUTHORS

Gilbert, Sandra M., and Susan Gubar. <u>The Madwoman in the Attic: The Woman Writer and the Nineteenth-Century Literary Imagination</u>. New Haven: Yale UP, 1979.

Note that the subtitle is included, set off from the main title by a colon. The second author's name is not inverted, and abbreviations are used for *University Press* to provide a shortened form of the publisher's name. For books with three authors, put commas after the names of the first two authors (invert the name of the first author); separate the second two authors with a comma followed by *and*.

C. EDITED BOOK

Stout, Janis, ed. <u>Willa Cather and Material Culture</u>. Tuscaloosa: U of Alabama P, 2005.

D. BOOK WITH MORE THAN THREE AUTHORS OR EDITORS

Black, Laurel, et al., eds. <u>New Directions in Portfolio Assessment: Practice, Critical Theory, and Large-Scale Scoring</u>. Portsmouth: Boynton, 1994.

Give the name of the first author or editor only, and add the abbreviation *et al.*

E. SUBSEQUENT EDITIONS OF A BOOK

Tate, Gary, Edward P. J. Corbett, and Nancy Myers, eds. <u>The Writing Teacher's Sourcebook</u>. 3rd ed. New York: Oxford UP, 1994.

F. WORK IN AN ANTHOLOGY

Owens, Derek. "Sustainable Composition." <u>Ecocomposition: Theoretical and Pedagogical Approaches</u>. Eds. Christian R. Weisser and Sidney I. Dobrin. Albany: State U of New York P, 2001. 27–38.

Note that a period comes after the title of the selection but before the second quotation marks. A period is also used to separate the date of publication from the page reference, which is followed by a period.

G. TRANSLATED BOOK

Eco, Umberto. <u>The Aesthetics of Thomas Aquinas</u>. Trans. Hugh Bredin. Cambridge: Harvard UP, 1988.

H. WORK IN MORE THAN ONE VOLUME

Leckie, Robert. <u>The Wars of America</u>. 2 vols. New York: Harper, 1992.

I. INTRODUCTION, PREFACE, FOREWORD, OR AFTERWORD

Dove, Rita. Foreword. <u>Jonah's Gourd Vine</u>. By Zora Neale Hurston. New York: Harper, 1990. vii–xv.

J. ARTICLE IN AN ENCYCLOPEDIA

Daniels, Robert V. "Marxism." <u>The Encyclopedia Americana</u>. 1999 ed.

In citing material from well-known encyclopedias, give the author's name first, then the article title. If material is arranged alphabetically within the source, which is usually the case, there is no need to include volume and page numbers. You should give the full title of the encyclopedia, the edition (if it is stated), and the year of publication (for example, 11th ed. 1996). When no edition number is stated, identify the edition by the year of publication (for example, 1996 ed.). If the author of the article is identified only by initials, look elsewhere within the encyclopedia for a list identifying the names these initials stand for. If the article is unsigned, give the title first. (Note: This same form can be used for other reference books, such as dictionaries and the various editions of *Who's Who*.) For an example of how to cite an electronic encyclopedia, see Sections T and U.

K. GOVERNMENT PUBLICATION

> United States. Federal Bureau of Investigation. <u>Handbook of Forensic Science</u>.
> Washington: GPO, 1994.

For many government publications the author is unknown. When this is the case, the agency that issued the publication should be listed as the author. State the name of the government (for example, United States, Florida, or United Nations) followed by a period. Then give the name of the agency that issued the work, using abbreviations only if you can do so clearly (for example, Bureau of the Census, National Institute on Drug Abuse, or Dept. of Labor) followed by a period. The underlined title of the work comes next, followed by another period. Then give the place of publication, publisher, and date. Most federal publications are printed in Washington by the Government Printing Office (GPO), but you should be alert for exceptions. (Note: Treat a government pamphlet just as you would a book.)

L. JOURNAL ARTICLE WITH ONE AUTHOR

> Hesse, Douglas. "The Place of Creative Nonfiction." <u>College English</u> 65 (2003):
> 237–241.

The volume number comes after the journal title without any intervening punctuation. The year of publication is included within parentheses after the volume number. A colon separates the year of publication and the page reference. Leave one space after the volume number and one space after the colon.

M. JOURNAL ARTICLE PAGINATED ANEW IN EACH ISSUE

> Hershon, Joanna. "Crawl." <u>Virginia Quarterly Review</u> 81.3 (2005): 63–77.

In this case the issue number is included immediately after the volume number, and the two are separated by a period without any intervening space.

N. ARTICLE FROM A MAGAZINE ISSUED MONTHLY

> Rhodes, Richard. "Living with the Bomb." <u>National Geographic</u> Aug. 2005: 98–113.

Instead of citing the volume number, give the month and year of the issue. Abbreviate the month when it has more than four letters. (May, June, and July are spelled out.) For an example of how to list an article from a magazine published monthly that was obtained through a computer database, see Section R.

O. ARTICLE FROM A MAGAZINE ISSUED WEEKLY

> Kalb, Claudia. "Get Up and Get Moving." <u>Newsweek</u> 20 Jan. 2003: 59–64.

The form is the same as for an article in a magazine issued monthly, but you add the day immediately before the month. Note that a dash between page numbers indicates consecutive pages. When an article is printed on nonconsecutive pages—beginning on page 34, for example, and continuing on page 78—give only the first page number and a plus sign: 34+.

P. ARTICLE FROM A DAILY NEWSPAPER

> Raspberry, William. "Poverty and the Father Factor." Washington Post 1 Aug. 2005, District & Maryland ed., A17.

If more than one edition is available on the date in question, specify the edition immediately after the date. If the city of publication is not part of a locally published newspaper's name, identify the city in brackets after the newspaper title. Because newspapers often consist of separate sections, you should cite the section letter if each section has separate pagination. If a newspaper consists of only one section or if the pagination is continuous from one section to the next, then you do not need to include the section letter. If the article is unsigned, begin the entry with the title of the article; alphabetize the article under its title, passing over small words such as "a" and "the." For an example of how to cite a newspaper article accessed through a subscription service such as LexisNexis, see Section U.

Q. EDITORIAL

> Terzian, Philip. "Armed Forces Work Just Fine without Draft." Editorial. Albany Times Union 14 Jan. 2003: A14.

Editorials are identified as such between the title of the article and the title of the newspaper or magazine.

R. PRINTED MATERIAL ACCESSED FROM A PERIODICALLY PUBLISHED DATABASE ON CD-ROM

Many periodicals and reference works such as bibliographies are now available on CD-ROMs, which are sometimes updated. Here's an example of a print article from a journal called *Managing Office Technology* that was found on a CD-ROM issued by UMI-ProQuest:

> Holtzman, Henry. "Team Management: Its Time Has Come . . . Again." Managing Office Technology Feb. 1994: 8. ABI/Inform. CD-ROM. UMI-ProQuest. Oct. 1994.

Notice that this entry includes the same information that would be provided for a magazine or journal article: author (if known), article title, journal title, date of print publication, and page reference. In addition, cite the database you used (in this case, ABI/ Inform), the medium through which you accessed it (CD-ROM), and, if available, the vendor that made this medium available (here, UMI-ProQuest). Conclude with the date of electronic publication.

S. EXCLUSIVELY ELECTRONIC MATERIAL ACCESSED FROM A PERIODICALLY PUBLISHED DATABASE

Many reference works today are published exclusively in electronic form on media such as CD-ROM and computer diskettes:

> African Development Bank. "1995 AFDB Indicative Learning Program." National Trade Data Bank. CD-ROM. U.S. Commercial Service. Mar. 1996.

Give the author's name (a corporate author in this case), the title of the material in quotation marks, the title of the database (here, *National Trade Data Bank*), the publication medium (in this case, CD-ROM), the vendor (here, U.S. Commercial Service), and the date it was published electronically. Note that the title of the database is underlined.

T. NONPERIODICAL PUBLICATION ON CD-ROM

Encyclopedias and similar nonperiodical reference works are now regularly available on CD-ROM. Here is an entry for an article from *The Academic American Encyclopedia* on CD-ROM:

> Hogan, Robert. "Abbey Theater." <u>The Academic American Encyclopedia</u>. CD-ROM. Danbury: Grolier, 1995.

If no author is identified, begin with the work's title; if no author or title is available, begin with the title of the product consulted.

If you are citing an article from an encyclopedia available online, use the format for an article accessed through an online database (see Section U).

U. PRINTED PUBLICATION ACCESSED THROUGH A DATABASE SUBSCRIPTION SERVICE

> Jeffers, Thomas L. "Plagiarism High and Low." <u>Commentary</u> 114.3 (2002): 54–61. LexisNexis. State U of New York-Albany Lib. 28 Dec. 2002.

Follow the same pattern you would for the print equivalent (in this case, a magazine article), then add the underlined title of the database (if known), the name of the service (in this case, LexisNexis), and how you accessed it (in this example, through the SUNY-Albany Libraries). Then include the date you accessed the article, followed by the URL of the service's home page (if known) in angled brackets < >. Break the URL only where there is a slash.

V. ARTICLE FROM AN ONLINE PERIODICAL

> Sands, Peter. "Pushing and Pulling Toward the Middle." Kairos 7.3 (2002). 15 Oct. 2002, <u><http://english.ttu.edu/kairos/7.3/binder2.html?coverweb.html#de.></u>

Cite the article as you would for a print article, but add the date you accessed the article just after the publication date (which is in parentheses followed by a period). Then add the URL in angled brackets. Remember to place a period at the end of the entry.

Follow this pattern for articles from any online periodicals, whether they are from newspapers, popular magazines, or scholarly journals: cite the article as you would a print article, then add the date you accessed it and the URL. The pattern holds for online books.

W. THESIS PUBLISHED ONLINE

Increasingly, authors make their work available on websites. Citing these websites can be tricky because you do not always have access to all publication information. Here's an entry for a thesis that the author published on a website:

> Formaro, Tom. "Argumentation on the World Wide Web." MA thesis. Some Random Stuff (and a Thesis). 9 May 2001. 17 Nov. 2002 <u><http://users.rcn.com/mackey/thesis/thesis.html.></u>

Notice that this entry follows the same pattern as an online periodical (see Section V): the author's name first, followed by the title of the work and of the website, the date of publication, the date you accessed the text, and the URL (in angled brackets). If there is no date of publication, use *n.d.* for "no date." Break the URL only where there is a slash.

X. ARTICLE ON A WEBSITE

There are many kinds of websites where you can find useful information about a topic. Many sites are maintained by advocacy groups, government or nongovernment organizations, and educational institutions. If you are using information from such a website, follow the same basic principles for citing the source that you would follow for more conventional print sources. Here's an entry for an article found on the website for an advocacy group called the Center for a New American Dream:

> "In the Market? Think Green: The Center for a New American Dream's Guide to Environmentally Preferable Purchasing." Center for a New American Dream. 8 Aug. 2001 <http://www.newdream.org/buygreen/index.html.>

Notice that because there is no author listed on the site, the title of the article is listed first, in quotation marks. The organization hosting the website is listed next, followed by the date of access and the URL of the article being referenced.

Y. PERSONAL HOME PAGE

> White, Crystal. Home page. 13 Jan. 2003. 22 June 2003 <http://www.geocities.com/lfnxphile/.>

Z. INTERVIEW

> Scheurer, Erika. Personal interview. 16 Jan. 2006.

If you interview someone, alphabetize the interview under the surname of the person interviewed. Indicate whether it was a personal interview, telephone interview, or e-mail interview.

AA. NEWSGROUP, MAILING LIST, OR DISCUSSION BOARD POSTING

There are several different kinds of online discussion forums, including mailing lists and newsgroups. This example is from a Web-based discussion board:

> Mountainman72. "Re: Avalanche Question." Online posting. 10 Jan. 2003. NEice Talk. 12 Jan. 2003 <http://www.neice.com/cgi-bin/ultimatebb.cgi?ubb=forum&f=1.>

Notice that the author's name (or pseudonym) is first, followed by the title of the posting, the description *Online posting*, the date of the posting, the name of the forum (if known), the date of access, and the URL.

For a mailing list or newsgroup posting, include the name of the mailing list or newsgroup after the date of the posting, as follows:

> Fleischer, Cathy. "Colearn Logins." Online posting. 9 Dec. 2002. CoLEARN Research
>
> Team Discussion List. 5 Jan. 2003 <researchteam@serv1.ncte.org.>

APA-Style Documentation

As in the preceding discussion of MLA-style documentation, this section begins with how to cite sources parenthetically within the text of an argument and then turns to how to cite sources in a bibliography.

The APA Author/Year Style   The American Psychological Association (APA) requires that in-text documentation identify the author of the work and the year in which the work was published; where appropriate, page numbers are also included, preceded by the abbreviation *p.* or *pp.* This information should be provided parenthetically; it is not necessary to repeat any information already provided directly in the sentence.

A. WORK BY ONE AUTHOR

If you wished to cite a book by Alan Peshkin titled *Places of Memory,* published in 1997, you might do so as follows:

> Native American students face the challenge of trying to maintain their cultural heritage while assimilating into mainstream American culture (Peshkin, 1997).

or

> Peshkin (1997) has argued that the pressures on Native American students to assimilate into mainstream American culture can contribute to poor academic performance.

If the reference is to a specific chapter or page, that information should also be included. For example:

> Peshkin's (1997) study focuses on what he calls the "dual-world character of the students' lives" (p. 5).

Note that the date of publication (in parentheses) follows the author's name; the page reference (also in parentheses) is placed at the end of the sentence. If the author's name is not included in the sentence, it should be included in the parentheses:

> The "dual-world character" of the lives of many Native American students can create obstacles to their academic success (Peshkin, 1997, p. 5).

B. WORK WITH TWO OR MORE AUTHORS

If a work has two authors, you should mention the names of both authors every time a reference is made to their work:

> A recent study of industry (Cole & Walker, 1997) argued that . . .

or

> More recently, Cole and Walker (1997) have argued that . . .

Note that the ampersand (&) is used only within parentheses.

Scientific papers often have multiple authors because of the amount of research involved. In the first reference to a work with three to five authors, you should identify each of the authors:

> Hodges, McKnew, Cytryn, Stern, and Kline (1982) have shown . . .

Subsequent references to the same work should use an abbreviated form:

> This method was also used in an earlier study (Hodges et al., 1982).

If a work has six authors (or more), this abbreviated form should be used even for the first reference. If confusion is possible because you must refer to more than one work by the first author, list as many coauthors as necessary to distinguish between the two works.

C. WORK WITH A CORPORATE AUTHOR

When a work has a corporate author, your first reference should include the full name of the corporation, committee, agency, or institution involved. For example, if you were citing the *Buying Guide 2002,* published by Consumer Reports, you might do so like this:

> There are several strategies you can use to protect yourself when ordering merchandise online (Consumer Reports, 2002, pp. 11-12).

If the corporate name is long, you can abbreviate subsequent references to the same source. If you were citing a report from the Fund for the Improvement of Postsecondary Education (FIPSE), for example, you would use the full name when you first cited it, then use FIPSE for any subsequent references.

D. REFERENCE TO MORE THAN ONE WORK

When the same citation refers to two or more sources, the works should be listed alphabetically, according to the first author's surname, and separated with semicolons:

> Several studies have examined the social nature of literacy (Finders, 1997; Heath, 1983; Street, 1984; Young, 1994).

If you are referring to more than one work by the same author(s), list the works in the order in which they were published.

> The validity of this type of testing is now well established (Collins, 1988, 1994).

If you refer to more than one work by the same author published in the same year, distinguish individual works by identifying them as *a, b, c,* and so on:

> These findings have been questioned by Scheiber (1997a, 1997b).

References in APA Style In APA style, the bibliography is arranged alphabetically by the author's last name. The date of publication is emphasized by placing it within parentheses immediately after the author's name. The APA *Publication Manual* (5th ed.) recommends a hanging indent style of a half-inch, or five spaces, which is what is shown in the following illustrations.

Here are the main things to keep in mind when preparing a bibliography in APA style:

- Provide the author's surname, followed by an initial for the first name.
- Place the date in parentheses and follow it with a period; the date should always be the second element in an entry.
- Capitalize only the first word and any proper nouns of any title and subtitle (if there is one) in the entry.
- Italicize titles of books, journals, magazines, and newspapers.
- Do *not* place quotation marks around the titles of articles or chapters and do not italicize or underline them.

In APA style, a typical entry for a single-authored book looks like this:

> Geertz, C. (2000). *Available light: Anthropological reflections on philosophical topics.*
> Princeton, NJ: Princeton University Press.

Here are the important parts of the entry:

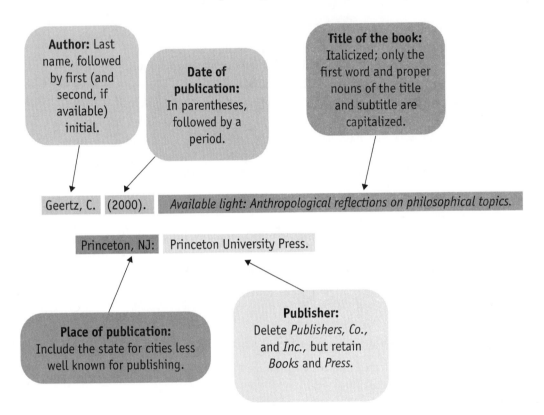

Author: Last name, followed by first (and second, if available) initial.

Date of publication: In parentheses, followed by a period.

Title of the book: Italicized; only the first word and proper nouns of the title and subtitle are capitalized.

Geertz, C. (2000). *Available light: Anthropological reflections on philosophical topics.*

Princeton, NJ: Princeton University Press.

Place of publication: Include the state for cities less well known for publishing.

Publisher: Delete *Publishers, Co.,* and *Inc.,* but retain *Books* and *Press.*

Here is an entry for a journal article:

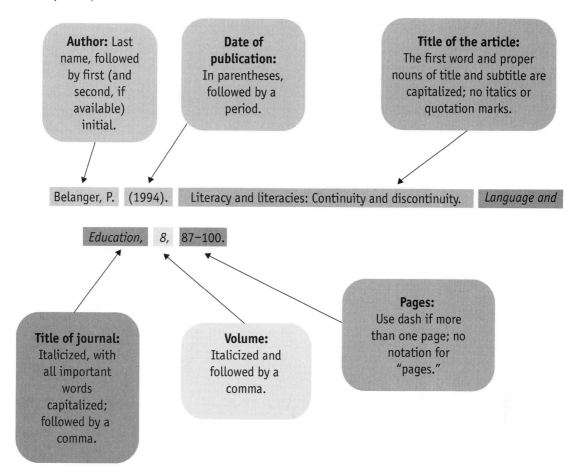

Notice the differences between the entry for a journal article and the following example of an entry for a newspaper article:

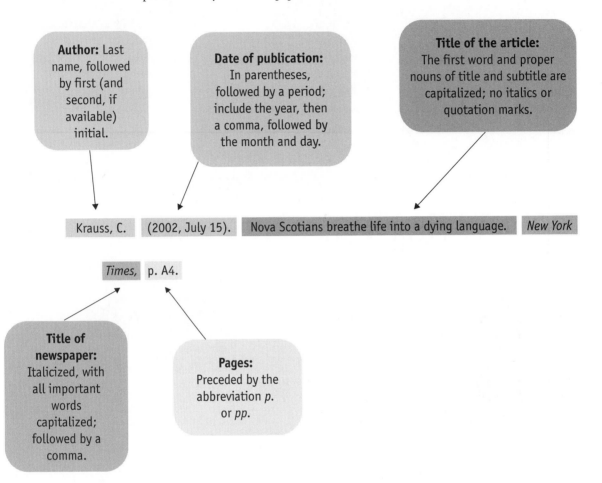

Author: Last name, followed by first (and second, if available) initial.

Date of publication: In parentheses, followed by a period; include the year, then a comma, followed by the month and day.

Title of the article: The first word and proper nouns of title and subtitle are capitalized; no italics or quotation marks.

Krauss, C.   (2002, July 15).   Nova Scotians breathe life into a dying language.   *New York*

Times,   p. A4.

Title of newspaper: Italicized, with all important words capitalized; followed by a comma.

Pages: Preceded by the abbreviation *p.* or *pp.*

Notice that for newspaper articles the date includes the month and day, along with the year, in parentheses; for monthly magazines, include only the year and month. Notice, too, that the page numbers are preceded by an abbreviation, unlike the entry for a journal article.

If you were citing a newspaper article that you retrieved from a database subscription service, your entry would look like this:

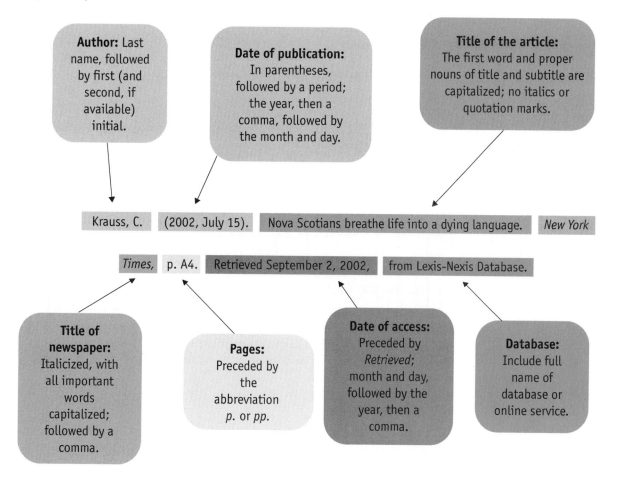

A. BOOK WITH ONE AUTHOR

Loy, D. (1998). *Nonduality: A study in comparative philosophy.* Amherst, NY: Humanity Books.

Note that the author's first name is indicated only by an initial. Capital letters are used only for the first word of the title and the first word of the subtitle if there is one. (But when a proper name appears within a title, it retains the capitalization it would normally receive; for example: *A history of ideas in Brazil.*) The name of the publisher, Humanity Books, is given in its entirety. A period comes after the parentheses surrounding the date of publication and after the title and the publisher.

B. BOOK WITH TWO OR MORE AUTHORS

Blitz, M., & Hurlbert, C. M. (1998). *Letters for the living: Teaching writing in a violent age.* Urbana, IL: National Council for Teachers of English.

An ampersand (&) is used to separate the names of two authors. When there are three or more authors, separate their names with commas, keeping each name reversed, and put an ampersand immediately before the last author's name.

C. EDITED BOOK

Street, B. V. (Ed.). (2001). *Literacy and development: Ethnographic perspectives.* New York: Routledge.

The abbreviation for editor is *Ed.;* it should be capitalized and included within parentheses between the name of the editor and the date of publication. The abbreviation for editors is *Eds.* Give the names of all editors, no matter how many there are.

D. ARTICLE OR CHAPTER IN AN EDITED BOOK

Faigley, L. (1999). Beyond imagination: The internet and global digital literacy. In G. E. Hawisher & C. L. Selfe (Eds.), *Passions, pedagogies, and 21st-century technologies* (pp. 129–139). Logan, UT: Utah State University Press.

Notice that the editor's name is not inverted when it is not in the author's position. Notice, too, that the title of the article or chapter is *not* placed in quotation marks. Use a comma to separate the editor from the title of the edited book. The pages between which the material can be found appear within parentheses immediately after the book title. Use *p.* for page and *pp.* for pages.

E. TRANSLATED BOOK

Calasso, R. (1993). *The marriage of Cadmus and Harmony* (T. Parks, Trans.). New York: Random. (Original work published 1988).

Within parentheses immediately after the book title, give the translator's name followed by a comma and the abbreviation *Trans.* If the original work was published earlier, include this information at the end.

F. SUBSEQUENT EDITIONS OF A BOOK

Hopkins, B. R. (1993). *A legal guide to starting and managing a nonprofit organization* (2nd ed.). New York: Wiley.

The edition is identified immediately after the title. Note that edition is abbreviated *ed.*—with a lowercase "e"—and should not be confused with *Ed.* for editor; it is also placed in parentheses.

G. BOOK WITH A CORPORATE AUTHOR

American Red Cross. (1993). *Standard first aid.* St. Louis, MO: Mosby.

H. MULTIVOLUME WORK

Eisenstein, E. (1979). *The printing press as an agent of change: Communications and cultural transformations in early-modern Europe* (Vol. 2). Cambridge, England: Cambridge University Press.

The volume number is included within parentheses immediately after the title.

I. JOURNAL ARTICLE WITH ONE AUTHOR

Butler, A. C. (1996). The effect of welfare benefit levels on poverty among single-parent families. *Social Problems, 43,* 94–115.

Do not use quotation marks around the article title. Capitalize all important words in the journal title and italicize. Put a comma after the journal title and then give the volume and page numbers. Abbreviations are not used for "volume" and "page." To distinguish between the numbers, italicize the volume number and put a comma between it and the page numbers.

J. JOURNAL ARTICLE WITH MORE THAN ONE AUTHOR

Nugent, J. K., Lester, B. M., Greene, S. M., Wieczorek-Deering, D., & O'Mahoney, P. (1996). The effects of maternal alcohol consumption and cigarette smoking during pregnancy on acoustic cry analysis. *Child Development, 67,* 1806–1815.

Note that all authors' names are listed in the same format: last name followed by a comma and then the first (and second, if available) initial; commas separate all names.

K. JOURNAL ARTICLE PAGINATED ANEW IN EACH ISSUE

Major, B. (1993). Gender, entitlement, and the distribution of family labor. *Journal of Social Issues, 49*(3), 141–159.

When each issue of a journal begins with page 1, include the issue number in parentheses immediately after the italicized volume number. Do not italicize the issue number.

L. ARTICLE FROM A MAGAZINE ISSUED MONTHLY

Baker, K. (1997, February). Searching the window into nature's soul. *Smithsonian, 745,* 94–104.

Include the month of issue after the year of publication in parentheses immediately after the author's name. Include the volume number. Follow the same form for an article in a weekly magazine issued on a specific day, but add the day after the month:

Hazen, R. M. (1991, February 25). Why my kids hate science. *Newsweek, 331,* 7.

M. ARTICLE FROM A DAILY NEWSPAPER

Bishop, J. E. (1996, November 13). Heart disease may actually be rising. *The Wall Street Journal,* p. B6.

Place the exact date of issue within parentheses immediately after the author. After the newspaper title, specify the page number(s). Include *The* if it is part of the newspaper title.

N. GOVERNMENT DOCUMENT

> U.S. Department of Labor. (1993). *Teaching the scans competencies.* Washington, DC: U.S. Government Printing Office.

List the agency that produced the document as the author if no author is identified. Within parentheses immediately after the document title, give the publication number (which is assigned to the document by the government), if available.

O. ANONYMOUS WORK

> A breath of fresh air. (1991, April 29). *Time, 187,* 49.

Alphabetize the work under the first important word in the title, and follow the form for the type of publication in question (in this case a magazine published weekly).

P. JOURNAL ARTICLE RETRIEVED ONLINE

If the article you are citing is from a print journal that also appears online, then cite the article as you normally would but indicate that you viewed the electronic version, as follows:

> Smith, K. (2001). Critical conversations in difficult times [Electronic version]. *English Education, 33*(2), 153–165.

However, if the article you are citing might be different online (for instance, it includes additional text or charts) or if it has no page numbers, then indicate when you accessed it and include the URL:

> Smith, K. (2001). Critical conversations in difficult times. English Education, 33(2), 153–165. Retrieved December 12, 2002, from http://www.ncte.org/pdfs/subscribers-only/ee/0332-jan01/EE0332Critical.pdf

Notice that there is no period after the URL.

Q. ONLINE JOURNAL ARTICLE

For an article from a journal that appears only online (and not in print form), include the date of access and the URL of the site where the article was located:

> Lassonde, C. A. (2002). Learning from others: Literacy perspectives of middle-school English teachers. Networks, 5(3). Retrieved January 15, 2003, from http://www. oise.utoronto.ca/~ctd/networks/journal/Vol%205(3).2002dec/Lassonde.html

R. INTERVIEW

Interviews are not considered recoverable data and should not be included in the References.

A Checklist for Documentation

1. Remember to document any direct quotation, any idea that has come from someone else's work, and any fact or statistic that is not widely known. **2.** Be sure to enclose all quotations in quotation marks. **3.** Make sure that paraphrases are in your own words but still accurately reflect the content of the original material. **4.** Remember that every source cited in your text should have a corresponding entry in the bibliography. **5.** Try to vary the introductions you use for quotations and paraphrases. **6.** When you mention authorities by name, try to identify who they are so that your audience can evaluate the source (for example, "According to Ira Glasser, Executive Director of the American Civil Liberties Union, recent congressional legislation violates . . ."). However, you need not identify well-known figures. **7.** If in doubt about whether to document a source, you would probably be wise to document it. But be careful not to overdocument your paper.

Preparing Your Final Draft

After investing considerable time in researching, drafting, and revising your paper, be sure to allow sufficient time for editing your final draft. If you rush this stage of the process, the work that you submit for evaluation might not adequately reflect the investment of time you gave to the project as a whole. Unless instructed otherwise, you should be guided by the rules in the following checklist.

A Checklist for Manuscript Form

1. Papers should be typed or word processed. Use nonerasable 8 1/2-by-11-inch white paper. Type on one side of each page. Double-space all lines, leaving a margin of one inch on all sides. **2.** In the upper left corner of page 1 or on a separate title page, include the following information: your name, your instructor's name, the course and section number, and the date the essay is submitted. **3.** Number each page in the upper right corner, 1.2 inches from the top. If using MLA-style documentation, type your last name immediately before the page number. If using APA-style documentation, type a shortened version of the title (one or two words) before the number. **4.** Make sure that you consistently follow a documentation style that is acceptable to your instructor. **5.** Any quotation of more than four lines in an MLA-style paper or more than forty words in an APA-style paper should be set off from the rest of the text. Begin a new line, indenting one inch (or ten spaces) to form the left margin of the quotation. The indention means that you are quoting, so additional quotation marks are unnecessary in this case (except for quotations within the quotation). **6.** Proofread your paper carefully. If your instructor allows ink corrections, make them as neatly as you can. Redo any page that has numerous or lengthy corrections. **7.** If you have used a word processor for your paper, be sure to separate pages that have been printed on a continuous sheet. Use a paper clip or staple to bind the pages together.

Negotiating Differences

8 ■ Ownership

9 ■ Body Image

10 ■ Relationships

11 ■ Education

12 ■ American National Identity

13 ■ Environments

8

Ownership

Cluster 1

WHO OWNS WORDS AND IDEAS?

① Jay Mathews, "Standing Up for the Power of Learning"

② Ralph Caplan, "What's Yours? (Ownership of Intellectual Property)"

③ David Gibson, "Copyright Crusaders"

④ Angela Lipson and Sheila M. Reindl, "The Responsible Plagiarist"

CON-TEXT
**What Is
Fair Use?**

Cluster 2

WHO OWNS MUSIC?

① Janis Ian, "Free Downloads Play Sweet Music"

② Tom Lowry, "Ringtones: Music to Moguls' Ears"

③ James Surowiecki, "Hello, Cleveland"

④ Tom McCourt, "Collecting Music in the Digital Realm"

CON-TEXT
**The Importance
of Music**

Cluster 3

WHO OWNS THE MEDIA?

① Jenny Toomey, "Empire of the Air"

② Gal Beckerman, "Tripping Up Big Media"

③ Laura Peterson, "The Moguls Are the Medium"

④ Tom Lowry and Ron Grover, "Breaking Up Is Easy to Do"

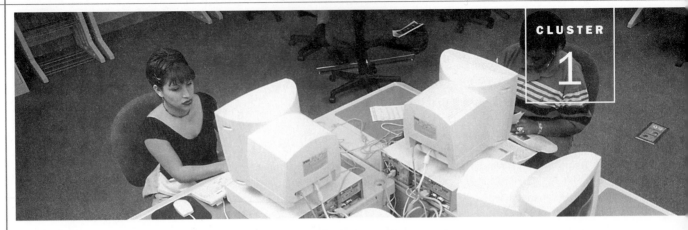

Who Owns Words and Ideas?

For students, plagiarism is usually a straightforward matter: If you present someone else's words or ideas as your own, you have plagiarized. In most schools, if you are caught doing so, the consequences can be severe, including even dismissal from school. The whole matter of plagiarism rests on an assumption that each of us has our own ideas and is responsible for our own words. In this sense, we "own" those words and ideas; we "own" our intellectual work. And we're not allowed to "steal" others' words or ideas. But the ownership of intellectual work—the matter of intellectual property—is not as straightforward as it might seem. It's easy to see plagiarism when a student hands in a paper written by someone else; in effect, that student is submitting as his or her own someone else's intellectual property. But what if you asked a roommate or a relative for help with an essay you are writing for one of your classes? What if that person suggested a way for you to reword a few sentences or a paragraph? Or that person advised you to reorganize your essay to make it more coherent and effective? If you did so and then submitted your essay to your teacher, is that essay yours? Or does it belong partly to the roommate or relative who helped you? Who owns the ideas and words in that essay? ■ This example suggests how difficult it can be to determine the source—or "owner"—of an idea or a phrase. It also suggests how little of what we tend to think of as our own intellectual work really is the result of an exclusively individual effort. It's common to ask a friend how a sentence sounds when you are writing an essay or a letter. It's also common for students to work together on projects, problems, or laboratory experiments. And if it's common for students to do so, it's even more common for professionals in many fields. Scientists rarely work alone, and even those who do usually draw on the previous experiments of other scientists. The same is true of professionals in every kind of field or business. Collaboration is the norm in many settings. And when people collaborate, the matter of whose intellectual property results becomes complicated. ■ Moreover, the ideas that are available to us often come from somewhere else altogether. For example, if you are writing a poem about an ill-fated romantic relationship, where did the idea for that poem come from? From your experience? From your imagination? From a movie you happened to see? From a story a friend told you? Are you "stealing" someone else's intellectual property because you have read dozens of love poems written by others? And if you write that poem in an established poetic format, such as a sonnet, are you stealing that format because you didn't create it yourself? ■ Intellectual property, of course, is not just an ethical matter; it is a legal and economic matter as well. The U.S. Constitution provides for the establishment of copyright laws to protect the creators of intellectual property. Copyright laws have existed since 1790, when Congress first passed a law decreeing that an author or artist "owned" a work he or she created for fourteen years. But even when intellectual property is defined legally, questions inevitably arise about who owns specific words or ideas and who has the right to use them. The idea of the "fair use" of copyrighted materials, for example, provides for exceptions to protected works. But even when such a principle is spelled out in the legal code, it can never answer all questions that might arise when determining who owns specific words or a specific idea. ■ Despite these difficulties, the fact that we live in a culture based on private property often means that we have to try to determine the ownership of intellectual property. The authors of the essays in this section all address this need as it emerges in schools and in the commercial culture. They examine questions of the ownership of words and ideas in ways that may help you appreciate the complexity of intellectual property and consider the many interests that people have in trying to determine who owns words and ideas. As a group, these essays also raise a broader question about intellectual property: Is it really possible for anyone to "own" words or ideas?

CON-TEXT

What Is Fair Use?

1 Congress favored nonprofit educational uses over commercial uses. Copies used in education, but made or sold at monetary profit, may not be favored. Courts also favor uses that are "transformative" or that are not mere reproductions. Fair use is more likely when the copyrighted work is "transformed" into something new or of new utility, such as quotations incorporated into a paper, and perhaps pieces of a work mixed into a multimedia product for your own teaching needs or included in commentary or criticism of the original. For teaching purposes, however, multiple copies of some works are specifically allowed, even if not "transformative." The Supreme Court underscored that conclusion by focusing on these key words in the statute: "including multiple copies for classroom use." . . .

Many characteristics of a work can affect the application of fair use. For example, several recent court decisions have concluded that the unpublished "nature" of historical correspondence can weigh against fair use. The courts reasoned that copyright owners should have the right to determine the circumstances of "first publication." The authorities are split, however, on whether a published work that is currently out of print should receive special treatment. Courts more readily favor the fair use of nonfiction rather than fiction.

SOURCE: "What is 'Fair Use'?" The Consortium for Educational Technology for University Systems.

① JAY MATHEWS, "Standing Up for the Power of Learning"

In the fall of 2001, a student at the Georgia Institute of Technology was accused of cheating because he had discussed an assignment in his computer science course with a friend. By talking about the assignment, the student violated an honor code in that computer science course that prohibits collaboration among students. According to that honor code, "at no time is it acceptable for you to share your solutions to the homework assignments with other students, whether these solutions are complete or partial, nor is it acceptable to compare your solutions with other students." On the surface, such a stipulation might seem reasonable, because students are usually graded on their ability to do the required work in a course. But as Jay Mathews suggests in the following essay, a closer look at this case raises some tricky questions. For one thing, is it cheating if a student learns by working with a classmate? Do students always learn by themselves? And if a student learns by getting help from someone else, does that mean that the work the student submits to a teacher—such as the solution to a problem in computer science—does not "belong" to that student? In writing about the incident at Georgia Tech, and in praising that university's willingness to change its policy as a result of the incident, Mathews argues for a position on cheating that tries to hold students accountable for doing their own work yet acknowledges the reality that learning is often not an exclusively individual activity. As you read, consider whether Mathews's position on this issue is realistic. Is it possible to distinguish between collaboration and cheating in the way he suggests? Do schools have any choice but to do so? Mathews reports on education for the *Washington Post* and is the author of *Class Struggles: What's Right (and Wrong) with America's Best Public Schools* (1998). This essay appeared in his column in the *Washington Post* in 2002.

Standing Up for the Power of Learning

JAY MATHEWS

1 I am barely capable of booting up my office computer in the morning. One of those neighborhood computer consultants just paid a house call because I can't get my new CD burner even to acknowledge my existence. But that did not stop me from telling Georgia Tech in a recent column how to monitor homework in its freshman course, Computer Studies 1321.*

I had help from one of the students in the course, a graduate of one of the Washington area's best high schools, who had the disagreeable experience of finding this e-mail addressed to him just before he was to leave on a family skiing vacation last December: "Your name has been turned into the Associate Dean of Students, Karen Boyd, for suspicion of academic misconduct."

A computer check designed to catch cheaters had found similarity between his answers and that of a classmate with whom he had discussed a CS 1321 homework assignment. He had worked hard to earn a B in a course that had started disastrously for him. He could have punted the assignment. It was only 2 percent of his grade. But he wanted to get ready for the final exam. He was eager to learn, which was his big mistake.

The CS 1321 honor code said "at no time is it acceptable for you to share your solutions to the homework assignments with other students, whether these solutions are complete or partial, nor is it acceptable to compare your solutions with other students." Students complained of the reign of terror atmosphere the rule encouraged—don't say anything to anybody because if your approach pops up on their homework, you're screwed.

5 My informant thought it made no sense for the course to prohibit students from working together and from consulting outside materials when dealing with difficult homework assignments. He thought his discussion with a classmate was useful discourse that could only make them better students. And now, it turns out, he was right. Acting like the great university it is, Georgia Tech ordered a study of the course. With astonishing speed, it announced Thursday that it was changing the rules in just the way the freshman told me they ought to be changed.

News stories on the university's announcement missed the importance of this. They emphasized that three fourths of the 187 Georgia Tech students ac-

cused of cheating on CS 1321 homework last fall were found guilty and punished with everything from a zero on the assignment to suspension. Everybody knew weeks ago that was going to happen. Many freshmen, like my informant, accepted the university's strong recommendation that they swallow their punishment, in his case a C in the course, and move on, even though they felt they had done nothing wrong.

Other universities, such as MIT, do not prohibit students from working together on difficult assignments. They are simply required to mark the places where they collaborated. That makes sense to me. Every successful educational enterprise I know encourages student discussion and cooperation. The anti-collaboration rule was even unusual for Georgia Tech, and only found in that freshman course. I suggested the computerized copying checks be reserved for

*Computer Science 1321, Introduction to Computers, is described in the Georgia Tech catalog as follows: "Foundations of computing with an emphasis on the design, construction, and analysis of algorithms. Laboratory-based instruction to computers and software tools."

COLLABORATIVE LEARNING

Also referred to as "cooperative learning," collaborative learning has been extensively studied by education researchers. Although there are different kinds of collaborative learning and there is disagreement among scholars on some of the specifics of such learning, most agree that collaborative learning benefits students. Many studies show positive results—including higher academic achievement—when students work together. According to Roger T. Johnson and David Johnson, researchers who have studied cooperative learning, "The fact that working together to achieve a common goal produces higher achievement and greater productivity than does working alone is so well confirmed by so much research that it stands as one of the strongest principles of social and organizational psychology. Cooperative learning is indicated whenever learning goals are highly important, mastery and retention are important, a task is complex or conceptual, problem solving is desired, divergent thinking or creativity is desired, quality of performance is expected, and higher-level reasoning strategies and critical thinking are needed" ("Cooperative Learning: An Overview").

people interested in this stuff. (Some messages also discussed my peculiar views on cheating, a separate issue which I will take up in a future column.)

Interestingly, the students, teachers and experts who sent the e-mails were split evenly on the no-collaboration and no-outside-materials rules. Stephen Miller, a senior technical specialist for FleetBoston Financial, said, "Restricting student access to resources in their effort to maximize their learning potential is simply unbelievable. Decreeing that the only valid resources are Georgia Tech staff or course materials is the height of arrogance. To forbid Computer Science students from seeking any help from other students on their homework is to remove one of the prime and fundamental learning tools. Collaboration and cooperation, especially in the computer science field, is one of the tried and true ways of advancement and improvement."

10 But Meredith Skeels, an undergraduate at the University of Washington, said it was vitally important to struggle through your coding assignments on your own, at least while you are learning. "Programming is all about problem solving," she said. "I will be the first to say that it can be very frustrating when you just cannot get the code to work. It drives you crazy. You

tests, the proper place to determine what a student has learned. Forcing undergraduates to watch what they say to friends about their homework sounded too much like the rules for discourse in the Chinese universities I used to visit.

The column produced an extraordinary volume of e-mail. That was another sign of my ignorance. I had no idea there were so many

walk to class thinking about it and you wake up in the morning thinking of some new way to fix it. That is part of the process that makes you a good programmer."

I had expected Georgia Tech to appoint a committee, give it several months to work up some recommendations, and then stick the results in a drawer until the dean in charge pulled them out to read during a vacation as an excuse to limit conversation with his mother-in-law. That is the way such matters would be handled by some of our better known liberal arts universities, the ones thick with Georgian architecture and administrators who used to be lawyers, economists or English professors. I figured it would be a year before any decisions were made, long after most people had forgotten the cheating charges of 2001.

Imagine my shock to learn Thursday that Georgia Tech's task force on introductory computer science courses had already made its recommendations, and many had been implemented immediately. It must be nice to have engineers in charge. They seem more interested in getting things done than making certain all the bureaucratic niceties are observed.

In its report, the task force acknowledged that "individual programming skills are the foundation upon which successful group programming projects are based" but "we also know that collaboration supports learning." The nine-member group said "many of us have had the experience of having a 'bug' in our program, explaining the program to another person in hopes that he or she might tell us what is wrong, and in the process of explaining, suddenly understanding why the program does not work!"

The most feasible way to check on student programming skills, the report said, was interactive testing in a computer lab. As for homework in CS 1321, it recommended that "any and all kinds of collaboration be allowed . . .

including sharing portions of others' programs if that is what is needed for a student to learn to develop a working solution to the assignment." Using such help, as well as outside sources, would be fine "so long as attribution is made."

15 And that, said Bob McMath, a member of the task force and the vice-provost for undergraduate studies, is the way it is going to be, starting right now. "This incident has caused the Georgia Tech community to look closely at the way we teach and the way we hold each other accountable for our actions," he said in a statement. "Because of the serious and thoughtful efforts of many people, I believe that we are coming out of this experience a stronger and better university."

The freshman who told me his story still declines to be identified and is not happy that the university has not wiped clean the records of the many students who, he feels, were punished for doing the best job they could under rules that made no sense.

"I do not like the idea that for the rest of my academic career I will have to explain what happened to me," he said. He is so sour on Georgia Tech that he is transferring to another school, but he said he is "glad that the policy is changed for all of the students that are now going to take the computer science courses."

I think the freshman, and the many parents, students, teachers and alumni who protested the non-collaboration rule, should be proud of standing up for the power of learning from one's peers. And I can think of several other universities who might benefit from studying how Georgia Tech handled this. Its administrators wasted no time in disassembling the trouble-prone course, examining each of its parts, and putting it back together in a way that will help young people come to understand the mysteries of the digital world with a minimum of confusion and trauma.

CONTEXT

As of fall 2002, the collaboration policy in Computer Science 1321 at Georgia Tech stated, "Because homework assignments are now not used for assessment, we can now greatly relax the constraints on collaboration with respect to these assignments. Effective this semester, any and all forms of collaboration between students in CS 1321 are permitted, including the sharing of solutions if that is what is needed for a student to learn to develop a working solution to a given homework problem. . . . As has always been the case, however, plagiarism is not allowed. If you use sources other than those provided for everyone in the course (i.e., instructors, teaching assistants, the textbook, the course web site, the course newsgroups, the lectures, or the recitations), you must give appropriate credit to those sources. Note that so long as you give credit where credit is due, your grade will not be affected nor will you be charged with academic misconduct. On the other hand, a failure to give appropriate credit to sources of help (other than course materials or personnel as noted above) will be treated as plagiarism, a violation of Georgia Tech's Student Conduct Code."

Questions for Discussion

1. Why do you think Mathews begins this essay by admitting that he hired a consultant to help him with his computer? How does that anecdote relate to his overall argument?

2. Mathews includes quotations from two e-mail messages he received from readers of his column. What purpose do these messages serve in his argument? Assess the effectiveness of these e-mail messages as evidence.

3. Why is Mathews "shocked" when he learns that Georgia Tech quickly addressed the issue of collaboration raised by this incident? What does his reaction suggest about his opinion of universities? Do you agree with him? Why or why not?

4. Consider your own experiences with collaborative learning, either in school or in some other setting where you worked with others. Have those experiences been beneficial to you? Explain. How might those experiences influence the way you respond to Mathews's views about collaboration? What pros and cons can you see in collaborative learning?

5. Do you think the original collaboration policy for Computer Science 1321 at Georgia Tech was a fair and reasonable one? Why or why not? Do you think students should always work individually? Is that possible, in your view? If so, how should that be enforced? If not, how might universities deal with cheating?

② **RALPH CAPLAN,** "What's Yours? (Ownership of Intellectual Property)"

"It isn't always so easy to know what belongs to us." So writes Ralph Caplan in the following essay. Caplan, an expert in architectural design, is referring to ideas. More specifically, he wonders how to determine when someone owns an idea for the design of a building or a mechanical device. In raising this question, Caplan helps demonstrate that arguments about intellectual property are not limited to words, music, or images, which are often the focus of copyright lawsuits. Here, Caplan explores how abstract ideas for something like the design of a building can also be "owned" through copyright and patent laws. As is often the case in disputes about intellectual property, patents for designs involve money. But Caplan asks whether questions about the ownership of such ideas go beyond the matter of who is paid for them. In this sense, his essay, which was published in 1998 in *Print* magazine, suggests that arguments about intellectual property are really about the fundamental value of fairness and about how people wish to share ideas and abilities with one another. Caplan is the author of *By Design: Why There Are No Locks on the Bathroom Doors of the Hotel Louis XIV and Other Object Lessons* (1982).

What's Yours? (Ownership of Intellectual Property)

RALPH CAPLAN

1 Victor Papanek was our most fervent practitioner and preacher of alternative design. By the time of his death earlier this year, he had seen many of his most hotly disputed ideas become accepted design wisdom, if not design practice. One of them, however, remains fiercely controversial. Believing that "there is something basically wrong with the whole concept of patents and copyrights," Papanek declined to patent his designs. His critics scoffed that no one would bother stealing them anyway. Actually, they were ripped off in large numbers, for personal use as well as for profit. "If I design a toy that provides therapeutic exercise for handicapped children, then I think it is unjust to delay the release of the design by a year and a half, going through a patent application," Papanek wrote. "I feel that ideas are plentiful and cheap, and it is wrong to make money off the needs of others."

I don't know how money is ever made except off the needs (real or imagined) of others, but the issue here is not money but the rights to what it can't entirely buy.

The late Dr. Gerald Fagan, a resident psychiatrist at a boys' school, relieved the guilt of students who masturbated by reminding them: "It's yours, isn't it?" But it isn't always so easy to know what belongs to us. The protection, and even the identification, of what's yours has been vastly complicated by technology. As media for distributing ideas are multiplied, amplified, and reduced in price, ownership of so-called intellectual property becomes increasingly ambiguous. Even the ownership of hard goods has been softly defined for generations. In Arthur Miller's *Death of a Salesman*, Willie Loman's refrigerator and car are falling apart at the same time as he is. "Once in my life I would like to own something outright

VICTOR PAPANEK

Victor Papanek (1926–1998) was a renowned and sometimes controversial expert in architectural design. In his groundbreaking book *Design for the Real World: Human Ecology and Social Change* (1971), he questioned conventional beliefs about industrial and architectural design and argued for an approach to design that focused on making the world a better place. His proposals for design were based on his study of indigenous peoples and their relationship to their environments. His last book, *The Green Imperative: Natural Design for the Real World* (1995), was an ardent call to designers and architects to become more environmentally conscious and for people to live in more ecologically and socially responsible ways.

before it's broken!" Willie cries. "They time those things. They time them so when you finally paid for them, they're used up." In the audience we smile and nod in recognition, for we are an audience and a society of renters.

The rights to what we do own are subject to interpretation. When film mavens objected to Ted Turner's colorizing black-and-white movie classics, he replied, "The last time I looked, I owned them"—his way of saying he was entitled to make them all mauve if he wished, or keep anyone else from seeing them.

5   Are there public rights to private property? The nadir of my adolescence was not acne, or being turned down by May Allen for the senior prom, or even being suspended from high school. It was a strike by ASCAP—the American Society of Composers, Authors and Publishers—and until it was settled radio stations were prohibited from broadcasting music or lyrics produced by its members. I don't remember exactly how long it lasted, but for what seemed like forever the only songs we heard were in the public domain, usually by Stephen Foster. We understood dimly that the rights of creators to the material they had created were at stake, but we wanted the music back. If the concept of intellectual property was in legal vogue then, none of us would have thought it applied to "Darn That Dream" or "Flat Foot Floogie with the Floy Floy."

The inheritance of intellectual property is more problematic. The son of a vaudeville comedian, having been given his father's name at birth and taken over his father's act when the old man died, proudly advertised in the trade papers: "This act is not a copy. It is a legacy." Today, Dickensian court battles rage over whether families own in perpetuity the images of their celebrity ancestors. I love a Gershwin tune, but if I can't play one without paying, whom do I pay? Not George and Ira, who have no further use for royalties. The Gershwin Family Trust? Well, why not? If families can inherit money, why shouldn't they inherit cultural resources that can be turned into money?

One reason is that cultural resources not only enrich us but enrich each other through us. Our copyright laws have always acknowledged this by providing only temporary coverage, after which the private holdings become public domain. * But temporary anything has a way of becoming at least semi-permanent. Copyright law has been extended over the years, and there is a good chance it will now be extended for another two decades. (Had that been in effect during the ASCAP revolt of my youth, nothing but Baroque would have been public domain.) A Gershwin trustee warned that without such protection, "someone could turn Porgy and Bess, into rap music." A dreadful prospect, I guess, but folklorist Steve Zeitlin, noting that Gershwin's opera itself drew on African-American musical traditions, asks, "What could be more appropriate?" Zeitlin finds it similarly ironic that Disney, having used "Snow White" and other public domain materials for major productions, anxiously seeks to protect forever the sanctity of Mickey Mouse, which strikes some people as a Mickey Mouse idea.

Designers know the danger of letting work go unprotected—the danger not only of theft by competitors but of erosion through the negligence of managers who can't see, don't care, or have designs (and designers) of their own. The elaborate graphics standards manuals, devised as security systems, have often been ineffective because the people who understood them were not in control of their implementation.

Intellectual property implies the commodification of what cannot be commodified. If we protect it, why not protect emotional property as well? When William Styron wrote about the Nat Turner uprising, blacks challenged his right to write about the slave experience, on the grounds that it belonged to them collectively and exclusively. A comparable possessiveness attaches to the Holocaust as a phenomenon uniquely applicable to Jews but not to the Gypsies and gays who were also sent to Nazi death camps, or to the Armenians and Rwandans slaughtered at other times under other auspices. When David Leavitt based a novel on the homoerotic autobiographical writing of Stephen Spender, the elderly poet sued, telling Leavitt to get his own sex life instead of

appropriating someone else's old one.

10 But Leavitt was writing fiction, in which personal experience may be transferable. In Charles Williams's Descent into Hell, Pauline tells Peter about a recurring event that terrifies her. He can't do anything about the recurring event, but he offers to carry the fear for her, just as he would carry a parcel or her books. It's still her fear, he explains, but with him as designated schlepper, she won't have to do the fearing.

No one has yet copyrighted an idiosyncrasy or patented a neurosis, but James Thurber has shown us the way: A character in a Thurber story steals another man's dream. Another character in a Thurber cartoon has a friend accompany him to the doctor's office, where he registers the unprecedented medical complaint, "I've got Bright's disease and he's got mine."

"What's mine is yours" is the posture of a saint. "What's yours is mine" is the ideology of a mugger. Frankly, I do not know how to reconcile them. I think I understand rights and privileges in respect to owning things—whether one-of or mass produced. If I find a rock, it's mine. If I fashion it into a tool, it is more decisively mine, because my hands shaped it and my imagination told them how. If it is mine, then, because I am no saint, it is not yours. You therefore have been served with a moral injunction not to covet my rock and a criminal code forbidding you to take it if you do covet it. However, if I give it to you or leave it to you, the rock is yours, with all the rights and privileges pertaining thereto.

Thereto is the rub. What rights and privileges pertain to the rocks in your head? And where do they go when your head is gone? Some things that are yours are part of you. No one can take them from you, but it hurts when they try. To be plagiarized is, as Steve Heller in-

*The term public domain refers to the status of a creative work or invention that is not protected by copyright or patent law and is freely available to anyone to use or copy. A work is considered to be "in the public domain" if the creator or inventor does not properly register it for copyright or patent protection or if that protection expires.

*American philosopher Suzanne Langer (1895–1985) was well known for her ideas about aesthetics and, in particular, for her writings about language and music. She believed that music was a form of expression of human feelings that cannot adequately be expressed in language.

dicated recently in *PRINT,* to be "violated." This can be accomplished with dazzling chutzpah, as when someone overseas used a couple of pages from an article of mine without attribution, then quoted an additional paragraph from the same article, as if I had written it, which of course I had. Thus he put me in the curious position of agreeing with myself.

Sometimes what looks like plagiarism is simply coincidence. But not all coincidence is entirely coincidental. After driving to Wesleyan University to hear the brilliant Suzanne Langer* lecture on signs and symbols, I was disappointed to find that she really had nothing more to say on the subject than I had already said in a lecture of my own. Driving home, I figured out why. My ideas were as good as hers because they were hers to start with! I had absorbed them from reading her books.

Questions for Discussion

1. Caplan argues that music and stage acts are cultural resources that should be available to the public. What support does he offer for this point? How persuasive do you think Caplan is on this point?

2. Caplan writes, "Intellectual property implies the commodification of what cannot be commodified." What does he mean by that statement? In what way is that statement important to his main argument?

3. What examples does Caplan offer as evidence of the ambiguity of determining the ownership of intellectual property? How effective do you think these examples are in illustrating his point?

4. Summarize Caplan's main point in this essay. How does his anecdote of attending a lecture by Suzanne Langer reinforce this main point? Do you agree with Caplan? Why or why not? What counterarguments could you offer in response to his position?

5. Caplan's essay might be seen as an example of an argument to inquire (see pages 11–12). Evaluate its effectiveness as such an argument. Does his argument help clarify the issues related to intellectual property rights that he addresses? Explain.

③ **DAVID GIBSON,** "Copyright Crusaders"

An award-winning writer who focuses on religious issues, David Gibson worked in Rome for Vatican Radio and has produced television documentaries about Catholicism for CNN. "Copyright Crusaders" was originally published by *Fortune* in May 2005. A widely distributed magazine on business, *Fortune* was created by Henry Luce—who also created *Time* magazine and *Sports Illustrated.* Consider this context as you read what Gibson has to say about the intersection of faith and business—specifically, about how a religious story of questionable origin has generated a battle for the revenues created by it through the sale of products such as greeting cards and coffee mugs. By doing so, Gibson demonstrates how concerns about "ownership"—in this case an issue of "intellectual property"—are so pervasive today that they occur in unexpected situations. Because of the copyright controversy reported by Gibson, the religious story in question is not reprinted here. But if you are not already familiar with it, you will be able to understand what it involves through the summary Gibson provides in his opening paragraph.

Copyright Crusaders

DAVID GIBSON

1   In the warm and frothy bubble bath that is American spirituality today, it's hard to think of anything quite as familiar and comforting as the mini-homily known as "Footprints in the Sand." For anyone who has somehow managed to avoid the gantlet of Footprints mugs, calendars, greeting cards, and mousepads—to name just a few of its incarnations—the poem is a soft-focus retrospective that imagines life as a walk on the beach with Jesus, a pilgrimage traced by two sets of footprints, the Savior's and the narrator's. The reverie is interrupted by the narrator's shock that at his lowest moments there was just a single set of footprints, indicating that Jesus had bolted when he was needed most. Catharsis comes with the Lord's soothing assurance that he did not abandon his follower during the dark night. Rather, there was only one set of prints because "it was then that I carried you." Or as Jesus put it elsewhere, "O ye of little faith."

The story can be read generously as a haiku of Christian belief vanquishing doubt, or perhaps as proof that there is more unalloyed emotion in religion than in any other field of human expression. But this being America, you can't get something for nothing, and that goes for piety as much as widgets. Hence the rather unseemly legal wrangling over this irenic tale, which is pitting three main contenders (there are apparently dozens of pretenders) for the right to claim authorship of "Footprints"—along with millions of dollars in licensing fees on all those Footprints tchotchkes.

The three claimants are the estate of Mary Stevenson, who died in 1999 at age 76 and said she wrote a version of the poem in 1936 in Chester, Pa.; Margaret Fishback Powers, a poet and co-founder of a children's ministry in Canada, who says she composed "Footprints" in 1964; and Carolyn Carty, a New Jersey woman and self-described "child prodigy" who says she wrote her version in 1963 when she was 6.

Go figure. Each author copyrighted her version (they differ in small details, most significantly in Carty's use of the third person over the first person of the other two), and each has a different tale of the story's genesis. Stevenson told her biographer she was a 14-year-old Philadelphia showgirl during the Depression when she was locked out of her house on a wintry night and was inspired by the sight of a cat leaving paw prints in the snow. Powers cites a stroll on an Ontario beach with her prospective husband during a troubled time in their lives as her inspiration. And Carty's donnée was the death of her grandfather; her role models, she says, were Longfellow and John F. Kennedy.

5 Powers has been most successful in marketing "Footprints." She has signed licensing agreements with Hallmark cards and wrote a 1993 book about the poem, along with a series of devotionals. But Carty told Beliefnet.com, which has a lengthy and illluminating column on the competing claims, that she is planning to sue Powers for infringement while at the same time seeking redress from companies that have used her copyrighted version. "I figure they owe me at least $500,000 in back royalties," she told Beliefnet in regard to one calendar maker. Royalties for Stevenson's version were the subject of a six-year legal battle between her son and a friend who for years had sold Footprints products and signed licensing agreements on the late claimant's behalf.

The legal maneuverings and marketing campaigns and megabucks deals are enough to make one yearn for the innocent moralism of "Footprints" itself, yet the story is depressingly familiar. In America today, God is too often turned into mammon,* and it seems no good deed—or inspirational thought—goes unsold, no profit uncontested.

Even religious teachings are becoming a source of copyright infringement battles rather than universal enlightenment. In an article in

Buffalo Law Review, a professor at Washington College of Law, Walter Effross, has detailed how many religious groups, especially New Age ones, have sought legal recourse to classify their teachings as "intellectual property" that cannot be used by others without permission. Among the justifications for spiritual secrecy that Effross identifies is the claim that people who use teachings without proper supervision could suffer psychological harm. In other words, "Don't try this at home."

Effross cites the case of the Arica Institute, which created the nine-pointed enneagram personality test based on what it says was ancient wisdom, and has sued Jesuits who often use the enneagram as an evaluation tool for novices. He also describes how a religious group known as Star's Edge has sought to prevent the unauthorized use of its Avatar courses. These groups are even using nondisclosure agreements so that students do not share what they learn.

The problem for many of these religions, Effross says, is that their "teachings" are often so profound or so mundane that they contain "near-universal elements" that cannot be copyrighted. Not surprisingly, there is nothing new under the sun (that's Ecclesiastes, not me) when it comes to spiritual insight, and so piety increasingly becomes a matter of repackaging products in different forms—old wine in new wineskins, to upend another bit of holy writ—and then zealously guarding them to maintain your brand identity and market share.

10 It wasn't always this way. Take the Serenity Prayer: "God, give us grace to accept with serenity the things that cannot be changed, courage to change the things that should be changed, and the wisdom to distinguish the one from the other." Quick: Who wrote it? A common answer is St. Francis, while some trace it back to Cicero or Sanskrit texts. Others attribute it to an 18th-century German pietist, Friedrich Oetinger,† which might account for its regular appearance beside Dürer's "Praying Hands" engraving.

*mammon
Often translated as "riches" or "wealth," mammon appears in the New Testament, Matthew 6:24 and Luke 16:9, 11, 13. Because mammon is personified by Luke, the word also appears as *Mammon,* a devil-like deity associated with the pursuit of wealth.

†Friedrich Oetinger (1702–1782) is the author of numerous works on theology and philosophy. As a "pietist" he argued for the importance of attention to the Bible and individual conscience as opposed to automatic obedience to Church authority.

The correct answer is Reinhold Niebuhr, the great 20th-century Protestant theologian, although even he conceded his inspiration could have gone back further. Niebuhr said he wrote the prayer in 1943 as a "tag line" to a sermon. He had no interest in copyrighting anything that could be dispersed widely to provide comfort to others, so when Alcoholics Anonymous approached him about using the Serenity Prayer, he quickly agreed. AA has made the prayer a hallmark of its philosophy, while Hallmark cards, and many others, have made the prayer into cash in the form of refrigerator magnets, teddy bears, serving trays, and the like.

Likewise, the ubiquitous WWJD slogan ("What would Jesus do?") never brought any fortune to its author, Charles M. Sheldon, a minister who coined the phrase in an 1896 book, *In His Steps,* in which a fictional pastor uses the phrase to challenge complacent Christians. Sheldon couldn't find a publisher for the book, so he had it serialized in a local newspaper, and it fell into the public domain.

A century later when Janie Tinklenberg, a youth pastor in Michigan, rediscovered Sheldon's book, she hit upon the idea of making WWJD wristbands for the teens in her charge. The idea swept the nation, but like her predecessor, Tinklenberg did not think about merchandising first, and so she watched while retailers raked in millions on WWJD kitsch. Tinklenberg won a victory of sorts in 2000 when the U.S. Patent and Trademark Office awarded her the trademark for "WWJD." But she decided not to invest a small fortune trying to enforce her claim or to set up a manufacturing business because the phrase is already so popular in the marketplace.

And after all, isn't that where religious truths—even spiritual bromides—belong? Certainly Christianity is defined by its commitment to spreading the "good news," or evangelion in Greek, the root of today's regnant Evangelicalism. And offering spiritual goods at a price has only gotten Christians in trouble in the past.

15 But historians of religion like to say that Christianity was born in the Middle East as a religion, moved to Greece and became a philosophy, journeyed to Rome and became a legal system, spread through Europe as a culture—and when it migrated to America, Christianity became big business.

The observation is so true today that it probably belongs on a coffee mug or calendar. I just hope it's not under copyright.

Questions for Discussion

1. Gibson writes about "the warm and frothy bubble bath that is American spirituality today" and refers to its "soothing assurance." What kind of spirituality does he have in mind? To what extent should Christianity—or other faiths—be soothing?

2. How appropriate, in your opinion, is it to put prayer on mugs and mousepads? What does Gibson imply when he refers to such items as "tchotchkes"?

3. How seriously do you take Carty's claim that Hallmark and other companies owe her "at least $500,000 in back royalties"? Why do you take this position?

4. Consider the "justification for spiritual secrecy" offered in paragraph 7: "that people who use teachings without proper supervision could suffer psychological harm." Do you agree? If so, would copyright law protect people from such harm?

5. Gibson concludes his argument by claiming that Christianity in the United States has become a "big business." Is this conclusion justified by the evidence he has cited?

④ **ABIGAIL LIPSON AND SHEILA M. REINDL,** "The Responsible Plagiarist"

Given how strongly organizations such as the Modern Language Association oppose plagiarism (see page 163), the title of the following argument may seem paradoxical. How could a plagiarist be "responsible"? Isn't any plagiarist irresponsible or worse? But as authors Abigail Lipson and Sheila Reindl demonstrate, students plagiarize for different reasons—and, ironically, some of these reasons are related to the desire to do what they believe is expected of them. This argument was written for an audience of teachers—but it may be interesting to hear how teachers discuss students when concerned about improving teaching methods. A graduate of Hampshire College with a Ph.D. from Duke University, Lipson is a clinical psychologist who directs the American University Counseling Center in Washington, D.C. Reindl majored in biology at Radcliff College and earned an Ed.D. in counseling and counseling psychology from Harvard's Graduate School of Education. She is director of the Harvard Writing Center. "The Responsible Plagiarist" was first published in *About Campus* during the summer of 2003. According to its website, "*About Campus* is a professional magazine designed to serve as a catalyst for educators in colleges and universities to thoughtfully examine a variety of issues, policies, and practices and how they affect the quality of undergraduate education and student learning."

The Responsible Plagiarist

ABIGAIL LIPSON AND SHEILA M. REINDL

1 In the academic community, there may be no higher crime or baser act than plagiarism. The word *plagiarist* comes from the Latin word for "kidnapper"—to plagiarize is to steal someone's brainchild. Most universities address the issue of academic integrity by providing students with thorough orientations, required writing courses, and clearly articulated honor codes. Indeed, there is a virtually uniform understanding among college students that plagiarism is wrong. Nevertheless, each year students are brought before their institutions' disciplinary boards on charges that they have misused sources in their schoolwork. We have to wonder, *What were they thinking?*

Universities tend to rely on three explanations for academic conduct violations:

1. *Criminal plagiarism* describes the actions of students who knowingly and intentionally claim others' work as their own. Most universities handle incidents of criminal plagiarism on a case-by-case basis, taking care both to preserve the academic standards of the institution and to address the (often dire) circumstances of the student. A student found responsible for criminal plagiarism typically earns a failing grade, a notation on his or her record, and perhaps a required leave or expulsion.
2. *Sloppy scholarship* describes the actions of students who know the rules for proper citation and don't intend to deceive but nevertheless engage in

scholarship of inexcusable carelessness (for example, when citations are unintentionally "lost" in a cut-and-paste or notemaking process). The work of these students may look like criminal plagiarism, but they have committed a negligent act of omission rather an intentional act of commission. Universities tend to treat sloppy scholarship as a serious breach of academic responsibility, despite the lack of criminal intent.

3. *Ignorance of the rules* is considered a weak explanation given the pains taken to ensure students' awareness of the importance and mechanisms of proper citation. Occasionally, though, it becomes clear that a student really is at a loss regarding the basic conventions of source use, perhaps because of poor precollege preparation or widely divergent cultural assumptions about the nature of knowledge or the role of a student. In such instances, students are generally still held accountable for their inappropriate use of sources while their knowledge gaps and cultural adjustments are addressed with remedial instruction or counseling.

In most cases, criminal plagiarism, sloppy scholarship, or ignorance of the rules provides an entirely satisfactory explanation for a student's conduct. Yet there remain students for whom these standard explanations just don't seem to suffice. We hear from these students that their intentions were straightforward and honest: they did not engage in criminal plagiarism. They were fully alert to the basic rules of citation: they did not act out of ignorance. And they were being careful and deliberate: they were not being sloppy. These students claim, in fact, that as they did their work they were conducting themselves in a most responsible manner.

And we believe them. We believe that their actions made sense to them at the time—not good sense, but their own internal coherent sense. They were taking their academic responsibilities very seriously. It seems that the question to ask about these students is not, "*Were* they behaving responsibly?" but rather, "To *what* were they trying to be responsible?"

MODELS OF RESPONSIBILITY

5 To understand students' private logic, we must listen closely to their descriptions of how they went about their work. Following are outlines of three models of responsibility that stand out especially clearly in our students' self-descriptions. Each model embodies assumptions that students hold about their proper role in the educational process. Each implies a set of responsibilities that students are doing their best to honor. And each results in the unintentional yet sometimes egregious misuse of sources.

The Responsible Apprentice. Sometimes students cast themselves in the role of Responsible Apprentice. Their job is to model their products after those of the masters, so they learn the canon, "lip-synch" the voices of their teachers, and use their readings to reproduce as professional-*looking* a product as they can. They figure that someday they may produce original work of their own, but for now their task is merely to mimic expert examples. One could easily imagine Responsible Apprentices forgetting to sign their names to their essays. They feel no need to sign work that is not their own creation. The notion of academic learning as a form of apprenticeship has been explored by a number of scholars, including Allan Collins, John Brown, and Susan Newman in their work on the craft of teaching.

Responsible Apprentices are particularly susceptible to appropriating language, sans citation, in their written work. They feel that this is an entirely legitimate aspect of their job. So when they are accused of *mis*using sources, they feel tricked: "Wait a minute! I was being responsible! The teacher knows full well where my material came from! All I did was try to do the assignment!"

The Responsible Truth Seeker. Sometimes we hear in our students' voices a joy in searching for the truth and a delight in finding it; they have cast themselves in the noble role of Truth Seeker. In going about their studies, Responsible Truth Seekers are smitten by a particular idea. It rings so true! It is so compellingly right! Responsible Truth Seekers adopt other scholars' material with the certainty that they are simply accepting the Truth—not Author X's truth, which they must attribute to Author X, but Truth itself.

Responsible Truth Seekers are likely to misuse sources in a slightly different way than Responsible Apprentices do. They are more likely to appropriate a whole argument or an entire line of reasoning. They freely use ideas from their reading in their writing, without citation. They assume that even when particular phrases need to be properly cited, the Truth to which the words refer doesn't belong to anybody—it is simply true.

10 When Responsible Truth Seekers find themselves accused of misusing sources, they are likely to react with dismay and disillusionment. They think, "Why should Author X's name be attached to this idea? Author X is just doing the same thing I'm doing—recognizing the Truth and embracing it for what it is." To the Responsible Truth Seeker, quibbling over who is cited as the author of the Truth is irrelevant to the student's primary responsibility: to be passionate and unflagging in the search for Truth itself.

The Responsible Tax Preparer. Sometimes students document a text as though it is a good-faith effort to prepare a tax return. In the role of Responsible Tax Preparer, students are trying to be fair: to credit others with what is rightfully theirs and themselves with what is rightfully their own. They do not claim to be professionals, merely well-meaning laypersons trying to follow the authorities' very complicated code. They get frustrated when there isn't a definitive rule for every possible circumstance, or when different authorities offer inconsistent advice on how to handle the very same citation. They have no basis on which to make judgment calls—they are guided only

by their sense of responsibility to dutiful rule-following.

Responsible Tax Preparers' myopic focus on the rules leaves them in danger of *mis*citation, for example, by carefully citing a primary source for material actually found in a secondary source. Their rule-boundness can also result in *over*citation—not a code violation but nevertheless a poor use of sources. When faced with what feel like risky judgments, Responsible Tax Preparers decide, "When in doubt, footnote!"

When Responsible Tax Preparers find themselves accused of misusing sources, they are likely to feel profoundly unappreciated. "Can't you see I was faithfully following the rules? The rules aren't always so clear, you know! I had, like, thirty footnotes in there—how much more responsible could I have been?!" To be accused of ignorance or neglect or dishonesty, given their extraordinary diligence, feels deeply unjust.

The students' responses to these accusations make some sense. They are all trying to be responsible to some value that they think the academic community holds. In fact, the academic community does share their values, to a degree. A willingness to apprentice oneself to the work of masters, a deep engagement in the quest for truth, a diligent effort to comply with the conventions of text preparation—all of these are indeed important values.

15 So let's grant that the students we have described here are not being entirely irresponsible, nor responsible to entirely unworthy aims. We can still conclude that they are misusing sources. These "responsible" plagiarists have failed to be responsible to a core value that the academic community holds even more dear.

THE COMMUNITY OF THE MIND

The responsibility that these students have failed to meet is the scholar's responsibility to *a set of relationships or connections* between the scholar's own ideas and the ideas of others. As scholars, we have a responsibility to our sources (to acknowledge our indebtedness to them), to our readers (to let them know what our sources were and how they informed us), and to ourselves (to declare our own contributions). Proper documentation traces a family tree of intellectual kinship, in which we place our own ideas and text in *context*. When students misuse sources, they violate not merely a set of rules but a set of relationships.

Richard Marius, a past director of Harvard's writing program, put it this way:

It is always important to think of the intellectual world as a community of mutual dependence, mutual helpfulness, mutual protectiveness, and common delight. We take ideas from others; we give ideas to others. We are indebted to others, and others are indebted to us. In sharing and acknowledging the community, we define ourselves more certainly as individuals. The ability to describe our sources is also an ability to recognize our own originality and our own selves. All communities depend on generosity, trust, and definition, and the proper use of sources is part of the mortar that holds the community of the mind together.

A scholar's primary responsibility is to this community of the mind to which every one of us belongs—whether student or professor, believer or heretic, expert or novice.

This notion that we all belong to one community of the mind is heartwarming, but problematic. What community? Does a modern-day Brazilian engineering professor belong to the same community of the mind as a Zhou dynasty* Chinese poet? Sometimes it's hard enough to imagine that two faculty members in the same department of the same North American university belong to one community of mind, when they subscribe to different journals, attend different conferences, and use different theoretical frameworks and languages.

In actuality, we each belong to many neighboring and nested communities of the mind. On a fairly local level, present-day North American academia is a community defined by some shared values and conventions regarding scholarly conduct. Even more locally, an academic discipline or an academic institution constitutes a community of the mind. On the most global level, the community of the mind consists of the constantly evolving network of relationships among all scholars, across time and place. The human activities of reading and writing, and listening and speaking, continue to hum along, even as the players change and despite sometimes impassable gulfs between languages, ideologies, eras, and cultures. As scholars, our academic integrity depends on honoring our intellectual interconnectedness on all levels, whether reckoning with the nitty-gritty of citation formats or orienting our intellectual constructions in their particular cultural and historical context.

20 The word *integrity* is particularly apt here because of its two equally important meanings. It refers in one sense to personal trustworthiness, good character, moral uprightness. It refers to individual scholars' professional conduct, the soundness of their scholarship, their intellectual honesty. Responsible scholars speak truthfully, fairly represent the work of fellow scholars, and claim their own work, and only their own work, as theirs.

The second meaning of the word *integrity* refers to a wholeness, an entirety. We can apply this meaning to the enterprise of human inquiry itself, the collective process and progress of human understanding. This process has its own intactness, its own enduring and continuing life. It is sustained and defined by its members-of-the moment, but its existence predates the individual scholar and will continue afterward. The integrity of human inquiry in this broad and collective sense refers to the complex interconnectedness of all scholarship.

Integrity on both levels is represented in the efforts of a responsible scholar to document a text in such a way as to ensure the readers' ability to evaluate the scholar's work independently. Readers can reanalyze the writer's

*Zhou dynasty
The Zhous ruled much of what is now China for more than 500 years, from approximately 1040 BCE to 479 BCE. By contrasting a modern-day Brazilian engineer with a Zhou dynasty poet, the authors contrast not only professions but also the modern with the ancient, in addition to contrasting countries from the northern and the southern hemispheres, one of which is in the east and one of which is in the west.

sources, see the larger body of data from which the writer selected material, and find in the original sources confirming or discrepant statements. By inviting readers to join in a mutual intellectual discourse, the writer helps preserve and promote the continuity of the conversation in the community of the mind.

Every scholar is, of course, both a reader and a writer. There is a wonderful recursiveness and simultaneity at work here as the human species constructs a collective if multiplistic conversation. The spirit of this conversation springs from the twin desires to learn and to create—to find inspiration in others and to make our own contributions. In practice, there is no choice between these priorities. Both the intellectual effort of the individual and the intellectual evolution of the community rely on the interplay between the two. This is how human knowledge, on the personal and the collective levels, is preserved and advanced: in the intricate dance between what we believe we already know and what we dare to speculate.

VOICELESSNESS

Everyone who has ideas, reactions, beliefs, and musings—in short, everyone—belongs by definition to the community of the mind in its broadest sense. One need not apply for membership and one cannot be thrown out. Every scholar, reader, and student stands *somewhere* in relationship to the texts being read or the words being heard and has *some* response—whether inspiration or outrage, interest or boredom, agreement or disagreement, confusion or conversion. This response is the scholar's voice, the scholar's contribution to the larger conversation.

Some of the students who get into trouble for misusing sources clearly do not experience themselves as members of the community of the mind. It is not simply that they consider themselves to be novice thinkers, or fear that their thinking is different or inadequate. Rather, they do not consider themselves to be thinkers at all; they feel they know only what they are told by others.

Because they experience themselves as voiceless, at least in the domain of their academic work, the voices of these students are missing from the papers they write. As Pat Hoy, at the time a writing teacher at Harvard University, remarked to one of us, it's not just that these students don't know how to *use* a source; it's that they don't know they *are* sources. This may explain in part why some students who have been thoroughly taught the conventions of source use have not learned them. They cannot make clear the relationship between their own ideas and the ideas of others because in their experience they do not have their own ideas, and therefore there is no relationship. They misappropriate their sources' ideas or words because, being voiceless themselves, they default to a master, a truth, or a (poorly understood) rule in performing what they see as their scholarly responsibilities.

One way we can understand the voicelessness of our students is in terms of their intellectual development. Many university educators are familiar with William G. Perry's longitudinal research with Harvard undergraduates, which demonstrated that students' assumptions about the nature of knowledge and the locus of authority change as they develop intellectually during the college years. Initially, students tend to see knowledge as discrete and indisputable facts and to see authorities as the possessors of those facts. As they develop, they come to regard knowledge as contextually determined and to regard themselves as constructors and authors of knowledge. Their focus as learners shifts from an effort to amass information to an effort to make meaning. Students in the midst of this developmental process, who have not yet come to regard themselves as makers of meaning, don't experience their own voices as voices of authority.

Another way to understand students' voicelessness is as a function of context and power. For all of us there are some contexts in which we feel confident of our voice and empowered to speak and other contexts in which we feel unsure, unsafe, or unwelcome, and in effect

WHAT CAN WE DO?

1. **Emphasize the spirit as well as the letter of the law.**

   Teach students to ask spirit-oriented questions about their use of sources (for example, Can my readers tell which ideas belong to whom? Am I clear about how I have used others' ideas in service to my own inquiry?) rather than rule-oriented questions (such as, Are my citations in the right format? Do I have enough footnotes?).

   Help novice writers learn how to specify their sources clearly; for example, have students read one another's papers and respond sentence by sentence only to the question, Whose thoughts or words are these and why do I think so?

2. **Make explicit any assumptions about the various roles that students play as learners and scholars; serve as a guide and informant regarding the culture of scholarship.**

   Help students identify the problematic assumptions they may hold about using sources. Explicitly introduce the concept of academic integrity and the notion that to use sources properly one must also recognize oneself as a source.

   Show students both *by* and *with* examples what responsible documentation means. Review examples of proper and improper attribution, quotation choices, paraphrases, and judgment calls.

   Be alert to the ways in which an assignment may elicit a particular metaphoric approach (for example, an essay assignment based on limited sources may elicit the Truth Seeker approach, or an assignment that calls for recitation of canon may elicit a Responsible Apprentice approach).

3. **Acknowledge the complexity of the task of documentation.**

   Let students know how challenging it is to represent others' work fairly in the context of their own. Summarizing and paraphrasing require translating another's language into one's own with minimal distortion of meaning; even the perfect gem of a quotation must be precisely set into one's own text. These basics are important skills, learned and developed through practice.

   Introduce students to the different conventions employed in different fields and to the personal judgment exercised in every field. While there may be simple answers to hypothetical documentation questions, and uniform agreement about a few documentation decisions, in practice documentation is a complex task.

   Illustrate for students the ways in which all writers struggle with such questions as *What is common knowledge? How do I know what is "enough" documentation? If a classmate or colleague and I have a generative discussion, to whom does our shared conversation belong?* Discuss your own real-world documentation dilemmas with your students.

4. **Treat students as the sources they are; demonstrate that the academic community includes them and values their contributions.**

   Ask students questions that will help them find words for their unvoiced thoughts: What implicit thinking guided their selection of a quotation? What in those words moved them, or inspired them, or bothered them?

   Help students identify instances of their own sense-making. When they point out a problematic assumption, reframe an issue, make an analogy, or note an oversight or counterexample, we need to point this out to them. By doing so we acknowledge their natural efforts at authority, help them recognize their own voices, and teach them how to identify various thinking tools and techniques.

   Let students know that their sense-making contributes to our own. When we learn something new from our students, we need to tell them, so they can know that their voice is effective. When we help students experience their voice as having power, we help them recognize their role in the community of the mind.

silenced. The less at home we feel in a given context—that is, the more foreign we feel—the more likely it is that we will experience intellectual voicelessness. Of course, *what* is foreign to *whom* is a matter of perspective.

The culture of North American academia can feel foreign to students in various ways. Students who come from a context of origin that does not place a premium on intellectual activity may be unpracticed in declaring their views and opinions on intellectual matters. Students from a culture of origin that values community participation over individual expression may regard such declarations as arrogant or inappropriate. Students might feel that their own culturally based ideas or viewpoints will be discounted or dismissed by the dominant culture. Students whose home culture regards intellectual material as publicly held (belonging to everyone or no one) may be disoriented in an academic community that regards such material as privately owned (and thus requiring attribution). Students might also feel foreign in a linguistic sense, whether the foreign tongue is English, the language of academic discourse in general, or the jargon of a particular field. Imitation and parroting are essential to learning a new language, but these very activities can leave student writers vulnerable to overrelying on and misappropriating others' voices.

The experience of voicelessness and foreignness can leave students vulnerable to the intense desperation that contributes to sloppy scholarship or criminal plagiarism. Because difficult coursework is even more difficult when it is in a foreign language or context, students adjusting to such circumstances may feel especially overwhelmed and fearful of failing, and thus be at risk for panic and poor judgment regarding source use. Fear and panic are heightened if a student's personal or familial expectations make the prospect of academic failure—or anything short of perfection—intolerable, such as for students who feel trapped in the familial role of trailblazer, redeemer, or shining hope.

TEACHING FOR AUTHORITY AND AUTHORSHIP

Most policy and instruction regarding the use of sources focuses primarily on the legalities of making correct citations and the penalties for failing to do so. In the process, students learn a hidden lesson: the proper use of sources is a matter of avoiding plagiarism (and therefore punishment), which is in turn a matter of complying with specific rules of citation.

When this is the primary lesson we teach our students, we almost guarantee that they will fail to behave as responsible members of the community of the mind. Even if they learn and try to comply with every rule we teach them, they will not necessarily recognize, value, or honor their responsibility to the integrity of human inquiry. They will have learned nothing about their own authority as thinkers and writers and about their own interests in the shared conversation that defines the community of the mind.

For students to behave as truly responsible members of the community of the mind, they need to experience *themselves* as members of that community. They need to know that that community includes them and values their participation. They need to recognize themselves as contributing thinkers, as makers of meaning. They need to understand that what they violate when they plagiarize is not a rule but a relationship. Only then can they appropriately use others' thinking in the service of, not instead of, their own thinking, and appropriately honor the relationships between their own work and the work of others. Recalling the words of Pat Hoy, we must teach our students not merely how to use sources but how to *be* sources.

Every time a scholar puts pencil to paper or fingers to keyboard, that scholar has to do the difficult work of documentation. We as teachers shouldn't misrepresent this work as a matter of simply avoiding plagiarism. We must teach our students the hows and whys of expressing their own voices, tracing their intellectual kinships, and honoring their intellectual debts. . . .

We can appreciate the attitude of Martin Price, who in the preface to his book *To the Palace of Wisdom* acknowledges the complexity and ambiguity inherent in documentation. He notes, "I have tried to specify particular sources from which I have drawn. I regret the omissions I have most certainly made, and I would ask in turn the charitable recognition that not all resemblances need represent indebtedness" (p. viii). A sampling of our office bookshelves reveals that many authors, both popular and academic, preface their work with similar statements—not to belittle the importance of proper documentation or to excuse themselves from their responsibilities, but rather to affirm their commitment to the community of the mind while openly acknowledging the difficulties of the task of thorough documentation. We can ask no more and no less of our students.

NOTES

Collins, A., Brown, J. S., and Newman, S. E. "Cognitive Apprenticeship: Teaching the Craft of Reading, Writing, and Mathematics." In L. B. Resnick (ed.), *Knowing, Learning, and Instruction* (pp. 453–494). Hillsdale, N.J.: Erlbaum, 1989.

Hjortshoj, K. *Transition to College Writing.* New York and Boston: Bedford/St. Martin's Press, 2001.

Marius, R. "The Use of Sources for Papers in Expository Writing." Pamphlet. Cambridge, Mass.: Harvard University, 1982.

Morrow, L. "Kidnapping the Brainchildren." *Time,* Dec. 3, 1990, p. 126.

Perry, W. G., Jr. *Forms of Intellectual and Ethical Development in the College Years: A Scheme.* Austin, Tex.: Holt, Rinehart and Winston, 1970.

Price, M. *To the Palace of Wisdom: Studies in Order and Energy from Dryden to Blake.* Garden City, N.Y.: Doubleday, 1964.

Questions for Discussion

1. In their opening paragraph, Lipson and Reindl claim that "academic integrity" is usually explained to students during orientation and that many schools have "clearly articulated honor codes." What is your school's position on academic integrity? How was it made known to you?

2. Of the three kinds of plagiarism identified by the authors, which do you think is the most pervasive?

3. Consider the distinction in paragraph 4 "It seems that the question to ask about these students is not, '*Were* they behaving responsibly?' but rather, 'To *what* were they trying to be responsible?'" What is the difference between these two questions? Why is it useful for the authors to contrast the two?

4. According to the authors, "Proper documentation traces a family tree of intellectual kinship . . ." What do they mean by this?

5. Why is it problematic to assume that all students (or scholars) "belong to one community of the mind"?

6. One reason students may plagiarize, according to the authors, is that "they do not consider themselves to be thinkers at all; they feel they know only what they are told." Have you met students like this? Are there circumstances under which teachers can make students feel incapable of independent thought?

7. What penalty do you think would be appropriate if you deliberately submitted as your own an essay that you did not compose? What penalty would be appropriate if you drew on sources that you did not acknowledge or that you acknowledged but did so incorrectly?

DIFFERENCES

NEGOTIATING

The essays in this section indicate that "intellectual property" is a broad and complex category encompassing words, ideas, and symbols, among other things. Moreover, they raise the tricky question of who should own an idea or a phrase. As a student, you must sometimes confront questions about the ownership of words or ideas when you are completing school assignments that require you to draw on sources. And if you have used the Internet to find information, as most of us do today, then you may have encountered additional uncertainties, since much of the information on the Internet is questionable and its origin unknown. If you have ever been tempted to use a sentence or phrase or idea that you found on an obscure web page without acknowledging that source, then you know how easy it can be to violate intellectual property standards.

With this in mind, review the policies of your college or university regarding academic dishonesty and intellectual property. (Most schools post such policies on their websites, but you can usually also find them in the school's library.) Examine these policies to see what standards for the ownership of words and ideas your school applies to student work. Then write an essay in which you either argue in favor of these policies or question them. In your essay, be sure to summarize the main points of your school's policies regarding intellectual property and academic dishonesty, then explain why you agree or disagree them. Try to identify the principles of fairness and ownership that you hold as a basis for your argument. And try to address the matter of the consequences that students suffer when they are found to have violated your school's policies: What are those consequences? Are they fair? If not, why not? And what alternatives would you provide? Try also to account for new technologies, like those associated with the Internet, and how they might affect intellectual property.

If your teacher allows it, consider working together with several classmates to review your school's policies and collaboratively draft your essay.

Who Owns Music?

In January 2003, in a case known as *Eldred* v. *Ashcroft,* the U.S. Supreme Court upheld a law that extended the term for copyrights for books, movies, music, and other intellectual property for twenty years beyond the fifty years that previous laws already provided for. The case was considered to be one of the most important decisions involving intellectual property in recent decades, and the intense debate surrounding it reflects the importance of copyright law in the United States and the deep concerns many citizens have about it. Those concerns seem especially deep when it comes to copyrights involving music. ■ Although creative works of all kinds are protected under copyright law, music seems to generate particularly intense controversy. Perhaps that's because music is so much a part of the lives of most people; for many people, music is not so much a product as a cultural treasure to which everyone has a right. (See Con-Text on page 238.) It can also be difficult to distinguish among the many different forms of music and the variety of media in which it exists. For example, is a song that is played on the radio subject to the same copyright rules as a song that is played on a CD in a private home? ■ *Eldred* v. *Ashcroft* highlighted the complexity of questions about who owns music and controls its distribution. Representatives of media corporations praised the ruling as an important protection for songwriters and musicians, but others complained that the ruling would prevent the public from enjoying the benefits of musical works. Some scholars believe that the framers of the Constitution intended copyright to encourage scientific and creative work and to ensure that such work would eventually benefit the public. But copyright law can also mean profits. It gives songwriters and musicians—and the media companies that produce and distribute their work—the right to earn money from their songs or performances, and it prevents others from profiting unfairly from copyrighted music. And the great popularity of music means that there is a great deal of money at stake. ■ Recent technological developments have added to the difficulty of sorting through these issues. The capabilities of new computer technologies have made it easier than ever for consumers to reproduce and share music. Like millions of other consumers, you might have visited a website where you can download, free of charge, copies of your favorite songs that someone else has made available on that site. Such capabilities raise questions about when a copy of a song is being used illegally. Is it a violation of copyright law to download a music file that was copied from a CD that another person legally purchased and then made available on a private website? Or is downloading a file the same thing as letting a friend borrow a CD you have purchased so that he or she can record it? The media companies supporting the decision in *Eldred* v. *Ashcroft* believe that they are losing profits whenever someone downloads a song in this way. Others argue that consumers have the right to share music through the Internet. Although the copyright to a song indicates clearly who "owns" that song, it is less clear how far that copyright extends. Must be permission be granted every time that song is played or copied, no matter what the circumstances? Such questions involve legal and economic complexities that will become even more difficult to sort out as new technologies develop. ■ But as the essays in this section indicate, controversies involving the ownership of music are not limited to legal or economic issues. Music can also be considered an expression of cultural identity. But who owns that identity? That question emerged as hip hop and rap music gained popularity in the 1980s and 1990s. ■ These musical forms "borrowed" from other kinds of music in the form of sampling, a practice whereby an artist incorporates or "quotes" from other songs. Some artists believe that such sampling requires payment, because parts of songs are protected by copyright law. In turn, rap music, which many consider to be a form of Black cultural expression, influenced other musicians, who then "borrowed" from rap—raising questions about whether such borrowing is simply the influence of one form of music on another or constitutes "stealing" an artist's racial or cultural identity. ■ Like certain written works, music has also been subject to censorship in the United States and elsewhere in the world. Sometimes such censorship is based on concerns about morality; sometimes it is driven by political beliefs. Whatever the case, censoring music raises questions not only about free speech but also about who has the right to control artistic expression. ■ Obviously, as such an important and widespread part of culture, music is much more than entertainment. Thus, the questions about the ownership of music raised by the essays in this section reflect important social, legal, economic, and even moral concerns that affect all of us, regardless of our musical tastes. These essays might not provide answers to the kinds of difficult questions regarding intellectual property and music discussed here. But they can help you understand the issues so that you can seek your own answers in a more informed manner.

CON-TEXT

The Importance of Music

1 Music is a basic function of human existence, arising from the physiological, psychological, and sociological needs of human kind. As such, the value of musical pursuit derives not only from the endeavor to achieve the highest forms of the musical art according to socially accepted norms, but also from the everyday musical encounters of every person. To this end, music is a necessary, life-enhancing experience which should be nurtured in all individuals, not only in those gifted with musical aptitude.

Music is an invariant. It has been present in all cultures, at all times, and throughout the known historical development of the human species, facilitating emotional, physical, and social expression. Music satisfies the human need for aesthetic enjoyment, provides for communication of cultural ideals, integrates, and enculturates.

SOURCE: Kenneth Liske, "Philosophy of Music Education."

① **JANIS IAN,** "Free Downloads Play Sweet Music"

In the late 1990s, as digital technologies began to influence the consumer market for music, listeners began to take advantage of the capabilities of the Internet to share music with each other. With powerful new computer technologies, a consumer could purchase a CD by a favorite musician, copy a song from that CD to a computer hard drive, then send that song to a friend—and to many other people—through the Internet. Eventually, websites were established that became clearinghouses for music, usually as MP3 files, a digital format well suited to reproducing sound. The best-known of these websites was Napster, which at the height of its popularity was visited by hundreds of thousands of users each day, many of whom would download music files using Napster's peer-to-peer software. But even after a legal suit curtailed much of the file-downloading activity enabled by Napster's software in 2000, consumers have continued to find ways to share music files digitally, raising concerns among some musicians and among media companies about copyright violations and about lost profits. As media companies seek ways to prevent the exchange of music files, advocates of free speech and privacy—including some musicians, like Janis Ian—argue that music should be freely available on the Internet, even if that music is protected by copyright. In the following essay, Ian, an accomplished musician and recording artist who has won two Grammy awards, argues that musicians and consumers can benefit from free music downloads; moreover, she suggests that free downloads are good for the art itself by making music more widely available. Her essay encourages you to consider some of the economic issues involving music downloads. But her argument might also be cause to wonder about who should control the distribution of music once a song has been protected by copyright. This article appeared on ZDNet, an Internet technology network, in 2002. It is a shorter version of the original article, which was published in *Performing Songwriter Magazine* in 2002.

Free Downloads Play Sweet Music

JANIS IAN

1 When researching an article, I normally send e-mails to friends and acquaintances, who answer my request with opinions and anecdotes. But when I said I was planning to argue that free Internet downloads are good for the music industry and its artists, I was swamped.

I received over 300 replies—and every single one from someone legitimately in the music business.

Even more interesting than the e-mails were the phone calls. I don't know anyone at the National Academy of Recording Arts & Sciences (NARAS, home of the Grammy

*According to its website, "The Recording Industry Association of America is the trade group that represents the U.S. recording industry. Its mission is to foster a business and legal climate that supports and promotes our members' creative and financial vitality. Its members are the record companies that comprise the most vibrant national music industry in the world. RIAA© members create, manufacture and/or distribute approximately 90% of all legitimate sound recordings produced and sold in the United States." The RIAA filed the lawsuit against Napster that ended Napster's online music sharing service.

Awards), and I know Hilary Rosen (head of the Recording Industry Association of America, or RIAA)* only in passing. Yet within 24 hours of sending my original e-mail, I'd received two messages from Rosen and four from NARAS, requesting that I call to "discuss the article."

Huh. Didn't know I was that widely read.

5 Ms. Rosen, to be fair, stressed that she was only interested in presenting RIAA's side of the issue, and was kind enough to send me a fair amount of statistics and documentation, including a number of focus group studies RIAA had run on the matter.

However, the problem with focus groups is the same problem anthropologists have when studying peoples in the field: the moment the anthropologist's presence is known, everything changes. Hundreds of scientific studies have shown that any experimental group *wants to please the examiner.* For focus groups, this is particularly true. Coffee and donuts are the least of the payoffs.

The NARAS people were a bit more pushy. They told me downloads were "destroying

sales," "ruining the music industry," and "costing *you* money."

Costing *me* money? I don't pretend to be an expert on intellectual property law, but I do know one thing. If a music industry executive claims I should agree with their agenda because it will make me more money, I put my hand on my wallet . . . and check it after they leave, just to make sure nothing's missing.

Am I suspicious of all this hysteria? You bet. Do I think the issue has been badly handled? Absolutely. Am I concerned about losing friends, opportunities, my 10th Grammy nomination, by publishing this article? Yeah. I am. But sometimes things are just wrong, and when they're that wrong, they have to be addressed.

10 The premise of all this ballyhoo is that the industry (and its artists) are being harmed by free downloading.

Nonsense.

Let's take it from my personal experience. My site gets an average of 75,000 hits a year. Not bad for someone whose last hit record was in 1975. When Napster was running full-tilt, we received about 100 hits a month from people who'd downloaded "Society's Child" or "At Seventeen" for free, then decided they wanted more information. Of those 100 people (and these are only the ones who let us know how they'd found the site), 15 bought CDs.

Not huge sales, right? No record company is interested in 180 extra sales a year. But that translates into $2,700, which is a lot of money in my book. And that doesn't include the people who bought the CDs in stores, or came to my shows.

RIAA, NARAS and most of the entrenched music industry argue that free downloads hurt sales. More than hurt—it's destroying the industry.

15 Alas, the music industry needs no outside help to destroy itself. We're doing a very adequate job of that on our own, thank you.

The music industry had exactly the same response to the advent of reel-to-reel home tape recorders, cassettes, DATs, minidiscs, videos, MTV ("Why buy the record when you can tape it?") and a host of other technological advances designed to make the consumer's life easier and better. I know because I was there.

The only reason they didn't react that way publicly to the advent of CDs was because they believed CDs were uncopyable. I was told this personally by a former head of Sony marketing, when they asked me to license *Between the Lines* in CD format at a reduced royalty rate. ("Because it's a brand new technology.")

Realistically, why do most people download music? To hear new music, and to find old, out-of-print music—not to avoid paying $5 at the local used CD store, or taping it off the radio, but to hear music they can't find anywhere else. Face it: Most people can't afford to spend $15.99 to experiment. And an awful lot of records are out of print; I have a few myself!

Everyone is forgetting the main way an artist becomes successful—exposure. Without exposure, no one comes to shows, no one buys CDs, no one enables you to earn a living doing what you love.

20 Again, from personal experience: In 37 years as a recording artist, I've created 25-plus albums for major labels, and I've *never* received a royalty statement that didn't show I owed *them* money. Label accounting practices are right up there with Enron. I make the bulk of my living from live touring, doing my own show. Live shows are pushed by my website, which is pushed by the live shows, and both are pushed by the availability of my music, for free, online.

Who gets hurt by free downloads? Save a handful of super-successes like Celine Dion, none of us. We only get helped.

Most consumers have no problem paying for entertainment. If the music industry had a shred of sense, they'd have addressed this problem seven years ago, when people like Michael Camp were trying to obtain legitimate licenses for music online. Instead, the industrywide attitude was, "It'll go away." That's the same attitude CBS Records had about rock 'n' roll when Mitch Miller was head of A&R. (And you wondered why they passed on The Beatles and The Rolling Stones.)

NARAS and RIAA are moaning about the little mom-and-pop stores being shoved out of business; no one worked harder to shove them out than our own industry, which greeted every new mega-music store with glee, and offered steep discounts to Target, WalMart, et al, for stocking their CDs. The Internet has zero to do with store closings and lowered sales.

And for those of us with major label contracts who want some of our music available for free downloading . . . well, the record companies own our masters, our outtakes, even our demos, and they won't allow it. Furthermore, they own our voices for the duration of the contract, so we can't post a live track for downloading even if we want to. 25 If you think about it, the music industry should be rejoicing at this new technological advance. Here's a foolproof way to deliver music to millions who might otherwise never purchase a CD in a store. The cross-marketing opportunities are unbelievable. Costs are minimal, shipping nonexistent—a staggering vehicle for higher earnings and lower costs. Instead, they're running around like chickens with their heads cut off, bleeding on everyone and making no sense.

There is *zero* evidence that material available for free online downloading is financially harming anyone. In fact, most of the hard evidence is to the contrary.

NAPSTER

An Internet service for sharing music files (in MP3 format), Napster was founded in 1999 by a college student named Shawn Fanning, who established a website where users could exchange their private music files. Napster quickly became an Internet phenomenon as thousands of users began to use Napster's file-sharing software to share music. As many as 60 million users were visiting the site by early 2001. In 2000, the Recording Industry Association of America (RIAA) filed suit against Napster, alleging copyright infringement, and a drawn-out court battle ensued. A court ruled in favor of the RIAA in 2000 and stopped the free exchange of copyrighted files using Napster's software, but Napster continued to operate in a more limited way until 2002, when additional court rulings finally shut it down. But the issues regarding intellectual property, copyright law, and consumer privacy that the Napster case raised generated intense debate that continued well after Napster ceased its operations.

CONTEXT

Born in 1951, singer and songwriter Janis Ian released the first of her seventeen albums in 1967. Her 1975 hit song "At Seventeen" earned her the first of two Grammy awards. She has recorded music for many movie soundtracks, and she has received acclaim as a jazz musician, as well as for her children's music. Despite her success, she has been an outspoken critic of many of the practices of the music industry.

The RIAA is correct in one thing—these are times of great change in our industry. But at a time when there are arguably only four record labels left in America (Sony, AOL Time Warner, Universal, BMG—and where is the RICO act when we need it?), when entire genres are glorifying the gangster mentality and losing their biggest voices to violence, when executives change positions as often as Zsa Zsa Gabor changed clothes, and "A&R" has become a euphemism for "Absent & Redundant," we have other things to worry about.

We'll turn into Microsoft if we're not careful, folks, insisting that any household wanting an extra copy for the car, the kids, or the portable CD player, has to go out and "license" multiple copies.

As artists, we have the ear of the masses. We have the trust of the masses. By speaking out in our concerts and in the press, we can do a great deal to dampen this hysteria, and put the blame for the sad state of our industry right back where it belongs—in the laps of record companies, radio programmers, and our own apparent inability to organize ourselves in order to better our own lives—and those of our fans.

30 If we don't take the reins, no one will.

Questions for Discussion

1. Ian draws heavily on her experience as a musician and a recording artist to support her position on music downloads. Evaluate her use of personal experience as evidence. How effective do you think it is? Is it adequate for her main argument? Do you think she could have used other kinds of evidence to support her argument? Explain. (In answering these questions, you might wish to review the discussion of appraising evidence on pages 80–86).

2. Ian begins her essay by telling an anecdote about the number of messages she received from people who learned that she was writing about free music downloads. Why do you think she begins her essay in this way? Do you think this beginning is an effective way for her to introduce her subject? Explain.

3. Ian writes, "There is *zero* evidence that material available for free online downloading is financially harming anyone. In fact, most of the hard evidence is to the contrary." To what extent do you think Ian provides such "hard evidence" in her essay? Do you think she is persuasive on this point? Why or why not?

4. How would you describe Ian's writing style in this essay? In what ways do you think her style might make her argument more effective? What sort of persona, or ethos (see pages 72–80) does her style establish? How might her background and experience as a recording artist contribute to that persona?

5. Ian devotes a considerable amount of her essay to discussing the positions of music industry people who oppose free music downloads. Why do you think she does so? Do you think she presents their concerns fairly? Explain. How does she characterize the music industry people who oppose her position? In what ways might her argument be strengthened—or weakened—by the way she characterizes these people and their interests?

6. This essay was published in ZDNet, a network of Internet sites that is, according to its website, intended for "IT [information technology] professionals and business influencers" and "provides an invaluable perspective and resources so that users can get the most out of their investments in technology." In what ways do you think Ian addresses this audience? Do you think she does so effectively? Explain.

② TOM LOWRY, "Ringtones: Music to Moguls' Ears"

If you venture into almost any public space today—be it a coffee shop, a mall, or even a park or a theater, you are likely to find people using their cell phones. Because of the importance some people attach to their phones, and the possibility of several phones ringing within earshot at the same time, users often like to customize their phones by programming them to play a specific melody or sound. The business of producing and selling these sounds, called *ringtones,* is becoming lucrative, as the following selection by Tom Lowry shows. "Ringtones" was originally published in *Business Week* during the spring of 2005. Media editor for *Business Week,* Lowry has also written about business for *USA Today* and the *New York Daily News.* He is a graduate of the University of Delaware and studied business and economic journalism as a Bagehot fellow at Columbia University.

Ringtones: Music to Moguls' Ears

TOM LOWRY

*50 Cent
With a violent criminal past upon which he draws for many of his songs, Curtis Jackson (under the name 50 Cent) became one of the most popular gangster rappers in the world during the first decade of this century, presenting himself as an authentic representative of a street culture other rappers never experienced.

1 Earlier this year, as the rapper 50 Cent* was putting the finishing touches on his second album, *The Massacre,* for Interscope Records, the Jamaica (N.Y.) sensation carved out time from his studio schedule for an important task: recording a voice tone and a voice ringback. Those snippets would eventually let cell-phone users paying a one-time fee of $2 to hear him when they received or placed a call. Then a musical ditty from the single, "Candy Shop," was converted into a ringtone, making 50 Cent ubiquitous in wireless—just as *The Massacre* topped the charts in March.

For music executives still stung by Internet piracy and slammed for not moving quickly enough to exploit the Net, the industry is going to great lengths not to blow it with new wireless technologies. They're seeing that cell phones are just as important as CD and MP3 players, radio, and music videos. And ensuring that breakout artists like 50 Cent have content tailored for mobile phones is now a must, not just for the sake of promotion but as a critical new source of revenue.

Increasingly, selling $13 CDs at retail stores is the old-fashioned way to make money on music. Now there's a host of fresh possibilities, from video game soundtracks to preloaded artist catalogs on hard drives in cars—imagine an Elvis Cadillac or a Britney BMW. Meanwhile, lawyers are working overtime on new publishing, royalty, and licensing agreements for the nascent business models. Cell phones now represent enough promise for all the major music companies to be setting up mobile-business divisions. "With 180 million handsets in the U.S., how could we not be bullish on the mobile market, especially now that downloads to phones are possible?" says Thomas Hesse, president of global digital business at Sony BMG Music Entertainment.

But no matter how many new businesses emerge, music execs still face an uphill battle competing with free. After the first uptick in music sales in years in 2004, the figures dropped again—by 6%—in the first quarter of 2005, to 134.8 million albums, according to Nielsen SoundScan. About 750 million songs are still being swapped unauthorized or free on the Internet every month, according to file-sharing tracker Big Champagne. To understand the magnitude of the threat, consider that the most successful legal download service, Apple Computer Inc.'s iTunes Music Store, has sold less than half of the illegal monthly volume, 300 million songs, since its launch two years ago.

Spinning Faster

5 What's more, digital-music sales are still a tiny sliver of the overall pie. Digital music, mostly made up of downloads on the Internet and tones on cell phones, accounts for roughly 2% of the $30 billion global music business. But executives see a quick ramp-up. Alain Levy, CEO of EMI Music, for one, has said that digital sales could be 25% of his company's total in five years, with cell-phone downloads and subscriptions making up a big chunk. In the first six months of its fiscal year ending last November, EMI reported digital sales that doubled year-on-year, to $37.8 million, still just a fraction of its $1.6 billion in total revenues. Much of the digital gain was attributable to online sales in America, mobile revenues in Japan, and ringtone revenues at EMI Publishing.

Ringtones are driving most of the mobile-music business today. The replication of songs into a series of tones costs customers $1 to $3 apiece. As their sound quality improves, so will demand, say executives. If there was any doubt of their importance to the future of music, the industry's stalwart trade magazine, *Billboard,* now compiles a regular chart of the 20 "Hot Ringtones." Thanks to teenagers who sometimes swap out ringtones as many as three to four times a week, they will become a nearly $9.4 billion business in 2008, estimates consultant Strategy Analytics Inc. "Ringtones are all about personalization. They are self-expression," says Rio Caraeff, vice-president of Universal Mobile Music. "You buy a ringtone for a different reason than you buy a download of a song." How about Joss Stone's "You Had Me" as the ring for an ex-husband, or

Sinatra's "New York, New York" for a cousin in Manhattan? Assigning a tune to a caller is an expressive way to make a statement about a person or a relationship.

The fact that the industry is embracing all kinds of new formats for selling music might be the one good thing to come from the nightmare of the past several years, says Mark Harrington, a media analyst at Bear, Stearns & Co. in London. "The music industry is where the movie business was 20 years ago—trying to figure new revenue streams. For Hollywood, it was establishing [staggered] releases to VHS, then DVD, to premium cable, to now [video on demand]." Up until then, film libraries had little value, he says, but now they are being thoroughly mined in a booming DVD market. The message for music and its catalogs is parallel: The new technologies are making it possible to wring even more profit from the industry's vast song libraries. Music execs should no longer care about where revenues come from, says Harrington, especially since operating margins for digital music sales are expected to be 18%, vs. about 12% for CDs. What has music moguls even more upbeat on cell phones is the relative security they offer compared with the Internet, they say. "Cell phones are a closed system," says Sony BMG's Hesse. "And a payment system through credit-card billing is built into the device."

Nobody understands the prospects for digital music better than the publishing side of the business, which collects money for the rights of songwriters from radio plays, live performances, TV commercials, and movies—and now ringtones. Publishing has always been a high-margin part of the business, but it stands to make a killing in this new world because of all the new ways for music to reach fans. "We love additive products, believe me," says Martin Bandier, CEO of EMI Music Publishing, the world's largest music publisher, with a catalog of more than 1 million songs. "It's like we are in the bread-crumb business. Sooner or later, you get a loaf of bread." Bandier says his company collects about 10% of the retail price of ringtones. The songwriter gets paid a royalty from that.

Despite the payoffs, threats still loom. There's new software, Xingtones, costing $20, that converts MP3 files to ringtone formats, pushing once again into the realm of free. Even so, the trick for the music industry will be to learn from the past—that new technologies mean new opportunities. Just ask 50 Cent.

Pennies From Heaven

10 The music industry got burned by the Internet but is now getting a lift from cell phones. Down the road, there's a rosy future in wireless downloads of entire songs. But now, the big bucks are in ringtones.

Monophonic Ringtones   These are the most prevalent now, but higher-quality tones will be available soon. They play one note at a time and sound like a series of beeps. Music publishers take about 10% of price.
TOTAL RETAIL REVENUES, IN BILLIONS
2004: $0.671
2008*: $0.042

Polyphonic Ringtones   They combine up to 16 notes, providing for a richer sound. Music publishers take about 10% of price.
TOTAL RETAIL REVENUES, IN BILLIONS
2004: $4.1
2008*: $2.6

True Tones   The master recording of a song. Music companies can take up to 30%; publishers get a 10% cut, as well.
TOTAL RETAIL REVENUES, IN BILLIONS
2004: $0.565
2008*: $4.5

Ringback Tones   Instead of the ring-ring, caller can hear a song of choice when dialing a certain person. The music-industry take depends on terms of the subscription plans offered by cell-phone operators.
TOTAL RETAIL REVENUES, IN BILLIONS
2004: $0.436
2008*: $2.3

TOTALS, IN BILLIONS

2004: $5.8
2008*: $9.4
*Estimates
Data: Strategy Analytics: BusinessWeek

Questions for Discussion

1. With so many musicians to choose among, why do you think Lowry chose to open his argument by using the rapper 50 Cent as an example?

2. Why are music executives increasingly interested in generated revenues from ringtones?

3. According to Lowry, teenagers can change the ringtones on their cell phones as often as three or four times a week. What would motivate this kind of behavior? Have you seen evidence of it?

4. Consider the quotation in paragraph 6: "Ringtones are all about personalization. They are self-expression." In your opinion, is the sound made by a telephone a genuine form of self-expression?

5. Cell phones are described as "a closed system." In what sense are they closed? And if credit-card billing is built into the system, how might such billing affect how people use their cell phones?

③ JAMES SUROWIECKI, "Hello, Cleveland"

A graduate of the University of North Carolina at Chapel Hill who then did graduate work at Yale University, James Surowiecki was financial editor of online magazine *Slate* before becoming a writer for the *New Yorker* in 2000. Respected for its high editorial standards, and known for its witty cartoons, the *New Yorker* publishes award-winning fiction, poetry, and nonfiction prose in weekly issues. "Hello, Cleveland" originally appeared in the issue of May 16, 2005. The title evokes what an announcer or lead singer might say to a concert audience at the beginning of a performance, signaling that the article is about the music-concert-touring business. When discussing his *New Yorker* column, Surowiecki described it as "a rigorous, demanding process." Surowiecki has also written for *Fortune,* the *New York Times Magazine,* the *Wall Street Journal,* and *Wired.* His books include *Best Business Crime Writing of the Year* (2002) and *The Wisdom of Crowds: Why the Many Are Smarter than the Few and How Collective Wisdom Shapes Business, Societies, and Nations* (2003).

Hello, Cleveland

JAMES SUROWIECKI

*Led by the vocalists Carleton Coon (1894–1932) and Joe Sanders (1896–1965), the Coon-Sanders Original Nighthawk Orchestra was broadcast nationally in the 1920s by NBC radio, which was then a new medium. Their best known song was "Yes, Sir, That's My Baby"—a big hit in 1925.

†Jules Stein (1896–1981) founded the Music Corporation of America, commonly referred to as MCA. By 1941, it was the country's largest agency for booking band concerts. Today, it is one of the largest and most powerful corporations in the entertainment business.

1   In the summer of 1924, a Kansas City band called the Coon-Sanders Original Nighthawk Orchestra* did something unusual: it went on tour. Popular as live music was, bands in those days tended to serve as house orchestras or to play long stands in local clubs; there was hardly even a road to go on. But Jules Stein,† a booking agent from Chicago, convinced the Nighthawk Orchestra that it could make more money by playing a different town every night. The tour, which lasted five weeks, was a smash. Soon, bands all over the country were hitting the road to play ballrooms and dance halls.

Stein's original version hasn't changed much, despite some modifications over the years—parking lots, hair spray, the disposable lighter. Consider Metallica, the Coon-Sanders Original Nighthawk Orchestra of our day. Though Metallica still sells a fair number of CDs from its back catalogue (it has made just

one album in the past six years), it makes most of its money from concerts. Two years ago, the band brought in almost fifty million dollars with its Sanitarium tour. Last year, it brought in sixty million with its Madly in Anger with the World tour. God knows what it would take to make Metallica happy.

The music industry may be in crisis, what with illegal file-sharing, stagnant CD sales, and the decline of commercial rock radio, but the touring business is as sturdy as ever. In some ways, it is healthier than some of the mediums (radio, recorded music) that at one point or another were supposed to render it obsolete. Since 1998, annual concert-tour revenue has more than doubled, while CD sales have remained essentially flat. Last year, thirteen different artists grossed more than forty million dollars each at the box office. (Prince made eighty-seven million.) Consumers who seem reluctant to spend nineteen dollars for a CD apparently have few qualms about spending a hundred bucks or more to see a show.

There are still artists who make huge sums of money selling records, but they are the lucky few. A longtime recording-industry rule of thumb holds that just one in ten artists makes money from royalties. Today, it's probably less than that. So the best model, if you're in it for the money, may be the Grateful Dead. Although the Dead didn't sell many records or get much airplay, they worked the big stadiums and arenas long enough and often enough to become one of the most profitable bands out there. As in politics and sales, nothing beats meeting the people face to face.

5 Most musicians, from a business perspective, at least, would wish it otherwise. Selling CDs is, as economists say, scalable: you make one recording, and you can sell it to an unlimited number of people for an unlimited amount of time, at very little cost. A tour, on the other hand, is work. You have to perform nearly every night, before a limited number of people, for hours at a time. You can knock a few seconds off each song, fire a percussionist, or sell more T-shirts, but in the end efficiencies are hard to come by.

The trick is that musicians get a much higher percentage of the money from concerts and merchandise than they do from the sale of their CDs. An artist, if he's lucky, gets twelve percent of the retail price of a CD. But he doesn't get any royalties until everything is paid for—studio time, packaging costs, videos—which means that he can sell a million records and make almost nothing. On tour, though, he often gets more than half of the box-office, so even if he grosses less he can profit more.

Traditionally, tours were a means of promoting a record. Today, the record promotes the tour. The decline in record sales has shrunk the size of the pie for labels and artists to fight over, so they've had to find new ways to make money, and artists have come to see how lucrative touring can be, given what people will pay to see them live. (Ticket prices for the top hundred tours doubled between 1995 and 2003.) And, while high prices may be starting to put a dent in attendance, the dollars keep pouring in. Last summer's concert season was considered a dismal one, yet, according to *Pollstar,* the industry's trade magazine, concert revenues rose for the year.

Inevitably, touring rewards some artists better than others—graying superstars, for example, with their deep-pocketed baby-boomer fans and set lists fulls of sing-along hits. The economist Alan Krueger has estimated that the top one percent of performers claim more than half of all concert revenues. But even indie rockers are reaping the benefits, with bands like Wilco and Modest Mouse selling out venues like Radio City Music Hall, at decidedly non-indie prices.

The upshot is that the fortunes of musicians and the fortunes of music labels have less and less to do with each other. This may be the first stage of what John Perry Barlow, a former lyricist for the Dead, once called the shift from "the music business" to "the musician business." In the musician-business, the assets that once made the major labels so important—promotion, distribution, shelf space—matter less than the assets that belong to the artists, such as their ability to perform live. As technology has grown more sophisticated, the ways in which artists make money have grown more old-fashioned. The value of songs falls, and the value of seeing an artist sing them rises, because that experience can't really be reproduced. It's funny that, in an era of file-sharing and iPod-stealing, the old troubadour may have the most lucrative gig of all. But then Metallica knew it all along. "Send me money, send me green," the group sang in "Leper Messiah," twenty years ago. "Make a contribution, and you'll get a better seat."

Questions for Discussion

1. What does Surowiecki accomplish by opening his argument with a reference to a band that was popular in the 1920s?

2. According to Surowiecki, "annual concert-tour revenue . . . more than doubled" between 1998 and 2005. What factors do you think led to this increase in revenue?

3. Why would consumers be willing to spend a hundred dollars to attend a concert but be reluctant to spend nineteen dollars for a CD?

4. If touring awards "graying superstars," what effect could "the musician business" have on "the music business"?

5. Where does Surowiecki make concessions that keep him from oversimplifying what is happening in the music business today?

6. As noted on page 247, this argument originally appeared in the *New Yorker.* Within that context, how would the title sound? How does it sound within the context of this book?

④ **TOM McCOURT,** "Collecting Music in the Digital Realm"

People have been collecting music for centuries, but these collections initially took the form of sheet music from which individuals could then play songs and other forms of music composed by others. In the late nineteenth century, however, the invention of the gramophone and other mechanisms made it possible for people to start collecting cylinders and then vinyl records from which music created by others could be played. Ever since, music lovers have collected recordings in the various forms—such as LPs, cassettes, and CDs—that technology has developed. But how will music collecting change now that so much music can be stored digitally on devices such as an iPod? This is the question that Tom McCourt sets out to answer in "Collecting Music in the Digital Realm," an argument first published in the academic journal *Popular Music and Society* in May 2005. McCourt, who has a Ph.D. from the University of Texas at Austin, teaches communication at the University of Illinois at Springfield. (Note: This argument also provides an example of MLA-style documentation. See pages 185–195.)

Collecting Music in the Digital Realm

TOM McCOURT

1 Musical recordings have a relatively short history, and their evolving physical forms have shaped our interactions with them and our perceptions of their value. For example, the "album" originated with collections of 78 rpm discs that featured elaborate, bulky packaging.

These discs were limited to three or four minutes per side, which shaped the contours of the modern pop song. The storage limitations of the 78 disc also explain why the solos of early jazz recordings were compressed, and why these recordings often ended abruptly with cymbal crashes. Each subsequent format has less physical presence while allowing for more storage and greater possibilities for user programming. The LP and cassette allowed for two contiguous halves of up to 24 and 45 minutes per side respectively, each largely self-contained, while CDs accommodate 78 minutes per disc arranged in a long ebb and flow, while a few scraps as bonuses at the end (Strauss 29). An iPod can store up to ten thousand songs in a gleaming white box smaller than a pack of cigarettes.

As recordings shed their mass and/or physicality, their visual and tactile aspects also are reduced. This reduction is particularly pro-

CONTEXT

The first record disc was created by Emil Berliner in 1884, and he secured patents for the record and the gramophone in 1887. Because they were easier to store and more economical to produce, these discs—or records, as they came to be called—gradually replaced the cylinders on which the first recordings had been made available by inventors such as Thomas Edison. By 1910, technology allowed records to rotate 78 or 80 times per minute, and the "78" became the industry standard from the late 1920s to the late 1940s, when Columbia Records introduced long-playing (LP) records with up to 30 minutes of playing time per side thanks to the use of very fine grooves. As McCourt notes, LPs eventually became capable of storing 45 minutes per side, but they fell out of favor when the introduction of CDs allowed more music to be stored on a smaller object.

nounced in the transition from LPs to CDs. Vinyl could be shaped, colored, or embedded with pictures; apart from "box sets," specialty packaging has largely been abandoned with CDs. Each format also has reduced the listener's physical interaction with music, which allows music to acquire an increasingly ambient status. A listener would have to rise from their chair to change an LP, turn over a cassette, or load a CD player, but an iPod can be programmed to play until its battery expires. While LPs and CDs allow the user to determine their flow, the work as a whole must initially be engaged on the creator's terms. With an iPod, flow is determined exclusively by the user. Some argue that through digital formats, music may return to an intangible essence altogether, in which it "would stop being something to collect and revert to its age-old transience: something that transforms a moment and then disappears like a troubadour leaving town" (Pareles 22).

CDs have a physical presence of plastic and metal, enhanced by packaging. They retain "aura," although this aura is diminished. Browsing a record collection is emotionally gratifying; it is visual and tactile at the same time. We pore over the jacket art and liner notes. We determine the value of the recording by gauging the wear on the jacket and disc. Browsing a CD collection, on the other hand, is less satisfying. The medium's size limits its visual appeal, and the plastic of the jewel box degrades the tactile sensation. Digital sound files lack potential emotive contexts altogether. They are just data, metadata, and a thumbnail, and therefore emotionally less valuable than a medium you can hold in your hands. Through their immateriality, digital files cannot contain their own history. Unless they are burned onto a CD, they have no physical manifestation. No history is encoded on their surfaces, since they have no surfaces. If a digital product is enshrined in a physical form, like an LP or CD, it is regarded as being valuable. When a product is delivered in a string of bits, rather than presenting itself in a physical form, it appears to

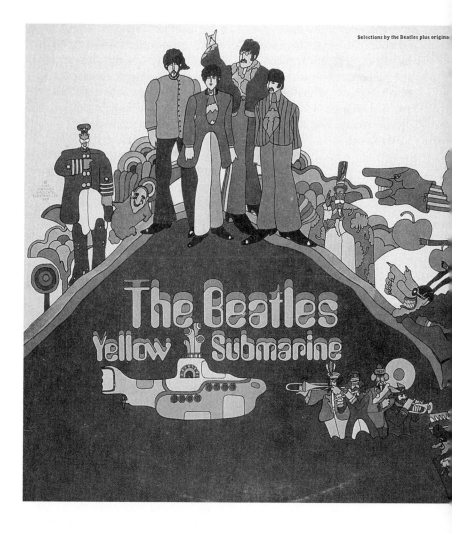

Selections by the Beatles plus origina

have less value. The result is that the world of commodities and the world of things continues to separate and our notions of value become separated from the material purchased. Diminished or nonexistent physical property undermines the notion of intellectual property—hence the widespread illicit copying of software and public support of file sharing.

Paradoxically, the lack of materiality in digital files heightens our sense of "ownership," as well as our desire to sample, collect, and trade music in new ways. Possessing digital files is a more intense and intimate experience than owning physical recordings, based on three things:

Mashup describes the product that results from using digital software to place the vocal from one song over the music of another, a process created in 2003 by Jeremy Brown, also known as DJ Reset.

5 ■ The desire for compacting. "Compacting," or compression, is integral to digital media. Codecs pare away a digital signal, in ways that allegedly are imperceptible to listeners or viewers, to facilitate their processing. Similarly, the appeal of digital collecting is predicted in part on the ability to contain huge amounts of data in a small area (witnessed by the popularity of iPods, which heighten the "geek" thrill of massive storage) despite the limited sound quality of MP3s and other file formats.

■ The desire for immediacy, in which the ability to sort and regroup files effortlessly transforms the listening experience. A collection of digital files in a hard drive becomes what one writer termed "an ocean of possibility [in which] daily life gets a different kind of soundtrack, endlessly mutable and instantly reconfigurable" (Moon 36). Fluidity becomes more prized than history; speed itself becomes a fetish.

■ The desire to customize, which is heightened by the malleability of digital media. Customization via digital software is expedient, efficient, and accomplished at physical remove (although software nomenclature implies otherwise: we "grab" cuts and personalize collections via "drag and drop" applications). Mix cassettes, on the other hand, are inefficient. They require the precision of starting and stopping, monitoring levels, erasing and re-cuing in real-time.

The popularity of MP3 files and related formats, as well as music in the form of telephone ring tones, indicates that access and convenience are increasingly more important than artifact and sound quality. Greater possibilities for user programming result in music increasingly approached in terms of utility, rather than aesthetics; it is "less about an artist's self-expression than a customer's desire for self-reflection" (Goldberg). Fluidity, rather than integrity, is the defining characteristic of digital technology. While mechanical technology enhances the possibilities for reproducing an original artifact, digital technology increases the possibilities for modifying an original (witness the popularity of "mashups"* and other recombinant recordings). Digital content is not static or universally commodifiable; instead, we engage in "dialogues" with a work by altering the artifact itself or recontextualizing it through mix CDs or playlists. While most of us lack the talent and abilities required for mixing and matching vocals and instrumental tracks into mashups, playlists increasingly serve as a form of personal expression. In cyberspace, people collect lists rather than objects. These lists may be geared to a theme, an event, an experience, a relationship. They also serve as a sort of "branding" for the creator, akin to DJ practices.

As aesthetic imagined communities, or "taste tribes," become more formalized and concretized via online tools, playlists may serve the function that CDs serve now. For example, the Rhapsody online music service's playlist function allows users to readily e-mail playlists to other users. If the recipient is a Rhapsody subscriber, he or she can click on an attachment, which will download the playlist. Playlists also reflect a key aspect of the relations of production in cyberspace, which increasingly rely on voluntary and unwaged "free labor" through the creation of web sites and other forms of user-provided content, modifying software packages, and viral marketing (Terranova). Nevertheless, as the historical record reveals, no new technology entirely substitutes for an older technology. Format obsolescence has been crucial to record companies, as it allows them to recycle their catalogs (which is where the industry draws much of its profit). Each new format is marketed as value-added by the record companies: The latest example is the (so far unsuccessful) shift to SACD and DVD-Audio, which are touted as offering improved sound quality as well as visuals, data, and interactivity to create multi-media experiences. The shift to these new formats allows the Big Four record companies to maintain bundled "albums" as a higher price point in the hard goods market, and is intended to counter the evolution of unmoored digital files in peer-to-peer systems. However, these "hard-good" formats have had limited success with consumers to date. Digital files enable heightened utility, power, and control for their users. As one reporter noted, "My records dissolved into the liquid-crystal order of a database. Organizing them was suddenly more than easy. It was a game" (Dibbell).

10 The disappearance of hard goods, in the form of physical recordings, heightens the transition from a world of cultural goods to a world of cultural services. The result is that "value" is not an inherent character of the product, but the manner in which it reaches the consumer. The popularity of song files indicates that digital value is created through mutability and process, rather than the existence of objects; therefore, the necessity to create value for something that has no physical presence accelerates the need for and process of circulation. As Marx reminds us, the status of commodities depends on movement. In cyberspace, the old market-based economy of buyers and sellers is replaced by a new network-based economy of servers and clients. Rifkin claims that "In markets, the parties exchange property. In networks, the parties share access to services and experiences . . . [it will be] a new kind of economic system based on network relationships, 24/7 contractual arrangements and access rights." This trend is reflected in the growing configuration of on-line music retailing as a service, rather than a product, in which licensing, rather than sale, provides a direct link between vendor and purchasers, making it easier to enforce limitations on use.

To compensate for their lack of materiality, digital music providers tout greater selectivity, personalization, and community as "value-added" features. In the absence of tangible commodities, the support structure itself, cyberspace, becomes the commodity. In cyberspace, collecting becomes based not on the linkage of people to objects, but of the linkage of individuals to others, realizing Stallabrass's prediction that "Experience will become a substance and a commodity" (63). As goods lose their physicality, they are imbued with greater and greater amounts of constructed value. The digital commodity is refigured continuously, emblematic of the ability of capitalism to endlessly reinvent itself.

ACKNOWLEDGMENTS

Thanks to Patrick Burkart and Rob Drew for ideas and inspiration.

WORKS CITED

Dibbell, Julian. "Unpacking My Record Collection." *Feed* Mar. 2000. 17 Oct. 2004. <http://www. juliandibbell.com/ texts/feed_records.html>.

Goldberg, Michelle. "Mood Radio: Do On-line Make-Your-Own Radio Stations Turn Music Into Muzak?" *San Francisco Bay Guardian* 6. Nov. 2000. 5 July 2001. <http:// sfbg.com/noise/05/mood.html>.

Marx, Karl. *Grundrisse.* Harmondsworth: Penguin, 1973. 533–34. (Cited in Stallabrass 62).

Moon, Tom. "Mix Master iPod Opens Up a World of Sound." *Chicago Tribune* 16 Jan. 2003: 36.

Pareles, Jon. "With a Click, a New Era of Music Dawns." *The New York Times* 15 Nov. 1988: 22.

Rifkin, Jeremy. "Where Napster Has Gone, Others Will Follow." *Los Angeles Times* 21 Aug. 2000. 21 Mar. 2001. <http://www. latimes.com/news/comment/2000821/ t000078663.html>.

Strauss, Neil. "The MP3 Revolution: Getting With it." *The New York Times* 18 Jul. 1999. Sec. 2: 29.

Stallabrass, Julian. *Gargantua: Manufactured Mass Culture.* New York: Verso, 1996.

Terranova, Tiziana. "Free Labor: Producing Culture for the Digital Economy." *Social Text* 18.2 (2000): 33–58.

DIFFERENCES

NEGOTIATING

The writers in this cluster have all addressed how corporations and performers try to profit from music, whereas individuals seek to enjoy it—by purchasing it, downloading it for free, hearing it as ringtones, or hearing it live at concerts.

Given these differences, conflicts of interest could easily emerge—as some of the readings collected here clearly indicate. But such conflicts may not be inevitable. Janis Ian, for example, argues that she is not hurt by free downloads of her music. And James Surowiecki argues that concert revenues can be more important for musicians than the royalties they earn by selling CDs.

Because the ways in which people access music are changing so rapidly, this assignment does not require you to formulate a policy that could resolve one of the problems that had already emerged at the time this book went to press. Instead, it simply asks you to research how music is most frequently heard and best enjoyed by a representative group of students at your own school and then to report your findings. When completing this assignment, you can talk informally to students, or you can conduct more formal research by conducting interviews or surveys. Consider the following options:

- Inspired by the arguments of Janis Ian and Tom McCourt, you can focus on the procedures and standards used by the people in your survey group when

Questions for Discussion

1. What does McCourt achieve by opening his argument with a summary of the history of the physical forms of musical recordings?

2. Why is McCourt drawn to the physical appeal of an LP jacket? If you have seen LP jackets, how do they compare, in your opinion, with the way CDs are packaged?

3. Why is it significant that the presentation of music is shifting from the creator's terms to those of the user?

4. How have changes in the way music is recorded and marketed contributed to the theft of intellectual property?

5. Why is it useful for McCourt to recognize that digital files have appeal? Does he do justice to this appeal?

6. When discussing the appeal of digital recordings, McCourt says, "Fluidity becomes more prized than history; speed itself becomes a fetish." Could this claim be made about other aspects of contemporary culture? What is the relationship, suggested by McCourt's allusion to Karl Marx, between speed and capitalism?

7. What does McCourt mean when he writes that the music business is in "transition from a world of cultural goods to a world of cultural services"?

they collect music—especially if they download recordings from the Internet or reproduce recordings for friends. What do they think about the question, "Who owns the music?"

- You can focus on the cultural implications of listening to music through headphones while waking across campus or waiting for a class to begin. How many students in your sample do so? And do they ever wonder if enjoying music this way inhibits social interaction with others?

- Drawing on the article by James Surowiecki, you can explore why people enjoy going to concerts even if it means paying for tickets that are priced much more highly than tickets for other events. Ask how much the people in your research group would be willing to pay to attend a live performance by one of their favorite groups, as well as what kind of pricing strikes them as fair

Whatever specific issue you choose to focus upon, think of this assignment as an argument to inquire. And be sure to indicate how you selected the students for the sample you studied, as well as how many students were in that sample.

Who Owns the Media?

If you are interested in music, current events, or entertainment such as movies or television shows, then you can benefit from learning and reflecting about how media ownership can affect what you hear or see. Take a simple example: if you read a newspaper owned by a conservative like Rupert Murdoch (see page 272) or get your news from Fox, a television network that he owns, then you will likely be exposed to editorials reflecting a conservative point of view. But could the presentation of the news be affected in ways that are not easily discernable? Some news may go unreported—or be buried in a back section—if it is news that could challenge the ideology of the paper's owner, but other news may be emphasized because it reinforces the owner's agenda. And what happens when a large number of radio stations are owned by a big corporation that also owns a music company or a movie studio? Could performers who can enrich another part of the company be played more frequently on its radio stations than performers who have no connection to the company? Questions such as these have grown urgent in recent years as media ownership has become concentrated in fewer hands—causing commentators to wonder not only about the potential abuse of power but also about the threat to diversity. If all newspapers in a city are owned by the same company or all radio stations within range are owned by one or two corporations, then the opportunity to learn or hear something different may be diminished. Three of the arguments in this cluster focus on the potential for problems such as these. The fourth argues that concentrating too many media outlets within a single corporation can lead to business difficulties.

① **JENNY TOOMEY,** "Empire of the Air"

If you have had the opportunity to travel from one part of the United States to another, you probably noticed that wherever you were, you could usually find a radio station similar to your favorite hometown radio station. One reason for the similarities among radio stations across the country is that an increasing number of them are owned by a few large media companies. Jenny Toomey thinks that is cause for concern. She isn't worried so much that radio stations today tend to play similar music by the same artists; rather, she is concerned that such similarity reflects a concentration of control of the radio airwaves in the United States. As she points out in her essay, which appeared in the public affairs magazine the *Nation* in 2003, a majority of radio stations are now owned by a small number of media companies. According to Toomey, such a concentration of many stations in the hands of a few companies gives those companies too much control over what people hear on the radio. She argues that radio is not just a business but also a public asset. Whether or not you share Toomey's concerns, her essay asks you to consider who should have control over what people hear on the radio. A musician and leader of the band Tsunami, Toomey is the former owner of the Simple Machines record label and the founder and executive director of the Future of Music Coalition, an advocacy group that works on behalf of musicians.

Empire of the Air

JENNY TOOMEY

1 For too long, musicians have had too little voice in the manufacture, distribution and promotion of their music and too little means to extract fair support and compensation for their work. The Future of Music Coalition was formed in June 2000 as a not-for-profit think tank to tackle this problem, advocating new business models, technologies and policies that would advance the cause of both musicians and citizens. Much of the work the FMC has done in the past two years has focused on documenting the structures of imbalance and inequity that impede the development of an American musicians' middle class, and translating legislative-speak into language that musicians and citizens can understand. Our most challenging work, however, and the project of which we are most proud, is our analysis of the effects of radio deregulation on musicians and citizens since the passage of the 1996 Telecommunications Act.*

Radio is a public resource managed on citizens' behalf by the federal government. This was established in 1934 through the passage of the Communications Act, which created a regulatory body, the Federal Communications Commission, and laid the ground rules for the regulation of radio. The act also determined that the spectrum would be managed according to a "trusteeship" model. Broadcasters received fixed-term, renewable licenses that gave them exclusive use of a slice of the spectrum for free. In exchange, they were required to serve the "public interest, convenience and

*In 1996 Congress passed the Telecommunications Act, which was intended to update the original Communications Act of 1934 that established laws regarding broadcasting and communications. One provision of the 1996 act is "to make available, so far as possible, to all the people of the United States without discrimination on the basis of race, color, religion, national origin, or sex a rapid, efficient, nation-wide, and world-wide wire and radio communication service with adequate facilities at reasonable charges." As Toomey notes in her essay, the effects of this and related provisions of the act are still a matter of much debate.

necessity." Though they laid their trust in the mechanics of the marketplace, legislators did not turn the entire spectrum over to commercial broadcasters. The 1934 act included some key provisions that were designed to foster localism and encourage diversity in programming.

Although changes were made to limits on ownership and FCC regulatory control in years hence, the Communications Act of 1934 remained essentially intact until it was thoroughly overhauled in 1996 with the passage of the Telecommunications Act. But even before President Clinton signed the act into law in February 1996, numerous predictions were made regarding its effect on the radio industry:

■ The number of individual radio-station owners would decrease. Those in the industry with enough capital would begin to snatch up valuable but underperforming stations in many markets—big and small.

5 ■ Station owners—given the ability to purchase more stations both locally and nationally—would benefit from economies of scale. Radio runs on many fixed costs: Equipment, operations and staffing costs are the same whether broadcasting to one person or 1 million. Owners knew that if they could control more than one station in a local market, they could consolidate operations and re-

duce fixed expenses. Lower costs would mean increased profit potential. This would, in turn, make for more financially sound radio stations, which would be able to compete more effectively against new media competitors: cable TV and the Internet.

■ There was a prediction based on a theory posited by a 1950s economist named Peter Steiner that increased ownership consolidation on the local level would lead to a subsequent increase in the number of radio format choices available to the listening public. (Steiner, writing in 1952, was not talking about oligopolistic control of the market by a few firms, as we have in the United States; rather, he was basing his predictions on an analysis of BBC radio, which is a nationally owned radio monopoly, not an oligopoly.) According to Steiner's theory, a single owner with multiple stations in a local market wouldn't want to compete against himself. Instead, he would program each station differently to meet the tastes of a variety of listeners.

But what really happened?

Well, one prediction certainly came true: The 1996 act opened the floodgates for ownership consolidation. Ten parent companies now dominate the radio spectrum, radio listenership and radio revenues, controlling two-thirds of both listeners and revenue nationwide. Two parent companies in particular—Clear Channel and Viacom—together control 42 percent of listeners and 45 percent of industry revenues.

Consolidation is particularly extreme in the case of Clear Channel. Since passage of the Telecommunications Act, Clear Channel has grown from forty stations to 1,240 stations—thirty times more than Congressional regulation previously allowed. No potential competitor owns even one-quarter the number of Clear Channel stations. With more than 100 million listeners, Clear Channel reaches more than one-third of the US population.

10 Even more bleak is the picture at the local level, where oligopolies control almost every market. Virtually every local market is dominated by four firms controlling 70 percent of

market share or greater. In smaller markets, consolidation is more extreme. The largest four firms in most small markets control 90 percent of market share or more. These companies are sometimes regional or national station groups and not locally owned.

Only the few radio-station owners with enough capital to buy additional stations have benefited from deregulation. Station owners have consolidated their operations on a local level, frequently running a number of stations out of a single building, sharing a single advertising staff, technicians and on-air talent. In some cases, radio-station groups have further reduced costs by eliminating the local component almost entirely. Local deejays and program directors are being replaced by regional directors or even by voice-tracked or syndicated programming, which explains a marked decrease in the number of people employed in the radio industry.

Prior to 1996, radio was among the least concentrated and most economically competitive of the media industries. In 1990 no company owned more than fourteen of the more than 10,000 stations nationwide, with no more than two in a single local market. But we found that local markets have now consolidated to the point that just four major radio groups control about 50 percent of the total listener audience and revenue. Clearly, deregulation has reduced competition within the radio industry.

As a result, listeners are losing. With an emphasis on cost-cutting and an effort to move decision-making out of the hands of local station staff, much of radio has become bland and formulaic. Recall Steiner's hopeful theory that an owner would not want to compete against his own company and would therefore operate stations with different programming. We found evidence to the contrary: Radio companies regularly operate two or more stations with the same format—for example, rock, country, adult contemporary, top 40—in the same local market. In a recent *New York Times* article, "Fewer Media Owners, More

CLEAR CHANNEL COMMUNICATIONS

Clear Channel Communications is the largest owner of radio stations in the United States, with more than 1,200 stations of its own and 100 shows on its Radio Premier Network, which reaches an additional 6,600 stations. It claims to reach 54 percent of all people between the ages of eighteen and forty-nine in the United States. However, it has been the target of much criticism and several lawsuits as a result of its business practices. According to Eric Boehlert, who wrote a series of reports about the company for *Salon* magazine, "radio has never seen anything quite like Clear Channel, which has swallowed up nearly 1,200 radio stations while putting its unique—and some say nasty—stamp on the business. In a series of recent *Salon* reports, insiders from the radio, record and concert industries have voiced concerns about the juggernaut's unmatched power, and how the company uses it."

Media Choices," FCC chairman Michael Powell denied this, propping up Steiner's theory by saying things like, "Common ownership can lead to more diversity—what does the owner get for having duplicative products?" But we found 561 instances of format redundancy nationwide—a parent company operating two or more stations in the same market, with the same format—amounting to massive missed opportunities for variety.

Still, from 1996 to 2000, format variety—the average number of formats available in each local market—actually increased in both large and small markets. But format variety is not equivalent to true diversity in programming, since formats with different names have similar playlists. For example, alternative, top 40, rock and hot adult contemporary are all likely to play songs by the band Creed, even though their formats are not the same. In fact, an analysis of data from charts in *Radio and Records* and *Billboard's Airplay Monitor* revealed considerable playlist overlap—as much as 76 percent—between supposedly distinct formats. If the FCC or the National Association of Broadcasters are sincerely trying to measure programming "diversity," doing so on the basis of the number of formats in a given market is a flawed methodology.

15 This final point may be the most critical one as we face an FCC that is poised to deregulate media even further in the next few months. (In September [2002], the commissioners voted unanimously to open review of the FCC's media ownership rules.) It is time to put to bed the commonly held yet fundamentally flawed notion that consolidation promotes diversity—that radio-station owners who own two stations within a marketplace will not be tempted to program both stations with the same songs. There's a clear corporate benefit in "self-competition," and it's time we made regulatory agencies admit that fact.

Even in the beginning, radio was regulated to cultivate a commercial broadcast industry that could grow to serve the greatest number of Americans possible. As the decades have passed, most calls for deregulation have come from incumbent broadcasters interested in lifting local and national ownership caps that protect against the competitive pressures of other media.

While the effects of deregulation have been widely studied and discussed, scrutiny is focused on the profitability of the radio industry. But the effect of increased corporate profitability on citizens is rarely, if ever, discussed. Radical deregulation of the radio industry allowed by the Telecommunications Act of 1996 has not benefited the public. Instead, it has led to less competition, fewer viewpoints and less diversity in programming. Substantial ethnic, regional and economic populations are not provided the services to which they are entitled. The public is not satisfied, and possible economic efficiencies of industry consolidation are not being passed on to the public in the form of improved local service. Deregulation has damaged radio as a public resource.

Musicians are also suffering because of deregulation. Independent artists have found it increasingly difficult to get airplay; in payola-like schemes, the "Big Five" music companies, through third-party promoters, shell out thousands of dollars per song to the companies that rule the airwaves. That's part of why the Future of Music Coalition undertook this research. We at the FMC firmly believe that the music industry as it exists today is fundamentally anti-artist. In addition to our radio study, our projects—including a critique of standard major-label contract clauses, a study of musicians and health insurance, and a translation of the complicated Copyright Arbitration Royalty Panel proceedings that determined the webcasting royalty rates—were conceived as tools for people who are curious about the structures that impede musicians' ability to both live and make a living. Understanding radio deregulation is another tool for criticizing such structures. We have detailed the connections between concentrated media ownership, homogenous radio programming and restricted radio access for musicians. Given that knowledge, we hope artists will join with other activists and work to restore radio as a public resource for all people.

CONTEXT

The 1996 Telecommunications Act is one of many efforts by U.S. lawmakers since the early 1980s to reduce federal regulation of the radio industry. In part as a response to the kinds of the concerns about deregulation that Toomey expresses in this essay, a bill titled "The Competition in Radio and Concert Industries Act of 2002" was introduced to the U.S. Senate in July 2002. The American Federation of Television and Radio Artists (AFTRA) endorsed the legislation as a way to curtail the consolidation of the radio industry, which AFTRA argued has hurt both the public and the artists whose music is played on radio stations. Supporters of deregulation maintain that the industry today is vibrant and profitable, with fierce competition for listeners in urban markets that benefits consumers by providing them with many choices addressing their listening interests. In 2003, Congress relaxed regulations on all media companies, making it easier for companies to acquire additional media outlets, including radio stations.

Questions for Discussion

1. In the first sentence of her essay, Toomey unequivocally states her position regarding who should control music. Evaluate the effectiveness of this approach to introducing her subject. How might Toomey's introduction enhance the effectiveness of her argument? In what ways might it weaken her argument? What other strategies might she have used to introduce her argument?

2. Why does Toomey believe that "listeners are losing" as a result of the consolidation of the radio industry? Do you agree with her? Why or why not?

3. According to Toomey, the deregulation of the radio industry as a result of the 1996 Telecommunications Act has not benefited citizens, even though it has resulted in greater profits for companies. On what grounds does she make that claim? How convincing do you think Toomey is on this point?

4. Toomey structures her essay around several predictions that were made about the effect of the 1996 Telecommunications Act on the radio industry in the United States. Do you think this approach to structuring her essay makes her argument persuasive?

5. Evaluate Toomey's use of statistical information as evidence for her claims. How appropriate to her argument are the kinds of statistics she cites? How do those statistics affect her argument?

6. Toomey's essay can be considered an example of an argument based on deductive reasoning. (See pages 88–93 for an explanation of this kind of argument.) What is the basic principle or belief on which Toomey bases her argument? Does she state this principle overtly anywhere in her essay? What syllogism does her argument rest on? (See pages 90–91 for a discussion of the syllogism.)

② GAL BECKERMAN, "Tripping Up Big Media"

How effective can organized citizens be when opposing a government policy that they object to? That question is at the heart of the following argument by Gal Beckerman, first published in 2003 by the *Columbia Journalism Review* when she was an assistant editor there. The answer to this question varies according to the policy, the strength of the government, and the government's commitment to the policy. But it is also determined by how active and articulate the opposition can be—as well as by the size and diversity of the opposition. As you can tell by the title, "Tripping Up Big Media," Beckerman is not sympathetic to large corporations, a sign that her argument will emphasize the case brought against big media companies by the opposition upon which she focuses. Her argument originally appeared with the following two sentences between the title and the author's name: "One of the strangest Left-Right coalitions in recent memory has challenged a free-market FCC. What's the glue that holds it together?" You may find it useful to keep that question in mind as you read Beckerman's work.

Tripping Up Big Media

GAL BECKERMAN

1 The angels of the public interest, with large pink wings and glittering halos, descended on Michael Powell* this fall, five years after he had, somewhat sarcastically, first invoked them.

That was back in April 1998, when Powell was speaking to a Las Vegas gathering of lawyers. Only a few months had passed since his appointment to one of the five spots on the Federal Communications Commission, and the new commissioner had been invited to speak about a longstanding and contentious issue: Was it the FCC's responsibility to keep the media working toward the public good?

Powell made clear that he placed his faith in the invisible hand of the market: the business of the FCC, he said, was to resolve "matters that predominantly involve the competing interests of industry" and not some vague "public interest." The FCC had no role in deciding whether to give free airtime to presidential

*Michael Powell
The son of former Secretary of State Colin Powell and a Republican, Michael Powell served for four years as chairman of the Federal Communications Commission under President George W. Bush before resigning in 2005, before his term was set to expire. In addition to attempting to reduce FCC regulations concerning the number of broadcasting stations an individual or corporation could own, he increased fines for "broadcast indecency" after singer Janet Jackson experienced what was called a "wardrobe malfunction" during the halftime performance of the 2004 Super Bowl. (One of her breasts became exposed—either accidentally, as implied by "wardrobe malfunction," or deliberately as part of a publicity stunt.)

CONTEXT

Sponsored by Columbia University, which has one of the best journalism schools in the country, the *Columbia Journalism Review* is a bimonthly magazine directed to an audience of professional journalists. Committed to promoting better journalism, *CJR* publishes articles about media trends, examinations of professional ethics, and stories about how the news that is reported was discovered and selected for publication or broadcast.

candidates, for example, or in forcing television channels to carry educational or children's programming. "Even if what is portrayed on television encourages or perpetuates some societal problem, we must be careful in invoking our regulatory powers," Powell insisted.

To highlight the point, Powell used biblical imagery. "The night after I was sworn in, I waited for a visit from the angel of the public interest," Powell said. "I waited all night but she did not come. And, in fact, five months into this job, I still had no divine awakening."

5 This September 4 the angels finally arrived.

Fifteen women dressed entirely in fluorescent pink and spreading frilly wings emblazoned with the words "Free Speech" stood on the sidewalk outside the large glass doors of the FCC. They banged on bongos and shouted chants, unfurling a large pink scroll containing their demands: full repeal of the new rules that Michael Powell had just shepherded into existence.

By this time, Powell had become FCC chairman and had overseen the biggest relaxation of media ownership rules in over thirty years. . . . But the day before, a federal appeals court in Philadelphia had granted an emergency stay barring the FCC from putting his new rules into effect. The court gave as one of its reasons "the magnitude of this matter and the public's interest in reaching the proper resolution." So the angels were celebrating, and they were not alone.

The massive public response to the rule changes, in fact, had been unprecedented. For months before and after the new rules were announced on June 2, opposition had been loud, passionate, and active. Hundreds of thousands of comments were sent to the FCC, almost all in opposition. It was the heaviest outpouring of public sentiment the commission had ever experienced.

Even more striking was the makeup of this opposition, what the *New York Times* called "an unusual alliance of liberal and conservative organizations." Together in the mix, along with Code Pink, the activists in angel wings, were

the National Rifle Association, the National Organization for Women, the Parents Television Council (a conservative group focused on indecency in television), every major journalism association, labor groups like the Writers and Screen Actors Guilds, and a collection of liberal nonprofit organizations that had been focused on media issues for decades.

10 It is not every day that the ideological lines get redrawn over an issue, let alone an issue that had been destined to remain obscure and complex for all but telecommunications experts to debate. What's the glue that has held this unlikely coalition together?

Victoria Cunningham is the twenty-four-year-old national coordinator of Code Pink, a grass-roots women's organization that engages in wacky direct action. Code Pink has sung Christmas carols outside Donald Rumsfeld's home and arrived at Hillary Clinton's Senate office wearing underwear over their clothing to deliver her a "pink slip" of disapproval for her early support of the war in Iraq. I met with her a month after her group's boisterous visit to the FCC. Code Pink's office is little more than a broom closet on the fifth floor of a building a few blocks from the White House. Pink beads and rainbow flags cram the walls. Cunningham was wearing—what else?—a very pink shirt.

Why were her members, who number in the thousands, so interested in this issue? "Our people are informed enough that they understand what happens when there are only one or three or four companies that are controlling the information we get," Cunningham said. "A lot of our people would love to turn on the evening news and see a variety of opinions coming out."

Like everyone I talked to who was involved in the opposition to the FCC rules, Cunningham spoke of the intuitive understanding most people had of an issue that seems complex on the surface. Over and over, as I attempted to understand what it was that was holding together this diverse coalition, I heard the same phrase: "People just get it." And I heard this from groups both left and right. The oddest invitation Cunningham said she had received in the last few months was to appear on Oliver North's* conservative radio talk show to debate the FCC issue. "And when we talked about that," she said, "we just couldn't say anything bad to each other."

Next, I made my way to a rather different scene, the headquarters of the United States Conference of Catholic Bishops, to talk with Monsignor Francis J. Maniscalco, its director of communications. No broom closet, the conference's home is in a giant modern Washington building behind a large sculpture of Jesus pointing to the sky.

15 Monsignor Maniscalco, a clerical collar under his soft, round face, spoke like a weathered telecommunications professional about his opposition to the FCC's new rules. The bishops are concerned about the loss of religious shows, like Catholic mass on television—but also the loss of a time when, he says, in order for broadcasters to keep their licenses they had to "prove they were being responsive to the local community." The further consolidation of the media that would be spurred by the new FCC rules, he said, would only increase the lack of responsiveness to community needs. "We see the media as being very formational of people, formational of a culture, formational of people's attitudes," he said, "and if certain strains of community life are not on television they are, by that very reason, considered less important, less vital to society."

Even though he and the conference had always opposed media consolidation, Maniscalco said, until recently they felt they were working in a vacuum. When the monsignor began talking about the current effort, though, he visibly brightened. His eyebrows, which are red, lifted, and he rolled forward in his chair. "The consumption of media is a passive consumption, it is a passive act in itself," he said. "And it is a passive audience that has said, 'We just have to take what they give us.' But interestingly enough, this seems to be something that has finally caught people's imagination, that they could make a difference

*Oliver North

A native of San Antonio who experienced combat as a U.S. Marine, Colonel Oliver North is best known for his work on the staff of the National Security Council under President Ronald Regan. From 1985 to 1986, he helped coordinate the sale of $48 million dollars of U.S. arms to Iran, in violation of the government's publicly stated policy of refusing to aid Iran or to bargain with terrorists. North helped channel a portion of these funds to guerrillas fighting in Nicaragua, violating a law passed by Congress in 1984. When these illegal activities were discovered, North lost his job and President Reagan's image was tarnished. North subsequently transformed himself into a speaker and author popular with conservative audiences.

†Trent Lott

An attorney who represented Mississippi in the House of Representatives from 1973–1989, Trent Lott subsequently became a senator and served as Republican party whip (1995–1996) and majority leader (2001–2003). A well-known conservative, Lott was forced to step down as majority leader after remarking that the country would have benefited from the election of Strom Thurmond as President in 1948. A Democrat who later became a Republican, Thurmond ran as an independent in 1948 on a platform that opposed civil rights for African Americans.

in terms of turning back these rules and saying no, we don't see that as being very helpful to our situation."

Media industry insiders were taken by surprise at how fast these groups managed to come together and exercise political influence. In addition to the emergency stay issued by the Philadelphia federal appeals court on the day before Powell's six new rules were to go into effect, Congress has responded with zeal to their demands. Consider: on July 23, only a month after the rules were approved, the House of Representatives voted 400 to 21 to roll back the ownership cap to 35 percent. Then, on September 16, the coalition had an even greater success. The Senate used a parliamentary procedure, called a resolution of disapproval—used only once before in history— to pass a bill repealing all the new regulations. It passed 55 to 40, and was supported by twelve Republicans, and cosponsored, astonishingly, by none other than Trent Lott.† Such quick legislative action has generated excitement, but it is unlikely that the coalition will find such easy victory in the future. The Senate bill must now face House Republican leaders who have vowed to prevent the measure from going to a vote, partly to keep this political hot potato away from the president during an election year. The court case that has put the new rules on hold, meanwhile, promises a complicated legal contest when it takes place next year.

But these challenges don't take away from what has been achieved. Such ideologically disparate groups rarely find common cause. As Powell himself has pointed out, the reasons behind most of these groups' opposition are parochial and narrow. The unions are worried that more consolidation will lead to fewer jobs; the left-leaning groups are still shivering from what they saw as nationalistic coverage of the war; groups like the Parents Television Council want less *Buffy the Vampire Slayer* and more *Little House on the Prairie.* Yet there they were, at countless public hearings over the last half-year, the bishop sitting next to the gun lobbyist sitting next to a woman from NOW, all united around some common denominator.

To get a better idea of what that common denominator might be, I went to visit Andrew Schwartzman, the fifty-seven-year-old president of the Media Access Project, a small public-interest law firm that has been fighting big media and the FCC for more than three decades. Schwartzman was the lead lawyer in the case that led to the September 4 emergency stay.

20 A week after that triumph, he looked exhausted, his bloodshot eyes contrasting with his white hair and bushy moustache. He looked a little like Mark Twain—a very tired Mark Twain. He spoke slowly and deliberately. "Michael Powell has significantly misunderstood what this is about, to his detriment" Schwartzman said. "He repeatedly says, somewhat disdainfully, that all the disparate organizations are unhappy about what they see on the air. The right-wingers think the media is liberal and the left-wingers think the media is a corporate conspiracy, and they all can't be right. This is a way of dismissing and trivializing their position. For me, what these groups have in common is that they represent people who are within the relatively small group of Americans who choose to be active participants in the political process, the people who exercise their First Amendment rights aggressively. And even where their principal areas of interest may be the Second Amendment or other things, they understand the importance of the electronic mass media in the democratic process. And Michael Powell hasn't understood that."

What unites these groups, he told me, is that they all generally believe that the media are limited, and that this limitation comes from the face that there is too much control in too few hands. This leads to a lack of diversity of voices, to programming that is out of touch with local concerns, to increasingly commercial and homogenized news and entertainment. And this is what has triggered people's passions. It is not the fear that their own voice won't echo loud enough, he said, but that further consolidation will produce media in which only the powerful few will be heard at all.

But why now? Neither Schwartzman nor anyone else I talked to could explain why, coming from so many different directions, all these groups landed in the same place at the same time. After all, this is not the first time that free-market enthusiasts have smashed up against the defenders of the public interest.

The 1980s saw a major crack in the idea that the public interest was the top priority for the FCC. President Reagan's FCC chairman, Mark Fowler, presided over the death of the Fairness Doctrine, which required broadcast stations to provide airtime for opposing voices in controversial matters of public importance. Then in 1996 Congress passed, and President Clinton signed, a major overhaul of U.S. telecommunications law, permitting greater media concentration. Radio was significantly deregulated, leading to the growth of companies such as Clear Channel, which now operates more than 1,200 stations in more than 300 markets. It was in that period that the national ownership cap for television stations went from 25 percent to 35 percent.

Such developments happened away from the public eye, in a place where only members of Congress and lobbyists roam. According to Celia Wexler, director and researcher for Common Cause, the nonpartisan citizens' lobby, those past fights were "very much inside the Beltway. It was very complicated, and there were no groups able to tell the story in a way that really made people understand what was at stake. There were media reformers who understood, who wanted a discussion of the public-interest obligations of broadcasters. But it didn't really catch fire."

25 At a morning session on media issues at a Common Cause conference, I saw how dramatically the situation had changed. Seats to the event were in hot demand. Next to me an elderly couple sat clutching newspaper clippings, one of which was headlined NEW FCC RULES SAP DIVERSITY IN MEDIA OWNERS.

Wexler, a small woman with the air of a librarian, was sitting on stage in a panel that included Gloria Tristani, a former FCC commissioner, who said of Michael Powell at one point: "I think he has lost touch with people or maybe never had touch with people in this country." The star of the morning, though, was John Nichols, a *Nation* Washington correspondent, who, together with Robert McChesney, another media reformer, this year started an

organization called Free Press. Nichols has a professional air, but he started his talk so dramatically that the couple next to me started nodding furiously.

He contended that, in the wake of September 11 and in the buildup to the war in Iraq, Americans had come to realize how shallow and narrow were their media. "People said maybe I support this war, maybe I oppose it, but I would like to know a little more about who we're going to bomb," Nichols said. "And I would like to know more about what came before and how this works—not just cheerleading. And all of that churned, combined, to have a profound impact."

This was an explanation I had heard from other liberal groups involved in the media movement. But it still didn't explain why conservatives had chosen this particular moment to join this coalition. As with the liberals, there have always been conservative groups that have opposed media deregulation, most notably the Catholic Church, but the message never resonated widely.

That, too, has changed. Take, for example, the Parents Television Council, an organization with 800,000 members that monitors indecency. The group regularly sends letters to the FCC when a show contains what they call "foul language" or racy subject matter. In August, L. Brent Bozell, the council's president joined Gene Kimmelman of Consumers Union, a longtime advocate of media reform, in an editorial that was published in the *New York Daily News,* writing that in spite of their ideological differences they "agree that by opening the door to more media and newspaper consolidation, the FCC has endangered something that reaches far beyond traditional politics: It has undermined the community-oriented communications critical to our democracy."

30 Conservatives see a link between the growth of big media and the amount of blood and skin they see on television. The smaller and more local that media are, the argument goes, the more attuned to community standards of decency. If local stations could preempt what was being fed from New York and Los Angeles, then programming could be more reflective of family values. Here again, the sense is that media have become too large and all-encompassing and lost touch with their audience.

Melissa Caldwell, director of research at the council, points out that the new ownership rules were a way for big media companies to buy up even more local stations. This is worrisome, she explained, because locally owned broadcast affiliates tend to be more responsive to community standards of decency. The council's surveys, Caldwell says, show that network-owned stations almost never preempt network shows, "whereas locally owned and operated stations were more likely to do so. We don't want to see the networks become even less responsive to community concerns than they already are."

By the end of September, with his rules in deep freeze, Powell, speaking to the *New York Times,* expressed exasperation with the effectiveness of the opposition. "Basically, people ran an outside political campaign against the commission," Powell was quoted as saying. "I've never seen that in six years."

At the core of this "campaign" were four groups—Consumers Union, led by Kimmelman, and the Consumer's Federation of America, represented by Mark Cooper, as well as Andrew Schwartzman's Media Access Project and the Center for Digital Democracy, run by Jeffrey Chester. The four men (who often referred to themselves as the "four Jewish horsemen of the apocalypse") played the central role in translating the growing anger and frustration of the Left and the Right into a cohesive movement.

Early on, these groups realized that to fight the FCC they would need more political power than their dependable but small progressive base could offer. One of their first steps, in addition to beginning a conversation with conservative groups like Parents Television Council, was to call on labor organizations like the Writers Guild and AFTRA, which could provide the resources and the manpower to get the message out.

35 By the beginning of 2003, a loose coalition was in place. And at that point, Powell's personality, of all things, began to play a galvanizing role. In pronouncement after pronouncement, he trumpeted the importance of these new rules—highlighted by his decision to vote on all of them in one shot. He insisted that their rewriting would be based purely on a scientific examination of the current broadcasting world.

It was true, as Powell claimed, that reexamining the rules was not his idea. The District of Columbia Court of Appeals, interpreting the 1996 Telecommunications Act, had ordered him to conduct a biennial assessment. But Powell had many chances to include the public in this review, and he did not. No public hearings were necessary, he said; the facts would do the talking, and would point to the rightness of his free-market convictions. "Michael Powell deserves a public-interest medal because he practically single-handedly created this enormous opposition," said Jeffrey Chester.

In December, Powell announced a single public hearing, to be held in what one opponent jokingly referred to as "the media capital" of Richmond, Virginia. Soon, groups who had been only peripherally involved in the loose coalition became increasingly angered by Powell's intransigence. One story often invoked to illustrate the unifying power of Powell's stubbornness involves a meeting that took place between members of the Hollywood creative community and labor groups, including producers and writers, and Kenneth Ferree, the chief of the media bureau at the FCC. According to several people present at the gathering, when a request for public hearings was made, Ferree was dismissive and rude, saying he was only interested in "facts," not "footstomping." "The sense of helplessness and anger that he generated by that meeting was enormous," said Mona Mangan, executive director of Writers Guild East.

If Powell's refusal to hold public hearings galvanized the opposition in one direction, the desire of another commissioner, Michael J. Copps, to engage with the public on this issue also played a key role. Copps, one of the two Democrats on the FCC, was unhappy with Powell's insistence on keeping the issue within the Beltway. When Powell finally announced that the number of public hearings would be limited to one, Copps issued a statement that read like the complaints of the growing grassroots opposition. "At stake in this proceeding are our core values of localism, diversity, competition, and maintaining the multiplicity of voices and choices that undergrid our marketplace of ideas and that sustain American democracy," he said.

"The idea that you are changing the basic framework for media ownership and you don't really want to make this a public debate was a reflection of Powell's own sort of arrogant, narrow mind-set" said Chester. "He didn't understand that this is about journalism, this is about media. No matter what the outcome, you have to go the extra mile to encourage a serious national debate."

40 Through the winter and early spring, Copps organized unofficial hearings around the country in collaboration with groups like the Writers Guild, earning the nickname Paul Revere in some quarters. As media reform groups searched for a wide range of witnesses to speak at these hearings, the coalition grew to include groups like the National Rifle Association and the National Organization for Woman. Out of the meetings came the first sense that this issue could resonate.

In the spring, after Powell refused to delay the June vote for further discussion, the FCC was flooded with calls and letters. Petitions were signed with hundreds of thousands of names and comments. Something was happening. Despite the scant press coverage, citizens were responding. The Internet helped to make this response immediate and numerous, mostly through an Internet-based public interest group called MoveOn.org, which had been an organizing force against the Iraq war, capable of turning out thousands upon thousands of signatures and donations in a matter of days. Now it turned its attention to media reform, and the result surprised even its organizers.

"We thought it was just kind of a weird issue because it's this wonky regulatory thing, it's not a typical MoveOn issue like stopping the drilling in the Arctic," said Eli Pariser, MoveOn's young national campaigns director. "After we heard from a critical mass of people we decided to pursue it and see what happened. And when we went out with our petition we got this amazing response."

A few days before the September 16 Senate vote on the resolution of disapproval, I accompanied lobbyists from Consumers Union and Free Press as they delivered a huge MoveOn petition. Lining one of the halls in the Hart Senate Office Building were stacks upon stacks of paper, 340,000 names in all. It was the quickest and largest turnover MoveOn had ever experienced, including its antiwar effort.

As the activists, young and in rumpled, ill-fitting suits, delivered these petitions to Senate aides, everyone was struck by the fact that they were more than just names printed on paper, more than a rubber-stamp petition drive. Many of the statements seemed heartfeld. Sometimes they were only a line, "I want more diversity and freedom of speech," and sometimes long letters, taking up whole pages. People expressed their personal dissatisfaction with what they saw when they turned on the TV. But mostly, they expressed passion. It popped off the page. People in Batesville, Arkansas, and Tekamah, Nebraska, were angry. Media had become a political issue, as deeply felt as the economy, health care, or education. Senate Republicans and Democrats alike understood this. A few days later, they voted to repeal all the new regulations.

45 When I asked the coalition partners how long their alliance could last beyond the battle over the ownership rules, their answers were uniform: not long. If the Parents Television Council and the Writers Guild ever sat down and tried to figure out rules for TV, the decency monitors would demand stricter limits on sex and violence, and the screenwriters who make up the guild would recoil in horror, shouting about the First Amendment.

But on the question of what these groups' larger and long-term objectives were for the media, I did get some kind of consensus. At the most fundamental level, there is a demand for a forum, for a place where diverse ideas can be heard and contrasted. The ideal seemed to be media that better reflect America, with its diversity, its ideological contentiousness, its multitude of values and standards.

When I asked Monsignore Maniscalco how he would want broadcasters to act in an ideal world, I assumed he would posit some narrow vision of an all-Catholic twenty-four-hour news channel, but he didn't.

"We would like them to take a chance on things that are noncommercial, that are simply not on television," the monsignor said. "Not for the sake of how much money they can make, but because they represent significant aspects of the community. We would really like to see the concept of broadcasting in the public interest be recognized by these people as a legitimate aspect of their work."

When I posed the problem of whether he could eventually agree to share airtime with all the groups in this coalition, groups like NOW with which he had fundamental and deep disagreements, Monsignor Maniscalco had a simple answer: "You could say that the goal is for the media to give us access so we can finally have a space to argue amongst ourselves."

Questions for Discussion

1. When reading about business or the economy, how do you interpret "the invisible hand of the market"? Why is that hand "invisible"? Is it a hand that can be trusted?

2. Consider the quotation from Michael Powell in paragraph 4. How would you describe its tone? What does it convey about him?

3. Why did the FCC rule change described in this argument generate such a strong public response?

4. Based on the information reported by Beckerman, what do you think of Code Pink?

5. One of the arguments against media mergers is that diverse opinions can be stifled. Do you think that breaking up large media holdings is sufficient to guarantee diversity of opinion?

6. According to a clergyman quoted in paragraph 16, "The consumption of media is a passive consumption, it is a passive act in itself." Do you agree? Do some forms of media require a more active response than others?

7. The American media is described as "shallow and narrow" in paragraph 27. Can you identify shows or publications that deserve this judgment? Can you think of exceptions?

8. Why do you think Powell scheduled the only public hearing on the FCC changes as a meeting in Richmond, Virginia? Beckerman uses punctuation to imply that Richmond is not a "media capital." What are the media capitals within the United States? Should hearings have been held there, or should they have been scheduled in cities across the nation?

9. Beckerman goes into much detail about how activists from all sides of the political spectrum organized their campaign against the FCC rule changes. Why is this example worth exploring in detail? What are the implications of this example?

③ **LAURA PETERSON**, "The Moguls Are the Medium"

A graduate of the University of California at Santa Cruz, Laura Peterson worked for eighteen months in Sarajevo, Bosnia, and Herzegovina as a correspondent and editor for the *San Francisco Chronicle*. She has also reported from Turkey for publications such as the *Christian Science Monitor* and *American Journalism Review*. Since 2003, she has been an associate editor of *Foreign Policy*, an award-winning magazine on global politics, economics, and ideas published in Washington, D.C., by the Carnegie Endowment for International Peace. *Foreign Policy* published the following argument at the end of 2004. In it, Peterson argues that the economics of media ownership have not changed even if popular anxiety about such ownership has increased. As you read her argument, note how she draws upon her interest in foreign affairs.

The Moguls Are the Medium

LINDA PETERSON

1 It's not easy being Rupert Murdoch.* Over the years the billionaire mogul has become the poster boy for the evils of media consolidation. With each new addition to his empire, Murdoch's critics grow in size and volume, angrily decrying the insidious danger of one person wielding so much influence over so many. But a CEO as reviled as Murdoch might take comfort in knowing he is just one man in a long history of cable barons. To be sure, these captains of the media industry ruled over a very different kingdom a century ago. But they cut a similar figure in the public imagination: the controlling oligarch holding information captive.

The cable companies of the mid-19th century—that is, the telegraph cable companies—were "interconnected in a complex series of monopolies and cartel arrangements" centered in London. Company officers held stakes in and sat on the boards of each other's companies, pooling resources and quashing competition. This "cable cartel" was an instrument of the British Empire's power and influence. In the 1850s, Britain funded cable companies to ensure priority for government messages, and from the mid-1870s subsidized cable construction to strategically important areas of the world.

Ownership of telegraph cables, like ownership of the airwaves today, was power. British cartels charged new services such as the Associated Press astronomical prices. Because the British news agency Reuters was able to use the imperial cable system under more favorable terms, it soon became the portal for all foreign news. Even in U.S. territories such

*Rupert Murdoch
Born in Australia, Rupert Murdoch is a naturalized citizen of the United States and arguably the most powerful media owner in the world. Controlling media in three continents, Murdoch's American properties include the **New York Post,** the New York Magazine Corporation, the **San Antonio Express,** and Fox Television Network. His conservative political views shape opinion in the media he controls. For example, when he acquired the **New York Post,** it changed from being New York's most liberal newspaper to its most conservative. Now one of the richest men in the world, Murdoch set a record when he paid $44 million for a penthouse apartment in New York City in December 2004—at the time, the highest price ever paid for a residence in that city.

as the Philippines news from the United States had to pass through Reuters.

The rise of these British syndicates sparked the first media reform movement, which pushed for greater state ownership and regulation of rates. U.S. President Woodrow Wilson only realized the extent of the problem when a European news agency mangled the translation of one of his speeches. Alarmed by Britain's media juggernaut, Wilson created the Committee of Public Information in 1917 to distribute U.S.-produced news, and he placed Chicago newspaperman and lawyer Walter Rogers at the agency's helm. Like the idealistic media protesters of his day, Rogers believed that affordable cable access would expand peoples' access to information and thereby improve the conduct of states.

5 Sadly, the world doesn't work that way. Canada-based scholars Robert Pike and Dwayne Winseck, in a recent article appearing in the British journal *Media, Culture & Society*, offer an impressive historical account of this early moment in media consolation. They ultimately conclude that would-be reformers such as Rogers—or for that matter, today's critics of media conglomerates—fail to grasp the "reality that corporate power, in league with the state, [has] made a mockery of prospects for a democratic global media system." For the authors, media consolidation is not another malefic product of modern globalization. As they point out, the U.S. radio industry subsequently followed a similar pattern of monopolization in the 1920s. What we are witnessing—then and now—is the ebb and flow of markets, and nothing more.

Pike and Winseck's history lesson ultimately tells us less about today's global media consolidation than about popular anxiety over it. They identify issues of ownership and control, cost, and technological entrenchment as the "cornerstones" of what would become an enduring debate about the politics of global media. The proliferation of news sources through media such as the Internet and cable television have now largely neutralized reformers' concerns about technology—and, to some extent—cost. But fears over ownership still resonate for today's media reformers, who see access to information suppressed by what media critic Ben Bagdikian calls the "Big Five" media companies: Time Warner, Disney, News Corporation, Viacom, and Bertelsmann.

The authors might argue that this anxiety flies in the face of studies showing that the portion of global media that multinational companies control remains relatively small. Still, modern critics have a point: The media barons of the 19th century wielded political power by controlling the means of transmitting information—and that's about it. Today's media behemoths control the distribution and content for global news operations their predecessors could never have imagined.

Woodrow Wilson did, however, anticipate these tensions. Pike and Winseck note that the Wilson administration understood that the drive to use information technologies could serve either "purely selfish national purposes," or "the equal benefit of all nations and all people." Substitute the world "national" for "corporate," and those sentences could appear in any media watchdog missive today—and suggest Wilson wouldn't have liked Rupert Murdoch, either.

COMPLICATION

The Committee of Public Information was founded, as Peterson notes, in 1917—but that was the year that the United States entered the First World War. The Committee's primary function was to use propaganda and public-relations techniques to rally support for U.S. involvement in a war President Woodrow Wilson had promised to avoid when campaigning for reelection in 1916. The work of this committee did much to shape subsequent propaganda campaigns. Although considerable opposition existed in the United States against entering a European war being fought among a number of empires, the Committee of Public Information helped create a climate in which the war was defined as a "war to end all wars," and Germany was perceived as the principal threat to peace and civilization. As a result, the teaching of German was temporarily eliminated from public schools and German Americans were subject to violence.

Questions for Discussion

1. What does Peterson achieve by beginning with a reference to Rupert Murdoch?

2. How did ownership of cable companies contribute to the power of the British empire during the nineteenth and early twentieth century? How relevant is this example to corporate ownership of information technologies today?

3. According to Peterson, does history support the idea that "affordable cable access would expand people's access to information and thereby improve the conduct of states"?

4. If media ownership becomes consolidated and then breaks apart, can these changes be attributed entirely to "the ebb and flow of markets," or does Peterson reveal other factors that affect how markets function?

5. What distinction does Peterson recognize between the media giants of the nineteenth century and those operating today?

6. Why does Peterson close with references to both Woodrow Wilson and Rupert Murdoch?

④ **TOM LOWRY AND RON GROVER,** "Breaking Up Is Easy to Do"

Although many critics of media mergers were concerned primarily with the political and social implications of concentrating media ownership within a relatively few number of hands, Tom Lowry and Ron Grover focus on whether the building of media empires was a sound business practice and argue that breaking up some of these large companies can actually benefit shareholders. "Breaking Up Is Easy to Do" was first published on March 17, 2005, by *Business Week Online,* the electronic version of *Business Week,* a well-known magazine for which Lowry is the media editor. (An argument by Lowry appears on pages 244–246.) Grover writes for the online version of the magazine. The collaboration between the two writers suggests that the story was considered too important or too complex to be reported by a single author—and this practice is not uncommon in journalism, especially when journalists are located in different cities or interview different sources. Even if you are not normally drawn to reading business news, you may find the following piece of interest given what it reports about the ownership of such companies as MTV, Comedy Central, and properties held by Walt Disney.

Breaking Up Is Easy to Do

TOM LOWRY AND RON GROVER

1 Viacom, Disney, and Liberty Media are all spinning off businesses. It may just be the only way to recapture the Street's respect.

The media moguls built them up and now they are breaking them apart. After a decade of unprecedented consolidation, massive media conglomerates with stagnant stock prices are looking to break off pieces of their companies in an attempt to unlock value.

On Mar. 16, Viacom* (VIA) confirmed that it was considering splitting the $22.5-billion-a-year company. One piece might comprise CBS, Infinity Broadcasting, and outdoor advertising, say sources, while the other would consist of red-hot MTV, its other cable networks, and the Paramount studio. Its theme park and book-publishing businesses may be put on the block. Wall Street applauded the news, with the stock rising $2.70, to $37.

Viacom is among a growing number of media outfits that feel frustrated by how the markets perceive their businesses. Of late, investors have been less than enthusiastic about the industry. In the past year, the Bloomberg Media Index, made up of 37 companies,

*Viacom
One of the largest media companies in the world, Viacom continues to change its holdings. But it has simultaneously owned CBS, MTV, Spike TV, Showtime, Nickelodeon, Paramount Pictures, and the publishing house of Simon & Schuster. Critics of media consolidation ask whether the synergy created by such diverse holdings could be used to manipulate public opinion—wondering, for example, if a talk show broadcast on CBS could be used to promote movies made by Paramount or books published by Simon & Schuster, benefiting the parent company in ways the average consumer would not detect.

posted a 3% return, vs. a 10% gain for the benchmark Standard & Poor's 500 Index.

Redstone's Example?

5 "These companies feel misunderstood and undervalued," says Gigi Johnson, executive director of the Entertainment and Media Management Institute at the UCLA Anderson School of Management. "There was a time when size mattered more than consistency, but it turns out it's hard for investors to decipher these companies and assess their business risks on their own. If you are buying Viacom today, you're buying an overly diversified media company, one in almost every sector of the industry's future."

The moguls are conceding that it's time to try a new strategy. "For whatever reason, [media stocks] have fallen out of favor with Wall Street, and I can't explain that," says Viacom Chairman Sumner Redstone who, over the course of 50 years, built his family owned drive-in operation into the huge corporation it is today. "As Shakespeare said, 'A rose by any other name is just as sweet.' Now I'll have two roses."

Does Redstone think other outfits will follow Viacom's lead? "Every media company is facing the same thing right now," he says. "I don't know if any of them will do what we have done, but I know that every one of them will be considering it."

They have already started. Just a day before Viacom's announcement, John Malone's Liberty Media (L), a holding company of sorts with a jumble of investments in various media companies, announced plans to spin off its 50% stake in cable networks Discovery Communications, along with a Hollywood post-production outfit, Ascent Media.

Garage Sales?

On Feb. 25, Walt Disney (DIS) sold off its Mighty Ducks hockey team for $60 million, a paltry gain on the $50 million the company spent to launch the team in 1992. This follows last November's sale by Disney of its U.S. chain of 400 stores to The Children's Place

(PLCE). The Mouse House is also considering exploring the sale of its European chain of retail stores, which it valued at $36 million as of last September.

10 And consider the poster child of media merger mania: Time Warner (TWX), which agreed to sell itself to America Online in 2000 at the height of the Internet boom for $130 billion, a record deal. It created a $40-billion-a-year company that was widely viewed as having too many disparate pieces.

After the stock of what was then called AOL Time Warner took a beating in the market, newly appointed CEO Richard Parsons began in 2002 to sell off what would eventually total more than $5 billion in assets, including the Warner Music Group, a CD manufacturing business, a 50% stake in Comedy Central, and two Atlanta sports teams. Now the company, whose stock has risen 80%—to about $18—in two years, is mulling a public offering of its cable business.

"Synergy" Discredited?

There's a huge catalyst for splitting these companies: the current abundance of private equity money looking for investment opportunities. It makes for an enticement to executives seeking to jettison declining but steady cash-flow businesses. Private equity firms have been gobbling up media companies from Warner Music to PanAmSat to Hollywood Entertainment, as well as taking a major position in a Sony (SNE)/MGM (MGM) venture.

After years of bombardment with unrelenting sales pitches from media companies about the importance of scale and "synergies," should investors now feel duped as they witness the companies pull themselves apart? "In the end, it's probably a good thing for shareholders that this is happening," says UCLA's Johnson.

It was Wall Street that dictated to the media companies what they wanted to see, not vice versa, says Robert Kindler, global chief of mergers and acquisitions at JPMorgan Securities, which is advising Barry Diller's Interactive Corp. (IAC) on its spin-off of online travel business Expedia. "The best companies are the ones responding to what investors want. And investors today want more focused businesses. They have less faith in conglomerates."

15 Yet it's far too early to know whether media deconsolidation will benefit investors in the long run. The only guaranteed winners will surely be investment bankers like Kindler, who get the fat fees whether they're putting companies together or taking them apart.

Questions for Discussion

1. To what does the title of this article allude? How does the title apply to the content?

2. In the opening, Lowry and Grover refer to "the Street"—as opposed to "Wall Street" as in paragraph 6. What does this writing decision reveal about their sense of audience? Do you detect a difference in how "the Street" sounds when compared with "Wall Street"?

3. Why have large media companies fallen out of favor with investors, and why are these large companies able to find buyers for units they had acquired?

4. The authors refer to Time Warner as "the poster child of media merger mania." What does it mean to be a "poster child"? What does this description convey about Time Warner?

5. If the break up of large media companies benefits investment bankers and some shareholders, is anyone likely to suffer from these changes?

6. Based on what the authors report about media mergers and breakups, what conclusions would you draw about how to run a profitable business?

DIFFERENCES

NEGOTIATING

The writers in this cluster have emphasized the dangers of concentrating the ownership of media within relatively few hands. Their objections include the risk of losing diversity in programming—as well as balanced coverage of the news—and of investors coming to believe that a company has weakened itself by acquiring too many properties. A third argument notes that the concentration of media ownership is not a new phenomenon.

It would be easy to write an argument recycling these views. But how many people are aware of who owns their local newspaper or television station? In some cases, the answer is obvious: the *New York Times* is owned and published by the New York Times Company. This prestigious paper has a long history and stands alone as a corporate entity. The *Washington Post,* also a well-respected paper, is published by

the same company that publishes *Newsweek*—information that would surprise many readers.

Media ownership will most likely become an issue in your own community if there is a pending transfer of media ownership. To cite a simple example: Until recently, the Twin Cities of Minneapolis and St. Paul were served by two radio stations affiliated with National Public Radio—one based in St. Paul and one based in Northfield, Minnesota, a nearby college town. Both stations broadcast many of the same programs because they were NPR programs—shows such as *All Things Considered, Car Talk,* and *A Prairie Home Companion.* Although both stations broadcast some jazz and popular music, they primarily broadcast classical music—part of NPR's mission because commercial radio stations are more likely to broadcast rock or country music. The difference was that the station based in St. Paul tended to broadcast well-known pieces of classical music and the station based in Northfield tended to broadcast lesser-known pieces. When the college that sponsored the Northfield station decided that it could no longer afford to own it, the NPR station in St. Paul acquired it. Lovers of classical music were disappointed and feared they would be less likely to hear new or unfamiliar pieces. This fear proved justified.

Now imagine a situation that could occur in the future: There are two newspapers in the city in which you have chosen to live. One tends to be liberal, and one tends to be conservative. Both do a good job of reporting local news but tend to rely heavily on wires services such as the Associated Press and nationally syndi-

cated columnists for national and international news. Both papers have been published for a long time, and both were commercially successful. But because the Internet and other forms of technology have made it easy to obtain news without subscribing to a newspaper, both papers have seen their circulations shrink and may not be profitable much longer. The owners of the conservative paper enter negotiations to acquire the liberal paper. As a member of this community, what counsel would you offer the owners of the former if they succeed in acquiring the latter? Because your focus is on *negotiating differences,* think in terms of what would be best for the community as a whole—as opposed to what would best suit your political philosophy.

9

Body Image

Cluster 1

HOW DO THE MEDIA INFLUENCE BODY IMAGE?

1. Sascha de Gersdorff, "Fresh Faces"

2. Graham Lawton, "Extreme Surgery"

3. Joyce McMillan, "The Brutality of Celebrity Culture"

4. Marika Tiggemann, "Media Influences on Body Image Development"

Cluster 2

WHY ARE SO MANY AMERICANS OVERWEIGHT?

1. Susan Brink and Elizabeth Querna, "Eat This Now!"

2. Barbara Wickens, "How Your Brain Makes You Fat"

3. W. Wayt Gibbs, "Obesity: An Overblown Epidemic?"

4. Jeffrey P. Koplan, Catharyn T. Liverman, and Vivica I. Kraak, "Preventing Childhood Obesity"

Cluster 3

WHEN DOES BEING "FIT" BECOME "UNFIT"?

1. Heather Beresford, "I Was an Idiot to Take It So Far"

2. Christopher McDougall and Lou Schuler, "Buyin' Bulk"

3. Harrison G. Pope Jr., Katharine A. Phillips, and Roberto Olivardia, "The Adonis Complex"

4. Sarah Grogan, Ruth Evans, Sam Wright, and Geoff Hunter, "Femininity and Muscularity: Accounts of Seven Women Body Builders"

How Do the Media Influence Body Image?

In earlier generations, media such as film and television conveyed an ideal of feminine beauty that was voluptuous. In the 1930s, Mae West was an icon for sexuality despite having a figure that would be perceived as fat today. And as late as the 1950s, Marilyn Monroe was widely considered extraordinarily beautiful despite having a fuller figure than many movie stars today. During these decades, male stars such as Cary Grant and Gregory Peck were admired because they were good looking and well mannered, not because they could flex massive muscles, show off perfect abs, and be filmed naked. Following an adage that holds "you can never be too thin or too rich," standards of feminine beauty changed in the 1960s, when a celebrity called "Twiggy" could be admired—as her name suggests—for being exceptionally thin. By the 1980s, men began to feel more pressure to have trimmer waistlines and to build muscle by lifting weights. Arnold Schwarzenegger may be the perfect representative for this cultural shift in the media's presentation of a male aesthetic for what it means to look buff today: His credentials as a world-class body builder led to a successful career as an actor, and his success as an actor led to his election as governor of California, largely on his fame and rugged good looks. By looking strong, and with the help of widespread media coverage, he could be perceived as a potentially strong leader.

What are the implications of this cultural shift for average Americans? Many commentators believe that women feel under increasing pressure to be thin and that this pressure can generate eating disorders, among other problems. Although women were the first to feel media pressures to perfect their bodies, men are now affected as well—with growing numbers of men falling victim to eating disorders or becoming obsessed with working out. But as the readings in this cluster demonstrate, media influences on body image are not limited to making people worry about how thin their waist is or how broad their shoulders are. A series of popular television shows have increased interest in cosmetic surgery. And once a man or a woman has turned to surgery to look better, and thus have higher self-esteem, it can be all too tempting to schedule additional procedures.

① SASCHA DE GERSDORFF, "Fresh Faces"

In "Fresh Faces," Sascha de Gersdorff reports on the rise of cosmetic surgery among teenagers, an increase attributed at least partly to "reality" television shows that focused on how surgeons could remake someone's appearance. Although she does not argue for or against these procedures, she does reveal why both parents and physicians have reason to be concerned about this trend. A graduate of Colgate University and the Medill School of Journalism at Northwestern University, de Gersdorff is a regular contributor to *Boston Magazine,* which published "Fresh Faces" in May 2005—hence the references you will find to Boston College and individuals in the Boston area. As you read this article, consider how you would respond to a teenager arguing that she or he needs cosmetic surgery to have the right look. Consider also how you would feel about parents who encourage their children to have cosmetic surgery.

Fresh Faces

SASCHA DE GERSDORFF

1 Kristin wanted a new nose. A better nose. A resculpted, slightly smaller version of the original, with no bump on its bridge and a shorter, perkier tip. It wasn't that she was ugly, or that her nose was so terrible: Kristin just wanted her features to be symmetrical. But doctors said she would have to wait at least a year before considering cosmetic surgery. After all, she was only 14.

At 15, Kristin got her wish. A Boston plastic surgeon performed the long-awaited rhinoplasty during her school's spring break. The petite, blond Newton native couldn't be happier with the results. "It turned out exactly how I wanted it," Kristin, now 17, says, "I feel like my face finally fits together."

Others agreed. Most girls at her west suburban high school told her she looked pretty and praised her new look. And, influenced by a youth culture that is increasingly open to all things cosmetic, some did a little resculpting of their own. "My best friend just got her nose done last summer," says Kristin (whose name,

> ### CONTEXT
>
> Makeover shows like ABC's *Extreme Makeover* and Fox's *The Swan* promise participants that their dreams will come true through plastic surgery and other changes in lifestyle. On its website, ABC touts "more emotion, tears and joy as life long dreams and fairy tale fantasies come true." Cecile Frot-Coutaz, CEO of the FremantleMedia NA production company, the producer of *The Swan,* has said, "With *The Swan,* we're offering the kind of dream makeover that's normally available only to the rich and famous. This is a positive show where we want to see how these women can make their dreams come true once they have what they want." MTV's *I Want a Famous Face,* on the other hand, makes no such dream promises to the show's participants and attempts to merely document the process and procedure of the surgeries. Dave Sirulnick, executive vice president of MTV News and Production, was quoted in *USA Today* in 2004 saying, "There is no guarantee for success. There is no guarantee you are going to look like anything close to what you think you are going to look like. It seemed to us that young MTV viewers were not getting that." What, if any, responsibilities do you think these networks have when airing such shows?

like those of other young patients quoted in this story, has been changed). "And my other best friend is planning on doing it as soon as she can."

Plastic surgery is a national hot topic, thanks in no small part to television show like ABC's *Extreme Makeover,* Fox's *The Swan,* MTV's *I Want a Famous Face,* and a veritable bonanza of other media attention. Everywhere they look, young Americans are bombarded with promises of planned perfection. Ads for cosmetic procedures pepper magazines and newspapers, toned Hollywood actors sport wrinkle-free figures, and celebrity rags rave over young starlets with impossible combinations of tiny waists and huge breasts.

5 The pressure to look young and beautiful is at an all-time high, and more and more people are picking up the phone to schedule surgical enhancements. Americans spent $12.5 billion on cosmetic procedures last year, according to the American Society for Aesthetic Plastic Surgery. Since 1997, the number of both surgical and nonsurgical procedures performed annually has increased by a whopping 465 percent.

"The television shows have really captured the country's imagination and attention," says Dr. James May, director of plastic surgery at Massachusetts General Hospital. "The sensationalism of those programs has brought plastic surgery to the minds of young people and their parents. It's now a dinner-table conversation."

And the nation is changing its perspective. Whereas some Americans used to keep their tummy tucks and Botox shots a secret, they're now showing them off with pride. Today, 60 percent of women approve of cosmetic surgery, while 82 percent say they would not be embarrassed by other people knowing that they'd had some. And these aren't just aging narcissists: 34 percent of 18- to 24-year-olds say they would definitely consider surgery for themselves, the highest proportion of all age groups.

Many teens like Kristin already have. The plastic surgery society notes that Americans 18 and younger had 46,198 chemical peels, 17,233 rhinoplasties, 4,211 breast augmentations, and 4,074 Botox injections last year alone. All in all, teenagers underwent nearly a quarter million cosmetic procedures last year.

"Teenagers are the new market," says Sharlene Hesse-Biber, professor of sociology at Boston College. "Magazines have pushed the envelope on what it means to be beautiful, and surgery is now a way to deal with body issues. We're a very visual and quick-fix society. Young people are now getting the quick fix, that instant body."

10 When he was 16, Brian started thinking about enhancing his appearance. He had breathing problems and was unhappy with his nose. So he did something about it. A surgeon performed a rhinoplasty. That same year, Brian paid for a chin implant. "What's great about cosmetic surgery," says Brian, who went on to attend Boston University, is that "you have the ability to change what couldn't otherwise be changed." He says he'd recommend surgery to other young people as a "self-esteem boost."

"All you have to do is watch any television show, and you will see relatively uncovered, young, supposedly ideal-looking Americans," says Chestnut Hill's SkinCare Physicians co-director Dr. Jeffrey Dover. "Twenty years ago, liposuction didn't even exist, but now young women are coming in for it. They're looking at all the magazines, from *People* to *Vogue* to *Seventeen.* Large breasts with skinny bodies are very popular right now. Look at Christina Aguilera. She has very large breasts in a tiny body, and teenagers want to look like her."

It's not just girls feeling the pressure. Young men, inspired by the metrosexual* movement, are also taking shortcuts to better looks. Dover says his practice has seen a dramatic increase in the number of 16- to 19-year-old males who come in for laser hair removal. He says they might be prompted by *GQ* and *Men's Health,* whose cover models sport nary a hair on their bodies.

*Metrosexual refers to a male who, as Dan Peres, editor in chief of *Details* magazine, described in a 2003 online interview with **Washingtonpost.com**, "is a straight, urban-based man who is extremely comfortable and passionate about pursuing his interests in things like design, architecture, fashion, dining, grooming. The sorts of things that just a few years ago the same men would have been labeled a 'sissy' for doing." The term originated in England in the 1990s.

Newbury Street surgeon Dr. Ramsey Alsarraf agrees that cosmetically enhanced celebrities' looks are affecting the way teenagers view themselves. "I've had young boys bring in 10 pictures of Brad Pitt and his nose from different angles and say 'I want to look like this.' Those are unrealistic expectations. Generally if someone says they want to look like Britney Spears or J.Lo, that puts up a red flag."

Lisa sees red flags, too. Now a 21-year-old college senior at the University of Maryland, Lisa had plastic surgery as a teenager. She, too, is pleased with the results of her rhinoplasty, which she'd been contemplating since middle school. But she says she's seen the cosmetic culture shift since then. Lisa thinks more people find surgery acceptable and that invasive procedures have become "easier than the alternatives, such as making an effort to accept yourself as beautiful or physically working hard to lose weight." Teenagers who want to look like models or celebrities they see should think again, she says.

That's what many plastic surgeons say, too. But all too often, they say, teenagers brush off any long-term implications in favor of immediate results. This blasé attitude, coupled with widening acceptance, helps young people gloss over the potentially ugly details of surgical procedures. Nor do many Boston doctors outright refuse to perform most such surgery on teenagers, though some ask the kids to wait a few years.

15 "I want a 17-year-old to understand that if she's going to have breast implants, she might need a new procedure at age 27," May says. "Then at age 47 she might have another revision. I would say the likelihood of her needing to have these other procedures is around 50 percent. It's very important to send the message loud and clear that surgery early in life is heading the patient down the pathway of having more operations."

Some wonder if even teenagers who have smaller, noninvasive procedures such as laser hair removal or microdermabrasion might be-

come mentally predisposed to surgery. While there is no solid research to support this theory, the notion that kids can become "addicted" to cosmetic alteration doesn't come as a surprise to sociologist Hesse-Biber.

"We're entering this cult-like status," she says. "Every time we have a little wrinkle, we want to run in for some Botox. We're becoming addicted. I'm not saying that women shouldn't look beautiful, but when surgery becomes the fix and you still don't feel good about yourself, what then?"

Alarmed parents are asking similar questions in response to a perceived nationwide increase in teenage plastic surgeries. And the media is fueling the fire. Nearly every major American newspaper and magazine has run stories on teenage breast augmentations and liposuctions, or procedures gone horribly wrong.

The attention rose to such heights that in February the American Society of Plastic Surgeons released a statement attributing the teenage cosmetic surgery "epidemic" to overblown media hype. A recent study found that only 5 percent of college-aged women have had cosmetic surgery. But that same study revealed that more than 60 percent of the same group surveyed could see themselves having at least one procedure in their lives.

20 Back in Boston, teenagers' cravings for physical perfection appear not quite as high as those of teens in places like Miami and Los Angeles, where breast augmentations are reported to be popular high-school graduation gifts. Despite its liberal arts, Boston remains steeped in conservative tradition and shrouded by a hush-hush mentality about cosmetic surgery. Many people here still consider cosmetic procedures déclassé. But local doctors say they have many teenagers come in for rhinoplasties, hair removal, and Botox, though requests from teens for breast augmentation are rare. Even rarer are doctors who would perform the procedure the Food and Drug Administration does not approve for girls under 18.

"You'd have to look hard in Boston for someone who's pushing breast implants on 16-year-old girls," Alsarraf says. "If you can't vote or smoke, should you really be able to have a synthetic piece of plastic put into your chest? That doesn't make much sense to me."

It doesn't make much sense to Kristin either. But while her mother says she would be shocked by a high school student having a breast augmentation, Kristin seems nonplused. "At my school, it doesn't happen enough for people not to be surprised," she says. "But it wouldn't be like 'Oh my God!'" Cosmetic procedures have simply become part of the culture, something she says her friends all talk about briefly before moving on to the next topic.

Kristin's mother admits she knows at least one parent who would let her own daughter get much-desired bigger breasts. And May says that although the media reports may be exaggerated, all the fuss does represent a fear that soon kids will be planning their dream bodies at an alarmingly young age.

Asked if she would consider having additional cosmetic procedures, Kristin nods enthusiastically. "Yeah, definitely," she says. She says there's nothing wrong with wanting to feel better about yourself. "I'm not going out searching for things to do, but if there was something I wanted to change, wanted to be different, I would do it."

Questions for Discussion

1. At what age would you allow a child of your own to have cosmetic surgery?

2. Why are teenagers "the new market" for such surgery?

3. Consider the statistics in paragraph 5. What do they say to you?

4. According to de Gersdorff, cosmetic surgery is still considered "déclassé" by some in Boston—or something that signified behavior associated with a class lower than one's own. Why do you think that is the case? Why would cultural expectations be changing to the point that people draw attention to the procedures they have undergone? Can you point to other behavior that might be described as "déclassé"? What assumptions about social class are embedded in this term?

5. Why would young men want to have laser hair removal? Why would a smooth body be considered more attractive than a hairy body? What cultural forces are encouraging men to try to perfect their bodies?

6. Why are some parents and surgeons concerned about the increasing popularity of cosmetic surgery with adolescents? What are the potential risks of such procedures?

② GRAHAM LAWTON, "Extreme Surgery"

Graham Lawton is a senior writer for *New Scientist*, a weekly magazine based in London and published in British, Australian, and U.S. editions. Although it is not a peer-reviewed journal, it is well respected and read by both scientists and people who want to know about current events in science and technology. As the title suggests, "Extreme Surgery" (first published in October 2004) focuses on how some surgeons are pushing their professional skills to the limits in an attempt to satisfy demands from people who want more than one simple procedure when determined to look attractive. Like Sascha de Gersdorff in "Fresh Faces" (pages 283–286), Lawton reports rather than argues. But his report suggests that cosmetic surgery can become an obsession, with one procedure generating the desire for another. As you read it, consider how far you would go to look "perfect" if world-class surgeons offered their services to you. Consider also how long you would be willing to remain under anesthesia while the surgeons worked on you.

Extreme Surgery

GRAHAM LAWTON

1   Unhappy with your body? Join the club. And I don't mean the gym or health club. Exercise and diet, it seems, are too much like hard work. These days, cosmetic surgery is the way to go.

In the US, surgeons carried out 1.8 million cosmetic procedures in 2003, the largest number ever recorded and nearly double the 1997 figure. The numbers considering surgery were also at record levels—not just among adult women but also men and teenagers. And as acceptance of cosmetic surgery grows, costs fall and techniques improve, the chances are that having our bodies tweaked to make them more to our liking will become increasingly common.

The list of body alterations we can choose from is growing ever more extensive and radical. A few years ago, it was all about fixing one or two irregular features with a nose job or facelift. These days, it focuses on "harmonising" the "aesthetic units" of your face and

> ### CONTEXT
>
> The years during and after World War I catapulted the use of plastic surgery because of the number of soldiers maimed by weaponry of the time. Surgeons used reconstructive procedures mainly to repair injuries to the head. During this same period, surgeons began to perform operations not as a result of injuries suffered but rather for purely aesthetic purposes, using the techniques that had been advanced through the treatment of soldiers.
>
> According to the website of the American Society of Plastic Surgeons (ASPS), "Mankind's essential nature entails self-improvement. Without the individual's pursuit of learning and enlightenment, peace with his or her neighbors and more efficient means to work, progress would stop. Because human beings have always sought self-fulfillment through self-improvement, plastic surgery—improving and restoring form and function—may be one of the world's oldest healing arts."
>
> Do you think the ASPS is justified in placing plastic surgery in the list of actions people have taken throughout time toward self-fulfillment? Should plastic surgery have been restricted to necessity, rather than a means to an aesthetic end?

THE SURGICAL WAY TO STANDING TALL

It can put you in a wheelchair for up to a year, but if you want it desperately enough there is a way to add 10 centimeters to your height.

Here's how it's done. A surgeon breaks both the patient's lower legs in two places—below the knee and above the ankle—and rigs up a traction device that pulls the broken ends apart by about 1 millimeter a day. The healing process does the rest.

Leg-lengthening surgery was invented in the 1950s for treating childhood deformities and short stature arising from genetic abnormalities. But an increasing number of people who just happen to want to be taller are choosing to pay up to $75,000 for the procedure in the belief that it will change their lives. "Many people feel inadequate due to their height," says Dror Paley, co-director of the International Center for Limb Lengthening in Baltimore, Maryland. "Lengthening surgery cures them." Paley receives some 50 inquiries each year about the procedure, and he operates on about 12 people.

The Baltimore centre is among 25 or so worldwide that will perform cosmetic leg lengthening. One of the busiest is the Beijing Institute of External Skeletal Fixation Technology in China. It claims to have carried out more than 2000 operations, many of them on people who see gaining an extra few centimeters as the key to a successful career.

body by working on them all at the same time. Some surgeons are happy to perform four or five procedures at once. At the extreme end of this trend is a controversial practice known as the total body overhaul.

In the past such radical reshaping would have taken months or years. Now cosmetic surgeons are getting the job done in weeks. Two American TV networks ran reality shows this year about cosmetic surgery, both promoting the idea of rapid, radical transformation. Fox Broadcasting's *The Swan* took 17 "average girls"—"ugly ducklings" presumably being a bit too near the knuckle—and turned them into beauty queens in six weeks. ABC's *Extreme Makeovers* transformed 24 men and women in a similar time.

5   Thirty-two-year-old Cindy from San Diego in California was a typical *Swan* contestant. At school she was teased because of her droopy nose; as a grown-up with two children she felt unattractive and frumpy. Sex happened with

the light off. Not any more. For the first time Cindy feels beautiful. She has a new nose, built from cartilage that used to be in her ear, plus a facelift, chin refinement, breast implants, tummy tuck, liposuction, lip augmentation, a brow lift and laser surgery on her eyes, not to mention non-surgical treatments including laser hair removal and cosmetic dentistry, all in the space of a few weeks. If you were an old friend of Cindy's, you might be forgiven for not recognising her in the street. And that, presumably, is the point.

Cindy is clearly happy with her new look, as are the majority of people who have cosmetic surgery. But the extent of the TV makeovers has whipped up a controversy. The shows' producers claim they are only reflecting what many people and their cosmetic surgeons are already doing, but many other surgeons are horrified. The very idea of a total body overhaul is wild exaggeration, they warn. In fact, it is positively dangerous. "Someone will die," warns Norman Waterhouse, a London-based surgeon and former president of the British Association of Aesthetic Plastic Surgeons (BAAPS).

But is there really a trend towards this sort of radical makeover, or is it just a TV phenomenon? It's hard to be certain. Statistics compiled by the American Society for Aesthetic Plastic Surgery (ASAPS) and other professional bodies record only the number of operations performed, not on whom and in what combination. But anecdotally, some practitioners in the US confirm that combination surgeries are on the increase. "There is a trend towards multiple procedures," says Michael McGuire, associate professor of plastic surgery at the University of California, Los Angeles. "There's an increasing realisation that it's not just one aspect of your appearance that is inadequate. Unattractive teeth will still ruin your face even if you have a nose job."

The watchword is "harmony." A facelift that improves matters above the chin might make a sagging neck more obvious, so many surgeons now do a neck lift at the same time. Another popular combination is facelift, brow lift and eyelid surgery. And for new mothers who want to get back into shape quickly, tummy tuck plus breast lift is the must-have combo. Some surgeons have even taken to working in pairs, one taking on the face while the other handles the body. And with big improvements in the safety of anaesthesia over the past 10 years, surgeons are increasingly prepared to keep patients under for longer in order to make time for extra procedures.

"In 7 hours you could get a facelift, eyelid surgery and an eyebrow lift plus a chemical peel, collagen injection or Botox," McGuire says. With a second surgeon working on your body at the same time, you are looking at a sizeable alteration in appearance. It's not exactly a total body overhaul. And it's not quite overnight; even the most minor cosmetic surgery takes days to heal. But it will be a noticeable and rapid change nonetheless.
10 So what is the limit? "I wouldn't exceed 7 or 8 hours," McGuire says. "After that you are not getting the surgeon's best work." Some surgeons go longer, he says, driven by competition or patients' demands. "It's not emergency surgery," McGuire points out, "but some people think it is."

Despite the increasing popularity of multiple procedures, most surgeons dispute the idea that a patient can walk into a clinic as an ugly duckling and walk out as a swan. "It's not possible, it's not safe and it's misleading," McGuire says. Waterhouse is more forthright. "I feel strongly that this trivialises and sensationalises surgery. It grotesquely distorts perceptions of what aesthetic surgery is about." He also considers it potentially dangerous. If you prolong operation time there is a massive increase in the risk of deep vein thrombosis and blot clots in the lungs, which can be life-threatening, he says.

Surgeons also worry that the promise of an as-seen-on-TV makeover distorts people's ex-

CONTEXT

According to its website, the British Association of Aesthetic Plastic Surgeons (BAAPS) was established for, among other reasons, the "advancement of education in, and the practice of, Aesthetic Plastic Surgery for public benefit, in particular: to promote an interchange of knowledge for the advancement of Aesthetic Plastic Surgery among suitably qualified surgeons; . . . to develop and encourage the practice of high standards of personal, professional and ethical conduct among members; . . . to advise those who wish to obtain information about Aesthetic Plastic Surgery; [and] to promote better understanding of Aesthetic Plastic Surgery among General Practitioners." Likewise, the mission of the American Society for Aesthetic Plastic Surgery (ASAPS), as stated on its website, is "to advance the science, art, and safe practice of aesthetic (cosmetic) plastic surgery among qualified plastic surgeons through medical education and research; to promote ethical conduct and responsible patient care; to serve the public by providing accurate and timely information regarding aesthetic (cosmetic) plastic surgery . . .; [and] to advance the medical profession and plastic surgery specialty."

pectations. According to Stanley Klatsky, editor-in-chief of *Aesthetic Surgery Journal,* increasing numbers of would-be patients are turning up at clinics asking to be made over from head to toe overnight. Adam Searle, current president of the BAAPS, says the same is happening in the UK. People are starting to see cosmetic surgery as equivalent to a trip to the salon. "This is a major surgical procedure, not a hairdo," he points out.

According to an ASAPS survey last year, 34 percent of women in the US and 14 percent of men were considering having cosmetic surgery. If the rest of us are tempted to sneer at such vanity, it is also important to remember that cosmetic surgery can have real benefits. Ted Grossbart, a psychologist at Harvard Medical School, says the majority of patients are pleased with the results and consequently feel happier and more self-confident. "It can change lives," Searle says.

Questions for Discussion

1. Consider the generalization with which Lawton opens his report. How reasonable does it seem to you?

2. Do you agree that acceptance of cosmetic surgery is growing? How would it be perceived in your family or community? What procedure would be the most likely to be accepted? What would generate the most concern?

3. How have cosmetic-surgery procedures been changing in recent years?

4. To what extent is the media responsible for increasing interest in cosmetic surgery? What other cultural pressures could be contributing to the increase in cosmetic surgery?

5. Why is it that the completion of one kind of surgery can lead to the desire for another?

6. Although Lawton raises concerns about the increasing popularity of cosmetic surgery, and the length of operations, he closes with a quotation that emphasizes the benefits of such surgery. How does this quotation contribute to his report? How appropriate is it as a conclusion?

③ JOYCE McMILLAN, "The Brutality of Celebrity Culture"

The following selection was first published in June 2005 in the *Scotsman,* a newspaper in Edinburgh, Scotland. Because it was written for a British audience, you may not recognize some of the allusions. On the other hand, you are likely to recognize those that are the most important. For example, Sarah Ferguson, Duchess of York, has appeared in Weight Watcher ads in this country. And Camilla Parker-Bowles, now Duchess of Cornwall, was often photographed when at the side of Charles, Prince of Wales. In a broader sense, however, the situation Joyce McMillan describes affects American celebrities, as well as those on the other side of the Atlantic. When someone famous gains a lot of weight or is caught poorly dressed, there's a good chance that an unflattering picture will appear in the tabloids or jokes will be made on late-night television. In other words, although discussion of the media's effect on body image often focuses on how celebrities are presented as glamorous ideals that cannot be equaled by the average person, celebrities themselves can be victims of the media's emphasis on beauty. Chief theater critic for the *Scotsman,* McMillan is also a member of the Scottish Arts Council and involved in European campaigns for human rights. As you read her argument, consider how it reflects an interest in human rights.

The Brutality of Celebrity Culture

JOYCE McMILLAN

1 It was Earl Spencer's* speech at the funeral of Diana, Princess of Wales, that finally put into words, for me, the nature of the quiet cultural revolution that had been sweeping Britain for a decade or two before her death. It was an impassioned speech, you'll remember, powerfully written, full of bitterness and grief. And it ended—before that famous roar of popular applause—with a memorable call to continue to cherish the memory of one "whose beauty," said the Earl, "both internal and external, will never be extinguished from our minds."

As a child born into the Britain of the early 1950s, after all, I had been brought up—almost without considering it—to see external beauty as the enemy of internal sweetness and virtue, rather than its partner and outward reflection. I lived, along with everyone else, in a slightly dowdy postwar British culture—heavily influenced, I suppose, by the dominant Protestant tradition both north and south of the Border—which strongly favoured the word over the image, the substance over the appearance; and which mistrusted those who tried to claim authority or pre-eminence by dazzling the eyes, rather than appealing to the mind. And I remember with great clarity the strong disapproval which that culture bestowed on women who seemed too concerned with their own appearance. Too much make-up, too fancy a hairstyle, too much glamour in the clothes, shoes, stockings—all

*Charles, Earl Spencer, gave the principal eulogy at the funeral for his sister Diana, Princess of Wales. This eulogy—which was broadcast live around the world—included an attack upon the royal family. Spencer described Diana as "a truly British girl who . . . needed no royal title to continue to generate her particular brand of magic"—a reference to the German background of the House of Windsor and how the queen had denied Diana the title "Her Royal Highness" after Diana and the heir to the throne divorced. Spencer subsequently concluded with a pledge from "we, your blood family" to raise her children so that they could "sing openly" and not be stifled by official duties.

that was for film stars, not real people; a vain preoccupation at best, and at worst, a sign of bad moral character.

But now—well, how very different is the culture of today's Big Brother Britain, driven by a popular media for whom failing to look good—for which read thin, buffered to perfection, dressed by a leading designer, and never older than 35—seems to have become the one unforgivable sin. It's not that the anti-beauty culture is entirely dead. If you look closely, for example, at any crowd of middle-aged and elderly British female peace campaigners or committed hillwalkers or retired lecturers, you will still find plenty who see personal adornment as no business of theirs, and who favour the same spiky grey haircuts, shapeless cardigans, flat shoes and cheerfully wrinkled faces innocent of make-up, that you might have seen on their great-aunts 40 years ago. But it is increasingly difficult to imagine how this breed of cheerfully unconcerned woman can long survive, in a world where celebrities like Elizabeth Hurley* denounce the "ugly" with all the moral righteousness of latterday bishops deploring sin. This week, Hurley apparently gave her opinion that fat women in tight clothes ought to be the first targets of the fashion police; not, mind you, because she is opposed to tight clothes—obviously not—but because she regards fatness as the cardinal sin of modern beauty culture.

Nor is this kind of hate-speak confined to fat or unattractive women in general; celebrity after celebrity, these days, is singled out for a personal slapping-around by the body-police of our visually obsessed age. Cherie Blair, who has made plenty of serious misjudgments and poor decisions as the Prime Minister's wife, is most widely condemned in popular culture not for her private financial dealings, but for her personal appearance, which is deemed slightly strange, and for the size of her hips, which the body cops apparently find excessive. The Duchess of York, Sarah Ferguson, who was once slightly overweight for a month or two after one of her babies was born, is still widely referred to as a notorious and embarrassing

tub of lard, despite the evident fact that she is now stick-thin, and extremely glamorous.

5   And as for the general run of public comment on the new Duchess of Cornwall, as she takes her place in the official royal images of Ascot and Trooping the Colour, it seems to me to border on the insane. Camilla, after all, has committed acts which many find morally questionable. But what do the popular media have to say against her? Mainly that she's old, ungorgeous, and looks like a horse. None of these comments is remotely true, of course. Camilla looks exactly what she is, which is a happy, attractive and well-dressed woman of 58. But somehow, the accusation of ugliness has become the catch-all criticism behind which every form of fear and loathing takes refuge. "Oh, I don't like her, I'm a young girls' bloke," says the cheeky thirtysomething Asian guy at the corner shop; as if Camilla's main flaw was simply, and absolutely, her age.

Nor is it wise to dismiss all this as the mere froth and nonsense of a trivial media culture; because this is the public realm into which our young people are growing up, and it is increasingly drenched in values which are at best shallow, and at worst plain vicious. Just for a start, it is profoundly self-destructive, and a recipe for endless future misery, for an ageing society like ours to allow such rampant age discrimination, and such widespread public abuse on the grounds of age.

Secondly, it is immensely cruel for children and young teenagers, whose bodies in any cases are changing at disturbing speed, to grow up surrounded by images of a physical perfection with which they cannot hope to compete, and which is presented to them not only as an example of spectacular good luck in the looks department, but as an outward and visible sign of grace and worthiness.

This cultural obsession with physical appearance plays its part in the rising incidence of anorexia, bulimia, self-harm, depression and suicide among vulnerable young people; and it is no longer good enough for the media to claim innocence over the role they play in perpetuating it.

*A model turned actress and producer, Elizabeth Hurley is widely considered both beautiful and well dressed. When she condemned the "ugly" she was probably not being self-critical—although she has been involved in activities, including a paternity battle, that might not be seen as pretty.

And thirdly, we need to consider exactly what our cult of physical-perfection-as-virtue means for those whose bodies fail to fit the norm, not only because of age, but because of illness or disability.

10 Robert Rae, the director of Scotland's Theatre Workshop company, which includes many actors with disabilities, talks about the growing "body fascism" of our culture; and perhaps he is right to remind us explicitly of the horrific treatment of disabled people under Nazism, where health and beauty became a political cult, and physical disability savagely victimised as an outward sign of decadence and depravity.

For all it sounds like trivial stuff, the endless sniggering banter about people's appearance, size, teeth, hair, age, shampoo and beauty products that trickles through Big-Brother-style television stands out like a streak of sour milk. But in the increasing absence of any more civilised or sophisticated consensus about how to assess people and their worth, the values of the sad young showbiz victims who appear on these shows are now coming to dominate our public space to a frightening extent.

After a few centuries of denial about the importance of physical beauty, personal adornment, visual gorgeousness and sensual pleasure, there probably was a deep need for some rebalancing of the culture, here in northern Europe; and in a society increasingly threatened by obesity and unhealthy eating patterns, it's no bad thing to try to stay fit. But to live out our lives in a celebrity magazine world, where virtue and entitlement is signalled by the ability to look great in carefully staged photographs, is to swing the pendulum much too far; not only towards silliness and triviality, but towards the brutal and the primitive, and the kind of dehumanising cruelty the world thought it had vanquished for good, 60 years ago this summer.

Questions for Discussion

1. How does McMillan describe the cultural values that shaped her childhood, and what evidence does she provide that these values are disappearing?

2. Consider McMillan's use of "hate-speak" in paragraph 4. What does this term mean to you? Under what circumstances does "fat" become of "hate-speak"? Can you provide other examples of "hate-speak"?

3. How would you describe McMillan's characterization of the Duchess of Cornwall—Camilla Parker-Bowles, the long-time mistress of the Prince of Wales, whom she married in 2005? How does this characterization compare with the treatment of Cherie Blair, wife of Prime Minister Tony Blair?

4. Why does McMillan believe that there are serious consequences to the media's emphasis on celebrity beauty?

5. Writing in June 2005, McMillan concludes her argument with a reference to "the kind of dehumanising cruelty the world thought it had vanquished for good, 60 years ago this summer." To what is she referring, and how has she prepared her audience for this reference?

④ MARIKA TIGGEMANN, "Media Influences on Body Image Development"

For the last few decades, it has often been asserted that advertisements and television programs showing unusually thin women have contributed to the lowering of self-esteem that many women experience when they compare their bodies with those that seem to be the cultural ideal. But does research support this claim? This is one of the questions Marika Tiggemann sets out to answer in the following selection. In addition to researching body image, Tiggemann studies women's health issues—including dieting. She teaches psychology at Flinders University in Australia, where she is working on a project about "the role of the media (focusing on television) in adolescent body image and self-esteem." The following article, "Media Influences on Body Image Development," was first published in 2002 in a collection of current scholarship on the theory, research, and clinical practice of body image. As you read her argument, you will find that Tiggemann is concerned with Western media, including U.S. media. In other words, her research and findings are not limited to Australia. You will also find that she has an APA-style reference list at the end of her argument.

Media Influences on Body Image Development

MARIKA TIGGEMANN

1 The mass media pervade the everyday lives of people living in Western societies. Most adults read newspapers daily, and magazines have huge circulations. Media surveys indicate that fashion magazines, in particular, are read by the majority of women and girls (estimates up to 83%). Virtually every home has a television set, switched on for an average of 7 hours per day, with individuals each watching 3 or 4 hours. Over a year, children and adolescents spend more time watching television than in any activity other than sleeping. Such high consumption is likely to affect the consumers in some way. This chapter describes the influences of various media on body image development and difficulties.

Avenues of Influence
Media Content
There is no doubt that current societal standards for female beauty inordinately emphasize the desirability of thinness—and thinness at a level that is impossible for most women to achieve by healthy means. In their pervasiveness, the mass media are powerful conveyors of this sociocultural ideal. A casual flick through any fashion magazine reveals a preponderance of young, tall, long-legged, and extremely thin women. Formal content analyses of visual media document this trend toward thinness in all of women's magazines, film, and television (including children's television). It has been argued that this media presentation of thin images as the ideal is a major

contributor to current high levels of body dissatisfaction and eating disorders in women.

For men, there is evidence that the cultural norm for the ideal body has become increasingly muscular during the 1990s, with some male ideals exceeding the upper limit of muscularity attainable without the use of anabolic steroids. Young, lean, and muscled male bodies are becoming more common in fashion magazines and advertising. Thus men and boys are also increasingly subject to media images that prescribe an ideal body shape: in their case, mesomorphic, broad shouldered, well-developed upper body, flat stomach, and narrow hips.

Influence Processes

The media's omnipresent idealized depiction of thin female figures may influence women's body image in a number of ways. Similar processes potentially operate in mediating the influence of muscular ideals in men. In increasing scope of influence, these processes include social comparison, internalization of the thin ideal, and investment in appearance for self-evaluation. When women compare their body with an image presented in the media, they almost invariably find themselves wanting. Repeated exposure to such images may lead women to internalize the thin ideal such that it becomes accepted by them as the reference point against which to judge themselves. Furthermore, thin ideals are not offered in a void but rather as part of complex cultural scripts that link thinness and attractiveness to happiness, desirability, and status. Acceptance of this cultural schema—that appearance and thinness are absolutely vital for success and happiness—means that self-worth becomes equated with a woman or girl's self perceived attractiveness. Thus appearance becomes a core basis of self-evaluation, with self-worth contingent on meeting the societal ideals. This schema is likely to exert particular salience in adolescence, when the major developmental task is the establishment of identity and when puberty moves girls away from, rather than toward, the thin ideal.

5 These three processes have perceptual, affective, cognitive,* and behavioral consequences for body image. There may be perceptual distortion whereby women view themselves as fat when they are not. In the affective realm, the failure to meet important but unrealistic size and weight goals leads to body dissatisfaction and negative mood. In the cognitive domain investment in appearance as the central criterion of self-evaluation results in selective attention to appearance messages. In terms of behavior, women typically pursue the thin ideal through dieting or other weight loss measures. Indeed, studies confirm that social comparison, internalization of the thin ideal, and investment in appearance are related to body dissatisfaction and disturbed eating in adult and adolescent women and girls as young as 8.

Not only do media influence behavior indirectly, they also offer explicit instruction on how to attain the beauty ideal. Leading women's magazines contain a large number of diet and exercise articles. In accord with the muscular male ideal, advertisements and articles in men's magazines focus more on changing body shape than losing weight. These all promote the belief that people can, and indeed should, control their body shape and weight. The methods (and accompanying beliefs) are also taught implicitly through modeling and vicarious reinforcement. An analysis of prime-time situation comedies found that 12% of female characters dieted, with many making negative comments about themselves.

Empirical Evidence of Media Effects on Body Image

A number of different evidentiary sources—women's own accounts, correlational studies of media exposure, and experimental studies of the immediate impact of idealized images—

*Cognitive means being capable of thinking. When used with behavioral (as in "cognitive-behavioral techniques"), the term describes how learning new and healthier patterns of thinking can lead to behavior that is more satisfying and generates better results.

converges to provide strong evidence for a link between the images presented in the media and women's negative body experience.

Perceived Media Pressure

Certainly women themselves say that their body image is adversely affected by idealized images portrayed in the media. For example, in Garner's large 1997 survey of 4,000 readers of the magazine *Psychology Today,* nearly half the women (and one-third of the men) reported that very thin or muscular magazine models make them feel insecure and want to lose weight. In open-ended interviews with young women, the media and fashion models are spontaneously nominated as the most potent source of the pressure to be thin; disclosures are usually accompanied by considerable anger, frustration, and hurt. Women with diagnosed eating disorders also often point to the models in fashion magazines as a trigger for their disorder.

A large prospective study of more than 12,000 children, ages 9–14 years, demonstrated that media involvement actually preceded the development of weight concerns.

Alison Field and her colleagues found that both girls and boys who reported making considerable effort to look like their same-sex figures in the media were more likely than their peers to have become very concerned about their weight over a 1-year period. For girls, these efforts were also predictive of beginning to purge at least monthly, and for boys, of starting to think frequently about wanting bigger muscles.

Media Exposure and Body Image

10 A number of studies has examined the relationship between women's body image and independently assessed indicators of media exposure, such as frequency of magazine reading or hours spent watching television. Both composite and specific measures of media use are correlated with a variety of body image indices, including body dissatisfaction, perceptions of over weight, and eating disorder symptomatology. More sophisticated statistical modeling by Stice and his colleagues found a direct link between media exposure and eating disorder symptoms, as well as an indirect pathway between internalization off the thin-ideal standard and the experience of body dissatisfaction.

However, other studies have found no relationship or inconsistent relationships. In one study, magazine reading but not television exposure was related to eating disorder symptomatology, with the opposite pattern for body dissatisfaction. Studies of adolescent girls find that time spent watching specific programs, particularly music videos, rather than total television-watching time, is related to weight and appearance concerns. Music videos may be a potent source of modeling; content analyses reveal high levels of eroticism and sex role stereotyping, with women usually depicted as thin, beautiful, and often scantily clad.

As a whole, the research supports a link between media exposure and body image. However, effect sizes are small and dependent on the specific measures. Although these results are generally taken to support the position that exposure to a large dose of idealized images leads to negative body experience, the converse casual assumption is equally plausible: That is, those women and girls who are most dissatisfied or invested in appearance seek out particular media content. This assumption is particularly likely in regard to the consumption of those types of media such as fashion magazines (and perhaps music videos) that offer explicit depictions of beauty and instruction on appearance enhancement, but less likely for television programs such as situation comedies and movies where thin ideal messages are implicit.

Experimental Studies

In an attempt to determine the direction of causation, several experiments have manipulated exposure to idealized images of thinness and assessed the immediate impact. Although an earlier comprehensive review by Levine and Smolak concluded that there was little support for the proposition that viewing photographs of thin models makes girls and women immediately feel worse about their bodies, a sizeable amount of research demonstrating negative impact has accumulated.

Brief exposure to print media images of thin female models from fashion magazines has been shown to produce a number of immediate negative effects, including greater concern about weight, body dissatisfaction, self-consciousness, negative mood, and decreased perception of self-attractiveness. Some studies have found effects only for some groups of women—those who are heavier, more concerned with self-presentation, and have high levels of trait-body dissatisfaction. In one study similar effects were found for men exposed to photographs of stereotypically attractive male fashion models, although the response was less than that of the female participants.

15 Given the ubiquity of television, it is surprising that there have been fewer studies of exposure to televised images. Among studies that compared the effects of appearance-related commercials (containing women who epitomize societal ideals of thinness and beauty) with non-appearance-related commercials, four out of five experiments reported negative consequences for at least some participants: specifically, greater anger, anxiety, depressed mood, and appearance dissatisfaction; more self-to-model comparisons; and self-perception of increased body size. Similar negative effects on body image have been found for appearance messages presented in auditory (radio-like) format.

Although not all women are equally affected, there is now sufficient evidence to conclude that brief exposure to idealized media images (less than one night's television viewing or a single issue of a fashion magazine) does have short-term deleterious effects on mood and body satisfaction. It seems likely that naturally occurring episodes of brief media exposure serve continually to maintain and reinforce levels of insecurity and concern about shape and weight.

Individual Differences

The pervasiveness of the media ensures that nearly all girls and women are exposed to a substantial dose of idealized images of thinness and beauty, yet not all develop extreme preoccupation with their weight and only a minority develops clinically diagnosable eating disorders. Similarly, the experimental studies show that not all women are equally vulnerable to adverse effects when exposed to media images. These studies have identified a number of individual characteristics that determine or moderate responsiveness to media images: weight (heavier women are more negatively affected by media images), disordered-eating symptomatology, trait-body dissatisfaction, self-consciousness, a tendency toward social comparison, and high dispositional levels of internalization regarding thinness ideals.

Some body image researchers have suggested that this list of characteristics can be subsumed under the concept of "appearance schematicity." *Appearance schemas* refer to cognitive structures concerning appearance that organize and determine the processing of self-relevant information. People for whom appearance is crucial and integral to the self-concept ("appearance schematics") selectively attend to the appearance-related aspects of any presented material. In particular, their more complex and highly developed appearance schemas are readily activated by idealized media images. This hypothesis was confirmed in two experiments, which found that appearance schematic women suffered greater negative consequences of media exposure than did their aschematic peers. In sum, the research indicates that it is those women already most heavily invested in their appearance who are the most vulnerable to the effects of idealized media images. This suggests a downward spiral in which negative body image is exacerbated by further exposure to idealized media images. Conversely, those women with low investment in their appearance are relatively immune to media effects.

Unanswered Research Questions

At a practical level, there is an urgent need for systematic research in several areas. Media impact on the body image of men and boys awaits investigation; the lean but muscular male ideal increasingly portrayed in advertising and other media may be as harmful for men as thin ideals are for women. In another arena, most of the experimental research has been conducted with college students. Similar research with adolescents and children should focus on identifying the variables that mediate and moderate the potentially adverse effects of exposure to idealized images of thinness for young people.

20 At a theoretical level, identifying the causal direction of media effects remains a challenge. The experimental studies show that brief exposure to idealized thin media images of thinness does have short-term deleterious consequences. Here the casual direction is clear: *from* media *to* body image (moderated by various individual characteristics).

*Image distortion techniques are possible through computer software that allows photographs to be easily altered. In some cases, a face may be attached to someone else's body—or an aspect of someone's body may be artificially enhanced in the image being created.

Unfortunately, however, this research finding does not address the development of body image, which necessarily takes place over time. Naturally occurring media exposure cannot be manipulated experimentally. What is required to clarify the media's role is *prospective research* that traces the development of both variables (body image and media exposure) over time, as well as their relationship to the mediating processes of internalization and investment in appearance. Most likely, the media play multiple and differing roles at different times in the development process. Ideally, to capture important developmental transitions, such investigations should begin in early childhood and proceed through late adolescence.

Clinical Implications
for Treatment and Prevention

The evidence shows that media images contribute to negative body image. The most obvious preventive strategy would be to reduce exposure to idealized images of thinness by encouraging the media to present a wider and more realistic range of female body shapes as acceptable and even beautiful. Surveys indicate that women and girls, as well as more formal advocacy groups, are calling for this change. However, economic pressures make it unlikely that such input will be heeded in the short-term. Women and girls can also reduce their own exposure to potentially damaging images, for example, by not buying or reading fashion magazines.

An alternative strategy is to equip young people with media literacy skills that make them resistant to media images. These skills need to go beyond the ability to recognize airbrushing and other image distortion techniques.* Young people need to be able to think critically, to deconstruct the images and messages presented to them—specifically, those glorifying slenderness and harmful practices such as dieting. To be successful as a preventive measure, such media literacy needs to begin in childhood, before beauty ideals are internalized and appearance becomes crucial for self-evaluation.

Further, the moderators identified by the experimental work (e.g., appearance schematicity) offer targets for intervention in the treatment of women with negative body image. Cognitive-behavioral techniques challenging underlying assumptions that appearance is central to identity can be used to reduce investment in appearance, self-monitoring, and comparison with others' bodies. These approaches do not attack the media directly but do serve to make people less vulnerable to negative effects of media images.

Research shows that the media are a potent force in the development of body image. In principle, then, it should be equally possible to use the media to promote a positive body image. Large-scale media-based interventions promoting healthy body image have the potential to reach farther and have greater impact than other methods.

Informative Readings

Berel, S., & Irving, L. M. (1998). Media and disturbed eating: An analysis of media influence and implications for prevention. *Journal of Primary Prevention, 18,* 415–430.—A review of media effects, including a feminist perspective.

Field, A. E., Camargo, C. A., Taylor, C. B., Berkey, C. S., Roberts, S. B., & Colditz, G. A. (2001). Peer, parent, and media influences on the development of weight concerns and frequent dieting among preadolescent and adolescent girls and boys. *Pediatrics, 107,* 54–60.—One of several reports on a large prospective cohort study.

Garner, D. M. (1997, January/February). The 1997 Body Image Survey results. *Psychology Today,* 30–44, 75–80, 84.—A survey of 4,000 people showing widespread body dissatisfaction.

Grogan, S. (1999). *Body image.* London: Routledge.—Contains a review of media effects on body image, including original research (Chapter 5).

Hargreaves, D., & Tiggemann, M. (2002). The effect of television commercials on mood and body dissatisfaction: The role of appearance-schema activation. *Journal of Social and Clinical Psychology, 21,* 328–349.—An experimental study of the effects of televised images from a schema perspective.

Harrison, K., & Cantor, J. (1997). The relationship between media consumption and eating disorders. *Journal of Communication, 47,* 40–67.—A correlational study of magazine and television exposure and disordered eating in women and men.

Leit, R. A., Pope, Jr., H. G., & Gray, J. J. (2001). Cultural expectations of muscularity in men: The evolution of *Playgirl* centerfolds. *International Journal of Eating Disorders, 29,* 90–93.—A study of the male models in *Playgirl* magazine, from 1973 to 1997, confirming increasingly muscular ideals of the male body.

Levine, M. P., & Smolak, L. (1996). Media as a context for the development of disordered eating. In L. Smolak, M. P. Levine, & R. Striegel-Moore (Eds.), *The developmental psychopathology of eating disorders: Implications for research, prevention, and treatment* (pp. 235–257). Mahwah, NJ: Erlbaum.—A comprehensive review from a developmental perspective.

Stice, E., Schupak-Neuberg, E., Shaw, H. E., & Stein, R. I. (1994). Relation of media exposure to eating disorder symptomatology: An examination of mediating mechanisms. *Journal of Abnormal Psychology, 103,* 836–840.—Structural equation modeling of direct and indirect effects of media exposure on body dissatisfaction and eating disorder symptomatology.

Thompson, J. K., Heinberg, L. J., Altabe, M., & Tantleff-Dunn, S. (1999). *Exacting beauty, Theory, assessment, and treatment of body image disturbance.* Washington, DC: American Psychological Association.—Contains a comprehensive review of the media as a sociocultural influence on body image (Chapter 3).

Tiggemann, M., Gardiner, M., & Slater, A. (2000). "I would rather be size 10 than have straight A's": A focus group study of adolescent girls' wish to be thinner. *Journal of Adolescence, 23,* 645–659.—A qualitative study highlighting the importance of perceived pressure from the media.

Questions for Discussion

1. Tiggemann opens her argument with a claim she expects her audience to accept with "no doubt." Do you accept this claim? What are the advantages and risks of opening with a claim that could be seen as widely accepted as true?

2. Do you agree with Tiggemann that the standard for thinness presented by the media "is impossible for most women to achieve by healthy means"? If so, on what do you base this belief?

NEGOTIATING DIFFERENCES

The authors in this cluster agree that the media can have a negative effect on body image. But even if the media overemphasize standards of physical perfection that are impossible to attain, images of attractive people can encourage people to take more trouble about their appearance. There is, of course, a big difference between deciding to lose some weight and becoming an anorexic or between dressing a little better and becoming obsessed with shopping. And in daily life, people may need to strike a balance between such extreme positions as "ignore what the media convey about beauty" and "do whatever it takes to honor the messages about beauty conveyed by the media."

Two the arguments in this cluster—"Fresh Faces" and "Extreme Surgery"—focus on what seems to be a growing trend: using cosmetic surgery to achieve what cannot be accomplished by working out, going to a good hair stylist, and making good choices when shopping for clothes. Both note that people who are pleased with the results of one procedure are often tempted to have another.

Now imagine the following situation: You are a marriage counselor, and a couple comes to see you because of a conflict about cosmetic surgery. The husband had his nose reshaped because he had been self-conscious about it for a long time. His wife supported this decision not because his nose displeased her but because she understood that the surgery was likely to improve his self-esteem. Pleased with the results of this procedure,

3. In paragraph 3, Tiggemann recognizes that the media influence how men and boys perceive their bodies, but most of her argument focuses on women. Was she wise to recognize that the media influence both genders, or do you think she should have kept her focus on women?

4. According to Tiggemann, media images are only "part of complex cultural scripts." What does she mean by this? Is your own life being shaped to some extent by a "cultural script" that has been imposed on it?

5. What kinds of women are especially vulnerable to media messages about body image?

6. Why would music videos be especially influential for adolescent girls? To what do you attribute the popularity of this medium?

7. According to Tiggemann, what does research about the influence of the media upon body image prove so far, and what remains to be established?

8. How effectively has Tiggemann incorporated sources into her argument?

the man then had a face-lift so that he would look younger—justifying this procedure on the grounds that it would give him a competitive advantage in the workplace because, in his view, looking old could lead to being perceived as looking tired or out-of-date. His wife reluctantly accepted this choice but reminded her husband that a face-lift can look artificial and cosmetic surgery was not covered by their health insurance. Now, a year later, the husband wants to undergo a more radical procedure: having his legs lengthened. The wife strongly objects. She argues that he is becoming obsessed about his appearance, spending too much money on unnecessary surgery, and proposing a procedure that should be reserved—if used at all—for someone who is unusually short, not someone who is already reasonably tall. He answers that she does not understand him and is failing to be a supportive partner. They have come to you in the hope of reconciling a conflict that has put their relationship at risk.

Write an argument in which you develop what you imagine to be the views they share with you when you meet with them individually after the initial session. Then conclude with a proposition that seems likely to reduce marital tension by helping the couple get past the conflict currently absorbing so much of their energy—a proposition that you will share with them when they return to your office as a couple.

Why Are So Many Americans Overweight?

It is one of the great ironies of our time that obesity seems to be on the rise in an era when diet products line grocery-store shelves, books on diet and fitness have their own section in bookstores, and health clubs are packed during peak hours with men and women working out as new and larger clubs continue to open. Why then is fat so much in evidence? There are almost certainly numerous factors, among them the rising popularity of fast food (a trend that can be attributed partly to people leading lives that are increasingly busy), the overly large portions of food served by many chains and restaurants, the temptation to snack when at work, the nature of work itself (which often has people sitting at desks rather than bailing hay or lifting loads of lumber), and the human tendency to use food as a kind of drug—a drug to ease frustration or disappointment or, on the other hand, to mark celebration. And the fatter people become, the more natural it can seem to be fat. North Americans do not have a monopoly on this problem. There is evidence that obesity is on the rise around the world, especially in prosperous nations where chains like McDonald's and Kentucky Fried Chicken have taken the North American menu overseas. But assuming that obesity is a problem—an assumption that one of the writers in this cluster questions—then determining the causes of the problem is essential to figuring out a cure. When making generalizations about people who are "overweight" or "obese," you need to think critically about what such terms mean. Is there a fixed measurement for being overweight that carries over from one generation to another and that people of diverse cultural backgrounds agree upon? Can doctors and dieticians define what it means to be an overweight child or an obese adult? Fat can certainly be measured in pounds and ounces. And you can easily see that some people weigh more than others. But is the nature of being overweight or obese to some extent a social construction—that is, something that people have temporarily agreed upon as opposed to something that exists as an absolute and unchanging truth? And does being overweight necessarily pose a health risk, or could it simply indicate that someone is enjoying the pleasure—and nutrition—of good food?

① SUSAN BRINK AND ELIZABETH QUERNA, "Eat This Now!"

In March 2005, *U.S. News & World Report* published the following article by reporters Susan Brink and Elizabeth Querna. It provides a useful introduction to contemporary concerns about the rise of obesity in the United States. As you read it, you will find that experts disagree about how serious the problem is but that there seems to be widespread agreement that U.S. citizens are overeating and underexercising. As Brink and Querna report, temptations to snack abound, portion sizes are growing, and too much of what is eaten consists of food with little nutritional value. As their title suggests, many people may be interested in eating quickly than in eating wisely. A weekly newsmagazine, *U.S. News & World Report* is perceived as politically more conservative than its larger rivals, *Time* and *Newsweek*. So when you read "Eat This Now!" you might consider whether it reflects conservative values.

Eat This Now!

SUSAN BRINK AND ELIZABETH QUERNA

1 It's everywhere. Tank up your car, and you walk past soft pretzels with cheese sauce. Grab a cup of coffee, and you see doughnuts, danishes, and cookies the size of hubcaps. Stop at Staples for an ink cartridge, and you confront candy bars at the register.

Stroll past the receptionist's desk at the office, and find somebody's leftover Christmas cookies, Valentine's Day candy, Easter Peeps, birthday cake, or vacation saltwater taffy. "We're just surrounded. Food is available every time you turn around," says Marilyn Tanner, dietitian at Washington University School of Medicine in St. Louis.

Overeating and its lethal companion underexercising are the recognized culprits in this country's rise in obesity rates. Today, two thirds of American adults are obese or overweight. A national team of researchers reported in last week's *New England Journal of Medicine* that obesity already reduces the current life expectancy in the United States by four to nine months.

What's worse, they project that the rise in obesity rates among children and teens could knock off as many as five years from today's average of 77 years as overweight people in that generation grow up and die prematurely. Diseases associated with obesity, such as diabetes, heart disease, kidney disease, and some cancers, are likely to strike at younger ages. It would be the first time in 200 years that children would be statistically likely to live shorter lives than their grandparents.

5 It's a controversial prediction, called speculative and "excessively gloomy" by Samuel Preston, a demographer at the University of Pennsylvania.

And the outcome is far from inevitable. All it would take to change that dire prediction is to have millions of people change their habits. That means diet, exercise, and a strong will within every individual to pass up high-calorie temptations. Right?

It's not that easy, as every failed and yo-yo dieter knows. The playing field is heavily tilted—

CONTEXT

A professor at the Catholic University of America asks on its website, "Why does a glossy magazine photo of a chocolate layer cake conjure up images of Mom and home? What does an ad for lime-green Jell-O say about American life in the 1950s? 'Food and Media' . . . seeks to answer those questions by exploring the media's role in shaping our perceptions of food. The course also examines how factors like class, gender and ethnicity play a role in our food choices." What other examples can you think of that show food in media conjuring up specific images or feelings? Would you be interested in taking a course that focused on how eating habits are shaped not only by the media but also by class, gender, and ethnicity? Why do you think such a course is being offered at a faith-based institution?

by advertising, fast-paced lives, convenience foods, and treats every time you turn around—away from healthful eating choices. Many experts in nutrition, public health, and law believe that the national obesity problem doesn't simply come down to millions of failures of individual will.

Attitude Shift

A generation ago, it was considered rude to eat in front of others. Now, Americans eat everywhere, all day long—an average of five meals a day, counting snacks. Cars have cupholders, but they arguably need trays, too. Americans eat 30 meals a year in their vehicles. "That's the average. I'm sure it's higher when it comes to people driving to work," said Harry Balzer, vice president of the NPD Group, a consumer marketing research firm that tracks how Americans eat. "Look at our cars. They look like restaurants."

Riddled with anxiety, we take our meals with equal parts pleasure and guilt. We might say an internal no a dozen times a day, then give in to the Krispy Kreme near the bus stop on the way home. Or if we pass up the doughnut shop, we get home only to find that the latest issue of Cooking Light has arrived in the mail—with a cover photo of pecan pie. We have few common rituals around dining but a common hurried pace through eating. All of these triggers and gustatory seductions play into an obesity epidemic—even as the messages manipulate the national obsession with health.

10 Food is more than a way of staying alive, more than an edible commodity. "Food is never just the physical product itself," says Stephanie Hartman, who teaches a course at Catholic University of America in Washington, D.C., called "Food and Media." "It's invested with national meanings, associated with comfort and nostalgia. There are class associations. Food can be elegant or cultured." Or it can carry a reverse snobbery. Where once the elite sampled truffles, today they might seek

the best barbecued ribs or the richest macaroni and cheese.

Certainly, the descendants of immigrants may still prepare pasta or pirogi recipes handed down from the old country, but Americans as a whole don't have shared food values. We don't all cook with the same oil, have an attachment to a certain variety of plum, or dine with predictable ceremony. Such culinary eclecticism may make us uniquely vulnerable to fads. "We don't have a culture of eating, a national cuisine, a traditional way of eating that guides us," says Tanner. "So we fall prey to the latest fad or scientific pronouncement. The fact that we're more responsive to medical trends makes us more responsive to marketing." As soon as science tells us that oat bran is good for preventing heart disease, people start buying potato chips sprinkled with oat bran. "This is who we are. We're always looking for the newest way to attack this problem. We're going to try to figure out this health issue by eating," says Balzer.

Why, even when we know better, do we succumb to the lure of rich desserts and nutritionally empty snacks? Why is the look—even stronger, the smell—of the forbidden so compelling? "I've seen evidence that bakeries and supermarkets pipe faked aromas out in the store," says Doug Kysar, a professor at Cornell Law School who teaches consumer law and studies deceptive advertising. "Things like taste and smell and sight can overcome one's awareness. The classic example is the candy gantlet at the supermarket. We have a long-term desire to maintain a healthful life, but the short-term desire can trump the long-term."

Marketers know what works. They tell us we're worth it, that we deserve it. "Magnify that by 45,000 different products, add in the fake bakery smell, the mood music in supermarkets calculated to lower blink rates to a somnolent state, the way the aisles are set up to keep people in the store for a longer time—that's an enormous amount of situational forces to weaken the will," says Kysar.

Food to Sell

America is truly a horn of plenty. In the early 1980s, food production came to an average of 3,300 calories a day available to every person. Then farm policy changed, and farmers no longer plowed food under or slaughtered animals to be entitled to subsidies. Today, American produces enough food to allow every man, woman, and child 3,900 calories a day.* "That additional food production had to be sold," says Marion Nestle, professor in the department of nutrition at New York University and author of *Food Politics.* "One of the first things that happened was portion sizes started getting bigger."

15 Many Americans feel entitled to big servings on a top-of-the-line chocolate bar as a way to get some short-term happiness. "You walk past a doughnut shop, and you say, 'Yum. Doughnuts.' Part of you says, 'No, I'll get fat.' But another part is like Scarlett O'Hara saying, 'Tomorrow is another day.' This feels good now," says Gail Saltz of the New York Psychoanalytic Institute.

Almost all of us are prone to comfort ourselves with food when we feel deprived in other ways. Many families have forsaken the shared meal and the long time of food preparation, dining, and cleanup as a communal effort. Along with it, they've lost an important psychological support. "If we take a good hour and a half to talk about our day, go slowly through the meal, maybe have a glass of wine—we're much more psychologically filled at the end of that meal than if I decide to eat alone. Then, I'm going to grab a hamburger and some chips," says psychoanalyst Kathryn Zerbe, vice chair for psychotherapy at Oregon Health and Science University.

Of course, we can just say no. But it's a David and Goliath fight. We're battling an entire environment, massive societal change, government policy, and billions of dollars in advertising.

*Percent Daily Values on food labels are based on a 2,000 calorie diet. Daily caloric intake varies widely based on a person's weight and activity level. Nevertheless, 3,900 calories a day is excessive except in extremely rare cases.

THE EXPERTS' TIPS

- Don't walk into a bakery or chocolate shop without a buddy who might sober you up enough to keep your order from getting out of hand.
- Know that what you buy at the grocery store will get eaten. Some 37 percent of dinner menus are planned spontaneously with what's available in the house, says Harry Balzer, vice president of the NPD Group. So don't bring fattening or unhealthful foods home.
- If you eat out a lot, it's no longer a special occasion. Don't order as if it's a party.
- Be aware of how advertising is trying to manipulate your need for comfort, quick gratification, or self-indulgence. "The only way to outsmart them is to know what they're tapping into and not have it go directly to your unconscious," says Gail Saltz, a psychoanalyst with the New York Psychoanalytic Institute.
- Cleaning your plate will not help starving children in the Third World. If you've been served too hefty a portion, it's better to scrape it into the garbage than shovel it into your stomach.

Questions for Discussion

1. Do you agree that we live in a culture in which temptations to snack or overeat abound? Have you seen evidence of this in your home, dormitory, or workplace? Do you feel pressured at times to snack even when you are not hungry?

2. Why is there reason to believe that children may eventually suffer more serious consequences from obesity than those currently experienced by adults?

3. What does it mean to be a "yo-yo dieter"?

4. According to the authors, it used to be considered rude to eat in front of others. Have you seen students eating in front of classmates before or during a class session—or witnessed people carrying food or drink into a shop at a mall? If so, how do you account for this behavior?

5. What cultural factors could make Americans especially vulnerable to overeating?

6. If you have traveled in another country, have you seen evidence supporting the claim that Americans expect larger portions of food than those served in other nations? If you have not traveled outside the United States, have you seen evidence within the country that portion size is increasing?

7. In what sense is the struggle to overcome obesity "a David and Goliath fight"?

② **BARBARA WICKENS, "How Your Brain Makes You Fat"**

Although people regularly make choices about what they eat, and some people make healthier choices than others, the human brain can contribute to obesity, according to the following report by Barbara Wickens, a senior editor for *MacLean's* magazine—one of the most widely distributed magazines in Canada. How then can studying the brain help researchers discover ways in which more people would regularly make healthy choices about diet? Because she is writing for a Canadian audience, Wickens makes a number of references to individuals and programs in that country—beginning in her opening paragraph, in which she refers to a program called *Les ateliers cinq epices,* which is French for "workshops of the five spices"—a title that suggests that well-flavored food does not have to be fattening. But as you read, be alert for how Wickens incorporates references to research being done in the United States so that Canadian research is placed in a larger scientific context.

How Your Brain Makes You Fat

BARBARA WICKENS

1   The students in the combined grades 4, 5 and 6 cooking class of Ste Odile may not know it, but they're part of a grand experiment. They're participating in a pilot project, Les ateliers cinq épices, that sends dietitians to eight Montreal elementary schools. Their job: to teach kids how to cook foods that are lower in salt, fat and sugar than the highly processed snacks they're used to eating. Just as important is making sure that, as these youngsters bake yummy cookies and cut fruits and veggies into weird shapes, they enjoy their break from the regular classroom routine. As program director Manon Paquette puts it, "We're hoping to make healthy eating fun." The kids are, in effect, learning nutrition through stealth. And there's new evidence that they may even be rewiring their brains in the process.

Thanks to advances in neural imaging techniques, we can see the brain at work in a way that was not possible even a decade ago. And in light of mounting concerns about the increasing prevalence of obesity, this is good news. According to data released last week by the World Health Organization, 4.1 percent of Canada's teenagers are obese (19.3 were found to be merely overweight). This makes the Canadians the fourth most obese teens in the world, behind Malta, the United States and Britain. The WHO, in fact, describes obesity as a global epidemic. And the traditional approach to weight loss—hoping individuals can muster enough willpower to stick to a low-calorie diet and get a little exercise—clearly hasn't worked. But by scanning the brains of the obese and the lean, science is coming to a new understanding about how the brain, body and food interact.

There is still much to be learned, but one thing already seems clear: humans are hard-wired to prefer, maybe even crave, the very foods that today cause us so many problems. No surprise, they're sweet, salty and/or high in fats and calories (the body's way of storing energy for future use). But new data is revealing that the brain is also more malleable than

CONTEXT

The World Health Organization, the United Nations' specialized agency for health, uses the body mass index (BMI) to find the prevalence of overweight and obesity. To measure BMI, divide weight in pounds by height in inches squared and multiply the result by 703. In adults a BMI over 25 is defined as overweight and a BMI over 30 as obese. BMI for children and teens is gender and age specific, according to the Centers for Disease Control and Prevention.

previously thought, even in adults. Lay down the right neural pathways and you can hook people—especially those under 21, whose brains are still growing and maturing—on a handful of crunchy carrots rather than a bag of nachos.

In North America, where 23,000-odd diet books have been published in the past three decades, the new research has far-reaching implications for parents, legislators and school administrators, not to mention the purveyors of fast food. Doctors, psychologists, nutritionists and others interested in weight control are just starting to use brain scans to answer such questions as: which regions are activated when you show someone food? Is the result different in obese and thin people? Where do cravings originate? Which part controls impulses? The knowledge gained from such testing, scientists hope, will be used to make and keep people healthy. If your brain can make you fat, maybe—if you can push the right buttons—it can also make you thin.

5 Earlier research had already mapped the vital organ's basic structures and developed crude maps of what went on where. But as technology improved, increasingly detailed pictures of the brain emerged. Positron emission tomography uses increases in blood flow associated with increased activity to give a sense of which brain cells are at work. But it takes radioactive markers to do this, and a PET scan* can take up to an hour. Then in the mid-1990s, the introduction of functional magnetic resonance imaging even allowed researchers to peer into the brain while it was performing some sort of mental task. An MRI detects the minute changes in magnetism that indicate blood flow to active parts of the brain. Those spots, which appear as brighter colours on the image, are giving scientists a much clearer picture of what the human mind goes through when it calculates a mathematical formula, recognizes different words—or contemplates a bar of chocolate.

The brain has yet to give up all its secrets. It has, after all, some 100 billion neuron cells extending through its different regions. Still, studies are indicating that brain chemistry strongly affects body weight. The neurons communicate with one another via a number of chemical messenger called neurotransmitters. One of these is dopamine, which is key to the brain's internal reward system. Thanks to dopamine's cheerful role in allowing us to feel pressure, some researchers hope it can be enlisted in the fight against fat.

Dopamine is also known to be a culprit in cocaine and nicotine addiction, but as obesity researchers Marcia Levin Pelchat points out, "this brain circuitry did not evolve for the purpose of recreational drug use." It seems designed to ensure that basic functions like eating, drinking and reproducing are more likely to be repeated if they're pleasurable.

So does this mean food can be addictive? It may be for some overweight individuals, says Pelchat, a scientist at the Monell Chemical Senses Center in Philadelphia. A series of studies has shown that some people who overeat may have less dopamine in their system, or fewer receptors for it. The theory is that they might be eating more in an effort to boost the pleasure they derive from food. Pelchat recommends the development of new behavioural methods or drugs that can help these people enjoy a more normal reward from eating. What's the alternative, she asks: "Are we going to outlaw pleasure?"

As brain chemicals go, dopamine is a pretty important player: it reaches into the brain's emotional centres, such as the hypothalamus, which is involved in memory, reward the learning; and rational centres such as the prefrontal cortex, where problem solving, planning and decision making occur. Willpower, a front brain function, is what helps a person resist immediate temptation—I want these new shoes now—in favour of a long-term goal, as in, I want my money in the bank to grow. But when it comes to food, the short-term almost always trumps the long-term, according to Antoine Bechara, a former Torontonian who is now associate neurology professor at the

*In positron emission tomography—or a PET scan—a very small dose of radioactive chemical is injected into a vein and then absorbed into organs and tissues. Patients are then placed on an examination table and moved into a machine that, together with a computer, generates three-dimensional images that can help physicians detect problems.

University of Iowa. And this may have something to do with our deepest ancestral instincts. Think of it this way the next time you grab a burger and fries at the nearest drive-through. Your conscious mind might register, I should've ordered a salad instead. But somewhere in its primordial parts your brain is cheering, Yippee! Mastodon meat! Tubers! Scarf 'em down quick before a sabre-toothed tiger comes by.

10 For millennia, our ancestors literally didn't know where their next meal was coming from. With food being scarce, and often requiring great effort to track down, the biggest bang for the hunter-gatherer's buck was a meal as high in calories as possible. This meant foods high in fats and sugars. Foods that fit the bill, like fruits and meat, were also rich in nutrients. Today, in the developed world at least, we have a cheap and plentiful food supply that's no farther than the nearest convenience store—but not necessarily nutritious. While some fatty foods, such as olive oil, nuts, avocado and fish, can be part of a healthy diet, there's very little nourishment, for instance, in a candy bar. To make matters worse, we have too few reasons to exercise. In evolutionary terms, these are such new developments that our brains haven't had time to adapt.

Until recently, little effort was spent on trying to understand why people became fat. Wasn't the answer simple? They ate more calories than they burned off. Anybody who failed obviously wasn't trying hard enough. The equation hasn't changed, but that single-minded focus on willpower clearly has not worked. And considering that obesity puts people at greater risk for other serious ailments such as type 2 diabetes, heart disease and stroke, as well as some types of cancer, the potential costs to the health-care system—not to mention the toll in human suffering—are staggering. The time is overdue to take a more sophisticated approach.

That's exactly what happened in early April, when the faculties of medicine and business management at Montreal's McGill University brought together an unusual cross-section of scientists and health and marketing experts from North America and Europe to brainstorm. The challenge, according to conference chairwoman Laurette Dubé, a McGill marketing professor, was to examine whether it is possible to fight today's fat society by better understanding when, why and how people make certain food choices. "We have looked too much to the rational side," said Dubé "No one serves a drink to an alcoholic and says the guy should resist."

Still, as one participant noted, understanding how the brain and body respond to food in a healthy person at a healthy weight, let alone in someone who is obese, "isn't rocket science, it's more complex than that." This complexity means that there will likely never be a single magic bullet for weight loss, but that a number of solutions may work. Some of the problems, it turns out, may be in your genes. There are at least 430 of them associated with obesity, says Diane Finegood, scientific director of the Institute of Nutrition, Metabolism and Diabetes, part of the Canadian Institutes of Health Research.

Some people may be more susceptible than others to putting on weight. Angelo Del Parigi wasn't specifically looking at that issue, but research he did at the U.S. National Institutes of Health in Phoenix, Ariz., may shed light on it. Using PET scans, Del Parigi studied the neurology of hunger and satiety—medical jargon for "had enough." In the scans of both lean and obese people during and after a 36-hour fast, hunger showed up broadly in the hypothalamus and other limbic areas, while satiety was represented in the prefrontal cortex. However, the obese had a number of abnormal responses in both areas, which seems to indicate that they feel hungry more often and take longer to feel full. People who had lost weight, however, still showed abnormalities in their scans, indicating that even though their bodies were leaner, their brains remained "fat." Del Parigi said that neural responses to hunger and satiety may be a warning sign that someone is predisposed to obesity. One tantalizing question for further research, however, is whether the abnormalities caused the weight gain, or the weight gain caused the abnormalities.

15 Still, there is positive news in the fight against obesity—in the form of clear evidence the palate can be re-educated to enjoy healthier foods. Over the past five years, Danone Canada quietly reduced the sugar content of its yogurt by 15 percent. And, notes company president and CEO Louis Frenette, it accomplished this not only with no complaints, but sales in that period actually increased. Also, Dr. David Ludwig, director of the obesity program at Boston's Children's Hospital, said that youngsters who come from outside North America often find fast food distasteful. They have to learn to like it. And that presumably means others can learn how not to like it.

Iowa's Bechara has done research that also supports that contention. His studies indicate that the willpower to override impulses is influenced by what children are taught as they grow up. This suggests that if adults make eating healthy food a rewarding experience, children will develop a better ability to control their food impulses. Of course, he didn't study the particular kids in Montreal's Les ateliers cinq épices program. And there's no evidence that such early interventions will have an effect over a lifetime. But until researchers can tease more secrets from the tangle of neurons that make up our internal reward system, encouraging brains and taste buds to enjoy healthy food looks to be the best weapon yet in the battle of the bulge.

Questions for Discussion

1. Wickens opens with a reference to a project being conducted in a French-speaking part of Canada. How does she subsequently use this project to apply to the rest of North America?

2. According to Wickens, the United States is the second most obese country in the world, followed by Britain and Canada. (Malta, the most obese, is a small island that was formerly part of the British empire.) What does this hierarchy suggest?

3. What is the function of dopamine, and why is it significant in research into the causes of obesity?

4. Where in her argument does Wickens recognize that there are still unanswered questions about the causes of obesity?

5. Based on what is now understood about the brain's role in "making fat," what can be done to promote healthy eating?

6. Consider how Wickens concludes with a reference to "weapon" followed by "battle of the bulge." To what is she alluding, and is this allusion appropriate for her audience and context?

③ **W. WAYT GIBBS, "Obesity: An Overblown Epidemic?"**

There have been so many reports about the rise of obesity in the United States and so many assumptions that this rise, if accurately measured, constitutes a public health crisis that critical thinking demands considering whether these reports could be misleading. As the title of the following argument suggests, W. Wayt Gibbs believes that concerns about the medical consequences of obesity have been exaggerated. In taking this position, he does not argue that obesity is desirable, but he does urge caution when it comes to using a word like *epidemic*. His argument was first published in the June 2005 issue of *Scientific American,* a well-respected monthly magazine read by both scientists and people who are interested in learning about current work in science. Gibbs is a senior writer and member of the editorial board at *Scientific American.* As you read his work, be alert for how he draws upon numerous sources when making his case. Note also how he uses sources to challenge conventional thinking instead of doing so directly on his own.

Obesity: An Overblown Epidemic?

W. WAYT GIBBS

1 Could it be that excess fat is not, by itself, a serious health risk for the vast majority of people who are overweight or obese—categories that in the U.S. include about six of every 10 adults? Is it possible that urging the overweight or mildly obese to cut calories and lose weight may actually do more harm than good?

Such notions defy conventional wisdom that excess adiposity kills more than 300,000 Americans a year and that the gradual fattening of nations since the 1980s presages coming epidemics of diabetes, cardiovascular disease, cancer and a host of other medical consequences. Indeed, just this past March the *New England Journal of Medicine* presented a "Special Report," by S. Jay Olshansky, David B. Allison and others that seemed to confirm such fears. The authors asserted that because of the obesity epidemic, "the steady rise in life expectancy during the past two centuries may soon come to an end." Articles about the special report by the *New York Times,* the *Washington Post* and many other news outlets emphasized its forecast that obesity may shave up to five years off average life spans in coming decades.

And yet an increasing number of scholars have begun accusing obesity experts, public health officials and the media of exaggerating the health effects of the epidemic of overweight and obesity. The charges appear in a recent flury of scholarly books, including *The Obesity Myth,* by Paul F. Campos (Gotham Books, 2004); *The Obesity Epidemic: Science, Morality and Ideology,* by Michael Gard and Jan Wright (Routledge, 2005); *Obesity: The Making of an American Epidemic,* by J. Eric Oliver (Oxford University Press, August 2005); and a book on popular misconceptions about diet and weight gain by Barry Glassner (to be published in 2006 by HarperCollins).

These critics, all academic researchers outside the medical community, do not dispute

CONTEXT

A component of the U.S. Department of Health and Human Services, The Centers for Disease Control and Prevention (CDC) is an important site for medical research, especially research that relates to public health. Founded in 1946, it also designs and implements programs intended to improve public health and respond to health emergencies. It is headquartered in Atlanta.

surveys that find the obese fraction of the population to have roughly doubled in the U.S. and many parts of Europe since 1980. And they acknowledge that obesity, especially in its extreme forms, does seem to be a factor in some illnesses and premature deaths.

5 They allege, however, that experts are blowing hot air when they warn that overweight and obesity are causing a massive, and worsening, health crisis. They scoff, for example, at the 2003 assertion by Julie L. Gerberding, director of the Centers for Disease Control and Prevention, that "if you looked at any epidemic—whether it's influenza or plague from the Middle Ages—they are not as serious as the epidemic of obesity in terms of the health impact on our country and our society." (An epidemic of influenza killed 40 million people worldwide between 1918 and 1919, including 675,000 in the U.S.)

What is really going on, asserts Oliver, a political scientist at the University of Chicago, is that "a relatively small group of scientists and doctors, many directly funded by the weight loss industry, have created an arbitrary and unscientific definition of overweight and obesity. They have inflated claims and distorted statistics on the consequences of our growing weights, and they have largely ignored the complicated health realities associated with being fat."

One of those complicated realities, concurs Campos, a professor of law at the University of Colorado at Boulder, is the widely accepted evidence that genetic differences account for 50 to 80 percent of the variation in fatness within a population. Because no

CONTEXT

The World Health Organization (WHO) is an agency of the United Nations. Created in 1945, a few months after the end of World War II, the United Nations replaced an earlier international organization that had been designed to foster peace: the League of Nations. The League never achieved any notable successes, however, partly because Congress voted against U.S. membership even though the League was an important project of President Woodrow Wilson. Locating the United Nations in New York City signaled, among other things, that the United States was ready to participate actively in international efforts to prevent future wars. The WHO was established in 1948. Governed by 192 member states, it works to promote health—which it defines as "a state of complete physical, mental, and social well-being and not merely the absence of disease or infirmity."

safe and widely practical methods have been shown to induce long-term loss of more than about 5 percent of body weight, Campos says, "health authorities are giving people advice—maintain a body mass index in the 'healthy weight' range—that is literally impossible for many of them to follow." Body mass index, or BMI, is a weight-to-height ratio.

By exaggerating the risks of fat and the feasibility of weight loss, Campos and Oliver claim, the CDC, the U.S. Department of Health and Human Services and the World Health Organization inadvertently perpetuate stigma, encourage unbalanced diets and, perhaps, even exacerbate weight gain. "The most perverse irony is that we may be creating a disease simply by labeling it as such," Campos states.

A Body to Die For

On first hearing, these dissenting arguments may sound like nonsense. "If you really look at the medical literature and think obesity isn't bad, I don't know what planet you are on," says James O. Hill, an obesity researcher at the University of Colorado Health Sciences Center. New dietary guidelines issued by the DHHS and the U.S. Department of Agriculture in January state confidently that "a high prevalence of overweight and obesity is of great public health concern because excess body fat leads to a higher risk for premature death, type 2 diabetes, hypertension, dyslipidemia [high cholesterol], cardiovascular disease, stroke, gall bladder disease, respiratory dysfunction, gout, osteoarthritis, and certain kinds of cancers." The clear implication is that any degree of overweight is dangerous and that a high BMI is not merely a marker of high risk but a cause.

10 "These supposed adverse health consequences of being 'overweight' are not only exaggerated but for the most part are simply fabricated," Campos alleges. Surprisingly, a careful look at recent epidemiological studies and clinical trials suggest that the critics, though perhaps overstating some of their accusations, may be onto something.

Oliver points to a new and unusually thorough analysis of three large, nationally representative surveys, for example, that found only a very slight—and statistically insignificant—increase in mortality among mildly obese people, as compared with those in the "healthy weight" category, after subtracting the effects of age, race, sex, smoking and alcohol consumption. The three surveys—medical measurements collected in the early 1970s, late 1970s and early 1990s, with subjects matched against death registries 9 to 19 years later—indicate that it is much more likely that U.S. adults who fall in the overweight category have a lower risk of premature death than do those of so-called healthy weight. The overweight segment of the "epidemic of overweight and obesity" is more likely reducing death rates than boosting them. "The majority of Americans who weigh too much are in this category," Campos notes.

Counterintuitively, "underweight, even though it occurs in only a tiny fraction of the population, is actually associated with more excess deaths than class I obesity," says Katherine M. Flegal, a senior research scientist at the CDC. Flegal led the study, which appeared in the Journal of the American Medical Association* on April 20 after undergoing four months of scrutiny by internal reviewers at the CDC and the National Cancer Institute and additional peer review by the journal.

These new results contradict two previous estimates that were the basis of the oft-repeated claim that obesity cuts shorts 300,000 or more lives a year in the U.S. There are good reasons to suspect, however, that both these earlier estimates were compromised by dubious assumptions, statistical errors and outdated measurements.

When Flegal and her co-workers analyzed just the most recent survey, which measured heights and weights from 1988 to 1994 and deaths up to 2000, even severe obesity failed to show up as a statistically significant mortality risk. It seems probable, Flegal speculates, that in recent decades improvements in med-

ical care have reduced the mortality level associated with obesity. That would square, she observes, with both the unbroken rise in life expectancies and the uninterrupted fall in death rates attributed to heart disease and stroke throughout the entire 25-year spike in obesity in the U.S.

15 But what about the warning by Olshansky and Allison that the toll from obesity is yet to be paid, in the form of two to five years of life lost? "These are just back-of-the-envelope, plausible scenarios," Allison hedges, when pressed. "We never meant for them to be portrayed as precise." Although most media reports jumped on the "two to five years" quote, very few mentioned that the paper offered no statistical analysis to back it up.

The life expectancy costs of obesity that Olshansky and his colleagues actually calculated were based on a handful of convenient, but false, presuppositions. First, they assumed that every obese American adult currently has a BMI of 30, or alternatively of 35—the upper and lower limits of the "mild obesity" range. They then compared that simplified picture of the U.S. with an imagined nation in which no adult has a BMI of more than 24—the upper limit of "healthy weight"—and in which underweight causes zero excess deaths.

To project death rates resulting from obesity, the study used risk data that are more than a decade old rather than the newer ratios Flegal included, which better reflect dramatically improved treatments for cardiovascular disease and diabetes. The authors further assumed not only that the old mortality risks have remained constant but also that future advances in medicine will have no effect whatsoever on the health risks of obesity.

If all these simplifications are reasonable, the Marach paper concluded, then the estimated hit to the average life expectancy of the U.S. population from its world-leading levels of obesity is four to nine months. ("Two to five years" was simply a gloomy guess of what could happen in "coming decades" if an increase in overweight children were to fuel

*The *Journal of the American Medical Association,* or *JAMA,* is the most widely circulated publication among physicians in the United States.

*Triggered by earthquakes, volcanic eruptions, or meteoritic impacts, a tsunami (from the Japanese for "harbor wave") begins beneath the surface of the ocean. Mild ones may go unnoticed, but severe ones create enormous surface waves that can have devastating effects. In December 2004, for example, a tsunami in Southeast Asia killed approximately 200,000 people and destroyed many communities.

additional spikes in adult obesity.) The study did not attempt to determine whether, given its many uncertainties, the number of months lost was reliably different from zero. Yet in multiple television and newspaper interviews about the study, co-author David S. Ludwig evinced full confidence as he compared the effect of rising obesity rates to "a massive tsunami* headed toward the United States."

Critics decry episodes such as this one as egregious examples of a general bias in the obesity research community. Medical researchers tend to cast the expansion of waistlines as an impending disaster "because it inflates their stature and allows them to get more research grants. Government health agencies wield it as a rationale for their budget allocations," Oliver writes. (The National Institutes of Health increased its funding for obesity research by 10 percent in 2005, to $440 million.) "Weight-loss companies and surgeons employ it to get their services covered by insurance," he continues. "And the pharmaceutical industry uses it to justify new drugs."

20 "The war on fat," Campos concurs, "is really about making some of us rich." He points to the financial support that many influential obesity researchers receive from the drug and diet industries. Allison, a professor at the University of Alabama at Birmingham, discloses payments from 148 such companies, and Hill says he has consulted with some of them as well. (Federal policies prohibit Flegal and other CDC scientists from accepting nongovernmental wages.) None of the dissenting authors cities evidence of anything more than a potential conflict of interest, however.

Those Confounded Diseases

Even the best mortality studies provide only a flawed and incomplete picture of the health consequences of the obesity epidemic, for three reasons. First, by counting all lives lost to obesity, the studies so far have ignored the fact that some diversity in human body size is normal and that every well-nourished population thus contains some obese people. The "epidemic," refers to a sudden increase in obesity, not its mere existence. A proper accounting of the epidemic's mortal cost would estimate only the number of lives cut short by whatever amount of obesity exceeds the norm.

Second, the analyses use body mass index as a convenient proxy for body fat. But BMI is not an especially reliable standin. And third, although everyone cares about mortality, it is not the only thing that we care about. Illness and quality of life matter a great deal, too.

All can agree that severe obesity greatly increases the risk of numerous diseases, but that form of obesity, in which BMI exceeds 40, affects only about one in 12 of the roughly 130 million American adults who set scales spinning above the "healthy" range. At issue is whether rising levels of overweight, or of mild to moderate obesity, are pulling up the national burden of heart disease, cancer and diabetes.

In the case of heart disease, the answer appears to be no—or at least not yet. U.S. health agencies do not collect annual figures on the incidence of cardiovascular disease, so researchers look instead for trends in mortality and risk factors, as measured in periodic surveys. Both have been falling.

25 Alongside Flegal's April paper in *JAMA* was another by Edward W. Gregg and his colleagues from the CDC that found that in the U.S. the prevalence of high blood pressure dropped by half between 1960 and 2000. High cholesterol followed the same trend—and both declined more steeply among the overweight and obese than among those of healthy weight. So although high blood pressure is still twice as common among the obese as it is among the lean, the paper notes that "obese persons now have better [cardiovascular disease] risk profiles than their leaner counterparts did 20 to 30 years ago."

The new findings reinforce those published in 2001 by a 10-year WHO study that examined 140,000 people in 38 cities on four continents. The investigators, led by Alun Evans of the Queen's University of Belfast, saw broad increases in BMI and equally broad declines in high blood pressure and high cholesterol. "These facts are hard to reconcile," they wrote.

It may be, Gregg suggests, that better diagnosis and treatment of high cholesterol and blood pressure have more than compensated for any increases from rising obesity. It could also be, he adds, that obese people are getting more exercise than they used to; regular physical activity is thought to be a powerful preventative against heart disease.

Oliver and Campos explore another possibility: that fatness is partially—or even merely—a visible marker of other factors that are more important but harder to perceive. Diet composition, physical fitness, stress levels, income, family history and the location of fat within the body are just a few of 100-odd "independent" risk factors for cardiovascular disease identified in the medical literature. The observational studies that link obesity to heart disease ignore nearly all of them and in doing so effectively assign their causal roles to obesity. "By the same criteria we are blaming obesity for heart disease," Oliver writes, "we could accuse smelly clothes, yellow teeth or bad breath for lung cancer instead of cigarettes."

As for cancer, a 2003 report on a 16-year study of 900,000 American adults found significantly increased death rates for several kinds of tumors among overweight or mildly obese people. Most of these apparently obesity-related cancers are very rare, however, killing at most a few dozen people a year for every 100,000 study participants. Among women with a high BMI, both colon cancer and postmenopausal breast cancer risks were slightly elevated; for overweight and obese men, colon and prostate cancer presented the most common increased risks. For both women and men, though, being overweight or obese seemed to confer significant protection against lung cancer, which is by far the most commonly lethal malignancy. That relation held even after the effects of smoking were subtracted.

Obesity's Catch-22

30 It is through type 2 diabetes that obesity seems to pose the biggest threat to public health. Doctors have found biological connections between fat, insulin, and the high blood sugar levels that define the disease. The CDC estimates that 55 percent of adult diabetics are obese, significantly more than the 31 percent prevalence of obesity in the general population. And as obesity has become more common, so, too, has diabetes, suggesting that one may cause the other.

Yet the critics dispute claims that diabetes is soaring (even among children), that obesity is the cause, and that weight loss is the solution. A 2003 analysis by the CDC found that "the prevalence of diabetes, either diagnosed or undiagnosed, and of impaired fasting glucose did not appear to increase substantially during the 1990s," despite the sharp rise in obesity.

"Undiagnosed diabetes" refers to people who have a single positive test for high blood sugar in the CDC surveys. (Two or more positive results are required for a diagnosis of diabetes.) Gregg's paper in April reiterates the off-repeated "fact" that for every five adults diagnosed with diabetes, there are three more diabetics who are undiagnosed. "Suspected diabetes" would be a better term, however, because the single test used by the CDC may be wildly unreliable.

In 2001 a French study of 5,400 men reported that 42 percent of the men who tested positive for diabetes using the CDC method turned out to be nondiabetic when checked by a "gold standard" test 30 months later. The false negative rate—true diabetics missed by the single blood test—was just 2 percent.

But consider the growing weights of children, Hill urges. "You're getting kids at 10 to 12 years of age developing type 2 diabetes. Two generations ago you never saw a kid with it."

35 Anecdotal evidence often misleads, Campos responds. He notes that when CDC researchers examined 2,867 adolescents in

the [National Health and Nutrition Examination survey] NHANES survey of 1988 to 1994, they identified just four that had type 2 diabetes. A more focused study in 2003 looked at 710 "grossly obese" boys and girls ages six to 18 in Italy. These kids were the heaviest of the heavy, and more than half had a family history (and thus an inherited risk) of diabetes. Yet only one of the 710 had type 2 diabetes.

Nevertheless, as many as 4 percent of U.S. adults might have diabetes because of their obesity—if fat is in fact the most important cause of the disease. "But it may be that type 2 diabetes causes fatness," Campos argues. (Weight gain is a common side effect of many diabetes drugs.) "A third factor could cause both type 2 diabetes and fatness." Or it could be some complex combination of all these, he speculates.

Large, long-term experiments are the best way to test causality, because they can alter just one variable (such as weight) while holding constant other factors that could confound the results. Obesity researchers have conducted few of these so-called randomized, controlled trials. "We don't know what happens when you turn fat people into thin people," Campos says. "That is not some oversight; there is no known way to do it"—except surgeries that carry serious risks and side effects.

"About 75 percent of American adults are trying to lose or maintain weight at any given time," reports Ali H. Mokdad, chief of the CDC's behavioral surveillance branch. A report in February by Marketdata Enterprises estimated that in 2004, 71 million Americans were actively dieting and that the nation spent about $46 billion on weight-loss products and services.

Dieting has been rampant for many years, and bariatric surgeries have soared in number from 36,700 in 2000 to roughly 140,000 in 2004, according to Marketdata. Yet when Flegal and others examined the CDC's most recent follow-up survey in search of obese se-

*H. L. Mencken (1880–1956) was a respected critic and editor who was especially influential in the early twentieth century.

nior citizens who had dropped into a lower weight category, they found that just 6 percent of nonobese, older adults had been obese a decade earlier.

40 Campos argues that for many people, dieting is not merely ineffective but downright counterproductive. A large study of nurses by Harvard Medical School doctors reported last year that 39 percent of the women had dropped weight only to regain it; those women later grew to be 10 pounds heavier on average than women who did not lose weight.

Weight-loss advocates point to two trials that in 2001 showed a 58 percent reduction in the incidence of type 2 diabetes among people at high risk who ate better and exercised more. Participants lost little weight: an average of 2.7 kilograms after two years in one trial, 5.6 kilograms after three years in the other.

"People often say that these trials proved that weight loss prevents diabetes. They did no such thing," comments Steven N. Blair, an obesity researcher who heads the Cooper Institute in Dallas. Because the trials had no comparison group that simply ate a balanced diet and exercised without losing weight, they cannot rule out the possibility that the small drop in subjects' weights was simply a side effect. Indeed, one of the trial groups published a follow-up study in January that concluded that "at least 2.5 hours per week of walking for exercise during follow-up seemed to decrease the risk of diabetes by 63 to 69 percent, largely independent of dietary factors and BMI."

"H. L. Mencken* once said that for every complex problem there is a simple solution—and it's wrong," Blair muses. "We have got to stop shouting from the rooftops that obesity is bad for you and that fat people are evil and weak-willed and that the world would be lovely if we all lost weight. We need to take a much more comprehensive view. But I don't see much evidence that that is happening."

Questions for Discussion

1. Consider the questions with which Gibbs opens his argument. What is the advantage of opening with a question—and, in this case, defying "conventional wisdom"?

2. Gibbs emphasizes that research challenging the danger of obesity is coming from "outside the medical community." How does this information affect the credibility of his argument?

3. In paragraph 5, Gibbs uses the expression "blowing hot air" when referring to experts who raise concerns about obesity. Is this language appropriate for his audience and purpose?

4. How much evidence does Gibbs supply to support the claim he reports, in paragraph 6, that many researchers are "directly funded by the weight loss industry"?

5. What can contribute to obesity besides diet?

6. Is there any reason to believe that research emphasizing the dangers of obesity may be flawed because it misattributes causation?

7. If it is true, as claimed in paragraph 14, that "improvements in medical care have reduced the mortality level associated with obesity," could there be other costs to both obese people and society as a whole?

8. Based on the evidence provided by Gibbs, how convinced are you that concerns about the health risks of obesity have been exaggerated?

④ **JEFFREY P. KOPLAN, CATHARYN T. LIVERMAN, AND VIVICA I. KRAAK, "Preventing Childhood Obesity"**

The following article originally appeared in *Issues in Science and Technology* (Spring 2005), a journal designed to help experts communicate with a broad audience. According to its website, the journal's mission is "idealistic but vital: to improve the effectiveness of public and private policy in making a better world and to raise the level of debate and mutual respect among all those who appreciate the critical contributions of science and technology." The team of authors who collaborated on "Preventing Childhood Obesity" has distinguished credentials. Formerly director of the Centers for Disease Control and Prevention and a U.S. assistant surgeon general, Jeffrey Koplan teaches medicine at Yale University. The author of more than 190 scientific papers and a Master of the American College of Physicians, he has received many awards from national and international organizations. In addition to his medical degree, he holds a master's degree in public health from Harvard University. Catharyn Liverman is a senior program officer at the Institute of Medicine, a division of the National Academy of Sciences, which advises the government on scientific and technological issues. A graduate of Wake Forest University and the University of Maryland, she specializes in medical library science and formerly worked at the Naval War College Library. Vivica Kraak is a registered dietician and a program officer at the Institute of Medicine.

Preventing Childhood Obesity

JEFFREY P. KOPLAN, CATHARYN T. LIVERMAN, AND VIVICA I. KRAAK

1   After improving dramatically during the past century, the health of children and youth in the United States now faces a dangerous setback: an epidemic of obesity. It is occurring in boys and girls in every state, in younger children and adolescents, across all socioeconomic strata, and among all ethnic groups. Traditionally, most people have considered weight to be a personal statistic, of concern only to themselves or, on occasion, to their physicians. Both science and statistics, however, argue that this view must change. As researchers learn even more about the health risks of obesity, the rise in the prevalence of obesity in children—and in adults as well—is increasingly becoming a major concern to society at large and hence a public health problem demanding national attention.

Since the 1970s, when the epidemic began to take hold, the prevalence of obesity has nearly tripled for children aged 6 to 11 years (from 4 percent to 15.3 percent), and it has more than doubled for youth aged 12 to 19 years (from 6.1 percent to 15.5 percent) and for children aged 2 to 5 years (from 5 percent to 10.4 percent). Although no demographic group is untouched, some subgroups have been affected more than others. Children in certain minority ethnic populations (including African Americans, American Indians, and Hispanics), children in low-income families, and children in the country's southern region tend to have higher rates of obesity than the rest of the population.

Today, more than 9 million children over age 6 are considered obese, which means that they face serious immediate and long-term health risks. They are at increased risk as they grow older of a number of diseases, including type 2 diabetes, cardiovascular disease, hypertension, osteoarthritis, and cancer. By being obese in a society that stigmatizes this condition, they also may develop severe psychosocial burdens, such as shame, self-blame, and low self-esteem, that may impair academic and social functioning and carry into adulthood.

Pared to its core, the solution is simple: Preventing obesity will require ensuring that children maintain a proper energy balance. This means that each child will consume enough of the right kinds of food and beverages and get enough physical activity to maintain a healthy weight while supporting normal growth and development and protecting overall health. Although this "energy intake = energy expenditure" equation may appear fairly simple, in reality it is extraordinarily complex. At work are a multitude of factors—genetic, biological, psychological, sociocultural, and environmental—acting independently and in concert.

5 Thus, combating the epidemic will be challenging. But there is precedent for success in other public health endeavors of comparable complexity and scope. Major gains have been made, for example, in reducing tobacco use, including preventing youth from smoking, and in improving automobile safety, including promoting the use of car seats and seatbelts to protect young passengers. Some lessons can be drawn from these efforts, past and current, and many new ideas and approaches will be needed to meet conditions specific to the task at hand. One overarching principle is clear: Preventing childhood obesity on a national scale will require a comprehensive approach that is based soundly on science and involves government, industry, communities, schools, and families.

Such an approach is detailed in *Preventing Childhood Obesity: Health in the Balance,* issued by the Institute of Medicine in September 2004. The report examines the various factors that promote childhood obesity, identifies promising methods for prevention, describes continuing research needs, and assigns responsibilities for action across a broad sweep of society. Its recommendations, when implemented together, will help keep the vast majority of the nation's children physically active and healthy. Some highlights of the report are offered in the following sections.

Strengthening Political Muscle

As many other public health programs have demonstrated, catalyzing national action to prevent childhood obesity will require the full commitment of government at all levels. The federal government should take the lead by declaring this a top public health priority and dedicating sufficient funding and resources to support policies and programs that are commensurate to the scale of the problem. The government also should ensure that prevention efforts are coordinated across all departments and agencies, as well as with state and local governments and various segments of the private sector.

Toward this end, the president should request the Department of Health and Human Services (DHHS) to convene a high-level task force (including the secretaries or senior officials of all departments and agencies whose work relates in any way to childhood obesity) to be responsible for establishing priorities and promoting effective collaborations. In order to foster full and free communication, the task force should meet regularly with local and state officials; representatives from nongovernmental organizations, including civic groups, youth groups, advocacy groups, and foundations; and representatives from industry.

In addition to providing broad leadership, the federal government should take a variety of specific steps. For example, funding should be increased for surveillance and monitoring systems that gather information needed for tracking the spread of childhood obesity and for designing, conducting, and evaluating prevention programs. In particular, the National Health and Nutrition Examination Survey, which for years has been used to monitor the population through home interviews and health examinations, should be strengthened, with more attention being paid to collecting and analyzing data that will inform prevention efforts. Special efforts should be made through this and other surveillance systems to better identify and monitor the populations most at risk of childhood obesity, as well as the social, behavioral, and environmental factors contributing to that elevated risk.

10 Among other steps, the government should increase support for public and private programs that educate children, youth, and their families about the importance of good nutrition and regular physical activity. Similarly, federal nutrition assistance programs, including the Department of Agriculture's (USDA's) Food Stamp Program and the Special Supplemental Nutrition Program for Women, Infants, and Children,* should be expanded to include obesity prevention as an explicit goal. Congress should request independent assessments of these assistance programs to ensure that each provides adequate access to healthful dietary choices for the populations served. In addition, pilot studies should be expanded within these programs to identify new ways to promote a healthful diet and regular physical activity behaviors. Ideas include using special vouchers or coupons for purchasing fruits, vegetables, and whole-grain baked goods; sponsoring discount promotions; and making it possible to use electronic benefit transfer cards at farmers' markets or community-supported agricultural markets. Test programs that prove successful should be scaled up as quickly as possible.

*According to the USDA, "The Special Supplemental Nutrition Program for Women, Infants, and Children—better known as the WIC Program—serves to safeguard the health of low-income women, infants, & children up to age 5 who are at nutritional risk by providing nutritious foods to supplement diets, information on healthy eating, and referrals to health care."

Congress also should call for an independent assessment of federal agricultural policies, including subsidies and commodity programs that may affect the types and quantities of foods available to children through food assistance programs. For example, concern has been expressed about whether the increasing amounts of caloric sweeteners (primarily derived from sugarcane, beets, and corn) that people are consuming are contributing to the obesity epidemic, and whether subsidies for these crops are promoting the production of inexpensive caloric sweeteners. These possible relationships warrant further investigation. If problems are confirmed in this or other cases, then the government should revise its policies and programs to promote a U.S. food system that supports energy balance at a healthy weight.

For their part, state and local governments should join in, making the prevention of childhood obesity a priority by providing the leadership—and resources—needed to launch and evaluate a slate of programs and activities that promote physical activity and healthful eating in communities, neighborhoods, and schools. One important step, for example, will be for governments to strengthen their public health agencies. As the front line of the public health system, these agencies are ideally positioned to assess the childhood obesity epidemic; to identify local conditions that are fueling it; and then to develop, implement, and evaluate prevention programs. In order to perform most effectively, however, many agencies will need restructuring to make them better able to work collaboratively with diverse community partners. Such partners can include schools, childcare centers, nutrition services, civic and ethnic organizations, faith-based groups, businesses, and community planning boards.

Harnessing the Market

Children, youth, and their families are surrounded by a commercial environment that strongly influences their purchasing and consumption behaviors as well as the choices they make in how to spend their leisure time. Thus, a variety of industries (including the food, beverage, restaurant, entertainment, leisure, and recreation industries) must share responsibility for preventing childhood obesity. Government can help strengthen industry efforts by providing technical assistance, research expertise, and, as necessary, targeted support and regulatory guidance.

As a general goal, industries should develop and promote products, opportunities, and information that will encourage healthful eating behaviors and regular physical activity. In order to improve the "expenditure" side of the energy balance equation, the leisure, entertainment, and recreation industries should step up efforts to promote active leisure-time pursuits and to develop new products and markets. Such efforts can help to reverse the recent trend that has seen people spending more time in passive sedentary pursuits and less in active leisure activities. Some companies already are setting the pace, apparently convinced that fostering physical activity will help to create significant markets for their products. For example, Nike, a manufacturer of athletic apparel, provides funding to build or refurbish sports courts and other public athletic facilities nationwide and supports physical education classes in elementary schools, among other projects. More projects of this kind are needed.

15 In order to improve the "intake" side of the equation, the food and beverage industries should put more effort into developing products that have low energy densities and are appealing to consumers. Foods with low energy densities, such as fruits and vegetables, promote safety and reduce total caloric intake, but they sometimes meet resistance in the marketplace, especially among people who have become used to foods of higher energy densities. Manufacturers, perhaps motivated by some form of government incentive, should continue to push for healthful new products that are more appealing to a range of people. They also should speed up modify-

CONTEXT

Nike programs include NikeGO Afterschool, which brings physical activity programs to after-school programs such as Boys and Girls Clubs; NikeGO Head Start, a physical education program for students in Head Start programs, along with their families; and NikePE2GO, which provides training and equipment to teachers in schools where physical education has been severely cut. Nike has this to say about physical activity and children: "As a sports and fitness company, we know first-hand the value that daily physical activity can offer—both to kids and adults. And we recognize that through the power of our brand, we are in an excellent position to help tackle this issue. But we realize that as passionate as we are about getting kids active, we simply can't do this alone. That is why we created a long-term, multi-stakeholder initiative to address youth inactivity called NikeGO. We have partnered with organizations whose expertise brings greater impact to the programs we build for inactive kids and the parents, teachers and coaches who influence their behavior. . . . These programs often target underserved kids in our largest cities, including Los Angeles, Chicago [and] New York, and are particularly focused on youth at higher risk for overweight and inactive lifestyles. All NikeGO programs are designed to teach kids about healthy lifestyles and the joy of physical activity."

ing existing products—for example, by replacing fat with protein, fruit or vegetable puree, fiber, or even air—to reduce energy density but maintain palatability without substantially reducing product size. As another line of attack, manufacturers should develop new forms of product packaging that would help consumers choose smaller, standard serving sizes without reducing product profitability.

Full-service and fast-food restaurants have important roles to play as well, given that people are consuming an increasing share of their meals and snacks outside of the home. Among a range of steps they should take, restaurants should continue to expand their healthier meal options by offering more fruits, vegetables, low-fat milk, and calorie-free beverages, and they should mount information campaigns to provide consumers at the point of purchase with easily understandable nutrition information about all of their products. The industry also should explore price incentives that encourage consumers to order smaller meal portions.

Industry also should make better use of nutrition labeling, which has been mandatory since 1990, to provide parents and youth with clear and useful information that will enable them to compare products and make informed food choices. Here, government can help. The Food and Drug Administration (FDA) should modify the nutrition facts panels—the familiar information charts printed on food products—to more prominently display the calorie content of a standardized serving size and the percent daily value (the percent of nutrients contained in a single serving, based on a 2,000-calorie-per-day diet) of key nutrients. But in many instances, people consume all at once quantities that are much larger than a standardized serving size. This is often the case for vending-machine items, single-serving snack foods, and ready-to-eat foods purchased at convenience stores. Such consumers are left on their own to calculate the nutritional content of their purchases. To help them out, the FDA should mandate that manufacturers prominently add the total calorie content to the nutrition facts panels on products typically consumed at one eating occasion.

Of course, any consideration of industry's impact on the choices that families and children make about eating and engaging in physical activities cannot overlook the role of advertising. Together, these industries are the second-largest advertising group in the U.S. economy, after the automotive industry, and young people are a major target. Current evidence suggests that the quantity and nature of advertisements to which children are exposed daily, reinforced through multiple media channels, appear to contribute to choices that can adversely affect their energy balance. Thus, industry has an important responsibility and opportunity to help foster healthier choices.

As a catalyst, DHHS should convene a national conference, bringing together representatives from industry, public health organizations, and consumer advocacy groups, to develop guidelines for the advertising and marketing of foods, beverages, and sedentary entertainment directed at children and youth. The guidelines would cover advertising content, promotion, and placement. They should pay particular attention to protecting children under the age of 8, as they are especially susceptible to the persuasive intent of advertising. Industry would then be responsible, on a voluntary basis, for implementing the guidelines. However, the Federal Trade Commission should be given the authority and resources to monitor compliance and to propose more stringent regulations if industry fails in its actions.

Building Healthy Communities

20 Many factors in the community setting affect the overall health and fitness of children and youth. Writ large, a community can be a town, city, or other type of geographic entity where people share common institutions and, usually, a local government. In turn, each of these communities contains many interdependent smaller networks of residential communities, faith-based communities, work communities, and social communities. Thus, there is a host of leverage points at which communities can help foster social norms that promote attitudes and behaviors that will help

their young members maintain a healthy weight.

In one approach, community groups—or, ideally, community coalitions—should expand current programs and establish new ones that widen children's opportunities to be physically active and maintain a balanced diet. Many youth organizations, such as Boys and Girls Clubs, Girl Scouts, Boy Scouts, and 4H, already have a number of programs under way that illustrate the gains possible. In one Girl Scout program, for example, girls who participated with their troops in nutrition classes, which included tasting sessions and sending foods home, were found to consume more fruits and vegetables on a regular basis. Youth groups also can help get more kids involved in physical activity by pursuing innovative approaches that reach beyond traditional competitive sports. These sports are not of interest to everyone, so it will be important for communities to expand their range of offering to include noncompetitive team and individual sports as well as other types of physical activities, such as dance and martial arts. To ensure equal access to physical activity programs, communities should help families overcome potential obstacles by providing transportation, paying fees, or providing special equipment.

Communities also should take a hard look at their built environments and expand the opportunities for children to be physically active outside, especially in their neighborhoods. Creating places to walk, bike, and play will require not only providing adequate space but also reducing risks from traffic or crime. Local governments, private developers, and community groups should work collaboratively to develop more parks, playgrounds, recreational facilities, sidewalks, and bike paths. It will be especially important for communities to ensure that children and youth have safe walking and bicycling routes between their homes and schools and that they are encouraged to use them. Making such improvements often will require local governments to revise their development plans, zoning and subdivision

ordinances, and other planning practices, and to prioritize the projects in their capital improvement programs.

Similarly, communities should expand efforts to provide their residents with access to healthful foods within walking distance, particularly in low-income and underserved neighborhoods. Some promising approaches include offering government financial incentives, such as grants, loans, and tax benefits, to stimulate the development of neighborhood grocery stores; developing community and school gardens; establishing farmers' markets; and supporting farm-to-school and farm-to-cafeteria programs.

It is within local communities, of course, where most health care is provided, and health care professionals have an influential role to play in preventing childhood obesity. As advisors to children and their parents, they have the access and influence to make key suggestions and recommendations on dietary intake and physical activity throughout children's lives. They also have the authority to elevate concern about childhood obesity and advocate preventive efforts. By conducting workshops at schools, testifying before legislative bodies, working in local organizations, or speaking out in any number of other ways, health care professionals can press for changes within their communities that support and facilitate healthful eating and physical activity.

25 In their everyday practices, health care professionals (pediatricians, family physicians, nurses, and other clinicians) should routinely measure the height and weight of their patients and track their body mass indices (BMIs). They then should carefully communicate the results to the children themselves, in an age-appropriate manner, and to their parents or other caregivers; provide information that the families need to make informed decisions about nutrition and physical activity; and explain the risks associated with childhood overweight and obesity.

In order to make sure that health care professionals are well prepared to provide quality services, medical and nursing schools should incorporate training with regard to nutrition, physical activity, and counseling on obesity prevention into their curricula. Training should happen at all levels, from pre-clinical science through the clinical training years and into postgraduate training programs and continuing medical education programs for practicing clinicians. Health care professional organizations also should make obesity prevention a high priority. Actions they should take to back up their commitment include creating and disseminating programs to encourage their members to be role models for proper nutrition and physical activity. In addition, accrediting organizations should add obesity prevention skills, such as tracking BMIs and providing needed counseling, to the measures they routinely assess.

Health insurers and group health plans can make valuable contributions as well. Indeed, the high economic costs of obesity provide them with major incentives to encourage healthful lifestyles. Creative options may include providing member families with incentives to participate in regular physical activity, perhaps by offering discounted fees for joining health clubs or participating in other exercise programs. It will be particularly important for insurers and health plans to consider incentives that are useful to high-risk populations, who often live in areas where easy access to recreational facilities is lacking or costs are prohibitive.

Lessons for Schools
Given that schools are one of the primary locations for reaching children and youth, it is critically important that the total school environment—cafeteria, playground, classrooms, and gymnasium—be structured to promote healthful eating and physical activity. Needs abound.

Schools, school districts, and state educational agencies should ensure that all meals served in schools comply with the DHHS and USDA's Dietary Guidelines for Americans, which recommend that no more than 30 percent of an individual's calories come from fat and less than 10 percent from saturated fat. Further, USDA should conduct pilot studies to evaluate the costs and benefits of providing full funding for breakfasts, lunches, and snacks in schools with a large percentage of children at high risk of obesity.

30 Increasingly, students are getting more of their foods and beverages outside of traditional meal programs. Many of these "competitive" foods, which are sold in cafeterias, vending machines, school stores, and fundraisers, or provided as snacks in classrooms and after-school programs, are high in calories and low in nutritional value. Current federal standards for such items are minimal. USDA, with independent scientific advice, should establish nutritional standards for all food and beverage items served or sold in schools. In turn, state education agencies and local school boards should adopt these standards or develop stricter standards for their schools. Enforcing such schoolwide standards not only will pro-

mote student health but help establish a broader social norm for healthful eating behaviors.

Schools also need to reinvigorate their commitments to providing students with opportunities to be physically active. Many schools have cut physical education classes or shrunk recess times, often as a result of budget cuts or pressures to increase academic offerings. Students are paying the price. Schools should ensure that all children and youth participate in at least 30 minutes of moderate to vigorous physical activity during the school day. This goal is equally important for young children in child development centers and other preschool and child-care settings. Congress, state legislatures and education agencies, local governments, school boards, and parents should hold schools responsible for providing students with recommended amounts of physical activity. Concurrently, they should ensure that schools have the resources needed to do the job properly.

Among the actions that schools can take to get students more active, they should provide physical education classes of 30 minutes to an hour on a daily basis, and they should examine ways to incorporate into these classes innovative activities that will appeal to the broad range of student interests. Elementary schools, middle schools, and child development centers should provide equal amounts of recess. Schools also should offer a broad array of after-class activity programs, such as intramural and interscholastic sports, clubs, and lessons that will interest all students. In addition, schools should be encouraged to extend the school day as a means of providing expanded instructional and extracurricular physical activity programs.

Schools offer many other opportunities as well to help students avoid developing weight problems. They should ensure that nutrition, physical activity, and wellness concepts are taught throughout the curriculum from kindergarten through high school, and they should incorporate into health classes evidence-based programs that teach behavioral skills that students can use to make better choices about foods and physical activity. Federal and state departments of education, along with education and health professional organizations, can support this effort. These organizations should develop, implement, and evaluate pilot programs that use innovative approaches for teaching about wellness, nutrition, physical activity, and making choices that promote wellness, as well as for recruiting and training teachers to meet expanding needs.

Health clinics and other school-based health services also can play a prominent role in prevention efforts. In particular, they should measure yearly each student's weight, height, and gender- and age-specific BMI percentile and make this information available to parents and to the student (when age-appropriate). It will be important that such data be collected and reported validly and appropriately, with the utmost attention to privacy concerns. The Centers for Disease Control and Prevention can help in this regard by developing guidelines that schools can follow in gathering information and communicating the results.

Family Matters

35 Parents, defined broadly to include primary caregivers, have a profound influence on their children by fostering values and attitudes, by rewarding or reinforcing specific behaviors, and by serving as role models. The family is a logical target for interventions designed to prevent childhood obesity. This focus is made even more important by changes in society in recent decades that are adding pressures on parents and children that can adversely affect choices about food and physical activity. For example, with the frequent need for both parents to work long hours, it has become more difficult for many parents to play with or monitor their children and to prepare home-cooked meals for them.

Along with challenges, however, come opportunities and responsibilities. In order to promote healthful food choices, parents should make available in the home foods such as fruits and vegetables that are nutritious and have low energy densities and should limit purchases of items characterized by high calorie content and low nutritional value. Parents also should assist and educate their children in making good decisions regarding types of foods and beverages to consume, how often, and in what portion size. Similarly, parents should encourage their children to play outdoors and to participate in other forms of regular physical activity. By the same token, they should discourage their children from participating excessively in sedentary pursuits by, for example, limiting television viewing and other recreational screen time, such as playing video games, to less than two hours per day.

Among other actions, parents should consider the weight of their children to be a critically important indicator of health. Just as vaccination schedules require parental intervention during childhood, parents should be discussing the prevention of obesity with their health care providers to make sure that their child is on a healthy growth track. In practice, parents should have a trained health professional regularly (at least once a year) measure their child's height and weight in order to track his or her BMI percentile. School health programs may be of critical help here, because many families lack insurance for preventive health services and cannot afford regular health screening. Underlying all of these efforts, parents should try their best to serve as positive role models by practicing what they are preaching.

Moving Ahead

The epidemic of childhood obesity, long overlooked, now looms as a major threat to the nation's health. Many stakeholders, public and private, are starting to take action to help slow and ultimately reverse its course. *Preventing Childhood Obesity* reviews progress and outlines a way to move forward in what must be viewed as a collective responsibility and an energetic and sustained effort. Some of the steps can be implemented immediately and will cost little. Others will cost more and will require a longer time for implementation and to see the benefits of the investment. Some actions will prove useful, either quickly or over the longer term, whereas others are likely to prove unsuccessful.

But the nation cannot wait to design a "perfect" prevention program in which every intervention has been scientifically tested ahead of time to guarantee success. Wide-ranging intervention programs are needed now, based on the best available evidence. At the same time, research must continue to refine efforts. Briefly, research is needed to evaluate the effectiveness, including the cost-effectiveness, of prevention programs; to better understand the fundamental factors involved in changing personal dietary behaviors, physical activity levels, and sedentary behaviors; and to explore the range of population-level factors that drive changes in the health of communities and other large groups of people.

40 Thus, the path ahead will involve surveillance, trial, measurement error, success, alteration, and dissemination of the knowledge and practices that prove successful. The key is to move ahead, starting immediately, on every front. As institutions, organizations, and individuals across the nation begin to make changes, social norms are also likely to change, so that obesity in children and youth will be acknowledged as an important and preventable health outcome, and healthful eating and regular physical activity will be the accepted and encouraged standard. Given that at stake is the health of today's children and youth, as well as the health of future generations, the nation must proceed with all due urgency and vigor.

Questions for Discussion

1. Have the authors of this argument convinced you that childhood obesity is an "epidemic"—as they claim in their opening sentence?

2. After claiming that obesity occurs across "all socioeconomic strata, and among all ethnic groups" in paragraph 1, the authors then identify ethnic and economic groups that are affected more than others. Why do you think some children are at greater risk than others?

3. Why do the authors believe that the federal government must be actively involved in the fight against obesity? Do you agree that this is an appropriate responsibility for the government?

4. Why do you think people are consuming increasing numbers of meals outside the home, and why do these meals contribute to obesity?

5. When discussing the role of communities in ensuring healthy lifestyles, the authors recommend easy access to walking and biking paths, as well as parks and playgrounds. How accessible are such facilities in the community where you now live? If they are available, do you take advantage of them? If they are not available, what do you think has kept them from being developed?

6. How healthy were the meals served when you were in secondary school? How healthy are the dining options at the school you currently attend?

7. How adequate was the physical education program at schools you have attended?

8. The authors of this argument indicate early on that the "solution" to the problem that concerns them is "extraordinarily complex." By the time they have concluded, they have called for numerous changes. In your opinion, does this approach effectively demonstrate that the problem must be addressed by multiple efforts, or are you left with so many recommendations that you have difficulty prioritizing them?

DIFFERENCES

NEGOTIATING

As the authors in this cluster point out, we live in a culture in which it is easy to become obese. They may differ in what they emphasize as the cause of obesity or how serious this condition is, but no one questions the fact that many Americans are overweight and at risk of becoming obese—and that children are especially at risk.

Now imagine the following situation: You are the parent of a twelve-year-old girl who is seriously overweight. She was pudgy as a child and never lost what you once called "baby fat." You love her deeply and have never wanted her to become self-conscious about her appearance or turn into a kind of Barbie doll. Without nagging her about her weight, you have encouraged her to have a healthy diet by serving low-fat meals with plenty of vegetables and reserved desert for special occasions. You have also encouraged her to be physically active by teaching her how to play volleyball and soccer. She's willing to play volleyball at family reunions, but she was not able to sustain an interest in soccer. And within the last few years, she has begun to gorge on sweets.

There is a limit to how much you can control her diet. Some foods served for lunch at her school—such as French fries—are fattening. She is entitled to an allowance because she needs some spending money and earns it by doing chores around the house. But that money can easily be turned into candy money, because there are vending machines at her school and a convenience store a block from where the bus drops her off. You know that she is consuming large quantities of candy in the privacy of her room because you discover the wrappings in the trash. You also know that she loves to go to McDonald's and may be doing so on her own between meals. During the past year, she has gained thirty pounds. She is being teased at school, and she responds to this teasing by eating even more of her comfort foods.

You believe that your daughter now faces the risk of both emotional and physical harm. Offering broccoli and controlling portion size at home is not going to solve the problem. You need to intervene but to do so in a way that will make you seem like an ally rather than an opponent.

With this situation in mind, write the argument that would motivate this girl to lose some weight without causing her to think that she is unloved or that she must abandon food that gives her pleasure.

When Does Being "Fit" Become "Unfit"?

Responding to various social and cultural pressures, increasing numbers of people have become concerned with watching what they eat and exercising as a way of being physically fit. For some people, this process comes naturally. When they are young, they acquire healthy eating habits and an interest in sports that keep them active in their spare time. For others, however, healthy habits must be acquired with some difficulty because of a history of eating fatty foods and a preference for watching television rather than biking or running daily. The impulse to become more physically fit may be generated by the simple desire to be healthier—a desire stimulated by a visit to a doctor or a frank conversation with a mate. This impulse can also be triggered by the desire to find or retain a mate—the focus of two of the clusters in Chapter 10. Although people may know that inner beauty and strength of character are more important than outward appearance, how they appear can make a big difference in terms of whether or not they are considered attractive. And, unfortunately, whether or not people are considered attractive sometimes limits how well others get to know their inner strengths. So the desire to be fit is closely associated with the desire to be attractive, and what kind of "fitness" is attractive may be changing. Authors in this cluster explore how men are using steroids to build muscle, how men and women disagree about how much muscle is attractive, and how women have taken up weight lifting—an activity traditionally associated with men but one that can be seen as a natural extension from working out in a gym. The first reading in the cluster describes a condition in which the desire to eat only healthy foods can become an obsession bordering on a disorder. None of the authors included here question the value of being fit. But they do question the extent to which some people focus on fitness—in some cases developing emotional and physical problems as they pursue perfection. In short, this cluster invites you to consider when behavior that should be healthy degenerates into the unhealthy because an obsession with taking control of one's own body leads to behavior that is out of control.

① HEATHER BERESFORD "I Was an Idiot to Take It So Far"

There is a cliché in English about "having too much of a good thing." Could it apply to the effort to eat a healthy diet? Could something normally considered virtuous become a problem when carried to excess? In the following article, which was first published in the London *Times* in September 2003, Heather Beresford argues that this can be the case. In it, Beresford reports on an obsession that experts are not ready to call an eating disorder but nevertheless raises cause for concern—an obsession in which people may be putting their overall health at risk because of their determination to avoid consuming anything that could be considered unhealthy. The *Times* is widely considered the best newspaper in Great Britain and one of the best in the world. Beresford writes regularly about health-related issues.

I Was an Idiot to Take It So Far

HEATHER BERESFORD

1   Tuck in to a full English fry-up with a double helping of black pudding and you know it's bad for you. But surely an organic wheat-free, fat-free, sugar-free muffin, washed down with a soya milk, decaf, GM-free* latte is a passport to living to 106?

Certainly, a growing number of super-health-conscious people in the UK seem to think so, as they nibble through life on increasingly abstemious and restricted diets in a quest to achieve optimum health and ward off illness.

A balanced healthy diet is clearly a good thing, but many experts believe that widespread obsession with the nutritional quality of food—be it unprocessed, organically grown, GM-free or linked into a diet to reduce allergies—is a growing problem in our information-rich society. Many nutritionists are reporting a marked increase in the number of patients coming to them with a virtual phobia of unhealthy foods.

The repercussions are potentially dire. Not only can a desire to eat the perfect healthy diet become such an overwhelming obsession that people make themselves ill with worry. But cutting out "harmful" food, such as meat or dairy, often leads to a lack of crucial nutrients, putting children at risk of poor growth and the entire family at risk of a debilitating illness, such as osteoporosis. In the most extreme cases, the obsession can trigger an eating disorder.

5   The problem has become very widespread and the condition has now been dubbed "orthorexia nervosa"† by worried nutritionists.

Dr Steven Bratman, co-author of *Health Food Junkies—Orthorexia Nervosa: Overcoming the Obsession with Healthful Eating,* describes obsessive healthy eating as "a disease disguised as a virtue." He says: "For many people eating 'correctly' has become a harmful obsession—one that causes them to adopt progressively rigid diets that not only eliminate crucial nutrients and food groups, but ultimately cost them their overall health, personal relationships and emotional wellbeing."

Steve Bloomfield, from the Eating Disorders Association, agrees: "Something that starts as

*GM-free means to be without genetic modification.

†Similar to anorexia nervosa in that sufferers follow strict rules and are bombarded with guilt when those rules are not followed, *orthorexia nervosa* focuses on the quality rather than the quantity of food. The term, coined by Dr. Steven Bratman in 1997, comes from the Greek *orthos* and *orexis,* the former meaning "right and correct" and the latter meaning "appetite."

TELL-TALE SIGNS OF OBSESSION

1. You ring the host before a dinner party with anxious questions about ingredients.
2. You dread eating at restaurants—the food could come from anywhere.
3. Fellow diners lose the will to live while you subject the waiter to a prolonged briefing on your must-have specialist ingredients.
4. When eating out, you sometimes take your own food.
5. There are more "must not eat" foods than "must eats" in your diet.
6. Your supplements bill is bigger than your food bill.
7. You feel scared about certain foods.
8. You care more about the virtue of what you are eating than the pleasure you get from eating it.
9. As the quality of your diet has "improved," the quality of your life has diminished.
10. You keep getting stricter with yourself.
11. You feel a greater sense of self-esteem when you eat healthy food and immensely superior to anyone who you see wolfing down chips.
12. You feel guilt or self-loathing when you stray from your diet.

a desire to eat well can grow into a full-blown eating disorder where sufferers show all the same obsessive-compulsive characteristics as people suffering from bulimia or anorexia nervosa."

Many people also become their own doctor, believing they can treat their health problems through diet. They read a generic article about food allergies, watch half a documentary and perhaps see an alternative therapist. On the basis of this largely unreliable diagnosis they decide which foods they are allergic to, and never touch them again. Wheat, dairy, white processed food, soya, fish/shellfish and eggs are usually the first to be eliminated.

Only 2 percent of the population are allergic to wheat or dairy, yet experts say that a staggering proportion of people think they are, and change their diet accordingly.

10 "The increasing emphasis on eating healthy and organic foods gives people another reason to restrict their diets and more vulnerable people can quickly develop an

obsessive-compulsive tendency to negate groups of foods that are not wholly pure or health enhancing," says Vicki Edgson, a nutritionist and naturopath and co-author of *The Food Doctor: Healing Foods for Mind and Body.* "Most of the people who become obsessive about food are subconsciously concerned about their body image and are using healthy eating as a cover to avoid fattening food."

Few nutritionists are ready to brand our new-found food obsession an eating disorder but most are worried about the trend.

"It's hard for people not to become concerned," says Susie Orbach, author of *Fat is a Feminist Issue,* and *Susie Orbach on Eating.* "Industrial production produces dreadful food and many people live on fairly unhealthy diets. So they read around the subject and take control of the situation by excluding food groups. Imposing a set of limits makes people feel safer."

The problem becomes even more serious when people start restricting their children's diet as well.

"Parents who are uptight and obsessive about food can easily pass this negative relationship on to their children, which can be very harmful," says Orbach. "Not only can it affect their relationship with food for life, but it can seriously damage their long term health."

15 Paul Sacher, specialist dietician at Great Ormond Street Hospital for Children, agrees. "Parents are desperate to prevent their children from becoming obese," he says.

"They are also worried about allergies because they are more common among children now. But it is too easy to start obsessing about feeding the family properly. Many parents eliminate what they perceive to be harmful foods, but don't bother to replace them with alternative sources of nutrients. This can be very harmful for children, putting them at risk of malnutrition, anaemia and even osteoporosis later in life. People must remember that only a small percentage of children are genuinely allergic."

Experts are already predicting an osteoporosis explosion in the UK because children take so little exercise and rarely eat calcium rich foods—a killer combination for the skeleton.

"People also overdose on vitamin supplements, scooping up a whole handful every day and exceeding the recommended dose," says Sacher. "Over time this can build up to toxic levels, which will damage the kidneys and liver."

Not only can eliminating food groups wreak havoc, but the sheer stress involved in eating perfectly healthy food all the time can make people ill, causing anything from gastric upsets and headaches to IBS and inflamed skin conditions. People try to treat their symptoms with a healthier diet, become more stressed when they don't feel better, which in turn causes their symptoms to become even worse—a vicious circle it can be difficult to break.

Questions for Discussion

1. What are the potentially dangerous consequences of becoming obsessed with eating only food that you feel sure is healthy?

2. Can you think of other examples of "a disease disguised as a virtue"?

3. Why is it dangerous to take vitamins at doses above recommended levels?

4. Writing for a British newspaper, Beresford focuses on dietary concerns with the United Kingdom (as Great Britain is sometimes called). Have you seen evidence in the United States of the behavior she describes? If so, to what do you attribute this behavior?

5. How useful is the list which Beresford includes in her article?

② CHRISTOPHER McDOUGALL AND LOU SCHULER, "Buyin' Bulk"

That steroids are widely used in professional sports comes as no surprise today. But how widely are they used by the guy next door—the apparently clean-cut and honest guy who, come to think of it, stays in exceptionally good shape? This question is at the heart of the following article by Christopher McDougall and Lou Schuler. Although McDougall writes regularly about fitness for magazines such as *Esquire, Men's Health,* and *Bicycling*—in addition to contributing to *GQ* and *Men's Journal*—he also served as an overseas correspondent for the Associate Press, covering fighting in Angola and massacres in Rwanda. His work was recognized by a Carion Award in 2002. Schuler often writes about body building. He is the coauthor of *Men's Health: The Book of Muscle, The Testosterone Advantage Plan,* and *Essential Chest and Shoulders.* The following article, which is the result of collaboration between the two writers, first appeared in *Men's Health* in March 2003. *Men's Health* is a monthly magazine designed for men concerned about being and looking fit. It was published with the following subhead: "You think pro athletes are the only ones pumping up their bodies with steroids? Take a closer look at the guy next to you in the gym."

Buyin' Bulk

CHRISTOPHER McDOUGALL AND LOU SCHULER

*According to a report by Tom Farrey on **ESPN.com** "Under Mexican law, steroids, too, are supposed to be sold only with prescription. . . . But those regulations are like red lights in Rome—they routinely are ignored."

1 Unless he changes his mind and makes a U-turn in the next 15 seconds, Bill is about to make the leap from average guy to federal felon.

A 45-year-old southern California sales executive, Bill has nearly a thousand dollars' worth of illegal steroids bolted inside the armrest of his SUV, and only one car to go before the drug-sniffing dogs swarm around him at the Tijuana checkpoint. So does he wheel his vehicle around, dump his stash, and come home the law-abiding guy he was when he left the house this warm summer morning? Or does he risk jail time and rap sheet that could snuff his career and his marriage?

It's worth it, Bill tells himself. He cranks up the air conditioner, eases his foot off the brake pedal, and glides up to the border patrolman and his choke-chained German Shepherd.

"What were you doing in Mexico?" the patrolman asks.

5 "Just buying some presents for my wife," Bill answers, holding up some handicraft jewelry he snuck out of his wife's jewelry box. In fact, after making the drive to Tijuana, Bill bought steroids at a downtown pharmacy,* then removed the four bolts that secure the SUV's center console. He crammed the steroids inside, bolted the console back in place, and put a half-empty soda in the cupholder on top as camouflage.

"Are you carrying any prescription drugs?" the officer asks.

He knows, Bill worries. Why else would a muscular American businessman be making a 1-hour trip to Mexico during a workday?

"No," Bill says.

"Pop your trunk," the officer commands. Bill obliges, then stares straight ahead while the dogs snuffle frantically around his gym bag and spare quart of 40-weight. The officer returns to the driver's side window, and Bill braces himself for the inevitable "Step out of the vehicle."

10 But seconds later, he's on his way, a freshly minted criminal with a grin on his face and just enough time, he realizes as he checks his watch, to make it back to his office before anyone realizes he's gone. By the next morning, he'll be injecting his way to a bigger, better body.

It's no secrete anymore that just about anyone who wrestles in a cage, flexes in a Speedo, or hits a heck of a lot more home runs than he did last year owes his extra power and thigh-size biceps to illegal anabolic steroids. But recently, another group has quietly joined the ranks of the 'roided. They're Wall Street brokers, cops, software developers—regular guys like Bill, in other words—who want to add muscle and melt fat, and don't mind a little chemical help. They're not out to be Smackdown champs or simulated Schwarzeneggers*—they just want to look as good at age 30 or 40 as Mark Wahlberg† did at 20.

"I call them 'politely 'roided,'" says Harrison Pope, M.D., a Harvard Medical School specialist in steroid abuse and author of *The Adonis Complex.* "Steroids used to be the province of a certain small group, the people you'd think of as muscle freaks. That was in the '70s and '80s." Over the past few years, however, the abuse has spread to mainstream men. They're not the kind of guys who are bursting out of triple-X shirts, so they're not so easily identifiable.

Dr. Pope is no envious, whining egghead. He's been a gym rat himself for over 20 years, and it shows: With forearms bulging from his rolled-up sleeves, the 55-year-old doctor looks if he could crank out set of one-handed chinups in the doorway of his office.

He started lifting at age 33 and became so "addicted," he says, that he still slips out of his office nearly every midday for an hour or longer workout session.

15 So Dr. Pope knows what's going on, despite the weight room's mighty code of silence. And he estimates that as many as 1 million to 2 million Americans may have had juice in their veins at some time—a number that would ordinarily place steroid abuse in the epidemic category. But there's no completely reliable data, because juicers have basically been overlooked, says Jack Stein, Ph.D., deputy director of science policy for the National Institute on Drug Abuse (NIDA). "Unlike, say, crack addicts, the men who take steroids are basically healthy, clean-living people," Stein explains. "We've been preoccupied with more immediate threats, like crack and heroin."

Studies are still continuing to verify estimates on adult steroid abusers, but Stein sees no reason to doubt Dr. Pope's numbers. Lax law enforcement, America's growing obsession with overgrown bodies, and the availability of steroids just across the border—and over the Internet—has created the steroid equivalent of a perfect storm. "In some of the gyms I've visited, I've been surprised by the sheer predominances of men on steroids," says Stein, who's also a personal trainer. "People don't see steroids as such a risk anymore."

In fact, some see them as essential to a perfect body. Though health concerns compelled the U.S. government to classify steroids as a controlled substance in 1991, they haven't discouraged many body-conscious men—the very ones who would never smoke, drink, or allow chicken skin to pass their lips—from accepting steroids as little more than souped-up, fat-burning vitamins. "There's a widespread belief that steroids are part of a healthy regimen," confirms Dr. Pope, "like eating well and working out, and that they can be controlled through moderation."

Is it just a gym rat's fantasy, this idea that hormone-jangling drugs can actually be food

*Before becoming an international action movie star and going on to be elected governor of California, Arnold Schwarzenegger was one of the top body builders in the world, winning such titles as Mr. Universe and Mr. Olympia.

†Actor Mark Wahlberg was first thrust into fame by modeling underwear for Calvin Klein and by embarking on a rap career, in which he was known as Marky Mark with a backing band called the Funky Bunch. In the video for the single "Good Vibrations," Wahlberg was seen shirtless and working out.

for you? Not necessarily. There's no question that large doses of steroids can cause any number of nasty side effects—from shrunken testicles to large breasts. What's more, doctors have speculated that steroids may increase your risk of stroke, heart attack, liver disease, and prostate cancer, and lead to the superaggressive behavior known as 'roid rage.

But the truth is, the medical community actually knows very little for certain about the long-term effects of steroid use—no one has done any large scientific studies. This is particularly true of the moderate doses favored by many of today's casual users. And since steroids can be medicinal—doctors use them to treat certain types of anemia and several other conditions—there's a growing belief in America's gyms that little bit of juice may be just what a body needs.

20 "In moderate dosages over the short term, can they be used safely?" asks Charles Yesalis, Sc.D., a Penn State professor of health policy and sports science, and author of *The Steroids Game.* "Probably. Yet, the truth of the matter is that the majority of these performance-enhancing drugs have been cleared for medical use. So, clearly, they can be used safely."

That's not to say the long-term health concerns are false—it just means that no one has bothered to find out whether they're true. Meanwhile, Arnold still strolls the Earth with a stogie in his hand and a smile on his face, a larger-than-life argument for steroids that no government agency has yet come up with the goods to refute.

While baseball's steroid boom has been fueled by the quest for better numbers and bigger contracts, the average-guy juicing trend is less about performance than about looks. Take Bill. He's also a recovering alcoholic, who became serious about bodybuilding 7 years ago, at age 38. (He figured that double sessions in the gym each day would keep his mind off booze.) Six months of intense lifting left his 6-foot, 5-inch frame looking better than it had in years. But one thing frustrated him: "I just

couldn't get any bigger," he says. "Maybe it was an age thing—the body produces less testosterone as you grow older—but I maxed out at 212 pounds and couldn't put on any more muscle."

It didn't take him long to find a solution. He'd never tried steroids before, but he quickly found a huge amount of information on the Internet, which in the past several years has become a vast, if not always reliable, repository for steroid data. Bill wavered for about a year before deciding to try his first "cycle," a period of use (usually injections, pills, or ointments) that typically lasts 6 to 12 weeks, followed by downtime. First, however, he got a thorough physical. "I was pretty up front with my doc, and he was real cool about it," Bill says. "He said as a doctor he couldn't condone it, but he had a lot of patients on steroids. He didn't try to talk me out of it."

Bill's new message-board buddies steered him toward a reliable supplier, a U.S.-based black marketeer who demanded cash in advance but always delivered the drugs, by mail, within a week. Following another tip he'd gotten online, Bill had the package delivered to his doorstep, then "accidentally" kicked it into the shrubs and let it sit there a few days, thinking that would somehow fool the cops if he were being watched.

25 For his first "stack"—a combination of different steroids—Bill decided to go with the basics: two weekly injections to increase muscle mass, a shot of the hormone HCG to keep his testicles from shrinking too much while his body's own testosterone was in chaos, and an oral dose of tamoxifen to help with enlarged breasts ("bitch tits," as they're commonly called). Steroids, after all, are basically synthetic testosterone: Flooding your bloodstream with them can fool the body into thinking it has enough of the real thing, so natural testosterone production shuts down.

Bill had never given an injection before, so at dawn one morning he sneaked out of bed before his wife was awake and practiced jabbing a needle into an orange. When he had the hang of it, he fitted a fresh needle onto the syringe and carefully sucked in 250 milligrams (mg) of Sustanon, a mixture of four different synthetic testosterones and big favorite among juicers, since it's widely available and known for fast muscle-mass gains. Bill swabbed a butt cheek with alcohol, braced himself, and plunged the needle home.

Damn! Good thing he'd been warned not to inject it into his shoulder; Sustanon can leave a nodule the size of a tennis ball. As soon as he stopped wincing, Bill followed the Sus with 200 mg of Deca-Durabolin, another favorite that helps the muscles absorb protein. One more shot to go: HCG, a natural hormone distilled from the urine of pregnant women.

And so, with a huge lump on his ass and pregnant-women urine splashing around inside him, Bill headed off to the gym. "The first couple of days, I didn't feel a thing," he recalls. "If anything, I was a little tired and depressed." But within 2 weeks, he felt a huge surge of strength, and after a month, his waist was shrinking and his chest expanding.

By the end of his 12-week cycle, Bill had aided 80 pounds to his bench press, jacking it from 245 pounds to 325. His biceps had swollen from 16 inches to $18^1/_2$, and his waist had slimmed from a size 36 to a 34. In short, he's given himself a radically larger, stronger, and leaner body in just 3 months. He was so big that his wife demanded to know what was going on. "She was freaked out at first," Bill admits, "She insisted I go right out and buy more health insurance."

30 Despite his wife's anxiety, Bill was ready to cycle again 8 months later. Since then, he has done at least one cycle a year for the past 6 years. He now weighs 265 pounds, with a very low, 12 percent body-fat ratio. He's suffered no hint of 'roid rage, he says, and his blood and liver enzymes are normal. "I got a little acne on my chest and back," Bill shrugs. "Otherwise, I'm rockin'."

Scientists have been searching for a magic, superman drug for more than 100 years, ever since a French researcher tried injecting himself with an extract of dog and guinea-pig testicles. The results of that experiment were disappointing—his special blend turned out to have no active hormones—but it didn't prevent other scientists from continuing to search the scrotum for its secrets.

German scientists finally came up with a successful formula in the 1930s, when they found a way to chemically reproduce the original testosterone molecule. Early results were fantastic: The new über-hormones helped double the size of skeletal muscle and increased endurance and aggression. Some of these protosteroids were reportedly administered to Hitler's troops in the 1940s, and later to Soviet athletes in the 1950s.

Soon after Iron Curtain powerlifters began annihilating their competition in the 1960s, anabolic steroids became the go-to drug for many elite athletes. Some negative side effects appeared, such as baldness, rampant acne, and plummeting sex drive. Even worse were the wild mood swings and frightening bursts of anger. Adolescents were suffering stunted growth, while female juicers saw their breasts flatten, their clitorises distend, and their faces sprout whiskers.

But there seemed to be little solid evidence, either then or in the decades that followed, that large numbers of 'roided men were collapsing from strokes or other potentially fatal afflictions. On the contrary, some of the most prominent musclemen of the '60s and '70s—the heavily juiced Pumping Iron era—have passed into middle age with few discernible consequences of their track-marked youth. (Schwarzenegger's 1997 heart surgery was to repair a congenital defect.) As for heart attacks and diseased prostates, to this day there's no definitive link between these diseases and steroids. "We just don't have the data," says Dr. Yesalis. "Even though steroids have been epidemic in elite sports since the '50s, we have yet to do the same epidemiological studies on them that we've done on tobacco, alcohol, and cocaine."

35 Nor has law enforcement been trained to crack down on juicers. "When you look at what we have to deal with across the board, steroids are our responsibility but not our priority," admits Will Glaspy, a spokesman for the U.S. Drug Enforcement Agency.

No wonder so many average guys are acting as if the liquor store was left unlocked. "Look, more than 60 percent of the American population is overweight," argues Mick Hart, the British fitness guru whose steroid-promoting web site, **mickhart.com**, has made him an Internet hero to thousands of American steroid users. "If they can burn fat and add muscle by combining hard work with a little 'gear,' what's the harm?" To back his point, Hart even put his 23-year-old son, Chris, on steroids, transforming him from a lumpy young man into a grinning, flexing hunk.

Judging by subscription rates for *No Bull,* Hart's online steroid newsletter marketed toward middle-aged men, the juice business is booming, especially among Boomers. Last May, *No Bull* signed on 3,000 new subscribers.

"I get more than 200 e-mails a day from men all over the world," Hart says. "Know what they all say? 'I can't wait to get started.'"

Francis, a member of various anabolic chat rooms, is a 35-year-old New Yorker who is about to begin his second cycle with his lifting partner, a 37-year-old Wall Street broker. Francis first tried steroids 2 years ago, when the clerk at a national supplement-store chain startled him by saying he was wasting his time with legal supplements. "I was about to buy a testosterone booster called 1AD," Francis recalls, "and the guy said I'd have to take 10 to 15 doses a day, which would do far more damage than a proper cycle."

40 "If you're going to do this stuff," the clerk told him, "you might as well do steroids." Francis spent 4 years reading detailed analyses of steroid composition and its effects, and finally decided the gains were worth the risks. "I don't drink or smoke, and there is no history of heart disease or liver problems in my fam-

ily," he explains. Same for his broker buddy. Plus, their goals were modest—each just wanted to add a few inches to his chest and arms—so they felt confident they could keep their steroid use under control.

"We're not muscle freaks," Francis says. "In 2 years, this is only my second 8-week cycle on steroids." All he wants to do, Francis says, is bulk up just enough to fill out his 6'4" frame. "I've been lifting since I was 17 and taking every supplement under the sun, and I finally realized that at 220 pounds, I'd gotten as big as I could naturally."

Two hundred twenty pounds on a six-four frame? And he's worried that he's not big enough?

That, believes Dr. Pope, is cause for concern. In some men, once that hunger takes hold, there's no satisfying it. "These men feel they never look good enough, and begin sacrificing their relationships, their careers, their peace of mind—because they are never satisfied with their bodies."

This obsession has become so common that Dr. Pope has come up with a term for it: Adonis Complex. What fuels it, he says, are the ridiculously outsized bodies purveyed by Hollywood, magazine covers, and even action-toy manufacturers (just check out the size of G.I. Joe these days). "One of the biggest lies being handed to American men today is that you can somehow attain by natural means the huge shoulders and pectorals of the biggest men in the magazines," says Dr. Pope. "Generations of young men are working hard in the gym and wondering what on earth they're doing wrong. They don't realize that the 'hypermale' look that's so prevalent these days is essentially unattainable without steroids."

45 Steroids have become so common, in fact, that Dr. Pope believes most of us no longer recognize a steroid-enhanced body when we see one. They're all around us, bulging with injection-enhanced muscle but posing as clean. Because there are certain dimensions that cannot be attained without chemical help, Dr. Pope adds, he can walk through the mall or grab a stack of magazines and swiftly pick out many of the steroid users. The numbers, he says, are astonishingly high: "I once grabbed six men's magazines at random, and I'm certain that more than half of them had steroid-enhanced men on the covers.

"No one wants to reveal that much of his impressive body is due to injections," he continues. "I have met guys who would sooner tell you they had knocked over a convenience store or raped a girl in her dorm room than admit they had taken steroids."

Tragically, too many steroid users are guilty of just those crimes, and worse. As both a psychiatrist and a steroid expert, Dr. Pope has consulted in numerous criminal cases in which normally peaceful men, with no history of psychiatric problems, have suddenly gone berserk after a few cycles of steroids. In one case, a frail and timid 14-year-old boy began taking steroids to bulk up. He started having fits of anger so extreme that his mother took him to the emergency room to be examined. Two years later, at age 16, he stabbed his 14-year-old girlfriend to death with a carving knife while on a cycle of steroids.

There have been no systematic studies on steroid among adult males, however, so there is still debate about the exact prevalence of 'roid rage and no clear understanding of its causes. However, Dr. Pope has no doubt that somewhere there is a cause and effect between synthetic testosterone and heightened aggression. "I've seen far too many examples of 'roid rage for this to be a coincidence," Dr. Pope says. Even in sedate lab studies, steroid users have had violent reactions; in one early

clinical test at the National Institute of Mental Health, for instance, a volunteer who'd taken a dose lower than used by the average bodybuilder became so out of control that he asked to be placed in the ward seclusion room.

Granted, medical science has yet to determine the long-term physiological risks or explain the cause of psychological flare-ups. But in the meantime, is it worth becoming a self-appointed guinea pig just to add a few inches of unnecessary bulk?

50 "My fear," Dr. Pope says, "is that one day, we'll look back on this period in steroid history the way smokers are looking back on the 1950s, before the link to lung cancer was well understood. Sometime in the future, many steroid users could be in trouble from some unforeseen long-term consequences of these drugs and wishing they'd known more in advance."

Bill's wife still wants him to stop, but unlike in his drinking days, she hasn't given him the ultimatum. Bill knows why. "If she did," he says, "she'd lose." Steroids, he feels, have changed his life. Alcohol was an escape; steroids are who he is. "This is the body I was meant to have," he explains. "It just took a little help to get there." Currently, he's in the midst of a new cycle, this time experimenting with Dianabol and Equipoise, a veterinary steroid designed for horses.

"I've never been healthier in my life," Bill concludes. There's no denying the joy in his voice—but his final comment is a chilling echo of Dr. Pope's warning about size obsession. "I feel like an Adonis!" Bill thunders.

SPOT THE JUICER!

How to tell if the guy in the next squat rack is natural or artificially enhanced

SKULL: Steroids may or may not increase the size of the skull; the effect is more often attributed to human growth hormone, which is sometimes taken in conjunction with anabolic steroids.

SKIN: Bodybuilders' skin sometimes takes on a reddish glow, since steroids cause water retention, which raises blood pressure. One writer described 'roided bodybuilders as resembling walking erections, "all veiny and red."

DELTOIDS, TRAPS: Supersized muscles surrounding the shoulders—trapezius, lats, pectorals, deltoids, biceps, and triceps—are a good clue that Mr. Needle has been introduced to Mr. Buttock. Even if the lower body is normal size, upper-body muscles tend to be inflated.

CHEST: One of the few consistent results of steroid studies is an increase in bench-press strength. When an experienced lifter makes sudden, dramatic strength gains, assume pharmacological intervention.

BACK: Upper-body acne is a common side effect in adults using steroids.

NIPPLES: By any other name, gynecomastia is a bitch. Steroid-induced breast tissue can only be removed surgically.

LATS: Lifters can increase muscle mass by up to 25 percent with 10 weeks of steroid use, so stretch marks on biceps and pectorals are common.

FOREARMS: This is anecdotal, but some have observed that the best natural bodybuilders have a thick bone structure. When you see a guy with huge forearm muscles rising off relatively small bones, it's a pretty good sign he's been hitting the Vitamin S.

BICEPS: Another way to tell the difference between natural and unnatural lifters: The juicers look as if they have more muscle fibers as well as bigger fibers. Steroids seem to trigger a process called hyperplasia, in which the body produces new muscle cells.

ABS: Steroids help reduce body fat even as they promote muscle growth. A guy who gains a lot of muscle quickly without steroids will also tend to add fat. Only a juicer can get substantially bigger in the chest and shoulders while losing fat from his waist.

HANDS: Sportswriters are fond of saying steroids won't help you hit a fastball. But, since testosterone regulates the nervous system, steroids are thought to increase quickness by decreasing reaction time. Next stop, McCovey Cove.

THIGHS: Anabolic steroids don't reduce inflammation, but they can help torn muscles recover their strength. On the other hand, corticosteroids, which are commonly used to reduce inflammation quickly, can cause damage to a muscle's structure and tissue regrowth.

KNEES: Sports-medicine physicians have long suspected that steroids damage tendons and ligament. Animal studies from the '80s show that the damage to joints begins within a few days of steroid use, and that exercise combined with steroid use makes it worse. The lab animals ended up with stiffer, weaker tendons.

TESTICLES: With artificial testosterone injected into your body, your testicles don't need to make their own, so the assembly line shuts down, and the testes shrink.

PENIS: Waldo goes wild, even while his two nutty friends turn into shrinking violets. Steroid users often develop voracious sexual appetites (despite the fact that they're actually producing less sperm), along with feelings of euphoria and boundless energy.

—Lou Schuler

Questions for Discussion

1. Consider the extent to which the authors rely upon a narrative about a 45-year-old sales executive. How compelling is this story, and how effective is it in setting up an argument against the use of steroids?

2. In paragraph 11, the authors claim that anabolic steroids are widely used in professional sports and that their use has spread to men in other professions. Have you read or seen evidence of this outside of this argument?

3. The authors draw heavily upon research done by Dr. Harrison Pope Jr.—the coauthor of a piece included later in this cluster of readings. How effectively have they integrated this source into their work? Have they relied too much upon a single source?

4. What are the risks of giving yourself an injection with a syringe—regardless of what that syringe contains?

5. In paragraph 28, the authors describe the drug Bill is using as "pregnant-women urine." What is such language meant to accomplish?

6. The authors point to a case in which a man put his son on steroids. Would you do that to a child of your own? What kind of message would doing so send?

7. Why do you think there has been so little research into the long-term effects of steroid use? What does this signify?

8. Why is the quotation with which the authors conclude significant?

③ HARRISON G. POPE, JR., KATHERINE A. PHILLIPS, AND ROBERTO OLIVARDIA, "The Adonis Complex"

The following selection consists of most of the first chapter of the book that brought the emerging crisis in male body image to national attention upon its publication in 2000. (To conserve space, a section on steroid abuse has been edited out; that topic is addressed in the preceding article by Christopher McDougall and Lou Schuler, two authors who were influenced by *The Adonis Complex*.) Harrison Pope Jr. is professor of psychiatry at Harvard Medical School and chief of the Biological Psychiatry Laboratory at McLean Hospital—a hospital long-recognized as one of the nation's best for the treatment of mental illness. Katharine Phillips is also a medical doctor. She teaches psychiatry at Brown University School of Medicine and directs the body dysmorphic disorder program at Butler Hospital in Providence, Rhode Island. At the time this work was first published, Roberto Olivardia was a Clinical Fellow at Harvard Medical School. He has a Ph.D. in psychology.

The Adonis Complex

HARRISON G. POPE JR., KATHERINE A. PHILLIPS, AND ROBERTO OLIVARDIA

1   It is 6 P.M. on a warm spring evening in a small city ten miles west of Boston. In an industrial part near the highway, the two-storied, white-brick Olympic Gym is surrounded by nearly half an acre of parking, but the lot is overflowing with cars. Some are old Fords and Chevys belonging to students at the nearby college; others are the pickups and delivery trucks of tradesmen and service men who've stopped to lift weights after work. There are also pristine Corvettes and Porsches, a Mercedes or two, and half a dozen BMWs. Every social class in America has come here to work out.

Inside, the frenetic beat of "Get Ready for This" is punctuated by the occasional clanging of a weight stack on a machine, or a 45-pound plate being loaded onto a bar. Although the gym has half an acre of floor space, it still seems crowded. Groups of weightlifters cluster around the cables and the squat racks; others

wait to use the lat pull-down machine or the Roman chair. A blond-haired twenty-six-year-old trainer instructs a prominent Boston attorney on the fine points of abdominal exercises. The gym's owner is out on the floor, giving a tour of the facilities to two young high school students who want to sign up. Wide-eyed and slightly frail-looking, they glance furtively at two big bodybuilders doing shoulder presses at the dumbbell rack nearby. Dozens of treadmills, Stair-Masters, stationary bicycles, and ergometers hum and whir on the balcony overhead. At the front counter, a handsome, highly muscular staff member, still in his teens, smiles brightly and mixes protein shakes in a blender as groups of clients joke together, read magazines, and search for their car keys among the hundreds of key rings hanging on the big pegboard on the wall. And this is only the evening crowd. At five-thirty tomorrow morning, twenty or thirty people will line up at the door, waiting eagerly for the gym to open. A hundred more will show up over the next couple of hours to lift weights before work. They will be followed by dozens of lunchtime regulars, with many stragglers in between.

The Olympic Gym has 2,400 members, and it is only one of several gyms in this small city of 60,000. All over the United States, in small towns, suburbs, and cities, big gyms like this one have their own large and faithful followings. In greater Boston alone, the major gyms collectively count well over 100,000 members—and some metropolitan areas have far more. As recently as twenty or thirty years ago, you would hardly ever see a crowd like this at any gym, with the possible exception of a few hard-core bodybuilding establishments in Southern California. But over the last two decades, gym memberships have exploded across America.

More than two-thirds of the people working out at the Olympic Gym tonight are men. Some wear old T-shirts and dirty cutoff shorts; others are carefully dressed in striped workout pants and Olympic Gym sweatshirts; a few wear deep-cut tank tops and tight spandex shorts, carefully chosen to show off their musculature. But the "muscleheads" are only a small minority of the gym community. Most of the members are ordinary-looking guys: they're a slice of America, ranging from squeaky-voiced boys of twelve or thirteen to gray-haired elders in their seventies.

5 You would think that the men at the Olympic Gym, or any gym, would be happy with their bodies. After all, they're getting in shape rather than vegetating on the couch watching TV after work. But surprisingly, many aren't content at all. Many, in fact, harbor nagging anxieties about how they look. They don't talk about it publicly—and they may not even admit it to themselves—but they suffer silently from chronic shame and low self-esteem about their bodies and themselves. And many are obsessed with trying to change how they look. Beneath the seemingly benign exterior of this scene at Olympic, and among millions of other men around the country, a crisis is brewing.

If we begin to look carefully around the gym, we see hints of this crisis everywhere. John and Mark, both twenty-four-year-old graduate students at a nearby university, are at the counter debating what kinds of protein supplements to buy from the bewildering display of boxes that crowd the wall. Many of the boxes boast "supermale" images: photographs of smiling body builders with massive shoulders, rock-hard pectorals, and impossibly sculptured and chiseled abdominal muscles. All of the supermales exude health, power, and sexuality. Not even the biggest bodybuilder at the Olympic Gym resembles these images, and John and Mark don't come close—even though they've been lifting weights for years and have spent thousands of dollars on nutritional supplements they hoped would thin their waists, stomachs, and buttocks, while swelling their chests, arms, and thighs. Privately, John and Mark are slightly embarrassed that they don't even begin to look like the guys in the pictures. But they've never admitted these concerns to anyone.

Supermale images appear not only on the boxes of protein powder, but throughout the gym. They're on magazine covers in the waiting area, on posters on the walls, and on a clothes advertisement posted on the bulletin board. John examines a magazine showing amazing "before" and "after" pictures of a middle-aged man who appears to have transformed in three months from a couch potato into a muscle-bound hunk, allegedly with the help of the food supplement advertised. John has tried a lot of food supplements himself, and he wonders why he still hasn't achieved the same Herculean image. All of these displays convey the same message to men: *If you're a real man, you should look bigger and better than you do.*

While John may feel as though he's the only guy at the gym who's so worried about his appearance and size, in reality he's surrounded by many others with similar secret feelings. But lost in his own thoughts of insecurity, John doesn't seem to notice all the other men who are covertly checking out their reflections in the big mirrors that line the walls. When they're sure that nobody is looking, some flex their arms, puff out their chests, or suck in their stomachs, almost as a reflex gesture. They don't say anything, of course. But many, like John, can't stop thinking about the discrepancy between the image in the mirror and the one they desperately want.

Alan, a math teacher from nearby Cambridge, notices, for the tenth or the twentieth time that day, the stubborn ring of fat that has accumulated around his abdomen in the years since college. Bob, a truckdriver, wears a baseball cap with the visor turned back, even though he's thirty-eight years old and the baseball-cap look is usually reserved for teenagers. But he'd rather wear the cap than expose his "prematurely" receding hairline. Meanwhile, John himself wears three layers of shirts—a T-shirt, then a regular shirt on top, and then a sweatshirt on top of that. He's sweating inside all of those layers, but they make him look bigger, and he's ashamed of how small he'd look without them. Bertrand, an attorney in his fifties who arrived a few minutes earlier in an immaculate, six-foot-high sport utility vehicle, despondently eyes his unappealing reflection in the mirror next to the drinking fountain. Above the drinking fountain, a poster of a famous bodybuilder twice his size, majestically posing on a rocky summit in the desert, stares back at him.

10 These are men who have achieved success in their careers; some are leaders in their community. They come from different classes, races, and sociological backgrounds. But they are all victims of a relentless message: *You don't look good enough.* Most of the time, men are unable to talk to each other about this message and the inferiority it makes them feel. So the message gets louder, the problem becomes bigger, and the isolation grows deeper.

Three college students arrive and head into the locker room. They're laughing and joking with each other, exchanging gossip about a party last weekend, while they get ready to go out onto the gym floor. But once they're in the locker room, none of them actually takes off his clothes in front of the others. Although they haven't shared their feelings with one another, one of the young men is terribly ashamed of the acne scars on his back. Another is convinced he's too fat, and he's especially upset at the "female" fat that he thinks has accumulated under his nipples. The third privately worries that his penis is too small. Even though they've been good friends for years, none of these young men has felt comfortable enough to reveal these secret concerns to any other person.

Male Body Image Obsession: A Troubling Double Bind

In our research at Harvard and Brown Medical Schools, and in studies collaborating with scientists across the country and overseas, the three of us have met countless otherwise "normal" boys and men who share these same feelings of inadequacy, unattractiveness, and even failure. By interviewing hundreds of men working out at gyms, and compiling our collective clinical experience with the hundreds more who have seen us at our offices, we've learned that men like John, Alan, Bob, Bertrand, and the three college students represent a broad and growing group who feel insecure and anxious—even paralyzed—by how they look. Society is telling them now, more than ever before, that their bodies define who they are as men. Because they find it impossible to meet this supermale standard, they are turning their anxiety and humiliation inward.

On the surface, most of the boys and men we've talked with, and the millions of other men like them across the country and around the globe, lead what appear to be regular, well-adjusted lives. In fact, the vast majority would never dream of going to see a mental health professional. But behind the smiling, behind the cheerful athletic bravado, many of these men worry about their looks and their masculinity. Some are even clinically depressed, and many are intensely self-critical. Because these men carry a secret that they're uncomfortable sharing even with their closest loved ones, their self-doubts can become almost toxic, insidiously eating away at their self-esteem and self-confidence as men.

Indeed, many of these men, we believe, are caught in a double bind they can neither understand nor escape. On the one hand, they're increasingly surrounded with media images of masculine perfection—not just here in the gym, but in advertisements, on television, in the movies. And if this alone weren't enough to make them feel inadequate about their bodies, they're also bombarded with messages from burgeoning multibillion-dollar industries that capitalize upon their body insecurities. These "male body image industries"—purveyors of food supplements, diet aids, fitness programs, hair-growth remedies, and countless other products—now prey increasingly on men's worries, just as analogous industries have preyed for decades on the appearance-related insecurities of women.

15 But the problem gets compounded further. Women, over the years, have gradually learned—at least to some extent—how to confront society's and the media's impossible ideals of beauty. Many women can now recognize and voice their appearance concerns, speaking openly about their reactions to these ideals, rather than letting them fester inside. But men still labor under a societal taboo against expressing such feelings. Real men aren't supposed to whine about their looks; they're not even supposed to worry about such things. And so this "feeling and talking taboo" adds insult to injury: to a degree unprecedented in history, men are being made to feel more and more inadequate about how they look—while simultaneously being prohibited from talking about it or even admitting it to themselves.

And so, trapped between impossible ideals on the one side and taboos against feeling and talking on the other, millions of boys and men are suffering. For some, body image concerns have grown into outright psychiatric disorders, ruining their own lives and often the lives of those who care about and love them. And for every boy or man with a full-scale body image disorder, there are many more with milder cases of the same body obsessions—not disabling in any way, but still enough to hurt.

The Adonis Complex: Men Unhappy with Their Bodies

We call this syndrome the "Adonis Complex." In greek mythology, Adonis was half man and half god—the ultimate in masculine beauty. So beautiful was his body that he won the love of Aphrodite, queen of the gods. But Persephone, who had raised Adonis, refused to give him up to Aphrodite. So Zeus, the king of the gods, brokered a deal: Adonis would spend four months out of every year in the underworld with Persephone, four months with Aphrodite, and four months on his own. It is said that he chose to spend his own personal four months with Aphrodite as well.

Throughout the centuries, many a great artist has attempted to depict the physical perfection of Adonis. Most famously, the Renaissance painter Titian* shows him about to go hunting with his dogs, with Aphrodite clutching his body in her arms. The body of Adonis presumably represents the ultimate male physique imaginable to a sixteenth-century artist—but Titian's Adonis looks fat and out of shape in comparison to the men pictured on the boxes of protein powder at the Olympic Gym.

We should note that "Adonis Complex" isn't an official medical term, and it doesn't describe any one body image problem of men. We use it . . . to refer to an array of usually secret, but surprisingly common, body image concerns of boys and men. These concerns range from minor annoyances to devastating and sometimes even life-threatening obsession—from manageable dissatisfaction to full-blown psychiatric body image disorders.

*Titian—or Tiziano Vecellio— was one of the greatest painters of the Italian Renaissance. His work can be found in museums throughout the world and at many sites in Venice, the city with which he is most closely associated. Although the date of his birth is not certain, he died in Venice in 1576 when he was over 80, so he had an unusually long career for a sixteenth-century artist.

In one form or another, the Adonis Complex touches millions of boys and men—and inevitably, the women in their lives.

20 Nowadays, it seems, increasing numbers of boys and men, including some of those lifting weights tonight at the Olympic Gym, have become fixated on achieving a perfect, Adonis-like body. Take Scott, for example. He's twenty-six-year-old personal trainer at the gym. Right now, he isn't training anybody because it's his own time to lift. He's just started his leg routine—three sets of squats, two sets of leg presses, two or three sets of leg extensions on a Nautilus machine, three sets of leg curls on another machine, and then on to some hack squats, leg abductions, and side leg raises. The whole routine will take him an hour and a half, and then he still has to do his calves for another half hour after that. He's working out alone, because he doesn't like any distractions to come between him and the weights.

To a casual observer, Scott seems like a perfect picture of fitness and health. Five feet nine inches tall, with shortly cropped dark brown hair and handsome facial features, Scott weighs 180 pounds and has only 7 percent body fat, making him leaner than at least 98 percent of American men his age. Beneath his worn gray sweatpants and sweatshirt, he has the proportions of a Greek statue. He has a 31-inch waist, a "six-pack" of sculptured abdominal muscles, a 46-inch chest, and shoulders as big as grapefruits. But surprisingly, and unknown to even many of his closest friends, Scott constantly fears that he isn't big enough.

As a result, Scott has surprisingly low self-esteem. He puts all his hopes and dreams into his workouts and not into his daily life. This makes him withdraw from others and hold himself back from social situations he would otherwise enjoy. Although women are enormously attracted to Scott, he secretly thinks he isn't really big enough or masculine enough to appeal to them. In fact, he doesn't have a girlfriend right now, partly because his self-image is so poor and his confidence about dating so crippled.

Scott came to see us at our research laboratory in response to a notice we put on the bulletin board at the Olympic Gym, looking for body-builders who weren't satisfied with their physiques. In this study, we were comparing male bodybuilders who were insecure about their appearance with those who felt comfortable with how they looked. The study involved an office visit in which we measured each man's height, weight, and body fat, had him fill out some questionnaires, and then interviewed him about his body image and other psychological issues.

When Scott arrived for his interview, he was ill at ease, almost embarrassed to be coming to see us for such a study. "You've really had a lot of guys who've called about your ad?" he asked. He was surprised when we told him that we'd already seen many men like himself.

25 Scott took a chair, seeming a little relieved. He wore loose cotton pants with a drawstring at the waist, and an oversized blue sweatshirt with a bodybuilding logo on the back. The words TAKE NO PRISONERS were emblazoned under a figure of a muscled bodybuilder wearing combat fatigues.

Scott soon grew relaxed and told us his story in a warm, soft-spoken, almost self-effacing manner. An honors graduate of a prestigious New England college and holder of a business degree, Scott was highly educated. But his heart, it turned out, had never been in business.

"I started going to the gym fairly regularly when I was in college," he said. "But I don't think it was until I started business school that it became an obsession. I remember, one day when I was in business school, looking at myself in the mirror and hating how I looked. I started wondering how I'd ever tolerated what I looked like when I was back in college. Gradually, I got more and more fixated on getting my time in the gym each day, and I got more and more impatient with all of the demands at school. The other guys were all talking about companies that they wanted to work for, and how much money they were going to make, but I could never seem to get into it."

By the time Scott graduated from business school, his body obsession dominated his life. "I had several good job offers," he continued, "but I just couldn't picture myself working in an office. I was afraid that if I was forced to sit behind a desk all day, I'd turn into a fat slob. In fact, even at school, I couldn't sit in front of a computer screen for more than about fifteen minutes before I started worrying that I wasn't getting any exercise."

During his graduate studies, Scott worked as a personal trainer at a local health club. After business school, it became his full-time job. "This probably sounds strange," he said, "but it was the only job I could think of that gave me enough time to do my own training."

30 He paused and studied our faces for several seconds, seeming to fear we would have a negative reaction to what he had said. Instead, we asked questions to hear more about and understand his concerns.

"Did people criticize you for not going on to a business career?" we asked.

"Everybody," he said with resignation. "Especially my mother, and also my girlfriend at that time. They just couldn't understand why I'd throw away my years of education to work at a gym. I guess it does seem a little weird. But I couldn't imagine going back to a business job now. I guess I've just become too wrapped up with working out."

As the interview progressed, Scott began to reveal the full extent of his preoccupations. "If you could see what I was thinking about during the day, ninety percent of the time it would have something to do with either my weightlifting, my diet, or the way I look. I can't go past a mirror without posing just for a minute to check out my body—as long as I'm sure nobody's watching. I even check myself out when I see my reflection in a store window or car window." He laughed nervously. "Sometimes when I'm in a restaurant, I even study my reflection in the back of a spoon."

Most of the time, Scott explained, he sees his reflection as small and puny, even though he's actually massively built. "I know it sounds silly," he said, "but there are times that even on hot summer days, after getting a bad shot of myself in the mirror, I'll put on heavy sweatshirts to cover up my body because I think I don't look big enough." For the same reason, he explained that he almost always wears heavy sweats when working out at the gym. He sometimes even turns down invitations to go to a swimming pool or the beach, for fear that when he takes his shirt off, people will notice him and think he's too small.

35 "How would you feel if you were forced to miss working out for a day?" we asked.

He looked shocked. "I'd probably go bananas and start breaking things. In fact, one day last winter there was a blizzard and I couldn't get out of my house to go to the gym. I felt trapped. I got so frustrated from not being able to work out that I put on my weight belt and started bench-pressing the furniture in my living room. My girlfriend thought I was crazy."

"Has your relationship with your girlfriend been affected by your weightlifting preoccupations?"

Scott fell silent, and for a brief moment, tears seemed to form in his eyes. "Actually, my girlfriend broke up with me because of my weightlifting. It got to be too much for her. Sarah could never really understand why I needed to go to the gym or why it mattered so much to me what I looked like. I'd ask several times a day whether she thought I looked big enough or muscular enough. I guess she got pretty tired of my asking her. She also complained a lot because she said I was too inflexible. She'd want to go out and do something, and I'd say that I couldn't because I needed to go to the gym and train. But I'd warned her that I was that way. I told her that when we first started living together: the gym comes first, my diet second, and she was third. I guess she couldn't take being in third place anymore. And I don't really blame her.

"It's weird," he continued. "I think the truth is that I actually thought Sarah would break up with me if I didn't work out enough. I actually thought she'd leave me for some bigger guy. But the real reason she left me was because I was so caught up in working out that I didn't do anything or go anyplace with her. She told me that I was screwed up and that our relationship was getting 'lost.' When I think about it, I guess maybe she was right."

40 "Why do you think you have such intense feelings about your body and about working out?" we asked.

"I don't know. I guess I've really never stopped to think about just how much this muscle thing has affected my life. At first, it was a healthy thing, wanting to pursue a healthy lifestyle and be in shape. But now, it's

gotten out of control. It's a trap. I can't get out of it."

"Have you ever considered some type of therapy to look at your feelings about your body?"

"Yeah, I've thought about it sometimes, but it would never work. Someone who doesn't lift weights himself would never understand." As he spoke, Scott flexed his arm unconsciously.

Over the last several years, we've interviewed many men with Scott's condition. We call it "muscle dysmorphia"—an excessive preoccupation with body size and muscularity. Many of these men, like Scott, revealed that this preoccupation had spiraled out of control and profoundly affected their lives—causing them to change their careers, or destroying relationships with people they loved. But practically none of them had sought treatment for their condition—usually because they doubted that any type of professional would actually understand or be able to help them.

Muscle Dysmorphia: "Puniness" in the Mind
45 The body image distortions of men with "muscle dysmorphia" are strikingly analogous to those of women (and some men) with anorexia nervosa. In fact, some people have colloquially referred to muscle dysmorphia as "bigorexia nervosa" or "reverse anorexia." People with anorexia nervosa see themselves as fat when they're actually too thin; people with muscle dysmorphia feel ashamed of looking too small when they're actually big. A recent study of ours illustrates these parallels. In this study, we compared interview and questionnaire responses from twenty-four young men with muscle dysmorphia, recruited from gymnasiums in the Boston area; thirty young men without muscle dysmorphia, recruited from the same gymnasiums; twenty-five college men with eating disorders such as anorexia nervosa and bulimia nervosa (binge eating and vomiting); and twenty-five ordinary college men without eating disorders. On question after question, the men with muscle dysmorphia showed levels of pathology similar

to the college men with eating disorders. In particular, the men from these two groups shared a need to exercise every day, shame about their body image, feelings of being too fat, dislike of their bodies, and often, lifetime histories of anxiety and depression. By contrast, the group of weightlifters without muscle dysmorphia closely resembled the ordinary college men on all of these same indices. In other words, men with muscle dysmorphia report that they are suffering just as badly as men with anorexia nervosa.

Also like people with anorexia nervosa, men with muscle dysmorphia often risk physical self-destruction. Frequently, they persist in compulsive exercising despite pain and injuries, or continue on ultra low-fat, high-protein diets even when they are desperately hungry. Many take potentially dangerous anabolic steroids and other drugs to bulk up, all because they think they don't look good enough.

But these men's nagging worries are rarely relieved by increasing their bodybuilding. In psychological terms, we call such persistent worries "obsessions." And in response to these obsessions, people are driven to repetitive behaviors—in Scott's case, constant weightlifting—which, in turn, we call "compulsions." Though people may realize, on one level, that their obsessive beliefs are irrational and their compulsive behaviors futile, they still cannot "shut off" their endless and often self-destructive behaviors. Scott is a case in point. Although his feelings of self-criticism were utterly irrational, Scott was so convinced of his deficiencies that, at the end of the day, he chose catering to his muscle obsession over maintaining his relationship with Sarah.

The sources of Scott's muscle obsessions and weightlifting compulsions are not known with absolute certainty, but most likely are threefold. First, there's almost certainly a genetic, biologically based component. In other words, some people like Scott inherit a chemical predisposition to developing obsessive-compulsive symptoms. But genetics do not act alone. The second likely component is

psychological—obsessive and compulsive behavior stems, in part at least, from one's experiences growing up, such as being teased. Scott still remembers being called "dorky" and "wimpy" in school, and these memories still fuel his muscle obsession and his compulsion to work out. And finally, we believe that society plays a powerful and increasing role, by constantly broadcasting messages that "real men" have big muscles—just like the bodybuilders in the pictures on the walls of the Olympic Gym. Men like Scott have been exposed to these images ever since they were small boys, thus laying the groundwork for muscle dysmorphia and other forms of the Adonis Complex in adulthood.

THE SPIRIT OF CONQUEST

KOUROS
EAU DE TOILETTE

SAINT LAURENT

Body-Dissatisfied Men: A Silent Epidemic

Cases as severe as Scott's may be uncommon. But for every man with severe muscle dysmorphia, dozens of others experience at least some distress about their muscularity. For example, a 1997 study found that an amazing 45 percent of American men were dissatisfied with their muscle tone—almost double the percentage found in the same survey in 1972. Thus, we can calculate that there are presently well over 50 million muscle-dissatisfied men in our country. And these millions of men are surrounded by many millions of very perplexed family members, friends, and loved ones, who probably can't quite understand what this anxiety about bigness and muscles is all about.

50 Why is muscle dissatisfaction, together with other body-appearance preoccupations, becoming so common among modern men?

Our grandfathers didn't seem to worry about how muscular they looked. They didn't do bench presses or abdominal exercises three days a week, or go to the gym to work out on the StairMaster, or worry about their percentage of body fat. Why has the Adonis Complex infected so many men over the last thirty years or so?

One reason is that our grandfathers were rarely, if ever, exposed to the "supermale" images—aside from Charles Atlas on an occasional matchbox cover—that Scott and his friends see every day. In modern society, these images aren't confined to pictures in the gym—they're everywhere. Look at television over the last several decades. The hardbodied lifeguards in *Baywatch* are viewed by over 1 billion viewers in 142 countries—figures unmatched by any previous television series. Or look at the movies. Hollywood's most masculine men of the 1930s, 1940s, and 1950s—John Wayne, Clark Gable, Gregory Peck—look like wimps in comparison to modern cinema's muscular action heroes—Arnold Schwarzenegger, Sylvester Stallone, or Jean-Claude van Damme. Today, while growing up, a young man is subjected to thousands and thousands of these supermale images. Each image links appearance to success—social, financial, and sexual. But these images have steadily grown leaner and more muscular, and thus more and more remote from what any ordinary man can actually attain. And so society and the media preach a disturbing double message: a man's self-esteem should be based heavily on his appearance, yet by the standards of modern supermale images, practically no man measures up.

It becomes understandable, then, that millions of modern American men are unhappy with how they look. And it isn't surprising that among these millions, we are seeing increasing numbers of serious casualties—men like Scott, whose lives have been damaged by these trends. Growing up in the 1970s and '80s, Scott steadily absorbed the stream of supermale images from the modern media. In

fact, he described to use how he watched *Rambo* movies and Schwarzenegger action thrillers and, even as a child, fantasized that he would someday look like those heroes. Gradually, body appearance became the dominant basis—and ultimately the only basis—for his self-esteem. To lose even a little of that muscle, or to gain even a little body fat, brought him instant shame and humiliation. For Scott, a muscled body became more important, much more important, than being a successful businessman. It became so important that it brought him nearly complete social isolation and even cost him his relationship with the woman he loved.

105 For every severe or dangerous case, such as Scott . . . there are dozens of less severe cases—men who cope quietly with emotional pain about some aspect of how they look. The suffering affects not only men who go to gyms like Olympic, but millions more who are too embarrassed about their appearance to be seen at a gym in the first place. In extreme cases, men may become so concerned about parts of their bodies—a balding head, a potbelly, a small penis, or some other perceived deficiency—that they do their best to avoid being seen in any public settings at all.

As clinicians and researchers in psychiatry and psychology, we've witnessed this growing male distress more and more in recent years. We've seen how the Adonis Complex can affect the lives of ordinary American men, young and old, producing a crippled masculine identity, chronic depression, compulsive behaviors, and often seriously impaired relationships with family members and loved ones.

What's particularly worrisome is that so many of these men are unaware of the societal forces that are constantly undermining their self-esteem. Boys and men have grown so accustomed to the constant barrage of supermale images in the media, and in advertising by the male body image industries, that they don't stop to question them. Rarely do they realize the extent to which they have accepted these Herculean images as sensible representations of male beauty. Instead, they change their behavior to try to make their own bodies conform to the new standard. Rarely do they consider that no previous generation in history was ever assaulted with comparable images—partly because it was impossible to create many of these modern supermale bodies before the availability of anabolic steroids. Rarely, also, do modern men fully acknowledge, even to themselves, how much their self-esteem and sense of masculinity is linked to their body image concerns. As a result of these feelings, they may become increasingly focused on deficiencies in their bodies, without really understanding why.

The starting place for healing this crisis of male body obsession—a crisis that extends across race, nationality, class, and sexual orientation—is to help men understand that they are not alone with these feelings, that millions of others share the same concerns and tribulations. It is time to help men appreciate the underlying social forces that contribute to their negative feelings about their bodies. Men must learn to acknowledge and talk about these feelings, to overcome the "feeling and talking taboo" that society has long imposed on them. And in our society, it is time to create widespread awareness about body-appearance concerns in men, and allow men to voice these concerns to those who care about and love them. We need to expose the societal and cultural forces that are inculcating new unattainable male body standards, and share the stories and voices of scores of men who have become frustrated and ashamed by their failure to meet these standards . . . . We hope to help men achieve the freedom and relief that has been attained by many women with eating disorders and other body image concerns: the ability to acknowledge their problems, seek new ways of perceiving their bodies and themselves, and find new paths toward self-confidence andfulfillment.

Questions for Discussion

1. The authors center their discussion by describing men who work out in a gym in an unnamed city west of Boston. Why not Boston itself? What is the advantage of using an anonymous "small city" as their site?

2. Although the men the authors describe are of different ages and engage in different behaviors, what do they have in common?

3. What factors contribute toward making men become obsessed about their appearance, especially whether they look big and strong enough?

4. Where do the authors reveal that their research extends beyond observing and interviewing men from the Olympic Gym? Why is it important for them to establish this?

5. Do you agree that it is easier for women to discuss concerns about their appearance than it is for men to do so?

6. How would you define *muscle dysmorphia*? Do you know anyone who may be suffering from this condition?

7. At the end of this selection, which is part of the first chapter of their book, the authors claim that male body obsession "extends across race, nationality, class, and sexual orientation." Do the examples they have used so far support this claim? Does it seem likely to be true? In your experience, how diverse are the men who become obsessed with trying to perfect their appearance?

④ **SARAH GROGAN, RUTH EVANS, SAM WRIGHT, AND GEOFF HUNTER,** "Femininity and Muscularity: Accounts of Seven Women Body Builders"

When women first entered the world of competitive body building, they were often perceived as entering a world that belonged to men—and thus stepping outside the boundaries of what it means to be "feminine." But after decades in which women athletes have achieved recognition in numerous sports, could those women who choose to lift weights and develop muscles now enjoy wider acceptance—and, most importantly, improved self-esteem? Researchers Sarah Grogan, Ruth Evans, Sam Wright, and Geoff Hunter set out to discover how women body builders feel about themselves. Grogan is principal lecturer in health psychology at Staffordshire University. She is currently investigating body image in women body builders, women who have had cosmetic surgery, and women who have tattoos and body piercing. Ruth Evans is a speech and language therapist. At the time of this research she was working at Manchester Metropolitan University. She remains interested in body image and other issues relating to women's health. Sam Wright was employed as Research Fellow at the Centre for Social Research into Health and Substance Abuse at Manchester Metropolitan University at the time of this project. She now works as senior research and evaluation specialist at NACRO, a crime reduction charity, in Sheffield. Geoff Hunter is a registered general nurse working as criminal justice team leader at Salford Drug Advisory Service. He is a former competitive body builder and until recently was a professional heavyweight boxer. He was team leader on a government Challenge Fund project that involved produced a guide for professionals on anabolic steroid use. As you read their argument, note that the authors follow a method of organization commonly used in writing within the social and natural sciences: beginning with an abstract (or summary), explaining their methodology, and setting off their conclusions in a separate section.

Femininity and Muscularity: Accounts of Seven Women Body Builders

SARAH GROGAN, RUTH EVANS, SAM WRIGHT, AND GEOFF HUNTER

Abstract:

In this study, we interviewed an opportunity sample of seven women body builders, who all compete (or have competed in the past) in Physique-level body building competitions. They were asked about training details, and motivations for body building including social pressures to become more muscular (and not to become more muscular). Women's accounts were complex and in some cases apparently contradictory, for while emphasising freedom to choose to be muscular within a cultural context where slimness is the norm, they stressed the importance of aspects of traditional femininity. Women's accounts are discussed in relation to Western cultural pressure on women to be slender. It is argued that these women had shifted their body-shape ideal to a more muscular figure, and their primary social reference group to those within the body building community. Women experienced pressures from within the body building community defining the acceptable size and appearance of their bodies. They were engaged in a "balancing act" where they were trying to attain a body that was muscular but not too muscular, and that maintained some aspects of traditional "feminine" appearance. It is concluded that women who engage in Physique-level body building face complex layers of social pressure from within and outside the body building community.

1 It is generally accepted that the ideal body shape for women in Western cultures is very slim. In Western societies, slimness is a valued attribute for women, and is associated with attractiveness, self-control, social skill, occupational success, and youth (Bordo, 1993; Grogan, 2000). Studies of body satisfaction in Britain, the United States and Australia have reliably found that women of all ages mostly wish to be thinner. When women have been asked to pick silhouette figures representing their current and ideal body size, American,

Australian, and British women and girls reliably pick thinner sizes for their ideal than their current size (Lamb et al., 1993; Tiggemann & Pennington, 1990; Wardle et al., 1993), and interview work substantiates these findings (Marchessault, 2000). Muscularity is generally seen as inappropriate for women (Choi, 2000). In interviews with girls as young as eight, we have found that they are as scared of becoming muscular as they are of becoming fat (Grogan & Wainwright, 1996). So women who aim for a muscular physique are transgressing current Western cultural norms.

Women's body building is a relatively new cultural phenomenon, and has shown a significant increase in popularity since the 1980s. Body building has traditionally been seen as a male-appropriate activity, and various authors have documented the struggle faced by pioneering women body builders as they entered the competitive body building world in the 1970s. Gold's Gym* is said to have prided itself on being "ovary free" until the late 1970s (St Martin & Gavey, 1996). The first widely publicised women's body building event was held in 1979 in Los Angeles (previously the only choice for women body builders was the "beauty pageant" added on to the men's competitions). In the 1980s, the Ms Olympia competition started in the US, and in the UK, NABBA (National Amateur Body Building Association) renamed its "Miss Bikini International" competition "Ms Universe." In 1986, the Ms Universe competition was divided into Physique and Figure classes. Physique class caters for those who are aiming for a more muscular physique and less traditionally feminine presentation (minimal make-up, bare feet), and the Figure for those who want traditionally feminine presentation (moderate degrees of muscularity, high shoes, g-strings, make-up). In the 1990s, two new competitions were set up: Natural Body Building competitions for men and women who choose not to use steroids, and Ms Fitness, for those women who engage in weight training as part of a general fitness regime.

Fitness competitors engage in an aerobic performance as well as posing to reveal body shape and tone.

Feminist authors have taken opposing positions on body building. Sandra Bartky (1990) sees it as an empowering practice that challenges the cultural association of muscularity (and strength) with masculinity. Leena St Martin and Nicola Gavey (1996) also argue that body building can be a way to challenge dominant ideologies that represent women as physically weak. For many women it could be an effective way to increase strength and to develop a more positive body image, with all the attendant positive effects on health (St Martin & Gavey, 1996). Other authors have seen body building as merely another way of persuading women to change their bodies in line with a cultural ideal that stresses the importance of avoiding fleshiness. Susan Bordo (1990) likens the female body builder to the anorexic, since she says that both are "united in battle against a common platoon of enemies; the soft, the loose, unsolid excess flesh." She denies that body building is an empowering practice for women, noting that the muscular body is simply a new ideal for women to aim for. Although her arguments have some credibility in relation to Figure and Fitness competitors, they do not ring true in relation to Physique-level competitors. Women in the Physique class are not merely toned and muscular. Their bodies are built up to look large and powerful and strong, and (to the untrained eye) look similar to the bodies of male body builders. It is important in this context to remember that body building is not a unitary phenomenon.

In this study, we interviewed an opportunity sample of women body builders, who all compete (or have competed in the past) in Physique-level competitions. They were asked about training details, and motivations for body building. In particular, social pressures to body build (and not to body build) were investigated. We were interested in investigating women's motivations for body building.

Non–body building women tend to want to be more slender than they are. Body building women (especially those in the Physique class) are engaging in behaviours that place them outside the mainstream norms for how it is appropriate for women to look. They are managing to resist the social pressures (that other women report) to be more slender, and we were interested in what motivated them to start body building and what maintained their body building. Given that mainstream Western culture expects women's bodies not to "take up space" (Orbach, 1993), we were also interested in these women's experience of other people's reactions to their increased size. We wondered how they experienced the reactions of those outside, and also inside the body building world, and what sources of social support these women used.

Method

5 Seven women were interviewed as part of this study. All were resident in the UK at the time of the study and all were white. We contacted them through "snowball sampling." The first interviewee was known to the fourth author. She put us in contact with the second interviewee who helped us to contact other women competing at Physique level. Pseudonyms are used here to protect the identity of the participants.

"Jane" was 26 years old, manages a fitness centre, and trains four or five times per week for one hour per session. She started training 13 years before the study, had competed as a Physique competitor in the past, but did not intend to compete again.

*"Anabolic steroids," as described by the National Institute on Drug Abuse, "is the familiar name for synthetic substances related to the male sex hormones (androgens). They promote the growth of skeletal muscle (anabolic effects) and the development of male sexual characteristics (androgenic effects). . . . [T]he proper term for these compounds is 'anabolic-androgenic' steroids."

"Paula" was 39 years old, worked as a personal trainer, had used anabolic steroids,* and had been body building for about 10 years. She competed as an amateur athlete until she was prevented from continuing due to physical injury. She trained twice a day, six days a week, with each session lasting about an hour, plus an hour of aerobics workout. She had competed as a Physique body builder in the past, and intended to compete again in the near future.

"Sarah" was 43 years old, works as manager of a fitness centre, and trained five times per week for 45 minutes to one hour per session. She started training 13 years before the interview, had competed in Physique class in the past, and competed in the Fitness class at the time of the interview.

"Sharon" was 22 years old, a health care professional, had used anabolic steroids, and had been training for 7.5 years and body building for 5.5 years. She started training at 15 years old, and trained five days a week—45 minutes with weights and 20–40 minutes cardiovascular work at the time of the interview. She had entered five body building competitions as a Physique competitor, and planned to compete again at some point in the future. 10 "Samantha" was 34 years old, a gym owner, had used anabolic steroids, and had been body building for five years. She trained four times a week, or six days a week when in preparation for a show, training for about an hour each time. She also did aerobics six days a week. She initially competed as a Figure competitor, the year after starting to body-build, and then changed to Physique competitions the following year, and she intended to compete again in the near future.

"Ruth" was 26, a fitness instructor, had used (and was using) anabolic steroids, and had been training for three years, training every day. She had entered one Physique competition and planned to compete again.

"Emma" was 24 years old, a factory worker, had used (and was using) anabolic steroids, and had been training for six years, training

seven times per week for about 90 minutes. She had entered competitions as a Physique competitor and intended to compete again in the future.

We used an interview schedule with a structured section at the beginning, asking specific questions about their training history, followed by some ideas for questions to be used in a semi-structured interview, covering topics such as motivations to start and continue training, responses by friends and family to training, responses of those outside the body building community, and changes in body image resulting from training. We produced the schedule based on previous work involving open- and closed-ended questionnaires, which were completed by 15 body building women (Wright et al., 2000) and on discussions with a woman who is a Physique body builder. We wanted to ensure that we would be asking questions that would be relevant to the women we were talking to, and that they would be likely to be able to answer. We also wanted to leave space to allow women to talk about experiences that we had not predicted prior to the interviews themselves.

Each woman was interviewed by the second author, using a semi-structured format, except for "Sharon" who was interviewed by "Paula" (who is her training partner). Women were interviewed at times and place that were convenient to them, and all interviews were conducted in quiet places with reasonable privacy. Women were assured of anonymity prior to the interviews taking place, and the limits of confidentiality of data were explained (i.e., they were warned that quotes from interviews would be used in reports). Interviews started with a series of demographic-type questions (age, length of training, etc.), designed to start the conversation and to put women at ease. This was followed by a semi-structured interview on a series of topics that were of interest to us (motivations to start and continue training, responses by friends and family to increased muscularity, responses of those outside the body building community, and change in body image resulting from increased muscularity), designed to allow women flexibility to talk around each topic for as long as they liked, and to introduce new topic areas. Each interview lasted between 30 minutes and an hour. Interviews were transcribed and analysed thematically following Stenner (1993).

Thematic Analysis

15 Each interview transcript was read and re-read with particular questions in mind. We wanted to focus on the ways that women talked about their motivations to increase their muscularity, to try to understand why they had started body building, and which factors influenced their continuation in the sport. We were particular interested in what women told us about social support for body building. What follows is a summary of what women told us about their experiences of body building and increased muscularity, arranged under theme headings. We will not specify who said what to protect the identify of the respondents. Women's Physique body building is a small community in the United Kingdom (there are currently about 30 women who compete on the amateur circuit), and we are concerned to preserve the anonymity of the women who spoke to us.

Countering Pressures to Be Slender

Pressure for Western women to be slender has been well documented by feminist authors (Bartky, 1990; Brook, 1999; Bordo, 1993; Marchessault, 2000; Wolf, 1991) who have argued that women objectify and separate from our material bodies, criticising them when they do not conform to the slender ideal that we think is preferred by men. Women are socially pressured into maintaining a slender body through the media and fashion industries (the "fashion-beauty complex," Bartky, 1990) and through pressure from peers and family (Marchessault, 2000). We were particularly interested in how women who body-build manage to resist these cultural pressures to be slender.

Firstly we were interested in our respondents' experiences of interacting with those outside the body building community, because we expected that women may have experienced negative reactions (given that their bodies transgressed what is acceptable for women). In fact, women presented generally positive reports of interactions with non-body building men and women: "They basically tell you you are looking well and you are looking good."

These kinds of experiences seem to run counter to suggestions of other authors (e.g. Aoki, 1996) that women who body build are faced routinely with negative social reactions. However, the very fact that most of the women we interviewed reported that strangers commented spontaneously on the look of their bodies is significant in itself. All women said that strangers regularly commented on their bodies, causing some of them to hide their bodies under baggy "sweats" to avoid attention. This was particularly problematic when women were in situations where it was difficult to hide their bodies, such as on beach holidays where they felt that they were stared at:

> If I go on holiday or out like that. The people always look at you like you've got two heads or something when you go out in your thong. But once they have got used to seeing you then they start to ask about things. They just stare. You know. You know when you are being stared at.

20 This contributed to women feeling different from non-body building women, whom they identified as "the general public." This functioned to place them outside the body rule system for non-body building women:

> I got a lot more comments from the general public last year . . . people were coming up to me, just general women by chance: "How do you get your waist like that?" sort of comment, and I would turn around and say "Well actually I'm a body builder."

They also represented themselves as "other" through giving examples of how men were threatened by their muscularity:

> I've had men come up to me and sort of squeeze my arm which I don't like very much, and sort of make comments like "I wouldn't mess with you" sort of thing. Now obviously they are finding it an insecurity problem. They obviously do look at me differently.

Representing themselves as different in this way functioned to increase women's perceptions of power in these situations. It is not surprising that feeling that men were threatened by one's muscularity would be seen as an empowering experience. Women are often encouraged to feel powerless in relation to men, especially in relation to the size of our bodies (Brownmiller, 1986). Positioning themselves as "different" also functioned to render irrelevant the views of "the general public" when they were not positive. When asked explicitly about how they felt about negative reactions from people outside the body building community, all women argued that they ignored negative reactions from "the general public," as these demonstrated a lack of understanding of the sport of body building. The reference group that was presented as the crucial judges, whose opinions of their bodies mattered, were others in the body building community (especially other body builders and judges in body building competitions): "The people, who understand, that matter, respect me and support me. And anyone else doesn't matter to me any way, so it's irrelevant."

25 Women redefined the importance of other people's reactions so that those who would be most likely to find their bodies acceptable become their reference group. This is an effective way of avoiding negative effects of social stigma (Goffman, 1984), and may have the effect of maintaining their high levels of body satisfaction and self-esteem relative to women outside the body building community. By clearly representing themselves as "different"/ "other" they explicitly placed themselves outside the normal rule system that applied to "the general public" where women were expected to be slender.

Alternative Images of the Ideal Body

The women we interviewed had a clear ideal of how their bodies should look which differed from the mainstream slender ideal discussed by authors such as Susan Bordo (1993), Gail Marchessault (2000), and Fabienne Darling-Wolf (2000). Ideals cited were muscular women body builders in magazines or competitions. The ideal body was described as "athletic," "toned," "healthy." Interestingly, none of the women we interviewed mentioned "large" or "highly muscled" as part of their ideal. This contrasted markedly with interviews with male body builders where being "huge," "enormous," and adding muscle bulk were represented as central to the male body building ideal (Wright *et al.,* 2001). Being "athletic" and "toned" are feminine-appropriate (Bordo, 1993), so these women are maintaining feminine discourses in relation to their stated ideals, although the women body builders cited as role models are highly muscled.

> I mean their bodies are beautiful. Their shape. Like the Figure and the Fitness, and your Americans—Universe and Miss Galaxy. They're beautiful, and this is what people are looking for now. That athletic shape of the female. The waist, and the toned, and umm you know that. But healthy.

Most of the women had started off trying to become moderately muscular, and had developed their ideals to a more muscular shape as they had progressed with their training regimes. Seeing other women highly muscled may have shifted these women's perceptions of what is acceptable for the female form. For instance, one woman noted how she thought her internal norms had changed through being exposed to the body building culture, so that she was used to seeing highly muscled women, and that muscularity had become her norm:

> We are used to it. We get *Muscle and Fitness* [magazine]. We get *Flex* [magazine]. We read them monthly. We get them every day and we have become conditioned to see the female body like that. It doesn't look any different to us. So, when you are in that environment, unless you are huge you're not going to be, if you like, a freak to them.

30 The acceptable degree of muscularity was clearly limited, as being "huge" would mean that you were seen as a "freak" even in the narrow confines of the body building community. The discourses presented here are similar to acceptable mainstream feminine discourses of wanting to be toned and athletic-looking (Bordo, 1993). What makes these accounts different is that these women are clearly aiming for a heavier and more muscular ideal than is acceptable in mainstream Western culture. In order to define muscles as feminine appropriate, body building women may have to shift their perceptions of women's bodies. Seeing positive images of well-muscled women (in magazines, in competition) may have helped to shift women's ideal image of the feminine body to a more muscular shape. However, their discourses maintain traditionally feminine elements, stressing tone and athleticism rather than muscle bulk.

Femininity and Muscularity

Some of the women were clearly uncomfortable with the Western cultural link between muscles and masculinity (Choi, 2000), and were keen to be seen to be "feminine" as well as muscular. Here "feminine" was used by all the women to refer to having "a good/nice shape," which normally meant a visible waist, breasts, and being less muscular than male body building competitors.

> I think I look feminine on stage. I'll never be the biggest girl on stage but do you know what I mean. I think I've got a nice

shape and still look feminine and that's what I base it on.

This "femininity" discourse was presented by most of the women. Women used "femininity" to signify "not looking like a man." All women argued that being muscular did not in itself detract from their perceptions of feeling feminine. For instance, one woman stressed that muscles and femininity were not incompatible, and that both were important to her. She wanted to look both "muscular" and "like a woman," which had informed her decision not to take anabolic steroids:

> If they said to me I had to look like a man and you had to take loads of neat steroids and all that. No so your face goes. You've seen them. I would say sorry I ain't doing it. I like to look like a muscular woman.

35 Being a "muscular woman" was linked with not getting "huge," and having a feminine shape (retaining a visible waist and breast tissue). This association of "femininity" and "muscularity" is explicitly encouraged in body building competitions. Competition rules for the International Federation of Body Builders (IFBB) say:

> First and foremost the judge must bear in mind that this is a woman's body building competition and that the goal is to find an ideal female physique. Therefore the most important aspect is shape, a *muscular yet feminine* shape. The other aspects are similar to those described for the male physique but muscular development must not be carried to such an excess that it resembles the massive musculature of the male physique.

(**http://www.ifbb.com/amarules**)

Women who compete in body building competitions are expected to look acceptably "feminine" as defined within the community by having a "feminine shape" (maintaining breast tissue or having breast implants, having a visible waist), and being smaller than male competitors. So although women explicitly rejected pressures to be thin, and the views of "the general public," they were still subject to pressures to restrict the degree of muscularity and to present as "feminine."

Sexuality and Muscularity

Women reported that they took a pride in their muscular bodies, representing them as feminine and sexual, and saying that they felt more sexually attractive and more sensual when they were "trained." Many of the women presented accounts where they had active sex lives (mostly) with men, and many argued that their sex lives had improved since starting to body-build.

> Physically, I feel more sexy and sensual and umm better about myself trained.
> Now I feel stronger in myself I feel fitter. I have more energy. I just feel more shapely about myself. I feel more sensual as well. I'm more aware of my body now—how it feels.

40 Feeling more sensual when you are muscular means developing a radical view of women's sexual attractiveness that challenges dominant concepts of the sexually attractive woman as slender and large breasted. These women were neither slender nor large breasted, and focused on how they felt in their bodies (more sexy, more sensual, more aware) as a signifier of sexiness, rather than how they looked. Women's sexuality is socially constituted and managed, and recognition of sexual desire and pleasure is not generally seen as feminine appropriate except in proscribed settings (Brook, 1999; Wolf, 1991). By recognising their sexual desires these women are transgressing these "feminine" norms (Bartky, 1990; Goffman, 1984; Tseelon, 1995). This discourse also serves to explicitly reject mainstream cultural perception of women body builders as "other," "unattractive to men" and "unfeminine." Sandra Bartky (1990) and Janet

Holland *et al.* (1998) have argued that most heterosexual women have a "Male in the Head" who judges our bodies in terms of sexual attractiveness. In rejecting mainstream "general public" norms of how women's bodies should look, heterosexual body building women may be faced with conflict over whether or not they are still sexually attractive to men. By emphasising how their sex lives have improved since getting more muscular they explicitly reject notions that they are not attractive to men. Though not a traditional "feminine" discourse (since sexual pleasure is mentioned explicitly), there are elements of the traditionally feminine in the desire to be seen as sexually attractive by men (Brownmiller, 1986).

Muscularity and Self-Confidence

Increasing muscularity was explicitly linked with greater self-confidence and self-esteem. Some of the women had started to body-build at times when they had felt unhappy or low in self-esteem, and where they felt that they needed to exert control over their lives, and spoke about the ways that body building increased confidence:

> Definitely got better self-esteem definitely more confident, and umm you are better able to deal with things in a silly way but you are.
> [I'm] a lot more confident. I think more than anything it builds your self-esteem.

In a culture where women are expected to be physically weak (Choi, 2000), and where physical weakness is often linked with mental weakness (Orbach, 1993) it is perhaps not surprising that these women experienced increased self-esteem when they became stronger and more muscular. All the women we interviewed said that they felt more confident and able to cope with challenges in their lives once they started to build muscle: "I actually feel better when I'm training. I feel better physically and mentally when I am training."

Increased self-confidence was linked with perceptions of increased physical strength, which women represented as masculine. Physical power was linked with mental power, and women drew explicitly on discourses associating femininity with physical weakness: "Women are not, like, supposed to be physically strong, and when you are you feel you can cope with anything."

45 This increase in physical and mental well-being has been associated with other sports. Adrian Furnham and colleagues (1994) found that exercising women tended to have a more positive perception of their own bodies than those who did not exercise, and that physical mastery increased self-esteem. Certainly, these women reported feeling generally better about themselves through training. This may be partly an effect of physical activity itself, which has frequently been documented as a source of well-being (Choi, 2000). However, women's accounts suggested that their well-being was the result of more than the physical exertion involved in training, stressing that they were "taking control" of their bodies. Taking control of the body, and being strong physically was related to being in control of their lives, and being mentally "strong" and able to cope with difficult situations. "Taking control of the body" is a common Western discourse, particularly in relation to women's bodies. Fabienne Darling-Wolf (2000) argues that women are encouraged to objectify and control our bodies, and to gain self-esteem through denial of bodily needs. Denial of the materiality of the body, and control of the body are central to Western post-modern ideology which represents the body as under human control, and control of the body as being crucial to presenting as "feminine" (Bordo, 1993). Susan Bordo (1993) argues that a controlled body (contained, firm, with no obvious fleshiness) represents internal control for women within Western cultures.

The women interviewed here presented traditionally feminine discourses where being in control (of their bodies, their eating and train-

ing, their lives) was represented positively, and where feeling in control was central to feeling good about themselves. However, although these women were drawing on traditionally feminine discourses of bodily control, they were also challenging traditional cultural concepts of what it means to be "feminine." They were controlling their bodies in ways that transgressed the feminine norm as they were building them up rather than scaling them down. Also, their bodies were not just toned (which may be seen as feminine appropriate; Darling-Wolf, 2000). They had built significant muscle mass that went far beyond the "solid, muscular, athletic" look described by Susan Bordo (1993); a look that was sufficiently "different" to attract comments from strangers, and that placed them clearly outside mainstream norms for how women's bodies should look.

Conclusions

When we designed this study we were primarily interested in how women who were engaged in Physique level body building experienced increased muscularity within a mainstream culture that promotes and values extreme slenderness for women. The women we interviewed presented discourses where they represented themselves as feeling good about their bodies, and about themselves generally, and more sensuous than in their pre–body building days. These discourses run counter to those reported in studies on non–body building women where the body is generally seen as cause for dissatisfaction and low self-esteem (Grogan, 1999; Marchassault, 2000), and where sensuality is rarely discussed except under proscribed circumstances (Brook, 1999). Their discourses also stressed control and mastery over the body. This is a traditional feminine discourse, drawing on notions of restraint and control of the female body (Bordo, 1993), although in this case women were talking about increasing rather than reducing the size of their bodies.

These women clearly had to negotiate a feminine identity within a mainstream culture, which prescribes quite a different ideal of feminine attractiveness compared to that to which they aspire. It seems likely that these women had shifted their internal body-shape ideal (with support from within the body building community) to a more muscular figure, and that the only reference group whose reactions really concerned them was the body building community (other body builders, competition judges). This effectively negated the importance of reactions from those who may not find a hard and muscular body appealing, enabling these women to feel physically and mentally strong, and raising their self-esteem and self-confidence. However, they were still under considerable constraint from the body building community in terms of what size was acceptable, which restricted how muscular they could get and still be able to succeed in competition.

This raises the crucial question of whether these women should be seen as complying with mainstream social pressures to be "feminine," as Jane Ussher (1997) puts it, to "do girl"; or whether, as Sandra Bartky (1990) and Leena St Martin and Nicola Gavey (1996) argue, they are resisting these pressures. We believe that they are doing both. In actively changing their bodies to be "unacceptably" muscular, and by explicitly rejecting the judgements of mainstream ("general public") views of their bodies, these women are resisting mainstream cultural norms. However, they are complying with a narrower set of ideals, determined by the largely male body building community. If we had interviewed women who have not competed then we may have identified more evidence of resistance and individuality, since they are likely to be under less pressure from the body building community (see Guthrie & Castelnuovo, 1992). The women interviewed here were engaged in a complex balancing act where they want to be muscular, toned and athletic looking, but not to get unacceptably muscular. Although they may be rejecting mainstream cultural ideals, they are nonetheless not completely free to evolve their own ideals.

50 While women body builders restrict the degree of muscular development for competitions, and whilst acceptable appearance is policed from within the body building community then the idealised model of resistance described by Sandra Bartky (1990) will not become a reality. However, these women's experiences provide a model of how women can resist mainstream cultural pressures to be slender, providing they have support from a salient sub-cultural group. They show that contesting the dominant slender ideal can lead to feelings of empowerment and the forging of alternative body ideals. The fact that these women are subject to alternative pressures from within the body building community to present as "feminine" should not detract from the fact that they have found a way to resist mainstream pressure to be slim, and to feel good about the look and feel of their bodies.

References

Aoki, D. (1996) "Sex and muscle: The female body builder meets Lacan," *Body and Society,* Vol. 2, pp. 45–57.

Bartky, S. (1990) *Feminity and Domination: Studies in the Phenomenology of Oppression,* Routledge, New York.

Bordo, S. (1990) "Reading the slender body," in *Body Politics,* eds M. Jacobus, E. Fox Keller & S. Shuttleworth, Routledge, New York.

Bordo, S. (1993) *Unbeatable Weight: Feminism, Western Culture, and the Body,* University of California Press, Berkeley.

Brook, B. (1999) *Feminist Perspectives on the Body,* Longman, London.

Brownmiller, S. (1986) *Femininity,* Paladin, London.

Choi, P. (2000) *Femininity and the Physically Active Woman,* Routledge, London.

Darling-Wolf, F. (2000) "From airbrushing to liposuction: The technological reconstruction of the female body," in *Women's Bodies Women's Lives,* eds B. Miedema, J. Stoppard & V. Anderson, Sumach Press, Toronto.

Furnham, A., Titman, P. & Sleeman, E. (1994) "Perception of female body shapes as a function of exercise," *Journal of Social Behaviour and Personality*, Vol. 9, pp. 335–352.

Goffman, E. (1984) *Stigma—Notes on the Management of Spoiled Identity*, Penguin, Harmondsworth.

Grogan, S. (1999) *Body Image: Understanding Body Dissatisfaction in Men, Women and Children*, Routledge, London.

Grogan, S. (2000) "Women's body image," in *Women's Health Reader*, ed J. Ussher, BPS Books, London.

Grogan, S. & Wainwright, N. (1996) "Growing up in the culture of slenderness: Girls' experiences of body dissatisfaction," *Women's Studies International Forum*, Vol. 19, pp. 665–673.

Guthrie, S. R. & Castelnuovo, S. (1992) "Elite women body builders: Models of resistance or compliance?" *Play and Culture*, Vol. 5, pp. 401–408.

Holland, J., Ramazanoglu, C., Sharpe, S. & Thomson, R. (1998) *The Male in the Head: Young People, Heterosexuality and Power*, The Tufnell Press, London.

http://www.ifbb.com/amarules (2002) International Federation of Body Building Competition Rules. Site accessed on 28 July 2002.

Lamb, S., Jackson, L., Cassiday, P. & Priest, D. (1993) "Body figure preferences of men and women: A comparison of two generations," *Sex Roles*, Vol. 28, no. 3, pp. 45–358.

Marchessault, G. (2000) "One mother and daughter approach to resisting weight preoccupation," in *Women's Bodies Women's Lives*, eds B. Miedema, J. Stoppard & V. Anderson, Sumach Press, Toronto.

Orbach, S. (1993) *Hunger Strike: The Anorectic's Struggle as a Metaphor for our Age*, Penguin, London.

St Martin, L. & Gavey, N. (1996) "Women's body building: Feminist resistance and/or femininity's recuperation?" *Body and Society*, Vol. 2, pp. 45–59.

Stenner, P. (1993) "Discoursing jealousy," in *Discourse Analytic Research: Repertoires and Readings of Texts in Action*, eds E. Burman & I. Parker, Routledge, London.

Tiggemann, M. & Pennington, B. (1990) "The development of gender differences in body-size dissatisfaction," *Australian Psychologist*, Vol. 25, pp. 306–313.

Tseelon, E. (1995) *The Masque of Femininity*, Sage, London.

Ussher, J. (1997) *Body Talk: The Material and Discursive Regulation of Sexuality, Madness and Reproduction*, Routledge, London.

Wardle, J., Bindra, R., Fairclough, B. & Westcombe, A. (1993) "Culture and body image: Body perception and weight concern in young Asian and Caucasian British women," *Journal of Community and Applied Social Psychology*, Vol. 3, pp. 173–181.

Wolf, N. (1991) *The Beauty Myth: How Images of Beauty are Used Against Women*, Vintage Books, London.

Wright, S., Grogan, S. & Hunter, G. (2000) "Motivations for anabolic steroid use among body builders," *Journal of Health Psychology*, Vol. 5, pp. 566–572.

Wright, S., Grogan, S. & Hunter, G. (2001) "Body builders attitudes towards steroid use," *Drugs: Education, Prevention and Policy*, Vol. 8, pp. 91–97.

Questions for Discussion

1. The authors open with a generalization about "the ideal body shape for women in Western cultures." What does "Western cultures" mean today, in an era of increasing globalization? Are there non-Western cultures that have different standards for judging the body shape for women?

2. What motivated the authors to undertake their research? Did they learn what they set out to learn?

3. The women interviewed for this study were identified through what the authors call "snowball sampling" in paragraph 5. What is the advantage of this method? Could there be any disadvantages?

4. Drawing upon a 1986 study, the authors claim, "Women are often encouraged to feel powerless in relation to men, especially in relation to the size of our bodies." Do you think this is still true?

5. How do the women in this study define *femininity*?

6. What is the relationship between body building and control? Why is "taking control" an issue for people today? How would you define it?

7. After reading this study, would you be inclined to encourage women to engage in body building?

NEGOTIATING DIFFERENCES

Few would deny that it is good for people to be physically fit, but as the authors in this cluster demonstrate, "fitness" can become an unhealthy obsession. That obsession can take the form of developing anxiety about food, turning to steroids to develop muscles, or simply spending too much time at the health club. On the other hand, the borderline between "being fit" and becoming "obsessed with fitness" is not entirely clear—especially when it comes to something like building muscle—as a team of authors demonstrates in "Femininity and Muscularity: Accounts of Seven Women Body Builders." Gender and age may be factors when people determine acceptable limits. For example, is it more acceptable for a man to work at building muscle than it is for a woman? Is concern for fitness more natural for someone in his twenties than in his sixties?

Whatever the answers to questions such as these, imagine the following situation: You are the parent of a seventeen-year-old boy. When he was a child, he was never especially interested in sports, although he occasionally tossed a football around with his buddies. Since he entered junior high, however, he has become obsessed with working out, using this as an alternative to playing team sports. Over the last three years, he has developed a fine physique through weight lifting and using various exercise machines at the health club where you have a family membership. You rarely go to the club as a family, however, because you have busy individual schedules—and when you try to go as a family, your son wants to stay at the club much longer than you do. You have become increasingly concerned about the amount of time he spends in what is essentially a solitary activity (working out while wearing headphones that signal he is in his own world where he should not be disturbed). And you note with particular concern that his GPA is falling. It looks as if he is now spending so much time working out that he is not spending enough time studying.

His birthday is approaching in two weeks. He has asked for a subscription to *Men's Health,* a large container of protein supplement, and a gift certificate for laser hair removal. You have decided to honor two of these requests but to substitute a board game for the third (a game that he would have to play with others). And once his birthday has passed, you have resolved to sit down and talk with him about time management.

Imagine that this young man has a short attention span, especially when it comes to listening to you. Compose a short argument in which you secure his attention by praising what you see as praiseworthy, then explain why you did not give him all of the gifts he had asked for and negotiate a plan that would allow him to pursue his passion but scale back the time he devotes to it so that he would have more time to study and to interact with others.

10

Relationships

Cluster 1

IS ANYONE REALLY "DATING" ANYMORE?

① Beth Bailey, "From Front Porch to Back Seat: A History of the Date"

② Darryl James, "Get Your Hand Out of My Pocket"

③ Vigen Guroian, "Dorm Brothel"

④ Phillip Vannini, "Will You Marry Me? Spectacle and Consumption in the Ritual of Marriage Proposals"

Cluster 2

WHAT DOES MARRIAGE REQUIRE?

① Stephanie Coontz, "Great Expectations"

② Christina Nehring, "Fidelity with a Wandering Eye"

③ Jonathan Rauch, "A More Perfect Union"

④ Phillip Hodson, "Baby, This Is For Ever"

Cluster 3

WHAT DOES IT MEAN TO BE A GOOD PARENT?

① Maureen Freely, "Designer Babies and Other Fairy Tales"

② Wendy McElroy, "Victims from Birth"

③ Anna Quindlen, "The Good Enough Mother"

④ Steven E. Rhoads, "What Fathers Do Best"

Is Anyone Really 'Dating' Anymore?

The question around which the readings in this cluster are organized may seem odd at first glance. You probably see couples in restaurants who look as if they are on a date; someone may have asked you for a date, or you may have asked someone on a date. But "dating" is a relatively modern concept. It began when bicycles made it possible to leave the parlor or porch where a watchful parent was close at hand and accelerated when automobiles made it even easier "to take someone out." But "dating" is not encouraged in all cultures. In some countries, couples who are to be married meet for the first time on their wedding day. And in the United States, it is not always possible to tell if you are or aren't on a date. Is an invitation to share a meal necessarily a sign of romantic intent, or could it simply be a friendly gesture? And is "the date" as a concept increasingly old-fashioned in a time when it is easy for people to meet online or at a party and have sex the same day—an era in which taking someone home is replacing taking someone out? In other words, has hooking up replaced going out—as one of the authors in this cluster argues? Or, if dating still exists, what are its rules? Are men still expected to take the initiative in setting up a date, or can women do so with equal ease? If one person is picking up the bill, is there sometimes an implicit understanding that paying expenses calls for compensation of some kind? How can you tell if dating is heading to a serious relationship? If it leads to a marriage proposal, what should the date be like when that proposal is made? Even if you think your own dating days are over, understanding the evolving nature of going out on a date can help keep you in touch with popular culture and recognize what social conventions seem to be prevailing when it comes to looking for short- or long-term companionship.

① **BETH BAILEY, "From Front Porch to Back Seat: A History of the Date"**

Although the rituals of courtship—or the process through which someone woos a potential lover or mate—can be traced back to antiquity, the phenomenon known as "dating" is relatively new and may already be starting to disappear. The following article by Beth Bailey will give you information upon which you can draw when composing an argument on dating. A cultural and social historian, Bailey teaches at Temple University. Her books include *Sex in the Heartland* (1999) and *From Front Porch to Back Seat: Courtship in Twentieth-Century America* (1988). The article you are about to read is adapted from that latter work for publication in *OAH Magazine of History,* where it appeared in the July 2004 issue. OAH is the Organization of American Historians. The illustrations accompanying Bailey's article are those that appeared upon publication in *OAH.* If you are interested in dating in terms of what it reveals about American culture, you might be alert for additional photographs or other art that illustrate or challenge the points Bailey makes.

From Front Porch to Back Seat: A History of the Date

BETH BAILEY

1 One day, the 1920s story goes, a young man came to call upon a city girl. When he arrived, she had her hat on. The punch line is completely lost on twenty-first-century readers, but people at the time would have gotten it. He came on a "call," expecting to sit in her parlor, be served some refreshments, perhaps listen to her play the piano. She expected to go out on a date. He, it is fairly safe to surmise, ended up spending a fair amount of money fulfilling her expectations (1).

In fact, the unfortunate young man really should have known better. By 1924, when this story was current, "dating" had almost completely replaced "calling" in middle-class American culture. The term appeared in *The Ladies' Home Journal,* a bastion of middle-class respectability, several times in 1914—set off by quotation marks, but with no explanation of its meaning. One article, written in the then-exotic voice of a college sorority girl, began:

CONTEXT

First published in 1883, *Ladies' Home Journal (LHJ)* remains one of the country's principal magazines designed for an audience of women. As its title suggests, it was originally aimed at middle- and upper-class women—women who would like to consider themselves "ladies"—who were not working outside the home, hence the need for news to be brought to them at home. At the beginning of the twentieth century, it featured articles by social reformers like Jane Addams, who had done pioneering work among the poor in Chicago. And its advertising code—which prohibited the publication of ads for fraudulent products—contributed to the political pressures that led to the passage of the Federal Food and Drugs Act in 1906. More recently, *LHJ* has focused on residential architecture and domestic life. It currently enjoys a circulation of more than 4 million. The passage quoted by Bailey reflects how *LHJ* tries to address social concerns without offending readers concerned about respectability.

One beautiful evening in the spring term, when I was a college girl of eighteen, the boy whom, because of his popularity in every phase of college life, I had been proud gradually to allow the monopoly of

In the 1930s, Lewis B. Simon established a "necking grounds" on his Delaware township farm near Camden, New Jersey. A large sign at the entrance to his property welcomed "spooners" and admonished authorities to stay away. (Image donated by Corbis-Bettman.)

my 'dates,' took me unexpectedly into his arms. As he kissed me impetuously I was glad, from the bottom of my heart, for the training of that mother who had taught me to hold myself aloof from all personal familiarities of boys and men (2).

Despite the sugarcoating provided by the tribute to motherhood and virtue, dating was a problematic new practice for the middle classes. Its origins were decidedly not respectable; they lay in the practices of "treating" and the sexual exchanges made by "charity girls." The very term "date" came from prostitution. While the urban working class and frankly sexual origins of dating were fairly quickly obscured, not only by such tributes to virtue but also by the increasingly common belief that young people began "going out" because automobiles made it possible, notions of exchange lingered. The same author who recorded the story about the frustrated caller and the woman in the hat made sense of dating this way: In dating, a man is responsible for all expenses. The woman contributes only her company. Of course, the man contributes his company also, but since he must "add money to balance the bargain," his company must be worth less than hers (3). Thus, according to this economic understanding, she is selling her company to him. Some men declared, flat out, that the exchange was not eq-

uitable, that men were operating at a loss. Others, of course, imagined ways to balance the equation: Man's Company + Money = Woman's Company + ?

5   Dating, which emerged from working class urban culture, became a key ritual of youth culture in the 1920s and was unquestionably the dominant form of "courtship" by the beginning of World War II. Certainly not all American youth participated in the rituals of dating. But those who did not, whether by choice, exclusion, or ignorance of the dominant custom, often still felt the weight of a set of expectations that were enacted in high school peer cultures and even written into school curriculums. For the great majority of youth who did date, the highly personal emotions and experiences of dating were shaped, at least in part, through an increasingly powerful and far-reaching national culture that defined the conventions of dating and lent meaning and coherence to individual experience.

While dating remained "the way of American youth," in the words of one sociologist, it took radically different forms during its roughly forty-five-year heydey from the mid-1920s through the 1960s. In the years before World War II, American youth prized a promiscuous popularity, demonstrating competitive success through the number and variety of dates they commanded. After the war, youth turned to "going steady," arguing that the system provided a measure of security from the pressures of the postwar world.

In the 1930s, a sociologist gave the competitive system a name: the dating and rating complex. His study of a college campus revealed that the system was based on notions of popularity. To be popular, men needed outward, material signs: an automobile, the right clothing, and money. Women's popularity depended on building and maintaining a reputation for popularity. They had to *be seen* with many popular men in the right places, indignantly turn down requests for dates made at the "last minute," which could be weeks in advance, and cultivate the impression that they were greatly n demand (4). Thus, in *Mademoiselle's* 1938 college issue, a Smith College senior advised incoming freshmen to cultivate an "image of popularity." "During your first term," she wrote, get "home talent" to ply you with letters, telegrams, and invitations. College men will think, "She *must* be attractive if she can rate all that attention" (5). At Northwestern University in the 1920s, the competitive pressure was so intense that co-eds made a pact not to date on certain nights of the week. That way they could find time to study, secure in the knowledge they were not losing out to others in the race for popularity by staying home (6).

The new conventions held sway well beyond the gates of colleges. The *Woman's Home Companion* explained the modern dating system—with no mention of college campuses—for its non-elite readers: "No matter how pretty you may be, how smart your clothes—or your tongue—if you have no dates your rating is low. . . . The modern girl cultivates not one single suitor, but dates, lots of them. . . . Her aim is not a too obvious romance but general popularity" (7). Writing to *Senior Scholastic,* a magazine for high school classrooms, a girl from Greensboro, North Carolina, summed it all up:

> Going steady with one date Is okay, if that's
> all you rate (8).

10 Rating, dating, popularity, and competition: catchwords hammered home, reinforced from all sides until they seemed a natural vocabulary. You had to rate in order to date, to date in order to rate. By successfully maintaining this cycle, you became popular. To stay popular, you competed. In the 1930s and 1940s, this competition was enacted, most publicly, on the dance floor—whether in private dancers, col-

lege formats, or high school parties. There success was a dizzying popularity that kept girls whirling from escort to escort. One etiquette book advised young women to strive to become "once-arounders" who never completed a turn around the dance floor before another man "cut in" on her partner (9). Dancing and cutting in were governed by strict protocol: The man had to ask the woman to dance and was responsible for her until she was taken over by another partner. On no account could he leave her stranded on the dance floor or alone on the sidelines. "Getting stuck" with a partner was taken quite seriously as a sign of social failure—even if it was with one's escort. Though a 1933 advice book told the story of a girl who, catching her partner waving a dollar bill behind her back as an inducement to cut in, offered. "Make it five and I'll go home" (10), a more serious suggestion for handling the situation appeared in *Mademoiselle,* "Keep smiling if it kills you" (11).

By 1950, that system had almost completely disappeared. A girl in Green Bay, Wisconsin, reported that her parents were "astonished" when they discovered that she had not danced with anyone but her escort at the high school formal. "The truth was," she admitted, "that I wasn't aware that we were supposed to" (12). This 180-degree reversal signaled not simply a change in dancing etiquette but a complete transformation of the dating system. Definitions of social success as promiscuous popularity based on strenuous competition had given way to new definitions, which located success in the security of a dependable escort.

How did such an entrenched system change so quickly? It was in large part because of World War II. With virtually all physically fit men between the ages of eighteen and twenty-six inducted into the military by 1943, a system already strained to provide multiple male escorts for every woman foundered. Though some women, near military bases, found an overbundance of men seeking companionship, in much of the nation the complaint was, in the words of the popular song, "There is no available male."

As war disrupted one pattern of courtship, it also changed priorities for many of the nation's youth. During the war, the rate at which Americans married jumped precipitously. That made sense—many young couples, facing an uncertain future, including the possibility the man might not survive the war, married in haste. Marriage rates also rose because the war revived the American economy; many couples had delayed marriage during the Depression, so there was a backlog of couples waiting to marry. But the high rate of marriages continued on well past the end of the war. And most strikingly, the average age at marriage plummeted. In 1939, the average age of marriage for women was 23.3. By 1959, fully 47 percent of brides married before they turned nineteen (13).

Before the war, when discussions of courtship centered on rating and dating, marriage had few cheerleaders. It is not that people did not intend to marry. They did. But marriage and the dating system were two quite different things. Dating was about competition within the peer culture of youth; marriage was the end, not the culmination, of participation in youth culture. By the time World War II drew to a close, however, American culture had begun celebrating marriage for youth. And the dating system was no longer a competitive struggle for popularity within youth culture, but instead preparation for an early marriage.

15 This new model had some unusual results. If girls were to marry at eighteen and boys at twenty, the preparation for marriage had to begin earlier than before. Experts told parents to help their children become datable, warning that a later start might doom their marriage prospects. Thirteen-year-olds who did not yet date were called "late daters;" magazines recommended formal sit-down birthday dinners and dances for ten-year-old boys and their dates. A 1961 study found that 40 percent of the fifth-graders in one middle-class Pennsylvania district were already dating (14).

In the prewar years, high school students had emulated the dating-rating system of their elders. As conventions changed for older youth, the younger group tried to keep up. As their slightly older peers married, younger teens developed a parallel convention: going steady. In earlier times, "keeping steady company" was understood as a step along the way to marriage (15). Going steady meant something quite different by the 1950s. Few steady couples really expected to marry one another—especially the twelve-year olds—but, for the duration, they acted as if they *were* married. Going steady had become a sort of play marriage, a mimicry of the actual marriage of their older peers (16).

The new protocol of going steady was every bit as strict as the old protocol of rating and dating, with the form of going steady mirroring teenagers' concepts of young marriage. To go steady, the boy gave the girl some visible token—class ring, letter sweater, etc.—or they exchanged identical tokens, often gold or silver friendship rings worn on the third finger of the left hand. Customs varied locally, as *Life* magazine reported: in Birmingham, Michigan, the girl wore the boy's ID bracelet, but never his letter sweater. In rural Iowa, the couple wore matching corduroy "steady jackets," but in the far West, any couple wearing matching clothing was sure to be laughed at (17).

As long as they went steady, the boy had to call the girl a certain number of times a week and take her on a certain number of dates a week—but numbers were subject to local convention. Neither boy nor girl could date anyone else or pay too much attention to anyone of the opposite sex. While either could go out with friends of the same sex, each must always know where the other was and what he or she was doing. Going steady meant a guaranteed date, but it also meant that the girl had to help her boyfriend save up for big events by budgeting "their" money, even if it meant sitting home together. Going steady also implied, as parents quickly figured out, greater sexual intimacy—either more necking or "going further" (18).

Despite the intense monogamy of such relationships, few saw going steady as a precursor to marriage. One study of 565 seniors in a suburban high school in the East found that 80 percent of them—or approximately 452 seniors—had gone or were going steady, but only 11 of them planned to marry their steadies (19). In New Haven, Connecticut, girls wore "obit bracelets": each time they broke up with a boy they added a disc (engraved with his name or initials to the chain. So temporary were such arrangements that a teen advice book from the mid-1950s suggested girls engrave a "Puppy Love Anklet" with "Going Steady" on one side and "Ready, Willing, 'n Waiting' on the other (20).

20 Harmless as this system sounds today, especially compared to the rigors of rating and dating, going steady precipitated an intense generational battle. The key issue, predictably, was sex. A popular advice book for teenage girls argued that going steady inevitably led girls to heavy necking and thus to guilt for the rest of their lives. Better to date lots of strangers, the author insisted, than end up necking with a steady boyfriend (21). Adults who advocated the old system as somehow sexually safer, however, had selective memories. The days of promiscuous popularity were also the days of "petting parties," and young people had worried endlessly about how "far" to go with a date. And who knew whether a stranger, parked on a dark road, would listen to a young woman's "firm but polite" NO (22)?

Promiscuous dating and going steady held different dangers. Consent was the difference. A beleaguered system of sexual control based on the resolve of girls and young women to say no—at least to the final step of sexual intercourse—was further breaking down in the new system of going steady. As going steady was a simulated marriage, relationships could and did develop within its even short-term security, monogamy, and, sometimes, love. Parents thought it was easier for girls to say no to the rapid successtion of boys who were, at some level, markers for popularity—even when

Young couple dine at the Busy Bee Restaurant in Radford, Virginia, 1940. (John Vachon, photographer. Image courtesy of the Library of Congress.)

the young men insisted, as one did in the pages of *Senior Scholastic,* that the $1.20 he spent on the date should entitle him to at least a little necking (23). Adults were afraid it was harder for girls to say no to a steady.

In some ways parents were right, but it was youth themselves, not parental complaints, that would transform the dating system once again. By the late 1960s, the system of sexual exchange that underlay both dating systems was in tatters, undermined by a widespread sexual revolution. In the 1970s, many young people rejected the artificialities of dating, insisting that it was most important to get to know one another as *people.* And a great many women, recognizing the implied exchange in Man's Company + Money = Woman's Company + ?, rejected that sort of bargain altogether for a variety of arrangements that did not suggest an equation in need of balancing. Since the early 1970s, no completely dominant national system of courtship has emerged, and the existing systems are not nearly so clear in their conventions and expectations as were the old systems of dating. Not always knowing "the rules" is undoubtedly harder than following the clear script of the traditional date, but those critics who are nostalgic for the good old days should first understand the complicated history of the date.

Endnotes

1. Alexander Black, "Is the Young Person Coming Back?" *Harper's,* August 1924, 340. The author of *Ladies' Home Journal's* (*LHJ*) "Good Manners and Good Form" column advised a young woman who had been invited to the theater to greet her escort with her hat on, though without her wrap and gloves. Mrs. Burton Kingsland, *LHJ,* August 1909, 39.

2. "How May a Girl Know?" *LHJ* January 1914, 9. See also a letter to Mrs. Stickney Parks, "Girls' 'Affairs,'" *LHJ.* May 1914, 58.

3. Black, 342.

4. Willard Waller, "The Rating and Dating Complex," *American Sociological Review* 2 (1937): 727–34. Women's popularity was described as associational— she received status as the object of men's choice. Undoubtedly, the right clothes, the right connections, and all the intangibles that come from the right background purchased male attention in the first place, but popular and scholarly experts consistently slighted this angle.

5. Mary Ellen Green, "Advice to Freshmen," *Mademoiselle,* August 1939, 8.

6. Paula Fass. *The Damned and the Beautiful* (New York: Oxford University Press, 1977), 200. Fass found the Northwestern arrangement reported in the *UCLA Daily* (November 13, 1925). I found an apocryphal version of the story in "If Your Daughter Goes to College," *Better Homes and Gardens* (*BH&G*), May 1940.

7. Anna Streese Richardson, "Dates in Christmas Socks," *Woman's Home Companion* (*WHC*). January 1940, 7.

8. "Jam Session," *Senior Scholastic* (*SS*). February 28-March 4, 1944, 32.

9. Elizabeth Eldridge, *Co-ediquette* (New York: E.P. Dutton & Company, 1936). 203. The author based her book on personal research and experience at several U.S. colleges and universities.

10. Alice Leone Moats, *No Nice Girl Swears* (New York: Alfred A. Knopf, 1933) 84-5.

11. Virginia Hanson, "Party-Girl—Princeton Style," *Mademoiselle,* May 1938, 46.

12. Jan London. "The Dateline: Every Dance With the Same Boy?" *Good Housekeeping* (*GH*), March 1955, 100. In the South, the cut-in system persisted longer, but as *Esquire* noted in 1958, "Cutting is the outer limit of poor form almost everywhere else in America" (Nicholas David, "Courtship on the Campus," *Esquire,* February 1958, 49).

13. See Phyllis I. Rosenteur. *The Single Woman* (Indianapolis, IN: Bobbs-Merrill Co., 1961), 58: James H.S. Bossard, "The Engagement Ring—A Changing Symbol," *New York Times Magazine,* September 14, 1958, 74: "The Family Woman's World," *Time,* June 14, 1963, 66.

14. Ruth Imler, "The Sub-Deb: The Late Dater," *LHJ,* September 1955, 54: Dorothy Barclay, "When Boy (Age Twelve) Meets Girl," *New York Times Magazine,* January 23, 1955, 39: "The Pre-Teens," *Time,* April 20, 1962, 68, "Going Steady at Twelve," *Newsweek,* December 18, 1961, 90. See also David R. Mace, "Let's Take a Sane Look at the Hysterical

Young couple on porch of suburban home, ca. 1906. (Image donated by Corbis-Bettman.)

Quest for a Husband," *McCall's*, September 1962, 54.

15. See, for example, G. O. Schultz, "Are Our High Schoolers Snobs?" *BH&G*, February 1941, 86; and Henrietta Ripperger, "Maid in America: Going Steady—Going Where?" *GH*, April 1941, 70. In the 1930s and early 1940s, *Senior Scholastic* argued that going steady would divert teens from achieving their ambitions. A 1939 argument against going steady went: "In our modern, highspeed civilization, it is safe to say that physical maturity usually arrives long before emotional maturity . . . and before most young men are vocationally established and capable of supporting a wife, let alone a family. The educational process for professional or business success today often requires the full concentration of thought and energies for a long time before love and marriage can be seriously considered" ("Readers' Forum," *SS*, February 11, 1939, 3).

16. Psychologists warned that going steady (unless leading directly to marriage) could have a "permanent emotional effect that makes later marriage anti-climactic, since it is 'make believe'" ("Going Steady . . . a National Problem," *LHJ*, July 1949, 131.)

17. For descriptions of the protocol of going steady, see "Going Steady," *LHJ*, 44; Betty Coe Spicer, "If You Don't Go Steady You're Different," *LHJ*, December 1955, 68-9; Cameron Shipp, "The Strange Custom of Going Steady," *WHC*, March 1956, 4; "Profile on Youth Iowa Teenagers Step Out," *LHJ*, July 1949, 42; Jan Landon, "The Date Line," *GH*, October 1956, 21; Thomas B. Morgan, producer, "How American TeenAgers Live," *Look*, July 1957, 21-32.

18. Ibid; see especially the articles in the *Ladies' Home Journal.*

19. Maureen Daly, ed., *Profile of Youth* (New York: J.B. Lippincott Co., 1949), 30. Also quoted in E.E. LeMasters, *Modern Courtship and Marriage* (New York: Macmillan, 1957) 123.

20. Jan Landon, "The Date Line," *GH*, June 1957, 20; Landon, "The Date Line," *GH*, October 1954, 18; Beverly Brandow, *Date Data* (Dallas, TX: Banks Upshaw & Co., 1954), 100.

21. Helen Louise Crounse, *Joyce Jackson's Guide to Dating* (Englewood Cliffs, NJ: Prentice-Hall, 1957), 101. Crounse's name appears nowhere on the book—it was supposedly written by teenage Joyce Jackson.

22. For example, see Gay Head, "Boy Dates Girl Fresh Date," *SS*, February 18, 1939, 31.

23. Gay Head, "Boy Dates Girl Jam Session," *SS*, December 1943, 45.

Questions for Discussion

1. Consider the passage quoted in paragraph 2. If you remove the "sugarcoating," what does it reveal about the girl in question?

2. What does Bailey mean by "notions of exchange"? How was "exchange" historically expected on a date? Do expectations differ today?

3. What is the relationship between social class and dating? Why do you think it emerged from "working class urban culture"?

4. Consider how "popularity" was accessed in the 1930s according to Bailey. Do you see people today engaging in similar behavior in the hope of being perceived as "popular"?

5. How did the Second World War affect national dating patterns?

6. It is often stated that kids today are growing up faster than ever and being sexualized at earlier ages than had been the case in the past. Does Bailey provide any evidence that complicates this version of the past?

7. Bailey remarks that adults sometimes have "selective memories" about dating. What do you think people are most likely to forget about this process?

8. In your experience, are many people still "dating" today, or is it a system of courtship that is passing away?

② DARRYL JAMES, "Get Your Hand Out of My Pocket"

The founder of *Rap Sheet* and the author of *Bridging the Black Gender Gap,* Darryl James writes a syndicated column called "The Bridge." The following argument originated as one of his columns, and it is reprinted here as it appeared in the *Los Angeles Sentinel* in March 2005. In this piece, you will find that James takes a provocative position—a position signaled by his title. He argues that women should pay their own way on dates and that women who expect men to pick up the tab should make that clear right away. "Perhaps some men will simply offer you a flat fee," he suggests, "to get right to what they want." In addition to his work on gender, James has written about race riots in Los Angeles in a work that won the 2004 nonfiction award at the Seventh Annual Black History Book Fair.

Get Your Hand Out of My Pocket

DARRYL JAMES

1 The lady was smart, pretty and in very good shape. We had been dating for a few weeks and I was enjoying the conversations with her.

We talked about our goals in life and we shared a great deal about ourselves with each other. We both recognized that sharing up front can prevent confusion later on down the line.

We began talking about what we really wanted in relationships when she went there—she said she wanted a man who was "generous." Now, the word itself may seem innocent enough, but let's really take a look at what it means.

When a woman says that she wants a man to be generous, she is typically referring to the dating process—she wants gifts, and she wants to be courted in a lavish manner.

5 We're not talking about some third world nation where women are denied employment and treated as property, we are talking about so-called "independent women" in the good old U.S. of A, who fought and still fight to be treated as equals with all the rights that men have—except in dating.

As an independent woman, you should have no problem picking up the check or at least paying your way. Otherwise, stop saying that you are independent, and stop saying you want a good man. What you want is a sucker and your honesty will be appreciated.

As far as finances are concerned, anything above wanting someone to carry their own weight is unreasonable.

In addition, there are so many other things to be concerned about that have value, that finances should be last on the list, because at the end of the day, when the conversation turns to finance, most men are turned off.

Being single and dating gets rough enough without all of the confusion of financial expectations. For any rational adult, it makes no sense to expect someone to spend money to entertain your grown behind. That's like saying you want all of the fun but none of the responsibility, and it's a poor way to begin a relationship.

10 A few years back, I was dating a woman who I really believed could have been my soul mate. We communicated beautifully, we were both from Chicago, and we liked the same things. We both had the same method of accepting the things about each other that were divergent from our own individual experiences. However, there was one thing that she presented that I ultimately could not get beyond.

She couldn't stop begging.

Yes, I said begging. It wasn't that I didn't have the money. I was making plenty of cash, but at every turn, she was asking me for money to go out, money to buy new shoes, money to buy birthday gifts for friends and money to spend at the mall.

The thing that was most disturbing was that she didn't even ask for bills or other necessities, she would ask for trinkets and trash just to see what she could get.

It's even difficult sometimes to sit at a bar and exchange conversation without the expectation of drink purchases. Why would any otherwise self-respecting woman want to diminish herself to a common "drink whore"? Be offended, but if you are selling your conversation and/or company for the price of a drink, this is what it amounts to.

15 There is already enough stress involved in trying to merge two individual personalities, which may be divergent based on religion, education, in addition to gender. Add finance to the mix and it's all bad.

It's just sad to watch beautiful sisters who claim to want a real relationship start things off with a focus on avoiding financial responsibility.

Here's another horrible example: One of my close friends in Chicago was scheduled to meet a young lady at a local hangout for drinks. Each time they went out, she created diversions when it was time to pay, or simply stared at the check, leaving him to pay. Once, he asked her to split the check and she claimed to have left her money at home. Outside of her difficulty with paying for her own entertainment, she was actually a nice young lady and my friend liked her very much.

CONTEXT

First published in 1933, the *Los Angeles Sentinel* is a weekly newspaper directed toward an audience of African Americans. With a circulation of 125,000, it is one of the oldest media outlets under black ownership in the western United States.

He arranged to meet her again and purposely arrived after she did. She had already ordered a few drinks and food. My friend sat down and ordered water. He declined any food, but otherwise, maintained the same kind of conversation as on previous dates. When the check came at the end of the evening, his date slid it across the table in front of him.

Quick—what would YOU do? Here's what my friend did: He politely slid the check back to her and stated: "I didn't eat or drink anything, so you should go ahead and take care of it." Her reply: "Why would you ask to spend time with me, if you don't want to treat me like a lady?"

20 Ladies, if there is a cost for your time, please make that clear up front. Perhaps some men will simply offer you a flat fee to get right to what they desire. If you are not for sale, you should take the price off of your company.

Now, here's the sad part: When I write pieces like this and give such examples, some sisters say that it's only the circles I run in, but those circles seem to be all across the nation, because not only are my brothers lodging numerous complaints, but many of my honest sisters who pay their own way are aware of the offending behavior as well.

The bottom line is that no matter how you couch it, coming after a man financially is unattractive. Phrase it as "generous," but if you expect to be paid for, then you are practicing a form of prostitution. Don't be surprised or angry if you get some of the same results.

Dating is an expensive venture and difficult to launch properly. In my lectures, my most salient piece of advice to single women is to be unafraid of initiating contact and open to sharing the financial burden of dating.

The dating process should allow two people to get to know each other, ostensibly before making a commitment. A relationship is about partnership and dating should not be any different. In fact, since dating may not turn out to be anything permanent, there should be no substantial financial investment. At the end of something that doesn't work out, both people can walk away undiminished.

25 So, ladies, please focus on a man's character, not his wallet, and maybe you will find something to have and to hold. When you approach a man keep your eyes on the prize.

And keep your hand out of my pocket.

COMPLICATION

Women may view an upcoming date from a perspective very different from James's. Consider the following advice from Doug Veith, author of *Win Her with Dinner*, as edited by Liesa Goins for publication in a 2004 issue of *Men's Health:*

Recipe for Romance

IMPRESS YOUR DATE: When cooking a romantic dinner, there are so many potential pitfalls—singed eyebrows, scalded crotch. We recommend oven mitts and these tips, . . .

TIME IT WELL. The third date is when the good stuff often happens, says Veith, so it's smart to be close to home. But anniversaries and Fridays are also good times.

AVOID SURPRISES. Always clear the proposed meal with the proposed woman ahead of time, says Veith. Make sure she doesn't have any allergy or diet issues.

IMPROVE THE SETTING. If you have a dining room, great. Otherwise, dress up any flat surface with a tablecloth, cloth napkins, and matching salad and dinner plates. To upgrade the setting, Veigh suggests sunflowers—an innocent and safe flower—and unscented candles.

PLAY MUSIC. Try to pair the song selection with your menu. For a classic American dinner like New York strip steak, try Billie Holiday. For an Italian supper, spin Paolo Conte. Good Charlotte doesn't go with anything. But the book has plenty of other pairing suggestions.

DON'T FORGET DESSERT. At the least, she'll leave with a good taste in her mouth.

Questions for Discussion

1. James describes the first woman in his argument as a "lady" and subsequently refers to other single women as "ladies." How do you interpret his use of this term? How do you respond when he subsequently switches to a phrase like "your grown behind"?

2. Do you agree that being "up front" on a date "can prevent confusion later on down the line"? What can keep people from being honest with each other in the early stages of dating?

3. How would you define a "drink whore"? Is there a male equivalent?

4. James anticipates the argument that women behave the way he describes only in his own circle. How well does he respond to this with his counterargument?

5. What does James expect from dating? To what extent does it correspond with your expectations?

6. How would you describe a "generous" person? Under what circumstances, in dating, can generosity be welcome? Under what circumstances would it make you uncomfortable?

③ VIGEN GUROIAN, "Dorm Brothel"

What happens when a college professor grows upset by what he perceives as sexual promiscuity on his campus—the campus of a faith-based college—and these perceptions are reinforced by stories from his college-age children? The following argument by Vigen Guroian demonstrates how one man responds under such circumstances. The author of *Rallying the Really Human Things: The Moral Imagination in Politics, Literature, and Everyday Life,* Guroian teaches theology at Loyola College in Baltimore—and you will find several references to Loyola in his work. You will also find references that reflect his interests in theology and literature. Whether or not you agree that sex is rampant in college dormitories—as the title suggests—understand that Guroian is raising a serious question about the nature of the relationship between a college and its students. Should college administrators assume that students are adults entitled to their own private lives, or should colleges honor a principle largely abandoned a generation ago: *in loco parentis,* which means that the college or university assumes parental responsibilities for students while their real parents are elsewhere—and often unaware of what life is really like in a college dormitory?

Dorm Brothel

VIGEN GUROIAN

*Born in Birmingham, Walker Percy (1916–1990) won the National Book Award for his first novel, *The Moviegoer,* in 1961. *The Last Gentleman* focuses on an issue that runs through much of Percy's work—man's difficulty fitting into the modern world that surrounds him. Well versed in theology and philosophy, he is considered by critics to be one of the most thoughtful fiction writers of the mid- to late-twentieth century.

"The so-called sexual revolution is not, as advertised, a liberation of sexual behavior but rather its reversal. In former days, even under Victoria, sexual intercourse was the natural end and culmination of heterosexual relations. Now one begins with genital overtures instead of handshake, then waits to see what will turn up (e.g., might become friends later). Like dogs greeting each other nose to tail and tail to nose."

THE LAST GENTLEMAN (1966) **WALKER PERCY**

1   Nineteen sixty-six, the year in which Walker Percy's* *The Last Gentleman* was published,

is also the year I entered as a first-year-man at the University of Virginia. We did not stoop to the State U level of referring to ourselves as freshmen, sophomores, and such—not at "The University." We were all men at U.Va.—"gentlemen," we were told. Young women visited on weekends from Sweet Briar and Randolph-Macon, Mary Washington, and Hollins College. But they did not stay in the dormitory or the fraternity house. They stayed in college-approved housing, more often than not the home of a widow who had a few rooms to let and happily accepted a delegation from the colleges to assume the responsibilities of *in loco parentis.*

Parental rules were enforced even in the fraternity houses—self-enforced by those of us who lived in them. Young women were not permitted in the bedrooms and had to be out of the house by a certain hour. We dated, blind-dated often. We did not know what "hooking up" was. We had never heard of date rape either, though some of us may have committed it. It could happen in the back seat of a car, a cheap motel, a cow pasture, or a Civil War battlefield, but not in a college dormitory or fraternity house bedroom, not yet at least; it was not until the end of the decade that all the rules and prohibitions came tumbling down and the brave new world of the contemporary coeducational college commenced.

Back then, and from the immemorial, so far as I knew, there were the "easy" girls. We had a provocative name or two for them, and they were quickly sorted out from the "other" girls. Word got around fast. These were not young women one seriously considered marrying, and most of us expected and hoped to find a mate in college. If, however, a guy got especially "hungry" or "horny," there was no special stigma attached to taking advantage of what the easy girls had to offer.

The gentlemen of the University of Virginia lived by a double standard, but there were standards. There was little doubt about that. The arrangements the colleges provided for the sexes to meet and mix, strict dorm-visitation hours, approved housing, curfews for female visitors, and the like made that abundantly clear. When we set off on a road trip to a girls school, either by hitchhiking or jamming six or eight into a car, and arrived at the dorm, we did not just mosey on up to our dates' rooms and hang out. We waited, garbed in coat and tie, in the big informal parlor until our dates made their entrance.

5 My college classmates and fraternity brothers at the University of Virginia and I were certainly not Victorians, but we were not post-Christian and postmodern young men either, not quite yet. Maybe we were the last gentlemen, which certainly should not be interpreted to mean that we always behaved like gentlemen, just that we had some appreciation for the meaning of the word and maybe even aspirations to become what it signified.

Furthermore, we knew what the opposite of a gentleman was. In fact, in those days "The University" was often called, proudly by some, the Playboy School of the South. So we were gentlemen and playboys both, spirited by our friend Jack Daniels. We knew there was a contradiction in being a gentleman and a Don Juan at the same time. But being a Don Juan or playboy has significance only in a world in which the idea of the gentleman exists, in which fidelity is acknowledged as a virtue, and in which sex is considered most appropriate to the marital union. We had absorbed these notions from a culture that had not yet abandoned them. We knew the game had to end eventually, probably when we met the right girl and got married, and most of us got married by the age of 23 or 24, many to our college sweethearts.

One could say that in 1966, what men and women called dating was a late—and as I look back on it, probably also tenuous—version of courtship. We understood, at least implicitly, that there was an important difference between going whoring and dating. Treating a young woman like a whore was what a Don Juan would do, but not the mark of a gentleman, especially one looking for a future wife. But today is entirely different. My grown children tell me so, as do my students at Loyola College,* and much has been written on the subjects of dating, courtship, and the sexual attitudes of our youth that confirms their testimony. But why is dating, as a form of courtship, an endangered practice?

Experts identify a variety of reasons and causes, but I do not pretend to address the subject scientifically or dispassionately. I will not review this literature here. Nor do I have a sentimental attachment to a remembered past. Lest I be misunderstood, I do not call for a return to the "good old days" of dating as it was when I was a youth anymore than I would advocate a return to arranged marriages. As a college professor and father of a college-age daughter, however, I am outraged by the complicity of my college and most other schools

*Loyola College's mission states, "Loyola College in Maryland is a Jesuit Catholic university committed to the educational and spiritual traditions of the Society of Jesus and to the ideals of liberal education and the development of the whole person. Accordingly, the College will inspire students to learn, lead and serve in a diverse and changing world."

*Doane College's website tells visitors, "'We Build on Christ.', . . . [T]his phrase reminds us of how Doane got its start through the efforts of the local Congregational pastor and Thomas Doane, chief engineer of the Burlington Railroad. Doane maintains its relationship with the church, now called the United Church of Christ (UCC)."

in the death of courtship and the emergence of a dangerous and destructive culture of "hooking up."

Doane College* in Nebraska recently mailed a recruiting postcard that showed a man surrounded by women, with a caption that read that students at this college have the opportunity to "play the field." After a public outcry last December, administrators hastily withdrew the marketing campaign, explaining that the postcard was harmless and a metaphor for exploring a variety of education options. But the very fact that the campaign was conceived and approved in the first place speaks volumes. The sexual revolution, if that is an appropriate title, was not won with guns but with genital groping aided and abetted by colleges that forfeited the responsibilities of *in loco parentis* and have gone into the pimping and brothel business.

Sex Carnival

I do not use these words lightly or loosely, and rarely is a college so blatantly suggestive as was Doane, although this attitude about the commendability of sexual experimentation has become an orthodoxy among many who hold positions as deans of student life at our colleges. Of course, some colleges take concrete steps to resist this revolution of morals. Still, in most American college coed dorms, the flesh of our daughters is being served up daily like snack jerky. No longer need young men be wolves or foxes to consume that flesh. There are no fences to jump or chicken coops to break into. The gates are wide open and no guard dogs have been posted. It is easy come and easy go. Nor are our daughters the only ones getting hurt. The sex carnival that is college life today is also doing great damage to our sons' characters, deforming their attitudes toward the opposite sex. I am witnessing a perceptible dissipation of manly virtue in the young men I teach.

10 Nevertheless, my more compelling concern about this state of affairs is for the young women, our daughters. Since my student

years, colleges have abandoned all the arrangements that society had once put in place to protect the "weaker sex" so they could say "no" and have a place to retreat if young men pressed them too far. And although even when these arrangements were in place, one could not always say with confidence that the girl was the victim and the boy the offender, the contemporary climate makes identifying predator and prey even trickier. The lure and availability of sexual adventure that our colleges afford is teaching young women also to pursue sexual pleasures aggressively. Yet, based on my own conversations and observations, there is no doubt that young women today are far more vulnerable to sexual abuse and mistreatment by young men than when I was a college student, simply because the institutional arrangements that protected young women are gone and the new climate says everything goes.

In 1966, my fraternity brothers and I were caught up in a monumental shift in relations between the sexes that Will Barrett, the young protagonist of Walker Percy's tale, struggles to understand and come to terms with. One evening, Will and his love interest, Kitty Vaught, retreat to a cramped camper. They try to dance and then lie together in a bunk with all the expectations ignited by young flesh pressed against young flesh. A conversation ensues that is profoundly emblematic of what my generation went through. Prompted by the intimacy and abandon of the situation, Will tells Kitty a story about how his grandfather took his father to a whorehouse at the age of 16. Kitty asks Will if his father did the same for him. Will answers that he did not. Then, after some chatter about the meaning of love and the difficulty of it, Kitty says to Will, "Very well, I'll be your whore." Will does not protest, so Kitty injects,

"Then you think I'm a whore?"

"No," that was the trouble. She wasn't. There was a lumpish playfulness, a sort of literary gap in her whorishness.

"Very well, I'll be a lady."

15 "All right."

"No, truthfully. Love me like a lady."

"Very well."

He lay with her, more or less miserably, kissed her lips and eyes and uttered sweet love murmurings into her ear, telling her what a lovely girl she was. But what am I, he wondered: neither Christian nor pagan nor proper lusty gentleman, for I've never really got the straight of this lady-and-whore business. And that is all I want and it does not seem much to ask: for once and all to get the straight of it.

This is what dating was becoming back then, as young men and women without traditional adult oversight started to entrust themselves to one another. A clear sense of the formal stages of courtship had faded and authoritative rules of conduct were dissolving. Percy's scene is not wholly foreign to my students. But neither is it typical. The culture has changed dramatically.

Literary Hook-Ups

20 When, in Tom Wolfe's* most recent novel, *I Am Charlotte Simmons,* Charlotte's mother asks her during Christmas break where students go on dates at Dupont University, Charlotte responds: "Nobody goes out on a date. The girls go out in groups and the boys go out in groups, and they hope they find somebody they like." This is Charlotte Simmons's description of "hooking up." "Hooking up" has replaced traditional courtship and dating among today's college students. "Hooking up" is dating sans courtship or expectations of a future relationship or commitment. It is strictly about user sex. I use you and you use me for mutual pleasure. And liquor is more often than not the lubricant that makes things go.

We all are familiar with contemporary sitcoms and so-called reality television shows that bring young men and women together with precisely the intent of getting them to eye each other's genitals like candy at a convenience store, respond to each other's sexual nature in animal fashion, and hop in bed together with no regrets. There are no evident prohibitions or taboos. The comic or dramatic plot is all about sexual adventure and getting as much pleasure from the experience as possible. The rules are strictly instrumental. Often, they are made up along the way merely to facilitate the smooth going of the "game" or "hunt," as it might more appropriately be called. There is no right and wrong.

I cannot say for sure whether these shows influence real life or whether it is the other way around. In the end, it does not much matter. What I do know is that a latter-day Walker Percy could not write the scene I have cited with the belief that it faithfully depicts how contemporary young men and women meet or what is at issue between them.

Take, for another example, the benchmark movies of the '60s about young men and women coming of age, such as *The Graduate* or Francis Ford Coppola's *You're a Big Boy Now.* They are now passé. The sexual innocence depicted and the presence of adult supervision, limited or mocked, against which the young protagonists struggle, are no longer realistic. Frank Capra's classic romantic comedy *It Happened One Night,* released in 1934,

*Born March 2, 1931, Tom Wolfe is a novelist widely recognized as the leader of the New Journalism of the 1960s. He may be best known for his 1968 work *The Electric Kool-Aid Acid Test,* but he remains a productive writer and a fashionable figure, famous for wearing immaculate white suits.

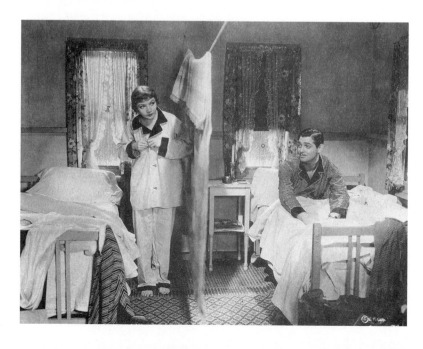

CONTEXT

Film director Frank Capra (1897–1991) won an Oscar for his film *It Happened One Night*. He also directed *Mr. Deeds Goes to Town*, *Mr. Smith Goes to Washington*, and *It's a Wonderful Life*. You may well have seen *It's a Wonderful Life* on television, because this film about a small-town banker rescued by his guardian angel just in time to celebrate Christmas is broadcast almost every December. But Capra's funniest film is *It Happened One Night*. In this film, a reporter, portrayed by Clark Gable, tracks down a wealthy heiress, played by Claudette Colbert, who has run away from home rather than marry a stuffy millionaire. The reporter and the heiress eventually fall in love, but they are careful not to act upon that love while on the road together. Two scenes from this movie are especially famous. In one, the character played by Colbert teaches the character played by Gable how to hitchhike when she lifts her skirt a few inches after he has failed to get a ride by sticking out his thumb. In the other, the character played by Gable carefully hangs a blanket to divide the motel room they are forced to share when they are running out of cash. That's the night that gives the movie its title.

contrasts even more strikingly with contemporary sexual mores. In that movie, a newspaper reporter named Peter Warne, played by Clark Gable, heroically and humorously lives up to the standard of a gentleman in his behavior toward a rebellious young heiress named Ellie Andrews, played by Claudette Colbert. Occasions arise that certainly present Peter with opportunities to make sexual advances. But Peter does not take advantage of these occasions, despite his increasing desire for a woman whom at first he disdained. Only after these two spirited combatants of the war between the sexes get wed is it suggested that they are sexually intimate. At the end of the film, a symbolic trumpet sounds, announcing that the "walls of Jericho" are falling.

Over the years, I have asked my students whether they have seen this movie. Only a handful of the students in my course on theology and literature acknowledge even having heard of it. If they were to watch *It Happened One Night*, I do not doubt that some of my students would enjoy it and highly appreciate its artistry and humor. Yet I hardly think many would identify strongly with the characters and

their situation. In simple terms, the symbolic curtain that Peter builds from a clothesline and a blanket in order to separate two twin beds in a rented room is hardly the correlative of life in coed college dormitories and apartments.

25 The nature and depth of this cultural disconnect is illustrated by a scene in Aldous Huxley's *Brave New World*, published just two years after *It Happened One Night* premiered. John, the so-called Savage, is brought to London from the Indian reservation. During a conversation with Helmholtz Watson, a young author of radio jingles and touchy-feely movie scripts, John recites lines from *Romeo and Juliet*, a play that has been banned and is unknown to the inhabitants of *Brave New World*. Despite the fact that Helmholtz rebels against the shallowness of life in *Brave New World*, the plot of Shakespeare's play puzzles him. After listening to the scene of the lovers' first meeting, he wonders what the fuss is all about. He does not understand the nature of the tragedy because he has no knowledge of courtship or the roles of parental and filial love and fidelity in Shakespeare's world.

> Getting into such a state about having a girl—it seemed rather ridiculous . . . The mother and father (grotesque obscenity) forcing the daughter to have someone she didn't want! And the idiotic girl not saying that she was having someone else whom (for the moment, at any rate) she preferred! In its smutty absurdly the situation was irresistibly comical.

It Happened One Night was filmed more than 300 years after Shakespeare wrote his plays. Nevertheless, its humor and ennobling power rest on standards of propriety and courtship nearer to the 16th century than to Huxley's futuristic London or even today's hook-up culture. The reading public of the first decades of the 20th century might find the abolition of courtship and marriage in *Brave New World* interesting and remote, but my students readily admit the possibility of such a future. I recently gave a lecture at Loyola on *Brave New World*. During the question-and-answer period, there was a brief discussion about the similarities of dormitory life with *Brave New World.* I opined that whatever the resemblances, there is a clear difference between the two: Sexual promiscuity and hooking up among college students is voluntary, I said, whereas in *Brave New World* this behavior is mandatory. A young woman and dormitory resident adviser walked up to me afterwards and chided me: "Dr. Guroian, you are mistaken about that. The peer pressure and the way things are set up make promiscuity practically obligatory. It doesn't matter what the school says officially. The rules are to be broken. This freedom can make girls dizzy and unsure of whatever else they believe about ' saving oneself for marriage.' When it seems like everyone else is 'doing it,' it is hard to say no. It is more like *Brave New World* here than you think. I deal with it or, more frequently, turn my eyes from it, every day as an RA."

During the spring semester, this same young woman, who was enrolled in one of my classes, wrote a brief exposé on what goes on at Loyola College and other colleges. She explains the sundry distinctions today's young men and women make in relationships and sexual liaisons.

> It may not be that dating is at the brink of extinction, but . . . it has taken a back seat in the modern-day lives of students. Hooking up, going out, going steady, and dating, contrary to what some may think, are not the same thing . . . If you are "going out" with someone it means that you have a boyfriend or a girlfriend, you are in a "steady" relationship with that person. However, a couple needn't actually go anywhere [go on dates together] to be in this kind of relationship. Hooking up is basically dating without the romance. It has become customary for young adults to simply cut to the chase, the sexual . . . part of a relationship. A hook-up can be a onetime thing, as it most often is, or it can be a semi-regular thing, but not a full relationship. Although it may take on the signs of one.

30 One might conclude that modern day youth have simply gotten lazy and careless.

Most . . . are not looking for a romantic relationship; they see the new freedom and plethora of sexual opportunities and simply take what they can get. They get to college, and it's an amusement park with so many different enticing rides, one would be missing out on the whole experience to settle with the first one they tried. And why should they bother with the responsibility and formalities of a date when they have a better chance of getting immediate satisfaction after buying a few drinks at a bar?

I could have foregone quoting this young coed to cite any number of studies that describe these phenomena more "scientifically." These studies try hard to be "objective," but as a result they cannot convey the immediacy and passion of this young woman's narrative or the matter-of-fact manner in which she draws connections between the breakdown of courtship, the rise of a hook-up culture, and what we used to call pimping and prostitution. "Coed dormitories," she continues, "are they an ideal situation or a sad form of prostitution? You go out with your friends on your terms, after a few drinks you're both attracted. . . . Interested and lonely, you go together, no obligations, no responsibilities, and no rules. Then there is that late-night 'booty call.' This has become such a custom of the college lifestyle [that] most have come to accept it, although maybe not respect it. If it were really the ideal situation, the walk home the next day [to one's own room] wouldn't be called 'the walk of shame.'" At Loyola College, the vast majority of students live on campus, and since the college has bought up a number of neighboring high-rise and garden apartments, after the freshman year the "walk of shame" need not even be made. It may be only a few steps from the boy's apartment to one's own, or better yet, from the boy's room to one's own.

The Culpable College
The campaign against alcohol and drugs, which it seems every American college has proudly announced it is waging, is a smoke-

CONTEXT

Brave New World by Aldous Huxley was first published in 1933. It envisions a future world in which procreation is managed at a Hatching and Conditioning Center that produces thousands of nearly identical embryos. Children born and raised in this center are conditioned to dislike books, obey the government, repress personal feelings, and become docile consumers. The book reflected the modern fascination with science and the emergence of totalitarian states in Russia and in Germany. (Hitler came to power in 1933 and would demonstrate deadly interest in producing and conditioning a master race, as well as subordinate races that would serve that master race.) The development of biotechnology at the end of the twentieth century—which continues to raise social and ethical concerns—makes Huxley's book of interest to many contemporary readers.

screen that covers the colleges' great sin. Regulating a substance like alcohol on an urban campus like Loyola's cannot succeed unless there is radical reform of the whole of college life. Nothing that the college does to limit alcohol consumption can make a significant difference until the major incentives to drink are removed, beginning with coed dormitories and apartments. Many of my students have explained to me that drinking, especially binge drinking, serves as the lubricant for the casual sex that living arrangements at Loyola invite and permit. There is no need to find the cheap hotel of yesterday. The college provides a much more expensive and available version of it.

The sexual adventures that follow can take a variety of paths, but what this young Loyola man describes is not atypical.

> True story: I woke up at three in the morning one day last year to my roommate having sex in his bed five feet away from me. Taking a moment to actually wake up, I realized what was going on. I got up . . . heard what was going on, and . . . recognized the voice of the girl . . . I had two classes with her the semester before and one that semester . . . The next morning . . , there was no awkward exchange. No childish giggling. I simply told him that I could not believe that she didn't mind having sex with someone for the first time while someone else was in the room sleeping. I also couldn't believe that she hadn't stopped and covered herself up when I had walked out of the room. My roommate looked at me with a casual smile, the same smile I'd seen when talking about the Mets or Red Sox, the same smile I'd seen at our dining-room table over Taco Bell, and he said to me, "Whatever, she's a college girl."

5 This is a disturbing description of the demise of decency and civility between the sexes for which the American colleges are culpable and blameworthy. It is not that what this student describes was unheard of in the late 1960s. Frankly, I can tell similar stories about my college experience. Nevertheless, this was the exception rather than a commonplace oc-

currence. For colleges made it clear to young men and women that such behavior was unacceptable, and had in place living arrangements with rules and sanctions that discouraged it.

There is nothing new or novel about human depravity or debauchery. Outrage over debauchery is deserved. Nevertheless, as I have suggested already, my outcry is not directed at the debauchery among college students, but rather at the colleges themselves. Today colleges not only turn a blind eye to this behavior, but also set up the conditions that foster and invite it. I am concerned about the young men and women who wish to behave differently, but for whom this is made especially difficult by the living conditions their colleges provide and often insist upon.

In *I Am Charlotte Simmons,* a fictitious counterpart of the young woman and resident advisor whom I cited earlier says to the new freshmen under her supervision, "The university no longer plays the role of parents." She means sex is permitted. The satiric irony is that there are rules against keeping or consuming alcohol in the dorms. Is that not also *in loco parentis?* Charlotte quickly learns, however, that all of these rules are made to be broken and that being "sexiled," which means being expelled from one's room so that the roommate may have sex, is routine and obligatory at Dupont University.

In the new culture that our colleges incubate and maintain, everyone is a "guy." Everyone is "familiar." Young men and women who have never seen anyone of the opposite sex naked or in underwear, other than family members, now must get used to being seen by and seeing others—perfect strangers—in just such a state. Everyone is available to everyone else. It would be antisocial not to be.

Under such conditions, how could dating and courtship possibly survive? How could traditional marriage survive, in the long term? Courtship and dating require an inviolable private space from which each sex can leave at appointed times to meet in public and enjoy the other. In other words, in a courtship culture it ought to be that two people who are "serious" actually do "go out" together and do not merely cohabit in a closeted dormitory or apartment. Yet over the past 40 years, American colleges have created a brave new unisex world in which distinctions between public and private, formal and familiar, have collapsed. The differences between the sexes are now dangerously minimized or else just plain ignored because to recognize them is not progressive or politically correct. This is manifestly the case with coed dorm floors and shared bathrooms and showers. These give the lie to official college rules against cohabitation. They are the wink and nod our colleges give to fornication and dissipation. Even in 1957, when he was chancellor of the University of California at Berkeley, Clark Kerr was almost prophetic when he stated humorously that his job responsibilities were "providing parking for faculty, sex for students, and athletics for the alumni."

40 Loyola College and a great many other colleges and universities simply do not acknowledge, let alone address, the sexualization of the American college. Rather, they do everything possible to put a smiley face on an unhealthy and morally destructive environment, one that—and this is no small matter—also makes serious academic study next to impossible. Most of the rhetoric one hears incessantly from American colleges about caring for young men and women and respecting their so-called freedom and maturity is disingenuous. Should we really count it to their credit that colleges are spending more and more resources on counseling and therapy when the direct cause of many wounds they seek to heal is the brave new world that they have engineered, sold as a consumer product, and supervised?

To serve *in loco parentis* involves caring for the whole student not as an employer or client but as parent. In its statement "Vision and Values: A Guide for the Loyola College Community," Loyola says it holds to "an ideal

of personal wholeness and integration." The college aims "to honor, care for, and educate the whole person," enjoining the entire college community "to strive after intellectual, physical, psychological, social, and spiritual health and well-being." The statement correctly associates these goals of education with the Roman Catholic faith and the liberal-arts tradition. Many other colleges and universities issue similar statements of aim and purpose on both religious and secular grounds. Yet the climate at Loyola College—and many, many others—produces the antithesis of these aims. It fosters not growth into wholeness but the dissolution of personality, not the integration of learning and everyday living but their radical bifurcation. It most certainly does not support the church's values of marriage and family.

Young men and women are being enticed to think of themselves as two selves, one that is mind and reason in the classroom and another self, active "after hours," that is all body and passion. They begin to imagine—though few entirely believe it—that they can use (that is, abuse) their bodies as they please for pleasure, and that choosing to do so has nothing to do with their academic studies or future lives. In reality, they are following a formula for self-disintegration and failure.

This is the grisly underbelly of the modern American college; the deep, dark, hidden secret that many parents suspect is there but would rather not face. The long-term damage to our children is difficult to measure. But it is too obvious to deny. I remember once hearing that the British lost the empire when they started sending their children away to boarding schools. I do not know whether anyone has ever seriously proposed that thesis. I am prepared, however, to ask whether America might not be lost because the great middle class was persuaded that they must send their children to college with no questions asked, when in fact this was the near-equivalent of committing their sons and daughters to one of the circles of Dante's *Inferno*.

I have lived long enough to understand and be thankful for the fact that the sins and indiscretions of youth may be forgiven and overcome. Nevertheless, the behavior of our American colleges and universities is inexcusable. Their mendacity is doing great harm to our children, whom we entrust to them with so much love, pride, and hope for the future.

Questions for Discussion

1. What does Guroian achieve by opening with a quotation from Walker Percy's novel *The Last Gentleman*? How does he use this reference in the argument that follows?

2. When Guroian writes that the men of his generation "lived by a double standard, but there were standards," is he implying that a double standard is better than no standard? What is your understanding of a "double standard"?

3. How does Guroian see contemporary young women? Why does he believe they need protection?

4. What is the implication of calling a female undergraduate a "coed"?

5. Guroian states that he is drawing upon stories his children have told him, as well as an "exposé" written by one of his students. How credible do these sources seem to you? Have you witnessed the kind of behavior they describe?

6. Is it true that "hooking up" has come to replace "dating" on college campuses?

7. What rules do you think a college should enforce in its dormitories? How would this enforcement take place?

8. As he concludes his argument, Guroian claims that American parents, when sending children off to college "with no questions asked," are doing "the near-equivalent of committing their sons and daughters to one of the circles of Dante's *Inferno*." How do you respond to this language?

9. To what extent is this argument informed by values determined by religion, gender, class, and sexual orientation?

④ **PHILLIP VANNINI, "Will You Marry Me? Spectacle and Consumption in the Ritual of Marriage Proposals"**

"Dating" as it is commonly understood concludes when a couple either breaks up or undertakes a commitment ceremony such as marriage. When moving from the concept of "dating" to that of "marriage," it can be useful for people to remember that it is possible to take a spouse or partner out on a date—that whatever romance associated with dating need not come to an abrupt end. Nevertheless, as some individuals prepare for the transition from dating to marriage, they feel that the occasion on which they propose must be the most special and memorable date in the history of the relationship. As Phillip Vannini shows in the following argument, which was first published in a 2004 issue of the *Journal of Popular Culture,* the Internet and other forms of mass communication are contributing pressures to turn "popping the question" into a public spectacle and to substitute objects for expressions of love. Vannini teaches sociology at the University of Victoria in Canada, where he specializes in media, music, and popular culture. The *Journal of Popular Culture* is published both in the United States and in Great Britain. Like other scholarly journals, it appears quarterly.

Will You Marry Me? Spectacle and Consumption in the Ritual of Marriage Proposals

PHILLIP VANNINI

1 Joel Fernghetti has been dating Annie Fredericks for over four years. Joel is a simple and honest man who shares a wonderful relationship with Annie. The two met on a summer night at a country fair in southern Alberta, where they were both born and raised. Introduced by common high school friends, they danced, talked, and kissed the night away. Now, Joel has held a regular job for quite some time and feels ready to "pop" the question to Annie. Bedeviled by his insecurities and motivated by the will to make a nice and lasting impression on his girlfriend, Joel decides to log on to the Internet to search for some inspiration. At **http://www.storybehindthe-rock.com**, one of the dozens of burgeoning Web sites specializing in engagement services,

Joel finds:

> You'll need a bag of Hershey kisses, and a lot of roses, some scented candles, etc. First set up the candles in the bathroom, low lighting helps. Then decorate the bathtub all over with the roses and its petals, especially the tub! Then leave a trail of Hershey kisses from the door of the bedroom (or wherever) to the bathroom. Leave a card to wherever you finally lead her that says: "Now that I have kissed the ground you walk on, and showered you with roses" . . . (you take it from there!!). ("Story Behind the Rock")

This sure sounds like a nice shopping list to Joel, a good place to start. The shopping list, to be sure, also should include at least one of the scores of advice books on the sub-

*Born in Morocco in 1961, Eva Illouz received her Ph.D. in 1991 from the University of Pennsylvania. She is a professor at the Hebrew University of Jerusalem. In 2003 her book *Oprah Winfrey and the Glamour of Misery: An Essay on Popular Culture* was published by Columbia University Press.

†Jean Baudrillard is a professor of philosophy of culture and media criticism at the European Graduate School (EGS) in Saas-Fee, Switzerland. Visitors to the EGS website learn that "Baudrillard's philosophy centers on the twin concepts of 'hyperreality' and 'simulation.' These terms refer to the virtual or unreal nature of contemporary culture in an age of mass communication and mass consumption."

‡The social scientist Erving Goffman (1922–1982) taught at the University of Pennsylvania and served for many years as president of the American Sociological Association. In *Gender Advertisements* (1979)—in which he analyzed how advertisements construct what it means to be "masculine" or "feminine"—he helped launch the field now known as gender studies. His best known work, however, is *The Presentation of Self in Everyday Life* (1959), and it is this work that influenced Vannini's argument.

ject, a book on engagement rings, perhaps the services of a professional photographer, a groom survival kit, a financial assessment by a private auditing firm that should give him an idea whether he is financially ready . . . you get the picture. Romance, as every relationship in a capitalist society, has been permeated by the logic of exchange.

Love, as Eva Illouz* writes in *Consuming the Romantic Utopia,* has been increasingly commodified with the advent and growth of capitalism and consumer culture. A host of novels, movies, paperbacks, DIY guides, songs, and ads have created the image of romance as a service to be offered and purchased for a price. Romantic love, as she suggests, reflects the democratic inclusion of all people into the ideology of romance, and the division of lovers into socioeconomic classes. If romance ceases to be an authentic expression of intimate sentiments, researchers must understand its impact at a macro level and analyze the cultural logic of romance production and reproduction. In this article, I attempt to examine romantic love as a cultural rather than an interpersonal phenomenon. In particular, I intend to focus on the ritual of marriage proposal as a reflection of the commodification of human feelings. Even though marriage and romantic relationships have been given much research attention, no academic work has yet explored marriage proposals. Marriage proposals represent an important step in an intimate relationship. Upon engagement, couples shift the nature of their rapport from casual or steady dating to projection toward marriage. Just as our hypothetical friend Joel would have done, I spent some time on the Internet researching stories of marriage proposals narrated by the individuals and couples who enacted them. I offer my analysis of such shared experiences by integrating the theoretical work of Guy Debord, Jean Baudrillard,† and Erving Goffman‡ into my own thinking. I offer a collection of themes and excerpts from proposal narratives to synthesize and exemplify such experiences. My reader may or may not agree

that these proposals are representative. The very fact that they were posted on the Web, my detractor might argue, testifies for their originality. Personally, I do not believe that this is the case. I have discussed the nature and form of marriage proposals with many people before embarking on this research project, and therefore I have attempted to select narratives that are representative and particularly illustrative. Of course, my purely exploratory approach should be justifiable in light of the fact that no previous empirical research whatsoever exists.

Consuming Romance

5   Feeling is a social act. Linguistic conventions and cultural habits allow us to make sense of social contexts and interaction and respond in socially appropriate ways (Shweder). When someone asks us to marry him or her, for example, we may respond with shame, surprise, joy, anxiety, or mixtures of similar emotions, but it is very doubtful that we will react with envy and respond by asking for a basket of fried chicken to go. By learning to express ourselves emotionally and to perceive emotions in a socially appropriate way, we become integral members of our society.

Romantic love is one of the defining sentiments of our culture. The ideology of romance has undergone tremendous changes over time. It has moved, for example, from a courtly idea of love as painful longing and idolization to the expression of spiritual purity typical of the Victorian era, and on to the hedonistic quest for self-fulfillment of our days (Branden, 33–51). Although many remark on the rampant individualism of contemporary love, Francesca Cancian suggests that love is moving away from self-fulfillment and toward the idea of androgynous interdependence. Illouz instead sees romance undergoing a different set of changes. Two interconnected processes are at work: the romanticization of commodities and the commodification of romance. As production and consumption have expanded, mass communication has been transmitting to the public a visual idea of love as spectacle. The romanticization of commodities occurs when media portray certain products and services as romantic. A cheap fast-food meal is not romantic, but the consumption of a candle-lit three-course meal at a French restaurant is. As Illouz points out, this "oblique consumption" is invested of typically postmodern values such as leisure, intensity, glamour, elegance, and beauty. When leisure and romance become intertwined, love turns into conspicuous consumption and entertainment. Beside self-expression, romance allowed those who have learned how to consume it properly to feel liberated from the drudgery of work. This is the image of the "date" as an outing to a restaurant, a movie theater, or a romantic getaway at the seaside or at a luxurious (and romantic) hotel. These consumption practices commodify romance by incorporating it into the public econoscope of consumer logic. Because of its important role in the new democratic ethic of consumption of leisure, romance is also used to market commodities; this process is known as the commodification of romance.

In *Motivation and Personality,* Abraham Maslow* identifies love as a third-order need, preceded in the hierarchy by physiological and safety needs. What Maslow did not foresee, according to Baudrillard's critique, is that in the contemporary phase of late capitalism he calls affluent society, needs cease to be merely psychologically motivated. In *The Mirror of Production* and *For a Critique of the Political Economy of the Sign* Baudrillard argues that in an affluent society, consumers can never become satisfied or saturated. Needs are no longer rooted in instinct but rather embedded in the relations among consumer goods and manipulated by the arrangement of commodities. Whereas in the past, humans were surrounded by other humans, Baudrillard argues, now we are surrounded by objects. This new morality of consumption restructures contemporary life and organizes our social identity as our place in the relation among objects and people. Leisure and work,

nature and culture—once dichotomous entities now become intermixed and user-friendly for our shopping comfort. Following Roland Barthes, Baudrillard understands fashion to pervade lifestyle. Fashion is first and foremost a system of signs that dictates an abstract code of distinction and consumption. In this sense, objects lose their original functionality, and as signs, become invested with sign exchange. In other words, objects no longer are privately consumed and exchanged to satisfy needs or pleasure, but rather consumed (often conspicuously) because they allow us to satisfy "needs" of social differentiation. Baudrillard identifies this new ethic order, the "fun morality," as responsible for the consumer's sense of duty to strive after happiness and pleasure. Romance, as we shall see, is far from being exempt from such logic. Marriage proposals reflect this ethic of entertainment of consumption very clearly.

How to "Pop the Question"

I invite the reader to pay a brief visit to some of the Web sites that discuss marriage proposals.[2] Some of these are personal Web pages designed by individuals and couples, and others specialize in offering a host of services and advice on dating, engagement, and the wedding process. I collected approximately 300 narratives of marriage proposals and consulted the nature of the services offered and pieces of advice posted online. Instead of offering a taxonomy of the various proposals, I chose to identify the components constituting each narrative. Although I am aware of the limitations of a discourse analysis of narratives based on short and often decontextualized text, I still believe that I may offer the reader an idea of the main characteristics of these marriage proposals. The reader should keep in mind that by no means am I trying to generalize my observations to the greater population of engaged couples. My selection is not based on a probability sample, but I believe that it is comprehensive. Individuals' and couples' paths toward married life differ considerably, yet the

*Abraham Maslow (1908–1970) was an influential American psychologist who believed in the importance of achieving "self-actualization" through understanding and attaining what he called a "hierarchy of human needs." He presented these needs as a pyramid. At the base of this pyramid were the physiological needs (such as food and water) necessary for survival; immediately above them were needs associated with safety and security. Once that layer had been achieved, one could move to the layer in which needs for love and belonging could be satisfied. That layer led, in turn, to a layer in which self-esteem can be attained. This achievement then leads to the apex of the pyramid: actualization, or the state in which anxiety disappears because all needs have been met.

*Telos is a Greek word meaning "ending" or "goal."

presence of agreement—or even consensus—on what makes a marriage proposal romantic and successful is a phenomenon worthy of sociological attention. Notwithstanding my unawareness of the life trajectories and individual idiosyncrasies of these romantic partners, I believe that I may interpret the significance of these rituals in light of the greater sociocultural and historical contexts in which they are embedded.

I speak of marriage proposals as social and symbolic rituals because such acts are staged and scripted in relation to greater social environments that influence the couple's rapport, their connection with a larger community, their social identity, and their meaningful interaction. My viewing of marriage proposal as ritual and performance is not incidental. Consider the following proposal:

10 We arrived (in New York City) on a Saturday and I had told my husband I always wanted to skate in Rockefeller Center. So our first mission was to go skating . . . After 20 minutes or so, my husband skated around me, got down on one knee and proposed. With the lights glimmering gloriously around us, I said yes and he slipped the ring on my finger. Everyone standing above us started clapping and cheering. Christmas of that year, I opened a beautifully wrapped box. It turned out my husband hired a photographer to take pictures of us and of him asking for my hand in marriage. ("Story Behind the Rock: Proposals")

People's narratives of their marriage proposals invoke a dramaturgical telos* of a common resolution: the "popping" of the question. The word "popping," often used in this context, evokes the idea of a sharp sound, a blast, a loud surprise. Such surprise is far from being limited to the members of the couple. The loud surprise is often a show, a spectacle staged for the amusement of an audience. Members of such an audience may include uninvolved bystanders such as those who walked by a gigantic city square billboard featuring the image of a man asking for his girlfriend's hand, and audience members who may play a confederate role or be acquaintances of the couple:

As [James] Yuhasz's brother, Michael, videotaped the couple . . . [Gemella] Pinto had just received a larger-than-life billboard marriage proposal from Yuhasz. He had escorted a blindfolded Pinto from his truck, leading her to a 12- by 25-foot billboard on Northampton Street next to the Taco Bell in Wilson. The billboard has a green background (her favorite color), two rings intertwined and, printed in gold lettering, "Gemella, will you marry me? Forever, James." "I think it's romantic, to see your name bigger than life on a 12-foot by 25-foot structure. It's a private moment, but he wants everybody to know this is the woman I love, and I'm asking her to marry me," DeNardo [a passer-by] said. ("Story Behind the Rock: Proposals")

The work of Erving Goffman is helpful here. In *The Presentation of Self in Everyday Life*, Goffman discusses his dramaturgical approach to interaction. Goffman argues that individuals are social actors concerned with the modes of self-presentation they choose to employ, and their meaning in the broader social context. Goffman sees interaction as a performance that is inevitably shaped by the greater sociocultural environment in which it is enmeshed and by the audience present. Social actors enact their performances to manage and provide their audiences with impressions that meet the

desired goals of the actor. An important concept in Goffman's dramaturgical approach is that of the "front." An actor's social identity is established and maintained through the presentation of the front, "that part of the individual's performance which regularly functions in a general and fixed fashion to define the situation for those who observe the performance" (22). The front is a "collective representation" that establishes a proper "setting," "appearance," and "manner" for the role staged by the social actor (27). Goffman calls this process dramatic realization, a set of activities focused on strategies of "impression management," or the control of information through the social performance (208). Actors attempt to be believable and acceptable by staging ideal versions of their fronts, consistent with the norms, mores, and laws of society.

Even though Goffman's approach is clearly microsociological, he argues that greater social and cultural processes are created, enacted, and negotiated in group interaction. Goffman's ideas are clearly important if we wish to understand the interactive dynamics of the ritual of marriage proposal, yet we need a critical approach to the concept of culture to understand why it is that late modern proposal rituals take the form they do. The idea that a late capitalist and consumer society and culture has assumed the logic of spectacle can be found in the work of Guy Debord. Debord emerged as the prominent figure of the Situationist movement during the times of political unrest of the late 1960s in France and Europe.

15 Debord, [Henri] Lefebvre, and the Situationists argued that the increasing division of labor and mindless work specialization had transformed work into meaningless drudgery. By transcending [Karl] Marx, they theorized that the expansionary logic of capitalism had created pseudoneeds to increase consumption. In this system, identity and consciousness were created at the point of consumption, not production. What matters most here is that such consumption needs to be

spectacular in order to court and seduce the consumer. In *The Society of the Spectacle,* Debord affirms that the consumer economy had transcended the idea of the degradation of being into having, and shifted from having into merely appearing. This criticism is, I believe, important for understanding the spectacular logic of some contemporary marriage proposals:

> I sat down and ordered a drink, just relieved to be inside and sitting down. Out of the corner of my eye I see this guy dressed in armor coming towards me. I think, "weird, what is it? Send in the Clowns day at T. J. Baxter's?" and turn back to the people at my table. That's when he stops in front of me and lifts the visor. Recognizing him yet confused, I say calmly "Hi honey." He then gets down on one knee and it hits me: HE'S GOING TO PROPOSE!! He says: "If you'll be my princess, I'll be your knight in shining armor and will love you forever. Will you marry me?" I was in SHOCK. . . . I kept saying "oh my god" over and over . . . for about three minutes. He then nudges me and whispers: "You haven't answered yet." OH NO! So . . . I decide to be emphatic, and in front of the whole restaurant staff and patrons who have crowded around us. . . . I yelled: "Hell, yes!" ("World's Greatest Marriage Proposals")

If we understand these marriage proposals to be spectacular illusionary displays of signification of love through representation and consumption, we may arrive at a description of the logic of such rituals. Following Goffman, I argue that these marriage proposals should be analyzed by looking at five aspects: the collective representation (the drama), the front, the setting, the appearance, and the manner.

The Drama
Through drama, social actors assign meaning to the situation, their audience, and themselves. For a performance to be impressive, actors must manage their impressions in accordance with the demands and restrictions of the situation, as well as the possibilities it offers. The marriage proposal drama revolves around its resolution, when the question is "popped."

There are mainly two types of resolutions: the climax and the shock. A climactic resolution occurs when a build-up of clues is constructed by the performer (usually the man) and/or his confederates.

> The night Rob proposed was absolutely perfect. We had a romantic dinner at a favorite restaurant. Mom Chaffee's. We had been planning dinner so it didn't seem out of the ordinary. I was diverted to the Reading Sheraton to seemingly pick up a friend of Rob's, who was in town (he wasn't really). We went up to "his" room, which was in the tower penthouse suite in the front of the hotel. The room had a breathtaking view over looking the city. When we entered the room it was like walking into a magical fairy tale. The room was lit by candlelight and covered in rose petals. There were roses, champagne, wine, chocolate covered strawberries, and a beautiful view of the city lights. Our song, Valentine by Martina McBride, was playing softly in the background. Rob then asked me to dance. He guided me to the window, and then asked me, on bended knee, to spend my life with him and for my hand in marriage. I said Yes! We danced, kissed, laughed, and cried. We visited my parents, his parents, called family and then visited with some special friends. It was truly a magical night. ("The World's Greatest Marriage Proposals")

20 These clues, as I will discuss later, are essential components of the setting, yet they play a crucial part in structuring the drama itself. Clues are, of course, signifiers of the "specialness" of the event. I speak of specialness and not uniqueness because there is little that is unique about both the signifiers themselves and the signified to which they refer. Commodities such as chocolate, meals, and hotel bedrooms offering scenic views have been romanticized, as Illouz suggests, and are mass marketed, mass produced, and still consumed as endowed with an aura of uniqueness. As Baudrillard suggests, consumption is always consumption of signs; objects are parts of a greater system of categories of objects inducing categories of persons. It is this system

of objects that organizes social difference. Hence, the construction of a marriage proposal drama must depend on particular relations among objects as signs and that to which they refer. The rose petal becomes a functional component of the drama, of the specialness of the story and the situation because, as Baudrillard would suggest, as a sign it connotes prestige, romance, and distinction (from the drudgery of a flowerless routine). When the commodity is invested of such significance, it allows its consumers to operate a Gestalt-like switch and interpret the story of an evening as "a magical fairy tale." The drama then becomes a playful performance *of* commodities, consumer products invested of particular significance.

The second type of resolution is the shock. Men sometimes pop the question out of the blue without first setting up the necessary elements of a performance. This is often risky behavior that may appear as kitsch and clumsy, as in the following:

> I took my soon to be fiancée on my boat to go fishing. We found a secluded spot in the Raritan Bay in NJ to begin our fishing trip. I proceeded to rig her fishing pole. I was a little nervous because I had the ring in the tackle box and she kept coming over by me. I told her to go to the front of the boat and begin fishing while I rig my pole. So with my shaking hands, I put the ring on my fishhook and walked up behind her. I said, "Kendra, I don't want to fish anymore." She replied, "We just started!" and I said, "But I already caught the BEST fish in the sea!" She turned around and the ring was dangling in front of her face. ("Story Behind the Rock: Proposals")

A surprise resolution is not necessarily bad, however. Among the numerous suggestions offered by supposed experts in shock resolutions include:

> Put an ad in a newspaper; Via email or on the Web; Ask a DJ on the radio to ask for you; At a sports event; Top of the Empire State Building or other tall building; At Disneyworld or Disneyland; In a restaurant. ("Proposal Ideas")

25 Regardless of whether the plot is intricate, the logic of the drama is that it be a spectacle. Not all marriage proposals are made in public, of course, but both public and private proposals must be performed as a special event. As remarked, its specialness is guaranteed by the consumption of romanticized commodities.

The Setting

As Goffman suggests, the front is always presented in a particular setting whose structure must be taken into careful consideration by the actor if a credible and acceptable impression is to be managed. The setting may include props, beautiful scenery, a particular location, and so on. As Illouz argues, the romanticization of nature and travel originated with the growth of the leisure ethic. Because people associate the home and the workplace with routine and dullness, evasion or escape to the "great outdoors" has been invested with the aura of specialness discussed previously. Very few of the proposals I surveyed occurred within the confines of the familiar. The logic of the spectacle demands that the setting be "romantic":

> He planned a weekend snowboarding trip at Mammoth, where we stayed at a cute B & B. On the first night, a snow storm hit, but it was beautiful! He took me for a walk in the knee-high snow, brought a blanket and camera. He had me sit on the blanket for a picture, and then pulled out the ring. After I said yes, he pulled out two wine glasses and a bottle of our favorite wine. Beautiful! ("World's Greatest Marriage Proposals")

Often the setting is public:

> For my 20th birthday, my mom and dad took me and my fiancé to New York City. The first night we were there, we went to the Empire State Building. When we got to the top I put a quarter into the telescope machine to take a look at the Statue of Liberty. When the quarter dropped into the machine, my fiancé grabbed my left hand, got down on one knee, and proposed to me in front of hundreds of people!!! It was so romantic. . . . Just like in the movies. ("World's Greatest Marriage Proposals")

30 The last sentence is very important. Movies, along with TV, ads, magazines, and novels, have provided us with clear visual ideas of romance (Illouz 33). Movie stars epitomize beauty, love, passion, "youth, glamour, wealth, conspicuous consumption, and relentless excitement" (33); in other words, the perfect romance. A billboard "larger than life," a "tall building," or a big "rock" render the marriage proposal somewhat of a quantifiable entity. As Baudrillard argues, outside the denotative function of objects (their function), objects can be substituted with one another because as signs they are free to circulate and be interchangeable. We play with these signs by consuming them as props for performances such as a marriage proposal. The very idea that the building on top of which (not somewhere in the middle) a proposal is made reminds us of the consumer desire for distinctive accumulation, for what social actors lack is always invested in the object.

Actors are aware of not "being" in the movies, yet the distinction from reality is blurred by the illusory convention that the simulated can replace the real. An example should clarify this point. Consider the following message posted on an Internet discussion board on marriage proposals:

> I think it's acceptable to have a faux diamond IF the girl knows and is ok with it. He certainly shouldn't try to "fool" her because that is no way to start out a marriage! And she WILL find out, I guarantee it! I'd suggest that they choose an emerald, sapphire or ruby center stone surrounded by accent diamonds. Also, many places offer payment plans . . . ("Story Behind the Rock: Proposals")

This way they are both fooled. In the past, Baudrillard argues, class chasms separated consumers from commodities. A Chippendale farm table could only be purchased by a noble, whereas today a Chippendale table imitation can be purchased by any consumer at a moderate price. What the consumer is purchasing is the "faux," the simulation—in other words, the sign. It is lack of resources, not structural class restrictions, that limits lovers and consumers. The meaning of the faux is generated from the differential relation of it, as a sign, with other signs. Therefore, in a sense, we may say that the setting is staged through the use of props as signs. These signs signify social distinction from others. This is perhaps why the declaration of love implied or explicitly contained in a marriage proposal is often public. On one hand, the man, by declaring, claims the woman as property; on the other hand (upon the utterance of the fatal "Yes!"), both man and women claim their "possession" of romance, a commodity that is highly priced in our society. In sum, it matters little that one feel real or like "in the movies" or in "a fairy tale," because what matters is that the impression of the spectacle be carefully staged.[3]

The Front, the Appearance, and the Manner
By now the reader should be able to easily interpret the logic and the characteristics of impression management of the front, its appearance in front of an audience, and the manner in which the role should be played. For clarity, let us further define these elements of dramaturgical performance. Goffman argues that expectations about appearance are regulated by cultural and social norms and mores. Appearance, of course, works ritualistically to signify the performer's status. In private performance, the question is popped by the man in front of the woman alone. The appearance of the man, in a consumer society, should reflect his socioeconomic status and his gender-specific potential. By gender-specific potential I intend to suggest that the man should present a "sensitive" front, a front that reveals his romantic and emotionally expressive side. An example will clarify:

35 On Valentine's Day I surprised Kathleen by sending her a dozen red roses. That night we planned to go out for a nice romantic dinner at Potowmack Landing. I walked Kathleen outside and she asked me where my car was. I then pointed to the white stretch limo I rented and told her that was our ride for tonight. Kathleen loved the limo. We had champagne and enjoyed the ride. The dinner at Potowmack Landing was great. We both love seafood and we ate plenty of it. The atmosphere was very romantic. We had a candlelit dinner, a strolling violinist and a great view of the Potomac River . . . ("Story Behind the Rock: Groom Survival")

It is through the conspicuous consumption of romanticized commodities that the man shows the woman his sensitive side and his distinctive economic means. This points to the Goffmanian idea of the manner, how we play our role, the personal touch we give our performance. The idea of manner is also synonymous with the value of spontaneity and originality. It is, however, notably difficult to be spontaneous in a society that offers (and imposes) all sorts of mass-market romantic commodities and teaches how by offering advice books on how to propose. *The Story Behind the Rock: The World's Most Creative Directory of Romantic and Surprising Engagement Ideas* by John Anthony Pagliaro, Jr., along with its corresponding Web site, offers all a groom-to-be needs to know before and after popping the question, including honeymoon services, engagement ring information, gifts for both him and her, and the Groom Survival Kit, "the only computer-based, groom wedding planning stress relief" computer game ("Story Behind the Rock: Groom Survival"). This is so that consumer's and performer's risk is minimized and the front is presented appropriately and ideally, conforming to conventions and stage demands. Consider these "Do's and Don't's" offered to grooms:

Do smile during your Jack and Jill party, rehearsal dinner, wedding ceremony, and especially at the reception. If your guests see that you're having a good time then so will they!
Don't get drunk before or at the wedding reception.
("Story Behind the Rock: Do's and Don't's")

40 The contemporary idea of a romantic manner or manners can be tied to the normative

aspects of the contemporary "political economy of romance": The class relationships that made possible and sustained the incorporation of romance within the economic practices of the sphere of consumption (Illouz 66).

Manner, therefore, is now the proper consumption style. Given the association of the idea of romance with leisure and entertainment—and therefore with conspicuous consumption—aesthetically "poor" romance is now economically poor romance as well:

> I dated my then boyfriend for 7 years patiently waiting for the day he would finally propose. One day after making a trip to what I thought was the grocery story, Steve walked through the door empty handed and announced "Hey, there's something for you on the backseat of the car." Thinking this was his sly way of getting me to bring in the groceries I went out to the car to retrieve the bags. To my surprise there was just this one very small paper bag, sitting on the seat. Well, I'm sure by now you have figured out that the bag contained the long awaited engagement ring! Hey, they say it's the thought that counts, right? LOL ("Story Behind the Rock: Proposals")

Surely the thought is what counts, but few would agree that this proposal is romantic by any means. Lack of manners in a marriage proposal can therefore be identified with lack of financial means. Appearance reflects one's distinctive status (or illusion thereof) within the stratified structure of the political economy of romance.

A few more words must be added to the Goffmanian idea of the front. Goffman's main contention is that the front be credible. Credibility, Goffman argues, is established through both verbal and nonverbal signifiers that satisfy the duties of a particular role and remain consistent with the audience's expectations and performer's traits. Credibility is of tremendous importance in the ritual of a marriage proposal. Throughout their relationship, partners may speak of marriage at several points prior to the formal engagement. Occasionally the man may even utter semiseri-

ous requests or demands such as, "Are you going to marry me one day?" or "Do you think we will get married?" Yet these preliminary explorations are far from constituting the actual marriage proposal ritual. These "performances" lack credibility because the front presented in these circumstances lacks the romantic signifiers required for the enactment of a believable ritual.

> **45** "Women can always tell when the guy is going to propose," she bragged. "They have a limo arrive or they take you to a restaurant that is incredibly expensive or they just plan something that is way out of the ordinary and get real nervous just before they pop the question." . . . One Saturday in April we dimmed the lights and snuggled up on the couch for what she thought was going to be an ordinary evening of watching television. Yeah . . . right! We began watching one of the two movies I had rented. . . . We had gotten quite comfortable with each other and the movie when all of sudden my face is on the TV screen—SURPRISE! My image on the screen told her that this was the evening I was going to ask her to marry me and how much I love her. Through the screen I asked her to sit back and enjoy the next few moments I had put together for her on the video. The tape then went into several minutes of romantic clips from her favorite movies such as "It's A Wonderful Life," "When Harry Met Sally," "Music From Another Room," "Jerry McGuire" and "You've Got Mail." When the clips were finished I opened up the lid to my coffee table in front of us to pull out a vase of her favorite flowers, tulips, and two candlesticks to set the mood even more. In the candle light I then proceeded to get on one knee not merely to ask her to marry me, but to ask her to marry me in a song I wrote for her and sang to her while playing my acoustic guitar. The last line of the last verse quietly asked, "Will you marry me?" I set the guitar on the floor and pulled the ring out from a nearby cabinet and held it between the two of us now close together. She said "yes" with tears in her eyes and a smile on her face! ("Story Behind the Rock: Proposals")

Romance, as I argued, must follow the logic of both spectacle and consumption because the ethos of interpersonal relationships

CONTEXT

In "Wedding Bell Blues Being Sung by Guests," an article published September 11, 2005, in the *Minneapolis Star Tribune*, reporter Thomas Lee writes, "Over the past 15 years, the average cost of a wedding has grown 75 percent to $26,326, according to a recent survey by the Fairchild Group, which publishes *Modern Bride*, *Brides*, and *Elegant Brides* magazines. Since 2002, the amount of money spent annually on weddings in this country has increased by $5 billion, to $125 billion." The same article reports that the average costs for wedding guests have increased as more couples throw destination weddings that call for airfare and hotel expenses in addition to the usual expenses for clothing and gifts. Attending weddings can become a financial burden for recent college graduates when many of their friends marry within a relatively short period. One of the women interviewed in this article claimed that the expenses she had incurred attending weddings during the first two years after her graduation from college had come to equal the size of her student loans.

has been increasingly intermixed with the ethic of consumer culture. Aware that a specific setting must be in place, the aforementioned performer becomes an entertainer, a representation of himself, and proposes to his girlfriend while playing the role of a Hollywood actor and that of a singer. The front becomes credible and real when the setting is magic, the appearance and manner illusory, and the drama "movie-like."

Conclusion

In this brief article, I have attempted to provide the reader with an introductory understanding of the dynamics of the ritual of marriage proposal. Because of the absolute lack of previous studies on the matter, I believe that my observation represents an important yet exploratory contribution to the sociological understanding of this phenomenon. Future studies could investigate marriage proposals in a dual fashion. At the micro level, there is a strong need to investigate the phenomenological significance of a marriage proposal for both the individuals involved in it and the life course of the couple. At the macro level, perhaps through in-depth studies of engagement narratives based on probability samples, social researchers should arrive at a taxonomic description of marriage proposals to better understand the links between individual choices for the characteristics of certain rituals, personal and social identity, and cultural and structural norms.

Hitherto, I have argued that our culture, and in particular our late modern consumer culture, plays an important part in defining the modalities of the marriage proposal ritual. Without pretending to offer sweeping generalizations to all marriage proposals, I have described this ritual by referring to Goffman's work on the presentation of the self, and provided a link to the macro level by using the work of Baudrillard on representation and signification, the idea of the Spectacle as presented by Guy Debord, and the influential and empirically-based reflections on Romance pro-

posed by Illouz. The idea that the micro level—dyadic or group—of the ritual of marriage proposals can be linked to greater cultural and semiotic processes operating at the macro level is, I believe, an important one for our understanding of symbolic interaction, and definitely for our future understanding of family and relationship processes.

NOTES

1. By oblique consumption, Illouz means the consumption of what the product signifies rather than the product in itself.

2. See the following: http://dir.yahoo.com/Society_and_Culture/Relationships/Marriage/Marriage_Proposals/, http://marriage.about.com/cs/proposals/a/proposing.htm, http://www.thestorybehindtherock.com, http://www.firstdance.com/mp1.htm, and http://dir.yahoo.com/Society_and_Culture/Weddings/Wedding_Experiences/.

3. I will leave it to the reader to consider whether, by the virtue of such marriage proposals, actors truly express their love or merely manifest an empty representation of it.

Works Cited

Barthes, Roland. *The Fashion System*. Trans. Matthew Ward and Richard Howard. London: Jonathan Cape, 1983.

Baudrillard, Jean. *The Mirror of Production*. St. Louis, MO: Telos Press, 1975.

———. *For a Critique of the Political Economy of the Sign*. Trans. Charles Levin. St. Louis, MO: Telos Press, 1981.

Branden, Nathaniel. *The Psychology of Romantic Love: What Love Is, Why Love Is Born, Why it Sometimes Grows, Why it Sometimes Dies*. Los Angeles: J. P. Tarcher, 1980.

Cancian, Francesca. *Love in America: Gender and Self-development*. Cambridge: Cambridge, UP, 1987.

Debord, Guy. *The Society of the Spectacle*. Detroit, MI: Black and Red, 1977.

Goffman, Erving. *The Presentation of Self in Everyday Life*. Garden City, NY: Doubleday Anchor Books, 1959.

Illouz, Eva. *Consuming the Romantic Utopia: Love and the Cultural Contradictions of Capitalism*. Berkeley: U of California P, 1997.

Maslow, Abraham. *Motivation and Personality*. New York: Harper, 1954.

Pagliaro, John Anthony, Jr. *The Story Behind the Rock: The World's Most Creative Directory of Romantic and Surprising Engagement Ideas*. West Springfield, MA: Pagliaro Publishing, 1999.

Shweder, Richard. *Thinking Through Cultures: Expeditions in Cultural Psychology*. Cambridge, MA: Harvard UP, 1991.

Stritof, Sheri, and Bob Stritof. "Proposal Ideas." 2004. About.com. 8 Jan. 2004 (http://marriage.about.com/cs/proposals/a/proposalideas.htm).

Webb, Michael, "The Story Behind the Rock." 1995, The Romantic.com. 15 Nov. 2001 (http://www.thestorybehindtherock.com).

———. "The Story Behind the Rock: Groom Survival." 1995. TheRomantic.com. 15 Nov. 2001 (http://www.thestorybehindtherock.com/groomsurvival.html).

———. "The Story Behind the Rock: Proposals." 1995. TheRomantic.com. 15 Nov. 2001 (http://www. thestorybehindtherock.com/proposals. html).

"The World's Greatest Marriage Proposals." 2004. FirstDance.com. 8 Jan 2004 (http://www.firstdance.com/mpl.htm).

Questions for Discussion

1. What can you infer about someone who needs to do research on the Internet to decide how to propose marriage?

2. Consider how Vannini describes his research methodology in paragraph 4. How seriously do you take his research? How effectively has he responded to critics who might question his scholarship?

3. What does it mean to "commodify" love? Can you point to examples that you have observed?

4. What does Vannini mean when he writes, "Feeling is a social act"?

5. How has mass communication contributed to the emergence of "love as spectacle"?

6. In addition to marriage proposals becoming public spectacles, are other forms of behavior once reserved for private settings becoming public?

7. Consider the passage quoted in paragraph 15 What does the punctuation reveal about the woman being quoted?

8. Have you ever engaged in "impression management"? If so, how did you go about it?

9. What does a title like "Groom Survival Kit" imply about gender and marriage?

10. In your opinion, how wise is it to raise the possibility of marriage before actually proposing it? If you sensed that you were going to receive a proposal you could not accept, what would you do?

DIFFERENCES

NEGOTIATING

As all of the authors in this cluster note, conventions about "dating" are changing—but as Beth Bailey helps explain, many of those conventions are relatively new, and different kinds of dating have been the norm in different decades. One of these conventions is that the man is expected to pay the expenses incurred on a date. This convention assumes that two people of the opposite sex have gone out on a date and that men have either more money than women or, at least, are able to undertake financial responsibility. Most of us are now aware, however, that people of the same biological gender can date (which makes the old convention useless) and that many women are strong and financially independent as a result of a good education and advances in the workplace. In "Get Your Hand Out of My Pocket," Darryl James takes a simple position: When dating, both individuals should pay their own way. But could this position be a little too simple to be useful in all contexts—as simple as assuming the "man" should always pay the expenses of a date?

Imagine the following situation: You are friends with Sally and Bill, a young couple who have been dating for six months. You were friends with each of them before they started dating. Now you see them primarily when they are together. But to sustain your friendship, you occasionally get together for coffee or lunch with each of them independently. When alone with you within the past month, they have each confided in you—sharing different perspectives on the same issue: who pays for what. Sally is concerned that Bill insists on paying for everything. At the beginning of their relationship, she repeatedly offered to pay her own way, but Bill insisted on picking up the tab and she went along because of a time-honored convention. She thinks that the time has come to get past this convention; failure to do so would fix her in an unequal position. Moreover, although she loves Bill and does not want to cause a crisis, she feels that he has become increasingly controlling—partly because of the money he has spent on her. Bill, on the other hand, is aware that Sally wants to pay her own way, and he thinks she is becoming increasingly irritable. From his point of view, her wish to pay her own way signals a lack of commitment. Indeed, he fears that she is getting ready to break up with him.

As a good friend, you listen carefully to their concerns but don't plunge right into offering advice. And mindful that you are not a counselor, you have no intention of seeing them as a couple to help them resolve their differences. But you assure both of them that you have heard their concerns and will see if there is anything you can do.

You want to give this problem some thought and then offer some good counsel when you next see each of them alone—not because you want to side with one at the expense of the other but because you want each of your friends out of harm's way in case one of them becomes visibly upset by what you recommend.

Write an argument addressed to the people you envision as Sally and Bill that summarizes their individual concerns and then recommends a position that can help them move successfully beyond the problem that troubles them. You do not plan to mail this argument to them, nor do you intend to memorize it. But understanding that writing is a form of cognition—which means that writing can help you generate ideas and think clearly—you see this writing exercise as essential preparation for the meetings that you will be having with them.

What Does Marriage Require?

Some people tell themselves that they would be happy if only they could get married. Others tell themselves they would be happy if only they could get divorced. Happiness, of course, depends upon many factors. But there are deeply rooted cultural reasons for associating it with marriage. There are, for example, all those fairy tales that end not only with a marriage but also with the assurance that the couple "lived happily ever after." And that idea is implicit in many novels—especially those written in the eighteenth and nineteenth century (and romance novels written today). In novels such as *Pride and Prejudice* (by Jane Austen), or *Jane Eyre* (by Charlotte Brontë), the female protagonist eventually marries her ideal mate despite numerous complications along the way. Similarly, in novels such as *Tom Jones* (by Henry Fielding) and *Nicholas Nickleby* (by Charles Dickens) the male protagonist settles down by getting married at the conclusion of his adventures. When building up to marriage as the conclusion of a novel, writers such as these were satisfying the expectations of readers. But few people really believed that married couples live in complete and everlasting happiness every day, and novelists gradually came to challenge the "lived happily ever after" myth. *Anna Karenina* (by Leo Tolstoy), for example, ends when a married woman commits suicide by throwing herself under a train after she has been abandoned by her lover. Still, old ideas linger—especially in a culture where people are encouraged to marry for love. In some cultures, marriages are arranged by parents, who are interested in finding a suitable match in terms of education, income, and class. Romance is not a factor. But in many western nations, such as the United States, popular culture links marriage with romance. Women are expected to find "Mr. Right" or "the man of their dreams"; magazines devoted to wedding preparations circulate widely, and weddings are becoming more expensive and elaborate. This could mean that romance is alive and well, but when you consider how high the divorce rate now is, other possibilities emerge. Could the fuss over weddings indicate that people want to play out a romantic fantasy before reality hits them once the honeymoon is over? Or are people trying to buy a kind of insurance—as if a perfectly planned wedding will ensure a perfectly happy marriage? Whatever the case, it is clear that a successful marriage requires more than having a great gown, a delicious cake, and well-chosen wedding gifts. Two of the authors in this cluster explore why marriage can be at risk. Another focuses on who should have the right to marry, and a fourth focuses on what kind of commitment to raising children is implicit when two people make a commitment to each other.

① STEPHANIE COONTZ, "Great Expectations"

Great Expectations is the title of a famous novel by Charles Dickens—the story of a young man whose life is shaped by the hope of inheriting a fortune and winning the approval of a beautiful but cruel woman. In adopting that title for her argument on marriage, Stephanie Coontz signals that people may be putting themselves at risk by expecting too much from that institution. A graduate of the University of California at Berkeley, Coontz is the author of two well-received books on the American family: *The Way We Never Were: American Families and the Nostalgia Trap* and *The Way We Really Are: Coming to Terms with America's Changing Families.* She teaches history and women's studies at Evergreen State College in Olympia, Washington. The following argument appeared in the *Baltimore Sun* in June 2005 and was reprinted in several other newspapers.

Great Expectations

STEPHANIE COONTZ

1 The problem with modern marriage, according to conventional wisdom, is that today's couples don't make marriage their top priority and put their relationship above all else. As one of my students once wrote, "People nowadays don't respect the marriage vowels." Perhaps she meant IOU.

But my research on the history of marriage convinces me that people now place a higher value on marriage than ever before in history. In fact, that's a big part of the problem.

One reason marriage is fragile today is that we expect so much more of it than we used to, and many of our expectations are contradictory.

Most people recognize that marriage takes sacrifice, hard work and the ability to put up with the bad in your partner as well as the good.

5 But they also expect marriage to be the ultimate source of their happiness and the most fulfilling, passionate relationship in their lives.

When Arkansas Gov. Mike Huckabee "upgraded" his marriage vows on Valentine's Day before an audience of 5,000 enthusiastic marriage advocates, a banner reading "Passion Transformation Intimacy Oneness Covenant" summed up their case for marriage. Unfortunately, people who expect to find passion, transformation, intimacy and oneness in their marriages often end up disappointed in their covenant, and the higher their expectations, the greater their disappointment.

Europeans and Americans used to view marriage as a work relationship in which passion took second place to practicality and intimacy never interfered with male authority. As that view of marriage has changed over the past 100 years, the divorce rate* has risen steadily.

For most of history people had modest expectations of marital happiness. The upper classes of Europe in the Middle Ages, who arranged their marriages for political and economic gain, believed that true love and passion could only exist outside marriage, in an adulterous affair.

10 In the 18th and 19th centuries, conventional wisdom among middle-class men was that the kind of woman you'd want for a wife was incapable of sexual passion. One marital

*According to the website Infoplease.com, citing the U.S. Department of Health and Human Services, the divorce rate has risen to 3.7 per every 1,000 in 2004 from 0.7 per every 1,000 in 1900.

CONTEXT

On Valentine's Day, 2005, Arkansas Governor Mike Huckabee and his wife Janet performed vows that made their marriage a covenant marriage, which is described by Rick Lyman in the *New York Times* as "a legally binding contract available only in Arkansas and Louisiana.... A covenant marriage commits a couple to counseling before any separation and limits divorce to a handful of grounds, like adultery or abuse." Covenant marriage is predominantly a conservative movement.

*Among other things, Lillian Rubin has been a senior research associate for the Institute of Scientific Analysis and for the Institute for the Study of Social Change at the University of California at Berkeley. Of her book *Intimate Strangers: Men and Women Together,* a reviewer at *Ms.* magazine said, "Once again, Lillian Rubin decodes human behavior better than anyone else, and she does it with a lively combination of intuitive skill, scholarship and the sound of women's and men's voices sharing their lives."

advice expert even wrote that frigidity was a virtue to be cultivated in women. When wives wrote about their husbands in diaries, they were much less likely to describe intimate conversations than to record a persistent feeling of loneliness. A successful marriage was more often based on resigned acceptance than on transformation.

In the early 20th century, people came to expect marriage to be based on love, sexual attraction and personal fulfillment. But women often settled for less because of their economic dependence on men.

As late as the 1960s, polls found that nearly three-fourths of college women said they would marry a man they didn't love if he met their other criteria. In the 1970s, the working-class women interviewed by psychologist Lillian Rubin* defined a good husband in terms that had little to do with intimacy or passion. "He's a steady worker; he doesn't drink; he doesn't hit me. That's a lot more than my mother had."

Today, by contrast, the desire for a "soul mate" is nearly universal. Eighty percent of women say it's more important to have a husband they can confide in than one who earns a good living. And more than two-thirds of men say they want a more rounded relationship with their wife than their father had with their mother, one marked by passion, intellectual equality, intimacy and shared interests.

Recognizing the potential for disillusion in such high hopes, some people counsel couples to tamp down their expectations of personal fulfillment and happiness. Certainly, anyone who expects each day with his or her spouse to be filled with passion, joy and transcendent oneness will be disappointed a lot of the time.

15 But having spent many years researching the low-expectation marriages of the past, I don't think high expectations are such as bad thing. True, they raise the risk of disappointment and disillusionment when one or both partners refuse to work on problems in the relationship. But they also motivate many people to put more energy into their relationships than couples did in centuries past.

When a marriage works well today, it works better than anyone in the past ever dared to dream. When it doesn't work well, people have more options to leave. And when people have doubts about their future, they have the option not to marry at all.

We may not always approve of the choices that people make and the relations they aspire to. But in marriage, as in politics, that is the price of democracy. People have the right to change their minds. We cannot foreclose people's choices and tamp down their aspirations without losing most of the things that make modern marriage so rewarding.

Questions for Discussion

1. Why do people expect more from marriage than they had in the past? Is this necessarily a bad thing?

2. What are the risks of expecting a spouse to be a "soul mate" and marriage to be the ultimate source of happiness?

3. How appropriate is the joke with which Coontz opens her argument?

4. What do you think of a public figure who renewed his marriage vows before an audience of 5,000 people? Is this a good model for fostering intimacy?

5. On what grounds other than romantic love can a marriage be based? Do you think such marriages can be successful?

6. To what extent is the divorce rate related to changes in gender expectations and economic opportunity as opposed to excessively high expectations for marriage?

② CHRISTINA NEHRING, "Fidelity with a Wandering Eye"

The following argument what written in response to a book by Diana Smith called *Undressing Infidelity: Why More Wives Are Unfaithful.* It is, in fact, a review of that book—hence the number of references that you will find to Smith—and demonstrates how argument can take the form of a book review. The review was first published in a 2004 issue of the *Atlantic,* one of the country's oldest and most prestigious magazines. In addition to writing for the *Atlantic,* Christina Nehring writes for *Harper's,* the *Nation,* and *London Review of Books.* She is currently working on *Women in Love: A Feminist Defense of Romance.* When you read her argument, you will find that it includes allusions to many writers—so be alert for how those allusions contribute to her case.

Fidelity with a Wandering Eye

CHRISTINA NEHRING

The American Association of Retired Persons (AARP) is, as its mission statement says, "a nonprofit, nonpartisan membership organization for people age 50 and over [that] is dedicated to enhancing quality of life for all as we age." The AARP is prominent in influencing legislation that affects the lives of older people in the United States.

1 It's official: the conventional wisdom is false. It's not men who leave their wives for younger, blonder temptresses; it's women who leave their husbands for—well, just about anybody. Or nobody. The fact is, women initiate 66 percent of divorces between partners over forty. That, at least, is what they reported during a major AARP* study, released last year. That is also the impression one gleans when contemplating a new spate of books and shows, from ABC's already classic *Desperate Housewives* to hot spring titles including most notably *Undressing Infidelity: Why More Wives Are Unfaithful.*

This is refreshing news—in some senses, at least. It puts a great big dent in sexual stereotypes with which we have been too long saddled: the security-besotted, marriage-angling, nest-squatting female and her counterpart, the freedom-loving, wild-oat-sowing male. Steppenwolf. They made for an insipid image all along, but everybody seemed to conspire in it, from self-help authors (who assumed that their female readers wanted nothing more than tips on how to "catch" and "tame" a husband) to family counselors, magazine pundits,

and, of course, evolutionary psychologists (who say it's all biology: girls are made to sit in the straw and warm their eggs; guys are made to fly through the heavens and spread their seed). Women have been told they are helpless and dependent for so long that we have begun to believe it—and to object vociferously when we are not treated as such. If men whose company we enjoy don't assume we want to be their wives and thus propose in short order, we consider it "an insult" (in the approving words of the sexpert-rabbi Shmuley Boteach†) and declare ourselves aggrieved. The result? Women have grown dull while men have grown smug, offering their hands (when they do) as one might bestow a winning lottery ticket: "There you go, honey, I guess I've made your life." Having given that, they too often feel they have given all; they've done their bit in the kingdom of relationships, and their companions may now live happily ever after.

Only they generally don't, as the books and studies make all too clear. Women need more than security to thrive, it seems. In fact, they often court the square opposite of security, as Diane Shader Smith learned when she began interviewing women for *Undressing Infidelity.* They court risk; they court intensity, variety, novelty, and disaster—very much like men. It is a peculiarity of our age to portray one sex as nature's safe and law-abiding partner—to cast it as the erotically muted, risk-averse nanny to man. A few hundred years before Jesus Christ, Aristophanes‡ presented women as rowdy and ebullient sexual predators, righting uninhibitedly over access to handsome boys. Utopia, as described by Aristophanes' *Congresswomen,* consists of "free fornication," with no grandma left behind. Nubile young girls can legally be seduced "only after the male adolescent has first applied his resources to the full satisfaction of a bona fide senile female." Ovid§ expends many lives in his *Art of Love* warning men against underestimating the ladies' amorous adventurism. In Dante's *Inferno* the circle of hell for sins of the flesh is populated in great part by women. It is the lust of a mother (not, say, an uncle) that so tortures Shakespeare's Hamlet ("Frality, thy name is woman"), a girl's sexual fickleness that takes out the hero in *Troilus and Cressida,* a queen's love for an ass that brings down the house in *A Midsummer Night's Dream.* The greatest adulterers in the Western canon—Emma Bovary, Anna Karenina, Molly Bloom, Carmen—have, in fact, been adulteresses. Each had a faithful husband at home.

Why do women leave? "Verbal, physical or emotional abuse" is the first reason cited in the AARP study by wives who initiated divorces. And yet "abuse" played little role in the decisions of Smith's interviewees to risk their unions, most of which sound altogether more docile than violent. So why did they do it? Smith herself is remarkably unhelpful on this score. "The reasons women cheat," she concludes, "are as varied as the women themselves." Fair enough. But surely more-provocative hypotheses might be floated. Mary Wollstonecraft, the author of *A Vindication of the Rights of Woman,* proffered a few as early as the end of the eighteenth century, and her words still resonate today. Women, she de-

clared, are reared for love: the novels they read, the fairy tales they hear, all prepare them for a future of fiery sentiments and gallant attentions. But "a husband cannot long pay those attentions with the passion necessary to excite lively emotions, and the "female" heart, accustomed to lively emotions, turns to a new lover, or pines in secret."

5   Is this so far wrong today? Don't women even now harbor romantic ideals that are tangibly more central to their lives than to men's, and thus more easily (and disastrously) disappointed? A man may dream of a passionate soulmate, as a woman does, but if he does not find one, he will rechannel that desire into his work, his sports, his substance abuse, his war-making—all things that define a man's identity more commonly than do his emotional efforts. A woman has these occupations open to her as well, but rightly or wrongly (and I think rightly) they are often subordinated to the love plot in her life. This is something a certain kind of feminist has lamented—and a certain kind of moralist might reasonably find dangerous, since it does indeed make women more sensitive to marital dissatisfaction. But on balance it is a noble hierarchy.

Romantic love has suffered a demotion following the wars of the sexes in recent decades, with the result that we've forgotten it is the source of some of our civilization's greatest acts of heroism and genius. For what else did knights slay dragons in the Middle Ages, did Petrarch‖ write poetry, did Dante take on *The Divine Comedy,* Zeus turn himself into a swan, and Penelope weave her gorgeous web? Even evolutionary psychologists say we are never so strong as when we are in love, never so poised for high achievement or fierce battle. (It has to do with dopamine levels, apparently.) Instead of trying to curb the power of this love plot in one of the sexes, as feminists like the late Carolyn Heilbrun have done, might it not be better to re-sanction it in both?

But why re-sanction romantic love if it leads not merely to maladaptive perfectionism but also to a propensity for homewrecking? The

†Online magazine *Slate* describes Shmuley Boteach this way: "Shmuley—he is known universally by his first name—is the best-selling author of *Kosher Sex* and has marketed himself as a rabbi to the stars and an expert on Jewish attitudes toward relationships and marriage." Once a spiritual adviser to Michael Jackson, Boteach has authored 15 books and has a nationally syndicated talk show.

†Born in 448 BCE, Aristophanes is thought to have been the greatest of the ancient Greek writers of comedy. He wrote more than 35 comedies. In *Lysistrata,* his best known work, women decide to bring an end to war by refusing to have sex with their husbands until they agree to declare peace. Aristophanes died around 385 BCE.

§Born in 43 BCE, Publius Ovidius Naso (Ovid) was a Roman epic poet. Considered one of the great writers of antiquity, he is best known for *Metamorphosis* and *The Art of Love.*

‖Italian Francesco Petrarch (1304–1374) is considered one of the greatest love poets of all time. His accomplishments include creating a form of the sonnet, a fourteen-line poem with a strict pattern of organization still used by poets today.

easy answer is that it doesn't. If women initiate 66 percent of divorces, they also initiate probably 96 percent of marriage counseling. For every new door they open to love, they have made several attempts to fix the old. That's what you do when you care about eros: you work on all fronts. The hard answer is that sometimes it's okay to wreck a home. Sometimes divorce is the brave and not the cowardly option. We all know couples who shouldn't be together but stay together anyway—excruciatingly, eternally, disastrously. The human animal is no more frivolous and irresponsible than fearful and lethargic. For every person who throws out a sublime relationship, there are two who masochistically cling to a visibly destructive one. (Note the wild success of books like *He's Just Not That Into You* and *How to Break Your Addiction to a Person.*)

Further, women are more frustrated with their marriages than men for myriad reasons—and only one (albeit a big one) is romantic idealism. Another is family culture. If the customer is supposedly king in American stores, the child is incontrovertibly king in American families. Of the women Smith describes in her book, many are overworked soccer moms. She interviews one as she drives—interminably—around town dropping and fetching her kids at after-school enrichment activities. Smith herself mentions in passing that she cooks and serves not three meals a day but three or more dietary regimens.

> Mediterranean for my husband Mark; red meat every two hours for our fourteen-year-old son, Micah; and four hot meals a day for our twelve-year-old daughter, Mallory. And then there are the kids' friends, who show up almost every day with their insatiable, and often picky, teenage appetites.

How can one doubt that these women—all of them attractive, we hear, and not long ago accustomed to lavish attention themselves—fantasize about escape? A place where they can be not just cogs in the domestico-pedagogic machine but colorful individuals, sexual entities, and romantic agents? A woman "cannot

contentedly become . . . an upper servant after being treated as a goddess," Wollstonecraft observed. And in today's superchild culture the typical wife is not what Wollstonecraft (with her French maid, her cook, and her habit of calling children "animals") would have considered an "upper servant"; she's a lot more like a galley slave.

10 Abjection to children often correlates directly with churlishness to mates. Children are extensions of our egos, so we dote on them, but spouses are often merely co-managers of a home business. As such, they are part of the same unsentimental consumer culture that defines our relationship to, say, submarine sandwiches or coffee drinks. The explosion of Internet dating, in which you announce the traits you want in a lover as you'd announce the ingredients you want in a latte, and remorselessly exchange him if he's not made to specifications, has hastened still further the commodification of romance—and its desanctification.

This, alas, is the worst of the many reasons that modern women trade partners at such a clip: not because they are into ethereal romance but because they are into eternal choice. The mystery and the altruism of love have been subsumed into the ruthless commerce of self-gratification. "I was looking for three things when I married Don," says one woman Smith interviews. "I wanted children, I wanted a house, and I wanted someone I could talk to. Don said he would give me all that . . ." We are intended to admire this self-knowledge, because it gets the speaker off compulsive affairs and up to the altar. But it does not do so in a way that could ever be moving—or flattering—to her mate. She might as easily have said, "I wanted a South Seas cruise, a masseur, and someone to keep me in Chanel"—and the person in her arms would have been another man entirely (as, for that matter, the man who fulfilled her domestic and maternal wishes could have been, too). Most of the extramarital relations in Smith's book are, in fact, shallow, opportunistic affairs. What makes them cut so deep is the price at which they come.

Almost all affairs, or all that don't occur in what used to be called an open marriage, are cause for deception. And deception—far more than extracurricular sex alone—is the cardinal relationship killer. If a lover has a single vast advantage over a spouse, it is not that he is newer or more attractive to the woman who takes him; it is that she can be honest with him. He knows about her husband; her husband does not know about him. Result: she feels closer to the person who knows her most fully—her lover. With the man at her hearth she feels the way one feels with all people one tricks: either superior, because of one's imagined cleverness, or inferior, because of one's ostensible guilt. Or both. But what she rarely feels, either at the moment of deception or afterward, is joined. (All this, of course, is equally true when the sexes are reversed.)

Lightly started, affairs become heavy barriers between partners. If they do not destroy a marriage, as they did for several of Smith's subjects, they take the sap and spark out of it. They turn a soulmate into a dupe, a friend into a jailer, conjugal pleasure into conjugal duty.

At its best, matrimony is a quixotic proposition. The odds that it will go well—or, at least, very well—are slim. The best minds over time (and also the worst) have studied alternatives to it, official and unofficial, public and private. The medieval courtier wed one person and wooed another. Such Romantic writers as Shelley and Byron inaugurated a high-minded promiscuity that took little notice of who was joined to whom. A generation later the long and quietly married Emerson came down hard against formalized vows: "No love can be bound by oath or covenant to secure it against a higher love." Emerson's wilder-eyed contemporary, the Utopian Charles Fourier, spent decades formulating theories of democratic sex—as non-possessive as it was non-marital. Even today social scientists who, like Helen Fisher, inform us that amorous loyalty does not

naturally exceed twelve to thirty-six months predict a transition to different kinds of unions—for example, marriages contracted for one to five years and, like magazine subscriptions, renewable.

15 And yet for all the rational appeal of such a proposition, no one who has ever been in love, who has ever felt the transformative wand of passion tap his or her shoulder, wants to go to the altar and say "For better or worse, until the next Olympics do us part." The very concept of love brings with it intimations of eternity, even allusions to death. Lovers don't want only to live together; they want to die together. How diminishing it is to let our prudent, miserly reason trump our brave-hearted, generous passion. Perhaps in this case we should let instinct prevail over argument.

A second marriage, as Samuel Johnson* observed, represents "the triumph of hope over experience." The experience of marriage is one of conflict between ideals: the ideal of loving companionship and that of erotic intensity; the ideal of unflagging devotion to a single person and that of emotional responsiveness to many. And yet some of these ideals are not as irreconcilable—or as irreconcilable with marriage—as they appear. Unshakable loyalty to a central partner does not preclude passionate responses to other people. If it seems that way, it is only because of the puritanism, the pious emotional parsimony, of our American era.

Diane Shader Smith's book provides, ironically, a perfect example of this. Her introduction is an alarmist confession of her attraction to a man other than her husband. She recounts in detail her nervousness around him, her supposedly dangerous fascination with his charm. She criminalizes her feelings. And so, one might add (albeit more understandably, since she has led the way), does her husband. In a different culture her attraction would be viewed by her readers, herself, and her husband as perfectly natural and even commendable. What sort of a creature would you be if, having once found a human being who stirs your heart (and whom you marry, if you follow

*Samuel Johnson (1709–1784), English author and wit, is best known for having composed the first dictionary of the English language and having inspired one of the most memorable biographies in British literature: James Boswell's *The Life of Samuel Johnson.* Fastidious about language, but often careless about his personal appearance, Johnson is the subject of many stories. Here is one: A young girl climbed on his lap and said, "You smell." "No, my dear," he corrected, "I stink; you smell."

*Jorge Luis Borges (1899–1986) was an Argentine writer whose works are considered classics of twentieth-century world literature. He excelled in both poetry and fiction and influenced many other writers, especially in South America.

Rabbi Boteach's example, by age twenty-one), you were never stirred again?

The key is to incorporate chemistry into our marital lives, not to snuff it out. We are erotic and emotional animals, and when we react most fully to people, we react to them erotically and emotionally. We react this way to teachers and to students; to pop stars and to politicians; to interns, novelists, and waiters; to our elders and our juniors. It is a part of what allows us to relate to human beings across the social, political, and cultural spectrums. To demonize this responsiveness is to truncate our sensibility, our humanity. Better to share our passing fancies with our mates, to turn them like colored glass in the light, lest they become blades in our pockets. For this we need mag-

nanimous partners. And we need an 18-karat commitment to those partners, who over the years will inevitably seem less perfect than those glinting shards of novelty in the corner of our sight.

"To fall in love is to create a religion that has a fallible god," said Jorge Luis Borges.* To love truly is to stay in love after the fall. It is to love more gratefully, more potentially, because our god has come down to earth: the spirit has been made flesh and now walks—and slips, and flounders, and slouches—among us. 20 It's a delicate proposition—counterintuitive, presumptuous, heady, unreasonable. And yet therein lies its nobility and, perhaps, its necessity.

Questions for Discussion

1. Why does Nehring find it "refreshing" to learn that women initiate most divorces? How does she put a positive spin on what could be used against women?

2. What are the implications of using a word like "catch" when describing courtship? Would you like to be perceived as a "good catch"?

3. According to Nehring, what do women need to thrive in a relationship?

4. What social and cultural forces contribute to the frustration many women feel about their marriages?

5. Nehring writes that "sometimes it's okay to wreck a home. Sometimes divorce is the brave and not the cowardly option." Can you describe a situation in which divorce would be the brave option?

6. Consider the various diets, in paragraph 8, offered by the author of the book Nehring is reviewing. What would you say to this woman if you were her friend?

7. What does Nehring mean when she writes of the challenge of "eternal choice"?

8. Why does deception undermine a marriage?

9. Nehring makes many allusions in this argument, referring, for example, to classical myths and to eighteenth- and nineteenth-century writers. How were you affected by the allusions?

③ JONATHAN RAUCH, "A More Perfect Union"

The following argument was first published in the *Atlantic* in 2004, shortly after the Massachusetts Supreme Court declared that the state's marriage laws were unconstitutional because they limited the right to a civil marriage to people of different genders who are assumed to be heterosexual. The state legislature was required to amend the law, and it did so—making Massachusetts the first state in which men could marry men and women could marry women. This change subsequently became an issue in that year's Presidential election, in which President George W. Bush defeated Senator John Kerry of Massachusetts, partly because Kerry was associated with a state that was seen as too liberal. During that election, eleven states passed initiatives to amend their constitutions so that marriage would be confined to a union between a man and a woman. Since then, however, both Canada and Spain have legalized gay marriage. And in September 2005, the California legislature voted to legalize it in that state. So it seems clear that the public debate over gay marriage is likely to continue for some time. A senior writer for *National Journal* and a correspondent for the *Atlantic*, Jonathan Rauch is a Yale University graduate who has published in numerous magazines and newspapers. In 1996, he coauthored a report for the U.S. Treasury Department on the future of the financial-services industry, reflecting his interest in economic issues. Marriage may seem unrelated to the economy, but those who are allowed to marry enjoy several economic benefits. "A More Perfect Union"—a title that comes from the Preamble of the U.S. Constitution—is an excerpt from Rauch's most recent book: *Gay Marriage: Why It Is Good for Gays, Good for Straights, and Good for America* (2004).

A More Perfect Union

JONATHAN RAUCH

1 Last November the Supreme Judicial Court of Massachusetts ruled that excluding gay couples from civil marriage violated the state constitution. The court gave the legislature six months—until May—to do something about it. Some legislators mounted efforts to amend the state constitution to ban same-sex marriage, but as of this writing they have failed (and even if passed, a ban would not take effect until at least 2006). With unexpected urgency the country faces the possibility that marriage licenses might soon be issued to homosexual couples. To hear the opposing sides talk, a national culture war is unavoidable.

But same-sex marriage neither must nor should be treated as an all-or-nothing national decision. Instead individual states should be left to try gay marriage if and when they choose—no national ban, no national mandate. Not only would a decentralized approach be in keeping with the country's most venerable legal traditions; it would also improve, in three ways, the odds of making same-sex marriage work for gay and straight Americans alike.

COMPLICATION

Opponents of gay marriage argued that it was an issue that should be decided by state governments rather than by the courts. Yet when the California Senate and House of Representatives voted to legalize gay marriage in September 2005, Governor Arnold Schwarzenegger vetoed the legislation on the ground that it was a matter that the people of the state should decide by direct ballot. This raises at least two questions: If neither courts nor state legislatures can be trusted to act on behalf of the people's good, what is their function? And how many issues should be decided directly by the people instead of by the representatives they have chosen—representatives, you might assume—who have the responsibility for being well informed on the issues of the day?

CONTEXT

In the 1973 *Roe* v. *Wade* decision by the Supreme Court, it was ruled that, as National Public Radio (NPR) put it on the thirtieth anniversary of the decision, "the relationship between a woman and her doctor was a private affair, not subject to governmental interference. Written by Justice Harry A. Blackmun, the ruling declared that the guarantee of liberty in the Fourteenth Amendment to the U.S. Constitution extends a right to privacy 'broad enough to encompass a woman's decision whether or not to terminate her pregnancy,'" thus making the procedure legal in all states.

First, it would give the whole country a chance to learn. Nothing terrible—in fact, nothing even noticeable—seems to have happened to marriage since Vermont began allowing gay civil unions, in 2000. But civil unions are not marriages. The only way to find out what would happen if same-sex couples got marriage certificates is to let some of us do it. Turning marriage into a nationwide experiment might he rash, but trying it in a few states would provide test cases on a smaller scale. Would the divorce rate rise? Would the marriage rate fall? We should get some indications before long. Moreover, states are, as the saying goes, the laboratories of democracy. One state might opt for straightforward legalization. Another might add some special provisions (for instance, regarding child custody or adoption). A third might combine same-sex marriage with counseling or other assistance (not out of line with a growing movement to offer social-service support to so-called fragile families). Variety would help answer some important questions: Where would gay marriage work best? What kind of community support would it need? What would be the avoidable pitfalls? Either to forbid same-sex marriage nationwide or to legalize it nationwide would be to throw away a wealth of potential information.

Just as important is the social benefit of letting the states find their own way. Law is only part of what gives marriage its binding power; community support and social expectations are just as important. In a community that looked on same-sex marriage with bafflement or hostility, a gay couple's marriage certificate, while providing legal benefits, would confer no social support from the heterosexual majority. Both the couple and the community would be shortchanged. Letting states choose gay marriage wouldn't guarantee that everyone in the state recognized such marriages as legitimate, but it would pretty well ensure that gay married couples could find some communities in their state that did.

5   Finally, the political benefit of a state-by-state approach is not to be underestimated. This is the benefit of avoiding a national culture war.

The United States is not (thank goodness) a culturally homogeneous country. It consists of many distinct moral communities. On certain social issues, such as abortion and homosexuality, people don't agree and probably never will—and the single political advantage of the federalist system is that they don't have to. Individuals and groups who find the values or laws of one state obnoxious have the right to live somewhere else.

The nationalization of abortion policy in the Supreme Court's 1973 *Roe* v. *Wade* decision created a textbook example of what can happen when this federalist principle is ignored. If the Supreme Court had not stepped in, abortion would today be legal in most states but not all; prolifers would have the comfort of knowing they could live in a state whose law was compatible with their views. Instead of endlessly confronting a cultural schism that affects every Supreme Court nomination, we would see occasional local flare-ups in state legislatures or courtrooms.

America is a stronger country for the moral diversity that federalism uniquely allows. Moral law and family law govern the most intimate and, often, the most controversial spheres of life. For the sake of domestic tranquility, domestic law is best left to a level of government that is close to home.

So well suited is the federalist system to the gay-marriage issue that it might almost have been set up to handle it. In a new land whose citizens followed different religious traditions, it would have made no sense to centralize marriage or family law. And so marriage has been the domain of local law not just since the days of the Founders but since Colonial times, before the states were states. To my knowledge, the federal government has overruled the states on marriage only twice. The first time was when it required Utah to ban polygamy as a condition for joining the union—and note that this ruling was issued before Utah became a state. The second time was in 1967, when the Supreme Court, in *Loving* v. *Virginia,* struck down sixteen states' bans on interracial marriage. Here the court said not that marriage should be defined by the federal government but only that states could not define marriage in ways that violated core constitutional rights. On the one occasion when Congress directly addressed same-sex marriage, in the 1996 Defense of Marriage Act, it decreed that the federal government would not recognize same-sex marriages but took care not to impose that rule on the states.

10 Marriage laws (and, of course, divorce laws) continue to be established by the states. They differ on many points, from age of consent to who may marry whom. In Arizona, for example, first cousins are allowed to marry only if both are sixty-five or older or the couple can prove to a judge "that one of the cousins is unable to reproduce." (So much for the idea that marriage is about procreation.) Conventional wisdom notwithstanding, the Constitution does not require states to recognize one another's marriages. The Full Faith and Credit clause (Article IV, Section 1) does require states to honor one another's public acts and judgments. But in 1939 and again in 1988 the Supreme Court ruled that the clause does not compel a state "to substitute the statutes of other states for its own statutes dealing with a subject matter concerning

CONTEXT

In 1996 President Bill Clinton signed into law the Personal Responsibility and Work Opportunity Reconciliation Act. Paired with the Balanced Budget Act of 1997, also signed by President Clinton, this act made moving the population receiving welfare into work one of the main goals of the federal welfare system. The Welfare-to-Work program officially ended in 2004. How well do you think this "experiment" worked? Has poverty disappeared from the United States? Does everyone who wants to work succeed in finding a job? In that same year, President Clinton signed the Defense of Marriage Act, legislation passed by Congress that defines *marriage* under federal law as "a legal union of one man and one woman as husband and wife" and defines *spouse* as "a person of the opposite sex who is a husband or a wife." The act also allowed each state to recognize or refuse to recognize a marriage performed in another state. What are the implications of thinking of a man or a woman as "the opposite sex"? What does it say about marriage to think that it requires an act of Congress to defend it? Do you think such an act would indeed protect marriage as an institution?

which it is competent to legislate." Dale Carpenter, a law professor at the University of Minnesota, notes that the Full Faith and Credit clause "has never been interpreted to mean that every state must recognize every marriage performed in every other state." He writes, "Each state may refuse to recognize a marriage performed in another state if that marriage would violate the state's public policy." If Delaware, for example, decided to lower its age of consent to ten, no other state would be required to regard a ten-year-old as legally married. The public-policy exception, as it is called, is only common sense. If each state could legislate for all the rest, American-style federalism would be at an end.

Why, then, do the states all recognize one another's marriages? Because they choose to. Before the gay-marriage controversy arose, the country enjoyed a general consensus on the terms of marriage. Interstate differences were so small that states saw no need to split hairs, and mutual recognition was a big convenience. The issue of gay marriage, of course, changes the picture, by asking states to reconsider an accepted boundary of marriage. This is just the sort of controversy in which the Founders imagined that individual states could and often should go their separate ways.

Paradoxically, the gay left and the antigay right have found themselves working together against the center. They agree on little else, but where marriage is concerned, they both want the federal government to take over. To many gay people, anything less than nationwide recognition of same-sex marriage seems both unjust the impractical. "Wait a minute," a gay person might protest. "How is this supposed to work? I get married in Maryland (say), but every time I cross the border into Virginia during my morning commute, I'm single? Am I married or not? Portability is one of the things that make marriage different from civil union. If it isn't portable, it isn't really marriage; it's second-class citizenship. Obviously, as soon as same-sex marriage is approved in any one state, we're going to sue in federal court to have it recognized in all the others."

"Exactly" a conservative might reply. "Gay activists have no intention of settling for marriage in just one or two states. They will keep suing until they find some activist federal judge—and there are plenty—who agrees with them. Public-policy exception and Defense of Marriage Act notwithstanding, the courts, not least the Supreme Court, do as they please, and lately they have signed on to the gay cultural agenda. Besides, deciding on a state-by-state basis is impractical; the gay activists are right about that. The sheer inconvenience of dealing with couples who went in and out of matrimony every time they crossed state lines would drive states to the lowest common denominator, and gay marriages would wind up being recognized everywhere."

Neither of the arguments I have just sketched is without merit. But both sides are asking the country to presume that the Founders were wrong and to foreclose the possibility that seems the most likely to succeed. Both sides want something life doesn't usually offer—a guarantee. Gay-marriage supporters want a guarantee of full legal equality, and gay-marriage opponents want a guarantee that same-sex marriage will never happen at all. I can't offer any guarantees. But I can offer some reassurance.

15 Is a state-by-state approach impractical and unsustainable? Possibly, but the time to deal with any problems is if and when they arise. Going in, there is no reason to expect any great difficulty. There are many precedents for state-by-state action. The country currently operates under a tangle of different state banking laws. As any banker will tell you, the lack of uniformity has made interstate banking more difficult. But we do have interstate banks. Bankers long ago got used to meeting different requirements in different states. Similarly, car manufacturers have had to deal with zero-emission rules in California and a few other states. Contract law, property law, and criminal law all vary significantly from state to state. Variety is the point of federalism. Uniform national policies may be convenient, but they risk sticking us with the same wrong approach everywhere.

My guess is that if one or two states allowed gay marriage, a confusing transitional period, while state courts and legislatures worked out what to do, would quickly lead in all but a few places to routines that everyone would soon take for granted. If New Jersey adopted gay marriage, for instance, New York would have a number of options. It might refuse to recognize the marriages. It might recognize them. It might honor only certain aspects of them—say, medical power of attorney, or inheritance and tenancy rights. A state with a civil-union or domestic partner law might automatically confer that law's benefits on any gay couple who got married in New Jersey. My fairly confident expectation is that initially most states would reject out-of-state gay marriages (as, indeed, most states have pre-emptively done), but a handful would fully accept them, and others would choose an intermediate option.

For married gay couples, this variation would be a real nuisance. If my partner and I got married in Maryland, we would need to be aware of differences in marriage laws and make arrangements—medical power of attorney, a will, and so on—for whenever we were out of state. Pesky and, yes, unfair (or at least unequal). And outside Maryland the line between being married and not being married would be blurred. In Virginia, people who saw my wedding band would be unsure whether I was "really married" or just "Maryland married."

Even so, people in Virginia who learned that I was "Maryland married" would know I had made the strongest possible commitment in my home state, and thus in the eyes of my community and its law. They would know I had gone beyond cohabitation or even domestic partnership. As a Jew, I may not recognize the spiritual authority of a Catholic priest, but I do recognize and respect the special commitment he has made to his faith and his community.

In much the same way, even out-of-state gay marriages would command a significant degree of respect.

If you are starving, one or two slices of bread may not be as good as a loaf—but it is far better than no bread at all. The damage that exclusion from marriage has done to gay lives and gay culture comes not just from being unable to marry right now and right here but from knowing the law forbids us ever to marry at all. The first time a state adopted same-sex marriage, gay life would change forever. The full benefits would come only when same-sex marriage was legal everywhere. But gay people's lives would improve with the first state's announcement that in this community, marriage is open to everyone.

20 Building consensus takes time. The nationwide imposition of same-sex marriage by a federal court might discredit both gay marriage and the courts, and the public rancor it

The Normality of Gay Marriages

There's nothing like a touch of real-world experience to inject some reason into the inflammatory national debate over gay marriages. Take Massachusetts, where the state's highest court held in late 2003 that under the State Constitution, same-sex couples have a right to marry. The State Legislature moved to undo that decision last year by approving a proposed constitutional amendment to ban gay marriages and create civil unions as an alternative. But this year, when precisely the same measure came up for a required second vote, it was defeated by a thumping margin of 157 to 39.

The main reason for the flip-flop is that some 6,600 same-sex couples have married over the past year with nary a sign of adverse effects. The sanctity of heterosexual marriages has not been destroyed. Public morals have not gone into a tailspin. Legislators who supported gay marriage in last year's vote have been re-elected. Gay couples, many of whom had been living together monogamously for years, have rejoiced at official recognition of their commitment.

As a Republican leader explained in justifying his vote switch: "Gay marriages has begun, and life has not changed for the citizens of the commonwealth, with the exception of those who can now marry who could not before." A Democrat attributed his change of heart to the beneficial effects he says "when I looked in the eyes of the children living with these couples." Gay marriage, it turned out, is good for family values. . . .

unleashed might be at least as intense as that surrounding abortion. My confidence in the public's decency and in its unfailing, if sometimes slow-acting, commitment to liberal principles is robust. For me personally, the pace set by a state-by-state approach would be too slow. It would be far from ideal. But it would be something much more important than ideal: it would be right.

Would a state-by-state approach inevitably lead to a nationwide court mandate anyway? Many conservatives fear that the answer is yes, and they want a federal constitutional amendment to head off the courts—an amendment banning gay marriage nationwide. These days it is a fact of life that someone will sue over anything, that some court will hear any lawsuit, and that there is no telling what a court might do. Still, I think that conservatives' fears on this score are unfounded.

Remember, all precedent leaves marriage to the states. All precedent supports the public-policy exception. The Constitution gives Congress a voice in determining which of one another's laws states must recognize, and Congress has spoken clearly: the Defense of Marriage Act explicitly decrees that no state must recognize any other state's same-sex marriages. In order to mandate interstate recognition of gay marriages, a court would thus need to burn through three different firewalls—a tall order, even for an activist court. The current Supreme Court, moreover, has proved particularly fierce in resisting federal incursions into states' rights. We typically reserve constitutional prohibitions for imminent threats to liberty, justice, or popular sovereignty. If we are going to get into the business of constitutionally banning anything that someone imagines the Supreme Court might one day mandate, we will need a Constitution the size of the Manhattan phone book.

Social conservatives have lost one cultural battle after another in the past five decades: over divorce, abortion, pornography, gambling, school prayer, homosexuality. They have seen that every federal takeover of state and local

powers comes with strings attached. They have learned all too well the power of centralization to marginalize moral dissenters—including religious ones. And yet they are willing to risk federal intervention in matrimony. Why?

Not, I suspect, because they fear gay marriage would fail. Rather, because they fear it would succeed.

25 One of the conservative arguments against gay marriage is particularly revealing: the contention that even if federal courts don't decide the matter on a national level, convenience will cause gay marriage to spread from state to state. As noted, I don't believe questions of convenience would force the issue either way. But let me make a deeper point here.

States recognized one another's divorce reforms in the 1960s and 1970s without giving the matter much thought (which was too bad). But the likelihood that they would recognize another state's same-sex marriages without serious debate is just about zero, especially at first: the issue is simply too controversial. As time went on, states without gay marriage might get used to the idea. They might begin to wave through other states' same-sex marriages as a convenience for all concerned. If that happened, however, it could only be because gay marriage had not turned out to be a disaster. It might even be because gay marriage was working pretty well. This would not be contagion. It would be evolution—a sensible response to a successful experiment. Try something here or there. If it works, let it spread. If it fails, let it fade.

The opponents of gay marriage want to prevent the experiment altogether. If you care about finding the best way forward for gay people and for society in a changing world, that posture is hard to justify. One rationale goes something like this: "Gay marriage is so certain to be a calamity that even the smallest trial anywhere should be banned." To me, that line of argument smacks more of hysteria than of rational thought. In the 1980s and early 1990s some liberals were sure that reforming the welfare system to emphasize work would put millions of children out on the street. Even trying welfare reform, they said, was irresponsible. Fortunately, the states don't listen. They experimented—responsibly. The results were positive enough to spark a successful national reform.

Another objection cites not certain catastrophe but insidious decay. A conservative once said to me, "Changes in complicated institutions like marriage take years to work their way through society. They are often subtle. Social scientists will argue until the cows come home about the positive and negative effects of gay marriage. So states might adopt it before they fully understood the harm it did."

Actually, you can usually tell pretty quickly what effects a major policy change is having—at least you can get a general idea. States knew quite soon that welfare reforms were working better than the old program. That's why the idea caught on. If same-sex marriage is going to cause problems, some of them should be apparent within a few years of its legalization.

30 And notice how the terms of the discussion have shifted. Now the anticipated problem is not sudden, catastrophic social harm but subtle, slow damage. Well, there might be subtle and slow social benefits, too. But more important, there would be one large and immediate benefit: the benefit for gay people of being able to get married. If we are going to exclude a segment of the population from arguably the most important of all civic institutions, we need to be certain that the group's

participation would cause severe disruptions. If we are going to put the burden on gay people to prove that same-sex marriage would never cause even any minor difficulty, then we are assuming that any cost to heterosexuals, however small, outweighs every benefit to homosexuals, however large. That gay people's welfare counts should, of course, be obvious and inarguable; but to some it is not.

I expect same-sex marriage to have many subtle ramifications—many of them good not just for gay people but for marriage. Same-sex marriage would dramatically reaffirm the country's preference for marriage as the gold standard for committed relationships. Of course there might be harmful and neutral effects as well. I don't expect that social science would be able to sort them all out. But the fact that the world is complicated is the very reason to run the experiment. We can never know for sure what the effects of any policy will be, so we conduct a limited experiment if possible, and then decide how to proceed on the basis of necessarily imperfect information.

If conservatives genuinely oppose same-sex marriage because they fear it would harm straight marriage, they should be willing to let states that want to try gay marriage do so. If, on the other hand, conservatives oppose same-sex marriage because they believe that it is immoral and wrong by definition, fine—but let them have the honesty to acknowledge that they are not fighting for the good of marriage so much as they are using marriage as a weapon in their fight against gays.

Questions for Discussion

1. Why does Rauch believe that the legality of gay marriage is something best determined on a state-by-state level? How do you respond to the news about gay marriage in Massachusetts, as reported in the box on page 415?

2. What role does the Supreme Court's 1973 decision in *Roe* v. *Wade* play in this argument?

3. By writing "some of us" in paragraph 3, Rauch discloses his sexual orientation. How does this disclosure affect his ethos? Why make it so simply?

4. "The United States is not (thank goodness) a culturally homogeneous country," writes Rauch. What are the advantages of cultural—and moral—diversity?

5. According to Rauch, what does the gay left have in common with the antigay right?

6. Does Rauch recognize that there are any risks to experimenting with marriage laws?

7. Why do you think people want to amend the U.S. Constitution to prohibit gay marriage? What assumptions are they making about the nature of the Constitution and the role of the federal government in the lives of citizens?

8. Consider Rauch's conclusion. Do you think that the debate over who gets to marry in the United States is truly about marriage law, or could the debate signal larger differences?

④ **PHILLIP HODSON, "Baby, This Is For Ever"**

Discussion of marriage as "commitment" usually focuses on the nature of the commitment between the people exchanging vows. But what is the commitment they subsequently have to the children that result from their union, and how does this commitment to children manifest itself in an era when divorce is increasingly common? Questions such as these shape the following argument by Phillip Hodson, a Fellow of the British Association for Counseling and the author of eleven books—the titles of which include *How to Make Great Love to a Man* and *How to Make Great Love to a Woman.* In Great Britain, he is also known for his appearances on television and radio. In the United States, he has contributed to publications such as *Psychology Today, Cosmopolitan,* and *Family Circle.* "Baby, This Is For Ever" first appeared in February 2005 in the *Times* of London, Britain's oldest and most influential newspaper.

Baby, This Is For Ever

PHILLIP HODSON

1 This year my partner and I will celebrate 30 years of living in sin. In fact, we've been happily unmarried for so long that I am thinking of applying for heritage status with the Office of National Statistics. According to official figures, we represent a considerable anomaly. Despite having raised one boy and step-parented two others, our union should by now have foundered on the very rocks of cohabitation that we innocently regard as its strengths.

The real victims of unorthodox unions such as ours, apparently, are the children.

The suggested solution is to tax cohabitation off the planet and start marriage classes in kindergarten. The assumptions behind this policy will do little for the children who need to be put at the heart of our social concerns, while stimulating the righteous into a dangerous frenzy.

New research says that unmarried parents are five times more likely to break up than married ones; that 75 percent of all family breakdowns where there are young children now involve unmarried parents, and that "Family failure is no longer driven by divorce but by the collapse of unmarried partnerships" (*The Times,* February 5, 2005). This has caused more excitement among family fundamentalists than the second coming of George Bush.

5 As a therapist, I understand the reasons why most of my fellow citizens will decide to marry. It is a traditional institution with something to recommend it.

At the very least, you end up being called husband and wife instead of that litany of uncertainties commencing with "partner" and ending in "whatsit."

However, I object to matrimonial ideology. Traditional marriage strikes me as an implicit cause of divorce. The terms of the marital contract are grandiose, sketchy and in some cases impossible to fulfill. You cannot promise to be the same person for the next five years let alone for the rest of your days. The basic causes of domestic friction are never

*Born in 1925, Margaret Thatcher rose from being a member of Parliament to leader of the Conservative Party and the first woman to serve as Prime Minister. Closely associated with President Ronald Reagan, many of whose values she shared, Thatcher served as prime minister from 1979 to 1990. She is best known for having privatized several state industries, having led her country to war against Argentina in a dispute over the Falkland Islands, and having worked with President Reagan to challenge the power of the Soviet Union. Her opponents called her the "Iron Lady."

addressed. Where in the contract does it tell you whether to have one bank account or two? Or who takes the children to school? Who loads and empties the dishwasher?

As for sex, the traditional ideal, while silent on the need for good pillow books, manages to make a fetish of phallic penetration. Apparently, oral sex and mutual masturbation won't do. Church and state require intromission. This is a distasteful invasion of personal liberty.

Underpinning such objections, I suspect, are contemporary philosophic shifts away from the official regulation of private feelings or personal morality. I have never believed my domestic sleeping arrangements are the business of any man or woman from any ministry. I "married" my partner, as it were, in the act of choosing to make a home with her, as she did with me. Today, fully one third of men and a quarter of all women prefer to cohabit. This to me represents the most truly authentic "deregulation" of the Thatcher* era—the "privatisation of marriage."

10 To those who still promote the research on marriage's greater durability, I ask which university of the blindingly obvious did they attend? The state of marriage, by definition, attracts all those who believe in lifelong monogamy, including heavy-duty Catholics, Jews and Muslims. Cohabitation, on the other hand, include those who say things like "Well, why don't you move in for a bit and we'll see how it goes, but no great dramas if we split up, eh?" When you compare apples with pears you get sour grapes.

To those who claim that marriage offers more security because it's harder to wriggle out of, let me break the sad news that one third of all new marriages still manage to end in divorce within the first five years. In fact, more than 430 marriages in England and Wales die daily. If, as a cohabitee, I find myself in similar perils, a divorce process would of course prove unnecessary, but do you imagine for one moment that there are no emotional,

legal, family and social ties, not to mention ties of outright blackmail, that after a number of years bind and secure two people just as tightly—or rather loosely—as those stemming from a wedding?

I am, therefore, truly bemused by the huzzas from the New Nuptial Movement. Why seek to replace one allegedly failing institution (cohabitation) with an incontrovertibly failing one (marriage)? I firmly believe that what is being overlooked is the probability that any statistical association between cohabitation and family breakup is coincidental instead of causal. I suspect that the real culprit is nothing to do with marital status but with a widespread absence of modern parenting skills in a state-financed sub-culture of recklessly unplanned birth.

Our obsession with weddings distracts attention from the one really portentous vow we ever have to make in life, namely our decision to reproduce. I find it scandalous that we make so much relative fuss about the scale of pre and extramarital sex while remaining utterly blase when parents enter a second union before they have finished looking after the children from the first. I would prefer to live in a society where anyone who caused a birth was deemed to be legally, morally and fiscally "married" to that child for 20 years at least. This is where legal and ideological reforms need to bite. Technically, you can never divorce your children, nor should you try. But in our society men, in particular, sometimes dump their offspring in order to achieve a more gratifying relationship.

What we seem to have overlooked is something that wolves and tigers never forget.

15 We need to suffer for our offspring, to lose body fat if necessary, to come second, third and fourth in the pecking order, put careers on hold, sacrifice sleep, slog on when depression is a visitor and accept that there will be an inevitable deterioration in the quality of our spousal union, as the pertinent research always attests, because having children is ex-

pensive and they make you tired. When children need you most, as teenagers, they show it least. This is the time you will be told to f- off by the unpleasant Kevin inside every tormented pubescent and you need to hold the boundaries of decency, taste and commitment throughout these perils. This is exactly the time NOT to split up.

To this end, we should update our folklore. The narrative mantra ought to run: "You go into puberty. You eventually have safe sex. Then you have some more. You leave education. You grow up. You shack up. You break up. You settle into your career zone. You live with someone else. And then comes your truly, madly, deeply BIG DAY. Shall we have a baby?"

I believe all the emphasis in our legislative and tax system, as well as the organisation of private ceremonies, should be poured into this single, defining moment. The state ought to be preoccupied with parenting, not partnering. The vital question for any responsible adult is mating, not marriage. Ring out those natal bells!

Questions for Discussion

1. Hodson opens by announcing that he and his partner have been "living in sin" for thirty years—as opposed to stating that their thirtieth anniversary is approaching. How do you take this remark? What do you think motivated it?

2. What does Hodson achieve by disclosing that he is a therapist?

3. What do you think Hodson means by "matrimonial ideology" and an "obsession with weddings"? How applicable are these statements to U.S. culture?

4. What is Hodson saying about sex in paragraph 13—and the relationship between sex and marriage?

5. What does Hodson propose to provide greater security for children in an era when increasing numbers of marriages seem at risk?

6. To what extent is this argument designed for an audience capable of having children? How helpful would others find it?

DIFFERENCES

NEGOTIATING

The standard wedding vows in Christian services include lines in which both the bride and the groom promise that they will forsake all others, remain faithful in sickness and in health, and not part until death. The spirit of these vows can be found in ceremonies within other faith traditions. Many people taking such vows sincerely believe that they will honor them. Others are marrying for a second or third time, and some have had love affairs when previously married, so they signal a good intention but realize deep down that their vows may be broken. Indeed, the divorce rate, as three of the authors in this cluster point out, and uncertainty about marriage have led some couples to sign legally binding prenuptial agreements spelling out what will happen as a result of infidelity or if the marriage ends in divorce—a document that often runs contrary to the vows these individuals will exchange in public.

Imagine now that you are deeply in love with someone who is smart, brave, funny, good looking, and well employed. This person has many strengths. You have dated long enough, however, to be aware of some weaknesses—a tendency to forget a promise to call, for example, or a tendency to have what Christina Nehring calls "a wandering eye." You want to marry, but you think it best to do so with a clear agreement of what you expect.

You have little money and see no likelihood of earning much in the foreseeable future. Moreover, hiring a lawyer to help plan your wedding strikes you as likely to generate bad karma. So instead you decide to draft a document outlining your expectations of your future spouse and yourself. You both understand that the final draft of this document will incorporate revisions suggested and agreed upon by you and your future spouse. Moreover, you decide to write your own wedding vows so that you are both sure you are making promises you can honor.

Write the first draft of the agreement you want your future spouse to honor and can promise to honor yourself. Include what you are sure you can contribute to the marriage, as well as what your limits might be. Also include the strengths you perceive in your future spouse, what you expect this person to be able to bring to the marriage you build, and the expectations you believe this person has in marrying you. Add what forms of behavior would disappoint you and what would be unacceptable. When you have finished your draft, add as an appendix a draft of the wedding vows you think you can both honor. Remember that your goal in this project is to create a clear understanding with someone you care about by recognizing differences within a positive context. If you turn this project into a document praising yourself and attacking your future mate, you are more likely to increase differences than to negotiate a way around them.

What Does It Mean to Be a Good Parent?

The rules governing the relationship between parents and children seemed relatively simple in the past. For example, there is an old adage that "children should be seen but not heard." And even when children were much loved, they were expected to honor their parents (as the fifth Commandment holds and other religious texts convey)—which means not only obeying parents but also respecting them and caring for them in old age. Beginning in the late eighteenth century, however, childhood was reconstructed. The Romantics believed that "the child is father to the man," as the poet William Wordsworth wrote in 1802—that, in other words, children are born with innate wisdom and imagination and are superior to adults in some respects because they are not yet corrupted by experience in the world. From this concept, increasing deference toward children began to emerge, and rather than take children for granted as "little adults" parents began to become concerned with what their offspring need besides food, shelter, and authority. Many parents simply wing it on their own, learning how to parent (or how not to parent) by taking things one day at a time and never thinking deeply about what they are doing. Others, however, take parenting classes and read much of the literature on parenting that can be found in books and magazines. Of this literature, the various editions of Dr. Benjamin Spock's *Baby and Child Care* have probably had the most influence. First published in 1946, it appeared just in time for the "baby boom" that began after the end of the Second World War and continued until the early 1960s. Thousands of young parents, many of them living far from their own parents, needed up-to-date advice about how to raise a healthy child. Concerned with questions such as "Should babies be picked up whenever they cry?" and "Is it better to breast feed or to use baby formula?" these parents turned to Dr. Spock—whose work, updated, remains in print. But the American family has changed dramatically over the last fifty years. Increasing numbers of children are being raised in families in which both parents work outside the home, by a single parent, or in reconfigured families when one of their parents remarries. Moreover, modern science has made conception possible for many couples that would not have been able to have children in the past. It has also made it possible for some potential parents to design the kind of children they wish to have—a topic addressed by the first two arguments in this cluster. The other two respond to the increasing complexity of parenting by focusing on the most important things that mothers and fathers can do.

① **MAUREEN FREELY, "Designer Babies and Other Fairy Tales"**

Because matters of human reproduction are both complex and, to many people, sacred, arguments about reproductive issues can become especially intense. They can encompass medical, economic, ethical, legal, and moral considerations. For example, a couple faced with the prospect of having a baby with a serious genetic disorder must confront the economic question of who will pay the enormous costs of caring for the child once it is born. Physicians may face legal questions if they advise the couple to perform a risky medical procedure on the unborn baby. Others may question the morality of such procedures. Writer Maureen Freely appreciates the complexity of such issues. In fact, she argues that the many different kinds of arguments made about such situations complicate the already difficult decisions facing parents and others who may be involved. Drawing on a reproductive case that caused a sensation in Great Britain in 2002, Freely sorts through the many different voices in debates about reproductive medicine, and she asks you, as a reader, to focus on *how* the issues are being debated. She encourages thinking of these issues as social issues that everyone has a stake in—whether you will ever face reproductive decisions yourself. And because these are social rather than private matters, they should properly be debated—and decided—publicly in democratic fashion. As you read, consider how Freely compares the way these issues are addressed in Great Britain to the way they are addressed in the United States. Her essay appeared in the British magazine the *New Statesman* in 2002.

Designer Babies and Other Fairy Tales

MAUREEN FREELY

1 Meet Raj and Shahana Hashmi. Their gorgeous three-year-old son, Zain, has a serious blood disorder. He needs a cell transplant, and if they do not find a suitable donor he could die. On 22 February, the Human Fertilisation and Embryology Authority (HFEA)* gave the Hashmis permission to try to create that donor. Shahana is to have IVF (in vitro fertilization)† . . . treatment. Any embryos that result will be subjected to genetic diagnosis. The hope is that the couple will find an embryo that could become the child with the bone marrow that will save Zain's life.

The odds are not in their favour. The success rate for a single course of IVF treatment is less than one in three. The likelihood of Shahana Hashmi creating a genetically suitable embryo is one in 16. So she and her husband must have a hard time understanding why so many people think they're playing God. If only, they must be thinking. All they want is to take this one-in-about-50 chance to keep their son alive.

How strange it must be for them to open the paper and read that they are symbols of moral decay. No one is quite ready to con-

*The Human Fertilisation and Embryology Authority, established in 1990, regulates reproductive research and therapies in Great Britain.

†In vitro fertilization is a process by which eggs are removed from a woman, fertilized with male sperm in a laboratory, and implanted in the woman's uterus, where they can potentially develop into human embryos. The first "test-tube baby" was born as a result of this technique in 1978 in England. Although the procedure is now common and used by women who have not been able to conceive a child by other means, typically fewer than one third of the women who undergo the procedure actually become pregnant.

demn them outright. No one who wants to avoid a writ, anyway. No, almost everyone is sure that the Hashmis will love any second child just as much as they love their first. Some have gone on the record to say we can count on this even if something goes amiss and their second born turns out not to be Zain's saviour. But what about the six other couples who have already announced they will be following in the Hashmis' footsteps? What about all the faceless others who are bound to follow them? What if the rules get looser still and this sort of thing becomes standard practice? When we work ourselves up into a moralistic froth about reproductive technology, what exactly are we talking about?

The short answer is that we are talking about too many things at once, and in a very muddled way. The dirge gets played out on the lowest keys on the piano. Many of the fears it evokes are, however, worthy of attention. There is, for example, the entirely legitimate fear of the new—or of the social havoc that can result when new technology makes false claims, or gives people more power than they know how to use, or changes the rules by which we procreate. There is religious fear—about hubris,

damnation, sacrilege and playing God. There is the fear of eugenics trying to "get in through the back door." There is the free-floating fear of the wrong people being in control. We are afraid of doctors taking control of our bodies to create a master race, of parents buying into the fantasy of perfection, of babies being turned into consumer products. And what if something goes wrong? What if, instead of creating the perfect baby, the scientists accidentally create a monster?

5 One of the most interesting things about the debate on reproductive medicine is its heavy reliance on the language of fairy tales. There are spectres, monsters and bogeymen, wishes and dreams and magic cures. Babies are not just babies, but potent symbols of our cultural future—what we want to pass on, what we stand to lose if the story goes the wrong way. When people talk about designer babies, they're not just talking about the manipulation of genes. They are talking about the next generation and who gets to shape it.

If they sometimes forget that they are talking in symbols and fall too easily into magical thinking, if their ideas about "suitable candidates for treatment" are arch-conservative, and even racist, it is also true that they are asking important questions. A society is not a society unless it can reproduce itself. The social regulation of fertility, the system of controls and supports that decides who gets to have children, and who does not, is what makes a society what it is. Every time a society changes its system, everyone and everything in that society feels the effects. The faster the change, the bigger the disruption.

In the past generation, we have seen one of the most dramatic changes ever. The regulation of fertility is less and less a private matter: increasingly, it is decided in the public domain. When fertility goes public, the game changes utterly.

Let me give a very obvious example—I cannot live as a free woman, in control of my body, in charge of my choices, unless I live in

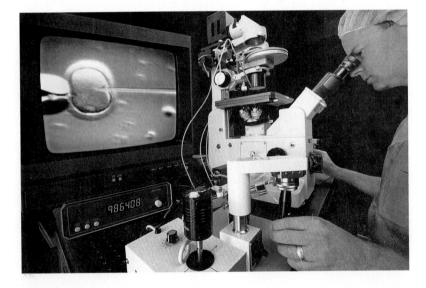

a society which supports that freedom with affordable, accessible contraception. I depend on the state to make sure that the services I use are regulated and staffed with real doctors. I need to have the right to complain if I find the service poor. I need to know that I can campaign for changes in legislation as and when they seem necessary. I need to bear in mind that other parties are free to do the same, which is why my right to birth control is something I should never take for granted.

As with birth control, so with birth. I need to bear in mind that my right to have a child at all is also subject to political control. If I live in a democratic society, I can fight my corner. If I happen to be in China in the time of the one-child policy, I cannot. If I live in any of the countries that condone the use of sex selection technologies to favour boys and weed out girls, my ability to protest against that policy will depend on the political system within which I am operating.

10 Wherever I am, whatever aspect of reproductive medicine I am talking about, the questions are the same. Who decides? And what ideological agenda are those people serving? Thus, Nazi eugenics was evil because it served Nazi ideals. It was dangerous because it was backed up by a fascist state.

If reproductive medicine is properly regulated and democratically debated, if the use of new technology is overseen by a regulatory agency with a clear ethical framework, it does not lead inexorably to the same place. Our own HFEA is far from perfect, but you have only to look at the chaotic, under-regulated United States to see how lucky we are. In Britain, at least, we have rules and principles. We can harness change, make sure it is not open to abuse, or slow it down so that we have time to think about it.

The HFEA's slow but steady move to a stance in favour of "eugenics for sound medical reasons" is a case in point. Most experts in the field predict that public attitudes will follow suit. But that is only a tiny part of the pic-

COMPLICATION

A private matter? In 1994, the International Conference on Population and Development was held in Cairo, Egypt, amid great controversy. Among the declarations made at that conference was the following statement:

> Women have the individual right and the social responsibility to decide whether, how and when to have children and how many to have; no woman can be compelled to bear a child or be prevented from doing so against her will. All women regardless of age, marital status or other social conditions have a right to information and services necessary to exercise their reproductive rights. (SOURCE: WOMEN AGAINST FUNDAMENTALISMS.)

Religious groups have mixed and often conflicting views about these issues, but many religious thinkers see reproduction as a private matter for a woman to decide according to her faith. Reverend Jim Eller of the All Souls Universalist Unitarian Church in Kansas City, Missouri, speaking about the controversy regarding the use of tissue from unborn fetuses for medical research, stated,

> Reproductive decisions should be a private matter, a concern of conscience. These decisions should be made by a woman in consultation with her doctor, and if she desires with her minister and her partner or husband. These choices should not be a matter of public policy and/or a concern into which the government inserts itself.

CHINA'S ONE-CHILD POLICY

Established in 1979, the one-child policy of the government of the People's Republic of China restricts most Chinese couples to having one child. The policy, which was adopted as a measure to control China's rapidly growing population, has been controversial in the decades since it was first implemented. Some human rights observers have charged that the Chinese government has subjected women to forced sterilizations and abortions in carrying out the policy. As a result of the policy, the ratio of males to females in China is 118 to 100 (compared to the average ratio of 105 males to 100 females). In 2003, the Chinese government announced plans to relax the policy.

ture. The larger, cultural implications of reproductive technology will continue to trouble. Every new technique will challenge power relations within families and kinship networks, and therefore the way we bring up children. Wherever the family loses power over an individual's right to become a parent, the advantage goes not just to the individual but to the medical profession, big business and the state. Is this what we want? If we do not, we are going to have to fight it out politically. But first, we need a more rational debate.

Questions for Discussion

1. Freely asserts that the public debates about reproductive situations like that of the Hashmis get "muddled" because people "are talking about too many things at once." What does she mean by that statement? How does that point relate to the main argument of her essay?

2. Freely concedes that many of the concerns expressed by people on various sides of the reproductive controversy involving the Hashmis are valid concerns. She even concedes that people who have racist ideas are asking important questions about this controversy. Why do you think Freely makes these concessions? In what ways might these concessions strengthen her main argument?

3. A central point that Freely makes in this essay is that "the regulation of fertility"—and reproductive issues in general—are increasingly public, rather than private, issues. What counterarguments could you offer to that point?

4. A British writer, Freely writes, "You have only to look at the chaotic, under-regulated United States to see how lucky we are. In Britain, at least, we have rules and principles. We can harness change, make sure it is not open to abuse, or slow it down so that we have time to think about it." She favors deliberate regulation of the technology based on "rules and principles." What purpose does this comparison to the United States serve? Do you think such a comparison is effective, given her audience? (Remember that Freely was writing this essay for a British magazine.) How did you react to this comparison? Does your reaction reflect your own nationality or ethnicity in any way? Explain.

5. Freely ends her essay by stating that "we need a more rational debate" about reproductive issues. On the basis of her essay, what do you think she means by a "rational debate"? Do you think her essay is an example of an argument that would be part of such a debate? Explain, citing specific examples from her essay to support your answer.

② WENDY McELROY, "Victims from Birth"

The capability to "engineer" a baby through certain medical reproductive techniques is often described by proponents as a way to avoid serious birth defects and to ensure that a child will be born healthy. But what if a couple wishes their child to be born with what most people consider a disability? Do those parents have the right to "engineer" such a child? Do they "own" that child's physical identity to the extent that they can use medical science to give that child certain characteristics that others find undesirable? In the following essay, feminist activist Wendy McElroy says no. She discusses an unusual case involving two women who used reproductive techniques to make it more likely that the child they would have would be deaf, just like the two of them. As McElroy notes in her essay, these parents believe that deafness is not a disability but a culture, and they wished their child to be part of that culture. But McElroy wonders whether the child would have chosen to be deaf—if allowed such a choice. She argues that the choice should have been the child's. Despite her unequivocal position on this case, McElroy complicates the already difficult questions surrounding genetics and reproductive issues. In a sense, she asks you to consider who owns physical identities in an age when medical science makes it possible to alter and even to determine those identities. Wendy McElroy writes a column for FoxNews.com and has authored many books and articles, including most recently *Individualist Feminist and the Nineteenth Century* (2001) and *Liberty for Women: Freedom and Feminism in the 21st Century* (2002). She is a research fellow at the Independent Institute, a public policy think tank.

Victims from Birth

WENDY McELROY

1 When Sharon Duchesneau gave birth on Thanksgiving Day to a deaf son, she was delighted.

Duchesneau and her lesbian partner, Candace McCullough, had done everything they could to ensure that Gauvin would be born without hearing. The two deaf women selected their sperm donor on the basis of his family history of deafness in order, as McCullough explained, "to increase our chances of having a baby who is deaf."

So they consciously attempted to create a major sensory defect in their child.

Scientists and philosophers have been debating the morality of new reproductive technologies that may allow us to design "perfect" human beings. Advocates dream of eliminating conditions such as spina bifida; critics invoke images of Nazis creating an Aryan race.*

5 But what of prospective parents who deliberately engineer a genetic defect into their offspring?

Why? Duchesneau illustrates one motive.

She believes deafness is a culture, not a disability. A deaf lifestyle is a choice she wishes to make for her son and his older sister

*Adolf Hitler's infamous ideas about a "master race" were based in part on a belief that a tribe of Indo-Europeans called Aryans invaded and subdued the Indian subcontinent around 1700 BCE. These Aryans were thought to be Nordic in appearance, which contributed to Hitler's belief that Germans were descended from this tribe. Historians and anthropologists generally dismiss the notion that Aryans existed or that any such tribe conquered parts of Eurasia.

Jehanne. McCullough said she and her partner are merely expressing the natural tendency to want children "like them."

"You know, black people have harder lives," she said. "Why shouldn't parents be able to go ahead and pick a black donor if that's what they want?"

Passing over the problem of equating race with a genetic defect, McCullough seems to be saying that deafness is a minority birthright to be passed on proudly from parent to child. By implication, those appalled by their choice are compared to bigots.

10 Some in the media have implicitly endorsed their view.

On March 31st, the *Washington Post Magazine* ran a sympathetic cover story entitled "A World of Their Own" with the subtitle, "In the eyes of his parents, if Gauvin Hughes McCullough turns out to be deaf, that will be just perfect." The article features Gauvin's birth and ends with the two women taking him home. There they

tell family and friends that, "He is not as profoundly deaf as Jehanne, but he is quite deaf. Deaf enough." The article does not comment critically on the parents' decision not to fit Gauvin with a hearing aid and develop whatever hearing ability exists.

The Duchesneau case is particularly troubling to advocates of parental rights against governmental intrusion. The moral outrage it elicits easily can lead to bad law—laws that may hinder responsible parents from using genetic techniques to remedy conditions such as cystic fibrosis in embryos. Selective breeding, after all, is a form of genetic engineering. The Duchesneau case, then, brings all other forms of genetic engineering into question.

The championing of deafness as a cultural "good" owes much to political correctness or the politics of victimhood, which view group identity as the foundation of all political and cultural analysis.

Disabled people used to announce, "I am not my disability." They demanded that society look beyond the withered arm, a clubbed-foot, or a wheel chair and see the human being, a human who was essentially identical to everyone else.

15 Now, for some, the announcement has become, "I am my deafness. That is what is special about me."

Society is brutal to those who are different. I know. As a result of my grandmother contracting German measles, my mother was born with a severely deformed arm. She concealed her arm beneath sweaters with sleeves that dangled loosely, even in sweltering weather. She hid.

Embracing a physical defect, as Duchesneau and McCullough have done, may be a more healthy personal response. Certainly they should be applauded for moving beyond the painful deaf childhoods they describe.

However, I remember my mother telling me that the birth of her children—both healthy and physically unremarkable—were the two happiest moments of her life. I contrast this with Duchesneau who, knowing the pain of growing

COMPLICATION

"In the case of Duchesneau and McCullough, there is no ethical issue—the couple have the right to procreate with whomever they want. And many couples with a family history of deafness or disability seek to have a child without that disability. But some deaf couples have expressed the desire to use prenatal genetic testing of their fetus or in vitro fertilisation and preimplantation genetic diagnosis to select a deaf child. These choices are not unique to deafness. Dwarves may wish to have a dwarf child. People with intellectual disability may wish to have a child like them. Couples of mixed race may wish to have a light skinned child (or a dark skinned child, if they are mindful of reducing the risk of skin cancer in countries like Australia)."

SOURCE: Julian Savulescu, "Deaf Babies, 'Designer Disability', and the Future of Medicine." *British Medical Journal* (October 2002).

up deaf, did what she could to impose deafness upon her son.

Deafness is not fundamentally a cultural choice, although a culture has sprung up around it. If it were, deafness would not be included in the Americans with Disabilities Act*—a source of protection and funding that deaf-culture zealots do not rush to renounce. 20 But if deafness is to be considered a cultural choice, let it be the choice of the child, not the parents. Let a child with all five senses decide to renounce or relinquish one of them in order to embrace what may be a richer life. If a child is rendered incapable of deciding "yes" or "no," then in what manner is it a choice?

CONTEXT

McElroy's essay was published in 2002 on a website called iFeminists.com, which describes itself as "an all-inclusive online center where people looking for a new way to approach feminism can gather online, learn, and access a wealth of information. iFeminists.com offers in-depth resources and portal-like tools for everyone: activists and scholars, experts and beginners, women and men." "iFeminism," according to the site, refers to "independent feminism," which "calls for freedom, choice, and personal responsibility." iFeminists believe that "freedom and diversity benefit women, whether or not the choices that particular women make are politically correct. They respect all sexual choices, from motherhood to porn. As the cost of freedom, iFeminists accept personal responsibility for their own lives. They do not look to government for privileges any more than they would accept government abuse." In what sense does McElroy's argument in this essay reflect an iFeminist philosophy?

---

*According to the U.S. Department of Justice, the Americans with Disabilities Act (ADA), passed in 1990, "gives civil rights protections to individuals with disabilities similar to those provided to individuals on the basis of race, color, sex, national origin, age, and religion. It guarantees equal opportunity for individuals with disabilities in public accommodations, employment, transportation, State and local government services, and telecommunications."

Questions for Discussion

1. On what grounds does McElroy criticize Duchesneau and McCullough's efforts to have a deaf child?

2. Why does McElroy reject the view that deafness is a culture? How convincing is her argument against that view?

3. Why is this case troubling for advocates of parental rights who resist government intrusion on parenting decisions, according to McElroy? In what sense is this point important to McElroy's main argument about this case?

4. In making a point about how difficult it is to be different in a society, McElroy refers to her mother's disability. Evaluate the effectiveness of this use of personal experience. Is McElroy's analogy between her mother's disability and the birth of the deaf child she describes in this essay relevant to her point? Explain.

5. McElroy's essay can be described as an argument based on deductive reasoning (see pages 88–93). On what fundamental belief or principle does McElroy base her argument? Do you agree with her? Why or why not?

③ ANNA QUINDLEN, "The Good Enough Mother"

Through her column in the *New York Times*—which won her a Pulitzer Prize in 1992—as well as her column in *Newsweek,* Anna Quindlen is one of the best known journalists in the country. In addition to publishing collections of her nonfiction, she is the author of four novels and two children's books, *The Tree Came to Stay* and *Happily Ever After.* The following argument—which draws upon her experience as a child and as a mother—originally appeared in *Newsweek* during the winter of 2005. When composing this column, Quindlen knows that it must fit on a single magazine page—a case in which the medium for publication helps determine the content of an argument. As you prepare to read "The Good Enough Mother," think about how this title signifies that Quindlen is not likely to make a case for being a supermom.

The Good Enough Mother

ANNA QUINDLEN

1 There was a kind of carelessness to my childhood. I wandered away from time to time, rode my bike too far from home, took the trolley to nowhere in particular and back again. If you had asked my mother at any given time where I was, she would likely have paused from spooning Gerber's peas into a baby's mouth or ironing our school uniforms and replied, "She's around here somewhere."

By the new standards of mothering, my mother was a bust. Given the number of times I got lost when I was young, she might even be termed neglectful. There's only one problem with that conclusion. It's dead wrong. My mother was great at what she did. Don't misunderstand: she didn't sit on the floor and help us build with our Erector sets, didn't haul us from skating rink to piano lessons. She couldn't even drive. But where she was always felt like a safe place.

The idea that that's enough is a tough sell in our current culture, and not simply because if one of my kids had been found wandering far from our home there would have been a caseworker and a cop at the door. We live in a per-

fection society now, in which it is possible to make our bodies last longer, to manipulate our faces so the lines of laughter and distress are wiped out. We believe in the illusion of control, and nowhere has that become more powerful—and more pernicious—than in the phenomenon of manic motherhood. What the child-care guru D. W. Winnicott once called "the ordinary devoted mother" is no longer good enough. Instead there is an uber-mom who bounces from soccer field to school fair to play date until she falls into bed at the end of the day, exhausted, her life somewhere between the Stations of the Cross and a decathlon.

A perfect storm of trends and events contributed to this. One was the teeter-totter scientific argument of nature versus nurture. When my mother was raising kids, there was a sub rosa assumption that they were what they were. The smart one. The sweet one. Even the bad one. There was only so much a mother could do to mold the clay she'd been dealt.

5 But as I became a mother, all that was changing. Little minds, we learned from researchers, were infinitely malleable, even be-

fore birth. Don't get tense: tense moms make tense infants. (That news'll make you tense!) In a prenatal exercise class, I remember lying on the mat working on what was left of my stomach muscles, listening to the instructor repeating, "Now hug your baby." If I had weak abs, did that mean my baby went unhugged? Keeping up with the Joneses turned into keeping up with the Joneses' kids. Whose mothers, by the way, lied. I now refuse to believe in 9-month-olds who speak in full sentences. But I was more credulous, and more vulnerable, when I had a 9-month-old myself.

This craziness sounds improbable in the face of the feminist revolution that transformed the landscape of America during our lifetime. But at some level it is the fruit of that revolution, a comeuppance cleverly disguised as a calling. Every time we take note of the fact that work is not a choice but an economic necessity—"most women have to work, you know"—it's an apology for freedom. How better to circumvent the power of the new woman than with, the idea of mothering not as care but as creation? Every moment for children was a teachable moment—and every teachable moment missed was a measure of a lousy mom.

My baby-boomer* friends and I were part of the first generation of women who took for granted that we would work throughout our lifetime, and like most pioneers we made it up as we went along. In 1976, Dr. Spock[†] revised his bible of child care to say that it was all right if we worked and had children as well. There was a slapdash approach to melding these disparate roles, usually reflected in the iconic woman at a business meeting with spit-up on her shoulder. My first sitter was the erstwhile manager of a cult punk band. She was a good sitter, too. We got by.

But quicker than you could say nanny cam, books appeared, seminars were held and modern motherhood was codified as a profession. Professionalized for women who didn't work outside the home: if they were giving up such great opportunities, then the tending of kids needed to be made into an all-encompassing job. Professionalized for women who had paying jobs out in the world: to show that their work was not bad for their kids, they had to take child rearing as seriously as dealmaking. (Fathers did not have to justify themselves; after all, no man has ever felt moved to say that most guys have to work, you know.)

It's not just that baking for the bake sale, meeting with the teachers, calling the other mothers about the sleepover and looking at the SAT camp made women of both sorts crazy, turning stress from an occasional noun into an omnipresent verb and adverb. A lot of this was not particularly good for kids. If your mother has been micromanaging your homework since you were 6, it's hard to feel any pride of ownership when you do well. You can't learn from mistakes and disappointments if your childhood is engineered so there aren't any.

10 So much has been written about how the young people of America seem to stay young longer now,[†] well into the years when their grandparents owned houses and had families. But their grandparents never had a mother calling the teacher to complain about a bad grade. And hair-trigger attention spans may be less a function of PlayStation and more a function of kids who never have a moment's peace. I passed on the weekend roundelay of kiddie-league sports so our three could hang out with one another. I told people I hoped it would cement a bond among them, and it did. But I really wanted to be reading rather than standing on the sidelines pretending my kids were soccer prodigies. Maybe I had three children in the first place so I wouldn't ever have to play board games. In my religion, martyrs die.

Our oldest child wrestled custody of his life away from me at a fairly early age, perhaps inspired by an epic bout in which I tried to persuade him to rewrite a perfectly good fourth-grade paper to turn it into an eight-grade paper. Perhaps I'd been addled by the class art projects, some of which looked like the work of a crack graphics design team—and

*According to *Encyclopaedia Britannica,* "For many industrialized countries, the period after World War II was marked by a 'baby boom.' One group of four countries in particular—the United States, Canada, Australia, and New Zealand—experienced sustained and substantial rises in fertility from the depressed levels of the prewar period. In the United States, for example, fertility rose by two-thirds, reaching levels in the 1950s not seen since 1910."

[†]Dr. Benjamin Spock (1903–1998) was a pediatrician and psychoanalyst whose book *Baby and Child Care,* first published in 1946, is referenced here as "his bible of child care." Spock's ideas on parenting focused on care of the child and common sense of the parents. In *Baby and Child Care* he writes, "You know more than you think you know . . . trust your own instincts."

[†]Among other names, adults who rely on their parents longer into their "adult" years than generations past have been labeled *boomerang kids,* referring to the trend of people in their twenties and thirties moving in and out of their parents' homes.

were. I asked the other day about his memories of my mothering. "You sorta freaked out during the college application process," he noted accurately. But then he wrote, "What I remember most: having a good time." You can engrave that on my headstone right this minute.

There's the problem with turning motherhood into martyrdom. There's no way to do it and have a good time. If we create a never-ending spin cycle of have-tos because we're trying to expiate senseless guilt about working or not working, trying to keep up with the woman at school whose kid gets A's because she writes the papers herself, the message we send our children is terrible. By our actions we tell them that being a mom—being their mom—is a drag, powered by fear, self-doubt and conformity, all the things we are supposed to teach them to overcome. It just becomes a gloss on that old joke: Enough about me. What about you? How do you make me feel about myself? The most incandescent memories of my childhood are of making my mother laugh. My kids did the same for me. A good time is what they remember long after toddler programs and art projects are over. The rest is just scheduling.

Questions for Discussion

1. How does Quindlen manage to praise her mother while recognizing that she operated according to a model of parenting different from what many mothers are urged to follow today? To what extent did Quindlen follow this model when she became a mother?

2. What problems does Quindlen see when mothers becoming overly involved in raising their children?

3. What does the "nature versus nurture" debate have to do with what Quindlen calls the codification of motherhood "as a profession"?

4. Quindlen observes that stress has gone "from an occasional noun into an omnipresent verb and adverb." Can you demonstrate what she means by using stress as three different parts of speech in three sentences?

5. How do you respond to Quindlen's speculations about attention span in paragraph 10?

6. Writing as a Catholic, Quindlen concludes paragraph 10 with the line, "In my religion, martyrs die." How does this line apply to being a mother?

7. In your opinion, what does it mean to be a good mother?

④ **STEVEN E. RHOADS** "What Fathers Do Best"

A graduate of Princeton University, where he majored in history, and with a Ph.D. in government from Cornell University, Steven Rhoads teaches politics at the University of Virginia. The author of *Taking Sex Differences Seriously,* he published the following argument shortly before Father's Day in 2005 in the *Weekly Standard,* a magazine owned by Rupert Murdoch and a highly influential medium for neoconservative values—the kind of values that inspired many of the policies pursued by President George W. Bush. In addition to circulating in print, the *Weekly Standard* can be found on the Internet. Knowing the context in which "What Fathers Do Best" first appeared should help you understand that Rhoads is likely to advocate qualities traditionally considered masculine.

What Fathers Do Best

STEVEN E. RHOADS

1 Father's Day no longer arrives without the national media highlighting Mr. Moms. The year before last, for example, Lisa Belkin of the *New York Times* described the life of one Michael Zorek, whose only job was taking care of his 14-month-old son Jeremy. Zorek, whose wife brought home a good salary as a corporate lawyer, felt he had become "remarkably good" at shopping, at cooking, and at entertaining his energetic toddler. He was angry at a parents' magazine whose essay contest was open only to mothers. "I'm the one who does the shopping, and I'm the one who does the cooking," he reasoned. "Why is it only sexist when women are excluded?"

This year the homemaking fathers even got to horn in on Mother's Day. On May 8, the *Washington Post's* Sunday Outlook section featured William McGee, a single dad who "couldn't help feeling excluded" by all the ads for products that "moms and kids" would both love. He mentioned, for example, the classic peanut butter ad, "Choosy Moms Choose Jif." McGee wanted advertisers to know that he is "one of many caring dads" who are choosy, too.

Brace yourselves for an onslaught of such features this week, even though, in the real world, there are still 58 moms staying home with minor children for every dad who does so. This is not just an accidental social arrangement, to be overcome once the media have sufficiently raised our consciousness about the joys of stay-at-home fatherhood. Mothers are loaded with estrogen and oxytocin, which draw them to young children and help induce them to tend to infants. And the babies themselves make it clear that they prefer their mothers. Even in families where fathers have taken a four-month-long paid parental leave to tend to their newborns, the fathers report that the babies prefer to be comforted by their mothers.

The problem with honoring fathers who do what mothers usually do—what used to be called "mothering"—is this: it suggests that fathers who do what *most* fathers do aren't contributing to their children's well-being. Yet we know this can't be true. Children who grow up in fatherless families are poorer, less healthy, less educated. They die much earlier, commit

*After receiving her Ph.D.
in economics from the
University of Rochester in
1980, Jennifer Roback Morse
went on to teach economics
for fifteen years at Yale
University and George Mason
University. Her book *Love and
Economics: Why the Laissez-
Faire Family Doesn't Work*
argues that the modern substitutes for the family, including the government and
single parents, are really no
substitutes. In 1997 she became a research fellow of
the Hoover Institution at
Stanford University—a conservative think tank.

†According to their website,
"The Board on Children,
Youth, and Families ad-
dresses a variety of policy-
relevant issues related to the
health and development of
children, youth, and families.
It does so by convening experts to weigh in on matters
from the perspective of the
behavioral, social, and health
sciences."

more crimes, and give birth to more babies
out of wedlock.

5   What do most real-world dads do? When
the kids get old enough, they teach them how
to build and fix things and how to play sports.
They are better than moms at teaching children how to deal with novelty and frustration,
perhaps because they are more likely than
mothers to encourage children to work out
problems and address challenges themselves—from putting on their shoes to operating a new toy.

When the kids become older still, Dad is
usually better than Mom at controlling unruly
boys. Jennifer Roback Morse* notes that all
the surveys of who does what around the
house never mention one of her husband's
most important functions—he is responsible
for glaring. When their son acts up, his glares
just seem to have more effect than hers do.

Similarly, a fascinating study in the journal
Criminology finds that female social ties in a
neighborhood—borrowing food, helping with
problems, having lunch together—are associated with much lower crime rates. Male social
ties in the neighborhood have no effect on
crime rates. But the beneficial effect of female
ties almost completely disappears in communities dominated by fatherless families! You
need husbands and fathers—what the authors
call "family rooted men"—if the crime-fighting
females ties are really to be effective. Perhaps
mothers still say, "Just you wait until your father
gets home," or its 21st-century equivalent.

Sometimes moms worry that their rough-
housing husbands are making their boys more
aggressive. But, in fact, fathers are teaching
their sons how to play fight—don't bite, don't
kick, stay away from the eyes—a form of play
enjoyed by most boys around the world. On
the playground, boys without fathers in the
home are unpopular because they respond in
a truly aggressive manner when other boys try
to initiate rough-and-tumble play. A committee

brought together by the Board on Children,
Youth, and Families of the National Research
Council† has concluded that "fathers, in effect,
give children practice in regulating their own
emotions and recognizing others' emotional
cues."

Of course, dads do a lot for their daughters
as well. For example, by providing a model of
love for and fidelity to their wives, dads give
teenage girls confidence that they can expect
men to be interested in them for reasons beyond sex.

10   We could begin to do dads justice if we
realized that their nature makes it unlikely
that they will like intensive nurturing in the
way that most mothers do. Testosterone inhibits nurturing. In both men and women high
levels of testosterone are associated with
less interest in babies. Low levels of testosterone are associated with a stronger than
average interest in nurturing. If you inject a
monkey mother with testosterone, she becomes less interested in her baby. And men
have much more testosterone than women.
Thus, in those two-career families where husband and wife are determined to share domestic and paid work equally, a common
argument ensues because dads typically suggest that they get more paid child-care help;
moms typically want less paid help and more
time with their children.

If dads were as tormented as moms by
prolonged absence from their children, we'd
have more unhappiness and more fights over
who gets to spend time with the children. By
faithfully working at often boring jobs to provide for their families, dads make possible
moms who can do less paid work and thereby
produce less stressed and happier households. Dads deserve a lot of credit for simply
making moms' nurturing of children possible.
On Father's Day we should more often notice,
and then honor, typical fatherly virtues and declare vive la difference.

Questions for Discussion

1. The original publication of this argument was planned to correspond with Father's Day, as established by a reference in paragraph 3. To what extent can it be read as celebrating the idea and practice of being a father?

2. Rhoads makes unsupported claims about how men and women differ in their capacity for nurturing because of estrogen, oxytocin, and testosterone. Could he safely assume that his audience would accept these claims as common knowledge, or should he have provided support for them?

3. Similarly, Rhoads makes an unsupported claim about the children of fatherless families, stating that they are "poorer, less healthy, less educated." Does this seem likely to be true? What factors could cause these problems regardless of the number of parents at home?

4. Rhoads describes how fathers teach their sons how to be aggressive and their daughters how to be respected. What assumptions about gender expectations are built into this argument?

5. In his conclusion, Rhoads evokes an image of fathers "faithfully working at often boring jobs to provide for their families." To what extent does this claim correspond with your observations about men at work?

DIFFERENCES

NEGOTIATING

June Cleaver lives on—but primarily on cable television. Many wives and mothers now work outside the home. Those who choose to be stay-at-home moms are unlikely to wear a perfectly ironed dress all day and wear earrings even at breakfast. Nor are they likely to be "at home" much of the day. They are more likely to be grocery shopping, doing volunteer work for a school, and hurrying to pick up one child from soccer practice after dropping off another at a ballet lesson. Similarly, fewer fathers are likely to come home promptly at the same hour every day, in an unwrinkled suit, ready to offer wise counsel to Wally and the Beaver. Perhaps most seriously, few families sit down to have dinner together as the Cleavers do. Busy schedules and conflicting interests all too often have different members of a family eating alone at different times—and the family dinner,

such as it is, often is reduced to occasions when everyone is free to go out to a restaurant together.

Imagine now that you are a fifteen-year-old boy in a heavily scheduled family. You like having a high degree of independence and the freedom to do things your parents are not around to see. You also enjoy some activities that take you outside the home, especially basketball practice. Your parents have often said that they would be at one of your games but backed out at the last minute. They've always had a good reason, such as an unexpected business trip out of town, but you have been disappointed nevertheless. They've also missed some teacher–parent conferences, and neither seems to have a clue that your sister is going to sex parties and has hosted one in your home. Plus now you are dating a girl from a family that sits down and eats dinner together most of the time, and your family's eating habits have begun to look a little weird. You find yourself spending more time alone in your room when you are home, but part of you hopes someone will knock on the door and ask what's wrong. What's wrong, in your view, is that your family is barely functioning because your parents are too caught up in their own lives. You don't expect your parents to be perfect, and you do not want them to be on your back all the time, but you do want what Anna Quindlen calls a "good enough mother"—and a good enough father.

Eventually the knock on the door comes. Your mother wants to know what is bothering you. You could avoid this conversation by saying, "Nothing." But you want to say more than that. You acknowledge that something is wrong, but when prompted to

say more manage only, "It's hard to talk about." Surprisingly, your mother asks if you would write a letter to her about what's on your mind—not an email, but a real letter. You say that you will.

What will you put in that letter? You could devote a couple of pages to complaining and try to make your parents feel as bad as possible. Or you could write a letter that shows you understand the complexity of their lives, praises them for the times they have been there for you, but asks for more of their attention—maybe by designating two or three nights a week as family nights upon which nonfamily activities cannot intrude. Whether you say anything about what your sister is up to remains to be determined.

Sit down now and write that letter.

11

Education

Cluster 1

WHAT SHOULD STUDENTS BE TAUGHT?

1. Rick Livingston, "The Humanities for Cocktail Parties and Beyond"

2. Stanley N. Katz, "Liberal Education on the Ropes"

3. Ronald Takaki, "An Educated and Culturally Literate Person Must Study America's Multicultural Reality"

4. Stephen L. Trainor, "Designing a Signature General Education Program"

Cluster 2

HOW SHOULD STUDENTS BE TAUGHT?

1. Bill Coplin, "Lost in the Life of the Mind"

2. Mano Singham, "Moving Away from the Authoritarian Classroom"

3. bell hooks, "Toward a Radical Feminist Pedagogy"

4. Lewis Thomas, "The Art of Teaching Science"

Cluster 3

HOW SHOULD LEARNING BE MEASURED?

1. Patricia Williams, "Tests, Tracking, and Derailment"

2. Gregory Cizek, "Unintended Consequences of High-Stakes Testing"

3. Bertell Ollman, "Why So Many Exams? A Marxist Response"

4. Peter Elbow, "Getting Along without Grades—and Getting Along with Them, Too"

What Should Students Be Taught?

The question of what should be taught in schools is as old as formal education itself. In the United States the emergence of the public school in the nineteenth century was accompanied by intense debates about the nature and content of the curriculum. Some argued that schools should impart values, as well as knowledge; others believed that schools should focus on teaching students the skills needed to be productive workers; still others saw schools as places where immigrants could learn to become Americans. And many believed that public education is central to American democracy; the curriculum, therefore, should foster good citizens. One influential voice who supported this connection between education and democracy was philosopher John Dewey, who argued that the school curriculum should do more than supply students with practical knowledge. For Dewey, schools were places where students learned how to live and work together, where they learned about democracy as a way of life rather than an idea or a set of principles (see Context on page 452). Accordingly, Dewey believed that *how* students are taught is as important as what they are taught. ■ Nearly a century after Dewey formulated his extensive philosophy of education, many Americans share his belief in the connection between education and democracy, even if they do not share his vision for a progressive public school system. It might be that this deeply held belief in education as central to democracy is a reason that education has been such a fierce political battleground in the United States. Conflicts about what students should be taught have been waged in classrooms, town halls, school board meetings, state legislatures, and the U.S. Congress. Sometimes these conflicts focus on a specific idea or theory, such as the long-standing debates about the teaching of evolution as opposed to creationism in science courses. Sometimes, conflicts arise around a particular book that students are asked to read; for example, *The Adventures of Huckleberry Finn* by Mark Twain and *The Diary of Anne Frank* are commonly challenged by groups that believe, for various religious or political reasons, that these books should not be required reading in U.S. schools. Other debates focus on how students should be taught—what teaching methods are likely to be most effective. The testing of students has also caused conflict among parents, educators, government officials, and scholars. ■ In one way or another, all of these battles are about the purpose of education. As the authors of the essays in this section suggest, to make an argument about what to teach students is to make a statement about what you believe education is—or should be—for.

If Dewey was correct in believing that education is ultimately about democracy, then one question to be answered is "What kind of democracy do we want?" There is rarely unanimous agreement among Americans about how to answer that question. As you read the following essays, think about how you might answer it. These writers make arguments about specific issues or ideas that should be taught in American classrooms, but their arguments all rest on beliefs—implied or explicitly stated—about the kind of society people want schools to help them build. Their views will help you appreciate the always political nature of formal education; they might also help them see common beliefs about education that can become the basis for curriculum reform in the twenty-first century.

① RICK LIVINGSTON, "The Humanities for Cocktail Parties and Beyond"

Rick Livingston is associate director of the Institute for Collaborative Research and Public Humanities and a senior lecturer in comparative studies at Ohio State University at Columbus. The argument you are about to read was first published in the *Chronicle of Higher Education* during the winter of 2005. College professors and administrators usually read journals focused on their specialty areas, but the *Chronicle* cuts across disciplinary lines, reaching a wide audience of anyone in higher education who is concerned about large issues, such as academic freedom, teaching practices, and curriculum reform. With this audience in mind, Livingston focuses on defending the value of the required courses in humanities—that is, courses in disciplines such as English, philosophy, and art history—in an era when many students want to focus on taking courses that clearly relate to career preparation and many professors want students to be able to take additional courses in majors that have become increasingly demanding. A shallow rationale for studying the humanities—and one not likely to be made by professors committed to them—is that they provide people with a cultural background upon which they can draw when chatting at cocktail parties. One of the problems with this rationale is that conversation at cocktail parties could easily focus on sports, fashion, movies, or politics—rather than on an exhibit at a nearby museum or a new production of a play by Shakespeare. A more serious problem is how the image of a cocktail party associates the humanities with both alcohol and small talk—marginalizing these areas of academic inquiry instead of seeing them as something that could enrich lives in diverse situations. So the key word in Livingston's title is "beyond." As you read his argument, be alert for how he attempts to establish that studying the humanities can be central to having a higher education—even if you are majoring in accounting or engineering.

The Humanities for Cocktail Parties and Beyond

RICK LIVINGSTON

*The expression "elephant in the room" is an idiom for describing an important and timely subject that a group of people are aware of but determined to ignore because they think discussing it would be problematic. Successfully ignoring this subject for an extended period is no more likely than being able to ignore for long the presence of an elephant in the room where these people have gathered.

1 In any introductory-humanities course, there is an elephant-in-the-room* question. I try to wait at least three weeks into the term before asking my students to face it squarely: Why study the humanities?

The students' first response, of course, is because they have to. Most of my courses fulfill one of the general-education requirements at Ohio State University, and I usually have a healthy mix of precocious freshmen and procrastinating seniors.

If I go on to ask why the students think the university has such requirements, they are initially baffled. After trying out a few wiseacre responses ("Because they want our tuition money!"), they almost always say—wait for it—that the humanities help you make small talk at cocktail parties.

With any luck we go on to talk seriously about common knowledge and cultural expectations. But the cocktail-party comment tends to hang in the air like secondhand smoke, clouding the intellectual atmosphere. It suggests that our primary subject is petty snobbery and chitchat. The comment is a cliché, obviously, but one I have to confront every year.

5 Thinking about the cliche sent me back to T. S. Eliot's 1950 play, The Cocktail Party. Eliot portrays social life as a series of hypocrisies, deceptions, and embarrassments, redeemable only by religious conversion. Theological insight alone, the play suggests, can help us endure the unending round of mannered niceties that make up an ordinary life.

My students tend to shut down when I start talking about their souls, or they consult the syllabus to see whether I've included a conversion experience among the course requirements. In confronting the cocktail-party cliché, I've had to consider how to convey the value of the humanities without resorting to divine intervention.

Luckily my position as associate director of a humanities institute on my campus has allowed me to experiment with alternative ways of engaging students in humanistic inquiry. One of the institute's missions is to bring students and faculty members together outside traditional classroom settings, as an antidote to the sometimes intimidating experience of attending one of the country's largest universities. Over the years we've learned that it is in such informal settings that students often begin to tie together the different subjects they've been studying. Connecting the dots allows them to get a larger picture of the education they've been receiving. That's why we've come up with a program we call (only half-jokingly) Big Ideas.

Here's how it works: Each quarter we choose a topic big enough to accommodate a range of approaches and cover more than one discipline. Past examples include evil, passion, war, and cities. We invite both faculty members and outside guests to have dinner with students and to give us their thoughts about the topics. Brief presentations are followed by open conversation, with students taking the lead in raising questions and responding.

Although we do bring in some of the best teachers at the university, the goal of Big Ideas is not really to teach the students specific facts. It is to give them practice in taking ideas seriously and to allow them to experience interesting conversations.

10 You're probably thinking: "Shouldn't they be doing that on their own? When I was in college, we would stay up late talking about ideas. What's wrong with these kids?"

But conversation about ideas seldom happens naturally, and nowadays it is rarer than ever. As historians of talk like Theodore Zeldin and Peter Burke have observed, conversation is not a spontaneous outpouring of well-formed sentences. It is a specific form of social behavior, with its own settings, tacit rules, and strategies. Like any social skill, it improves with practice.

Students today have few chances to practice serious talking. Our most visible examples of conversation come from TV: the political debate that is little more than a shouting match, and the celebrity interview. What students lack is experience with grown-up conversation, in which curiosity and respect can lead to self-discovery and mutual illumination.

At their best, the Big Ideas classes get students involved in such conversations. Our course on evil, for instance, picked up on a President Bush's use of a morally charged vocabulary (the "axis of evil") to orient U.S. foreign policy. We brought in four guest speakers: a philosopher, a historian of religion, a theologian, and a judge. Then students talked about personal experiences with evil, ranging from anger to sexual abuse, and about evil in the world—including terrorism and the Holocaust. In the process, students confronted their own

CONTEXT

On January 29, 2002, President George W. Bush, in his State of the Union address, said: "North Korea is a regime arming with missiles and weapons of mass destruction, while starving its citizens. Iran aggressively pursues these weapons and exports terror, while an unelected few repress the Iranian people's hope for freedom. Iraq continues to flaunt its hostility toward America and to support terror. . . . States like these, and their terrorist allies, constitute an axis of evil, arming to threaten the peace of the world."

Considering the amount of coverage given to and the tensions surrounding the war in Iraq since it began in 2002, do you think programs like "Big Ideas" are necessary to facilitate discussion of such topics among college students?

beliefs about God and human nature, and tested their intuitions about differences among the illegal, the immoral, and the downright evil. Nothing was resolved, of course, but the students get a clearer sense of the necessity—and the difficulty—of making such distinctions.

In our course on cities, we began by talking about the places where we had grown up, and how they had changed over our lifetimes. We met with an architect to talk about high rises and skylines. Ideas about consumerism and sustainability became the focus of a class with an urban planner, and a sociologist talked with us about the effects of globalization on the shape of cities. Finally, an artist who is designing a waterfront park came to discuss ideas about making public art in and out of neglected urban spaces. Students learned a vocabulary for talking about the changes they can see happening in their neighborhoods as well as in the world at large.

15 Inevitably, there is a certain amount of overlap among the sessions; predictably, discussions sometimes meander and leave the topic altogether. But most of the sessions include a moment when some of the students catch fire and carry the rest of us forward, or when someone gets the idea of dialogical inquiry and asks more, and better, questions. Sometimes students discover that their intuitions don't match their convictions. Most inter-

esting, however, are the times when, as in the discussion of war and peace during the run-up to the invasion of Iraq, we find ourselves trying hard to make sense of the world together.

I've thought a lot about what makes the courses work. The topics belong to no one field: Different disciplines may contribute perspectives to the issues we cover, but when faced with the problem of evil, for instance, we are all amateurs. We use no set body of material, and students' own experiences and examples often become common points of reference.

Each course is for one academic credit—enough to make the students take the class seriously; but the grade is pass or fail, so students don't need to demonstrate mastery of a subject. To keep the atmosphere informal, we meet in a dining hall rather than a classroom. And mixing up faculty members with outside guests shows that ideas can live off campus, too.

Maybe the most unexpected lesson of Big Ideas, however, is that professors appreciate making conversation, too. It can be thought to step out of the comfort zones of our expertise, to let go of disciplinary jargon. But the opportunity to speak, not as a professional to novices, but as a citizen with other (albeit younger) citizens, can be liberating. It's not just a cocktail party—and that, I think, is the main point.

Questions for Discussion

1. Livingston writes that he waits three weeks into a course before asking students to address the purpose of studying in the discipline he is teaching. Why do you think he waits so long? How receptive would students be to this question during the first week? Should students have to figure out the rationale for why they are required to take certain courses, or should teachers simply explain the rationale to them?

2. Can you imagine going to a cocktail party where the conversation concerns knowledge about the humanities? What do people talk about at the parties you currently attend? What kind of parties do you imagine in your future?

3. In your opinion, how important is the relationship between setting and learning? If asked to engage in the free exchange of ideas, what kind of room would you be most comfortable in? Is there any kind of room that would make you uncomfortable?

4. Do you agree with Livingston's claim that contemporary students "have few chances to practice serious talking"? What kind of social or cultural forces could disrupt or inhibit serious talk? How serious is the "talk" that can be found in an Internet chat room?

5. What do you think of the "Big Ideas" forums described by Livingston? Would you be interested in participating in one? What would it take for your school to sponsor a program along these lines?

② STANLEY N. KATZ, "Liberal Education on the Ropes"

As the title of the following article suggests—evolving from an image in boxing, in which a fighter pressed against the ropes that surround the ring is in a vulnerable position—Stanley Katz is seriously concerned about the future of liberal education (which means an education that attempts to address the whole person through an emphasis on developing critical thinking and acquiring broad knowledge as opposed to mastering the details of a single field). He had the benefit of one, graduating magna cum laude from Harvard University, where he majored in English history and literature before going on to earn his Ph.D. in history at Harvard. The author of many books and articles, he is currently doing research on how constitutional democracies could be created in the Middle East and Central Asia. In addition to being an active scholar who holds honorary degrees from several universities, Katz is director of Princeton University's Center for Arts and Cultural Policy Studies. He is also president emeritus of the American Council of Learned Societies. As you read the following argument—which was first published in the *Chronicle of Higher Education* in April 2005—note why Katz believes that liberal education is at risk and see whether he provides any ideas about how it can return to the center of the ring.

Liberal Education on the Ropes

STANLEY N. KATZ

CONTEXT

The Association of American Colleges and Universities (AAC&U) claims to have four broad goals it works around. One of these is "Taking Responsibility for the Quality of Every Student's Liberal Education," which AAC&U describes this way: "Throughout its history, AAC&U has called upon the academy to take responsibility for the quality of student learning in college. AAC&U consistently stresses the importance of clearly articulating the qualities of a well-educated person, creating coherent educational programs that cultivate those qualities, and assessing to determine if they have been achieved."

1 Surely "liberal education" is the most used and abused phrase in the rhetoric of higher education. Just as surely it has no universal meaning. The Association of American Colleges and Universities recently launched a 10-year campaign to "champion the value of a liberal education"—and to "spark public debate" about just what that is. But the concept may be more alive and well in four-year liberal-arts colleges than it is in our great research universities that are setting the agenda for higher education today. Those institutions are my concern: I fear that undergraduate education in the research university is becoming a project in ruins.

Last year we heard of the renewal of interest in liberal education at those institutions when Harvard University announced that it was reforming its "core curriculum." The obvious question that wasn't asked in all the newsprint devoted to Harvard's statement is whether research universities can purport to offer undergraduates a liberal education. Furthermore, the questions that were asked indicate just how contested the meaning of liberal education is at research universities. Should the core curriculum offer common knowledge? Or a way of learning? Should it require set courses, or provide student choice? Focus on big questions, or on specialized exploration in a variety of disciplines?

It seems that we have not traveled very far in defining a liberal education at research universities. Not in the last year. Not, perhaps, in the last 100 years.

Reliable truisms are available. The association of colleges and universities currently defines liberal education as: "a philosophy of education that empowers individuals, liberates the mind from ignorance, and cultivates social responsibility. Characterized by challenging encounters with important issues, and more a way of studying than specific content, liberal education can occur at all types of colleges and universities." While the association's new campaign seeks to unite that philosophy with what it calls "practical education," the elements of the definition that have been at the heart of the most important ambitions of liberal education for the last century are likely to remain—empowering students, liberating their minds, preparing them for citizenship. In short, a process rather than a substantive orientation.

5 Through most of the 20th century, liberal education was more or less exclusively identified with the four-year liberal-arts colleges and a handful of elite universities. Both the institutions and its advocates were avowed educational elitists. But times have changed—hence the attempt of the association of colleges and universities to universalize liberal education across all types of institutions. But liberal education is being asked to carry more freight than it did a century ago, and it is not clear that it can succeed.

As it has expanded throughout higher education, it has suffered inevitable losses and unresolved tensions. As it spread from what were once primarily church-related colleges, for example, it lost its focus on moral values. But even the surviving emphasis on an orientation that stresses general values has been an uncomfortable fit in the modern research university, which has increasingly stressed the production of scientific knowledge over the transmission of culture.

Many of the attempts to package liberal education in the modern university have centered on "general education." The idea of general education derives from Matthew Arnold, and it was picked up and Americanized in the United States early in the 20th century. Although we seldom recognize the fact, there were actually three streams in American thinking at the time.

The first stream is perhaps one of the oldest, but still continues. It has been the self-conscious rejection of specific courses in favor of a vague notion of enforced diversity of subject matter, to be provided by regular disciplinary departments. Here the pre-eminent example is, alas, my own university, Princeton. Under the leadership of James McCosh* in the late 1880s, Princeton developed the "distribution" system that is still all we have to provide structured liberal education at Old Nassau.

At Princeton it was not necessary to offer special courses or designate faculty members to provide the content of liberal education—just to ensure that students did not concentrate too narrowly by requiring a variety of what McCosh called "obligatory and

*James McCosh (1811–1894) was the eleventh president of Princeton University.

CONTEXT

Matthew Arnold (1822–1888) was an English poet and critic. The ideas of "general education" brought up here come from his idea of learning "the best that is known and thought in the world, and thus [establishing] a current of fresh and true ideas." One of the most influential writers of his time, Arnold was deeply troubled by the problems that were arising because of rapid industrialization, the movement of rural populations to cities that were growing haphazardly, and the demands for education that would be designed primarily to train people to be good employees. Although it is easy to think of the Victorian period as one of gentility and gingerbread, people were struggling with many of the issues they continue to face today. Moreover, the threat of political revolution was almost always in the air during the nineteenth century. Unsuccessful revolutions broke out throughout Europe in 1848, and many prominent leaders would be assassinated toward the end of Arnold's life. This background can help you understand the title of one of Arnold's most famous works, *Culture and Anarchy*—a work in which he argued that the kind of culture that comes from a liberal education not only enriches the individual but also stabilizes society. (For an example of Arnold's poetry, see page 450 and consider how it works as an argument.)

By Matthew Arnold

Dover Beach

The sea is calm tonight,
The tide is full, the moon lies fair
Upon the straits; on the French coast the light
Gleams and is gone; the cliffs of England stand,
Glimmering and vast, out in the tranquil bay.
Come to the window, sweet is the night air!

Only, from the long line of spray
Where the sea meets the moon-blanched land,
Listen! you hear the grating roar
Of pebbles which the waves draw back, and fling.
At their return, up the high strand,
Begin, and cease, and then again begin,
With tremulous cadence slow, and bring
The eternal note of sadness in.

Sophocles long ago
Heard it on the Agean, and it brought
Into his mind the turbid ebb and flow
Of human misery; we
Find also in the sound a thought,
Hearing it by this distant northern sea.

The Sea of Faith
Was once, too, at the full, and round earth's shore
Lay like the folds of a bright girdle furled.
But now I only hear
Its melancholy, long, withdrawing roar,
Retreating, to the breath
Of the night wind, down the vast edges drear
And naked shingles of the world.

Ah, love, let us be true
To one another! for the world, which seems
To lie before us like a land of dreams,
So various, so beautiful, so new,
Hath really neither joy, nor love, nor light,
Nor certitude, nor peace, nor help for pain;
And we are here as on a darkling plain
Swept with confused alarms of struggle and flight,
Where ignorant armies clash by night.

1867

disciplinary" courses. With the exception of a sequence of humanities courses and a large program of freshman seminars, present-day Princeton still has neither nondepartmental general-education courses nor any structured mechanism for thinking about the broader contours of undergraduate liberal education. We review the program periodically, but we seem always to conclude that McCosh had it right. Well, perhaps.

10 The most obvious and most highly publicized example of the next stream began at Columbia University as the United States was entering World War I. This was an attempt to ensure that undergraduates in an increasingly scientific university would be broadly educated across the fields of the liberal arts and to integrate their increasingly fragmented selection of courses into some coherent form. (Admittedly, it was also fueled by a felt need to promote Western civilization in the face of German barbarism.) Combining new synthetic courses outside the disciplinary-obsessed department structure with the inculcation of a notion of democratic citizenship, the curriculum was organized around surveys of "Contemporary Civilization." In essence, the Columbia sequence humanized the now-secular university curriculum by broadly historicizing it. As time passed, most other elite institutions did the same.

In the 1930s Robert Maynard Hutchins and Mortimer J. Adler* at the University of Chicago launched an important experiment in this approach. It was complex and somewhat inwardly self-contradictory, but the bottom line was an insistence on the centrality of the Greek classics and other Great Books to undergraduate education, later supplemented by the construction of a "core curriculum" to educate undergraduates across the liberal-arts subjects and to force them to think through and across traditional disciplinary approaches.

In 1945 Harvard, under James Bryant Conant,† issued *General Education in a Free Society*, commonly known as the Harvard Red Book. I still have my copy, for it was the basis

of my undergraduate education at Harvard beginning in 1951, when as a freshman I took a "Natural Sciences" course in the general-education sequence taught by President Conant, a stunning chemistry professor named Leonard Nash, and an obscure assistant professor of physics named Thomas S. Kuhn. I never had a better undergraduate course. The political rationale for the Red Book was grander than Columbia's or Chicago's, but the basic principles of general education were not that different, based on sweepingly synthetic historical approaches to classically great ideas. The attempt to give all undergraduates at least a taste of different disciplines is now one of the unchallenged principles of general education.

The third stream, which in some ways has had a more profound influence on our actual educational practices, was that championed by John Dewey and Arthur O. Lovejoy. This effort focused on cognitive development and individual student growth, and its key was the idea of reflective thinking as a goal of liberal education. That concept was institutionalized at

*Robert Maynard Hutchins (1899–1977) began serving as president of the University of Chicago in 1929 at the age of 30. He remained in that post until 1945. After receiving his Ph.D. in psychology in 1928, Mortimer J. Adler (1902–2001) was invited by Hutchins to start the Great Books program at Chicago.

†James Bryant Conant (1893–1978) served as the president of Harvard University from 1933 to 1953.

COMPLICATION

The idea of basing education upon the study of "great books" assumes that there is wide agreement about which books are great in the sense that they have had a profound and lasting affect upon civilization. Plato's *Republic* or Chaucer's *The Canterbury Tales* might be considered such a work. For many years in the west, numerous scholars and educators believed that such works could be identified and agreed upon. They thought that although different individuals might compose different lists of the best books of all times, there would be considerable overlap—and often this proved to be the case, because programs such as the one at the University of Chicago were created and lists of this kind were used to shape the education of many students. The process of establishing a list of great works is referred to by contemporary scholars as *canon formation*. But most scholars now agree that canon formation is problematic. For example, because "the canon" was formed by men of European descent such as Mortimer J. Adler, it tended to emphasis works by what some contemporary critics call "dead white men." The canon has been widely challenged during the last thirty years by scholars and teachers determined to make it more culturally diverse. Can you identify a work that is "canonical" within American literature and one that is "noncanonical" but deserves to be taught?

Columbia under the leadership of Dewey and at the Johns Hopkins University under Lovejoy. This approach was entirely cognitive, lacking in specific education content. To this day it forms the basis of the stress on process at the heart of approaches to liberal education.

To be sure, there have been many other approaches to liberal education over the years. Until recently, many liberal-arts colleges used both sophisticated distribution systems and a variety of innovative course designs. Many still continue to innovate. As Ernest L. Boyer forcefully noted in *College: The Undergraduate Experience in America,* first published in 1987, some such colleges have become university wannabes or citadels of preprofessional education. In any case, in most of the major four-year institutions that are educating a larger and larger proportion of undergraduates, the challenge has seemed to be modifying the historical principles of general education in order to bring them up to date.

15 Harvard, as usual, got the most publicity, first for the creation of its "core curriculum" in the 1970s—another attempt to problematize and repackage general-education courses in a

manner consistent with the epistemology and intellectual progress of the era. This twist on general education dehistoricized it, organizing the curriculum around abstract concepts like "moral reasoning," "quantitative reasoning," or "social analysis."

Last year Harvard seemed to concede the failure of that approach and has begun to consider what I would call "Core Two." According to the dean of the faculty of arts and sciences, William C. Kirby, reporting to the faculty, the aim is to empower students to "grasp the importance and relevance of fields to which they do not themselves owe personal allegiance and in which they have not developed special expertise" so that they may "understand, criticize, and improve our world constructively."

Harvard is adding to its definition of general education a focus on international studies and one on scientific literacy. New "Harvard College Courses" are proposed to supply the new approaches, along with courses already in the curriculum. Freshman seminars are suggested and other small-group learning engagements for the final three years of college. A parallel aim of the new curriculum is to limit the student's concentration (Harvardese for "major"), by changing when undergraduates begin to major in a particular field from freshman year to the middle of the sophomore year (talk about epicycles!), and to limit the requirements for concentrators. The report also suggests that the university facilitate undergraduate research opportunities. Not one of those seems like either a new or very exciting idea.

The Harvard document, when it is completed and put into effect, will predictably be the most discussed document on liberal education over the next few years. I have no doubt that it will, if put into practice in anything like a full-blooded fashion, significantly improve general education at Harvard. But it is a modest, reformist document.

It defines liberal education in an altogether traditional manner, and each of its proposed reforms is mostly familiar. After all, internationalization has been on everyone's mind for some time, and there has not been a moment in the last century during which some group has not lamented that we are not doing a good job of conveying science to the nonscientist. Similarly, freshman seminars are hardly a new idea (I taught one the first year they were offered at Harvard, in 1961), nor is the call for more small-group instruction or for more undergraduate research. Three years is arguably too long for an undergraduate to major in a discipline. Undergraduates already do research and take courses in professional schools (if, perhaps, that has just been harder at Harvard than at comparable institutions). For those of us at other institutions who are long-term observers of liberal education, there does not seem to be a lot to learn from Harvard.

20 My intention is not to attack any particular definition of liberal education. It is to suggest that we have not traveled far in our definitions over the past 100 years. Until we do, we can do little to fundamentally improve undergraduate education at research universities.

Moreover, whatever the definition, we all face a dilemma. As I've suggested for a number of years, the real problem is that both long-term changes to the social, political, and economic environment for higher education and the recent internal restructuring of the university make it difficult—if not impossible—to achieve a satisfactory liberal education for undergraduates. Even if Dean Kirby can persuade his university significantly to increase the number of faculty members to help teach general-education courses (and President John E. Sexton of New York University is making a similar proposal), what are the odds (a) that Harvard or NYU can afford it, and (b) that they can and will hire the sorts of faculty members competent (and inclined) to be superior undergraduate teachers? Does anyone believe that possible? I do not.

The modern university has been in tension with the liberal-arts college it harbors within its bosom for years. We are at a point in the history of the research university at which, in all likelihood, curriculum reform can no longer plausibly produce what we are looking for, despite the best efforts of admirable administrators like Bill Kirby or John Sexton. That is why I fear that liberal education for undergraduates in the research university, despite the recent hoopla, is in ruins.

There are two ways of thinking about why that is so. The first is the intellectual task of reconceptualizing what the content and curricular mechanisms should be at the beginning of the second century of modern liberal education. The second approach is to consider the structural changes in the modern research university that are relegating undergraduate education to the margins.

I will not attempt more than to gesture at what seem to me the contours of the intellectual problem. The overriding difficulty is the vast expansion of the domains of knowledge from the late 19th century to the early 21st century. After all, the by-now-traditional academic disciplines only took shape from the 1880s to the 1920s. The social sciences, in particular, were very much the original product of that period, and one of the original objectives of general education was to locate the social sciences within the new sociology of knowledge (itself a creation of the first half of the 20th century).

25 As undergraduates increasingly "majored" in a single discipline, the question was how they could relate what they were learning to the larger intellectual cosmology. That was what Columbia and other elite colleges were addressing. But the intellectual panorama was already changing rapidly. By the 1940s, when Harvard introduced its undergraduate curriculum, atomic physics was most obviously where the action was, but the revolution in cell biology was quietly beginning and, with it, the total transformation of the life sciences. New forms and combinations of knowledge were being institutionalized in the natural sciences along the model that had produced biochemistry in the

1930s. What had begun a a private philanthropic initiative in the 1920s and 1930s was suddenly overwhelmed by the entrance of the federal government following World War II, especially through the mechanisms of the National Science Foundation and the National Institutes of Health. There would soon be no such thing as the generally educated scientist, much less the generally scientifically literate undergraduate student. There was simply too much to know because of the range, depth, and quantity of new scientific scholarship, and of the increasing centrality of complex mathematics to scientific understanding.

Change was afoot in the humanities and social sciences as well. Those were more complicated and subtle stories, but the larger outlines seem clear enough. The social sciences became more complex theoretically, more scientific in their methodology, and more wide-ranging in their ambitions. They became less focused on understanding the problems of building democracy in the United States (as they had begun to do in the 1920s and 1930s), and more interested in fostering both economic and political development abroad, especially in the "underdeveloped" areas of the world. As in every other disciplinary domain, the traditional social-science disciplines splintered, sprouted new lines, and recombined in novel ways.

In the humanities, the focus moved from studies of Europe (especially classical Europe) and America to contemplation of the rest of the world. We discovered world literature, philosophy, history, and music. New subdisciplines developed (the history of everything in the social sciences and humanities, for instance), new languages were studied, new techniques were employed. And the relevance of the humanities to politics became a problem and an opportunity.

For undergraduate education, the center simply could not hold. There were many attempts to identify an essential core of knowledge, and many new attempts will

undoubtedly be made. I think them unlikely to succeed given the breadth and complexity of the intellectual content students now confront.

Nor do we seem to have the educational leaders capable of defining new content. Let me say that I do not think the blame should fall on university presidents and deans. It should be assigned to research faculties for whom thoughtful consideration of undergraduate education is simply not on the agenda. They are dominated by scholars committed to disciplinary approaches, who would mostly prefer to teach graduate students and, increasingly, postgrads. The professional schools at least claim to prefer to admit generally educated students, but what about graduate departments? Can we simply presume that the products of American secondary education are already liberally educated? To ask the question is to answer it.

30 And that brings me to my second concern: the extent to which structural changes in the university, especially the research university, tend to marginalize undergraduate education generally and, more important, make it difficult to theorize and put into effect anything like liberal education. Some of those factors also affect colleges and general universities, but the problem is worst in the research universities. Quite apart from the intellectual transformation I have just described, the most important thing that has changed for higher education is the entirety of the social and political environment in which it is situated.

The most significant shift is from elite to democratic higher education, which began in the 1930s and took off after World War II, heralded by the GI Bill. Since then the numbers of undergraduate students in four-year institutions have expanded exponentially, and student bodies have come to resemble the diversity of the general population of the country. Of course, pluralism requires something less morally prescriptive, less tailored, more diverse, and more practical than the elite higher education of the early-20th century. Notions of democratic higher education originated a century ago, but they took on new urgency and complexity after World War II. That is why Harvard went to such lengths to explore the democratic character of general education in its postwar Red Book.

None of us wants to go back to traditional educational elitism. I assume that the "best" institutions these days aspire to meritocratic elitism, leavened by diversity programs aimed at casting a broad net, and compensating for past deficiencies where necessary. However, in all but the most selective institutions, students have a broad range of motivations for "going to college," and many (if not most of them) cannot choose freely to construct their educations. They are older, part time, and financially hard pressed. That does not mean that they are narrowly preprofessional or unreceptive to the need for a liberal education, but that they are obviously very different sorts of candidates for general education than students of my own or earlier generations.

Over time the social and political pressures that shaped the modern research university have shaped the way that undergraduate education is conceptualized. It is at least arguable that the early research universities genuinely thought of themselves as collegiate institutions—by which I mean a university surrounding an undergraduate college. That is still embodied in institutions such as Harvard and Yale University, where the phrase "the college" has some meaning. The term "Harvard graduate" (or "Yale graduate") still means someone who has completed the undergraduate program. But the fuller notion that the liberal arts are the core of the university has eroded badly—mainly, I think, in response to the university's attempt to satisfy concrete and immediate pragmatic social demands.

My contention is that we have gone so far down this road in the major universities that we have reversed our priorities and now give precedence to research and graduate and professional training—in the kind of faculty members we recruit, in the incentives (light or nil teaching loads) we offer them, and even in the teaching we value (graduate over undergraduate students). Our research faculty members have little interest in joining efforts to build core or general-education programs, much less in teaching in them. Moreover, can we be confident that those prized faculty recruits are sufficiently liberally educated to participate in general education? The same is true of our fractionalizing of universities into research centers. Those increasingly become pawns in the faculty recruiting game—we will finance a research center for you, help you recruit postdocs and graduate students to do the research—with little room or thought to undergraduate education.

35 Another problem, though one hard to document and discuss, is the difficulty of financing the humanities and soft social sciences, the fields in which so many undergraduates find their most important liberal-education experiences. We all know that faculty members in those fields teach more, get paid less, and have fewer resources for research than their colleagues in the natural sciences and hard social sciences. They have less leverage in the institution to get what they want, from secretarial services and office space to computers. They are also, on balance, the faculty members most likely to be concerned with undergraduate education, but they are in a weak position to influence decisions within their universities.

Perhaps most important, those who administer our research universities are less and less likely to be well-known teachers, especially collegiate teachers. Presidents have less and less time to worry about education problems, and even provosts and deans of faculty are incredibly hard pressed to keep the lights on and the laboratories functioning. They themselves seldom teach. Such administrators are often forced to prize efficiency in undergraduate education—the more bodies in a classroom the better, and cheaper. It may well be that in most American universities the economic realities are such that the administrators have few alternatives.

I think I would know what to do about the plight of liberal education in the modern research university if I were offered the magic wand. We all have lovely theories. But none of us, and no university president, has such power. That makes it all the more important that we be conscious of the nature of the task at hand. I asked my friend Charles S. Maler, a professor of history at Harvard who has been working on its curricular review, about the university's recent proposal. "I do think it's a step in the right direction to bury the Core, which essentially said students should understand how scholars do scholarship. The Gen Ed that you and I took was a far more humanist enterprise. But by the early 1970s, faculties no longer had confidence in Values and thus turned toward Expertise," he told me. "At least we now have a sense that Values—aesthetic, civic, moral—are important again, even if we don't have confidence we know which values are important."

I believe he's right. Lest we continue to be mired in incremental reforms, we need to be clearer about the larger function of general education. If we believe that values do have a role in education, then the challenge may be to rehistoricize and rehumanize the underclass curriculum. That does not mean going back to Contemporary Civilization courses or the Red Book. It does mean rethinking the content of knowledge appropriate for our contemporary society, and summoning the intellectual courage to embolden students to make qualitative judgments about the materials they are required to engage with in their underclass years.

Of course, that will not be possible unless we are safely beyond the conflicts of the culture wars of the 1980s and 1990s. That seems to me problematic at the current moment in American history, but perhaps I am too pessimistic.

40 Even if we are able to open a new discussion about reforming the curriculum, however, we will still fall unless we take seriously the structural constraints on higher education today. At best we have been taking those constraints for granted; at worst, enthusiastically embracing them.

The changing structure of the university is the place we may need to start the discussion. A great deal is at stake for undergraduate education, and for the country. If we believe, as so many of the founders of liberal education did, that the vitality of American democracy depends upon the kind of liberal education undergraduates receive, we need to put the reimagination of liberal education near the top of our agenda for education in our research universities.

Questions for Discussion

1. Although Katz focuses on the status of liberal education at research universities, is there reason to believe that such education is at risk elsewhere?

2. At your school, are you required to take courses outside of your major? Is doing so useful? If there is a core curriculum or set of requirements that all students must fulfill, how long has it been in place? How well does it suit the present climate at your school?

3. In paragraph 13, Katz describes a cognitive approach to liberal learning. In your opinion, how important is the acquisition of academic skills such as critical thinking as opposed to the acquisition of specific knowledge?

4. Why do you think Katz provides so much history about the evolution of liberal education during the last century? How does this history contribute to his argument?

5. If there is, as Katz, claims, "too much to know," does that in itself provide a rationale for not learning broadly? There has been, without question, a rapid acceleration in the amount of information available to people today, but how well do you think undergraduates a century ago really got to know what was available then?

6. Do you think it is fair to blame faculty for the decline in liberal education? What could motivate faculty to focus on research rather than teaching?

7. Why do you think English teachers and history teachers usually earn considerably less than faculty in the natural sciences? What economic forces determine faculty salaries? Do other factors contribute to salary inequity?

8. Do you think an undergraduate education should convey values, as well as expertise? If so, what values? If not, why not?

③ **RONALD TAKAKI,** "An Educated and Culturally Literate Person Must Study America's Multicultural Reality"

To what extent should schools teach Americans about their own diversity? In a sense, the emergence of multicultural education in the United States in the past two decades is an answer to that question. When Ronald Takaki published the following essay in 1989, many American colleges and universities were beginning to require students to take courses in which they learned about other cultures. The purpose of such requirements, as Takaki suggests, was to help students understand diversity to be able to live and work together. More than a decade after Takaki's essay was published, such diversity requirements are common, suggesting that multicultural education has become widely accepted by Americans. Yet these requirements continue to spark controversy. Perhaps that is because they force people to reconsider beliefs about the purpose of education, or perhaps these requirements do not fit in with what people believe schools should teach. Whatever the case, Takaki's argument about the importance of multicultural education is part of the larger discussion that Americans continue to have about what should be taught in schools. Ronald Takaki is professor of ethnic studies at the University of California at Berkeley and the author of many books about race, ethnicity, and education, including *A Different Mirror: A History of Multicultural America* (1993) and *From Different Shores: Perspectives on Race and Ethnicity in America* (1994). This essay was first published in the *Chronicle of Higher Education*.

An Educated and Culturally Literate Person Must Study America's Multicultural Reality

RONALD TAKAKI

1   In Palolo Valley, Hawaii, where I lived as a child, my neighbors were Japanese, Chinese, Portuguese, Filipino, and Hawaiian. I heard voices with different accents and I heard different languages. I played with children of different colors. Why, I wondered, were families representing such an array of nationalities living together in one little valley? My teachers and textbooks did not explain our diversity.

After graduation from high school, I attended a college on the mainland where students and even professors would ask me how long I had been in America and where I had learned to speak English. "In this country," I would reply. "I was born in America, and my family has been here for three generations."

Today, some twenty years later, Asian and also Afro-Americans, Chicano/Latino, and Native-American students continue to find themselves perceived as strangers on college campuses. Moreover, they are encountering a new campus racism. The targets of ugly racial slurs and violence, they have begun to ask critical questions about why knowledge of their histories and communities is excluded from the curriculum. White students are also realizing the need to understand the cultural diversity of American society.

In response, colleges and universities across the country, from Brown to Berkeley, are currently considering requiring students to take courses designed to help them understand diverse cultures.

5 The debate is taking place within a general context framed by academic pundits like Allan Bloom and E. D. Hirsch.* Both of them are asking: What is an educated, a culturally literate person?

I think Bloom is right when he says: "There are some things one must know about if one is to be educated. . . . The university should try to have a vision of what an educated person is." I also agree with Hirsch when he insists that there is a body of cultural information that "every American needs to know."

But the question is: What should be the content of education and what does cultural literacy mean? The traditional curriculum reflects what Howard Swearer, former president of Brown University, has described as a "certain provincialism," an overly Eurocentric perspective. Concerned about this problem, a Brown University visiting committee recommended that the faculty consider requiring students to take an ethnic-studies course before they graduate. "The contemporary definition of an educated person," the committee said, "must include at least minimal awareness of multicultural reality."

This view now is widely shared. Says Donna Shalala, chancellor of the University of Wisconsin at Madison: "Every student needs to know much more about the origins and history of the particular cultures which, as Americans, we will encounter during our lives."

This need is especially felt in California, where racial minorities will constitute a majority of the population by 2000, and where a faculty committee at the University of California at Berkeley has proposed an "American-cultures requirement" to give stu-

dents a deeper understanding of our nation's racial and cultural diversity. Faculty opposition is based mainly on a disdain for all requirements on principle, an unwillingness to add another requirement, an insistence on the centrality of Western civilization, and a fear that the history of European immigrant groups would be left out of the proposed course.[†]

10 In fact, however, there are requirements everywhere in the curriculum (for reading and composition, the major, a foreign language, breadth of knowledge, etc.). The American-cultures requirement would not be an additional course, for students would be permitted to use the course to satisfy one of their social-sciences or humanities requirements. Western civilization will continue to dominate the curriculum, and the

*Influential scholars Allan Bloom and E. D. Hirsch achieved national prominence during the 1980s by arguing that U.S. colleges were failing to produce culturally literate citizens. Bloom is best known for *The Closing of the American Mind* (1987), Hirsch for *Cultural Literacy: What Every American Needs to Know* (1987).

†The proposal for an American-cultures requirement to which Takaki refers in this essay was subsequently passed and adopted by the University of California at Berkeley. Since 1993 all students entering the university have had to satisfy this requirement by taking an approved course focusing on issues of race, culture, and ethnicity in American society.

CONTEXT

According to the U.S. Census Bureau, as of 2000, 49.9 percent of the 33.1 million residents of California were classified as White, 31.6 percent were Latino, 11.4 percent were Asian, 6.7 percent were Black, and fewer than 1 percent were Native American. During the 1990s the Latino population in California grew by 35 percent, and the Asian population grew by 36 percent. These figures mirrored population changes in the United States as a whole: Nationally, the Latino population grew by 38.8 percent during the 1990s, and the Asian population grew by 43 percent; during the same period the White population increased by 7.3 percent.

proposed requirement would place the experiences of racial minorities within the broad context of American society. Faculty support for some kind of mandatory course is considerable, and a vote on the issue is scheduled this spring.

But the question often asked is: What would be the focus and content of such multicultural courses? Actually there is a wide range of possibilities. For many years I have been teaching a course on "Racial Inequality in America: A Comparative Historical Perspective." Who we are in this society and how we are perceived and treated have been conditioned by America's racial and ethnic diversity. My approach is captured in the phrase "from different shores." By "shores," I intend a double meaning. One is the shores that immigrants left to go to America—those in Europe, Africa, Latin America, and Asia. The second is the different and often conflicting shores or perspectives from which scholars have viewed the experiences of racial and ethnic groups.

In my course, students read Thomas Sowell's *Ethnic America: A History* along with my *Iron Cages: Race and Culture in 19th-Century America.* Readings also include Winthrop Jordan on the colonial origins of racism, John Higham on nativism, Mario Barrera on Chicanos, and William J. Wilson on the Black underclass. By critically examining the different "shores," students are able to address complex comparative questions: How have the experiences of racial minorities such as Blacks and Asians been similar to, and different from, one another? Is "race" the same as "ethnicity"? How have race relations been shaped by economic developments, as well as by culture? What impact have these forces had on moral values about how people should think and behave, beliefs about human nature and society, and images of the past as well as the future?

Other courses could examine racial diversity in relation to gender, immigration, urbanization, technology, or the labor market. Courses could also study specific topics such

as Hollywood's racial images, ethnic music and art, novels by writers of color, the civil rights movement, or the Pacific Rim. Regardless of theme or topic, all of the courses should address the major theoretical issues concerning race and should focus on Afro-Americans, Asians, Chicanos/Latinos, and Native Americans.

Who would teach these courses? Responsibility could be located solely in ethnic-studies programs. But this would reduce them to service-course programs and also render even more remote the possibility of diversifying the traditional curriculum. The sheer logistics of meeting the demand generated by an institution-wide requirement would be overwhelming for any single department.

15 Clearly, faculty members in the social sciences and humanities will have to be involved. There also are dangers in this approach, however. The diffusion of ethnic studies throughout the traditional disciplines could undermine the coherence and identity of ethnic studies as a field of teaching and scholarship. It could also lead to area-studies courses on Africa or Asia disguised as ethnic studies, to revised but essentially intact Western-civilization courses with a few "non-Western" readings tacked on, or to amorphous and bland "American studies" courses taught by instructors with little or no training in multicultural studies. Such courses, though well-intentioned, could result in the unwitting perpetuation of certain racial stereotypes and even to the transformation of texts by writers and scholars of color into "mistexts." This would only reproduce multicultural illiteracy.

But broad faculty participation in such a requirement can work if there is a sharply written statement of purpose, as well as clear criteria for courses on the racial and cultural diversity of American society. We also need interdisciplinary institutes to offer intellectual settings where faculty members from different fields can collaborate on new courses and where ethnic-studies scholars can share their expertise. More importantly, we need to develop and strengthen ethnic-studies programs and departments as academic foundations for this new multicultural curriculum. Such bases should bring together a critical mass of faculty members committed to, and trained in, ethnic studies and should help to preserve the alternative perspectives provided by this scholarly field.

In addition, research must generate knowledge for the new courses, and new faculty members must be trained for ethnic-studies teaching and scholarship. Berkeley already has a doctoral program in ethnic studies, but other graduate schools must also help prepare the next generation of faculty members. Universities will experience a tremendous turnover in teachers due to retirements, and this is a particularly urgent time to educate future scholars, especially from minority groups, for a multicultural curriculum.

The need to open the American mind to greater cultural diversity will not go away. We can resist it by ignoring the changing ethnic composition of our student bodies and the larger society, or we can realize how it offers colleges and universities a timely and exciting opportunity to revitalize the social sciences and humanities, giving both a new sense of

purpose and a more inclusive definition of knowledge.

If concerted efforts are made, someday students of different racial backgrounds will be able to learn about one another in an informed and systematic way and will not graduate from our institutions of higher learning ignorant about how places like Palolo Valley fit into American society.

COMPLICATION

Cultural critic Dinesh D'Souza has been a consistent critic of the kind of multicultural requirements that Ronald Takaki advocates in this essay. According to D'Souza, such requirements undermine traditional liberal education in American colleges and universities:

An academic and cultural revolution has overtaken most of our 3,535 colleges and universities. It's a revolution to which most Americans have paid little attention. It is a revolution imposed upon the students by a university elite, not one voted upon or even discussed by the society at large. It amounts, according to University of Wisconsin-Madison Chancellor Donna Shalala, to "a basic transformation of American higher education in the name of multiculturalism and diversity." The central thrust of this "basic transformation" involves replacing traditional core curricula—consisting of the great works of Western culture—with curricula flavored by minority, female, and Third World authors.

Questions for Discussion

1. Takaki opens his essay by drawing on personal experience from twenty years earlier. In what ways is this experience relevant to his main argument? How effective is his use of personal experience in helping him make his argument?

2. Why does Takaki believe that a required course in American cultures is important? How does he establish the need for such a requirement?

3. What risks does Takaki see in giving responsibility for such courses to a single department? Why is he concerned about locating such courses within traditional academic disciplines?

4. Why do you think Takaki chooses Brown and Berkeley as examples of "colleges and universities across the country"? Does his use of these examples strengthen or weaken his argument? Explain.

5. In his essay, Takaki refers to two scholars—Allan Bloom and E. D. Hirsch—who have criticized multicultural education. Why does he do so? What do you think he accomplishes with these references?

④ **STEPHEN L. TRAINOR,** "Designing a Signature General Education Program"

If you are attending a school that requires you to take courses outside of your major, you may question the rationale for these requirements and wonder if they are subject to change. At most schools, considerable effort is invested in determining what courses should be required of all students. But because curriculum reform is labor-intensive and carries with it the possibility of triggering conflict among various departments, schools often leave their core curriculum in place for years. When a review of the curriculum is mandated for some reason, different constituencies are likely to have different proposals about what courses should be required, how many requirements there should be, and how many options students should have in selecting courses that fulfill a requirement within a specific discipline. In the following selection from 2004, which first appeared in *Peer Review,* a publication of the Association of American Colleges and Universities, Stephen Trainor argues that the key to successful reform is the process a school uses. To illustrate what proved to be a successful process, he focuses upon what was done at Salve Regina University, where he is dean of undergraduate studies. As you read it, think about what advice you might offer authorities at your school if they undertake a similar process.

Designing a Signature General Education Program

STEPHEN L. TRAINOR

1 Notoriously contentious and protracted, efforts to reform general education curricula can prove frustrating for the participants, and they often end in failure. In particular, the goal of producing a signature program—a curriculum that captures the distinctive mission and essence of an institution—often remains elusive, sacrificed to the exigencies of political compromise or financial constraints. The source of the problem usually can be traced to the process involved in a given curricular reform. In its effort to develop a new signature general education curriculum, Salve Regina University was able to avoid many of the usual pitfalls by adopting a formal problem-solving model that emphasizes creativity and involves the entire faculty in the process.

How Does the Process Affect the Outcome?
The problem is not that colleges and universities do not pay attention to process; rather, difficulties arise from their failure to anticipate the results a given process is likely to produce. In designing a signature program, the typical procedure is to appoint a committee to produce a curricular model and then present it to the entire faculty for consideration, debate, and a vote. Great care is taken to ensure that all viewpoints are represented on this committee, in the hope that the final model will produce consensus among the larger faculty. While it seems plausible on the surface, this process is, for a variety of reasons, unlikely to produce a distinctive signature program.

Precisely because they were chosen as representatives, the committee members are concerned to speak for their constituents' interests—the liberal arts, the professional programs, the humanities or the social sciences, the territory of a single department or discipline. It is the rare faculty member who can transcend his or her own area and speak for the institution as a whole. Thus, this typical process practically guarantees that the committee will be at odds with itself in most of its deliberations.

To produce a model that will achieve consensus among the faculty is a laudable goal; the core curriculum should have widespread support. Yet in striving to reach this elusive goal, the committee may be forced to sacrifice the more distinctive elements of any signature model in favor of domestic harmony. Accordingly, the most likely outcome is a least-common-denominator model designed to offend no one and to garner the necessary votes from the wider faculty.

5 Because they are established up front and the model is developed to satisfy them, the criteria for the new curriculum actually are design elements in disguise. As such, these restrictive criteria can undermine the committee's ability to come up with a distinctive signature program. Finally, since the committee's task is to produce a single model, the voting faculty's only comparative frame of reference is the current core curriculum (aka the devil that you know).

A Creative Problem-Solving Model

At Salve Regina University, we were able to avoid many of these problems by adopting a problem-solving model outlined by Vincent Ryan Ruggiero* (2003). Ruggiero's model calls for a progression of four stages: (1) *being aware,* which involves gathering information and defining the problem; (2) *being creative,* which asks the problem-solvers to generate as many creative solutions as possible; (3) *being critical,* which asks participants to set aside

the proposed solutions while they develop the criteria by which the solutions will be judged; and (4) *communicating* or *acting,* which calls for the selection of a solution based on the criteria and implementing that solution.

This model posits a process that is, in a number of ways, counterintuitive but that nonetheless effectively addresses the process problems discussed above. Rather than a representative committee, the process adopted at Salve Regina calls for multiple design teams brought together by common interests and vision. Every faculty member, either individually or in groups, is invited to propose a model curriculum. Rather than developing a compromise model designed to build consensus, the process calls for choosing whichever model receives a majority of the faculty votes; presumably, that model best represents the university's idea of an integrated signature curriculum.

In order to foster creativity, Ruggiero's model reverses the anticipated order of activities by placing the development of criteria after the brainstorming of solutions. Faculty are thus free to focus on developing a distinctive "dream" curriculum without the usual constraints. The development of a variety of models offers the faculty a broader range of choices than the "take it or leave it" approach implied in the single committee, single curriculum process.

At Salve Regina, we considered a common understanding of the process to be so important that we asked the faculty to endorse it in a formal vote, at which point the stages were linked to a strict timetable designed to get to a decision by the time of the faculty's annual post-commencement meeting in May. A steering committee, composed of eight faculty members and the undergraduate dean, was established to oversee the process and to ensure adherence to the schedule. The process itself suggested a variety of questions along the way, questions worth considering in the development of any signature program.

*Widely recognized as a leader in placing critical thinking at the forefront of education, Vincent Ryan Ruggiero has published more than fifteen books and upward of seventy articles. His books include *Beyond Feelings: A Guide to Critical Thinking* and *The Art of Thinking: A Guide to Critical and Creative Thought.*

Stage One: What Is the Problem You Want to Solve?

10 The first task of the steering committee was to define the problem clearly. One aspect of the problem turned on the question of mission. The university community recently had completed a two-year process to develop a new mission statement, and many perceived a cognitive disconnect between the new mission and the set of distribution requirements in place at the time. A second aspect of the problem turned on integrative learning. The distribution requirements had no internal frame of reference or connection; there was no philosophy, no theme, no developmental structure, no interdisciplinary cooperation.

In the end, the steering committee was able to articulate the general dissatisfaction with the current core in a way that gave shape and direction to the problem-solving process. It proposed to the faculty assembly the following clearly defined task; to create a core curriculum of liberal arts and sciences that includes explicit goals and measurable objectives and that is (1) grounded in the university's mission as a Catholic institution founded by the Sisters of Mercy, "to work for a world that is harmonious, just, and merciful," and that is (2) integrated by cooperation.

Stage Two: How Can You Tap into the Creativity of the Faculty?

Ruggiero's model fosters creativity by reversing the anticipated order of events. Instead of specifying criteria first and then tailoring the solution to fit them, the process asks participants to generate solutions before criteria are established. This is particularly challenging for academics who, usually more critical than creative by training, are apt to want to know the criteria first. But it is Ruggiero's particular insight to see that *a priori* criteria can be thought-stoppers. If one begins with a given set of constraints—e.g., the core will have an upper limit of thirty-nine credit hours; the core will be delivered by the current faculty; the

core will not touch the current requirements in English, or history, or modern languages; the core must be completed by the end of sophomore year; the core will not cost any more money than the current curriculum—one can with some accuracy predict the outcome, which is likely to bear a striking resemblance to the status quo. Ruggiero avoids this problem by proscribing the creation of criteria until a number of creative solutions have been generated. Liberated from considerations of staffing and cost (which are administrative problems, anyway) and from the need to achieve consensus on credit allocations (which are turf matters rather than curricular principles), faculty are free to focus on their real task: designing a signature curriculum that reflects the mission and character of the institution.

By the deadline established by Salve Regina's steering committee, five fully developed models and some eighteen focused suggestions had emerged. Two of the models were proposed by individuals, three by teams of two to seven faculty members. The range of approaches and educational philosophies put forth is suggested by the titles of the five models:

- The Seven Frames of Salve Regina University
- The Millennium Core
- Classics Program
- Preparation for Lifelong Learning and World Citizenship
- Searching for a Meaningful Life

The focused suggestions ranged from recommendations about information literacy to competency in the sciences to the inclusion of service learning. The models and the suggestions were collected in a packet and presented, with an opportunity for questions and discussion, at an open session attended by the faculty, the academic administration, and the university's president. The presentation of five fully developed models created a sense of

CONTEXT

Almost every school has a mission statement, and you might benefit from studying the mission statement of your school, if you have not already done so. To help you understand how the faculty at Trainor's school wanted a curriculum that would be in keeping with the school's mission statement, here is an excerpt from how Salve Regina University defines its mission. According to the school's website, Salve Regina seeks to educate "men and women for responsible lives by imparting and expanding knowledge, developing skills, and cultivating enduring values. Through liberal arts and professional programs, students develop their abilities for thinking clearly and creatively, enhance their capacity for sound judgment, and prepare for the challenge of learning throughout their lives."

excitement about the process and confidence about the future. The general consensus was that any one of the new models would be much better than the status quo.

Stage Three: How Do You Evaluate the Proposed Models?

15 At this stage of the process, participants set aside the solutions proposed in Stage Two and develop the criteria by which those solutions will be judged. The challenge is to create a set of criteria independent of the existing possible solutions: This is particularly difficult in smaller problem-solving processes where the participants involved in developing Stage Three criteria are the same as those who proposed solutions in Stage Two. At Salve Regina, these difficulties were addressed by a division of labor between the steering committee and the self-generated design teams. Before the solutions were proposed, the steering committee, whose members were not permitted to participate in model design, had set about developing criteria but kept them in strict confidence.

After the five proposed models were presented to the full faculty and academic administration, the steering committee publicly presented its criteria to the faculty assembly. Their original proposal included the following points:

- How is the proposed curriculum based on the concept of the liberal arts and sciences?
- How will the university be able to measure the extent to which the explicit goals and outcomes of the proposal are being achieved?
- How does the proposal implement the university's mission to encourage students to seek wisdom and to "work for a world that is harmonious, just, and merciful"?
- How is the proposed curriculum integrated by cooperation?

In the discussions on the floor of the assembly, various other criteria were proposed and debated; ultimately, two more were added:

- How does the proposed curriculum present all undergraduates with expectations and standards that promote the development of intellect and character?
- How does the proposed curriculum prepare students for a lifetime of learning, service, and career choices?

The faculty involved in developing the five models were asked to explain in writing how their proposals addressed the criteria, and their answers were collected and published to the faculty at large. These faculty also were free to amend their original proposals to address the criteria; however, it was important for the process that they were under no obligation to do so.

Stage Four: Which Model Do You Want?

The final stage calls for judging the proposed solutions against the established criteria and selecting a model. Rather than merely using the criteria as a checklist, Stage Four involves choosing the model that is deemed the most effective and attractive in terms of the criteria. Rather than compromising the overall integrity of the model to match the list of criteria perfectly, it may be advisable to overlook weaknesses in satisfying one criterion in view of strengths in satisfying others.

At Salve Regina, the final selection of the model took place over two days at a post-commencement faculty meeting conducted by the officers of the faculty assembly. At this stage in the process, all members of the faculty were vitally engaged in the discussions and debates. For example, the faculty in the professional departments, who had not been extensively involved in proposing possible models, now emerged as important decision makers. They critiqued the various models and argued for or against them. In a straw poll taken at the end of the first day, two models clearly were shown to have widespread support. On the next day, the faculty formally endorsed the model that had garnered the most votes in the straw poll. This model still needed much work; indeed, it required two more years of development before the first courses were offered. Nonetheless, a distinctive, signature curricular model had been selected over the course of a single academic year.

Conclusion

20 Institutions about to embark on a general education curricular revision should give careful attention to process, and particularly to the kind of outcomes a given process is likely to produce. While consensus is a laudable goal in the selection of a model, it can be an impediment at the design level, especially if the goal is to design a distinctive signature program. The Ruggiero problem-solving model used at Salve Regina University had the effect of tapping into faculty creativity by inviting a variety of groups and individuals to propose curricular models and deferring the definition of selection criteria until after the models were published. Thus, faculty members were free to concentrate on mission, content, skills, and pedagogy without worrying about pleasing all possible constituencies and interest groups. When the time came to select a model, the faculty assembly had five distinctive programs to choose from, and the model selected clearly reflected the university mission statement in a high-profile, signature design.

Reference

Ruggiero, Vincent Ryan. 2003. *The Art of Thinking: A Guide to Critical and Creative Thought.* New York: Longman.

Questions for Discussion

1. When Trainor opens his argument by claiming that efforts to reform an undergraduate curriculum are not only "frustrating" but also "notoriously contentious and protracted," what assumptions is he making about his audience? What kind of readers would be likely to accept this as a reasonable claim—the definition of a problem in need of a solution?

2. Why is "process" so important, in Trainor's view? How did the process used at his university differ from those widely used elsewhere? What was the advantage of allowing faculty to think about what an ideal curriculum would look like without feeling constrained by predetermined guidelines?

3. Why would a school's mission statement be essential when evaluating or reforming its curriculum? How well do the requirements at your school match its mission statement? If you do not know the mission statement, how do you think you could find it?

NEGOTIATING DIFFERENCES

The writers in this cluster address issues that continue to generate intense discussion and directly affect the lives of students. In some cases, the debate focuses on what courses should be retained from the models of liberal or general education widely used in the past. For example, should all students be required to take at least one course in English or history? The arguments by Rick Livingston and Stanley Katz focus not only on the merits of a liberal education but also on why such an education is frequently challenged. In other cases, the debate focuses on reshaping the curriculum to include new courses. Ronald Takaki, for example, refers to a proposal for a required multicultural course in the University of California system. Since he wrote the piece included in this section, scholars have continued to discuss whether students are best introduced to issues of cultural diversity in a course specifically designed for that purpose or whether a multicultural perspective should be expected in a range of courses.

In the final section within this cluster, Stephen Trainor describes the process used at his school to review and reform its general education program—the core courses that all students are required to take regardless of the major or minor they choose. Imagine now that your college or

4. What is your understanding of "integrative learning" (to which Trainor refers in paragraph 10)?

5. According to Trainor, a steering committee at his school was secretly developing criteria by which new proposals would be evaluated, and these criteria were not disclosed to the faculty until new models were presented. He offered a rationale for this process. Do you see any risk to it? How, say, would you feel about learning the evaluation criteria for a project you were completing only after you had submitted it?

6. Trainor states that a two-day faculty meeting was held after commencement to select which proposal to adopt. What does the length of this faculty meeting and its timing imply? Why do you think faculty from professional departments were encouraged to speak?

7. Trainor concludes by restating points that he had already made. Is this an effective conclusion given the length and context of his argument?

university has decided to revise its curriculum. You have been given the opportunity to participate in the review process and offer a student perspective on what should be retained, eliminated, or added to the current curriculum. As a representative of other students, it is your responsibility to consider whether the curriculum serves the needs of the students who attend your school—not just whether it suits you.

Your task now is to write an essay in which you propose or justify one change in the curriculum or argue on behalf of retaining one of the current requirements. To make your argument, you will need to consider not only your school's curriculum but also its mission statement. You should also consider the kinds of students who attend your school and the reasons they do so. And you should think about what purpose your school serves in the community. Finally, you should imagine that your argument will be read by faculty and administrators who may differ from you in terms of what they consider important. You will need their support if proposing a significant change. So if you are writing, for example, to recommend the elimination of a history requirement, imagine that historians sit on the committee charged with the responsibility for curriculum review.

How Should Students Be Taught?

By This point in your education, you have probably experienced different kinds of teaching methods: lectures, discussions, research with a lab partner, collaborative learning within small groups, and maybe even service learning—a process in which students learn through doing volunteer work in their communities. Different teaching methods—or pedagogies, as educators call them—appeal to different kinds of teachers, as well as different kinds of students. Some professors are at their best in a lecture hall, commanding the attention of a large audience; others do their best work by facilitating discussion in which students engage in the open exchange of ideas. Most educators would agree that no single teaching method should be imposed on all teachers. How teachers proceed in the classroom must be informed by the nature of the discipline in which they are teaching, their own strengths, and the kinds of students they have. ■ But underlying the decisions that educators need to make about "how students should be taught" are some fundamental questions: To what extent is the teacher an authority who should be in command within the classroom? To what extent should students have a voice in determining how they learn? Should teaching be designed to pass knowledge on to students who passively receive it, or should teachers encourage active learning in which students question what has been previously believed to be true? Answering questions such as these calls for considering another: Is it more important for students to leave college with knowledge of facts and figures or with skills such as critical thinking and writing? And if both of these goals are desirable, is it possible for teachers to give equal emphasis to both? As you read the selections in this cluster, you will find diverse views. One author emphasizes the importance of learning skills that are useful in the workplace, two argue on behalf of giving students power in the classroom, and one emphasizes the importance of engaging the attention of students by focusing on what remains to be discovered rather than on what is already known.

① BILL COPLIN, "Lost in the Life of the Mind"

Educators traditionally value what can be called "the life of the mind," or the kind of interior life that can be fostered through serious reflection. But as the title of the following argument suggests, it might be possible to dwell so long in the mind that you become "lost" there—either entangled in thoughts that do not lead to resolution or so much at home in this life of the mind that it becomes hard to connect with the realities of daily life. So to what extent should higher education focus on helping students learn how to apply what they learn or develop skills for which there are demands in the workplace? Bill Coplin teaches public affairs at the Maxwell School and the College of Arts and Sciences at Syracuse University, where he was recently awarded a Chancellor's Citation for Exceptional Educational Achievement. In "Lost in the Life of the Mind," Coplin argues that professors sometimes allow the passion they have for their own areas of scholarship to obscure what might be in the best interest of students. This argument was first published in the *Chronicle of Higher Education* in September 2004. (For information about the *Chronicle of Higher Education,* see page 444.) As you read, consider whether Coplin is addressing issues that you have experienced in courses you were required to take.

Lost in the Life of the Mind

BILL COPLIN

1 "Bait and switch" is usually used to describe the sleazy telephone sales rep who starts, "This is your lucky day. You are the winner of a free vacation in the Bahamas." Schnooks take the bait only to find out the hidden costs.

I felt like a schnook after my second week as an undergraduate in 1956 at Washington College in Chestertown, Md. After a year, I transferred to the Johns Hopkins University, where the switch was even more apparent. My parents, relatives, high-school teachers, and guidance counselor had said, "You are college material," so I thought I'd go to college and live happily ever after.

However, I quickly realized that I had been a victim of a gigantic conspiracy on the part of colleges that was unwittingly supported by the rest of society in the name of the American

dream, unfettered social mobility. I took the bait that college would lead to a high-paying and rewarding job. Once there, the switch was on. My role was to please the faculty by showing them I wanted to learn everything they loved to learn. It wasn't until getting my Ph.D. in international relations from American University that I was told by a wise professor, "A college degree and four quarters will get you a dollar."

I thought taking English meant improving my writing skills, that taking Spanish meant that when I went to Mexico I'd be able to converse, that studying history would be an exercise in learning about the past. Wrong on all three counts!

5 English courses at that time were about appreciating literature. (Now many are about deconstructing text and going off on ideological

*Charles Beard (1874–1948) was an American historian whose book *An Economic Interpretation of the Constitution of the United States* (1913) created controversy because in it Beard argued that the writers of the Constitution wrote it for the economic interests of land-owning white males.

†Geoffrey Chaucer (1342–1400) is best known for having written *The Canterbury Tales,* a work about thirty people on a religious pilgrimage to Canterbury, the site of an important cathedral. To pass the time during this long trip, the travelers tell each other stories about who they are and what they have experienced. These stories, or tales, provide a rich and diverse portrait of English life in the late Middle Ages. Because Chaucer wrote in a version of English that is no longer spoken, professors assigning *The Canterbury Tales* must decide whether to teach it as it was originally composed or to assign an edition that translates Chaucer's language into contemporary English.

rants). Spanish taught language that would permit me to read great Spanish novelists and thinkers, not close a deal. History was a study of the study of history—discussion, for instance, of Charles Beard's* economic interpretation of the Constitution rather than of what the founding fathers actually did.

I was impressed by my English professor's passion and excitement. Wish I could have been as excited about Chaucer,† or even figured out what the hell he was saying. If you haven't had the pleasure, here is a short quote out of Bartlett's Familiar Quotations: "feeld hath eyen, and the wode has eres."

The first thing that strikes you is that if you had this on Microsoft Word, there would be red squiggles under half of it. I had to learn a foreign language called 14th-century English. The professor subjected me to this because he was a professional scholar saying, in essence, "Be like me."

I could not blame him for his missionary zeal because that is why he went into academe in the first place, and what his Ph.D. trained him for. However, I was plenty angry at a system that treated all students as if they were in college to learn for the sake of learning when in fact the vast majority wanted college to prepare them for a successful career. I wanted to learn about life; they wanted me to lose myself in the life of the mind.

Not much has changed over the past 48 years, and with devastating results, if a recent conversation I had with Joe, let's call him, is any indication. I met Joe in the late 1980s when he was 12 years old in a program in which my undergraduates worked with at-risk youth. Joe adopted me as his mentor because, despite a serious speech impediment, he liked to argue politics. He didn't want to end up, like many of his friends had, in jail or dead, and he didn't want to be on welfare like his parents were.

10 However, Joe could not pass the New York State standardized tests required for graduation. He went into the Job Corps, where he got his GED, became a professional house painter,

joined the Army, completed basic training at the top of his class, served overseas, and eventually left the military. He decided he wanted to be a policeman and did OK on the civil-service exam.

He called me in 2003 to tell me that he was in a local community college to study criminal justice and get an associate degree. During the course of the conversation, he said, "Coplin, how come I got to learn the MLA, the APA, and the Chicago style? Can't they make up their minds?"

I told Joe that the college curriculum, even at a community college serving students who don't necessarily want to go on to a four-year liberal-arts degree, was designed to prepare professional scholars. Moreover, the inability to select one citation form was evidence that college faculty members can't reach a consensus on even the most trivial of educational goals. I advised him to play the game. He said, "No problem, I learned to do that in the Army."

Joe would have been far better served if he had spent his time learning to write and speak more clearly and with better grammar. It's tempting to dismiss him as an example because of his socioeconomic background and the faults of the public-school system. But poor oral and written communication skills are rampant no matter what the educational background of the student or the ranking of the college.

According to employers, college students are not prepared for the work force because they lack the skills and character needed to succeed. Our best and brightest students might take statistics in college and score A's on the tests that measure their ability to solve some abstract problem about white and black Ping-Pong balls, but cannot figure out how to set up a bar graph to display real-world data. They learn calculus, but they can't make budget projections.

15 They learn shortcuts to jump the academic hurdles with a minimum of effort, but not much about honesty and work ethic. A director of sales and marketing for a media com-

pany wrote me: "What I found from my hiring—the higher the GPA and the more prestigious the school, the less prepared for the real world the grad was. I was amazed at the basics that these 22- and 23-year-olds lacked. Real basic—like how about we wake up every day and show up for work on time!"

Liberal-arts leaders have no choice but to continue setting the bait. It's a matter of economic survival. Most students and their parents will pay as much as $160,000 only if they believe a college experience will lead to a better economic future.

The important question is to what degree colleges will deliver what they promise. Teaching critical thinking and fostering intellectual well-roundedness are important goals, but too general and self-serving. Faculties need to take more responsibility for helping students acquire the skills employers want. The list needs to be specific enough so that professors can assess skill levels but general enough so that the skills cut across all academic programs.

Those skills include dependability, attention to detail, teamwork, obtaining and analyzing information, problem solving, and writing clearly. Such a list can be found in my recent book *10 Things Employers Want You to Learn in College*. Similar lists can be found in a study in 2002 that the National Association of Colleges and Employers based on surveys of 457 employers, or in work from the early 1990s by the Department of Labor's Secretary's Commission on Achieving Necessary Skills, or in the 2003 Business-Higher Education Forum report, "Building a Nation of Learners."

The focus on general professional skills would allow liberal-arts faculties to have their cake and eat it too. On one hand, they would be free to choose whatever curricular content they want. On the other, they would provide students with the opportunity to practice and improve the skills employers expect. Professors just need to keep their eye on the target and to be as rigorous about students' skills as they are about their own research. Whatever content they teach should be applicable beyond the confines of their disciplines. They can do that by incorporating more fieldwork and active learning into their courses.

20 For example, students from a class studying *The Canterbury Tales* could rewrite one of them in a modern setting (active learning) or present one to a 12th-grade English class in a local high school (fieldwork). Instructors teaching methods in various social sciences could require students, as I have since 1979 in my methods course, to complete a client survey for a community agency serving youth.

Liberal-arts professors will have to accept the implicit social contract with their students. They need to treat undergraduates as clients who learn not only from what is said, assigned, and tested, but also from the professor's own behavior. For their part, students must recognize professors' expertise in their subjects, but also their importance as professional-skills coaches. That means seeking constructive criticism rather than worrying only about grades, and working hard to master the material rather than cramming before tests.

Over the past 30 years, service learning, internships, computer-based instruction, team projects, and problem-based interdisciplinary courses have become more widespread. However, they remain the exceptions, helping admissions officers better set the bait. Liberal-arts institutions over all need to embrace a skills perspective to minimize the switch.

COMPLICATION

Scholars often refer to work that they have published because doing so can alert their audience to sources that provide additional information about their research or views. Providing a record of publication can also be useful when establishing ethos (see pages 72–80). But are there circumstances in which it might be inappropriate to direct attention to a prior publication? Consider Coplin's reference to his book *10 Things Employers Want You to Learn in College*. Is it contributing to his argument or distracting from it?

Questions for Discussion

1. Coplin begins his argument with a reference to a disreputable sales practice in which an attractive but insincere offer is used to lure consumers who, once caught, are maneuvered into accepting a different deal. Have telemarketers ever tried to use this practice on you? Have there been other situations in which you have experienced or observed a "bait and switch"? Has anyone at your school done that to you?

2. When drawing on his own undergraduate experience, Coplin emphasizes what he remembers of English. To what extent has your experience in college English been similar? Has the focus been on developing your writing skills, appreciating literature, or something else? Are you being trained to be a "professional scholar"?

3. What harm can be done when a professor conveys, "Be like me"? Could harm be done if professors are not role models to some extent? At what point, in your opinion, should professors back off and let you be yourself?

4. What does the phrase "real world" mean to you? Is school part of the real world or separate from it?

5. How does Coplin believe students should be taught? Why do you think he puts more emphasis on the development of professional skills than on the acquisition of specific knowledge?

6. To what extent are you responsible for your education?

7. How would you describe the tone of this argument?

8. In his conclusion, Coplin returns to the images with which he opened his argument, this time noting that "admissions officers . . . set the bait." How much influence do you think faculty members have on how admissions officers market schools? If schools are promising more than they can deliver, or something other than they can deliver, who do you think is responsible for sending that message?

② **MANO SINGHAM,** "Moving Away from the Authoritarian Classroom"

As the title of the following argument suggests, Mano Singham is interested in working collaboratively with students instead of wielding absolute power in the classroom. Singham teaches physics at Case Western Reserve University and serves as a member of Ohio's science advisory board, which drafted guidelines for the teaching of science in that state—no easy task given how rapidly new discoveries are being made in the sciences and how some aspects of science (such as evolutionary biology) have been attacked by social conservatives. If you are interested by the following article—first published in a 2005 issue of *Change*—and would like to read more of Singham's work, you might enjoy the web journal he regularly posts (http://blog.case.edu/mxs24/). A July 2005 entry in that journal offers insight into what motivates him as a writer. After noting that he used to let ideas "swirl around in my head, without putting them down in concrete form," only to later forget them and be left with a "nagging feeling of dissatisfaction that I should have explored the ideas further and written them down," Singham states, "It is easy to delude yourself that you understand something when you have the idea only in your mind. Putting those ideas to paper (or screen) has the startling effect of revealing gaps in knowledge and weaknesses of logic and reasoning, thus forcing re-evaluation of one's ideas. So writing is not a one-way process from brain to screen/paper. It is a dialectic process. Writing reveals your ideas but also changes the way you think."

Moving Away from the Authoritarian Classroom

MANO SINGHAM

1 The professor at the conference handed around a copy of his class syllabus to illustrate how he had implemented his teaching innovation. He seemed a gentle, polite, and concerned teacher, someone who would be well liked by his students. And yet, viewed through the lens of his syllabus, he appeared a tyrant.

The arrogant tone of the document was all too familiar. Instructions to the students read like imperial commands: "You will submit three projects . . ," "You will make a five-minute report. . . ." His institution's policy on electronic submission of assignments, quoted in the syl-

labus, was even sterner. "Students bear sole responsibility for ensuring that papers or assignments submitted electronically to a professor are received in a timely manner" and are "obliged to have their e-mail client issue a receipt verifying that the document has been received." Indeed, they should "retain a copy of the dated submission on a separate disk," presumably as proof of having met the deadline.

The school's policy on disabilities was yet more legalistic. "Students with a documented disability must inform the instructor at the close of the first class meeting. . . . If you do not consult with the instructor and follow up at the Student Support Services office during the first two weeks of classes . . . you will thereby waive any claim to a disability and the right to any accommodation pertaining thereto."

This harshness is, unfortunately, not uncommon in syllabi. At a subsequent faculty discussion of power in the classroom at my own university, I quoted these sections of the syllabus as examples of an authoritarian faculty mindset. There were embarrassed smiles of recognition all around. One faculty member, also a kindly and concerned teacher, shamefacedly admitted that those phrases could have been lifted directly from her own syllabus. She hadn't realized until that moment how rude they might sound to students.

5 But the sad fact is that students don't seem to be offended by being ordered around in course syllabi. Cynics might argue that this is because no student actually reads them. But even if they do, by the time they come into our college classroom, students have received many similar edicts. They have probably come to think of them as the normal way of doing things.

I find it hard to believe that teachers always treated students so rudely in their syllabi or that syllabi were always so detailed and legalistic, trying to cover almost every eventuality. It is likely that the authoritarian syllabus is just the visible symptom of a deeper underlying problem, the breakdown of trust in the student–teacher relationship. When and why did this state of affairs arise, and how did it become so widespread?

One reason for this breakdown is undoubtedly the lengthening reach of local and national legislatures into the classrooms. For example, a faculty member at my university was surprised to be told that he had been reported for violating the law by leaving graded homework outside his office for students to pick up at any time. He contacted my office to find out if such an arrangement, convenient for both instructor and students, was indeed illegal. (These issues are dealt with in my own institution's *Undergraduate Instructor's Manual*,

but faculty ignore this document the way students ignore syllabi.)

I checked the manual and found that it was: "Graded exams, papers, and homework should never be left outside of office doors or otherwise unattended for students to claim; this is a violation of FERPA and an invitation to theft. Instructors should return graded material to students individually, in class or in office hours, or should arrange to mail final material to students once the semester has ended."

FERPA, as we all come to know sooner or later, stands for Family Educational Rights and Privacy Act, federal legislation that governs the privacy of student educational records.

10 So it has come to this, that the innocuous act of returning homework to students is now overseen by federal statute.

College faculty across the country are probably routinely violating this law one way or another, wittingly or not. For example, in my own 200-student physics course, I had been assigning homework for each class (which met three times a week). The assignments were handed in at the beginning of each class, graded, and returned at the beginning of the subsequent class.

This resulted in a lot of paper moving around: at the beginning of each class, 200 students had to hand in their new homework and pick up their graded assignments. In order to manage this process efficiently, I sorted the graded homework into assigned groups of four and placed the piles in front of the class, so that any one member could pick them up for the entire group before class began. The system worked so well that I did not lose any instructional time at all, despite the seeming complexity of the operation.

But was I breaking the law? Possibly. I was, after all, not returning homework individually, and students were picking up someone else's homework in addition to their own. But after doing this for 10 years for a total of about 4,000 students, I have not heard one student complaint. Maybe the students did not know about FERPA. But even if they knew, they did not care. I think that most students understand when something is done to advance legitimate educational goals, and they will look for rules to invoke only if they feel that the teacher does not have their best interest in mind. It is when that sense of trust is broken that rules and laws become important.

If we were to take the number of rules in a typical syllabus as a measure of that lack of trust, we would have to conclude that at present the college classroom is in a very sorry state indeed. Of course we need some rules and policies at the institutional level. But there should also be room for common sense and judgment about what is and is not appropriate in the classroom, and good learning practices should be the driving force. My concern is that trust, respect, and judgment are being squeezed out by an increasingly adversarial relationship between teachers and students.

15 There is no doubt that in the college classroom, the teacher wields a great deal of institutional power, and students have very little. College ideals about academic freedom are for the benefit of the faculty, and students know this. As long as we are not capricious, abusive, or flagrantly unjust, we can pretty much set the rules of the classroom, and students have to live with them. The problem is that many teachers are not using this flexibility to explore teaching methods that might enhance learning. Instead, we defend ourselves against potential challenges to our authority by wielding the course syllabus, our chief instrument of power, like a club.

My own institution's *Undergraduate Instructor's Manual* is full of useful information on how to prepare course materials, prepare and conduct exams, deal with students with disabilities, respect confidentiality, etc. All these issues are presented with the aim of helping the instructor—especially the novice— avoid the kind of blunders that might generate disputes.

But the tone of the sections that deal with course syllabi are formal and defensive, as if a committee had looked at all the possible

CONTEXT

FAMILY EDUCATIONAL RIGHTS AND PRIVACY ACT (FERPA)

The Family Educational Rights and Privacy Act (FERPA) (20 U.S. C. § 1232g; 34 CFR Part 99) is a Federal law that protects the privacy of student education records. The law applies to all schools that receive funds under an applicable program of the U.S. Department of Education.

FERPA gives parents certain rights with respect to their children's education records. These rights transfer to the student when he or she reaches the age of 18 or attends a school beyond the high school level. Students to whom the rights have transferred are "eligible students."

- Parents or eligible students have the right to inspect and review the student's education records maintained by the school. Schools are not required to provide copies of records unless, for reasons such as great distance, it is impossible for parents or eligible students to review the records. Schools may charge a fee for copies.
- Parents or eligible students have the right to request that a school correct records which they believe to be inaccurate or misleading. If the school decides not to amend the record, the parent or eligible student then has the right to a formal hearing. After the hearing, if the school still decides not to amend the record, the parent or eligible student has the right to place a statement with the record setting forth his or her view about the contested information.
- Generally, schools must have written permission from the parent or eligible student in order to release any information from a student's education record. However, FERPA allows schools to disclose those records, without consent, to the following parties or under the following conditions (34 CFR § 99.31):

  ❏ School officials with legitimate educational interest;
  ❏ Other schools to which a student is transferring;
  ❏ Specified officials for adult or evaluation purposes;
  ❏ Appropriate parties in connection with financial aid to a student;
  ❏ Organizations conducting certain studies for or on behalf of the school;
  ❏ Accrediting organizations;
  ❏ To comply with a judicial order or lawfully issued subponea;
  ❏ Appropriate officials in cases of health and safety;
  ❏ State and local authorities, within a juvenile justice system, pursuant to specific State law.

Schools may disclose, without consent, "directory" information such as a student's name, address, telephone number, date and place of birth, honors and awards, and dates of attendance. However, schools must tell parents and eligible students about directory information and allow parents and eligible students a reasonable amount of time to request that the school not disclose directory information about them. Schools must notify parents and eligible students annually of their rights under FERPA. The actual means of notification (special letter, inclusion in a PTA bulletin, student handbook, or newspaper article) is left to the discretion of each school.

things that could go wrong and all the possible laws that might apply, and then had devised rules to prevent disaster. New faculty are also given friendly advice by academic administrators that the syllabus is like a legally binding contract, so they should put in it everything that they expect of students and go over it on the first day of class.

I have before me a legal newsletter from another university in which the author clearly lays out the implied contractual nature of the syllabus:

> The most common of these types of implied agreements, at least from the faculty perspective, is the written syllabus and/or oral recitation of the rules, policies, procedures, and expectations given to students by faculty at the beginning of each academic course. When a dispute arises with a student over course requirements, satisfactory resolution of the dispute frequently rests on the legal enforceability of the terms and conditions of these implied agreements.

20 The author then proceeds to describe what a faculty member needs to put in the syllabus in order to have a solid legal case in the event that a dispute with a student should go to court.

Given this attitude, it should not be surprising that the classroom has become a quasi-courtroom. I have seen course syllabi that extend over 20 pages. A colleague told me the he spent almost all the time of his first three-hour class walking the students carefully through the syllabus, because otherwise he could not be sure that they were aware of all the rules he had established for them to follow. But the result of such an attitude is that we end up viewing all students as potential courtroom adversaries.

I am sure that it is not pleasant for students or teachers or universities to have to go through judicial proceedings because of some classroom disagreement. But why do we assume that this is the worst thing that could

happen and must be avoided at all costs? If the price that we pay for our legal protection is the creation of a controlling classroom atmosphere that stifles learning, isn't that a much worse result? Repeated questions by students such as "Will this be on the test?" and "Do we have to know this?" are symptoms of the extent to which following rules has replaced learning as the chief goal in the classroom.

To begin to understand the phenomenon of creeping authoritarianism, I need go no further than my own courses and syllabi and see how they have evolved over the years. When I started teaching my large introductory physics courses, I was convinced that the only way to keep on top of things and maintain clarity, fairness, and uniformity was to be highly organized.

So my syllabi were very detailed, laying out what topics would be covered and when, all the deadlines for homework and dates for exams, detailed penalties for missing anything, and the exact format for writing papers (down to page length, fonts, and font sizes). I even had instructions for how the homework sheets were to be folded before being handed in, and students lost points if they folded them incorrectly or not at all.

25 What is telling is that my monster syllabus came about even though I wasn't trying to prevent legal actions. I had a good educational reasons for all the rules, and for dealing efficiently with large classes I can still justify a few of them. But the list of rules grew year by year, driven by its own internal logic. Initially, for example, I had no penalties for missing deadlines, since I assumed students would meet them. When a significant number of students did not, my syllabus the following year had penalties that increased each day that the assignment was late.

I also didn't have penalties for papers that had typographical or grammatical errors; I simply assumed that students would proofread anything they handed in. When that didn't happen, I introduced detailed penalties for those infractions too. Each added rule produced requests for exceptions from students who couldn't meet it. So other rules were tacked on to deal with the possible range of exceptions. And so on. Like Abou Ben Adham,* my name led all the rest when it came to comprehensive, detailed, and authoritarian syllabi.

I confess that my system worked extremely well. The papers came in on time, carefully proofread and edited. Homework was handed in like clockwork, folded correctly. I, like so many teachers before me, had discovered the power of the detailed syllabus to achieve precisely targeted goals. That power went to my head, like power usually does, and I began to think that I could create a rule to achieve whatever I wanted. Some departmental colleagues, marveling at the smoothness with which my course was run, adopted many features of my syllabus for their own courses. Thus are the viruses of complex syllabi spread through academia.

But I discovered that there were important things that I just could not do with my syllabus. I could not make students care about the work, be creative and original, be considerate of others, or write and speak well. All I could do was force them to do very specific things. As I started reading the research literature on good teaching practices, I came to realize that this failure was not due to my technical inability to devise ingenious rubrics to add to my syllabus to achieve those more worthwhile goals. Rather, it was that the very act of creating detailed course requirements and forcing students to obey them actually worked against the higher goal of learning.

The emphasis on tight classroom management, although widespread, goes counter to some of the most compelling research on learning. In *The Learner-Centered Classroom*, Maryellen Weimer argues that learning ensues when instructors relinquish much of their power and cede some decisionmaking power to students. Alfie Kohn, in *Punished by Rewards*, points out that student motivation is enhanced when rewards and punishments are minimized, students are given choices about what and how they learn, and students and teachers collaborate in classroom-policy decisionmaking.

30 In *Power in the Classroom*, Virginia Richmond and James McCroskey emphasize that students have more power than we realize and that the more we try to exercise direct authority, the more likely it is that they will devise ways to thwart us, leading to reduced learning. Robert Boice's work on classroom incivilities in *Advice for the New Faculty Member* shows how student resistance to learning is not necessarily innate but arises from the atmosphere created early on in the classroom.

All this made sense, once I realized what I should have known all along, that learning is an inherently voluntary act that you can no more force than you can force someone to love you. Authoritarianism and fostering a love of learning just do not go together. If they did, the best learning should occur in prison education programs, where the "students" can be coerced to do almost anything.

When I stepped back and looked at my syllabus in the light of this new understanding, it appeared completely foreign to my conception of what an ideal teacher–student relationship should be. Somewhere along the way, I had lost sight of the fact that a learning community has to be a community in the best sense of the word. I had made my classroom into a dictatorship. But it was a dictatorship nonetheless, since I unilaterally made all the decisions that affected the students. My focus on having the trains run on time had prevented me from achieving more fundamental and important learning goals.

I became increasingly uncomfortable with the way my classroom was structured. So when I had the chance to teach a new seminar on the evolution of scientific ideas to a much smaller class of 17 sophomores, I decided that the time had come to make changes. But rather than make incremental changes I decide—like an addict who concludes that the only way to become free of the dependency is

*"Abou Ben Adhem" is the name of a poem written by James Henry Leigh Hunt (1784–1859), the last stanza of which reads, "The next night/ [The Angel] came again with a great wakening light,/ And showed the names whom love of God had blessed,/ And lo! Ben Adhem's name led all the rest."

to make a clean break—to dispense with a formal written syllabus altogether.

I walked into the first class with only a reading list and a tentative schedule of readings for the first few weeks. We did not talk about rules or grades at all; instead we went straight into a discussion of the course subject matter. While I felt almost naked going into the class with no syllabus in my hand or already posted on the Web, the students did not seem to be at all concerned by its absence. No one mentioned it, lending further support to the thesis that no student ever reads it.

35 It was only after about five weeks into the course, when the students were getting their essays returned with detailed feedback, that one asked whether the essays would be eventually assigned a grade. It was then that we had a class discussion on the topic of course requirements. I told them what my learning goals for the seminar were and said that I was open to discussing how they would be evaluated. However, I also said that I had an ethical obligation to my institution to ensure that the grades were meaningful measures of learning, and also to my discipline to ensure that the course was advancing knowledge in that area.

Within those constraints, we reached a consensus on what the students would need to do to reach the learning goals and to earn their course grades. We selected a fairly traditional mix of short essays, a research paper, a formal presentation, and participation. We also decided on the approximate weights of the assignments, with some flexibility for individual choice.

We reached an agreement about broad criteria for evaluating each item in the mix, with the consensus being that they would leave it up to me to make the final judgment based on my experience and expertise. What was especially interesting to me was that they did not want a reductionist, detailed, itemized scoring of class participation (such as keeping track of how many times each person spoke, the quality of what they said, etc.), which is exactly the

kind of thing a legalistic syllabus might spell out. They felt that this led to artificial, points-related behavior and hindered genuine discussion and learning.

They preferred that I make a holistic judgment. I told them that ultimately, assigning a grade has an unavoidably subjective component and that the system would work only if they trusted that I would judge them fairly. The students seemed to treat that statement as if it were obvious, and it went unchallenged. (This is another example of the differences between student and teacher perceptions. While we go to great lengths to persuade students that our grading is objective they, despite our protestations, seem to assume that it is quite subjective.)

We also set up a schedule of deadlines for assignments, again with some flexibility built in to accommodate the students' individual schedules (we sometimes forget that students have other courses and even personal lives outside of our classes) and with respect for mine (I have a life too).

40 In about 30 minutes we thus jointly created a de-facto syllabus. There was no controversy, though the students were extremely surprised that they were being given such leeway in setting up the structure of the course. The course has ended, and so far no one has sued me or even complained about grades or course requirements. A few students missed some of their self-determined deadlines, but only by a few days, and they were profusely apologetic. The students came to class, discussed serious topics in a relaxed way, and wrote excellent papers on topics they chose for themselves and seemed really to care about. In fact, the end of the semester brought with it genuine sadness that we were going our separate ways. It really felt like a community, and the semester was one of the most enjoyable teaching experiences of my life.

Will this idyllic result occur every time? Probably not. When I speak about my experience with colleagues, I am asked what I would do if a student consistently missed deadlines or took advantage in some way of the flexibility and freedom I provided. I say I don't know. I would deal with such situations on an ad hoc, case-by-case basis, because each such case is likely to be caused by factors unique to that individual student. Tolstoy's famous opening line in Anna Karenina* that "all happy families resemble one another, but each unhappy family is unhappy in its own way" applies to students too.

By devising complex general rules to cope with any and all anticipated behavior, we tend to constrain, alienate, and dehumanize students, and we remove a great deal of the enjoyment from the learning experience. Surely students are like us in flourishing under conditions of freedom. Why is it that given the choice between creating a freer classroom atmosphere that risks the occasional problem and establishing an authoritarian classroom that tries to anticipate and thwart any and all problems, we choose the latter? Surely creating learning conditions that benefit almost all students should be preferred to those aimed at protecting ourselves against the occasional malcontent.

The syllabus has also become a defensive shield against grade complaints. It is rare that students will complain directly to the professor that they did not learn much in the course. They might make this serious charge to their peers, but complaints to teachers are almost always about grades or other sanctions. The formal written syllabus, with all the lists of things that students must and must not do and highly detailed grading schemes that outline how students are to be evaluated, is the teacher's preemptive strike against such complaints.

At some level, we know that grading is an art, not a science. We should come to our judgments with great care and all the expertise, objectivity, and honesty we can muster, but they are judgments nonetheless. Elaborate grading schemes merely create an illusion of

objectivity and hide that judgment under a shroud of numbers. If a student complains, the syllabus with its formulas can provide a spurious precision that can mute criticism. We can sigh regretfully and tell the student. "You needed to get an 80 to get a B and unfortunately you scored only 78.6."

45 Complex and precise grading schemes remind me of the highly dramatic ritual that occurs in football games if there is doubt as to whether the ball has been advanced the required 10 yards. A hush falls on the stadium as the game is halted and two officials are called from the sidelines to carefully place the 10-yard chains on the field. The referee then signals that either the effort to advance the ball 10 yards has failed by a few inches or has just barely succeeded. That this is an elaborate farce can be appreciated by noting that where the ball is spotted at the end of the play is only a rough approximation, as are the estimations of the starting point and of the distances advanced in previous plays. But the players and fans accept the result unquestioningly, cowed by the solemnity of the ritual.

The research of Patricia King and Karen Strohm Kitchener, summarized in their book Developing Reflective Judgment, indicates that our incoming college students tend to be largely pre-reflective in their thinking. They view knowledge in black/white, right/wrong terms, and colleges do not do particularly well in nudging them to take a more nuanced view of knowledge or in teaching them how to weigh evidence and arguments in order to arrive at reasoned judgments. When we try to hide the role that judgment makes in our own decisions, we may be inadvertently reinforcing their low-level view of knowledge.

If we dispense with the authoritarian syllabus as a weapon, then the challenge for teachers is to give students confidence that we have the competence to make judgments about their performance, that we have meaningful criteria for doing so, that our assessments are meaningful measures of important

*Widely considered a masterpiece of world literature, Leo Tolstoy's Anna Karenina was first published in 1877. It tells the story of a beautiful woman who is a member of the social elite in St. Petersburg, Russia, until she leaves her husband to live with a handsome military officer, Count Vronsky. Her husband refuses to give her a divorce and keeps her from seeing their son. Eventually, Vronsky loses interest in Anna. Abandoned by her lover and unwilling to return to a husband she detests, Anna commits suicide by throwing herself under a train.

learning, and that we have the impartiality to make honest judgments. This is a harder task than creating a watertight syllabus, primarily because it requires a change in mindset on the part of teachers. But in the long run it results in a much more rewarding experience for both teachers and students.

If we are not to be adversaries in the classroom, then what is the appropriate relationship between teachers and students? As I see it, it is that of good neighbors in a small community. The classroom works best when students and teachers perceive it as a place where there is a continuing conversation among interested people, similar to what one might have with neighbors and friends. A sense of community is not created by rules and laws but by a sense of mutual respect and tolerance. Good neighborliness cannot be legislated—it can only be learned by example and experience, and it flourishes in an atmosphere of trust and acceptance of differences.

Can we recover the ideal of the classroom as a collegial conversation among faculty and students where the role of the instructor is to provide the insight that experience and expertise provides, without invoking the institutional power vested in us to coerce students? Or have we gone too far down the path of authoritarian, adversarial classrooms to regain that level of trust, assuming we did have it at some point?

50 When I tell people of my attempts to create a freer classroom atmosphere, I am reminded of those political discussions in which the future of this or that authoritarian country is discussed, and the question is raised as to whether the people of that country are "ready for democracy."

I am asked, are students mature enough to deal with such freedom responsibly? Will they take advantage of the situation to not do any serious work? Might they even sue because the teacher did something that was not in the syllabus? All these things might happen, but this is a chance that I have to take. The possibility that my students may not be ready for democracy worries me a little, but the thought that they should be ready for and accepting of authoritarianism troubles me a great deal more.

I am looking forward to teaching the seminar again. And once more I will start without a syllabus.

Questions for Discussion

1. Singham writes that "students don't seem to be offended by being ordered around in course syllabi." Has this been true in your experience? How carefully do you read the syllabi you receive? At what point would you feel a teacher is patronizing you by spelling out rules that should be common sense? How would you feel about taking a class in which the instructor did not distribute a syllabus?

2. What do you think of the FERPA policy that prohibits instructors from leaving graded assignments unattended? How would you respond if you volunteered to take a paper to an absent classmate you would see later that day and the instructor refused to give the paper to you? Why do you think the federal government has come to have the power of deciding how an instructor can return an assignment to a student?

3. What does Singham mean by "creeping authoritarianism"? How does he illustrate it?

4. To what extent is the need for rules conditioned by class size? If a class should be like a small "community," how large could it grow before community broke down?

5. Singham writes that detailed syllabi "tend to constrain, alienate, and dehumanize students." Can you identify other practices in higher education that have this effect?

6. Consider the football ritual to which Singham devotes paragraph 45. Can you think of other rituals that don't make sense once you examine them critically but that nevertheless reassure people? What does this suggest about the nature of ritual?

7. Consider paragraph 51 of this argument. What are the questions within it designed to achieve? What assumptions about audience inform Singham's position that it is better to offer democracy prematurely than to become authoritarian?

③ BELL HOOKS, "Toward a Radical Feminist Pedagogy"

In the late 1970s and early 1980s colleges and universities began to establish new programs in Women's Studies. These programs, which grew out of the feminist movement, encouraged students to examine the role of gender and power relations in society and challenged long-standing ideas about teaching and learning in American education. But like the women's movement itself, Women's Studies faced resistance and often struggled to gain acceptance as a legitimate academic discipline. That sense of struggle is a central part of the vision of feminist teaching presented in the following essay by scholar and writer bell hooks. hooks argues for a kind of education that is both collaborative and confrontational, one that intentionally challenges convention. The very title of hooks's essay is provocative, suggesting that the purpose of her approach to education is radical change. Perhaps it is that sense of purpose that continues to invite controversy, because despite the growth of Women's Studies programs in American higher education and despite the acceptance of feminism as a school of thought, both Women's Studies and feminist theory continue to face criticism inside and outside educational circles. A distinguished professor of English at City College of New York, hooks has been an insistent voice for a progressive view of education based on feminist theory. Her many books about education and culture focus attention on issues of race, gender, and social class. As you read the following essay, which was published in 1989 in her book *Talking Back*, compare her sense of the purpose of education to your own view.

Toward a Radical Feminist Pedagogy

BELL HOOKS

1 My favorite teacher in high school was Miss Annie Mae Moore, a short, stout black woman. She had taught my mama and her sisters. She could tell story after story about their fast ways, their wildness. She could tell me ways I was like mama, ways I was most truly my own self. She could catch hold of you and turn you around, set you straight (these were the comments folk made about her teaching)—so that we would know what we were facing when we entered her classroom. Passionate in her teaching, confident that her work in life was a pedagogy of liberation (words she would not have used but lived instinctively), one that

would address and confront our realities as black children growing up in the segregated South, black children growing up within a white-supremacist culture. Miss Moore knew that if we were to be fully self-realized, then her work, and the work of all our progressive teachers, was not to teach us solely the knowledge in books, but to teach us an oppositional world view—different from that of our exploiters and oppressors, a world view that would enable us to see ourselves not through the lens of racism or racist stereotypes but one that would enable us to focus clearly and succinctly, to look at ourselves, at the world around us, critically—analytically—to see ourselves first and foremost as striving for wholeness, for unity of heart, mind, body and spirit.

It was as a student in segregated black schools called Booker T. Washington and Crispus Attucks that I witnessed the transformative power of teaching, of pedagogy. In particular, those teachers who approached their work as though it was indeed a pedagogy, a science of teaching, requiring diverse strategies, approaches, explorations, experimentation, and risks, demonstrated the value—the political power—of teaching. Their work was truly education for critical consciousness. In these segregated schools, the teachers were almost all black women. Many of them had chosen teaching at a historical moment when they were required by custom to remain single and childless, to have no visible erotic or sexual life. Among them were exceptional teachers who gave to their work a passion, a devotion that made it seem a true calling, a true vocation. They were the teachers who conceptualized oppositional world views, who taught us young black women to exult and glory in the power and beauty of our intellect. They offered to us a legacy of liberatory pedagogy that demanded active resistance and rebellion against sexism and racism. They embodied in their work, in their lives (for none of them appeared as tortured spinsters estranged and alienated from the world around them) a feminist spirit. They were active participants in black community, shaping our futures, mapping our intellectual terrains, sharing revolutionary fervor and vision. I write these words, this essay to express the honor and respect I have for them because they have been my pedagogical guardians. Their work has had a profound impact on my consciousness, on my development as a teacher.

During years of graduate schools, I waited for that phase of study when we would focus on the meaning and significance of pedagogy, when we would learn about teaching, about how to teach. That moment never arrived. For years I have relied on those earlier models of

excellent teaching to guide me. Most specifically, I understood from the teachers in those segregated schools that the work of any teacher committed to the full self-realization of students was necessarily and fundamentally radical, that ideas were not neutral, that to teach in a way that liberates, that expands consciousness, that awakens is to challenge domination at its very core. It is this pedagogy that Paulo Freire calls "education as the practice of freedom." In his introduction to Freire's *Pedagogy of the Oppressed,* Richard Shaull writes:

> Education either functions as an instrument which is used to facilitate the integration of the younger generation into the logic of the present system and bring about conformity to it, or it becomes "the practice of freedom," the means by which men and women deal critically and creatively with reality and discover how to participate in the transformation of their world.

A liberatory feminist movement aims to transform society by eradicating patriarchy, by ending sexism and sexist oppression, by challenging the politics of domination on all fronts. Feminist pedagogy can only be liberatory if it is truly revolutionary because the mechanisms of appropriation within white-supremacist, capitalist patriarchy are able to co-opt with tremendous ease that which merely appears radical or subversive. Within the United States, contemporary feminist movement is sustained in part by the efforts academic women make to constitute the university setting as a central site for the development and dissemination of feminist thought. Women's Studies has been the location of this effort. Given the way universities work to reinforce and perpetuate the status quo, the way knowledge is offered as commodity, Women's Studies can easily become a place where revolutionary feminist thought and feminist activism are submerged or made secondary to the goals of academic careerism. Without diminishing in any way our

CONTEXT

One of the most influential educational theorists of the twentieth century, Paulo Freire (1921–1997) was a teacher, activist, and writer whose many books and articles outlined a revolutionary theory of education. Born in Brazil, Freire developed his early ideas about "liberatory education" by working with illiterate Brazilian peasants, for which he was jailed and then exiled in 1964. He returned to Brazil in 1979 and later served as minister of education. His best known book is *Pedagogy of the Oppressed* (1970), in which he describes his theory of education as a means of personal and political transformation. Some scholars consider Freire's ideas to be the basis for feminist education of the kind that hooks describes in this essay.

Feminist education is a general term referring to an approach to teaching based on feminist theory. Often, programs based on feminist theory are called Women's Studies programs. According to the Center for Women's and Gender Studies at the University of Texas at Austin, there are more than 600 Women's Studies programs in the United States. The center defines the purposes of Women's and Gender Studies as fostering "multi-disciplinary research and teaching that focuses on women, gender, sexuality, and feminist issues [and supporting] the intersections of the above with age, class, race, ethnicity, and nationality."

struggle as academics striving to succeed in institutions, such effort is fully compatible with liberatory feminist struggle only when we consciously, carefully, and strategically link the two. When this connection is made initially but not sustained, or when it is never evident, Women's Studies becomes either an exotic terrain for those politically chic few seeking affirmation or a small settlement within the larger institutional structure where women (and primarily white women) have a power base, which rather than being oppositional simply mirrors the status quo. When feminist struggle is the central foundation for feminist education, Women's Studies and the feminist classroom (which can exist outside the domain of Women's Studies) can be places where education is the practice of freedom, the place for liberatory pedagogy.

5   At this historical moment, there is a crisis of engagement within universities, for when knowledge becomes commoditized, then much authentic learning ceases. Students who want to learn hunger for a space where they can be challenged intellectually. Students also suffer, as many of us who teach do, from a crisis of meaning, unsure about what has value in life, unsure even about whether it is important to stay alive. They long for a context where their subjective needs can be integrated with study, where the primary focus is a broader spectrum of ideas and modes of inquiry, in short a dialectical context where there is serious and rigorous critical exchange. This is an important and exciting time for feminist pedagogy because in theory and practice our work meets these needs.

Feminist education*—the feminist classroom—is and should be a place where there is a sense of struggle, where there is visible acknowledgement of the union of theory and practice, where we work together as teachers and students to overcome the estrangement and alienation that have become so much the norm in the contemporary university. Most importantly, feminist pedagogy should engage students in a learning process that makes the world "more rather than less real." In my classrooms, we work to dispel the notion that our experience is not a "real world" experience. This is especially easy since gender is such a pressing issue in contemporary life. Every aspect of popular culture alerts us to the reality that folks are thinking about gender in both reactionary and progressive ways. What is important is that they are thinking critically. And it is this space that allows for the possibility of feminist intervention, whether it be in our classroom or in the life of students outside the classroom. Lately there has been a truly diverse body of students coming to my classes and other feminist classes at universities all around the United States. Many of us have been wondering "what's going on" or "why are all these men, and white men, in the class." This changing student body reflects the concern about gender issues, that it is one of the real important issues in people's private lives that is addressed academically. Freire writes, "Education as the practice of freedom—as opposed to education as the practice of domination—denies that we are abstract, isolated, independent, and unattached to the world; it also denies that the world exists as a reality apart from us."

To make a revolutionary feminist pedagogy, we must relinquish our ties to traditional ways of teaching that reinforce domination. This is very difficult. Women's Studies courses are often viewed as not seriously academic because so much "personal stuff" is discussed. Fear that their courses will be seen as "gut" classes has led many feminist professors to rely more on traditional pedagogical styles. This is unfortunate. Certainly, the radical alternative to the status quo should never have been simply an inversion. That is to say, critical of the absence of any focus on personal experience in traditional classrooms, such focus becomes the central characteristic of the feminist classroom. This model must be viewed critically because a class can still be reinforcing domination, not transforming consciousness about gender, even as the "personal" is the ongoing topic of conversation.

To have a revolutionary feminist pedagogy we must first focus on the teacher–student relationship and the issue of power. How do we as feminist teachers use power in a way that is not coercive, dominating? Many women have had difficulty asserting power in the feminist classroom for fear that to do so would be to exercise domination. Yet we must acknowledge that our role as teacher is a position of power over others. We can use that power in ways that diminish or in ways that enrich and it is this choice that should distinguish feminist pedagogy from ways of teaching that reinforce domination. One simple way to alter the way one's "power" as teacher is experienced in the classroom is to elect not to assume the posture of all-knowing professors. This is also difficult. When we acknowledge that we do not know everything, that we do not have all the answers, we risk students leaving our classrooms and telling others that we are not prepared. It is important to make it clear to students that we are prepared and that the willingness to be open and honest about what we do not know is a gesture of respect for them.

To be oppositional in the feminist classroom one must have a standard of valuation that differs from the norm. Many of us tried new ways of teaching without changing the standards by which we evaluated our work. We often left the classroom feeling uncertain about the learning process or even concerned that we were failing as teachers. Let me share a particular problem I have faced. My classroom style is very confrontational. It is a model of pedagogy that is based on the assumption that many students will take courses from me who are afraid to assert themselves as critical thinkers, who are afraid to speak (especially students from oppressed and exploited groups). The revolutionary hope that I bring to the classroom is that it will become a space where they can come to voice. Unlike the stereotypical feminist model that suggests

COMPLICATION

Feminist education and Women's Studies programs have long been the object of intense criticism, which often focuses on the charge that such programs do not have the same kind of intellectual foundation that more traditional disciplines in the sciences and the humanities have. In 1993 writer Karen Lehrman reignited the controversy with an article in *Mother Jones* magazine in which she examined the state of Women's Studies programs in the United States. She wrote,

> In many classes discussions alternate between the personal and the political, with mere pit stops at the academic. Sometimes they are filled with unintelligible post-structuralist jargon; sometimes they consist of consciousness-raising psychobabble, with the students' feelings and experiences valued as much as anything the professor or texts have to offer. Regardless, the guiding principle of most of the classes is oppression, and problems are almost inevitably reduced to relationships of power. "Diversity" is the mantra of both students and professors, but it doesn't apply to political opinions.
>
> Not every women's studies course suffers from these flaws. In fact, the rigor and perspective of individual programs and classes vary widely, and feminist academics have debated nearly every aspect of the field. But it seems that the vast majority of women's studies professors rely, to a greater or lesser extent, on a common set of feminist theories. Put into practice, these theories have the potential to undermine the goals not only of a liberal education, but of feminism itself.

Lehrman's article provoked much debate about Women's Studies programs. Since her article was published, many critics have continued to charge that Women's Studies programs lack intellectual rigor.

women best come to voice in an atmosphere of safety (one in which we are all going to be kind and nurturing), I encourage students to work at coming to voice in an atmosphere where they may be afraid or see themselves at risk. The goal is to enable all students, not just an assertive few, to feel empowered in a rigorous, critical discussion. Many students find this pedagogy difficult, frightening, and very demanding. They do not usually come away from my class talking about how much they enjoyed the experience.

10 One aspect of traditional models of teaching that I had not surrendered was that longing for immediate recognition of my value as a teacher, and immediate affirmation. Often I did not feel liked or affirmed and this was difficult for me to accept. I reflected on my student experiences and the reality that I often learned the most in classes that I did not enjoy and complained about, which helped me to work on the traditional assumption that immediate positive feedback is a signifier of worth. Concurrently, I found that students who often felt that they hated a class with me would return later to say how much they learned, that they understood that it was the different style that made it hard as well as the different demands. I began to see that courses that work to shift paradigms, to change consciousness, cannot necessarily be experienced immediately as fun or positive or safe and this was not a worthwhile criteria to use in an evaluation.

In the feminist classroom, it is important to define a term of engagement, to identify what we mean when we say that a course will be taught from a feminist perspective. Often the initial explanations about pedagogy will have a serious impact on the way students experience a course. It is important to talk about pedagogical strategy. For a time, I assumed that students would just get the hang of it, would see that I was trying to teach in a different way and accept it without explanation. Often, that meant I explained after being criticized. It is important for feminist professors to explain

not only what will differ about the classroom experience but to openly acknowledge that students must consider whether they wish to be in such a learning space. On a basic level, students are often turned off by the fact that I take attendance, but because I see the classroom experience as constituting a unique learning experience, to miss class is to really lose a significant aspect of the process. Whether or not a student attends class affects grading and this bothers students who are not accustomed to taking attendance seriously. Another important issue for me has been that each student participate in classroom discussion, that each student have a voice. This is a practice that I think is important not because every student has something valuable to say (this is not always so), but often students who do have meaningful comments to contribute are silent. In my classes, everyone's voice is heard as students read paragraphs which may explore a particular issue. They do not have the opportunity to refuse to read paragraphs. When I hear their voices, I become more aware of information they may not know that I can provide. Whether a class is large or small, I try to talk with all students individually or in small groups so that I have a sense of their needs. How can we transform consciousness if we do not have some sense of where the students are intellectually, psychically?

Concern with how and what students are learning validates and legitimates a focus, however small, on personal confession in classroom discussions. I encourage students to relate the information they are learning to the personal identities they are working to socially construct, to change, to affirm. If the goal of personal confession is not narcissism, it must take place within a critical framework where it is related to material that is being discussed. When, for example, I am teaching Toni Morrison's novel, *The Bluest Eye,* I may have students write personal paragraphs about the relationship between race and physical beauty, which they read in class. Their paragraphs may reveal pain, woundedness as they explore and express ways they are victimized by racism and sexism, or they may express ideas that are racist and sexist. Yet the paragraphs enable them to approach the text in a new way. They may read the novel differently. They may be able to be more critical and analytical. If this does not happen, then the paragraphs fail as a pedagogical tool. To make feminist classrooms the site of transformative learning experiences, we must constantly try new methods, new approaches.

Finally, we cannot have a revolutionary feminist pedagogy if we do not have revolutionary feminists in the classroom. Women's Studies courses must do more than offer a different teaching style; we must really challenge issues of sexism and sexist oppression both by what we teach and how we teach. This is truly a collective effort. We must learn from one another, sharing ideas and pedagogical strategies. Although I have invited feminist colleagues to come and participate in my classes, they do not. Classroom territoriality is another traditional taboo. Yet if we are to learn from one another, if we are to develop a concrete strategy for radicalizing our classrooms, we must be more engaged as a group. We must be willing to deconstruct this power dimension, to challenge, change and create new approaches. If we are to move toward a revolutionary feminist pedagogy, we must challenge ourselves and one another to restore to feminist struggle its radical and subversive dimension. We must be willing to restore the spirit of risk—to be fast, wild, to be able to take hold, turn around, transform.

Questions for Discussion

1. What crisis does hooks see in education? How can Women's Studies programs help address that crisis, in her view?

2. What does hooks mean when she writes that knowledge has become a commodity? What evidence does she offer to support this assertion? Do you agree with her? Why or why not?

3. Why does hooks teach in a way that is confrontational? What is the goal of such an approach to teaching? hooks states that many students find her approach uncomfortable. Why does it not concern her that some of her students do not enjoy her classes? Should it concern her, in your view? Explain.

4. hooks argues that personal experience should be the central focus of the kind of feminist classroom she advocates. Evaluate the way in which hooks uses her experience as a student and a teacher to help her make her argument. How effective is her use of personal experience in this essay?

5. hooks has been both praised and criticized for her unconventional writing style as a scholar. How would you characterize her style? In what ways might her writing style be considered appropriate for the argument she is making about education in this essay?

6. How effectively does hooks address possible objections to her view? What questions would you raise about hooks's approach to education? What might your reaction to her essay reveal about your views regarding the purpose of education?

④ LEWIS THOMAS, "The Art of Teaching Science"

Lewis Thomas (1913–1993) lived through a period when the practice of medicine underwent dramatic changes as physicians became more specialized, more able to draw upon new procedures and medications, and less likely to visit patients in their homes. A graduate of Harvard Medical School, Thomas was active as both a physician and a researcher who specialized in immunology. He taught medicine at Tulane University, New York University, and Yale University in addition to being an administrator. At New York University he was dean of the School of Medicine, and he later became president of the Sloan-Kettering Institute in New York, making it one of the world's most prominent sites for cancer research. But throughout his busy life Thomas found time to write. As a student at Harvard during the great economic depression of the 1930s, he helped support himself by writing poems that were published in the *Atlantic Monthly, Harper's Bazaar,* and the *Saturday Evening Post.* And in 1971 he accepted an invitation from the editor of the prestigious *New England Journal of Medicine* to contribute a short essay about biology each month. The terms of this offer were simple: Thomas would not be paid for his writing, but his essays would be published without editorial interference. Three years later, twenty-nine of these essays were published in a book, *The Lives of the Cell,* and Thomas began to attract a national audience of readers interested in science and engaged by his reflections. He subsequently contributed to many periodicals and published six additional volumes of essays. "The Art of Teaching Science" was first published in the *New York Times Magazine* in 1982. As you read it, consider the extent to which your education in science was shaped by the practices to which Thomas objects.

The Art of Teaching Science

LEWIS THOMAS

1 Everyone seems to agree that there is something wrong with the way science is being taught these days. But no one is at all clear about when it went wrong or what is to be done about it. The term "scientific illiteracy" has become almost a cliché in educational circles. Graduate schools blame the colleges; colleges blame the secondary schools; the high schools blame the elementary schools, which, in turn, blame the family.

I suggest that the scientific community itself is partly, perhaps largely, to blame. Moreover, if there are disagreements between the world of the humanities and the scientific enterprise as to the place and importance of science in a liberal-arts education and the role of science in 20th-century culture, I believe that the scientists are themselves responsible for a general misunderstanding of what they are really up to.

During the last half-century, we have been teaching the sciences as though they were the same collection of academic subjects as always, and—here is what has really gone wrong—as though they would always be the same. Students learn today's biology, for example, the same way we learned Latin when I was in high school long ago: first, the fundamentals; then, the underlying laws; next, the essential grammar and, finally, the reading of texts. Once mastered, that was that: Latin was Latin and forever after would always be Latin. History, once learned, was history. And biology was precisely-biology, a vast array of hard facts to be learned as fundamentals, followed by a reading of the texts.

Furthermore, we have been teaching science as if its acts were somehow superior to the facts in all other scholarly disciplines—more fundamental, more solid, less subject to subjectivism, immutable. English literature is not just one way of thinking; it is all sorts of ways; poetry is a moving target; the facts that underlie art, architecture and music are not really hard facts, and you can change them any way you like by arguing about them. But science, it appears, is an altogether different kind of learning: an unambiguous, unalterable and endlessly useful display of data that only needs to be packaged and installed somewhere in one's temporal lobe in order to achieve a full understanding of the natural world.

5 And, of course, it is not like this at all. In real life, every field of science is incomplete, and most of them—whatever the record of accomplishment during the last 200 years—are still in their very earliest stages. In the fields I know best, among the life sciences, it is required that the most expert and sophisticated minds be capable of changing course—often with a great lurch—every few years. In some branches of biology the mind-changing is occurring with accelerating velocity. Next week's issue of any scientific journal can turn a whole field upside down, shaking out any number of

immutable ideas and installing new bodies of dogma. This is an almost everyday event in physics, in chemistry, in materials research, in neurobiology, in genetics, in immunology.

On any Tuesday morning, if asked, a good working scientist will tell you with some self-satisfaction that the affairs of his field are nicely in order, that things are finally looking clear and making sense, and all is well. But come back again on another Tuesday, and the roof may have just fallen in on his life's work. All the old ideas—last week's ideas in some cases—are no longer good ideas. The hard facts have softened, melted away and vanished under the pressure of new hard facts. Something strange has happened. And it is this very strangeness of nature that makes science engrossing, that keeps bright people at it, and that ought to be at the center of science teaching.

The conclusions reached in science are always, when looked at closely, far more provisional and tentative than are most of the assumptions arrived at by our colleagues in the humanities. But we do not talk much in public about this, nor do we teach this side of science. We tend to say instead: These are the facts of the matter, and this is what the facts signify. Go and learn them, for they will be the same forever.

By doing this, we miss opportunity after opportunity to recruit young people into science, and we turn off a good many others who would never dream of scientific careers but who emerge from their education with the impression that science is fundamentally boring.

Sooner or later, we will have to change this way of presenting science. We might begin by looking more closely at the common ground that science shares with all disciplines, particularly with the humanities and with social and behavioral science. For there is indeed such a common ground. It is called bewilderment. There are more than seven times seven types of ambiguity in science, all awaiting analysis. The poetry of Wallace Stevens is crystal clear alongside the genetic code.

*As Thomas implies, the "age of reason" is often used to describe the eighteenth century, a period in which the educated believed in the excellence of the human mind and optimistically thought that intelligence—informed by knowledge and shaped by logic—could solve almost any problem. This phrase also provided the title for a work published in the late eighteenth century, *The Age of Reason* (1795), by the American patriot Thomas Paine.

†F. R. Leavis (1895–1978) and Edmund Wilson (1895–1972) were important literary critics. Leavis was an influential advocate of what is called "New Criticism," which was an approach to literature emphasizing that the meaning of a work could be determined exclusively from the text of that work. During the 1920s, Wilson's reviews of writers such as Ernest Hemingway, F. Scott Fitzgerald, and Eugene O'Neill helped build their reputations. John Ruskin (1819–1900) was the most important art critic in the English-speaking world during much of his lifetime, and the college of art at Oxford University—where he taught for many years—is named after him. What all three men have in common is that they eventually turned to what today would be called *cultural criticism*, publishing books that called attention to social injustice and explored the challenges of contemporary life.

10 One of the complaints about science is that it tends to flatten everything. In its deeply reductionist way, it is said, science removes one mystery after another, leaving nothing in the place of mystery but data. I have even heard this claim as explanation for the drift of things in modern art and modern music: Nothing is left to contemplate except randomness and senselessness; God is nothing but a pair of dice, loaded at that. Science is linked somehow to the despair of the 20th-century mind. There is almost nothing unknown and surely nothing unknowable. Blame science.

I prefer to turn things around in order to make precisely the opposite case. Science, especially 20th-century science, has provided us with a glimpse of something we never really knew before; the revelation of human ignorance. We have been accustomed to the belief, from one century to another, that except for one or two mysteries we more or less comprehend everything on earth. Every age, not just the 18th century, regarded itself as the Age of Reason,* and we have never lacked for explanations of the world and its ways. Now, we are being brought up short. We do not understand much of anything, from the episode we rather dismissively (and, I think, defensively) choose to call the "big bang," all the way down to the particles in the atoms of a bacterial cell. We have a wilderness of mystery to make our way through in the centuries ahead. We will need science for this but not science alone. In its own time, science will produce the data and

some of the meaning in the data, but never the full meaning. For perceiving real significance when significance is at hand, we will need all sorts of brains outside the fields of science.

It is primarily because of this need that I would press for changes in the way science is taught. Although there is a perennial need to teach the young people who will be doing the science themselves, this will always be a small minority. Even more important, we must teach science to those who will be needed for thinking about it, and that means pretty nearly everyone else—most of all, the poets, but also artists, musicians, philosophers, historians and writers. A few of these people, at least, will be able to imagine new levels of meaning which may be lost on the rest of us.

In addition, it is time to develop a new group of professional thinkers, perhaps a somewhat larger group than the working scientists and the working poets, who can create a discipline of scientific criticism. We have had good luck so far in the emergence of a few people ranking as philosophers of science and historians and journalists of science, and I hope more of these will be coming along. But we have not yet seen specialists in the fields of scientific criticism who are of the caliber of the English literary and social critics F. R. Leavis and John Ruskin or the American literary critic Edmund Wilson.† Science needs critics of this sort, but the public at large needs them more urgently.

I suggest that the introductory courses in science, at all levels from grade school through college, be radically revised. Leave the fundamentals, the so-called basics, aside for a while, and concentrate the attention of all students on the things that are not known. You cannot possibly teach quantum mechanics without mathematics, to be sure, but you can describe the strangeness of the world opened up by quantum theory. Let it be known, early on, that there are deep mysteries and profound paradoxes revealed in distant outline by modern physics. Explain that these can be approached more closely and puzzled over, once the language of mathematics has been sufficiently mastered.

15 At the outset, before any of the fundamentals, teach the still imponderable puzzles of cosmology. Describe as clearly as possible, for the youngest minds, that there are some things going on in the universe that lie still beyond comprehension, and make it plain how little is known.

Do not teach that biology is a useful and perhaps profitable science; that can come later. Teach instead that there are structures squirming inside each of our cells that provide all the energy for living. Essentially foreign creatures, these lineal descendants of bacteria were brought in for symbiotic living a billion or so years ago. Teach that we do not have the ghost of an idea how they got there, where they came from, or how they evolved to their present structure and function. The details of oxidative phosphorylation and photosynthesis can come later.

Teach ecology early on. Let it be understood that the earth's life is a system of interdependent creatures, and that we do not understand at all how it works. The earth's environment, from the range of atmospheric gases to the chemical constituents of the sea, has been held in an almost unbelievably improbable state of regulated balance since life began, and the regulation of stability and balance is somehow accomplished by the life itself, like the autonomic nervous system of an immense organism. We do not know how such a system works, much less what it means, but there are some nice reductionist details at hand, such as the bizarre proportions of atmospheric constituents, ideal for our sort of planetary life, and the surprising stability of the ocean's salinity, and the fact that the average temperature of the earth has remained quite steady in the face of at least a 25 percent increase in heat coming in from the sun since the earth began. That kind of thing: something to think about.

Go easy, I suggest, on the promises sometimes freely offered by science. Technology relies and depends on science these days, more than ever before, but technology is far from the first justification for doing research, nor is it necessarily an essential product to be expected from science. Public decisions about the future of technology are totally different from decisions about science, and the two enterprises should not be tangled together. The central task of science is to arrive, stage by stage, at a clearer comprehension of nature, but this does not all mean, as it is sometimes claimed to mean, a search for mastery over nature.

Science may someday provide us with a better understanding of ourselves, but never, I hope, with a set of technologies for doing something or other to improve ourselves. I am made nervous by assertions that human consciousness will someday be unraveled by research, laid out for close scrutiny like the workings of a computer, and then—and *then* . . . ! I hope with some fervor that we can learn a lot more than we now know about the human mind, and I see no reason why this strange puzzle should remain forever and entirely beyond us. But I would be deeply disturbed by any prospect that we might use the new knowledge in order to begin doing something about it—to improve it, say. This is a different matter from searching for information to use against schizophrenia or dementia, where we are badly in need of technologies, indeed likely one day to be sunk without them. But the ordinary, everyday, more or less normal human mind is too marvelous an instrument ever to be tampered with by anyone, science or no science.

20 The education of humanists cannot be regarded as complete, or even adequate, without exposure in some depth to where things stand in the various branches of science, particularly, as I have said, in the area of our ignorance. Physics professors, most of them, look with revulsion on assignments to teach their subject

*Francis Cornford (1874–1943) was an influential literary scholar—or, more precisely, a classical scholar, because his work focused on the literature of ancient Greece. He was a member of a group known as the Cambridge Realists, scholars who drew upon anthropology and philology when interpreting literature because they believed that the key to understanding ancient literature was understanding the cultural rituals and myths to which writers were responding. By citing Cornford, Thomas is providing another example of a scholar with multidisciplinary interests.

to poets. Biologists, caught up by the enchantment of their new power, armed with flawless instruments to tell the nucleotide sequences of the entire human genome, nearly matching the physicists in the precision of their measurements of living processes, will resist the prospect of broad survey courses; each biology professor will demand that any student in his path master every fine detail within that professor's research program.

The liberal-arts faculties, for their part, will continue to view the scientists with suspicion and apprehension. "What do the scientists want?" asked Cambridge professor in Francis Cornford's* wonderful "Microcosmographia Academica." "Everything that's going," was the quick answer. That was back in 1912, and scientists haven't much changed.

But maybe, just maybe, a new set of courses dealing systematically with ignorance in science will take hold. The scientists might discover in it a new and subversive technique for catching the attention of students driven by curiosity, delighted and surprised to learn that science is exactly as the American scientist and educator Vannevar Bush described it: an "endless frontier." The humanists, for their part,

might take considerable satisfaction in watching their scientific colleagues confess openly to not knowing everything about everything. And the poets, on whose shoulders the future rests, might, late nights, thinking things over, begin to see some meanings that elude the rest of us. It is worth a try.

I believe that the worst thing that has happened to science education is that the fun has gone out of it. A great many good students look at it as slogging work to be got through on the way to medical school. Others are turned off by the premedical students themselves, embattled and bleeding for grades and class standing. Very few recognize science as the high adventure it really is, the wildest of all explorations ever taken by human beings, the chance to glimpse things never seen before, the shrewdest maneuver for discovering how the world works. Instead, baffled early on, they are misled into thinking that bafflement is simply the result of not having learned all the facts. They should be told that everyone else is baffled as well—from the professor in his endowed chair down to the platoons of postdoctoral students in the laboratories all night. Every important scientific advance that has come in looking like an answer has turned, sooner or later—usually sooner—into a question. And the game is just beginning.

If more students were aware of this, I think many of them would decide to look more closely and to try and learn more about what *is* known. That is the time when mathematics will become clearly and unavoidably recognizable as an essential, indispensable instrument for engaging in the game, and that is the time for teaching it. The calamitous loss of applied mathematics from what we might otherwise be calling higher education is a loss caused, at least in part, by insufficient incentives for learning the subject. Left by itself, standing there among curriculum offerings, it is not at all clear to the student what it is to be applied to. And there is all of science, next door, looking like an almost-finished field reserved only for chaps who want to invent or apply new

CONTEXT

Vannevar Bush (1890–1974) was an influential scientist and inventor, especially in the 1930s and 1940s. Interested in the possibilities of microfilm, he is best known for his work on what he called the *memex*—a system that would allow individuals to conveniently and compactly store all of the information they needed. This concept eventually contributed to the development of the World Wide Web. Bush was also politically active. In 1941, the year in which the United States entered the Second World War, he was appointed head of the National Defense Research Committee, which sponsored—among other programs—the Manhattan Project, the program that produced the first atomic bomb. It was Bush who recommended the creation of what is now called the National Science Foundation. But an allusion to him is problematic in the context of this argument. Although Bush believed that science was an "endless frontier" (as Thomas points out), he had contempt for the humanities and cut off funding for them when in a position to do so. And his own research was hampered by his unwillingness to learn from people who were not scientists or engineers.

technologies. We have had it wrong, and presented it wrong to class after class for several generations.

25 An appreciation of what is happening in science today, and how great a distance lies ahead for exploring, ought to be one of the rewards of a liberal-arts education. It ought to be good in itself, not something to be acquired on the way to a professional career but part of the cast of thought needed for getting into the kind of century that is now just down the road. Part of the intellectual equipment of an educated person, however his or her time is to be spent, ought to be a feel for the queernesses of nature, the inexplicable thing, the side of life for which informed bewilderment will be the best way of getting through the day.

Questions for Discussion

1. Consider the claim with which Thomas opens this argument. Who would be included in "everyone"—every person alive or every person of a certain kind? To what extent are you included in that "everyone"? Do you agree that science is not taught as well as it could be—especially to students who are unlikely to major in one of the sciences?

2. Consider the analogy Thomas makes in paragraph 3 between studying Latin and studying biology. What makes biology so different from Latin that it cannot be taught in the same way?

3. In paragraph 6, Thomas asks you to imagine a scientist who is happy with his work but subsequently learns that new discoveries have undermined the foundation of his research. What are the implications of this scenario for the arguments you write?

4. Thomas refers to poets more than once. The last of these references is in paragraph 22: "poets, on whose shoulders the future rests. . . . " Isn't this an odd statement to come from a scientist? What do you make of it? How could the future depend upon poets and what they write?

5. Thomas claims that the fun has gone out of science and that teachers need to convey that sense of fun in what he calls "the game." How is science like a game? Under what circumstances would it be fun to play it? Under what circumstances, if any, should fun be constrained when working in the sciences?

6. How does Thomas's ethos contribute to this argument? Would its effect be different if the argument was composed by a poet rather than by a physician?

DIFFERENCES

When asked to evaluate a course at the end of a semester, students sometimes record significantly different responses. For example, one student might object to the amount of class time devoted to discussion—indicating that the professor is the authority and more time devoted to lecturing would have facilitated learning because more information would have been transmitted. Another student in the same class might note that the professor dominated discussion and express the wish that more student voices be heard. Good teachers usually consider evaluations such as these when planning how to teach in the future. They also consider the ideas of other teachers—such as those who have work included in this cluster.

Without asking you to speak for all students, this assignment gives you the opportunity to develop your thinking about effective teaching in more detail than you would have when completing a standard evaluation form. Write an argument in response to one of the following questions:

- To what extent should teachers make sure that students see the connection between what they are learning in the classroom and the skills they will need in their professional lives?

- Should teachers and students collaborate when constructing a syllabus or planning specific assignments?
- To what extent can professors challenge students without intimidating them?
- What do you expect from a good teacher? If you are required to attend class, what expectations should the professor fulfill when you arrive?

- How well—and why—is science being taught to nonmajors?

When composing your essay, draw on your own experiences as well as at least one of the sources included in this cluster. Consider also the learning style that works best for you and how you have come to discover that style.

Imagine that your audience consists of at least one teacher with whom you will work next semester—a teacher who will give careful consideration to your views when planning the course in question.

How Should Learning Be Measured?

Learning can too easily be confused with grading. Although students are sometimes puzzled by how their grades are determined, teachers can be frustrated by questions such as "Will this be on the test?"—as if only the material that will be part of a formal assessment matters. Students, on the other hand, have a right to understand how their learning will be assessed—and to be dismayed if tested on material that seems to come out of nowhere or if graded by arbitrary standards. To take an example, what is the difference between a paper that receives an A and one that receives a B? In some cases, the answer may be easy because an instructor has posted clear evaluation criteria and offered a thoughtful response in addition to a grade. In other cases, the answer may be obscure. Such confusion may cause students to worry about grades—worry too much in the view of many educators (although from a student perspective, this might be "easy for them to say"). ■ Regardless, many teachers invest considerable time in determining how learning can be measured. The most common assessment instruments are tests and papers. One form of testing—the multiple choice test—has the merit of being easy to score. On the other hand, it reduces learning to determining the correct from the incorrect, and that kind of distinction is not always possible in serious inquiry. (Indeed, bright students sometimes score poorly on multiple choice tests because they can imagine circumstances under which more than one answer can be correct.) Essay tests allow students to explore and develop ideas, but the criteria for evaluating them can be more subjective. And out-of-class papers have the merit of allowing additional time for drafting and revising (as well as for research), but they carry higher stakes: the more time you have for a project, the more it might be expected to count in your final grade. Aside from determining what kinds of instruments to use for measuring what students have learned, teachers must consider the frequency with which students should be tested. How useful, for example, is a pop quiz? And how many tests can you take before you feel like you are on a treadmill? Issues such as these are addressed by the writers in this cluster. Three focus on testing, and one focuses on alternative methods for evaluating student writing.

① PATRICIA WILLIAMS, "Tests, Tracking, and Derailment"

If you have gone to school in the United States, chances are that you have encountered some form of tracking: Advanced Placement or honors classes, special education programs for students with special needs, remedial courses for struggling students, enrichment programs for gifted and talented students. Even if you were not tracked into such a program, it is likely that your school's curriculum offered different options for college-bound students and students who did not intend to go to college. The purpose of all these educational tracks is to match the curriculum to students' needs and abilities. But tracking has always been controversial, in part because it is not clear that special programs or tracks serve their intended purposes. Writer Patricia Williams, for example, believes that tracking students—for whatever purpose—ultimately leads to more problems than it solves. In her essay, which was published in the *Nation* in 2002, she traces what she sees as some of those problems and argues that educational resources can be better spent to ensure that all children benefit from schooling. In one sense her essay suggests that debates about how to allocate educational monies inevitably raise larger questions about the goals of schooling. As you read, consider how Williams's sense of the purpose of education informs her argument against educational tracking.

Tests, Tracking, and Derailment

PATRICIA WILLIAMS

1 As state budgets around the country are slashed to accommodate the expense of the war on terror, the pursuit of educational opportunity for all seems ever more elusive. While standardized tests are supposed to be used to diagnose problems and facilitate individual or institutional improvement, too often they have been used to close or penalize precisely the schools that most need help; or, results have been used to track students into separate programs that benefit the few but not the many. The implementation of gifted classes with better student–teacher ratios and more substantial resources often triggers an unhealthy and quite bitter competition for those unnaturally narrowed windows of opportunity. How much better it would be to have more public debate about why the pickings are so slim to begin with. In any event, it is no wonder there is such intense national anxiety just now, a fantastical hunger for children who speak in complete sentences by the age of six months.

A friend compares the tracking of students to the separation of altos from sopranos in a choir. But academic ability and/or intelligence is both spikier and more malleably constructed than such an analogy allows. Tracking students by separating the high notes from the low only works if the endgame is to teach all children the "Hallelujah Chorus." A system that teaches only the sopranos because no parent wants their child to be less than a diva is a system driven by the shortsightedness of narcissism. I think we make a well-rounded

IQ, or intelligence quotient, is a measure of intelligence based partly on the ideas of nineteenth century French psychologist Alfred Binet. Drawing on his observations of children with and without various disabilities, Binet developed a test to measure a child's "mental age." His test was adapted by several American psychologists and used by the U.S. Army to measure the intelligence levels of its recruits during the First World War. IQ tests have long been criticized as inaccurate and unfair, and criticisms of the tests as racially biased intensified in the 1960s and 1970s.

society the same way we make the best music: through the harmonic combination of differently pitched, but uniformly well-trained voices.

A parsimony of spirit haunts education policy, exacerbated by fear of the extremes. Under the stress of threatened budget cuts, people worry much more about providing lifeboats for the very top and containment for the "ineducable" rock bottom than they do about properly training the great masses of children, the vibrant, perfectly able middle who are capable of much more than most school systems offer. In addition, discussions of educational equality are skewed by conflation of behavioral problems with IQ,*and learning disabilities with retardation. Repeatedly one hears complaints that you can't put a gifted child in a class full of unruly, noisy misfits and expect anyone to benefit. Most often it's a plea from a parent who desperately wants his or her child removed from a large oversubscribed classroom with a single, stressed teacher in an underfunded district and sent to the sanctuary of a nurturing bubble where peace reigns because there are twelve kids in a class with two specialists and everyone's riding the high of

great expectations. But all children respond better in ordered, supportive environments; and all other investments being equal, gifted children are just as prone to behavior problems—and to learning disabilities—as any other part of the population. Nor should we confuse exceptional circumstances with behavior problems. The difficulty of engaging a child who's just spent the night in a homeless shelter, for example, is not productively treated as chiefly an issue of IQ.

The narrowing of access has often resulted in peculiar kinds of hairsplitting. When I was growing up, for example, Boston Latin School was divided into two separate schools: one for boys and one for girls. Although the curriculum was identical and the admissions exam the same, there were some disparities: The girls' school was smaller and so could admit fewer students; and the science and sports facilities were inferior to those of the boys.

5 There was a successful lawsuit to integrate the two schools about twenty years ago, but then an odd thing happened. Instead of using the old girls' school for the middle school and the larger boys' school for the new upper school, as was originally suggested, the city decided to sever the two. The old boys' school retained the name Boston Latin, and the old girls' school—smaller, less-equipped—was reborn as Boston Latin Academy. The entrance exam is now administered so that those who score highest go to Boston Latin; the next cut down go to what is now, unnecessarily, known as the "less elite" Latin Academy.

One of the more direct consequences of this is that the new Boston Latin inherited an alumni endowment of $15 million dollars, much of it used to provide college scholarships. Latin Academy, on the other hand, inherited the revenue of the old Girls' Latin alumni association—something under $200,000. It seems odd: Students at both schools are tremendously talented, the cutoff between them based on fairly insignificant scoring differences. But rather than pool the resources of the combined facilities—thus maximizing edu-

CONTEXT

In 1972, in response to a state law ending gender-based discrimination in Massachusetts schools, Girls' Latin Academy was changed to Boston Latin Academy and began accepting boys. That same year, girls were accepted into Boston Latin School, which describes itself as the oldest school in America, founded in 1635.

cational opportunity, in particular funding for college—the resolution of the pre-existing gender inequality almost purposefully reinscribed that inequality as one driven by wealth and class.

There are good models of what is possible. The International Baccalaureate curriculum, which is considered "advanced" by most American standards, is administered to a far wider range of students in Europe than here, with the result that their norm is considerably higher than ours in a number of areas. The University of Chicago's School Mathematics Project, originally developed for gifted students at the Chicago Lab School, is now recommended for all children—all children, as the foreword to its textbooks says, can "learn more and do more than was thought to be possible ten or twenty years ago." And educator Marva Collins's widely praised curriculum for inner-city elementary schools includes reading Shakespeare.

Imparting higher levels of content requires nothing exceptional but rather normal, more-or-less stable children, taught in small classes by well-trained, well-mentored teachers who have a sophisticated grasp of mathematics and literature themselves. It will pay us, I think, to stop configuring education as a battle of the geniuses against the uncivilized. We are a wealthy nation chock-full of those normal, more-or-less stable children. The military should not be the only institution that teaches them to be all that they can be.

INTERNATIONAL BACCALAUREATE CURRICULUM

This curriculum is based on guidelines from the International Baccalaureate Organization (IBO), founded in Geneva, Switzerland, in 1968. According to its website, the IBO "grew out of international schools' efforts as early as 1924 to establish a common curriculum and university entry credential. The schools were also motivated by an idealistic vision. They hoped that critical thinking and exposure to a variety of points of view would encourage intercultural understanding by young people." The IBO diploma program is a rigorous curriculum of six academic subjects based on well-established criteria for assessing students' knowledge of those subjects. As of 2002, there were 1,376 authorized IBO schools in 114 countries.

CONTEXT

According to its website, "*The Nation* will not be the organ of any party, sect, or body. It will, on the contrary, make an earnest effort to bring to the discussion of political and social questions a really critical spirit, and to wage war upon the vices of violence, exaggeration, and misrepresentation by which so much of the political writing of the day is marred." Founded in 1865, the *Nation* is a respected magazine of political affairs that is generally considered to espouse a liberal viewpoint. In what ways does Patricia Williams's argument against tracking reflect the editorial slant of this magazine and its expressed purpose?

Questions for Discussion

1. Williams compares tracking to separating the singers in a choir. How effectively do you think this comparison helps Williams make her point about the disadvantages of tracking? What does this comparison reveal about her beliefs about the purposes of schooling?

2. Williams refers to "the great masses of children, the vibrant, perfectly able middle who are capable of much more than most school systems offer." What evidence does she offer to support this assertion? Do you think she is right? Why or why not?

3. What point does Williams use the example of the Boston Latin School to illustrate? How effectively does this example help her make her point? How does it contribute to her main argument about tracking?

4. In her final paragraph Williams argues that we should not think of education "as a battle of the geniuses against the uncivilized." To what extent do you think Bertell Ollman and Gregory Cizek, whose essays appear later in this chapter, would agree with Williams? Cite specific passages from their essays to support your answer.

5. Williams's essay might be considered an essay based on inductive reasoning (see pages 86–88). How effective do you think her essay is as such an argument? How persuasively does she compile evidence to reach her conclusion?

② GREGORY CIZEK, "Unintended Consequences of High-Stakes Testing"

As author Gregory Cizek notes, the title of the following essay is misleading. We tend to think of "unintended consequences" as negative. But Cizek makes a vigorous case in favor of standardized testing, arguing that high-stakes tests lead to a number of important and beneficial consequences for students, schools, and teachers alike. Like many proponents of such tests, Cizek believes that carefully constructed standardized tests are a crucial element in efforts to improve public education. As you read through his discussion of the benefits of testing, consider what his list of these benefits reveals about his view of the purpose of formal education. Consider, too, the extent to which his fundamental beliefs about education match—or diverge from—the views of the other writers in this section. Gregory Cizek is an associate professor of education at the University of North Carolina and the author of *Detecting and Preventing Classroom Cheating* (1999). This essay originally appeared in 2002 at **EducationNews.org**, an online news service devoted to educational issues.

Unintended Consequences of High-Stakes Testing

GREGORY CIZEK

1 It's eschatological.* In one tract after another, the zealous proclaim that there is a dire threat posed by the anti-Christ of postmodern education: testing. To be more precise, the Great Satan does not comprise *all* testing, only testing *with consequences*—consequences such as grade retention for students, salaries for educators, or the futures of (in particular) low-performing schools. In this fevered and frenzied battle, what is clear is that any sort of high-stakes test is the beast. On the side of the angels are those who take the path of beast-resistance.

   As I reflect on my own writing here, I wondered if I would need to make a confession for the sin of hyperbole. Then I re-read some of the sacred texts. According to Alfie Kohn in a recent issue of the *Kappan,* we must "make the fight against standardized tests our top priority . . . until we have chased this monster from our schools."[1] A companion article in the same issue discussed high-stakes testing in an article titled "The Authentic Standards Movement and Its Evil Twin."[2] Still another canonized a list of 22 martyrs and described their sacrifices of resistance to testing.[3] I concluded that there was no need for me to repent.

   In addition to the zealotry, there is also heresy. This article is one example. Testifying to the truth of that label, I confess that the very title of this article is somewhat deceptive. Perhaps many readers will, like me, recall having reviewed several articles with titles like the one used here. In those epistles the faithful are regaled with the travails of students who were denied a diploma as a result of a high-stakes test. They illustrate how testing narrows the curriculum, frustrates our best teachers, produces gripping anxiety in our brightest students, and makes young children vomit or cry,

Eschatology **is a branch of theology concerned with the end of the world or of humankind.**

COMPLICATION

Alfie Kohn, to whom Cizek refers several times in this essay, is one of the most visible and respected (or vilified) critics of high-stakes tests in the United States. He has argued against such tests on the grounds that their popularity is driven by profits for testing companies and by the desire for votes among political officials who publicly call for "accountability" in education. In one article (which Cizek cites in his essay), Kohn argues that in addition to several other flaws, standardized tests do not accurately measure student achievement:

The central problem with most standardized tests, however, is simply that they fail to assess the skills and dispositions that matter most. Such tests are generally contrived exercises that measure how much students have managed to cram into short-term memory. Reading comprehension exams usually consist of a concatenation of separate questions about short passages on unrelated topics that call on students to ferret out right answers rather than to engage in thoughtful interpretation. In mathematics, the point is to ascertain that students have memorized a series of procedures, not that they understand what they are doing. Science tests often focus on recall of vocabulary, stressing "excruciatingly boring material," failing to judge the capacity of students to think, and ultimately discouraging many of them from choosing a career in the field, according to Bruce Alberts, president of the National Academy of Science.

In light of all this, it should not be surprising—but it is seldom realized—that the students who perform well on tests are often those who are least interested in learning and least likely to learn deeply. Studies of elementary, middle school, and high school students have found a statistical association between high scores on standardized tests and relatively superficial thinking. (From Alfie Kohn, "Burnt at the High Stakes.")

"The Case for National Standards and Assessments."[4] The other nominally favorable article simply reviewed surveys of public opinion about high-stakes tests and concluded that broad support for such tests persists.[5] The other 57 entries reflected the accepted articles of faith concerning high-stakes tests. Examples of the titles of these articles include:

"Excellence in Education versus High-Stakes Testing"[6] (which carries the obvious implication that testing is antithetical to high-quality education);

"The Distortion of Teaching and Testing: High-Stakes Testing and Instruction"[7] (ditto);

"Burnt at the High Stakes"[8] (no explanation required);

"Judge's Ruling Effectively Acquits High-Stakes Test: To the Disadvantage of Poor and Minority Students in Texas"[9] (personally, I thought that the less equivocal title "Analysis Reveals High-quality Test: Everyone Gets the Shaft" could have been used); and

"I Don't Give a Hoot If Somebody Is Going to Pay Me $3600: Local School District Reactions to Kentucky's High-Stakes Accountability Program."[10]

The Roots of All Evil

5 There have always been high-stakes tests. Testing history buffs have traced high-stakes testing to civil service examinations of 200 B.C., military selection dating to 2000 B.C., and Biblical accounts of the Gilead guards. Mehrens and Cizek relate the story of the minimum competency exam that took place when the Gilead guards challenged the fugitives from the tribe of Ephraim who tried to cross the Jordan river.

"Are you a member of the tribe of Ephraim?" they asked. If the man replied that he was not, then they demanded, "Say Shibboleth." But if he couldn't pronounce the H and said Sibboleth instead of Shibboleth he was dragged away and killed. So forty-two thousand people of Ephraim died there."[11]

or both. This article will not repeat any of those parables, either in substance or perspective. We now turn to the apocrypha.

Reports from the Battlefield

If nothing else, published commentary concerning high-stakes testing has been remarkable for its uniformity. The conclusion: high-stakes tests are uniformly bad. A recent literature search to locate information about the effects of high-stakes tests turned up 59 entries over the last 10 years. A review of the results revealed that only 2 of the 59 could even remotely be categorized as favorably inclined toward testing. The two entries included a two-page, 1996 publication in a minor source, which bore the straightforward title,

In the scriptural account of this assessment, nothing is reported concerning the professional and public debates that may have occurred regarding: what competencies should have been tested; how to measure them; how minimally-proficient performance should be defined; whether paper/pencil testing might have been cheaper and more reliable than performance assessment; whether there was any adverse impact against the people of Ephraim; or what remediation should be provided for those judged to be below the standard. Maybe the Gilead guards should have abandoned their test altogether because it was unclear whether Ephraimites really had the opportunity to learn to pronounce "shibboleth" correctly, because the burden of so many oral examinations was a top-down mandate, or because listening to all those Ephraimites try to say "shibboleth" reduced the valuable instructional time available for teaching young members of the tribe of Gilead the real-life skills of sword fighting and tent making.[12]

While it is certain that high-stakes testing has been around for some time, it is curious that current high-stakes tests in American education face such an inquisition from, primarily, educators. Ironically, for this, too, we should blame those in the field of testing. Those who know and make high-stakes tests have done the least to make known the purposes and benefits of testing. The laws of physics apply: for every action in opposition to tests, there has been and equal and opposite silence.

A Revelation

One assumption underlying high-stakes testing has received particularly scant attention: the need to make decisions. There is simply no way to escape making decisions about students. These decisions, by definition, create categories. If, for example, some students graduate from high school and others do not, a categorical decision has been made, even if a graduation test was not used. (The decisions were, presumably, made on *some* basis.) High school music teachers make decisions such

as who should be first chair for the clarinets. College faculties make decisions to tenure (or not) their colleagues. We embrace decision making regarding who should be licensed to practice medicine. All of these kinds of decisions are unavoidable; each should be based on sound information; and the information should be combined in some deliberate, considered fashion.

10 It is currently fashionable to talk as if high-stakes tests are the *single* bit of information used to make categorical decisions that wreak hellacious results on both people and educational systems. But simple-minded slogans like "high stakes are for tomatoes" are, well, simple-minded. One need only examine the context in which high-stakes tests are given to see that they are almost never the single bit of information used to make decisions. In the diploma example, multiple sources of information are used to make decisions, and success on each of them is necessary. For instance: So many days of attendance are required. Just one too few days?: No diploma. 2) There are course requirements. Didn't take American Government?: No diploma. 3) There are credit hour requirements.

Missing one credit?: No diploma. 4) And, increasingly, there are high-stakes tests. Miss one too many questions on a test?: No diploma. Categorical decisions are made on each of these four criteria. It makes as much sense to single out a single test as the sole barrier as it does to single out a student's American Government examination as "the single test used to make the graduation decision."

We could, of course, not make success on each of the elements essential. One could get a diploma by making success on, say, three out of the four. But which three? Why three? Why not two? The same two for everyone? That seems unfair, given that some people would be denied a diploma simply on the basis of the arbitrary two that were identified. Even if all other criteria were eliminated, and all that remained was a requirement that students must attend at least 150 out of 180 days in their senior year to get a diploma, then what about the student who attends 149 and is a genius? In the end, as long as any categorical decisions must be made, there is going to be subjectivity involved. If there is going to be subjectivity, most testing specialists—and most of the public—simply favor coming clean about the source and magnitude of the subjectivity, and trying to minimize it.

In the end, it cannot be that high-stakes tests themselves are the cause of all the consternation. It is evident that categorical decisions will be made with or without tests. The real reasons are two-fold. One reason covers resistance to high-stakes testing within the education profession; the second explains why otherwise well-informed people would so easily succumb to simplistic rhetoric centering on testing. On the first count, the fact that high-stakes tests are increasingly used as part of accountability systems provides a sufficient rationale for resistance. Education is one of the few (only?) professions for which advancement, status, compensation, longevity, and so on are not related to personal performance. The entire accountability movement—of which testing has been the major element—has been vigorously resisted by many in the profession. The rationale is rational when there is a choice between being accountable for performance or maintaining a status quo without accountability.

Two Tables of Stone

There is much to be debated about professionalization of teaching and its relationship to accountability. My primary focus here, however, is on the second count—the debate about testing. As mentioned previously, those who know the most about testing have been virtually absent from the public square when any criticism surfaces. In response to 57 bold articles nailed to the cathedral door, 2 limp slips of paper are slid under it. The benefits of high-stakes tests have been assumed, unrecognized, or unarticulated. The following paragraphs present 10 unanticipated consequences of high-stakes testing—consequences that are actually *good* things that have grown out of the increasing reliance on test data concerning student performance.[13]

I. Professional Development I suspect that most educators painfully recall what passed as professional development in the not-too-distant past. Presentations with titles like the following were all-too-common:

- Vitamins and Vocabulary: Just Coincidence that Both Begin with "V"?
- Cosmetology across the Curriculum
- Horoscopes in the Homeroom
- The Geometry of Rap: 16 Musical Tips for Pushing Pythagoras
- Multiple Intelligences in the Cafeteria

In a word, much professional development was spotty, hit-or-miss, of questionable research base, of dubious effectiveness, and thoroughly avoidable.

15 But professional development is increasingly taking a new face. Much of it is considerably more focussed on what works, curriculum-relevant, and results-oriented. Driven by the demands of high-stakes tests, the press toward professional development that helps educators hone their teaching skills and content area expertise is clear.

II. Accommodation Recent federal legislation enacted to guide the implementation of high-stakes testing has been a catalyst for increased attention to students with special needs. Describing the impact of that legislation, researchers Martha Thurlow and James Ysseldyke observe that, "Both Goals 2000* and the more forceful IASA indicated that high standards were to apply to *all* students. In very clear language, these laws defined 'all students' as including students with disabilities and students with limited English proficiency."[14]

Because of these regulations applied to high-stakes tests, states across the US are scurrying to adapt those tests for all students, report disaggregated results for subgroups, and implement accommodations so that tests more accurately reflect the learning of all students. The result has been a very positive diffusion of awareness. Increasingly, at the classroom level, educators are becoming more sensitive to the needs and barriers faced by special needs students when they take tests— even the ordinary assessments they face in the classroom. If not forced by the context of once-per-year, high-stakes tests, it is doubtful that such progress would have been witnessed in the daily experiences of many special needs learners.

III. Knowledge about Testing For years, testing specialists have documented a lack of knowledge about assessment on the part of many educators. The title of a 1991 *Kappan* article bluntly asserted educators' "Apathy toward Testing and Grading."[15] Other research has chronicled the chronic lack of training in assessment for teachers and principals and has offered plans for remediation.[16] Unfortunately, for the most part, it has been difficult to require assessment training for preservice teachers or administrators, and even more difficult to wedge such training into graduate programs in education.

Then along came high-stakes tests. What faculty committees could not enact has been

accomplished circuitously. Granted, misperceptions about tests persist (for example, in my state there is a lingering myth that "the green test form" is harder than "the red one"), but I am discovering that more educators know more about testing than ever before. Because many tests now have stakes associated with them, it has become *de rigeur* for educators to inform themselves about their content, construction, and consequences. Increasingly, teachers can tell you the difference between a norm-referenced and a criterion-reference test; they can recognize, use, or develop a high-quality rubric; they can tell you how their state's writing test is scored, and so on. In this case, necessity has been the mother of intervention.

20 IV and V. Collection and Use of Information Because pupil performance on high-stakes tests has become of such prominent and public interest, there has been an intensity of effort directed toward data collection and quality control that is unparalleled. As many states mandate the collection and reporting of this information (and more),

*Goals 2000 refers to the Educate America Act, passed by the U.S. Congress in 1994 and intended to promote coherent educational standards for K–12 schools by supporting efforts in individual states to set standards for student learning. IASA, or the Improving America's Schools Act, which was also passed in 1994, is broad legislation that provided funding and other kinds of support for various initiatives, including improving services for students with disabilities, enhancing basic educational programs, upgrading technology, and strengthening substance abuse prevention efforts.

unparalleled access has also resulted. Obtaining information about test performance, graduation rates, per-pupil spending, staffing, finance, and facilities is, in most states, now just a mouse-click away. How would you like your data for secondary analysis: Aggregated or disaggregated? Single year or longitudinal? PDF or Excel? Paper or plastic? Consequently, those who must respond to state mandates for data collection (i.e., school districts) have become increasingly conscientious about providing the most accurate information possible—sometimes at risk of penalties for inaccuracy or incompleteness.

This is an unqualified boon. Not only is more information about student performance available, but it is increasingly used as part of decision making. At a recent teacher recruiting event, I heard a recruiter question a teacher about how she would be able to tell that her students were learning. "I can just see it in their eyes," was the reply. Sorry, you're off the island. Increasingly, from the classroom to the school board room, educators are making use of student performance data to help them refine programs, channel funding, and identify roots of success. If the data weren't so important, it is unlikely that this would be the case.

VI. Educational Options Related to the increase in publicly-available information about student performance and school characteristics is the spawning of greater options for parents and students. Complementing a hunger for information, the public's appetite for alternatives has been whetted. In many cases, schools have responded. Charter schools, magnet schools, home schools, and increased offerings of honors, IB and AP courses,* have broadened the choices available to parents. And, research is slowly accumulating which suggests that the presence of choices has not spelled doom for traditional options, but has largely raised all boats.[17] It is almost surely the case that legislators' votes and parents' feet would not be moving in the direction of expanding alternatives if

not for the information provided by high-stakes tests—the same tests are being used to gauge the success or failure of these emerging alternatives.

VII. Accountability Systems No one would argue that current accountability systems have reached a mature state of development. On the contrary, nascent systems are for the most part crude, cumbersome, embryonic endeavors. Equally certain, though, is that even rudimentary accountability systems would not likely be around if it weren't for high-stakes tests. For better or worse, high-stakes tests are often the foundation upon which accountability systems have been built. This is not to say that this relationship between high-stakes tests and accountability is right, noble, or appropriate. It simply recognizes the reality that current accountability systems were enabled by an antecedent: mandated, high-stakes tests.

To many policy makers, professionals, and the public, however, the notion of introducing accountability—even just acknowledging that accountability is a *good* innovation—is an important first step. That the camel's nose took the form of high-stakes tests was (perhaps) not recognized or (almost certainly) viewed as acceptable. Debates continue about the role of tests and the form of accountability.

25 A memory that has helped me to understand both sides of accountability debates involves high school sports physicals. I have vivid memories evoked to this day whenever I drive by a marquee outside a high school on which the notice appears: Boys' Sports Physicals Next Tuesday. As an adolescent male trying out for a high-school baseball team, I recall that event as one at which dozens of similarly situated guys would line up mostly naked and be checked over by a hometown physician, who volunteered his time to poke, prod, and probe each potential player. The characteristics of the event included that it was: a) somewhat embarrassing; b) performed by an external person; c) somewhat invasive; d) and had the possibility of denying individu-

*IB refers to International Baccalaureate programs, which are described on page 501. AP refers to Advanced Placement programs, which are rigorous high school courses that can lead to college credit. Founded in 1955, the AP program standards are set by the College Board, which also administers the AP exams that students who complete AP courses must usually take to earn college credit.

als access to an opportunity. I think that these same four characteristics help explain the reaction of many educators to high-stakes tests.

But the analogy can be extended. At the time—and still—I can see that the physicals were necessary to identify small problems, and to prevent potentially bigger problems. But here's the big difference with high-stakes tests: if one of the players was found to have a heart murmur, it was acknowledged that he had a problem and something was done about it. In education, if a student fails a high-stakes test, we assail the test. Now, we all know that achievement tests aren't perfect, but neither are medical tests. Pregnancy tests are often wrong; blood pressure readings are subjective and variable within an individual; even with DNA tests, experts can only say things like "there is 99.93% chance that the DNA is a match." Yet nobody reports their blood pressure as 120/80 with an associated standard error. Maybe I don't really have high blood pressure. Maybe my pressure is 120/80 plus or minus 17.

People seem inclined to accept medical measurements as virtually error-free because there's no finger pointing, only therapy. Maybe his blood pressure is high because he failed to heed the physician's orders to lay off the salt and lose some weight. Maybe her pregnancy test was positive because she was sexually active. Who should be held accountable for the results of the pregnancy test or blood pressure but the person? We seem resigned to accountability in this context.

Don't get me wrong. When a defective medical measuring device is identified, it gets pulled by the FDA. If there were intolerable error rates in home pregnancy test kits, it would create a stir, and the product would be improved, or fall out of use. In education, however, if a pupil doesn't pass a high-stakes test, there are a lot of possible (and confounded) explanations: lack of persistence, poor teaching, distracting learning environment, inadequate resources, lack of prerequisite skills, poorly-constructed test, dysfunctional home

situation, and so on. We know that all of these (and more) exist to greater or lesser extents in the mix. Who should be accountable? The teacher for the quality of instruction? I think so. The student for effort and persistence? Yes, again. Administrators for providing safe learning environment? Yep. Assessment specialists for developing sound tests? Bingo. Communities for providing adequate resources? Sure. Parents for establishing a supportive home environment? Yessirree. The key limitation is that we can only make policies and products to address those factors that are legitimately under governmental control. And, in education, we understand that intervention may or may not prove effective.

Thus, although high-stakes tests have made a path in the wilderness, the controversy clearly hinges on accountability itself. The difficult fits and starts of developing sound accountability systems may actually cause some hearts to murmur. Understanding the importance, complexity, and difficulties as the accountability infant matures will be surely be trying. How—or if—high-stakes tests will fit into the mature version is hard to tell, and the devil will be in the details. But it is evident that the presence of high-stakes tests have at least served as a conversation-starter for a policy dialogue that may not have taken place in their absence.

30 **VIII. Educators' Intimacy with Their Disciplines** Once a test has been mandated in, say, language arts, the first step in any high-stakes testing program is to circumscribe the boundaries of what will be tested. The almost universal strategy for accomplishing this is to empanel groups of (primarily) educators who are familiar with the ages, grades, and content to be tested. These groups are usually large, selected to be representative, and expert in the subject area. The groups first study relevant documentation (e.g. the authorizing legislation, state curriculum guides, content standards). They then begin the arduous, time-consuming task of discussing among themselves the

nature of the content area, the sequence and content of typical instruction, learner characteristics and developmental issues, cross-disciplinary relationships, and relevant assessment techniques.

These extended conversations help shape the resulting high-stakes tests, to be sure. However, they also affect the discussants, and those with whom they interact when they return to their districts, buildings, and classrooms. As persons with special knowledge of the particular high-stakes testing program, the participants are sometimes asked to replicate those disciplinary and logistic discussions locally. The impact of this trickling-down is just beginning to be noticed by researchers—and the effects are beneficial. For example, at one session of the 2000 American Educational Research Association conference, scholars reported on the positive effects of a state testing program in Maine on classroom assessment practices[18] and on how educators in Florida were assimilating their involvement in large-scale testing activities at the local level.[19]

These local discussions mirror the large-scale counterparts in that they provide educators with an opportunity to become more intimate with the nature and structure of their own disciplines, and to contemplate interdisciplinary relationships. As Martha Stewart would say: it's a good thing. And the impulse for this good thing is clearly the presence of a high-stakes test.

IX. Equity There is a flip-side to the common concern that high-stakes tests result in the homogenizing of education. The flip-side is that high-stakes tests promote greater homogeneity of education. Naturally, we should be vigilant about the threat posed by common *low* standards that could be engendered, and it is right to worry about gravitating to the lowest common denominator.[20] On the other hand, there is something to be said for increased equity in expectations and experiences for all students. As a result of schools' aligning their curricula and instructional focus more closely to outcomes embodied in high-

stakes tests, the experiences of and aspirations for children in urban, suburban, and rural districts within a state are more comparable than they have been in the recent past.

Surely, inequalities—even savage ones—persist. However, some movement toward greater consistency is perceptible. And, the press toward more uniformity of expectation and experience may be particularly beneficial in an increasingly mobile society. The seamlessness with which a student can move from one district to another—even one school to another within a district—may well translate into incremental gains in achievement sufficient enough to spell the difference between promotion and graduation, or retention and dropping out.

35 X. Quality of Tests The final benevolent consequence is the profoundly positive effect that the introduction of high-stakes consequences has had on the tests themselves. Along with more serious consequences has come heightened scrutiny. The high-stakes tests of today are surely the most meticulously developed, carefully constructed, and rigorously reported. Many criticisms of tests are valid, but a complainant who suggests that today's high-stakes tests are "lower-order" or "biased" or "not relevant" are most likely unfamiliar with that which they purport to critique.

If only for its long history and ever-present watch-dogging, high-stakes tests have evolved to a state of being: highly reliable; free from bias; relevant and age appropriate; higher order; tightly related to important, public goals; time and cost efficient; and yielding remarkably consistent decisions. It is fair to say that one strains the gnat in objecting to the characteristics of high-stakes tests, when the characteristics of those tests is compared to what a child will likely experience in his or her classroom the other 176 days of the school year. It is not an overstatement to say that, at least on the grounds just articulated, the high-stakes, state test that a student takes will, by far, be the best assessment that student will see all year.

A secondary benefit of the quality of typical high-stakes tests is that, because of their perceived importance, they become mimicked at lower levels. It is appropriate to abhor teaching to the test. However, it is also important to recognize the beneficial effects of exposing educators to high-quality writing prompts, document-based questions, constructed-response formats, and even challenging multiple-choice items. It is not cheating, but the highest form of praise when educators then rely on these exemplars to enhance their own assessment practices.

Keepin' It Real

It would be foolish to ignore the shortcomings and undesirable consequences of high-stakes tests. Current discussions and inquiries are essential, productive, and encouraging. However, amidst the consternation about high-stakes tests, it is equally inappropriate to fail to consider the unanticipated positive consequences, or to fail to incorporate these into any cost-benefit calculus that should characterize sound policy decisions.

Vigorous debates about the nature and role of high-stakes tests and accountability systems are healthy and needed. To these frays, the protestants may bring differing doctrinal starting points and differing conceptions of the source of salvation. It is an exhilarating time of profound questioning. High-stakes tests: we don't know how to live with them; we can't seem to live without them. The oft-quoted first sentence of Charles Dickens' *A Tale of Two Cities* ("It was the best of times, it was the worst of times") seems especially relevant to the juncture at which we find ourselves. The remainder of Dickens' opening paragraph merely extends the piquant metaphor:

It was the age of wisdom, it was the age of foolishness, it was the epoch of belief, it was the epoch of incredulity, it was the season of Light, it was the season of Darkness, it was the spring of hope, it was the winter of despair, we had everything before us, we had nothing before us, we were all going direct to Heaven, we were all going direct the other way.[21]

Notes

1. Alfie Kohn, "Fighting the Tests: A Practical Guide to Rescuing Our Schools," *Phi Delta Kappan*, vol. 82, 2001, p. 349.
2. Scott Thompson, "The Authentic Standards Movement and Its Evil Twin," *Phi Delta Kappan,* vol. 82, 2001, pp. 358–362.
3. Susan Ohanian, "News from the Test Resistance Trail," *Phi Delta Kappan,* vol. 82, 2001, p. 365.
4. Diane Ravitch, "The Case for National Standards and Assessments," *The Clearing House,* vol. 69, 1996, pp. 134–135.
5. Richard Phelps, "The demand for standardized student testing," *Educational Measurement: Issues and Practice,* vol. 17, no. 3, 1998, pp. 5–23.
6. Asa Hilliard, "Excellence in Education versus High-Stakes Testing," *Journal of Teacher Education,* vol. 51, 2000, pp. 293–304.
7. George Madaus, "The Distortion of Teaching and Testing: High-Stakes Testing and Instruction," *Peabody Journal of Education,* vol. 65, 1998, pp. 29–46.
8. Alfie Kohn, "Burnt at the High Stakes," *Journal of Teacher Education,* vol. 51, 2000, pp. 315–327.
9. Karin Chenoweth, "Judge's Ruling Effectively Acquits High-Stakes Test: To the Disadvantage of Poor and Minority Students in Texas," *Black Issues in Higher Education,* vol. 51, 2000, p. 12.
10. Patricia Kannapel and others, "I Don't Give a Hoot If Somebody Is Going to Pay Me $3600: Local School District Reactions to Kentucky's High-Stakes Accountability Program." Paper presented at the annual meeting of the American Educational Research Association, April 1996, New York, (ERIC Document No. 397 135).

CONTEXT

A web portal devoted to education news, **EducationNews.org** describes itself as "the Internet's leading source of education news." It claims to provide more balanced coverage of education issues than more traditional media, and it seeks to use Internet technologies "to increase interest and subsequent involvement in education reform."

11. Judges 12:5-6, *The Living Bible;* cited in William Mehrens and Gregory Cizek, "Standard Setting and the Public Good: Benefits Accrued and Anticipated," in G. J. Cizek (Ed.), *Setting Performance Standards: Concepts, Methods, and Perspectives* (Mahwah, NJ: Lawrence Erlbaum, 2001).

12. Mehrens and Cizek, pp. 477–478.

13. Ordinarily, the 10 items should probably be presented with appropriate recognition of their downsides, disadvantages, etc. However, for the sake of clarity, brevity, and because most readers are probably already all too aware of the counterarguments, I have chosen to avoid any facade of balanced treatment.

14. Martha Thurlow and James Ysseldyke, "Standard Setting Challenges for Special Populations," in G. J. Cizek (Ed.), *Setting Performance Standards: Concepts, Methods, and Perspectives* (Mahwah, NJ: Lawrence Erlbaum, 2001), p. 389.

15. John Hills, "Apathy toward Testing and Grading," *Phi Delta Kappan,* vol. 72, 1991, pp. 540–545.

16. See, for example, Rita O' Sullivan and Marla Chalnick, "Measurement-Related Course Requirements for Teacher Certification and Recertification," *Educational Measurement: Issues and Practice,* vol. 10, 1991, pp. 17–19, 23; Richard Stiggins, "Assessment Literacy," *Phi Delta Kappan,* vol. 72, 1991, pp. 534–539; and James Impara and Barbara Plake, "Professional Development in Student Assessment for Educational Administrators," *Educational Measurement: Issues and Practice,"* vol. 15, 1996, pp. 14–20.

17. Chester Finn, Jr., Bruno V. Manno, and Gregg Vanourek, *Charter Schools in Action: Renewing Public Education* (Princeton, NJ: Princeton University Press, 2000).

18. Jeff Beaudry, "The Positive Effects of Administrators and Teachers on Classroom Assessment Practices and Student Achievement." Paper presented at the annual meeting of the American Educational Research Association, April 2000, New Orleans, LA.

19. Madhabi Banerji, "Designing District-Level Classroom Assessment Systems." Paper presented at the annual meeting of the American Educational Research Association, April 2000, New Orleans, LA.

20. Actually, the concern about low expectations may have passed and, if the experiences of states like Washington, Arizona, and Massachusetts are prescient, the concern may be being replaced by a concern that content or performance expectations (or both) are too high and coming too fast. See http://seattletimes.nwsource. com/news/local/html98/test_19991010. html; http://www.edweek. org/ew/ewstory.cfm?slug=13ariz.h20; and Donald C. Orlich, "Education Reform and Limits to Student Achievement," *Phi Delta Kappan,* vol. 81, 2000, pp. 468–472.

21. Charles Dickens, *A Tale of Two Cities* (New York: Dodd, Mead, and Company, 1925), p. 3.

Questions for Discussion

1. Examine the way in which Cizek opens this essay, noting especially his use of religious metaphors. How, specifically, does he introduce his subject and establish his own stance toward it? How does he set the tone for his argument? How effective do you think his introduction is in setting up his argument? In your answer, cite specific words and phrases from his introductory paragraphs.

2. Cizek devotes much of his essay to summarizing and responding to the arguments of those who are opposed to testing. Evaluate his use of his references to his opponents. How effective are these references in helping him make his own argument in favor of standardized testing? Do you think he represents his opponents fairly?

3. In paragraph 25, Cizek recalls his own experience as a student to introduce an analogy in which he compares high school physical exams to standardized testing. What point does Cizek use this analogy to make? How effectively do you think this analogy helps Cizek make his point? Would the analogy have been less effective if Cizek had not referred to his own experience as a student? Explain.

4. In many ways, Cizek's writing style is unusual for a scholarly essay, especially his use of figurative language. How would you describe Cizek's writing style? In what ways do you think it strengthens or weakens his argument? Cite specific passages from his essay in your answer.

5. Cizek describes the way in which curriculum standards are typically set by panels of experts who determine the appropriate content for specific grade levels in specific subjects. He declares this to be a "good thing." What are some pros and cons that you see in this approach to developing curriculum? Do you think Cizek's discussion of this process enhances his argument?

6. Near the end of his essay, Cizek states that vigorous debates about testing "are healthy and needed" and that it is an "exhilarating time of profound questioning" about testing. Do you agree? Why or why not? To what extent do you think Cizek's essay contributes positively to this ongoing debate?

③ **BERTELL OLLMAN, "Why So Many Exams? A Marxist Response"**

Complaints about public education in the United States are so common that the view that schools are in crisis seems to be almost universal. Rarely does anyone describe the schools as working. Critic Bertell Ollman is someone who does. But he doesn't think that's a good thing. Ollman believes that despite constant criticism of schools and calls for reform, public education in the United States effectively serves the basic economic system on which American society is based: capitalism. In his view, the many problems typically associated with schools reflect of the needs of capitalism rather than the needs of individual students. More specifically, standardized testing is necessary to prepare students for their roles in a capitalist system, and as long as that system remains in place, neither standardized tests nor the problems associated with schooling will go away. Whether or not you agree with Ollman's view of capitalism or his position on testing, his essay is a good example of an argument that reflects a specific theory or political ideology (in this case, Marxism). It suggests as well that educational issues such as testing are related in complex ways to individuals' political and economic lives. Bertell Ollman is a professor of political science at New York University. A well-known Marxist scholar, he has written many books and essays about political and social issues, including *Dialectical Investigations* (1993) and *How to Take an Exam . . . and Remake the World* (2001). The following essay was published in 2002 in *Z Magazine*.

Why So Many Exams? A Marxist Response

BERTELL OLLMAN

1 Psychologist Bill Livant has remarked, "When a liberal sees a beggar, he says the system isn't working. When a Marxist does, he says it is." The same insight could be applied today to the entire area of education. The learned journals, as well as the popular media, are full of studies documenting how little most students know and how fragile are their basic skills. The cry heard almost everywhere is "The system isn't working."

Responding to this common complaint, conservatives—starting (but not ending) with the Bush administration—have offered a package of reforms in which increased testing occupies the central place. The typical liberal

and even radical response to this has been to demonstrate that such measures are not likely to have the "desired" effect. The assumption, of course, is that we all want more or less the same thing from a system of education and that conservatives have made an error in the means they have chosen to attain our common end. But what if students are already receiving—more or less—the kind of education that conservatives favor? This would cast their proposals for "reform" in another light. What if, as Livant points out in the case of beggars, the system is working?

Before detailing what young people learn from their forced participation in this educational ritual, it may be useful to dispose of a number of myths that surround exams and exam taking in our society.

(1) *Exams are a necessary part of education.* Education, of one kind or another has existed in all human societies, but exams have not; and the practice of requiring frequent exams is a very recent innovation and still relatively rare in the world.

5 (2) *Exams are unbiased.* In 1912, Henry Goddard, a distinguished psychologist, administered what he claimed were "culture free" IQ * tests to new immigrants on Ellis Island and found that 83 percent of Jews, 80 percent of Hungarians, 79 percent of Italians, and 87 percent of Russians were "feebleminded," adding that "all feebleminded are at least potential criminals." IQ tests have gotten better since then, but given the character of the testing process, the attitudes of those who make up any test, and the variety of people—coming from so many different backgrounds—who take it, it is impossible to produce a test that does not have serious biases.

(3) *Exams are objectively graded.* Daniel Stark and Edward Elliot sent two English essays to 200 high school teachers for grading. They got back 142 grades. For one paper, the grades ranged from 50 to 99; for the other, the grades went from 64 to 99. But English is not an "objective" subject, you say. Well, they did the same thing for an essay answer in mathematics and got back grades ranging from 28 to 95. Though most of the grades they received in both cases fell in the middle ground, it was evident that a good part of any grade was the result of who marked the exam and not of who took it.

(4) *Exams are an accurate indication of what students know and of intelligence in general.* But all sorts of things, including luck in getting (or not getting) the questions you hoped for and one's state of mind and emotions the day of the exam, can have an important effect on the result.

(5) *All students have an equal chance to do well on exams. . . .* [E]ven major differences in their conditions of life have a negligible impact on their performance. There is such a strong correlation between students' family income and their test scores, however, that the radical educational theorist, Ira Shor, has suggested (tongue-in-cheek) that college applications should ignore test scores altogether and just ask students to enter their family income. The results would be the same—with relatively few exceptions, the same people would get admitted into college, but then, of course, the belief that there is equality of opportunity in the classroom would stand forth as the myth that it is.

(6) *Exams are the fairest way to distribute society's scarce resources* to the young, hence the association of exams with the ideas of meritocracy and equality of opportunity. But if some students consistently do better on exams because of the advantages they possess and other students do not outside of school, then directing society's main benefits to these same people compounds the initial inequality.

10 (7) *Exams, and particularly the fear of them, are necessary in order to motivate stu-*

*See the margin gloss on IQ tests on page 500.

dents to do their assignments. Who can doubt that years of reacting to such threats have produced in many students a reflex of the kind depicted here? The sad fact is that the natural curiosity of young people and their desire to learn, develop, advance, master, and the pleasure that comes from succeeding—which could and should motivate all studying—has been progressively replaced in their psyches by a pervasive fear of failing. This needn't be. For the rest, if the only reason a student does the assignments is that he/she is worried about the exam, he/she should not be taking that course in the first place.

(8) *Exams are not injurious, socially, intellectually, and psychologically.* Complaining about exams may be most students' first truly informed criticism about society because they are its victims and know from experience how exams work. They know, for example, that exams don't only involve reading questions and writing answers. They also involve forced isolation from other students, prohibition on talking and walking around and going to the bathroom, writing a lot faster than usual, physical discomfort, worry, fear, anxiety, and often guilt.

They are also aware that exams do a poor job of testing what students actually know. But it is here that most of their criticisms run into a brick wall, because most students don't know enough about society to understand the role that exams—especially taking so many exams—play in preparing them to take their place in it.

But if exams are not what most people think they are, then what are they? The short answer is that exams have less to do with testing us for what we are supposed to know than teaching us what the other aspects of instruction cannot get at (or get at as well). To understand what that is we must examine what the capitalist* class require from a system of education. Here, it is clear that capitalists need a system of education that provides young people with the knowledge and skills necessary for their businesses to function and prosper. But they also want schools to give youth the

beliefs, attitudes, emotions, and associated habits of behavior that make it easy for capitalists to tap into this store of knowledge and skills. They need all this not only to maximize their profits, but to help reproduce the social, economic, and even political conditions and accompanying processes that allow them to extract profits. Without workers, consumers and citizens who are well versed in and accepting of their roles in these processes, the entire capitalist system would grind to a halt. It is here—particularly as regards the behavioral and attitudinal prerequisites of capitalist rule—that the culture of exams has become indispensable. So what do exams "teach" students?

(1) The crush of tests gets students to believe that one gets what one works for, that the standards by which this is decided are objective and fair, and therefore that those who do better deserve what they get; and that the same holds for those who do badly. After a while, this attitude is carried over to what students find in the rest of society, including their own failures later in life, where it encourages them to "blame the victim" (themselves or others) and feel guilty for what is not their fault.

15 (2) By fixing a time and a form in which they have to deliver or else, exams prepare students for the more rigorous discipline of the work situation that lies ahead.

(3) In forcing students to think and write faster than they ordinarily do, exams get them ready mentally, emotionally, and also morally for the speed-ups they will face on the job.

(4) The self-discipline students acquire in preparing for exams also helps them put up with the disrespect, personal abuse, and boredom that awaits them on the job.

(5) Exams are orders that are not open to question—"discuss this," "outline that," etc.—and taking so many exams conditions students to accept unthinkingly the orders that will come from their future employers.

(6) By fitting the infinite variety of answers given on exams into the straitjacket of A, B, C, D, and F, students get accustomed to the stan-

*The term *capitalism* can be used to refer to an economic system based on a free market in which supply and demand dictate the movement of goods and services. The term can be used more broadly to refer to a social system based on the ideas of individual rights and free choice.

dardization of people as well as of things and the impersonal job categories that will constitute such an important part of their identity later on.

20 (7) Because passing an exam is mainly good for enabling students to move up a grade so they can take a slightly harder exam, which—if they pass—enables them to repeat the exercise *ad infinitum,* they begin to see life as an endless series of ever more complicated exams, where one never finishes being judged and the need for being prepared and respectful of the judging authorities only grows.

(8) Because their teachers know all the right answers to the exams, students tend to assume that those who are above them in other hierarchies also know much more than they do.

(9) Because their teachers genuinely want them to do well on exams, students also mistakenly assume that those in relation of authority over them in other hierarchies are also rooting for them to succeed, that is, have their best interests at heart.

(10) Because most tests are taken individually, striving to do well on a test is treated as something that concerns students only as individuals. Cooperative solutions are equated with cheating, if considered at all.

(11) Because one is never quite ready for an exam, there is always something more to do, students often feel guilty for reading materials or engaging in activities unrelated to the exam. The whole of life, it would appear, is but preparation for exams or doing what is required in order to succeed (as those in charge define "success").

25 (12) With the Damocles* sword of a failing (or for some a mediocre) grade hanging over their heads throughout their years in school (including university), the inhibiting fear of swift and dire punishment never leaves students, no matter their later situation.

(13) Coupled with the above, because there is always so much to be known, exams—especially so many of them—tend to undermine students' self-confidence and to raise

their levels of anxiety, with the result that most young people remain unsure that they will ever know enough to criticize existing institutions and become even physically uncomfortable at the thought of trying to put something better in their place.

(14) Exams also play a key role in determining course content, leaving little time for material that is not on the exam. Among the first things to be omitted in this "tightening" of the curriculum are students' own reactions to the topics that come up, collective reflection on the main problems of the day, alternative points of view and other possibilities generally, the larger picture (where everything fits), explorations of topics triggered by individual curiosity, and anything else that is likely to promote creative, cooperative, or critical thinking.

(15) Exams also determine the form in which most teaching goes on, since for any given exam there is generally a best way to prepare for it. Repetition and forced memorization, even learning by rote, and frequent quizzes (more exams) leave little time for other more imaginative approaches to conveying, exchanging and questioning facts and ideas.

(16) Multiple exams become one of the main factors determining the character of the relation between students (with students viewing each other as competitors for the best grades), the relation between students and teachers (with most students viewing their teachers as examiners and graders first, and most teachers viewing their students largely in terms of how well they have done on exams), also the relation between teachers and school administrators (since principals and deans now have an "objective" standard by which to measure teacher performance), and even the relation between school administrations and various state bodies (since the same standard is used by the state to judge the work of schools and school systems). Exams mediate all social relations in the educational system in a manner similar to the way money mediates relations between people in the larger society with the same dehumanizing results.

*According to Roman myth, Damocles was a courtier in Syracuse, Greece, in the fourth century BCE who envied the life of his ruler Dionysius. Given the chance to experience that life, Damocles agreed until he realized that, once seated in the ruler's throne, a large sword was suspended over his head by a single horse hair. The experience prompted him to reevaluate his beliefs about what constitutes a good life.

30 While exams have been with us for a long time, socializing students in all the ways that I have outlined above, it is only recently that the mania for exams has begun to affect government policies. Why now? Globalization, or whatever it is one chooses to call this new stage, has arrived. But to which of its aspects is the current drive for more exams a carefully fashioned response? The proponents of such educational "reform" point to the intensified competition between industries and workers worldwide and the increasingly rapid pace at which economic changes of all kinds are occurring. To survive in this new order requires people, they say, who are not only efficient, but also have a variety of skills (or can quickly acquire them) and the flexibility to change tasks whenever called upon to do so. Thus, the only way to prepare our youth for the new economic life that awaits them is to raise standards of education, and that entails, among other things, more exams.

A more critical approach to globalization begins by emphasizing that the intensification of economic competition worldwide is driven by capitalists' efforts to maximize their profits. It is this that puts all the other developments associated with globalization into motion. It is well known that, all things being equal, the less capitalists pay their workers and the less money they spend on improving work conditions and reducing pollution, the more profit they make. Recent technological progress in transportation and communication, together with free trade and the abolition of laws restricting the movement of capital, allow capitalists to consider workers all over the world in making their calculations. While the full impact of these developments is yet to be felt, we can already see two of its most important effects in the movement of more and more companies (and parts of companies) out of the U.S. and a rollback of modest gains in wages, benefits, and work conditions that American workers have won over the last 50 years.

The current rage for more exams needs to be viewed as part of a larger strategy that includes stoking patriotic fires and chipping away at traditional civil liberties (both rationalized by the so-called war on terrorism), the promotion of "family values," restrictions on sexual freedom (but not, as we see, on sexual hypocrisy), and the push for more prisons and longer prison sentences for a whole range of minor crimes.

Is there a connection between exams and the privatization of public education? They appear to be separate, but look again. With new investment opportunities failing to keep up with the rapidly escalating surpluses in search of them (a periodic problem for a system that never pays its workers enough to consume all the wealth they produce), the public sector has become the latest "last" frontier for capitalist expansion. Given its size and potential for profit, what are state prisons or utilities or transport or communication systems or other social services next to public education? But how to convince the citizenry that companies whose only concern is with the bottom line can do a better job educating our young than public servants dedicated to the task? What seems impossible could be done if somehow education were redefined to emphasize the qualities associated with business and its

GLOBALIZATION

The term *globalization* has been used to refer to a complex set of political, social, and economic developments in the last decade or so that have made nations, societies, and regions of the world more interdependent. Commerce, communication, and travel between various regions of the world have increased, and international trade agreements have facilitated economic and social contacts across national borders. According to journalist Thomas Friedman, whose 1999 book *The Lexus and the Olive Tree* examines the effects of globalization, "Globalization is not a phenomenon. It is not just some passing trend. Today it is an overarching international system shaping the domestic politics and foreign relations of virtually every country, and we need to understand it as such." Whether or not globalization is a good thing is intensely debated. You can find a sampling of the debate at http://globalization.about.com/library/weekly/aa080701a.htm.

achievements. Then—by definition—business could do the "job" better than any public agency.

Enter exams. Standardization, easily quantifiable results, and the willingness to reshape all intervening processes to obtain them characterize the path to success in both exams and business. When that happens (and to the extent it has already happened), putting education in the hands of businesspeople who know best how to dispense with "inessentials" becomes a perfectly rational thing to do.

35 What should students do about all this? Well, they shouldn't refuse to take exams (unless the whole class gets involved) and they shouldn't drop out of school. Given the relations of power inside education and throughout the rest of society, that would be suicidal and suicide is never good politics. Rather, they should become better students by learning more about the role of education, and exams in particular, in capitalism. Nowhere does the contradiction between the selfish and manipulative interests of our ruling class and the educational and developmental interests of students stand out in such sharp relief as in the current debate over exams. Students of all ages need to get involved in this debate in order to raise the consciousness of young people regarding the source of their special oppression and the possibility of uniting with other oppressed groups to create a truly human society. Everything depends on the youth of today doing better on this crucial test than my generation did, because the price for failure has never been so high. Will they succeed? Can they afford to fail?

CONTEXT

Founded in 1987, *Z Magazine* describes its mission as follows: "Z is an independent monthly magazine dedicated to resisting injustice, defending against repression, and creating liberty. It sees the racial, gender, class, and political dimensions of personal life as fundamental to understanding and improving contemporary circumstances; and it aims to assist activist efforts for a better future." To what extent does Ollman's essay fit this mission? In what ways do you think Ollman's argument might be effective for a wider audience than the readers of *Z Magazine*?

Questions for Discussion

1. Ollman discusses eight "myths" that he believes surround testing in the United States. Evaluate his discussion of these "myths." How widespread do you think the eight beliefs he calls "myths" really are? How effectively does he dispel each of these beliefs? To what extent does his discussion of these beliefs—and his description of them as "myths"—enhance or weaken his argument? How does his discussion of these "myths" compare to Gregory Cizek's discussion of the ten benefits of standardized testing (see pages 503–511)?

2. Ollman asserts that "most students don't know enough about society to understand the role that exams . . . play in preparing them to take their place in it." How does this point contribute to his main argument about testing? How might it reflect his Marxist perspective? Do you agree with him?

3. Ollman claims that a capitalist system requires citizens with certain beliefs, attitudes, and skills who also accept specified roles in American society. He then offers a list of sixteen ways in which testing teaches students what they need to know to serve the capitalist system. How persuasive do you find this list? What responses might you offer to Ollman's lessons? Do you think Ollman expects most Americans to reject his list?

4. Why does Ollman believe that globalization is an important factor influencing standardized testing? What evidence does he offer in support of this position? Evaluate the effectiveness of that evidence. Do you agree with Ollman about the connection between globalization and testing? Why or why not?

5. Ollman offers advice to students about what they should do about standardized tests. In what ways do you think this advice might enhance the effectiveness of his argument? How realistic do you think his advice is?

6. Ollman's essay can be described as an argument based on deductive reasoning (see pages 88–93). What is the basic premise of his argument? Do you think most Americans would agree with him? Explain.

7. Using the Toulmin Model of argumentation (see pages 93–97), identify Ollman's central claim and the warrant (or warrants) on which that claim is based. Do you think most Americans would accept his warrant(s)? Explain.

④ **PETER ELBOW, "Getting Along without Grades—
and Getting Along with Them, Too"**

Peter Elbow is one of the most influential and most widely respected writing specialists in the country. After achieving national recognition with the 1973 publication of *Writing without Teachers,* he continued to be a prolific writer over the next three decades. This distinguished publication record was achieved while he was fulfilling many other responsibilities. Before joining the faculty of the University of Massachusetts, from which he recently retired, Elbow directed the writing program at the State University of New York at Stony Brook. A popular speaker and writing consultant, Elbow is also a regular contributor to journals such as *College English* and the *Journal of Advanced Composition.* The following argument is from *Everyone Can Write: Essays toward a Hopeful Theory of Writing and Teaching Writing.* As the subtitle suggests, much of Elbow's work is about hope. In addition to being hopeful about students, believing that they have ideas worth communicating and can succeed at expressing these ideas, he is hopeful for teachers, believing that they take their responsibilities seriously and are capable of growth. You will find signs of this hope, as well as references to two of the schools at which Elbow taught (Evergreen State College and the Massachusetts Institute of Technology), in the argument you are about to read. You will also find that he is aware that some people are inclined to dismiss his ideas as too hopeful or idealistic. You can judge for yourself. As you read the following pages, ask yourself if you would enjoy taking a class from a teacher with the ideas Elbow conveys here and the voice with which he conveys them.

Getting Along without Grades—
and Getting Along with Them, Too

PETER ELBOW

1 In this paper I am driven by the utopian impulse but also the impulse to tinker. On the one hand, I insist on the possibility of large change: grading is neither natural nor inevitable; we can avoid grading; we can step outside the mentality of evaluation; we can even change systems. Yet on the other hand, I insist on the importance of small, pragmatic changes—what some might call mere fiddling. Indeed, most of what I suggest here can be used within a conventional grading system. After all, most of us are obliged to do our evaluating within such systems (for now), and the human tendency to evaluate is inevitable. The utopian and the pragmatic impulses may seem at odds, but the common element is an insistence that things can be better. Change is possible.

My focus is on pedagogy, practice, and by implication, policy. My method is simply to try to think through my own evaluative practices since they are the practices all teachers engage in; this is a report on experience and thinking rather than on research.

When I speak of grades, I'm speaking of the quantitative, official grades that teachers commonly put on papers—and also the course grades we give at the end of the term and the holistic grades we use in large-scale writing assessments. I mean to distinguish between grading (quantitative marks) and the much larger and more various and multidemensional activity evaluation.

This essay is in three parts: first, suggestions for how to step outside of grading; second, suggestions for how to step outside of the very mentality of judging or evaluation; and third, suggestions for how to *use* grades more effectively.

1. Ways to Step Outside of Grading

5 If I am suggesting ways to step outside of grading, I suppose I'd better summarize my reasons for *wanting* to do so. Grades seem to me a problem for these reasons:

- They aren't trustworthy.
- They don't have clear meaning.
- They don't give students feedback about *what* they did well or badly.
- They undermine the teaching-and-learning situation in the following ways:
  - They lead many students to work more for the sake of the grade than for learning.
  - They lead to an adversarial atmosphere; students often resent or even fight us about grades; many students no longer feel the teacher as ally in the learning process and try to hide what they don't understand. (Think of patients hiding symptoms from doctors.)
  - They lead to a competitive atmosphere among students themselves.
- Figuring out grades is difficult, and the task often makes us anxious because fairness is so hard to achieve.

Conventional grading is so ubiquitous that people tend to see it as inevitable and to feel hopeless about making any changes.

Therefore, it's important to realize that grading is not built into the universe; grading is not like gravity—not "natural" or inevitable. If that sounds utopian, I can point to The Evergreen State College. I taught there for nine years. Since it started in 1971, faculty have given narrative evaluations instead of grades. The system works fine on all counts, including success in helping students enter high quality professional and graduate school. Where Evergreen is a nonelite state college in Washington, Hampshire College is an elite private institution here in Amherst, Massachusetts, that also has a solid history of success with no grades. So we mustn't forget that educational institutions *can* get along just fine without grades. The pressure for grades is probably greatest at the secondary level since grades seem so central to the college admissions process; yet there are secondary schools that prosper without grades.

But discussions of institutions like Evergreen and Hampshire tend to trap people into either/or thinking: whether or not to have grading at all; whether or not to transform the entire curriculum as they've done at Evergreen or Hampshire. Let's wrest the discussion out of this binary rut. Instead of fighting about *Yes* or *No,* let's discuss *When?* and *How much?* I am interested in exploring temporary time-outs from grading, even while operating under a conventional grading system.

And let's jump from the largest scale to the smallest: *freewriting.* To freewrite for ten minutes is to step outside of grading for ten minutes. When I get students to freewrite, I am using my authority to create unusual conditions in order to contradict or interrupt the pervasive feeling in the air that writing is always evaluated. What is essential here are the two central features of freewriting: that it be private (thus I don't collect it or have students share it with anyone else); and that it be nonstop (thus there isn't time for planning, and control is usually diminished). Students quickly catch on and enter into the spirit. It's sad if teachers use freewriting in thoughtless or mechanical ways: just ten minutes now and then for no good reason—and sadder if teachers call it freewriting but collect it and read it. Still, most freewriting is a common instance of a kind of writing that is not really so rare: *nongraded* writing.

Every time teachers get students to do nongraded writing, they are inviting students to notice that the link between writing and grading can be broken: it is possible to write and not worry about how the teacher will grade it; it is possible to write in pursuit of one's own goals and standards and not just someone else's. When teachers assign journal writing and don't grade it, this too is an important time-out from grading.

10 A bigger time-out from grading is the single *nongraded assignment.* These can be "quick-writes" or sketches done in class or for homework; sometimes they are simply "ungraded essays." In either case they are usually unrevised. These writings carry more weight than freewritings if the teacher reads them or asks students to read them to each other, but still they break the link between writing and grading. (It helps to say out loud to the students that this writing is ungraded. Occasionally, students write *as though* it were a graded exercise. And indeed, many students have had the experience of being *told* that something was ungraded and then being surprised.)

These are small time-outs—ten minutes, one or two hours. What if we have *ten days of nongraded writing?* We can do that and still work solidly within a grading system. Many teachers start the semester with this kind of orgy of nongraded writing, and it has a deep effect on students' and teachers' relationship to writing. It improves students' fluency and enlivens their voices on paper; it helps them learn to take risks in writing; and it permits us to assign *much* more writing than we usually can in two weeks.

Portfolios. Portfolios are a way to refrain from putting grades on individual papers: for a while we can just write comments and students can revise. Grading can wait till we have more pieces of writing in hand—more data to judge. By avoiding frequent ranking or grading, we make it *somewhat* less likely for students to become addicted to oversimple numerical rankings—to think that evaluation always translates into a simple number. Portfolios permit me to refrain from grading individual papers and limit myself to writerly evaluative comments—and help students see this as a positive rather than a negative thing, a chance to be graded on a body of their best work that can be judged more fairly. Portfolios are particularly helpful as occasions for asking students to write extensive and thoughtful explorations of their own strengths and weaknesses.

Contracts for a Grade. For the last few years, this has been my favorite way to step outside of most grading while still working within a regular grading system. Contracts provide a way to avoid trying to *measure* the quality of work or learning and yet still arrive at a grade for the course. A contract says, "If you do *x, y,* and *z,* you can count on such and such a grade." For me, the pedagogical principle in using contracts is this: I don't trust my efforts to *measure* learning or quality of writing, and I hate pretending to do so. I'd rather put my efforts into something I do trust and

---

CONTEXT

If Elbow touched only briefly on portfolios here, it was because he could assume that his original audience was already familiar with them. He had advocated their use for twenty years before publishing this piece.

Portfolios can be designed in different ways. But here is the basic concept: instead of being graded on each paper after it has been submitted and judged as a final product, students submit work that is evaluated and then are given the option to revise. A portfolio—or a collection of work—is submitted at the end of the semester (and sometimes at midsemester as well). It contains final drafts in addition to other material—such as earlier drafts and a self-assessment. This process encourages students to think critically about their work, as well as about how they wish to present themselves. This method of presenting representative work is not altogether different from how artists or photographers might prepare a portfolio containing work in which they take pride when seeking a commission.

enjoy: trying to specify activities and behaviors that will *lead* to learning and good writing.

Most often I have used what might be called a limited or impure or timid contract—a contract that spells out the many, many activities that seem most central to producing learning for the course, and then says, "If you do all these, you are guaranteed a course grade of B." But the contract goes on to say, "If you want an A, I have to judge most of your papers or your portfolio to be excellent." Thus I am not getting rid of all official measurement of quality. But I am vastly reducing it.[1]

15 Contracts highlight the distinction between evaluation and grading. My contract minimizes grading (and a full contract eliminates it altogether), but in doing so it *helps evaluation to be more effective.* That is, even though a contract permits me to cut back on evaluation when I find that helpful, I continue to give lots of evaluation, and the contract permits me to make blunter criticisms or pushier suggestions and have students listen to them better. They know that my responses have nothing to do with their grade (up to a B). Students needn't go along with what I say in order to get a good grade. I've set up the contract so that they cannot refrain from making significant revisions, but I emphasize to them that they can revise entirely differently from how I might have suggested or implied—and they don't have to make their revisions necessarily better, just substantively different. In short, by decoupling evaluation from grading, I think we can make it healthier and more productive.

I like the learning situation my contract puts my students into: they have to listen to my reactions, evaluation, and advice, yet they get to make up their own mind about whether

to go along with what I say. Their decision will have no effect on their grade (up to a B). This means they have to *think* about my response on its own terms—listen to me as reader and human being—instead of just reacting to me in the thoughtless and habitual ways in which so many students understandably react to teacher feedback. That is, students too often feel, "Of course my teacher is right," or else, "Well that's the kind of junk that *this* teacher wants, so I guess I'll do it for my grade." Either way, these students don't really wrestle in their minds with the crucial question of whether my reactions or comments actually make sense to them. In the end I think my contract gets students to listen to me better. (Of course, students occasionally tell me that they *feel* pressure to go along with my comments—even though they can see that it really won't help their grade. This provides fruitful occasions for me to help students explore their learning process and how they deal with the role of being a student: how they tend to feel and react to teacher comments and grades.) So whereas some people say that teachers are evading their intellectual responsibility if they don't grade, I would argue that we can create *more* intellectual engagement by minimizing grades and highlighting evaluation.

I hear an objection:

But we need grades for motivation—to get students to work hard.

But notice how *indirectly* grades motivate students. The casual link between grading and student work is very tenuous. We hope that by awarding fair grades, we will cause students to exert themselves to engage in the learning activities we want them to engage in. But our hope is dashed as often as it is fulfilled. Some students get good grades without much work; some have given up trying to get good grades; a few don't care what grade they get; still others work only to psych out the teacher rather than to learn (and a few of these even cheat or plagiarize*). I prefer the way a contract is more direct and simply requires the activities I

*For information about plagiarism, see pages 163–165 and 226–233.

1. Perhaps I should say that I am still grading, but that my only grades are *excellent, acceptable* and *not acceptable for the terms of the contract,* but the procedure feels more like not grading. Perhaps, in addition, I should not use the word "contract" since I impose this policy unilaterally rather than letting students have a choice about whether to enter into it; and I don't ask students to sign anything. But the word is a convenient shorthand that suggests the general approach.

think will lead to learning. I'd rather put my time and effort into trying to figure out which activities will in fact help them learn and grow rather than into trying to measure the exact degree of quality of the writing they turn in and hope that my grade leads to effort.

Do I find that using a contract makes everything perfect? No. I think my contract leads to a bit *more* work from the class as a whole, more tasks accomplished by more people. But I think it also leads to a bit *less* pushing, struggle, or strain from a number of students. This disappoints me, but I have to accept the fact that my real goal is not struggle for its own sake but struggle that comes *from them*—from intrinsic motivation. When students are habituated to struggling mostly or even only for grades, it's not surprising that they have a hard time coming up with this rarer and more precious kind of struggle. Gradually, pieces of self-motivation begin to kick in, and when that happens it's very exciting for both them and me. But I have to settle for less.

2. Ways to Step Outside of the Mentality of Evaluation

20 I want to up the ante. If we step outside of grading, we may not be stepping outside the mentality of evaluation or judging. After all, we sometimes read an ungraded assignment and say, "I'm sure glad I don't have to grade this because it really stinks." Is it *possible* to stop judging or seeing writing in terms of quality? Yes. In fact, it's not so unusual. That is, even though it is inevitable that humans *often* look at things through the lens of judgment or quality, sometimes they don't.

The most obvious example is when we like or love. Sometimes we like or dislike a person, an object, a work of art—and more to the point here, a piece of writing—without any judgment of its quality. We know this can happen because sometimes we are even aware of the two mentalities at once: we like it but we know it is not good—or we dislike it but we know it is good. We often love someone or something

because we "value" them, not because we "evaluate" them. The loving or "valuing" is something we do or give or add; we don't necessarily base it on our judgment of the "value" or "quality" of the person or object.

I'm not saying that we always take off the judging lens when we like or love, for sometimes our liking or loving is indeed based on our evaluation of quality. ("It's so great I love it.") I'm simply insisting that liking or loving *can* operate outside of judging—and often do. When I began to realize this, I found myself liking more often—students and students' writing—without wearing my judging hat. Thus we can get better at liking students and their writing; it's a skill. . . . My main claim, then, is limited, but important: I'm insisting on the empirical observation that it is not unusual for us to spend some time outside the evaluative mentality.

I find it a great relief to do this now and then. It seems to me that these time-outs from the evaluative mentality help my teaching. I think they foster an atmosphere of support and appreciation that helps students flourish, think well, and stretch themselves.

I am not denying that there is a different and more obvious kind of stretching that comes from the opposite atmosphere of judging, evaluating, and criticizing. Many people testify with appreciation to how a tough teacher's evaluative criticism made them stretch. But this stretching-through-evaluative-criticism does not negate the quite different and more delicate kind of stretching that can occur when we reduce or remove the pressure of judgment and evaluation. Sometimes people don't take risks or try out their own values or start to use their own internal motivation until critical thinking is turned off and even nonsense and garbage are welcomed. In such a setting people sometimes think themselves into their best thinking or imagine themselves into being more of who they could be. Nonevaluative support and acceptance are common in the family, especially toward infants and young children, but the evaluative

*Because the words "great works" are in quotation marks in this context, they evoke an association with the great works of literature, history, theology, and philosophy that scholars once thought could be identified and listed. See page 451.

mentality is pervasive in school and college settings. Of course, banishing evaluation does not always lead to this delicate stretching—but then neither does evaluation always lead to that other kind of stretching.

25 This talk of liking and loving tends to sound soft, fuzzy, and unintellectual. I don't want to run away from that most dreaded indictment, *soft!* It's time to insist openly that there's nothing wrong with time-out zones from what is critical, hard, cool, and detached—not just in elementary school but in higher education. We need it, even for good thinking.

Nevertheless, I want to cut through the shallow-minded association between not being evaluative and not being intellectual. That is, we can have time-outs from the evaluative mentality itself and still operate in a fully intellectual, cognitive, academic spirit. We can do so through the use of certain questions about texts—especially about student writing.

Admittedly, the questions we most often ask of student writing are quality questions: "How good or bad is it? What are its strengths and weaknesses? How can it be better?" But these are not the only questions to ask of a text, and indeed they are not the most common questions we ask of important texts in literature, history, biology, or physics—whether in teaching or scholarship. In studying important texts we tend to ask questions like these:

> What does the text say? What does it imply or entail? What are its consequences? What does the writer assume? What is the writer's point of view or stance? Who does the text speak to? How does the text ask me to see the world? What would I do if I believed it?

Nothing should stop us from using these questions on student writing. They are simple, obvious, and important questions that have no inherent connection to quality or value. They are all requests to summarize, explicate, or extend the paper (or, carried out step further, to play the "believing game" with it).

Admittedly, when we use these questions on professional writing, we tend to *assume* value—sometimes even that these are "great works"* and so don't need evaluating. And with student writing, many of these neutral questions have taken on evaluative freight. "What is this paragraph saying?" often means, "I don't think it is saying anything" or "You are confused."

30 But we don't *need* to use these questions in this way, and it's not hard to answer them without saying anything about a paper's quality. A careful summary of a bad paper need not reveal anything of its badness. Yes, we *can* summarize a paper by saying, "It says X—which is absurd," or "It says both X an not X—which is self-contradictory." or "It says X and P and there is no relation between them." But we don't need to put a judgmental spin on summaries. For the fact remains that plenty of *excellent* papers say things that seem absurd or logically contradictory or seemingly unrelated. Some people can't summarize without praising or criticizing, but that's because they've never practiced.

There is one kind of badness that might seem unavoidable in a summary: if a paper simply doesn't say much at all, a careful summary will contain damningly little. But even this kind of badness will not show up when we answer the other questions: "What does the paper imply or entail, what does the writer assume?" Besides, some *excellent* papers say remarkably little.

So if we learn how to answer these kinds of questions about our students' writing without a habitual edge of evaluation (and it's not so hard) and if we train our students to answer them about each others' writing, we will be doing something perfectly intellectual, academic, cognitive, hard, and detached. We will not be giving in to the dread disease of "softness." Yet we will still be stepping outside of the mentality of judgment. Most of us have done this if only now and again, perhaps inadvertently. As with loving and liking, these questions don't *force* us out of the mentality of evaluation, but they *invite* us—if we are willing—to take off the lens of judging for a while. We discover it is possible to have long discussions of the meaning and implications of a paper and find we have wholly forgotten about the question of how good it is.

The same goes for other interesting questions we can ask of any text:

How does the paper relate to other events or values in the culture? How does it relate to what other students are writing—or other texts around us? How does this text relate to other things the student has written?

There are related questions that, interestingly, we can't usually answer without the writer's help:

How does the paper relate to events in the writer's life? Why did the writer write these words?

Yet these questions are no less intellectual or analytic or interesting. We often ask published writers to answer them. Why not ask our students too?

35 It's a bit harder to strip away our habits of judgment from some of the most interesting and pointed questions about craft and structure in a paper:

How is the text organized or put together? How does the text function so as to say what it says and do what it does?

But even these questions *can* be answered in a non-evaluative fashion.

Finally, I would call attention to the most bluntly simple, obvious, and frequently asked questions about a text, and insist that it is also, in fact, entirely irrelevant to quality:

As reader, what are my thoughts on the topic? Where do I agree or disagree?

For even if I disagree completely with everything the paper says, it does not follow that I consider the paper bad. We often disagree with excellent writing. Even more frequently, we agree with terrible writing. It turns out not to be so very hard simply to talk about our agreement or disagreement and to give our thoughts, and not enter at all into the realm of judgment. If I simply *engage* the issue of the paper and tell my thoughts, I need not be playing the quality game.

Many students have never had a teacher take their message seriously enough to engage with it by saying, "Here are *my* thoughts about your issue." For this reason, students will often *infer* value judgments even if we are not making them. But they can gradually catch on to this more frankly intellectual way of talking about texts—and will be grateful to do so. When teachers talk only about how good or bad a paper is or talk only about its strengths and weaknesses, making suggestions for improvement, this can function as a way to *avoid* engagement with the topic or the writer.

None of these analytic, academic questions are inherently evaluative, yet they are much more intellectually interesting than questions about quality. In the end, then, I conclude that the *least* interesting questions we can ask of any text—by students or by published authors—are questions of quality or evaluation. The most intellectually interesting work comes from asking and answering many of our most common analytic and academic questions—questions that invite us (though they do not require us) to step outside the mentality of evaluation.

3. Ways to Use Grades More Effectively

I turn now to the nitty-gritty: grading itself. The essential fact about grades is that they are one-dimensional. Grades are simply numbers and the essence of numbers is very austere: N is wholly defined as "greater than $N - 1$ and less than $N + 1$." B has no other meaning than "worse than A and better than C." Conventional grades demarcate ten or eleven levels of "pure quality"—wholly undefined and unarticulated. We can visualize the one-dimensional essence of grading quite literally with a simple vertical line. Such a line is pure verticality; it is entirely lacking in the horizontal dimension.

40 This pure, numerical, one dimensional verticality—no words or concepts attached—is the main reason why conventional grades are untrustworthy if they are used as descriptors for *complex* human performances—and thus why grading leads to such difficulty and dispute. We see even more unrelenting verticality when faculty members grade essays on a scale of 1 to 100 (which is, amazingly, not so uncommon, for example, in some law schools).

In this section, I am suggesting two ways to deal with this unrelenting verticality: (A) reduce it somewhat by using fewer grades—what I call "minimal grading"; (B) add a bit of the horizontal dimension by using criteria.

(A) Minimal Grading—Reducing the Vertical

We can reduce the verticality of conventional grades by simply using a scale with fewer levels. Most of us use minimal grades when we make low-stakes assignments and grade them pass/fail or else use $\sqrt{}$ and $\sqrt{+}$ and $\sqrt{-}$. But we tend to assume that if an assignment is important and we want students to take it more seriously and work harder on it, we should use conventional grades with their ten or more levels of quality.

But this assumption is misleading and counterproductive. It rests on a failure to distinguish between *stakes* and *levels.* Every act of grading involves two very different questions: "How much credit is at stake in this performance?" "How many levels of quality shall I use on my evaluation scale?" When students take an assignment more seriously and work harder, it usually has little to do with our having added levels to our grading scale, and much more to do with our having raised the stakes and made the assignment *count* for more of the final grade. Few students will struggle hard for an A that doesn't count much for their final grade. (A few students have become obsessive about *any* A; a few others will struggle on a low-stakes assignment—not for

the grade but because they are particularly interested in the issue.)

Thus the most reliable way to use grades to make students work harder is to raise the stakes—as long as we make the passing level high enough. Even a two-level scale can be very demanding if we put the bar at a high level. At M.I.T. for the last twenty years or so, faculty have given nothing but Pass and Fail as final grades to all first year students in all courses. The stakes are very high indeed and so are the standards, but only two levels are used. We need only increase the number of levels to three or four if we want to give less-skilled students a goal of "pretty good"—or to spur those students who are hungry to distinguish their work as superior. If we use three levels, we have even more scope for making strategic decisions about where to place the bars.

45 But there *is* something we reliably achieve by increasing the number of grading levels: we make *our* work harder. Think of the difference between reading a stack of paper in order to give them conventional grades, versus reading them so as only to pick out those that stand out as *notably weak* or *notably strong.*

I'm suggesting, then, that we can get what we need from the grading of important or high-stakes assignments if we use just three (or at most four) levels and make *pass* hard enough to get. Most of our difficulties with grading come from having too many levels—too much verticality:

- The more levels we use, the more untrustworthy and unfair the results. We know what the history of literary criticism has shown (along with informal research by students turning in the same paper to multiple teachers): good readers do not agree in their rankings of quality: Your A paper is liable to become a B in my hands—or vice versa. Diederich provides the classic research on this matter.)

- The more levels we use, the more chances students have to resent or even dispute those fine-grained distinctions we struggled so hard to make in the first place. (Think of the resentment-laden arguments that occur about a plus or a minus!) Thus the more levels we have, the more we slide toward an adversarial student/teacher relationship and consequently the more damage to the teaching/learning climate. Yes, as long as there are *any* distinctions or levels at all, *some* students will be disappointed or resentful at not getting the higher level they were hoping for. But fewer levels means fewer borderline performances.

- The more levels we use, the more we establish a competitive atmosphere among students and a pecking order culture.

- The more levels we use, the more work for us. It's *hard* making all those fine distinctions—say between A and A minus or B plus and B. If we use just three levels all we need to do is pick out papers that *stand out* as notably strong and notably weak.

In short, boundary decisions are always the most untrustworthy and arguable. Fewer boundaries mean fewer boundary decisions (see the highly useful pieces by Haswell and Wyche-Smith).

Let me consider some objections to minimal grading.

> But how can we compute a final grade for the semester using eleven levels, if our constituent grades use only three levels?

This is a problem if we only have a couple of constituent grades to work with at the end of the semester, for example, one paper and two exams. But if we have a fair number of papers, exercises, quizzes, or tests on a

CONTEXT

Paul Diederich—whose work is cited at the end of this argument—wrote, "As a test of writing ability, no test is as convincing to English teachers, to teachers in other disciplines, and to the public as actual samples of each student's writing, especially if done under test conditions in which one can be sure that each sample is the student's own unaided work." This statement was published in 1974. If it now seems obvious, it is because decades of work by composition scholars and hard-working English teachers has established that writing ability cannot be accurately accessed by tests that are easy to score—such as multiple choice or true/false tests or those that invite students to identify errors in a sample passage. From today's perspective, the phrase "unaided work" seems problematic, because many scholars and teachers now believe in collaborative learning and the importance of procedures such as peer review. But Diederich's stance was determined not only by the era in which he wrote but also by his work for the Educational Testing Service, the company that creates and distributes tests such as the SAT—tests designed to identify what an individual knows and understands.

three-level scale, we can use some mathematical formula to calculate the final grade by simply counting up points (perhaps with different weighings according to how important the assignments are): 3 for a Strong, 2 for Satisfactory, and 1 for Weak. Alternatively, if there are a lot of low-stakes assignments graded Satisfactory/Unsatisfactory, we can decide that students with Satisfactory on all their low-stakes assignments start off with a foundation of B. Then their final grade is pulled up or down by Strongs or Weaks on their high-stakes assignments. Or vice-versa: we can average the high-stakes pieces, and if the result is some kind of "satisfactory" or "2"—let low-stakes pieces decide the gradations between C and B. A multitude of scoring systems are possible—and I haven't even mentioned other factors that most teachers count in their final grading, such as attendance, participation, effort, and improvement.

> We already use minimal grading: most faculty already give nothing but As and Bs.

Yes, many faculty have fallen into this practice. When some faculty members give a full range of grades and others give mostly As and Bs, we have a situation of semantic chaos. The grade of B has become particularly ambiguous: readers of a transcript have no way of knowing whether it denotes good strong competent work (many college catalogues define it as an "honors grade") or disappointing, second-rate work. C might mean genuinely satisfactory work or virtually failing work. Critics of "grade inflation" charge that even "A" has lost its meaning of genuine excellence (though some research undercuts that charge, see U.S. Department of Education). If instead of using symbols like A, B, and C, teachers used meaningful words like "excellent," "honors," "outstanding," "strong," "satisfactory," "weak," "poor," "unsatisfactory," all parties to grading would have a better understanding of the message.

Some teachers will probably still give mostly Excellent or Strong.

Inevitably so. But the point here is to have teachers take responsibility for signing their names to *words* rather than to completely ambiguous letter grades. And in truth it can happen that most of the performances on an essay or even for the whole course are indeed genuinely excellent or strong, and therefore, we want to sign our name honestly to that assertion. But with conventional grading, when a teacher gives mostly As and B pluses, no one knows whether she is saying, "This was a remarkable outcome" or "I just don't want to make it too hard to get a good grade in my course."

I actually have some hope that we'd see a bit less grade inflation in a three-level scale, where teachers had to use a word like "excellent" or "honors" for the top grade rather than just A— or A. If a program or school really wanted to get rid of too many high grades, they could even insist on a term like "top 10%" or "top quarter" for the top grade.

50 And surely the *worst* grade inflation is at the bottom, not the top. Most teachers give passing grades and even Cs to performances that they consider completely unsatisfactory. Grades would be much more meaningful if we had to decide between the categories of "satisfactory" vs. "unsatisfactory" or "unacceptable."

But minimal grading won't solve the problem of meaninglessness. Grades are just as ambiguous if most students get Satisfactory.

Not really. That is, even though minimal grading will probably give most students the grade of Satisfactory, we will have *clearly communicated* to readers, by the fact of our three-level scale and the use of this word "satisfactory," that this single grade *is* being used for a wide range of performances. This result is *not* so ambiguous as with conventional grading, where no one knows whether B is being used for a wide range or a restricted range of performances.

But you're still evading the main problem of all. Sure, sure, it may be technically "unambiguous" to give most of the class a grade like Satisfactory, but the term still remains empty. It doesn't tell us enough. It's too unsatisfying to leave so many students in one undifferentiated lump.

Yes, "unsatisfying" is exactly the right word here. For it's a crucial fact about minimal grade that they carry *less information:* conventional grades records more distinctions. By sorting students into more groups that are thus more finely differentiated, conventional grades give students a sense of seeing themselves as better and worse in relation to more of their peers. Conventional grades *feel* more precise than minimal grades at the job of telling students exactly how well or how badly they did.

Thus students will tend, at first anyway, to experience minimal grading as *taking something away from them,* and they will be correct—even though what is being taken away from them is bad information. Information itself feels precious; distinctions themselves feel valuable, even spurious precision is missed. When students contemplate moving to minimal grading, they often put out of their minds what most of them actually do know at some level: that this information was bad and this precision was spurious. People are easily seduced into wanting to see themselves sorted into levels—*even* people who have a pretty good idea that they will find the information painful. "Doctor, I need you to tell me if I have cancer." "Teacher/examiner, I need you to tell me *exactly* how bad my paper is." There may be trustworthy precise knowledge about the cancer, but there can be no trustworthy *precise one-dimensional, numerical* knowledge about how bad a paper is. (Consider further that there often is *not* trustworthy knowledge even about the cancer. Thus, if we *really* want accuracy and precision in grading, perhaps we should makes grades more analogous to the outcomes of much medical evaluation: "Based on my long training in composition and my extensive experience in teaching writing and my careful examination of your paper, I feel quite confident in saying that there is a 70 percent likelihood that it is a C plus.")

Even if the additional information and precision of conventional grades were entirely trustworthy and accurate, there would still be serious problems. Neither the students nor any other readers of the grades would benefit from the potential information carried by this precision unless they saw all the grades for the whole class. "B minus" means virtually nothing unless we see what grade everyone else got. In addition, that precise, accurate, and trustworthy grade would tell the students nothing at all about *what it is* they did well or badly.

(B) Using Explicit Criteria in Grading— Adding the Horizontal

I turn now to the second suggestion I am making in this essay. When I argued above for minimal grading, I might have seemed to be pleading for less information. No. I was arguing for less *bad* information. If the only grades we can give are purely one-dimensional or vertical, the only honest recourse is to cut back on information and go for minimal grades. But minimal grading is not our only option. My larger purpose is not to reduce information but to increase it. In this section I want to show that when we take away *bad information* from students by moving to minimal grading, we can give them *better information* in return. We can make minimal grades *more* full of meaning than conventional grades if we find a way to tell students what they are actually weak, satisfactory, or excellent *at*. To do so, we need to work out the *criteria* for our minimal grades.

That is, up till now I've been arguing only for less verticality. But using criteria, we can add a crucial *horizontal* dimension to grades. By spelling out the various features of writing that we are looking for when we grade, we are saying that "quality in writing" is not a single, monolithic, one-dimensional entity. And, of course, we are giving more information and meaning to our grades and making them less mysterious.

55 How do we name criteria? The simplest criteria are the traditional and commonly used pair, *form* and *content*. The distinction is surely useful in grading. Despite some criticism of the distinction as old fashioned or even theoretically suspect, students obviously benefit from knowing our different judgments about these two general areas: ideas-and-thinking versus clarity-organization-mechanics. Almost as commonly used in evaluating is a more elaborated set of criteria with elements like these: *ideas, organization, syntax/wording, mechanics.* Furthermore, many teachers like to specify in their evaluation the intellectual operation that is most central to a particular assignment by using criteria like these: *analysis, details, persuasion, research, documentation.* I have been naming textually oriented criteria. But some teachers use some rhetorically oriented or even process-oriented criteria like these: *connecting with the subject, connecting to an audience, voice, substantive revision.* The important principle here is that we do well to

CONTEXT

For the last twenty years, increasing numbers of English teachers have devoted time to teaching and encouraging the use of "writing process"—which means moving from model in which an assignment was given, submitted, and graded to a model in which students are encouraged to engage in prewriting activities (such as brainstorming), share early drafts of their work, and then revise after they have had the benefit of learning how their audience has responded to their initial drafts. Teachers using a process model often incorporate peer review, usually within small groups, into the writing process and try to keep reviewers focused on big issues such as organization and development rather than editing issues such as spelling and punctuation. When well done, the process model can help students earn higher grades than they might otherwise earn—because their final drafts are stronger than their early drafts. But the principal reason for teaching along these lines is to establish a process that students can use long after the course in which it was required: sharing their work with others and taking their responses into account rather than writing entirely on their own and hoping for the best.

name and acknowledge and communicate the features of writing that influence our judgments. Since scholars and critics have failed to agree on what "good writing" really is, we get to decide what we are actually looking for and admit it openly to our students.

If we have a large number of papers to grade and we are assigning lots of papers—or if we are teaching a large class that doesn't center on writing and we have little or no help in grading—we probably need to resort to the simplest, least time-consuming way to use criteria: just give one overall grade (or perhaps form/content grades)—yet nevertheless, spell out explicitly for students the other features or characteristics of writing that we are looking for when we grade. Thus we might announce, "In grading this set of papers I will try to count these four criteria equally: . . ." Or "I will grade most on the strength of your argument, but I'll also take some account of these other three criteria: . . ." If our criteria are at all complicated, we can explain and describe them in a handout. And in order to help students do the

best job of *meeting* our criteria, we need to announce them when we announce the assignment—before they write—and not wait till afterward when we hand back the graded papers.

The point is that even if we give nothing but a single minimal grade, we can make that grade carry much more information and meaning if we spell out our criteria in public. And using criteria even in this minimal way helps us grade more fairly. For the process of figuring out criteria and announcing them publicly renders us less likely to be unduly swayed if one particular feature of the writing is terrible or wonderful. For example, teachers often get annoyed by papers that are full of grammar and spelling mistakes and nonmainstream dialect, and consequently overlook virtues in information, ideas, or reasoning in such papers—and give them unreasonably low grades. We are less likely to slip into this unfairness if we have specifically announced our criteria.

However, we get the most benefit from criteria if we can actually give a grade on each one. We tell each student how well we think he or she did on each of the features of writing we are looking for. In doing this we are making *multiple vertical judgments* of quality.

But this will make grading too much work!

The principle of minimal grading comes to our rescue here. For just as it isn't so hard to read through a set of papers and merely note the ones that stand out as weak or strong, so it isn't so much harder merely to notice if an essay seems notably weak or notably strong on the criteria we have named as important. We hold each criterion in mind for a moment and see if that feature of the paper stands out for being strong or weak. In my efforts not to make it too onerous to use criteria, I even announce to students that Satisfactory is the "default" grade and so I will make a notation *only* if I find something notably strong or weak. If we use criteria in this more complete fashion, we have a kind of grid, and our "grade" on a paper might look something like this:

Weak	Satisfactory	Strong	(Note: No check means "satisfactory.")
			Genuine revision, substantive changes, not just editing
		√	Ideas, insight, thinking
√			Organization, structure, guiding the reader
			Language, sentences, wording
√			Mechanics: spelling, grammar, punctuation, proofreading
√			Overall

This is the form a grid might take when I photocopy a set of blank ones and make check marks. I often write a comment in addition: something more "readerly" and less evaluative—some comment about the responses and reactions I had at various points in reading. I think these discursive comments actually do more good in the long run than quantified evaluations. Indeed, I came to use grids when I gradually realized that my readerly comments were leaving students too dissatisfied, but I didn't want to give a regular grade. Grids were a way to give a bit of quantified evaluation but not on just one dimension.[2]

60 When I write comments on a computer—as I now prefer to do—I put the grid on a tiny file or even a "macro." Then, when I start to write a comment, I bring in the file or macro. This way I can write in little comments about a criterion. If I were using my computer on the same paper as above, my grid response might look like this:

GENUINE REVISION, SUBSTANTIVE CHANGES, NOT JUST EDITING:
IDEAS, INSIGHTS, THINKING: *Strong. I liked the way you complicated things by exploring points that conflict with your main point.*
ORGANIZATION, STRUCTURE, GUIDING THE READER: *Weak. I kept feeling confused about where you were going—though also sensing that my confusion came from your process of complicating your thinking. This confusion would be good if it weren't a final draft.*
LANGUAGE, SENTENCES, WORDING:
MECHANICS: SPELLING, GRAMMAR, PUNCTUATION, PROOFREADING: *Weak. Because of all the mistakes, this paper doesn't fulfill the contract and is not acceptable. I'll call it acceptable this first time IF you give me a fully cleaned up version by next class.*
OVERALL: *Unsatisfactory for now.*

2. Unfortunately, the spatial orientation of my grid works at crosspurposes with my metaphor of vertical and horizontal, but it's easier to represent quality horizontally from left to right if we want to use words to name criteria.

And of course I might write an additional discursive comment at the end.

When we use criteria in this fuller way and make *multiple judgments*, we finally make our grades carry explicit meaning—rather than letting them remain mysterious or magical. And we finally give students some valuable feedback on the particular strengths and weaknesses in their writing—feedback that they don't get from conventional grades. Indeed, mere checkmarks on a grid (perhaps with a few short comments) are sometimes clearer and more useful to students than the longer comments we write in our unrevised prose—especially when it's late at night and we are tired.

Grids are particularly useful for responding to a revised final version when we have already given plenty of feedback to a draft. After all, extended commenting makes more sense at the draft stage: we can give encouragement ("Here's what you need to work on to make it better") instead of just giving an autopsy ("Here's what didn't work"). For the final version, we can read through quickly and then check off criteria on a grid and give no comments at all. We give students better help if we assign papers and give full feedback on drafts and only grid check marks on final versions, than if we assign fewer papers and give full feedback on both drafts and revisions.

Let me explore the interesting issue of figuring out one's criteria. When students ask me, "What are you looking for?" I sometimes feel some annoyance—though I don't think my reaction is quite fair. But I enjoy it when *I* ask the question of myself: "What actually *are* the features in a piece of writing that make me value it?" If I try to answer this question in an insecure, normative way, I tie myself in knots: "What *ought* I to value in student essays?" But we are professionals in our fields and so we get to ask the question in an *empirical* way: "What *do* I value in writing?" For there *is* no Platonic correct answer to the question, "What is good writing?"

This process of empirical self-examination can be intellectually fascinating. We learn to

notice more clearly how we read—and this can even lead to some *change* in how we read. For example, some faculty members discover that they are giving more weight than they realized to certain criteria (e.g., to matters of style or correct restatement of textbook and lecture material or correct mechanics)—and this realization leads them to attend more to other criteria. Or they discover that they use different criteria for student writing than for professional writing (e.g., that in student writing they disapprove of the use of first person writing or personal anecdote, but in published professional writing in their field they value it).

65 The use of criteria has a powerful added benefit because it helps students engage in valid and productive *self-evaluation*. When we ask students to give or suggest a conventional grade for themselves, we are putting them in an unhelpfully difficult spot. There are too many unstated criteria to sum up into one number and it's hard for them not to translate the question into characterological and almost moral terms: "Am I an A person or a B person?" It's much easier and more valid for students to grade themselves with a system of minimal grades and multiple criteria. When they rate themselves as strong, satisfactory, or weak on a wide range of skills or abilities, their answers are more likely to be honest and accurate. I ask such questions at the beginning of the semester ("As we start this course, do you rate yourself Strong, OK, or Weak on the following skills or abilities or areas of knowledge?"). This helps them set goals. I ask the questions again at midsemester. Most important, I ask them at the end ("Do you think your performance has been strong, satisfactory, or weak on these criteria this semester?") Also, I find it very productive to ask students themselves to generate the criteria that they think are important—again at the beginning, middle, and end of the semester.

The Institutional Dimension
In the third and final section of this essay, I've suggested two ways to make grades

more trustworthy and meaningful—while still working within a conventional grading system: using minimal grades as a way to reduce the bad information in conventional grades; using multiple explicit criteria as a way to make grades more informative and useful as feedback.

But minimal grades and explicit criteria are not just useful *within* a conventional grading system. They could vastly improve institutional grading itself. At present, a transcript consists of countless single letter grades that no reader can trust since faculty members have such different standards. When a student gets a B, it can mean anything from good honors work to disappointing work. Nor can readers translate those grades into meaningful or useful information. Even when a student gets an A, we don't have any idea what skills or kinds of writing the student is good at—and inevitably, not so good at.

Transcripts would be much more useful if they respresented a different deployment of energy and ambition. On the one hand, we should be *less* ambitious and stop pretending that we can reliably sort students into eleven vertical levels of quality—or that we can reliably sort students into eleven vertical levels of quality—or that the sortings would mean the same thing in different teachers' hands and in different readers' minds. Transcripts would be more honest, accurate, and trustworthy if we settled for recording only three levels, say, *Honors, Satisfactory, Unsatisfactory* (or at most four: *Honors, Strong, Fair, Unsatisfactory*).

But on the other hand, it is feasible to be far *more* ambitious where it counts, and to give grades on *criteria* for each course. Thus, at the end of a course, we would provide the registrar with a small grid of grades for each student. There would be a grade for the student's overall performance—using three or at most four levels. But we would also list the three to six criteria that we think are most important, and for each we would tick off whether we thought this student's work was satisfactory or notably weak or notably strong.

70 Faculty members need not be forced to use the same criteria. There could be a large list of criteria to choose from: textual criteria like *clarity* and *organization;* process criteria like *generating, revising,* and *working collaboratively;* rhetorical criteria like *awareness of audience* and *voice;* and genre-related criteria like *analysis* and *argument.* Teachers could even create their own criteria. Indeed, there's no reason why teachers should be obliged to use the same criteria for every student in a course. After all, we might want to bring in certain criteria only for certain students (*creative* or *diligent*—or *unable to meet deadlines*) yet not want to speak about these criteria for all students.

This procedure sounds complicated, but given computers, it would not be hard to manage—both for giving course grades and in producing a transcript. (Elementary school report cards have long used this approach; and many high school teachers now have a list of fifty or more criteria they can add electronically to grades on report cards.) Readers of the transcript would finally get useful information about substance and be spared the untrustworthy information about levels of quality.

I have been suggesting a visual metaphor: Minimal grading asks for less of the vertical; using criteria means more of the horizontal. But my suggestions also imply a move away from the tradition of *norm-based* or *measuring* assessment toward the tradition of *criterion-based* or *mastery* assessment. Norm-based or measuring assessment involves making single, complex, all-determining decisions about each student: all are strung out along a single vertical line—each at an exact distance above or below every other student. Criterion-based or mastery assessment, on the other hand, implies multiple simpler decisions about each student: all are placed in a complicated multi-dimensional space—each student being strong in certain abilities, okay in others, and weak in yet more, with different students having different constellations of strengths and weaknesses. (See D. C. McClelland for the classic formulating essay in the criterion-based tradition. This tradition is also represented in the "New Standards Project," for which see Myers and Pearson.)

In this paper I am trying to get outside the either/or debates around grading. We can look for ways to step temporarily outside of grading and even of the mentality of evaluations; and we can look for better *ways* to grade and not grade. We can make small pragmatic improvements, but also push for large utopian change. The human impulse to judge or evaluate is inevitable and useful, but we also need to find ways to bypass that impulse. It won't be so hard, really, to have assessments that lead to a healthier climate for teaching and learning, and that give us a more accurate picture of student achievement.

Works Cited

Belanoff, Pat, Peter Elbow, and Sheryl Fontaine. *Nothing Begins with N: New Investigations of Freewriting.* Carbondale: Southern Illinois UP, 1991.

Diederich, Paul. *Measuring Growth in English.* Urbana, IL: NCTE, 1974.

Elbow, Peter. "Ranking, Evaluating, Liking: Sorting Out Three Forms of Judgment." *College English* 55.2 (February 1993) 187–206.

Haswell, Richard and Susan Wyche-Smith. "Adventuring into Writing Assessment." *CCC* 45.2 (May 1994): 220–36.

_____. "A Two-Tier Rating Procedure for Placement Essays: Washington State University." *Assessment in Practice: Putting Principles to Work on College Campuses.* San Francisco: Jossey-Bass, 1996. 204–07.

Lakoff, George and Mark Johnson. *Metaphors We Live By.* Chicago: U of Chicago P, 1980.

McClelland, D. C. "Testing for Competence Rather than for Intelligence." *American Psychologist* 28 (1973): 1–14.

Myers, Miles and P. David Pearson. "Performance Assessment and the Literacy Unit of the New Standards Project." *Assessing Writing* 3.1 (1996): 5–29.

U.S. Department of Education. *The New College Course Map and Transcript Files: Changes in Course-Taking and Achievement, 1972–1992.* Washington, DC: Office of Educational Research and Improvement, 1996.

Questions for Discussion

1. What is your understanding of a "utopian impulse"? What does Elbow accomplish by raising both the "utopian and the pragmatic impulses" in his opening paragraph?

2. Consider the list of objections to grades that Elbow includes in paragraph 5. Drawing upon your experience as someone who has been receiving grades for years, how do you respond to the claims in this list? Do they reflect your experience, or are they at odds with it?

3. In paragraphs 8–11, Elbow moves from raising the possibility of ten minutes without grades to considering ten days without them. What do you think motivated this sequence? How long would you feel comfortable in a course in which grading was suspended or deferred?

4. Have you ever been graded on an assignment that you thought was not going to be graded? Have you ever been given the opportunity to revise a paper after it has been graded?

5. Consider Elbow's discussion of portfolios and the context box on page 523. Given that portfolios can be labor-intensive for both students and professors, under what kind of conditions are they most likely to be used? Would you like to be in a course in which your final grade was determined by a portfolio? Or do you prefer the clarity of having fixed grades as you make your way through a course?

6. What do you think of Elbow's proposal for contract grading?

7. In paragraphs 21–25, Elbow uses words such as "liking" and "loving," which he recognizes could seem "soft, fuzzy, and unintellectual" to his audience. Why does he believe such language is appropriate for the case he is making? How do you respond to it?

8. "The grade of B," Elbow writes, "has become particularly ambiguous." Have you had to work harder for a B in some courses than in others? If so, was it because of the subject matter or the standards set by the instructor (or both)? How high, in your opinion, is a grade of B?

9. Consider the evaluation forms on page 533. Would you be content with the first grid, or would you also like comments? Would you recommend any changes to this method of evaluation?

10. This is one of the longest selections in the book. What do you think motivated Elbow to write at such length? What does it imply about his sense of audience? What can you infer from the decision to reprint this piece within the book?

NEGOTIATING DIFFERENCES

Suppose that you have been doing well in a course until you get to the final exam. It was your impression—and you have a record of this in your notes—that the final exam would be based exclusively on material covered since midterm. Upon receiving the exam, you discover that it is cumulative, and you score poorly because you had not reviewed material that you thought was going to be excluded from the exam. Several of your classmates report the same problem based on the same information, which can be traced to a remark made by the instructor in class in response to a question. The instructor claims that she made no such remark and points to the syllabus, which clearly indicates that the final exam would be cumulative. You would doubt your own impression but trust the judgment of those students who heard what you heard. You wonder if the instructor misspoke in class or forgot what she had said. In any case, a good third of the class now has a problem; these students are about to receive significantly lower grades in the course than they had anticipated receiving because the final exam—fair or unfair—counts for 30 percent of the final grade. You have already emailed the instructor and been referred to the syllabus. You do not want to be drawn into a conflict with her. She still has to determine your final grade, after all, and you are expecting to take a course with her next semester. But your GPA matters to you, and you believe that you are the victim of a genuine misunderstanding. You are tempted to bring the problem to the department chairperson but recognize that doing so can escalate the problem. The chairperson would be thrust into a position of mediating a dispute that involved your word versus your instructor's word. You know that this is still an option for you but decide that it would be best to approach the instructor one more time. Accordingly, you schedule an appointment to meet with her. That appointment has now arrived. What argument can you make that will lead to a resolution respectful to all concerned?

American National Identity

Cluster 1

WHO GETS TO BE AN AMERICAN?

1. Celia C. Perez-Zeeb, "By the Time I Get to Cucaracha"

2. Peter Brimelow, "A Nation of Immigrants"

3. Jacob G. Hornberger, "Keep the Borders Open"

4. Steven Camarota, "Too Many: Looking Today's Immigration in the Face"

CON-TEXT
The New Colossus

Cluster 2

WHAT DOES IT MEAN TO BE A GOOD AMERICAN CITIZEN?

1. John Balzar, "Needed: Informed Voters "

2. Wilfred M. McClay, "America: Idea or Nation?"

3. Michael Kazin, "A Patriotic Left"

4. Josiah Bunting, III, "Class Warfare"

CON-TEXT
John F. Kennedy's Inaugural Address 1961

Cluster 3

WHAT KIND OF POWER SHOULD WE GIVE OUR GOVERNMENT?

1. Martin Luther King, Jr., "Letter from a Birmingham Jail"

2. Heather Green, "Databases and Security vs. Privacy"

3. Alan M. Dershowitz, "Why Fear National ID Cards?"

4. David J. Barron, "Reclaiming Federalism"

CON-TEXT
The Declaration of Independence

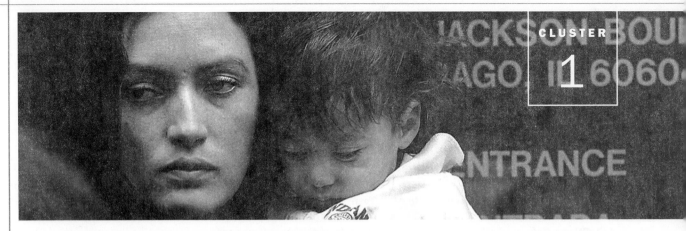

Who Gets to Be an American?

According to the U.S. Census Bureau, more than 13 million legal and illegal immigrants entered the United States between 1990 and 2000. The Center for Labor Market Studies at Northeastern University determined that immigrants accounted for 50 percent of the 16 million new workers who entered the workforce during the 1990s. Those numbers indicate the significant impact that immigrants can have on the U.S. economy. In fact, Andrew Sum, the director of the Center for Labor Market Studies, speaking in 2002 about his center's study of immigrant labor, declared that "the American economy absolutely needs immigrants." ■ Not everyone would agree. The impact of immigrants on U.S. society has long worried many Americans. As Peter Brimelow, whose essay appears on pages 549–552, points out, Americans seem fond of declaring that "we are a nation of immigrants." Indeed, the famous poem inscribed on the Statue of Liberty seems to say unequivocally that America will accept all those who seek a better life here (see *Con-Text* on page 543). Nevertheless, concerns about the effects of immigration on U.S. economic and cultural life have always fueled debates about the extent to which the United States should open its borders to immigrants. Although the patterns of immigration might change from one era to another, the issues surrounding immigration do not. In the late nineteenth and early twentieth centuries, when millions of people came to the United States from eastern European and Mediterranean countries, most of them hoping to escape poverty or political conflict, many Americans saw these new arrivals as a threat to economic stability and even to the values that had shaped the U.S. legal and political systems. As you read through the essays in this section, you will encounter some of those same concerns, expressed more than a century later, at a time when increasing numbers of immigrants are arriving from South America and Asia. ■ But arguments about immigration are not just about policy matters or economic worries. They reflect deeper and more complicated concerns about American identity: What exactly does it mean to be an American? Who decides? And *how* should we decide who will become an American? The authors of the essays in this section address these questions, sometimes focusing on policy and sometimes on ethnicity, race, gender, or national origin. These authors represent a range of views on immigration, but perhaps more important is the fact that their essays reveal how complex the questions about immigration and American national identity can be. In a sense, these authors all seek the same thing: immigration policies that contribute to a society that is consistent with American ideals. The real challenge, though, might be reaching agreement on those ideals. As you read these essays, consider the extent to which these authors help us meet that challenge.

CON-TEXT

"The New Colossus"

This is the famous poem that appears on the pedestal of the Statue of Liberty in New York Harbor:

The New Colossus

by Emma Lazarus

Not like the brazen giant of Greek fame, With conquering limbs astride from land to land;

Here at our sea-washed, sunset gates shall stand
A mighty woman with a torch, whose flame
Is the imprisoned lightning, and her name
Mother of Exiles. From her beacon-hand
Glows world-wide welcome; her mild eyes command
The air-bridged harbor that twin cities frame.

"Keep ancient lands, your storied pomp!" cries she
With silent lips.

"Give me your tired, your poor,
Your huddled masses yearning to breathe free,
The wretched refuse of your teeming shore.

Send these, the homeless, tempest-tost to me,
I lift my lamp beside the golden door!"

① CELIA C. PEREZ-ZEEB, "By the Time I Get to Cucaracha"

Current debates about immigration often focus on the problem of illegal immigrants entering the United States from Mexico and other Central and South American countries. Critics of U.S. immigration policy sometimes charge that the high numbers of illegal immigrants from these countries place a burden on schools and other social services paid for by U.S. taxpayers; they also contend that because these immigrants are willing work for low wages, they weaken the job market for legal citizens. These concerns tend to cast the debates about immigration in economic terms. Writer Celia Perez-Zeeb, however, believes that concerns about immigration might have more to do with race and gender than with jobs and taxes. In the following essay she focuses attention on the laws governing marriages between immigrants and American citizens, and she points out how those complicated laws can place women at a disadvantage. She also examines the role that ethnic stereotypes about Hispanic people play in public debates about immigration. Although she focuses her argument on how Hispanic people are portrayed in these debates and in the popular media, you might consider whether her argument would apply to other ethnic groups associated with immigration. This essay appeared in *Bad Subjects* in 2002.

By the Time I Get to Cucaracha

CELIA C. PEREZ-ZEEB

*"Green cards" grant noncitizens the right to live permanently in the United States. (See www.ftc.gov/bcp/conline/pubs/alerts/lottery.htm.)

1 I was watching NBC's *Will and Grace*. It's a show about a woman, Grace, who leaves her fiancé at the chapel on their wedding day and runs off to live with her gay best friend, Will. In this particular episode Karen, Grace's extremely obnoxious socialite assistant, was upset because her housekeeper, Rosario, was going to be deported. In order to keep her in the country they hatched up the old green card* scam, and picked Will's gay friend, Jack, to be the groom. In one scene Karen and Rosario, who have one of those wacky love-hate relationships, are arguing and Karen says to Rosario, "If it wasn't for this you'd be flying back to Cucaracha on Air Guacamole with live chickens running up and down the aisle!"

I almost fell off the bed. I could not believe my ears.

The people involved in the creation of the show probably justify such blatantly unfunny and racist remarks by making the Karen character super-annoying, self-absorbed and materialistic, thus excusing her ignorance. Maybe they feel they have a little bit of leeway since they have (gasp!) gay characters in the show, and so, of course, they cannot possibly be racist or discriminatory. But, frankly, I think it's messed up that the maid "just happens" to be Latina because, hey, guess what, Latinas are capable of being more than some yuppie's housekeeper! And that said, we should be grateful to all the women, Latina or otherwise, who earn or have earned a living as housekeepers. My mom was a housekeeper when she first came to this country.

Most of the mainstream media seem to believe it's okay to portray Latinos like dirtballs.

Not to mention the fact that Latino characters are usually depicted as being in this country illegally. There are plenty of people out there who already view Latinos as hailing from "Cucaracha" without having their beliefs reinforced by the almighty television. If you think we Latinos have made amazing progress and have many Latino actors on television and in movies that aren't portrayed negatively, how about watching the ALMA awards? It pains me to see the association grasping at straws to have a category in which there are more than two actors and to see how, in most cases, the nominees for awards are supporting actors. Characters not unlike Rosario.

5 But, when I see shows like *Will and Grace,* I wonder where the outrage is? Maybe the right people weren't watching that particular episode and so there was no uproar about it (unlike the whole Taco Bell Chihuahua controversy), but I think there's also something to be said about the fact that people tend to forget that groups other than African-Americans are discriminated against in this country and are often portrayed as racist stereotypes by the media. If the maid had been African-American and "Karen" had made a similarly insulting comment, all hell probably would have broken loose. However, NBC wouldn't have had the balls to even allow such a comment against a black character to air, because it is widely acknowledged that this country has treated black people terribly. And, perhaps more importantly, there are a lot of black activists and groups who would protest. Whatever the reason, it definitely seems to be more acceptable to make fun of certain groups than others.

What's more, pulling this tired and deceptive green card story line is ignorant and misleading. They assume (a) that it's easy to become a legal immigrant in such a manner and (b) that illegal immigrants are gaining residency left and right by marrying for green cards. I think it's fucked up that NBC can get away with letting something so insulting and demeaning to Latinos air, but, frankly, I'm not surprised. I'd seen that story line way too many times already in now-defunct shows like *Jesse* and *Beverly Hills 90210.* It's always portrayed as quick, easy, funny, and oh so romantic. Oh look at this wonderful American marrying this poor wetback just so she can stay in the country. How sweet. Yeah, well it isn't.

The rules governing the attainment of residency by non-citizens married to U.S. citizens are not necessarily clear and not necessarily easy to follow. According to U.S. law, marriages between a citizen and non-citizen must be entered into in "good faith." Then, just before a couple's two year anniversary, they must undergo an interview with an immigration officer, who attempts to make sure their union isn't a sham. The "investigation" includes weird, personal questions like: what side of the bed does your mate sleeps on? Or, What kind of underwear do they wear? During this two-year period the marriage cannot be annulled or terminated unless the spouse dies. And no, permanent resident status isn't automatically granted after two years. A petition has to be entered in order to terminate immigrant status. If it isn't filed then the person can be sent back to their country of origin, unless there's a really good reason for not having filed the petition.

AMERICAN LATINO MEDIA ARTS (ALMA) AWARDS

The ALMA awards were created in 1995 as part of an effort among advocacy groups to promote fair, accurate, and balanced portrayals of Latinos in television, film, and music. Born as a direct response to negative stereotyping of Latinos in entertainment, these awards honor Latino performers for their outstanding artistic achievement and for enhancing the image of Latinos. The name ALMA, which is Spanish for "spirit" or "soul," is intended to represent the determined spirit of the Latino people, as well as, the scope of the awards program.

THE TACO BELL CHIHUAHUA CONTROVERSY

In 1998 the fast-food company Taco Bell ran a series of advertisements featuring a talking chihuahua that spoke with a pronounced Spanish accent. Despite the ad campaign's apparent commercial success, many people condemned the ads as insulting to Latino people. One critic of the ads was Gabriel Cazares, the mayor of Clearwater, Florida, who was also a former president of the Tampa, Florida, chapter of the League for United Latin American Citizens. Cazares told an interviewer,

> I think it was an unfortunate commercial. I think that the use of a dog to depict Mexicans was very demeaning. If Taco Bell wanted to depict someone that would reflect Mexican culture we have many live, two-legged artists, singers, dancers, musicians—some great people in America that could have been selected to give a testimonial for Taco Bell (and) say, 'Yo quiero un taco.' And that wouldn't have been offensive.

*Passed by Congress in 1986, the Immigration Marriage Fraud Amendment was intended to deter illegal immigration that occurred through fraudulent marriages between American citizens and immigrants seeking legal status in the United States. The act requires the U.S. citizen and his or her foreign spouse to prove two years of valid marriage before the foreign spouse can apply to become a permanent U.S. resident, except under certain special circumstances.

An article in the *Yale Journal of Law and Feminism,* "The Gender Dimensions of U.S. Immigration Policy," argues that female immigrants tend to be at a disadvantage because their entrance into the country often depends more on family ties than other more "legitimate" reasons for entry. For example, employment-based immigration is dominated by men because it tends to favor people who already have advanced degrees in their field, are wealthy, or have much sought after scientific or technological skills. The number of "unskilled" workers who are allowed to enter the country has been lowered; therefore, immigrant women, who tend to come to work as housekeepers or child care providers, have a more difficult time having a "legitimate" reason to enter the United States.

Don't get me wrong, though! The United States does love its immigrants. Of course, on the condition that they can do something for the economy. They don't want to hear about your poverty and persecution, but if you have money or special skills, well, that's a different story. Immigrants are allowed to enter the country legally if they make an outrageous monetary donation. Supermodels are also given special visas as entertainers and as possessors of specialized skills (being skinny and being able to pout on cue, I guess).

10 In 1986 the Immigration Marriage Fraud amendment* was passed by Congress. This is the amendment that made the two-year minimum marriage period mandatory before a person could be considered for permanent resident status. The *Yale Law* article argues that this piece of legislation gives the spouse who is a citizen, most often the male, excessive power over the immigrant spouse because, believe it or not, after the two-year period is over, if the citizen spouse chooses not to sign the petition for resident status then the immigrant spouse and children, if there are any, can be removed from the United States. So for at least two years an immigrant woman can be at the mercy of whatever her spouse wishes.

You get a whole other story from the senators who spoke at the July 26, 1985, session of Congress for the Subcommittee on Immigration and Refugee Policy. According to Senator Alan K. Simpson (chairman of the subcommittee), "United States citizens legitimately petition for 'mail order brides' advertised in the backs of magazines and tabloids sold at the checkout lines of supermarkets. The alien admitted as a fiancé will go through the appearance of wanting to marry and build a future life until after the actual wedding ceremony. The alien then promptly abandons his or her spouse." Now, come on. It's okay for these men to order brides through the mail, but god forbid someone try to marry in order to stay in this country and hope for a better life? Does the idea of ORDERING a bride not seem even slightly disturbing to Senator Simpson?

Throughout his speech Alan Simpson made it seem like those who marry immigrants do so either because they "feel sorry" for them or because they are being coerced to do so. The "alien" (what's up with that label?) is portrayed as the scheming good-for-nothing, while the United States citizen is just a poor little lamb who is being manipulated. Simpson states that, "Because the alien and the arranger are well aware of the risks and penalties of disclosure . . . , they feel no compunction in intimidating their United States citizen or resident alien spouses or fiancés." Simpson referred to immigrants who sought marriage for residency as "smooth-talking alien(s)" who made it a practice to convince the citizen that they were going into the marriage out of love and then once they obtained their resident status, they dumped the spouse.

It took Simpson awhile, but he eventually got his main concern off his chest when he argued that most of the illegal immigrants attempting to gain residency through marriage were doing so because they could not obtain residency otherwise. The reasons for their inability to obtain visas, according to Simpson, was because "most aliens" have broken the law in some manner—through illegal entry, or due to the fact that they are terrorists, criminals, narcotics users/dealers, or prostitutes. Note the words "MOST ALIENS."

In the early '80s, before the 1986 amendment was passed, the INS [Immigration and Naturalization Service] estimated that nearly 30% of the cases in which an immigrant had gained resident status through marriage were involved in "suspect marital relationships." When this estimate was revised, the figure was much closer to 8%.

15 Television and movies portray things as if there really are hundreds of thousands of immigrants in the United States getting hitched left and right in order to stay in the country, which is not true. The media makes it seem like a piece of cake to just up and marry and all of a sudden you're an American, which is also not true. Even sadder is that the media completely trivializes the reasons why people come to this country, or why some women might be so desperate not to return to their countries that they would be willing to marry someone they don't know and potentially endure abuse.

The media rarely, if ever, mentions that many of the Central and South American countries these people are fleeing have been historically terrorized by U.S. supported regimes. The media never bothers to mention that the United States quite often turns a blind eye to the terrorism, the disappearances, the tortures, the rapes, and other abuses being suffered by people who come to this country. Apparently, immigrants are most useful to the U.S. when they are performing backbreaking labor or being the brunt of jokes.

CONTEXT

This essay appeared in 2002 in *Bad Subjects: Political Education for Everyday Life*, a journal published by a nonprofit organization that describes itself as "a collective that . . . seeks to revitalize progressive politics in retreat." According to its website, *Bad Subjects* believes that "too many people on the left have taken their convictions for granted. So we challenge progressive dogma by encouraging readers to think about the political dimension to all aspects of everyday life. We also seek to broaden the audience for leftist and progressive writing, through a commitment to accessibility and contemporary relevance" (see http://eserver.org/bs/faq/). In what ways do you think this essay addresses the political viewpoints of people who are likely to read this journal?

Questions for Discussion

1. What is Perez-Zeeb's main point is this essay? Where in the essay does she state that point most directly?

2. Using specific examples of Perez-Zeeb's language to support your answer, describe the tone of this essay. Do you think the tone is appropriate to Perez-Zeeb's argument?

3. Perez-Zeeb objects to the humor involving Latinos on U.S. television shows, and she specifically criticizes an episode of the television show *Will and Grace* in which a marriage is arranged between two characters, one who is a Latina immigrant and one who is an American citizen. What problem involving immigrants does Perez-Zeeb use this episode to introduce? Do you think her criticism of this television show is an effective strategy, given her main argument? Why or why not?

4. Perez-Zeeb refers several times to an article from the *Yale Journal of Law and Feminism*. What do you think she accomplishes by making these references? How might these references enhance (or weaken) her argument?

5. Does the fact that Perez-Zeeb is Latina have any effect on her argument?

② PETER BRIMELOW, "A Nation of Immigrants"

Born and educated in Great Britain, Peter Brimelow now lives and works in the United States. A senior editor of *Forbes* magazine, he is the author of *Alien Nation: Common Sense About America's Immigration Disaster* (1995), *The Patriot Game: Canada and the Canadian Question Revisited* (1987), and *The Wall Street Gurus: How You Can Profit from Investment Newsletters* (1986), among other books. "A Nation of Immigrants" is an editor's title for the following short excerpt from a long, controversial article on immigration that Brimelow published in 1992 in *National Review,* a monthly magazine that reflects politically conservative opinions. Although Brimelow addresses the political debate about immigration policy that was occurring in the early 1990s, his argument goes beyond policy issues to the complicated question of what constitutes a nation. Does it have to do with ethnic or racial identity? Or is it a matter of political borders and geographic location? Such questions, Brimelow suggests, must be answered if there is to be any acceptable resolution to the continuing conflicts regarding immigration policy in the United States.

A Nation of Immigrants

PETER BRIMELOW

1 Everyone has seen a speeded-up film of the cloudscape. What appears to the naked eye to be a panorama of almost immobile grandeur writhes into wild life. Vast patterns of soaring, swooping movement are suddenly discernible. Great towering cumulo-nimbus formations boil up out of nowhere, dominating the sky in a way that would be terrifying if it were not, in real life, so gradual that we are barely aware that anything is going on.

This is a perfect metaphor for the development of the American nation. America, of course, is exceptional. What is exceptional about it, however, is not the way in which it was created, but the speed.

"We are a nation of immigrants." No discussion of U.S. immigration policy gets far without someone making this helpful remark. As an immigrant myself, I always pause respectfully. You never know. Maybe this is what they're taught to chant in schools nowadays, a sort of multicultural Pledge of Allegiance.

But it secretly amuses me. Do they really think other nations sprouted up out of the ground? ("Autochthonous" is the classical Greek word.) The truth is that *all* nations are nations of immigrants. But the process is usually so slow and historic that people overlook it. They mistake for mountains what are merely clouds.

5 This is obvious in the case of the British Isles, from which the largest single proportion of Americans are still derived. You can see it in the place-names. Within a few miles of my parents' home in the north of England, the names are Roman (Chester, derived from the Latin for camp), Saxon (anything ending in *-ton,* town, like Oxton), Viking (*-by,* farm, like Irby), and Norman French (Delamere). At times, these successive waves of peoples were

clearly living cheek by jowl. Thus among these place-names is Wallesey, Anglo-Saxon for "Island of the Welsh"—Welsh being derived from the word used by low-German speakers for foreigners wherever they met them, from Wallonia to Wallachia. This corner of the English coast continued as home to some of the pre-Roman Celtic stock, not all of whom were driven west into Wales proper as was once supposed.

The English language that America speaks today (or at least spoke until the post-1965 fashion for bilingual education) reflects the fact that the peoples of Britain merged, eventually; their separate contributions can still be traced in it. Every nation in Europe went through the same process. Even the famously homogeneous Japanese show the signs of ethnically distinct waves of prehistoric immigration.

But merging takes time. After the Norman Conquest in 1066, it was nearly three hundred years before the invaders were assimilated to the point where court proceedings in London were again heard in English. And it was nearly nine centuries before there was any further large-scale immigration into the British Isles—the Caribbean and Asian influx after World War II. Except in America. Here the process of merging has been uniquely rapid. Thus about 7 million Germans have immigrated to the U.S. since the beginning of the nineteenth century. Their influence has been profound—to my British eye it accounts for the odd American habit of getting up in the morning and starting work. About 50 million Americans told the 1980 Census that they were wholly or partly of German descent. But only 1.6 million spoke German in their homes.

So all nations are made up of immigrants. But what is a nation—the end product of all this merging? This brings us into a territory where words are weapons, exactly as George Orwell pointed out years ago. "Nation"—as suggested by its Latin root *nascere,* to be born— intrinsically implies a link by blood. A nation is an extended family. The merging process through which all nations pass is not merely cultural, but to a considerable extent biological, through intermarriage.

Liberal commentators, for various reasons, find this deeply distressing. They regularly denounce appeals to common ethnicity as "nativism" or "tribalism." Ironically, when I studied African history in college, my politically correct tutor deprecated any reference to "tribes." These small, primitive, and incoherent groupings should, he said, be dignified as "nations." Which suggests a useful definition: tribalism/nativism is nationalism of which liberals disapprove.

10 American political debate on this point is hampered by a peculiar difficulty. American editors are convinced that the term "state" will confuse readers unless reserved exclusively for the component parts of the United States— New York, California, etc. So when talking about sovereign political structures, where the British would use "state," the Germans "*Staat,*" and the French "*l'état,*" journalists here are compelled to use the word "nation." Thus in the late 1980s it was common to see references to "the nation of Yugoslavia," when Yugoslavia's problem was precisely that it was not a nation at all, but a state that contained several different small but fierce nations—Croats, Serbs, etc. (In my constructive way, I've been trying to introduce, as an alternative to "state," the word "polity"—defined by Webster as "a politically organized unit." But it's quite hopeless. Editors always confuse it with "policy.")

This definitional difficulty explains one of the regular entertainments of U.S. politics: uproar because someone has unguardedly described America as a "Christian nation." Of course, in the sense that the vast majority of Americans are Christians, this is nothing less than the plain truth. It is not in the least incompatible with a secular *state* (polity).

But the difficulty over the N-word has a more serious consequence: it means that American commentators are losing sight of the concept of the "nation-state"—a sovereign structure that is the political expression of a specific ethno-cultural group. Yet the nation-state was one of the crucial inventions of the modern age. Mass literacy, education, and mobility put a premium on the unifying effect of cultural and ethnic homogeneity. None of the great pre-modern multinational empires have survived. (The Brussels bureaucracy* may be trying to create another, but it has a long way to go.)

This is why Ben Wattenberg is able to get away with talking about a "Universal Nation." On its face, this is a contradiction in terms. It's possible, as Wattenberg variously implies, that he means the diverse immigrant groups will eventually intermarry, producing what he calls, quoting the English poet John Masefield, a "wondrous race." Or that they will at least be assimilated by American culture, which, while globally dominant, is hardly "universal." But meanwhile there are hard questions. What language is this "universal nation" going to speak? How is it going to avoid ethnic strife? Dual loyalties? Collapsing like the Tower of Babel? Wattenberg is not asked to reconcile these questions, although he is not unaware of them, because in American political discourse the ideal of an American nation-state is in eclipse.

Ironically, the same weaknesses were apparent in the rather similar concept of "cultural pluralism" invented by Horace M. Kallen at the height of the last great immigration debate, before the Quota Acts of the 1920s.[†] Kallen, like many of today's pro-immigration enthusiasts, reacted unconditionally against the cause for "Americanization" that the 1880-to-1920 immigrant wave provoked. He argued that any unitary American nationality had already been dissipated by immigration (sound familiar?). Instead, he said the U.S. had become merely a political state (polity) containing a number of different nationalities.

15 Kallen left the practical implications of this vision "woefully undeveloped" (in the words of the *Harvard Encyclopedia of American Ethnic Groups*). It eventually evolved into a vague approval of tolerance, which was basically how Americans had always treated immigrant

groups anyway—an extension, not coincidentally, of how the English built the British nation.

But in one respect, Kallenism is very much alive: he argued that authentic Americanism was what he called "the American Idea." This amounted to an almost religious idealization of "democracy," which again was left undeveloped but which appeared to have as much to do with non-discrimination and equal protection under the law as with elections. Today, a messianic concern for global "democracy" is being suggested to conservatives as an appropriate objective for U.S. foreign policy.

And Kallenism underlies the second helpful remark that someone always makes in any discussion of U.S. immigration policy: "America isn't a nation like the other nations—it's an idea."

Once more, this American exceptionalism is really more a matter of degree than of kind. Many other nations have some sort of ideational reinforcement. Quite often it is religious, such as Poland's Roman Catholicism; sometimes cultural, such as France's ineffable Frenchness. And occasionally it is political. Thus—again not coincidentally—the English used to talk about what might be described as the "English Idea": English liberties, their rights as Englishmen, and so on. Americans used to know immediately what this meant. As Jesse Chickering wrote in 1848 of his diverse fellow Americans: "English laws and institutions, adapted to the circumstances of the country, have been adopted here. . . . The tendency of things is to mold the whole into one people, whose leading characteristics are English, formed on American soil."

What is unusual in the present debate, however, is that Americans are now being urged to abandon the bonds of a common ethnicity and instead to trust entirely to ideology to hold together their state (polity). This is an extraordinary experiment, like suddenly replacing all the blood in a patient's body. History suggests little reason to suppose it will succeed. Christendom and Islam have long ago been sundered by national quarrels. More recently, the much-touted "Soviet Man," the

*The "Brussels bureaucracy" to which Brimelow refers in this paragraph is the European Community (now called the European Union), which has its administrative offices in the city of Brussels, Belgium.

[†]The Immigration Quota Acts of 1921 and 1924 established the first limits to the number of legal immigrants who were allowed to enter the United States each year. These laws tended to place greater restrictions on immigration from southern and eastern European countries and fewer restrictions on Nordic and Anglo-Saxon nations.

have been considered absurd throughout most of American history.

John Jay in *The Federalist Papers* wrote that Americans were "one united people, a people descended from the same ancestors, speaking the same language, professing the same religion, attached to the same principles of government, very similar in their manners and customs." Some hundred years later, Theodore Roosevelt in his *Winning of the West* traced the "perfectly continuous history" of the Anglo-Saxons from King Alfred to George Washington. He presented the settling of the lands beyond the Alleghenies as "the crowning and greatest achievement" of "the spread of the English-speaking peoples," which—though personally a liberal on racial matters—he saw in explicit terms: "it is of incalculable importance that America, Australia, and Siberia should pass out of the hands of their red, black, and yellow aboriginal owners, and become the heritage of the dominant world races."

Roosevelt himself was an example of ethnicities merging to produce this new nation. He thanked God—he teased his friend Rudyard Kipling—that there was "not a drop of British blood" in him. But that did not stop him from identifying with Anglo-Saxons or from becoming a passionate advocate of an assimilationist Americanism, which crossed ethnic lines and was ultimately to cross racial lines.

And it is important to note that, at the height of the last great immigration wave, Kallen and his allies totally failed to persuade Americans that they were no longer a nation. Quite the contrary: once convinced that their nationhood was threatened by continued massive immigration, Americans changed the public policies that made it possible. While the national origins quotas were being legislated, President Calvin Coolidge put it unflinchingly: "America must be kept American."

Everyone knew what he meant.

*Fought in 1415, the Battle of Agincourt was one of the key battles in what has become to be known as the Hundred Years War between France and England. King Henry V of England led an invading army into France over a land dispute and defeated an apparently stronger French force near a fortified town named Agincourt. His exploits were immortalized in Shakespeare's *Henry V*.

creation of much tougher ideologists using much rougher methods than anything yet seen in the U.S., has turned out to be a Russian, Ukrainian, or Kazakh after all.

20 Which is why Shakespeare has King Henry V say, before the battle of Agincourt,* not "we defenders of international law and the dynastic principle as it applies to my right to inherit the throne of France," but

We few, we happy few, we band of brothers.

However, although intellectuals may have decided that America is not a nation but an idea, the news has not reached the American people—especially that significant minority who sternly tell the Census Bureau their ethnicity is "American." (They seem mostly to be of British origin, many generations back.) And it would

ASSIMILATION

Often, debates about immigration policy in the U.S. focus on the issue of *assimilation,* which refers to the process by which immigrants become American by adopting the values, traditions, ideals, and even the language of the United States. Sometimes, the metaphor of the "melting pot" is used to describe this process: people of many different backgrounds and identities are mixed together to form a single American nation. When Brimelow describes Theodore Roosevelt as an "advocate of an assimilationist Americanism" he is also referring to a belief in the importance of assimilation in maintaining American identity. When he states in paragraph 11 that "the vast majority of Americans are Christians," he is partly defining that American identity. When he refers in paragraph 19 to "a common ethnicity," he is referring to the same Anglo-Saxons that he tells us Roosevelt aligned himself with—an ethnic group that, for Brimelow, constitutes the American identity. However, in the last few decades, many Americans, especially those from minority groups, have questioned this idea of one nation in which one's ethnic, racial, and religious identities become subsumed by his or her identity as an "American." Instead, arguing that diversity rather than assimilation is what makes America unique and strong, these critics have proposed the metaphor of a mosaic, in which each person retains his or her racial or ethnic identity while becoming a piece of the larger American cultural "mosaic."

Questions for Discussion

1. In his essay, Brimelow describes words as weapons. What does he mean? In what way is his concern about language—and about the definitions of specific terms—central to his argument?

2. Brimelow distinguishes between *nation* and *state*. Why does he believe that the distinction is important? How does he use that distinction in building his argument?

3. According to Brimelow, how has the debate over immigration changed? Why is he concerned about this change? Do you think his concern is justified? Why or why not?

4. In paragraphs 21 and 22, Brimelow appeals to American figures of historical importance, such as John Jay and Theodore Roosevelt. Has he strengthened his case by making these references? Explain. In what ways might he have left himself open to counterargument on this point?

5. Brimelow asserts that Americans do not agree with the statement that America is an idea, not a nation. Why is this point important to Brimelow? Do you think he is right? Why or why not?

6. Brimelow concludes by stating that "everyone" knew what it meant to be American in the 1920s. What is Brimelow implying here? How effective is that statement as a conclusion to his argument?

7. Does the fact that Brimelow was born in England influence the way you read his argument? Does it give him more or less credibility, in your view? Explain.

③ JACOB G. HORNBERGER, "Keep the Borders Open"

Arguments about immigration in the United States often focus on concerns about jobs and money. Many Americans worry that immigrants will take jobs away from them; some fear that immigrants will strain city and state budgets for education and unemployment benefits, resulting in higher taxes. These are valid and serious concerns, and Jacob Hornberger acknowledges them in the following essay. But unlike many critics of U.S. immigration policy, Hornberger is concerned about a more basic issue: individual freedom. He makes his argument in favor of an open immigration policy from his perspective as a libertarian (see the sidebar on page 556). Hornberger is founder of the Future of Freedom Foundation, an organization that advocates in favor of libertarian positions on issues such as immigration. As you read his essay, pay attention to the way he builds his argument on his fundamental libertarian views about individual citizens and the role of the state. Consider how those views might make his argument more or less effective among readers who have allegiances to other political perspectives.

Keep the Borders Open

JACOB G. HORNBERGER

1 In times of crisis, it is sometimes wise and constructive for people to return to first principles and to reexamine and reflect on where we started as a nation, the road we've traveled, where we are today, and the direction in which we're headed. Such a reevaluation can help determine whether a nation has deviated from its original principles and, if so, whether a restoration of those principles would be in order.

It is impossible to overstate the unusual nature of American society from the time of its founding to the early part of the 20th century. Imagine: no Social Security, Medicare, Medicaid, income taxation, welfare, systems of public (i.e., government) schooling, occupational licensure, standing armies, foreign aid, foreign interventions, or foreign wars. Perhaps most unusual of all, there were virtually no federal controls on immigration into the United States.

With the tragic and costly exception of slavery, the bedrock principle underlying American society was that people should be free to live their lives any way they chose, as long as their conduct was peaceful. [See "Libertarianism" on page 556.] That is what it once meant to be free. That is what it once meant to be an American. That was the freedom that our ancestors celebrated each Fourth of July.

Let's examine the issue of immigration because it provides a good model for comparing the vision of freedom of our ancestors with that which guides the American people today.

5 In economic terms, the concept of freedom to which our Founders subscribed entailed the right to sustain one's life through labor by pursuing any occupation or business without government permission or interference, by freely entering into mutually beneficial exchanges with others anywhere in the world, accumulating unlimited amounts of wealth arising from those endeavors, and freely deciding the disposition of that wealth.

LIBERTARIANISM

Hornberger's statement that "the bedrock principle underlying American society was that people should be free to live their lives any way they chose, as long as their conduct was peaceful" reflects his Libertarian beliefs. According to its website, the Libertarian Party "is committed to America's heritage of freedom: individual liberty and personal responsibility; a free-market economy of abundance and prosperity; a foreign policy of non-intervention, peace, and free trade" (see www.lp.org). In short, libertarians believe in maximizing individual freedom and minimizing the power of the state. This political philosophy has a long history in American society. Although the Libertarian Party itself does not have sufficient membership to challenge the Democrats and Republicans in national elections, it plays an important political role in some states, and many Americans share its views on issues such as immigration and foreign policy.

*In 1939 the S.S. *St. Louis* sailed for Cuba from Germany carrying 900 Jewish passengers who were fleeing Nazi persecution and who hoped eventually to enter the United States. The passengers were refused entry into Cuba, and after several weeks the ship was forced to return to Germany. The incident came to be known as the "voyage of the damned."

The moral question is: Why shouldn't a person be free to cross a border in search of work to sustain his life, to open a business, to tour, or simply because he wants to? Or to put it another way, under what moral authority does any government interfere with the exercise of these rights?

Most Americans like the concept of open borders within the United States, but what distinguished our ancestors is that they believed that the principles of freedom were applicable not just domestically but universally. That implied open borders not only for people traveling inside the United States but also for people traveling or moving to the United States.

One important result of this highly unusual philosophy of freedom was that throughout the 19th century, people all over the world, especially those who were suffering political tyranny or economic privation, always knew that there was a place they could go if they could succeed in escaping their circumstances.

The American abandonment of open immigration in the 20th century has had negative consequences, both morally and economically. Let's consider some examples.

10 Prior to and during World War II, U.S. government officials intentionally used immigration controls to prevent German Jews from escaping the horrors of Nazi Germany by coming to America. Many of us are familiar with the infamous "voyage of the damned,"* where U.S. officials refused to permit a German ship to land at Miami Harbor because it carried Jewish refugees. But how many people know that U.S. officials used immigration controls to keep German Jews and Eastern European Jews from coming to the United States even after the existence of the concentration camps became well known?

Indeed, how many Americans know about the one million anti-communist Russians whom U.S. and British officials forcibly repatriated to the Soviet Union at the end of World War II, knowing that death or the gulag awaited them?

Ancient history, you say? Well, consider one of the most morally reprehensible policies in the history of our nation: the forcible repatriation of Cuban refugees into communist tyranny, a practice that has been going on for many years and that continues to this day.

Let me restate this for emphasis: Under the pretext of enforcing immigration laws, our government—the U.S. government—the same government that sent tens of thousands of American GIs to their deaths in foreign wars supposedly to resist communism, is now forcibly returning people into communism.

We have seen the establishment of Border Patrol passport checkpoints on highways and airports inside the United States (north of the border), which inevitably discriminate against people on the basis of skin color. We have seen the criminalization of such things as transporting, housing, and hiring undocumented workers, followed by arbitrary detentions on highways as well as raids on American farms and restaurants.

15 We have seen the construction of a fortified wall in California. This wall, built soon after the fall of the ugliest wall in history, has resulted in the deaths of immigrants entering the country on the harsh Arizona desert. Would Washington, Jefferson, or Madison have constructed such a wall?

We have come a long way from the vision of freedom set forth by our Founding Fathers. Let's consider some of the common objections to open immigration:

1. *Open immigration will pollute America's culture.* Oh? Which culture is that? Boston? New York? Savannah? New Orleans? Denver? Los Angeles? I grew up on the Mexican border (on the Texas side). My culture was eating enchiladas and tacos, listening to both Mexican and American music, and speaking Tex-Mex (a combination of English and Spanish). If you're talking about the danger that my culture might get polluted, that danger comes from the north, not from the south. America's culture has always been one of liberty—one in which people are free to pursue any culture they want.

2. *Immigrants will take jobs away from Americans.* Immigrants displace workers in certain sectors but the displaced workers benefit through the acquisition of higher-paying jobs in other sectors that expand because of the influx of immigrants. It is not a coincidence that historically people's standard of living has soared when borders have been open. Keep in mind also that traditionally immigrants are among the hardest-working and most energetic people in a society, which brings a positive vitality and energy to it.

3. *Immigrants will go on welfare.* Well maybe we ought to reexamine whether it was a good idea to abandon the principles of our ancestors in that respect as well. What would be wrong with abolishing welfare for everyone, including Americans, along with the enormous taxation required to fund it? But if Americans are in fact hopelessly addicted to the government dole, there is absolutely no reason that the same has to happen to immigrants.

U.S. IMMIGRATION POLICY ON CUBA

According to the Close Up Foundation, a nonpartisan citizen education organization,

The island nation of Cuba, located just ninety miles off the coast of Florida, is home to 11 million people and has one of the few remaining communist regimes in the world. Cuba's leader, Fidel Castro, came to power in 1959 and immediately instituted a communist program of sweeping economic and social changes. Castro allied his government with the Soviet Union and seized and nationalized billions of dollars of American property. U.S. relations with Cuba have been strained ever since. A trade embargo against Cuba that was imposed in 1960 is still in place today. . . . All aspects of U.S. policy with Cuba, such as the current trade embargo, immigration practices, and most recently the possibility of a free exchange by members of the media, provoke heated debates across the United States. . . . Some believe that the country's current policy toward Cuba is outdated in its Cold War approach and needs to be reconstructed. However, many still consider Fidel Castro a threat in the hemisphere and a menace to his own people and favor tightening the screws on his regime even more.

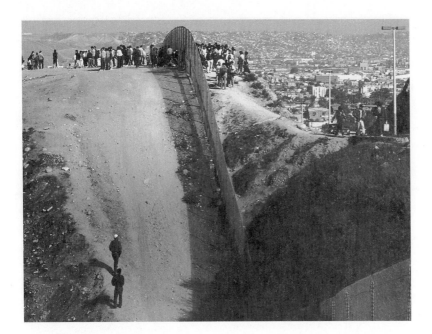

Part of the new border fence in California. (Photo by Nic Paget-Clarke.)

free market to make such a determination be more consistent with our founding principles? Immigrants go where the opportunities abound and they avoid areas where they don't, just as Americans do.

6. *Open immigration will permit terrorists to enter our country.* The only permanent solution to terrorism against the United States, in both the short term and long term, is to abandon the U.S. government's interventionist foreign policy, which is the breeding ground for terrorism against our country. No immigration controls in the world, not even a rebuilt Berlin Wall around the United States, will succeed in preventing the entry of people who are bound and determined to kill Americans.

Therefore, the answer to the welfare issue is not to control immigration but rather to deny immigrants the right to go on the government dole. In such a case, however, wouldn't it be fair to exempt them from the taxes used to fund the U.S. welfare state?

4. *Immigrants will bring in drugs.* Lots of people bring in drugs, including Americans returning from overseas trips. Not even the harshest police state would ever alter that fact. More important, why not legalize drugs and make the state leave drug users alone? Is there any better example of an immoral, failed, and destructive government program than the war on drugs? Why should one government intervention, especially an immoral, failed one, be used to justify another?

5. *There will be too many people.* Oh? Who decides the ideal number? A government board of central planners, just like in China? Wouldn't reliance on the

More than 200 years ago, ordinary people brought into existence the most unusual society in the history of man. It was a society based on the fundamental moral principle that people everywhere are endowed with certain inherent rights that no government can legitimately take away.

Somewhere along the way, Americans abandoned that concept of freedom, especially in their attachment to such programs and policies as Social Security, Medicare, Medicaid, income taxation, economic regulation, public (i.e., government) schooling, the war on drugs, the war on poverty, the war on wealth, immigration controls, foreign aid, foreign intervention, and foreign wars—none of which our founders had dreamed of.

20 The current crisis provides us with an opportunity to reexamine our founding principles, why succeeding generations of Americans abandoned them, the consequences of that abandonment, and whether it would be wise to restore the moral and philosophical principles of freedom of our Founders. A good place to start such a reexamination would be immigration.

Questions for Discussion

1. On what fundamental principle does Hornberger rest his main argument about immigration? Do you share his belief in this principle? Do you think most Americans do?

2. What main reasons does Hornberger cite in support of his position on immigration? Identify the kinds of evidence he provides (see "Appraising Evidence" on pages 80–86). Do you find his reasons persuasive? Why or why not?

3. Hornberger is a libertarian (see the sidebar on page 556 Identify specific points in his article that reveal his libertarian views. To what extent do you think most Americans would agree with his views?

4. Hornberger identifies six main arguments against immigration and offers a rebuttal to each one. Do you think this way of addressing the position of those who oppose immigration is an effective one? Why or why not?

5. Hornberger's essay is an example of an argument based on deductive reasoning (see pages in Chapter 4). What is the fundamental belief or principle on which he bases his argument? How effective do you think this strategy for argumentation is in the issue of immigration?

④ **STEVEN CAMAROTA,** "Too Many: Looking Today's Immigration in the Face"

Steven Camarota is the director of the Center for Immigration Studies (CIS), a nonprofit organization devoted to analyzing the effects of immigration on the United States and generally favoring greater restrictions on immigration to the United States (see **www.cis.org/**). He is a well-known voice in public discussions about immigration. The following essay, which first appeared in 2002 in *National Review,* a respected politically conservative magazine, lays out his position on immigration in detail. In his essay Camarota addresses the main issues that often emerge in debates about immigration: concerns about jobs, schools, taxes, and poverty. But in addressing those issues and providing extensive factual evidence to support his points about each, Camarota is also presenting a view of what he believes America should be. As you read, pay attention to how his vision of America emerges in his essay—and how that vision shapes his argument about U.S. immigration policy.

Too Many: Looking Today's Immigration in the Face

STEVEN CAMAROTA

1 When the history of the 1990s is written, the most important story may not be the GOP takeover of Congress, the boom economy, or the Clinton impeachment. The big story may be the decade's unprecedented level of immigration: a social phenomenon of enormous significance, affecting everything from the nation's schools to the political balance between the two parties.

Newly released census figures show that the foreign-born population reached 31.1 million in 2000 (including some 7 to 8 million here illegally). This is by far the largest immigrant population in U.S. history, and represents a 57 percent increase from 1990. The rate of increase is itself unprecedented: Even during the great wave of immigration from 1900 to 1910, the foreign-born population grew by only about 31 percent (from roughly 10 million to 13.5 million). Over the past 30 years, the number of immigrants in the U.S. has tripled. If current trends are allowed to continue, the foreign-born share of the population will in fact pass the all-time high by the end of this decade. Many defenders of high immigration argue that the current immigration is not really unusual, because although the numbers and growth are without precedent, the total U.S. population was smaller 100 years ago and immigrants constituted a larger share of the total. It is true that the 11.1 percent of the nation's population that is foreign-born today is lower than the all-time high of nearly 15 percent reached in 1910. But one may ask why 1910 should be the benchmark by which to judge today's immigration. In evaluating its effect on modern society, it seems more reasonable to compare today's immigration with that of the more recent past. And in that context, today's figures represent a fundamental break with prior decades: From 1940 to 1990 the foreign-born population averaged less than 7 percent, and as recently as 1970 it was less than 5 percent.

The implications for American society are enormous. For example, a good deal of attention has been given to the fact that the number of people who live in poverty did not decline in the 1990s, despite a strong economy. What has generally not been reported is that new immigrants and their U.S.-born children accounted for the nation's stubborn poverty rate. The primary reason so many immigrant families live in poverty is that a large percentage have very little education. Newly arrived adult immigrants, for example, are more than three times as likely as natives to lack a high-school education.

Immigrants and their children also account for nearly two-thirds of the increase in the population lacking health insurance over the last decade. By dramatically increasing the uninsured population, immigration creates significant costs for taxpayers, and it drives up costs for insured Americans as providers pass along the costs of treating the uninsured to paying customers. The central role immigration has played in creating the nation's health-insurance quandary has largely gone unreported.

5 The impact on public schools is even more significant. In the last 20 years the school-age population has grown by roughly 8 million. Most observers agree that this increase has strained resources in districts across the country. What most media accounts of this growth leave out is that census data indicate that there are about 8 million school-age children from immigrant families—and, because they are much poorer on average than natives, this increase in enrollment has not been accompanied by a corresponding increase in local tax revenue. Moreover, because of language barriers, the children of immigrants often cost significantly more to educate than those of natives. Most news coverage of the issue discusses how to meet the needs of these children, but fails to point out that federal immigration policy created the problem in the first place.

Despite the clear implications mass immigration has for the future of American society, many boosters still argue that today's immigration is very much like that of 1910. No doubt, there are similarities, but the differences are profound and striking to even the casual observer. America is a fundamentally different place than it was 100 years ago, and today's immigration is also very different.

As far as assimilation is concerned, numbers matter at least as much as percentages. For example, a quarter of a million immigrants in a metropolitan area are enough to create linguistic isolation: neighborhoods where immigrants can live and work without ever learning much English. Large numbers also create politically influential ethnic organizations whose leaders often adhere

COMPLICATION

From *Immigration Policy Reports,* a project of the American Immigration Law Foundation:

With 56 million, or 20 percent of the current U.S. population estimated as foreign-born, the Census Bureau's report claims these numbers are the highest in history. However, past demographic data shows otherwise. For example, at the turn of the century when the total foreign-born percentage was 13, the first and second generation accounted for nearly 35 percent of the U.S. population—much higher than today's 20 percent. In fact, from 1870 through 1930, the combination of these two generations was even larger, totaling $\frac{1}{3}$ of the total population.

schools, neighborhoods, entire metropolitan areas, and even whole states.

One institution that helped immigrants and their children acquire an American identity in the past was public education. Schools brought children from different immigrant backgrounds into contact with natives and helped to forge a common American culture. But today, basic demographics makes this much more difficult. Unlike in the past, immigrants now have many more children on average than natives, which means kids from immigrant families very quickly predominate in public schools. For example, although about a quarter of California's total population is foreign-born, half of the school-age population is from immigrant families. In many districts in high-immigration states, immigrant families now account for more than 80 percent of school kids.

10 Of course, neighborhood schools in 1910 saw heavy immigrant concentrations. But because of the large differences in fertility rates, immigration today creates many more districts in which the cultural norms are set by children from immigrant families, who have relatively little contact with their counterparts from native families.

There is, of course, another problem with expecting public schools to play the role they did in the past of assimilating immigrants: Schools don't want to. A very significant share of the U.S. elite has embraced the anti-assimilation ethos, which regards America as a collection of peoples, each with its own distinct culture, which vie for political power as groups. America's educational establishment has embraced this multicultural vision. This is why history textbooks look as they do, and why bilingual education remains widely popular among educators. This trend shows no signs of abating; in fact, the growing number of immigrants only feeds the multiculturalist perspective. Immigration provides further justification for it by creating an ever larger aggrieved class, whose cultures must be preserved in the face of an oppressive majority culture.

to an anti-assimilation multicultural ideology. Whether the immigrants in question represent 10 percent or 30 percent of a city's population is not so important; it's the raw numbers that count, and the numbers are already well over twice what they were in 1910.

In one sense, today's immigrants are more diverse than ever before, in that significant numbers arrive from all continents and races. But in a more important sense, today's immigration wave is considerably less diverse than those of the past, because Spanish speakers dominate in a way no other group ever did before. While German speakers accounted for a little over a quarter of all immigrants in the late 1800s and Italians for about one-fifth in the first decades of the 1900s, such concentrations were transitory. In contrast, the domination of immigrants from Latin America has grown steadily. In 1970, 19 percent of the foreign-born were from Latin America; by 2000, it was more than half. One ethnolinguistic group can now predominate in

Of course, some form of assimilation does take place, even in the modern public school. While language acquisition almost certainly has slowed in recent years, most immigrants learn to speak at least some English. But assimilation is much more than learning to speak English, or driving on the right side of the road. It involves what John Fonte of the Hudson Institute calls "patriotic assimilation," the belief that American history is one's own history. A century ago it meant that immigrants and their children came to see America's past as something "we" did, not something "they"—white people of European ancestry—did. To the extent that immigrants are assimilating they are doing so, in many cases, as "multicultural" Americans.

Some conservatives, and even some liberals, have a different conception of assimilation, but it is not at all clear that those who wish to see a more robust love of country inculcated in our children (immigrant or native) are winning the debate. It simply makes no sense, therefore, for a society that cannot agree on its own history or even what it means to be an American to welcome over a million newcomers each year from outside.

Technology is another obstacle to assimilation. It is now possible to call—or even to visit—one's home country with a frequency that was inconceivable even 50 years ago. One can listen to a hometown radio station or read the local newspapers on the Internet. The costs of travel and communication are now so low that many wealthier immigrants can live in two countries at the same time, traveling back and forth with ease. In such a world, it is less likely that immigrants will develop a deep attachment to the U.S.

15 The American economy is also fundamentally different, with serious consequences for the assimilation process. A century ago, manufacturing, mining, and agriculture employed the vast majority of the workforce, creating plentiful work for unskilled immigrants. These jobs eventually led to solid working-class incomes for immigrants and their children. (In fact, most native-born Americans a century ago worked in the same kinds of jobs.) Though most people were poor by today's standards, most historians agree that there was not a very large economic gap between the standard of living of natives and that of immigrants; this was because, on average, immigrants were not that much less skilled than natives. Data are limited, but in terms of years of schooling or literacy, immigrants 100 years ago were roughly equal to natives.

This is no longer the case. While a number of today's immigrants are quite skilled, immigrants overall are significantly less educated than natives. As a result, when it comes to average income, poverty rates, welfare use, and other measures of economic well-being, today's immigrants are much worse off than natives. Unlike that of 1910, today's U.S. economy offers very limited opportunity for those with little education, and this creates a very sizable gap between the two groups.

Another important change since 1910 is the profound expansion in the size and scope of government. Spending on everything from education to infrastructure maintenance is many times greater than it was back then. With federal, state, and local government now eating up roughly one-third of GDP, the average individual must be able to pay a good deal in taxes to cover his use of public services. In practice, the middle and upper classes pay most of the taxes; the poor, immigrant or native, generally consume significantly more in public services than they pay in taxes.

This means that the arrival of large numbers of relatively poor immigrants has a significant negative effect on public coffers in a way that was not the case in the past. In 1997 the National Academy of Sciences estimated that immigrant households consumed between $11 and $20 billion more in public services than they were paying in taxes each year. (Other estimates have found this deficit to be even higher.) A smaller government may well

CONTEXT

In 1995 education scholar Mike Rose reported on the increasing diversity of American public schools. At Pasadena High School in California, for example, more than thirty-eight different languages were spoken by students enrolled there.

SOURCE: *Possible Lives* (1995).

be desirable, but it is politically inconceivable that we would ever return to the situation of 100 years ago, when government accounted for a tiny fraction of the economy. Thus, continually allowing in large numbers of unskilled immigrants has very negative implications for taxpayers.

The situation of today's immigrants is, then, dramatically different from what it was at the turn of the last century. But even if one ignores all these differences, one undeniable fact remains: The last great wave of immigration was stopped, as an act of government policy. World War I, followed by restrictive legislation in the early 1920s, dramatically reduced immigration to about a quarter of what it had been in previous decades. This immigration pause played a critically important role in turning yesterday's immigrants into Americans. So if the past is to be our guide, then we should significantly reduce immigration numbers.

20 If we don't, the assimilation problem will only get worse. We know from experience that it is often the children of immigrants who have the greatest difficulty identifying with America. While their parents at least know how good they have it, the children tend to compare their situation to that of other Americans, instead of that in their parents' homeland. Unless the gap between themselves and other Americans has been closed in just one generation, something few groups have been able to

accomplish, this can be a source of real discontent. Moreover, it is children born in the U.S. to immigrant parents who often feel caught between two worlds and struggle with their identity.

What we should do is call a halt to the current heedless increase in annual immigration, and reduce the numbers to something like their historical average of 300,000 a year. In the mid 1990s, the bipartisan immigration-reform panel headed by the late Barbara Jordan suggested limiting family immigration to the spouses and minor children of U.S. citizens and legal non-citizens, and to the parents of citizens. However, we should probably eliminate the preferences for the spouses and minor children of non-citizens, since these provisions apply to family members acquired after the alien has received a green card but before he has become a citizen. If we also eliminated the parents of U.S. citizens as a category, family immigration would fall to less than half what it is today. The Jordan panel also wisely suggested eliminating the visa lottery and tightening up the requirements for employment- and humanitarian-based immigration.

These changes would, taken together, reduce legal immigration to roughly 300,000 annually. Only if we get the numbers down to this reasonable level can we begin the long process of assimilating the huge number of immigrants and their children who are already here.

Questions for Discussion

1. Examine the way in which Camarota uses statistical information as evidence to support his argument, especially in paragraph 2. What specific point do these statistics help him make? How effectively do you think he uses these statistics?

2. Camarota asserts that "America is a fundamentally different place than it was 100 years ago, and today's immigration is also very different." What does he mean? What evidence does he offer to support this assertion? Do you think he is right? Why or why not?

3. What is Camarota's view of the assimilation of immigrants into U.S. society? What does he mean when he refers to "the assimilation problem"? Why is his view of assimilation important to his overall argument? Do you agree with him about this issue? Why or why not? How might your views about immigration affect your reaction to Camarota's point about assimilation?

4. Camarota writes that "in terms of years of schooling or literacy, immigrants 100 years ago were roughly equal to natives." How does he arrive at this conclusion? What evidence does he present? Do you think he makes a persuasive case that this point is valid? Explain.

5. Evaluate the way in which Camarota uses history to make his argument about what should be done about immigration today. What historical events or developments does he cite? How does he use these historical references to build his argument? What do you think is his general view of America's past? How does that view influence his use of historical references in his argument? Identify specific passages in his essay to illustrate your answer.

6. Several times in his essay Camarota refers to "liberals" and to "boosters"—that is, people who favor immigration. Who exactly are these boosters? Where in the essay are they described or identified? Does Camarota see any common ground between him and boosters of immigration?

NEGOTIATING DIFFERENCES

Each of the authors in this section presents an argument about immigration policy in the United States. But each author also presents a vision of what America is—and what it should be. Part of the challenge in sorting through debates about immigration policy is understanding the way these visions of America inform the views of participants in these debates. Ultimately, decisions about immigration policy reflect some general agreement about what America is and who Americans are. In other words, when laws governing immigration are passed by the U.S. Congress, or when policies regarding immigrants are adopted by schools or state agencies, these laws are implicitly saying, "This is the kind of nation or society we believe we want to have."

With that in mind, imagine that you are part of a committee created by your state government to examine the impact of immigration on your state. Your committee's task is to draft a report to the governor in which you present and justify a general immigration policy in your state. That task requires you to investigate immigration in your state: who the immigrants in your state are; where they have come from and why; how many there are; and what impact they have on schools, jobs, and social life. It also requires you to consider your own views about what kind of society you be-lieve America should be and who should be allowed to become an American.

Working by yourself or with a group of your classmates, write a report to your governor in which you make an argument for a general immigration policy for your state. In your report, you might draw on the perspectives presented in the four essays in this section and on any other relevant material.

CLUSTER
2

What Does It Mean to Be a Good American Citizen?

In a famous line from his inaugural address, President John F. Kennedy challenged Americans: "Ask not what your country can do for you. Ask what you can do for your country." (See Con-Text on page 569.) His challenge implied a sense of duty that he hoped all Americans would feel. It was a time of political uncertainty and tension between the United States and the Soviet Union, both of which possessed nuclear weapons of fearful power—a time that seemed to require Americans to put their own desires aside to help protect their nation. To be a good citizen, Kennedy seemed to be saying, means placing the nation's good before your own. ■ Many Americans have shared Kennedy's belief in this sense of duty, especially in times of war and crisis. But the question of what it means to be an American citizen has never been simple and has at times created great conflict. During the Vietnam War, for example, some Americans believed fervently that it was their patriotic duty to serve their country by fighting with the U.S. armed forces in southeast Asia. Others believed just as fervently that the demands of citizenship required them to oppose their country's involvement in Vietnam through protest and resistance to the draft. Still others supported the American war effort in Vietnam despite genuine misgivings about it. The deep divisions among Americans caused open conflict, as well, as soul-searching about what it meant to be a good citizen. ■ Of course, debate and conflict about citizenship and patriotism date back to the beginnings of the United States. During the Revolutionary War many Americans remained loyal to the British Crown as their rightful government. The Civil War highlighted the conflicting loyalties that many Americans felt to their states and to their national government. In our own time a different kind of war—what many call the "war on terror"—has again provoked debate about citizenship, patriotism, and duty in the aftermath of September 11, 2001. As several of the writers in this section demonstrate, those events have prompted Americans to examine not just their opinions about their government's response to terrorism but also their most fundamental beliefs about citizenship, patriotism, and American identity. Once again, young Americans are being asked to risk their own lives for their country. Such great sacrifice inevitably causes Americans to pause and think hard about what they must do—and what they *should* do—as citizens. ■ Although these questions about citizenship might emerge most provocatively during war and crisis, they are not questions *about* war or crisis. Even in peacetime Americans wrestle with the idea of citizenship, which sometimes seems to conflict with beliefs about individual freedom and self-determination that run deep in U.S. culture. As the following essays suggest, the problem of defining what it means to be a good citizen can emerge in such seemingly common activities as voting or expressing political opinions. It might be that these more mundane acts of citizenship can give Americans cause to wonder about the relationship between their duties as citizens and their religious or ethnic loyalties, as Wilfred McClay reminds us in his essay. ■ In the end, the question of what it means to be a good citizen is a complicated and difficult one in part because it can be answered in so many different ways. As you engage the various arguments about citizenship in this section, you might ask yourself how your view of what it means to be an American shapes your sense of duty as a citizen—and how you would respond to President John F. Kennedy's challenge.

CON-TEXT

President John F. Kennedy's 1961 Inaugural Address

1. . . . In your hands, my fellow citizens, more than mine, will rest the final success or failure of our course. Since this country was founded, each generation of Americans has been summoned to give testimony to its national loyalty. The graves of young Americans who answered the call to service surround the globe.

Now the trumpet summons us again—not as a call to bear arms, though arms we need—not as a call to battle, though embattled we are—but a call to bear the burden of a long twilight struggle, year in and year out, "rejoicing in hope, patient in tribulation"—a struggle against the common enemies of man: tyranny, poverty, disease and war itself.

Can we forge against these enemies a grand and global alliance, North and South, East and West, that can assure a more fruitful life for all mankind? Will you join in that historic effort?

In the long history of the world, only a few generations have been granted the role of defending freedom in its hour of maximum danger. I do not shrink from this responsibility—I welcome it. I do not believe that any of us would exchange places with any other people or any other generation. The energy, the faith, the devotion which we bring to this endeavor will light our country and all who serve it—and the glow from that fire can truly light the world.

5 And so, my fellow Americans: ask not what your country can do for you. Ask what you can do for your country.

My fellow citizens of the world: ask not what America will do for you, but what together we can do for the freedom of man.

Finally, whether you are citizens of America or citizens of the world, ask of us here the same high standards of strength and sacrifice which we ask of you. With a good conscience our only sure reward, with history the final judge of our deeds, let us go forth to lead the land we love, asking His blessing and His help, but knowing that here on earth God's work must truly be our own.

① JOHN BALZAR, "Needed: Informed Voters"

The right to vote is a fundamental right guaranteed to Americans by the U.S. Constitution. It is a hallmark of the political system, central to the workings of democracy. But it is a right that has not always been enjoyed by all Americans. Women were not allowed to vote in the United States until 1920, and African Americans were often prevented from voting by local and state restrictions even after Congress passed the Voting Rights Act in 1963. Perhaps Americans take this hard-won right for granted, because only about half of eligible voters usually turn out for presidential elections and often fewer than half vote in local and state elections. As reporter John Balzar notes in the following essay, political commentators routinely lament these low voter turnouts, suggesting that low participation in American political campaigns weakens democracy. Balzar has a somewhat different view. He believes not only that voting is a right but also that it entails responsibility; in his view, it is not enough simply to show up at the polling place to vote. Citizenship requires more than that. As you engage his argument, consider your views about voting. How important is the right to vote? What responsibilities come with that right? Does being an American *require* you to vote? Or does it mean that you can choose *not* to exercise that right?

Balzar has covered politics and served as a foreign correspondent for the *Los Angeles Times.* The author of *Yukon Alone* (1999), Balzar has won the Scripps-Howard Foundation Prize for his human interest and adventure stories.

Needed: Informed Voters

JOHN BALZAR

*Considered by some critics to be America's first successful novelist, James Fenimore Cooper (1789–1851) is best known today for his novel *The Last of the Mohicans* (1826). But like Mark Twain, author of *The Adventures of Huckleberry Finn* (1884), Cooper was also widely known in his day as a social and political critic whose writings about American democracy were often controversial.

1   More than 150 years ago, the writer James Fenimore Cooper* put it this way: "The man who can right himself by a vote will seldom resort to a musket."

Cooper found agreement on the point even with his old nemesis, Mark Twain, who set aside humor to observe: "Where every man in a state has a vote, brutal laws are impossible."

Ah, voting. When you read through American civics, you find that almost everybody who presumed to comment on our nation had something celebratory to say about the franchise.

The United States, no one should forget, pioneered the idea of self-governance on a grand scale by way of popular elections.

5   Only elections aren't so popular anymore. In the 2002 primaries, 83 percent of eligible Americans exercised their rights as free citizens and chose not to vote. Far more people stake their hopes on playing the Lotto than on participating in democracy. We now bemoan the results: With the onset of autumn, the public begins to lay eyes on the matchups of candidates chosen by tiny fractions of their neighbors.

Yikes.

Our normal suspicions about those who seek political office turn into outright alarm. Consequently, fewer people muster the enthusiasm to drive down the block and cast a vote in the election.

Two truths: I've never met anyone who would forfeit his or her right to vote. Likewise, everyone knows that the United States would be a much different country if everyone availed himself of the opportunity and actually cast an informed vote.

So, do we have a crisis on our hands? Instinctively, we are conditioned to say yes. But I don't think it's quite as simple as that. 10 The hand-wringers have been telling us for decades now that something must be way wrong in the land for participation to be so low. Yet many nonvoters I know are not distraught, but content.

We live in an age of decidedly centrist politics, driven in large measure by personality. Most candidates are foursquare in favor of a full-employment economy, equal opportunity, a healthy environment, good schools and health care. Thus, political differences boil down to the tactics and philosophy of governance, and for a good number of people, it's enough to leave that choice to others.

There's another matter, usually too delicate to be discussed directly. That's the distinction between voting and voting wisely.

For as long as I've covered politics, I've listened to experts say that we need to make registration and voting simpler, easier. In truth, registration has never been simpler in most places, and it's getting more so all the time.

The real difficulty in voting is the preparation involved. To cast an intelligent ballot requires more than casual exposure to TV commercials. 15 Many Americans have lost faith in those who offer considered election guidance, whether political parties, newspaper editorials or interest groups. Thus the rise of the vaunted "independent voter."

Sounds lofty. But in truth, the homework necessary to inform oneself about the issues and candidates in most elections is no less than that faced in an upper-division college class.

From what I can tell, many Americans aren't up to the task. Reading through opinion surveys is always as amusing as it is sobering.

Almost half the nation believes that the communist creed "from each according to his abilities, to each according to his needs" is spelled out in the U.S. Constitution. And although 66 percent of adults can identify Regis Philbin as host of a TV game show, only 6 percent can name Dennis Hastert, R-Ill., as speaker of the U.S. House of Representatives.

So, would our democracy be better served if more people voted? As I said, it's not as simple as answering yes.

INDEPENDENT VOTERS

When he refers to the "independent voter," Balzar is invoking the belief that Americans tend to vote for their favored candidates regardless of party affiliation. In other words, especially in presidential elections, voters will vote for the candidate they like best, whether or not that candidate represents their own party. According to the Center for Voting and Democracy, 64 percent of voting-age Americans were registered with a political party in 2002. In the eighteen states that require voters to register with a party to vote, 34.1 percent of voting-age individuals were registered as Democrats, 22.6 percent as Republicans, and 17.4 percent as independent or with a third party—an increase from 15.8 percent in 1998. (See www.fairvote.org/turnout/csae2002.htm.)

COMPLICATION

Balzar asserts that being an informed voter requires "homework" equivalent to the work required in "an upper-division college class." Is he right? According to political commentator Thomas Sowell,

Ideally, each citizen should both become informed about issues and candidates and go to the polls on Election Day. But the real question is what to do in a world that is seldom ideal. Even informed voters sometimes have trouble understanding that they can only choose among alternatives actually available. Some voters vote—or don't vote—according to whether their elected officials have lived up to all their hopes. Seldom can any officials in a democracy do that ("High Stakes Elections," 2002).

According to Martin Wattenberg, Americans who choose not to vote tend to have less education than those who do vote. In 1998 U.S. college graduates voted at 36 percent above the national average; those with "some high school" voted at 43 percent below it. (source: *Where Have All the Voters Gone?* 2002.)

In 1849 Henry David Thoreau wrote in his famous essay "Civil Disobedience,"

All voting is a sort of gaming, like checkers or backgammon, with a slight moral tinge to it, a playing with right and wrong, with moral questions; and betting naturally accompanies it. . . . Even voting *for the right* is *doing* nothing for it. It is only expressing to men feebly your desire that it should prevail. A wise man will not leave the right to the mercy of chance, nor wish it to prevail to the power of the majority.

Questions for Discussion

1. What do you think Balzar accomplishes with his references in paragraphs 1 and 2 to two well-known American writers from the nineteenth century, James Fenimore Cooper and Mark Twain? How do those references relate to his main argument?

2. Why does Balzar disagree with political commentators who believe there is a crisis among U.S. voters because of low turnout rates for elections? What support does he offer for his position on voter turnout rates in the United States?

3. Balzar states that "we live in an age of decidedly centrist politics." What does he mean? Do you agree with him that politics today are "driven in large measure by personality"? Explain.

4. What evidence does Balzar offer for his assertion that "many Americans aren't up to the task" of informing themselves on the issues and candidates in most elections? Do you find his evidence convincing? Why or why not?

5. What do you think are the implications of Balzar's argument? What might his view of U.S. voters say about democracy? What might it suggest about how elections should be run? What response would you offer to his argument?

② WILFRED M. McCLAY, "America: Idea or Nation?"

The question that Wilfred McClay poses in the title of the following essay is perhaps misleading because it suggests that the answer must be that the United States is *either* an idea *or* a nation. But in his carefully reasoned essay, McClay makes it clear that the issue is more complicated than that. He makes it clear, too, that because understanding America as an idea *and* a nation can be challenging, patriotism is also a challenging concept. McClay explores what it means to be a patriot in a nation that is a powerful symbol of democracy both for its own citizens and for citizens of other nations. In exploring the symbolic importance of America, McClay refuses to simplify the issue of patriotism. The complexity of his argument might be appropriate, because McClay believes that many Americans have not thought carefully enough about what it means to be a patriotic citizen. His essay challenges you to reflect on your own patriotism and how it relates to your sense of identity. McClay is the SunTrust Bank Chair of Excellence in Humanities and a professor of history at the University of Tennessee at Chattanooga; he is also the author of *The Masterless: Self and Society in Modern America* (1994) and a contributing editor of *Touchstone: A Journal of Mere Christianity*. The following essay was published in the *Public Interest* in 2001.

America: Idea or Nation?

WILFRED M. McCLAY

1   At first glance, American patriotism seems a simple matter. But it is simple only until one actually starts to think about it, inquire after its sources, and investigate its manifestations. Consider a small but significant case in point, an observation recently made by a distinguished rabbi who serves a large and prosperous Reform congregation in the New York suburbs. This man takes the business of premarital counseling very seriously, and therefore gets to know many of his congregation's younger members in a fairly intimate way. In the course of interviewing and counseling them over the years, he has discovered an interesting pattern: a high correlation between the level of these young people's patriotic sentiments and the extent of their opposition to intermarriage, meaning marriage to non-Jews. In other words, those with the strongest love of country were also those most firmly committed to marrying only within the Jewish faith. Conversely, those most indifferent or hostile to patriotism were also most likely to have no reservations about intermarriage—and most likely to find fault with those who do.

Loyalties Large and Small

The rabbi's observation rings true to me. And yet if it is true, it would seem to throw much of our conventional wisdom about patriotism into a cocked hat. Don't we generally assume that loyalty to the nation is a form of belonging that tends, as it intensifies, to divert, diminish, or even swallow up lesser loyalties and more particular affiliations? Doesn't the study of European history indicate precisely this, that the modern nation-state* grew in power and prestige at the expense of local and regional

*The Merriam-Webster dictionary defines *nation-state* as "a form of political organization under which a relatively homogeneous people inhabits a sovereign state; especially: a state containing one as opposed to several nationalities."

identities and affinities, including those of religion? Wouldn't it therefore be more reasonable to predict that observant American Jews would value their nation less, because they value their faith more—particularly when theirs is a faith that sets them apart from the vast majority of Americans? And by the same token, wouldn't it stand to reason that intensely patriotic American Jews would see an act of such primal loyalty to the Jewish community, particularly on a matter as personal and intimate as the question of a marriage partner, as an atavism and a betrayal of the American promise of universal liberty and equality?

Reasonable guesses all, except that they happen not to be borne out by this rabbi's experiences. To be sure, this seeming paradox may have a lot to do with the history and current state of the factions within American Jewry. But it also is wonderfully illustrative of a more general truth, which is this: A considerable part of the genius of American patriotism resides in the fact that being a proud and loyal American does not require one to yield up all of one's identity to the nation. On the contrary, American patriotism has generally affirmed and drawn upon the vibrancy and integrity of other, smaller-scale, and relatively independent loyalties. Far from weakening American national sentiment, or causing it to be half-hearted or anemically "thin," these other traditions have strengthened it immeasurably. Nor is this ideal a recent innovation, brought on by the nation's growing ethnic diversity and the vogue of multiculturalism. Instead, it is an ideal as old as the nation itself, going back to the fundamental concept of a federated republic, which consisted of free and self-governing states, counties, and townships, and which loomed so large in the minds of the nation's Founders.

Needless to say, it has not been an easy ideal to realize or sustain, as recurrent crises in American history from the Whiskey Rebellion to the Civil War to the post–World War II conflicts over school desegregation and voting rights have shown. America's national government has grown steadily in power and influence, and the political, economic, legal, technological, and social forces tending to impose homogeneity upon the national culture are stronger than ever. Yet there is an enduring power in this more diffuse patriotic ideal, which seats the general in the local, and asserts that one does not become more of an American by becoming less of something else—less Southern, less Virginian, less small-town, less black, less Jewish, less whatever.

5   Of course, there will always be instances in which certain profound loyalties come into conflict, in ways that cannot be reconciled. Such is the human condition, and such is the stuff of civil wars, religious martyrdoms, and Sophoclean tragedies. But the American patriotic ideal has generally been wise and generous about granting the widest possible berth to our disparate loyalties and in assuming a certain respect for the multiplicity of the person. Loyalty, like love, is not necessarily a zero-sum game, in which any loyalty accorded to X is thought to take away from what Y might have received. A husband does not love his wife less because he also loves his children; if anything, the opposite is the case. And, as Burke and Tocqueville* both well understood, something of the same is true of political and social life. By giving as free a hand as possible to the "little platoons," local institutions, and independent associations in a free society, the nation not only makes it possible for many citizens to be meaningfully involved in the work of public life but also elicits from them a deep, unfeigned, and uncoerced patriotism. In a word, the health of local and particular freedoms strengthens the nation. . . .

The Problems of Commerce
So where will the next generation of American patriots come from? The particulars of the situation are not terribly encouraging. There is no iron-clad guarantee that there will even be such a generation. The heart of the problem is the well-known fact that the cultivation of pa-

*French political writer Alexis de Tocqueville (1805–1859) examined the characteristics of the American political system and the American people in his classic book *Democracy in America* (1835). He argued that a crucial component of democracy is "self-interest rightly understood," which refers to a citizen's understanding that acting in ways that society deems good is actually in one's own self-interest.

triotic virtue does not come naturally to a commercial society such as the United States. When the self-interested pursuit of material well-being, rather than the inculcation of public-spiritedness, has become the glue of social cohesion and the chief engine of social progress, where can such a society catch a glimpse of broader and longer horizons, or find compelling rationales for sacrificial acts devoted to the common good? Tocqueville showed persuasively how far the principle of "self-interest rightly understood" could go in reproducing many of the salutary effects of virtue. Rather than appealing to an obsolete standard of noble thoughts and character, the principle of "self-interest rightly understood" succeeded by persuading citizens that it was both prudent and useful for them to behave in outwardly virtuous ways. But even that principle has its limits, and it reaches those limits at precisely the moment when the utilitarian pay-off for virtuous behavior is no longer so plainly evident.

The martial virtues fall first. How can the principle of self-interest serve to persuade a soldier to lay down his life for his country or to risk life and limb by withholding confidential information when he is held prisoner? Or, on a less heroic level, how does this principle command sufficient loyalty from the general populace to fight an extended, costly war, or form affective bonds that will take precedence over self-interest in moments of national crisis? Even the self-restraints entailed by more commonplace virtues such as thrift, modesty, and marital fidelity are likely to weaken when there is no obvious utility in respecting them, and no obvious risk in disdaining them. In any event, the broad spirit of patriotism, which blends the martial virtues with the commonplace ones, cannot thrive without being nourished by moral sources, ones that the principle of self-interest cannot provide. Finding and sustaining those alternative sources turns out to be one of the perennial problems of American society. It is a problem very much facing us in the prosperous present.

Happily complicating the matter, however, is the undeniable fact that the United States has managed to produce more than its share of genuine patriots—warriors and heroes great and small, gallant and unprepossessing, romantic and gritty, aristocratic and plebeian, all united by a willingness to put their lives on the line for their country. How then, in light of the formidable obstacles mentioned above, has the United States managed to bring forth such patriots? And how can it find the means to honor them properly in the present, and—most important of all—produce more of them in the future? The answers to these questions have never been obvious, either to the generation of the Founders or to our own, but a great deal hangs upon the way they are answered, or not answered. Hence it is a fortunate event that Walter Berns, one of our most thoughtful political philosophers, has come forward with a lucid new book, *Making Patriots,* the fruit of his many years of reflection on the American polity and society, to address precisely these questions. "Designing a public-spirit curriculum for such a people" is, Berns writes, "no easy task." But few are better qualified to help initiate the process.

MAKING PATRIOTS BY WALTER BERNS

"The Founders . . . knew, and accepted as a fact, that the nation was formed by self-interested men, men, as John Locke puts it, naturally in a 'state of perfect freedom to order their actions and dispose of their possessions and persons as they think fit . . . without asking leave or depending on the will of any other man.' But they also knew, as Locke knew, that these men ceased to be autonomous, or simply self-interested men, when they entered civil society and agreed to be governed. That agreement made them citizens, and a citizen is obliged to think of his fellows and of the whole of which he is a part. This requires that he possess certain qualities of character, or virtues, and, as Madison says in Federalist 55, 'republican government presupposes the existence of these qualities in a higher degree than any other form [of government].' Because these qualities cannot be taken for granted, they must somehow be cultivated" Source: *Making Patriots* (2001).

American Exceptionalism

To begin with, Berns argues, we need to recognize that patriotism in America is an entirely different animal from patriotism in other times and places. The ancient Greek city-state of Sparta, for example, which Berns takes to represent the apex of the classical world's understanding of patriotism, was legendary for its public-spirited citizenry. But it achieved that distinction at far too high a cost, at least according to our standards, by imposing a comprehensive regime of severe, near-totalitarian control upon its people. Every aspect of life, from education to marriage to childrearing to eating, fell under the state's purview. Ruthlessly obliterating any elements of privacy or individuality in its citizen's lives, or any of the institutions that mediated between the state and the individual, Sparta sought to achieve a homogeneous, mobilized, martially virtuous populace, imbued with an overwhelming sense of duty to the collective whole, and rendered invulnerable to the siren songs of self-interest and self-gratification. All private sentiments became displaced onto the state itself, so that self-love was sublimated and absorbed entirely into the love of Sparta. Such discipline made for a mighty and disciplined war machine. But it neglected nearly every other aspect of human potentiality and would be entirely inappropriate as a model of patriotism or patriot-formation for the American republic.

10 This is true in part because the American polity would emphasize commerce over war-making, and protection of men's natural rights over enforcement of their social obligations. But it also is true, Berns points out, because the classical model had long before been shattered by the advent of Christianity, which separated the spiritual duties of men from their political ones and the things of God from the things of Caesar. This decisively changed the nature of patriotism, driving a wedge between the private and public virtues, and demoting the latter to a decisively subordinate role. If Sparta had made the cultivation of

public virtue and patriotic sentiment the be-all and end-all of social existence, then Christianity did something like the opposite, downgrading the sentiment of patriotism and presenting it with an enduring dilemma. Would patriotism become conflated with religious sentiment, and thereby absorbed into the vision of a crusading worldly theocracy? Or would it remain aloof from religious sentiment, and thereby run the risk of becoming the distant junior partner of a gnostic, otherworldly faith?

The American solution, which could not have been arrived at without the clarifying help of centuries of European religious wars, managed to split the difference, with a decisive move in the direction of separation, though also with a healthy expression of generalized Protestant civil religion undergirding and enlivening the whole. It is a settlement that defies easy formulation and is more fragile than many Americans appreciate. Berns overstates matters a bit in asserting baldly that the Founders "consigned [religion] to the private sphere." In fact, that prospect didn't come fully into view until the century just past, and its effects have always been highly controversial. But Berns is right, in the end, to say that the Constitution the Framers devised did not envision the United States government as the custodian of men's souls. That was to be the task of other entities. Instead, the Constitution was designed to free men to engage in the self-interested pursuits of a bourgeois society.

Which brings us back to the central problem: How does a republic that is based upon cupidity and self-seeking make public-spirited patriots? Thomas Jefferson, like [Jean-Jaques] Rousseau before him, was himself dubious about the possibility, which was one reason why he preferred the agrarian ideal of a virtuous landowning yeomanry over the Hamiltonian vision of a restless and inventive commercial class of continental-minded men.* A farmer, after all, lived a settled life and had a citizen's substantial stake in the land he inhabited and cultivated. But what

*Important figures in the founding of the United States as a nation, Thomas Jefferson and Alexander Hamilton held different ideals for American democracy. Jefferson believed that democracy could be fostered through a society of land-owning farmers whose stake in preserving their land and their way of life would ensure good citizenship. Hamilton envisioned a nation built on commerce driven by American entrepreneurship that is regulated by a strong central government.

about the holder of stocks, bonds, and bank notes? He was a man ever on the move, a citizen of no place, a man whose only home was the market.

Yet Jefferson was also principal author of the document that, for Berns, provides the one sure basis for American patriotism: the Declaration of Independence. The key to American patriotism, in Berns's view, is that it is twofold, entailing not only devotion to one's country but also devotion to the principles upon which that country had been founded and to which it was consecrated. These principles are not peculiar to Americans, but are thought to be universal in scope, grounded self-evidently in human nature. First among these principles are the famous assertions that all men are created equal, that they are endowed by their Creator with certain inalienable rights, including life, liberty, and the pursuit of happiness, and that governments derive their legitimacy from the consent of the governed and are instituted for the purpose of securing these rights. From these principles may be derived a more generalized commitment to democratic self-government, which Lincoln called government "of the people, by the people and for the people." This is the creed to which Americans assent, Berns argues, and it is out of admiration for these ideals, and not merely out of filial loyalty to "their" country, that American patriots derive their animating sentiments.

The figure of Abraham Lincoln looms especially large for Berns. He is "patriotism's poet," the uncommon common man whose words and personal example offer eloquent testimony to the possibilities of American democracy. Hence Berns twice cites words from Lincoln's 1852 eulogy to Henry Clay* as a definitive statement on the shape of American patriotism. Clay, Lincoln said, "loved his country partly because it was his own country, but mostly because it was a free country; and he burned with a zeal for its advancement, because he saw in such, the advancement, prosperity, and glory of human liberty, human right,

and human nature." It was this sense of America's mission, as the carrier and leading advocate for universal ideals, and not merely as another nation seeking to preserve its territory or expand its place in the sun, that animated Clay and Lincoln. And, Berns argues, it has animated the generations of American patriots who fought to preserve the Union and to defeat the totalitarian powers of the twentieth century.

15 Berns does not deny the stains on the national record, particularly the institution of slavery and its aftermath. But he is determined that those failures be estimated properly, as the ex-slave Frederick Douglass himself did, as remediable defects in an otherwise admirable and promising structure, rather than be exaggerated and used to denigrate the whole. Berns endorses Lincoln's contention that America represents "the last, best hope of earth," with all the enormous responsibilities that that entails. And he concludes by insisting that it is all-important to defend the legitimacy of America's liberal democracy and the ideal it embodies against the armies of its postmodernist, relativist, and multiculturalist detractors. For once this legitimacy is damaged, and once the foundational truths are no longer regarded as self-evident by the citizenry, then the American nation will be uprooted and fatally undermined to the detriment not only of America but of all humanity.

Dangerous Abstractions
Berns is himself a member of the generation of patriots, now gradually disappearing from our midst, that fought in the war against Hitler. That poignant fact echoes through his pages, subtly but unmistakably, giving an added measure of authority to his words. He has written a deeply moving book, personal without being the least bit mawkish or confessional and vibrant with the full range of human emotions—pride, reverence, tenderness, and occasional flashes of anger. This is, after all, his country that he is writing about. He manages to convey a keen sense of connection to the American

CONTEXT

To read part of *The Declaration of Independence,* see *Con-Text* on page 599.

*Henry Clay (1777–1852) served for many years as Speaker of the House. A skillful legislator, he worked hard to mediate political differences before the Civil War.

past, a sense that is much more than merely historical. There is a feeling of urgency, too, a concern that the rising generations have not been taught about what they have inherited, about what their inheritance cost—and about those who were willing to pay the price for it. "Ours is not a parochial patriotism," Berns insists, because "it comprises an attachment to principles that are universal." Anything less would be "un-American."

One hopes there will be young readers of Berns's book who will find themselves stirred by such a full-throated and unabashed endorsement of America's sense of heroic mission. But there will be other readers, even ones as admiring as this reviewer, who may want to pause at such words and the argument they embody. For there is a danger in coming to regard America too exclusively as an idea, the carrier of an idea, or the custodian of a set of principles, rather than as a real nation that exists in a world of other nations, with all the features and limitations of a nation, including its particular history, institutions, and distinctive national character.

To be sure, Berns is right to stress the twofold character of American patriotism: The patriot loves America partly because it is his own country and partly because of his love for the ideals for which the country stands. The two motives are in tension, but they also are inseparable and mutually indispensable. America is not a class-ridden traditional society or a homogeneous blood-and-soil nation-state, but neither is it a universalistic ideological crusade. What is worrisome and lopsided in Berns's account of American patriotism is the near-exclusive weight he gives to the abstract and ideological dimensions of American patriotism, to the virtual exclusion of all other elements.

Indeed, at one point in his book he unfairly ridicules (and misquotes) a famous toast delivered in 1815 by the heroic American naval officer Stephen Decatur, declaring the words to be unpatriotic, even "un-American," because of their failure to endorse abstract universal principles of political right. The toast goes like this:

"Our country! In her intercourse with foreign nations may she always be in the right; but our country, right or wrong!" In his rendering, Berns omits the words "In her intercourse with foreign nations," which changes the meaning of the quote rather dramatically. But even in its truncated form, the quote does not deserve the scorn Berns heaps upon it. For patriotism, like any love, withers and dies if it is not accorded some degree of instinctive assent. Berns's position could be interpreted to be that our country deserves our support only when its motives are demonstrably pure and its course of action demonstrably unassailable, that our loyalty to it is always revocable, that the nation stands every day freshly before the bar of judgment, to be assessed solely on the basis of its consonance that day with the universal principles of political right. This is much too brittle and unstable a foundation for any durable patriotism—particularly, one might add, in a nation's intercourse with foreign nations.

20 Berns, of course, is not advocating any such thing. But his words inadvertently point to the problem with interpreting America exclusively as an idea. Obviously, no decent patriotism can ever be completely unconditional, blindly loyal on all occasions, deaf to the claims of morality. That way lies tyranny and human degradation. But compelling reasons of state do not always translate into readily apprehended principles of universal morality, and there are times when being a patriot means being like a soldier, following leaders who have had to make complex judgments beyond the soldier's ken. Even Berns's beloved Lincoln is vulnerable to the charge that the human rights of slaves and such fundamental rights as habeas corpus were less important to him than the preservation of the Union, that the Emancipation Proclamation was primarily a cynical and calculated war measure, and that only the relentless pressure of events and other men led Lincoln to end slavery. If those charges sound familiar, it is because they are the same charges that two generations of morally indignant historians have hurled at Lincoln, convicting him by reference to a universalistic (and

unrealistic and ungenerous) standard very much like the one Berns advocates.

We Are Family?

So how might one arrive at a more complex understanding of the mixed nature of American patriotism? One might find some insight in an analogy to marriage, an institution in which something very much like Berns's twofold division of motives obtains. The parallels are suggestive. A man is devoted to his wife partly because she is admirable—and partly because she is his. And it is easy to see how, in a marriage, one cannot separate these two things in practice. A man may perhaps initially fall in love with a woman because she is admirable and lovely. But it is an entirely different matter to explain why he stays married and faithful to her, even when he knows full well that she is not always admirable and lovely. Should a man continue to love and honor his wife only if she is always admirable? Of course not. We all recognize that only a very shallow and insubstantial love would express itself in this way. Are there not occasions when a good husband honors and defends his wife, even when she may be in the wrong, simply because she is his and he is hers? Is there not a mutual obligation subsisting between them, far more deep-seated than any transient wrong? Obviously. Are there times when the strict pursuit of justice in a marriage takes a back seat to the preservation of the union? Yes. Can a happy and healthy marriage endure when justice is always subordinated to the preservation of the union? No.

In other words, the nature of the commitment made in a good marriage is a complex blend of motives, ideal and primal, extrinsic and intrinsic, practical and impractical. It would be unthinkable, and in fact somewhat ludicrous, to imagine that one set of motives could exist without the counterbalance of the other. There is merit in a love that is directed toward a person who possesses abundant admirable qualities. But there is even more merit in a love that is able, over time, and within the enclosure of a mutual commitment, to ac-

knowledge and accept—up to a point—what is less than fully admirable, what is all-too-human, about the otherwise admirable other. Where that point is located and when it is reached are questions almost impossible to answer in any general way. [Leo] Tolstoy, wrong in so many other things, was also wrong in proposing that happy families are always the same. *General principles may be helpful, but they always have to be weighed against other considerations.

One might also extend the analogy to encompass other relationships within the family. If a country is like a spouse, it is also like a parent, since it constitutes one of the irreducible sources of one's being. One's gratitude to one's forebears is very much like the gratitude a patriot should feel toward those, like Walter Berns, who fought to preserve their nation. So then: Is it a good thing to admire one's father (and to be an admirable father)? Of course. Should one's love for one's father be conditional upon his always having been an admirable person and having always done admirable things? Of course not. Should one love one's father even when he has behaved shamefully, as a criminal or a traitor? That is more difficult. Perhaps even then, though only up to a point. But then, who is to say? The truth of the matter is buried in the particulars.

Like all analogies, these marital and familial ones break down at some point. Mario Cuomo's famous words notwithstanding, a nation is not a family. Indeed, the analogy becomes problematic when overtaxed precisely because (as Berns points out) Americans have never spoken of their country as a "fatherland," in the way so many Europeans spoke of their own nations in the pre-European Union era. In fact, it might be said that America was the country one came to in order to escape from one's father, both literally and figuratively. It was the country where one put aside the heavy lumber of inherited identity and tradition, and was freed to begin again. Hence Berns much prefers G. K. Chesterton's† notion that America, far from being a fatherland, is "the only nation in the

*Tolstoy's *Anna Karenina* (1877), one of the great novels of the nineteenth century, begins: "Happy families are all alike; every unhappy family is unhappy in its own way."

†Poet, novelist, playwright, and journalist G. K. Chesterton (1874–1936) was also a Catholic who unabashedly argued for a moral political philosophy based on Christian values.

CONTEXT

This essay was published in the fall 2001 edition of the *Public Interest,* which likely means that it was written before the September 11, 2001, attacks. After those attacks, patriotism became an important topic of discussion among many Americans. How might the September 11 attacks change the way readers respond to McClay's argument about patriotism? Does his argument become stronger or weaker in light of those attacks?

world that is founded on a creed," and is therefore "a nation with the soul of a church." To be an American, in this view, is not a matter of whose child you are but of what principles you accept. It is a nation of the twice-born, politically and culturally, a nation founded not upon descent but consent.

A Creedal Nation?

25 There is profound truth in this, but it is not the whole of the matter. The Chestertonian analogy breaks down too—or more precisely, it tells us more than was intended. Indeed, it goes directly to the heart of what is so troubling about Berns's view of American patriotism. For a church is much more than its creed. The creed is indispensable, as an intellectual guidepost, a check upon heresy, a means of instructing the young, and a handy distillation of church doctrine. Documents like the Westminster Confession are masterpieces of theological clarity and concision. But a church that had only a creed would be no church at all. One need only visit an old churchyard and see the gravestones of several generations of a family clustered together to understand how this is so. All churches, even the most nouveau-Protestant ones, possess a rich storehouse of conscious and unconscious traditions, liturgies, songs, rituals, and customs. Over time these become inseparable in the minds and hearts of the worshipers from the content of their faith. Creeds are useful, but the Biblical and liturgical texts and the sacraments and rituals are not finally reducible to propositional statements; they are not reducible to anything less than themselves. There is a seamless web that unites every piece of church life with every other, for better or worse. This is why any changes in the pattern of church life become fraught with peril: Such changes may seem to disturb the bones of the dead and tamper with the very structure of the cosmos.

So a creed can be useful to shake up the musty complacency and cultural stasis that can creep into such a hidebound environment. It may also have defensive uses, as a means

of keeping the train from going off the tracks. But it is not the soul of a church or a nation. Or, to put it another way, a living creed is a distillation and codification of beliefs that are grounded elsewhere—embodied in the habits and mores and institutions of the people. The words have to be made flesh and dwell among us. Without such quickening, a creed soon becomes a dead letter.

And for the same reasons, indoctrination into the principles of the Declaration of Independence alone will not make our young Americans into patriots. It is a beginning, but only a beginning. As both Thomas Jefferson and John Adams made clear, the Americans of the Revolutionary generation did not need instruction in what their Declaration declared. Their Declaration was mainly a press release to the world which attempted to put into words what most Americans already believed and embodied in their way of life. For our young people to know about it is, in the end, indispensable. But what is just as needful—perhaps even more so—is a recognition that there can be no meaningful patriotism in a society whose most privileged young people know nothing, remember nothing, respect nothing, cherish nothing, feel responsible for nothing, and are grateful for nothing.

This litany is not meant as a disparagement of the young but of those adults who have abdicated their responsibility for the young's formation, setting them free to be shaped by cable television, shopping malls, Internet chat rooms, and all the other flotsam of our feckless commercial culture. That irresponsibility, I think, is what has produced the conditions that sadden, anger, and worry Walter Berns, as they should all of us. But if no grand national program of ideological revitalization can rebuild what has been eroded, there is still hope for America in the patriotism of those young Jews mentioned earlier who have chosen to swim against the tide by paying homage to their birthright. A second birth does not have to renounce the first, and faithfulness in large things begins with faithfulness in smaller ones. The genius of American patriotism resides here just as much as it does in the Declaration of Independence. And if taken seriously, it will do far more to change the way Americans live.

A final image. When Lincoln wondrously invoked the "mystic chords of memory" in his first inaugural address, he envisioned them as the emanations of musical strings, "stretching from every battlefield and patriot grave to every living heart and hearthstone all over this broad land." It is an amazingly rich and well-considered image. We should not miss the fact that the strings are held in place not only by the deeds of warriors at one end but also by the domestic world, the world of family and home, at the other. Gratitude to one's country, however principled, must also draw upon forms of gratitude that are more primary—upon the things that are personal, particular, and singular. The things, in short, that are one's own. Without them, there can be no music, no memory, and no chorus of the Union.

Questions for Discussion

1. What is the central problem that McClay believes faces the United States when it comes to encouraging a patriotic citizenry? Why, in McClay's view, does the United States face this problem?

2. McClay devotes much of his essay to discussing the ideas of Walter Berns in the book *Making Patriots* (see the sidebar on page 575). Why does McClay discuss Berns's book at such length? What main points does he use Berns's ideas to make? Do you think this is an effective strategy on McClay's part? What other strategies might be used to make these points?

3. What is the danger that McClay sees in thinking of the United States as an idea and a set of principles rather than as a real nation that exists in the world?

4. McClay has divided his essay into six main sections. What point does he make in each of these sections? How does each of these main points fit together to help McClay make his main argument about patriotism? Do you think his way of organizing his argument is effective? Why or why not?

5. How would you describe the tone and style of this essay? Compare McClay's tone and style to those of the other writers in this section. In what ways do his tone and style contribute to the main argument of this essay?

6. In his essay McClay makes many references to young Americans, as well as to older Americans. How does he characterize young Americans? Do you think his characterization is accurate and fair? Given these references to young Americans, whom do you think McClay imagined as his primary audience for this essay? To whom is his argument primarily addressed? Do you think his argument is effective for that audience? Why or why not? Cite specific passages from his essay to support your answer.

7. McClay uses several analogies in his essay. For example, he compares patriotism to the loyalty two married people feel toward each other. Evaluate McClay's use of these analogies. What do they contribute to his main argument? How effectively do they help him make his points?

③ MICHAEL KAZIN, "A Patriotic Left"

It is an old practice in American politics for a candidate to question an opponent's patriotism during an election. It is also common for those who question U.S. policies or actions to be called unpatriotic. As Michael Kazin suggests in the following essay, Americans with leftist political views not only seem to regularly endure the accusation of being unpatriotic but also reject patriotism as a kind of blind loyalty to the United States. Whether it is true or not that left-leaning Americans are more commonly charged with being unpatriotic than are their fellow citizens with more moderate or conservative views, Kazin believes that patriotism is an important element in political debate. As an avowed leftist, he refuses to accept the criticism that leftists are unpatriotic because of their willingness to question their government. For Kazin, patriotism is more complicated than loyalty or love of country. It involves a deep sense of duty founded on the moral and ethical principles implicit in the U.S. Constitution. That duty might sometimes require the true patriot to question or criticize the government, as many important political figures in America's history have done. In making his argument, Kazin looks to those figures in America's past—people such as Frederick Douglass, Mother Jones, and Eugene Debs—to highlight the long tradition in American politics of patriots criticizing the U.S. government in their efforts to create a more just America. You might disagree with Kazin's politics, but consider how his argument can help you clarify your sense of what it means to be a patriot. Kazin serves on the editorial board of *Dissent* magazine, in which this essay was published in 2002.

A Patriotic Left

MICHAEL KAZIN

The term American exceptionalism refers to the idea that the United States is unique among nations because of the special circumstances of its beginnings as a democracy that was built on the principles of individual liberty and self-determination.

1 I love my country. I love its passionate and endlessly inventive culture, its remarkably diverse landscape, its agonizing and wonderful history. I particularly cherish its civic ideals— social equality, individual liberty, a populist democracy—and the unending struggle to put their laudable, if often contradictory, claims into practice. I realize that patriotism, like any powerful ideology, is a "construction" with multiple uses, some of which I abhor. But I persist in drawing stimulation and pride from my American identity.

Regrettably, this is not a popular sentiment on the contemporary left. Antiwar activists view patriotism as a smokescreen for U.S. hegemony, while radical academics mock the notion of "American exceptionalism"* as a relic of the cold war, a triumphal myth we should quickly outgrow. All the rallying around the flag after September 11 increased the disdain many leftists feel for the sentiment that lies behind it. "The globe, not the flag, is the symbol that's wanted now," scolded Katha Pollitt in the *Nation*. Noam Chomsky described patriotic blather as simply the governing elite's way of telling its subjects, "You shut up and be obedient, and I'll relentlessly advance my own interests."

Both views betray an ignorance of American history, as well as a quixotic desire to leap from a distasteful present to a gauzy future liberated from the fetters of nationalism. Love of country was a demotic faith long before September 11, a fact that previous lefts understood and attempted to turn to their advantage. In the United States, Karl Marx's dictum that the workers have no country has been refuted time and again. It has been not wage earners but the upper classes—from New England gentry on the Grand Tour a century ago to globe-trotting executives and cybertech professionals today—who view America with an ambivalent shrug, reminiscent of Gertrude Stein's line, "America is my country, Paris is my hometown."

One can, like [authors Katha] Pollitt and [Noam] Chomsky, curse as jingoistic all those "United We Stand" and "God Bless America" signs and hope somehow to transcend patriotism in the name of global harmony. Or one can empathize with the communal spirit that animates them, embracing the ideals of the nation and learning from past efforts to put them into practice in the service of far-reaching reform.

5 An earlier version of American patriotism was a forerunner of the modern genre: pride in the first nation organized around a set of social beliefs rather than a shared geography and history. In its novelty, Americanism gave citizens of the new republic both a way to understand and to stand for purposes that transcended their self-interest. Of course, these purposes were not always noble ones. As historian Gary Gerstle points out in his recent book *American Crucible,* "racial nationalism" dominated much of American life through the nineteenth century and into the early decades of the twentieth. It led some white Americans to justify exterminating Indians, others to hold slaves, and still others to bar immigrants who did not possess "Anglo-Saxon" genes. But the tolerant alternative, which Gerstle calls "civic nationalism," also inspired many Americans in the modern era to help liberate Europe from

fascism and Stalinism and to organize at home for social and economic justice.

For American leftists, patriotism was indispensable. It made their dissent and rebellion intelligible to their fellow citizens—and located them within the national narrative, fighting to shape a common future. Tom Paine praised his adopted homeland as an "asylum for mankind"—which gave him a forum to denounce regressive taxes and propose free public education. Elizabeth Cady Stanton issued a "Woman's Declaration of Rights" on the centennial of the Declaration of Independence and argued that denying the vote to women was a violation of the Fourteenth Amendment. Union activists in the Gilded Age such as Eugene Debs and Mother Jones accused employers of crushing the individuality and self-respect of workers. When Debs became a socialist, he described his new vision in the American idiom, as "the equal rights of all to manage and control" society. Half a century later, Martin Luther King, Jr., told his fellow bus boycotters, "If we are wrong, the Supreme Court of this nation is wrong" and proclaimed that "the great glory of American democracy is the right to protest for right."

One could easily list analogous statements from such pioneering reformers as Jane Addams and Betty Friedan, unionists Sidney Hillman and Cesar Chavez, and the gay liberationist Harvey Milk. Without patriotic appeals, the great social movements that attacked inequalities of class, gender, and race in the United States—and spread their messianic rhetoric around the world—would never have gotten off the ground.

Even slavery couldn't extinguish the promise radicals found in the American creed. On Independence Day, 1852, Frederick Douglass gave an angry, eloquent address that asked, "What to the slave is the Fourth of July?" Every account quotes the fugitive-turned-abolitionist speaking truth to white power: "Your celebration is a sham; your boasted liberty, an unholy license; your national greatness, swelling vanity; your sounds of rejoicing are empty and heartless; your denunciations of tyrants, brass fronted impudence; your shouts of liberty and equality, hollow mockery." But fewer commentators note that when, at the end of his speech, Douglass predicted slavery's demise, he drew his "encouragement from the Declaration of Independence, the great principles it contains, and the genius of American Institutions," as well as from a spirit of enlightenment that he believed was growing on both sides of the Atlantic. After emancipation, Douglass never stopped condemning the hypocrisy of white Americans—or continuing to base his hopes for equality on traditions he and they held in common.

A self-critical conception of patriotism also led Americans on the left to oppose their leaders' aggressive policies abroad. Anti-imperialists opposed the conquest of the Philippines after the war of 1898 by comparing President William McKinley to King George III. Foes of U.S. intervention in World War I demanded to know why Americans should die to defend European monarchs and their colonies in Africa and Asia. In 1917, a mass movement led by socialists and pacifists called for a popular referendum on the question of going to war. Neither group of resisters succeeded at the time, but each gained a mass hearing and saw its arguments incorporated into future policies. Congress promised independence to the Philippines sooner than colonial officials favored. And, challenged by such antiwar voices as Debs, Robert LaFollette, and William Jennings Bryan, Woodrow Wilson proclaimed national self-determination to be the core principle of a new world order.

10 A good deal that we cherish about contemporary America was thus accomplished by social movements of the left, speaking out for national ideals. It may be, as the idiosyncratic Trotskyist Leon Samson argued in 1935, that Americanism served as a substitute for social-

THE FOURTEENTH AMENDMENT

Adopted in 1868, the Fourteenth Amendment to the U.S. Constitution addresses issues related to voting, such as the number of congressional representatives each state should have. When Elizabeth Cady Stanton, a nineteenth-century activist who campaigned for women's right to vote, invoked this amendment in her famous "Women's Declaration of Rights," she was referring to Section 1, which states,

All persons born or naturalized in the United States, and subject to the jurisdiction thereof, are citizens of the United States and of the state wherein they reside. No state shall make or enforce any law which shall abridge the privileges or immunities of citizens of the United States; nor shall any state deprive any person of life, liberty, or property, without due process of law; nor deny to any person within its jurisdiction the equal protection of the laws.

ism, an ideology of self-emancipation through equal opportunity that inoculated most citizens against the class-conscious alternative. But leftists made what progress they did by demanding that the nation live up to its stated principles, rather than dismissing them as fatally compromised by the racism of the founders or the abusiveness of flag-waving vigilantes. After all, hope is always more attractive than cynicism, and the gap between promise and fulfillment is narrower for Americanism than it is for other universalist creeds such as communism, Christianity, and Islam.

It's difficult to think of any radical or reformer who repudiated the national belief system and still had a major impact on U.S. politics and policy. The movement against the Vietnam War did include activists who preferred the Vietcong's flag to the American one. But the antiwar insurgency grew powerful only toward the end of the 1960s, when it drew in people who looked for leadership to liberal patriots such as King, Walter Reuther, and Eugene McCarthy rather than to Abbie Hoffman and the Weathermen.

Perhaps one exception to this rule was Malcolm X, who stated, in 1964, that he was a "victim of Americanism" who could see no "American dream," only "an American nightmare." But Malcolm was primarily a spokesman for black anger and pride, not a builder of movements or a catalyst of reforms to benefit his people.

He was, however, a prophetic figure. Soon after Malcolm's death, many on the left, of all races, began to scorn patriotic talk and, instead, to celebrate ethnic and sexual differences. In 1970, writer Julius Lester observed, "American radicals are perhaps the first radicals anywhere who have sought to make a revolution in a country which they hate." At the time, there were certainly ample reasons to consider Americanism a brutal sham. After World War II, the word itself became the property of the American Legion, the House Un-American Activities Committee,

and the FBI. In the 1960s, liberal presidents bullied their way into Indochina in the name of what Lyndon Johnson called "the principle for which our ancestors fought in the valleys of Pennsylvania." Fierce love for one's identity group—whether black, Latino, Asian, Native American, or gay or lesbian—seemed morally superior to the master narrative that had justified war abroad and racial exclusion at home.

Yet the history of the last thirty years has also exposed the outsized flaw in such thinking. Having abandoned patriotism, the left lost the ability to pose convincing alternatives for the nation as a whole. It could take credit for spearheading a multicultural, gender-aware revision of the humanities curriculum, but the right set the political agenda, and it did so in part because its partisans spoke forcefully in the name of American principles that knit together disparate groups—anti-union businesspeople, white evangelicals, Jewish neoconservatives—for mutual ends.

15 In the face of such evidence, many leftists would respond that civic idealism should not be confined within national borders. In a provocative 1994 essay, philosopher Martha Nussbaum argued that patriotism is "morally dangerous" because it encourages Americans to focus on their own concerns and minimize or disregard those of people in other lands. "We should regard our deliberations," she wrote, "as, first and foremost, deliberations about human problems of people in particular concrete situations, not problems growing out of a national identity that is altogether unlike that of others." Echoing her words, activists and intellectuals talk of challenging global exploitation with some form of global citizenship.

As an ethicist, Nussbaum is certainly on solid ground. Americans ought to take a massacre in Africa as seriously as one that takes place in lower Manhattan and demand that their government move rapidly to halt it. But she offers no guidance for how global leftists

"PATRIOTISM AND COSMOPOLITANISM"

In making his argument, Kazin refers to a well-known essay by legal scholar Martha Nussbaum, stating that Nussbaum sees patriotism as "morally dangerous." However, in her essay Nussbaum does not say that *all* patriotism is morally dangerous, only some types of patriotism, and only insofar as patriotism is incompatible with a decent concern for the rights of people everywhere. She writes, "I believe . . . that this emphasis on patriotic pride is both morally dangerous and, ultimately, subversive of some of the worthy goals patriotism sets out to serve—for example, the goal of national unity in devotion to worthy moral ideals of justice and equality. These goals, I shall argue, would be better served by an ideal that is in any case more adequate to our situation in the contemporary world, namely the very old ideal of the cosmopolitan, the person whose primary allegiance is to the community of human beings in the entire world. . . .

As students here grow up, is it sufficient for them to learn that they are above all citizens of the United States, but that they ought to respect the basic human rights of citizens of India, Bolivia, Nigeria, and Norway? Or should they, as I think—in addition to giving special attention to the history and current situation of their own nation—learn a good deal more than is frequently the case about the rest of the world in which they live, about India and Bolivia and Nigeria and Norway and their histories, problems, and comparative successes? . . . Most important, should they be taught that they are above all citizens of the United States, or should they instead be taught that they are above all citizens of a world of human beings, and that, while they themselves happen to be situated in the United States, they have to share this world of human beings with the citizens of other countries?" (from Martha Nussbaum, "Patriotism and Cosmopolitanism," 1994).

CONTEXT

According to its website, "A magazine of the left, *Dissent* is also a magazine of independent minds. A magazine of strong opinions, *Dissent* is also a magazine that welcomes the clash of strong opinions." Does Kazin's essay, which appeared in *Dissent* in 2002, fit this description?

can get the power to achieve their laudable objectives. A planetary government is hardly on the horizon, and rich nations would no doubt hog its agenda if it were.

In the meantime, Americans who want to transform the world have to learn how to persuade the nation. At minimum, this means putting pressure on the national government, organizing coalitions of people from different regions and backgrounds, and debating citizens who think their tax money ought to be spent only at home. Disconnected as they are from any national or local constituency, global leftists now live at risk of being thrust to the margins—abstract sages of equity, operatives of nongovernmental organizations engaged in heroic but Sisyphean tasks, or demonstrators

roving from continent to continent in search of bankers to heckle.

In the wake of September 11, the stakes have been raised for the American left. Even if the "war against terrorism" doesn't continue to overshadow all other issues, it will inevitably force activists of every stripe to make clear how they would achieve security for individual citizens and for the nation. How can one seriously engage in this conversation about protecting America if America holds no privileged place in one's heart? Most ordinary citizens understandably distrust a left that condemns military intervention abroad or a crackdown at home but expresses only a pro forma concern for the actual and potential victims of terrorism. Without empathy for one's neighbors, politics becomes a cold, censorious enterprise indeed.

There's no need to mouth the Pledge of Allegiance or affix a flag pin to your lapel or handbag. But to rail against patriotic symbols is to wage a losing battle—and one that demeans us and sets us against the overwhelming majority of Americans for no worthwhile moral or political purpose.

20 Instead, leftists should again claim, without pretense or apology, an honorable place in the long narrative of those who demanded that American ideals apply to all and opposed the efforts of those who tried to reserve them for favored groups. When John Ashcroft denies the right of counsel to a citizen accused of terrorism or a CEO cooks the books to impress Wall Street, they are soiling the flag and ought to be put on the patriotic defensive. Liberals and radicals are the only people in politics who can insist on closing the gap between America as the apotheosis of democratic strivings and the sordid realities of greed and arrogance that often betray it.

There is really no alternative. In daily life, cultural cosmopolitanism is mostly reserved to the rich and famous. Radical environmentalists and anti-IMF [International Monetary Fund] crusaders seek to revive the old dream of internationalism in a version indebted more to

John Lennon's "Imagine" than to V. I. Lenin's *Comintern.* But three years after bursting into the headlines from the streets of Seattle, that project seems stalled indefinitely in the Sargasso Sea that lies between rhetorical desire and political exigency.

In hope of a revival, left patriots might draw inspiration from . . . the white, conservative skeptic George Santayana, [who] observed that "America is the greatest of opportunities and the worst of influences. Our effort must be to resist the influence and improve the opportunity." . . .

Throughout our history, and still today, the most effective way to love the country is to fight like hell to change it.

"The protesters object to what they see as unfair IMF policies that benefit wealthier nations at the expense of developing nations. The IMF disagrees, saying it is the poor of the world who are benefited by its policies." (FROM **CNN.com**, SEPTEMBER 27, 2002.)

Questions for Discussion

1. In the opening paragraphs of his essay, Kazin summarizes some of the criticisms of leftists who dismiss American patriotism. On what grounds does Kazin disagree with these leftists? What benefit might there be to debating this issue with others who share your political views?

2. Evaluate Kazin's introduction to this essay. What does he accomplish by beginning his argument with the statement that he loves his country? What audience do you think Kazin was primarily addressing with this introduction?

3. Kazin makes many references in this essay to historical events and people, tracing the history of several important political developments in the United States in the eighteenth, nineteenth, and twentieth centuries. What role does history play in Kazin's argument? How effectively do you think he uses history to help him make his main argument? (You might compare the way Kazin uses history to Steven Camarota's use of history in his essay on pages 560–564.)

4. How does Kazin define *patriotism* in this essay? Does his understanding of patriotism differ from the ideas of Wilfred McClay whose essay appears earlier in this section? Explain. Do you think most Americans would agree with Kazin about what it means to be patriotic? Do you agree with him? Why or why not?

5. Kazin is a leftist, but he expresses concern about the views of other leftists about patriotism. He is concerned as well about the way those on the political right understand patriotism. Do you think he offers a compelling alternative to the views of the leftists and rightists he criticizes? On the basis of your answer to that question, how effectively do you think his essay works as an example of a Rogerian argument? (See pages 131–137 for a discussion of Rogerian argument.)

④ JOSIAH BUNTING, III, "Class Warfare"

The nature of American military service underwent a profound shift in the late 1960s—a shift that became formalized when President Richard Nixon abolished the draft in 1973. Many commentators had observed that the war in Vietnam, which began in the early 1960s but escalated dramatically in 1965, was conducted disproportionately by men of color, of limited financial means, and of limited political influence. Deferments from service were available to college and graduate students, and the cost of the war was impressed upon many Americans only after deferments had expired and White, middle-class soldiers were coming home in body bags. Through these years, some of the richest and most powerful young men in the country were able to avoid serving in Vietnam. The creation of an all-volunteer army seemed to eliminate the political difficulties that arise from mandatory service. But social inequities remained. The all-volunteer army would draw many of its members from segments of the American population that had fewer educational and economic choices than those who are privileged at birth by race or class. After President George W. Bush ordered the invasion of Iraq in 2003—and that war dragged on for years, with National Guard troops and private contractors taking unprecedented responsibility for overseas military action—opponents of the war noted that neither of the President's daughters volunteered for military service. It was within this context that Josiah Bunting, III composed the following argument, which was originally published in the winter of 2005 in *American Scholar,* the journal of the Phi Beta Kappa Society. A lieutenant general, Bunting has been deeply involved in American education and the military. Currently superintendent of Virginia Military Institute, he was previously headmaster of the Lawrenceville School—an elite boarding school located near Princeton, New Jersey. He also taught history and social sciences at U.S. Military Academy at West Point. A Rhoades scholar, Bunting was educated at Oxford University, where he received both his B.A. and M.A., and he is the author of several novels. For his service in Vietnam, he was awarded the Bronze Star, and he has received the Army Commendation Medal, among other awards.

Class Warfare

JOSIAH BUNTING, III

It may be laid down as a primary position, and the basis of our system, that every Citizen who enjoys the protection of a free Government, owes not only a proportion of his property, but even of his personal services to the defence of it.

—George Washington, "Sentiments on a Peace Establishment"

1 For some years I worked as headmaster of a large boarding school. By that time, the late 1980s and early '90s, "chapel" had become a weekly, not a daily, ritual—although the usages of custom and of a certain civic religion sometimes brought the school together in chapel on other days. Sunday chapel rites were mainly Anglican in tone, despite the school's Presbyterian heritage: lordly preludes and processionals, antique calls to worship, lessons that concluded with "endeths," hymns from a confident epoch in British history. The ambience remained very much that of the nineteenth-century school, redolent with the communicated sense of duty to the less fortunate and less privileged—the nave hung with banners and heraldic flags, its walls studded with bronze plaques offering the Loyola Prayer for Generosity and tributes to deceased masters and alumni. Among them there was a testimonial to a master who had given his life to the school and who had lived "a life of Christian self-forgetfuness." I remember phrases and verses from certain favored hymns: "Noble mirth." What was that? "Who follows in his train?" "Faint not, nor fear!"—the exclamation mark communicating to the congregant it's all right, you'll be fine! "By the light of burning martyrs, Christ, Thy bleeding feet I track." And from Scripture: "Where moths and rust doth corrupt, and where thieves break through and steal." Most particularly I remember four flags of scarlet, white, and gold, rectangular in shape, that hung before us, on either side of the altar. These were memorial flags that commemorated graduates of the school who had died in four wars: 1917–1918; 1941–1945; 1950–1953; 1965–1973. They framed a great gold altar cross on which was inscribed: I WILL LIFT UP MY EYES UNTO THE HILLS.

Lifting my eyes up to the flags and their rows of stars, one star for each child of the school who had been killed Fighting For Our Country, I used to consider not only what the stars signified but also what they meant: what the young men thought they might have to die for what they gave up in losing their lives, and what the shattered families learning of their deaths felt. These were boys (all in the school then were boys) who had sat where my wife and I were sitting now, who had sung the same hymns and recited the same comforting creeds, who had dispersed out onto the virid Frederick Olmsted Circle and come to our house for coffee and singing—songs from Gilbert and Sullivan, Cole Porter, Rodgers and Hammerstein. Chapel itself always ended with a brisk, triumphant postlude, a Handel or a Widor anthem. Once, I remember, it ended with "Stout-Hearted Men." The intention and the consequence were to uplift us.

The business of war was fully remote from these proceedings, and remote increasingly from a particular segment of the American people. For the memorial flags told another story, a kind of second lead. In World War I, some forty sons of the school, which then enrolled about four hundred students, had been killed. Pershing's army had fought only one really large campaign, the Meuse-Argonne offensive, and that was late in the war. Its butcher's bill, combined with our losses earlier in places with such names as Cantigny, Belleau Wood, St. Mihiel, exceeded 350,000 killed and wounded.

For World War II there were approximately sixty stars on the flag. United States forces were engaged for about forty-five months, not counting the service of those who had volunteered and gone off to fight for Canada or Britain. For Korea, ten stars: three years' fighting, but a much smaller American force serving in a much smaller theater. Finally, Vietnam: only five stars for eight years of war; at its height the American force "in country" was about 550,000. I do not know how many graduates of the school died in Desert Storm, or have died to date in the present fighting in Iraq and Afghanistan. None, I hope; very few, I imagine—even as I ponder the ageless fact of war: that overwhelmingly those we send off to die are but a year or two, perhaps five, from the ages of the children who sat with my wife

CONTEXT

The Frederick Olmsted Circle refers to part of the landscaping design for the Lawrenceville School created by Frederick Law Olmsted (1822–1903), who is widely considered the greatest and most influential landscape architect in American history. Olmsted's most famous creation is Central Park in New York City—a large and magnificent park that he created out of an environmental wasteland. With his partner Calvert Vaux, he also created Prospect Park in Brooklyn; the park systems for Boston, Massachusetts, and Buffalo, New York; the grounds of the Vanderbilt mansion in North Carolina; and the landscaping for the 1893 World's Fair in Chicago—a vast and dazzling project created on swampland at the shore of Lake Michigan.

and me in the Lawrenceville Chapel singing "I sing a song of the saints of God."

5 The flags commemorate terrible but noble deaths.* *Dulce et decorum est pro patria mori.* That is some recompense, I suppose. But there is, as I say, a second story here. The diminishing numbers of war dead disclose another phenomenon: the withdrawal of the American clerisy (I will call it, after Coleridge[†]), the privileged intellectual and professional and commercial classes, and their novitiates and children, from the active military service of our country. It is dangerous, it is unworthy, it is wrong. When I hear U.S. Representative Charles Rangel, his voice passionate and cracking, demand that the country begin drafting young people for the armed forces, I know exactly what he means.

"I no longer take the cigarette out of my mouth when I write 'deceased' over their names," wrote the English poet and lieutenant Wilfred Owen near the end of World War I. Owen was himself killed a few days afterward. He had become, almost, inured to such deaths, just as we are inured to, and so terribly removed from, the deaths of our soldiers in Iraq. But few, very few indeed, of these are the deaths of children of those who lead our country, who control its resources and institutions, direct and inflect its tastes and opinions, batten most avidly upon its treasures and most lavishly upon its expensive entertainments. No one wants any American to die in a war. But if there is harm's way to tread, should not all who are our national bounty's beneficiaries tread it together or, at least, be liable to be asked by their country to do so?

Representative Rangel's message might be communicated in a twenty-first-century adaptation of the peppery, flag-snapping Victorian jingle:

1895 We don't want to fight by Jingo
But by Jingo if we do
We've got the men, and we've got the ships
And we've got the money too!

2005 We don't want to fight by Jingo,
But by Jingo if we do
The smart and privileged people,
They'd better join us, too!

I mean "smart" not in the sense of the social éclat of places like San Francisco or New York, but as the easy synonym Americans use for academic success: intelligence as it is measured in rankings and grades, acceptances and advancement to, and within, these nurseries for the most privileged young people, the great boarding schools and revered public high schools (say, New Trier or Bronx Science) and the famous private universities and colleges of the coasts. For it is in these places, and the culture that nourishes them, that ignorance of military service is so deep-seated as to be, almost, unconscious. He went where? Into the marines? These places, once the veriest source of eager and idealistic young military leaders and volunteers in 1898, 1917, and 1941, are fully settled in 2004 in their contempt or condescension for the profession of arms. And it has been so since the mid-1960s for reasons that are perfectly obvious.

You may not be interested in war, observed Trotsky,[‡] but war is interested in you. The issue of military conscription is deeply controversial, of course; and it is one of a family of public policy questions, recurrent and vexed, upon whose difficulties people advance, make ner-

*"***Dulce et decorum est pro patria mori***" are the first lines in an ode by Horace, a great poet in ancient Rome. Translated from the Latin, the words mean "It is sweet and right to die for one's country." But Bunting's reference to the English poet Wilfred Owen (1893–1918) establishes that he is aware that this statement can be a "lie." Owen's poem, which incorporated the line in question, appears on page 592. It was written at the end of what was then called the Great War, a war that had produced slaughter beyond what anyone entering it in 1914 could possibly have imagined.

[†]English poet Samuel Taylor Coleridge (1772–1834) was a major figure in Romanticism, an artistic movement that began in the late eighteenth century. His most famous poems include "Kubla Khan" and "The Rhime of the Ancient Mariner"—the latter of which includes the often-quoted line "Water, water every where,/Nor any drop to drink."

[‡]A close associate of Vladimir Ilyich Lenin, Leon Trotsky (1879–1940) was a leader of the Communist revolution in Russia. After Lenin's death in 1924, Trotsky lost political control of what was by then the Soviet Union to Joseph Stalin and was later exiled and assassinated in Mexico City. Marxists who were alarmed by the mass murder conducted by Stalin liked to argue that the Soviet Union would have been a better nation if Trotsky had prevailed over Stalin, but many scholars dispute this claim.

DULCE ET DECORUM EST

Wilfred Owen

Bent double, like old beggars under sacks,
Knock-kneed, coughing like hags, we cursed through sludge,
Till on the haunting flares we turned our backs
And towards our distant rest began to trudge.
Men marched asleep. Many had lost their boots
But limped on, blood-shod. All went lame; all blind;
Drunk with fatigue; deaf even to the hoots
Of tired, outstripped Five-Nines that dropped behind.

Gas! Gas! Quick, boys!—An ecstasy of fumbling,
Fitting the clumsy helmets just in time;
But someone still was yelling out and stumbling,
And flound'ring like a man in fire or lime . . .
Dim, through the misty panes and thick green light,
As under a green sea, I saw him drowning.
In all my dreams, before my helpless sight,
He plunges at me, guttering, choking, drowning.

If in some smothering dreams you too could pace
Behind the wagon that we flung him in,
And watch the white eyes writhing in his face,
His hanging face, like a devil's sick of sin;
If you could hear, at every jolt, the blood
Come gargling from the froth-corrupted lungs,
Obscene as cancer, bitter as the cud
Of vile, incurable sores on innocent tongues,
My friend, you would not tell with such high zest
To children ardent for some desperate glory,
The old Lie; Dulce et Decorum est
Pro patria mori.

asked of it. And it is not certain, in a world of competing sovereignties—many of them hostile to us, some close to being able to deploy nuclear weapons—what may be asked, or required, of it in the future.

What is certain is how distant all things military, all the appurtenances and actions and needs of war and warriors, have become from the informed and thoughtful consideration of those to whom our commerce and culture have given the most. When a successful National Football League athlete, having left his sport and its gigantic emoluments to enlist in the army and serve in the active theater of operations, is killed in combat, his death is not only mourned. That he went off to serve at all strikes people as flat-out astounding. How could a young American abandon the pursuit of those two things Americans most deeply venerate, money and celebrity, to join the army? Not very long ago, the Northwestern University sociologist Charles Moskos reminds us, a Princeton graduating class, his own, sent 400 of its number (of 900) into the military, some volunteers, some drafted, within a year or two of graduation. That was in 1956. Thus far in 2004 the same university has sent, of a class of 1,110, nine.

10 The continuing allure of the generations that led and served in the Second World War testifies to our national uneasiness about the profoundly unequal sharing of the military burden in the early years of the twenty-first century. A veteran of the landings on Normandy or Tarawa is about eighty years old today. His generation, modest and reticent about its time in uniform, refers to that period of their lives simply as the service. "I was in the service." The consequent phrase is omitted: ". . . of my country."

Of the enduring cultural testimonials to that service—novels, plays, movies, most of them celebratory—the universal expression of the American experience is the polyglot infantry squad: by honest happenstance, eight or ten Americans, eighteen or twenty years old, are thrown together in basic training. The tired

vous reconnaissances, and then withdraw, unwilling to engage them fully. It is also an issue that excites a multiplicity of opinions that seem unhinged from regular political affiliations, parties, and philosophies. I have never met anyone able to consider the question with anything approaching disinterestedness. There are, of course, many approaches to it, not the least of them, in 2005, the fact that the armed force is far too small to do what is being

melting-pot metaphor is for once apt. Birth, creed, color, and wealth are no longer the criteria of judgment, acceptance, or advancement. The student of architecture and the Navajo, the college boy and the Italian American from Oakland are wonderfully commingled in a transcending mission. The survivors—most survive—are immensely the better for their service together. All have won through to a new quality—moral, intellectual, temperamental all at once—which is judgment, a kind of canny wisdom, that will make them better citizens for the rest of their lives. (Of that sense of national commonality, we in our turn experienced a frission in the week or so after 9/11. It has not lasted.)

The point is that many went into the military and learned from the experience. Today when we watch a dusty squad of nineteen-year-old marines moving along a street in Fallujah, windswept and sere, and we hear a chirping MSNBC voice-over use language like "The artillery has already softened up" the area, we know we are listening to someone mouthing words whose meaning he cannot possibly guess. He doesn't really know, nor can he really communicate to us, what is happening, but he feels obliged to try. The young marines are of the same métier as their World War II grandfathers—but now the college boy and the senator's kid are missing.

World War II is called a good war. No war is a good war, though some, patently, are more necessary than others. The war in Iraq, terribly controversial like the police action in Korea and the war in Vietnam, has splintered away from the conscious concern of most of those in whose behalf it is said to be prosecuted; and since such wars, not to say the "war on terror," are the template for future conflict, it seems unlikely that this will change. "The abuse of greatness is when it disjoins remorse from power"; the line from *Julius Caesar* makes the predicament plain. Those for whom the war is being waged are disjoined from its costs.

In another Shakespeare play, *Henry V,* the physical and moral devastation of France has

led, a speaker remarks, to a terrible coarsening of its life and landscape. Things now grow "as soldiers will, that nothing do but mediate on blood." My sense of the generation that led the soldiers of World War II, particularly of that generation's professional soldiers, is very different. Its most senior officers, most born between 1875 an 1890, nowadays subsist in the common memory as awkward clusters of attendant lords, gathered about the seated icons of Allied leadership, Churchill, Stalin, Roosevelt, and later Atlee and Truman. They appear preternaturally calm and self-possessed, anything but warlike in appearance; dutiful, forbearing, wise and weary. These leaders are models of a certain kind of disinterestedness, their counsel offered (as U.S. Grant's was provided Lincoln) without reference to themselves or their advancement. With a couple of famous exceptions, they were uneasy in a celebrity they had certainly not sought. They embodied a kind of mature civic wisdom, not measurable in the ways our age defines "leadership ability" or cleverness, and they were far from the caricature of militarism and its punctilios the clerisy imputes to today's soldiers. **15** We see men like George Marshall, Hap Arnold, Dwight D. Eisenhower, and Admirals

Ernest King and William Leahy as heirs to the tradition of U.S. Grant and Robert E. Lee: functional soldiers, noble and dutiful, devoted only to the mission, leaders to whom citizens might safely entrust the services of their children, men for whom the attractions of money and fame were nonexistent. (It was not proper, Marshall believed, for him to write his memoirs; these would invariably give pain to those he would be obliged to mention. Nor indeed was it proper for him to allow himself to receive any American decoration during the course of the war, because the soldiers he led were having a far harder, more dangerous time of it than he.)

Such leaders in their day defined civil society's expectations of wartime military commanders. They were themselves distant cousins of our clerisy. Most were products of the American heartland, of villages and farms. But their families did venerate learning, strong exemplary tutelage, and advancement to secure professional careers. No brassy vocation to soldier had called them to West Point. They went to the academies because the academies were free and provided a good education. These leaders seemed the best expressions of a moral democracy; they weren't commanders coarsened and insensitive to the value of what they had been called upon to destroy. They were fatherly in their concern, in their love, for their soldiers. Their commitment to their profession, too, their allegiance to the principle embodied in such commitment, had kept them in uniform through the long, bleak winter of the 1920s and 1930s: unpromoted, ill paid, often in assignments that seemed far beneath their talents.

That generation is gone, tone and tint, and those who served in the ranks, 1941–1945, are leaving us each month by the tens of thousands. But a citizen who sees and acknowledges the deepening chasm that is separating those who serve from those whom they serve (which no number of eyewitness news teams and Veterans Day editorials can usefully bridge) can only deplore a civic culture that removes the burdens of military service from those it

has blessed most abundantly. We may be grateful, we may even rejoice, when we see fewer and fewer stars on the memorial flags that hang from the walls of the chapels and halls of the nurseries of the American clerisy, of the schools of privilege earned and unearned. But our own education in these places, moral, liberal, civic, has failed us terribly if we do not also remember that such stars are accumulating somewhere: only somewhere else. Fifty-one Americans died in Fallujah in eleven days. More than four hundred were wounded. Those are mounting numbers, and each number, each star, is a devastation—but each is a devastation out there, just not where we are.

Twenty years ago a young woman named Wendy Kopp graduated from Princeton. By passionate and focused effort she founded and has led a remarkable program called Teach for America. Idealistic and bright graduates of universities like Princeton and Stanford and Brown are recruited to teach, for two years and for a small stipend, in public schools that badly need teachers: most of them in difficult places, hardscrabble, sometimes in violent neighborhoods. At a meeting, a questioner wondered whether Kopp expected her young volunteers to make careers of teaching in such places. No, she said, probably not. But someday they will be forty or fifty years old. They will serve on school boards. They will be appointed or elected to offices. They will carry the inestimable benefit of having themselves done what they will be asking another young generation to do; they will know the costs and difficulties and sometimes dangers of such duties. So it should be with—to use a word that has gone utterly out of fashion—soldiering in behalf of the American republic. It is not idle of us to remind a new generation of undergraduates and those educating them, not to say their own families, that this generation in its turn will ask young men and women to wear the uniform of our country, to serve in harm's way, and that it is—there is no other word for it—better that they themselves have something to remember about what it is that a private or a second lieutenant does in a war. In the service.

Questions for Discussion

1. What does Bunting achieve by opening with a description of an elite boarding school? Why do you think he chose not to name the school at first?

2. Note how the second paragraph opens with a reference to "each child of the school" and concludes with a reference to a song called "Stout-Hearted Men." What is Bunting implying about the relationship between military service and adolescence?

3. Consider the numbers Bunting provides in paragraphs 3, 4, and 9. What do these numbers signify? To what extent do you think they are representative of other schools?

4. Bunting declares that in 2005 "the armed force is far too small to do what is being asked of it." Have subsequent events justified this claim?

5. Without calling for a return of the draft, an issue that he describes as "deeply controversial," Bunting clearly believes that military service has value. What is the nature of that value? Why is it important for men and women of diverse backgrounds—including diverse social classes—to serve in the military? Are you prepared to do so? If so, why? If not, why not?

6. Bunting raises, in paragraph 16, the idea of "moral democracy." What does that phrase mean to you? How would a moral democracy be different from a political democracy? How would it be similar?

7. What does the story of Wendy Kopp contribute to this argument? Why do you think Bunting chose to use it for his conclusion? How well does it work as a conclusion?

DIFFERENCES

NEGOTIATING

In his essay in this section, Michael Kazin refers explicitly to the events of September 11, 2001, and suggests that those events underscore the importance of examining the question of what it means to be patriotic. He argues that being a patriot requires more than loyalty to America, more than even a willingness to go to war. Wilfred McClay reinforces this idea by asking how people justify the decision to fight and perhaps even to die for their country. John Balzar shows that even the act of voting, which Americans may take for granted, places a responsibility on citizens that goes beyond simply expressing an opinion. And Josiah Bunting argues that America's elite should share the responsibility carried by citizens who are less privileged. In short, these essays suggest that citizenship is more than a matter of which country you

happen to live in; they challenge you to think about what citizenship requires of each citizen, including yourself.

After September 11, 2001, these questions about citizenship and patriotism have understandably preoccupied many Americans. On many college campuses, controversies have arisen when professors or students have openly criticized the U.S. government's actions in its efforts to fight terrorism. In a few cases, faculty members have been sanctioned by their schools for such criticisms. In other cases, some courses have been criticized because they seem to be sympathetic to the views of America's enemies.

Imagine that such a controversy has emerged at your college or university. A professor has been publicly criticized for teaching a course that seems to be sympathetic to the point of view of groups that openly espouse violence against Americans. In response to the controversy, your school's administration has decided to address the issue by reexamining the school's curriculum. One proposal that is under consideration would require all students to take a newly designed course in citizenship. In effect, the course would teach students how to be good citizens. Not surprisingly, this proposal has generated further controversy as students, faculty, and community members debate what such a course should include and even whether such a course should be required. In the wake of this controversy, students have been invited to express their views about the proposal in writing.

Write an essay in which you present your position on the question of whether students should be required to take a course in citizenship. In your essay, define what you believe a good citizen is, and discuss what responsibilities citizens have. Using the essays in this section and any other relevant sources you find, make a case for or against the proposed course in citizenship, or suggest some alternative way of addressing the school's concerns about encouraging students to become good citizens. Keep your audience in mind as you construct your argument: the administrators of your school, as well as students who attend the school. Try to construct your argument in a way that might address their concerns and help your school community find a solution to the controversy about the proposed course.

What Kind of Power Should We Give Our Government?

Americans consider the Declaration of Independence to be a sacred document (see Con-Text on page 599). American children learn in school that the Declaration, written mostly by Thomas Jefferson, was a catalyst for the American Revolutionary War. Its presentation to King George III of England made it clear that the American colonists were rejecting the British government that had ruled them. What students often overlook is how radical a step the colonists had taken. In the eighteenth century the idea that citizens, rather than governments, ultimately hold political power was almost unheard of—an idea that flew in the face of the established order, under which people were viewed as the subjects of their rulers. But in the Declaration of Independence, Jefferson and his cosigners stated unequivocally that it should be the other way around: Leaders served at the behest of citizens; if those leaders should compromise the inherent rights of the citizens, then citizens were legally and morally justified in removing those leaders. Power to the people. ■ In this sense the founding of the United States ushered in a new era in which the whole idea of government was redefined, but it also created a new set of questions about the relationship between a government and its citizens. If political power ultimately resides in the people, then what is the role of government? How is that role determined? And how much power should a government have over citizens? These questions are not answered in the Declaration of Independence except in the abstract. Jefferson and his cosigners famously declared that government exists to secure the rights of citizens to "Life, Liberty, and the pursuit of Happiness," but they left it up to later generations to define exactly what "life, liberty, and the pursuit of happiness" means. And each generation has wrestled with the question of how much power government should have to fulfill that purpose. ■ The essays in this section reveal some of the ways in which Americans have confronted this question. In his famous "Letter from a Birmingham Jail," Martin Luther King, Jr. refers directly to the Declaration of Independence to make his argument that citizens are morally justified—and even obligated—to disobey laws that are unjust. The entire civil rights movement of the 1960s, in which King was such an important figure, rested largely on that very idea. After September 11, 2001, Americans revisited some of the same questions that civil rights activists and protesters against the Vietnam War raised about granting government too much power over individual citizens. In the wake of the September 11 terrorist attacks, the U.S.

government took several actions to protect the nation against additional attacks. But many Americans believed that the government overstepped its legal powers and compromised the rights of its own citizens. Fierce debates ensued about how much freedom citizens should give up so that their government could better protect them. The essays in this section reveal the complexity and intensity of those debates. ■ As a group, these essays provide various perspectives on the relationship between a government and its citizens. They also suggest that Americans are still trying to answer the same questions Thomas Jefferson and others raised when they signed the Declaration of Independence more than 225 years ago.

CON-TEXT

"The Declaration of Independence"

1 When in the Course of human events, it becomes necessary for one people to dissolve the political bands which have connected them with another, and to assume among the powers of the earth, the separate and equal station to which the Laws of Nature and of Nature's God entitle them, a decent respect to the opinions of mankind requires that they should declare the causes which impel them to the separation.

We hold these truths to be self-evident, that all men are created equal, that they are endowed by their Creator with certain unalienable Rights, that among these are Life, Liberty and the pursuit of Happiness. That to secure these rights, Governments are instituted among Men, deriving their just powers from the consent of the governed. That whenever any Form of Government becomes destructive of these ends it is the Right of the People to alter or to abolish it, and to institute new Government, laying its foundation on such principles and organizing its powers in such form, as to them shall seem most likely to effect their Safety and Happiness. Prudence, indeed, will dictate that Governments long established should not be changed for light and transient causes; and accordingly all experience has shown, that mankind are more disposed to suffer, while evils are sufferable, than to right themselves by abolishing the forms to which they are accustomed. But when a long train of abuses and usurpations, pursuing invariably the same Object evinces a design to reduce them under absolute Despotism, it is their right, it is their duty, to throw off such Government, and to provide new Guards for their future security. Such has been the patient sufferance of these Colonies; and such is now the necessity which constrains them to alter their former Systems of Government. . . .

① MARTIN LUTHER KING, JR., "Letter from a Birmingham Jail"

Martin Luther King, Jr. (1929–1968) was the most important leader of the movement to secure civil rights for Black Americans during the mid-twentieth century. Ordained a Baptist minister in his father's church in Atlanta, Georgia, King became the founder and director of the Southern Christian Leadership Conference, an organization he continued to lead until his assassination in 1968. He first came to national attention by organizing a boycott of the buses in Montgomery, Alabama (1955–1956)—a campaign that he recounts in *Stride Toward Freedom: The Montgomery Story* (1958). An advocate of nonviolence who was jailed fourteen times in the course of his work for civil rights, King was instrumental in helping secure the passage of the Civil Rights Bill in 1963. His efforts on behalf of civil rights led to many awards, most notably the Nobel Peace Prize in 1964. "Letter From a Birmingham Jail" was written in 1963, when King was jailed for eight days as the result of his campaign against segregation in Birmingham, Alabama. In the letter, King responds to White clergymen who had criticized his work and blamed him for breaking the law. But "Letter From a Birmingham Jail" is more than a rebuttal of criticism; it is a well-reasoned and carefully argued defense of civil disobedience as a means of securing civil liberties. In justifying his refusal to obey what he believed were unjust laws, King invokes a high moral standard by which to judge a government's actions. His famous essay thus should prompt you to consider the limits of governmental power and the responsibilities of citizens in supporting or opposing that power.

Letter from a Birmingham Jail

MARTIN LUTHER KING, JR.

April 16, 1963

My Dear Fellow Clergymen:

1 While confined here in the Birmingham city jail, I came across your recent statement calling my present activities "unwise and untimely." Seldom do I pause to answer criticism of my work and ideas. If I sought to answer all the criticisms that cross my desk, my secretaries would have little time for anything other than such correspondence in the course of the day, and I would have no time for constructive work. But since I feel that you are men of genuine good will and that your criticisms are sincerely put forth, I want to try to answer your statement in what I hope will be patient and reasonable terms.

I think I should indicate why I am here in Birmingham, since you have been influenced by the view which argues against "outsiders coming in." I have the honor of serving as president of the Southern Christian Leadership Conference, an organization operating in every southern state, with headquarters in Atlanta, Georgia. We have some eighty-five affiliated organizations across the South, and one of them is the Alabama Christian Movement for Human Rights. Frequently we share staff, educational, and financial resources with our affiliates.

Several months ago the affiliate here in Birmingham asked us to be on call to engage in a nonviolent direct-action program if such were deemed necessary. We readily consented, and when the hour came we lived up to our promise. So I, along with several members of my staff, am here because I was invited here. I am here because I have organizational ties here.

But more basically, I am in Birmingham because injustice is here. Just as the prophets of the eighth century B.C. left their villages and carried their "thus saith the Lord" far beyond the boundaries of their home towns, and just as the Apostle Paul left his village of Tarsus and carried the gospel of Jesus Christ to the far corners of the Greco-Roman world, so am I compelled to carry the gospel of freedom beyond my own home town. Like Paul, I must constantly respond to the Macedonian call for aid.

Moreover, I am cognizant of the interrelatedness of all communities and states. I cannot sit idly by in Atlanta and not be concerned about what happens in Birmingham. Injustice anywhere is a threat to justice everywhere. We are caught in an inescapable network of mutuality, tied in a single garment of destiny. Whatever affects one directly, affects all indirectly. Never again can we afford to live with the narrow, provincial, "outside agitator" idea. Anyone who lives inside the United States can never be considered an outsider anywhere within its bounds.

5 You deplore the demonstrations taking place in Birmingham. But your statement, I am sorry to say, fails to express a similar concern for the conditions that brought about the demonstrations. I am sure that none of you would want to rest content with the superficial kind of social analysis that deals merely with effects and does not grapple with underlying causes. It is unfortunate that demonstrations are taking place in Birmingham, but it is even more unfortunate that the city's white power structure left the Negro community with no alternative.

In any nonviolent campaign [see "Nonviolence" on page 602], there are four basic steps: collection of the facts to determine whether injustices exist; negotiation; self-purification; and direct action. We have gone through all these steps in Birmingham. There can be no gainsaying the fact that racial injustice engulfs this community. Birmingham is probably the most thoroughly segregated city in the United States. Its ugly record of brutality is widely known. Negroes have experienced grossly unjust treatment in courts. There have been more unsolved bombings of Negro homes and churches in Birmingham than in any other city in the nation. These are the hard, brutal facts of the case. On the basis of these conditions, Negro leaders sought to negotiate with the city fathers. But the latter consistently refused to engage in good-faith negotiation.

Then, last September, came the opportunity to talk with leaders of Birmingham's economic community. In the course of the negotiations, certain promises were made by the merchants—

NONVIOLENCE

Inspired by the ideas of Mahatma Gandhi, whose nonviolent movement helped end the British rule of India, King developed a philosophy of nonviolent resistance based on the Christian ideal of brotherly love. In an essay published in 1960, King wrote that "the Christian doctrine of love operating through the Gandhian method of nonviolence was one of the most potent weapons available to oppressed people in their struggle for freedom." In a related essay, King responded to a critique of pacifism by Christian philosopher Reinhard Neibuhr by arguing that "pacifism is not unrealistic submission to evil power, as Niebuhr contends. It is rather a courageous confrontation of evil by the power of love." King's philosophy was put to the test in 1956 during the bus boycott in Montgomery, Alabama, during which Blacks and civil rights activists were harrassed and sometimes physically attacked. In the end, King's nonviolent protest movement resulted in a Supreme Court decision that declared segregation on public buses unconstitutional.

for example, to remove the stores' humiliating racial signs. On the basis of these promises, the Reverend Fred Shuttlesworth and the leaders of the Alabama Christian Movement for Human Rights agreed to a moratorium on all demonstrations. As the weeks and months went by, we realized that we were the victims of a broken promise. A few signs, briefly removed, returned; the others remained.

As in so many past experiences, our hopes had been blasted, and the shadow of deep disappointment settled upon us. We had no alternative except to prepare for direct action, whereby we would present our very bodies as means of laying our case before the conscience of the local and the national community. Mindful of the difficulties involved, we decided to undertake a process of self-purification. We began a series of workshops on nonviolence, and we repeatedly asked ourselves: "Are you able to accept blows without retaliating?" "Are you able to endure the ordeal of jail?" We decided to schedule our direct-action program for the Easter season, realizing that except for Christmas, this is the main shopping period

of the year. Knowing that a strong economic-withdrawal program would be the byproduct of direct action, we felt that this would be the best time to bring pressure to bear on the merchants for the needed change.

Then it occurred to us that Birmingham's mayoral election was coming up in March, and we speedily decided to postpone action until after election day. When we discovered that the Commissioner of Public Safety, Eugene "Bull" Connor, had piled up enough votes to be in the run-off, we decided again to postpone action until the day after the run-off so that the demonstrations could not be used to cloud the issues. Like many others, we waited to see Mr. Connor defeated, and to this end we endured postponement after postponement. Having aided in this community need, we felt that our direct-action program could be delayed no longer.

10 You may well ask, "Why direct action? Why sit-ins, marches, and so forth? Isn't negotiation a better path?" You are quite right in calling for negotiation. Indeed, this is the very purpose of direct action. Nonviolent direct action seeks to create such a crisis and foster such a tension that a community which has constantly refused to negotiate is forced to confront the issue. It seeks so to dramatize the issue that it can no longer be ignored. My citing the creation of tension as part of the work of the nonviolent resister may sound rather shocking. But I must confess that I am not afraid of the word "tension." I have earnestly opposed violent tension, but there is a type of constructive, nonviolent tension which is necessary for growth. Just as Socrates felt that it was necessary to create a tension in the mind so that individuals could rise from the bondage of myths and half-truths to the unfettered realm of creative analysis and objective appraisal, so must we see the need for nonviolent gadflies to create the kind of tension in society that will help men rise from the dark depths of prejudice and racism to the majestic heights of understanding and brotherhood.

The purpose of our direct-action program is to create a situation so crisis-packed that it will inevitably open the door to negotiation. I therefore concur with you in your call for negotiation. Too long has our beloved Southland been bogged down in a tragic effort to live in monologue rather than dialogue.

One of the basic points in your statement is that the action that I and my associates have taken in Birmingham is untimely. Some have asked: "Why didn't you give the new city administration time to act?" The only answer that I can give to this query is that the new Birmingham administration must be prodded about as much as the outgoing one, before it will act. We are sadly mistaken if we feel that the election of Albert Boutwell as mayor will bring the millennium to Birmingham. While Mr. Boutwell is a much more gentle person than Mr. Connor, they are both segregationists, dedicated to maintenance of the status quo. I have hoped that Mr. Boutwell will be reasonable enough to see the futility of massive resistance to desegregation. But he will not see this without pressure from devotees of civil rights. My friends, I must say to you that we have not made a single gain in civil rights without determined legal and nonviolent pressure. Lamentably, it is an historical fact that privileged groups seldom give up their privileges voluntarily. Individuals may see the moral light and voluntarily give up their unjust posture; but, as Reinhold Niebuhr* has reminded us, groups tend to be more immoral than individuals.

We know through painful experience that freedom is never voluntarily given by the oppressor; it must be demanded by the oppressed. Frankly, I have yet to engage in a direct-action campaign that was "well timed" in the view of those who have not suffered unduly from the disease of segregation. For years now I have heard the word "Wait!" It rings in the ear of every Negro with piercing familiarity. This "Wait" has almost always meant "Never." We must come to see, with one of our distinguished jurists, that "justice too long delayed is justice denied."

We have waited for more than 340 years for our constitutional and God-given rights. The nations of Asia and Africa are moving with jetlike speed toward gaining political independence, but we still creep at horse-and-buggy pace toward gaining a cup of coffee at a lunch counter. Perhaps it is easy for those who have never felt the stinging darts of segregation to say, "Wait." But when you have seen vicious mobs lynch your mothers and fathers at will and drown your sisters and brothers at whim; when you have seen hate-filled policemen curse, kick, and even kill your black brothers and sisters; when you see the vast majority of your twenty million Negro brothers smothering in an airtight cage of poverty in the midst of an affluent society; when you suddenly find your tongue twisted and your speech stammering as you seek to explain to your six-year-old daughter why she can't go to the public amusement park that has just been advertised on television, and see tears welling up in her eyes when she is told that Funtown is closed to colored children, and see ominous clouds of inferiority beginning to form in her little mental sky, and see her beginning to distort her personality by developing an unconscious bitterness toward white people; when you have to concoct an answer for a five-year-old son who is asking, "Daddy, why do white people treat colored people so mean?"; when you take a cross-country drive and find it necessary to sleep night after night in the uncomfortable corners of your automobile because no motel will accept you; when you are humiliated day in and day out by nagging signs reading "white" and "colored"; when your first name becomes "nigger," your middle name becomes "boy" (however old you are) and your last name becomes "John," and your wife and mother are never given the respected title "Mrs."; when you are harried by day and haunted by night by the fact that you are a Negro, living constantly at tiptoe stance, never quite knowing what to expect next,

*Reinhold Niebuhr (1892–1971) was a Protestant theologian who explored how Christianity related to modern politics and diplomacy (see www.newgenevacenter.org/biography/niebuhr2.htm).

Now, what is the difference between the two? How does one determine whether a law is just or unjust? A just law is a man-made code that squares with the moral law or the law of God. An unjust law is a code that is out of harmony with the moral law. To put it in the terms of St. Thomas Aquinas: An unjust law is a human law that is not rooted in eternal law and natural law. Any law that uplifts human personality is just. Any law that degrades human personality is unjust. All segregation statutes are unjust because segregation distorts the soul and damages the personality. It gives the segregator a false sense of superiority and the segregated a false sense of inferiority. Segregation, to use the terminology of the Jewish philosopher Martin Buber, substitutes an "I–it" relationship for an "I–thou" relationship and ends up relegating persons to the status of things. Hence segregation is not only politically, economically, and sociologically unsound, it is morally wrong and sinful. Paul Tillich has said that sin is segregation. Is not segregation an existential expression of man's tragic separation, his awful estrangement, his terrible sinfulness? Thus it is that I can urge men to obey the 1954 decision of the Supreme Court, for it is morally right; and I can urge them to disobey segregation ordinances, for they are morally wrong.

Let us consider a more concrete example of just and unjust laws. An unjust law is a code that a numerical or power majority group compels a minority group to obey but does not make binding on itself. This is *difference* made legal. By the same token, a just law is a code that a majority compels a minority to follow and that it is willing to follow itself. This is *sameness* made legal.

Let me give another explanation. A law is unjust if it is inflicted on a minority that, as a result of being denied the right to vote, had no part in enacting or devising the law. Who can say that the legislature of Alabama which set up that state's segregation laws was democratically elected? Throughout Alabama all sorts of devious methods are used to prevent Negroes

and are plagued with inner fears and outer resentments; when you are forever fighting a degenerating sense of "nobodiness"—then you will understand why we find it difficult to wait. There comes a time when the cup of endurance runs over, and men are no longer willing to be plunged into the abyss of despair. I hope, sirs, you can understand our legitimate and unavoidable impatience.

15 You express a great deal of anxiety over our willingness to break laws. This is certainly a legitimate concern. Since we so diligently urge people to obey the Supreme Court's decision of 1954 outlawing segregation in the public schools, at first glance it may seem rather paradoxical for us consciously to break laws. One may well ask: "How can you advocate breaking some laws and obeying others?" The answer lies in the fact that there are two types of laws; just and unjust. I would be the first to advocate obeying just laws. One has not only a legal but a moral responsibility to obey just laws. Conversely, one has a moral responsibility to disobey unjust laws. I would agree with St. Augustine that "an unjust law is no law at all."

from becoming registered voters, and there are some counties in which, even though Negroes constitute a majority of the population, not a single Negro is registered. Can any law enacted under such circumstances be considered democratically structured?

Sometimes a law is just on its face and unjust in its application. For instance, I have been arrested on a charge of parading without a permit. Now, there is nothing wrong in having an ordinance which requires a permit for a parade. But such an ordinance becomes unjust when it is used to maintain segregation and to deny citizens the First-Amendment privilege of peaceful assembly and protest.

20 I hope you are able to see the distinction I am trying to point out. In no sense do I advocate evading or defying the law, as would the rabid segregationist. That would lead to anarchy. One who breaks an unjust law must do so openly, lovingly, and with a willingness to accept the penalty. I submit that an individual who breaks a law that conscience tells him is unjust, and who willingly accepts the penalty of imprisonment in order to arouse the conscience of the community over its injustice, is in reality expressing the highest respect for law.

Of course, there is nothing new about this kind of civil disobedience. It was evidenced sublimely in the refusal of Shadrach, Meshach, and Abednego to obey the laws of Nebuchadnezzar,* on the ground that a higher moral law was at stake. It was practiced superbly by the early Christians, who were willing to face hungry lions and the excruciating pain of chopping blocks rather than submit to certain unjust laws of the Roman Empire. To a degree, academic freedom is a reality today because Socrates practiced civil disobedience. In our own nation, the Boston Tea Party represented a massive act of civil disobedience.

We should never forget that everything Adolf Hitler did in Germany was "legal" and everything the Hungarian freedom fighters did in Hungary[†] was "illegal." It was "illegal" to aid and comfort a Jew in Hitler's Germany. Even

BROWN V. BOARD OF EDUCATION

On May 17, 1954, Chief Justice Earl Warren read the decision of the unanimous U.S. Supreme Court in the case of *Brown v. Board of Education* of Topeka, Kansas, which overturned the previous policy of providing "separate but equal" education for Black children:

We come then to the question presented: Does segregation of children in public schools solely on the basis of race, even though the physical facilities and other "tangible" factors may be equal, deprive the children of the minority group of equal educational opportunities? We believe that it does. . . . We conclude that in the field of public education the doctrine of "separate but equal" has no place. Separate educational facilities are inherently unequal. Therefore, we hold that the plaintiffs and others similarly situated for whom the actions have been brought are, by reason of the segregation complained of, deprived of the equal protection of the laws guaranteed by the Fourteenth Amendment.

(For information about the Fourteenth Amendment, see the sidebar on page 584.)

so, I am sure that, had I lived in Germany at the time, I would have aided and comforted my Jewish brothers. If today I lived in a Communist country where certain principles dear to the Christian faith are suppressed, I would openly advocate disobeying that country's anti-religious laws.

I must make two honest confessions to you, my Christian and Jewish brothers. First, I must confess that over the past few years I have been gravely disappointed with the white moderate. I have almost reached the regrettable conclusion that the Negro's great stumbling block in his stride toward freedom is not the White Citizen's Counciler or the Ku Klux Klanner, but the white moderate, who is more devoted to "order" than to justice; who prefers a negative peace which is the absence of tension to a positive peace which is the presence of justice; who constantly says, "I agree with you in the goal you seek, but I cannot agree with your methods of direct action"; who paternalistically believes he can set the timetable for another man's freedom; who lives by a mythical concept of time and who constantly

*Nebuchadnezzar, King of Babylon, destroyed the temple at Jerusalem and brought the Jewish people into captivity. He set up a huge image in gold and commanded all to worship it. Shadrach, Meshach, and Abednego refused and were thrown into a fiery furnace from which they emerged unscathed. (See *Daniel* 3.)

[†]In 1956 Hungarian citizens temporarily overthrew the communist dictatorship in their country. Unwilling to confront the Soviet Union, Western democracies stood by when the Red Army suppressed the revolt by force.

advises the Negro to wait for a "more convenient season." Shallow understanding from people of good will is more frustrating than absolute misunderstanding from people of ill will. Lukewarm acceptance is much more bewildering than outright rejection.

I had hoped that the white moderate would understand that law and order exist for the purpose of establishing justice and that when they fail in this purpose they become the dangerously structured dams that block the flow of social progress. I had hoped that the white moderate would understand that the present tension in the South is a necessary phase of the transition from an obnoxious negative peace, in which the Negro passively accepted his unjust plight, to a substantive and positive peace, in which all men will respect the dignity and worth of human personality. Actually, we who engage in nonviolent direct action are not the creators of tension. We merely bring to the surface the hidden tension that is already alive. We bring it out in the open, where it can be seen and dealt with. Like a boil that can never be cured so long as it is covered up but must be opened with all its ugliness to the natural medicines of air and light, injustice must be exposed, with all the tension its exposure creates, to the light of human conscience and the air of national opinion, before it can be cured.

25 In your statement you assert that our actions, even though peaceful, must be condemned because they precipitate violence. But is this a logical assertion? Isn't this like condemning a robbed man because his possession of money precipitated the evil act of robbery? Isn't this like condemning Socrates because his unswerving commitment to truth and his philosophical inquiries precipitated the act by the misguided populace in which they made him drink hemlock? Isn't this like condemning Jesus because his unique God-consciousness and never-ceasing devotion to God's will precipitated the evil act of crucifixion? We must come to see that, as the federal courts have consistently affirmed, it is wrong to urge an individual to cease his efforts to gain his basic constitutional rights because the quest may precipitate violence. Society must protect the robbed and punish the robber.

I had also hoped that the white moderate would reject the myth concerning time in relation to the struggle for freedom. I have just received a letter from a white brother in Texas. He writes: "All Christians know that the colored people will receive equal rights eventually, but it is possible that you are in too great a religious hurry. It has taken Christianity almost two thousand years to accomplish what it has. The teachings of Christ take time to come to earth." Such an attitude stems from a tragic misconception of time, from the strangely irrational notion that there is something in the very flow of time that will inevitably cure all ills. Actually, time itself is neutral; it can be used either destructively or constructively. More and more I feel that the people of ill will have used time much more effectively than have the people of good will. We will have to repent in this generation not merely for the hateful words and actions of the bad people, but for the appalling silence of the good people. Human progress never rolls in on wheels of inevitability; it comes through the tireless efforts of men willing to be coworkers with God, and without this hard work, time itself becomes an ally of the forces of social stagnation. We must use time creatively, in the knowledge that the time is always ripe to do right. Now is the time to make real the promise of democracy and transform our pending national elegy into a creative psalm of brotherhood. Now is the time to lift our national policy from the quicksand of racial injustice to the solid rock of human dignity.

You speak of our activity in Birmingham as extreme. At first I was rather disappointed that fellow clergymen would see my nonviolent efforts as those of an extremist. I began thinking about the fact that I stand in the middle of two opposing forces in the Negro community. One is a force of complacency, made up in part of Negroes who, as a result of long years of oppression, are so drained of self-respect and a sense of "somebodiness" that they have adjusted to segregation; and in part of a few middle-class Negroes who, because of a degree of academic and economic security and because in some ways they profit by segregation, have become insensitive to the problems of the masses. The other force is one of bitterness and hatred, and it comes perilously close to advocating violence. It is expressed in the various black nationalist groups that are springing up across the nation, the largest and best-known being Elijah Muhammad's Muslim movement. Nourished by the Negro's frustration over the continued existence of racial discrimination, this movement is made up of people who have lost faith in America, who have absolutely repudiated Christianity, and who have concluded that the white man is an incorrigible "devil."

I have tried to stand between these two forces, saying that we need emulate neither the "do-nothingism" of the complacent nor the hatred and despair of the black nationalist. For there is the more excellent way of love and nonviolent protest. I am grateful to God that, through the influence of the Negro church, the way of nonviolence became an integral part of our struggle.

If this philosophy had not emerged, by now many streets of the South would, I am convinced, be flowing with blood. And I am further convinced that if our white brothers dismiss as "rabble-rousers" and "outside agitators" those of us who employ nonviolent direct action, and if they refuse to support our nonviolent efforts, millions of Negroes will, out of frustration and despair, seek solace and security in black-nationalist ideologies—a development that would inevitably lead to a frightening racial nightmare.

30 Oppressed people cannot remain oppressed forever. The yearning for freedom eventually manifests itself, and that is what has happened to the American Negro. Something within has reminded him of his birthright of freedom, and something without has reminded

him that it can be gained. Consciously or unconsciously, he has been caught up by the *Zeitgeist,* and with his black brothers of Africa and his brown and yellow brothers of Asia, South America, and the Caribbean, the United States Negro is moving with a sense of great urgency toward the promised land of racial justice. If one recognizes this vital urge that has engulfed the Negro community, one should readily understand why public demonstrations are taking place. The Negro has many pent-up resentments and latent frustrations, and he must release them. So let him march; let him make prayer pilgrimages to the city hall; let him go on freedom rides—and try to understand why he must do so. If his repressed emotions are not released in nonviolent ways, they will seek expression through violence; this is not a threat but a fact of history. So I have not said to my people, "Get rid of your discontent." Rather, I have tried to say that this normal and healthy discontent can be channeled into the creative outlet of nonviolent direct action. And now this approach is being termed extremist.

But though I was initially disappointed at being categorized as an extremist, as I continued to think about the matter I gradually gained a measure of satisfaction from the label. Was not Jesus an extremist for love: "Love your enemies, bless them that curse you, do good to them that hate you, and pray for them which despitefully use you, and persecute you." Was not Amos an extremist for justice: "Let justice roll down like waters and righteousness like an everflowing stream." Was not Paul an extremist for the Christian gospel: "I bear in my body the marks of the Lord Jesus." Was not Martin Luther an extremist: "Here I stand; I cannot do otherwise, so help me God." And John Bunyan: "I will stay in jail to the end of my days before I make a butchery of my conscience." And Abraham Lincoln: "This nation cannot survive half slave and half free." And Thomas Jefferson: "We hold these truths to be self-evident, that all men are created equal. . . ." So the question is not whether we will be extremists, but what kind

CONTEXT

Elijah Muhammad was a charismatic leader of the Nation of Islam who advocated an ideology of Black superiority and urged Blacks to reject Christianity, which he described as a tool for the enslavement of Blacks by Whites. Muhammad and his followers criticized King, for his nonviolent philosophy, arguing that violent resistance is necessary to defeat White racism and achieve freedom for Blacks. King's letter was addressed to White ministers who criticized his Birmingham campaign, but he surely knew that members of the Nation of Islam would read it, too.

COMPLICATION

King describes a number of revered historical figures, including Thomas Jefferson, Abraham Lincoln, and even Jesus, as "extremists" for love and justice. In 1964, a year after King wrote this letter, Arizona Senator Barry Goldwater, then running for nomination as the Republican Party's candidate for president, said in a speech at the Republican Party's national convention, "Extremism in the defense of liberty is no vice"—a statement for which he was severely criticized by many. In 2001 the men who carried out the attacks on the United States on September 11 were routinely described in the press and by U.S. government officials as "extremists." To what extent are all of these uses of the term *extremist* similar? To what extent are they different? To what extent is the effectiveness of King's use of this term dependent on the time in which he wrote his essay?

of extremists we will be. Will we be extremists for hate or for love? Will we be extremists for the preservation of injustice or for the extension of justice? In that dramatic scene on Calvary's hill three men were crucified. We must never forget that all three were crucified for the same crime—the crime of extremism. Two were extremists for immorality, and thus fell below their environment. The other, Jesus Christ, was an extremist for love, truth, and goodness, and thereby rose above his environment. Perhaps the South, the nation, and the world are in dire need of creative extremists.

I had hoped that the white moderate would see this need. Perhaps I was too optimistic; perhaps I expected too much. I suppose I should have realized that few members of the oppressor race can understand the deep groans and passionate yearnings of the oppressed race, and still fewer have the vision to see that injustice must be rooted out by strong, persistent, and determined action. I am thankful, however, that some of our white brothers in the South have grasped the meaning of this social revolution and committed themselves to it. They are still all too few in quantity, but they are big in quality. Some—such as Ralph McGill, Lillian Smith, Harry Golden, James McBride Dabbs, Ann Braden, and Sarah Patton Boyle—have written about our struggle in eloquent and prophetic terms. Others have marched with us down nameless streets of the South. They have languished in filthy, roach-infested jails, suffering the abuse and brutality of policemen who view them as "dirty nigger-lovers." Unlike so many of their moderate brothers and sisters, they have recognized the urgency of the moment and sensed the need for powerful "action" antidotes to combat the disease of segregation.

Let me take note of my other major disappointment. I have been so greatly disappointed with the white church and its leadership. Of course, there are some notable exceptions. I am not unmindful of the fact that each of you has taken some significant stands on this issue. I commend you, Reverend Stallings, for your Christian stand on this past Sunday, in welcoming Negroes to your worship service on a nonsegregated basis. I commend the Catholic leaders of this state for integrating Spring Hill College several years ago.

But despite these notable exceptions, I must honestly reiterate that I have been disappointed with the church. I do not say this as one of those negative critics who can always find something wrong with the church. I say this as a minister of the gospel, who loves the church; who was nurtured in its bosom; who has been sustained by its spiritual blessings and who will remain true to it as long as the cord of life shall lengthen.

35 When I was suddenly catapulted into the leadership of the bus protest in Montgomery, Alabama, a few years ago, I felt we would be supported by the white church. I felt that the white ministers, priests, and rabbis of the South would be among our strongest allies. Instead, some have been outright opponents, refusing to understand the freedom movement and misrepresenting its leaders; all too many others have been more cautious than courageous and have remained silent behind the anesthetizing security of stained-glass windows.

In spite of my shattered dreams, I came to Birmingham with the hope that the white religious leadership of this community would see the justice of our cause and, with deep moral concern, would serve as the channel through which our just grievances could reach the power structure. I had hoped that each of you would understand. But again I have been disappointed. . . .

There was a time when the church was very powerful—in the time when the early Christians rejoiced at being deemed worthy to suffer for what they believed. In those days the church was not merely a thermometer that recorded the ideas and principles of popular opinion; it was a thermostat that transformed the mores of society. Whenever the early Christians entered a town, the people in power became disturbed and immediately sought to convict the Christians for being "disturbers of the peace" and "outside agitators." But the Christians pressed on, in the conviction that they were "a colony of heaven," called to obey God rather than man. Small in number, they were big in commitment. They were too God-intoxicated to be "astronomically intimidated." By their effort and example they brought an end to such ancient evils as infanticide and gladiatorial contests.

Things are different now. So often the contemporary church is a weak, ineffectual voice with an uncertain sound. So often it is an archdefender of the status quo. Far from being disturbed by the presence of the church, the power structure of the average community is consoled by the church's silent—and often even vocal—sanction of things as they are.

But the judgment of God is upon the church as never before. If today's church does not recapture the sacrificial spirit of the early church, it will lose its authenticity, forfeit the loyalty of millions, and be dismissed as an irrelevant social club with no meaning for the twentieth century. Every day I meet young people whose disappointment with the church has turned into outright disgust.

40 Perhaps I have once again been too optimistic. Is organized religion too inextricably bound to the status quo to save our nation and the world? Perhaps I must turn my faith to the inner spiritual church, the church within the church, as the true *ekklesia**** and the hope of the world. But again I am thankful to God that some noble souls from the ranks of organized religion have broken loose from the paralyzing chains of conformity and joined us as active partners in the struggle for freedom. They have left their secure congregations and walked the streets of Albany, Georgia, with us. They have gone down the highways of the South on torturous rides for freedom. Yes, they have gone to jail with us. Some have been dismissed from their churches, have lost the support of their bishops and fellow ministers. But they have acted in the faith that right defeated is stronger than evil triumphant. Their witness

has been the spiritual salt that has preserved the true meaning of the gospel in these troubled times. They have carved a tunnel of hope through the dark mountain of disappointment.

I hope the church as a whole will meet the challenge of this decisive hour. But even if the church does not come to the aid of justice, I have no despair about the future. I have no fear about the outcome of our struggle in Birmingham, even if our motives are at present misunderstood. We will reach the goal of freedom in Birmingham and all over the nation, because the goal of America is freedom. Abused and scorned though we may be, our destiny is tied up with America's destiny. Before the pilgrims landed at Plymouth, we were here. Before the pen of Jefferson etched the majestic words of the Declaration of Independence across the pages of history, we were here. For more than two centuries our forebears labored in this country without wages; they made cotton king; they built the homes of their masters while suffering gross injustice and shameful humiliation—and yet out of a bottomless vitality they continued to thrive and develop. If the inexpressible cruelties of slavery could not stop us, the opposition we now face will surely fail. We will win our freedom because the sacred heritage of our nation and the eternal will of God are embodied in our echoing demands.

Before closing I feel impelled to mention one other point in your statement that has troubled me profoundly. You warmly commended the Birmingham police force for keeping "order" and "preventing violence." I doubt that you would have so warmly commended the police force if you had seen its dogs sinking their teeth into unarmed, nonviolent Negroes. I doubt that you would so quickly commend the policemen if you were to observe their ugly and inhumane treatment of Negroes here in the city jail; if you were to watch them push and curse old Negro women and young Negro girls; if you were to see them slap and kick old Negro men and young boys; if you were to observe them, as they did on

*Ekklesia **is a Greek word meaning assembly, congregation, or church.**

*In the fall of 1962 James Meredith became the first black student to enroll at the University of Mississippi. His act, which sparked riots on the university's campus that resulted in two deaths, is widely considered an important event in the civil rights movement.

two occasions, refuse to give us food because we wanted to sing our grace together. I cannot join you in your praise of the Birmingham police department.

It is true that the police have exercised a degree of discipline in handling the demonstrators. In this sense they have conducted themselves rather "nonviolently" in public. But for what purpose? To preserve the evil system of segregation. Over the past few years I have consistently preached that nonviolence demands that the means we use must be as pure as the ends we seek. I have tried to make clear that it is wrong to use immoral means to attain moral ends. But now I must affirm that it is just as wrong, or perhaps even more so, to use moral means to preserve immoral ends. Perhaps Mr. Connor and his policemen have been rather nonviolent in public, as was Chief Pritchett in Albany, Georgia, but they have used the moral means of nonviolence to maintain the immoral end of racial injustice. As T. S. Eliot has said, "The last temptation is the greatest treason: To do the right deed for the wrong reason."

I wish you had commended the Negro sit-inners and demonstrators of Birmingham for their sublime courage, their willingness to suffer, and their amazing discipline in the midst of great provocation. One day the South will recognize its real heroes. They will be the James Merediths,* with the noble sense of purpose that enables them to face jeering and hostile mobs, and with the agonizing loneliness that characterizes the life of the pioneer. They will be old, oppressed, battered Negro women, symbolized in a seventy-two-year-old woman in Montgomery, Alabama, who rose up with a sense of dignity and with her people decided not to ride segregated buses, and who responded with ungrammatical profundity to one who inquired about her weariness: "My feets is tired, but my soul is at rest." They will be the young high school and college students, the young ministers of the gospel and a

host of their elders, courageously and nonviolently sitting in at lunch counters and willingly going to jail for conscience's sake. One day the South will know that when these disinherited children of God sat down at lunch counters, they were in reality standing up for what is best in the American dream and for the most sacred values in our Judeo-Christian heritage, thereby bringing our nation back to those great wells of democracy which were dug deep by the founding fathers in their formulation of the Constitution and the Declaration of Independence.

45 Never before have I written so long a letter. I'm afraid it is much too long to take your precious time. I can assure you that it would have been much shorter if I had been writing from a comfortable desk, but what else can one do when he is alone in a narrow jail cell, other than write long letters, think long thoughts, and pray long prayers?

If I have said anything in this letter that overstates the truth and indicates an unreasonable impatience, I beg you to forgive me. If I have said anything that understates the truth and indicates my having a patience that allows me to settle for anything less than brotherhood, I beg God to forgive me.

I hope this letter finds you strong in the faith. I also hope that circumstances will soon make it possible for me to meet each of you, not as an integrationist or a civil-rights leader but as a fellow clergyman and a Christian brother. Let us all hope that the dark clouds of racial prejudice will soon pass away and the deep fog of misunderstanding will be lifted from our fear-drenched communities, and in some not too distant tomorrow the radiant stars of love and brotherhood will shine over our great nation with all their scintillating beauty.

Yours for the cause of Peace and Brotherhood, Martin Luther King, Jr.

Questions for Discussion

1. What reason does King give for writing this letter? What justification does he provide for its length? In what ways might these explanations strengthen his argument?

2. One of the many charges brought against King at the time of his arrest was that he was an "outsider" who had no business in Birmingham. How does he justify his presence in Birmingham? How convincing do you think his justification is?

3. What does King mean by nonviolent "direct action"? Why did he believe that such action was necessary in Birmingham? How does he build his case for the nonviolent campaign in Birmingham? Do you think he does so convincingly? Why or why not?

4. Examine the images that King invokes in paragraph 14. What does he accomplish with these images? How do they contribute to his overall argument? Do you think he is intentionally making an emotional appeal here? What does he achieve by including an unusually long sentence in this paragraph?

5. How does King distinguish between a just and an unjust law? Why is this distinction important for his main argument? What evidence does King provide to support his contention that unjust laws must be broken? Do you think King's original audience of White ministers would have found his argument on this issue convincing?

6. What specific features of King's letter reveal that it was written originally for an audience of White Christian ministers? What strategies does King employ that might be effective for such an audience? Do you think King intended his letter *only* for that audience?

7. At one point in his essay King explains that one purpose of the campaign in Birmingham was "to create a situation so crisis-packed that it will inevitably open the door to negotiation." Do you think King's letter itself is intended to lead to negotiation? Explain, citing specific passages in his letter to support your answer.

8. King had much experience as a preacher when he wrote this famous letter. Is there anything about its style that reminds you of oratory? How effective would this letter be if delivered as a speech?

② HEATHER GREEN, "Databases and Security vs. Privacy"

Concerns about threats to their country's—and their personal—security after September 11, 2001, led many Americans to reexamine an idea that has been debated in the United States for many years: the establishment of a national identification card system. Such a system would, in effect, require all Americans to carry an authorized identification card to be used for important but routine transactions, such as withdrawing money from a bank account; paying a bill; visiting a doctor; boarding an airplane or train; entering a government building; and purchasing a variety of items, including medications, alcohol, ammunition, knives, or fertilizer. To an extent, some kind of official identification is already required for many of these activities. For example, when you withdraw money from your bank account, you usually must present a photo ID such as a driver's license. A national ID card system, however, would centralize this process and place it in the hands of the federal government. That worries many critics, including business reporter Heather Green, who sees in such ID cards the potential for the abuse of the privacy of individual Americans. As Green points out in the following essay, which was first published in *Business Week* in 2002, the debate over national ID cards is really a broader debate about the extent to which Americans are willing to sacrifice some of their rights to privacy for greater security in a dangerous world. In this respect, the controversy about ID cards is also part of a debate about how much power the government should have over its citizens.

Databases and Security vs. Privacy

HEATHER GREEN

1   The debate about whether or not the U.S. should or would adopt a national identification-card system has emerged with a jolting intensity. Jolting because even through world wars and a cold war, in which the U.S. feared an enemy within the country as much as the armies outside, Americans resisted the creation of a national ID that they would carry to prove their citizenship. Now, however, public surveys, congressional speeches, and remarks by high-profile CEOs are bringing the issue to the forefront, causing everyone to consider whether America is ready to adopt a card ID system—like those widely used in other countries—at the expense of our privacy.

The problem is, the debate over trading security provided by card IDs for a lower standard of privacy focuses on the wrong issue. The federal government and law enforcement don't need national ID cards. Indeed, the Bush Administration stated publicly last month that it had no intention of pushing for cards. Instead, law-enforcement and intelligence agencies can achieve many of the same goals of an ID card by increasing the collection and sharing of data among federal and state agencies, banks, transportation authorities, and credit-card companies.

People concerned about balancing privacy and security need to focus on this point and not get caught up in the red herring* debate around the ID cards themselves.

Robust Resource

After all, the U.S. already is a database nation. In the corporate world, the push to gather, store, and trade information about individuals' daily lives, habits and tastes, families, purchases, health, and financial standing has steadily increased as database software and hardware, data-mining technology, and computer networks have become cheaper to run and connect.

5 The FBI, Central Intelligence Agency, Federal Aviation Administration, Immigration & Naturalization Service, port authorities, and state motor vehicle departments could possibly take a page from Corporate America. By creating data-gathering systems in the background that pull together information about people—including their travel plans, frequent-flier info, license certification, border crossings, and financial records—law-enforcement and intelligence agencies can run a robust national ID system without the card itself.

Two questions: Would government in the U.S. really be able to implement a system of databases, and why have other countries avoided this path? First, commercial databases are a particularly American heritage. We're concerned about privacy, but not urgently. Most believe that if we personally think it's important, we can set limits on how our information is used: We can call a number provided by the Direct Marketing Assn., say, to get ourselves off catalog lists. And we accept that some benefits and efficiency come from providing data to companies, including health insurers, credit-card issuers, and airlines. So a huge system of commercial databases has been created.

Highly Protected

Second, Europe has a different, more tragic historical perspective. The Nazis used personal information culled from commercial and government files, including telephone and bank

records, to track down Jews, communists, resistance fighters, and the mentally ill. As a direct result of that experience, privacy is very highly protected in countries such as Germany and France.

That doesn't mean these countries aren't interested in protecting security. It simply means that instead of amassing huge amounts of information in databases, these countries favor national ID cards. According to privacy group Privacy International, most of the Western European countries that have strict controls protecting the privacy of personal information—including Germany, France, Belgium, Greece, Luxembourg, Portugal, and Spain—have compulsory national ID systems.

So, Americans need to get more sophisticated and realize that, in the interest of security, law-enforcement and intelligence agencies are likely to start beefing up their databases on citizens. We need to be on guard and informed about this eventuality. Despite how difficult it might be to make these databases work effectively, you have to believe that security officials view networked databases as key to their war on terrorism.

Overstepped Boundaries

10 Facing this likelihood, citizens need to know and make clear what the rules are under which people land in these databases and are flagged as suspects, who gets to look at the information, and what protections can be established so that information collected for one purpose isn't used for another without some kind of oversight. America needs clear definitions about what terrorism is, so that someone who is protesting against U.S. policies isn't labeled a terrorist out of hand. This is where the true privacy vs. security battlefield will be in the future.

After September 11, it's only natural that the nation would search for ways to increase its security. But law enforcement has overstepped the boundaries of acceptable surveillance of Americans in the past. Widespread wiretapping of civil-rights leaders, including

*A red herring is something that distracts attention from the real issue at hand. The term comes from an old practice of dragging a smoked, or "red," herring across a trail to confuse hunting dogs.

COMPLICATION

Established in 1917, the Direct Marketing Association (DMA) claims to be the oldest and largest trade association for direct marketing. It provides a service by which consumers can ask to have their names removed from the lists used by DMA member businesses to market directly to consumers through telephone calls and mailings. In 1995 DMA was the focus of a lawsuit challenging its practice of distributing names of consumers among its member businesses. Documents filed in that case indicated that as of 1995, DMA had more than 3.2 million names of consumers in its databases. The suit led to several bills in Congress that were intended to protect consumers from direct marketing practices that they believe violate their rights to privacy by sharing information about them without permission.

Martin Luther King, as well as Vietnam war dissidents including Jane Fonda and John Lennon during the 1960s and early 1970s led to stricter controls over the kind of information intelligence agencies could gather and the type of broad investigations they could conduct.

Just because we depend on the government to protect us doesn't mean that it will always respect our individual rights. That's the contest that has always been waged in a democracy: the rights of individuals against the safety of the community. Individuals have a duty to be aware of the steps a security-focused government will contemplate and to fight for the protection of rights that they believe are the foundation of a democracy. Privacy is a civil liberty worthy of protection.

Questions for Discussion

1. Why does Green believe that the debate about national ID cards focuses on the wrong issue? On what point, according to Green, should Americans focus instead?

2. Green calls the United States a "database nation." What does she mean by that phrase? What evidence does she offer to support that statement? Do you agree with her? Why or why not?

3. What is the main difference between European countries where ID cards are in use and the United States when it comes to information privacy, in Green's view? Why is this difference important to her main argument?

4. What is Green's primary concern regarding the use of a national ID card in the United States? What evidence does she present that such a concern is justified? Do you find this evidence persuasive? Why or why not?

5. How does the fact that Green is a business reporter—and that her essay was published in a business journal—affect your reaction to her argument? Do you think her identity as a business reporter enhances her credibility in making this argument? Explain.

③ ALAN M. DERSHOWITZ, "Why Fear National ID Cards?"

The right to individual liberty is guaranteed to U.S. citizens by the Constitution. But that right is more than a legal one; it also reflects a belief in individual freedom that runs deep in American culture. Perhaps that is one reason that the debate about national ID cards has been so intense in the United States. Any proposal that seems to compromise individual rights tends to make Americans suspicious. But balancing the rights of individuals with the well-being of all Americans is a challenge, in part because of the great diversity of the United States and in part because of the enormous difficulties of protecting citizens from harm. If, like Alan Dershowitz, you prefer "a system that takes a little bit of freedom from all to one that takes a great deal of freedom and dignity from the few," then perhaps you will agree with him that a national ID card is a worthwhile tradeoff. On the other hand, you might share the concerns of many Americans about the danger of giving up any of your freedoms to your government. As you read the following essay by this well-known lawyer and activist, consider how your views about individual liberties influence your reaction to his argument. Dershowitz is also a columnist and the author of many books on legal issues, including *Why Terrorism Works* (2002).

Why Fear National ID Cards?

ALAN M. DERSHOWITZ

CONTEXT

This essay was originally published in October 2001 on the editorial page of the *New York Times*, which has one of the largest national circulations of any publication in the United States. What audience do you think Dershowitz primarily intended to address with this essay? Do you think he addressed this audience effectively?

1 At many bridges and tunnels across the country, drivers avoid long delays at the toll booths with an unobtrusive device that fits on a car's dashboard. Instead of fumbling for change, they drive right through; the device sends a radio signal that records their passage. They are billed later. It's a tradeoff between privacy and convenience: the toll-takers know more about you—when you entered and left Manhattan, for instance—but you save time and money.

An optional national identity card could be used in a similar way, offering a similar kind of tradeoff: a little less anonymity for a lot more security. Anyone who had the card could be allowed to pass through airports or building security more expeditiously, and anyone who opted out could be examined much more closely.

As a civil libertarian, * I am instinctively skeptical of such tradeoffs. But I support a national identity card with a chip that can match the holder's fingerprint. It could be an effective tool for preventing terrorism, reducing the need for other law-enforcement mechanisms—especially racial and ethnic profiling—that pose even greater dangers to civil liberties.

I can hear the objections: What about the specter of Big Brother? † What about fears of identity cards leading to more intrusive measures? (The National Rifle Association, for example, worries that a government that registered people might also decide to register guns). (See "Complication" on page 618.) What about fears that such cards would lead to increased deportation of illegal immigrants?

5 First, we already require photo ID's for many activities, including flying, driving, drinking and check-cashing. And fingerprints differ from photographs only in that they are harder to fake. The vast majority of Americans routinely carry photo ID's in their wallets and pocketbooks. These ID's are issued by state motor vehicle bureaus and other public and private entities. A national card would be uniform and difficult to forge or alter. It would reduce the likelihood that someone could, intentionally or not, get lost in the cracks of multiple bureaucracies.

The fear of an intrusive government can be addressed by setting criteria for any official who demands to see the card. Even without a national card, people are always being asked to show identification. The existence of a national card need not change the rules about when ID can properly be de-

manded. It is true that the card would facilitate the deportation of illegal immigrants. But President Bush has proposed giving legal status to many of the illegal immigrants now in this country. And legal immigrants would actually benefit from a national ID card that could demonstrate their status to government officials.

Finally, there is the question of the right to anonymity. I don't believe we can afford to recognize such a right in this age of terrorism. No such right is hinted at in the Constitution. And though the Supreme Court has identified a right to privacy, privacy and anonymity are not the same. American taxpayers, voters and drivers long ago gave up any right of anonymity without loss of our right to engage in lawful conduct within zones of privacy. Rights are a function of experience, and our recent experiences teach that it is far too easy to be anonymous—even to create a false identity—in this large and decentralized country. A national ID card would not prevent all threats of terrorism, but it would make it more difficult for potential terrorists to hide in open view, as many of the Sept. 11 hijackers apparently managed to do.

A national ID card could actually enhance civil liberties by reducing the need for racial and ethnic stereotyping. There would be no excuse for hassling someone merely because he belongs to a particular racial or ethnic group if he presented a card that matched his print and that permitted his name to be checked instantly against the kind of computerized criminal-history retrieval systems that are already in use. (If there is too much personal information in the system, or if the information is being used improperly, that is a separate issue. The only information the card need

*A *civil libertarian* generally supports individual rights as opposed to state control. In the United States, civil libertarians are usually defenders of the specific rights guaranteed by the U.S. Constitution, including the right to free speech and protection against unreasonable search and seizure. The American Civil Liberties Union, the best known such organization, describes its mission as "fighting to ensure that the Bill of Rights will always be more than a 'parchment barrier' against government oppression and the tyranny of the majority." (See the sidebar on Libertarianism on page 556).

†*Big Brother* refers to the totalitarian government in George Orwell's novel *1984*. The term is generally used to describe an omnipotent and oppressive government or institution.

COMPLICATION

According to the National Rifle Association, "The language and intent of the framers of the Second Amendment were perfectly clear two centuries ago. Based on English Common Law, the Second Amendment guaranteed against federal interference with the citizen's right to keep and bear arms for personal defense. Also, the revolutionary experience caused the Founding Fathers to address a second concern—the need for the people to maintain a citizen-militia for national and state defense without adopting a large standing army, which was viewed as the bane of liberty."

contain is name, address, photo and print.) From a civil liberties perspective, I prefer a system that takes a little bit of freedom from all to one that takes a great deal of freedom and dignity from the few—especially since those few are usually from a racially or ethnically disfavored group. A national ID card would be much more effective in preventing terrorism than profiling millions of men simply because of their appearance.

Questions for Discussion

1. Notice the images Dershowitz describes in his opening paragraph. How do these images help him establish his position in the debate about national ID cards? Do you think the use of these images is a good strategy for introducing his argument? Explain.

2. Dershowitz describes himself as a "civil libertarian." Why do you think he does so? How might describing himself in this way affect his readers' response to his argument?

3. In his essay Dershowitz addresses several possible objections to his position on ID cards. What are those objections? Do you think Dershowitz answers them effectively? Evaluate the extent to which Dershowitz strengthens or weakens his argument by including these possible objections.

4. Dershowitz makes a distinction between the right to privacy and the right to anonymity. Why is this distinction important to his argument?

5. How does Dershowitz support his point that national ID cards could enhance civil liberties? Do you agree with him on this point? Why or why not? What counterarguments might you offer in response to this point?

④ DAVID J. BARRON, "Reclaiming Federalism"

"Federalism" describes an approach to government advocated by some of the founders of the United States. Simply put, it means limiting the power of the national government so that individual states can still have a high degree of political autonomy. In other words, "federalism" does not call for expanding the power of the federal government; instead it calls for seeing states as part of a federation. In the Declaration of Independence (see page 599), Thomas Jefferson referred to these "united States of America" using capitalization that shows a federalist influence; "united States" emphasizes "States," but "United States"—as the country is now referred to—emphasizes unity. Federalism made it possible for different states to take different positions on slavery, among other issues. In the 1960s, the phrase "state's rights" was federalist code for opposing racial integration. More recently, however, scholars have had reason to reconsider the balance of power in the United States. For example, in an argument you will find in Chapter 10 (pages 411–417), Jonathan Rauch argues that gay marriage should be determined by states rather than by the federal government. Former Chief Justice William Rehnquist (1924–2005) was a leading advocate of states' rights and had considerable influence in the 33 years he served on the Supreme Court. The following argument by David Barron was first published in 2005 shortly before Rehnquist's death. The issues raised by Barron are still relevant because Rehnquist was succeeded as Chief Justice by John Roberts, who had previously served as Rehnquist's clerk and shares many of the same views. Barron received both his B.A. and his law degree from Harvard University, where he currently teaches constitutional law and local government law, among other courses. His argument was first published in *Dissent,* a quarterly magazine that is associated with the left but also defines itself as a "magazine that welcomes the clash of strong opinions." According the *New York Times, Dissent* "ranks among the handful of political journals read most regularly by U.S. intellectuals."

Reclaiming Federalism

DAVID J. BARRON

1 The revival of states' rights may be the most substantial accomplishment of the Rehnquist Court's conservative majority. Cases concerning federalism do not regularly capture the newspaper headlines of hot-button constitutional disputes, but the jurisprudence of the Rehnquist majority has, in fact, been in retreat recently when it comes to affirmative action, abortion, school prayer, gay rights, and even the death penalty. In each area, conservative justices defected, creating de facto liberal majorities. When it comes to states' rights, by contrast, the conservative majority has changed constitutional law dramatically. Not long ago, few propositions could be asserted more confidently in law-school classrooms than that states enjoy almost no constitutional protection from congressional power. Now, the talk concerns increasing restraints on federal power. What may be called "Rehnquist Federalism" has not yet made a revolution, and defections occur in federalism cases, too. But Rehnquist Federalism has changed the legal landscape by limiting congressional efforts to provide everything from effective remedies against discrimination to enforcement of federal statutory guarantees of overtime pay—all in the name of

*The term *progressives* has been used since the late nineteenth century to describe political activists who favor using government as a means for remedying social abuse. Some of the early successes of the progressive movement were the creation of child labor laws and of building codes that would protect residents and workers. Historical events have sometimes played a key role in these changes. For example, the Triangle Shirt Waist Factory fire in 1911 shocked Americans when 146 seamstresses, most of whom were immigrants and locked inside the workplace by their employer, burned or jumped to their deaths. This fire inspired stricter fire codes and helped workers gain union representation. "Progressives" could be found in both of the major political parties. For example, President Theodore Roosevelt, a Republican, was widely considered a progressive.

CONTEXT

The New Deal describes the combination of domestic initiatives that President Franklin D. Roosevelt launched to fight the great economic depression that gripped the country when he took office in 1933. The most famous program to emerge from the New Deal is Social Security, which was designed to protect the elderly from poverty. Physical evidence of the New Deal can still be found in the nation's infrastructure. Many roads and buildings were constructed by the Works Progress Administration (WPA), and the Civilian Conservation Corps (CCC) improved national parks and forests. Another lasting legacy is the Tennessee Valley Authority (TVA), which brought electric power to millions of Americans in and near Tennessee. The New Deal was controversial at the time. Many critics argued that the federal government had no business becoming so actively involved in economic projects—and borrowing money to do so. But most Americans were relieved that the federal government was putting the destitute to work and making improvements that people could see. Partially because of these programs, Roosevelt was elected to four consecutive terms as President—the only President to serve more than two terms.

"state sovereignty" and despite the arguments of the four liberals on the Court.

Progressives* used to know what to think about states' rights. The idea was so thoroughly associated with opposition to the civil rights movement and resistance to the New Deal that it seemed to go hand in hand with conservatism. But since the "federalism" revival began in 1992, with a decision curtailing federal authority over hazardous-waste facilities, conservatives have gained control of Congress, regained control of the presidency, and retained their majority on the Supreme Court. With all three branches of the national government in conservative hands, progressives have begun to wonder whether federalism might be useful after all.

Salon† magazine reports the emergence of why-go-to-Canada-when-you-have-federalism discussions within lefty circles. Progressive icons from U.S. representative Barney Frank to the San Francisco city government use state rights' rhetoric to oppose a federal ban on gay marriage. Look for progressive policy making at the present moment and you are much more likely to find it in a city hall or a state capitol than in a federal agency or a Senate cloakroom. Is there something in a revival of federalism, then, that even a liberal could love? The short answer is, "The revival of federalism? Yes. Rehnquist Federalism? No." Let me explain.

There is no such thing as "federalism." There are only "federalisms," fashioned at specific times and for specific reasons, each necessarily reflecting the particular political vision of its authors. Rehnquist Federalism is not the same as alternative federalism that prevailed at other times in our history. Some of the framers of the Constitution, for example, favored limiting federal power in order to preserve liberty. They believed that the limited scope of Congress's "enumerated" (that is, explicitly stated) powers made a separate bill of rights unnecessary. The conservative justices on the present Court construe Congress's enumerated powers very narrowly, thus limiting the federal government's ability to give life to those same liberties. These justices have done so (they say) to preserve states' rights.

Limiting Federal Power

5 Before progressives address Rehnquist Federalism they need to understand its implications. A key dimension of the new federalism involves limiting national power in order to expand state and local authority. This entails three distinct lines of doctrine:

- The first concerns Congress's enumerated powers. Article I of the Constitution grants Congress the power to regulate "Commerce . . . among the several States" and the Fourteenth Amendment empowers Congress to "enforce" the constitutional guarantee of equal protection of the laws and other basic rights against state infringement. By the end of the 1960s, the Supreme Court had construed these powers to give Congress a great deal of authority and, in doing so, confirmed the legal foundations of both the New Deal and the civil rights era. Now, thanks to the Rehnquist Court's conservatives, Congress has much less power under the Commerce Clause[‡] to regulate matters that are not in some sense "economic" (even if they could be shown to have real impact on the national economy). And Congress has only limited power under Section 5 of the Fourteenth Amendment because the Court has taken a very narrow view of the legislature's power to "enforce" constitutional guarantees such as the right to the equal protection of the laws. For example, while the Rehnquist Court continues to permit Congress to prohibit race and sex discrimination, it holds that Section 5 does not give Congress the same power to prohibit state discrimination based on disability or age.
- The second line invokes vague principles of "federalism" in order to prohibit Congress from ordering states to implement federal regulatory programs.

Congress may preempt state and local actions by passing contrary federal laws, but it may not require state and local governments to become regulators.

- The third line protects "sovereign immunity," the right of a government to refuse to respond to a suit brought by a private party. It traces back to the idea that the king can do no wrong. Not surprisingly, no reference to such an immunity is set forth in the Constitution. The Rehnquist Court, however, calls it a "postulate" of our federal system. The practical result is that even when states clearly violate federal statutes, the Court says that they cannot be made to pay damages for the harm they cause.

Congress still has the ability to regulate. Many matters are directly economic, after all, and even if Congress cannot commandeer states, it can (at least for now) get them to do what it wants in other ways. It can, for example, threaten to take away their federal grants. But the real-world consequences of Rehnquist Federalism should not be understated. Here are some examples:

- It led to the invalidation of portions of the Violence Against Women Act, which enabled women alleging harms from gender-based violence to seek civil redress in federal court;
- It struck down parts of the Brady Act, which required local law enforcement actors to perform background checks on gun purchasers;
- It undermined numerous statutes authorizing damages actions against state governments, ranging from the Fair Labor Standards Act to the Americans With Disabilities Act.

Some Limits on States

In each of these instances, the Court's solicitude for the "dignity" of states trumped congressional attempts to protect the dignity of individuals. But these cases tell only half the

[†]*Salon* is an online magazine that includes sections on news, politics, arts, and technology. *Time* has said of *Salon,* "While many have tried, few have succeeded in building a truly compelling magazine on the Web. *Salon* has managed to move to the top of the Web's short mustread list."

[†]Article I, Section 8 of the Constitution says, "The Congress shall have Power To lay and collect Taxes, Duties, Imposts and Excises, to pay the Debts and provide for the common Defence and general Welfare of the United States; but all Duties, Imposts and Excises shall be uniform throughout the United States."

CONTEXT

Named after James Brady, the press secretary who was seriously wounded in an assassination attempt against President Ronald Reagan, the Brady Bill was signed into law by President Bill Clinton in 1993. It required a five-day waiting period for the purchase of a handgun from a dealer registered with the government agency responsible for the regulation of firearms. It also required a national background check on the purchaser during this period. No restrictions were placed on private sales. In 1997, the Rehnquist Court ruled that the background check was unconstitutional. The waiting period remained in effect and could discourage violence by someone buying a gun in a moment of passion. But without the background check that was to have occurred during the waiting period, the law lost most of its potential to reduce the sale of weapons to criminals and terrorists. Dealers are required, however, to see identification from their customers, and many states have provisions for restricting the sale of handguns within their borders.

story—the half that concerns what the Court thinks Congress cannot do and what is reserved to the states. The other half concerns what the federal government should do, and what states and local governments should not. In other words, Rehnquist Federalism also limits state and local power in certain ways in order to expand national authority.

For example, the same Court that waxes eloquent about the need to restrain national power in order to protect state dignity routinely interprets ambiguous federal statutes broadly in order to preempt state regulation of private business. Even without a new federal statute mandating tort reform, the Court's conservatives have engaged in a kind of ad hoc tort reform project of their own. It has displaced significant swaths of state consumer protection law, including some measures that would permit state residents to sue health maintenance organizations. Similarly, some of the Court's leading federalism proponents turn out to be great fans of the so-called "Dormant Commerce Clause." This is a judge-made doctrine that prohibits states and local governments from regulating in ways that might interfere with the free flow of commerce nationwide. For example, Justices Sandra Day

O'Connor and Anthony Kennedy helped to forge majorities to invalidate local business regulations on the grounds that they are unconstitutionally protectionist or obstructive of national markets.

Finally, Rehnquist Federalism has expanded the Constitution's "Takings Clause." Historically, that clause required the government to compensate private owners when it seized their land, but not when it merely regulated how they could develop it. Over the last decade or so, the Court has treated more and more land-use regulations—such as restrictions on beachfront development or requirements that developers take steps to limit the cost imposed on the public by new construction—as if they were outright land grabs. As a result, the government increasingly risks multimillion-dollar claims by developers. By changing constitutional doctrine in this way, the Court departs from its view of states and localities as autonomous sovereigns entitled to respect. Instead, it intimates at times that they are nothing more than petty extortionists seeking to rob private businesses.

10 Viewed as a whole, then, the current "federalism" revival does not simply protect states' rights. It reallocates powers between the federal government and state and local ones, simultaneously limiting and extending the scope of each. And it does so in a politically ingenious way. Rehnquist Federalism synthesizes the social-conservative, small-government, and pro-business philosophies of the Republican Party. When it comes to nonmarket social issues, the Court carves out a domain of state and local power that is immune to federal legislative interference because of the "economic" requirement. This shift empowers localities to implement extreme social policies—whether concerning abortion or gay rights—favored on the right. With respect to market matters, by contrast, the Court consistently decides against "overreaching" by states and localities and legitimates business-backed federal efforts to curb state and local regulations. So, the Court finds that federal statutes trump state consumer protection laws or that local government land-use measures are unconstitutional. Even the state sovereign immunity and anti-commandeering cases seem to comport with the Republican Party platform. They make it harder to force states to pay for the harms they cause and more difficult for the federal government to implement national programs that require state assistance. In doing so, they reflect contemporary conservative interests in preserving the state treasury and shrinking the size of government.

Which Federalism?
The overlap between the Court's decisions and conservative ideology is not perfect, and one cannot prove that it is intentional. The notion that there might be some federalism-based limits on national power, after all, is not senseless. But there is precious little in the Constitution's text or the history of its adoption that compels the particular conservative allocation of national and local powers favored by the Rehnquist Court.

That Rehnquist Federalism promotes a substantively conservative political philosophy should not be surprising. Nor should it be surprising that Rehnquist Federalism limits state power even as it protects it. No one who believes in states' rights believes in unlimited states' rights. Federalism presumes that states exist within a larger nation. Each form of "federalism," therefore, rests on a view of what it is that states should and should not be doing. Some constitutional lawyers say that the allocation between the federal and state levels can be made "neutrally." That is, one can try to discern what the Framers would have wanted or one can make technical judgments about the likely geographic impacts of a government's decision. But neither of these approaches is helpful. What the Framers wanted is arguable, and it is difficult to determine the "local" or "national" effects of state policies. When the highest court in Massachusetts ruled on same-sex marriage,* its decision applied only to the state's residents. Yet some analysts

think that decision also helped to decide the national presidential election. Thus, cultural, ideological, and social forces that are contemporary and political, rather than timeless or technical, are bound to shape judgments about whether an issue is "national" or "local." In other words, what is "truly local" or "truly national"—as the Rehnquist Court has famously described the two domains—is truly political.

To say that Rehnquist Federalism has a strong conservative flavor is not to say that it lacks conceptual integrity as a form of federalism. Roughly speaking, it allocates social regulation to the states and market regulation to the federal government. The Rehnquist Court's conservative majority seems committed to maintaining this boundary even though it may limit the ability of Congress to advance conservative policies in particular cases. Take same-sex marriage. Even though it is an A-list issue for social conservatives, the Court expressly identified marriage (in a recent Commerce Clause case) as a matter of "truly local" concern and not at all "economic." There is little reason to think the Court will back off on this, even if confronted by a federal statute banning same-sex marriage. The Rehnquist Court's federalism, then, is conservative without always generating a conservative outcome.

Federalism and Conservative Interests
Now that we have a better fix on what the new federalism is about, we can return to our initial question of how progressives should think about it. Clearly, there is a lot not to like, beginning with an allocation of national and local powers that promotes the interests of contemporary conservatism so well. In addition, Rehnquist Federalism seems to assume a zero-sum battle for power between national and local governments that is not justified. National legislation can enhance the ability of state and local governments to cope with very local problems. That's why some local officials filed briefs opposing the invalidation (on "federalism" grounds) of both the Brady Act and the

*In 2003 Massachusetts Supreme Court Justice C. J. Marshall wrote, "The question before us is whether, consistent with the Massachusetts Constitution, the Commonwealth may deny the protections, benefits, and obligations conferred by civil marriage to two individuals of the same sex who wish to marry. We conclude that it may not."

*Appointed to the U.S. Supreme Court in 1916 by President Woodrow Wilson, Louis Brandeis (1856–1941) supported most, though not all, New Deal legislation. As the *Encyclopaedia Britannica* puts it, "He believed that, to preserve federalism, state legislatures must be able to make laws suited to varied and changing needs, but he wished to restrict them when they interfered with the freedom to express ideas." Brandeis, who was the first Jewish American to serve on the Supreme Court, is widely regarded as having had one of the best minds in the court's history. Brandeis University, near Boston, is named after him.

Violence Against Women Act referred to earlier. **15** At the same time, progressives know well the virtues of local power and decentralization. Just ask Eliot Spitzer, New York State's activist attorney general, if he would favor congressional action to preempt state business regulation. Thus, the standard progressive approach to federalism—that national governmental institutions must be free to act as they wish and when they wish on any matter of their choosing—seems problematic. The Constitution separates powers not only horizontally among the three branches of the federal government, but also vertically between national and state and local institutions. It's time for a progressive vision that imagines all levels to be important actors and not just the national government.

Of course, securing that vision in constitutional terms is not easy. There are problems with judges' drawing lines between local and national authority. But there are also problems with judges' leaving it to Congress to decide the limits of national authority. With no constitutional limits on congressional power, a majority party can act without constraint. For example, the conventional progressive view of the power of Congress under the Constitution's Commerce Clause—that it covers almost any matter one can think of—would clearly authorize federal legislation banning same-sex marriage or state death-with-dignity laws. So there is, ironically, something attractive for progressives about the Rehnquist Court's defense of judicially enforceable limits on national power. There is also something admirable about its apparent willingness to accept some outcomes that are hardly conservative. This Court is not prone to the case-by-case, nuanced assessment of what makes "good" policy that progressives often favor but that makes them vulnerable to the criticisms that they have positions and no principles. Perhaps progressives should bite some bullets of their own.

For a Progressive Federalism

What would a progressive federalism look like? It might well be a mirror image of Rehnquist Federalism. It would give states and local governments much greater room to regulate the private market. This would check national and multinational business influence as Louis Brandeis* and earlier progressives once imagined. It would also give the national government much more power to regulate nonmarket social relations. This would give Congress the power to protect basic Fourteenth Amendment rights.

To expand the ability of states and local governments to regulate private business, progressive federalism would permit federal statutes to trump state regulations only when they were in clear conflict. In other words, states would get the benefit of the doubt in this area. A progressive federalism would also interpret the Takings Clause to give more deference to local efforts to make developers assume the costs of their development. And rather than characterizing state and local regulations as protectionist or as obstructive of the national market, as the Court often does in its Dormant Commerce Clause decisions, progressive federalism would permit sensible attempts by state and local governments to protect their communities from the harsh and dislocating effects of larger economic forces.

But progressive federalism would do more than free states from the limits imposed by Rehnquist Federalism. It would promote a different view of Congress's enumerated powers. It would reinforce Congress's Fourteenth Amendment power to "enforce" basic constitutional rights and thereby protect the prerogatives of national citizenship from threats posed by local prejudices. Among the highest priorities of progressive federalism would be to reverse the Rehnquist Court's unwarranted curtailing of this vital power.

20 Progressive federalism would not, however, view congressional power as unlimited. Consider Congress's power to grant copyrights. The Constitution authorizes Congress to give "exclusive Right[s]" to "authors" for "limited Times" in order to "promote the Progress of Science and useful Arts." But that grant of power was not intended to turn Congress into a lackey of the national entertainment industry. The Rehnquist Court recently upheld a federal statute—thanks to aggressive industry lobbying—that retroactively extends federal copyrights in creative works for life plus seventy years. This was a legislative giveaway to the Walt Disney Company and other large, national companies, and it hardly promotes the arts. Nor does it comply with the requirement that creative works can be locked up only for a "limited time." A narrower view of Congress's copyright power, therefore, might be quite progressive. It would respond to the concern that the national legislature is unusually likely to be captured by the national entertainment industry.

A progressive federalism might also embrace the Rehnquist Court's limited view of Congress's Commerce Clause power. Congress would retain its ability to regulate economic activity. It would not, however, possess a general power to regulate any matter chosen by a majority of its members.

Such a limit on the Commerce Clause power, moreover, would not prevent Congress from enforcing an inclusive vision of national citizenship. Congress could still act forcefully against discrimination by invoking its Fourteenth Amendment authority to protect rights to equality.

Some legal scholars would say, no doubt, that progressive federalism is "political" rather than constitutional. But it is no more political than Rehnquist Federalism, and it is just as defensible in legal terms. Progressive federalism would not guarantee a liberal outcome in every case any more than Rehnquist Federalism guarantees a conservative one. For instance, progressive federalism might permit some local anti-affirmative-action

CONTEXT

The Fourteenth Amendment was passed in 1866 and designed to protect the rights of recently freed slaves. It states, "All persons born or naturalized in the United States, and subject to the jurisdiction thereof, are citizens of the United States and of the State wherein they reside. No State shall make or enforce any law which shall abridge the privileges or immunities of citizens of the United States; nor shall any State deprive any person of life, liberty, or property, without due process of law; nor deny to any person within its jurisdiction the equal protection of the laws." The amendment was widely ignored during the century that followed, however. The landmark civil rights decision in *Brown v. Board of Education* can be traced partly to the Supreme Court's recognition that segregated schools violated the Fourteenth Amendment. The movement led by Martin Luther King, Jr. in the 1960s to gain civil rights for African Americans (see pages 600–610) also emphasized the importance of the Fourteenth Amendment. Congress would have to enact major legislation guaranteeing civil rights, however, before the promises of the Fourteenth Amendment could begin to become a reality. The amendment has implications for all minorities.

measures that would otherwise be deemed inconsistent with federal statutory requirements. And a requirement that Commerce Clause legislation target economic activity could jeopardize some applications of environmental regulations, notably to local wetlands. But progressive federalism would promote national/local relations consistent with a broader liberal political vision. That vision has a constitutional pedigree that is at least as legitimate as the conservative one it would displace. Progressive federalism, then, would have just as much—or as little—integrity as today's conservative federalism.

Progressives for too long have been strikingly unimaginative when it comes to federalism. They speak only in a national key. But it is clear that their faith in unlimited national authority was the contingent product of liberal control of national institutions. Circumstances have changed. We should now look at the Constitution's federalism with fresh eyes. Doing so would cast some much needed doubt on the stereotype that progressives love big government. If progressive federalism results in

COMPLICATION

As a principle, federalism is sometimes applied selectively. For example, conservatives who argue against the centralization of power in Washington, D.C., and who emphasize the importance of local decision making have nevertheless supported attempts to ban gay marriage nationwide. And in a highly controversial decision, the Supreme Court ruled in *Bush* v. *Gore* to stop the recount of ballots in Florida that had been ordered in that state by the Florida Supreme Court after George W. Bush narrowly carried the state in the 2000 presidential election. The Supreme Court stopped the recount in a 5-4 decision, with Chief Justice William Rehnquist casting one of the votes to stop the recount and Justice Sandra Day O'Connor—another advocate of federalism—casting another. What do you think motivates this kind of inconsistency?

judicial decisions that limit national power too much, there would still be recourse to constitutional amendments. Fighting for an amendment to authorize Congress to protect the environment might, for example, be quite good for a broader liberal agenda.

25 So, the next time you read a progressive trashing of the Rehnquist Court, resist the impulse to applaud the national government as our sole hope and savior. Federalism is what we make of it. Rehnquist and his conservative colleagues have been making the most of it for more than a decade. It's time for progressives to do the same.

Questions for Discussion

1. What does Barron mean when he writes, "There is no such thing as 'federalism.' There are only 'federalisms,' fashioned at specific times for specific reasons, each necessarily reflecting the particular political vision of its authors"? Can you provide an example of a federalist decision that could be considered politically conservative and one that could be considered politically liberal?

2. What is the relationship between federalism and commerce? Why might the federal government have a legitimate role in regulating interstate commerce? Do you think the term *interstate commerce* should apply only to goods shipped over state lines, or should it also apply to ideas transmitted from state to state through the Internet and other forms of mass communication?

3. Can you explain the principle of "sovereign immunity"? What are its advantages and disadvantages?

4. What decisions of the Rehnquist Court does Barron disagree with? At what points in his argument does he demonstrate that he also has respect for the Rehnquist Court?

5. How do you think your state would respond if the federal government declared it would take away grant money if the state did not make a specific change—such as denying federal funds for highway construction unless a change is made in a state motor vehicle law? How dependent is your state on grants from the federal government? Is the federal government supporting your school in any way? If so, would that give it the right to demand a change at your school?

6. Writing before Hurricane Katrina hit Louisiana and Mississippi in the fall of 2005, Barron declared, in paragraph 9, that "the government increasingly risks multimillion-dollar claims by developers" because the court had eased restrictions on beachfront property. Do you think the federal government has the responsibility for rescuing people who have been victims of a natural disaster? If so, would it follow that the federal government should also have some say in how and where land is developed?

7. Can the courts be nonpolitical? To what extent is the judiciary—and the Supreme Court in particular—influenced by principles that are political in nature?

8. How would you balance power among local, state, and federal governments?

9. Barron has clearly written for an audience of fellow progressives. This is established by the way he addresses progressives in the course of his argument and by the nature of the magazine in which he chose to publish it. How were you affected by this writing decision as you read "Reclaiming Federalism"? Did you feel included because you share similar political principles? Did you feel excluded because your politics are different from those of the author? Or are his ethos and logos sufficiently strong to hold your attention regardless of your politics?

DIFFERENCES

NEGOTIATING

In his famous "Letter from a Birmingham Jail," Martin Luther King, Jr. argues on moral grounds that citizens are justified and even obligated to resist their government if that government imposes unjust laws on them. Many people who resisted the military draft during the Vietnam War made the same argument, asserting that their government was forcing them to fight in an unjust war, so they were justified in defying the laws that required them to submit to the military draft. In a sense, arguments about U.S. government actions in response to the terrorist attacks on September 11, 2001, focus on the same basic question of the civic and moral responsibility of citizens. For most Americans these arguments about government power and individual responsibility can seem abstract. But they can become real when the government takes action that directly affects the lives of citizens, as the military draft did during the Vietnam War. Americans who have never faced such a situation might wonder, "What would *I* do?"

In 2003 the possibility that some Americans would have to answer that question arose in the form of a war with Iraq. The United States subsequently found itself in a protracted war. Because of the many demands placed on Armed Services, young men and women might eventually be subject to the military draft. They would, in effect, be asked to sacrifice their own safety and liberty for the sake of their government and other citizens.

What would you do in such a case? In an essay in which you draw on the readings in this chapter (and any other appropriate sources), put forth your position on the question of the government's authority to ask you to sacrifice your life for your country. Under what circumstances do you think the government is justified in compelling young men and women to serve in the military and possibly go to war? When is it acceptable for a government to ask you to sacrifice your health and maybe your life? When is it not acceptable? To what extent are you justified in blatantly disobeying the laws that would require you to serve in the military? On what moral or legal or philosophical grounds would you

do so? And do Americans have any special obligations to serve their country because of its history? In other words, how does your idea of America figure into your answer to these questions?

These are some of the questions you should try to address in your essay. In effect, you are writing a position paper on the military draft in which you make an argument about the extent and the limits of your government's power over you and other citizens.

Alternatively, you may make your argument about the use of national ID cards or other security measures enacted after September 11, 2001.

13

Environment

Cluster 1

HOW CAN WE IMPROVE THE CYBER ENVIRONMENT?

1. Cass Sunstein, "The Daily We: Is the Internet Really a Blessing for Democracy?"

2. Danny O'Brien, "How to Mend a Broken Internet"

3. Andrew K. Pace, "Surviving Chronic E-Mail Fatigue"

4. John Tierney, "Making Them Squirm"

Cluster 2

HOW DO WE DESIGN COMMUNITIES?

1. Stuart Meck, "Getting on the Case"

2. Jane Holtz Kay, "The Lived-In City: A Place in Time"

3. Donella Meadows, "So What Can We Do—Really Do—about Sprawl?"

4. Robert Wilson, "Enough Snickering. Suburbia Is More Complicated and Varied Than We Think"

CON-TEXT
A Beautiful Place Made Ugly

Cluster 3

WHAT IS OUR RELATIONSHIP TO NATURE?

1. Rachel Carson, "The Obligation to Endure"

2. Ronald Bailey, "Silent Spring at 40"

3. Jack Turner, "In Wilderness Is the Preservation of the World"

4. Charles Petit, "Hazy Days in Our Parks"

CON-TEXT
Thoreau's Wildness

How Can We Improve the Cyber Environment?

When people hear references to "the environment" in American English, they usually think of the outdoors. They are especially likely to picture those aspects of the outdoors—such as land, water, air, and wildlife—that have been at the center of debate about how to preserve the environment. These debates are of critical importance, and readings later in this chapter will address them. The focus of this cluster, however, is the environment in which increasing numbers of people live for large parts of their day: the cyber environment, or the world in which they dwell when they are at computers answering e-mail, engaging in online discussion forums, or doing research on the World Wide Web. Indeed, people may spend so much time in cyberspace that they might not notice they are missing an exceptionally beautiful day outside. So what is this cyber environment like? Is it fixed or constantly changing? Is it healthy or at risk and in need of environmental protection? And are people ever tempted to do things in the cyber environment that they would not do in what is sometimes called "real time"? The writers in this cluster address questions such as these. The first talks about how the Internet can lead some people to live in increasingly narrow worlds. The second discusses problems indicating that the Internet needs to be redesigned. The third discusses how e-mail can become an ideal tool for procrastinators, and the fourth takes a humorous approach to how hackers should be punished for spreading viruses and worms. As you read these selections, consider how they reflect or challenge your experience in the cyber environment.

① CASS SUNSTEIN, "The Daily We: Is the Internet Really a Blessing for Democracy?"

Democracy is based on the idea that citizens have the right to decide what is in the public interest. Yet studies regularly show that only about half of all eligible Americans vote in national elections and even fewer in local elections. You might put it this way: citizens have the power to determine what is in their interests as a society, but few exercise that power. Why? One answer might be that people do not have a genuine public forum in which they can debate the issues that affect common interests. That answer might seem surprising in an age characterized by new forms of technology and media that seem to keep people informed and connected "24-7." But Cass Sunstein suggests that despite the power of new media—specifically, the Internet—to inform and connect, people lack a true public sphere in which, as he writes, "a wide range of speakers have access to a diverse public." The Internet has the potential to be part of that public sphere, a commons for ideas, but according to Sunstein, for most Americans it has become a means for accessing only the information that interests them. As a result, it is not a forum for confronting the diversity of views on which a healthy democracy depends. Sunstein's well-documented argument rests on a particular vision of what a democracy should be. As you read, ask yourself whether you share his vision. Ask yourself, too, what role media like the Internet should play in a democracy. Sunstein is the Karl N. Llewellyn Distinguished Service Professor of Jurisprudence for the law school and department of political science of the University of Chicago. He has written widely on civil rights, technology, and social justice. The following essay is a slightly shortened version of an article that appeared in *Boston Review* in 2001.

The Daily We: Is the Internet Really a Blessing for Democracy?

CASS SUNSTEIN

1 Is the Internet a wonderful development for democracy? In many ways it certainly is. As a result of the Internet, people can learn far more than they could before, and they can learn it much faster. If you are interested in issues that bear on public policy—environmental quality, wages over time, motor vehicle safety—you can find what you need to know in a matter of seconds. If you are suspicious of the mass media, and want to discuss issues with like-minded people, you can do that, transcending the limitations of geography in ways that could barely be imagined even a decade ago. And if you want to get information to a wide range of people, you can do that via email and websites; this is another sense in which the Internet is a great boon for democracy.

But in the midst of the celebration, I want to raise a note of caution. I do so by emphasizing one of the most striking powers provided by emerging technologies: the growing power of consumers to "filter" what they see. As a result of the Internet and other technological developments, many people are increasingly engaged in a process of "personalization" that limits their exposure to topics and points of view of their own choosing. They filter in, and they also filter out, with unprecedented powers of precision. Consider just a few examples:

1. **Broadcast.com** has "compiled hundreds of thousands of programs so you can find the one that suits your fancy. . . . For example, if you want to see all the latest fashions from France 24 hours of the day you can get them. If you're from Baltimore living in Dallas and you want to listen to WBAL, your hometown station, you can hear it."

2. **Sonicnet.com** allows you to create your own musical universe, consisting of what it calls "Me Music." Me Music is "A place where you can listen to the music you love on the radio station YOU create. . . . A place where you can watch videos of your favorite artists and new artists."

3. **Zatso.net** allows users to produce "a personal newscast." Its intention is to create a place "where you decide what's news." Your task is to tell "what TV news stories you're interested in," and **Zatso.net** turns that information into a specifically designed newscast. From the main "This is the News I Want" menu, you can choose stories with particular words and phrases, or you can select topics, such as sports, weather, crime, health, government/politics, and much more.

4. Info Xtra offers "news and entertainment that's important to you," and it allows you to find this "without hunting through newspapers, radio and websites." Personalized news, local

weather, and "even your daily horoscope or winning lottery number" will be delivered to you once you specify what you want and when you want it.

5. TiVo, a television recording system, is designed, in the words of its website, to give "you the ultimate control over your TV viewing." It does this by putting "you at the center of your own TV network, so you'll always have access to whatever you want, whenever you want." TiVo "will automatically find and digitally record your favorite programs every time they air" and will help you create "your personal TV line-up." It will also learn your tastes, so that it can "suggest other shows that you may want to record and watch based on your preferences."

6. Intertainer, Inc. provides "home entertainment services on demand," including television, music, movies, and shopping. Intertainer is intended for people who want "total control" and "personalized experiences." It is "a new way to get whatever movies, music, and television you want anytime you want on your PC or TV."

7. George Bell, the chief executive officer of the search engine Excite, exclaims, "We are looking for ways to be able to lift chunks of content off other areas of our service and paste them onto your personal page so you can constantly refresh and update that 'newspaper of me.' About 43 percent of our entire user data base has personalized their experience on Excite."

Of course, these developments make life much more convenient and in some ways much better: we all seek to reduce our exposure to uninvited noise. But from the standpoint of democracy, filtering is a mixed blessing. An understanding of the mix will permit us to obtain a better sense of what makes for a well-functioning system of free expression. In a heterogeneous society, such a system requires something other than free, or publicly unrestricted, individual choices. On the contrary, it imposes two distinctive requirements. First, people should be exposed to materials that they would not have chosen in advance. *Unanticipated encounters,* involving topics and points of view that people have not sought out and perhaps find irritating, are central to democracy and even to freedom itself. Second, many or most citizens should have a range of *common experiences.* Without shared experiences, a heterogeneous society will have a more difficult time addressing social problems and understanding one another.

Individual Design

Consider a thought experiment—an apparently utopian dream, that of complete individuation, in which consumers can entirely personalize (or "customize") their communications universe.

5   Imagine, that is, a system of communications in which each person has unlimited power of individual design. If some people want to watch news all the time, they would be entirely free to do exactly that. If they dislike news, and want to watch football in the morning and situation comedies at night, that would be fine too. If people care only about America, and want to avoid international issues entirely, that would be very simple; so too if they care only about New York or Chicago or California. If people want to restrict themselves to certain points of view, by limiting themselves to conservatives, moderates, liberals, vegetarians, or Nazis, that would be entirely feasible with a simple point-and-click. If people want to isolate themselves, and speak only with like-minded others, that is feasible too.

At least as a matter of technological feasibility, our communications market is moving rapidly toward this apparently utopian picture. A number of newspapers' websites allow readers to create filtered versions, containing exactly what they want, and no more. If you are

interested in getting help with the design of an entirely individual paper, you can consult a number of sites, including **Individual.com** and **Crayon.net**. To be sure, the Internet greatly increases people's ability to expand their horizons, as millions of people are now doing; but many people are using it to produce narrowness, not breadth. Thus MIT professor Nicholas Negroponte refers to the emergence of the "Daily Me"—a communications package that is personally designed, with components fully chosen in advance.

Of course, this is not entirely different from what has come before. People who read newspapers do not read the same newspaper; some people do not read any newspaper at all. People make choices among magazines based on their tastes and their points of view. But in the emerging situation, there is a difference of degree if not of kind. What *is* different is a dramatic increase in individual control over content, and a corresponding decrease in the power of general interest intermediaries, including newspapers, magazines, and broadcasters. For all their problems, and their unmistakable limitations and biases, these intermediaries have performed some important democratic functions.

People who rely on such intermediaries have a range of chance encounters, involving shared experience with diverse others and exposure to material that they did not specifically choose. You might, for example, read the city newspaper and in the process come across a range of stories that you would not

CONTEXT

The First Amendment to the U.S. Constitution reads, "Congress shall make no law respecting an establishment of religion, or prohibit the free exercise thereof; or abridging the freedom of speech, or of the press; or of the right of the people peacefully to assemble, and to petition the government for a redress of grievances."

have selected if you had the power to control what you see. Your eyes may come across a story about Germany, or crime in Los Angeles, or innovative business practices in Tokyo, and you may read those stories although you would hardly have placed them in your "Daily Me." You might watch a particular television channel—perhaps you prefer Channel 4—and when your favorite program ends, you might see the beginning of another show, one that you would not have chosen in advance. Reading *Time* magazine, you might come across a discussion of endangered species in Madagascar, and this discussion might interest you, even affect your behavior, although you would not have sought it out in the first instance. A system in which you lack control over the particular content that you see has a great deal in common with a public street, where you might encounter not only friends, but a heterogeneous variety of people engaged in a wide array of activities (including, perhaps, political protests and begging).

In fact, a risk with a system of perfect individual control is that it can reduce the importance of the "public sphere" and of common spaces in general. One of the important features of such spaces is that they tend to ensure that people will encounter materials on important issues, whether or not they have specifically chosen the encounter. When people see materials that they have not chosen, their interests and their views might change as a result. At the very least, they will know a bit more about what their fellow citizens are thinking. As it happens, this point is closely connected with an important, and somewhat exotic, constitutional principle.

Public (and Private) Forums

10 In the popular understanding, the free speech principle forbids government from "censoring" speech of which it disapproves. In the standard cases, the government attempts to impose penalties, whether civil or criminal, on political dissent, and on speech that it considers dangerous, libelous, or sexually explicit.

The question is whether the government has a legitimate and sufficiently weighty basis for restricting the speech that it seeks to control.

But a central part of free speech law, with large implications for thinking about the Internet, takes a quite different form. The Supreme Court has also held that streets and parks must be kept open to the public for expressive activity.[1] Governments are obliged to allow speech to occur freely on public streets and in public parks—even if many citizens would prefer to have peace and quiet, and even if it seems irritating to come across protesters and dissidents whom one would like to avoid. To be sure, the government is allowed to impose restrictions on the "time, place, and manner" of speech in public places. No one has a right to use fireworks and loudspeakers on the public streets at midnight. But time, place, and manner restrictions must be both reasonable and limited, and government is essentially obliged to allow speakers, whatever their views, to use public property to convey messages of their choosing.

The public forum doctrine serves three important functions.[2] First, it ensures that speakers can have access to a wide array of people. If you want to claim that taxes are too high, or that police brutality against African Americans is common, you can press this argument on many people who might otherwise fail to hear the message. Those who use the streets and parks are likely to learn something about your argument; they might also learn the nature and intensity of views held by one of their fellow citizens. Perhaps their views will be changed; perhaps they will become curious, enough to investigate the question on their own.

Second, the public forum doctrine allows speakers not only to have general access to heterogeneous people, but also to specific people, and specific institutions, with whom they have a complaint. Suppose, for example, that you believe that the state legislature has behaved irresponsibly with respect to crime or health care for children. The public forum ensures that you can make your views heard by legislators simply by protesting in front of the state legislature building.

Third, the public forum doctrine increases the likelihood that people generally will be exposed to a wide variety of people and views. When you go to work, or visit a park, it is possible that you will have a range of unexpected encounters, however fleeting or seemingly inconsequential. You cannot easily wall yourself off from contentions or conditions that you would not have sought out in advance, or that you would have chosen to avoid if you could. Here, too, the public forum doctrine tends to ensure a range of experiences that are widely shared—streets and parks are public property—and also a set of exposures to diverse circumstances. In a pluralistic democracy, an important shared experience is in fact the very experience of society's diversity. These exposures help promote understanding and perhaps, in that sense, freedom. And all of these points are closely connected to democratic ideals.

15 Of course, there is a limit to how much can be done on streets and in parks. Even in the largest cities, streets and parks are insistently *local.* But many of the social functions of streets and parks as public forums are performed by other institutions, too. In fact, society's general interest intermediaries—newspapers, magazines, television broadcasters—can be understood as public forums of an especially important sort, perhaps above all because they expose people to new, unanticipated topics and points of view.

When you read a city newspaper or a national magazine, your eyes will come across a number of articles that you might not have selected in advance, and if you are like most people, you will read some of those articles. Perhaps you did not know that you might have an interest in minimum wage legislation, or Somalia, or the latest developments in the Middle East. But a story might catch your attention. And what is true for topics of interest is also true for points of view. You might think that you have nothing to learn from someone whose view you abhor; but once you come across the editorial pages, you might read what they have to say, and you might benefit from the experience. Perhaps you will be persuaded on one point or another. At the same time, the front-page headline or the cover story in *Newsweek* is likely to have a high degree of salience for a wide range of people.

Television broadcasters have similar functions. Most important in this regard is what has become an institution: the evening news. If you tune into the evening news, you will learn about a number of topics that you would not have chosen in advance. Because of their speech and immediacy, television broadcasts perform these public forum-type functions more than general interest intermediaries in the print media. The "lead story" on the networks is likely to have a great deal of public salience; it helps to define central issues and creates a kind of shared focus of attention for millions of people. And what happens after the lead story—dealing with a menu of topics both domestically and internationally—creates something like a speakers' corner beyond anything imagined in Hyde Park. As a result, people's interest is sometimes piqued, and they might well become curious and follow up, perhaps changing their perspective in the process.

None of these claims depends on a judgment that general interest intermediaries are unbiased, or always do an excellent job, or deserve a monopoly over the world of communications. The Internet is a boon partly because it breaks that monopoly. So too for the proliferation of television and radio shows, and even channels, that have some specialized identity. (Consider the rise of Fox News, which appeals to a more conservative audience.) All that I am claiming is that general interest intermediaries expose people to a wide range of topics and views and at the same time provide shared experiences for a heterogeneous public. Indeed, intermediaries of this sort have large advantages over streets and parks precisely because they tend to be national, even international.

ten *least* popular programs for whites. With respect to race, similar divisions can be found on the Internet. Not surprisingly, many people tend to choose like-minded sites and like-minded discussion groups. Many of those with committed views on a topic—gun control, abortion, affirmative action—speak mostly with each other. It is exceedingly rare for a site with an identifiable point of view to provide links to sites with opposing views; but it is very common for such a site to provide links to like-minded sites.

With a dramatic increase in options, and a greater power to customize, comes an increase in the range of actual choices. Those choices are likely, in many cases, to mean that people will try to find material that makes them feel comfortable, or that is created by and for people like themselves. This is what the Daily Me is all about. Of course, many people seek out new topics and ideas. And to the extent that people do, the increase in options is hardly bad on balance; it will, among other things, increase variety, the aggregate amount of information, and the entertainment value of actual choices. But there are serious risks as well. If diverse groups are seeing and hearing different points of view, or focusing on different topics, mutual understanding might be difficult, and it might be hard for people to solve problems that society faces together. If millions of people are mostly listening to Rush Limbaugh* and others are listening to Fox News, problems will arise if millions of other people are mostly or only listening to people and stations with an altogether different point of view.

We can sharpen our understanding of this problem if we attend to the phenomenon of *group polarization*. The idea is that after deliberating with one another, people are likely to move toward a more extreme point in the direction to which they were previously inclined, as indicated by the median of their predeliberation judgments. With respect to the Internet, the implication is that groups of people, especially if they are like-minded, will end up think-

Typically they expose people to questions and problems in other areas, even other countries.

Specialization and Fragmentation
In a system with public forums and general interest intermediaries, people will frequently come across materials that they would not have chosen in advance—and in a diverse society, this provides something like a common framework for social experience. A fragmented communications market will change things significantly.

20 Consider some simple facts. If you take the ten most highly rated television programs for whites, and then take the ten most highly rated programs for African Americans, you will find little overlap between them. Indeed, more than half of the ten most highly rated programs for African Americans rank among the

ing the same thing that they thought before— but in more extreme form.

Consider some examples of this basic phenomenon, which has been found in over a dozen nations.[3] (a) After discussion, citizens of France become more critical of the United States and its intentions with respect to economic aid. (b) After discussion, whites predisposed to show racial prejudice offer more negative responses to questions about whether white racism is responsible for conditions faced by African Americans in American cities. (c) After discussion, whites predisposed not to show racial prejudice offer more positive responses to the same question. (d) A group of moderately profeminist women will become more strongly profeminist after discussion. It follows that, for example, after discussion with one another, those inclined to think that President Clinton was a crook will be quite convinced of this point; that those inclined to favor more aggressive affirmative action programs will become more extreme on the issue if they talk among one another; that those who believe that tax rates are too high will, after talking together, come to think that large, immediate tax reductions are an extremely good idea.

The phenomenon of group polarization has conspicuous importance to the current communications market, where groups with distinctive identities increasingly engage in within-group discussion. If the public is balkanized,* and if different groups design their own preferred communications packages, the consequence will be further balkanization, as group members move one another toward more extreme points in line with their initial tendencies. At the same time, different deliberating groups, each consisting of like-minded people, will be driven increasingly far apart, simply because most of their discussions are with one another. . . .

25 Group polarization is a human regularity, but social context can decrease, increase, or even eliminate it. For present purposes, the most important point is that group polarization

will significantly increase if people think of themselves, antecedently or otherwise, as part of a group having a shared identity and a degree of solidarity. If, for example, a group of people in an Internet discussion group think of themselves as opponents of high taxes, or advocates of animal rights, their discussions are likely to move toward extreme positions. As this happens to many different groups, polarization is both more likely and more extreme. Hence significant movements should be expected for those who listen to a radio show known to be conservative, or a television program dedicated to traditional religious values or to exposing white racism.

This should not be surprising. If ordinary findings of group polarization are a product of limited argument pools and social influences, it stands to reason that when group members think of one another as similar along a salient dimension, or if some external factor (politics, geography, race, sex) unites them, group polarization will be heightened.

Group polarization is occurring every day on the Internet. Indeed, it is clear that the Internet is serving, for many, as a breeding ground for extremism, precisely because likeminded people are deliberating with one another, without hearing contrary views. Hate groups are the most obvious example. Consider one extremist group, the so-called Unorganized Militia, the armed wing of the Patriot movement, "which believes that the federal government is becoming increasingly dictatorial with its regulatory power over taxes, guns and land use." A crucial factor behind the growth of the Unorganized Militia "has been the use of computer networks," allowing members "to make contact quickly and easily with like-minded individuals to trade information, discuss current conspiracy theories, and organize events."[4] The Unorganized Militia has a large number of websites, and those sites frequently offer links to related sites. It is clear that websites are being used to recruit new members and to allow like-minded people to speak with one another and to reinforce or

*Balkanization is a term that is used to describe small-scale independence movements that divide countries into several nations. A clear example is Yugoslavia, located in the Balkans, which broke into the conflict-ridden states of Bosnia, Kosovo, Serbia, and Montenegro.

MILITIA GROUPS

Officials estimate that there are more than 400 militia groups active in the United States. Some are open, with their own websites; others are underground. Most are dedicated to the defense of individual liberty from what they perceive as the threat of an oppressive federal government. Some militia groups have been associated with terrorist attacks within the United States. Militia members, many of whom are on the extreme right, tend to see themselves as patriots. The FBI sees them as a threat to national security.

strengthen existing convictions. It is also clear that the Internet is playing a crucial role in permitting people who would otherwise feel isolated and move on to something else to band together and spread rumors, many of them paranoid and hateful. . . .

Of course we cannot say, from the mere fact of polarization, that there has been a movement in the *wrong* direction. Perhaps the more extreme tendency is better; indeed, group polarization is likely to have fueled many movements of great value, including the movement for civil rights, the antislavery movement, the movement for sex equality. All of these movements were extreme in their time, and within-group discussion bred greater extremism; but extremism need not be a word of opprobrium. If greater communications choices produce greater extremism, society may, in many cases, be better off as a result.

But when group discussion tends to lead people to more strongly held versions of the same view with which they began, and if social influences and limited argument pools are responsible, there is legitimate reason for concern. Consider discussions among hate groups on the Internet and elsewhere. If the underlying views are unreasonable, it makes sense to fear that these discussions may fuel increasing hatred and a socially corrosive form of extremism. This does not mean that the discussions can or should be regulated. But it does raise questions about the idea that "more speech" is necessarily an adequate remedy—especially if people are increasingly able to wall themselves off from competing views.

30 The basic issue here is whether something like a "public sphere," with a wide range of voices, might not have significant advantages over a system in which isolated consumer choices produce a highly fragmented speech market. The most reasonable conclusion is that it is extremely important to ensure that people are exposed to views other than those with which they currently agree, that doing so protects against the harmful effects of group polarization on individual thinking and on social cohesion. This does not mean that the government should jail or fine people who refuse to listen to others. Nor is what I have said inconsistent with approval of deliberating "enclaves," on the Internet or elsewhere, designed to ensure that positions that would otherwise be silenced or squelched have a chance to develop. Readers will be able to think of their own preferred illustrations. Consider, perhaps, the views of people with disabilities. The great benefit of such enclaves is that positions may emerge that otherwise would not and that deserve to play a large role in the heterogeneous public. Properly understood, the case of "enclaves," or more simply discussion groups of like-minded people, is that they will improve social deliberation, democratic and otherwise. For these improvements to occur, members must not insulate themselves from competing positions, or at least any such attempts at insulation must not be a prolonged affair.

Consider in this light the ideal of "consumer sovereignty," which underlies much of contemporary enthusiasm for the Internet. Consumer sovereignty means that people can choose to purchase, or to obtain, whatever they want. For many purposes this is a worthy ideal. But the adverse effects of group polarization show that, with respect to communications, consumer sovereignty is likely to produce serious problems for individuals and society at large—and these problems will occur by a kind of iron logic of social interactions. . . .

I hope that I have shown enough to demonstrate that for citizens of a heterogeneous democracy, a fragmented communications market creates considerable dangers. There are dangers for each of us as individuals; constant exposure to one set of views is likely to lead to errors and confusions, or to unthinking conformity (emphasized by John Stuart Mill). And to the extent that the process makes people less able to work cooperatively on shared problems, by turning collections of people into non-communicating confessional groups, there are dangers for society as a whole.

Common Experiences

In a heterogeneous society, it is extremely important for diverse people to have a set of common experiences.[5] Many of our practices reflect a judgment to this effect. National holidays, for example, help constitute a nation, by encouraging citizens to think, all at once, about events of shared importance. And they do much more than this. They enable people, in all their diversity, to have certain memories and attitudes in common. At least this is true in nations where national holidays have a vivid and concrete meaning. In the United States, many national holidays have become mere days-off-from-work, and the precipitating occasion—President's Day, Memorial Day, Labor Day—has come to be nearly invisible. This is a serious loss. With the possible exception of the Fourth of July, Martin Luther King Day is probably the closest thing to a genuinely substantive national holiday, largely because that celebration involves something that can be treated as concrete and meaningful—in other words, it is *about* something.

Communications and the media are, of course, exceptionally important here. Sometimes millions of people follow the presidential election, or the Super Bowl, or the coronation of a new monarch; many of them do so because of the simultaneous actions of others. The point very much bears on the historic role of both public forums and general interest intermediaries. Public parks are places where diverse people can congregate and see one another. General interest intermediaries, if they are operating properly, give a simultaneous sense of problems and tasks.

35 Why are these shared experiences so desirable? There are three principal reasons:

1. Simple enjoyment is probably the least of it, but it is far from irrelevant. People like many experiences more simply because they are being shared. Consider a popular movie, the Super Bowl, or a presidential debate. For many of us, these are goods that are worth less, and possibly worthless, if many others are not enjoying or purchasing them too. Hence a presidential debate may be worthy of individual attention, for many people, simply because so many other people consider it worthy of individual attention.

2. Sometimes shared experiences ease social interactions, permitting people to speak with one another, and to congregate around a common issue, task, or concern, whether or not they have much in common with one another. In this sense they provide a form of social glue. They help make it possible for diverse people to believe that they live in the same culture. Indeed they help constitute that shared culture, simply by creating common memories and experiences, and a sense of common tasks.

3. A fortunate consequence of shared experiences—many of them produced by the media—is that people who would otherwise see one another as unfamiliar can come to regard one another as fellow citizens, with shared hopes, goals, and concerns. This is a subjective good for those directly involved. But it can be objectively good as well, especially if it leads to cooperative projects of various kinds. When people learn about a disaster faced by fellow citizens, for example, they may respond with financial and other help. The point applies internationally as well as domestically; massive relief efforts are

often made possible by virtue of the fact that millions of people learn, all at once, about the relevant need.

How does this bear on the Internet? An increasingly fragmented communications universe will reduce the level of shared experiences having salience to a diverse group of Americans. This is a simple matter of numbers. When there were three television networks, much of what appeared would have the quality of a genuinely common experience. The lead story on the evening news, for example, would provide a common reference point for many millions of people. To the extent that choices proliferate, it is inevitable that diverse individuals, and diverse groups, will have fewer shared experiences and fewer common reference points. It is possible, for example, that some events that are highly salient to some people will barely register on others' viewscreens. And it is possible that some views and perspectives that seem obvious for many people will, for others, seem barely intelligible.

This is hardly a suggestion that everyone should be required to watch the same thing. A degree of plurality, with respect to both topics and points of view, is highly desirable. Moreover, talk about "requirements" misses the point. My only claim is that a common set of frameworks and experiences is valuable for a heterogeneous society, and that a system with limitless options, making for diverse choices, could compromise the underlying values.

Changing Filters

My goal here has been to understand what makes for a well-functioning system of free expression, and to show how consumer sovereignty, in a world of limitless options, could undermine that system. The point is that a well-functioning system includes a kind of public sphere, one that fosters common experiences, in which people hear messages that challenge their prior convictions, and in which citizens can present their views to a broad audience. I do not intend to offer a comprehensive set of policy reforms or any kind of

blueprint for the future. In fact, this may be one domain in which a problem exists for which there is no useful cure: the genie might simply be out of the bottle. But it will be useful to offer a few ideas, if only by way of introduction to questions that are likely to engage public attention in coming years.

In thinking about reforms, it is important to have a sense of the problems we aim to address, and some possible ways of addressing them. If the discussion thus far is correct, there are three fundamental concerns from the democratic point of view. These include:

(a) the need to promote exposure to materials, topics, and positions that people would not have chosen in advance, or at least enough exposure to produce a degree of understanding and curiosity;

(b) the value of a range of common experiences;

(c) the need for exposure to substantive questions of policy and principle, combined with a range of positions on such questions.

Of course it would be ideal if citizens were demanding, and private information providers were creating, a range of initiatives designed to alleviate the underlying concerns. Perhaps they will; there is some evidence to this effect. New technology can expose people to diverse points of view and creates opportunities for shared experiences. People may, through private choices, take advantage of these possibilities. But, to the extent that they fail to do so, it is worthwhile to consider private and public initiatives designed to pick up the slack.

40 Drawing on recent developments in regulation generally, we can see the potential appeal of five simple alternatives. Of course, different proposals would work better for some communications outlets than others. I will speak here of both private and public responses, but the former should be favored: they are less intrusive, and in general they are likely to be more effective as well.

Disclosure: Producers of communications might disclose important information on their own, about the extent to which they are promoting democratic goals. To the extent that they do not, they might be subject to disclosure requirements (though not to regulation). In the environmental area, this strategy has produced excellent results. The mere fact that polluters have been asked to disclose toxic releases has produced voluntary, low-cost reductions. Apparently fearful of public opprobrium, companies have been spurred to reduce toxic emissions on their own. The same strategy has been used in the context of both movies and television, with ratings systems designed partly to increase parental control over what children see. On the Internet, many sites disclose that their site is inappropriate for children. . . .

Self-Regulation: Producers of communications might engage in *voluntary self-regulation.* Some of the difficulties in the current speech market stem from relentless competition for viewers and listeners, competition that leads to a situation that many broadcast journalists abhor about their profession, and from which society does not benefit. The competition might be reduced via a "code" of appropriate conduct, agreed upon by various companies, and encouraged but not imposed by government. In fact, the National Association of Broadcasters maintained such a code for several decades, and there is growing interest in voluntary self-regulation for both television and the Internet. The case for this approach is that it avoids government regulation while at the same time reducing some of the harmful effects of market pressures. Any such code could, for example, call for an opportunity for opposing views to speak, or for avoiding unnecessary sensationalism, or for offering arguments rather than quick soundbites whenever feasible. On television, as distinct from the Internet, the idea seems quite feasible. But perhaps Internet sites could also enter into informal, voluntary arrangements, agreeing to create links, an idea to which I will shortly turn.

Subsidy: The government might *subsidize speech,* as, for example, through publicly subsi-

dized programming or publicly subsidized websites. This is, of course, the idea that motivates the Public Broadcasting System. But it is reasonable to ask whether the PBS model is not outmoded. Other approaches, similarly designed to promote educational, cultural, and democratic goals, might well be ventured. Perhaps government could subsidize a "**Public.net**" designed to promote debate on public issues among diverse citizens—and to create a right of access to speakers of various sorts.[6]

Links: Websites might use links and hyperlinks to ensure that viewers learn about sites containing opposing views. A liberal magazine's website might, for example, provide a link to a conservative magazine's website, and the conservative magazine might do the same. The idea would be to decrease the likelihood that people will simply hear echoes of their own voices. Of course many people would not click on the icons of sites whose views seem objectionable; but some people would, and in that sense the system would not operate so differently from general interest intermediaries and public forums. Here, too, the ideal situation would be voluntary action. But if this proves impossible, it is worth considering both subsidies and regulatory alternatives.

45 *Public Sidewalk:*

If the problem consists in the failure to attend to public issues, the most popular websites in any given period might offer links and hyperlinks, designed to ensure more exposure to substantive questions. Under such a system, viewers of especially popular sites would see an icon for sites that deal with substantive issues in a serious way. It is well established that whenever there is a link to a particular webpage

PBS

The Corporation for Public Broadcasting was created by Congress in 1967. According to its mission statement, "The fundamental purpose of public telecommunications is to provide programs and services which inform, enlighten and enrich the public. While these programs and services are provided to enhance the knowledge, and citizenship of all Americans, the Corporation has particular responsibility to encourage the development of programming that involves creative risks and that addresses the needs of unserved or underserved audiences, particularly children and minorities." Its best-known show for children is *Sesame Street.* Other popular programs have included *Nova, Masterpiece Theater,* and the *News Hour with Jim Lehrer.*

from a major site, such as MSNBC, the traffic is huge. Nothing here imposes any requirements on viewers. People would not be required to click on links and hyperlinks. But it is reasonable to expect that many viewers would do so, if only to satisfy their curiosity. The result would be to create a kind of Internet "sidewalk" that promotes some of the purposes of the public forum doctrine. Ideally, those who create websites might move in this direction on their own. To those who believe that this step would do no good, it is worth recalling that advertisers are willing to spend a great deal of money to obtain brief access to people's eyeballs. This strategy might be used to create something like a public sphere as well.

These are brief thoughts on some complex subjects. My goal has not been to evaluate any proposal in detail, but to give a flavor of some possibilities for those concerned to promote democratic goals in a dramatically changed media environment.[7] The basic question is whether it might be possible to create spaces that have some of the functions of public forums and general interest intermediaries in the age of the Internet. It seems clear that government's power to regulate effectively is diminished as the number of options expands. I am not sure that any response would be worthwhile, all things considered. But I am sure that if new technologies diminish the number of common spaces, and reduce, for many, the number of unanticipated, unchosen exposures, something important will have been lost. The most important point is to have a sense of what a well-functioning democratic order requires.

Beyond Anticensorship

My principal claim here has been that a well-functioning democracy depends on far more than restraints on official censorship of controversial ideas and opinions. It also depends on some kind of public sphere, in which a wide range of speakers have access to a diverse public—and also to particular institutions, and practices, against which they seek to launch objections.

Emerging technologies, including the Internet, are hardly an enemy here. They hold out far more promise than risk, especially because they allow people to widen their horizons. But to the extent that they weaken the power of general interest intermediaries and increase people's ability to wall themselves off from topics and opinions that they would prefer to avoid, they create serious dangers. And if we believe that a system of free expression calls for unrestricted choices by individual consumers, we will not even understand the dangers as such. Whether such dangers will materialize will ultimately depend on the aspirations, for freedom and democracy alike, by whose light we evaluate our practices. What I have sought to establish here is that in a free republic, citizens aspire to a system that provides a wide range of experiences—with people, topics, and ideas—that would not have been selected in advance.

Notes

1. *Hague v. CIO,* 307 US 496 (1939).
2. I draw here on the excellent treatment in Noah D. Zatz, "Sidewalks in Cyberspace: Making Space for Public Forums in the Electronic Environment," *Harvard Journal of Law and Technology* 12 (1998): 149.
3. For a general discussion, see Cass R. Sunstein, "Deliberative Trouble? Why Groups Go To Extremes," *Yale Law Journal* (2000).
4. See Matthew Zook, "The Unorganized Militia Network: Conspiracies, Computers, and Community," *Berkeley Planning Journal* 11 (1996), available at **http://socrates.berkeley.edu/zook/ pubs/Militia_paper.html** .
5. I draw here on Cass R. Sunstein and Edna Ullmann-Margalit, "Solidarity Goods," *Journal of Political Philosophy* (forthcoming in 2001).
6. See Andrew Shapiro, *The Control Revolution* (New York: Basic Books, 1999).
7. See Sunstein, **Republic.com** , for more detail.

Questions for Discussion

1. Early in his essay, Sunstein raises a warning about what he calls the "personalization" of the Internet. What does he mean by that term? Why is that idea of personalizing the Internet important to his main argument? Is his concern valid, in your view? Why or why not? To what extent do you think you "personalize" the Internet?

2. Notice that Sunstein opens his essay with a summary of the benefits of the Internet. How does this opening contribute to his main argument? What advantages and disadvantages do you see to this approach to opening his essay?

3. In paragraphs 24–29, Sunstein discussed the dangers of "group polarization." What does Sunstein mean by this term? In what ways is it important to his main argument? Have you experienced a situation in which group discussion led to reinforcement—or change—of a belief you already had? How might that experience influence your reaction to Sunstein's argument?

4. Sunstein offers five possible solutions to the problems he sees with current trends in media. How effective do you think these measures would be in addressing Sunstein's concerns? What does he achieve by presenting these measures as possibilities rather than certainties?

5. Although Sunstein describes this argument as "brief thoughts on some complex subjects," it nevertheless runs for many pages. Why is this argument so long? What strategies does Sunstein use to help readers make their way through it? Do you find those strategies effective? Explain.

6. At the end of his argument, Sunstein writes, "My principal claim here has been that a well-functioning democracy depends on far more than restraints on official censorship of controversial ideas and opinions. It also depends on some kind of public sphere, in which a wide range of speakers have access to a diverse public—and also to particular institutions, and practices, against which they seek to launch objections." To what extent does the argument as a whole depend on readers accepting this principle as a premise?

7. Sunstein's essay might be described as an argument based on inductive reasoning. (See pages 86–88 for a discussion of arguments based on inductive reasoning.) How effective do you think his essay is as such an argument? Does he offer sufficient evidence to lead you to his conclusions about the Internet as a public sphere in a democracy? Explain, citing specific passages from his essay in your answer.

② DANNY O'BRIEN, "How to Mend a Broken Internet"

Upsetting though it may be when a computer crashes or a system goes down, you can usually reassure yourself that the problem will be resolved within a day or two. But what if the Internet broke down? Because the Internet was designed thirty years ago and because it carries so much more traffic that its designers anticipated, there seems reason to question how long it can continue to fulfill its purpose. As Danny O'Brien argues in "How to Mend a Broken Internet," technology already exists for increasing the power and efficiency of the Internet, but change is hard to implement because so many people are using technology that is out of date. As you read the following selection, consider how serious the problem is and whether it would be better to redesign the Internet now or wait until the problem becomes more evident to the average person. This piece was first published in the November 2004 issue of *New Scientist*—a weekly magazine that, since 1956, has been reporting new developments in science and technology. With seven editorial offices around the world, it attracts an international audience.

How to Mend a Broken Internet

DANNY O'BRIEN

CONTEXT

What people have come to call the Internet can be traced back to research in the early 1960s at the Massachusetts Institute of Technology (MIT) and subsequently at the University of California at Los Angeles (UCLA) and the Rand Corporation, among other institutions. Much of this research was funded by the federal government, especially the Department of Defense, the Department of Energy, and the National Science Foundation—making the Internet a communications vehicle developed at the expense of U.S. taxpayers, who may therefore have a legitimate say in the future uses to which it is put. The key components for the Internet were in place by 1972, but it was only when personal computers became popular in the 1980s that the Internet began to become widely used. The technology for using the Internet, and the uses to which it can be put, continue to evolve.

1 The smart conference suite at Stanford University in California was packed with the cream of the computing community. They were there, earlier this year, to hear David Cheriton explain his vision of the future of the internet. If Cheriton is to be believed, the wired world we now know and rely on is on the brink of collapse. The internet, he insists, is broken.

How can this be? Emails still get through. The web seems to work well enough. Prophesies of doom might seem alarmist, even laughable. But Cheriton, a professor of computing at

Stanford, has played a leading role in computer networking for the best part of 20 years, and the networking community takes him seriously. Cheriton reckons that the internet is dangerously insecure, and it's a verdict that few internet experts would disagree with. What held the audience's rapt attention, however, was Cheriton's radical solution to the problem.

"Look at the way things are going," he says. From phone networks to banking, power distribution and air-traffic control systems, just about every critical communication network will soon rely on the internet. And that makes us all vulnerable. "Unless we do something soon, the internet will become the largest target of attack on the planet in terms of doing economic damage."

Hints of what may be in store are already emerging. Earlier this year, criminal gangs held several gambling websites to ransom, threatening to knock their servers off the web by flooding them with bogus traffic. Denial of service attacks like these now happen almost every week, and the internet's security monitoring organisation, CERT, has had almost 320,000 reports of malicious attacks since it began gathering statistics in 1988. Though police forces across the globe have set up dedicated units to tackle cybercrime, the pace is quickening, and more than a third of these attacks took place in 2003. . . .

5 The source of the problem is there for all to see. The internet was created at a time when no one dreamed its users would be anything other than benevolent. So it was designed to deliver its packets of digital data in the most straightforward way possible, without any thought of defeating spam, or defending its servers from malicious hackers or viruses.

Even the Internet Engineering Task Force (IETF), the internet's official guardian, acknowledges there are problems. But what should be done about it is still hotly disputed. Karl Auerbach, a computer engineer who has been involved with the internet since 1974, explains the caution: "There's a lot about the current internet we don't understand," he says. "You can bring down a net by trying to repair it."

On top of the net's poor security, there are other concerns that many internet experts consider equally pressing. Most high-tech manufacturers foresee a future in which everything from your car to your fridge will be connected to the net. The problem is how to give them all a unique address that will identify them on the net. Like an old telephone network in which the number of subscribers has outgrown the pool of available phone numbers, the existing design of the internet has too few addresses for all these devices.

The IETF's solution is a rewrite of the internet protocol (IP) on which the net is founded. Called IPv6, the rewrite was proposed as long ago as 1992 and it undeniably provides more numbers, or "IP addresses": up from the 4.5 billion available today to a staggering thousand billion billion billion billion. With IPv6, the IETF also took the opportunity to

defend the net against denial of service attacks by adding new security features such as encrypted signatures to authenticate packets of information and further encryption to prevent the packets being tampered with. Since then, IPv6 has been the net's big chance to improve itself.

But there's one big problem with IPv6. Even now, 12 years after it was introduced, most people are still not using it. And that highlights a problem with re-engineering the net: the pace of change is dictated by the most conservative users. Even when the people nominally in charge have agreed on a change, they have to persuade everyone else to switch. Upgrading to IPv6 means installing it on every part of the net, and while most modern computers support the new protocol, just one old machine on a route between two computers—be it a desktop PC, or one of the computers along the way that steers packets of data to their destination—will force the network to default to the old system.

10 To the dismay of IETF engineers, internet users are turning to an alternative—and many would say clunky—solution to their problems. Network Address Translation (NAT) is the most common, cheap fix to the shortage of IP numbers. It is a way of hiding several computers behind a single IP address. Think of it as like a telephone operator at a company with several phones but only one line to the outside world. Just as the operator switches calls to any number of internet extensions, so the NAT machine diverts packets from the internet to the computer that requested them. All traffic through these computers goes to and from the net via a single IP address, but because the internet uses packets rather than a continuous uninterrupted stream like a phone call, the NAT machine can juggle the data for hundreds of machines. It's a simple solution, with the advantage that no global upgrade is required. If you are using a local area network of broadband service to connect to the net, there's a good chance there's NAT between you and the global internet.

*A mountainous region in southeastern Europe, the Balkans were long dominated by two imperial powers: the Ottoman empire, ruled from the city once called Constantinople and now called Istanbul, and the Austro-Hungarian empire, ruled from Vienna. It has long been known for political instability. The First World War began after the heir to the Austrian throne was assassinated in Sarajevo, a city in what is now Serbia. After that war, several independent states emerged; some of these states, such as Albania, Bulgaria, and Yugoslavia, experienced temporary stability—at great cost—during the cold war when the Soviet Union dominated eastern Europe. After the collapse of the Soviet Union, nations such as Yugoslavia broke apart—so the Balkans now include smaller states such as Serbia, Croatia, and Macedonia. Violence continues to be part of life in the Balkans, and a former president of Serbia is now on trial for genocide practiced in the 1990s. To *balkanize* has thus come to mean "to break into smaller and less stable units."

†Found in Southeast Asia, white elephants were considered a source of sacred power that belonged to royalty. Kings in Burma and Siam collected white elephants, decorated them with jewelry, and maintained them in great comfort for use in ceremonies. Occasionally, a king would offer a white elephant as a gift when he wished to bestow a special favor. These gifts could be problematic, however, because anyone who received a white elephant would be expected to lavish attention upon it and not put it to work—a responsibility that could ruin someone who did not have considerable wealth. Accordingly, the phrase "white elephant" has come to mean a large burden that cannot be easily discarded. Real white elephants have become rare. In Cambodia, for example, the last sighting of one occurred in the 1960s.

The IETF hates NAT. What its engineers would like is for any computer on the internet to be able to address a data packet to any other, without the intervention of any machines on the way. That was the original mission of the internet engineers: and, for a brief period, they achieved it. Then NAT came along and spoilt it. "NAT's balkanise* the net," Auerbach says. Worse, by disguising the shortage of IP addresses, NAT has slowed down the switch to IPv6. "With NAT in place, there's no compelling reason for most users to switch."

This is where Cheriton disagrees with the IETF. Far from casting NAT as the villain of the peace, he sees it as the internet's potential saviour that will rescue us from what he says is the great IPv6 white elephant.† NAT and IPv6 have been around for about the same time, he points out. "They both had their chance, but NAT has succeeded," he says. "I'm a great believer in the survival of the fittest."

Controversially, he claims that NAT might do a better job of securing that net against malicious attack than IPv6's encryption features. "Encryption and authentication don't get you any safety," he says, as they rely on keeping the encryption key secret. "As soon as that secret is out—and all secrets leak in the end—the security vanishes."

Computers often receive unsolicited packets of information that pretend to be from a trusted or familiar source but in fact come from somewhere else. It is incredibly easy to fake the source of data in this way. Spammers do it, and malicious hackers do it to cover their tracks.

15 NAT could be made to stand guard against these rogue packets, keeping them out of local networks like a receptionist filtering calls, Cheriton says. Machines behind a NAT can't be reached directly; packets have to wait for the gatekeeping machine to explicitly permit them to enter before they can get through. Getting rid of NATs would make the net worse and more unstable, he argues.

His solution is to co-opt the NAT system to week out rogue packets. He wants to switch the NAT boxes from being enemy number one to the net's best citizen. Cheriton laid out his vision in an experimental networking project called TRIAD (or, in full, Translating Relaying Internetwork Architecture integrating Active Directories).

While IPv6 makes machines that are now hidden behind NATs visible to the internet at large, Cheriton's system goes one better. Unlike today's IP addresses, TRIAD data packets will have addressed that are hierarchical, like postal addresses: for example, "Fred's Machine, c/o the Stanford NAT." You can string these addresses together, so if you're Danny, say, and you're behind a NAT at *New Scientist*, a data packet from you to Fred carries the address "Fred, c/o the Stanford NAT box, c/o New Scientist NAT box/ from Danny." In this way, TRIAD allows computers behind NATs to become fully connected; they are as reachable as any other computer on the network. And because the addresses can be as long as you like, there is no limit to the maximum number of machines you can connect on the net. Number shortage solved.

Openness Is Key

But how do you find out what address to use to reach the destination you want? Under the existing internet system, a network of computers called domain name servers (DNSs) hold tables that translate addresses such as **www.newscientist.com** into IP addresses of the form 194.203.155.123, which are what the machines that route data round the net currently understand.

TRIAD will do away with DNS machines, and give NAT boxes the job of finding an address. The NAT boxes will talk amongst themselves like neighbourhood gossips to discover who is looking after a particular name. But crucially for Cheriton's idea of making the system secure, they will also share information about rogue data packets.

20 Cheriton likens TRIAD to the way the air traffic control system works. When an aircraft is given an instruction, it can be heard by all the other pilots in the area. If a pilot receives a command that conflicts with previous orders given to other pilots, then they will refuse the order and other pilots will immediately know that the controller is making errors, or maybe even acting maliciously. Openness is the key.

In the TRIAD world, say a terrorist wants to use a computer to pretend to be a machine that is authorised to close down a power station. The terrorist's machine would have to announce that it belonged to the power station's network to all the local TRIAD servers—including the one run by the power station. Such announcements would travel across the net in a matter of seconds, Cheriton says. The real

power station servers could then quickly put out a message—using one of the old routes that they know from experience they can trust—telling the world to ignore the impostor.

So instead of being the silent Balkanisers of the net, NAT boxes would become its chattiest and most dutiful citizens—a kind of online neighbourhood watch. Almost all the work of running the net would fall to them.

But what about the spoof packets that disguise their true origin? While today it is easy for a sender to fake a data packet's address, in TRIAD all packets are traceable. Each packet must carry the addresses of every machine it visits on route through the network. So packets from Transylvania will have "c/o Transylvanian NAT" on them. If a machine from the Transylvania NAT is suspect, every intermediary NAT in the network can be told to ignore packets winging in from Transylvania. Cheriton claims this will give the network an automatic ability to contain denial of service attacks almost instantly.

Many internet engineers see Cheriton as a maverick. And as he himself acknowledges, "there are a lot of wild crazies out there with ways to replace the net." But not many of them have his track record. His hunches on the future of networking, though often controversial at first, have usually proved right. In the late 1980s, when many in the networking world were abandoning the internet's TCP/IP system for a competing standard called Open Systems Interconnection (OSI), it was Cheriton who said that OSI was doomed to fail. Later, when telephone companies suggested that the internet's hardware would be rendered obsolete by a more telephone-friendly system called ATM, Cheriton declaimed against that, too—and started his own company, Granite, producing a new generation of high-speed internet hardware. That made him his first fortune, when he sold the company to internet hardware manufacturer Cisco. Five years ago, two students turned up at his house asking for seed money to start a company based on their PhD theses: Cheriton spotted the potential and wrote Larry Page and Sergy Brin their first investor's cheque. Their bright idea became Google, and when the company went public this year the *Washington Post* estimated Cheriton's stake at more than $300 million. **25** But re-engineering the internet will require more than the say-so of one man, no matter how impressive his credentials. What's more, TRIAD has its own problems. If the comparatively conservative IPv6 project ultimately fails because it requires so many potentially dangerous changes to the net, isn't the more radical TRIAD even more dangerous? Nearly three years since Cheriton began working on TRIAD, the organisations responsible for defining standards on the net continue to support IPv6, and have paid little attention to his warnings. But the idea is far from dead.

Research papers that adopt many of Cheriton's ideas are appearing in computing journals. IPv6 still isn't here. And the NAT keeps spreading.

"I'm an old guy," says Cheriton. "I remember back in 1980, when the phone companies thought they had the solution to everything, and the Internet engineers were the young Turks. Now, we're the ones who have become ossified."

While Cheriton acknowledges that his plan for TRIAD as it stands might never make it out of the labs, he believes that his ideas about NATs will win out over IPv6 in the end. He's banking that his students will go out into the world and propagate them. That's a long shot, but then again so were many of Cheriton's other high-tech gambles.

Questions for Discussion

1. How seriously does O'Brien take the idea that the Internet is "on the brink of collapse"? After reading this article, how convinced are you that major changes are necessary to make the Internet function better?

2. Why has the Internet become vulnerable to increasing numbers of threats? How can this vulnerability be traced to assumptions that governed its original design?

3. What has kept a solution designed by the Internet Engineering Task Force (IETF) from becoming widely used? Given what O'Brien reports about how the IETF's solution was received, how likely is it that users would adopt the solution advocated by David Cheriton and endorsed by O'Brien? What would it take to motivate people to embrace significant change?

4. Consider the analogies in paragraphs 10 and 20. How helpful were they to you? What do they reveal about O'Brien's sense of audience?

5. O'Brien acknowledges that Cheriton is seen as a "maverick." What does it mean to be a maverick? What are the advantages and disadvantages of playing that role?

③ ANDREW K. PACE, "Surviving Chronic E-Mail Fatigue"

E-mail offers tremendous advantages. Instead of searching for an appropriate piece of stationary, writing a document that will look well formatted and centered on the page, sliding it into an envelope, putting a stamp on it, and then taking it to a mailbox (after which days may pass before it reaches its recipient), you can instantly transmit a message without worrying about how to package it. It leaves your computer screen and arrives within seconds in an electronic mailbox anywhere on earth. Moreover—unlike a phone call—an e-mail message can be sent at any hour, without regard to whether it's a convenient moment for the recipient to be interrupted. If you are up late at night, for example, you can send a message to someone who is already asleep—confident that the recipient will open the message when prepared to do so. But is there a dark side to e-mail? Are some people turning a medium designed for sending quick messages into a means for sending long letters that might be more properly sent by "snail mail"? And, as Andrew Pace suggests in the following argument, are some people so addicted to e-mail that reading and writing messages interferes with their ability to complete other tasks? If you are not sure whether your use of e-mail may be excessive, Pace's argument may help you decide. Pace is head of the systems department at the North Carolina State University Library. "Surviving Chronic E-Mail Fatigue" was first published in *Computers in Libraries* in March 2005.

Surviving Chronic E-Mail Fatigue

ANDREW K. PACE

1   I'm too young to be nostalgic. At least, someone told me that once. But lately, technology has been making me nostalgic for a time when we used to communicate differently. I think I have Chronic E-Mail Fatigue (CEF), and I am desperate for a cure.

Fleeting Anonymity

If there were such a thing as an anti- "do not call" list, it would be what's created when you put your e-mail address on a web site. (Experts warn us not to do this anymore.) If you put your e-mail address on a web site, it will wind up on a spammer's mailing list. Well, for some of us, it's just too late. So, like all good systems folks, when the problem cannot be resolved upstream, we try to find some way to divert the problem downstream: filters, spam assassins, buddy lists, "whitelists," etc. There has to be a better way.

I like the dichotomy of spam solutions. On the one hand, you have filters and junk controls keeping all the bad stuff from getting through, as well as something as drastic as a spam assassin (**http://spamassasin. apache.org**), which works at the server level to, well, assassinate spam messages. (In actuality, it can be used to mark potential spam as well, allowing the end user to determine a filtering rule based on "spam probability.")

On the other hand, you have "allow" lists and buddies and known correspondents. Blacklists are too long to maintain; new so-called whitelists allow systems administrators

CONTEXT

The thirty-seventh President of the United States, Richard M. Nixon (1913–1994) left a controversial legacy. His advocates point to how he ended the draft, supported the creation of the Environmental Protection Agency, and—most famously—reopened diplomatic relations with China after decades of bad relations between that country and the United States. Critics argue that he prolonged the Vietnam War and repeatedly lied to the American people—denying, for example, that the United States was secretly bombing Cambodia when this was indeed occurring. Because evidence emerged showing that Nixon tried to cover up a scandal that began when Republican operatives broke into the headquarters of the Democratic National Committee in the Watergate complex, and was stretching the limits of his constitutional authority as President, he resigned in 1974 rather than face the impeachment that seemed inevitable by that point. Reporters covering how Nixon functioned while in the White House revealed that he kept an "enemies list." People on this list were targeted for audits by the IRS and monitoring by the FBI. It is this list that is being evoked by Pace.

to determine who's allowed to do something rather than keeping up with the much longer lists of enemies. If Nixon had known about whitelists, he probably could have kept a shorter list too.

Warning Sign: "Junk Volume"

5 The first symptom of CEF is when you get more spam than real mail. On a day like today (a Tuesday), I received 291 pieces of junk mail, roughly double the amount of bona fide mail (not counting listserv traffic). Of course, a corollary sign of CEF is knowing just how much e-mail and junk mail you get each day.

To play devil's advocate on the impact of spam, however, I once tried a little experiment. Sorting through a week's worth of paper mail, I was able to discard about 6 pounds of junk, while the amount I kept would not even register on my bathroom scales. Last time I checked, my e-mail junk mail weighed almost nothing, was much simpler to discard, and was in no danger of taking up space in a landfill somewhere.

Warning Sign: "Get Mail"

E-mail has got to be one of the most amazing procrastination tools ever invented. Although I was never lucky enough to live through the era of dictating a memo, I cannot imagine a manager trying to avoid bigger projects by composing a memo. That seems too much like work, and e-mail is too easy. Show of hands: How many of us hit the "Get Mail" button in our e-mail programs hoping that an incoming message will distract us, however fleetingly, from the rigors of real work?

I'm 600 words into this column, and I've already checked my e-mail four times. (OK, seven times, but three of those times I didn't have any new messages, so those don't count.) I'm having a tougher and tougher time convincing myself that there is any real work involved in e-mail, but I rest assured, as all rationalizing addicts do, that there are people out there worse off than I am.

Warning Sign: "The Fix"

"The fix" is a lot like the "Get Mail" syndrome. You can spot people looking to score a fix in public libraries, airports, and around any number of wireless hotspots. In an industry that has already taken to calling patrons "users," you'd think there'd be a way to make a small fortune dolling out dimebags of bandwidth to the network-addicted. There has to be a profit-making alternative to libraries giving away the goods for free and wireless hotspots charging outrageous fees for an activity that takes only seconds to garner user satisfaction.

10 Also, if you've ever smoked or known a smoker, then you're familiar with the rule of "last and first." That is, it's the last thing you do before you go to bed and the first thing you do when you wake up in the morning. Seriously, what could be so important about an e-mail that arrived between the hours of 11 P.M. and 6 A.M.? As guilty as I am of having this symptom of CEF, I can at least honestly say that I have never gotten up in the middle of the night to check my e-mail.

If these warning signs apply to you (I have all three), then a) you probably have Chronic E-Mail Fatigue, and b) you probably deserve spam. You also run the risk of turning to the "hard stuff," like blogs and instant messaging. These might look like cures for e-mail, but don't be fooled.

Don't Give Up Hope

Actually, I'm just kidding about that last part. While I do believe that e-mail has nearly outlived its usefulness as a productivity tool, there is some hope for newer communications technologies. If you missed "I've Gathered a Basket of Communication and Collaboration Tools" by May Chang in the September 2004 issue of *CIL,* you should go back and take a look. In it, she summarizes NCSU's success with using blogging, wikis, * online forums, and instant messaging software as new communication tools. Chang also gave a presentation on open source solutions for collaborative communication at the 2004 LITA Forum. A PDF version of that presentation is available at **http://www. ala.org/ala/lita/litaevents/2004Forum/ CS Open Source Applications.pdf**.

Chang's strategy at NCSU involved rapid prototyping of a solution to solve specific communications problems in the library. For example, a forum on the staff intranet could be much more effective than spamlike e-mails that leave out key staff and include others who would never participate in an online discussion thread. Blogs make excellent "news and events" tools. Wikis are great for group collaboration and information sharing when participants are spread far and wide. Finally, instant messaging is, well, instant. I know too many people who use e-mail as an instant messaging client, growing unduly frustrated at a message that goes unanswered for more than a couple of hours.

If you're feeling extra radical, you can always try that thing that sits next to your computer—you know, that thing with the buttons that you pick up and talk into? Yes, I'm talking about the telephone, that anathema to systems folk. If it makes you feel better to use one that can play games and take pictures, then a cell phone can ease you into this old-fashioned mode of communication.

Getting Some Rest
It seems obvious, but they say the best cure for fatigue is a little rest. I challenge you to close your e-mail client for a couple of hours and get some work done. Pick up the phone if you really need to. I won't go so far as to suggest writing letters. (I'm a systems librarian, not a mother.)

I remember in college someone told me not to study in bed because it might make me associate my bed with studying, making sleep more difficult. (This made sense, except I think by that age I was pretty safely associating my bed with sleep. So studying in bed actually made me fall asleep instead.) Similarly, I have come to associate my office with e-mail and phone work. I find when I need a rest from either, it's best to disappear for a while and get some work done away from the distractions of addictive communication tools.

Of course, a day will come when I really want and need e-mail again. At some point I might really need to m*Ort-gage my house to pay for all that V*i*c*o*d*i*n. If anyone has any POwerhouse investment OppOrtunities, please send them to andrew_pace "at" **ncsu.edu**.

*Software that allows users to create and edit websites, wikis have been in use since 1995. Ward Cunningham, a programmer involved in the development of wikis, defines them as "the simplest online database that could possibly work." Cunningham adds, "I really think programming is easy and fun. Those that think it hard and boring have only to collect some more experience."

Questions for Discussion

1. How does Pace present himself in this article? Writers sometimes create a "persona"—that is, a rhetorical or literary version of themselves that exaggerates or simplifies aspects of their real character. To what extent do you think his self-presentation reflects his true self?

2. In paragraph 6, Pace plays "devil's advocate." What does that role mean to you? What does this paragraph contribute to his piece as a whole?

3. Pace describes e-mail as "one of the most amazing procrastination tools ever invented." How actively do you use e-mail? Does e-mail ever interfere with your productivity?

4. What assumptions about his audience has Pace made when using language such as "score a fix" and "dimebags"? As someone who has now joined that audience, how do you feel about the way he addressed you?

5. Why might people prefer to use e-mail than to place a telephone call? Under what circumstances is a telephone call likely to produce better results than an e-mail would?

6. What do you make of Pace's conclusion? What are the references within it meant to convey? And why do you think he includes his e-mail address after disclosing that he is already relying excessively on e-mail?

④ **JOHN TIERNEY, "Making Them Squirm"**

Have you ever found yourself spending more time at your computer than is necessary—so much time that your productivity is being hampered? If you answer "yes," it may be for diverse reasons. But as John Tierney discusses in the following piece—first published in the *New York Times* in June 2005—hours of work time can be lost when computers crash, forcing users to invest additional hours in recreating their work. This problem is especially troubling when an entire system goes down because it has been infected by a virus or a worm. What does it say about the health of the cyber environment that some people, known as hackers, can find pleasure in demonstrating their technological expertise at the expense of others sometimes causing serious economic damage? This question is worth considering as you read the following selection that uses humor to discuss how convicted hackers should be punished.

Making Them Squirm

JOHN TIERNEY

1 Last year a German teenager named Sven Jaschan released the Sasser worm,* one of the costliest acts of sabotage in the history of the Internet. It crippled computers around the world, closing businesses, halting trains and grounding airplanes.

Which of these punishments does he deserve?

A) A 21-month suspended sentence and 30 hours of community service.

B) Two years in prison.

C) A five-year ban on using computers.

D) Death.

E) Something worse.

If you answered A, you must be the German judge who gave him that sentence last week.

If you answered B or C, you're confusing him with other hackers who have been sent to prison and banned from using computers or the Internet. But those punishments don't seem to have deterred hackers like Mr. Jaschan from taking their place.

5 I'm tempted to say that the correct answer is D, and not just because of the man-years I've spent running virus scans and reformatting hard drives. I'm almost convinced by Steven Landsburg's cost-benefit analysis showing that the spreaders of computer viruses and worms are more logical candidates for capital punishment than murderers are.

Professor Landsburg, an economist at the University of Rochester, has calculated the relative value to society of executing murderers and hackers. By using studies estimating the deterrent value of capital punishment, he figures that

*In May 2004, the Sasser worm caused hundreds of thousands of computers around the world to crash. The targets included major companies in Germany, Great Britain, and the United States. Although it did not cause permanent damage to the machines, the virus-like worm caused computers to continually crash and reboot—costing millions of dollars in lost productivity and a tremendous amount of frustration. Sasser spread rapidly because it did not require users to click on an e-mail attachment. Instead, it used the Internet to spread from any infected computer to others with the same vulnerability. The worm exploited a flaw in Microsoft Windows, and many commentators noted the risk posed to the world economy when so many people rely on a product from a single corporation.

executing one murderer yields at most $100 million in social benefits.

The benefits of executing a hacker would be greater, he argues, because the social costs of hacking are estimated to be so much higher: $50 billion per year. Deterring a mere one-fifth of 1 percent of those crimes—one in 500 hackers—would save society $100 million. And Professor Landsburg believes that a lot more than one in 500 hackers would be deterred by the sight of a colleague on death row.

I see his logic, but I also see practical difficulties. For one thing, many hackers live in places where capital punishment is illegal. For another, most of them are teenage boys, a group that has never been known for fearing death. They're probably more afraid of going five years without computer games.

So that leaves us with E: something worse than death. Something that would approximate the millions of hours of tedium that hackers have inflicted on society.

10 Hackers are the Internet equivalent of Richard Reid,* the shoe-bomber who didn't manage to hurt anyone on his airplane but has been annoying travelers ever since. When I join the line of passengers taking off their shoes at the airport, I get little satisfaction in thinking that the man responsible for this ritual is sitting somewhere by himself in a prison cell, probably with his shoes on.

He ought to spend his days within smelling range of all those socks at the airport. In an exclusive poll I once conducted among fellow passengers, I found that 80 percent favored forcing Mr. Reid to sit next to the metal detector, helping small children put their sneakers back on.

The remaining 20 percent in the poll (meaning one guy) said that wasn't harsh enough. He advocated requiring Mr. Reid to change the Odor-Eaters insoles of runners at the end of the New York City Marathon.

What would be the equivalent public service for Internet sociopaths? Maybe convicted spammers could be sentenced to community service testing all their own wares. The number of organ-enlargement offers would decline if a spammer thought he'd have to appear in a public-service television commercial explaining that he'd tried them all and they just didn't work for him.

Convicted hackers like Mr. Jaschan could be sentenced to a lifetime of removing worms and viruses, but the computer experts I consulted said there would be too big a risk that the hackers would enjoy the job. After all, Mr. Jaschan is now doing just that for a software security firm.

15 The experts weren't sure that any punishment could fit the crime, but they had several suggestions: Make the hacker spend 16 hours a day fielding help-desk inquiries in an AOL chat room for computer novices. Force him to do this with a user name at least as uncool as KoolDude and to work on a vintage IBM PC with a 2400-baud dial-up connection. Most painful of all for any geek, make him use Windows 95 for the rest of his life.

I realize that this may not be enough. If you have any better ideas, send them along.

*Richard Charles Reid, a British citizen, was arrested for terrorism December 22, 2001—only a couple of months after the deadly attacks on the World Trade Center and the Pentagon. He was traveling on an American Airlines flight en route from Paris, France, to Miami, Florida, when a flight attendant noted that he was trying to light a match on the tongue of his sneaker. She tried to stop him, but Reid—who is 6′ 3″—pushed her to the floor. When another flight attendant intervened, Reid bit her thumb. He was eventually subdued by other passengers on the plane, including doctors who were able to sedate him. Plastic explosives were subsequently found in the lining of his shoes. During his sentencing, he declared himself an enemy of the United States working in league with Osama bin Laden—the mastermind behind the September 11 attacks and other acts of terror. Travelers were astonished that Reid had passed through French security when the world was on heightened alert. The practice of requiring airline passengers to remove their shoes began shortly afterward. Reid remains in prison.

Questions for Discussion

1. What does Tierney accomplish by contrasting answer A with answers B and C? How seriously do you take his defense of answer D?

2. Tierney claims that most hackers are teenage boys. If this is true, what is the role of gender in trouble-making? Why might boys be more likely than girls to be hackers?

3. Joking aside, what is Tierney's point? Has humor helped convey it, or has it worked to obscure it? Was there any point in this piece where you were amused?

4. How comfortable are you knowing that a major hacker is now working for a software security firm?

5. What penalty, if any, would you advocate for a hacker who makes your computer go down just before you are about to print an important paper due within minutes?

NEGOTIATING DIFFERENCES

People sometimes feel free to behave in the cyber environment in a way that is different from the way they try to act in the real world. For example, would a teenage hacker who figures out how to cost a country tens of millions of dollars without leaving the comfort of his bedroom be likely to execute a real-time crime that would do so much damage? Would someone who has grown addicted to watching pornography on the Web devote as much time to this pursuit if the only other option was driving to what is so ironically called an "adult" bookstore and purchasing videos and magazines before being spotted by a neighbor or colleague? And would people address each other in person the same way they address strangers in chat rooms, on bulletin boards, or even in e-mail?

Because electronic messages are so easy to send, and because people are looking at a computer screen when they send them—not at the person or people to whom they are writing—it can be tempting to engage in a practice once known as *flaming*. This means sending a message so nasty that the recipient could feel scorched by the words received. Even if you have never received an e-mail that struck you as worded more harshly than necessary, imagine that you have been asked to draft a document that will establish a code of behavior for how a specific group will treat other members of this group when exchanging messages online. There will be fifty students in this group, all of whom are taking an online course together. They will meet in person only a few times during the semester. Most of the discussion they participate in will take place through an electronic bulletin board created by the professor. Messages on this site can be directed to the entire class or sent privately to the professor or to a single student. During the first real-time meeting of the class, held just as it was about to begin, the professor asked everyone present to have an honest exchange of ideas while conversing online but nevertheless treating each other with respect. To make sure that this advice was taken seriously, she asked everyone to post on the bulletin board a list of rules that should govern online class discussion. You have been advised that the list should focus on the rules you think are the most important and not to submit a list so long that people could end feeling afraid to say anything. All rules should be designed to promote the common good (rather than your personal likes and dislikes), and for every rule you post you must submit a paragraph-long rationale for it. This assignment is due within forty-eight hours. With this situation in mind, compose the document that you would send your professor and fellow students.

How Do We Design Communities?

Visitors to Washington, D.C., sometimes complain about how difficult it can be to drive in that city. The streets seem to be laid out in a confusing pattern, with several main thoroughfares cutting across otherwise parallel streets at odd angles. It might surprise those visitors to learn that Washington, D.C., was originally designed from scratch by French architect Pierre L'Enfant, who was commissioned by President Washington in 1791. If you look at a street map of the city, you can make out the main features of that original design. For instance, those angled thoroughfares radiate from the central location of the Capitol Building; the famous Mall in front of the Capitol reflects L'Enfant's vision for a wide, central avenue. L'Enfant's original design was changed in several ways even as the city was being built, and in the years since it was constructed, the city, like many American cities, has grown dramatically. The confusing street patterns partially reflect the lack of planning and regulation as the city has grown; other oddities have occurred as builders and city leaders have tried to accommodate the original design. For example, some buildings, such as the FBI Building and the East Building of the National Gallery of Art, are not square or rectangular but have unusual angles (such as a trapezoid) to fit into the odd-shaped city blocks created by those radiating thoroughfares. If you live in a city or town that has experienced recent growth, you might have seen the same phenomenon. ■ The growth of cities and towns tends to be seen as a good thing. But as the example of Washington, D.C., indicates, growth can create problems, too. As cities and towns expand, new residents and businesses require more services, which lead to even more growth. There is an increasing need for more energy and more space. Not surprisingly, such growth often occurs at the edges of cities, where farmland and rural communities once existed. Despite the economic benefits, residents sometimes resist growth because it inevitably changes the quality of life in their communities. Famous architect Frank Lloyd Wright, whose building designs reflected his belief that structures should be part of the natural environment where they are located, once scolded the people of Miami about the unnatural way in which their city developed (see *Con-Text* on page 661). Wright's argument was really a call to create livable communities that foster a certain kind of quality of life. But "quality of life" might not be the same for all people, and that is where conflicts can arise. Ultimately, growth raises questions about the kinds of communities people want. And how do they determine what kinds of communities they should have? ■ In a sense, all the essays in this section address that question. Ostensibly, these essays are about the problems associated with the growth of communities. A few of the writers discuss "sprawl," which is the rapid and seemingly unchecked growth of cities and towns into surrounding rural areas. Others describe the "smart growth" movement that emerged in the 1990s, partly as a reaction to sprawl. In making their arguments, these writers offer their respective visions for the kinds of communities people should have. Their essays are reminders that when you argue about practical problems such as sprawl, you are really addressing deeper—and often more difficult—questions about how people should live together.

CON-TEXT

"A Beautiful Place Made Ugly"

1 We were coming in on the plane looking over this great, marvelous and very beautiful plateau and what do we see? Little tiny subdivisions of squares, little pigeonholes, little lots, everything divided up into little lots, little boxes on little lots, little tacky things.

And you come downtown and what's happening? Plenty of skyscrapers. You call them hotels. You can't tell whether they're hotels or office buildings or something in a cemetery. They have no feelings, no richness, no sense of this region.

And that, I think is happening to the country. It's not alone your misfortune. . . .

You want to live in a way becoming to human beings with your spirit and a devotion to the beautiful, don't you? Well, why don't you? Why would you accept this sort of thing? Why would you let them put it over on you? You say because of economic reasons.

5 Well, if that's what this country talks about as the highest standard of living in the world, then I think it isn't at all the highest, it's only biggest—and quite ignorant.

Nature must be ashamed of these hotels that you're building down here. Nature must be ashamed of the way this place has been laid out and patterned after a checkerboard and parceled out in little parcels where you stand on each other's toes, face the sidewalk, your elbows in the next neighbor's ribs. . . .

SOURCE: Frank Lloyd Wright, public address, Miami, Florida (1955).

① STUART MECK, "Getting on the Case"

When cities are perceived as unsafe or unattractive, the blame is usually put upon two segments of the population: criminals (who make residents and visitors feel at risk) and police (who are not making residents and visitors feel safe). But is this fair? Are there other people who need to accept part of the responsibility for urban decline—such as mayors and city councils that have tolerated the construction of poorly designed neighborhoods? And what about the city planners who conceived those plans—plans that may have allowed interstate highways to cut through once healthy neighborhoods or allowed blocks of three-story buildings to be demolished and replaced with large housing towers in which vestibules and hallways can become ideal sites for criminal attacks upon some of the most vulnerable citizens? The following argument by Stuart Meck discusses how urban planners can create safer and more attractive spaces by following a few key design principles. Meck is a senior research fellow at the American Planning Association. His argument was first published in the 2005 issue of *Planning*—a journal published by that association. You will find that he also asks you to consider why housing has to be located in areas separate from where people want to live and work. He advocates a principle called "mixed use"—designs that allow housing, shops, and offices to be located on the same street.

Getting on the Case

STUART MECK

1 Like a lot of ideas that planners take for granted today, the concept of crime prevention through environmental design originated with Jane Jacobs, as a chapter in her provocative 1961 book, *The Death and Life of Great American Cities.* Jacobs, a journalist who now lives in Toronto, offered detailed observations about "what kinds of city streets are safe and what kinds are not; why some city parks are marvelous and others are vice traps and death traps."

   If anything, her ideas are even more influential today. Although Jacobs didn't use the phrase "crime prevention through environmental design" (CPTED came into currency a decade later), she set out the basic concepts that others later refined. Criminologists, sociologists, and planners have used her book as the starting point for an ongoing discussion of what makes places safe.

What Is a Safe Street?

Jacobs focused on sidewalks and city streets, human activity, and human watchfulness. A street needs three qualities to be safe, she said: a clear demarcation between public space and private space, "eyes upon the street," and sidewalks in continuous use. Constant activity adds to the number of effective eyes on the street, she said, because it induces people in nearby buildings to watch the sidewalks.

   Jacobs recognized that the sidewalks needed to be lively not only during the day, but also in the evening and at night. A mix of uses give both residents and strangers concrete reasons for using the sidewalks, Jacobs wrote.

5   Good lighting also encourages people to go out onto the street at night, making the eyes "count for more because their range is greater." But lighting alone did not make the gray areas of the city less crime ridden. Jacobs noted; rather, it was the interaction of lighting and street activity that did the trick.

Some Followers

For many years, Jane Jacobs lived in Greenwich Village, a lively neighborhood in lower Manhattan. By coincidence, two other residents of the area were also formulating theories of how crime can be controlled. Her themes were reflected in their writing.

The first was C. Ray Jeffery, who went on to become a professor of criminology at Florida State University in Tallahassee. Jeffery's work, *Crime Prevention Through Environmental Design,* first published in 1971, and revised and reissued in 1977, took a highly critical view of conventional approaches to crime control.

Historically, wrote Jeffery, there have been three models of crime control: retribution, deterrence, or treatment. He contended that both the retribution and deterrence models had been resounding failures, and that treatment had failed "because of lack of scientific knowledge about behavioral change and treatment methods." He advocated, in their place, a model of prevention that embraced not only architectural design, but also human behavior and learning theory.

According to Jeffery, crime prevention involved any activity that would reduce or eliminate a crime before it is committed. This included physical design measures for streets, parks, terminals, and residential and commercial buildings; changing the behavior of potential victims and potential criminals; alarm and surveillance systems; and addressing market forces to control white-collar or organized crime.

Defensible Space

10 The late Oscar Newman, an architect and planner who also lived in Greenwich Village in the early 1970s, published *Defensible Space* in 1972 and went on to write design manuals for the now-defunct Law Enforcement Assistance Administration in the U.S. Department of Justice and for the U.S. Department of Housing and Urban Development. He also worked as a CPTED consultant.

Newman developed a set of design principles aimed at reducing urban crime. In large measure, his work was a reaction against high-rise public housing such as Pruitt-Igoe in St. Louis and Chicago's Cabrini-Green.

"High-rise, elevator-service, double-loaded corridor apartment buildings for the use of low- and middle-income families have proven disastrous," Newman wrote. In these buildings, he said, elevators, fire stairs, hallways, and roofs—all screened from public view—"are freely roamed and ruled by criminals." By comparison, he said, low-rise buildings, where two or three families share a hallway, and six to 12 share an entrance, were much less vulnerable to crime, even when built at the same densities.

Newman defined defensible spaces as a range of mechanisms—real and symbolic barriers, defined areas of influence, and improved opportunities for surveillance—that combine to bring an environment under the control of its residents. His notion of defensible space included three principles:

■ **Zones of territorial influence.**
    Newman favored design approaches that give residents territorial prerogatives over certain spaces. These included letting the building shape define and enclose its grounds; subdividing streets to create territorially defined blocks and areas; interrupting, but not stopping, easy vehicular access; and creating symbolic barriers—interrupting movement along access paths that alert the user of the

CONTEXT

Alexander von Hoffman, a senior fellow at the Joint Center for Housing Studies at Harvard University, has described St. Louis's Pruitt-Igoe as "arguably the most infamous public housing project ever built in the United States. A product of the postwar federal public-housing program, this mammoth high-rise development was completed in 1956." Containing thirty-three eleven-story buildings, the project was razed in 1973 after the U.S. Department of Housing and Urban Development labeled it unsalvageable. Likewise, in a 2003 story on *60 Minutes*, CBS described Chicago's Cabrini-Green as "the nation's most infamous public housing project, synonymous with gangs, drugs, misery, and murder." In 1998 development began on plans to get rid of the high-rise "projects" and create mixed-income housing in the area.

Von Hoffman attributes the creation of projects such as Pruitt-Igoe and Cabrini-Green to a "new breed of big-city mayors who came to power in the postwar period. These mayors distanced themselves from the old-style political bosses and looked for support from downtown business interests. They campaigned for the revival of their aging cities and promoted large-scale physical building programs that included highways, airports, and especially downtown and neighborhood redevelopment." Elected in 1949, St. Louis Mayor Joseph Darst was one such mayor. Von Hoffman goes on: "Darst, in particular, considered the low-rise projects built by his predecessors to be ugly. Instead, he greatly admired the new high-rise public housing projects that New York Mayor William O'Dwyer had shown him on a visit to that city."

Cabrini-Green in Chicago.

SOURCE: "Why They Built the Pruitt-Igoe Project" by Alexander von Hoffman.

---

*According to the American Planning Association website (**www.planning.org**), the American Institute of Certified Planners (AICP) "is the American Planning Association's professional institute, providing recognized leadership nationwide in the certification of professional planners, ethics, professional development, planning education, and the standards of planning practice."

transition between public and private space.

- **Surveillance opportunities for residents.** Newman believed that lighting, windows, and the positioning of public areas should allow residents to see the common areas and convey the sense that one is continually under observation while on the grounds. For example, a lobby can be designed so that internal activity—such as getting mail and waiting for the elevator—can be seen from the streets and exterior grounds of the housing project.
- **Image and milieu.** To Newman, it was important to provide housing

with interior design finishes and furniture that would give housing projects a distinctive tone, not an institutional one. Another idea was to juxtapose residential areas with other safe functions such as commercial, institutional, industrial, entertainment uses, and safe streets. Today, we call this mixed uses.

Diane Zahm, AICP,* an associate professor of urban affairs and planning at Virginia Tech, Blacksburg, contrasts Jeffery's approach to that of Newman. "Jeffery is coming out of criminology and sociology; he's looking at the offender and the offender's environment," she says. "Newman is looking at the target or victim—what the people in the housing project can do by providing cues to the offender that this place is taken care of."

"Broken Windows"

15 A fourth perspective, the "broken windows" theory, was advanced by James Q. Wilson, a professor of government at Harvard University, and George Kelling, then a research fellow in Harvard's Kennedy School of Government, in an influential article in the *Atlantic Monthly* in March 1982. Disorder and crime "are usually inextricably linked, in a kind of developmental sequence," they wrote. "[I]f a window in a building is broken *and is left unrepaired,* all the rest of the windows will soon be broken."

To Wilson and Kelling, "one unrepaired broken window is a signal that no one cares, and so breaking more windows costs nothing." By the same token, they argued, "the unchecked panhandler is, in effect, the first broken window. Muggers and robbers, whether opportunistic or professional, believe they reduce their chances of being caught or even identified if they operate on streets where potential victims are already intimidated by prevailing conditions."

Thus, controlling crime required addressing what might be seen as low quality-of-life intrusions: panhandlers, abandoned buildings, drunkenness, littering, and loitering. In one sense, these intrusions, while not about architectual or site design, still speak to the physical environment, or at least individual response to its quality. When these instrusions occur, people fear the street and are reluctant to leave their homes.

Drunkenness and panhandling might be seen as individual acts that harm no one, Wilson and Kelling said. "But failing to do anything about a score of drunks or a hundred vagrants may destroy an entire community," they wrote.

While citizens can have an impact on crime, the police ought to protect communities as well as individuals, wrote Wilson and Kelling. They were skeptical about whether police forces were trained to recognize areas where public order is deteriorating and if they could respond appropriately. They noted that police departments were, in the early 1980s, suffering budgetary cutbacks that made the job more difficult.

20 Still, they suggested that police might be encouraged to go to and from duty stations on public transportation and, while on the bus or subway car, enforce rules about smoking, drinking, disorderly conduct, and the like. And they acknowledged that there might be areas of a city, like shopping centers and well-tended neighborhoods, where informal social control was so effective that police intervention needs were minimal.

Critics of Wilson and Kelling have cited that the police would prefer more leeway in enforcement even though that strategy raises the prospect of constitutional infractions through overzealousness. One of them, David Cole, a professor of law at Georgetown University Law Center, has written that if tolerating minor crimes leads to more serious crime on the street, "it would also follow that the toleration of minor law violations by the police will lead to more serious crime on the force." And in fact, that is exactly what is happening, says Cole.

More Police or Better Design?

Jack Nasar, AICP, a professor of city and regional planning at Ohio State University in Columbus and an environmental design researcher, believes that defensible space is a "long-term way of reducing crime and improving the look of the community." Although this means crime prevention is relatively inexpensive, "people are still talking about older and not-so-effective strategies like more police on the street, target hardening [refitting the physical environment with mechanisms that make it difficult for the criminal to enter, such as putting bars on windows], and the block watch."

Interviewed recently, C. Ray Jeffery, who is now retired, says that the retribution and deterrence models remain popular because they entail "more police, more judges." In contrast, the whole purpose of environmental design "is to reduce the number of crimes committed," he says.

But the preventive approach has not gained widespread acceptance. Jeffery asserts, because its supporters have less to gain economically and its detractors more. "As far as I can tell, I don't see any interest in it. If you prevent crime, what are the police going to do?"

25 Marcus Felson, a professor of criminology at Rutgers University in New Brunswick, New Jersey, writes and conducts research on crime prevention. He favors the design approach to averting crime, although he agrees that there is more money to be made through more intensive policing.

People-Centered Design

"A crime occurs," Felson says, when there is a convergence of three factors: an offender, a target, and lack of a guardian" (in other words, an opportunity). The guardian is not a police officer, he adds, but simply someone who watches the place. "You have to design buildings, facilities, and parks in ways that produce natural security," he says. "You don't want space that nobody owns, because the toughest and nastiest will take it over."

Privacy and crime prevention often conflict, he says. "The best design is a street with the houses lined up," so the entries can be seen, he adds. "You don't want to orient houses so no one can see one another. If the designer designs so much privacy that offenders can enjoy it, you'll have more crime."

Many planners believe the answer lies, in part, in rethinking postwar development patterns. A complicating factor is that suburban neighborhoods are now often devoid of adult residents during the day, since heads of household are at work—in contrast to the 1950s, when mothers were more inclined to stay at home and could monitor the neighborhood.

Al Zelinka, AICP, a planning consultant in Irvine, California, and coauthor (with Dean Brennan, AICP), of *SafeScape,* a book on CPTED published in 2001 by APA's Planner Press, believes the U.S. should return to "thoughtful, people-centered design, as op-posed to just accommodating the automobile or cost-engineering aspects of development."

30 Patricia Brantingham, a professor of criminology at Simon Fraser University in Vancouver, British Columbia, who has a doctorate in urban planning, contends that after World War II, the U.S. "developed a whole suburban environment that makes crime so easy that many teenagers are pulled into it." Instead, she says, we need "to create an environment that's attractive and dynamic" while paying more attention to conflicts (she terms them "nuisance behaviors") in the use of urban space.

Dean Brennan, a principal planner with the city of Phoenix, agrees. "Rather than creating an environment that separates people, we need opportunities for people to interact in public settings," he says. Crime prevention through environmental design, Brennan says, has become part of the mainstream design review processes in cities like Vancouver, Toronto, Tampa, Tucson, and Phoenix, where site plans and the buildings themselves are scrutinized for their compliance with CPTED principles.

To be effective, Zelinka believes, planners must form interdisciplinary partnerships involving police, engineers, lawyers, and others. "We can't just rely solely on our own discipline," he asserts, because the problems are too complex and planners must depend on others to help implement solutions. The benefits of cooperation can be significant, he says, especially the financial ones. "If through planning and design we can create communities that are self-policing, then the demand for police services is reduced, and economic vitality is enhanced in districts that would otherwise not be patronized."

The planner's special mandate, says Zelinka, is looking after the public realm, and not treating it as an afterthought. "If we focus on the intent of creating a public realm that is vital," he reflects, "then we will have safer communities."

In this, he agrees with Jane Jacobs: Mixed uses and lively streets make places safer.

Questions for Discussion

1. Meck opens his article by drawing upon scholarship from the 1960s and 1970s. Is there any risk to this approach? What is its advantage?

2. What does the concept of "mixed use" mean to you? Can you provide an example of it in the communities where you live, work, or attend school? Can you also provide an example of "defensible space"?

3. Assuming that it works, how would an emphasis on prevention of crime through design offer benefits that the models of retribution and deterrence cannot?

4. Consider the image of the Cabrini-Green housing project on page 664. How would you feel about living in or visiting such a space if you knew that there was a high crime rate in the area? What elements in the design strike you as things you'd want to avoid? Are there any elements that you associate with safety?

5. If eliminating panhandlers and drunks can make neighborhoods safer, what should be done with these people? Meck does not provide an answer. Assuming that you cannot simply move such people to another neighborhood, and that the cost of imprisoning them is both financially and morally high, what would you recommend?

6. Why does Meck think that strategies such as putting bars on windows are old and ineffective? Does he convince you that there are better alternatives? And for whom would these alternatives be available: urban designers or people whose income already restricts them to living in neighborhoods with a high crime rate?

7. Why has it become so easy to commit crime in suburbs? On what outdated assumption is much suburban design still based?

② **JANE HOLTZ KAY,** "The Lived-In City: A Place in Time"

Why would anyone want to live in a city, when the suburbs offer affordable housing, private yards, and convenient shopping—not to mention the reassuringly familiar flavors of chain restaurants such as TGIF, Perkins, and the Olive Garden? The city, on the other hand, can so easily be considered a place where it is hard to find a parking space and where you need to be alert for the presence of criminals whenever you go out for a stroll. But cities can also be sites for diversity, privacy, and excitement—as Jane Holtz Kay argues in the following piece, first published in a 2004 collection of essays on the urban experience. The challenge, as Kay argues, is how to design cities so that they remain vital and livable. The author of several books on urban planning, including *Lost Boston* and *Asphalt Nation,* Kay writes regularly about art, architecture, and natural environments for well-respected newspapers and magazines.

The Lived-In City: A Place in Time

JANE HOLTZ KAY

1   Robert, or rather Robairrrrrr, as even our monolingual lunch-goers managed to say, rolling his French forename with the same care he devoted to our sandwiches, was the host of our lunch hour. Endowed with the memory to recall three preferences while slicing and dicing a fourth, he was the maître d' of our neighborhood. ("So are you turkey rollup today or . . ." he would prompt one customer as he minced onions for a second while joshing along yet a third.) Time after time, he would jive us geographic provincals with a really bad joke about a trip he had just taken to his native Haiti . . . to play hockey, enlisting the assembled flock in his riff as the lines grew longer.

   Now, our spirited chef, our slicer-dicer, our Haitian-born master of ceremonies has left, was let go: axed with the speed of his dancing sandwich knife, it seemed. In a day, the deli counter at the 24-store where he worked was swiftly sanitized, all signs of unwrapped foodstuffs swept away. The gleaming silver counter was gone, the food trays vanished. Just a shelf of neon-toned bottles, snappleracklepop drinks parading behind the vacant cook 'n' serve space. And the Oasis 24-store was on to slicker things.

   In his stead, the next day, strangers handed out free sandwiches with every drink purchase, plastic-wrapped fare, thin and meager next to Robert's oozing composite sandwiches, customized for our daytime neighborhood. And the neighborhood he created missed more than the food. More than the eating, the absence was in the serving, the rock 'n' rolling repartee—the power to unite us odd-lot Bostonians: more folks of color, more mix in income than any other eatery around this downtown edge, from stiff-jawed suits to slackers jiving with idle chatter. More nodding and smiling customers than I had found before, or would again in its sanitized reincarnation. And the absence went beyond the loss and lack within our strange but powerful semi-demi neighborhood of city life. For what was lacking in the aftermath was what defines cities: the everyday urbanity that exists nowhere else.

So it ended, one day in late June, and, by now, the bustling "before" has become a sterile "after," as empty of life as the lost memory of our casual comrades in line those many months. Well, not quite comrades. For the urbanity that this corner collage boasted was based on the anonymity that defines a city. Oasis, unlike Cheers,* was actually the place where *nobody* knows your name. And that was just fine, thank you. We knew one another's faces, the banter, the menu, of course, but not much beyond. And as a city lover, delighting in the absentminded but congenial anonymity that is downtown's hallmark, I say thank God for that: sing a hymn for the hammering, clambering hammering of the city's impersonal connections. Casual discourse, casual multiracial, mixed-income elbowing of our neighbors is at a zero in most suburbs (and, admittedly, in parts of this town). So is walking, even talking. Here, we mingled and moved, rubbed elbows casually, not nervous in anonymous urbanity. And that was fine, too. For the strange pertinence of the city's everyday, predictable flux was the very definition the serious city: mixing ephemeral ease in everlasting surrounding the lived-in city shares space as it does the centuries.

5 Need I stress, then, that lived-in cities like Boston are not the place "where everybody knows your name"? That, in fact, they can be proud fortresses of *not* knowing your name? Only real cities can teach us the meaning of place and time that is the opposite of television's "have a-good-day" nonplaces like Cheers, which is now a tourist stop of T-shirts and trinkets tucked into the ground floor of an otherwise elegant Beacon Hill row house—a faux tourist place more faux than even television.

Is this the comment of a tourist xenophobe? Yes, I confess, but also of a partisan of the city, a visceral and intellectual city lover possessed of the conviction that cities, eternal cities, are, indeed—well—too grown up, too his-

torically genuine to turn a blind eye to Disney-style pastiche† inflated along the street.

Not all American cities are the inheritors of four centuries of comings and goings as Boston is, of course, but they have time on their side. Serious time. And it is that sense of permanence and flux growth and instability, tolerance and suspicion visible on their worm streets and sidewalks that lends character.

Diversity in place and time is just one of many partnerships it the city, of course. City life is the sharing of space with absentminded courtesy—the chance encounters of strangers and neighbors. (Check the subways to see how we suffer crowds politely, if not happily. Check the city, but not the suburbs, for acceptance of the Other, cheek to jowl, backpack to briefcase.) Urbanity is about mingling and hanging back, about civility and bellicosity, quirkiness and constancy. Above all, serious cities actively decline uniformity despite the Gaps—in both senses—that mar our streets: their flanks and facades offer an eclectic mingling that stands in contrast to the uniformity of the malls and supermalls that bloat the landscape in our new suburbs and outburbs.

Suburbanity, so to speak, is about another kind of civility, I concede: the civility of good schools and good roads, of manicured lawns and well-groomed street trees. It is, alas, about how the lopsided subsidies of our federal government have fed urban flight, promoting the pattern of settlement that breeds suburban wealth and urban poverty as Washington subsidized the highway exodus from downtown and dug our nation's Great Divide—urban versus suburban—and maintained it for a half century or more. Doubt it? Think, then: no one has yet to strive "toward a livable *suburb.*"

10 Strangely, even those who struggle for a livable planet, intermingling the built and natural environments in these days of global malaise and environmental activism, have yet to turn to the lived-in city to ally the green and the grid—the country and the city—as did our ancestors. Few follow the 150-year-old tradition of Frederick Law Olmsted's† masterworks of

*A televised situation comedy called *Cheers* was popular in the 1980s; in it a regular cast of characters met in a bar with that name, and the bar was supposed to exist in Boston. Tourists to Boston subsequently expected to find this bar, and entrepreneurs found a way to profit from this expectation.

†Both Disneyland and Disney World create idealized—and some would argue trivialized—representations of historic architecture, whether it be through the construction of a fake medieval castle or the sanitized version of a small-town American Main Street. *Pastiche* indicates pasted together, so part of the Disney experience is to move from one kind of architectural re-creation to another that bears no relation to it. "Disney-like," in this context, implies that this kind of cultural misrepresentation can be found in other settings.

†Arguably the most famous landscape architect in American history, Frederick Law Olmsted is best known for designing Central Park in New York City. He also designed a series of parks for Boston.

*After the construction of two dams in the early nineteenth century, a large swamp was created not far from Boston's most fashionable neighborhood. Considered a health hazard, the swamp was drained and developed as part of a carefully drawn plan for expanding the city. Although the plan took thirty years to implement, it transformed what people would now call wetlands into Back Bay, a large and elegant neighborhood filled with fine houses—and the churches and shops that the residents of them wanted close. Newberry Street continues to be known for fashionable shops and restaurants. Commonwealth Avenue, the widest street in the Back Bay, was designed to create the sense of a Parisian boulevard.

†French for "to allow to choose," *laissez-faire* has since the early nineteenth century described economic policies that promote free enterprise with minimal interference by government.

naturalizing the city and urbanizing the planet's biological systems; fewer peruse the more recent classics *Design with Nature* and *Granite Garden,* invoking the need for whole earth systems in our urban zones. Is the city cacophonous? Irritating? Disrupted? Yes. Is the glass half full? Half empty? Yes, of course, but, and at the same time. Name it what you will, but add one thing: it is also this fragile planet's last, best hope—the only alternative to settling on the ever-contracting fringes, consuming the last chance landscape, extinguishing resources and species. If we are ever to become ecofluent, as the green warriors put it, the strengthening of our lived-in cities is where it must take place.

To be sure, our livable cities tally wins along with losses; some big-box blanders along with a legion of local activists battle the most invasive attack of the chains in our nation's history. Meanwhile, an ethnic flavor continues to spice the eateries, and even the chains, in our quasi-cosmopolitan downtown and urban neighborhoods. Muslim women, their heads swathed in scarves, serve at Dunkin' Donuts. Newcomers from Afghanistan, El Salvador, and Algeria chat up customers at Bean and Leaf Café, as do two generations of Greeks under the Grecian blue letters of the Odysseus restaurant, inscribing their diversity in the architecture as it always has been: five centuries worth—from the Union Oyster House, solid as its colonial bricks, to the upscale anyplaces of contemporary cuisine, the newcomer Irish bars and after-work scenes.

And yet, the Anyplace USA establishments proliferate more rapidly than ever before: in the Franco-fake Bon Pain, the Starbucks and Wendy's, undercutting diversity, destroying vivacity, while neighborhood by neighborhood we fight the good fight. Since Staples superstore came downtown, stationery stores have dwindled. A month-at-a-glance pocket calendar is nowhere to be found, nor the chance to buy *one* pen, *one* pad of paper, *one* anything, it sometimes seems. In the Back Bay* row house world where I live, empty storefronts

have succumbed to soap and cell phone shops as rents rise and the economy slides. An eyeglass shop papered over with neon images stares like empty eyes. Chain stores sit in the old Prince School while the nearby Exeter Theatre, once the Spiritualist Temple, has fallen from grace over the years: a Friday's sits on one of its corners, an Internet company in the space above. And every site seems tentative.

Perhaps they always have. In the time line of the historic city, change is the constant. Yet the loss of flavor and the larger-scaled anonymity seem more rampant these days . . . the pace faster, bigger . . . the city planners more laissez-faire,† the renters greedier here now, as across the country. A Shakespeare and Company bookstore bowing to a New York Barnes & Noble has its counterparts, and, across the ocean, cities in "Old" Europe and old everyplace fail to ward off the monopolies in our sprawling, ever-globalizing world.

Change, as history teaches us, can be good and bad alike. The grand design of Paris by its great builder, Baron Von Haussmann, caused the ferocious leveling of its medieval, quirky, charming streets for the grand boulevards, which we also love. So, too, the filling of Boston's murky Back Bay following Von Haussmann's lead in splendid avenues would never pass an environmental impact statement. Yet the planners who filled the bay with pilings to create the mile-long stretch of streets shaped splendid structures on the French model, as they had created English housing modes atop Beacon Hill. Again, is the cup of city change half full or half empty? One must always ask.

15 Today, truth be told, the cup seems overflowing. The pace has quickened, and change—rightfully—alarms us. The props for greedy growth are strong, the planning weak, the scale of building grandiose. For all the landmark legislation and historic cache that make these surroundings livable, neither neighbors nor activists can ward off the construction booms that turn land to unminted gold and money to "serious money" for seri-

ous building—building too serious to fret about architecture's ease and accommodation with its surroundings. As pernicious as any suburban subdivider, today's city builders focus on the bottom line, caring little for proper fit and public process in a city where planning is a lost art and politicians pay back the piper. And so a new generation builds. Chunky, pricey postmodern buildings rise, stage sets of history for architectural appeasement flourish, and the tall towers for the rich rise above the church steeples where the homeless take an icy night's winter sleep beneath timeless porticoes.

In the lived-in, not always livable city, such issues become visible. That is the joy, and trial, of their heft and density. The city, as always, reflects "the times that try men's souls,"* and in these times of terror and increasing economic inequality, social malaise is manifest on its streets. The newly refurbished Bulfinch State House, with its 1789 golden dome and rolling front lawn, partakes of troubled times as they hide the security cameras that pry into passing sound and sights. The fear of terrorist attack combines with privatism to virtually bar access to the landmark Custom House tower whose once-public balcony offered a splendid view of the city's wraparound world of water.

Downtown, the alliance of politics and money dictates, and the city skyline soars. Towers break through barriers to appropriate the sky. Human scale is lost while the winds they churn affront walkers. Blank-walled facades squeeze out shops below and rising property values threaten old ethnic neighborhoods like Chinatown with high-rise holdouts for the rich. The hot spot seaport sites in South Boston are being sliced and diced to serve the upper income, not the long-time artists.

And yet, the paradox of urban life defies its shortcomings as restored buildings enliven main streets and bustling neighborhoods thrive with new ethnic vitality. The city survives with a novelty and energy that baffle expectations. For all our days deploring slapdash change, a visit to the area once dubbed the Combat Zone offers a new/old downtown in a new after-hours world. Plunging through the streets of the newly named Ladder Blocks, we seek a meal in Restaurant Land's new digs and find one: FELT (so-called) dazzles our eyes. Across from old Washington Street's decay, we enter a black, cavernous space, dazzles by designer lights and silver mirrors. Lofty ceilings rise high, offering images of James Bond to the Great God of Retro Chic . . . and good food. On the second and third floors above, billiard tables explain the "felt" nomenclature and more glitz offers the decor du jour. Soon, the floor above will echo to dancing bands. The crowd's average age is not much beyond the twenties. A minimiracle. How did this hip factor return again to the tired streets of the moribund picture palace world that headlined "Banned in Boston"? The endless city will survive a new generation, and surprise an old one.

Robert will survive, as well. His Oasis stand-ins say he has found work. In fact, from time to time, I have seen him in the Back Bay, driving by the Clarendon Street Baptist Church with his family, one of many immigrant and ethnic parishioners who have rescued this old Yankee edifice. In the shifting, lived-in city, the Back

CONTEXT

One of the most influential city planners in world history, Baron Georges-Eugene Haussmann (1809–1891) was commissioned by Emperor Napoleon III in 1853 to transform Paris into a modern and elegant city. Although there was great beauty to be found in Paris, it was also congested and lacked many of the services—such as good lighting and sanitation—that had become perceived as essential for urban life. To ease congestion and improve traffic flow, Haussmann destroyed much of the city's medieval architecture to create broad, tree-lined boulevards radiating from and toward major monuments such as the Arc de Triomphe. These new boulevards were lined with well-designed housing and shops, and a new water supply and a huge network of sewers was created below ground. New buildings such as the Paris Opera House and several railroad stations were strategically placed, and many new bridges were built across the Seine. His designs cost a fortune to implement and took years to complete. It was a plan that was highly controversial not only because of its financial cost but also because the extensive demolition and construction over decades was socially disruptive. Nevertheless, visitors to Paris today see a city shaped in good measure by Haussmann's vision and energy. He thus represents the kind of planner willing to destroy historic architecture and cause people enormous inconvenience to achieve a magnificent master plan.

*The first line in Thomas Paine's *The American Crisis* (1776) is "These are the times that try men's souls." Writing on the eve of the American Revolution, Paine continued, "The summer patriot and the sunshine soldier will, in this crisis, shrink from the service of his country, but he that stands it now deserves the love and thanks of man and woman." Both of these lines have often been quoted over the years.

Along Newbury street in the Back Bay neighborhood of Boston

Bay's volume of nineteenth-century churches is a loose-leaf scrapbook of change. Its "proper Bostonian" members drifted off to the suburbs long ago, leaving fraying carpets, crumbling brownstone facades, and shrinking budgets. Today's urban influx brings a fascinating miscellany of new members—secular condo dwellers, social do-gooders, and a colorful congregation of immigrants. Five earlier incarnations of the Baptist assemblage and more than 300 years stand between the first Clarendon Street Church and its ethnic rainbow of newcomers who fill the chambers on Sundays and celebrate their weddings in spring and summer as the celebratory stretch limos line the block and flower-strewn brides in white gowns reflect the world's outposts, from Haiti to Vietnam.

20 To me, a sometime historian of this evanescent city, the city is a tale to be twice or thrice told, depending on willing audiences, and this peripatetic church that finally lit here in 1872 is one of my favorites. The very early work of two geniuses, Henry Hobbs Richardson* and Frédéric Auguste Bartholdi,† its design is decidedly the best of neither. Richardson, the great architect of nineteenth-century America, launched his career here, and the marginal and not altogether pleasing proportions of the church show his unsure hand. Ah, that lumbering campanile. Bartoldi, too, better known (and better accomplished elsewhere) at the Statute of Liberty, arrived in 1871 and created the sculpture adorning its peak with dubious success. Alike, the Richardson building and the Bartoldi figure tooting its horn in an ungainly pose caused the locals to dub the structure the Church of the Holy Beanblower. The name stuck.

The New Land above the Back Bay pilings was a city of churches reflecting the flux of population from downtown to the burgeoning new town, and, though their congregations have fallen off, the new members reflect history's ever-constant vigor and diversity as the new gallery of worshippers offer music events and instill art galleries to pay the bills in myriad ways, adding new life to the old neighborhood. And more. The Unitarian-Universalist Arlington Street Church a few blocks from the Clarendon Street congregation continues the open-minded political policies demonstrated by its basement horde of Sandista papers exploded by counter-radicals a few decades ago. on a cold winter day, the front stairs are packed with singers bundled against the chill, and "If I Had a Hammer," the song of sixties activism, wafts from the front steps of the church—a countercry to the president's State of the Union call to invade Iraq. The spiritual and the political ally visibly here. Internet activism has an alternative in the city's public streets. "Life is not about speed," said the

*Henry Hobbs Richardson (1838–1886) was one of the most important American architects in the nineteenth century. Born in Louisiana and educated in Paris, he developed a style that draws upon the Romanesque architecture he saw in France but is nevertheless distinctively his own. Examples of his work can be found throughout New England and the Midwest, especially in Boston and Chicago.

†A prominent sculptor in the nineteenth century, Frédéric Auguste Bartholdi (1834–1904) is best known for designing and creating the Statue of Liberty in New York Harbor, a project to which he devoted enormous effort—effort that included raising the funds so that the statue could be completed and presented as a gift from the French people. In addition to the Boston church referred to by Kay, examples of Bartholdi's work can be found in New York's Union Square and the U.S. Botanic Garden in Washington, D.C.

church signboard, quoting Gandhi as its members prayed for peace and paid for restoring its Tiffany windows.

Still, God loses out to Mammon, that Syrian deity, in the embattled city, and even ecclesiastical masterpieces are not safe from his claims. In fact, a soaring twentieth-century version dedicated to the monetary diety—the one-hundred-story-high glass John Hancock tower—famously just about undid that bastion of the former, Trinity Church. Designed by Richardson, who, by a mathematical irony, began creating his masterpiece there in 1872, exactly a century before the insurance company did, the tower suffered assaults from the new building from the start. The glass rhomboid cresting upward seemed hellbound from the beginning, despite (because of ?) its proud and prestigious architect, I. M. Pei.* As a young architecture critic for the Boston Globe, I deplored (still do) the overweening height of the sixty-two-story structure looming over Copley Square, whiplashing its famous public space, creating hostile wind tunnels for pedestrians, and diminishing surrounding architectural marvels including the magnificent Boston Public Library by McKim, Mead and White.†

What ego! What arrogance, I thought, to break the barrier of this low-rise landscape, to create this antisocial climate change. And more, for suddenly it seemed that the skybreaking building had caused yet another phenomenon: the sun reflected in its mirror-glass walls was glaring at Mass. Turnpike drivers from miles away, blinding them. A hue. A stew. A cry. An article. But first, of course, a call to the public relations staff about what the new "sunset" was doing to the accident rate. Did a building have the right? I asked. "Would you ask God to stop the sunsets?" came the reply. Not even the Fountainhead school of ego architecture had prepared me for the conceit of someone equating an act of the Almighty with an insurance company's phallic gesture. It was a first but not a last.

Worse luck, the glass windows began to pop, and wooden panels replaced them. A

*Born in China in 1917, Ieoh Ming Pei came to the United States to study architecture when he was seventeen. He graduated from the Massachusetts Institute of Technology in 1940 and became a U.S. citizen in 1954. It was in 1964, however, that he first attracted national attention; that was the year Jacqueline Kennedy selected him to design the John F. Kennedy Library in Boston. Since then, he has been responsible for many important projects, the most successful of which may be the East Building of the National Gallery in Washington, D.C., and the expansion of the Louvre in Paris at the request of French President Francois Mitterrand. Critics consider the Hancock building in Boston one of his least successful designs.

†McKim, Mead, and White was one of the country's most prestigious architectural firms in the late nineteenth and early twentieth century. Examples of its work, such as the American Academy in Rome, can still be admired. Other works created by the firm were destroyed by developers before they became protected as national landmarks. Sadly, the firm's greatest accomplishment—Pennsylvania Station in New York City—was torn town in the 1960s, a loss still mourned by New Yorkers. (Indeed, it was the demolition of this station, more than any other event, that inspired citizens to press the government to preserve important architecture by designating such sites as historic landmarks.) Given the loss of Pennsylvania Station, Boston's Public Library, New York's Morgan Library, and the state capital building in Rhode Island are among the most important designs that remain in place.

strange patchwork indeed. "The U.S. Plywood Building," they called it, as lawyers scrapped and engineers hemmed and hawed and failed for a long time, a very long time, to fix it. Worse still, the wooden foundations that secured the adjacent Trinity Church's foundations in solid soil below its watery bed began to quiver from the insurance company's construction work while the elegant Copley Plaza Hotel, on the other side, next door, was wobbling . . . and . . .

25 To cut to the chase: they did it with dollars. You can say that a city is where everything has a price and nothing has a value, where everything is negotiated, not planned, but this was remarkable even in the annals of urban myths. After suits and a newspaper splash nationally, the Hancock's wealthy insurance folks bought

the Copley to salve the suit and forked out the funds to fix up the church. But not quickly. Only now, decades later, has the church opened its basement to reveal the repaired foundations and take tourists through the site . . . just in time, it seems, for the flagging insurance folks to put their falling business up for sale in—ahhh, the indignity of it!—a package with other relatively dwarfed buildings they owned totaling perhaps a billion dollars.

Ego rises, ego falls . . . likewise architecture in the lived-in city. Is it that nothing is sacred in the striving city? Or, more positively, that the city is—happily and by definition—a striving city: the place of all places where we try . . . and try . . . to get it right? Incredibly, too, the square where these structures sit has also gone through three lives in the same time span. The square's nineteenth-century shape, an erratic and triangular landscape in early postcards, became a subterranean plaza in the 1970s, which, in turn, became the local subterranean "needle park," which was, then, more positively, raised and fountained and tree-filled and paved with a potpourri of brick patterns, statuary, and grass. And, yet again in the restless, lived-in city, as summer nears, the square is being enlarged. A portion of a road that straddles its western side will expand the space. With any luck, we could live through still more evolutions by folks who think they've really, finally, definitely, absolutely got it right this time, in the endlessly striving, endlessly lived-in city.

And why not? Belief in striving for the New New Thing could be the city's most important product. Not just here, though, but everywhere. Our oldest, best, and brightest cities—San Francisco, Chicago, New York, you know them— grew because they were built by some folks with nothing left to lose and some folks with a lot to gain. (They are also best, of course, because they are oldest and bound by preindustrial, "natural" laws of craftsmanship and gravity and kinship to that nature.) Without the will to do better, and, of course, to do well in

the most brazen financial manner, cities would not grow. Without cities we would not have the coming together, the sense of history, the outrage that keeps us on edge. Only cities can teach us both the permanence and the impermanence of human handiwork. There is stability and its opposite, beauty and its lack, but always history in the midst of assault, creativity in the midst of destruction, and, for me, always stories to see and tell in the life and death, the liveliness and torpor, the wealth and poverty of their ever-shifting landscapes.

In the early morning hours, I hear a tinny rattle in the alley five flights below my bedroom window. A man with very white sneakers beneath a ragtag outfit and a silver shopping bag dangling from his hand has hit the heap of trash in the parking space beneath the alianthus. It is very, very cold and as I watch him make his way through our rejects, I calculate the rentals for such alley parking lots. The premium to rent this paved plot is three hundred dollars a month, about the same sum to bed and board this trash picker shuffling below the weed tree; the price to buy it is an astounding $129,000—offensive: "profane," as the sixties had it.

The city throws such inequities before public eyes, but not the suburbs. Is that why the deepest inhumanity, the inhumanity of indifference, lies in the isolated homes behind the greenest laws in those affluent outposts? You can run but you can't hide in the lived-in city. There is color as well as sorrow here, I think as I survey the sad scene amid the beauty and the affluence. For even the weed trees shade the brick buildings in the summer and blush their alleys with bounteous red berries in the fall.

30 Yet cities themselves rise and fall in time, on the small scale—the loss of Robert to the neighborhood, I think—and on the large as well, I muse, contemplating the rising sea levels that could wash over my neighborhood on its watery pilings. The city's sunrise is over in a minute in the long span of planetary life. Still,

ephemeral or not, I cling to the belief that cities are the finest record of human will and human creativity. In flux, yes, and flawed, but lived-in, they link their living neighbors and long-gone ancestors in a way that confirms our sense of community and the genius of humanity to create art from habitat.

Questions for Discussion

1. What does Kay accomplish by opening with the story of Robert—a story to which she returns toward the end of her argument? How do you picture his sandwiches and the atmosphere in which he makes them? How would it differ from buying a sandwich in a chain such as Subway or a convenience store in which plastic-wrapped sandwiches are already on hand?

2. What does Kay mean when she celebrates the city's "impersonal connections"? In what sense is the city "impersonal" and thus private? In what sense does it still offer daily opportunities for "connections"?

3. What do you make of Kay's capitalization in paragraph 8, when she refers to "Gaps" rather than "gaps"?

4. Kay claims that the federal government has "fed urban flight" by encouraging suburban growth through subsidies for highway construction. To what extent do you think the ongoing construction of highways has been good policy? What are the disadvantages of public policy that encourages people to live ever further from the urban center?

5. What kind of shops might you find in a city that you might not find in a suburban mall? Why do you think chains once located in the suburbs are moving into city centers?

6. What do you picture when Kay associates "pernicious" with "suburban subdivider"? How does greed also affect urban development?

7. What is the purpose of paragraph 18?

8. Consider the sign quoted in paragraph 21: "Life is not about speed." Why is this advice relevant to contemporary culture? Why do you think this message would be posted by a church?

9. At the end of her argument, Kay draws attention to a man going through the trash and notes that he is in an area where it costs $129,000 to buy a parking space. She then labels what she witnessed "profane." What is your understanding of the word "profane"? Why do you think Kay considers it an appropriate word for this context?

③ DONELLA MEADOWS, "So What Can We Do—
Really Do—about Sprawl?"

Debates about sprawl—a term that refers to the spread of housing developments, strip malls, and office buildings into rural areas—often focus on concerns about quality of life and environmental damage. But Donella Meadows demonstrates that sprawl is also a public policy issue. She is clearly an opponent of unchecked development, but she refuses simply to criticize developers. "We can't blame those who make the money," she writes. "They're playing the game according to the rules." For Meadows, combating sprawl means understanding—and changing—those rules, which include tax laws and zoning ordinances. Meadows refuses to reduce the problem of sprawl to a pro-versus-con debate. Everyone, she suggests, benefits from municipal services and economic development, no matter how fervently some might support environmental protection. So people cannot simply say that they are for or against development. Her argument encourages you to think about protecting the environment and enhancing quality of life in terms of such mundane (and perhaps dull) matters as taxes and zoning. In doing so, you might also think about your responsibilities—as consumer and as a citizen of a town or city—for the problems caused by sprawl. In this sense her essay is an effort to address a complex problem by understanding it rather than by opposing those who might disagree with her. Meadows, who died in 2001, was the director of the Sustainability Institute and an adjunct professor of environmental studies at Dartmouth College. Author or coauthor of nine books, including the best-selling *Limits to Growth* (1972), she was an internationally known voice for an environmentally conscious lifestyle. This essay appeared in her weekly "Global Citizen" column in 1999.

So What Can We Do—Really Do—about Sprawl?

DONELLA MEADOWS

1   In my mind St. Louis is the poster city for sprawl [see photo on page 677]. It has a glittering, high-rise center where fashionable people work, shop and party. Surrounding the center are blocks and blocks of empty lots, abandoned buildings, dying stores, a sad wasteland through which the fashionable people speed on wide highways to the suburbs. In the suburbs the subdivisions and shopping centers expand rapidly outward onto the world's best farmland.

When I imagine the opposite of sprawl, I think of Oslo, Norway [see photo on page 678]. Oslo rises halfway up the hills at the end of a fjord and then abruptly stops. What stops it is a huge public park, in which no private entity is allowed to build anything. The park is full of trails, lakes, playgrounds, picnic tables, and scattered huts where you can stop for a hot drink in winter or cold drink in summer. Tram lines radiate from the city to the park edges, so you can ride to the end of a line, ski or hike in a loop to the end of another line and ride home.

That is a no-nonsense urban growth boundary. It forces development inward. There are no derelict blocks in Oslo. Space no longer useful for one purpose is snapped up for another. Urban renewal goes on constantly everywhere. There are few cars, because there's hardly any place to park and anyway most streets in the shopping district are pedestrian zones. Trams are cheap and frequent and go everywhere. The city is quiet, clean, friendly, attractive and economically thriving.

How could we make our cities more like Oslo and less like land-gulping, energy-intensive, half-empty St. Louis? There is a long list of things we could do. Eben Fodor, in his new book *Better Not Bigger,* (the most useful piece of writing on sprawl control I've seen) organizes them under two categories: taking the foot off the accelerator and applying the brake.

5 The accelerator part comes from widespread public subsidies to sprawl. Fodor lists ten of them, which include:

- Free or subsidized roads, sewer systems, water systems, schools, etc. (Instead charge development impact fees high enough to be sure the taxes of present residents don't go up to provide public services for new residents.)
- Tax breaks, grants, free consulting services, and other handouts to attract new businesses. (There's almost never a good reason for the public to subsidize a private business, especially not in a way that allows it to undercut existing businesses.)
- Waiving environmental or land-use regulations. (Make the standards strong enough to protect everyone's air, water, views and safety and enforce those standards firmly and evenly.)
- Federally funded road projects. (The Feds pay the money, but the community puts up with the sprawl. And where do you think the Feds get the money?)

Urban growth accelerators make current residents pay (in higher taxes, lower services,

BETTER NOT BIGGER

"Our cities and towns keep growing and growing. 'To what end?' you might ask. Are big cities so much better than small cities that we should strive to convert every small city into a bigger one? It seems clear from looking at many of the world's largest cities that we have little reason to envy them. Maybe there is some ideal size where all the best qualities of a community come together to reach an optimal state of urban harmony? If there is such a size, would we know when we've reached it? Would we be less able to stop growing once we were there? The reality is that we just grow and grow, regardless of our community's size or whether further growth is good or bad for us. Endless growth is the only plan on the table."

SOURCE: Eben Fodor, *Better Not Bigger* (1999).

more noise and pollution and traffic jams) for new development. There is no legal or moral reason why they should do that. Easing up on the accelerator should at least guarantee that growth pays its own way.

Applying the brake means setting absolute limits. There are some illegal reasons for wanting to do this: to protect special privilege, to keep out particular kinds of persons; to take private property for public purpose without fair compensation. There are also legal reasons: to protect watersheds or aquifers or farmland or open space, to force growth into places where public services can be efficiently delivered, to slow growth to a rate at which the community can absorb it, to stop growth before land, water, or other resources fail.

Fodor tells the stories of several communities that have limited their growth and lists many techniques they have used to do so. They include:

- Growth boundaries and green belts like the one around Oslo.
- Agricultural zoning. Given the world food situation, not another square inch of prime soil should be built upon anywhere.
- Infrastructure spending restrictions. Why should a Wal-Mart that sucks in traffic

force the public to widen the road? Let Wal-Mart do it, or let the narrow road limit the traffic.
- Downzoning. Usually met with screams of protest from people whose land values are reduced, though we never hear objections when upzoning increases land values.
- Comprehensive public review of all aspects of a new development, such as required by Vermont's Act 250.
- Public purchase of development rights.
- Growth moratoria, growth rate limits, or absolute caps on municipal size, set by real resource limitations.

Boulder, Colorado, may be the American town that has most applied growth controls, prompted by a sober look at the "build-out" implications of the city's zoning plan. Boulder voters approved a local sales tax used to acquire greenways around the city. A building height limitation protects mountain views. Building permits are limited in number, many can be used only in the city center, and 75 percent of new housing permits must be allocated to affordable housing. Commercial and industrial land was downzoned with the realization that if jobs grow faster than housing, commuters from other towns will overload roads and parking facilities.

10 All that and more is possible in any city. But controlling growth means more than fiddling at the margins, "accommodating" growth, "managing" growth. It means questioning myths about growth, realizing that growth can bring more costs than benefits. That kind of growth makes us poorer, not richer. It shouldn't be celebrated or welcomed or subsidized or managed or accommodated; it should be stopped.

We have planning boards. We have zoning regulations. We have urban growth boundaries and "smart growth" and sprawl conferences. And we still have sprawl. Between 1970 and 1990 the population of Chicago grew by four percent; its developed land area grew by 46 percent. Over the same period Los Angeles swelled 45 percent in population, 300 percent in settled area.

Sprawl costs us more than lost farmland and daily commutes through landscapes of stunning ugliness. It costs us dollars, bucks straight out of our pockets, in the form of higher local taxes. That's because our pattern of municipal growth, especially land-intensive city-edge growth, consistently costs more in public services than it pays in taxes.

In his new book *Better Not Bigger,* Eben Fodor cites study after study showing how growth raises taxes. In Loudon County, Virginia, each new house on a quarter-acre lot adds $705 per year to a town budget (in increased garbage collection, road maintenance, etc. minus increased property tax). On a five-acre lot a new house costs the community $2232 per year. In Redmond, Washington, single-family houses pay 21 percent of property tax but account for 29 percent of the city budget. A study in California's Central Valley calculated that more compact development could save municipalities 500,000 acres of farmland and $1.2 billion in taxes.

There are dozens of these studies. They all come to the same conclusion. New subdivisions reach into the pockets of established residents to finance additional schools and services. Commercial and industrial developments sometimes pay more in taxes than they demand in services, but the traffic and pollution they generate reduces nearby property value. New employees don't want to live near the plant or strip, so they build houses and raise taxes in the NEXT town. Large, well-organized companies, such as sports teams and Wal-Mart, push city governments to widen roads, provide free water or sewage lines, offer property tax breaks, even build the stadium.
15 Given all the evidence to the contrary, it's amazing how many of us still believe the myth that growth reduces taxes. But then, every myth springs from a seed of truth. Municipal growth does benefit some people. Real estate agents get sales, construction companies get

jobs, banks get more depositors and borrowers, newspapers get higher circulations, stores get more business (though they also get more and tougher competition). Landowners who sell to developers can make big money; developers can make even bigger money.

Those folks are every town's growth promoters. Eben Fodor calls them the "urban growth machine" and cites an example of how the machine is fueled. Imagine a proposed development that will cost a community $1,000,000 and bring in $500,000 in benefits. The $500,000 goes to ten people, $50,000 apiece. The $1,000,000 is charged to 100,000 people as a $10 tax increase. Who is going to focus full attention on this project, be at all the hearings, bring in lawyers, chat up city officials? Who is going to believe sincerely and claim loudly that growth is a good thing?

Fodor quotes Oregon environmentalist Andy Kerr, who calls urban growth, "a pyramid scheme in which a relatively few make a killing, some others make a living, but most [of us] pay for it." As long as there is a killing to be made, no tepid "smart-growth" measures are going to stop sprawl. We will go on having strips and malls and cookie-cutter subdivisions and traffic jams and rising taxes as long as someone makes money from them.

We can't blame those who make the money. They're playing the game according to the rules, which are set mainly by the market,

PYRAMID SCHEMES

A *pyramid scheme* is a fraudulent way of making money through which someone creates the illusion of a profitable business by attracting new investment through false claims. Any "profits" are the result of new investment, not because the company is succeeding in producing or selling anything. New investment eventually dries up, and the pyramid collapses. To use a simple analogy, you might use a chain letter to convince five people to give you $1.00 each, promising that they will each receive $5.00 back once they recruit five more investors at a $1.00 apiece as the chain letter continues. Sooner or later, people stop writing back. For more information, visit http://skepdic.com/pyramid.html.

which rewards whomever is clever enough to put any cost of doing business onto someone else. They get the store profits, we build the roads. They hire the workers (paying as little as they can get away with, because the market requires them to cut costs), we sit in traffic jams and breathe the exhaust. They get jobs building the subdivision, we lose open lands, clean water, and wildlife. Then we subsidize them with our taxes. That, the tax subsidy, is not the market, it's local politics. Collectively we set out pots of subsidized honey at which they dip. We can't expect them not to dip; we can only expect them to howl if the subsidy is taken away.

The "we-they" language in the previous paragraph isn't quite right. They may profit more than we do, but we flock to the stores with the low prices. We buy dream homes in the ever-expanding suburbs. We use the services of the growth machine. (With some equally amateur friends I'm trying to create a 22-unit eco-development, and I'm learning to appreciate the skills needed and the risks borne by developers.) We want our local builders and banks and stores and newspapers to thrive.

20 So what can we do about this spreading mess, which handsomely rewards a few, which turns our surroundings into blight, which most of us hate but in which most of us are complicit—and which we subsidize with our tax dollars?

Concrete answers to that question take a long chapter in Fodor's book and will take another column here. The general answer is clear. Don't believe the myth that all growth is good. Ask hard questions. Who will benefit from the next development scheme and who will pay? Are there better options, including undeveloped, protected land? How much growth can our roads, our land, our waters and air, our neighborhoods, schools and community support? Since we can't grow forever, where should we stop?

Questions for Discussion

1. In her opening paragraphs, Meadows contrasts St. Louis and Oslo. How effective is this contrast? To what extent does her argument as a whole depend on comparison or contrast?

2. Meadows devotes much of her space to summarizing the work of Eben Fodor. Evaluate her use of Fodor's ideas. Does she tell you enough about his work that you can understand the principles he advocates? Does Meadows inspire sufficient confidence as a writer for you to believe that her summary of Fodor is accurate? In what ways do you think her argument about sprawl is strengthened or weakened by her use of Fodor's ideas?

3. Drawing on Fodor's work, Meadows uses the metaphors of growth accelerators and brakes to explain her concerns about sprawl. How effectively does this strategy enable her to review her concerns? Do you think the metaphors of accelerators and brakes are appropriate in this case? Explain.

4. Meadows asserts that there is "no legal or moral reason" current residents of an area should be compelled to pay for new development of that area. What does this assertion reveal about Meadows's fundamental beliefs and assumptions about communities and development? Do you agree with her? Why or why not?

5. Meadows cites various statistics related to development and growth, and she cites several studies. How persuasive is her use of such evidence to support her claims?

6. According to Meadows, who is responsible for urban sprawl? Do you agree? Why or why not?

7. Meadows ends her argument with a series of questions. How effectively do you think her questions conclude her argument? In what sense might they be appropriate, given her main argument about sprawl?

8. Meadows asserts that the problem of sprawl is not really a "we-they" problem. In other words, it is not possible to reduce the issue to two sides: one in favor and one against. She encourages you to consider how everyone involved has some responsibility for the problem. In this regard, her argument might be considered a Rogerian argument. Drawing on the explanation of Rogerian argument on pages 131–137, evaluate Meadows's essay as a Rogerian argument. Do you think it can justifiably be described as a Rogerian argument? Explain. How effective do you think it is as such an argument?

④ **ROBERT WILSON,** "Enough Snickering. Suburbia Is More Complicated and Varied Than We Think"

When people debate about sprawl, they usually talk about suburbs, since the growth that creates sprawl tends to occur there. But just what do they mean by the term *suburb*? Robert Wilson seeks to answer that question. He argues that people need to understand suburbs in part because they reflect values and visions for the lives these people wish to have. In the following essay, Wilson explores not only what suburbs are but also what they mean to our sense of ourselves as Americans. He reveals that, although he is not a big fan of the way suburbs have evolved since the early twentieth century, he sees suburbs as an important part of American culture. Furthermore, he points out, many people love them. Notice that Wilson approaches his subject from the perspective of a journalist and citizen deeply interested in preserving American culture. At the time this essay was published in the *Architectural Record* in 2000, he was the editor of *Preservation,* the magazine of the National Trust for Historical Preservation, which is devoted to preserving historically and culturally significant buildings and places.

Enough Snickering. Suburbia Is More Complicated and Varied Than We Think

ROBERT WILSON

1 As the editor of *Preservation* magazine, a publication that sees itself as being about place, I've realized recently that we have been overlooking a pretty significant subject: suburbia, the place where half of Americans live. We have run stories about sprawl and the New Urbanism and made the usual condescending references to cookie-cutter houses and place-less places. But we have failed to look at the suburbs with the same curiosity and courtesy that we've shown to Dubrovnik, say, or Sioux Falls or Paducah. "Why is that?" I now wonder. Snobbery is part of the answer. Nothing can be less hip than suburbia. At a time when our cities are showing new signs of life and our open space is still being chewed up at an exponential rate, whose imagination is going to catch fire over the problems of the suburbs?

Part of the answer is also linguistic. The s-word itself has become so ubiquitous and so baggage-laden that it barely means anything anymore. There is a paradox lurking here. The word suburbia has been used to describe the increasingly varied places where more and more of us live—gritty inner suburbs that share many of the problems of their urban neighbors, immigrant neighborhoods at every economic level, and new greenfield developments sporting one McMansion bigger than the next. Yet our definition of the word remains fixed in a former time, decades ago, when women worked at home and men commuted to work. The biggest problem with suburbia is that we are all so certain that we know what it means. We watched *Father Knows Best* and read our Updike,* and even a recent film like the

*Award-winning novelist John Updike is especially known for a series of novels focused on a character named Harry "Rabbit" Angstrom, who responds with mixed results to the opportunities and challenges of suburban, middle-class life.

Oscar-laden *American Beauty* confirms what we think we know: suburbia is a dull, sterile, unhappy place.

A Persistent Bias

As this suggests, the problem is also cultural. For the most part, American culture and opinion are still created, even in the Internet age, in cities at either edge of the continent. City dwellers, whether native born or the still more unforgiving recent converts, think of the suburbs as a mediocre place for mediocre people, a place where they will never venture or from which they have happily escaped. Even those who work in cities and live in suburbs (many of which now offer more urban amenities than nine-to-five cities) share this anti-suburban frame of mind. If intellectuals do deign to look at the suburbs—whether cleverly in a film like *American Beauty* or clumsily, as in another recent film, the ugly paranoid fantasy *Arlington Road*—they assume that so much banality must be hiding something deeply evil.

Beyond the Movies

I'm really not here to defend suburbia, only to suggest that it is a more complicated, more various, and more quickly evolving place than we think. Two writers I admire, Witold Rybczynski and Joel Garreau, have helped me reach this state of cautious curiosity. The former, in his recent biography of Frederick Law Olmsted* and elsewhere, has reminded me that the suburb was a noble idea that was often, in the first decades of its existence, nobly executed. Many of these places, such as Chevy Chase near Washington, D.C., continue to function admirably well. Garreau's insight is that Venice didn't become Venice the instant it was built, but developed over a period of centuries. If we remember that the suburbs, especially the postwar suburbs over which we do most of our hand-wringing, are still relatively new places, the question becomes not "Why are they so bad?" but, "What is the next step to making them better?"

Who's to Blame?

As a journalist, I am naturally filled with righteous indignation about the subject. My instincts are first to find someone to blame and second to flatter myself that I know the solution. So, here goes: One reason that the suburbs are not better is that the best minds in architecture abandoned them. Once, not just Olmsted but Frank Lloyd Wright, Le Corbusier, Clarence Stein,† and others considered, in an urgent and serious way, the questions of where and how people might live if they didn't live in cities or on farms. Am I wrong in believing that between the Garden City movement of the 1910s and 1920s and the New Towns of the 1960s there was a wasteland of ideas beyond the city limits—just as the suburbs began to lay waste to vast portions of the American landscape? And that there was precious little between the New Towns and the New Urbanists? Isn't this why the design and execution of suburbs have been so disappointing, because the field was abandoned to the merely avaricious? For anyone who is irritated by how much attention the New Urbanists get, here is the simple answer to their popularity with the media: However retrograde their ideas, however short their accomplishments to date might fall, at least they have an idea and at least they have acted upon it.

5 The New Urbanists spent a certain amount of time reacting to Vincent Scully's suggestion that they should really be thought of as the New Suburbanists, but in their new book, *Suburban Nation: The Rise of Sprawl and the Decline of the American Dream*, Andres Duany, Elizabeth Plater-Zyberk, and Jeff Speck frankly admit and defend their suburban focus. Whether they helped create the slow-growth, sustainable-growth, antisprawl movements

*Frederick Law Olmsted (1822–1903) is widely considered one of our country's most important landscape architects. With his partner Calvert Vaux, he created the winning design for the creation of Central Park in New York City. He also designed the grounds for the U.S. Capitol, among many other projects of national significance.

†Frank Lloyd Wright (1869–1959), Le Corbusier (1887–1967), and Clarence Stein (1882–1975) were influential architects in the early twentieth century. Stein, in particular, is associated with the Garden City movement, which sought to create beautifully landscaped communities within easy access of major cities.

NEW TOWNS AND NEW URBANISTS

The New Towns movement in regional planning gained popularity in the United States in the 1920s. It focused on carefully designed and largely residential communities located away from urban centers. These New Towns, also called "Garden Cities," sometimes developed into large suburban areas. New Urbanism, which emerged in the 1990s, is a reaction to the New Town idea of community planning. As an alternative to sprawl, New Urbanism emphasizes the integration of housing, workplaces, businesses, and recreation into small neighborhoods connected by public transportation. According to Ute Angleki Lehrer, a professor of urban and regional planning at the State University of New York at Buffalo, "By establishing specific rules for land use and building design, the architects of New Urbanism believe that they can create diversity and density in neighborhoods of both new suburban development and revitalization projects in existing urban areas."

that have captured the imagination of so many voters in recent elections at all levels of government, or whether they merely capitalized on these movements, their book seems timely. In a recent front-page article, the *New York Times* reported that academics have suddenly taken an urgent interest in suburbia. Other major newspapers across the country have latched on to the subject, perhaps as an outgrowth of the widening interest in sprawl.

Recent stories in *Preservation,* beginning with a cover story on the new suburban immigrants, have not thrilled hardcore preservationists, for whom suburbia has always been a particular bete noire. For me, this resistance is only a speed bump on the road to the movement's democratization.

Do I foresee the wholesale preservation of postwar suburbs? Probably not. Rapid evolution would be far more desirable. Still, alarms were sounded recently in Houston, where a whole neighborhood of brick ranch houses was under siege. The truth is that most people love their suburban homes and neighborhoods and will fight to save them. And if preservationists have learned anything in the last century or so, it is that the notion of what is worth preserving changes. Just recall how Victorian buildings were despised as recently as a few decades ago. Perhaps the split-level will be the retro rage in 2050.

Design Creeps In
As money and newly sophisticated consumers pour into the suburbs, good design and architecture are beginning to

follow. In my neck of suburbia, northern Virginia, where even a determined electorate has had trouble slowing sprawl, there are nonetheless hopeful signs that good ideas are arriving—from town-center schemes for shopping and living to interesting and appealing buildings for churches, college campuses, and office complexes.

Most welcome of all, perhaps, is the improved architecture for public buildings, including schools, which were the most bereft places we allowed to be built in the bad old days just ending. May all of you who read these words enthusiastically enter the fray, enriching yourselves even as you enrich a vast part of our landscape that urgently needs you.

Questions for Discussion

1. Wilson opens his argument by establishing that he is editor of *Preservation* magazine. To what extent does this information make him a credible source? When considering his argument as a whole, how would you evaluate his credibility?

2. On what grounds might preservationists try to protect suburban neighborhoods that some critics find ugly? Do you think Wilson does justice to a more positive view of suburban communities? Explain.

3. Wilson suggests in this essay that suburbs can be better. What does he mean? What does his position reveal about his beliefs regarding the ideal community? Do you agree with him? Why or why not?

4. Notice the many references Wilson makes in his essay to films, literature, historical developments, and social movements. What do these references suggest about the audience Wilson is addressing in this essay? Does that audience include you? Explain.

5. Wilson's essay raises questions about how people think about the communities they live in. How does his argument affect the way you think communities should be designed? Do you think he wishes to challenge conventional views about community design? Explain, citing specific passages from his essay to support your answer.

DIFFERENCES

NEGOTIATING

Urban sprawl can also damage inner cities as people move to distant suburbs and eventually work and shop many miles from the city center. Moreover, sprawl can affect older suburbs located at the inner ring around a city. According to one expert, "These are the patterns that many cities in the Rust Belt are carving out—entire rings spreading outward relentlessly, or pie-shaped pieces doing the same. Left behind are devastated neighborhoods in formerly industrial cities. So natural landscapes aren't the only victims of the public policies and private preferences that have suburbanized America. They've also taken a toll on aging built landscapes and the people remaining in them" (Deron Lovass, "Shrinking Cities, Growing Populations").

So sprawl can affect most Americans: city dwellers, suburbanites, and anyone living in a rural area within commuting distance of a metropolitan region.

Imagine now that you are at a public meeting at which a developer is seeking permission to build new housing on 500 acres of farmland an hour's drive from the center of the largest city in your state. This meeting has attracted environmentalists who are concerned about the consequences of development, commuters who are worried that highways are already overcrowded, and residents from the city and older suburbs who believe that continued growth will damage the areas in which they live. Other voices are heard at this meeting, however. Several people speak about an urgent need for safe, affordable housing, and others insist that additional development is essential for the economic well-being of the metropolitan area as a whole. Finally, someone else points out that new developments do not have to be ugly. On the contrary, they can be well designed and built in an environmentally responsible way.

With this scenario in mind, write an essay in which you advocate a specific plan for the land in question. In your essay, discuss what you see as the primary goals for the community that will be built—and for the use of such land in general. Also try to account for the various perspectives of people who are concerned about how that land will be used. Taking these matters into account, make an argument for what you believe should be done with the land. Ideally, your argument will address the various concerns expressed at the meeting, even if all parties involved would not agree with your proposal.

Alternatively, focus your essay on how a city in your area could be improved through better design.

What Is Our Relationship to Nature?

In his famous essay, "Walking" (see *Con-Text* on page 689), nineteenth-century American writer Henry David Thoreau announces, "Life consists with wildness. The most alive is the wildest. Not yet subdued to man, its presence refreshes him." Perhaps this idea that people require "the wild" to be truly alive helped make Thoreau a favorite writer of the environmental movement that emerged in the United States in the 1960s and 1970s. And perhaps it accounts for his high standing among environmentalists even today. Certainly, many people who support wilderness preservation and who venture into wilderness areas find solace and revitalization there. They argue that wilderness helps us understand who we are. ■ But in "Walking," Thoreau argues that wilderness doesn't help us understand who we are; for Thoreau wilderness *is* who we are. Indeed, Thoreau criticized the cultivation of farmland and the construction of cities and towns not because they destroyed wilderness areas but because they destroyed human life as he believed it should be lived: "Hope and the future for me are not in lawns and cultivated fields," he wrote, "not in cities and towns, but in the impervious and quaking swamps." This is a vision not so much of wilderness but of human life. For Thoreau the two—wilderness and humans—are not distinct but the same. ■ The essays in this section explore this connection between humans and wilderness. In one way or another these writers take up the challenge of defining our relationship to wilderness. It seems to be an especially important challenge at the beginning of the twenty-first century, because wilderness areas around the world are under great pressure from development and population growth, and many are disappearing altogether. The loss of such areas raises questions about their value. Is their value only a function of the economic benefit they might produce—such as the lumber from the trees removed from a wilderness area when it is developed? Or does the value of wilderness lie in something more than profit, as Thoreau believed? For some writers the answers to those questions require them and their readers to reexamine the very idea of wilderness. Some writers even suggest that the desire to preserve wilderness is really a reflection of Western cultural values—values that might be at odds with the values of people from other cultures. ■ As a group, then, these essays underscore the need to think carefully about the human relationship to wilderness as people address the difficult question of what to do about disappearing wilderness areas.

CON-TEXT

Thoreau's Wildness

1 Life consists with wildness. The most alive is the wildest. Not yet subdued to man, its presence refreshes him. One who pressed forward incessantly and never rested from his labors, who grew fast and made infinite demands on life, would always find himself in a new country or wilderness, and surrounded by the raw material of life. He would be climbing over the prostrate stems of primitive forest trees.

Hope and the future for me are not in lawns and cultivated fields, not in towns and cities, but in the impervious and quaking swamps. . . .

In short, all good things are wild and free. There is something in a strain of music, whether produced by an instrument or by the human voice—take the sound of a bugle in a summer night, for instance—which by its wildness, to speak without satire, reminds me of the cries emitted by wild beasts in their native forests. It is so much of their wildness as I can understand. Give me for my friends and neighbors wild men, not tame ones. The wildness of the savage is but a faint symbol of the awful ferity with which good men and lovers meet. . . .

SOURCE: Henry David Thoreau, "Walking," 1862.

① RACHEL CARSON, "The Obligation to Endure"

If the environmental movement in the latter part of the twentieth-century can be traced to any single work, it is probably *Silent Spring* (1962), Rachel Carson's widely read analysis of how pesticides and other chemicals were polluting the earth and endangering both wildlife and human life. An aquatic biologist with the U.S. Bureau of Fisheries, Carson (1907–1966) became the editor in chief of the publications of the U.S. Fish and Wildlife Service. The values that Carson espouses regarding the natural world—values that deeply influenced a generation of environmental advocates—emerge subtly but powerfully in her discussion of the physical and biological effects of chemicals in the environment. She writes as a scientist, but as you read, consider whether science is the primary perspective from which she examines the problem of pesticides. More important, perhaps, is what Carson conveys about our relationship with the earth. This remains complex and often troubled, which might account for the enduring popularity of Carson's book in the more than forty years since its publication. "The Obligation to Endure" is the second chapter of *Silent Spring*.

The Obligation to Endure

RACHEL CARSON

1   The history of life on earth has been a history of interaction between living things and their surroundings. To a large extent, the physical form and the habits of the earth's vegetation and its animal life have been molded by the environment. Considering the whole span of earthly time, the opposite effect, in which life actually modifies its surroundings, has been relatively slight. Only within the moment of time represented by the present century has one species—man—acquired significant power to alter the nature of his world.

During the past quarter century this power has not only increased to one of disturbing magnitude but it has changed in character. The most alarming of all man's assaults upon the environment is the contamination of air, earth, rivers, and sea with dangerous and even lethal materials. This pollution is for the most part irrecoverable; the chain of evil it initiates not only in the world that must support life but in living tissues is for the most part irreversible. In this now universal contamination of the environment, chemicals are the sinister and little-recognized partners of radiation in changing the very nature of the world—the very nature of its life. Strontium 90, released through nuclear explosions into the air, comes to earth in rain or drifts down as fallout, lodges in soil, enters into the grass or corn or wheat grown there, and in time takes up its abode in the bones of a human being, there to remain until his death. Similarly, chemicals sprayed on croplands or forests or gardens lie long in soil, entering into living organisms, passing from one to another in a chain of poisoning and death. Or they pass mysteriously by underground streams until they emerge and, through the alchemy of air and sunlight, combine into new forms that kill vegetation, sicken cattle, and work unknown harm on those who drink from once pure wells. As Albert Schweitzer has said, "Man can hardly even recognize the devils of his own creation."

It took hundreds of millions of years to produce the life that now inhabits the earth—eons of time in which that developing and evolving and diversifying life reached a state of adjustment and balance with its surroundings. The environment, rigorously shaping and directing the life it supported, contained elements that were hostile as well as supporting. Certain rocks gave out dangerous radiation; even within the light of the sun, from which all life draws its energy, there were shortwave radiations with power to injure. Given time—time not in years but in millennia—life adjusts, and a balance has been reached. For time is the essential ingredient; but in the modern world there is no time.

The rapidity of change and the speed with which new situations are created follow the impetuous and heedless pace of man rather than the deliberate pace of nature. Radiation is no longer merely the background radiation of rocks, the bombardment of cosmic rays, the ultraviolet of the sun that have existed before there was any life on earth; radiation is now the unnatural creation of man's tampering with the atom. The chemicals to which life is asked to make its adjustment are no longer merely the calcium and silica and copper and all the rest of the minerals washed out of the rocks and carried in rivers to the sea; they are the synthetic creations of man's inventive mind, brewed in his laboratories, and having no counterparts in nature.

5 To adjust to these chemicals would require time on the scale that is nature's; it would require not merely the years of a man's life but the life of generations. And even this, were it by some miracle possible, would be futile, for the new chemicals come from our laboratories in an endless stream; almost five hundred annually find their way into actual use in the United States alone. The figure is staggering and its implications are not easily grasped—

500 new chemicals to which the bodies of men and animals are required somehow to adapt each year, chemicals totally outside the limits of biologic experience.

Among them are many that are used in man's war against nature. Since the mid-1940s over 200 basic chemicals have been created for use in killing insects, weeds, rodents, and other organisms described in the modern vernacular as "pests"; and they are sold under several thousand different brand names.

These sprays, dusts, and aerosols are now applied almost universally to farms, gardens, forests, and homes—nonselective chemicals that have the power to kill every insect, the "good" and the "bad," to still the song of birds and the leaping of fish in the streams, to coat the leaves with a deadly film, and to linger on in soil—all this though the intended target may be only a few weeds or insects. Can anyone

NUCLEAR TESTING

More than 2,000 nuclear tests have been conducted since 1945, and more than 700 of them were conducted in the earth's atmosphere or under its oceans. When Carson wrote her argument in 1962, above-ground nuclear testing was routine. Since 1980 most nations have agreed to avoid above-ground nuclear testing, but tests are still conducted underground, under the ocean, and in space. In 1996 Greenpeace estimated that the tests that had been conducted by then had left 3,830 kilograms of plutonium in the ground and 4,200 kilograms of plutonium in the air.

*See Complication on page 698.

believe it is possible to lay down such a barrage of poisons on the surface of the earth without making it unfit for all life? They should not be called "insecticides," but "biocides."

The whole process of spraying seems caught up in an endless spiral. Since DDT* was released for civilian use, a process of escalation has been going on in which ever more toxic materials must be found. This has happened because insects, in a triumphant vindication of Darwin's principle of the survival of the fittest, have evolved super races immune to the particular insecticide used, hence a deadlier one has always to be developed—and then a deadlier one than that. It has happened also because, for reasons to be described later, destructive insects often undergo a "flareback," or resurgence, after spraying, in numbers greater than before. Thus the chemical war is never won, and all life is caught in its violent crossfire.

Along with the possibility of the extinction of mankind by nuclear war, the central problem of our age has therefore become the contamination of man's total environment with such substances of incredible potential for harm—substances that accumulate in the tissues of plants and animals and even penetrate the germ cells to shatter or alter the very material of heredity upon which the shape of the future depends.

10 Some would-be architects of our future look toward a time when it will be possible to alter the human germ plasm by design. But we may easily be doing so now by inadvertence, for many chemicals, like radiation, bring about gene mutations. It is ironic to think that man might determine his own future by something so seemingly trivial as the choice of an insect spray.

All this has been risked—for what? Future historians may well be amazed by our distorted sense of proportion. How could intelligent beings seek to control a few unwanted species by a method that contaminated the entire environment and brought the threat of disease and death even to their own kind? Yet

this is precisely what we have done. We have done it, moreover, for reasons that collapse the moment we examine them. We are told that the enormous and expanding use of pesticides is necessary to maintain farm production. Yet is our real problem not one of *overproduction?* Our farms, despite measures to remove acreages from production and to pay farmers *not* to produce, have yielded such a staggering excess of crops that the American taxpayer in 1962 is paying out more than one billion dollars a year as the total carrying cost of the surplus-food storage program. And is the situation helped when one branch of the Agriculture Department tries to reduce production while another states, as it did in 1958, "It is believed generally that reduction of crop acreages under provisions of the Soil Bank will stimulate interest in use of chemicals to obtain maximum production on the land retained in crops."

All this is not to say there is no insect problem and no need of control. I am saying, rather, that control must be geared to realities, not to mythical situations, and that the methods employed must be such that they do not destroy us along with the insects.

The problem whose attempted solution has brought such a train of disaster in its wake is an accompaniment of our modern way of life. Long before the age of man, insects inhabited the earth—a group of extraordinarily varied and adaptable beings. Over the course of time since man's advent, a small percentage of the more than half a million species of insects have come into conflict with human welfare in two principal ways: as competitors for the food supply and as carriers of human disease.

Disease-carrying insects become important where human beings are crowded together, especially under conditions where sanitation is poor, as in time of natural disaster or war or in situations of extreme poverty and deprivation. Then control of some sort becomes necessary. It is a sobering fact, however, as we shall presently see, that the method of massive chemical control has had only limited success, and also threatens to worsen the very conditions it is intended to curb.

15 Under primitive agricultural conditions the farmer had few insect problems. These arose with the intensification of agriculture—the devotion of immense acreages to a single crop. Such a system set the stage for explosive increases in specific insect populations. Single-crop farming does not take advantage of the principles by which nature works; it is agriculture as an engineer might conceive it to be. Nature has introduced great variety into the landscape, but man has displayed a passion for simplifying it. Thus he undoes the built-in checks and balances by which nature holds the species within bounds. One important natural check is a limit on the amount of suitable habitat for each species. Obviously then, an insect that lives on wheat can build up its population to much higher levels on a farm devoted to wheat than on one in which wheat is intermingled with other crops to which the insect is not adapted.

The same thing happens in other situations. A generation or more ago, the towns of large areas of the United States lined their streets with the noble elm tree. Now the beauty they hopefully created is threatened with complete destruction as disease sweeps through the elms, carried by a beetle that would have only limited chance to build up large populations and to spread from tree to tree if the elms were only occasional trees in a richly diversified planting.

Another factor in the modern insect problem is one that must be viewed against a background of geologic and human history: the spreading of thousands of different kinds of organisms from their native homes to invade new territories. This worldwide migration has been studied and graphically described by the British ecologist Charles Elton in his recent book *The Ecology of Invasions.* During the Cretaceous Period, some hundred million years ago, flooding seas cut many land bridges between continents and living things found themselves confined in what Elton calls

"colossal separate nature reserves." There, isolated from others of their kind, they developed many new species. When some of the land masses were joined again, about 15 million years ago, these species began to move out into new territories—a movement that is not only still in progress but is now receiving considerable assistance from man.

The importation of plants is the primary agent in the modern spread of species, for animals have almost invariably gone along with the plants, quarantine being a comparatively recent and not completely effective innovation [See "Context" on page 694.] The United States Office of Plant Introduction alone has introduced almost 200,000 species and varieties of plants from all over the world. Nearly half of the 180 or so major insect enemies of plants in the United States are accidental imports from abroad, and most of them have come as hitchhikers on plants.

In new territory, out of reach of the restraining hand of the natural enemies that kept

INSECTS AND AGRICULTURE

U.S. agricultural production more than doubled between the late 1940s and the 1980s, in part because of the increased use of pesticides to control insects that damaged some agricultural products and lowered agricultural yields. However, concerns about the health risks associated with pesticides grew in the years after *Silent Spring* was published. In addition, some insects have demonstrated resistance to pesticides. And despite increased use of pesticides, some studies show a slight rise in crop losses because of insects among major crops (such as corn) over the past century; these studies show such crop losses between 10 percent and 15 percent, with some estimates as high as 37 percent. These developments, along with the growing influence of the environmental movement in the 1970s and 1980s, have prompted some farmers to consider alternatives to conventional farming methods that rely on pesticides to control insects. "Organic" or "natural" farming uses a variety of methods to control insects, including crop rotation and biological controls (for example, introducing one kind of insect to control other insects that damage crops). Proponents of such methods argue that crop yields are not reduced when pesticide use is decreased or discontinued, and some studies actually show increased crop yields as a result of organic farming methods.

CONTEXT

More than forty years after the publication of *Silent Spring*, the importation of nonnative species, especially plants, remains a significant problem in the United States. One study estimated monetary losses caused by such species, which often overwhelm local ecosystems because of the lack of natural predators, at $123 billion.

down its numbers in its native land, an invading plant or animal is able to become enormously abundant. Thus it is no accident that our most troublesome insects are introduced species.

20 These invasions, both the naturally occurring and those dependent on human assistance, are likely to continue indefinitely. Quarantine and massive chemical campaigns are only extremely expensive ways of buying time. We are faced, according to Dr. Elton, "with a life-and-death need not just to find new technological means of suppressing this plant or that animal"; instead we need the basic knowledge of animal populations and their relations to their surroundings that will "promote an even balance and damp down the explosive power of outbreaks and new invasions."

Much of the necessary knowledge is now available but we do not use it. We train ecologists in our universities and even employ them in our governmental agencies but we seldom

take their advice. We allow the chemical death rain to fall as though there were no alternative, whereas in fact there are many, and our ingenuity could soon discover many more if given opportunity.

Have we fallen into a mesmerized state that makes us accept as inevitable that which is inferior or detrimental, as though having lost the will or the vision to demand that which is good? Such thinking, in the words of the ecologist Paul Shepard, "idealizes life with only its head out of water, inches above the limits of toleration of the corruption of its own environment. . . . Why should we tolerate a diet of weak poisons, a home in insipid surroundings, a circle of acquaintances who are not quite our enemies, the noise of motors with just enough relief to prevent insanity? Who would want to live in a world which is just not quite fatal?" Yet such a world is pressed upon us. The crusade to create a chemically sterile, insect-free world seems to have engendered a fanatic zeal on the part of many specialists and most of the so-called control agencies. On every hand there is evidence that those engaged in spraying operations exercise a ruthless power. "The regulatory entomologists . . . function as prosecutor, judge and jury, tax assessor and collector and sheriff to enforce their own orders," said Connecticut entomologist Neely Turner. The most flagrant abuses go unchecked in both state and federal agencies.

It is not my contention that chemical insecticides must never be used. I do contend that we have put poisonous and biologically potent chemicals indiscriminately into the hands of persons largely or wholly ignorant of their potentials for harm. We have subjected enormous numbers of people to contact with these poisons, without their consent and often without their knowledge. If the Bill of Rights contains no guarantee that a citizen shall be secure against lethal poisons distributed either by private individuals or by public officials, it is surely only because our forefathers, despite their considerable wisdom and foresight, could conceive of no such problem.

I contend, furthermore, that we have allowed these chemicals to be used with little or no advance investigation of their effect on soil, water, wildlife, and man himself. Future generations are unlikely to condone our lack of prudent concern for the integrity of the natural world that supports all life.

There is still very limited awareness of the nature of the threat. This is an era of specialists, each of whom sees his own problem and is unaware of or intolerant of the larger frame into which it fits. It is also an era dominated by industry, in which the right to make a dollar at whatever cost is seldom challenged. When the public protests, confronted with some obvious evidence of damaging results of pesticide applications, it is fed little tranquilizing pills of half truth. We urgently need an end to these false assurances, to the sugar coating of unpalatable facts. It is the public that is being asked to assume the risks that the insect controllers calculate. The public must decide whether it wishes to continue on the present road, and it can do so only when in full possession of the facts. In the words of Jean Rostand, "The obligation to endure gives us the right to know."

Questions for Discussion

1. What kinds of evidence does Carson present to support her claim that the environment is at risk? How persuasive do you find her evidence?

2. Carson asks, "How could intelligent beings seek to control a few unwanted species by a method that contaminated the entire environment and brought the threat of disease and death even to their own kind?" How would you answer her?

3. Ronald Bailey, whose essay begins on pages 697–701, asserts that the effectiveness of Carson's book was largely because of her language rather than the strength of her evidence. Evaluate Carson's writing style and tone in this essay. How effective do you find them? In what ways do you think they contribute to her argument? Do you think Bailey is right?

4. On the basis of the essay, what fundamental values do you think Carson holds about humans and their relationship to the environment? Do you think most Americans share these values today? Explain.

5. As the sidebar on page 694 indicates, crop losses because of insect damage can be significant for farmers, and many agricultural experts believe that the appropriate use of pesticides remains the best way to control insects. In what ways does Carson address this concern in her essay?

6. *Silent Spring* was published in 1962. What elements of Carson's argument do you think are still relevant? Do you think that any of the concerns raised by Carson have been resolved? Explain.

② RONALD BAILEY, "Silent Spring at 40"

Rachel Carson's best-selling and widely influential book *Silent Spring* (see pages 690–695) is usually thought of as a scientific work—a careful analysis of the effects of pesticides. In the following essay, Ronald Bailey suggests that it is something else. Its influence, he argues, lies in its persuasiveness as an argument more than in the quality of its scientific analysis. In fact, Bailey argues that Carson played fast and loose with scientific facts in making her argument against pesticide use, and he offers a detailed and extensive examination of those facts in an effort to call Carson's argument into question. In doing so, Bailey provides a reminder that any text can be understood as an argument and that even science relies on argument and rhetoric. Whether or not you agree with Bailey's critique of Carson, the real value of his essay might be in the way it reveals the rhetorical and argumentative character of scientific texts. He helps you see, too, that this is as it should be, because issues such as pesticide use are not just scientific issues but social and political issues that can directly affect lives. Argument, in other words, is one of the means by which people try to address these issues together. Bailey is the science correspondent for *Reason* magazine, in which the following essay appeared in 2002; he is also the editor of *Earth Report 2000: Revisiting the True State of the Planet.*

Silent Spring at 40

RONALD BAILEY

1 The modern environmentalist movement was launched at the beginning of June 1962, when excerpts from what would become Rachel Carson's anti-chemical landmark *Silent Spring* were published in *The New Yorker.* "Without this book, the environmental movement might have been long delayed or never have developed at all," declared then-Vice President Albert Gore in his introduction to the 1994 edition. The foreword to the 25th anniversary edition accurately declared, "It led to environmental legislation at every level of government."

In 1999 *Time* named Carson one of the "100 People of the Century." Seven years earlier, a panel of distinguished Americans had selected *Silent Spring* as the most influential book of the previous 50 years. When I went in search of a copy recently, several bookstore owners told me they didn't have any in stock because local high schools still assign the book and students had cleaned them out.

Carson worked for years at the U.S. Fish and Wildlife Service, eventually becoming the chief editor of that agency's publications. Carson achieved financial independence in the 1950s with the publication of her popular celebrations of marine ecosystems, *The Sea Around Us* and *The Edge of the Sea.* Rereading *Silent Spring* reminds one that the book's effectiveness was due mainly to Carson's passionate, poetic language describing the alleged horrors that modern synthetic chemicals visit upon defenseless nature and

From a public health statement by the Agency for Toxic Substances and Disease Registry (1989):

Short-term exposure to high doses of DDT affects primarily the nervous system. People who either voluntarily or accidentally swallowed very high amounts of DDT experienced excitability, tremors, and seizures. These effects on the nervous system appeared to be reversible once exposure stopped. Some people who came in contact with DDT complained of rashes or irritation of the eyes, nose, and throat. People exposed for a long-term at low doses, such as people who made DDT, had some changes in the levels of liver enzymes, but there was no indication that DDT caused irreversible harmful (noncancer) effects. Tests in laboratory animals confirm the effect of DDT on the nervous system. However, tests in animals suggest that exposure to DDT may have a harmful effect on reproduction, and long-term exposure may affect the liver. Studies in animals have shown that oral exposure to DDT can result in an increased occurrence of liver tumors. In the five studies of DDT-exposed workers, results did not indicate increases in the number of deaths or cancers. However, these studies had limitations so that possible increases in cancer may not have been detected. Because DDT caused cancer in laboratory animals, it is assumed that DDT could have this effect in humans.

hapless humanity. Carson was moved to write *Silent Spring* by her increasing concern about the effects of pesticides on wildlife. Her chief villain was the pesticide DDT.

The 1950s saw the advent of an array of synthetic pesticides that were hailed as modern miracles in the war against pests and weeds. First and foremost of these chemicals was DDT. DDT's insecticidal properties were discovered in the late 1930s by Paul Muller, a chemist at the Swiss chemical firm J.R. Geigy. The American military started testing it in 1942, and soon the insecticide was being sprayed in war zones to protect American troops against insect-borne diseases such as typhus and malaria. In 1943 DDT famously stopped a typhus epidemic in Naples in its tracks shortly after the Allies invaded. DDT was hailed as the "wonder insecticide of World War II."

5 As soon as the war ended, American consumers and farmers quickly adopted the wonder insecticide, replacing the old-fashioned arsenic-based pesticides, which were truly nasty. Testing by the U.S. Public Health Service and the Food and Drug Administration's Division of Pharmacology found no serious human toxicity problems with DDT. Muller, DDT's inventor, was awarded the Nobel Prize in 1948.

DDT was soon widely deployed by public health officials, who banished malaria from the southern United States with its help. The World Health Organization credits DDT with saving 50 million to 100 million lives by preventing

malaria. In 1943 Venezuela had 8,171,115 cases of malaria; by 1958, after the use of DDT, the number was down to 800. India, which had over 10 million cases of malaria in 1935, had 285,962 in 1969. In Italy the number of malaria cases dropped from 411,602 in 1945 to only 37 in 1968.

The tone of a *Scientific American* article by Francis Joseph Weiss celebrating the advent of "Chemical Agriculture" was typical of much of the reporting in the early 1950s. "In 1820 about 72 per cent of the population worked in agriculture, the proportion in 1950 was only about 15 per cent," reported Weiss. "Chemical agriculture, still in its infancy, should eventually advance our agricultural efficiency at least as much as machines have in the past 150 years." This improvement in agricultural efficiency would happen because "farming is being revolutionized by new fertilizers, insecticides, fungicides, weed killers, leaf removers, soil conditioners, plant hormones, trace minerals, antibiotics and synthetic milk for pigs."

In 1952 insects, weeds, and disease cost farmers $13 billion in crops annually. Since gross annual agricultural output at that time totaled $31 billion, it was estimated that preventing this damage by using pesticides would boost food and fiber production by 42 percent. Agricultural productivity in the United States, spurred by improvements in farming practices and technologies, has continued its exponential increase. As a result, the percentage of Americans living and working on farms has dropped from 15 percent in 1950 to under 1.8 percent today.

But DDT and other pesticides had a dark side. They not only killed the pests at which they were aimed but often killed beneficial organisms as well. Carson, the passionate defender of wildlife, was determined to spotlight these harms. Memorably, she painted a scenario in which birds had all been poisoned by insecticides, resulting in a "silent spring" in which "no birds sing."

10 The scientific controversy over the effects of DDT on wildlife, especially birds, still vexes researchers. In the late 1960s, some researchers concluded that exposure to DDT caused eggshell thinning in some bird species, especially raptors such as eagles and peregrine falcons. Thinner shells meant fewer hatchlings and declining numbers. But researchers also found that other bird species, such as quail, pheasants, and chickens, were unaffected even by large doses DDT.

On June 14, 1972, 30 years ago this week, the EPA banned DDT despite considerable evidence of its safety offered in seven months of agency hearings. After listening to that testimony, the EPA's own administrative law judge declared, "DDT is not a carcinogenic hazard to man . . . DDT is not a mutagenic or teratogenic hazard to man . . . The use of DDT under the regulations involved here [does] not have a deleterious effect on freshwater fish, estuarine organisms, wild birds or other wildlife." Today environmental activists celebrate the EPA's DDT ban as their first great victory.

Carson argued that DDT and other pesticides were not only harming wildlife but killing people too. The 1958 passage by Congress of the Delaney Clause, which forbade the addition of any amount of chemicals suspected of causing cancer to food, likely focused Carson's attention on that disease.

For the previous half-century some researchers had been trying to prove that cancer was caused by chemical contaminants in the environment. Wilhelm Hueper, chief of environmental cancer research at the National Cancer Institute and one of the leading researchers in this area, became a major source for Carson. Hueper was so convinced that trace exposures to synthetic chemicals were a major cause of cancer in humans that he totally dismissed the notion that smoking cigarettes caused cancer. The assertion that pesticides were dangerous human carcinogens was a stroke of public relations genius. Even people who do not care much about wildlife care a lot about their own health and the health of their children.

In 1955 the American Cancer Society predicted that "cancer will strike one in every four Americans rather than the present estimate of one in five." The ACS attributed the increase to

"the growing number of older persons in the population." The ACS did note that the incidence of lung cancer was increasing very rapidly, rising in the previous two decades by more than 200 percent for women and by 600 percent for men. But the ACS also noted that lung cancer "is the only form of cancer which shows so definite a tendency." Seven years later, Rachel Carson would call her chapter on cancer "One in Four." **15** To bolster her case for the dangers of DDT, Carson improperly cited cases of acute exposures to the chemical as proof of its cancer-causing ability. For example, she told the story of a woman who sprayed DDT for spiders in her basement and died a month later of leukemia. In another case, a man sprayed his office for cockroaches

and a few days later was diagnosed with aplastic anemia. Today cancer specialists would dismiss out of hand the implied claims that these patients' cancers could be traced to such specific pesticide exposures. The plain fact is that DDT has never been shown to be a human carcinogen even after four decades of intense scientific scrutiny.

Carson was also an effective popularizer of the idea that children were especially vulnerable to the carcinogenic effects of synthetic chemicals. "The situation with respect to children is even more deeply disturbing," she wrote. "A quarter century ago, cancer in children was considered a medical rarity. Today, more American school children die of cancer than from any other disease." In support of this claim, Carson reported that "twelve per cent of all deaths in children between the ages of one and fourteen are caused by cancer."

Although it sounds alarming, Carson's statistic is essentially meaningless unless it's given some context, which she failed to supply. It turns out that the percentage of children dying of cancer was rising because other causes of death, such as infectious diseases, were drastically declining.

In fact, cancer rates in children have not increased, as they would have if Carson had been right that children were especially susceptible to the alleged health effects of modern chemicals. Just one rough comparison illustrates this point: In 1938 cancer killed 939 children under 14 years old out of a U.S. population of 130 million. In 1998, according to the National Cancer Institute, about 1,700 children died of cancer, out of a population of more than 280 million. In 1999 the NCI noted that "over the past 20 years, there has been relatively little change in the incidence of children diagnosed with all forms of cancer; from 13 cases per 100,000 children in 1974 to 13.2 per 100,000 children in 1995."

Clearly, if cancer incidence isn't going up, modern chemicals can't be a big factor in cancer. But this simple point is lost on Carson's

heirs in the environmental movement, who base their careers on pursuing phantom risks. The truth is that both cancer mortality and incidence rates have been declining for about a decade, mostly because of a decrease in the number of cigarette smokers.

20 The Great Cancer Scare launched by Carson, and perpetuated by her environmentalist disciples ever since, should have been put to rest by a definitive 1996 report from the National Academy of Sciences, *Carcinogens and Anticarcinogens in the Human Diet.* The NAS concluded that levels of both synthetic and natural carcinogens are "so low that they are unlikely to pose an appreciable cancer risk." Worse yet from the point of view of anti-chemical crusaders, the NAS added that Mother Nature's own chemicals probably cause more cancer than anything mankind has dreamed up: "Natural components of the diet may prove to be of greater concern than synthetic components with respect to cancer risk."

Meanwhile, Carson's disciples have managed to persuade many poor countries to stop using DDT against mosquitoes. The result has been an enormous increase in the number of people dying of malaria each year. Today malaria infects between 300 million and 500 million people annually, killing as many 2.7 million of them. Anti-DDT activists who tried to have the new U.N. treaty on persistent organic pollutants totally ban DDT have stepped back recently from their ideological campaign, conceding that poor countries should be able to use DDT to control malaria-carrying mosquitoes.

So 40 years after the publication of *Silent Spring,* the legacy of Rachel Carson is more troubling than her admirers will acknowledge. The book did point to problems that had not been adequately addressed, such as the effects of DDT on some wildlife. And given the state of the science at the time she wrote, one might even make the case that Carson's concerns about the effects of synthetic chemicals on human health were not completely unwarranted. Along with other researchers, she was simply ignorant of the facts. But after four decades in which tens of billions of dollars have been wasted chasing imaginary risks without measurably improving American health, her intellectual descendants don't have the same excuse.

Questions for Discussion

1. Bailey begins this essay with a description of the impact that *Silent Spring* had—and continues to have—after its publication in 1962. He also discusses the praise Rachel Carson received for that book. Why do you think Bailey begins his essay, which is critical of Carson's *Silent Spring,* in this way? In what ways might this beginning help set up his main argument?

2. Bailey claims that the effectiveness of *Silent Spring* "was due mainly to Carson's passionate, poetic language describing the alleged horrors that modern synthetic chemicals visit upon defenseless nature and hapless humanity." What evidence does he provide to support that claim? Why, in Bailey's view, should people be concerned that *Silent Spring* was persuasive largely because of Carson's "passionate, poetic language"? Evaluate Bailey's use of language in this essay. To what extent does he employ some of the same argumentative strategies that he claims Carson used in her book? Cite specific passages from his essay to support your answer.

3. Bailey essentially accuses Carson either of ignoring important facts about the dangers or safety of DDT or of not telling the whole story. What specific kinds of evidence does he present to support this accusation? How persuasive is this evidence, in your view? Do you think Bailey's argument is influenced by his views about the environment, as he believes Carson's argument was influenced by her views about the environment? Explain, citing specific passages from the essay to support your answer.

4. In Bailey's view, what are the consequences of the problems that he describes with Carson's *Silent Spring*? Why is it important to understand these consequences? What should be done about this situation, in his opinion? Do you agree? Why or why not?

5. Bailey's essay was published in *Reason* magazine, which is considered libertarian in its viewpoint and which advocates liberty and individual choice. To what extent do you think Bailey's essay reflects the perspective of *Reason*? How effective do you think his argument would be for an audience that advocates environmental protection—for example, members of the Sierra Club? Do you think Bailey would be concerned if such readers were to dismiss his argument? Explain.

6. Given the intensity of arguments about environmental issues—and given the potential health and economic consequences of environmental damage—evaluate Bailey's contributions to the ongoing debates about protecting the environment. What value do you think Bailey's essay has in these debates? To what extent does Bailey's essay help people better address the challenge of finding fair and reasonable ways to protect the environment?

③ JACK TURNER, "In Wildness Is the Preservation of the World"

In the following essay from his book *The Abstract Wild* (1996), writer and environmentalist Jack Turner states that "most people no longer have much direct experience of wild nature." As a result, he suggests, neither those who seek to preserve wilderness areas nor those who oppose such preservation really know what they're talking about; they simply do not understand the *wild*. What's more, Turner contends, today's wilderness is not wild. Instead, it is packaged and managed in parks and preserves that are more like museums than genuine wild areas. In providing his reasons for his unconventional view, Turner challenges people to rethink not only their relationship to wilderness but also their understanding of what it means to be human. He advocates a sense of self as intimately part of the wild—in a physical sense. Only this direct experience of the wild—and this sense of self *as* wild—will lead to the kind of passionate commitment to wilderness that Turner believes is essential for preserving wilderness. Turner's argument might seem extreme at times, and you might wonder about the feasibility of the kind of direct experience of the wild that he advocates. Can everyone have such experience? Yet as extreme as his views might sometimes seem, Turner offers a reminder that all arguments about wilderness preservation are in a sense about how people understand themselves in relation to the natural world. A former philosophy professor, Turner is now a mountain guide and writer whose articles and books focus on environmental issues.

In Wildness Is the Preservation of the World

JACK TURNER

Created by President John F. Kennedy in 1962, Point Reyes National Seashore in the middle of California's coast is known for its biological diversity and panoramic views.

I wish my neighbors were wilder.

—Henry Thoreau

1 Hanging from the ceiling of the visitors center at Point Reyes National Seashore* are plaques bearing famous quotations about the value of the natural world. The one from Thoreau, from his essay "Walking," reads: "In Wilderness is the preservation of the World." This, of course, is a mistake. Henry didn't say "wilderness," he said "wildness." But the mistake has become a cliché, suitable for T-shirts and bumper stickers. I think this mistake is like a Freudian slip: it serves a repressive function, the avoidance of conflict, in this case the tension between wilderness as property and wildness as quality. I also think we are all confused about this tension. William Kittredge has been candid enough to admit that "For decades I misread Thoreau. I assumed he was saying wilderness. . . . Maybe I didn't want Thoreau to have said wildness, I couldn't figure out what he meant."[1] I agree.

I believe that mistaking wilderness for wildness is one cause of our increasing failure to preserve the wild earth and that Kittredge's honesty identifies the key issue: we are confused about what Thoreau meant by wildness, we aren't sure what we mean by wildness, and we aren't clear how or what wildness preserves.

If you study the indexes in the recent scholarly edition of Thoreau's works published by Princeton University Press, you will discover that "wild" and "wilderness" do not often occur. Nor do Thoreau's journal entries during the period he was writing "Walking," roughly the spring of 1851, explain what he might have meant. But after reading Richard C. Trench's *On the Study of Words,* published in 1852, Thoreau made the following important note in his "Fact-Book": "*Wild*—past participle of *to will,* self-willed."[2]

We are also confused about what Thoreau meant by "world." I do not believe he meant merely our planet, even in the fashionable sense of Gaia. Near the end of "Walking" he says, "We have to be told that the Greeks called the World Κόσμοδ, Beauty, or Order, but we do not see clearly why they did so, and we esteem it at best only a curious philological fact."[3] Our modern word is *cosmos,* and the most recent philological studies suggest the meaning of harmonious order.[4] So in the broadest sense we can say that Thoreau's "In Wildness is the preservation of the World" is about the relation of free, self-willed, and self-determinate "things" with the harmonious order of the cosmos. Thoreau claims that the first preserves the second. The problem is this: it is not clear to any of us, I think, how the wildest acts of nature—earthquakes, wildfires, the plagues, people being killed and eaten by mountain lions and grizzly bears, our lust, the open sea in storm—preserve a harmonious cosmic order.

5 I know of no author who directly addresses this issue, and a cursory examination of our environmental literature will convince anyone that we are not dealing with a saying that, for most preservationists, describes the heart of our ideology. Indeed, it was not until Gary Snyder published *The Practice of the Wild* that we had a general discussion of what nature, wildness, and wilderness mean and how they are connected. This situation shouldn't surprise us, because most people no longer have much direct experience of wild nature, and few meditate on the cosmos. Since language and communication are social phenomena that presume common, shared experience, it follows that clarity about the issue, perhaps even discourse, is impossible. I would go so far as to say that in many inner cities, here and in the developing world, people no longer have a concept of wild nature based on personal experience. Mostly, the wild is something bad reported by television. As a New York wit has it, "Nature is something I pass through between my hotel and my taxi." And, needless to say, a growing world population ignorant of the key concepts of our movement will hinder the cause of preservation and render its goals increasingly unrealistic.

"Walking," and also *Walden* and two other essays—"Resistance to Civil Government" (unfortunately called "Civil Disobedience" most of the time) and "Life without Principle"—express the radical heart of Thoreau's life's work, and since he revised "Walking" just before his death, we may assume it accurately represents his ideas.

The most notable fact about these works is that Thoreau virtually ignores our current concerns with the preservation of habitats and species. He would no doubt include them—he says "all good things are wild and free"—but he writes mainly about human beings, their literature, their myths, their history, their work

*Philosopher Ralph Waldo Emerson (1803–1882) is widely considered one of the most influential figures in the development of American ideas about education and nature. He is closely associated with Thoreau, whom he mentored.

†The Wilderness Act of 1964 defines *wilderness* as follows: "A wilderness, in contrast with those areas where man and his own works dominate the landscape, is hereby recognized as an area where the earth and its community of life are untrammeled by man, where man himself is a visitor who does not remain."

and leisure, and, of course, their walking. His question, which he got from Emerson,* is about human life: "How ought I to live?" Thoreau is unique because part of his answer to this old question involves wildness. In "Walking," he says, for instance, "Give me for my friends and neighbors wild men, not tame ones. The wildness of the savage is but a faint symbol of the awful ferity with which good men and lovers meet" (122). And listen to the essay's opening lines: "I wish to speak a word for Nature, for absolute freedom and wildness, as contrasted with a freedom and culture merely civil—to regard man as an inhabitant, or a part and parcel of Nature, rather than a member of society" (93). Absolute freedom. Absolute wildness. Human beings as inhabitants of that absolute freedom and wildness. This is not the usual environmental rhetoric, and Kittredge is surely correct: most of us simply don't know what Thoreau means.

What is equally confounding is that people who have led a life of intimate contact with wild nature—a buckaroo working the Owyhee country, a halibut fisherman plying the currents of the Gulf of Alaska, an Eskimo whale hunter, a rancher tending a small cow/calf op-

eration, a logger with his chain saw—often oppose preserving wild nature. The friends of preservation, on the other hand, are often city folk who depend on weekends and vacations in designated wilderness areas and national parks for their (necessarily) limited experience of wildness. This difference in degree of experience of wild nature, the dichotomy of friends/enemies of preservation, and the notorious inability of these two groups to communicate also indicate the depth of our muddle about wildness. We don't know what we mean, and those who have the most experience with the wild disagree with what we want to achieve.

We also presume that the experience of wildness and wilderness are related, and this is plausible (though it ignores elements of our personal lives that also might be thought of as wild: sex, dreams, rage, etc.). However, since wilderness is a place, and wildness a quality, we can always ask, "How wild is our wilderness?" and "How wild is our experience there?" My answer? Not very, particularly in the wilderness most people are familiar with, the areas protected by the Wilderness Act of 1964.†

10 There are many reasons for this. Some are widely acknowledged, and I will pass over them briefly, but there is one reason that is not widely accepted, a reason that is offensive to many minds, but one that goes to the heart of Thoreau's opening lines, namely, that human beings no longer accept their status as "part and parcel" of a biological realm that is self-willed, self-determined, self-ordered. Instead we have divided ourselves from that realm and make every attempt to control it for our own interests. Wilderness is one of the few places where we can begin to correct this division; hence, despite the rage for wilderness as a bastion for conserving biodiversity, I am inclined to think its primary importance remains what the founders of the conservation movement thought it was: a basis for an important kind of human experience. Without big, wild wilderness I doubt most of us will ever see ourselves as part and parcel of nature.

Why isn't our wilderness wild, and why is there so little experience of wildness there? Well, first of all, the wilderness that most people visit (with the exception of Alaska and Canada) is too small—in space and time. Like all experience, the experience of the wild can be a taste or a feast, and a feast presumes substance and leisure. Yet about a third of our legislated wilderness units are smaller than 10,000 acres, an area approximately four miles long on each side. An easy stroll. Some wilderness areas, usually islands, have fewer than 100 acres, and I have been told that Point Reyes now has meaningless "wilderness zones" measuring several hundred yards.

Even our largest wilderness areas are small. Only 4 percent are larger than 500,000 acres, an area 27 miles on a side, and since many follow the ridges of mountain ranges, they are so elongated that a strong hiker can cross one in a single day. True, some are adjacent to other wilderness areas and remote BLM lands and national parks, but compared to the Amazon, Alaska, the Northwest Territories, or the Himalayas, most Wilderness Act wilderness seems very small indeed.

Unfortunately, without sufficient space and time the experience of wildness in the wilderness is diminished or simply doesn't exist. Many people agree with Aldo Leopold that it should take a couple of weeks to pack across a true wilderness, something that probably isn't possible in the lower forty-eight now. The law is simple: The farther you are from a road, and the longer you are out, the wilder your experience. Two weeks is the minimum, a month is better. Until then the mind remains saturated with human concerns and blind to the natural world, the body bound to metronomic time and ignorant of natural biological rhythms. A traveler in small wilderness for a weekend backpack trip remains ignorant of these differences between short and long stays in wilderness, yet a long stay is fundamental to seeing ourselves as part of biological nature, for the order of nature is above all a rhythmic order.

Second, small wilderness units usually lack predators. Sometimes this is simply a function of their small size, but sometimes it's a function of artificial borders created according to economic and political, rather than ecological, criteria. The result is the same: the wilderness is tamed. Predators are perhaps our most accessible experience of the wild. To come upon a grizzly track is to experience the wild in a most intimate, carnal way, an experience that is marked by gross alterations in attention, perception, body language, body chemistry, and emotion. Which is to say you feel yourself as part of the biological order known as the food chain, perhaps even as part of a meal.

15 Third, this tameness is exacerbated by our current model for appropriate human use of the wild—the intensive recreation that requires trail systems, bridges, signs for direction and distance, backcountry rangers, and rescue operations that in turn generate activities that further diminish wildness—maps, guide books, guiding services, advertising, photography books, instructional films—all of which diminish the discovery, surprise, the unknown, and the often-dangerous Other—the very qualities that make a place wild. Each of these reductions tames and domesticates the wilderness and diminishes wild experience.

Fourth, intensive recreational use influences public policy, leading those with authority to institute artificial methods of control that benefit recreational use. Animal populations are managed by controlled hunting, wildfires are suppressed, predators moved, and humans treated in a manner best described by the word "surveillance." The wild becomes a problem to be solved by further human intervention—scientific studies, state and federal laws, judicial decision, political compromise, and administrative and bureaucratic procedures. Once this intervention begins, it never ends; it spirals into further and further human intrusion, rendering wilderness increasingly evaluated, managed, regulated, and controlled. That is, tamed. Nibble by nibble, decision by decision, animal by animal,

CONTEXT

The Bureau of Land Management (BLM) is a U.S. government agency in the Department of the Interior that manages 262 million acres of public land, mostly in western states. The BLM describes its mission in part as sustaining "the health, diversity, and productivity of the public lands for the use and enjoyment of present and future generations." Lands under BLM management are used for a variety of purposes, including grazing livestock, mining, logging, and recreation. The BLM's policies have often been the subject of criticism by environmentalists and by proponents of the development of wilderness areas.

COMPLICATION

Sometimes called "eco-tourism," wilderness tourism has become a multibillion-dollar industry in the past few decades. A study by the Council for Environmental Cooperation reported in 2000 that tourism was the largest industry worldwide and nature travel was the fastest-growing segment of that industry. A separate study estimated that nature travel accounted for $260 billion annually in revenues in the United States. Some proponents of wilderness tourism argue that it can support efforts to preserve the environment. For example, Ralph Keller, of the Eco-tourism Association of Vancouver (Canada), where conflicts have erupted between eco-tourism business and industries such as logging, argued in 1999 that "wilderness, worldwide, is disappearing at an astonishing rate. Those countries with enough foresight to protect wilderness will have a powerful economic edge in years to come."

fire by fire, we have diminished the wildness of our wilderness.

Thus diminished, wilderness becomes a special unit of property treated like a historic relic or ruin—a valuable remnant. It becomes a place of vacations (a word related to "vacant, empty"). Humans become foreigners to the wild, foreigners to an experience that once grounded their most sacred beliefs and values. In short, wilderness as relic leads to tourism, and tourism in the wilderness becomes the primary mode of experiencing a diminished wild.

Wilderness as relic always converts places into commodities, because tourism, in its various manifestations, is a form of commerce. All tourism is to some degree destructive, and wilderness tourism is no exception. Virtually everyone (including me) in "the Nature business" feeds (literally) on wilderness as commodity. We are enthralled with our ability to make a living with this exchange, but we tend to ignore the practical consequences for wilderness preservation and for ourselves. Wilderness tourism is not a free lunch. Its worse consequence is that it conceals what should be its primary use: the wild as a project of the self. Compared with residency in a wild biological realm, where the experience of wildness is part of everyday life, wilderness tourism is pathetic. It has had some very bad consequences, and we need to acknowledge them.

Wilderness tourism ignores, perhaps even caricatures, the experience that decisively marked the founders of wilderness preservation: Henry Thoreau, John Muir, Robert Marshall, Aldo Leopold, and Olaus Murie. * The

kind of wildness they experienced has become very rare—an endangered experience. As a result, we no longer understand the roots of our own cause. Reading the works of these men and then looking at an issue of, say, *Sierra* can cause severe disorientation. The founders had something we lack, something Thoreau called "Indian Wisdom." For much of their lives these men lived in and studied nature before it became a "wilderness area," and their knowledge came not from visitor centers and guidebooks but from intimate, direct personal experience.

20 Thoreau's knowledge of the lands surrounding Concord was so vast that some of the town's children believed that, like God, Henry had created it all. His knowledge of flora was so precise, a rare fern species not seen for a hundred years was recently rediscovered by examining his notes, and his examination of the succession of forest trees is a seminal essay for modern ecology. Muir spent months alone in the wild Sierra Nevada and made original contributions to the study of glaciers. The lives of Marshall, Leopold, and Murie similarly exhibit extensive personal experience and knowledge of wilderness and wildness. To a considerable degree their lives were devotions to wild nature. Without such devotion, I do not believe there would be Thoreau's epiphanies on Katahdin, Muir's mystical identification with trees, or Leopold's thinking like a mountain.

Wilderness tourism is completely different. It is devoted to fun. We hunt for fun, fish for fun, climb for fun, ski for fun, and hike for fun. This is the grim harvest of the "fun hog" philosophy that powered the wilderness-recreation boom for three decades, the philosophy of *Outside* magazine and dozens of its ilk, and there is little evidence that either the spiritual or scientific concerns of the original conservationists—or the scientific concerns of conservation biologists—have trickled down to most wilderness fun hogs.

Given the ignorance and arrogance of most fun hogs, it is understandable that those who stand to lose by increased wilderness designation—farmers, ranchers, loggers, commercial

*Sometimes called the father of our national park system, John Muir (1838–1914) is credited with inspiring President Theodore Roosevelt to found Yosemite National Park; Muir was also the founder of the Sierra Club. Robert Marshall (1906–1938) founded the Wilderness Society and fought to preserve wilderness in its natural state. Environmental activist Aldo Leopold (1887–1948) wrote *A Sand County Almanac* (1949), which promoted his idea of a "land ethic" and influenced the environmental movement in the 1960s and 1970s. Olaus Murie (1889–1963) helped establish Jackson Hole National Monument and led the campaign to establish the million 9-acre Arctic National Refuge in Alaska.

fishermen, American Indians—are often enraged. Instead of a clash of needs, the preservation of the wild appears to be a clash of work versus recreation. Lacking a deeper experience of wildness and access to the lore, myth, metaphor, and ritual necessary to share that experience, there is no communication, no vision, that might shatter the current dead-end of wilderness debate. Both groups exploit the wild, the first by consuming it, the second by converting it into a playpen and then consuming it. Worship of wilderness designation thus becomes idolatry, the confusion of a symbol with its essence. In either case the result is the same: destruction of the wild.

With wilderness tourism we also lose our most effective weapon for preserving what little remains of the natural world: emotional identification. At the bedrock level, what drives both reform environmentalism and deep ecology is a practical problem: how to compel human beings to respect and care for wild nature. The tradition of Thoreau and Muir says that the best way to do this is raw, visceral contact with wild nature. True residency in the wild brings identification and a generalized "not in my back yard," or NIMBY, response that extends sympathy to all the wild world. Without this identification, solutions are abstract and impotent—that is, impractical. But because so many of us are obsessed with fun in the wild, there is a lot of impractical, impotent stuff dominating environmental thought. We have fun and we have philosophy, but we have little serious use of wilderness to study our place in nature, to study, that is, the relation between freedom and the cosmos.

For example, giving trees and animals moral rights analogous to the rights of humans has bogged down in a morass of value theory. The aesthetic campaign to preserve the wild has done as much harm as good, since it suggests (especially in a nation of relativists) that preservation is a matter of taste, a preference no more compelling than the choice between vanilla and chocolate. It leads to tedious arguments that begin with "Who are you to say that we shouldn't have snowmobiles in the Teton wilderness?" on the model of "Who are you to say I shouldn't eat chocolate?" This, in turn, leads inevitably to questions of egalitarianism and elitism, and hence directly into the dismal swamp of politics, which, as Thoreau says in "Walking," is the most alarming of man's affairs. Politicians are invariably people of the *polis*—city slickers, those furthest removed from the natural order.

25 Philosophers have been no more helpful. Deep ecologists are desperately attempting to replace the philosophical foundations of a mechanical model of the world with those of an organic model of the world. Unfortunately, these new foundations are not at all obvious to the other philosophers, not to mention the lay public. The search for foundations—for science, mathematics, logic, or the social sciences—has been the curse of rationalism from Descartes to the present, and the foundations of deep ecology will not exorcise that curse. Many explications of deep ecology rely on some of the most obscure ruminations of Spinoza, Whitehead, and Heidegger. This bodes ill for big wilderness.

All these things are reasonable (sort of), but as Hume saw clearly, reason alone is insufficient to move the will. We should repeat this to ourselves every day like a mantra. Reason has not compelled us to respect and care for wild nature, and we have no basis to

DEEP ECOLOGY

The deep ecology movement, which grew out of the ideas of Norwegian philosopher Arne Naess, emphasizes a holistic view of the relationship between humans and environment. Deep ecologists embrace all manner of diversity and advocate a set of values that emphasizes harmony in human relationships to each other and to the natural world, of which humans are a part. According to philosophy scholar Alan Drengson, "Supporters of the deep ecology movement platform are committed to recognizing and respecting in word and deed the inherent worth of humans and other beings. This leads to actions that try to minimize our own impacts on ecological communities and other human cultures."

believe it will in the future. Philosophical arguments, moralizing, aesthetics, political legislation, and abstract philosophies are notoriously incapable of compelling human behavior. Given the choice, I would side with the fun hogs, who are at least out there connecting with the wild on some level.

Wilderness tourism also results in little art, literature, poetry, myth, or lore for many, if not most, of our wild places. In "Walking," Thoreau described "the West" as "preparing to add its fables to those of the East. The valleys of the Ganges, the Nile, and the Rhine, having yielded their crop, it remains to be seen what the valleys of the Amazon, the Platte, the Orinoco, the St. Lawrence, and the Mississippi will produce" (121). Well, nearly 150 years later, it still remains to be seen. If you ask for the art, literature, lore, myth, and fable of where I live, the headwaters of the Snake River, I would answer that we are working on it, but it might be awhile, because art that takes

a place as its subject is created by people who live in and develop a sense of that place. And this takes lots of time. This is true of both wilderness and civilization. Joyce grew up in Dublin, Atget lived in Paris, Muir and Adams lived in Yosemite, Henry Beston lived on Cape Cod. Many of our best writers on wilderness—Abbey, Snyder, Peacock—worked as fire lookouts for the U.S. Forest Service. (There is probably a doctoral dissertation here: "The Importance of Fire Lookouts in the Development of Western Nature Literature.") But if access to the wild world is limited to weekend tourism, we have no reason to expect a literature and lore of wild nature.

Yet most of us, when we think about it, realize that after our own direct experience of nature, what has contributed most to our love of wild places, animals, plants—and even, perhaps, to our love of wild nature, our sense of our citizenship—is the art, literature, myth, and lore of nature. For here is the language we so desperately lack, the medium necessary for vision. Mere concepts and abstractions will not do, because love is beyond concepts and abstractions. And yet the problem is one of love. As Stephen Jay Gould wrote, "We cannot win this battle to save species and environments without forging an emotional bond between ourselves and nature as well—for we will not fight to save what we do not love."[5] The conservation movement has put much thought, time, effort, and money into public policy and science, and far too little into direct personal experience and the arts. There is nothing wrong with public policy and science, but since they will not produce love, they must remain secondary in the cause of preservation.

And finally, wilderness tourism produces no phenology of wild places, the study of periodic phenomena in nature—bird migration, mating of animals, leafing of trees, the effects of climate. This is unfortunate, for phenology, as Paul Shepard has reminded us, is the study of the mature naturalist—the gate through which nature becomes personal.[6] Leopold published phenological studies of two counties in

Wisconsin, and Thoreau dedicated the last years of his life to studying the mysterious comings and goings of the natural world. Phenology* requires a complete immersion in place over time so that the attention, the senses, and the mind can scrutinize and discern widely—the dates of arrivals and departures, the births, the flourishings, the decays, and the deaths of wild things, their successions, synchronicities, dependencies, reciprocities, and cycles—the lived life of the earth. To be absorbed in this life is to merge with larger patterns. Here ecology is not studied, but felt, so that truths become known in the same way a child learns hot from cold—truths that are immune from doubt and argument and, most important, can never be taken away. Here is the common wisdom of indigenous peoples, a wisdom that cannot emerge from tourism in a relic wilderness.

30 We are left with the vital importance of residency in wild nature, and a visceral knowledge of that wildness, as the most practical means of preserving the wild. What we need now is a new tradition of the wild that teaches us how human beings live best by living in and studying the wild without taming it or destroying it. Such a tradition of the wild did exist; it is as old as the Pleistocene. Before Neolithic times, human beings were always living in, traveling through, and using lands we now call wilderness; they knew it intimately, they usually respected it, they often cared for it. It is the tradition of the people that populated all of the wilderness of North America, a tradition that influenced Taoism and Hinduism and informed major Chinese and Japanese poetic traditions. It is the tradition that emerged again with Emerson and Thoreau. In short, it is a tradition that could again compel respect, care, and love for wild nature in a way that philosophical foundations, aesthetics, moral theory, and public policy cannot. It is a tradition we need to re-create for ourselves, borrowing when necessary from native cultures, but making it new—a wild tradition of our own.

A wild bunch is forming, an eclectic tribe returning to the wild to study, learn, and express. From them will come the lore, myth, literature, art, and ritual we so require. Frank Craighead, John Haines, and Gary Snyder are among the elders of this tribe. There is also Richard Nelson on his island, Doug Peacock with his grizzlies, Terry Tempest Williams and her beloved birds, Hannah Hinchman and her illuminated journals, Gary Nabhan and his seeds, Dolores LaChapelle and her rituals, and many others—all new teachers of the wild. Their mere presence is not sufficient, however. It will not help us if this tradition is created for us, to be read about in yet another book. To create a wilder self, the self must live the life of the wild, mold a particular form of human character, a form of life. Relics will not do, tourism will not do, books will not do.

If we want this wilder self, we must begin, in whatever ways we can imagine, to rejoin the natural world. One way is to consider our bodies as food for others. Out there is the great feeding mass of beings we call the Earth. We incorporate, and are incorporated, in ways not requiring legal papers. We are creator and created, terrorist and hostage, victim and executioner, guest of honor and part of the feast. This system of food, which is hidden from the urban mind, is terrifying in its identity and reciprocity. It is a vision that could inform everything from our private spiritual matters to the gross facts of nourishment and death. It at least partly answers Thoreau's question, "How should I live?" Now we have to figure out how we can achieve it here and now, in this place, in these times.

I am convinced that such a life is still possible. I love my Powerbook, my Goretex gear, and my plastic kayak. But I also make a point to eat fritillaria, morels, berries, fish, and elk. I want to feed directly from my place, to incorporate it. When I die, I wish my friends could present my body as a gift to the flora and fauna of my home, Grand Teton National Park, because I want my world to incorporate me.

*Phenology is the study of periodic biological phenomena such as the flowering of trees and the migration of birds.

On my travels in Tibet I was always delighted by the tradition of sky-burial. The human body is cut up and the bones broken to the marrow and left for animals, mostly birds. Later the bones are pounded and mixed with tsampa—a roasted barley—and again offered to the animals. Finally everything is gone, gone back into the cycle. Recently, when a friend lost her beloved dog, she carried it out to a beautiful view of the mountains, covered it with wild flowers, and left it for the coyotes and ravens and bugs. We should have the courage to do the same for ourselves, to re-enter the great cycle of feeding.

35 The moose incorporates the willow, taking the life of the willow into its own life, making the wildness of the willow reincarnate. I kill the moose, its body feeds the willow and grouse wortleberries where it dies, it feeds my body, and in feeding my body, the willow and the moose feed the one billion bacteria that inhabit three inches of my colon, the one million spirochetes that live in my mouth, and the microscopic brontosaurus-like mites that live by devouring the goo on my eyelashes. This great feeding body is the world. It evolved together, mutually, all interdependent, all interrelating ceaselessly, the dust of old stars hurtling through time, and we are the form it chose to make it conscious of itself.

From this vision of a wild order in complete interdependence comes freedom, a freedom unlike our civil freedoms but, I think, close to what Thoreau imagined. Perhaps it is best expressed by the Taittiriya Upanishad:[7]

O wonderful! O wonderful! O wonderful!
I am food! I am food! I am food!
I eat food! I eat food! I eat food!
My name never dies, never dies, never dies!

I was born first in the first of the worlds, earlier than the gods, in the belly of what has no death!
Whoever gives me away has helped me the most!
I, who am food, eat the eater of food!
I have overcome this world!

He who knows this shines like the sun. Such are the laws of mystery!

Notes
1. Kittredge, William. "What Do We Mean?" *Northern Lights* 6 (Fall 1990).
2. See Sherman Paul, *The Shores of America: Thoreau's Inward Exploration* (University of Illinois Press, 1958), 412–17, and Robert D. Richardson, Jr., *Henry Thoreau: A Life of the Mind* (University of California Press, 1986), 224–27.
3. Thoreau, Henry David. "Walking." *The Natural History Essays* (Salt Lake City: Peregrine Smith Books, 1984), 130.
4. This is the meaning given by Eric Partridge in *Origins: A Short Etymological Dictionary of Modern English* (New York: Macmillan, 1958).
5. Gould, Stephen Jay. "Unenchanted Evening." *Natural History* (September 1991): 14.
6. Shepard, Paul. *Nature and Madness* (San Francisco: Sierra Club Books, 1982), 132.
7. Translated by Lewis Hyde and used as an epigraph for his book *The Gift: Imagination and the Erotic Life of Property* (New York: Random House, 1979).

Questions for Discussion

1. What is the importance of distinguishing *wilderness* from *wildness,* according to Turner? What would you have to do if you wanted to experience both? What does this distinction have to do with current debates about environmental preservation, as Turner sees it?

2. Turner gives a great deal of emphasis to the ideas of Henry David Thoreau in this essay (see the sidebar on page 703). Evaluate his use of Thoreau's work. What do you think he achieves by establishing that Thoreau's meaning is unclear? How does he use Thoreau's ideas to help make his main argument? What does this emphasis on Thoreau suggest about Turner's sense of audience?

3. Turner asserts that there are at least four reasons people have little true experience of the wild. What do these four reasons suggest about Turner's beliefs about wilderness? What do they suggest about Turner's values in general? Do you think Turner is right that people today have little genuine experience with the wild? Why or why not?

4. Why does Turner criticize wilderness tourism? How do these criticisms support his main argument? Do you agree with him? What benefits do you see to wilderness tourism that Turner overlooks?

5. Although he admits to wearing Goretex and having a plastic kayak, Turner is critical of "fun hogs," or people who spoil wilderness by using it as "a playpen." What does this imply about how he would like to see wilderness areas managed? How does his position about "fun hogs" influence your sense of him as a credible author?

6. Turner asserts that the kind of relationship to the wild that he advocates is still possible. Do you agree with him? Why or why not? What objections to his position can you offer? To what extent do you think Turner adequately addresses these objections?

④ CHARLES PETIT, "Hazy Days in Our Parks"

Discussion of "nature" is often based on assumptions that "nature" is found someplace other than where we are—in some remote part of the world, rather than in the blades of grass springing up between the cracks of a concrete sidewalk, in tomatoes ripening in a backyard garden, or in a park designed for the pleasure of visitors. Purists might argue that the way people experience "nature" when they visit a park is problematic, because nature has been groomed to suit human needs and is therefore inauthentic. But in an increasingly urban culture, in which suburbs sprawl out over what was once farmland, parks may be the most likely site where people are aware that they are encountering nature (even if that is different from experiencing a wilderness). Given these circumstances, what should public policy be in respect to national parks such as Yellowstone that have been popular destinations for years but are now at risk? For a student response to national park policy, see the essay by Tyler Sunderman (pages 127–131). For the views of a reporter who has interviewed both scientists and environmental activists, read the following piece by Charles Petit, which was first published in the June 2005 issue of *Smithsonian.* A contributing editor for *U.S. News & World Report,* and a freelance science writer, Petit lives in California—a state with more than one famous park.

Hazy Days in Our Parks

CHARLES PETIT

1 Big Band National Park's superintendent, John King, calls the 801,163-acre reserve on the West Texas border with Mexico a "destination park," meaning for most folks there's little other reason to venture into the area at all. Reaching it takes four hours on a two-lane road from Midland, the nearest major airport. In between is the flat, scraggly Permian Basin, the state's historic oil patch, dotted with dying and dead "horsehead" walking-beam pumps and filled with the pungent odor of black gold wafting from those still in production. But even in scorching summer heat, when temperatures average more than 90 degrees, the trip is worth it. Mesas and buttes pop up as one nears the oversize oxbow in the Rio Grande that gives the region its name, and the terrain turns to the classic Chihuahuan Desert of purple-tinged prickly pear, spiny ocotillo, sharp-barbed lechuguilla, and yuccas spikier on top than any punk rocker.

Since the late 1980s, the remote park has been plagued by an unexpected problem: haze. "I've had people come out, take a look around, and tell me they had to get going back to Houston for some clean air," says Big Bend's air quality technician, John Forsythe. Hall Hammond, a San Antonio jewelry sales consultant who has visited the park 60 times since 1969, is an activist with the private Friends of Big Bend National Park, a group that supports the Texas park. He remembers when he used to ask friends to float down the river with him and stare up from the canyon at what he called Big Bend blue. "The sky would just be cobalt," he recalls. But lately that hue is rarer and rarer. In 1998, Hammond hiked up Emory Peak in the Chisos Mountains, looked down from its 7,825-foot height and saw "this yellow layer sitting down on the desert to the north and east. It just completely threw me."

The air has been going bad in many parks for decades, affecting views and endangering the health of visitors, plants and wildlife. Last year, the National Parks Conservation Association (NPCA), a nonpartisan watchdog group based in Washington, D.C., listed the five most polluted national parks. Relying almost entirely on data from the National Park Service and the EPA,* the group says the parks with the worst visibility and most severe ozone and acid rain levels are the Great Smoky Mountains Park on the Tennessee–North Carolina border, followed by Mammoth Cave in Kentucky, Shenandoah in Virginia, Acadia on the Maine coast, and the jointly operated Sequoia and Kings Canyon National Parks in California's Sierra Nevada. Many parks have been hard hit by sulfur dioxide and nitrogen oxide from coal-fired power plants, which are responsible for nearly 70 percent of sulfur dioxide and 22 percent of nitrogen oxide emissions nationwide. The park service, while it disagrees with the way the NPCA assessed some of the pollution data, has little quarrel with the report's general tenor.

Eastern parks, many downwind from huge coal-fired power plants in the Ohio River Valley and elsewhere, are the worst hit, in keeping with national pollution patterns. Over the past century or so, man-made haze has cut average visibility in the eastern half of the country from 90 miles to between 75 and 25 miles. In the arid and naturally clearer western states, visibility has dropped from 140 miles to 35 to 90 miles. Parks famed for their views—Grand Canyon in Arizona, Yellowstone in Wyoming, Montana and Idaho, Yosemite in California, Colorado's Rocky Mountain, and Big Bend— have long bouts of murky, polluted air each year.

5 Because federal rules have long mandated that national parks and other wilderness areas should have the cleanest air in America, regulators have been authorized to take action against known polluters, typically by suing them for non-compliance. But as pollution-control laws have become increasingly complex, companies accused of violating park air-quality standards have gone to court to delay enforcement, stalling cleanup efforts. The Bush administration has proposed overhauling air pollution regulations, replacing the current, plant–specific air quality standards with a barter system; power plants would buy or trade pollution credits, allowing them to exceed pollutant limits in some places. Proponents say the administration's Clear Skies Initiatives† will ultimately improve air quality by lowering emissions. But critics say that the changes will reverse progress against dirty air—and allow egregious polluters to stay in operation.

The political debate over air pollution laws underscores the plight of the parks. "There is still that vision that you can go out to the parks and breathe fresh mountain air, and get away from the urban problems that we all see, and stand in that pristine natural word," says NPCA president Tom Kiernan, who worked from 1989 to 1992 as an EPA official in the first Bush administration. "Yet we see, by god, that we have some of the worst air in the country in the national parks."

Why? An extraordinary scientific study conducted in an isolated stretch of Texas is yielding some answers. The implications—for the regulatory debate, for the health of the parks, even for the health of parkgoers—give new meaning to the idea of far-reaching.

Big Bend is a historic place. Comanche, Apache and other tribes defied 300 years of Spanish and Mexican rule in the rugged badlands. It was the last redoubt of Indian warrior Victorio and his Mescalero Apache, finally scattered in 1880 by U.S. Army troops. The park's center is crowned by the rugged escarpments of the Chisos Mountains massif, giving it the look of a fortress.

*The Environmental Protection Agency (EPA) was created by the federal government in 1970 to address growing concerns about the pollution of soil, water, and air in the United States. Its mission is, as its name suggests, to protect the environment. In practice, however, the EPA has had different agendas and different degrees of political support depending upon who is President, because it is the President who appoints the head of the EPA.

†Announced by President George W. Bush in February 2002 and emphasized in his State of the Union Address in January 2003, the Clear Skies Initiative proposed replacing the Clean Air Act of 1970 with a law that would respond to new needs and new technologies. Critics argued that the administration was undermining—as a favor to big business—legislation essential to the nation's well-being. Part of the press release issued by the White House on the Clear Skies Initiative is reprinted on pages 716–717.

In the 1990s, Big Bend's growing haze spurred wide suspicion that the pollution originated across the river, 140 miles to the southeast. By 1995, two big coal-fired Mexican power plants, Carbon I and II, were generating 2,600 megawatts of electricity without significant emission controls.

10 In a joint effort, the EPA, the park service, the Texas Commission on Environmental Quality, the U.S. utility industry's Electric Power Research Institute and the National Oceanic and Atmospheric Administration launched the Big Bend Regional Aerosol and Visibility Observational (BRAVO) Study. From July through October 1999, a small tent and trailer city sprang up in a scrubby corner of the park. Instruments sprouted at dozens of locations in or near Texas. Scientists around the state injected different perfluorocarbon chemicals into the sky, and monitors in the park recorded the tracers as they arrived. Mexican officials, apparently afraid they were being set up to take the blame for Big Bend's bad air, had backed out of the study; so U.S. scientists, unable to put tracers directly into the Carbon plants' plumes as hoped, released them from a tower in the Texas border town of Eagle Pass, 20 miles from the plants.

The BRAVO researchers made their results public this past September. The short version? Don't blame Mexico. In fact, the park's worst haze comes from the eastern United States and East Texas. Mexico's Carbon I and II plants remain the biggest single contributors to Big Bend's sulfate haze. But on the haziest days, they contribute just 9 percent of the total, and the rest of Mexico another 7 percent. Texas adds 11 percent, the eastern United States 22 percent and the western United States 4 percent. The rest of the haze arises from wind-blown soil, smoke from agricultural and forest fires, manufacturing activities and vehicle exhaust. Mark Scruggs, assistant chief in the National Park Service's air resources division, which monitors pollution in the parks, says the big surprise was how much sulfate originates in the eastern United States, borne on prevail-

ing winds that blow across East Texas or loop down to the Gulf of Mexico and north trough the Mexican mainland. Mexican officials had been arguing since 1996 that Big Bend's problems came from north of the border—including a string of power plants along the Ohio River Valley—but the Americans were skeptical until the BRAVO data came in.

Ever since Congress created the first national park, at Yellowstone in 1872, the parks have enjoyed special legal protections. In 1916, the National Park Service was set up to maintain areas "unimpaired for the enjoyment of future generations." Additional legal backing came in 1977 when amendments to the Clean Air Act gave parks the highest priority, designating them as Class I areas. The law is emphatic: "Congress hereby declares as a national goal the prevention of any future, and the remedying of any existing, impairment of visibility in mandatory class I Federal areas which impairment results from manmade air pollution."

"It was visionary to try to protect these areas without even knowing how difficult it would be," says air resources division director Chris Shaver. The division has outfitted most major parks with filters to gather aerosols, or ultrafine solid and liquid particles in the air; nephelometers to measure how haze scatters sunlight; and transmissiometers that gauge scattering and absorption of light by pollution, dust, mist or other material in the air. Chemical samplers scrutinize the concentration of such problematic molecules as ozone, which can be harmful to humans at ground level.

Shaver remembers standing on the rim of the Grand Canyon with her then 6-year-old daughter, Courtney, in 1990. The girl looked at the barely visible cliffs on the other side and said, "Mom, I don't know how to tell you this, because I know how hard you are working, but you're not doing a very good job." Courtney graduated from college this year, and Shaver still sees haze in the park system. When researchers started measuring the Grand

Canyon's air quality in the 1970s, "Congress and most people thought we had a problem with [only] a few power plants in the four corners," she says of the region where Arizona, New Mexico, Colorado and Utah meet. Since then, while these power plants have slashed their overall sulfur emissions by 72 percent, the canyon's haze remains—evidence that the problem isn't merely local.

15 Whether the Bush administration's proposed air quality regulations will more effectively reduce pollution in the worst-hit parks is hotly debated. The present system "is tied up in the courts," says Jim Connaughton of the White House Council on Environmental Quality. The Clear Skies Initiative aims to replace the strict limits governing an individual power plant's emissions of sulfur dioxide and nitrogen oxides with a "cap-and-trade" system. A plant that exceeds a limit for a pollutant would buy or trade credits from an operator that was under the limit for the same compound, keeping the nation's overall pollution in check. Proponents, including many Republicans and most industry lobbies, say the plan is simpler, allows companies to be flexible, and lets some stay in business without buying expensive clean-up equipment. If a plant goes over its limit and has no credits to buy its way clear, EPA officials can levy fines with fewer hearings and lawsuits.

Connaughton also says that the proposal preserves long-term national goals on clean air and will improve visibility in the national parks. The proposal aims to reduce emissions of sulfur dioxide, a prime cause of haze and acid rain, by 73 percent by 2018—down 8 tons from the 11 million tons emitted in 2000. At the same time it would cut nitrogen oxides, a cause of ozone, by 67 percent.

But opponents see Clear Skies as a sellout to industry. They say the proposal is less aggressive than current regulations, and they complain that it would let dirty power plants operate as long as their owners buy credits elsewhere. Many environmental organizations have attacked the proposals. "Why is the Administration bragging about a plan that will actually result in more pollution than if we simply enforced the existing Clean Air Act?" the Sierra Club asks. In 2002, Eric Schaeffer quit his job a the EPA's regulatory enforcement head, protesting what he says is the Bush administration's soft approach to power company pollution. "If you allow them to buy their way out of reducing emissions, then the parks may not get better for a long time," he says. Clear Skies opponents also say the plan would put park air at risk because the cap-and-trade credit system takes the teeth out of the parks' Class I designation. Park superintendents would no longer have clear authority to demand that the EPA or other agencies go after individual polluters. The Clear Skies legislation is currently stalled in a Senate committee.

Bartering has worked in the past. Since 1990, power plants have been allowed to use a cap-and-trade system to help reduce acid rain, produced largely by coal-fired plants spewing nitrogen and sulfur. Consequently, sulfur emissions went from 17.3 million tons in 1980 to 10.6 million tons in 2003.

Park service expert Mark Scruggs is guardedly optimistic about the Clear Skies Initiative. "If the caps are stiff enough, sure, it will help a lot," he says. "A 70 percent cut in sulfur dioxide is going to make a difference, especially for the East Coast parks," But Scruggs says that when the current system is at its best—when agencies work together to prosecute individual polluters—results are impressive. EPA pressure on industry led to improvements in scrubber technologies, which reduce smokestack emissions, with 95 to 98 percent elimination of some pollutants now commonplace. Scruggs says similar improvements are possible for other pollutants.

20 But park lovers shouldn't expect big improvements soon. The EPA's deadline for returning park air to normal is 2064, a date instructive both in its temporal distance and legalistic precision. To be sure, there have been isolated gains. Sulfate haze tends to be dropping in the East, even as nitrate pollution and

CONTEXT

Founded in 1892, the Sierra Club is the nation's oldest and best known organization working to protect the environment. Its mission, as posted on its website, is to:

1. Explore, enjoy and protect the wild places of the earth.
2. Practice and promote responsible use of the earth's ecosystems and resources.
3. Educate and enlist humanity to protect and restore the quality of the natural and human environment.
4. Use all lawful means to carry out these objectives.

Executive Summary— The Clear Skies Initiative

February 14, 2002

Today, President Bush proposed the most significant step America has ever taken to cut power plant emissions, the Clear Skies Initiative. This new proposal will aggressively reduce air pollution from electricity generators and improve air quality throughout the country. The Clear Skies Initiative will cut air pollution 70 percent, using a proven, market-based approach that will save American consumers millions of dollars.

America needs a clean, secure, affordable, reliable energy supply in the years ahead. President Bush has often said that environmental protection and energy production are not competing priorities. This progressive plan shows how that objective can be reached. We can meet our environmental goals while providing affordable electricity for American consumers and American businesses.

America has made great progress in reducing air pollution. Over the last three decades, air pollution has declined by 29 percent, while our economy has grown nearly 160 percent. These gains have provided cleaner air for millions of people. Our understanding of science, technology, and markets has improved since the Clean Air Act was passed in 1970. We know more about the best way to reduce pollution, and how to do it cost effectively. The acid rain cap and trade program created by Congress in 1990 reduced more pollution in the last decade than all other Clean Air Act command-and-control programs combined, and achieved significant reductions at two-thirds of the cost to accomplish those reductions using a "command-and-control" system. It's time to take the best of what we have learned and modernize the Clean Air Act. That's why President Bush is proposing a new Clean Air Act for the twenty-first century.

The Clear Skies Initiative will:

- Dramatically cut power plants' emissions of three of the worst air pollutants:
  - Cut sulfur dioxide (SO_2) emissions by 73 percent, from current emissions of 11 million tons to a cap of 4.5 million tons in 2010, and 3 million tons in 2018.
  - Cut emissions of nitrogen oxides (NO_x) by 67 percent, from current emissions of 5 million tons to a cap of 2.1 million tons in 2008, and to 1.7 million tons in 2018.
  - Cutting mercury emissions by 69 percent—the first-ever national cap on mercury emissions. Emissions will be cut from current emissions of 48 tons to a cap of 2010, and 15 tons in 2018.
  - Emission caps will be set to account for different air quality needs in the East and the West.

Executive Summary— The Clear Skies Initiative—cont'd

- Use a new, market-based approach to clean air:
  - Protect Americans from respiratory and cardiovascular diseases by dramatically reducing smog, fine particulate matter, regional haze; and protect wildlife habitat and ecosystem health from acid rain, nitrogen and mercury deposition. NO_x and SO_2 emissions both contribute to fine particulate matter emissions and NO_x also contributes to ground-level ozone or smog.
  - Save Americans as much as $1 billion annually in compliance costs that are passed along to American consumers, while improving air quality and protecting the reliability and affordability of electricity for consumers.
  - Cut pollution further, faster, cheaper—and with more certainty— eliminating the need for expensive and uncertain litigation as a means of achieving clean air.
  - Build upon the 1990 Clean Air Act's acid rain program. America's most successful clean air law in the last decade, and encourage the use of new pollution control technologies.

President Bush has a strong track record on enacting far-reaching clean air initiatives. In 1999, then-Governor Bush signed legislation that permanently caps NO_x and SO_2 emissions from older power plants in Texas starting in 2003. The legislation was widely hailed as a model for the country. The Texas program is designed to reduce NO_x emissions by 75,000 per year, and SO_2 emissions by 35,000 tons per year, while giving utilities flexibility in determining how and where to achieve the reductions.

Continued

ozone are rising a bit in the West. In January the park service said it met its 2004 performance goal of achieving stable or improving air quality in at least 62 percent of monitored parks, with 15 getting cleaner and 16 staying the same. Still, 18 got worse—including high-profile destinations such as Acadia, Death Valley, Grand Canyon and Yellowstone.

"We're at the end of the tailpipe," says Ken Olson, president of the Friends of Acadia. Pollutants emitted as far away as the Ohio River Valley cook in the sun as they are blown east, their ozone and acid levels rising as they move. "We get days when the visibility is just terrible [and] palpably polluted," he says.

And don't let the Smoky Mountains' name fool you. The nation's most popular park, at 9.2 million visitors a year, once offered terrific views year-round. The "smoke," known to the Cherokee long before the Industrial Revolution, is a bluish haze of moisture and natural organic particles that hangs on the hills.

Today, one of the worst pollutant concentrations in any national park has created a more unwelcome haze. Jim Embry, an architect in the tourist-happy town of Gatlinburg, Tennessee, north of the park, built a house in 1966 on Mount Harrison, facing the park. Two walls are almost all glass, with a scenic vista of majestic 6,593-foot Mount LeConte. Good views of the mountains are less and less common, he says. "I am watching them disappear before my eyes."

The air in California's Sequoia and Kings Canyon National Parks is essentially hostage to geography and climate. In the southern Sierra overlooking California's broad San Joaquin Valley, the 865,952-acre pair of parks range from rolling foothills and oak woodlands to granite peaks. Founded in 1890, Sequoia is the nation's second-oldest national park, after Yellowstone. Its eastern border crosses the summit of Mount Whitney, at 14,494 feet the loftiest point in the 48 conterminous states. The parks hold 30 groves of giant sequoia, the world's largest tree. Many are thousands of years old, 30 feet or more across at chest level, and taller than a 26-story building.

25 In winter, when the air is clearest, the vista from a snowy scenic outlook toward the San Joaquin Valley seems etched in crystal. From late spring through fall, though, dawn typically brings an ugly sight: a gray-brown murk that rises like a tide as the day warms. The miasma, says air resources specialist Annie Esperanza, even looks like a river as it flows into the park. Natural visibility at Sequoia should be 122 to 158 miles, the EPA says. But summer views average less than 40 miles, and on the worst days can drop below 6.

Though the parks are just 230 miles from Los Angeles, the problem is not Southern California sprawl. Instead, scientists have found that the pollution originates as fresh air off the Pacific picks up pollutants from the urban industrial complex around San Francisco Bay. As the air spreads south into California's sun-blasted Central Valley, it picks up more fine aerosols, sulfur dioxide, soot, dust and ozone-making nitrogen compounds from fast-growing cities, intense agriculture, busy Interstate 5 and other highways crowded with cars and diesel tractor-trailer rigs. The air is walled in by the Coast Ranges to the west, the Sierra Nevada to the east and the Tehachapi Mountains to the south, creating an eddy of recirculating and concentrated pollution before it wafts into Sequoia and Kings Canyon.

Bill Tweed, Sequoia and Kings Canyon's chief park naturalist, figures that the southern San Joaquin Valley is the nation's most efficient smog pot. The air, Tweed says, "just cooks and cooks and cooks in a warm, summer, cloudless climate." To make things worse, the valley's population is on track to double over the next four decades, to more than seven million. "We've already gone from a broth to a stew, and if we're not careful our stew will turn into a chowder," Tweed says. "The best way to enjoy a park is to just go out and walk. You must get out of your car to enjoy a park. But on a fair number of days, it is not even healthy to get outside and walk. That is a most direct assault on our mission."

Ozone, park officials say, has hurt 90 percent of the parks' Jeffrey pines. So far, the mature giant sequoia appear to be OK, but their seedlings may be suffering. In the Foothill Visitors Center at Ash Mountain, park workers post air advisories for the public and staff. On bad days, a sign tells visitors to avoid extended hikes. On 52 days last year, the parks' ozone levels exceeded the EPA "unhealthy air" standard of 85 parts per billion for eight hours. And 2004 was a good year; 2002 saw 80 unhealthy days, contributing to a 305-day unhealthy air total for the span 1992–2003—just 68 fewer than Los Angeles.

"I can't even bring my kids up here unless I know we're going to have clean air," says Laura Whitehouse, NPCA's local representative. Her three children all have severe asthma. In May 2004, thinking the air would be tolerable, she took them into the park. Her 9-year-old son, Aaron, complained of chest pains in the parking lot and plunked down on a bench, wheezing badly. Paramedics had to bring a nebulizer to clear up the boy's lungs. "It's sometimes worse up here than in the valley," Whitehouse says.

30 In 1967, Bill Tweed was 18 and working as a bellboy at the lodge at Sequoia and Kings Canyon. With July 4 coming up, veteran employees let him in on a local tradition: load up backpacks with beer and other refreshments and scale Moro Rock, a bald monolithic knob near park headquarters. For generations, its lordly 6,725-foot-high view across the San Joaquin Valley to the west had provided a granite throne for simultaneously looking down on fireworks spouting from Fresno, Visalia, Dinuba and other communities. But that year not a flicker was to be seen. "Everybody said it had been happening more and more often," Tweed recalls. Within a few years, the Fourth of July climb was kaput, killed by haze.

As Tweed lists the man-made threats to the parks—climate change, invasive species, forests choked by overzealous fire suppression, nitrogen air pollutants that overfertilize ozone—he's not optimistic that Moro Rock Independence Day viewing will return any time soon. "We are making it harder and harder to carry out the legal mandate to maintain these parks in their natural state," Tweed says. "What we don't know now is, can we ever get it back?"

Questions for Discussion

1. Why do you think Petit chose to open his report with a description of Big Bend National Park in Texas rather than one of a more famous park, such as Yellowstone? What does this example establish?

2. What is contributing to the air pollution at Big Bend, and why is it worth understanding where these contributions originate?

3. Consider the statistics in paragraph 4. How do these statistics prepare the way for a discussion of visibility elsewhere in this piece? At what points is the change in visibility conveyed most dramatically to you?

4. Have you visited any of the parks mentioned in this piece? If so, what was your experience there? If not, do you feel motivated to visit them before conditions deteriorate further, or are you moved to stay away?

5. How diverse are the sources that Petit has drawn upon? Do you come away from this piece thinking that he has relied primarily on environmental activists or a broader segment of the population? Why do you think Petit took the trouble to establish that one of the activists he cites is a "jewelry sales consultant"?

6. What do you think it means to live in a "tourist-happy town"? Would such a town be likely to protect the surrounding environment?

7. Does Petit employ pathos—or an appeal to feeling—at any point in this piece?

8. Based on your reading of this piece, how would you respond to the question with which it concludes?

DIFFERENCES

NEGOTIATING

As the essays in this section indicate, environmental concerns have not disappeared since Rachel Carson's *Silent Spring* was published in 1962; rather, they have in many ways intensified, despite increasing awareness of some of the risks that Carson highlighted in her famous book. One of the challenges people now face is how to set environmental priorities and then use them to identify specific actions that can be undertaken to benefit the environment. Part of that challenge is deciding where to place responsibility for some of the environmental problems ahead. For example, whose responsibility is the increased air pollution and greater use of oil that result from the popularity of SUVs? The drivers who purchase such vehicles? The companies that manufacture and sell them? The U.S. government, whose policies allow SUVs to avoid the stricter emissions controls placed on cars? How should we determine that responsibility when so many different people seem to have a hand in environmental degradation?

With these points in mind, identify an environmental problem in your geographic region (or identify a national environmental issue that affects your region), and try to determine who is responsible for this problem. Using whatever sources seem appropriate, try to learn about the problem to identify the factors that seem to have helped create it. Look also for potential solutions to it. Then write an essay to a local audience (for example, the readers of your local newspaper or residents of an area affected by the problem) in which you argue for what you think is the most feasible solution to the problem. For example, if you were to write your essay about the problem of SUVs mentioned in the previous paragraph, you would want to learn about the environmental damage SUVs might cause, as well as related problems. And you would want to learn about the extent of those problems in your region. Whatever your topic, try to write an argument that would persuade environmentalists and others affected by the problem that your approach would be a reasonable one.

Credits

Chapter 2: p. 26: From "Beauty Face-Off" by Julia Storberg in HEALTH Magazine, October 2000, pp. 14–15.

Chapter 2: p. 28: "In a Chat Room, You Can Be NE1" by Camille Sweeney from NEW YORK TIMES Magazine, October 17, 1999. Copyright c 1999 The New York Times Co. Reprinted by permission.

Chapter 3: p. 38: Reprinted by permission of Christoph Niemann.

Chapter 3: p. 38: "The Ethicist" by Randy Cohen as appeared in THE NEW YORK TIMES Magazine, July 10, 2005. Copyright c 2005. Reprinted by permission of Randy Cohen.

Chapter 3: p. 42: "Whatever happened to all those heroes?" by Peter Lennon from THE GUARDIAN, 30 December 1998. Copyright Guardian Newspapers Limited 1998. Reprinted by permission.

Chapter 3: p. 46: "Torture Incarnate, and Propped on a Pedestal" by Sarah Boxer from THE NEW YORK TIMES, June 13, 2004. Copyright c 2004 The New York Times Co. Reprinted by permission.

Chapter 3: p. 52: "An Open Letter to the Community" by St. Lawrence Cement Company as appeared in ALBANY TIMES UNION, December 28, 2002, p. A7.

Chapter 4: p. 73: "Dummying Up: For Fear of Reading Book about the Koran" by Clarence Page, Tribune Media Services, July 1, 2002. Reprinted by permission of TMSReprints.

Chapter 4: p. 74: "A Farewell to Alms" by James Surowiecki from THE NEW YORKER, July 25, 2005. Copyright c 2005 Conde Nast Publications, Inc. Reprinted by permission. All rights reserved.

Chapter 4: p. 76: Letter to editor by Pamela G. Bailey from CLEVELAND PLAIN DEALER, September 4, 2002.

Chapter 4: p. 77: "Why You Can Hate Drugs and Still Want to Legalize Them" by Joshua Wolf Shenk. Reprinted with permission from THE WASHINGTON MONTHLY. Copyright by Washington Monthly Publishing, LLC, 733 15th St. NW, Suite 520, Washington, DC 20005. (202) 393–5155. Web site: www.washingtonmonthly.com

Chapter 4: p. 78: "Myers' Success Rests on Bad Humor" letter to editor by Keith Sollenberger from USA TODAY, August 2, 2002, p. 8A. Reprinted by permission of the author.

Chapter 4: p. 104: Excerpt from "Why Nick" by Jeanne Shields from NEWSWEEK, May 8, 1978, p. 23.

Chapter 4: p. 107: "Ronaldo Earns his Glory" by Filip Bondy, Knight Ridder/Tribune, July 1, 2002. Reprinted by permission of TMSReprints.

Photo Credits

Chapter 9: p. 280 and 330: Ronnie Kaufman/Corbis; **p. 282 and 296:** M. Nader/Getty Images; **p. 302 and 321:** Shakh Alvazov/AP Wide World Photos; **p. 323:** Homer Sykes/Alamy; **p. 346:** MedioImages Fresca Collection/Alamy; **p. 349:** The Advertising Archives; **p. 355:** UKraft/Alamy

Chapter 10: p. 366 and 369: Richard Flood/DK Stock/Getty Images; **p. 370:** Bettmann/Corbis; **p. 373:** Library of Congress. Courtesy of Ann Vachon; **p. 374:** Bettmann/Corbis; **p. 383:** Bettmann/Corbis; **p. 392 and 402:** AP Wide World Photos; **p. 424:** © Sheri Blaney; **p. 426:** Lester Lefkositz/Corbis; **p. 427:** Ariel Skelly/Corbis; **p. 430:** Reuters New Media Inc/Corbis

Chapter 11: p. 440: Louise Gubb/Corbis SABA; **p. 442 and 505:** Jose Luis Pelaez/Corbis; **p. 459:** Cindy Charles/PhotoEdit; **p. 470:** Michael Pole/Corbis; **p. 487:** Spencer Grant/PhotoEdit; **p. 498:** Bryn Colton/Corbis **p. 500:** Tom Stewart/Corbis; **p. 501:** Eric Fowke/PhotoEdit; **p. 507:** Spencer Grant/PhotoEdit; **p. 515:** Dennis Brack/IPN/Aurora; **p. 519:** Rob Lewis/Corbis

Chapter 12: p. 540: Scott Olson/AFP/Getty Images; **p. 543:** PhotoDisc/Getty Images; **p. 542 and 546:** Scott Olson/AFP/Getty Images; **p. 552:** Robert Essel/Corbis; **p. 553:** David Barber/PhotoEdit; **p. 557:** David McNew/Getty Images; **p. 558:** A. Ramey/PhotoEdit; **p. 561:** Bettmann/Corbis; **p. 562:** Will Hart/PhotoEdit; **p. 568:** Peter Turnley/Corbis; **p. 583:** Amy Etra/PhotoEdit; **p. 587:** Greg Newton/Reuters NewMedia Inc/Corbis; **p. 598:** Bettmann/Corbis; **p. 601 and 604:** Bettmann/Corbis; **p. 614:** Dylan Martinez/Reuters New Media/Corbis; **p. 617:** Mark Leffingwell/Getty Images

Chapter 13: p. 630 and 660: Taxi/Getty Images; **p. 638:** Royalty-Free Corbis; **p. 664:** Tim Boyle/Getty Images; **p. 672:** Ulrike Welsch Photography; **p. 677:** Royalty-Free Corbis; **p. 678:** Royalty-Free Corbis; **p. 684:** Topical Press Agency/Getty Images; **p. 685:** Wes Thompson/Corbis; **p. 688 and 699:** Cary Anderson/Aurora; **p. 691:** Justin Sullivan/Getty Images; **p. 693:** James Shaffer/PhotoEdit; **p. 695:** Bettmann/ Corbis; **p. 704:** Peter Essick/Aurora; **p. 708:** Layne Kennedy/Corbis

Index

A

"A Patriotic Left" (Kazin), 582–588
AAC&U, 448
AARP, 406
"Abou Ben Adhem" (Hunt), 479
About Campus, 226
Above-ground nuclear testing, 691
"Absent at What Price?" (Rivedal), 120–121
Abstract, 156
Abstract Wild, The (Turner), 702
Abstracting services, 174–175
Abu Ghraib prison, 46
Academic research. *See* Research
Academic Search Premier, 170
ACLU, 617
ACS Style Guide: A Manual for Authors and Editors, 183
Ad hominem argument, 100, 106
ADA, 431
Adbusters, 44
Addams, Jane, 584
Adirondack Mountains, 83
Adler, Mortimer J., 450
"Adonis Complex, The" (Pope et al.), 342–352
Advanced Placement programs, 508
Adventures of Huckleberry Finn (Twain), 442
Advertisement
    arguing to assert, 8
    argument, as, 8, 43–45
    politicians, 73
Advice for the New Faculty Member, 479

Afghanistan, 42
Age, 28–29
Age of reason, 492
Agricultural Act of 1956, 692
Agricultural zoning, 678
AICP, 664
AIP Style Manual, 183
Air pollution, 712–720
All-volunteer army, 589
ALMA awards, 545
"America: Idea or Nation?" (McClay), 160, 573–581
American Association of Retired Persons (AARP), 406
American Beauty, 683
American Civil Liberties Union (ACLU), 617
American Crisis, The (Paine), 671
American Crucible (Gerstle), 583
American exceptionalism, 582
American Heritage Dictionary, 122
American Institute of Certified Planners (AICP), 664
American Medical Association Manual of Style: A Guide for Authors and Editors, 183
American national identity, 540–629
    federalism, 619–627
    good American citizen?, 568–569
    immigration, 542–567. *See also* Immigration
    leftist political views, 582–588
    "Letter from Birmingham Jail" (King), 600–611
    national ID card, 612–618
    patriotism, 573–588
    power of government, 598–599

American national identity *(Continued)*
  student assignment, 566–567, 596–597, 628–629
  voting, 570–572
  war, 589–595
American Psychological Association (APA), 182. *See also* APA-style
    documentation
American Scholar, 589
American Society for Aesthetic Plastic Surgery (ASAPS), 289
American Society of Composers, Authors and Publishers (ASCAP),
    219
Americans with Disabilities Act (ADA), 431
Anabolic steroids, 334–341, 356
Analogy, 99
Analyzing your audience, 19–20
AND, 174
Anna Karenina (Tolstoy), 402, 481, 579
Annotated text, 158
Annotation, 156–158
Anorexia nervosa, 331, 344
Anthologies, 155
Anti-Vietnam War sentiment, 585
Anticipating the opposition, 167
Antiwar poster, 45
AP program, 508
APA-style documentation
  APA author/year style, 196–201
  references list, 201–204. *See also* APA-style references list
APA-style references list, 201–204
  anonymous work, 204
  book with one author, 201
  book with two/three authors, 202
  corporate author, 202
  edited book, 202
  example, 299–300
  government document, 204
  interview, 204
  journal article, 203
  magazine article, 203
  multivolume work, 203
  newspaper article, 203
  online journal article, 204
  subsequent editions of book, 202
  translated book, 202
Appeal to pity, 98
Appeal to prejudice, 99
Appeal to tradition, 99
Aquinas, Thomas, 62

Araton, Harvey, 23–25
Argument
  advertisement, 43–45
  art, 45–51
  assert, 4, 7–9
  context. *See* Contexts of argument
  culture, 23–26
  icons, 45
  inquire, 5, 11–12
  MLA-style bibliography, 193–195
  negotiate differences, 5–7, 13–15
  paintings, 45–48
  photograph, 39–42
  posters, 45, 48–51
  prevail, 4, 9–10
  strategies. *See* Strategies for argument
  websites, 61–62
Argument by analogy, 99–100
Argument to assert, 4, 7–9
Argument to inquire, 5, 11–12
Argument to negotiate differences, 5–7, 13–15
Argument to prevail, 4, 9–10
Aristophanes, 407
Aristotle, 71–72, 92, 147
Arnold, Matthew, 449, 450
Art, 45–51
  argument, as, 45–51
  paintings, 45–48
  posters, 45, 48–51
Art of Love (Ovid), 407
"Art of Teaching Science, The" (Thomas), 490–495
Article I, Section 8 of the Constitution, 621
Aryans, 430
ASAPS, 289
ASCAP, 219
Asian-American population, 460
Asian tsunami (2004), 314
Assert, argument to, 4, 7–9
Assessing students. *See* Grading
Assistive reproductive technologies, 425–431
Association of American Colleges and Universities (AAC&U), 448
Asynchronous forums, 63–65
Atlantic, 406
Attack ads, 73
Attacking character of opponent, 100
Attributing false causes, 100–101
Attributing guilt by association, 101

Audience
    analyzing the, 19–20, 115–122
    expectations, 117
    identify the, 115–116
    imagining the, 20–21
Audience analysis, 115–122
Audience expectations, 117, 147
Auerbach, Karl, 647
Author, 155
Authoritarian classroom, 471–483
Authority
    credibility, 76–80
    evidence, 84–85
Axis of evil, 446

B

BAAPS, 289
"Baby, This Is For Ever" (Hodson), 419–421
Baby and Child Care (Spock), 424, 433
Baby boom, 433
Back Bay, 670–672
Bad Subjects: Political Education for Everyday Life, 547
Bailey, Beth, "From Front Porch to Back Seat: A History of the
    Date," 369–376
Bailey, Pamela G., 77
Bailey, Ronald, "Silent Spring at 40," 697–701
Bait and switch, 471
Balanced Budget Act of 1997, 413
Balkanization, 639
balkanize, 648
Balkans, 648
Balzar, John, "Needed: Informed Voters," 570–572
Barron, David J., "Reclaiming Federalism," 619–627
Bartholdi, Frédéric Auguste, 672
Battle of Agincourt, 552
Baudrillard, Jean, 390, 391, 395
Beard, Charles, 472
Beckerman, Gal, "Tripping Up Big Media," 263–271
Begging the question, 101
Bell, George, 634
Beresford, Heather, "I Was an Idiot to Take It So Far," 331–334
Berliner, Emil, 250
Berns, Walter, 575
Better Not Bigger (Fodor), 677–679
Bibliography, 184. *See also* APA-style references list; MLA-style
    bibliography
Big Bend National Park, 712–714

Big Brother, 617
Big Five media companies, 273
Bigorexia nervosa, 348
Binet, Alfred, 500
Birkerts, Sven, 87
Blair, Cherie, 292
BLM, 705
Blogs, 653
Bloom, Allan, 459
Bluebook: A Uniform System of Citation, 183
BMI, 307
Board on Children, Youth, and Families, 436
Body fascism, 293
Body image, 280–365
    celebrity bashing, 291–293
    cosmetic surgery, 283–290
    fitness, 330–365. *See also* Fitness
    media influences, 282, 294–301
    student assignment, 300–301, 328–329, 364–365
    weight gain, 302–329. *See also* Obesity
Body mass index (BMI), 307
Bolter, Jay David, 11
Bondy, Filip, 107
Book review, 149–150, 406–410
Books, 175–176
Boolean operators, 174
Boomerang kids, 433
Borges, Jorge Luis, 410
Borowski, John, 148
Boston, 669–674
Boston Latin School, 500–501
Boston Review, 633
Boteach, Shmuley, 407
Boulder, Colorado, 678
Boulder County, 678
Boxer, Sarah, 46
Brady, James, 622
Brady Bill, 622
Brain and obesity, 307–310
Brandels, Louis, 624
Brantingham, Patricia, 666
Bratman, Steven, 331
Brave New World (Huxley), 384–385
BRAVO Study, 714
"Breaking Up Is Easy to Do" (Lowry/Grover), 275–277
Brennan, Dean, 666
Brimelow, Peter, "Nation of Immigrants, A," 549–554

Brin, Sergy, 650

Brink, Susan, "Eat This Now!", 303–306

British Association of Aesthetic Plastic Surgeons (BAAPS), 289

Broadcast indecency, 263

Broadcast.com, 634

Broken windows, 665

Brooks, David, 35

Brown, Jeremy (DJ Reset), 252

Brown v. Board of Education, 605, 625

Browning, Frank, 29

Brownmiller, Susan, 27

Brubaker, Kristen, 142–145

Bruce, Bertram, 635

Brussels bureaucracy, 551

"Brutality of Celebrity Culture, The" (McMillan), 291–293

Bryan, William Jennings, 584

Bunting, Josiah, III, "Class Warfare," 589–595

Bureau of Land Management (BLM), 705

Burkart, Patrick, 253

Bush, George W., 30, 39, 81, 263, 411, 435, 446, 589, 617, 713, 716–717

Bush, Vannevar, 494

Bush v. Gore, 626

Business Week Online, 275

"Buyin' Bulk" (McDougall/Schuler), 334–341

"By the Time I Get to Cucaracha" (Perez-Zeeb), 544–548

C

Cabrini-Green, 664

Camarota, Steven, "Too Many: Looking Today's Immigration in the Face," 560–565

Cambridge Realists, 494

Cancer, 700

Canon formation, 450

Canterbury Tales, The (Chaucer), 472

Capitalism, 514, 516

Caplan, Ralph, "What's Yours? (Ownership of Intellectual Property)," 217–221

Capra, Frank, 384

Carcinogens and Anticarcinogens in the Human Diet, 700

Carnegie, Andrew, 482

Carnegie Foundation, 482

Carson, Rachel, 697–701

"The Obligation to Endure," 690–696

Castro, Fidel, 557

Catalog, 175–176

Cats, 445

Cause-and-effect relationship, 100–101

Cazares, Gabriel, 545

CDC, 312

Celebrity bashing, 291–293

Cell phones, 244

Censorship, 237

Censorship of information on U.S. government websites, 96

Center for Immigration Studies (CIS), 560

Centers for Disease Control and Prevention (CDC), 312

Chang, May, 653

Change, 482

Character, 72–76, 80

Character witnesses, 73

Charity girls, 370

Chat rooms, 66, 67

Chaucer, Geoffrey, 472

Chavez, Cesar, 584

Checklist

documentation, 205

final draft, 205

Cheers, 669

Cheriton, David, 646–650

Chesterton, G. K., 579

Chicago Manual of Style, 183

Chickering, Jesse, 551

Childhood obesity, 318–327

China's one-child policy, 428

Chomsky, Noam, 582

Christ, Jesus, 608

Chronicle of Higher Education, 444, 448, 458, 471

Cicero, 127

Cigarette packages, 87

Circular reasoning, 101

CIS, 560

Cities. *See* Urbanization

Citing sources. *See* Documenting your sources

Citizenship. *See* American national identity

City planners, 662–675

"Civil Disobedience" (Thoreau), 571

Civil libertarian, 617

Civil rights movement, 600, 625

Cizek, Gregory, 149

"Unintended Consequences of High-Stakes Testing," 503–513

Claim, 93–97, 141

Class discussion, 11

"Class Warfare" (Bunting), 589–595

Classical arrangement, 126–131

Classical rhetoric, 126–127
Clay, Henry, 577
Clear Channel Communications, 259
Clear Skies Initiative, 713–717
Clinton, Bill, 413, 622
Cocktail party, 444
Cocktail Party, The (Eliot), 445
Code Pink, 264
Cognitive, 295
Cognitive-behavioral techniques, 295
Cohen, Randy, 37–39
Cole, David, 665
Cole, Thomas, 47
Coleridge, Samuel Taylor, 591
Collaborative learning, 214
"Collecting Music in the Digital Realm" (McCourt), 250–254
College: The Undergraduate Experience in America (Boyer), 452
College students' sexual exploits, 380–388
Colossal separate nature reserves, 693
Columbia Journalism Review, 263
Commentary, 147–148
Commerce Clause, 622, 624
Committee of Public Information, 273
Commondreams.org, 148
Competence, 79
Competition in Radio and Concert Industries Act of 2002, 261
Composing process, 113–123
Computerized catalogs, 175–176
Conant, James Bryant, 450
Concentration of ownership (media), 257–262
Concessions, 116–117
Concluding paragraph, 127
Confirmatio, 126
Congresswomen (Aristophanes), 407
Connaughton, Jim, 715
Constructing arguments, 110–151
    audience analysis, 115–122
    classical arrangement, 126–131
    concessions, 116–117
    defining your terms, 122–123
    language, 147–151
    lists, 116
    logical arrangement, 137–146
    outline, 124–125
    Rogerian argument, 131–137
    source material, 125
    structuring the argument, 123–146

    supporting evidence, 146–147
    topic, 113–115
Consumer sovereignty, 640, 642
Consuming the Romantic Utopia (Illouz), 390
Content notes, 183
Contexts of argument, 17–33
    cultural context, 22–30. *See also* Cultural context
    historical context, 30–32
    rhetorical situation, 18–22
Contract grading, 523–525
Coolidge, Calvin, 552
Coon, Carleton, 247
Coon-Sanders Original Nighthawk Orchestra, 247
Coontz, Stephanie, "Great Expectations," 403–405
Cooper, James Fenimore, 570
Cooperative learning, 214
Coplin, Bill, "Lost in the Life of the Mind," 471–474
Copyright
    fair use, 211
    legislation, 211
    Supreme Court decision, 219, 236
"Copyright Crusaders" (Gibson), 222–225
Cornford, Francis, 494
Corporate behavior, 20
Corporation for Public Broadcasting, 643
Cosmetic surgery, 283–290
Courtship, 368–379
Covenant marriage, 404
CPTED, 662, 666
Craighead, Frank, 709
Crayon.net, 635
Credibility
    arrogance, 79
    competence, 79
    establishing one's, 74–78
    medium, 66
    online forum, 66
    personal experience, 77–78
    questioning one's, 73–74
    reasonableness, 79
Cretaceous Period, 693
Crime prevention through environmental design (CPTED), 662, 666
Crime Prevention Through Environmental Design (Jeffrey), 663
Criminal plagiarism, 226
Critical language, 148
Critical reading, 154–155

Cultural context, 22–30
  age, 28–29
  culture in argument, 23–26
  gender, 26–28
  sexual orientation, 29–30
Cultural criticism, 492
Cultural difference in logical arguments, 93
Cultural pluralism, 551
Culture, 22–26
Culture and Anarchy (Arnold), 449
Cunningham, Ward, 653
Curriculum, 442–469
  humanities, 444–447
  liberal education, 448–457
  multicultural education, 458–462
  redesigning the, 463–469
  student assignment, 468–469
  what is the issue?, 442–443
  women's studies courses, 484–489
Cyber environment, 622–659
  e-mail, 651–654
  hackers, 655–657
  personalization, 633–645
  re-engineering the Internet, 646–650
  student assignment, 658–659
  what is the issue?, 622

D

Daily Me, 635
Damocles, 517
Darst, Joseph, 664
Data, 93, 140
"Databases and Security vs. Privacy" (Green), 612–615
Dating, 368–379
DDT, 698–700
de Gersdorff, Sascha, "Fresh Faces," 283–286
"Deaf Babies, 'Designer Disability,' and the Future of Medicine" (Savulescu), 430
Deafness, 429
Death and Life of Great American Cities (Jacobs), 662
Death of a Salesman (Miller), 217
Debs, Eugene, 584
Declaration of Independence, 31, 89, 158, 577, 598, 599, 619
Deductive reasoning, 88–93, 138–140
Deep ecology, 707
Defense of Marriage Act, 29, 413
Defensible space, 663–664

Defensible Space (Newman), 663
Defining your terms, 122–123
Delaney Clause, 699
Democracy, 633–645
Democracy in America (Tocqueville), 574
Dershowitz, Alan M., "Why Fear National ID Cards?", 616–618
Design for the Real World: Human Ecology and Social Change (Papanek), 218
"Designer Babies and Other Fairy Tales" (Freely), 425–428
"Designing a Signature General Education Program" (Trainor), 463–469
Desk dictionary, 122
Detective, 88
Developing Reflective Judgment (King/Kitchener), 481
Dewey, John, 442, 452
Diana, Princess of Wales, 291
Diary of Anne Frank, 442
Dictionary, 122
Diederich, Paul, 529
Diet. *See* Obesity
Digital technology, 175
Dionysius, 517
Direct Marketing Association (DMA), 613
Disney World, 669
Disneyland, 669
Dissent, 586, 619
Divorce rate, 403
DJ Reset, 252
DMA, 613
DNS, 649
Doane College, 382
Documenting your sources, 180–205
  APA-style documentation, 196–204. *See also* APA-style documentation
  bibliography, 184
  checklist, 205
  content notes, 183
  endnotes, 183–184
  footnotes, 183–184
  MLA-style documentation, 185–195. *See also* MLA-style documentation
  parenthetical citations, 184
  style manuals, 183
Domain, 169
Domain name server (DNS), 649
"Dorm Brothel" (Guroian), 380–388
Dormant Commerce Clause, 622, 624

Douglass, Frederick, 584
"Dover Beach" (Arnold), 450
Downzoning, 678
Drengson, Alan, 707
Drew, Rob, 253
Drunk driving, 9
D'Souza, Dinesh, 461
Duchesneau, Sharon, 429–431
Duchess of Cornwall (Camilla Parker-Bowles), 291, 292
Duchess of York (Sarah Ferguson), 291, 292
"Dulce et Decorum Est" (Owen), 592
Dulce et decorum est pro patria mori, 591

E

E-mail, 651–654
"Eat This Now!" (Brink/Querna), 303–306
Eating disorder, 331, 344
Eco-tourism, 706–708
Ecological Literacy (Orr), 84
Ecology of Invasions, The (Elton), 693
Edison, Thomas, 250
Educate America Act, 507
"Educated and Culturally Literate Person Must Study America's Multicultural Reality, An" (Takaki), 458
Education, 440–539
    assessment, 498–539. *See also* Grading
    curriculum, 442–469. *See also* Curriculum
    mission statement, 465
    purpose of, 442
    sexual promiscuity on campus, 380–388
    teaching methods, 470–497. *See also* Teaching methods
Educational Testing Service, 529
EducationNews.org, 511
ekklesia, 609
Elbow, Peter, "Getting Along without Grades—and Getting Along with Them, Too," 521–537
Eldred v. Ashcroft, 236
Electronic catalogs, 175–176
Electronic media. *See* Internet; Radio and Television
Electronic surveillance of personal mail, 18
Electroshock therapy, 21
Eliot, T. S., 445
Eller, Jim, 427
Ellipsis (...), 125
Elton, Charles, 693
Embry, Jim, 718
Emerson, Ralph Waldo, 704

Emory Peak, 713
Emotional arguments, 103–108
"Empire of the Air" (Toomey), 257–262
Empirical self-examination, 534
Endnotes, 183–184
"Enough Snickering. Suburbia Is More Complicated and Varied than We Think" (Wilson), 682–685
Enthymeme, 92
Environment, 630–721
    air pollution, 712–720
    Internet, 622–659. *See also* Cyber environment
    national parks, 712–720
    pesticides, 690–701
    student assignment, 658–659, 686–687, 720–721
    urbanization. *See* Urbanization
    wilderness, 688, 702–711
Environmental Protection Agency (EPA), 713
Environmentalist movement, 697
EPA, 713
Equivocation, 101
Eschatology, 503
Esperanza, Annie, 718
Essay tests, 498
et al., 185
Ethos, 72–80, 150
Eugenics, 427
European Union, 551
Evaluating Internet resources, 168
Evans, Ruth, "Femininity and Muscularity: Accounts of Seven Women Body Builders," 353–364
Evening news, 637
Everyone Can Write: Essays toward a Hopeful Theory of Writing and Teaching Writing (Elbow), 521
Evidence, 80–85
    authority, 84–85
    deduction, 88
    facts, 81–83
    induction, 88
    personal experience, 83–84
    supporting claims, 146–147
    values, 85
    visual form, 85
Excite, 634
Exercise, 330–365. *See also* Fitness
Exordium, 126
Expanded Academic ASAP, 169, 170
Experiments, 87

Extreme Makeover, 283
"Extreme Surgery" (Lawton), 287–290
Extremist, 608

F

Face-to-face discussion, 63
Facts as evidence, 81–83
Fahrenheit 9/11, 31
Fair use, 211
Fairness doctrine, 267
Fallacies. *See* Logical fallacies
False dilemma, 102, 117
Family Educational Rights and Privacy Act (FERPA), 477
Fanning, Shawn, 241
"Farewell to Alms?, The" (Surowiecki), 74–76
Farewell to Arms, A (Hemingway), 74
Farrey, Tom, 334
Fascism, 48
Fatherhood, 435–437
Fay, Brian, 23
FCC, 264
Federal Communications Commission (FCC), 264
Federalist Papers, The, 552
Felson, Marcus, 666
Female body builders, 353–364
Feminine beauty, 282
Femininity (Brownmiller), 27
"Femininity and Muscularity: Accounts of Seven Women Body Builders" (Grogan et al.), 353–364
Feminist education, 486
Ferguson, Sarah (Duchess of York), 291, 292
FERPA, 477
"Fidelity with a Wandering Eye" (Nehring), 406–410
50 Cent, 244
Figurative language, 149
Final draft, 205
Fire lookouts, 708
First Amendment, 636
Fitness, 330–365
   adonis complex, 342–352
   healthy diet as obsession, 331–333
   steroids, 334–341
   student assignment, 364–365
   what is the issue?, 330
   women body builders, 353–364
Fix-Masseau, Pierre-Félix, 48
Flame wars, 55, 67

Flaming, 658
FMC, 257–261
Fodor, Eben, 677–679
"Food and Media," 304
Footnotes, 183–184
For a Critique of the Political Economy of the Sign (Baudrillard), 391
Foreign aid, 74
Foreign Policy, 272
Formaro, Tom, 58
Forsythe, John, 712
Fortune, 222
Fourteenth Amendment, 584, 625
Fox News, 637
Frank, Barney, 620
Frederick Olmsted Circle, 590
"Free Downloads Play Sweet Music" (Ian), 239–243
Free speech principle, 636
Freely, Maureen, "Designer Babies and Other Fairy Tales," 425–428
Freewriting, 522–523
Freire, Paulo, 485
French State Railways, 48–49
"Fresh Faces" (de Gersdorff), 283–286
Friedan, Betty, 584
Friedman, Milton, 77
Friedman, Thomas, 518
"From Front Porch to Back Seat: A History of the Date" (Bailey), 369–376
Frot-Coutaz, Cecile, 283
Fun hog, 706
Future of Freedom Foundation, 555
Future of Music Coalition (FMC), 257–261

G

Garden Cities, 684
Garreau, Joel, 683
Gas out, 96–97
Gay adoption, 133–136
Gay marriage, 411–418
Gay Marriage: Why It Is Good for Gays, Good for Straights, and Good for America (Rauch), 411
Gender, 26–28
Gender Advertisements (Goffman), 390
"Gender Dimensions of U.S. Immigration Policy, The," 546
General audience, 21
General Education in a Free Society, 450
General interest intermediaries, 635, 637, 641

General Motors, 49
Generalization, 91
Genetic engineering, 429–431
Gerstle, Gary, 583
Gestalt theory, 394
Get Mail syndrome, 652
"Get Your Hand Out of My Pocket" (James), 377–379
"Getting Along without Grades—and Getting Along with Them, Too" (Elbow), 521–537
"Getting on the Case" (Meck), 662–667
Gibbs, W. Wayt, "Obesity: An Overblown Epidemic?", 311–317
Gibson, David, "Copyright Crusaders," 222–225
Globalization, 518
GM-free, 331
Goals 2000, 507
Goffman, Erving, 390, 392–393, 395, 397
Going steady, 373
Goins, Liesa, 379
Gold's Gym, 354
Goldwater, Barry, 608
"Good Enough Mother, The" (Quindlen), 432–434
Good Vibrations, 335
Google, 650
Gore, Albert, 697
Gould, Stephen Jay, 708
Government, power of, 598–599
Goya, Francisco José de, 45–47
Grade inflation, 530
Grading, 498–539
    alternative methods of, 521–537
    contract, 523–525
    criterion based assessment, 535–536
    explicit criteria, 534–535
    grid, 533–534
    institutional, 535–536
    Marxist response, 514–520
    minimal, 528–531
    myths (surrounding testing), 515–516
    nongraded writing, 523
    portfolio, 523
    standardized testing, 503–513
    student assignment, 537–538
    tracking, 499–502
    what is the issue?, 498
Graham, Mary, 96
Granite, 649
Grant, Cary, 282

Great books, 450
Great Cancer Scare, 700
"Great Expectations" (Coontz), 403–405
Great Expectations (Dickens), 403
Great works, 526
Green, Heather, "Databases and Security vs. Privacy," 612–615
Green card, 544
Green Imperative: Natural Design for the Real World (Papanek), 218
Greene, Cooper, 45
Grid, 533–534
Grogan, Sarah, "Femininity and Muscularity: Accounts of Seven Women Body Builders," 353–364
Group polarization, 638–639
Grover, Ron, "Breaking Up Is Easy to Do," 275–277
Guetter, Rachel, 125, 133–136
Guilt by association, 101
Gun control, 104–107
Guroian, Vigen, "Dorm Brothel," 380–388

H
Hackers, 655–657
Hadad, Amir, 24, 25
Hague v. CIO, 644
Haid, Saeed, 25
Haines, John, 709
Hamilton, Alexander, 576
Hamlet, 407
Hammond, Hall, 712–713
Harvard Red Book, 450
Hate groups, 639
Hate-speak, 292
Haussmann, Georges-Eugene, 671
"Hazy Days in Our Parks" (Petit), 712–720
Health Maintenance Organization (HMO), 324
"Hello, Cleveland" (Surowiecki), 247–249
Henry V, 552, 593
Hernandez, Daisy, 78
HFEA, 425, 427
Hierarchy of human needs, 391
High-stakes testing, 503–513
Highlighting, 157
Hilfiger, Tommy, 43
Hill, Grant, 73
Hillman, Sidney, 584
Hinchman, Hannah, 709
Hirsch, E. D., 459
Hirsch, Fred, 84

Hispanics, 460, 544–548

Historical context, 30–32

Hitler, Adolf, 48, 430

HMO, 324

Hodson, Phillip, "Baby, This Is For Ever," 419

hooks, bell, "Toward a Radical Feminist Pedagogy," 484–489

Hornberger, Jacob G., "Keep the Borders Open," 555–559

"How to Mend a Broken Internet" (O'Brien), 646

"How Your Brain Makes You Fat" (Wickens), 307–310

Huckabee, Mike, 403, 404

Hudson Valley School, 47

Human Fertilisation and Embryology Authority (HFEA), 425, 427

"Humanities for Cocktail Parties and Beyond, The" (Livingston), 444

Hume, David, 707

Hungarian freedom fighters, 605

Hunter, Geoff, "Femininity and Muscularity: Accounts of Seven Women Body Builders," 353–364

Hurley, Elizabeth, 292

Hutchins, Robert Maynard, 450

Hyperlinks, 57

Hyperreality, 390

Hypertext, 57

Hypertextual websites, 57–62

I

I Am Charlotte Simmons (Wolfe), 383, 386

I Want a Famous Face, 283

"I Was an Idiot to Take It So Far" (Beresford), 331–334

Ian, Janis, "Free Downloads Play Sweet Music," 239–243

IASA, 507

IB courses, 501

IBO diploma program, 501

Icons, 45

Identifying your audience, 115–116

IETF, 647–648

iFeminists.com, 431

Ignorance of the rules, 227

Ignoring the question, 101–112

Illegal immigrants, 544–548

Illouz, Eva, 390, 391, 395

Image distortion techniques, 298

Images. *See* Visual media

Imagining your audience, 20–21

Immigration, 542–567

    Brimelow article, 549–554

    illegal immigrants, 544–548

    libertarian view, 555–559

    restricted policy view, 560–565

    student assignment, 566–567

    what is the issue?, 542–543

Immigration Marriage Fraud Amendment, 546

Immigration Quota Acts, 551

Importation of plants, 693–694

Impotence, 44

Improving America's Schools Act (IASA), 507

In loco parentis, 387

In-text citations, 184

In vitro fertilization, 426

"In Wildness Is the Preservation of the World" (Turner), 702–711

Inaugural speech (Kennedy), 569

Independent voter, 571

Index (periodicals), 169–173

Individual.com, 635

Inductive leap, 88

Inductive reasoning, 86–88, 137–138

Inferno (Dante), 407

Infidelity, 406–410

Info Xtra, 634

Information Anxiety (Wurman), 635

Information overload, 635

Inquire, argument to, 5, 11–12

Insecticides, 690–701

Instant messaging, 66, 653

Institutional grading, 535–536

Intellectual property, 210–235

    Caplan article, 217–221

    collaborative learning, 212–216

    copyright, 211, 219

    fair use, 211

    Gibson article, 222–225

    Lipson/Reindl article, 226–233

    student assignment, 234–235

    what is the issue?, 210–211

Intelligence quotient (IQ), 500

Interlibrary loan, 175

International Baccalaureate curriculum, 501

International Conference on Population and Development, 427

Internet, 54–62

    evaluating sources, 168

    historical overview, 646

    hypertextual websites, 57–62

    online discussion forums, 62–67

    online versions of print arguments, 56–57

readings. *See* Cyber environment
research, 167–169
searching, 168, 169, 174
websites, 56–62
Internet directories, 168
Internet domain, 169
Internet Engineering Task Force (IETF), 647–648
Intertainer, Inc., 634
Interview, 176–177
Intimate Strangers: Men and Women Together (Rubin), 404
Introductory paragraph, 126, 132
Invention, 71
Investigator, 88
IP address, 647
IPv6, 647, 648
IQ, 500
IQ tests, 500, 515
Iran-Contra affair, 265
iRaq, 45
Iraq War, 589
It Happened One Night, 383–384
Italics, 184
It's a Wonderful Life, 384
"I've Gathered a Basket of Communication and Collaboration Tools" (Chang), 653

J

Jackson, Curtis (50 Cent), 244
Jackson, Janet, 263
Jacobs, Jane, 662–663
JAMA, 313
James, Darryl, "Get Your Hand Out of My Pocket," 377–379
Jane Eyre (Arantë), 402
Jay, John, 552
Jefferson, Thomas, 31, 38–89, 576, 598, 608, 619
Jeffery, C. Ray, 663, 665–666
Jesus, 608
Job application, 4
Johnson, Lyndon, 585
Johnson, Samuel, 409
Jones Act, 95
Jordan, Michael, 73
Journal articles, 169–173
Journal of Popular Culture, 389
Journal of the American Medical Association (JAMA), 313
Judgment, 114
Julius Caesar, 593

Jumping to conclusions, 88, 102
Junk e-mail, 651–652

K

Kairos, 30
Kallen, Horace M., 551
Kallenism, 551
Katz, Stanley N., "Liberal Education on the Ropes," 448–457
Kay, Jane Holtz, "The Lived-In City: A Place in Time," 668–675
Kazin, Michael, "A Patriotic Left," 582–588
"Keep the Borders Open" (Hornberger), 555–559
Keller, Ralph, 706
Kelling, George, 665
Kennedy, Anthony, 622
Kennedy, Jacqueline, 673
Kennedy, John F., 569, 702
Kerr, Andy, 679
Kerry, John, 411
Key word, 175
Kiernan, Tom, 713
King, John, 712
King, Martin Luther, Jr., 84–85, 584, 625
"Letter From a Birmingham Jail," 600–611
Kings, Canyon National Park, 718–719
Koplan, Jeffrey P., "Preventing Childhood Obesity," 318–327
Kopp, Wendy, 594
Kraak, Vivica I., "Preventing Childhood Obesity," 318–327

L

LaChapelle, Dolores, 709
Ladies' Home Journal (LHJ), 369
LaFollette, Robert, 584
laissez-faire, 670
"Laments of Commuting, The" (Hernandez), 78
Land ethic, 706
Landsburg, Steven, 655–656
Lange, Dorothea, 40, 41
Langer, Suzanne, 220
Language, 147–151
Last Gentleman, The (Percy), 380
Latino-Americans, 460, 544–548
Lawton, Graham, "Extreme Surgery," 287–290
Lazarus, Emma, 543
Le Corbusier, 683
League of Nations, 312
Learner-Centered Classroom, The (Weimer), 479
Leavis, F. R., 492

Lee, Thomas, 398
Leftist political views, 582–588
Leg-lengthening surgery, 288
Legal case, 9–10
Lehrer, Ute Angleki, 684
Lehrman, Karen, 487
L'Enfant, Pierre, 660
Length of a work, 155
Lengthening surgery, 288
Leopold, Aldo, 705, 706
Lester, Julius, 585
"Letter From a Birmingham Jail" (King), 84–85, 600–611
LexisNexis, 173
Lexus and the Olive Tree, The (Friedman), 518
"Liberal Education on the Ropes" (Katz), 448–457
Libertarian Party, 556
Library, 175
Life of Samuel Johnson, The (Boswell), 409
Limbaugh, Rush, 638
Lincoln, Abraham, 577, 608
Lipson, Abigail, "The Responsible Plagiarist," 226–233
List, 116
Listing, 124–125
Liverman, Catharyn T., "Preventing Childhood Obesity," 318–327
Lives of the Cell, The (Thomas), 490
Livingston, Rick, "The Humanities for Cocktail Parties and Beyond," 444
Logic, 80
Logical arguments
    deduction, 88–93
    induction, 86–88
    Toulmin model, 93–97
Logical arrangement, 137–146
Logical fallacies, 97
    appeal to pity, 98
    appeal to prejudice, 99
    appeal to tradition, 99
    argument by analogy, 99–100
    attacking character of opponent, 100
    attributing false causes, 100–101
    attributing guilt by association, 101
    begging the question, 101
    equivocation, 101
    ignoring the question, 101–112
    jumping to conclusions, 102
    opposing a straw man, 102
    presenting a false dilemma, 102
    reasoning that does not follow, 102–103
    sliding down a slippery slope, 103
Logos, 80–103
    cultural difference in logical arguments, 93
    evidence, 80–85. *See also* Evidence
    fallacies. *See* Logical fallacies
    logic, distinguished, 80
    logical arguments. *See* Logical arguments
London *Times,* 331
Long-playing (LP) records, 250
Lopresti, Mike, 149
Los Angeles Sentinel, 378
Los Angeles Times online, 56–57
"Lost in the Life of the Mind" (Coplin), 471–474
Lott, Trent, 265
Loudon County, Virginia, 679
Love and Economics: Why the Laissez-Faire Family Doesn't Work (Morse), 436
Loving v. Virginia, 413
Lowry, Tom, "Breaking Up Is Easy to Do," 275–277
Lowry, Tom, "Ringtones: Music to Moguls' Ears," 244–246
Loyola College, 381, 387
LPs, 250
Luce, Henry, 222
Lysistrata (Aristophanes), 407

M

MacLean's, 307
Magazine and journal articles, 169–173
Mailing lists, 63
Major premise, 90, 91, 92
Makeover shows, 283
Making Patriots (Berns), 575
"Making Them Squirm" (Tierney), 655–657
Malcolm X, 585
Mammon, 223
Mandela, Nelson, 14
Mapping, 125
Markham, Ken, 242
Marriage, 402–423
    commitment, as, 419–421
    expectations, 403–405
    gay, 411–418
    infidelity, 406–410
    proposing, 389–399
    student assignment, 422–423
    what is the issue?, 402

Marriage proposal, 389–399
Marshall, Robert, 706
Marx, Karl, 583
Marxism, 514
Masefield, John, 551
Mashup, 252
Maslow, Abraham, 391
Mastery assessment, 535
Mathews, Jay, "Standing Up for the Power of Learning," 212–216
MCA, 247
McClay, Wilfred M., "America: Idea or Nation?", 573–581
McCosh, James, 449
McCourt, Tom, "Collecting Music in the Digital Realm," 250–254
McCullough, Candace, 429–431
McDougall, Christopher, "Buyin' Bulk," 334–341
McElroy, Wendy, "Victims from Birth," 429–431
McIntosh, Katherine, 41–42
McKinley, William, 584
McLuhan, Marshall, 69
McMillan, Joyce, "The Brutality of Celebrity Culture," 291–293
Meadows, Donella, "So What Can We Do—Really Do—about Sprawl?", 676–681
Measuring assessment, 535
Meck, Stuart, "Getting on the Case," 662–667
Media consolidation, 257–262, 273
Media for argument, 34–69
    Internet, 54–62. *See also* Internet
    print media, 36–39
    radio and television, 67–69
    visual media. *See* Visual media
"Media Influences on Body Image Development" (Tiggemann), 294–301
Media ownership, 256–279
    big media as sound business practice?, 275–277
    concentration of ownership of radio stations, 257–262
    opposition to big media, 263–271
    student assignment, 278–279
    unchanging economic situation, 272–274
    what is the issue?, 256
Medical reproductive techniques, 425–431
Mencken, H. L., 316
Men's Health, 334
Meredith, James, 610
Merriam Webster's Collegiate Dictionary, 122
Metaphor, 149
Metrosexual, 283
Microform, 175

Midsummer Night's Dream, A, 407
"Migrant Mother" (Lange), 41
"Migrant Mother" postage stamp, 41
Militia groups, 640
Milk, Harvey, 584
Minimal grading, 528–531
Minor premise, 91–92
Mirror of Production, The (Baudrillard), 391
Mission statement (school), 465
Mitterand, Francois, 673
MLA-style bibliography, 188–195
    afterword, 191
    anthology, 191
    book with more than three authors, 191
    book with one author, 190
    book with two/three authors, 190
    CD-ROM, 193–194
    database subscription service, 194
    discussion board posting, 195
    edited book, 191
    editorial, 193
    electronic sources, 193–195
    encyclopedia, article in, 191–192
    example, 254
    foreword, 191
    government publication, 192
    home page, 195
    interview, 195
    introduction, 191
    journal article, 192
    magazine article, 192–193
    mailing list, 195
    multivolume work, 191
    newsgroup, 195
    newspaper article, 193
    online discussion forums, 195
    online periodical, 194
    preface, 191
    subsequent editions of book, 191
    thesis published online, 194–195
    translated book, 191
    Website, article on, 195
MLA-style documentation
    MLA author/work style, 185–187
    works cited, 188–195. *See also* MLA-style bibliography
Modern Language Association (MLA), 182. *See also* MLA-style documentation

"Moguls Are the Medium, The" (Peterson), 272–274
Monophonic ringtones, 246
Monroe, Marilyn, 282
Moore, Michael, 30–31
"More Perfect Union, A" (Rauch), 411–418
Moro Rock, 719
Morse, Jennifer Roback, 436
Moskos, Charles, 592
Mother Jones, 584
Motherhood, 432–434
Motivation and Personality (Maslow), 391
Mount Rushmore, 40
"Moving Away from the Authoritarian Classroom" (Singham), 475–483
"MP3s Great Technology, but Use Must Be Ethical" (Markham), 242
MUDs, 66
Muhammad, Elijah, 607
Muir, John, 706
Multicultural education, 458–462
Multiple choice test, 498
Multiuser domains (MUDs), 66
Murdoch, Rupert, 272
Murie, Olaus, 706
Muscle dysmorphia, 348–349
Muscle obsession, 342–352
Music, 236–255
   censorship, 237
   collecting, 250–254
   copyright, 236
   free downloads, 239–243
   importance, 238
   ringtones, 244–246
   sampling, 237
   student assignment, 254–255
   touring, 247–249
Music collecting, 250–254
Music-concert-touring business, 247–249
Music Corporation of America (MCA), 247
Mussolini, Benito, 48
Myers, Mike, 78

N

Nabhan, Gary, 709
Naess, Arne, 707
Napster, 239, 241
Narratio, 126

Nasar, Jack, 665
Naso, Publius Ovidius (Ovid), 407
NAT, 647–648
Nation, 502
"Nation of Immigrants, A" (Brimelow), 549–554
Nation-state, 573
National identity. *See* American national identity
National Park Service, 714
National parks, 712–720
National Parks Conservation Association (NPCA), 713
National Review, 549, 560
National Rifle Association, 618
National security, 95–96
Natural farming, 694
Nazi eugenics, 427
NCSU, 653
Nebuchadnezzar, 605
Necking grounds, 370
"Needed: Informed Voters" (Balzar), 570–572
Negotiate differences, argument to, 5–7, 13–15
Negroponte, Nicholas, 635
Nehring, Christina, "Fidelity with a Wandering Eye," 406–410
Network address translation (NAT), 647–648
"New Colossus, The" (Lazarus), 543
New Criticism, 492
New Deal, 620
New Scientist, 287, 646
New Towns, 684
New Urbanism, 683, 684
New York Post, 272
New York Times, 616
New Yorker, 247
Newman, Oscar, 663
News shows, 637
Newsgroup, 63–67
Newspaper column, 35–39, 56–57
Newspapers/Current Events database, 172
Newsweek, 432
Nicholas Nickleby (Dickens), 402
Niebuhr, Reinhold, 602–603
Nike, 51, 73, 321
NikeGO Afterschool, 321
NikeGO Head Start, 321
NikePE2GO, 321
1984 (Orwell), 617
Nixon, Richard M., 589, 652
Non sequitur, 102–103

Nongraded writing, 523
Norm-based assessment, 535
North, Oliver, 265
NOT, 174
Note card, 162
Note taking, 162
NPCA, 713
Nuclear testing, 691
Nuisance behaviors, 666
Nussbaum, Martha, 585, 586
Nutrition. *See* Obesity

O

OAH Magazine of History, 369
Obesity, 302–329
    Brink/Querna article, 303–306
    childhood, 318–327
    epidemic, as, 311–317
    human brain, 307–310
    prevention, 305, 318–327
    student assignment, 328–329
    what is the issue?, 302
"Obesity: An Overblown Epidemic?" (Gibbs), 311–317
Objectivity, 80
"Obligation to Endure, The" (Carson), 690–696
O'Brien, Danny, "How to Mend a Broken Internet," 646–650
Obsession, 332
O'Connor, Sandra Day, 622, 626
O'Dwyer, William, 664
Oetinger, Friedrich, 223
Olivardia, Roberto, "The Adonis Complex," 342–352
OLLC FirstSearch, 170
Ollman, Bertell, "Why So Many Exams? A Marxist Response,"
    514–520
Olmsted, Frederick Law, 590, 669, 683
Olson, Ken, 718
One-child policy (China), 428
Ong, Walter, 20
Online discussion forums, 62–67
Online versions of print arguments, 56–57
Open Systems Interconnect (OSI), 649
Opinion, 114
Opposing a straw man, 102
OR, 174
O'Reilly, Bill, 73–74
O'Reilly Factor, The, 73
Organic farming, 694

Orr, David, 84
Orthorexia nervosa, 331
Orwell, George, 550
OSI, 649
Oslo, Norway, 676–677, 678
Out-of-class papers, 498
Outline, 124–125
Overweight, 302–329. *See also* Obesity
Ovid, 407
Owen, Wilfred, 591, 592
Ownership, 208–279. *See also* individual subject headings
    intellectual property, 210–235
    media, 256–279
    music, 236–255, 256–279
Oxford English Dictionary, 122

P

p, 185
Pace, Andrew K., "Surviving Chronic E-Mail Fatigue," 651–654
Page, Clarence, 73–74
Page, Larry, 650
Paine, Tom, 583, 671
Paintings, 45–48
Papanek, Victor, 217–218
par., 187
Paragraph length, 156
Paraphrasing, 126, 157, 159
Parenthetical citations, 184
Parenting, 424, 432–437
Parents Television Council, 267
Paris, 671
Parker-Bowles, Camilla, 291–292
pars., 187
Partitio, 126
Post hoc reasoning, 100
Pathos, 103–108
Patriot movements, 639
Patriotism, 573–588
PBS, 643
Peacock, Doug, 709
Peck, Gregory, 282
Pedagogies, 470. *See also* Teaching methods
Pedagogy of the Oppressed (Freire), 485
Peer Review, 463
Pei, I. M., 673
Pennsylvania Station, 673
Percy, Walker, 380

Peres, Dan, 283

Perez-Zeeb, Celia C., "By the Time I Get to Cucaracha," 544–548

Periodicals, 169–173

Peroratio, 127

Personal digital assistant, 162

Personal experience
   credibility, 77–78
   evidence, 83–84

Personal preference, 114

Personal Responsibility and Work Opportunity Reconciliation Act, 413

Pesticides, 690–701

PET scan, 308

Peterson, Laura, "The Moguls Are the Medium," 272–274

Petit, Charles, "Hazy Days in Our Parks," 712–720

Petrarch, Francesco, 408

Phenology, 708–709

Philadelphia Extra Light cream cheese, 43, 44

Phillips, Katherine A., "The Adonis Complex," 342–352

Photographs, 39–42

Physical fitness, 330–365. *See also* Fitness

Physiological needs, 391

Pity, appeal to, 98

Plagiarism, 63–65, 163–165, 226–233

Planning, 662

Planning a paper, 124

Plastic surgery, 283–290

Pledge of Allegiance, 89, 90

Point Reyes National Seashore, 702

Political advertisements, 68

Political conventions, 68–69

Pollitt, Katha, 582

Polyphonic ringtones, 246

Pope, Harrison G., Jr., "The Adonis Complex," 342–352

Portfolio, 523

Positron emission tomography (PET scan), 308

Poster, 45, 48–51

Powell, Michael, 263–264, 268

Power in the Classroom (Richmond/McCroskey), 479

Power of government, 598–599

pp, 185

Practice of the Wild, The (Snyder), 703

Prejudice, appeal to, 99

Premise, 89–92, 138–140

Presentation of Self in Everyday Life, The (Goffman), 390, 392

Presenting a false dilemma, 102

Preservation, 682

Presidential election (2004), 411

Prevail, argument to, 4, 9–10

Preventing Childhood Obesity: Health in the Balance, 319

"Preventing Childhood Obesity" (Koplan et al.), 318–327

Previewing, 155–156

Pride and Prejudice (Austen), 402

Primary research, 154

Print media, 35–39, 56–57

Process model, 532

Progressive federalism, 624–625

Progressives, 620

Promiscuous dating, 373

Proof, 126

Proposition, 126

Provocative language, 148

Pruitt-Igoe, 664

Psychology & Counseling database, 172

PsycINFO, 170

Public Broadcasting System (PBS), 643

Public domain, 219

Public forum doctrine, 636–637

Public Interest, 573

Public newsgroups, 67

Public prominence, 77

Publisher, 156

Pumping Iron, 354

Punished by Rewards (Kohn), 479

Pyramid scheme, 679

Q

qtd. in, 186

Qualifiers, 94

Queer Geography, A (Browning), 29

Querna, Elizabeth, "Eat This Now!", 303–306

Question of judgment, 114

Quindlen, Anna, "The Good Enough Mother," 432–434

Quintillian, 72

Quotation, 125

Quotation within cited work, 186–187

Qureshi, Aisam ul-Haq, 24, 25

R

Racial nationalism, 583

Radio and television, 67–69

Radio stations, 257–262

Random House Dictionary, 122

Rangel, Charles, 591

Rauch, Jonathan, "A More Perfect Union," 411–418
Re-engineering the Internet, 646–650
Reading, 37–39, 154–155
Reagan, Ronald, 265, 420, 622
Reality television shows, 283
"Reasonable Approach to Gay Adoption, A" (Guetter), 133–136
Reasoning
   deduction, 88–93
   induction, 86–88
   Toulmin model, 93–97
Reasoning that does not follow, 102–103
"Reclaiming Federalism" (Barron), 619–627
Record of publication, 473
Recording Industry Association of America (RIAA), 240, 241
Red herring, 613
Redmond, Washington, 679
References list, 201–204. *See also* APA-style references list
Refutatio, 127
Refutation, 127
Rehnquist, William, 619, 626
Rehnquist Federalism, 620–623
Reid, Richard Charles, 656
Reindl, Sheila M., "The Responsible Plagiarist," 226–233
Relationships, 366–439
   college students' sexual exploits, 380–388
   dating, 368–379
   fatherhood, 435–437
   genetic engineering, 429–431
   marriage, 403–423. *See also* Marriage
   marriage proposal, 389–399
   motherhood, 432–434
   parenting, 424, 432–437
   recipe for romance, 379
   reproductive medicine, 425–431
   sexual promiscuity on campus, 380–388
   student assignment, 400–401, 422–423, 438–439
Reproductive medicine, 425–431
Research, 152–178
   abstracting services, 174–175
   annotation, 156–157, 158
   books, 175–176
   getting started, 166
   Internet, 167–169. *See also* Internet
   interview, 176–177
   magazine and journal articles, 169–173
   plagiarism, 163–165
   previewing, 155–156

   primary/secondary, 154
   reading critically, 154–155
   selective, 166–167
   summarizing, 157–159, 160
   survey, 177–178
   synthesizing, 159–161
   taking notes, 162
"Responsible Plagiarist, The" (Lipson/Reindl), 226–233
Reverse anorexia, 348
Revolutionary War, 568
Rhetoric, 71
Rhetoric (Aristotle), 72, 147
Rhetorical situation, 18–22
Rhetorical syllogism, 92
"Rhime of the Ancient Mariner, The" (Coleridge), 591
Rhoads, Steven E., "What Fathers Do Best," 435–437
RIAA, 240, 241
Richardson, Henry Hobbs, 672
Ringback tones, 246
"Ringtones: Music to Moguls' Ears" (Lowry), 244–246
Rivedal, Karen, 117–122
Roberts, John, 619
Roe v. Wade, 412
Rogerian argument, 13–14, 131–137
Rogers, Carl, 13–14, 131
Romanticism, 591
Romantics, 424
Ronaldo, 107–108
Roosevelt, Franklin D., 620
Roosevelt, Theodore, 552, 620, 706
Rose, Mike, 563
Rubin, Lillian, 404
Ruggiero, Vincent Ryan, 464
Ruskin, John, 492
Rybczynski, Witold, 683

S

Safe street, 662–663
SafeScape (Zelinka/Brennan), 666
Salon.com, 169, 621
Salve Regina University, 463–468
Same-sex marriage, 411–418
Sampling, 237
Samson, Leon, 584
San Joaquin Valley, 718
Sand County Almanac, A (Leopold), 706
Sanders, Joe, 247

Sasser worm, 655
School board example, 5–7
Schooling. *See* Education
Schuler, Lou, "Buyin' Bulk," 334–341
Schwarzenegger, Arnold, 282, 335, 412
Scientific American, 311
Scientific research, 87
Scientific Style and Format: The CBE Manual for Authors, Editors, and Publishers, 183
Scientific texts, 697
Scruggs, Mark, 714, 715
Search engine, 168
Searching the Internet, 168–169, 174
Second Amendment, 618
Secondary research, 154
Selective research, 166–167
Self-actualization, 391
Separation of church and state, 89–90
September 11 terrorist attacks, 30–31, 580, 598
Sequoia National Park, 718–719
Sexual orientation
    context, 29–30
    gay adoption, 133–136
Sexual promiscuity on campus, 380–388
Shared experiences, 641–642
Shaull, Richard, 485
Shaver, Chris, 714
Shenk, Joshua Wolf, 77–78
Shepard, Paul, 694, 708
Shields, Jeanne, 104–107
Shoe bomber (Richard Reid), 656
Sierra Club, 715
Silent Spring (Carson), 690–701
"Silent Spring at 40" (Bailey), 697–701
Simile, 149
Simon, Lewis B., 370
Simple Living, 97
Simpson, Alan K., 546–547
Simulation, 390
Singham, Mano, "Moving Away from the Authoritarian Classroom," 475–483
Sirulnick, Dave, 283
Situationists, 393
Sketches, 49
Skimming, 156
Slate, 169
Sliding down a slippery slope, 103
Slippery slope argument, 103

Sloan, Allan, 20
Sloppy scholarship, 226–227
Slouka, Mark, 55
Smith, Diana, 406
Smog, 712–720
Smoky Mountains, 718
"Snowmobiles in Yellowstone: The Case for Fair Access" (Sunderman), 127–131
Snyder, Gary, 709
"So What Can We Do—Really Do—about Sprawl?" (Meadows), 676–681
Soil Bank Act, 692
Sonicnet.com, 634
Source material, 125
Sowell, Thomas, 571
Spam, 651–652
Spam assassin, 651
Special Supplemental Nutrition Program for Women, Infants, and Children, 320
Specialized dictionaries, 122
Spencer, Earl, 291
Spock, Benjamin, 433
Spooners, 370
Sprawl, 676–681
Sprite, 73
S.S. *St. Louis,* 556
St. Lawrence Cement, 51–53
St. Louis, 556
St. Louis, Missouri, 676–677
St. Thomas, 61–62
Stalin, Joseph, 591
Standardized testing, 503–513
"Standing Up for the Power of Learning" (Mathews), 212–216
Stanton, Elizabeth Cady, 583, 584
Statement of background, 126
Statement of benefits, 132–133
Statement of understanding, 132
Statement of your position, 132
Statistics, 83
Statue of Liberty, 543
Stein, Clarence, 683
Stein, Jules, 247
Steroids, 334–341, 356
Stevens, Wallace, 491
Storm King Mountain, 47
Story Behind the Rock: The World's Most Creative Directory of Romantic and Surprising Engagement Ideas, The (Pagliaro), 396

Strategies for argument, 70–108
  ethos, 72–80
  logos, 80–103. *See also* Logos
  pathos, 103–108
Straw man fallacy, 102
Stride Toward Freedom: The Montgomery Story (King), 600
Strontium 90, 690
Structuring the argument, 123–146
Students' voicelessness, 230
Stupid White Men (Moore), 31
Style, 147–151
Style guides, 183. *See also* Documenting your sources
Subject, 113
Subtitles, 156
Suburban Nation: The Rise of Sprawl and the Decline of the American Dream (Duany et al.), 683
Suburbs, 669, 682–685
Suicide bombings, 93
Sullivan, R. Mark, 82, 83
Sum, Andrew, 542
Summarizing, 126, 157–160
Summary of opposing views, 132
Sunderman, Tyler, 127–131
Sunstein, Cass, "The Daily We: Is the Internet Really a Blessing for Democracy?", 633–645
Supporting evidence, 146–147
Surowiecki, James, 74–76
Surowiecki, James, "Hello, Cleveland," 247–249
Survey, 177–178
"Surviving Chronic E-Mail Fatigue" (Pace), 651–654
Swan, The, 283
Sweeney, Camille, 28
Sweeping conclusion, 88
Syllogism, 90–91
Synchronous forums, 66–67
Synthesizing, 159–161

T

Taco Bell Chihuahua controversy, 545
Takaki, Ronald, "An Educated and Culturally Literate Person Must Study America's Multicultural Reality," 458
Taking notes, 162
Takings Clause, 622
Tale of Two Cities, A (Dickens), 511
Taliban, 42
Talk radio, 67–68
Tape recorder, 177
Tax refund, 81

Teaching methods, 470–497
  authoritarian classroom, 471–483
  student assignment, 496–497
  teaching science, 490–495
  what is the issue?, 470
  women's studies courses, 484–489
Telecommunications Act, 258
Television, 67–69
Television commercials, 68
Telos, 392
10 Things Employers Want You to Learn in College (Coplin), 473
Test-tube baby, 426
Testing. *See* Grading
"Tests, Tracking, and Derailment" (Williams), 499–502
Thatcher, Margaret, 420
"The Daily We: Is the Internet Really a Blessing for Democracy?" (Sunstein), 633–645
"The Lived-In City: A Place in Time" (Kay), 668–675
Thomas, Lewis, 87
"The Art of Teaching Science," 490–495
Thoreau, Henry David, 151, 571, 688, 689, 702–704, 706–709
Thurmond, Strom, 265
Tierney, John, "Making Them Squirm," 655–657
Tiggemann, Marika, "Media Influences on Body Image Development," 294–301
Times, 331, 419
Titian, 345
Title, 155
TiVo, 634
"To Skip or Not to Skip: A Student Dilemma" (Rivedal), 118–119
Tocqueville, Alexis de, 574
Tom Jones (Fielding), 402
TomPaine.com, 81
Tone, 147–151
"Too Many: Looking Today's Immigration in the Face" (Camarota), 560–565
Toomey, Jenny, "Empire of the Air," 257–262
Topic, 113–115, 166
Topic sentence, 158
Toulmin, Stephen, 93
Toulmin model, 93–97, 140–145
"Toward a Radical Feminist Pedagogy" (hooks), 484–489
Tracking, 499–502
Tradition, appeal to, 99
Trainor, Stephen L., "Designing a Signature General Education Program," 463–469
Transcript, 535
TRIAD, 648–650

Triangle Shirt Waist Factory fire, 620
"Tripping Up Big Media" (Beckerman), 263–271
Troilus and Cressida, 407
Trotsky, Leon, 591
True tones, 246
Truth about Hillary: What She Knew, When She Knew It, and How Far She'll Go to Become President, The (Klein), 149
Tsunami, 314
Turner, Jack, "In Wildness Is the Preservation of the World," 702–711
Turner, Neely, 694
Turner, Ted, 218
TV, 67–69
Twain, Mark, 570
Tweed, Bill, 718, 719
Twiggy, 282
Twin Cities, 61

U

U.S. Army home page, 54
U.S. News & World Report, 303
Underlining, 184
Undressing Infidelity: Why More Wives Are Unfaithful (Smith), 406
"Unintended Consequences of High-Stakes Testing" (Cizek), 149, 503–513
Universal nation, 551
University of California at Berkeley, 459
University of St. Thomas, 61–62
University students' sexual exploits, 380–388
Unorganized Militia, 639
Urban growth accelerators, 677–678
Urban growth machine, 679
Urban planning, 662–675
Urban sprawl, 676–681
Urbanization, 660–687
  sprawl, 676–681
  student assignment, 686–687
  suburbs, 669, 682–685
  urban planning, 662–675
  what is the issue?, 660–661
USA Today, 19
Usenet newsgroup, 63–67

V

Values as evidence, 85
Vannini, Phillip, "Will You Marry Me? Spectacle and Consumption in the Ritual of Marriage Proposals," 389–399

Vecellio, Tiziano (Titian), 345
Veith, Doug, 379
Viacom, 275
"Victims from Birth" (McElroy), 429–431
Vietnam War, 568, 585, 589
Violence Against Women Act, 621
Virtual communities, 55
Visual media, 39–53
  advertisements, 43–45
  art, 45–51
  icons, 45
  integrating textual elements, 51–53
  paintings, 45–48
  photographs, 39–42
  poster, 45, 48–51
Vitamins, 333
Voicelessness, 230
von Hoffman, Alexander, 664
Voting, 570–572
Voyage of the damned, 556

W

Wahlberg, Mark, 335
"Walking" (Thoreau), 688, 689, 702–704, 707, 708
War, 589–595
War against terrorism, 568, 586
War bonds, 49, 50
War effort, 49–51
Wardrobe malfunction, 263
Warrant, 93–97, 141
Washington, D.C., 660
Washington, George, 589, 660
Watergate, 652
Wattenberg, Ben, 551
Wattenberg, Martin, 571
Web addresses, 169
Websites, 56–62
"Wedding Bell Blues Being Sung by Guests" (Lee), 398
Weekly Standard, 435
Welfare-to-work program, 413
West, Mae, 282
"What Fathers Do Best" (Rhoads), 435–437
"What's Yours? (Ownership of Intellectual Property)" (Caplan), 217–221
White elephant, 648
Whitehouse, Laura, 719
Whitelists, 651–652
WHO, 312

"Why Fear National ID Cards?" (Dershowitz), 616–618

"Why Nick?" (Shields), 104–106

"Why So Many Exams? A Marxist Response" (Ollman), 514–520

WIC Program, 320

Wickens, Barbara, "How Your Brain Makes You Fat," 307–310

Wikis, 653

Wilderness, 688, 702–711

Wilderness Act of 1964, 704

Wilderness tourism, 706–708

Wile, Joan, 81

Will and Grace, 544

"Will You Marry Me? Spectacle and Consumption in the Ritual of Marriage Proposals" (Vannini), 389–399

Williams, Patricia, "Tests, Tracking, and Derailment," 499–502

Williams, Terry Tempest, 709

Wilson, Edmund, 492

Wilson, James Q., 665

Wilson, Robert, "Enough Snickering. Suburbia Is More Complicated and Varied than We Think," 682–685

Wilson, Woodrow, 273, 312, 584, 624

Winning of the West (Roosevelt), 552

Wired, 147–148

Wolfe, Tom, 383

Woman's Declaration of Rights, 583, 584

Women body builders, 353–364

Women's studies courses, 484–489

Words and ideas. *See* Intellectual property

Wordsworth, William, 424

Works cited, 188–195. *See also* MLA-style bibliography

World Health Organization (WHO), 312

"World of Their Own, A," 430

World War II, 590, 593

World Wide Web, 55. *See also* Internet

Wright, Frank Lloyd, 660, 661, 683

Wright, Sam, "Femininity and Muscularity: Accounts of Seven Women Body Builders," 353–364

"Writer's Audience Is Always a Fiction, The" (Ong), 20

Writing process, 532

Writing Space (Bolter), 11

Wurman, Richard, 635

X

Xingtones, 246

Y

Yugoslavia, 639, 648

Z

Z Magazine, 519

Zahm, Diane, 664

Zatso.net, 634

ZDNet, 239

Zelinka, Al, 666

Zhou dynasty, 229

Zones of territorial influence, 663